The Millennium Reader

Fifth Edition

Stuart Hirschberg
Rutgers University

Terry Hirschberg

PEARSON

Prentice
Hall

Upper Saddle River, New Jersey 07458

In memory of Hans Ruesch (1913–2007).
The world's a lesser place now.

Library of Congress Cataloging-in-Publication Data
The millennium reader / [compiled by] Stuart Hirschberg, Terry Hirschberg.—5th ed.
  p. cm.
  Includes index.
  ISBN-13: 978-0-13-601738-7   ISBN-10: 0-13-601738-X
1. College readers. 2. English language—Rhetoric. I. Hirschberg, Stuart.
II. Hirschberg, Terry.
  PE1417.M4 S83 2009
  808'.0427—dc22   2007049198

Editorial Director: Leah Jewell
Senior Acquisitions Editor: Brad Potthoff
Editorial Assistant: Tracy Clough
Production Liaison: Joanne Hakim
Director of Marketing: Brandy Dawson
Senior Marketing Manager: Windley Morley
Marketing Assistant: Kimberly Caldwell
Senior Operations Supervisor: Sherry Lewis
Cover Art Director: Jayne Conte
Cover Design: Robert Aleman
Cover Image: © Bob Sacha/Corbis Corporation
Manager, Cover Visual Research & Permissions: Karen Sanatar

Director, Image Resource Center: Melinda Patelli
Manager, Rights and Permissions: Zina Arabia
Manager, Visual Research: Beth Brenzel
Photo Coordinator: Ang'john Ferreri
Photo Researcher: Melinda Alexander
Full-Service Project Management: Dennis Troutman/TexTech International
Composition: TexTech International
Printer/Binder: The Courier Companies
Cover Printer: The Courier Companies

Credits and acknowledgments borrowed from other sources and reproduced, with permission, in this textbook appear on pages 817–822.

Pearson Education LTD., London
Pearson Education Singapore, Pte. Ltd
Pearson Education, Canada, Ltd
Pearson Education—Japan
Pearson Education Australia PTY, Limited

Pearson Education North Asia Ltd
Pearson Educación de Mexico, S.A. de C.V.
Pearson Education Malaysia, Pte. Ltd
Pearson Education, Upper Saddle River, New Jersey

10 9 8 7 6 5

ISBN 13: 978-0-13-601738-7
ISBN 10:   0-13-601738-X

CONTENTS

Poetry

Connections for Chapter 1:
Reflections on Experience   100

Nonfiction

Fiction

Poetry

Connections for Chapter 2:
Memorable People and Places   160

Nonfiction

Fiction

Poetry

Connections for Chapter 3:
The Value of Education

4 PERSPECTIVES ON LANGUAGE

Nonfiction

Fiction

Poetry

Connections for Chapter 4:
Perspectives on Language

7   PAST TO PRESENT   439

Nonfiction

Fiction

Poetry

Connections for Chapter 7:
Past to Present   521

8 POWER AND POLITICS 523

Nonfiction

Fiction

Poetry

Drama

Connections for Chapter 8:
Power and Politics 605

9 SCIENCE AND TECHNOLOGY 607

Nonfiction

Fiction

RHETORICAL CONTENTS

ILLUSTRATION AND EXAMPLE

COMPARISON AND CONTRAST

PROCESS ANALYSIS

CLASSIFICATION

ARGUMENTATION AND PERSUASION

Arguments That Define and Draw Distinctions

Arguments That Establish Causes and Draw Consequences

Arguments That Make Value Judgments

Arguments That Propose Solutions

AUTOBIOGRAPHY

PREFACE

The fifth edition of *The Millennium Reader* is intended for first-year composition, intermediate, and advanced composition courses that consider the essay as a form of literature.

The book introduces students to major traditions in essay writing and explores the relationship between the writer's voice and stylistic features that express the writer's attitude toward his or her personal experiences. The text also provides guidance for students in developing skills in critical reading and writing, with a strong emphasis on argumentation.

The Millennium Reader provides thought-provoking and engaging models of writing by scholars, researchers, and scientists that show writing is essential to learning in all academic fields of study.

The eighty-eight nonfiction selections, thirty of which are new to this edition, have been chosen for their interest, reading level, and length and include a broad range of topics, authors, disciplines, and cross-cultural perspectives.

Many of the longer readings are included because of their value in allowing students to observe the development of ideas and to enhance their own skills in reading comprehension and writing their own essays.

The readings shed light on myriad subjects—from ancient Egypt to robots in the home; from the sinking of the *Titanic* to the Sistine Chapel; from the lowly pencil to high-powered lasers; from the American Civil War to the aftermath of September 11, 2001; from fast food to global warming; from ballet to tatooing; from autism to advertising; from martial arts to Harry Potter.

The text is thematically organized in order to bridge the gap between the expressive essays students traditionally read and their own life experiences. Selections drawn from memoirs, scholarly essays, and biographies illustrate how writers move through, and beyond, personal experiences and adapt what they write for different audiences.

The book includes 135 selections by classic, modern, and contemporary authors whose work, in many cases, provides the foundation of the broader intellectual heritage of a college education.

The chapters are organized by themes that have traditionally elicited compelling expressive essays and thoughtful arguments and include accounts of personal growth, nature writing, prison literature, and narratives of religious and philosophical exploration. *The Millennium Reader* is rich in a variety of perspectives by African-American, Native-American, Asian-American, and Hispanic writers and offers cross-cultural and regional works as well as a core of selections by classic authors.

The sixteen short stories (seven new to this edition), twenty-seven poems (eleven new to this edition), and two plays amplify the themes in each chapter in ways that introduce students to techniques and forms that writers have traditionally used in the fields of fiction, poetry, and drama.

NEW TO THIS EDITION

We have thoroughly updated all eleven chapters, expanded the introductions, and provided guidelines for reading the works in the chapters.

We have added thirty new illustrations (from photographs to billboard art, and from film stills to drawings, paintings, and other images) that enhance the impact of the themes and selections.

Also, we have expanded the end-of-selection questions by adding a new category ("Rhetorical Inquiry") that addresses specific features of style, tone, organization, context and mode to enable students to more fully understand the writers' strategies.

CHAPTER DESCRIPTIONS

The eleven chapters cover a wide range from the sphere of reflections on personal experience, family life, and influential people to descriptions of memorable places, discussions of the value of education and perspectives on language, consideration of issues in popular culture; various sections contemplate our place in nature, history in the making, the pursuit of justice, the impact of technology, the artistic impulse, and matters of ethics, philosophy, and religion.

Chapter 1, "Reflections on Experience," introduces candid, introspective reminiscences by writers who want to understand the meaning of important personal events that proved to be decisive turning points in their lives.

Chapter 2, "Memorable People and Places," introduces portraits of people important to the writers, presents an invaluable opportunity to study the methods biographers use, and explores the role that landscapes and natural and architectural wonders have played in the lives of the writers.

Chapter 3, "The Value of Education," attests to the value of literacy and looks at the role education plays in different settings as a vehicle for self-discovery, especially for marginalized citizens and questions raised by censorship.

Chapter 4, "Perspectives on Language," explores the social impact of language and how it defines ethnic identity; the importance of being able to communicate; and the dangers of the language used to manipulate attitudes, beliefs, and emotions, whether in the form of propaganda or advertising.

Chapter 5, "Everyday Matters," touches on broad issues of contemporary concern, including child abuse, AIDS, consumerism, eating disorders, addictions, the funeral industry, racism, and fast-food.

Chapter 6, "Our Place in Nature," offers investigations of animal behavior and parallels in humans, explores the complex interactions of living things, and presents different perspectives on global warming.

Chapter 7, "Past to Present," brings to life important social, economic, and political events of the past and addresses the question of how historians shape our perceptions of the past in ways that influence the present.

Chapter 8, "Power and Politics" draws on firsthand testimonies by writers whose accounts combine eyewitness reports, literary texts, and historical records in the continuing debate over the allegiance individuals owe their government and the protection of individual rights that citizens expect in return.

Chapter 9, "Science and Technology," examines the extent of our culture's dependence on technology and energy, and the mixed blessings that scientific innovations, including lasers, robots, and genetic engineering, will bequeath to future generations.

Chapter 10, "The Artistic Impulse," considers how artists deepen and enrich our knowledge of human nature and experience through their distinctive contributions in particular societies and how art changes from age to age and culture to culture.

Chapter 11, "The Ethical Dimension," focuses on universal questions of faith, good and evil, obedience to authority, and basic questions about the meaning and value of life as applied to specific contemporary issues of abortion, vivisection, religious tolerance, and ethical and personal choices.

EDITORIAL APPARATUS

An introduction, "Reading in the Various Genres," discusses the crucial skills of reading for ideas and organization and introduces students to the basic rhetorical techniques writers use in developing their essays. This introduction also shows students how to approach important elements in appreciating and analyzing short fiction, poetry, drama, and the rhetoric of visual texts.

Chapter introductions discuss the theme of each chapter and its relation to the individual selections and offer guidelines for discovering connecting themes. A biographical sketch preceding each selection gives background information on the writer's life and identifies the personal and literary context in which the selection was written. Prompts before each selection lead readers to consider issues that the selection develops.

Questions for discussion and writing at the end of each selection are designed to encourage readers to discover relationships between their personal experiences and those described by the writers in the text, to explore points of agreement in areas of conflict sparked by the viewpoint of the authors, and to provide ideas for further inquiry and writing. These questions ask students to think critically about the content, meaning, and purpose of each selection; students will evaluate the author's rhetorical strategy, voice projected in relationship to his or her audience, evidence cited, and underlying assumptions. The writing suggestions afford opportunities for personal and expressive writing as well as expository and persuasive writing.

Images within each chapter are accompanied by prompts or questions that ask students to connect that image to the corresponding selection or chapter theme.

Connection questions at the end of each chapter link each selection with other readings in that chapter and/or with readings throughout the book to afford students the opportunity to explore multiple perspectives on the same topic.

A rhetorical index is included to enhance the usefulness of the text by permitting students to study the rhetorical strategies of the selections as well as their content and themes.

INSTRUCTOR'S MANUAL

An accompanying Instructor's Manual provides (1) guidance on how to approach each selection; (2) sample syllabi and suggestions for organizing courses with different kinds of focus (argumentation, cultural studies, writing across the curriculum); (3) detailed answers to discussion questions; (4) additional essay topics for writing and research; (5) supplemental resources (bibliographies and Web sites) for students who wish to follow up on any of the authors or issues for in-depth study; and (6) alternative tables of contents by secondary themes, disciplines, and subjects.

MYCOMPLAB

MyCompLab is a Web application that offers comprehensive and integrated resources for every writer. With **MyCompLab,** students can learn from interactive tutorials and instruction; practice and develop their skills with grammar, writing, and research exercises; share and collaborate their writing with peers; and receive comments on their writing from instructors and tutors. Go to http://www.mycomplab.com to register for these premiere resources and much more!

ACKNOWLEDGMENTS

No expression of thanks can adequately convey our gratitude to all those teachers of composition who offered thoughtful comments and suggestions on changes for this edition: G. Douglas Atkins, University of Kansas; Mary Bishop, Holmes Community College; Richard Johnson, Kirkwood Community College; Charlene Keeler, California State University at Fullerton; Lisa Langstraat, Colorado State University; Hildy Miller, Portland State University; Elizabeth Oldfield, Southeastern Community College; Derek Soles, Drexel University; David Sullivan, Cabrillo Community College.

For their dedication and skill, we owe much to the able staff at Prentice-Hall, especially to our editor, Brad Potthoff, and his assistants, Megan Dubrowski and Tracy Clough. We were indeed fortunate to have Dennis Troutman as our production editor and Premlal Premkumar as our copyeditor.

Stuart Hirschberg
Terry Hirschberg

INTRODUCTION: READING IN THE VARIOUS GENRES

READING ESSAYS

As a genre, the essay harks back to the form invented four hundred years ago by the French writer Michel Montaigne, who called his writings *essais* (attempts) because they were intended less as accounts of objective truth than as personal disclosures of a mind exploring its own attitudes, values, and assumptions on a diverse range of subjects. The essayist speaks directly without the mediation of imagined characters and events.

Essayists invite us to share the dramatic excitement of an observant and sensitive mind struggling to understand and clarify an issue that is of great importance to the writer. We feel the writer trying to reconcile opposing impulses to evolve a viewpoint that takes into account known facts as well as personal values.

Reading for Ideas and Organization

One of the most important skills to have is the ability to survey unfamiliar articles, essays, or excerpts and come away with an accurate understanding of what the author wanted to communicate and of how the material is organized. On the first and in subsequent readings of any of the selections in this text, especially the longer ones, pay particular attention to the title, look closely at the introductory and concluding paragraphs (with special emphasis on the author's statement or restatement of central ideas), identify the headings and subheadings (and determine the relationship between these and the title), and locate any unusual terms necessary to fully understand the author's concepts.

As you first read through an essay, you might look for cues that enable you to recognize the main parts or help you to perceive its overall **organization.** Once you find the main **thesis,** underline it. Then work your way through fairly rapidly, identifying the main ideas and the sequence in which they are presented. As you identify an important idea, ask yourself how this idea relates to the thesis statement you underlined or to the idea expressed in the title.

Finding a Thesis

Finding a thesis involves discovering the idea that serves as the focus of the essay. This idea is often stated in the form of a single sentence that asserts the author's response to an issue that an **audience** might respond to in different ways. For example, in "The Lowest Animal" (Ch. 5), Mark Twain presents his assessment of human nature:

> In the course of my experiments I convinced myself that among the animals man is the only one that harbors insults and injuries, broods over them, waits till a chance offers, then takes revenge. The passion of revenge is unknown to the higher animals.

The main idea or thesis represents the writer's view of a subject or **topic** from a certain perspective. Here Twain states a view that serves as a focus for his essay.

Writers often place the thesis in the first paragraph or group of paragraphs so that the readers will be able to perceive the relationship between the supporting evidence and this main idea.

As you read, you might wish to underline the topic sentence or main idea of each paragraph or section (since key ideas are often developed over the course of several paragraphs). Jot it down in your own words in the margins, identify supporting statements and **evidence** (such as examples, statistics, and the testimony of authorities), and try to discover how the author organizes the material to support the development of important ideas. To identify supporting material, look for any ideas more specific than the main idea that is used to support it.

Pay particular attention to important transitional words, phrases, or paragraphs to better see the relationships among major sections of the selection. Noticing how certain words or phrases act as **transitions** to link paragraphs or sections together will dramatically improve your reading comprehension. Also look for section summaries, where the author draws together several preceding ideas.

Writers use certain words to signal the starting point of an **inductive** or **deductive** chain of reasoning. If you detect any of the following terms, look for the main idea they introduce:

since	as shown by	for the reason that
because	inasmuch as	may be inferred from
for	otherwise	may be derived from
as	as indicated by	may be deduced from
follows from	the reason is that	in view of the fact that

An especially important category of words includes signals that the author will be stating a conclusion. Words to look for are the following:

therefore	in summary
hence	which shows that
thus	which means that
so	and which entails

accordingly	consequently
in consequence	proves that
it follows that	as a result
we may infer	which implies that
I conclude that	which allows us to infer
in conclusion	points to the conclusion that

You may find it helpful to create a running dialogue with the author in the margins, posing and then trying to answer the basic questions *who, what, where, when,* and *why,* and to note your observations on how the main idea of the article is related to the title. You can later use these notes to evaluate how effectively any specific section contributes to the overall line of thought.

Organization of the Essay   Writers use a variety of means in an **introduction** to attract readers' interest, at the same time explicitly stating or at least implying the probable thesis. Some writers find that a brief story or anecdote is an ideal way to focus the audience's attention on the subject, as does Jill Nelson in "Number One!" (Ch. 1):

> That night I dream about my father, but it is really more a memory than a dream. "Number one! Not two! Number one!" my father intones from the head of the breakfast table. The four of us sit at attention, two on each side of the ten-foot teak expanse, our brown faces rigid. At the foot, my mother looks up at my father, the expression on her face a mixture of pride, anxiety and could it be, boredom? I am twelve. It is 1965.

Other writers use the strategy of opening with an especially telling or apt quotation. Writers may also choose to introduce their essays in many other ways, by defining key terms, offering a prediction, posing a thoughtful question, or providing a touch of humor.

Even though the introductory paragraph is the most logical place to state the thesis, one can also expect to find the central assertion of the essay in the title, as, for example, in Judy Blume's essay "Is Harry Potter Evil?" (Ch. 3), which decries banning Harry Potter books from school libraries.

The main portion of the essay presents and develops the main points the writer wishes to communicate. A wide range of strategies may be used, depending on the kind of point the writer is making and the form the supporting evidence takes to demonstrate the likelihood of the writer's thesis.

The **conclusion** of an essay may serve a variety of purposes. The writer may restate the thesis after reviewing the most convincing points or close with an appeal to the needs and values of the specific audience. This sense of closure can be achieved in many different ways. For instance, the conclusion can echo the ideas stated in the opening paragraph, or it can present a compelling image. Other writers choose to end on a note of reaffirmation and challenge or with irony or a striking **paradox.** The most traditional ending sums up points raised in the essay, although usually not in as impressive a fashion as does Robert Sapolsky's conclusion to "Bugs in the Brain" (Ch. 6):

> My reflection on a curbside puddle brought me to the opposite conclusion that Narcissus reached in his watery reflection. We need phylogenetic humility. We are certainly not the most evolved species around, nor the least vulnerable. Nor the cleverest.

Supporting Evidence   An important part of critical reading depends on your ability to identify and evaluate how the writer develops the essay in order to **support** the thesis. The most common patterns of thinking are known as the **rhetorical modes.** For example, writers might describe how something looks, narrate an experience, analyze how something works, provide examples, define important terms, create a classification, compare and contrast, create an analogy, or explore what caused something. To clarify and support the thesis, writers also use a wide variety of evidence, including examples drawn from personal experience, the testimony of experts, statistical data, and case histories.

Describing   Writers use **description** for a variety of purposes, ranging from portraying the appearance of people, objects, events, or scenes to revealing the writer's feelings and reactions to those people, objects, events, or scenes. Gayle Pemberton in "Antidisestablishmentarianism" (Ch. 2) accomplishes this in her description of her grandmother, an intimidating woman who taught Pemberton to be independent and think for herself:

> She disliked white people, black people in the aggregate and pretty much individually too, children—particularly female children—her daughter, her husband, my mother, Episcopalianism, Catholicism, Judaism and Dinah Shore. She had a hot temper and a mean streak. . . . Grandma scared the daylights out of me.

We learn that her grandmother's curmudgeon-like attitude proved invaluable in helping Pemberton deal with the white society in which she grew up.

Perhaps the most useful method of arranging details within a description is the technique of focusing on an impression that dominates the entire scene. This main impression can center on a prominent physical feature, a tower or church steeple, or a significant psychological trait, such as Pemberton's grandmother's "take no shit" attitude. A skillful writer will often arrange a description around this central impression, in much the same way a good photographer will locate a focal point for pictures. Jack London, who was a journalist and novelist, uses this technique in "The San Francisco Earthquake" (Ch. 7) in his description of how San Francisco residents reacted to the devastating earthquake of 1906:

> Before the flames, throughout the night, fled tens of thousands of homeless ones. Some were wrapped in blankets. Others carried bundles of bedding

and dear household treasures. Sometimes a whole family was harnessed to a carriage or delivery wagon that was weighted down with their possessions. Baby buggies, toy wagons, and go-carts were used as trucks, while every other person was dragging a trunk. Yet everybody was gracious. The most perfect courtesy obtained. Never, in all San Francisco's history, were her people so kind and courteous as on this night of terror.

A wealth of specific descriptive details re-creates the sights and sounds of the conflagration. Yet, the primary impression London communicates is that the citizens of San Francisco displayed forbearance and rare courtesy toward one another in the most trying of circumstances.

Description is more effective when the writer arranges details to produce a certain effect, such as **suspense,** empathy, or surprise. Agnes De Mille, a renowned choreographer, does this in "Pavlova" (Ch. 10) when she describes the great Russian ballerina, so that her readers can share the moment when De Mille decided to become a dancer herself. De Mille's description draws the reader's attention to Pavlova's physical appearance, gestures, style of performance, and the response she produced in her audiences. Through a multitude of evocative details we can "see" Pavlova's slight figure, minuscule slipper size, graceful limbs and neck, and accelerated hummingbird-like movements. De Mille carefully structures her description to present Pavlova first at rest, a diminuative figure who seems insignificant, and then to depict her in motion, when Pavlova magically becomes larger than life through her dancing.

Narrating Another essential technique often used by writers is **narration.** Narrative relates a series of events or a significant experience by telling about it in chronological order. The events related through narrative can entertain, inform, or dramatize an important moment. For example, in "West with the Night" (Ch. 1), Beryl Markham tells us of the moment on her epic cross-Atlantic flight when she faced a life-and-death decision. By relating the events of the flight as they led to this crucial moment, Markham provides her readers with a coherent framework in which to interpret the events of her story.

Effective narration focuses on a single significant action that dramatically changes the relationship of the writer (or main character) to family, friends, or environment. A significant experience may be defined as a situation in which something important to the writer or to the people he or she is writing about is at stake.

Narratives are usually written from the **point of view** of a **first-person** narrator, as in the case of Beryl Markham:

> It is dark already and I am over the south of Ireland. There are the lights of Cork and the lights are wet; they are drenched in Irish rain, and I am above them and dry.

Events can also be related through a second-person point of view (you) or through a more objective third-person (he, she, they) point of view.

Narration can take the form of an anecdote (such as Markham's) or as a historical account synthesized from journals, logs, diaries, and even interviews, such as that compiled by Hanson W. Baldwin (in "R.M.S. *Titanic*," Ch. 7). Baldwin's account of the events leading up to and after the moment when the *Titanic* struck an iceberg is shaped to emphasize the poignancy and irony of this catastrophe. For example, Baldwin recounts the following event:

> 12:45 A.M. Murdock, in charge on the starboard side, eyes tragic, but calm and cool, orders boat No. 7 lowered. The women hang back: they want no boat ride on an ice-strewn sea; the *Titanic* is unsinkable. The men encourage them, explain that this is just a precautionary measure: "We'll see you again at breakfast."

We notice how skillfully Baldwin creates a composite that includes the actions of those who were there along with what was actually said at the time. Baldwin uses narration to summarize, explain, interpret, and dramatize an important moment in history.

Narratives offer writers means by which they can discover the meaning of experiences through the process of writing about them. For Mikhal Gilmore (in "My Brother, Gary Gilmore," Ch. 2), the need to understand his family history became an overpowering motivation that led him to write his **autobiography**:

> Over the years, many people have judged me by my brother's actions as if in coming from a family that yielded a murderer I must be formed by the same causes, the same sins, must by my brother's actions be responsible for the violence that resulted, and bear the mark of a frightening and shameful heritage. It's as if there is guilt in the fact of the blood-line itself. Maybe there is.

In these more personal, autobiographical narratives (see, for example, Fritz Peters, Jill Nelson, Richard Rhodes, Agnes De Mille, and Sabine Reichel), the need to clarify and interpret one's past requires the writer to reconstruct the meaning and significance of experiences *whose importance may not have been appreciated at the time they occurred.*

Just as individuals can discover the meaning of past experiences through the process of writing about them, so writers use narration to focus on important moments of collective self-revelation. Sabine Reichel in "Learning What Was Never Taught" (Ch. 3) draws on records and eyewitness accounts (including her own memories) from the post-Nazi era for specific details to re-create the scene for her readers, and she summarizes necessary background information to provide a context for her account.

Illustrating with Examples   Providing good **examples** is an essential part of effective writing. A single well-chosen example or a range of illustrations can provide clear cases that illustrate, document, and substantiate a writer's thesis. The report of a memorable incident, an account drawn from records, eyewitness reports, and a personal narrative account of a crucial incident are all important ways examples can document the authenticity of the writer's thesis.

One extremely effective way of substantiating a claim is by using a **case history,** that is, an in-depth account of the experiences of one person that typifies the experience of many people in the same situation. Juliet B. Schor, an economist, uses this technique in her account "The Culture of Consumerism" (Ch. 5). The experience of Jeff Lutz stands for the experiences of many people who have voluntarily downsized their lifestyles and have found that they can be quite comfortable with less money and material possessions and more time for the things that really matter to them. Schor begins by telling us something about Jeff Lutz and then follows his activities as he attempts to make do with $18,000 a year:

> He says he does not feel materially deprived, and he is careful to point out that voluntary simplicity is not poverty. While he decided against the lattés, he does own a car and a computer, goes out to eat between one and three times a month, rents videos, has friends over for dinner, and buys his clothes both new and used.

By selecting one person to represent many who have left the rat race, Schor brings into human terms an idea that otherwise would be more difficult to grasp.

Defining Yet another rhetorical pattern often used by writers is **definition.** Definition is a useful way of specifying the basic nature of any phenomenon, idea, or thing. Definition is the method of clarifying the meaning of key terms, either in the thesis or elsewhere in the essay. In some cases, writers may develop an entire essay to explore the **connotations** accrued by an unusual or controversial term or to challenge preconceptions attached to a familiar term. Besides eliminating **ambiguity** or defining a term important to the development of the essay, definitions can be used persuasively to influence perceptions, as Jean-Paul Sartre does for the term *existentialism* in "Existentialism" (Ch. 11):

> Not that we believe that God exists, but we think that the problem of His existence is not the issue. In this sense existentialism is optimistic, a doctrine of action, and it is plain dishonesty for Christians to make no distinction between their own despair and ours and then to call us despairing.

Dividing and Classifying Writers also divide and classify a subject on the basis of important similarities. **Classification and division** is used to sort, group, and collect things into categories, or classes, that are based on one or more criteria. The criteria are features that members of the group all have in common. The purposes of the classifier determine which specific features are selected as the basis of the classification. Thus, classification is, first and foremost, an intellectual activity based on discovering generic characteristics shared by members of a group, according to the interests of the writer. Effective classifications shed light on the nature of what is being classified by identifying significant features, using these features as criteria in a systematic way, dividing phenomena into at least two different classes on the basis of these criteria, and presenting the results logically and consistently. For example, in "The Rhetoric of Advertising" (Ch. 4), Stuart Hirschberg classifies the techniques advertisers use according to the traditional rhetorical strategies identified by Aristotle:

> Seen in this way, ads appear as mini-arguments whose strategies and techniques of persuasion can be analyzed just like a written argument. We can discover which elements are designed to appeal to the audience's emotions (*pathos* according to Aristotle), which elements make their appeal in terms of reasons, evidence, or logic (*logos*), and how the advertiser goes about winning credibility . . . in terms of the spokesperson employed to speak on behalf of the product (the *ethos* dimension).

If we can identify the specific techniques advertisers use, the author believes, we will be less likely to be manipulated into buying things we don't need.

Comparing and Contrasting   Another way of arranging a discussion of similarities and differences relies on the rhetorical method of **comparison and contrast.** Using this method, the writer compares and contrasts relevant points about one subject with corresponding aspects of another. For example, in "Concerning Egypt" (Ch. 7), Herodotus compares unfamiliar Egyptian customs to the corresponding, but different, customs of his countrymen:

> In other countries the priests have long hair, in Egypt their heads are shaven; elsewhere it is customary, in mourning for near relations to cut their hair close: the Egyptians, who wear no hair at any other time, when they lose a relative, let their beards and the hair of their heads grow long.

The comparative method serves Herodotus well as a way of getting his audience to perceive basic differences between the two cultures (Egypt and Greece).

Comparisons may be arranged structurally in one of two ways. In one method, the writer discusses all the relevant points of one subject and then covers the same ground for the second. Writers may use transitional words like *although, however, but, on the other hand, instead of, different from,* and *as opposed to* to indicate contrast. Words used to show comparisons include *similarly, likewise,* and *in the same way.* Comparisons may also be arranged point by point to create a continual contrast from sentence to sentence between relevant aspects of two subjects. Comparisons may also evaluate two subjects. The writer contrasts sets of qualities and decides between the two on the basis of some stipulated criteria.

Dramatic contrast is a favorite device of satirists, who expose hypocrisy by reminding people of what they really do, as opposed to what they profess. In "The Lowest Animal" (Ch. 5), Mark Twain contrasts the behavior of humans with that of animals in comparable situations in order to deflate the high opinion the human species has of itself. Each of Twain's "experiments" is meant to show the preponderance in humans of such traits as greed and cruelty, and to **parody** the interpretation of Darwin's theory (then currently popular) that humans were the apex of all living species.

Although Twain's "experiments" are hypothetical and meant to underscore ironic insights, the comparative technique is indispensable as a way of structuring real scientific experiments. Such is the case in a fascinating study conducted by John M. Darley and Bibb Latané in "Why People Don't Help in a Crisis" (Ch. 11), which evaluated the behavior of subjects in response to what could be perceived of as an emergency. The researchers compared the responses and drew a surprising conclusion:

> As part of the study, we staged an emergency: smoke was released into the waiting room through a vent. Two thirds of the subjects who were alone noticed the smoke immediately, but only 25 per cent of those waiting in groups saw it as quickly. Although eventually all the subjects did become aware of the smoke . . . this study indicates that the more people present, the slower an individual may be to perceive an emergency and the more likely he is not to see it at all.

Darley and Latané's analysis of the different responses is developed through a comparison of striking dissimilarities in behavior between each of the groups in the study. For Darley and Latané, the measurable difference in the subjects' willingness to perceive an emergency provided evidence to support their "diffusion of responsibility" theory that the presence of nonresponsive others makes individuals less likely to define an event as an emergency.

Figurative Comparisons and Analogies   **Figurative language** rather than literal comparisons reveal the writer's feelings about the subject. Figurative comparisons can take the form of **metaphors** that identify two things with each other, as in Rick Bass's description in "A Fitting Desire" (Ch. 2): "The yellow sulphers dance and skitter across the fields from one buttery dandelion to the next."

They can also take the form of **similes** that use the word *like* or *as* to relate two seemingly unrelated things, as in Gayle Pemberton's description in "Antidisestablishmentarianism" (Ch. 2): "He was a thin, small-boned man who looked to me far more *like* an Indian chief than *like* a black man."

The ability to create compelling images in picturesque language is an important element in communicating a writer's thoughts, feelings, and experiences. Creating a vivid picture or image in an audience's mind requires writers to use metaphors, similes, and other figures of speech. **Imagery** works by evoking a vivid picture in the audience's imagination. A simile compares one object or experience to another by using *like* or *as*. A metaphor applies a word or phrase to an object it does not literally denote in order to suggest the comparison. To be effective, metaphors must look at things in a fresh light to let the reader see a familiar subject in a new way.

Analogy, which is a comparison between two basically different things that have some points in common, is an extraordinarily useful tool that writers use to clarify subjects that otherwise might prove to be difficult to understand, unfamiliar, or hard to visualize. The greater the numbers of similarities that the writer is able to draw between what the audience finds familiar and the newer complex idea the writer is trying to clarify, the more successful the analogy. For example, Garrett Hardin in "Lifeboat Ethics" (Ch. 11) compares an affluent country to a lifeboat that is already almost full of people and compares immigrants from poor countries to people in the water who desperately wish to get into the lifeboat: "Since the boat has an unused excess capacity of ten more passengers, we could admit just ten more to it. But which ten do we let in?"

Hardin's tactics are based on getting his audience to agree that a country has a limited capacity to support a population, just as there are only so many seats in a lifeboat, and that if those begging for admission are taken into "our boat," the boat will swamp and everyone will drown.

In addition to clarifying abstract concepts and processes, analogies are ideally suited to transmit religious truths in the form of parables and metaphors. An aptly chosen metaphor can create a memorable image capable of conveying truth in a way that is permanent and vivid.

An effective analogy provides a way to shed new light on hidden, difficult, or complex ideas by relating them to everyday human experience. One of the most famous analogies ever conceived, Plato's "The Allegory of the Cave" (Ch. 11), uses a series of comparisons to explore how lifelong conditioning deludes people into mistaking illusions for reality:

> Behold! Human beings living in an underground den, which had a mouth open toward the light and reaching all along the den; here they have been from their childhood, and have their legs and necks chained so that they cannot move, and can only see before them, being prevented by the chains from turning around their heads. Above and behind them is a fire blazing at a distance.

Plato explains that in this den the prisoners, who have never seen anything outside the cave, mistake shadows cast on the wall by reflected firelight for realities. If some were free to leave the cave, they would be dazzled by the sunlight. It is ironic, says Plato, that once their eyes had adjusted to the light, they would be unable, if they then returned to the cave, to see as well as the others. Moreover, if they persisted in trying to lead their fellow prisoners out of the cave into the light, the others would find their claim of greater light outside the cave ridiculous. Thus, each element in the analogy—the fire, the prisoners, the shadows, the dazzling light—offers an unparalleled means for grasping the Platonic ideal of truth as a greater reality beyond the illusory shadows of what we mistake as the "real" world.

Thus, analogies are extraordinarily useful to natural and social scientists, poets, and philosophers as an intellectual strategy and rhetorical technique for clarifying difficult subjects, explaining unfamiliar terms and processes, transmitting religious truths through parables, and spurring creativity in problem solving by opening the mind to new ways of looking at things.

Process Analysis   One of the most effective ways to clarify the nature of something is to explain how it works. **Process analysis** divides a complex procedure into separate and easy-to-understand steps in order to explain how something works, how something happened, or how an action should be performed. Process analysis requires the writer to include all necessary steps in the procedure and to demonstrate how each step is related to preceding and subsequent steps in the overall sequence. To be effective, process analysis should emphasize the significance of each step in the overall sequence and help the reader understand how each step emerges from the preceding stage and flows into the next.

For example, in "To Make Them Stand in Fear" (Ch. 8), Kenneth M. Stampp, a noted historian, investigates a past era in our country's history when blacks were brought to America as slaves. Stampp analyzes the instructions given by manuals that told slaveowners, step-by-step, how to break the spirit of newly transported blacks in order to change them into "proper" slaves:

> Here, then, was the way to produce the perfect slave: accustom him to rigid discipline, demand from him unconditional submission, impress upon him his innate inferiority, develop in him a paralyzing fear of white men, train him to adopt the master's code of good behavior, and instill in him a sense of complete dependence. This, at least, was the goal.

Stampp's analysis of source documents reveals that slaveowners used behavior modification techniques to produce "respectful" and "docile" slaves. The process began with a series of measures designed to enforce external discipline. Later on, attention shifted to measures designed to encourage psychological conditioning so that, in theory at least, the slave would control himself or herself through internalized perceptions of inferiority.

Causal Analysis   Whereas process analysis explains *how* something works, **causal analysis** seeks to discover *why* something happened, or why it will happen, by dividing an ongoing stream of events into causes and effects. Writers may proceed from a given effect and seek to discover what cause or chain of causes could have produced the observed effect, or to show how further effects will flow from a known cause.

Causal analysis is an invaluable analytical technique used in many fields of study. Because of the complexity of causal relationships, writers try to identify, as precisely as possible, the contributory factors in any causal sequence. The direct or immediate causes of the event are those most likely to have triggered the actual event. Yet, behind direct causes may lie indirect or remote causes that set the stage or create the framework in which the event could occur. By the same token, long-term future effects are much more difficult to identify than are immediate, short-term effects.

This technique of distinguishing between predisposing and triggering causes is used by Aldous Huxley, political essayist and author of *Brave New World* (1932), to answer the question of why one particular segment of the German population was so easily swayed by Hitler's rhetoric:

> Hitler made his strongest appeal to those members of the lower middle classes who had been ruined by the inflation of 1923, and then ruined all over again by the depression of 1929 and the following years. "The masses" of whom he speaks were these bewildered, frustrated and chronically anxious millions.

In this passage from "Propaganda under a Dictatorship" (Ch. 4), Huxley uses causal analyis to emphasize that the people most likely to yield to **propaganda** were those whose security had been destroyed by previous financial disasters. That is, previous cycles of financial instability (the disastrous inflation of 1923 and the depression of 1929) played a crucial role in predisposing the lower middle classes, those whose security was most affected by the financial turmoil, to become receptive to Hitler's propaganda. Hitler, says Huxley, used techniques of propaganda—mass marches, repetition of slogans, scapegoating—to manipulate the segment of the population that was the least secure and the most fearful.

It is most important that causal analysis demonstrate the means (sometimes called the *agency*) by which an effect could have been produced. Writers are obligated to show how the specific causes they identify could have produced the effects in question.

Solving a Problem   Although not a rhetorical strategy as such, writers use techniques for **problem solving** to identify difficulties and apply theoretical models. Defining constraints, employing various search techniques, and checking solutions against relevant criteria are an important part of all academic and professional research.

The problem-solving process usually involves recognizing and defining the problem, using various search techniques to discover a solution, verifying the solution, and communicating it to a particular audience, who might need to know the history of the problem, the success or failure of previous attempts to solve it, and other relevant information.

Recognizing the Existence and Nature of the Problem   The first step in solving a problem is recognizing that a problem exists. Often, the magnitude of the problem is obvious from serious effects that the problem is causing. For example, in his analysis of the dangers posed by deforestation, Joseph K. Skinner in "Big Mac and the Tropical Forests" (Ch. 6) describes the disastrous effects that have already beset the tropical forests of the world and alerts us to how vulnerable the ecosystem is, a concept that most people would be reluctant to believe:

> Hello, fast food chains.
>
> Goodbye, tropical forests.
>
> Sound like an odd connection? The "free-market" economy has led to results even stranger than this, but perhaps none have been as environmentally devastating.
>
> These are the harsh facts: the tropical forests are being leveled for commercial purposes at the rate of 150,000 square kilometers a year, an area the size of England and Wales combined.

Skinner uses dramatic evidence to persuade his readers to perceive the relationship of the destruction of tropical forests and raising cattle for cheap beef for fast-food chains.

Defining the Problem   When the problem has been clearly perceived, it is often helpful to present it with a single, clear-cut example. Robert W. Felix in "Fatal Flaw" (Ch. 6) does this to illustrate the disproportionate extinction of large mammals in the most recent ice age:

> Towering over them all, though, was the giant North American Ground Sloth. Heavier than a pickup truck (several thousand pounds), it wandered through ancient forests on skateboard feet up to three feet long, and stood as tall as a two-story house. You'd think an animal that big could name its own ticket. No such luck.

The way Felix frames this problem provides a context in which to understand it and a way to identify the most important criterion—the relative size of mammals—by which to evaluate theories as to why some became extinct.

Verifying the Solution   When at last a solution is found after researchers have used various search techniques, it must meet all the tests specific to the problem and take into account all pertinent data uncovered during the search. For example, Charles H. Townes reports in "Harnessing Light" (Ch. 9) that researchers had succeeded in stimulating emission of radiation to produce a coherent beam of laser light that would have a host of useful applications:

> Soon there were many variations on the laser theme, using different atoms or molecules and different methods of providing them with energy, but all used a mirrored chamber.

In his article, Townes describes how he and other scientists (1) analyzed the nature of the problem, (2) created a set of procedures to solve it, (3) allocated resources for the most productive investigations, and (4) verified the results of their experiments.

Argumentation and Persuasion   Some of the most interesting and effective writing you will read takes the form of **arguments** that seek to persuade a specific audience (colleagues, fellow researchers, or the general public) of the validity of a proposition or claim through logical reasoning supported by facts, examples, data, or other kinds of evidence.

The purpose of argument is the **persuasion** of an audience to accept the validity or probability of an idea, proposition, or claim. Essentially, a **claim** is an assertion that would be met with skepticism if it were not supported with sound evidence and persuasive reasoning. Formal arguments differ from assertions based on likes and dislikes or personal opinion. Unlike questions of personal taste, arguments rest on evidence, whether in the form of facts, examples, the testimony of experts, or statistics, which can be brought forward to objectively prove or disprove the thesis in question.

Readers expect that evidence cited to substantiate or refute assertions will be sound, accurate, and relevant and that conclusions will be drawn from this evidence according to the guidelines of logic. Readers also expect that the writer arguing in support of a proposition will acknowledge and answer objections put forth by the opposing side and will provide compelling evidence to support the writer's own position.

Although arguments explore important issues and espouse specific theories, the forms in which arguments appear vary according to the style and format of individual disciplines. Evidence in different fields of study can appear in a variety of formats, including laws, precedents, the interpretation of statistics, or the citation of authorities. The means used in constructing arguments depend on the audience within the discipline being addressed, the nature of the thesis being proposed, and the accepted methodology for that particular area of study.

In the liberal arts, critics evaluate and interpret works of fine art; review music, dance, drama, and film; and write literary analyses (see Aaron Copland's "Film Music," Ch. 10). Philosophers probe the moral and ethical implications of people's actions and advocate specific ways of meeting the ethical challenges posed by new technologies (see David Ewing Duncan's "DNA as Destiny," Ch. 9). Historians interpret political, military, and constitutional events; analyze their causes; and theorize about how the past influences the present (see Kenneth M. Stampp's "To Make Them Stand in Fear," Ch. 8).

In the political and social sciences, lawyers and constitutional scholars argue for specific ways of applying legal and constitutional theory to everyday problems (see Jonathan Kozol's "The Human Cost of an Illiterate Society," Ch. 3). Economists debate issues related to changes wrought by technology, distribution of income, unemployment, and commerce (see Juliet B. Schor's "The Culture of Consumerism," Ch. 5).

Political scientists look into how effectively governments initiate and manage social change, and they ask basic questions about the limits of governmental intrusion into individual rights (see Aldous Huxley's "Propaganda under a Dictatorship," Ch. 4). Sociologists analyze statistics and trends to evaluate how successfully institutions accommodate social change (see Barbara Ehrenreich's "Nickel-and-Dimed," Ch. 8).

In the sciences, biologists as well as biochemists, zoologists, botanists, and other natural scientists propose theories to explain the interdependence of living things with their natural environment (see Gunjan Sinha's "You Dirty Vole," Ch. 6). Psychologists champion hypotheses based on physiological, experimental, social, and clinical research to explain various aspects of human behavior. Physicists, as well as mathematicians, astronomers, engineers, and computer scientists, put forward and defend hypotheses about the basic laws underlying manifestations of the physical world, from the microscopic to the cosmic (see Donald A. Norman's "Emotional Robots" Ch. 9).

Evaluating Tone   An important ability to develop in critical reading is making inferences about the writer from clues in the text. Looking beyond the facts to see what those facts imply requires readers to look carefully at writers' word choices, their level of knowledge, their use of personal experience, and the skill with which various elements of an essay are arranged. Inferences about a writer's frame of reference and values go beyond what is on the page and can help us get a sense of what the writer is like as a person.

Tone is a crucial element in establishing a writer's credibility. Tone is produced by the combined effect of word choice, sentence structure, and the writer's success in adapting his or her particular **voice** to the subject, the audience, and the occasion. When we try to identify and analyze the tone of a work, we are seeking to hear the actual "voice" of the author in order to understand how the writer intended the work to be perceived. It is important for writers to know what image of themselves they project. Writers should consciously decide on the particular style and tone that best suit the audience, the occasion, and the specific subject matter of the argument.

For example, Martin Luther King, Jr.'s speech "I Have a Dream" (Ch. 8) was delivered when King led a march of 250,000 people through Washington, D.C., to the Lincoln Memorial on the centennial of Lincoln's Emancipation Proclamation. The persuasive techniques that King uses are well suited to adapt his message of nonviolent protest to both his audience and the occasion.

King reminds his audience that the civil rights movement puts into action basic ideas contained in the Constitution. King reaffirms minority rights as a way of renewing aspirations put forward by the Founding Fathers of the United States and uses figurative language drawn from the Emancipation Proclamation and the Bible to reinforce his audience's emotional resolve to continue in their quest for equal rights:

> I say to you today, my friends, even though we face the difficulties of today and tomorrow, I still have a dream. It is a dream deeply rooted in the American dream. I have a dream that one day this nation will rise up and live out the true meaning of its creed: "We hold these truths to be self-evident, that all men

are created equal." I have a dream that one day, on the red hills of Georgia, sons of former slaves and the sons of former slaveowners will be able to sit down together at the table of brotherhood.

The effectiveness of this speech depends in large part on the audience's sense of King as a man of high moral character. In arguments that appeal to the emotions as well as to the intellect, the audience's perception of the speaker as a person of the highest ethics, good character, and sound reason amplifies the logic of the discourse.

Irony, Humor, and Satire   A particular kind of tone encountered in many essays is called **irony**. Writers adopt this rhetorical strategy to express a discrepancy between opposites, between the ideal and the real, between the literal and the implied, and most often between the way things are and the way the writer thinks things ought to be.

Sometimes it is difficult to pick up the fact that not everything the writer says is intended to be taken literally. Authors occasionally say the opposite of what they mean to catch the attention of the reader. If your first response to an ironic statement is "Can the writer really be serious?" look for signals that the writer means the opposite of what is being said. One clear signal that the author is being ironic is a noticeable disparity between the tone and the subject. For example, Jonathan Swift in his essay "A Modest Proposal" (Ch. 8) presents a narrator who offers in a most reasonable, matter-of-fact way a proposal that Ireland solve its economic problems by slaughtering and exporting one-year-old children as foodstuffs.

Satire is an enduring form of argument that uses parody, irony, and caricature to poke fun at a subject, an idea, or a person. Tone is especially important in satire. The satirist frequently creates a mask, or **persona**, that is very different from the author's real self in order to shock the audience into a new awareness about an established institution or custom. Satirical works by Mike Adams (Ch. 3), Mark Twain (Ch. 5), and Jessica Mitford (Ch. 5) assail folly, greed, corruption, pride, vanity, hypocrisy, deceit, and other permanent targets of the satirist's pen.

Responding to What You Read

When reading an essay that seems to embody a certain value system, try to examine any **assumptions** or beliefs the writer expects the audience to share. How are these assumptions related to the author's purpose? If you do not agree with these assumptions, has the writer provided sound reasons and evidence to persuade you to change your mind?

You might describe the author's tone or voice and try to assess how much it contributed to the essay. How effectively does the writer use authorities, statistics, or examples to support the claim? Does the author identify the assumptions or **values** on which his or her views are based? Are they ones with which you would agree or disagree? To what extent does the author use the emotional connotations of language to try to persuade the reader? Do you see anything unworkable or disadvantageous about the solutions offered as an answer to the problem the essay addresses? All these and many other ways of analyzing someone else's essay can be used to create your own. Here are some specific guidelines to help you.

When evaluating an essay, consider what the author's **purpose** is in writing it. Is it to inform, explain, solve a problem, make a recommendation, amuse, enlighten, or achieve some combination of these goals? How is the tone, or voice, the author projects related to the purpose in writing the essay?

You may find it helpful to write short summaries after each major section to determine whether you understand what the writer is trying to communicate. These summaries can then serve as a basis for an analysis of how successfully the author employs reasons, examples, statistics, and expert testimony to support and develop main points.

For example, if the essay you are analyzing cites authorities to support a claim, assess whether the authorities bring the most timely opinions to bear on the subject or display any obvious biases, and determine whether they are experts in that particular field. Watch for experts described as "often quoted" or "highly placed reliable sources" without accompanying names, credentials, or appropriate documentation. If the experts cited offer what purports to be a reliable interpretation of facts, consider whether the writer also quotes equally trustworthy experts who hold opposing views.

If statistics are cited to support a point, judge whether they derive from verifiable and trustworthy sources. Also, evaluate whether the author has interpreted them in ways that are beneficial to the case, whereas someone who held an opposing view could interpret them quite differently. If real-life examples are presented to support the author's opinions, determine whether they are representative or whether they are too atypical to be used as evidence. If the author relies on hypothetical examples or analogies to dramatize ideas that otherwise would be hard to grasp, judge whether these examples are too far-fetched to back up the claims being made. If the essay depends on the stipulated definition of a term that might be defined in different ways, check whether the author provides clear reasons to indicate why one definition rather than another is preferable.

As you list observations about the various elements of the article you are analyzing, take a closer look at the underlying assumptions and see whether you can locate and distinguish between those assumptions that are explicitly stated and those that are implicit. Once the author's assumptions or **premises** are identified, you can compare them with your own beliefs about the subject, determine whether these assumptions are commonly held, and make a judgment as to their validity. Would you readily agree with these assumptions? If not, has the author provided sound reasons and supporting evidence to persuade you to change your mind?

Marking as You Read

The most effective way to think about what you read is to make notes as you read. Making notes as you read forces you to go slowly and think carefully about each sentence. This process is sometimes called *annotating the text,* and all you need is a pen or a pencil. There are as many styles of annotating as there are readers, and you will discover your own favorite technique once you have done it a few times. Some readers prefer to underline major points or statements and jot down their reactions to them in the margin. Others prefer to summarize each paragraph or section to help them follow the author's line of thinking. Other readers circle key words or phrases necessary to understand the main ideas. Feel free to use your notes as a kind of conversation with the text. Ask questions. Express doubts. Mark unfamiliar words or phrases to look up later. If the paragraphs are not already numbered, you might wish to number them as you go to help you keep track of your responses. Try to distinguish the main ideas from supporting points and examples. Most important, go slowly and think about what you are reading. Try to discover whether the author makes a credible case for the conclusions reached. One last point: Take a close look at the idea expressed in the title before and after you read the essay to see how it relates to the main idea.

Keeping a Reading Journal

The most effective way to keep track of your thoughts and impressions and to review what you have learned is to start a reading journal. The comments you record in your journal may express your reflections, observations, questions, and reactions to the essays you read. Normally, your journal would not contain lecture notes from class. A reading journal will allow you to keep a record of your progress during the term and can also reflect insights you gain during class discussions and questions you may want to ask, as well as unfamiliar words you intend to look up. Keeping a reading journal becomes a necessity if your composition course requires you to write a research paper that will be due at the end of the semester. Keep in mind that your journal is not something that will be corrected or graded, although some instructors may wish you to share your entries with the class.

Turning Annotations into Journal Entries   Although there is no set form for what a journal should look like, reading journals are most useful for converting your brief annotations into more complete entries that explore in depth your reactions to what you have read. Interestingly, the process of turning your annotations into journal entries will often produce surprising insights that will give you a new perspective.

Summarizing   Reading journals may also be used to record summaries of the essays you read. The value of summarizing is that it requires you to pay close attention to the reading in order to distinguish the main points from the supporting details. Summarizing tests your understanding of the material by requiring you to restate concisely the author's main ideas in your own words. First, create a list composed of sentences that express in your own words the essential idea of each paragraph or of each group of related paragraphs. Your previous underlining of topic sentences, main ideas, and key terms (as part of the process of critical reading) will help you follow the author's line of thought. Next, whittle down this list still further by eliminating repetitive ideas. Then formulate a thesis statement that expresses the main idea in the article. Start your summary with this thesis statement, and combine your notes so that the summary flows together and reads easily.

Remember that summaries should be much shorter (usually no longer than half a page) than the original text (whether the original is one page or twenty pages long) and should accurately reflect the central ideas of the article in as few words as possible. Try not to intrude your own opinions or critical evaluations into the summary. Besides requiring you to read the original piece more closely, summaries are necessary first steps in developing papers that synthesize materials from different sources. The test for a good summary, of course, is whether a person reading it without having read the original article would get an accurate, balanced, and complete account of the original material.

Using Your Reading Journal to Generate Ideas for Writing   You can use all the material in your reading journal (annotations converted to journal entries, reflections, observations, questions, rough and final summaries) to relate your own ideas to the ideas of the person who wrote the essay you are reading. Here are several different kinds of strategies you can use as you analyze an essay in order to generate material for your own:

1. What is missing in the essay? Information that is not mentioned is often just as significant as information the writer chose to include. First, you must already have summarized the main points in the article. Then, make up another list of points that are not discussed, that is, missing information that you would have expected an article of this kind to cover or touch on. Write down the possible reasons why this missing material has been omitted, censored, or downplayed. What possible purpose could the author have had? Look for vested interests or biases that could explain why information of a certain kind is missing.

2. You might analyze an essay in terms of what you already knew and what you didn't know about the issue. To do this, simply make a list of what concepts were already familiar to you and a second list of information or concepts that were new to you. Then write down three to five questions you would like answered about this new information and make a list of possible sources you might consult.

3. You might consider whether the author presents a solution to a problem. List the short-term and long-term consequences of the action the writer recommends. You might wish to evaluate the solution to see whether positive short-term benefits would be offset by possible negative long-term consequences not mentioned by the author. This might provide you with a starting point for your own essay.

4. After clearly stating what the author's position on an issue is, try to imagine other people in that society or culture who would view the same issue from a different perspective. How would the concerns of these people be different from those of the writer? Try to think of as many different people, representing as many different perspectives, as you can. Now, try to think of a solution that would satisfy both the author and at least one other person who holds a different viewpoint. Try to imagine that you are an arbitrator negotiating an agreement. How would your recommendation require both parties to compromise and reach an agreement?

READING FICTION

Works of **fiction** communicate intense, complex, deeply felt responses to human experiences that speak to the heart, mind, body, and imagination.

Although the range of situations that stories can offer is limitless, what makes any particular story enjoyable is the writer's capacity to present an interesting **plot,** believable characters, and convincing dialogue. The nature of the original events matters less than the writer's ability to make us feel the impact of this experience intellectually, physically, and emotionally. The writer who uses language in skillful and precise ways allows us to share the perceptions and feelings of people different from ourselves. Works of fiction not only can take us to parts of the world we may never have the opportunity to visit but can deepen our emotional capacity to understand what life is like for others in conditions very different from our own. We become more conscious of ourselves as individual human beings when our imaginations and emotions are fully involved. We value a story when through it we touch the aspirations, motives, and feelings of other people in diverse personal and cultural situations.

Works of fiction, as distinct from biographies and historical accounts, are imaginative works that tell a story. Fiction writers use language to recreate the emotional flavor of experiences and are free to restructure their accounts in ways that will create suspense and even build conflict. They can add to or take away from the known facts, expand or compress time, invent additional imaginative details, or even invent new characters or a narrator through whose eyes the story is told.

The oldest works of fiction took the form of **myths** and legends that described the exploits of heroes and heroines, gods and goddesses, and supernatural beings. Other ancient forms of literature include **fables** (stating explicit lessons using animal characters), **folk tales, fairy tales,** and **parables** (using analogies to suggest rather than state moral points or complex philosophical concepts) of the kind related by Jesus in the New Testament.

The modern short story differs from earlier narrative forms in emphasizing life as most people know it. The **short story** originated in the nineteenth century as a brief fictional prose narrative that was designed to be read in a single sitting. In a short story, all the literary elements of plot, **character(s)**, **setting,** and the author's distinctive use of language work together to create a single effect. Short stories usually describe the experiences of one or two characters over the course of a series of related events. Realistic stories present sharply etched pictures of characters in real settings reacting to kinds of crises with which readers can identify. The emotions, reactions, perceptions, and motivations of the characters are explored in great detail. **Realism** is reflected in short stories ranging from Kate Chopin's "Désirée's Baby" (Ch. 5), written in the nineteenth century, through Raymond Carver's "Neighbors" (Ch. 2) to, most recently, Irene Zabytko's "Home Soil" (Ch. 7).

Other writers, reacting against the prevailing conventions of realistic fiction, create a kind of story in which everyday reality is not presented directly but is filtered through the perceptions, associations, and emotions of the main character. In these *nonrealistic* stories, the normal chronology of events is displaced by a psychological narrative that reflects the ebb and flow of the characters' feelings and associations. Nonrealistic stories may include fantastic, bizarre, or supernatural elements as well. We can see this alternative to the realistic story in Kurt Vonnegut, Jr.'s "Harrison Bergeron" (Ch. 9).

Although it is something we have done most of our lives, when we look at it closely reading is a rather mysterious activity. The individual interpretations readers bring to characters and events in the text make every story mean something slightly different to every reader. There are, however, some strategies all readers use: We instinctively draw on our own knowledge of human relationships in interpreting characters and incidents, we simultaneously draw on clues in the text to anticipate what will happen next, and we continuously revise our past impressions as we encounter new information.

At what points in the work were you required to imagine or anticipate what would happen next? How did you make use of the information the author gave you to generate a **hypothesis** about what lay ahead? To what extent do your own circumstances—gender, age, race, class, and culture—differ from those of the characters in the story, poem, or play? How might your reading of the text differ from that of other readers? Has the writer explored all the possibilities raised within the work? Has the writer missed any opportunities that you as the writer would have explored?

The Millennium Reader offers works drawn from many cultural contexts reflecting diverse styles and perspectives. Fiction produced in the second half of the twentieth century differs in a number of important ways from that produced before World War II. Writers in this postmodern period avoid seeing events as having only one meaning and produce works that represent reality in unique, complex, and highly individual ways.

Contemporary writers have a great deal to say about the forces that shape ethnic, sexual, and racial identity in various cultural contexts. Unlike traditional works that presented social dilemmas in order to resolve them, **postmodernist** works underscore the difficulty of integrating competing ethnic, sexual, and racial identities within a single culture. This is especially apparent in Irene Zabytko's "Home Soil" (Ch. 7) and Andre Dubus's "The Fat Girl" (Ch. 1). Other writers address the ways different cultures define gender roles and class relationships in terms of power and powerlessness. These issues are explored in Edward P. Jones's The First Day" (Ch. 3), Gish Jen's "Who's Irish?" (Ch. 4), Kate Chopin's "Désirée's Baby," and Gloria Anzaldúa's "Cervicide" (Ch. 5).

READING POETRY

Poetry differs from other genres in that a **poem** achieves its effects with fewer words, compressing details into carefully organized forms in which sounds, words, and images work together to create a single intense experience. Poetry uses language in ways that communicate experience rather than simply give information. The difference between prose and poetry emerges quite clearly when you compare a **stanza** from Grace C. Kuhns's poem "Lisa's Ritual, Age 10" (Ch. 5) with the same words punctuated as a sentence in prose:

> The wall is steady while she falls away: first the hands lost arms dissolving feet gone the legs disjointed body cracking down the center like a fault she falls inside slides down like dust like kitchen dirt slips off the dustpan into noplace a place where nothing happens, nothing ever happened.

Notice how in this **free verse** stanza from the poem the arrangement of the words and lines creates an entirely different relationship:

The wall is steady
while she falls away:
   first the hands lost
arms dissolving feet gone
the legs dis-jointed
   body cracking down
     the center like a fault
      she falls inside
               slides down like
dust like kitchen dirt
           slips off
   the dustpan into
          noplace
   a place where
nothing happens,
nothing ever happened.

The way the words are arranged communicates the experience of the child's detachment, alienation, and sense of shock, whereas the same words in prose merely describe it.

Because it communicates an extraordinarily compressed moment of thought, feeling, or experience, poetry relies on figurative language, connotation, imagery, sound, and **rhythm.** Poetry evokes emotional associations through images whose importance is underscored by a rhythmic beat or pulse. Patterns of sounds and images emphasize and underscore distinct thoughts and emotions, appealing simultaneously to the heart, mind, and imagination. The rhythmic beat provides the sensuous element coupled with imagery that appeals to the senses and touches the heart. At the same time, the imagination is stimulated through unexpected combinations and perceptions and figurative language (similes, metaphors, **personification**) that allow the reader to see things in new ways. Because these effects work simultaneously, the experience of a poem is concentrated and intense.

Like fiction, poems may have a narrator (called a **speaker**), a particular point of view, and a distinctive tone and **style.**

Learning to enjoy what poetry has to offer requires the reader to pay close attention to specific linguistic details of sound and rhythm, **rhyme** and **meter, assonance** and **consonance, alliteration,** connotations of words, and the sensations, feelings, memories, and associations that these words evoke. After reading a poem, preferably aloud, try to determine who the speaker is. What situation does the poem describe? How might the title provide insight into the speaker's predicament? What attitude does the poet project toward the events described in the poem? Observe the language used by the speaker. What emotional state of mind is depicted? You might look for recurrent references to a particular subject and see whether these references illuminate some psychological truth.

Although it has a public use, poetry mainly unfolds private joys, tragedies, and challenges common to all people, such as the power of friendship, value of self-discovery, bondage of outworn traditions, delight in nature's beauty, devastation of war, achievement of self-respect, and despair over failed dreams. The universal elements in poetry bridge gaps in time and space and tie people together in expressing emotions shared by all people in different times, places, and cultures.

READING DRAMA

Drama, unlike fiction and poetry, is meant to be performed on a stage. The **script** of a play includes **dialogue** (conversation between two or more characters)—or a **monologue** (lines spoken by a single character to the audience)—and the playwright's stage directions.

Although the dramatist makes use of plot, characters, setting, and language, the nature of drama limits the playwright to presenting the events from an objective point of view. There are other important differences between short stories, novels, and drama as well. The dramatist must restrict the action in the play to what can be shown on the stage in two or three hours. Since plays must hold the attention of an audience, playwrights prefer obvious rather than subtle conflicts, clearly defined sequences of action, and fast-paced **exposition** that is not weighed down by long descriptive or narrative passages. Everything in drama has to be shown directly, concretely, through vivid images of human behavior.

The **structure** of most plays begins with an exposition or introduction that introduces the characters, shows their relationship to one another, and provides the background information necessary for the audience or reader to understand the main conflict of the play. The essence of drama is **conflict.** Conflict is produced when an individual pursuing an objective meets with resistance either from another person, from society, from nature, or from an internal aspect of that individual's own personality. In the most effective plays, the audience can see the central conflict through the eyes of each character in the play. As the play proceeds, complications make the problem more difficult to solve and increase suspense as to whether the **protagonist,** or main character, or the opposing force (referred to as the **antagonist**) will triumph. In the **climax** of the play, the conflict reaches the height of emotional intensity, and one side achieves a decisive advantage over the other. This **crisis** is often the moment of truth, when characters see themselves and the situation clearly for the first time. The end of the play, or conclusion, explores the implications of the nature of the truth that has been realized and what the consequences will be.

Reading the script of a play is a very different kind of experience from seeing it performed on the stage. From a script containing dialogue and brief descriptions, you must visualize what the characters look like and sound like and imagine how they relate to one another. For example, try to imagine the following scene from *Trifles* by Susan Glaspell (Ch. 8). It dramatizes the beginning of an investigation of the murder of Mr. John Wright under circumstances that seem to point to his wife.

COUNTY ATTORNEY.   And what did Mrs. Wright do when she knew that you had gone for the coroner?

HALE.   She moved from that chair to this one over here (*Pointing to a small chair in the corner.*) and just sat there with her hands held together and looking down. I got a feeling that I ought to make some conversation, so I said I had come in to see if John wanted to put in a telephone, and at that she started to laugh, and then she stopped and looked at me— scared. (*The County Attorney, who has had his notebook out, makes a note.*) I dunno, maybe it wasn't scared. I wouldn't like to say it was. Soon Harry got back, and then Dr. Lloyd came, and you, Mr. Peters, and so I guess that's all I know that you don't.

COUNTY ATTORNEY.   (*Looking around.*) I guess we'll go upstairs first— and then out to the barn and around there. (*To the Sheriff.*) You're convinced that there was nothing important here—nothing that would point to any motive.

SHERIFF.   Nothing here but kitchen things.

How do you stage this **scene** in your mind? What do the County Attorney, a neighboring farmer (Mr. Hale), and the Sheriff look like? What are they wearing? Keep in mind that Hale is a farmer and might be dressed in overalls while the County Attorney might be in a suit and the Sheriff in a uniform. What do their voices sound like? How do you imagine the interior of the farmhouse where this conversation takes place? What emotions are reflected in the faces of each at various points in the scene? In all of these and countless other details, the reader must play a vital role in bringing the scene to life by making the kinds of decisions that would be delegated to the director, the set designer, the costume designer, and the actors in a stage production.

LITERARY WORKS IN CONTEXT

Since no short story, poem, drama, or essay is written in a vacuum, a particularly useful way of studying works of **literature** entails discovering the extent to which a work reflects or incorporates the historical, cultural, literary, and personal contexts in which it was written. Although works vary in what they require readers to know already, in most cases knowing more about the **context** in which the work was written will enhance the reader's understanding and enjoyment. For this reason, the information contained in the biographical sketches that precede each selection can be quite useful.

Investigating the psychological or **biographical context** in which the work was written assumes that the facts of an author's life are particularly relevant to a full understanding of the work. For example, the predicament confronting the speaker in Linda Pastan's poem "Ethics" (Ch. 11) articulates a problem the poet confronted in her own life. Similarly, we can assume that Elizabeth Barrett Browning's poem "How Do I Love Thee?" (Ch. 1) grew out of the author's own experiences.

Despite the presumed relevance of an author's life, especially if the work seems highly autobiographical, we should remember that literature does not simply report events; it imaginatively re-creates experience.

The information that precedes each selection can be useful in a number of ways. For example, the reader can better understand a single story, poem, or play by comparing how an author has treated similar subjects and concerns in other works. Speeches, interviews, lectures, and essays by authors often provide important insights into the contexts in which a literary work was created. For example, Kurt Vonnegut's humanistic perspective in his essay "How to Write with Style" (Ch. 10) is also apparent in his short work of fiction "Harrison Bergeron" (Ch. 9).

Placing individual works within the author's total repertoire is another way of studying works in their context. You can compare different works by the same author or compare different stages in the composition of the same work by studying subsequent revisions in different published versions of a story, poem, or play. Authors often address themselves to the important political and social issues of their time. For example, Bruce Springsteen's song "Streets of Philadelphia" (Ch. 5) can be understood as a protest against society's treatment of those with AIDS in its poignant depiction of the consequences in the lives of those afflicted with this disease.

In studying the **social context** of a work, ask yourself what dominant social values the work dramatizes, and try to determine whether the author approves or disapproves of particular social values by the way in which the characters are portrayed. Or you might analyze how the author describes or draws upon the manners, mores, customs, rituals, or codes of conduct of a specific society at a particular time, as does Kate Chopin in "Désirée's Baby" (Ch. 5), a story that dramatizes the human consequences of racism in the South at the turn of the nineteenth century.

Studying the **historical context** in which a work is written means identifying how features of the work reveal important historical, political, economic, social, intellectual, or religious currents and problems of the time. Think how useful it would be, for example, to know what issues were at stake in Cyprus in the 1950s and how they are reflected in Panos Ioannides's story "Gregory" (Ch. 8).

In an analysis of any work, the title, names of characters, references to places and events, or topical **allusions** may provide important clues to the work's original sources. For example, has the writer chosen to interweave historical incidents and figures with characters and events of his or her own creation and, if so, to what effect? In any case, simply knowing more about the circumstances under which a work was written will add to your enjoyment and give you a broader understanding of the essay, short story, poem, or play.

READING AND ANALYZING VISUAL TEXTS

A prominent feature of this anthology is that visual images accompany some of the readings. They are quite similar to those you see every day, often without really noticing them. They can include items as diverse as pop-up ads on the Internet, book covers, photos in travel brochures, reproductions of works of art, still life photography, architectural layouts, greeting cards, postcards, editorial cartoons and caricatures, catalogue photos of products, magazine covers, ads for nonprofit organizations, spreads in fashion magazines, menu photos in restaurants, postage stamps, billboards, announcements on park benches and bus shelters, displays of childrens' drawings in banks and supermarkets, personal snapshots, photos that accompany articles in newspapers, bumper stickers, concert programs and playbills, CD covers, film posters, matchbook covers, designer logos, and, of course, images in textbooks like this one.

In addition to these purely visual images, we are innundated by images (on television, in films, and on Web pages) whose effectiveness is enhanced by sound and movement. Fortunately, many of the same considerations that help us analyze a written text can also serve us in analyzing the rhetoric of visual texts.

For every visual image, the first question to ask is, who is the likely *audience?* The general public? Or some specialized segment of the general population, such as children, teenagers, senior citizens, parents, young professionals, baby boomers, men, women, or particular ethnic or racial groups? What might this intended audience be expected to know, believe, or feel about this particular image? For example, if you compare the ads on different kinds of television shows—soap operas, late-night talk shows, Monday night football, Saturday morning cartoons, cooking shows—you will observe different kinds of products being advertised and, correspondingly, different marketing appeals targeted for specific audiences.

The next thing to determine is the *purpose* for which the visual image was created. As with written texts, images may explain or inform, persuade, or entertain. Unlike the case in written texts, however, one of these usually predominates. For example, news photographs are primarily intended to inform an audience by showing events and persons. Ads obviously are intended to persuade while most films and television shows are intended to entertain.

We can look at an image to see how it illustrates a *subject* or topic. Looked at in this way, the image serves the same function as clear-cut examples do in a written text. They clarify, illustrate, or support the main idea. For example, does a CD cover show a picture of the performer(s), or does it show an image that evokes a feeling or expresses a theme? Does an ad show a product in a literal way, or does it use images of celebrities, supermodels, or prominent athletes to promote the product's mystique? Or is the ad intended to offset criticism (as with oil or chemical companies) by highlighting the company's efforts to protect the environment?

In general, visual texts are much more closely tied to specific *occasions* than are written texts. For example, does a cartoon strip reflect a current issue? Is a billboard or bumper sticker part of a political campaign? Does an ad introduce a new product or take advantage of a current trend? Is a public sculpture intended to commemorate a famous person or notable event?

Last, what does the image suggest about the *artist or creator* who designed the image for a given audience, purpose, and occasion? This is analogous to analyzing a written text where the author is known, or at least is knowable.

ELEMENTS OF DESIGN

We analyze written texts in terms of rhetorical techniques. So, too, in understanding visual texts we can analyze the formal elements of design (balance,

proportion, movement, contrast, and unity) according to basic principles that determine how we "read" an image in both a literal and figurative sense.

Our feeling that a design is *balanced* is determined by how symmetrical or asymmetrical the image is; if the top and bottom or right and left sides are of equal proportion or mirror each other, the effect is one of stability or tension. For example, see the picture of a Tug of War team; its right and left sides mirror each other. The effect is formal and static (and aptly communicates the equally matched teams competing against each other).

By contrast, an asymmetrical design will suggest informality and dynamic movement, as does the publicity photo with Beyoncé.

Next, the relative size of elements in a design will create a sense of *proportion* and determine what we notice first, second, and so on. By adjusting these elements, the designer can suggest an implicit agenda as to what is most important and least important.

We are accustomed to reading a page of text, and our sense of *movement* is created by the fact that we read from left to right and from top to bottom. However, the size and arrangement of elements in a visual text can make us scan differently. Horizontal and vertical lines in a two-dimensional image will suggest stability and lack of movement, whereas diagonal or angular lines imply movement and energy. For example, Beyoncé's photo appears to catch her in a dynamic gesture that emphasizes her energy as both singer and dancer, whereas a static pose would have simply shown her as a singer.

Visual images can also suggest an agenda through *contrast* of size, shape, and color and by placing the subject in sharp focus in the foreground.

New York's Z100 Jingle Ball Concert 2004-Performance
R&B group "Destiny's Child" (L-R) Kelly Rowland, Beyoncé Knowles, and Michelle Williams perform during Z100's Jingle Ball 2004 concert at Madison Square Garden, in New York City.

When an image is effective, all the preceding elements (balance, proportion, movement, and contrast) work together to produce a feeling of *unity*, a sense that the image is complete in and of itself. Most ads are designed to function this way.

READING IMAGES AS CULTURAL SIGNS

Beyond these rhetorical elements (audience, purpose, topic, occasion, and designer or artist) and the principles of design that create moods and communicate messages, visual texts can also be **read** as signs for what they reveal about the surrounding **culture**. Cultural **signs** can include artifacts, objects, events, images, products, gestures, sounds, or indeed almost anything that when analyzed reveals something meaningful about a culture, its

assumptions, values, beliefs, and struggles. The process of "decoding" these underlying meanings requires us to move from a literal analysis of the design principles in art reproductions, photographs, advertisements, and cartoons in order to discover the explicit and implicit messages conveyed and to think critically about the agendas of those who wish to influence our behavior.

Semiotics

The study of images for what they suggest about our culture puts us in a situation similar to that of anthropologists who discover and try to decipher the meaning of artifacts. Just as anthropologists have to form hypotheses about the context within which these objects and artifacts have meaning, so practitioners of **semiotics** (the study of signs) always try to recontextualize the meaning of any single sign or image by putting it in a broader cultural context. We do this by identifying the current themes, and issues of the moment that are reflected in the image (or visual text) and by becoming aware of the underlying system in which the sign functions.

Analyzing Images

Just how this works can be seen by analyzing some rather interesting spoofs of ads posted on the Adbusters web site. The ad containing the question "Why Milk?" plays off against the popular "Got Milk" series of ads in which famous celebrities and athletes appear with milk mustaches to prove that drinking milk is chic, hip, and cool.

The design of the page is effective and features a photograph of an ordinary person who certainly is not a celebrity or star athlete. As we scan the page, we read the small text at the bottom and learn that the milk is not quite the wholesome beverage the other series of ads would have you believe. The text suggests a stark choice of drinking an unhealthy beverage produced by cows that have been treated with hormones and antibiotics or a soy drink that is natural and pure. The user's stance with her elbow extended and her hand on her hip projects a quiet confidence and sense of satisfaction. Her functional eyesglasses, unglamorous hairstyle, no-nonsense cardigan sweater and collared blouse and the just-visible wedding ring all create a down-to-earth person who wants the best for herself and her family.

Another spoof ad created by Adbusters puts us at eye level in front of a foot of someone who has died from alcoholism and wears a toe tag reading D.O.A. (dead on arrival).

The vertical highlighted sole of the foot is meant to remind us of the outline and contours of a brand of vodka bottle that is prominently displayed in a well-known series of ads. The words used in the ad "Absolute on Ice" echo those that might be found in any real ad, but here they have an ironic meaning. The image and the text function together to persuade us that drinking vodka to excess is not hip, cool, and stylish as the original ads would have us believe, but potentially lethal.

As cultural signs, these spoof ads make us reconsider assumptions that real ads would have us believe. They demonstrate our need to critically examine images as another form of text that tell us about ourselves, our culture, and our world.

1

REFLECTIONS ON EXPERIENCE

I am being frank about myself in this book. I tell of my first mistake on page 850.

Henry Kissinger, THE OBSERVER (London)

The authors of the essays in this chapter describe moments that were crucial in their lives. They are motivated by the desire to understand these life experiences and to share them with others. In each case, the writer reconstructs the meaning of important personal events, the full significance of which was not obvious at the time the events occurred. The advantage of these reminiscences is that they offer a means by which the authors can define themselves as individuals, distinct from the images fostered by societal or cultural stereotyping. The qualities of candor, honesty, and self-analysis these narratives display stem from the assumption that one's own life is an appropriate object of scrutiny. For example, essays by Fritz Peters and Douchan Gersi explore moments that proved to be decisive turning points in the authors' lives. Jill Nelson, Ruth Reichl, James Herriot, Dave Barry, and George Orwell recover pivotal memories that illuminate the directions their lives have taken. An essay by Beryl Markham provides an engaging and informative reflection on an experience that draws us into the private world of an aviator.

Stories differ from essays in important ways. A writer of fiction can add to the known facts, expand or compress the sequence of events, build suspense, and even invent characters and create a narrator to tell the story. For example, William Maxwell creates an ironic story about an American couple in France obsessed with finding the same gourmet meal sampled by their friends—and thus reveals the way food can come to embody social aspirations. Andre Dubus explores the lifelong consequences for a young girl of the social pressures to be thin. In both cases, the writers use the imaginative freedom of storytelling to more fully explore the meanings of experiences that seem true to life.

The poems in this chapter are first and foremost personal reminiscences. In them, we can hear the feelings and perceptions that allow us to identify with the speaker's reactions. In her sonnet, Elizabeth Barrett Browning discovers that love in its most idealized form sustains and redeems the world for her. By contrast, Sara Teasdale realizes that being independent and self-sufficient were the values she cherished most. The African-American poet Nikki Giovanni describes the sense of love and security her family provided for her despite their poverty.

As you read works in this chapter and prepare to discuss or write about them, you may wish to use the following questions as guidelines:

- How does the author frame the event that proved to be so important in his or her life?
- What motivates the author in telling his or her story?
- What does the writer believe is the most important aspect of his or her experience?
- Which of these writers changed the way you think about these experiences?
- Which conflict or issues raised by the writer are purely personal and which address important social themes?
- Based on reading any of these works, which of your past experiences would you want to reflect on and write about—would it be in the form of an essay, story, or poem?
- Which of the author's values seem closest to your own?

Nonfiction

GEORGE ORWELL

George Orwell was the pen name taken by Eric Blair (1903–1950), who was born in Bengal, India. Educated on a scholarship at Eton, he served as a British official in the police in Burma (1922–1927), and became disillusioned with the aims and methods of colonialism. He describes his struggle with poverty in his first book Down and Out in Paris and London *(1933), a gripping account of life on the fringe. In 1936, Orwell went to Spain to report on the Civil War and joined the Communist P.O.U.M. militia to fight against the Fascists. His account of this experience, in which he was severely wounded, titled* Homage to Catalonia *(1938), is an unflinching account of the bleak and comic aspects of trench warfare. In* Animal Farm *(1945), he satirized the Russian Revolution and the machinations of the Soviet bureaucracy. In his acclaimed novel,* Nineteen Eighty-Four *(1949), his distrust of totalitarianism emerged as a grim prophecy of a bureaucratic, regimented England of the future whose citizens are constantly watched by "big brother." Five collections of his essays have been published, including* Shooting an Elephant and Other Essays *(1946) where this selection first appeared.*

Before You Read

How do you understand the meaning of the term colonialism?

Shooting an Elephant

In Moulmein, in Lower Burma, I was hated by large numbers of people—the only time in my life that I have been important enough for this to happen to me. I was sub-divisional police officer of the town, and in an aimless, petty kind of way anti-European feeling was very bitter. No one had the guts to raise a riot, but if a European woman went through the bazaars alone somebody would probably spit betel juice over her dress. As a police officer I was an obvious target and was baited whenever it seemed safe to do so. When a nimble Burman tripped me up on the football field and the referee (another Burman) looked the other way, the crowd yelled with hideous laughter. This happened more than once. In the end the sneering yellow faces of young men that met me everywhere, the insults hooted after me when I was at a safe distance, got badly on my nerves. The young Buddhist priests were the worst of all. There were several thousands of them in the town and none of them seemed to have anything to do except stand on street corners and jeer at Europeans.

All this was perplexing and upsetting. For at that time I had already made up my mind that imperialism was an evil thing and the sooner I chucked up my job and got out of it the better. Theoretically—and secretly, of course—I was all for the Burmese and all against their oppressors, the British. As for the job I was doing, I hated it more bitterly than I can perhaps make clear. In a job like that you see the dirty work of Empire at close quarters. The wretched prisoners huddling in the stinking cages of the lock-ups, the grey, cowed faces of the long-term convicts, the scarred buttocks of the men who had been flogged with bamboos—all these oppressed me with an intolerable sense of guilt. But I could get nothing into perspective. I was young and ill-educated and I had had to think out my problems in the utter silence that is imposed on every Englishman in the East. I did not even know that the British Empire is dying, still less did I know that it is a great deal better than the younger empires that are going to supplant it. All I knew was that I was stuck between my hatred of the empire I served and my rage against the evil-spirited little beasts who tried to make my job impossible. With one part of my mind I thought of the British Raj[1] as an unbreakable tyranny, as something clamped down, in *saecula saeculorum,*[2] upon the will of prostrate peoples; with another part I thought that the greatest joy in the world would be to drive a bayonet into a Buddhist

---

[1] The imperial government of British India and Burma.   [2] Forever and ever.

priest's guts. Feelings like these are the normal by-products of imperialism; ask any Anglo-Indian official, if you can catch him off duty.

One day something happened which in a roundabout way was enlightening. It was a tiny incident in itself, but it gave me a better glimpse than I had had before of the real nature of imperialism—the real motives for which despotic governments act. Early one morning the sub-inspector at a police station the other end of the town rang me up on the phone and said that an elephant was ravaging the bazaar. Would I please come and do something about it? I did not know what I could do, but I wanted to see what was happening and I got on to a pony and started out. I took my rifle, an old .44 Winchester and much too small to kill an elephant, but I thought the noise might be useful *in terrorem*. Various Burmans stopped me on the way and told me about the elephant's doings. It was not, of course, a wild elephant, but a tame one which had gone "must."[3] It had been chained up, as tame elephants always are when their attack of "must" is due, but on the previous night it had broken its chain and escaped. Its mahout, the only person who could manage it when it was in that state, had set out in pursuit, but had taken the wrong direction and was now twelve hours' journey away, and in the morning the elephant had suddenly reappeared in the town. The Burmese population had no weapons and were quite helpless against it. It had already destroyed somebody's bamboo hut, killed a cow and raided some fruit-stalls and devoured the stock; also it had met the municipal rubbish van and, when the driver jumped out and took to his heels, had turned the van over and inflicted violences upon it.

The Burmese sub-inspector and some Indian constables were waiting for me in the quarter where the elephant had been seen. It was a very poor quarter, a labyrinth of squalid bamboo huts, thatched with palm-leaf, winding all over a steep hillside. I remember that it was a cloudy, stuffy morning at the beginning of the rains. We began questioning the people as to where the elephant had gone and, as usual, failed to get any definite information. That is invariably the case in the East; a story always sounds clear enough at a distance, but the nearer you get to the scene of events the vaguer it becomes. Some of the people said that the elephant had gone in one direction, some said that he had gone in another, some professed not even to have heard of any elephant. I had almost made up my mind that the whole story was a pack of lies, when we heard yells a little distance away. There was a loud, scandalized cry of "Go away, child! Go away this instant!" and an old woman with a switch in her hand came round the corner of a hut, violently shooing away a crowd of naked children. Some more women followed, clicking their tongues and exclaiming; evidently there was something that the children ought not to have seen. I rounded the hut and saw a man's dead body sprawling in the mud. He was an Indian, a black Dravidian coolie, almost naked, and he

---

[3] Gone into sexual heat.

could not have been dead many minutes. The people said that the elephant had come suddenly upon him round the corner of the hut, caught him with its trunk, put its foot on his back and ground him into the earth. This was the rainy season and the ground was soft, and his face had scored a trench a foot deep and a couple of yards long. He was lying on his belly with arms crucified and head sharply twisted to one side. His face was coated with mud, the eyes wide open, the teeth bared and grinning with an expression of unendurable agony. (Never tell me, by the way, that the dead look peaceful. Most of the corpses I have seen looked devilish.) The friction of the great beast's foot had stripped the skin from his back as neatly as one skins a rabbit. As soon as I saw the dead man I sent an orderly to a friend's house nearby to borrow an elephant rifle. I had already sent back the pony, not wanting it to go mad with fright and throw me if it smelt the elephant.

The orderly came back in a few minutes with a rifle and five cartridges,   5 and meanwhile some Burmans had arrived and told us that the elephant was in the paddy fields below, only a few hundred yards away. As I started forward practically the whole population of the quarter flocked out of the houses and followed me. They had seen the rifle and were all shouting excitedly that I was going to shoot the elephant. They had not shown much interest in the elephant when he was merely ravaging their homes, but it was different now that he was going to be shot. It was a bit of fun to them, as it would be to an English crowd; besides they wanted the meat. It made me vaguely uneasy. I had no intention of shooting the elephant—I had merely sent for the rifle to defend myself if necessary—and it is always unnerving to have a crowd following you. I marched down the hill, looking and feeling a fool, with the rifle over my shoulder and an ever-growing army of people jostling at my heels. At the bottom, when you got away from the huts, there was a metalled road and beyond that a miry waste of paddy fields a thousand yards across, not yet ploughed but soggy from the first rains and dotted with coarse grass. The elephant was standing eight yards from the road, his left side towards us. He took not the slightest notice of the crowd's approach. He was tearing up bunches of grass, beating them against his knees to clean them and stuffing them into his mouth.

I had halted on the road. As soon as I saw the elephant I knew with perfect certainty that I ought not to shoot him. It is a serious matter to shoot a working elephant—it is comparable to destroying a huge and costly piece of machinery—and obviously one ought not to do it if it can possibly be avoided. And at that distance, peacefully eating, the elephant looked no more dangerous than a cow. I thought then and I think now that his attack of "must" was already passing off; in which case he would merely wander harmlessly about until the mahout came back and caught him. Moreover, I did not in the least want to shoot him. I decided that I would watch him for a little while to make sure that he did not turn savage again, and then go home.

But at that moment I glanced round at the crowd that had followed me. It was an immense crowd, two thousand at the least and growing every minute. It blocked the road for a long distance on either side. I looked at the sea of yellow faces above the garish clothes—faces all happy and excited over this bit of fun, all certain that the elephant was going to be shot. They were watching me as they would watch a conjurer about to perform a trick. They did not like me, but with the magical rifle in my hands I was momentarily worth watching. And suddenly I realized that I should have to shoot the elephant after all. The people expected it of me and I had got to do it; I could feel their two thousand wills pressing me forward, irresistibly. And it was at this moment, as I stood there with the rifle in my hands, that I first grasped the hollowness, the futility of the white man's dominion in the East. Here was I, the white man with his gun, standing in front of the unarmed native crowd—seemingly the leading actor of the piece; but in reality I was only an absurd puppet pushed to and fro by the will of those yellow faces behind. I perceived in this moment that when the white man turns tyrant it is his own freedom that he destroys. He becomes a sort of hollow, posing dummy, the conventionalized figure of a sahib. For it is the condition of his rule that he shall spend his life in trying to impress the "natives," and so in every crisis he has got to do what the "natives" expect of him. He wears a mask, and his face grows to fit it. I had got to shoot the elephant. I had committed myself to doing it when I sent for the rifle. A sahib has got to act like a sahib; he has got to appear resolute, to know his own mind and do definite things. To come all that way, rifle in hand, with two thousand people marching at my heels, and then to trail feebly away, having done nothing—no, that was impossible. The crowd would laugh at me. And my whole life, every white man's life in the East, was one long struggle not to be laughed at.

But I did not want to shoot the elephant. I watched him beating his bunch of grass against his knees, with that preoccupied grandmotherly air that elephants have. It seemed to me that it would be murder to shoot him. At that age I was not squeamish about killing animals, but I had never shot an elephant and never wanted to. (Somehow it always seems worse to kill a *large* animal.) Besides, there was the beast's owner to be considered. Alive, the elephant was worth at least a hundred pounds; dead, he would only be worth the value of his tusks, five pounds, possibly. But I had got to act quickly. I turned to some experienced-looking Burmans who had been there when we arrived, and asked them how the elephant had been behaving. They all said the same thing. He took no notice of you if you left him alone, but he might charge if you went too close to him.

It was perfectly clear to me what I ought to do. I ought to walk up to within, say, twenty-five yards of the elephant and test his behavior. If he charged, I could shoot; if he took no notice of me, it would be safe to leave him until the mahout came back. But also I knew that I was going to do no such thing. I was a poor shot with a rifle and the ground was soft mud into which one would sink at every step. If the elephant charged and I missed him, I should have about as much chance as a toad under a steam-roller. But even then I was not thinking particularly of my own skin, only of the watchful yellow faces behind. For at that moment, with the crowd watching me, I was not afraid in the ordinary sense, as I would have been if I had been alone. A white man mustn't be frightened in front of "natives"; and so, in general, he isn't frightened. The sole thought in my mind was that if anything went wrong those two thousand Burmans would see me pursued, caught, trampled on and reduced to a grinning corpse like that Indian up the hill. And if that happened it was quite probable that some of them would laugh. That would never do. There was only one alternative. I shoved the cartridges into the magazine and lay down on the road to get a better aim.

The crowd grew very still, and a deep, low, happy sigh, as of people who   10
see the theatre curtain go up at last, breathed from innumerable throats. They were going to have their bit of fun after all. The rifle was a beautiful German thing with cross-hair sights. I did not then know that in shooting an elephant one would shoot to cut an imaginary bar running from ear-hole to ear-hole. I ought, therefore, as the elephant was sideways on, to have aimed straight at his ear-hole; actually I aimed several inches in front of this, thinking the brain would be further forward.

When I pulled the trigger I did not hear the bang or feel the kick—one never does when a shot goes home—but I heard the devilish roar of glee that went up from the crowd. In that instant, in too short a time, one would have thought, even for the bullet to get there, a mysterious, terrible change had come over the elephant. He neither stirred nor fell, but every line of his body had altered. He looked suddenly stricken, shrunken, immensely old, as though the frightful impact of the bullet had paralysed him without knocking him down. At last, after what seemed a long time—it might have been five seconds, I dare say—he sagged flabbily to his knees. His mouth slobbered. An enormous senility seemed to have settled upon him. One could have imagined him thousands of years old. I fired again into the same spot. At the second shot he did not collapse but climbed with desperate slowness to his feet and stood weakly upright, with legs sagging and head drooping. I fired a third time. That was the shot that did for him. You could see the agony of it jolt his whole body and knock the last remnant of strength from his legs. But in falling he seemed for a moment to rise, for as his hind legs collapsed beneath him he seemed to tower upward like a huge rock toppling, his trunk reaching skywards like a tree. He trumpeted, for the first and only time. And then down he came, his belly towards me, with a crash that seemed to shake the ground even where I lay.

I got up. The Burmans were already racing past me across the mud. It was obvious that the elephant would never rise again, but he was not dead. He was breathing very rhythmically with long rattling gasps, his great mound of a side painfully rising and falling. His mouth was wide open—I could see far down into caverns of pale pink throat. I waited a long time for him to die, but his breathing did not weaken. Finally I fired my two remaining shots into the spot where I thought his heart must be. The thick blood welled out of him like red velvet, but still he did not die. His body did not even jerk when the shots hit him, the tortured breathing continued without a pause. He was dying, very slowly and in great agony, but in some world remote from me where not even a bullet could damage him further. I felt that I had got to put an end to that dreadful noise. It seemed dreadful to see the great beast lying there, powerless to move and yet powerless to die, and not even to be able to finish him. I sent back for my small rifle and poured shot after shot into his heart and down his throat. They seemed to make no impression. The tortured gasps continued as steadily as the ticking of a clock.

In the end I could not stand it any longer and went away, I heard later that it took him half an hour to die. Burmans were bringing dahs[4] and baskets even before I left, and I was told they had stripped his body almost to the bones by the afternoon.

Afterwards, of course, there were endless discussions about the shooting of the elephant. The owner was furious, but he was only an Indian and could do nothing. Besides, legally I had done the right thing, for a mad elephant has to be killed, like a mad dog, if its owner fails to control it. Among the Europeans opinion was divided. The older men said I was right, the younger men said it was a damn shame to shoot an elephant for killing a coolie, because an elephant was worth more than any damn Coringhee coolie. And afterwards I was very glad that the coolie had been killed; it put me legally in the right and it gave me a sufficient pretext for shooting the elephant. I often wondered whether any of the others grasped that I had done it solely to avoid looking a fool.

Questions for Discussion and Writing

1. In what untenable position does Orwell find himself as a British official in Burma? How does he react to the task he is required to perform?
2. What different kinds of motivations—personal, political, circumstantial—prompted Orwell to shoot the elephant? In your view, which of these played the most decisive role?
3. How does Orwell's analysis of his motives and reactions illustrate his thesis that "when the white man turns tyrant it is his own freedom that he destroys"?
4. **Rhetorical inquiry:** How does Orwell frame his account so that his readers can understand why he became so disillusioned with the aims and methods of colonialism?

RUTH REICHL

Ruth Reichl, known for her delightful and informative restaurant reviews, is the editor-in-chief of Gourmet *magazine. She was the food critic for the* New York

---

[4] Butcher knives.

Times, *where her job required her to go undercover, an experience she describes in the following selection "Betty," the name of one of several personas she assumed, from her memoir* Garlic and Sapphires: The Secret Life of a Critic in Disguise *(2005). Her earlier memoirs include* Tender at the Bone: Growing Up at the Table *(1998) and* Comfort Me with Apples: More Adventures at the Table *(2001). Most recently, she has edited* History in a Glass: Sixty Years of Wine Writing from Gourmet *(2006).*

Before You Read

In a fancy restaurant, how does the way you dress translate into the kind of service you receive?

Betty

Michael and Nicky watched me dress.

"I think she looks like a very nice person," said Nicky loyally. "She looks like Matt's grandma."

"See," I said, turning to Michael, "you could come along and call me Mom."

"Thanks anyway," he said.

"What's your name?" asked Nicky.   5

"Betty," I said. "Betty Jones."

"How old are you?" he asked.

"Sixty-eight."

"You look older," he replied.

"I've had a hard life," I said.   10

"Don't you have any children?" he asked. Like all beloved children, he felt very sorry for childless grown-ups.

"No," I said, "I'm a spinster."

"Oh, too bad." And then, "What's a spinster?"

"A woman who's never been married."

"Poor you," he said. "No children. No husband. You must be lonely."   15

"Yes," I said.

"Are you poor too?"

"Pretty poor," I said. "At least not rich. Tonight Claudia is taking me out to dinner."

"Did you warn her?" asked Michael. "Does she know she has to pay the bill?"

"Yes," I said. "I told her to bring a credit card and I'd pay her back.   20
And I told her whom to expect. She's never met Chloe or Brenda, and I think she's sort of eager to see who I've managed to concoct without her help."

"Good luck," he said.

"'Night Mom," said Nicky. He examined Betty for a moment and added, "I'm glad you have someone to be nice to you."

I put on the shapeless black coat I had bought for Betty and threw a shawl over the gray wig. I pulled on sensible black wool gloves and picked up the square black pocketbook. Glancing in the mirror, I realized that only a few inches of the real me were visible, just below the glasses.

Still, I was not prepared for Gene's reaction. When the elevator door swung open, he didn't smile or say hello. He just stood there as I got on, waiting to close the door, and then allowed the car to descend. As we fell toward the ground he stared straight ahead, and when I exited, the "Good evening" he murmured was a mechanical response to my "Thank you." I couldn't help feeling that if I had remained silent, he would not have acknowledged me at all.

As I walked up Riverside Drive, not one of the many people walking dogs, wheeling strollers, or carrying briefcases glanced my way. No doorman tipped his hat as I went by. By the time I got to the corner, I felt as insubstantial as the wind; when people looked my way they saw only the buildings at my back. When I waved my hand the taxis hurtled past as if I were not there. I finally resorted to stepping into the middle of the street.

"Where to?" asked the driver, who had stopped to avoid hitting me.

"Tavern on the Green, please," I said, practicing my softest voice.

"Speak up," he said, and when I repeated myself he stepped on the gas so hard I was thrown back and pinned against the seat. The cabbie stared straight ahead, racing madly through the avenues as if he were piloting a bumper car in a small-town carnival ride. He shot through every light just as it turned, passed to the right of cars, swerved through intersections cutting off pedestrians. "Slow down!" I pleaded. In answer he stepped on the gas, narrowly averting a baby carriage that was nosing into a crosswalk.

"Please!" I shouted, but he did not acknowledge my alarm. Perhaps it was how he always drove, but it made me feel like an old boot, a piece of junk that he was desperate to deposit at its destination.

When we swerved into the driveway and shuddered to a halt in front of Tavern on the Green, I was very grateful. I pulled the door open and staggered onto the pavement. I was so shaken that my hands trembled as I counted out the money and pushed it through the window, feeling every minute as old as I looked.

Claudia was standing beneath the awning, her diminutive body dwarfed by a handsome hawk-faced woman with short blond hair who was clad entirely in cashmere and furs. As each taxi pulled up, Claudia studied its occupants. She stared at me for a moment, and I should have felt triumphant when her gaze moved on. Perversely I felt only sadness.

I limped morosely up to tap her on the arm; my shoes were too tight and my feet hurt. She turned toward me, considered my face, and asked, "Betty?"

As I nodded and bent to kiss her, she said, "I want you to meet my friend Helen. But come inside; it is frigid out here. You must be cold too." She took my arm and we walked into the fantasyland that is Tavern on the Green. Looking up at the lights twinkling in the foyer, I remembered how thrilled Nicky had once been by the tacky theatricality of the place.

"Oh," I whispered, trying for the reverent tone of a tourist walking into Chartres cathedral for the first time, "isn't this lovely?" My voice was filled with wonder as I scrutinized the overdone room. "It looks just like Christmas."

"Lovely," said the tall friend, casting a suspicious glance at Claudia, as if asking what on earth she meant by foisting such a peculiar person upon her. An elegant specimen, she made no attempt to disguise her disdain for this tawdry room—or for me for liking it. "It's a museum of things that should never have been made," she said fiercely, plowing through the crowd to initiate the process of checking us in. All around us heads swiveled to watch her progress, and I saw that she was an attention magnet. Had Claudia brought her along as a decoy?

"My compliments," Claudia whispered when she was gone. "You look quite remarkable."

"I know," I said in my most pathetic voice. "At the moment I am not feeling at all like myself. Oh, not in the least." And I threw back my head and opened my mouth, gazing up at the dangling ornaments with what I hoped looked like innocent awe.

The dining room was heaving with candles, balloons, plants, paintings, and chandeliers, but even their combined forces were not enough to combat the chill of a big glass edifice on a windy winter day. To my dismay the young hostess insisted that we check our coats and then led us inexorably through the urban greenhouse to a table right against a window. "Prime seating!" She smiled.

When I asked, "Do you think we might be able to sit somewhere a little warmer?" she did not trouble herself with an answer. Turning on her heel she left us to shiver on our narrow chairs.

"You have to be more forceful!" cried Helen. "You made it sound as if she'd be doing us a favor to give us another table. We're paying for this meal; it's her *job* to make us happy." The intensity of Helen's irritation made me realize that the Betty Joneses of the world are a particular trial to elegant older people. "A cup of tea," she announced now, waving her hand imperiously at the nearest waiter, "I must have a cup of tea." He ignored her.

Undaunted, Helen lifted her beringed fingers to the next passing person, who happened to be a busboy. He ignored her as well. At that Helen simply stood up and marched toward a waiter unwise enough to be standing idly, but visibly, nearby. He looked unhappy, but he moved off in the direction of the kitchen.

"Helen," Claudia told me, "is quite an expert on tea." She thought for a moment and added, "Actually, I think she considers herself an expert on everything."

"How do you know her?" I asked.

"She was an aspiring actress," Claudia replied, "who came to me for lessons. As an actress she was quite hopeless, but over the years I have found her to be a rather entertaining friend. Although"—she cast a dubious eye over me—"had I known that this was the role you had planned, I doubt that

I would have chosen her as our dinner companion. The wealthy, I find, can be quite obtuse and they often permit themselves to behave very badly."

"Our tea," said Helen, strolling back and seating herself with the smile   45
of a Cheshire cat, "will be here directly."

The tea arrived but there was nothing in its wake. "Have you ever seen such terrible service?" cried Claudia. "You could be wearing a sign that said, 'I am the restaurant critic of the *New York Times*,' and nobody here would give a fig."

"Oh, I doubt that," said Helen knowingly. "If that Ruth Reichl were here, I imagine things would be quite different."

"Do you?" asked Claudia. I peered at her face, which was alive with mischief, and realized that she had not let her friend in on my secret. All at once I began to understand why Helen was here. And in that moment I began to enjoy myself.

When the captain finally came to take our order, I gave it to him in my most timid tones. "I can't hear you," he shouted. "Speak up."

"It's so loud in here!" I repeated. To be honest, I could hardly hear   50
myself.

"Please, lady," said the captain, "talk louder. I'm not deaf, but you talk so soft."

"It's too loud!" I said again.

"You say you want the salad?" he asked.

"No," I said, raising my voice a bit, "the dumplings."

"Caesar, or beet and walnut?" he asked.   55

Helen watched in exasperation and then extracted a sterling silver pen from her pocketbook. "I," she announced to the waiter, "will write the order down for you." She glared at me.

"Thanks, lady," he said gratefully. "Makes my job easier." He pocketed the paper and moved off.

All around us people were videotaping each other, celebrating anniversaries and birthdays, so enchanted with Warner LeRoy's antic room that they didn't seem to mind the tardiness of the food.

At our table things were considerably less cheerful. The service was so slow that after a great deal of small talk and five pots of tea, I felt compelled to apologize. "I always seem to get bad service," I told Helen. "I don't know why."

"Well, I do," she snapped. "You look like an old lady. And waiters con-   60
sider old ladies their natural enemies. They think that they will complain constantly, order the cheapest dishes on the menu, and leave a six percent tip. I have found that it is essential to appear prosperous when going out to eat."

"I didn't know that," I said demurely. I was about to add that appearing prosperous was no problem for her, but fortunately the waiter chose that moment to arrive and ask, "Who gets the crab cakes?"

Helen took her irritation out on him. "Oh, do your job!" she snapped.

He looked at the order in his hand and plunked the crab ungraciously at her place.

"Those look good," I said. "And my dumplings are delicious. Would you like to try them?"

"I do not care for Chinese food," she said, waving it away.

"Taste it," I insisted, thrusting the plate under her nose. "It's not Chinese. It just looks it."

"No, thank you," she said firmly, pushing my arm away. I got the distinct feeling that she was reluctant to let her lips touch anything that had touched mine.

I took a bite of the dumpling and a robustly beefy flavor filled my mouth, quickly followed by the insistent prickle of horseradish. The two flavors grew stronger as I ate and before long the heat and richness were radiating down my throat and through my body.

"The crab cake *is* excellent," Helen conceded. And then, even more reluctantly, she added, "Would you like to try one?"

"Yes, please," I replied. It was a fine crab cake—generous lumps of fresh meat bound together with a bit of egg and a lot of faith.

"Do taste mine, too," said Claudia, cutting off a chunk of foie gras and topping it with a slice of poached pear. "So lovely. But is this goose or duck liver?"

"Duck," I replied, unthinking.

"How can you tell?" she asked.

"The taste," I said, "and the color. Goose liver is richer and smoother. The livers are bigger, which makes them easier to devein, and they have about thirty percent more fat, which gives them a smoother character. They're paler too."

Helen looked at me with grudging respect. "You're a cook?" she asked.

"Not exactly," I said. "You know there's a difference between French and domestic foie gras as well. I'm pretty sure this is domestic."

A series of emotions flitted across her face, and I saw that she was wondering if she might have misjudged me. For a moment I felt a slight softening of her attitude. But then the hostess led a distinguished gentleman with silver hair to a nearby table. He was accompanied by a beautiful young woman, his granddaughter most likely, because when he sat down he did nothing to hide the small appreciative nod he gave Helen. His eyes openly assessed the beige cashmere and good jewelry before moving on to Claudia. He quickly dismissed her, and then his gaze wandered in my direction. Instantly his face changed and he jerked backward, as if he would like to retract the nod. Helen caught that too, and immediately edged her chair away, trying to disown me.

The busboy cleared the table; the waiter brought our main courses. Helen took a bite of her fish and nodded thoughtfully. "I adore Chilean sea bass," she said in a voice meant to carry to the next table, "such a rich and elegant fish."

"Actually," I said, "that's not Chilean sea bass."

"Thank you very much," she replied indignantly, "I am quite aware of what I ordered."

"I know you ordered Chilean sea bass," I insisted, trying to reclaim a little dignity for poor Betty, "but there is no such thing. You are eating Patagonian toothfish."

"I couldn't be," she said.

"You are. I'm sure you won't be surprised to learn that it didn't sell very well under its own name. So they changed it."

"Really?" There was grudging respect in her voice. I thought I'd see if I could keep it. "May I taste those prosciutto-stuffed mashed potatoes?" I asked. She passed me a bite and I tasted, thoughtfully. "Good-quality prosciutto," I said.

"How do you know?" she asked.   85

"I can taste it. Real prosciutto, the kind they make in Parma, has a sweetness and a softness that others lack. Lesser prosciutto has a waxy quality, and it's often over-salted. The color's different too."

"How odd that someone like you should know so much," said Helen, giving me a long slow look.

"Yes," I said sweetly, "isn't it?" And I turned back to my food. Meanwhile Helen and the man at the next table kept exchanging glances, and Claudia sat there like a director admiring the scene she had created.

"Dessert, ladies?" asked the waiter.

"Oh, no," said Helen, "I never eat sweets." She glanced briefly at the   90
next table. The silver-haired man smiled. Claudia ordered gingerbread, and I pointed at a waiter walking cautiously across the room.

"Young man," I said, pointing at the drink the waiter was carrying with such care. It looked like a captive rainbow. "What is that beautiful concoction?"

"A pousse café, madam," he replied.

"A who?" I asked.

"It's a kind of cocktail."

"All those layers? How do they make it?"   95

"Carefully," he said, "very carefully. You see, different liqueurs weigh different amounts. So if you start with the heaviest, and then keep pouring a lighter liqueur on top, you can keep them from mixing. At least, a good bartender can."

"Isn't it difficult?" I asked.

"Oh yes, madam," he said, "very."

"What if you trip while you're carrying it?"

"The bartender kills you," he said solemnly. "And the court rules it jus-   100
tifiable homicide." This was clearly a joke he had made before.

"I'll have one," I decided.

As he walked away I murmured, "Grenadine, crème de cacao, maraschino, curaçao, crème de menthe, parfait amour, cognac."

"What's that?" asked Helen.

"The order of a pousse café. Red on the bottom, followed by brown, white, orange, green, violet, and finally the cognac on the top. They have to be made very, very slowly. Bartenders usually pour them over the back of a spoon to spread out the liquid. They're difficult to make correctly."

"I thought you didn't know what it was," she said, giving me another 105
long look.

"I was just testing him." I peeked at Claudia and saw that she was
enjoying herself hugely.

When the drink came, I held it out to Helen. "Would you care to taste it?"

"Oh no," she said. The silver-haired man was looking at her again and
she smiled—a little coyly I thought—and said, "Well, maybe just a sip."

She grimaced—the thing truly was horrid—and then there was a small
awkward silence. Helen was looking at me, clearly weighing whether or not
to say what was on her mind. Finally she decided. "May I speak frankly?"

"Certainly," I said.   110

"I don't know what to make of you, but you seem like a good enough
person. Why don't you take better care of yourself? A good haircut—and
perhaps a silver rinse—would do wonders. I have a facialist who could
improve your skin tone. And I could point you to a shop where a few chic
outfits would not cost much money. I just can't understand why anyone
would go through life looking so . . . pitiful." She looked at my face and
added, "I hope I have not offended you?"

"Not at all," I said. "That's very kind. I'd be very grateful for your
help." Claudia made a little choking sound.

"What, may I ask, is so funny?" asked Helen.

"Later, my darling," gasped Claudia, attempting to control her mirth.
"I will tell you later."

Helen looked miffed and Claudia abruptly changed the subject. "Have I 115
told you," she asked, "that I am moving to Los Angeles for a few months?"

"You didn't tell me that!" I said, so shocked that I used my own voice.
Helen's eyes narrowed. I lowered it to ask, "Why?"

"One of my old students has been given an excellent role in a big new
film, and he insists that I must come coach him. I thought it might be fun.
And I cannot deny that the notion of leaving New York for the duration of
the winter has enormous appeal."

"I'm going to miss you," I said.

"Don't worry, my darling," she said, patting my hand. "I will come
hurrying back. I could not bear to miss seeing the transformation Helen has
planned. I suspect you'll be an entirely different person. In fact, I'm sure of
it." She tried to catch Helen's eye but Helen was, once again, looking at the
man at the next table. I wondered if anything would come of it.

RESTAURANTS*

Patrick Clark is a terrific chef. Unfortunately, he is only human, and it 120
would take a magician to make food good enough to overcome the service
at Tavern on the Green.

---

* Here is the review Reichl wrote [Eds.].

Consider the meal I had in the spring, soon after Mr. Clark took over the kitchen of America's largest-grossing restaurant. We were seated at 7:30 P.M. By 8:30 we had eaten our way through the entire bread basket, visited the gift shop twice, taken a stroll through the gardens, admired the lanterns and the topiary. We begged for food. When we could find someone to beg. Once I looked across that vast windowed room, past the balloons, flowers and chandeliers, and counted only four service people. They were all studiously avoiding our waving hands.

Finally our first courses came. I relaxed as I tasted a fine shrimp cocktail with a jazzy smoked tomato rémoulade and a parsley-lemon salad. Crab cakes were impressively served with a spicy pumpkin seed sauce. I admired roasted chunks of lobster meat in a spicy red Thai curry sauce. Even plain old Caesar salad was dressed up with sheets of crisped Parmesan. There was just one problem: my asparagus soup was nowhere to be seen.

It took a while to attract someone's attention and point out that I had not been served. Ten minutes later, the soup showed up. No apology, but after the waiter had painstakingly poured it into my bowl, he proudly announced, "Not a drop!"

Then our entrées came so quickly that the appetizer plates were still on the table. "Hold that please," said the waiter, indicating that I was to pick up my soup bowl so he could put my entrée down. Meanwhile, my companions were clearing off the extra plates and stacking them on the floor.

For all that, the food was impressive. Mr. Clark is serving more than 1,500 meals a day, and he has carefully constructed his menu within the limits of quantity cooking. He builds each plate around a sturdy center-piece, starting with food that can take a little abuse and using imaginative accompaniments to perk it up. His grilled pork porterhouse, a robust portion, was served with a glorious mush of potatoes, bacon and cabbage. On the side, standing in for applesauce, was a zesty rhubarb-apple chutney. 125

Grilled swordfish steak was accented with sautéed pea greens and wild mushroom dumplings. He made salmon special by giving it a Moroccan glaze, setting it on a buttery bed of savoy cabbage and a cake of couscous. But he also knows when to leave well enough alone; his rotisserie chicken was sensibly plain, served with haricots verts and potatoes mashed with just a hint of green chilies.

Should we chance dessert? Anticipating another endless wait, we quit while we were ahead. There was, however, one bright point. As one friend noted, "They certainly didn't rush us."

Every restaurant has its off nights, but in my experience they are standard at Tavern on the Green. One recent night, we waited 40 minutes after placing our order before any food arrived. The captain acted as if he were bestowing a favor each time he honored us with his presence, and the waiters hardly deigned to glance our way. A request to take dessert home was met with this response: "We don't do that." But the worst thing was that after being requested to surrender our coats ($1 each), we found ourselves seated next to the window, freezing. We spent a small fortune on tea trying to get warm.

Still, the dinner was delicious. Short-rib-and-horseradish dumplings were a sly take on a Chinese dish. Soups were thick, a little too sweet, but satisfying. Crab cakes were filled with chunks of sweet crabmeat. And foie gras sautéed with pears was completely luxurious. 130

Grilled Chilean sea bass was nicely cooked; it's a very forgiving fish. A fine loin of venison was paired with a puree of squash and cranberry sauce. And a double rack of pork, another huge portion, came with irresistible cheese-filled mashed potatoes and braised red cabbage.

Desserts were good, too. I liked the cheesecake and the crème brûlée. But the dessert that seemed most appropriate to this gaudy, glitzy, enchantingly over-the-top room was the banana split, an exercise in American excess that is almost good enough to make you forget how shabbily you have been treated.

Looking around at that fairyland of lights, I felt a surge of rage. To thousands of visitors, Tavern on the Green is New York. They are so happy to be here that you see them all around the room, videotaping one another as they eat their meals. This is an expensive restaurant; does it really have to be such a blatant example of our famous rudeness?

No, it does not. I discovered that on my last visit when waiters and captains were suddenly hovering attentively over my table. The food came in a flash. It was warm in that inner circle of the Garden Room in more ways than one. Forgive me for thinking that I must have been recognized.

The evening seemed enchanted. I looked out over that splendidly silly space as I ate beautifully arranged poached shrimp in a lime, soy and ginger sauce. Orecchiette were beautifully cooked and tossed with broccoli rabe and sausage. And if the thick fillet of smoked salmon on truffle mashed potatoes seemed more appropriate as an entrée than an appetizer, who's to quibble with generosity? 135

Then there was moist turkey with stuffing, sweet potatoes, brussels sprouts and cranberry sauce: a holiday on a plate. Pork, one of Mr. Clark's best dishes, was as satisfying as it always is.

As I sat there, basking in the attention and enjoying the Christmas decorations, I looked around at the people seated on the edges of the room. I hoped they were having as nice a time as I was. I suspected they were not.

Questions for Discussion and Writing

1. Why was it important for Reichl to be anonymous when dining at Tavern on the Green? How did the persona she created named Betty make this possible?
2. How did the waiter treat "Betty" as compared with the women who accompanied her? What cues did he respond to that might explain this?

Lighted Trees Outside Tavern on the Green
How does this scene convey the glamour of this restaurant?

3. Have you ever gone to the same restaurant dressed differently and received treatment that corresponded to your appearance? Describe your experience.

4. **Rhetorical inquiry:** How does Reichl's review of Tavern on the Green take into account her experience as Betty and when she was recognized?

JILL NELSON

Jill Nelson, born in 1952, is a native New Yorker and a graduate of the City College of New York and Columbia University's School of Journalism. A journalist for fifteen years, she is a frequent contributor to Essence, U.S.A. Weekend, the Village Voice, *and* Ms. *In 1986 she went to work for* The Washington Post's *new Sunday magazine as the only black woman reporter in a bastion of elite journalism, an experience she described in* Volunteer Slavery: My Authentic Negro Experience *(1993). Her latest books are* Straight, No Chaser: How I Became a Grown-Up Black Woman *(1997),* Sexual Healing *(2003), and* Finding Martha's Vineyard *(2005). In "Number One!" she reflects on the importance of her father's influence on her life.*

Before You Read

What message have adults used to boost your self-esteem?

Number One!

That night I dream about my father, but it is really more a memory than a dream.

"Number one! Not two! Number one!" my father intones from the head of the breakfast table. The four of us sit at attention, two on each side of the ten-foot teak expanse, our brown faces rigid. At the foot, my mother looks up at my father, the expression on her face a mixture of pride, anxiety, and, could it be, boredom? I am twelve. It is 1965.

"You kids have got to be, not number two," he roars, his dark face turning darker from the effort to communicate. He holds up his index and middle fingers. "But number—" here, he pauses dramatically, a preacher going for revelation, his four children a rapt congregation, my mother a smitten church sister. "Number one!"

These last words he shouts while lowering his index finger. My father has great, big black hands, long, perfectly shaped fingers with oval nails so vast they seem landscapes all their own. The half moons leading to the cuticle take up most of the nail and seem ever encroaching, threatening to swallow up first his fingertips, then his whole hand. I always wondered if he became a dentist just to mess with people by putting those enormous fingers in their mouths, each day surprising his patients and himself by the delicacy of the work he did.

Years later my father told me that when a woman came to him with an infant she asserted was his, he simply looked at the baby's hands. If they lacked the size, enormous nails, and half-moon cuticles like an ocean eroding the shore of the fingers, he dismissed them.

Early on, what I remember of my father were Sunday morning breakfasts and those hands, index finger coyly lowering, leaving the middle finger standing alone.

When he shouted "Number one!" that finger seemed to grow, thicken and harden, thrust up and at us, a phallic symbol to spur us, my sister Lynn, fifteen, brothers Stanley and Ralph, thirteen and nine, on to greatness, to number oneness. My father's rich, heavy voice rolled down the length of the table, breaking and washing over our four trembling bodies.

When I wake up I am trembling again, but it's because the air conditioner, a luxury in New York but a necessity in D.C., is set too high. I turn it down, check on Misu,[1] light a cigarette, and think about the dream.

It wasn't until my parents had separated and Sunday breakfasts were no more that I faced the fact that my father's symbol for number one was the world's sign language for "fuck you." I know my father knew this, but I still haven't figured out what he meant by it. Were we to become number one and go out and fuck the world? If we didn't, would life fuck us? Was he intentionally sending his children a mixed message? If so, what was he trying to say?

---

[1] *Misu:* Nelson's daughter.

I never went to church with my family. While other black middle-class   10
families journeyed to Baptist church on Sundays, both to thank the Lord for
their prosperity and donate a few dollars to the less fortunate brethren they'd
left behind, we had what was reverentially known as "Sunday breakfast."
That was our church.

In the dining room of the eleven-room apartment we lived in, the only
black family in a building my father had threatened to file a discrimination
suit to get into, my father delivered the gospel according to him. The recurring
theme was the necessity that each of us be "number one," but my father
preached about whatever was on his mind: current events, great black heroes,
lousy black sell-outs, our responsibility as privileged children, his personal
family history.

His requirements were the same as those at church: that we be on time,
not fidget, hear and heed the gospel, and give generously. But Daddy's church
boasted no collection plate; dropping a few nickels into a bowl would have
been too easy. Instead, my father asked that we absorb his lessons and become
what he wanted us to be, number one. He never told us what that meant or
how to get there. It was years before I was able to forgive my father for not
being more specific. It was even longer before I understood and accepted that
he couldn't be.

Like most preachers, my father was stronger on imagery, oratory, and
instilling fear than he was on process. I came away from fifteen years of Sunday
breakfasts knowing that to be number two was not enough, and having no idea
what number one was or how to become it, only that it was better.

When I was a kid, I just listened, kept a sober face, and tried to understand what was going on. Thanks to my father, my older sister Lynn and
I, usually at odds, found spiritual communion. The family dishwashers, our
spirits met wordlessly as my father talked. We shared each other's anguish
as we watched egg yolk harden on plates, sausage fat congeal, chicken livers
separate silently from gravy.

We all had our favorite sermons. Mine was the "Rockefeller wouldn't   15
let his dog shit in our dining room" sermon.

"You think we're doing well?" my father would begin, looking into
each of our four faces. We knew better than to venture a response. For my
father, even now, conversations are lectures. Please save your applause—and
questions—until the end.

"And we are," he'd answer his own query. "We live on West End Avenue,
I'm a professional, your mother doesn't have to work, you all go to private
school, we go to Martha's Vineyard in the summer. But what we have, we
have because 100,000 other black people haven't made it. Have nothing! Live
like dogs!"

My father has a wonderfully expressive voice. When he said dogs, you
could almost hear them whimpering. In my head, I saw an uncountable
mass of black faces attached to the bodies of mutts, scrambling to elevate
themselves to a better life. For some reason, they were always on 125th

Street, under the Apollo Theatre marquee. Years later, when I got political and decided to be the number-one black nationalist, I was thrilled by the notion that my father might have been inspired by Claude McKay's[2] poem that begins, "If we must die, let it not be like dogs."

"There is a quota system in this country for black folks, and your mother and me were allowed to make it," my father went on. It was hard to imagine anyone allowing my six-foot-three, suave, smart, take-no-shit father to do anything. Maybe his use of the word was a rhetorical device.

"Look around you," he continued. With the long arm that supported   20
his heavy hand he indicated the dining room. I looked around. At the eight-foot china cabinet gleaming from the weekly oiling administered by Margie, our housekeeper, filled to bursting with my maternal grandmother's china and silver. At the lush green carpeting, the sideboard that on holidays sagged from the weight of cakes, pies, and cookies, at the paintings on the walls. We were living kind of good, I thought. That notion lasted only an instant.

My father's arm slashed left. It was as though he had stripped the room bare. I could almost hear the china crashing to the floor, all that teak splintering, silver clanging.

"Nelson Rockefeller wouldn't let his dog shit in here!" my father roared. "What we have, compared to what Rockefeller and the people who rule the world have, is nothing. Nothing! Not even good enough for his dog. You four have to remember that and do better than I have. Not just for yourselves, but for our people, black people. You have to be number one."

My father went on, but right about there was where my mind usually started drifting. I was entranced by the image of Rockefeller's dog—which I imagined to be a Corgi or Afghan or Scottish Terrier—bladder and rectum full to bursting, sniffing around the green carpet of our dining room, refusing to relieve himself.

The possible reasons for this fascinated me. Didn't he like green carpets? Was he used to defecating on rare Persian rugs and our 100 percent wool carpeting wasn't good enough? Was it because we were black? But weren't dogs colorblind?

I've spent a good part of my life trying to figure out what my father   25
meant by number one. Born poor and dark in Washington, I think he was trying, in his own way, to protect us from the crushing assumptions of failure that he and his generation grew up with. I like to think he was simply saying, like the army, "Be all that you can be," but I'm still not sure. For years, I was haunted by the specter of number two gaining on me, of never having a house nice enough for Rockefeller dog shit, of my father's middle finger admonishing me. It's hard to move forward when you're looking over your shoulder.

---

[2] *Claude McKay (1889–1948):* African-American poet.

When I was younger, I didn't ask my father what he meant. By the time I was confident enough to ask, my father had been through so many transformations—from dentist to hippie to lay guru—that he'd managed to forget, or convince himself he'd forgotten, those Sunday morning sermons. When I brought them up he'd look blank, his eyes would glaze over, and he'd say something like, "Jill, what are you talking about? With your dramatic imagination you should have been an actress."

But I'm not an actress. I'm a journalist, my father's daughter. I've spent a good portion of my life trying to be a good race woman and number one at the same time. Tomorrow, I go to work at the *Washington Post* magazine, a first. Falling asleep, I wonder if that's the same as being number one.

Questions for Discussion and Writing

1. What message did Jill Nelson's father wish to instill during their Sunday breakfasts?
2. How has Nelson's life been influenced by her attempt to understand and act on her father's advice?
3. Is there a member of your family who has been particularly influential in shaping your attitudes and expectations? Describe this person, and give some examples of how your life has been changed because of the expectations.
4. **Rhetorical inquiry**: What descriptive details does Nelson provide that enables her audience to gain a more accurate picture of her childhood environment? In what sense is her father's vision at odds with how the family actually lives?

FRITZ PETERS

Fritz Peters's (1916–1979) association with the philosopher and mystic George Gurdjieff began when Peters attended a school founded by Gurdjieff in Fontainebleau, France, where he spent four and a half years between 1924 and 1929. His experiences with Gurdjieff were always unpredictable and often enigmatic and rewarding. Peters wrote two books about his experiences, Boyhood with Gurdjieff *(1964) and* Gurdjieff Remembered *(1965). In the following essay, Peters reveals the highly unconventional methods Gurdjieff used to compel his protégé to develop compassion.*

Before You Read

What is the most memorable lesson you have learned about human nature?

Boyhood with Gurdjieff

The Saturday evening after Gurdjieff's return from America, which had been in the middle of the week, was the first general "assembly" of everyone at the Prieuré,[1] in the study-house. The study-house was a separate building, originally an airplane hangar. There was a linoleum-covered raised stage at one end. Directly in front of the stage there was a small, hexagonal fountain, equipped electrically so that various coloured lights played on the water. The fountain was generally used only during the playing of music on the piano which was to the left of the stage as one faced it.

The main part of the building, from the stage to the entrance at the opposite end, was carpeted with oriental rugs of various sizes, surrounded by a small fence which made a large, rectangular open space. Cushions, covered by fur rugs, surrounded the sides of this rectangle in front of the fence, and it was here that most of the students would normally sit. Behind the fence, at a higher level, were built-up benches, also covered with Oriental rugs, for spectators. Near the entrance of the building there was a small cubicle, raised a few feet from the floor, in which Gurdjieff habitually sat, and above this there was a balcony which was rarely used and then only for "important" guests. The cross-wise beams of the ceiling had painted material nailed to them, and the material hung down in billows, creating a cloud-like effect. It was an impressive interior—with a church-like feeling about it. One had the impression that it would be improper, even when it was empty, to speak above a whisper inside the building.

On that particular Saturday evening, Gurdjieff sat in his accustomed cubicle, Miss Madison sat near him on the floor with her little black book on her lap, and most of the students sat around, inside the fence, on the fur rugs. New arrivals and "spectators" or guests were on the higher benches behind the fence. Mr. Gurdjieff announced that Miss Madison would go over all the "offences" of all the students and that proper "punishments" would be meted out to the offenders. All of the children, and perhaps I, especially, waited with bated breath as Miss Madison read from her book, which seemed to have been arranged, not alphabetically, but according to the number of offences committed. As Miss Madison had warned me, I led the list, and the recitation of my crimes and offences was a lengthy one.

Gurdjieff listened impassively, occasionally glancing at one or another of the offenders, sometimes smiling at the recital of a particular misdemeanour, and interrupting Miss Madison only to take down, personally, the actual number of individual black marks. When she had completed her reading, there was a solemn, breathless silence in the room and Gurdjieff said, with a heavy sigh, that we had all created a great burden for him. He said then that

---

[1] *Prieuré:* a priory; a large chateau in Fountainebleau, France, where G. I. Gurdjieff conducted his school.

he would give out punishments according to the number of offences committed. Naturally, I was the first one to be called. He motioned to me to sit on the floor before him and then had Miss Madison re-read my offences in detail. When she had finished, he asked me if I admitted all of them. I was tempted to refute some of them, at least in part, and to argue extenuating circumstances, but the solemnity of the proceedings and the silence in the room prevented me from doing so. Every word that had been uttered had dropped on the assemblage with the clarity of a bell. I did not have the courage to voice any weak defence that might have come to my mind, and I admitted that the list was accurate.

With another sigh, and shaking his head at me as if he was very much   5
put upon, he reached into his pocket and pulled out an enormous roll of bills. Once again, he enumerated the number of my crimes, and then laboriously peeled off an equal number of notes. I do not remember exactly how much he gave me—I think it was ten francs for each offence—but when he had finished counting, he handed me a sizeable roll of francs. During this process, the entire room practically screamed with silence. There was not a murmur from anyone in the entire group, and I did not even dare to glance in Miss Madison's direction.

When my money had been handed to me, he dismissed me and called up the next offender and went through the same process. As there were a great many of us, and there was not one individual who had not done something, violated some rule during his absence, the process took a long time. When he had gone through the list, he turned to Miss Madison and handed her some small sum—perhaps ten francs, or the equivalent of one "crime" payment—for her, as he put it, "conscientious fulfilment of her obligations as director of the Prieuré."

We were all aghast; we had been taken completely by surprise, of course. But the main thing we all felt was a tremendous compassion for Miss Madison. It seemed to me a senselessly cruel, heartless act against her. I have never known Miss Madison's feelings about this performance; except for blushing furiously when I was paid, she showed no obvious reaction to anything at all, and even thanked him for the pittance he had given her.

The money that I had received amazed me. It was, literally, more money than I had ever had at one time in my life. But it also repelled me. I could not bring myself to do anything with it. It was not until a few days later, one evening when I had been summoned to bring coffee to Gurdjieff's room, that the subject came up again. I had had no private, personal contact with him—in the sense of actually talking to him, for instance—since his return. That evening—he was alone—when I had served him his coffee, he asked me how I was getting along; how I felt. I blurted out my feelings about Miss Madison and about the money that I felt unable to spend.

He laughed at me and said cheerfully that there was no reason why I should not spend the money any way I chose. It was my money, and it was a reward for my activity of the past winter. I said I could not understand why I should have been rewarded for having been dilatory about my jobs and having created only trouble.

Gurdjieff laughed again and told me that I had much to learn. 10

"What you not understand," he said, "is that not everyone can be troublemaker, like you. This important in life—is ingredient, like yeast for making bread. Without trouble, conflict, life become dead. People live in status-quo, live only by habit, automatically, and without conscience. You good for Miss Madison. You irritate Miss Madison all time—more than anyone else, which is why you get most reward. Without you, possibility for Miss Madison's conscience fall asleep. This money should really be reward from Miss Madison, not from me. You help keep Miss Madison alive."

I understood the actual, serious sense in which he meant what he was saying, but I said that I felt sorry for Miss Madison, that it must have been a terrible experience for her when she saw us all receiving those rewards.

He shook his head at me, still laughing. "You not see or understand important thing that happen to Miss Madison when give money. How you feel at time? You feel pity for Miss Madison, no? All other people also feel pity for Miss Madison, too."

I agreed that this was so.

"People not understand about learning," he went on. "Think necessary 15 talk all time, that learn through mind, through words. Not so. Many things can only learn with feeling, even from sensation. But because man talk all time—use only formulatory centre—people not understand this. What you not see other night in studyhouse is that Miss Madison have new experience for her. Is poor woman, people not like, people think she funny—they laugh at. But other night, people not laugh. True, Miss Madison feel uncomfortable, feel embarrassed when I give money, feel shame perhaps. But when many people also feel for her sympathy, pity, compassion, even love, she understand this but not right away with mind. She feel, for first time in life, sympathy from many people. She not even know then that she feel this, but her life change; with you, I use you like example, last summer you hate Miss Madison. Now you not hate, you not think funny, you feel sorry. You even like Miss Madison. This good for her even if she not know right away—you will show; you cannot hide this from her, even if wish, cannot hide. So she now have friend, when used to be enemy. This good thing which I do for Miss Madison. I not concerned she understand this now—someday she understand and make her feel warm in heart. This unusual experience—this warm feeling—for such personality as Miss Madison who not have charm, who not friendly in self. Someday, perhaps even soon, she have good feeling because many people feel sorry, feel compassion for her. Someday she even understand what I do and even like me for this. But this kind learning take long time."

I understood him completely and was very moved by his words. But he had not finished.

"Also good thing for you in this," he said. "You young, only boy still, you not care about other people, care for self. I do this to Miss Madison and you think I do bad thing. You feel sorry, you not forget, you think I do bad thing to her. But now you understand not so. Also, good for you, because you feel about other person—you identify with Miss Madison, put self in her place, also regret what you do. Is necessary put self in place of other person if wish understand and help. This good for your conscience, this way is possibility for you learn not hate Miss Madison. All people same—stupid, blind, human. If I do bad thing, this make you learn love other people, not just self."

Questions for Discussion and Writing

1. How did Gurdjieff's allotment of rewards violate conventional expectations? What consequences did this have in changing Peters's view of Miss Madison?
2. What knowledge of human nature is implied in Gurdjieff's ability to create such an emotionally challenging event?
3. Write about a personal experience that forced you to completely reevaluate your attitude toward another person or group.
4. **Rhetorical inquiry**: How is Peters's account structured to enhance the suspense of Gurdjieff's decision? Now, in retrospect, does Peters feel that he was manipulated? Why or why not?

BERYL MARKHAM

Beryl Markham (1902–1986) achieved renown when she became the first person to fly solo across the Atlantic from England to America (a journey of over twenty-one hours). Hemingway said of her, "She can write rings around all of us who consider ourselves as writers." In this final chapter of West with the Night *(1942), Markham describes the harrowing conditions of this flight.*

Before You Read

What challenges would face a woman who wanted to be a pilot?

West with the Night

I have seldom dreamed a dream worth dreaming again, or at least none worth recording. Mine are not enigmatic dreams; they are peopled with characters who are plausible and who do plausible things, and I am the most plausible amongst them. All the characters in my dreams have quiet voices like the voice of the man who telephoned me at Elstree one morning in September of nineteen-thirty-six and told me that there was rain and strong head winds over the west of England and over the Irish Sea, and that there were variable winds and clear skies in mid-Atlantic and fog off the coast of Newfoundland.

"If you are still determined to fly the Atlantic this late in the year," the voice said, "the Air Ministry suggests that the weather it is able to forecast for tonight, and for tomorrow morning, will be about the best you can expect."

The voice had a few others things to say, but not many, and then it was gone, and I lay in bed half-suspecting that the telephone call and the man who made it were only parts of the mediocre dream I had been dreaming. I felt that if I closed my eyes the unreal quality of the message would be re-established, and that, when I opened them again, this would be another ordinary day with its usual beginning and its usual routine.

But of course I could not close my eyes, nor my mind, nor my memory. I could lie there for a few moments—remembering how it had begun, and telling myself, with senseless repetition, that by tomorrow morning I should either have flown the Atlantic to America—or I should not have flown it. In either case this was the day I would try.

I could stare up at the ceiling of my bedroom in Aldenham House, which   5
was a ceiling undistinguished as ceilings go, and feel less resolute than anxious, much less brave than foolhardy. I could say to myself, "You needn't do it, of course," knowing at the same time that nothing is so inexorable as a promise to your pride.

I could ask, "Why risk it?" as I have been asked since, and I could answer, "Each to his element." By his nature a sailor must sail, by his nature a flyer must fly. I could compute that I had flown a quarter of a million miles; and I could foresee that, so long as I had a plane and the sky was there, I should go on flying more miles.

There was nothing extraordinary in this. I had learned a craft and had worked hard learning it. My hands had been taught to seek the controls of a plane. Usage had taught them. They were at ease clinging to a stick, as a cobbler's fingers are in repose grasping an awl. No human pursuit achieves dignity until it can be called work, and when you can experience a physical loneliness for the tools of your trade, you see that the other things—the experiments, the irrelevant vocations, the vanities you used to hold—were false to you.

Record flights had actually never interested me very much for myself. There were people who thought that such flights were done for admiration and publicity, and worse. But of all the records—from Louis Blériot's first crossing of the English Channel in nineteen hundred and nine, through and beyond Kingsford Smith's flight from San Francisco to Sydney, Australia— none had been made by amateurs, nor by novices, nor by men or women less than hardened to failure, or less than masters of their trade. None of these was false. They were a company that simple respect and simple ambition made it worth more than an effort to follow.

The Carberrys (of Seramai) were in London and I could remember everything about their dinner party—even the menu. I could remember June Carberry and all her guests, and the man named McCarthy, who lived in Zanzibar,[1] leaning across the table and saying, "J. C., why don't you finance Beryl for a record flight?"

I could lie there staring lazily at the ceiling and recall J. C.'s dry answer: 10 "A number of pilots have flown the North Atlantic, west to east. Only Jim Mollison has done it alone the other way—from Ireland. Nobody has done it alone from England—man or woman. I'd be interested in that, but nothing else. If you want to try it, Burl, I'll back you. I think Edgar Percival could build a plane that would do it, provided you can fly it. Want to chance it?"

"Yes."

I could remember saying that better than I could remember anything—except J. C.'s almost ghoulish grin, and her remark that sealed the agreement: "It's a deal, Burl. I'll furnish the plane and you fly the Atlantic—but, gee, I wouldn't tackle it for a million. Think of all that black water! Think how cold it is!"

And I had thought of both.

I had thought of both for a while, and then there had been other things to think about. I had moved to Elstree, half-hour's flight from the Percival Aircraft Works at Gravesend, and almost daily for three months now I had flown down to the factory in a hired plane and watched the Vega Gull they were making for me. I had watched her birth and watched her growth. I had watched her wings take shape, and seen wood and fabric moulded to her ribs to form her long, sleek belly, and I had seen her engine cradled into her frame, and made fast.

The Gull had a turquoise-blue body and silver wings. Edgar Percival had   15 made her with care, with skill, and with worry—the care of a veteran flyer, the skill of a master designer, and the worry of a friend. Actually the plane was a standard sport model with a range of only six hundred and sixty miles. But she had a special undercarriage built to carry the weight of her extra oil and petrol tanks. The tanks were fixed into the wings, into the centre section, and into the cabin itself. In the cabin they formed a wall around my seat, and each tank had a petcock of its own. The petcocks were important.

"If you open one," said Percival, "without shutting the other first, you may get an airlock. You know the tanks in the cabin have no gauges, so it may be best to let one run completely dry before opening the next. Your motor might go dead in the interval—but she'll start again. She's a De Havilland Gipsy—and Gipsys never stop."

I had talked to Tom. We had spent hours going over the Atlantic chart, and I had realized that the tinker of Molo, now one of England's great pilots, had traded his dreams and had got in return a better thing. Tom had grown older too; he had jettisoned a deadweight of irrelevant hopes and

---

[1] *Zanzibar:* an island off the east coast of Africa.

wonders, and had left himself a realistic code that had no room for temporizing or easy sentiment.

"I'm glad you're going to do it, Beryl. It won't be simple. If you can get off the ground in the first place, with such an immense load of fuel, you'll be alone in that plane about a night and a day—mostly night. Doing it east to west, the wind's against you. In September, so is the weather. You won't have a radio. If you misjudge your course only a few degrees, you'll end up in Labrador or in the sea—so don't misjudge anything."

Tom could still grin. He had grinned; he had said: "Anyway, it ought to amuse you to think that your financial backer lives on a farm called 'Place of Death' and your plane is being built at 'Gravesend.' If you were consistent, you'd christen the Gull 'The Flying Tombstone.'"

I hadn't been that consistent. I had watched the building of the plane 20
and I had trained for the flight like an athlete. And now, as I lay in bed, fully awake, I could still hear the quiet voice of the man from the Air Ministry intoning, like the voice of a dispassionate court clerk: ". . . the weather for tonight and tomorrow . . . will be about the best you can expect." I should have liked to discuss the flight once more with Tom before I took off, but he was on a special job up north. I got out of bed and bathed and put on my flying clothes and took some cold chicken packed in a cardboard box and flew over to the military field at Abingdon, where the Vega Gull waited for me under the care of the R.A.F. I remember that the weather was clear and still.

Jim Mollison lent me his watch. He said: "This is not a gift. I wouldn't part with it for anything. It got me across the North Atlantic and the South Atlantic too. Don't lose it—and, for God's sake, don't get it wet. Salt water would ruin the works."

Brian Lewis gave me a life-saving jacket. Brian owned the plane I had been using between Elstree and Gravesend, and he had thought a long time about a farewell gift. What could be more practical than a pneumatic jacket that could be inflated through a rubber tube?

"You could float around in it for days," said Brian. But I had to decide between the life-saver and warm clothes. I couldn't have both, because of their bulk, and I hate the cold, so I left the jacket.

And Jock Cameron, Brian's mechanic, gave me a sprig of heather. If it had been a whole bush of heather, complete with roots growing in an earthen jar, I think I should have taken it, bulky or not. The blessing of Scotland, bestowed by a Scotsman, is not to be dismissed. Nor is the well-wishing of a ground mechanic to be taken lightly, for these men are the pilot's contact with reality.

It is too much that with all those pedestrian centuries behind us we 25
should, in a few decades, have learned to fly; it is too heady a thought, too proud a boast. Only the dirt on a mechanic's hands, the straining vise, the splintered bolt of steel underfoot on the hanger floor—only these and such

anxiety as the face of a Jock Cameron can hold for a pilot and his plane before a flight, serve to remind us that, not unlike the heather, we too are earthbound. We fly, but we have not "conquered" the air. Nature presides in all her dignity, permitting us the study and the use of such of her forces as we may understand. It is when we presume to intimacy, having been granted only tolerance, that the harsh stick falls across our impudent knuckles and we rub the pain, staring upward, startled by our ignorance.

"Here is a sprig of heather," said Jock, and I took it and pinned it into a pocket of my flying jacket.

There were press cars parked outside the field at Abingdon, and several press planes and photographers, but the R.A.F. kept everyone away from the grounds except technicians and a few of my friends.

The Carberrys had sailed for New York a month ago to wait for me there. Tom was still out of reach with no knowledge of my decision to leave, but that didn't matter so much, I thought. It didn't matter because Tom was unchanging—neither a fairweather pilot nor a fairweather friend. If for a month, or a year, or two years we sometimes had not seen each other, it still hadn't mattered. Nor did this. Tom would never say, "You should have let me know." He assumed that I had learned all that he had tried to teach me, and for my part, I thought of him, even then, as the merest student must think of his mentor. I could sit in a cabin overcrowded with petrol tanks and set my course for North America, but the knowledge of my hands on the controls would be Tom's knowledge. His words of caution and words of guidance, spoken so long ago, so many times, on bright mornings over the veldt or over a forest, or with a far mountain visible at the tip of our wing, would be spoken again, if I asked.

So it didn't matter, I thought. It was silly to think about.

You can live a lifetime and, at the end of it, know more about other people than you know about yourself. You learn to watch other people, but you never watch yourself because you strive against loneliness. If you read a book, or shuffle a deck of cards, or care for a dog, you are avoiding yourself. The abhorrence of loneliness is as natural as wanting to live at all. If it were otherwise, men would never have bothered to make an alphabet, nor to have fashioned words out of what were only animal sounds, nor to have crossed continents—each man to see what the other looked like. 30

Being alone in an aeroplane for even so short a time as a night and a day, irrevocably alone, with nothing to observe but your instruments and your own hands in semi-darkness, nothing to contemplate but the size of your small courage, nothing to wonder about but the beliefs, the faces, and the hopes rooted in your mind—such an experience can be as startling as the first awareness of a stranger walking by your side at night. You are the stranger.

It is dark already and I am over the south of Ireland. There are the lights of Cork and the lights are wet; they are drenched in Irish rain, and I am above them and dry. I am above them and the plane roars in a sobbing world, but it imparts no sadness to me. I feel the security of solitude, the exhilaration of escape. So long as I can see the lights and imagine the people walking under them, I feel selfishly triumphant, as if I have eluded care and left even the small sorrow of rain in other hands.

It is a little over an hour now since I left Abingdon. England, Wales, and the Irish Sea are behind me like so much time used up. On a long flight distance and time are the same. But there had been a moment when Time stopped—and Distance too. It was the moment I lifted the blue-and-silver Gull from the aerodrome, the moment the photographers aimed their cameras, the moment I felt the craft refuse its burden and strain toward the earth in sullen rebellion, only to listen at last to the persuasion of stick and elevators, the dogmatic argument of blueprints that said she *had* to fly because the figures proved it.

So she had flown, and once airborne, once she had yielded to the sophistry of a draughtsman's board, she had said, "There: I have lifted the weight. Now, where are we bound?"—and the question had frightened me.

"We are bound for a place thirty-six hundred miles from here—two   35
thousand miles of it unbroken ocean. Most of the way it will be night. We are flying west with the night."

So there behind me is Cork; and ahead of me is Berehaven Lighthouse. It is the last light, standing on the last land. I watch it, counting the frequency of its flashes—so many to the minute. Then I pass it and fly out to sea.

The fear is gone now—not overcome nor reasoned away. It is gone because something else has taken its place; the confidence and the trust, the inherent belief in the security of land underfoot—now this faith is transferred to my plane, because the land has vanished and there is no other tangible thing to fix faith upon. Flight is but momentary escape from the eternal custody of earth.

Rain continues to fall, and outside the cabin it is totally dark. My altimeter says that the Atlantic is two thousand feet below me, my Sperry Artificial Horizon says that I am flying level. I judge my drift at three degrees more than my weather chart suggests, and fly accordingly. I am flying blind. A beam to follow would help. So would a radio—but then, so would clear weather. The voice of the man at the Air Ministry had not promised storm.

I feel the wind rising and the rain falls hard. The smell of petrol in the cabin is so strong and the roar of the plane so loud that my senses are almost deadened. Gradually it becomes unthinkable that existence was ever otherwise.

At ten o'clock P.M. I am flying along the Great Circle Course for   40
Harbour Grace, Newfoundland, into a forty-mile headwind at a speed of one hundred and thirty miles an hour. Because of the weather, I cannot be sure of how many more hours I have to fly, but I think it must be between sixteen and eighteen.

At ten-thirty I am still flying on the large cabin tank of petrol, hoping to use it up and put an end to the liquid swirl that has rocked the plane since my take-off. The tank has no gauge, but written on its side is the assurance: "This tank is good for four hours."

There is nothing ambiguous about such a guaranty. I believe it, but at twenty-five minutes to eleven, my motor coughs and dies, and the Gull is powerless above the sea.

I realize that the heavy drone of the plane has been, until this moment, complete and comforting silence. It is the actual silence following the last splutter of the engine that stuns me. I can't feel any fear; I can't feel anything. I can only observe with a kind of stupid disinterest that my hands are violently active and know that, while they move, I am being hypnotized by the needle of my altimeter.

I suppose that the denial of natural impulse is what is meant by "keeping calm," but impulse has reason in it. If it is night and you are sitting in an aeroplane with a stalled motor, and there are two thousand feet between you and the sea, nothing can be more reasonable than the impulse to pull back your stick in the hope of adding to that two thousand, if only by a little. The thought, the knowledge, the law that tells you that your hope lies not in this, but in a contrary act—the act of directing your impotent craft toward the water—seems a terrifying abandonment, not only of reason, but of sanity. Your mind and your heart reject it. It is your hands—your stranger's hands— that follow with unfeeling precision the letter of the law.

I sit there and watch my hands push forward on the stick and feel the Gull respond and begin its dive to the sea. Of course it is a simple thing; surely the cabin tank has run dry too soon. I need only to turn another petcock . . . 45

But it is dark in the cabin. It is easy to see the luminous dial of the altimeter and to note that my height is now eleven hundred feet, but it is not easy to see a petcock that is somewhere near the floor of the plane. A hand gropes and reappears with an electric torch, and fingers, moving with agonizing composure, find the petcock and turn it; and I wait.

At three hundred feet the motor is still dead, and I am conscious that the needle of my altimeter seems to whirl like the spoke of a spindle winding up the remaining distance between the plane and the water. There is some lightning, but the quick flash only serves to emphasize the darkness. How high can waves reach—twenty feet, perhaps? Thirty?

It is impossible to avoid the thought that this is the end of my flight, but my reactions are not orthodox; the various incidents of my entire life do not run through my mind like a motion-picture film gone mad. I only feel that all this has happened before—and it has. It has all happened a hundred times in my mind, in my sleep, so that now I am not really caught in terror; I recognize a familiar scene, a familiar story with its climax dulled by too much telling.

I do not know how close to the waves I am when the motor explodes to life again. But the sound is almost meaningless. I see my hand easing back on the stick, and I feel the Gull climb up into the storm, and I see the altimeter whirl like a spindle again, paying out the distance between myself and the sea.

The storm is strong. It is comforting. It is like a friend shaking me and   50
saying, "Wake up! You were only dreaming."

But soon I am thinking. By simple calculation I find that my motor had
been silent for perhaps an instant more than thirty seconds.

I ought to thank God—and I do, though indirectly. I thank Geoffrey De
Havilland who designed the indomitable Gipsy, and who, after all, must
have been designed by God in the first place.

A lighted ship—the daybreak—some steep cliffs standing in the sea. The
meaning of these will never change for pilots. If one day an ocean can be
flown within an hour, if men can build a plane that so masters time, the sight
of land will be no less welcome to the steersman of that fantastic craft. He
will have cheated laws that the cunning of science has taught him how to
cheat, and he will feel his guilt and be eager for the sanctuary of the soil.

I saw the ship and the daybreak, and then I saw the cliffs of Newfoundland wound in ribbons of fog. I felt the elation I had so long imagined, and
I felt the happy guilt of having circumvented the stern authority of the
weather and the sea. But mine was a minor triumph; my swift Gull was not
so swift as to have escaped unnoticed. The night and the storm had caught
her and we had flown blind for nineteen hours.

I was tired now, and cold. Ice began to film the glass of the cabin win-   55
dows and the fog played a magician's game with the land. But the land was
there. I could not see it, but I had seen it. I could not afford to believe that it
was any land but the land I wanted. I could not afford to believe that my
navigation was at fault, because there was no time for doubt.

South to Cape Race, west to Sydney on Cape Breton Island. With my
protractor, my map, and my compass, I set my new course, humming the ditty
that Tom had taught me: "Variation West—magnetic best. Variation East—
magnetic least." A silly rhyme, but it served to placate, for the moment, two
warring poles—the magnetic and the true. I flew south and found the lighthouse of Cape Race protruding from the fog like a warning finger. I circled
twice and went on over the Gulf of Saint Lawrence.

After a while there would be New Brunswick, and then Maine—and then
New York. I could anticipate. I could almost say, "Well, if you stay awake,
you'll find it's only a matter of time now"—but there was no question of staying awake. I was tired and I had not moved an inch since that uncertain
moment at Abingdon when the Gull had elected to rise with her load and fly,
but I could not have closed my eyes. I could sit there in the cabin, walled in
glass and petrol tanks, and be grateful for the sun and the light, and the fact
that I could see the water under me. They were almost the last waves I had
to pass. Four hundred miles of water, and then the land again—Cape Breton.
I would stop at Sydney to refuel and go on. It was easy now. It would be like
stopping at Kisumu and going on.

Success breeds confidence. But who has a right to confidence except
the Gods? I had a following wind, my last tank of petrol was more than

three-quarters full, and the world was as bright to me as if it were a new world, never touched. If I had been wiser, I might have known that such moments are, like innocence, short-lived. My engine began to shudder before I saw the land. It died, it spluttered, it started again and limped along. It coughed and spat black exhaust toward the sea.

There are words for everything. There was a word for this—airlock, I thought. This had to be an airlock because there was petrol enough. I thought I might clear it by turning on and turning off all the empty tanks, and so I did that. The handles of the petcocks were sharp little pins of metal, and when I had opened and closed them a dozen times, I saw that my hands were bleeding and that the blood was dropping on my maps and on my clothes, but the effort wasn't any good. I coasted along on a sick and halting engine. The oil pressure and the oil temperature gauges were normal, the magnetos working, and yet I lost altitude slowly while the realization of failure seeped into my heart. If I made the land, I should have been the first to fly the North Atlantic from England, but from my point of view, from a pilot's point of view, a forced landing was failure because New York was my goal. If only I could land and then take off, I would make it still . . . if only, if only . . .

The engine cuts again, and then catches, and each time it spurts to life   60
I climb as high as I can get, and then it splutters and stops and I glide once more toward the water, to rise again and descend again, like a hunting sea bird.

I find the land. Visibility is perfect now and I see land forty or fifty miles ahead. If I am on my course, that will be Cape Breton. Minute after minute goes by. The minutes almost materialize; they pass before my eyes like links in a long slow-moving chain, and each time the engine cuts, I see a broken link in the chain and catch my breath until it passes.

The land is under me. I snatch my map and stare at it to confirm my whereabouts. I am, even at my present crippled speed, only twelve minutes from Sydney Airport, where I can land for repairs and then go on.

The engine cuts once more and I begin to glide, but now I am not worried; she will start again, as she has done, and I will gain altitude and fly into Sydney.

But she doesn't start. This time she's dead as death; the Gull settles earthward and it isn't any earth I know. It is black earth stuck with boulders and I hang above it, on hope and on a motionless propeller. Only I cannot hang above it long. The earth hurries to meet me, I bank, turn, and side-slip to dodge the boulders, my wheels touch, and I feel them submerge. The nose of the plane is engulfed in mud, and I go forward striking my head on the glass of the cabin front, hearing it shatter, feeling blood pour over my face.

I stumble out of the plane and sink to my knees in muck and stand there   65
foolishly staring, not at the lifeless land, but at my watch.

Twenty-one hours and twenty-five minutes.

Atlantic flight, Abingdon, England, to a nameless swamp—nonstop.

A Cape Breton Islander found me—a fisherman trudging over the bog saw the Gull with her tail in the air and her nose buried, and then he saw me floundering in the embracing soil of his native land. I had been wandering for an hour and the black mud had got up to my waist and the blood from the cut in my head had met the mud halfway.

From a distance, the fisherman directed me with his arms and with shouts toward the firm places in the bog, and for another hour I walked on them and came toward him like a citizen of Hades blinded by the sun, but it wasn't the sun; I hadn't slept for forty hours.

He took me to his hut on the edge of the coast and I found that built 70 upon the rocks there was a little cubicle that housed an ancient telephone— put there in case of shipwrecks.

I telephoned to Sydney Airport to say that I was safe and to prevent a needless search being made. On the following morning I did step out of a plane at Floyd Bennett Field and there was a crowd of people still waiting there to greet me, but the plane I stepped from was not the Gull, and for days while I was in New York I kept thinking about that and wishing over and over again that it had been the Gull, until the wish lost its significance, and time moved on, overcoming many things it met on the way.

Questions for Discussion and Writing

1. What motivates Markham and explains her compulsion to succeed?
2. How would you characterize Markham's personality as it emerges in her account? What sort of relationship did she have with her fellow pilots?
3. Do you consider Markham a workaholic? What distinguishes workaholics from other hard workers? Would you consider yourself one? Why or why not?
4. **Rhetorical inquiry:** How does the structure of Markham's account beginning with the dream sequence that leads to a flashback preceding her flight allow the reader to join her on her journey?

How does Beryl Markham identify herself in this photo?

DAVE BARRY

Dave Barry, born in 1947, is a Pulitzer Prize-winning author whose nationally syndicated columns appear in The Miami Herald *and other newspapers and magazines. He received a B.A. in English from Haverford College and is the author of numerous books including* Dave Barry Is Not Making This Up *(1995),* Dave Barry's Complete Guide to Guys *(1996),* Dave Barry on Dads *(2007), and* Dave Barry Talks Back *(1991), in which "Just Say No to Rugs" first appeared. In this piece, Barry offers an ironic and whimsical account of the joys and tribulations of owning a pet.*

Before You Read

What are some of the joys and tribulations of being owned by a pet?

Just Say No to Rugs

Everybody should have a pet. And I'm not saying this just because the American Pet Council gave me a helicopter. I'm also saying it because my family has always owned pets, and without them, our lives would not be nearly so rich in—call me sentimental, but this is how I feel—dirt.

Pets are nature's way of reminding us that, in the incredibly complex ecological chain of life, there is no room for furniture. For example, the only really nice furnishing we own is an Oriental rug that we bought, with the help of a decorator, in a failed attempt to become tasteful. This rug is way too nice for an onion-dip-intensive household like ours, and we seriously thought about keeping it in a large safe-deposit box, but we finally decided, in a moment of abandon, to put it on the floor. We then conducted a comprehensive rug-behavior training seminar for our main dog, Earnest, and our small auxiliary dog, Zippy.

"NO!!" we told them approximately 75 times while looking very stern and pointing at the rug. This proven training technique caused them to slink around the way dogs do when they feel tremendously guilty but have no idea why. Satisfied, we went out to dinner.

I later figured out, using an electronic calculator, that this rug covers approximately 2 percent of the total square footage of our house, which means that if you (not you *personally*) were to have a random diarrhea attack in our home, the odds are approximately 49 to 1 against your having it on our Oriental rug. The odds against your having *four* random attacks on this rug are more than *five million to one*. So we had to conclude that it was done on purpose. The rug appeared to have been visited by a group of specially bred, highly trained Doberman Poopers, but we determined, by interrogating both dogs, that the entire massive output was the work of Zippy. Probably he was trying to do the right thing. Probably, somewhere in the Coco Puff-sized nodule of nerve tissue that serves as his brain he dimly remembered that The Masters had told him *something about the rug*, Yes! That's it! *To the rug*!

At least Zippy had the decency to feel bad about what he did, which is   5
more than you can say for Mousse, a dog that belonged to a couple named Mike and Sandy. Mousse was a Labrador retriever, which is a large enthusiastic bulletproof species of dog made entirely from synthetic materials. This is the kind of dog that, if it takes an interest in your personal regions (which of course it does) you cannot fend it off with a blowtorch.

So anyway, Mike and Sandy had two visitors who wore expensive, brand-new down-filled parkas, which somehow got left for several hours in a closed room with Mousse. When the door was finally opened, the visibility in the room had been drastically reduced by a raging down storm, at the center of which was a large quivering down clot, looking like a huge mutant duckling, except that it had Mousse's radiantly happy eyes.

For several moments Mike and Sandy and their guests stared at this apparition, then Mike, a big, strong, highly authoritative guy, strode angrily into the room and slammed the door. He was in there for several minutes, then emerged, looking very serious. The down clot stood behind him, wagging its tail cheerfully.

Source: Jeff MacNelly

"I talked to Mousse," Mike said, "and he says he didn't do it."

People often become deranged by pets. Derangement is the only possible explanation for owning a cat, an animal whose preferred mode of communication is to sink its claws three-quarters of an inch into your flesh. God help the cat owner who runs out of food. It's not uncommon to see an elderly woman sprinting through the supermarket with one or more cats clinging, leech-like, to her leg as she tries desperately to reach the pet-food section before collapsing from blood loss.

Of course for sheer hostility in a pet, you can't beat a parrot. I base this statement on a parrot I knew named Charles who belonged to a couple named Ed and Ginny. Charles had an IQ of 260 and figured out early in life that if he talked to people, they'd get close enough so he could bite them. He especially liked to bite Ed, whom Charles wanted to drive out of the marriage so he could have Ginny, the house, the American Express card, etc. So in an effort to improve their relationship, Ginny hatched (ha ha!) this plan wherein Ed took Charles to—I am not making this up—Parrot Obedience School. Every Saturday morning, Ed and Charles would head off to receive expert training, and every Saturday afternoon Ed would come home with chunks missing from his arm. Eventually Ginny realized that it was never going to work, so she got rid of Ed.

10

I'm just kidding, of course. Nobody would take Ed. Ginny got rid of Charles, who now works as a public-relations adviser to Miss Zsa Zsa Gabor. So we see that there are many "pluses" to having an "animal friend," which is why you should definitely buy a pet. If you act right now, we'll also give you a heck of a deal on a rug.

Questions for Discussion and Writing

1. How are Barry's aspirations of having the values of a higher social class negated by his dogs?
2. What effects result from the contrast between Barry's attempt to condition his dogs' behavior and what they actually do?
3. How have your pet-related experiences helped you to see the humor in this piece?
4. **Rhetorical inquiry:** How does Barry use irony and humor to satirize his futile efforts to have a trained pet dog and an expensive rug?

DOUCHAN GERSI

Douchan Gersi is the producer of the National Geographic *television series called* Discovery. *He has traveled extensively throughout the Philippines, New Zealand, the Polynesian Islands, the Melanesian Islands, the Sahara, Africa, New Guinea, and Peru. "Initiated into an Iban Tribe of Headhunters," from his book* Explorer *(1987), tells of the harrowing initiation process he underwent to become a member of the Iban tribe in Borneo. He subsequently wrote* Out of Africa *with Maroussia Gersi (1989). His works include* Faces in the Smoke: An Eyewitness Experience of Voodoo *(1991) and, most recently,* Une vie de maharajah [The Life of a Maharajah] *(2003). Gersi's account introduces us to the mode of life of the Iban, a people whose customs, including intertribal warfare and headhunting, have remained unchanged for centuries.*

An accomplished Iban man not only would be proficient in argument and courageous in hunting but also would be skillful in woodcarving. The traditional Iban dwelling is the longhouse (which is nearly always built by the bank of a navigable river), a semi-permanent structure housing twenty or more families in separate apartments. The longhouse is decorated with drums, gongs, weavings, and hanging skulls from days gone by.

Before You Read

What is the most harrowing initiation ritual you have experienced or have heard about?

Initiated into an Iban Tribe of Headhunters

The hopeful man sees success where others see shadows and storm.

—O. S. Marden

Against Tawa's excellent advice I asked the chief if I could become a member of their clan. It took him a while before he could give me an answer, for he had to question the spirits of their ancestors and wait for their reply to appear through different omens: the flight of a blackbird, the auguries of a chick they sacrificed. A few days after the question, the answer came:

"Yes . . . but!"

The "but" was that I would have to undergo their initiation. Without knowing exactly what physical ordeal was in store, I accepted. I knew I had been through worse and survived. It was to begin in one week.

Late at night I was awakened by a girl slipping into my bed. She was sweet and already had a great knowledge of man's morphology. Like all the others who came and "visited" me this way every night, she was highly skilled in the arts of love. Among the Iban, only unmarried women offer sexual hospitality, and no one obliged these women to offer me their favors. Sexual freedom ends at marriage. Unfaithfulness—except during yearly fertility celebrations when everything, even incest at times, is permitted—is punished as an offense against their matrimonial laws.

As a sign of respect to family and the elders, sexual hospitality is not openly practiced. The girls always came when my roommates were asleep and left before they awoke. They were free to return or give their place to their girlfriends.

The contrast between the violence of some Iban rituals and the beauty of their art, their sociability, their kindness, and their personal warmth has always fascinated me. I also witnessed that contrast among a tribe of Papuans (who, besides being headhunters, practice cannibalism) and among some African tribes. In fact, tribes devoted to cannibalism and other human sacrifices are often among the most sociable of people, and their art, industry, and trading systems are more advanced than other tribes that don't have these practices.

For my initiation, they had me lie down naked in a four-foot-deep pit filled with giant carnivorous ants. Nothing held me there. At any point I could easily have escaped, but the meaning of this rite of passage was not to kill me. The ritual was intended to test my courage and my will, to symbolically kill me by the pain in order for me to be reborn as a man of courage. I am not sure what their reactions would have been if I had tried to get out of the pit before their signal, but it occurred to me that although the ants might eat a little of my flesh, the Iban offered more dramatic potentials.

Since I wore, as Iban do, a long piece of cloth around my waist and nothing more, I had the ants running all over my body. They were everywhere. The pain of the ants' bites was intense, so I tried to relax to decrease the speed of my circulation and therefore the effects of the poison. But I couldn't help trying to get them away from my face where they were exploring every inch of my skin. I kept my eyes closed, inhaling through my almost closed lips and exhaling through my nose to chase them away from there.

I don't know how long I stayed in the pit, waiting with anguish for the signal which would end my ordeal. As I tried to concentrate on my relaxing, the sound of the beaten gongs and murmurs of the assistants watching me from all around the pit started to disappear into a chaos of pain and loud heartbeat.

Then suddenly I heard Tawa and the chief calling my name. I removed   10
once more the ants wandering on my eyelids before opening my eyes and seeing my friends smiling to indicate that it was over. I got out of the pit on my own, but I needed help to rid myself of the ants, which were determined to eat all my skin. After the men washed my body, the shaman applied an herbal mixture to ease the pain and reduce the swellings. I would have quit and left the village then had I known that the "pit" experience was just the hors d'oeuvre.

The second part of the physical test started early the next morning. The chief explained the "game" to me. It was Hide and Go Seek Iban-style. I had to run without any supplies, weapons, or food, and for three days and three nights escape a group of young warriors who would leave the village a few hours after my departure and try to find me. If I were caught, my head would be used in a ceremony. The Iban would have done so without hate. It was simply the rule of their life. Birth and death. A death that always engenders new life.

When I asked, "What would happen if someone refused this part of the initiation?" the chief replied that such an idea wasn't possible. Once one had begun, there was no turning back. I knew the rules governing initiations among the cultures of tradition but never thought they would be applied to me. Whether or not I survived the initiation, I would be symbolically killed in order to be reborn among them. I had to die from my present time and identity into another life. I was aware that, among some cultures, initiatory ordeals are so arduous that young initiates sometimes really die. These are the risks if one wishes to enter into another world.

I was given time to get ready and the game began. I ran like hell without a plan or, it seemed to me, a prayer of surviving. Running along a path I had never taken, going I knew not where, I thought about every possible way I could escape from the young warriors. To hide somewhere. But where? Climb a tree and hide in it? Find a hole and squeeze in it? Bury myself under rocks and mud? But all of these seemed impossible. I had a presentiment they would find me anyway. So I ran straight ahead, my head going crazy by dint of searching for a way to safely survive the headhunters.

I would prefer staying longer with ants, I thought breathlessly. It was safer to stay among them for a whole day since they were just simple pain and fear compared to what I am about to undergo. I don't want to die.

For the first time I realized the real possibility of death—no longer in a romantic way, but rather at the hands of butchers.

Ten minutes after leaving the long house, I suddenly heard a call coming from somewhere around me. Still running, I looked all around trying to locate who was calling, and why. At the second call I stopped, cast my gaze about, and saw a woman's head peering out from the bushes. I recognized her as one of my pretty lovers. I hesitated, not knowing if she were part of the hunting party or a goddess come to save me. She called again. I thought, God, what to do? How will I escape from the warriors? As I stood there truly coming into contact with my impossible situation, I began to panic. She called again. With her fingers she showed me what the others would do if they caught me. Her forefinger traced an invisible line from one side of her throat to the other. If someone was going to kill me, why not her? I joined her and found out she was in a lair. I realized I had entered the place where the tribe's women go to hide during their menstruation. This area is taboo for men. Each woman has her own refuge. Some have shelters made of branches, others deep covered holes hidden behind bushes with enough space to eat and sleep and wait until their time is past.

She invited me to make myself comfortable. That was quite difficult since it was just large enough for one person. But I had no choice. And after all, it was a paradise compared to what I would have undergone had I not by luck crossed this special ground.

Nervously and physically exhausted by my run and fear and despair, I soon fell asleep. Around midnight I woke. She gave me rice and meat. We exchanged a few words. Then it was her turn to sleep.

The time I spent in the lair with my savior went fast. I tried to sleep all day long, an escape from the concerns of my having broken a taboo. And

I wondered what would happen to me if the headhunters were to learn where I spent the time of my physical initiation.

Then, when it was safe, I snuck back to the village . . . in triumph. I arrived   20
before the warriors, who congratulated and embraced me when they returned. I was a headhunter at last.

I spent the next two weeks quietly looking at the Iban through new eyes. But strangely enough, instead of the initiation putting me closer to them, it had the opposite effect. I watched them more and more from an anthropological distance: my Iban brothers became an interesting clan whose life I witnessed but did not really share. And then suddenly I was bored and yearned for my own tribe. When Tawa had to go to an outpost to exchange pepper grains for other goods, I took a place aboard his canoe. Two days later I was in a small taxi-boat heading toward Sibu, the first leg in civilization on my voyage home.

I think of them often. I wonder about the man I tried to cure. I think about Tawa and the girl who saved my life, and all the others sitting on the veranda. How long will my adopted village survive before being destroyed like all the others in the way of civilization? And what has become of those who marked my flesh with the joy of their lives and offered me the best of their souls? If they are slowly vanishing from my memories, I know that I am part of the stories they tell. I know that my life among them will be perpetuated until the farthest tomorrow. Now I am a story caught in a living legend of a timeless people.

Questions for Discussion and Writing

1. What do the unusual sexual customs and hospitality bestowed on outsiders suggest about the different cultural values of the Iban? Do these customs suggest that the initiation would be harsher or milder than Gersi expected?

2. At what point did Gersi realize that his former ideas about being accepted by the tribe were unrealistic and that his present situation was truly life-endangering? How is the narrative shaped to put the reader through the same suspenseful moments that Gersi experienced? Speculate about why Gersi's life-and-death initiation, rather than bringing him closer to the Iban, as he expected, actually made him more distant from them.

3. Have you ever gone through an initiation ritual to become part of an organization, club, fraternity, or sorority? Describe your experiences and how you felt before, during, and after this initiation. How can other rituals, such as being confirmed in the Catholic church or becoming a bar or bat mitzvah in Judaism, be analyzed as an initiation rite?

4. **Rhetorical inquiry:** How does Gersi strengthen the irony of his predicament by first referring to it as a "hide and go seek" game? How does this make the reader share Gersi's naive expectations?

What does this group photo of the Iban tribe in their longhouse suggest about the life that might await Douchan Gersi?

JAMES HERRIOT

James Herriot, the renowned Scottish veterinarian (1916–1995), whose books and television series have made his experiences known and appreciated by millions, was born James Alfred Wight. He adopted as a pseudonym the name of a Birmingham soccer player he saw on television. His engaging autobiographical depictions of his life as a country veterinarian in the Yorkshire farmlands include All Creatures Great and Small *(1972),* All Things Bright and Beautiful *(1974),* All Things Wise and Wonderful *(1977),* The Lord God Made Them All *(1981),* Every Living Thing *(1922), and* James Herriot's Cat Stories *(1955). These stories affirm with compassion and humor the ups and downs of veterinary life and the relationships of the country people and their animals. "Rumenotomy on a Cow," from* All Creatures Great and Small, *is an ironic and amusing portrait of a country lad's first experience with animal surgery.*

Before You Read

What steps did you take to make a good impression on the first day of a new job?

Rumenotomy on a Cow

I have a vivid recollection of a summer evening when I had to carry out a rumenotomy on a cow. As a rule I was inclined to play for time when I suspected a foreign body—there were so many other conditions with similar symptoms that I was never in a hurry to make a hole in the animal's side. But this time diagnosis was easy; the sudden fall in milk yield, loss of cudding; grunting, and the rigid, sunken-eyed appearance of the cow. And to clinch it the farmer told me he had been repairing a hen house in the cow pasture—nailing up loose boards. I knew where one of the nails had gone.

The farm, right on the main street of the village, was a favourite meeting place for the local lads. As I laid out my instruments on a clean towel draped over a straw bale a row of grinning faces watched from above the half door of the box; not only watched but encouraged me with ribald shouts. When I was about ready to start it occurred to me that an extra pair of hands would be helpful, and I turned to the door. "How would one of you lads like to be my assistant?" There was even more shouting for a minute or two, then the door was opened and a huge young man with a shock of red hair ambled into the box; he was a magnificent sight with his vast shoulders and the column of sunburned neck rising from the open shirt. It needed only the bright blue eyes and the ruddy, high-cheekboned face to remind me that the Norsemen had been around the Dales a thousand years ago. This was a Viking.

I had him roll up his sleeves and scrub his hands in a bucket of warm water and antiseptic while I infiltrated the cow's flank with local anaesthetic. When I gave him artery forceps and scissors to hold he pranced around, making stabbing motions at the cow and roaring with laughter.

"Maybe you'd like to do the job yourself?" I asked. The Viking squared his great shoulders. "Aye, I'll 'ave a go," and the heads above the door cheered lustily.

As I finally poised my Bard Parker scalpel with its new razor-sharp blade over the cow, the air was thick with earthy witticisms. I had decided that this time I really would make the bold incision recommended in the surgery books; it was about time I advanced beyond the stage of pecking nervously at the skin. "A veritable blow," was how one learned author had described it. Well, that was how it was going to be.

I touched the blade down on the clipped area of the flank and with a quick motion of the wrist laid open a ten-inch wound. I stood back for a few second admiring the clean-cut edges of the skin with only a few capillaries spurting on to the glistening, twitching abdominal muscles. At the same time I noticed that the laughter and shouting from the heads had been switched off and was replaced by an eerie silence broken only by a heavy, thudding sound from behind me.

"Forceps please," I said, extending my hand back. But nothing happened. I looked round; the top of the half door was bare—not a head in sight. There was only the Viking spreadeagled in the middle of the floor, arms and legs flung wide, chin pointing to the roof. The attitude was so theatrical that I thought he was still acting the fool, but a closer examination erased all doubts: the Viking was out cold. He must have gone straight over backwards like a stricken oak.

The farmer, a bent little man who couldn't have scaled much more than eight stones, had been steadying the cow's head. He looked at me with the faintest flicker of amusement in his eyes. "Looks like you and me for it, then, guvnor." He tied the halter to a ring on the wall, washing his hands methodically and took up his place at my side. Throughout the operation, he passed me my instruments, swabbed away the seeping blood and clipped the sutures, whistling tunelessly through his teeth in a bored manner; the only time he showed any real emotion was when I produced the offending nail from the depths of the reticulum. He raised his eyebrows slightly, said "'ello, 'ello," then started whistling again.

We were too busy to do anything for the Viking. Halfway through, he sat up, shook himself a few times then got to his feet and strolled with elaborate nonchalance out of the box. The poor fellow seemed to be hoping that perhaps we had noticed nothing unusual.

Questions for Discussion and Writing

1. What diagnostic clues made Herriot believe that the cow needed an operation called a *rumenotomy?*
2. Why does Herriot decide to perform the operation in the most dramatic way possible?
3. How does the appearance of the "Viking" make his reaction to the rumenotomy all the more ironic?
4. **Rhetorical inquiry:** What descriptive details help transport the reader to the locale of the story? How does Herriot's keen ear for dialect give his audience a sense of the no-nonsense attitude of Yorkshire farmers, whose respect he is trying to earn.

Fiction

WILLIAM MAXWELL

While traveling in France, two U.S. tourists go to desperate lengths to obtain specific dishes recommended by their friends back home. In "The Pilgrimage" from Over the River and Other Stories *(1953), William Maxwell takes the reader along with Ellen and Ray on their quest to attain sophistication and social acceptance. This thought-provoking story asks why certain foods have come to represent refinement and upper-class values. Maxwell (1909–2000) was a prolific writer whose works include* Billie Byer and Other Stories *(1992) and* All the Days and Nights: The Collected Stories of William Maxwell *(1995).*

Before You Read

As you read Maxwell's story, pay particular attention to his tone: does he sympathize with Ray and Ellen's obsession?

The Pilgrimage

In a rented Renault, with exactly as much luggage as the back seat would hold, Ray and Ellen Ormsby were making a little tour of France. It had so far included Vézelay, the mountain villages of Auvergne, the roses and Roman ruins of Provence, and the gorges of the Tarn. They were now on their way back to Paris by a route that was neither the most direct nor particularly scenic, and that had been chosen with one thing in mind—dinner at the Hôtel du Domino in Périgueux. The Richardsons, who were close friends of the Ormsbys in America, had insisted that they go there. "The best dinner I ever had in my entire life," Jerry Richardson had said. "Every course was something with truffles." "And the dessert," Anne Richardson had said, "was little balls of various kinds of ice cream in a beautiful basket of spun sugar with a spun-sugar bow." Putting the two statements together, Ray Ormsby had persisted in thinking that the ice cream also had truffles in it, and Ellen had given up trying to correct this impression.

At seven o'clock, they were still sixty-five kilometres from Périgueux, on a winding back-country road, and beginning to get hungry. The landscape was gilded with the evening light. Ray was driving. Ellen read aloud to him from the "Guide Gastronomique de la France" the paragraph on the Hôtel du Domino: "*Bel et confortable établissement à la renommée bien assise et que Mme. Lasgrezas dirige avec beaucoup de bonheur. Grâce à un maître queux qualifié, vous y ferez un repas de grande classe qui vous sera servi dans une élégante salle à manger ou dans un délicieux jardin d' été. . . .*"[1]

As they drove through village after village, they saw, in addition to the usual painted Cinzano and Rasurel signs, announcements of the *spécialité*[2] of the restaurant of this or that Hôtel des Sports or de la Poste or du Lion d'Or—always with truffles. In Montignac, there were so many of these signs that Ellen said anxiously, "Do you think we ought to eat *here?*"

---

[1] A beautiful and comfortable, justifiably famous establishment that Madame Lasgrezas efficiently runs. Given such a proprietor, you will find meals of great quality, served in an elegant dining room or in a delightful summer garden.   [2] featured offering, specialty of the house.

"No," Ray said. "Périgueux is the place. It's the capital of Périgord, and so it's bound to have the best food."

Outside Thenon, they had a flat tire—the seventh in eight days of 5
driving—and the casing of the spare tire was in such bad condition that Ray was afraid to drive on until the inner tube had been repaired and the regular tire put back on. It was five minutes of nine when they drove up before the Hôtel du Domino, and they were famished. Ray went inside and found that the hotel had accommodations for them. The car was driven into the hotel garage and emptied of its formidable luggage, and the Ormsbys were shown up to their third-floor room, which might have been in any plain hotel anywhere in France: "What I'd really like is a roast chicken stuffed with truffles," Ellen said from the washstand. "But probably it takes a long time."

"What if it does," Ray said. "We'll be eating other things first."

He threw open the shutters and discovered that their room looked out on a painting by Dufy—the large, bare, open square surrounded by stone buildings, with the tricolor for accent, and the sky a rich, stained-glass blue. From another window, at the turning of the stairs on their way down to dinner, they saw the delicious garden, but it was dark, and no one was eating there now. At the foot of the stairs, they paused.

"You wanted the restaurant?" the concierge asked, and when they nodded, she came out from behind her mahogany railing and led them importantly down a corridor. The maître d'hôtel, in a grey business suit, stood waiting at the door of the dining room, and put them at a table for two. Then he handed them the menu with a flourish. They saw at a glance how expensive the dinner was going to be. A waitress brought plates, glasses, napkins, knives, and forks.

While Ellen was reading the menu, Ray looked slowly around the room. The *"élégante salle à manger"* looked like a hotel coffee shop. There weren't even any tablecloths. The walls were painted a dismal shade of off-mustard. His eyes came to rest finally on the stippled brown dado[3] a foot from his face. "It's a perfect room to commit suicide in," he said, and reached for the menu. A moment later he exclaimed, "I don't see the basket of ice cream!"

"It must be there," Ellen said. "Don't get so excited."   10

"Well, where? Just show me?"

Together they looked through the two columns of desserts, without finding the marvel in question. "Jerry and Anne were here several days," Ellen said. "They may have had it in some other restaurant."

This explanation Ray would not accept. "It was the same dinner, I remember distinctly." The full horror of their driving all the way of Périgueux in order to eat a very expensive meal at the wrong restaurant broke over him. In a cold sweat he got up from the table.

"Where are you going?" Ellen asked.

---

[3] lower broad part of an interior wall covered in wallpaper, paint, or fabric.

"I'll be right back," he said, and left the dining room. Upstairs in their   15
room, he dug the "Guide Michelin" out of a duffel-bag. He had lost all faith in
the "Guide Gastronomique," because of its description of the dining room; the
person who wrote that had never set eyes on the Hôtel du Domino or, probably,
on Périgueux. In the "Michelin," the restaurant of the Hôtel du Domino rated
one star and so did the restaurant Le Montaigne, but Le Montaigne also had
three crossed forks and spoons, and suddenly it came to him, with the awful
clarity of a long-submerged memory at last brought to the surface through layer
after layer of consciousness, that it was at Le Montaigne and not at the Hôtel du
Domino that the Richardsons had meant them to eat. He picked up Ellen's coat
and, still carrying the "Michelin," went back downstairs to the dining room.

"I've brought your coat," he said to Ellen as he sat down opposite her.
"We're in the wrong restaurant."

"We aren't either," Ellen said. "And even if we were, I've *got* to have
something to eat. I'm starving, and it's much too late now to go looking for—"

"It won't be far," Ray said. "Come on." He looked up into the face of
the maître d'hôtel, waiting with his pencil and pad to take their order.

"You speak English?" Ray asked.

The maître d'hôtel nodded, and Ray described the basket of spun sugar   20
filled with different kinds of ice cream.

"And a spun-sugar bow," Ellen said.

The maître d'hôtel looked blank, and so Ray tried again, speaking slowly
and distinctly.

"*Omelette?*" the maître d'hôtel said.

"No—ice cream!"

"*Glace,*" Ellen said.   25

"*Et du sucre,*"[4] Ray said. "*Une—*" He and Ellen looked at each other.
Neither of them could think of the word for "basket."

The maître d'hôtel went over to a sideboard and returned with another
menu. "*Le menu des glaces,*" he said coldly. "*Vanille,*" they read, "*chocolat,
pistache, framboise,*[5] *fraise*[6] *tutti-frutti, praliné . . .*"

Even if the spun-sugar basket had been on the *menu des glaces* (which it
wasn't), they were in too excited a state to have found it—Ray because of
his fear that they were making an irremediable mistake in having dinner at
this restaurant and Ellen because of the dreadful way he was acting.

"We came here on a pilgrimage," he said to the maître d'hôtel, in a
tense, excited voice that carried all over the dining room. "We have these
friends in America who ate in Périgueux, and it is absolutely necessary that
we eat in the place they told us about."

"This is a very good restaurant," the maître d'hôtel said. "We have many   30
spécialités. Foie gras truffé[7] *poulet du Périgord noir,*[8] *truffes sous la cendre*[9]—"

---

[4] and of sugar.   [5] raspberry.   [6] strawberry.   [7] goose liver with truffles (rare edible
mushrooms).   [8] chicken casserole with a dark brown Madeira sauce with chopped truffles.
[9] grilled truffles.

"I know," Ray said, "but apparently it isn't the right one." He got up from his chair, and Ellen, shaking her head—because there was no use arguing with him when he was like this—got up, too. The other diners had all turned around to watch.

"Come," the maître d'hôtel said, taking hold of Ray's elbow. "In the lobby is a lady who speaks English very well. She will understand what it is you want."

In the lobby, Ray told his story again—how they had come to Périgueux because their friends in America had told them about a certain restaurant here, and how it was this restaurant and no other that they must find. They had thought it was the restaurant in the Hôtel du Domino, but since the restaurant of the Hôtel du Domino did not have the dessert that their friends in America had particularly recommended, little balls of ice cream in—

The concierge, her eyes large with sudden comprehension, interrupted him. "You want truffles?"

Out on the sidewalk, trying to read the "Michelin" map of Périgueux by the feeble light of a tall street lamp, Ray said, "La Montaigne has a star just like the Hôtel du Domino, but it also has three crossed forks and spoons, so it must be better than the hotel."

"All those crossed forks and spoons mean is that it is a very comfortable place to eat in," Ellen said. "It has nothing to do with the quality of the food. I don't care where we eat, so long as I don't have to go back there."

There were circles of fatigue under her eyes. She was both exasperated with him and proud of him for insisting on getting what they had come here for, when most people would have given in and taken what there was. They walked on a couple of blocks and came to a second open square. Ray stopped a man and woman.

"*Pardon, m'sieur,*" he said, removing his hat. "*Le restaurant La Montagne, c'est par là*"—he pointed—"*ou par là?*"[10]

"*La Montagne? Le restaurant La Montagne?*" the man said dubiously. "*Je regrette, mais je ne le connais pas.*"[11]

Ray opened the "Michelin" and, by the light of the nearest neon sign, the man and woman read down the page.

"*Ooh, LE MONTAIGNE!*" the woman exclaimed suddenly.

"*LE MONTAIGNE!*" the man echoed.

"*Oui, Le Montaigne,*" Ray said, nodding.

The man pointed across the square.

Standing in front of LeMontaigne, Ray again had doubts. It was much larger than the restaurant of the Hôtel du Domino, but it looked much more like a bar than a first-class restaurant. And again there were no tablecloths. A waiter approached them as they stood undecided on the sidewalk. Ray asked to see

---

[10] Is La Montagne restaurant there . . . or over there?   [11] I'm sorry, but I never heard of it.

the menu, and the waiter disappeared into the building. A moment later, a second waiter appeared. *"Le menu,"* he said, pointing to a standard a few feet away. Le Montaigne offered many specialties, most of them *truffés,* but not the Richardson's dessert.

"Couldn't we just go someplace and have an ordinary meal?" Ellen said. "I don't think I feel like eating anything elaborate any longer."

But Ray had made a discovery. "The restaurant is upstairs," he said. "What we've been looking at is the café, so naturally there aren't any tablecloths."

Taking Ellen by the hand, he started up what turned out to be a circular staircase. The second floor of the building was dark. Ellen, convinced that the restaurant had stopped serving dinner, objected to going any farther, but Ray went on and, protesting, she followed him. The third floor was brightly lighted—was, in fact, a restaurant, with white tablecloths, gleaming crystal, and the traditional dark-red plush upholstery, and two or three clients who were lingering over the end of dinner. The maître d'hôtel, in a black dinner jacket, led them to a table and handed them the same menu they had read downstairs.

"I don't see any roast chicken stuffed with truffles." Ellen said.

"Oh I forgot that's what you wanted!" Ray said, conscience-stricken. 50 "Did they have it at the Domino?"

"No, but they had it *poulet noir*—and here they don't even have that."

"I'm so sorry," he said. "Are you sure they don't have it here?" He ran his eyes down the list of dishes with truffles and said suddenly, "There it is!"

"Where?" Ellen demanded. He pointed to *"Tournedos aux truffes du Périgord."* "That's not chicken," Ellen said.

"Well, it's no good, then," Ray said.

"No good?" the maître d'hôtel said indignantly. "It's *very* good! *Le* 55 *tournedos aux truffes du Périgord*[12] is a *spécialité* of the restaurant!"

They were only partly successful in conveying to him that that was not what Ray had meant.

No, there was no roast chicken stuffed with truffles.

No chicken of any kind.

"I'm very sorry," Ray said, and got up from his chair.

He was not at all sure that Ellen would go back to the restaurant in the 60 Hôtel du Domino with him, but she did. Their table was just as they had left it. A waiter and a busboy, seeing them come in, exchanged startled whispers. The maître d'hôtel did not come near them for several minutes after they had sat down, and Ray carefully didn't look around for him.

"Do you think he is angry because we walked out?" Ellen asked.

---

[12] beef tenderloin with truffles from the region of Perigord.

Ray shook his head. "I think we hurt his feelings, though. I think he prides himself on speaking English, and now he will never again be sure that he does speak it, because of us."

Eventually, the maître d'hôtel appeared at their table. Sickly smiles were exchanged all around, and the menu was offered for the second time, without the flourish.

"What is *les truffes sous la cendre?*" Ellen asked.

"It takes forty-five minutes," the maître d'hôtel said.   65

"*Le foie gras truffé,*" Ray said. "For two."

"*Le foie gras,* O.K.," the maître d'hôtel said. "*Et ensuite?*"[13]

"*Oeufs en gelée,*"[14] Ellen said.

"*Oeufs en gelée,* O.K."

"*Le poulet noir,*" Ray said.   70

"*Le poulet noir,*" O.K."

"*Et deux Cinzano,*" Ray said, on solid ground at last, "*avec un morceau de glace et un zeste de citron. S'il vous plaît.*"[15]

The apéritif arrived, with ice and lemon peel, but the wine list was not presented, and Ray asked the waitress for it. She spoke to the maître d'hôtel, and that was the last the Ormsbys ever saw of her. The maître d'hôtel brought the wine list, they ordered the dry white *vin du pays*[16] that he recommended, and their dinner was served to them by a waiter so young that Ray looked to see whether he was in knee pants.

The pâté was everything the Richardsons had said it would be, and Ray, to make up for all he had put his wife through in the course of the evening, gave her a small quantity of his, which, protesting, she accepted. The maître d'hôtel stopped at their table and said, "Is it good?"

"Very good," they said simultaneously.   75

The *oeufs en gelée* arrived and were also very good, but were they any better than or even as good as the *oeufs en gelée* the Ormsbys had had in the restaurant of a hotel on the outskirts of Aix-en-Provence was the question.

"Is it good?" the maître d'hôtel asked.

"Very good," they said. "So is the wine."

The boy waiter brought in the *poulet noir*—a chicken casserole with a dark-brown Madeira sauce full of chopped truffles.

"Is it good?" Ray asked when the waiter had finished serving them and   80
Ellen had tasted the *pièce de résistance.*[17]

"It's very good," she said. "But I'm not sure I can taste the truffles."

"I think I can," he said, a moment later.

"With the roast chicken, it probably would have been quite easy," Ellen said.

---

[13] and after that?   [14] eggs in aspic.   [15] Two Cinzanos (Italian red wine) with a little bit of ice and a lemon twist, if you please.   [16] local wine.   [17] the principal dish of a meal.

"Are you sure the Richardsons had roast chicken stuffed with truffles?" Ray asked.

"I think so," Ellen said. "Anyway, I know I've read about it."   85

"Is it good?" the maître d'hôtel, their waiter, and the waiter from a neighboring table asked, in succession.

"Very good," the Ormsbys said.

Since they couldn't have the little balls of various kinds of ice cream in a basket of spun sugar with a spun-sugar bow for dessert, they decided not to have any dessert at all. The meal came to an abrupt end with *café filtre*.

Intending to take a short walk before going to bed, they heard dance music in the square in front of Le Montaigne, and found a large crowd there, celebrating the annual fair of Périgueux. There was a seven-piece orchestra on a raised platform under a canvas, and a few couples were dancing in the street. Soon there were more.

"Do you feel like dancing?" Ray asked.   90

The pavement was not as bad for dancing as he would have supposed, and something happened to them that never happened to them anywhere in France before—something remarkable. In spite of their clothes and their faces and the "Michelin" he held in one hand, eyes constantly swept over them or past them without pausing. Dancing in the street, they aroused no curiosity and, in fact, no interest whatever.

At midnight, standing on the balcony outside their room, they could still hear the music, a quarter of a mile away.

"Hasn't it been a lovely evening!" Ellen said. I'll always remember dancing in the street in Périgueux."

Two people emerged form the cinema, a few doors from the Hôtel du Domino. And then a few more—a pair of lovers, a woman, a boy, a woman and a man carrying a sleeping child.

"The pâté was the best I ever ate," Ellen said.   95

"The Richardsons probably are in the garden," Ray said. "I don't know that the dinner as a whole was all *that* good," he added thoughtfully. And then, "I don't know that we need to tell them."

"The poor people who run the cinema," Ellen said.

"Why?"

"No one came to see the movie."

"I suppose Périgueux really isn't the kind of town that would support a   100 movie theatre." Ray said.

"That's it," Ellen said. "Here when people want to relax and enjoy themselves, they have an apéritif, they walk up and down in the evening air, they dance in the street, the way people used to do before there were any movies. It's another civilization entirely from anything we're accustomed to. Another world."

They went back into the bedroom and closed the shutters. A few minutes later, some more people emerged from the movie theatre, and some more, and some more, and then a great crowd came streaming out and, walking gravely, like people taking part in a religious procession, fanned out across the open square.

Questions for Discussion and Writing

1. In what ways can Ray and Ellen's quest to locate the restaurant and have the exact meal their friends described be characterized as a "pilgrimage"? Is Ray and Ellen's quest successful and to whom is this quest more important?

2. What details suggest that the rituals of eating in a fancy expensive French restaurant have acquired a quasi-religious aura, at least for Ellen and Ray?

3. Describe a visit to your favorite restaurant, including details drawn from all five senses. Analyze the decor, architecture, menu, and other features that have created its image. Do you go there only on special occasions or more frequently? What is the most memorable meal you have had there?

4. **Rhetorical inquiry:** What examples does Maxwell include to reveal the obstacles that Ray and Ellen must overcome to achieve their goal? For example, how successfully do they decipher obscure and unintelligible signs and symbols and converse with people whose language they do not understand? How would you describe Maxwell's tone and his attitude toward Ray and Ellen?

ANDRE DUBUS

Andre Dubus (1936–1999) was born in Lake Charles, Louisiana. He graduated from McNeese State College and joined the Marine Corps, in which he served until 1964. After studying creative writing at the University of Iowa, he taught at Bradford College in Massachusetts from 1966 until 1984. His many collections of short fiction include The Cage Keeper and Other Stories *(1989), and* Dancing After Hours *(1996). His short story "Killings" was adapted for the 2001 film* In the Bedroom. *"The Fat Girl" first appeared in* Adultery and Other Choices *(1975).*

Before You Read

Would you be sympathetic to a girl who lost weight to get married and then gained it back? Why or why not?

The Fat Girl

Her name was Louise. Once when she was sixteen a boy kissed her at a barbecue; he was drunk and he jammed his tongue into her mouth and ran his hands up and down her hips. Her father kissed her often. He was thin and kind and she could see in his eyes when he looked at her the lights of love and pity.

It started when Louise was nine. You must start watching what you eat, her mother would say. I can see you have my metabolism. Louise also had her mother's pale blond hair. Her mother was slim and pretty, carried herself erectly, and ate very little. The two of them would eat bare lunches, while her older brother ate sandwiches and potato chips, and then her mother would sit smoking while Louise eyed the bread box, the pantry, the refrigerator. Wasn't that good, her mother would say. In five years you'll be in high school and if you're fat the boys won't like you; they won't ask you out. Boys were as far away as five years, and she would go to her room and wait for nearly an hour until she knew her mother was no longer thinking of her, then she would creep into the kitchen and, listening to her mother talking on the phone, or her footsteps upstairs, she would open the bread box, the pantry, the jar of peanut butter. She would put the sandwich under her shirt and go outside or to the bathroom to eat it.

Her father was a lawyer and made a lot of money and came home looking pale and happy. Martinis put color back in his face, and at dinner he talked to his wife and two children. Oh give her a potato, he would say to Louise's mother. She's a growing girl. Her mother's voice then became tense: If she has a potato she shouldn't have dessert. She should have both, her father would say, and he would reach over and touch Louise's cheek or hand or arm.

In high school she had two girlfriends and at night and on weekends they rode in a car or went to movies. In movies she was fascinated by fat actresses. She wondered why they were fat. She knew why she was fat: she was fat because she was Louise. Because God had made her that way. Because she wasn't like her friends Joan and Marjorie, who drank milk shakes after school and were all bones and tight skin. But what about those actresses, with their talents, with their broad and profound faces? Did they eat as heedlessly as Bishop Humphries and his wife who sometimes came to dinner and, as Louise's mother said, gorged between amenities? Or did they try to lose weight, did they go about hungry and angry and thinking of food? She thought of them eating lean meats and salads with friends, and then going home and building strange large sandwiches with French bread. But mostly she believed they did not go through these failures; they were fat because they chose to be. And she was certain of something else too: she could see it in their faces: they did not eat secretly. Which she did: her creeping to the kitchen when she was nine became, in high school, a ritual of deceit and pleasure. She was a furtive eater of sweets. Even her two friends did not know her secret.

Joan was thin, gangling, and flat-chested; she was attractive enough and all she needed was someone to take a second look at her face, but the school was large and there were pretty girls in every classroom and walking all the corridors, so no one ever needed to take a second look at Joan. Marjorie was thin too, an intense, heavy-smoking girl with brittle laughter. She was very

5

intelligent, and with boys she was shy because she knew she made them uncomfortable, and because she was smarter than they were and so could not understand or could not believe the levels they lived on. She was to have a nervous breakdown before earning her Ph.D. in philosophy at the University of California, where she met and married a physicist and discovered within herself an untrammelled passion: she made love with her husband on the couch, the carpet, in the bathtub, and on the washing machine. By that time much had happened to her and she never thought of Louise. Joan would finally stop growing and begin moving with grace and confidence. In college she would have two lovers and then several more during the six years she spent in Boston before marrying a middle-aged editor who had two sons in their early teens, who drank too much, who was tenderly, boyishly grateful for her love, and whose wife had been killed while rock-climbing in New Hampshire with her lover. She would not think of Louise either, except in an earlier time, when lovers were still new to her and she was ecstatically surprised each time one of them loved her and, sometimes at night, lying in a man's arms, she would tell how in high school no one dated her, she had been thin and plain (she would still believe that: that she had been plain; it had never been true) and so had been forced into the weekend and night-time company of a neurotic smart girl and a shy fat girl. She would say this with self-pity exaggerated by Scotch and her need to be more deeply loved by the man who held her.

She never eats, Joan and Marjorie said of Louise. They ate lunch with her at school, watched her refusing potatoes, ravioli, fried fish. Sometimes she got through the cafeteria line with only a salad. That is how they would remember her: a girl whose hapless body was destined to be fat. No one saw the sandwiches she made and took to her room when she came home from school. No one saw the store of Milky Ways, Butterfingers, Almond Joys, and Hersheys far back on her closet shelf, behind the stuffed animals of her childhood. She was not a hypocrite. When she was out of the house she truly believed she was dieting; she forgot about the candy, as a man speaking into his office dictaphone may forget the lewd photographs hidden in an old shoe in his closet. At other times, away from home, she thought of the waiting candy with near lust. One night driving home from a movie, Marjorie said: "You're lucky you don't smoke; it's incredible what I go through to hide it from my parents." Louise turned to her a smile which was elusive and mysterious; she yearned to be home in bed, eating chocolate in the dark. She did not need to smoke; she already had a vice that was insular and destructive. . . .

She brought it with her to college. She thought she would leave it behind. A move from one place to another, a new room without the haunted closet shelf, would do for her what she could not do for herself. She packed her large dresses and went. For two weeks she was busy with registration, with shyness, with classes; then she began to feel at home. Her room was no longer like a motel. Its walls had stopped watching her, she felt they were her friends, and she gave them her secret. Away from her mother, she did not have to be as elaborate; she kept the candy in her drawer now.

The school was in Massachusetts, a girls' school. When she chose it, when she and her father and mother talked about it in the evenings, everyone so carefully avoided the word boys that sometimes the conversations seemed to be about nothing but boys. There are no boys there, the neuter words said; you will not have to contend with that. In her father's eyes were pity and encouragement; in her mother's was disappointment, and her voice was crisp. They spoke of courses, of small classes where Louise would get more attention. She imagined herself in those small classes; she saw herself as a teacher would see her, as the other girls would; she would get no attention.

The girls at the school were from wealthy families, but most of them wore the uniform of another class: blue jeans and work shirts, and many wore overalls. Louise bought some overalls, washed them until the dark blue faded, and wore them to classes. In the cafeteria she ate as she had in high school, not to lose weight nor even to sustain her lie, but because eating lightly in public had become as habitual as good manners. Everyone had to take gym, and in the locker room with the other girls, and wearing shorts on the volleyball and badminton courts, she hated her body. She liked her body most when she was unaware of it: in bed at night, as sleep gently took her out of her day, out of herself. And she liked parts of her body. She liked her brown eyes and sometimes looked at them in the mirror: they were not shallow eyes, she thought; they were indeed windows of a tender soul, a good heart. She liked her lips and nose, and her chin, finely shaped between her wide and sagging cheeks. Most of all she liked her long pale blond hair, she liked washing and drying it and lying naked on her bed, smelling of shampoo, and feeling the soft hair at her neck and shoulders and back.

Her friend at college was Carrie, who was thin and wore thick glasses   10 and often at night she cried in Louise's room. She did not know why she was crying. She was crying, she said, because she was unhappy. She could say no more. Louise said she was unhappy too, and Carrie moved in with her. One night Carrie talked for hours, sadly and bitterly, about her parents and what they did to each other. When she finished she hugged Louise and they went to bed. Then in the dark Carrie spoke across the room: "Louise? I just wanted to tell you. One night last week I woke up and smelled chocolate. You were eating chocolate, in your bed. I wish you'd eat it in front of me, Louise, whenever you feel like it."

Stiffened in her bed, Louise could think of nothing to say. In the silence she was afraid Carrie would think she was asleep and would tell her again in the morning or tomorrow night. Finally she said okay. Then after a moment she told Carrie if she ever wanted any she could feel free to help herself; the candy was in the top drawer. Then she said thank you.

They were roommates for four years and in the summers they exchanged letters. Each fall they greeted with embraces, laughter, tears, and moved into their old room, which had been stripped and cleansed of them for the summer. Neither girl enjoyed summer. Carrie did not like being at home because her parents did not love each other. Louise lived in a small city in Louisiana. She did not like summer because she had lost touch with Joan and Marjorie; they saw each other, but it was not the same. She liked being with her father but with no one else. The flicker of disappointment in her mother's eyes at the airport was a vanguard of the army of relatives and acquaintances who awaited her: they would see her on the streets, in stores, at the country club, in her home, and in theirs; in the first moments of greeting, their eyes would tell her she was still fat Louise, who had been fat as long as they could remember, who had gone to college and returned as fat as ever. Then their eyes dismissed her, and she longed for school and Carrie, and she wrote letters to her friend. But that saddened her too. It wasn't simply that Carrie was her only friend, and when they finished college they might never see each other again. It was that her existence in the world was so divided; it had begun when she was a child creeping to the kitchen; now that division was much sharper, and her friendship with Carrie seemed disproportionate and perilous. The world she was destined to live in had nothing to do with the intimate nights in their room at school.

In the summer before their senior year, Carrie fell in love. She wrote to Louise about him, but she did not write much, and this hurt Louise more than if Carrie had shown the joy her writing tried to conceal. That fall they returned to their room; they were still close and warm, Carrie still needed Louise's ears and heart at night as she spoke of her parents and her recurring malaise whose source the two friends never discovered. But on most weekends Carrie left, and caught a bus to Boston where her boyfriend studied music. During the week she often spoke hesitantly of sex; she was not sure if she liked it. But Louise, eating candy and listening, did not know whether Carrie was telling the truth or whether, as in her letters of the past summer, Carrie was keeping from her those delights she may never experience.

Then one Sunday night when Carrie had just returned from Boston and was unpacking her overnight bag, she looked at Louise and said: "I was thinking about you. On the bus coming home tonight." Looking at Carrie's concerned, determined face, Louise prepared herself for humiliation. "I was thinking about when we graduate. What you're going to do. What's to become of you. I want you to be loved the way I love you. Louise, if I help you, *really* help you, will you go on a diet?"

Louise entered a period of her life she would remember always, the way   15 some people remember having endured poverty. Her diet did not begin the next day. Carrie told her to eat on Monday as though it were the last day of her life. So for the first time since grammar school Louise went into a school cafeteria and ate everything she wanted. At breakfast and lunch and dinner she glanced around the table to see if the other girls noticed the food on her tray. They did not. She felt there was a lesson in this, but it lay beyond her grasp. That night in their room she ate the four remaining candy bars. During the day Carrie rented a small refrigerator, bought an electric skillet, an electric broiler, and bathroom scales.

On Tuesday morning Louise stood on the scales, and Carrie wrote in her notebook: *October 14: 184 lbs.* Then she made Louise a cup of black coffee and scrambled one egg and sat with her while she ate. When Carrie went to the dining room for breakfast, Louise walked about the campus for thirty minutes. That was part of the plan. The campus was pretty, on its lawns grew at least one of every tree native to New England, and in the warm morning sun Louise felt a new hope. At noon they met in their room, and Carrie broiled her a piece of hamburger and served it with lettuce. Then while Carrie ate in the dining room Louise walked again. She was weak with hunger and she felt queasy. During her afternoon classes she was nervous and tense, and she chewed her pencil and tapped her heels on the floor and tightened her calves. When she returned to her room late that afternoon, she was so glad to see Carrie that she embraced her; she had felt she could not bear another minute of hunger, but now with Carrie she knew she could make it at least through tonight. Then she would sleep and face tomorrow when it came. Carrie broiled her a steak and served it with lettuce. Louise studied while Carrie ate dinner, then they went for a walk.

That was her ritual and her diet for the rest of the year, Carrie alternating fish and chicken breasts with the steaks for dinner, and every day was nearly as bad as the first. In the evenings she was irritable. In all her life she had never been afflicted by ill temper and she looked upon it now as a demon which, along with hunger, was taking possession of her soul. Often she spoke sharply to Carrie. One night during their after-dinner walk Carrie talked sadly of night, of how darkness made her more aware of herself, and at night she did not know why she was in college, why she studied, why she was walking the earth with other people. They were standing on a wooden foot bridge, looking down at a dark pond. Carrie kept talking; perhaps soon she would cry. Suddenly Louise said: "I'm sick of lettuce. I never want to see a piece of lettuce for the rest of my life. I hate it. We shouldn't even buy it, it's immoral."

Carrie was quiet. Louise glanced at her, and the pain and irritation in Carrie's face soothed her. Then she was ashamed. Before she could say she was sorry, Carrie turned to her and said gently: "I know. I know how terrible it is."

Carrie did all the shopping, telling Louise she knew how hard it was to go into a supermarket when you were hungry. And Louise was always hungry. She drank diet soft drinks and started smoking Carrie's cigarettes, learned to enjoy inhaling, thought of cancer and emphysema but they were as far away as those boys her mother had talked about when she was nine. By Thanksgiving she was smoking over a pack a day and her weight in Carrie's notebook was one hundred and sixty-two pounds. Carrie was afraid if Louise went home at Thanksgiving she would lapse from the diet, so Louise spent the vacation with Carrie, in Philadelphia. Carrie wrote to her family about the diet, and told Louise that she had. On the phone to Philadelphia, Louise said: "I feel like a bedwetter. When I was a little girl I had a friend who used to come spend the night and Mother would put a rubber sheet on the bed and we all pretended there wasn't a rubber sheet and that she hadn't wet the bed. Even me, and I slept with her." At Thanksgiving dinner she lowered her eyes as Carrie's father put two slices of white meat on her plate and passed it to her over the bowls of steaming food.

When she went home at Christmas she weighed a hundred and fifty-five 20
pounds; at the airport her mother marveled. Her father laughed and hugged
her and said: "But now there's less of you to love." He was troubled by her
smoking but only mentioned it once; he told her she was beautiful and, as
always, his eyes bathed her with love. During the long vacation her mother
cooked for her as Carrie had, and Louise returned to school weighing a hundred and forty-six pounds.

Flying north on the plane she warmly recalled the surprised and con-
gratulatory eyes of her relatives and acquaintances. She had not seen Joan or
Marjorie. She thought of returning home in May, weighing the hundred and
fifteen pounds which Carrie had in October set as their goal. Looking toward
the stoic days ahead, she felt strong. She thought of those hungry days of fall
and early winter (and now: she was hungry now: with almost a frown, almost
a brusque shake of the head, she refused peanuts from the stewardess): those
first weeks of the diet when she was the pawn of an irascibility which still,
conditioned to her ritual as she was, could at any moment take command of
her. She thought of the nights of trying to sleep while her stomach growled.
She thought of her addiction to cigarettes. She thought of the people at school:
not one teacher, not one girl, had spoken to her about her loss of weight, not
even about her absence from meals. And without warning her spirit collapsed.
She did not feel strong, she did not feel she was committed to and within reach
of achieving a valuable goal. She felt that somehow she had lost more than
pounds of fat; that some time during her dieting she had lost herself too. She
tried to remember what it had felt like to be Louise before she had started living on meat and fish, as an unhappy adult may look sadly in the memory of
childhood for lost virtues and hopes. She looked down at the earth far below,
and it seemed to her that her soul, like her body aboard the plane, was in some
rootless flight. She neither knew its destination nor where it had departed
from; it was on some passage she could not even define.

During the next few weeks she lost weight more slowly and once for
eight days Carrie's daily recording stayed at a hundred and thirty-six. Louise
woke in the morning thinking of one hundred and thirty-six and then she
stood on the scales and they echoed her. She became obsessed with that
number, and there wasn't a day when she didn't say it aloud, and through
the days and nights the number stayed in her mind, and if a teacher had
spoken those digits in a classroom she would have opened her mouth to
speak. What if that's me, she said to Carrie. I mean what if a hundred and
thirty-six is my real weight and I just can't lose anymore. Walking hand-in-hand
with her despair was a longing for this to be true, and that longing angered
her and wearied her, and every day she was gloomy. On the ninth day she
weighed a hundred and thirty-five and a half pounds. She was not relieved;
she thought bitterly of the months ahead, the shedding of the last twenty
and a half pounds.

On Easter Sunday, which she spent at Carrie's, she weighed one hundred and twenty pounds, and she ate one slice of glazed pineapple with her

ham and lettuce. She did not enjoy it: she felt she was being friendly with a recalcitrant enemy who had once tried to destroy her. Carrie's parents were laudative. She liked them and she wished they would touch sometimes, and look at each other when they spoke. She guessed they would divorce when Carrie left home, and she vowed that her own marriage would be one of affection and tenderness. She could think about that now: marriage. At school she had read in a Boston paper that this summer the cicadas would come out of their seventeen-year hibernation on Cape Cod, for a month they would mate and then die, leaving their young to burrow into the ground where they would stay for seventeen years. That's me, she had said to Carrie. Only my hibernation lasted twenty-one years.

Often her mother asked in letters and on the phone about the diet, but Louise answered vaguely. When she flew home in late May she weighed a hundred and thirteen pounds, and at the airport her mother cried and hugged her and said again and again: You're so *beauti*ful. Her father blushed and bought her a martini. For days her relatives and acquaintances congratulated her, and the applause in their eyes lasted the entire summer, and she loved their eyes, and swam in the country club pool, the first time she had done this since she was a child.

She lived at home and ate the way her mother did and every morning she weighed herself on the scales in her bathroom. Her mother liked to take her shopping and buy her dresses and they put her old ones in the Goodwill box at the shopping center; Louise thought of them existing on the body of a poor woman whose cheap meals kept her fat. Louise's mother had a photographer come to the house, and Louise posed on the couch and standing beneath a live oak and sitting in a wicker lawn chair next to an azalea bush. The new clothes and the photographer made her feel she was going to another country or becoming a citizen of a new one. In the fall she took a job of no consequence, to give herself something to do.

Also in the fall a young lawyer joined her father's firm, he came one night to dinner, and they started seeing each other. He was the first man outside her family to kiss her since the barbecue when she was sixteen. Louise celebrated Thanksgiving not with rice dressing and candied sweet potatoes and mince meat and pumpkin pies, but by giving Richard her virginity which she realized, at the very last moment of its existence, she had embarked on giving him over thirteen months ago, on that Tuesday in October when Carrie had made her a cup of black coffee and scrambled one egg. She wrote this to Carrie, who replied happily by return mail. She also, through glance and smile and innuendo, tried to tell her mother too. But finally she controlled that impulse, because Richard felt guilty about making love with the daughter of his partner and friend. In the spring they married. The wedding was a large one, in the Episcopal church, and Carrie flew from Boston to be maid of honor. Her parents had recently separated and she was

25

living with the musician and was still victim of her unpredictable malaise. It overcame her on the night before the wedding, so Louise was up with her until past three and woke next morning from a sleep so heavy that she did not want to leave it.

Richard was a lean, tall, energetic man with the metabolism of a pencil sharpener. Louise fed him everything he wanted. He liked Italian food and she got recipes from her mother and watched him eating spaghetti with the sauce she had only tasted, and ravioli and lasagna, while she ate antipasto with her chianti. He made a lot of money and borrowed more and they bought a house whose lawn sloped down to the shore of a lake; they had a wharf and a boathouse, and Richard bought a boat and they took friends waterskiing. Richard bought her a car and they spent his vacations in Mexico, Canada, the Bahamas, and in the fifth year of their marriage they went to Europe and, according to their plan, she conceived a child in Paris. On the plane back, as she looked out the window and beyond the sparkling sea and saw her country, she felt that it was waiting for her, as her home by the lake was, and her parents, and her good friends who rode in the boat and waterskied; she thought of the accumulated warmth and pelf of her marriage, and how by slimming her body she had bought into the pleasures of the nation. She felt cunning, and she smiled to herself, and took Richard's hand.

But these moments of triumph were sparse. On most days she went about her routine of leisure with a sense of certainty about herself that came merely from not thinking. But there were times, with her friends, or with Richard, or alone in the house, when she was suddenly assaulted by the feeling that she had taken the wrong train and arrived at a place where no one knew her, and where she ought not to be. Often, in bed with Richard, she talked of being fat: "I was the one who started the friendship with Carrie, I chose her, I started the conversations. When I understood that she was my friend I understood something else: I had chosen her for the same reason I'd chosen Joan and Marjorie. They were all thin. I was always thinking about what people saw when they looked at me and I didn't want them to see two fat girls. When I was alone I didn't mind being fat but then I'd have to leave the house again and then I didn't want to look like me. But at home I didn't mind except when I was getting dressed to go out of the house and when Mother looked at me. But I stopped looking at her when she looked at me. And in college I felt good with Carrie; there weren't any boys and I didn't have any other friends and so when I wasn't with Carrie I thought about her and I tried to ignore the other people around me, I tried to make them not exist. A lot of the time I could do that. It was strange, and I felt like a spy."

If Richard was bored by her repetition he pretended not to be. But she knew the story meant very little to him. She could have been telling him of a childhood illness, or wearing braces, or a broken heart at sixteen. He could not see her as she was when she was fat. She felt as though she were trying to tell a foreign lover about her life in the United States, and if only she could command the language he would know and love all of her and she would feel complete. Some of the acquaintances of her childhood were her friends now, and even they did not seem to remember her when she was fat.

Now her body was growing again, and when she put on a maternity   30
dress for the first time she shivered with fear. Richard did not smoke and he asked her, in a voice just short of demand, to stop during her pregnancy. She did. She ate carrots and celery instead of smoking, and at cocktail parties she tried to eat nothing, but after her first drink she ate nuts and cheese and crackers and dips. Always at these parties Richard had talked with his friends and she had rarely spoken to him until they drove home. But now when he noticed her at the hors d'oeuvres table he crossed the room and, smiling, led her back to his group. His smile and his hand on her arm told her he was doing his clumsy, husbandly best to help her through a time of female mystery.

She was gaining weight but she told herself it was only the baby, and would leave with its birth. But at other times she knew quite clearly that she was losing the discipline she had fought so hard to gain during her last year with Carrie. She was hungry now as she had been in college, and she ate between meals and after dinner and tried to eat only carrots and celery, but she grew to hate them, and her desire for sweets was as vicious as it had been long ago. At home she ate bread and jam and when she shopped for groceries she bought a candy bar and ate it driving home and put the wrapper in her purse and then in the garbage can under the sink. Her cheeks had filled out, there was loose flesh under her chin, her arms and legs were plump, and her mother was concerned. So was Richard. One night when she brought pie and milk to the living room where they were watching television, he said: "You already had a piece. At dinner."

She did not look at him.

"You're gaining weight. It's not all water, either. It's fat. It'll be summertime. You'll want to get into your bathing suit."

The pie was cherry. She looked at it as her fork cut through it; she speared the piece and rubbed it in the red juice on the plate before lifting it to her mouth.

"You never used to eat pie," he said. "I just think you ought to watch it   35
a bit. It's going to be tough on you this summer."

In her seventh month, with a delight reminiscent of climbing the stairs to Richard's apartment before they were married, she returned to her world of secret gratification. She began hiding candy in her underwear drawer. She ate it during the day and at night while Richard slept, and at breakfast she was distracted, waiting for him to leave.

She gave birth to a son, brought him home, and nursed both him and her appetites. During this time of celibacy she enjoyed her body through her son's mouth; while he suckled she stroked his small head and back. She was hiding candy but she did not conceal her other indulgences: she was smoking again but still she ate between meals, and at dinner she ate what Richard did, and coldly he watched her, he grew petulant, and when the date marking the end of their celibacy came they let it pass. Often in the afternoons her mother visited and scolded her and Louise sat looking at the baby and said nothing until finally, to end it, she promised to diet. When her mother and father came for dinners, her father kissed her and held the baby and her mother said nothing about Louise's body, and her voice was tense. Returning from work in the evenings Richard looked at a soiled plate and glass on the table beside her chair as if detecting traces of infidelity, and at every dinner they fought.

"Look at you," he said. "Lasagna, for God's sake. When are you going to start? It's not simply that you haven't lost any weight. You're gaining. I can see it. I can feel it when you get in bed. Pretty soon you'll weigh more than I do and I'll be sleeping on a trampoline."

"You never touch me anymore."

"I don't want to touch you. Why should I? Have you *looked* at yourself?"   40

"You're cruel," she said. "I never knew how cruel you were."

She ate, watching him. He did not look at her. Glaring at his plate, he worked with fork and knife like a hurried man at a lunch counter.

"I bet you didn't either," she said.

That night when he was asleep she took a Milky Way to the bathroom. For a while she stood eating in the dark, then she turned on the light. Chewing, she looked at herself in the mirror; she looked at her eyes and hair. Then she stood on the scales and looking at the numbers between her feet, one hundred and sixty-two, she remembered when she had weighed a hundred and thirty-six pounds for eight days. Her memory of those eight days was fond and amusing, as though she were recalling an Easter egg hunt when she was six. She stepped off the scales and pushed them under the lavatory and did not stand on them again.

It was summer and she bought loose dresses and when Richard took   45 friends out on the boat she did not wear a bathing suit or shorts; her friends gave her mischievous glances, and Richard did not look at her. She stopped riding on the boat. She told them she wanted to stay with the baby, and she sat inside holding him until she heard the boat leave the wharf. Then she took him to the front lawn and walked with him in the shade of the trees and talked to him about the blue jays and mockingbirds and cardinals she saw on their branches. Sometimes she stopped and watched the boat out on the lake and the friend skiing behind it.

Every day Richard quarreled, and because his rage went no further than her weight and shape, she felt excluded from it, and she remained calm within layers of flesh and spirit, and watched his frustration, his impotence. He truly believed they were arguing about her weight. She knew better: she knew that beneath the argument lay the question of who Richard was. She thought of him smiling at the wheel of his boat, and long ago courting his slender girl, the daughter of his partner and friend. She thought of Carrie telling her of smelling chocolate in the dark and, after that, watching her eat it night after night. She smiled at Richard, teasing his anger.

He is angry now. He stands in the center of the living room, raging at her, and he wakes the baby. Beneath Richard's voice she hears the soft crying, feels it in her heart, and quietly she rises from her chair and goes upstairs to the child's room and takes him from the crib. She brings him to the living room and sits holding him in her lap, pressing him gently against the folds of fat at her waist. Now Richard is pleading with her. Louise thinks tenderly of Carrie broiling meat and fish in their room, and walking with her in the evenings. She wonders if Carrie still has the malaise. Perhaps she will come for a visit. In Louise's arms now the boy sleeps.

"I'll help you," Richard says. "I'll eat the same things you eat."

But his face does not approach the compassion and determination and love she had seen in Carrie's during what she now recognizes as the worst year of her life. She can remember nothing about that year except hunger, and the meals in her room. She is hungry now. When she puts the boy to bed she will get a candy bar from her room. She will eat it here, in front of Richard. This room will be hers soon. She considers the possibilities: all these rooms and the lawn where she can do whatever she wishes. She knows he will leave soon. It has been in his eyes all summer. She stands, using one hand to pull herself out of the chair. She carries the boy to his crib, feels him against her large breasts, feels that his sleeping body touches her soul. With a surge of vindication and relief she holds him. Then she kisses his forehead and places him in the crib. She goes to the bedroom and in the dark takes a bar of candy from her drawer. Slowly she descends the stairs. She knows Richard is waiting but she feels his departure so happily that, when she enters the living room, unwrapping the candy, she is surprised to see him standing there.

Questions for Discussion and Writing

1. What factors explain why being thin becomes so important to Louise? How do her mother and father communicate very different messages about this?
2. Why is Louise's relationship with Carrie one of the most important ones in her life?
3. Why does Louise return to being fat after she has married Richard and had a child and established a life she presumably wanted?
4. Write a caption to a snapshot or an e-mailed photo of a family member or friend, and then write a short paragraph describing the person, the circumstances, and how the picture and the caption work together.
5. **Rhetorical inquiry:** What means does Dubus use to make the reader aware of the hidden emotional costs of Louise's dieting regimen? For example, how does the imagery used to describe what Louise feels when she is taking a flight back to school express her ambivalence?

Poetry

Elizabeth Barrett Browning

Elizabeth Barrett Browning (1806–1861) was given a thorough education in Greek, Latin, French, Italian, German, and Spanish from tutors. She began writing poetry at the age of eight. Plagued by ill health, she settled in the family home in London in 1841 and devoted what energy she had to writing. A two-volume collection of her poems elicited a letter from Robert Browning that initiated their celebrated correspondence. In the Sonnets from the Portuguese,[1] *written during 1846, Elizabeth charts her growing love for him. Her father was violently opposed to their marrying, and so they eloped to Italy in 1846. Her poetry is not only about love but political change and social justice.*

Before You Read

Think about how love is similar to religious devotion.

How Do I Love Thee?

How do I love thee? Let me count the ways.
I love thee to the depth and breadth and height
My soul can reach, when feeling out of sight
For the ends of Being and ideal Grace.
I love thee to the level of every day's   5
Most quiet need; by sun and candlelight.
I love thee freely, as men strive for Right;
I love thee purely, as they turn from Praise.
I love thee with the passion put to use
In my old griefs, and with my childhood's faith,   10
I love thee with a love I seemed to lose
With my lost saints,—I love thee with the breath,
Smiles, tears, of all my life!—and, if God choose,
I shall but love thee better after death.

Questions for Discussion and Writing

1. In what ways does the speaker blend an idealized romantic love with an almost quasi-religious devotion?

---

[1] From *Sonnets from the Portuguese*, No. 43. These love poems addressed to Browning are lightly disguised as translations from a fictitious Portuguese source.

2. How does this sonnet develop the spacial metaphor of the second line? Beginning at line 10 the sonnet shifts to the temporal dimension referring to "old griefs," "childhood faith," and "lost saints" (line 12). How does this shift in focus amend the catalog listing "the ways of love"?

3. Do you believe that this idealized kind of love is capable of being sustained in the real world? Why or why not?

4. **Rhetorical inquiry:** How is the emotional logic of the poem designed to prepare the reader for a startling revelation that the lovers will exist as souls reunited after death? How does the theme of the poem continue the tradition of the Italian sonnet (originally developed by Petrarch 1304–1374)?

Sara Teasdale

Sara Teasdale (1884–1933) was raised and educated in St. Louis and traveled to Europe and the Near East. After returning to the United States, she settled in New York and lived a life very similar to the independent "solitary" she describes in this poem. Her published works include Rivers to the Sea *(1915) and* Love Songs *(1917).* Love Songs *went through five editions in one year and won Teasdale a special Pulitzer award, the first given to a book of poetry.*

Before You Read

Is it possible or even desirable to be completely independent?

The Solitary

My heart has grown rich with the passing of years,
    I have less need now than when I was young

To share myself with every comer
    Or shape my thoughts into words with my tongue.

It is one to me that they come or go   5
    If I have myself and the drive of my will,
And strength to climb on a summer night
    And watch the stars swarm over the hill.

Let them think I love them more than I do,
    Let them think I care, though I go alone;   10
If it lifts their pride, what is it to me
    Who am self-complete as a flower or a stone.

Questions for Discussion and Writing

1. In what way has the speaker changed from when she was young?
2. How does the speaker feel toward the way others perceive her?
3. Do you believe it is possible or desirable for someone to become as "self-complete as a flower or a stone"? Why, or why not? Alternatively, you might consider whether people become more self-sufficient as they grow older.
4. **Rhetorical inquiry:** Can we infer that the speaker has chosen two contrasting symbols (flowers open out to the world and the opposite might be said of stones) to express her ambivalence about how far she has come in achieving her goal of self-sufficiency? Is her new-found independence a pose? Why or why not?

NIKKI GIOVANNI

Nikki Giovanni was born in 1943 in Knoxville, Tennessee, the daughter of a probation officer and a social worker. She graduated with honors from Fisk University in 1967 and did postgraduate work at the University of Pennsylvania School of Social Work and Columbia University School of Fine Arts. She has taught black studies at Queens College, City University of New York, and English at Rutgers University (1968–1970). She is currently a professor of creative writing at Virginia Tech University. Giovanni attained prominence in the late 1960s and early 1970s with her poetry on the themes of racial pride and family values. Collections of her poetry include Black Judgement *(1968) in which Giovanni's reminiscences of her childhood, "Nikki-Rosa," first appeared. Her recent works include* Love Poems *(1997) and* Blues: For All the Changes: New Poems *(1999).*

Before You Read

What makes a happy childhood?

Nikki-Rosa

childhood remembrances are always a drag
if you're Black
you always remember things like living in Woodlawn[1]
with no inside toilet
and if you become famous or something   5
they never talk about how happy you were to have your mother
all to yourself and

---

[1] a predominantly black suburb of Cincinnati, Ohio.

how good the water felt when you got your bath from one of those
big tubs that folk in chicago barbecue in
and somehow when you talk about home   10
it never gets across how much you
understood their feelings
as the whole family attended meetings about Hollydale
and even though you remember
your biographers never understand   15
your father's pain as he sells his stock
and another dream goes
and though you're poor it isn't poverty that
concerns you
and though they fought a lot   20
it isn't your father's drinking that makes any difference
but only that everybody is together and you
and your sister have happy birthdays and very good christmasses
and I really hope no white person ever has cause to write about me
because they never understand Black love is Black wealth   25
and they'll
probably talk about my hard childhood and never understand that
all the while I was quite happy

Questions for Discussion and Writing

1. In what way did the speaker's childhood differ from how her biographers understand it? What preconceptions does Giovanni refute in this poem?
2. What details in the poem explore the question of what constitutes "true" wealth? How does the appearance of the lines and rhythms and pauses that they create underscore Giovanni's evolving argument?
3. How does this poem dramatize what artists do as compared with sociologists who chronicle facts about social conditions?
4. **Rhetorical inquiry:** How would you characterize the tone of the speaker? To what extent does her willingness to describe privations and setbacks make her overall conclusion more believable?

Connections for Chapter 1:
Reflections on Experience

1. **George Orwell,** *Shooting an Elephant*
   What complementary insights about life under colonialism are offered by Orwell and Fatima Mernissi ("Moonlit Nights of Laughter") in Chapter 2?

2. **Ruth Reichel,** *Betty*
   How do both Reichl's account and William Maxwell's story illustrate how dining in fine restaurants brings into play issues of status and social class and can have symbolic meaning?

3. **Jill Nelson,** *Number One!*
   In what ways do both Nelson and Judith Ortiz Cofer ("The Myth of the Latin Woman") in Chapter 5 strive to transcend socially restrictive expectations linked to race and ethnicity?

4. **Fritz Peters,** *Boyhood with Gurdjieff*
   Compare Gurdjieff's seemingly unfair method for teaching compassion with Jesus's teaching parable ("The Laborers in the Vineyard") in *The New Testament* in Chapter 11.

5. **Beryl Markham,** *West with the Night*
   Compare the reasons why Markham and Douchan Gersi subject themselves to life-endangering challenges that most people would not choose to encounter.

6. **Dave Barry,** *Just Say No to Rugs*
   Compare the perspectives of having a pet as expressed by Barry with those in "Cervicide" by Gloria Anzaldúa in Chapter 5.

7. **Douchan Gersi,** *Initiated into an Iban Tribe of Headhunters*
   Compare the experiences, expectations, and outcomes in Gersi's account with those of Herodotus in "Concerning Egypt" (Chapter 7).

8. **James Herriot,** *Rumenotomy on a Cow*
   Compare Herriot's account with the humanistic perspective of Alice Walker's essay "Am I Blue?" in Chapter 6.

9. **William Maxwell,** *The Pilgrimage*
   Contrast the elusive goal pursued in this story with the evolution of cuisine in America as described by Bill Bryson ("What's Cooking? Eating in America") in Chapter 5.

10. **Andre Dubus,** *The Fat Girl*
    Compare the effects of social pressures on the protagonist in this story with Rosalind Coward's analysis "The Body Beautiful" in Chapter 5.

11. **Elizabeth Barrett Browning,** *How Do I Love Thee?*
    Is Browning's poem as far from Gregory Corso's "Marriage" (Chapter 5) as it might seem at first glance?

12. **Sara Teasdale,** *The Solitary*
    How is the theme of self-reliance developed in Teasdale's poem and in Nasreddin Hodja's story ("Do As You Please") in Chapter 11?

13. **Nikki Giovanni,** *Nikki-Rosa*
    Compare Giovanni's childhood with that of Jill Nelson ("Number One!") in terms of empowerment and race.

2

MEMORABLE PEOPLE AND PLACES

Who shall set a limit to the influence of a human being?
Ralph Waldo Emerson, "Power", THE CONDUCT OF LIFE

The authors in this chapter reflect on the influence of parents, friends, teachers, and public role models in shaping their lives. As you read the accounts by Maya Angelou, Gayle Pemberton, Mikhal Gilmore, Fatima Mernissi, Richard Rhodes, you might ask yourself how much of your personality, outlook, and expectations are the direct result of knowing someone who was important to you.

The writers of the essays identify defining qualities and character traits, and they also relate important incidents that enable us to understand why each of the people they describe had such an impact on their lives. In other essays, unique locations play a decisive role in eliciting personal responses. The architectural wonders, landscapes, and natural settings, described by Rudolph Chelminski, Rick Bass, and Aldo Leopold, transport us to the Twin Towers, a meadow in bloom, and a mountain wilderness.

The stories by Raymond Carver and John Cheever offer dramatic examples of how the people we know and the places where we live can change our lives. In "Neighbors" a couple vicariously enter the lives of their friends for whom they are apartment sitting. In "Reunion" a father's boorish insensitivity undermines what was a much-anticipated get together.

The poems in this chapter deepen our emotional capacity to understand the often inexpressible dimensions of human relationships and present a variety of responses toward one's cultural heritage and nature. In Robert Hayden's poem "Those Winter Sundays" the speaker regrets that he has failed to appreciate his father's devotion and hard work. In "A Grave" Marianne Moore looks at humanity's feverish ambitions from the perspective of the ocean. William Carlos Williams, in "At the Ball Game," shows us how the innocent crowds at a sporting event contain the dynamics of mobs who change history.

As you read works in this chapter and prepare to discuss or write about them, you may wish to use the following questions as guidelines:

- Are memorable people described in positive or negative terms or in more complex ways?

- What is the author's chief purpose in writing about this person or place—to explain, to explore, or to persuade?
- Which of the memorable people remind you of someone you know?
- Which of the places the authors describe is connected to important social issues?
- What stylistic means does the writer use to evoke the person or place?
- Does the author support his or her conclusions with personal experiences that are appropriate and effective?
- How would you characterize the author's tone and his or her attitude toward the person or place?
- How has your view of this person or place been changed by the author's treatment?

Nonfiction

Maya Angelou

Maya Angelou was born in 1928 in St. Louis, Missouri, and attended public schools in Arkansas and California. In her widely varied career, she has been a streetcar conductor, a successful singer, an actress, and a teacher. She is the author of several volumes of poetry and ten plays for stage, screen, and television, but she is best known for her autobiography, a work still in progress (five volumes of which have been published). "Liked for Myself" originally appeared in the first volume of this autobiography, I Know Why the Caged Bird Sings *(1970). Her most recent works are* Angelina of Italy *(2004) and* Mother: A Cradle to Hold Me *(2006).*

Before You Read

Who has encouraged you to broaden your reading with challenging books?

Liked for Myself

For nearly a year, I sopped around the house, the Store, the school and the church, like an old biscuit, dirty and inedible. Then I met, or rather got to know, the lady who threw me my first life line.

Mrs. Bertha Flowers was the aristocrat of Black Stamps. She had the grace of control to appear warm in the coldest weather, and on the Arkansas summer

days it seemed she had a private breeze which swirled around, cooling her. She
was thin without the taut look of wiry people, and her printed voile dresses and
flowered hats were as right for her as denim overalls for a farmer. She was our
side's answer to the richest white woman in town.

Her skin was a rich black that would have peeled like a plum if snagged,
but then no one would have thought of getting close enough to Mrs. Flowers
to ruffle her dress, let alone snag her skin. She didn't encourage familiarity.
She wore gloves too.

I don't think I ever saw Mrs. Flowers laugh, but she smiled often. A slow
widening of her thin black lips to show even, small white teeth, then the slow
effortless closing. When she chose to smile on me, I always wanted to thank
her. The action was so graceful and inclusively benign.

She was one of the few gentlewomen I have ever known, and has   5
remained throughout my life the measure of what a human being can be. . . .

One summer afternoon, sweet-milk fresh in my memory, she stopped at the
Store to buy provisions. Another Negro woman of her health and age would
have been expected to carry the paper sacks home in one hand, but Momma
said, "Sister Flowers, I'll send Bailey up to your house with these things."

She smiled that slow dragging smile, "Thank you, Mrs. Henderson. I'd
prefer Marguerite, though." My name was beautiful when she said it. "I've
been meaning to talk to her, anyway." They gave each other age-group
looks. . . .

There was a little path beside the rocky road, and Mrs. Flowers walked
in front swinging her arms and picking her way over the stones.

She said, without turning her head, to me, "I hear you're doing very
good school work, Marguerite, but that it's all written. The teachers report
that they have trouble getting you to talk in class." We passed the triangular
farm on our left and the path widened to allow us to walk together. I hung
back in the separate unasked and unanswerable questions.

"Come and walk along with me, Marguerite." I couldn't have refused   10
even if I wanted to. She pronounced my name so nicely. Or more correctly,
she spoke each word with such clarity that I was certain a foreigner who
didn't understand English could have understood her.

"Now no one is going to make you talk—possibly no one can. But bear
in mind, language is man's way of communicating with his fellow man and
it is language alone which separates him from the lower animals." That was
a totally new idea to me, and I would need time to think about it.

"Your grandmother says you read a lot. Every chance you get. That's
good, but not good enough. Words mean more than what is set down on paper.
It takes the human voice to infuse them with the shades of deeper meaning."

I memorized the part about the human voice infusing words. It seemed
so valid and poetic.

She said she was going to give me some books and that I not only must
read them, I must read them aloud. She suggested that I try to make a sentence sound in as many different ways as possible.

"I'll accept no excuse if you return a book to me that has been badly   15
handled." My imagination boggled at the punishment I would deserve if in
fact I did abuse a book of Mrs. Flowers'. Death would be too kind and brief.

The odors in the house surprised me. Somehow I had never connected
Mrs. Flowers with food or eating or any other common experience of common
people. There must have been an outhouse, too, but my mind never recorded it.

The sweet scent of vanilla had met us as she opened the door.

"I made tea cookies this morning. You see, I had planned to invite you
for cookies and lemonade so we could have this little chat. The lemonade is
in the icebox."

It followed that Mrs. Flowers would have ice on an ordinary day, when
most families in our town bought ice late on Saturdays only a few times during the summer to be used in the wooden ice-cream freezers.

She took the bags from me and disappeared through the kitchen door.   20
I looked around the room that I had never in my wildest fantasies imagined
I would see. Browned photographs leered or threatened from the walls and
the white, freshly done curtains pushed against themselves and against the
wind. I wanted to gobble up the room entire and take it to Bailey, who
would help me analyze and enjoy it.

"Have a seat, Marguerite. Over there by the table." She carried a platter covered with a tea towel. Although she warned that she hadn't tried her
hand at baking sweets for some time, I was certain that like everything else
about her the cookies would be perfect.

They were flat round wafers, slightly browned on the edges and butter-
yellow in the center. With the cold lemonade they were sufficient for childhood's lifelong diet. Remembering my manners, I took nice little lady-like bites
off the edges. She said she had made them expressly for me and that she had a
few in the kitchen that I could take home to my brother. So I jammed one
whole cake in my mouth and the rough crumbs scratched the insides of my
jaws, and if I hadn't had to swallow, it would have been a dream come true.

As I ate she began the first of what we later called "my lessons in living." She said that I must always be intolerant of ignorance but understanding of illiteracy. That some people, unable to go to school, were more
educated and even more intelligent than college professors. She encouraged
me to listen carefully to what country people called mother wit. That in
those homely sayings was couched the collective wisdom of generations.

When I finished the cookies she brushed off the table and brought a
thick, small book from the bookcase. I had read *A Tale of Two Cities*[1] and
found it up to my standards as a romantic novel. She opened the first page
and I heard poetry for the first time in my life.

---

[1] *A Tale of Two Cities (1859):* written by Charles Dickens (1812–1870), one of the great
English writers of fiction, begins with the familiar lines "It was the best of times, it was the worst
of times"; set against the background of the French Revolution, which Dickens researched with
the aid of his friend Thomas Carlyle's *History of the French Revolution* (1837).

"It was the best of times and the worst of times . . ." Her voice slid in   25
and curved down through and over the words. She was nearly singing. I
wanted to look at the pages. Were they the same that I had read? Or were
there notes, music, lined on the pages, as in a hymn book? Her sounds began
cascading gently. I knew from listening to a thousand preachers that she was
nearing the end of her reading, and I hadn't really heard, heard to understand, a single word.

"How do you like that?"

It occurred to me that she expected a response. The sweet vanilla flavor
was still on my tongue and her reading was a wonder in my ears. I had to
speak.

I said, "Yes, ma'am." It was the least I could do, but it was the most also.

"There's one more thing. Take this book of poems and memorize one
for me. Next time you pay me a visit, I want you to recite."

I have tried often to search behind the sophistication of years for the   30
enchantment I so easily found in those gifts. The essence escapes but its aura
remains. To be allowed, no, invited, into the private lives of strangers, and
to share their joys and fears, was a chance to exchange the Southern bitter
wormwood for a cup of mead with Beowulf[2] or a hot cup of tea and milk
with Oliver Twist.[3] When I said aloud, "It is a far, far better thing that I do,
than I have ever done . . ." tears of love filled my eyes at my selfishness.

On that first day, I ran down the hill and into the road (few cars ever came
along it) and had the good sense to stop running before I reached the Store.

I was liked, and what a difference it made. I was respected not as
Mrs. Henderson's grandchild or Bailey's sister but for just being Marguerite
Johnson.

Childhood's logic never asks to be proved (all conclusions are absolute).
I didn't question why Mrs. Flowers had singled me out for attention, nor did
it occur to me that Momma might have asked her to give me a little talking
to. All I cared about was that she had made tea cookies for *me* and read to
me from her favorite book. It was enough to prove that she liked me.

Questions for Discussion and Writing

1. What insights about attitudes toward race at that time does Angelou's
   account provide, as revealed in the conversations between Marguerite
   and Mrs. Flowers?
2. What do you think Angelou means by "mother wit"? How does it differ
   from formal education?
3. How did the way Bertha Flowers treated Marguerite help her gain
   self-esteem?

---

[2] *Beowulf:* the oldest English epic, in alliterative verse, probably composed in the early eighth
century; drawn from Scandinavian history.   [3] *Oliver Twist (1838):* Dickens's second novel,
which tells the story of an orphan living in the seamy underside of London's criminal world.

4. **Rhetorical inquiry:** How does Angelou use the examples of classic works of literature to illustrate the kind of world that Mrs. Flowers introduced to Marguerite?

GAYLE PEMBERTON

Gayle Pemberton (b. 1948) is the William R. Kenan Professor of the Humanities at Wesleyan University and chair of the African-American Studies Department. She was raised in Chicago and Ohio, received a Ph.D. in English and American literature at Harvard University, and has served as the associate director of African-American Studies at Princeton University. Pemberton has taught at Smith, Reed, and Bowdoin Colleges. The following chapter, drawn from her memoir The Hottest Water in Chicago *(1992), recounts the influential role her grandmother played in her life.*

Before You Read

What family member encouraged you to think for yourself?

Antidisestablishmentarianism

Okay, so where's Gloria Lockerman?[1] I want to know. Gloria Lockerman was partially responsible for ruining my life. I might never have ended up teaching literature if it had not been for her. I don't want to "call her out." I just want to know how things are, what she's doing. Have things gone well, Gloria? How's the family? What's up?

Gloria Lockerman, in case you don't recall, won scads of money on "The $64,000 Question."[2] Gloria Lockerman was a young black child, like me, but she could spell anything. Gloria Lockerman became my nemesis with her ability, her a-n-t-i-d-i-s-e-s-t-a-b-l-i-s-h-m-e-n-t-a-r-i-a-n-i-s-m.

My parents, my sister, and I shared a house in Dayton, Ohio, with my father's mother and her husband, my stepgrandfather, during the middle fifties. Sharing is an overstatement. It was my grandmother's house. Our nuclear group ate in a makeshift kitchen in the basement; my sister and I shared a dormer bedroom, and my parents actually had a room on the main floor of the house—several parts of which were off-limits. These were the

---

[1] *Gloria Lockerman:* the African-American twelve-year-old from Baltimore who won $32,000 with her spelling abilities on *The $64,000 Question.*   [2] *The $64,000 Question* was a phenomenally popular big-money quiz show that aired in the mid-1950s. In the first six months of this show, the sales of Revlon (the show's sponsor) rose 54 percent. The following year, Revlon's sales tripled.

entire living room, anywhere within three feet of Grandma's African violets, the windows and venetian blinds, anything with a doily on it, the refrigerator, and the irises in the backyard.

It was an arrangement out of necessity, given the unimpressive state of our combined fortunes, and it did not meet with anyone's satisfaction. To make matters worse, we had blockbusted a neighborhood. So, for the first year, I integrated the local elementary school—a thankless and relatively inhuman experience. I remember one day taking the Sunday paper route for a boy up the block who was sick. It was a beautiful spring day, dewy, warm. I walked up the three steps to a particular house and placed the paper on the stoop. Suddenly, a full-grown man, perhaps sixty or so, appeared with a shotgun aimed at me and said that if he ever saw my nigger ass on his porch again he'd blow my head off, I know—typical American grandfather.

Grandma liked spirituals, preferably those sung by Mahalia Jackson.   5
She was not a fan of gospel and I can only imagine what she'd say if she were around to hear what's passing for inspirational music these days. She also was fond of country singers, and any of the members of "The Lawrence Welk Show." ("That Jimmy. Oh, I love the way he sings. He's from Iowa.") She was from Iowa, Jimmy was from Iowa, my father was from Iowa. She was crazy about Jimmy Dean too, and Tennessee Ernie Ford, and "Gunsmoke." She could cook with the finest of them and I wish I could somehow recreate her Parkerhouse rolls, but I lack bread karma. Grandma liked flowers (she could make anything bloom) and she loved her son.

She disliked white people, black people in the aggregate and pretty much individually too, children—particularly female children—her daughter, her husband, my mother, Episcopalianism, Catholicism, Judaism, and Dinah Shore. She had a hot temper and a mean streak. She also suffered from several nagging ailments: high blood pressure, ulcers, an enlarged heart, ill-fitting dentures, arteriosclerosis, and arthritis—enough to make anyone hot tempered and mean, I'm sure. But to a third grader, such justifications and their subtleties were ultimately beyond me and insufficient, even though I believe I understood in part the relationship between pain and personality. Grandma scared the daylights out of me. I learned to control my nervous stomach enough to keep from getting sick daily. So Grandma plus school plus other family woes and my sister still predicting the end of the world every time the sirens went off—Grandma threatened to send her to a convent—made the experience as a whole something I'd rather forget, but because of the mythic proportions of family, can't.

I often think that it might have been better had I been older, perhaps twenty years older, when I knew Grandma. But I realize that she would have found much more wrong with me nearing thirty than she did when I was eight or nine. When I was a child, she could blame most of my faults on my mother. Grown, she would have had no recourse but to damn me to hell.

Ah, but she is on the gene. Grandma did everything fast. She cooked, washed, cleaned, moved—everything was at lightning speed. She passed this handicap on to me, and I have numerous bruises, cuts, and burns to show for it. Watching me throw pots and pans around in the creation of a meal, my mother occasionally calls me by my grandmother's first name. I smile back, click my teeth to imitate a slipping upper, and say something unpleasant about someone.

Tuesday nights were "The $64,000 Question" nights, just as Sundays we watched Ed Sullivan and Saturdays were reserved for Lawrence Welk and "Gunsmoke." We would all gather around the television in what was a small, informal family section between the verboten real living room and the mahogany dining table and chairs, used only three or four times a year. I don't remember where I sat, but it wasn't on the floor since that wasn't allowed either.

As we watched these television programs, once or twice I sat briefly on   10
Grandma's lap. She was the world's toughest critic. No one was considered worthy, apart from the above-mentioned. To her, So-and-So or Whosits could not sing, dance, tell a joke, read a line—nothing. In her hands "Ted Mack's Amateur Hour" would have lasted three minutes. She was willing to forgive only very rarely—usually when someone she liked gave a mediocre performance on one of her favorite shows.

I must admit that Grandma's style of teaching critical thinking worked as well as some others I've encountered. My father had a different approach. Throughout my youth he would play the music of the thirties and forties. His passion was for Billie Holiday, with Ella Fitzgerald, Peggy Lee, Sarah Vaughan, and a few others thrown in for a touch of variety. He enjoyed music, and when he wanted to get some musical point across, he would talk about some nuance of style that revealed the distinction between what he called "really singing" and a failure. He would say, "Now, listen to that there. Did you catch it? Hear what she did with that note?" With Grandma it was more likely to be:

"Did you hear that?"

"What?" I might ask.

"That. What she just sang."

"Yes."   15

"Well, what do you think of it?"

"It's okay, I guess."

"Well, that was garbage. She can't sing a note. That stinks. She's a fool."

Message across. We all choose our own pedagogical techniques.

Game shows are, well, game shows. I turned on my television the other   20
day, and as I clicked through channels looking for something to watch I stopped long enough to hear an announcer say that the guest contestant was going to do something or other in 1981. Reruns of game shows? Well, why not? What difference does it make if the whole point is to watch people squirm, twist, sweat, blare, weep, convulse to get their hands on money and gifts, even if they end up being just "parting gifts?" (I won some of them myself once: a bottle of liquid Johnson's Wax, a box of Chunkies, a beach towel with the name of a diet soda on it, plus a coupon for a case of the stuff,

and several boxes of Sugar Blobs—honey-coated peanut butter, marshmallow, and chocolate flavored crispies, dipped in strawberry flavoring for that special morning taste treat!)

Game shows in the fifties were different, more exciting. I thought the studio sets primitive even when I was watching them then. The clock on "Beat the Clock," the coat and crown on "Queen for a Day"—nothing like that mink on "The Big Payoff" that Bess Meyerson modeled—and that wire card flipper on "What's My Line" that John Charles Daly used—my, was it flimsy looking. The finest set of all, though, was on "The $64,000 Question." Hal March would stand outside the isolation booth, the door closing on the likes of Joyce Brothers, Catherine Kreitzer, and Gloria Lockerman, the music would play, and the clock would begin ticking down, like all game show clocks: *TOOT-toot-TOOT-tootTOOT-toot-BUZZZZZZ.*

There were few opportunities to see black people on television in those days. I had watched "Amos 'n' Andy" when we lived in Chicago. But that show was a variation on a theme. Natives running around or jumping up and down or looking menacing in African adventure movies; shuffling, subservient, and clowning servants in local color movies (or any other sort); and "Amos 'n' Andy" were all the same thing: the perpetuation of a compelling, deadly, darkly humorous, and occasionally laughable idea. Nonfictional blacks on television were limited to Sammy Davis, Jr., as part of the Will Mastin Trio and afterward, or Peg Leg Bates on "The Ed Sullivan Show" on Sunday, or the entertainers who might show up on other variety shows, or Nat King Cole during his fifteen-minute program. Naturally, the appearance of Gloria Lockerman caused a mild sensation as we watched "The $64,000 Question," all assembled.

"Look at her," Grandma said.

I braced myself for the torrent of abuse that was about to be leveled at the poor girl.

"You ought to try to be like that," Grandma said.   25

"Huh?" I said.

"What did you say?"

"Yes, ma'am."

I was shocked, thrown into despair. I had done well in school, as well as could be hoped. I was modestly proud of my accomplishments, and given the price I was paying every day—and paying in silence, for I never brought my agonies at school home with me—I didn't need Gloria Lockerman thrown in my face. Gloria Lockerman, like me, on television, spelling. I was perennially an early-round knockout in spelling bees.

My sister understands all of this. Her own story is slightly different and   30
she says she'll tell it all one day herself. She is a very good singer and has a superb ear; with our critical training, what more would she need? Given other circumstances, she might have become a performer herself. When she was about eleven Leslie Uggams was on Arthur Godfrey's "Talent Scouts" and was soon to be tearing down the "Name That Tune" runway, ringing the bell and becoming moderately famous. No one ever held Leslie Uggams up to my

sister for image consciousness-raising. But my sister suffered nevertheless. She could outsing Leslie Uggams and probably run as fast; she knew the songs and didn't have nearly so strange a last name. But, there she was, going nowhere in the Middle West, and there was Leslie Uggams on her way to "Sing Along With Mitch." To this day, my sister mumbles if she happens to see Leslie Uggams on television—before she can get up to change the channel—or hears someone mention her name. I told her I saw Leslie Uggams in the flesh at a club in New York. She was sitting at a table, just like the rest of us, listening with pleasure to Barbara Cook. My sister swore at me.

Grandma called her husband "Half-Wit." He was a thin, small-boned man who looked to me far more like an Indian chief than like a black man. He was from Iowa too, but that obviously did not account for enough in Grandma's eyes. He had a cracking tenor voice, a head full of dead straight black hair, reddish, dull brown skin, and large sad, dark brown eyes. His craggy face also reminded me of pictures I'd seen of Abraham Lincoln—but, like all political figures and American forefathers, Lincoln, to my family, was fair game for wisecracks, so that resemblance did Grandpa no good either. And for reasons that have gone to the grave with both of them, he was the most thoroughly henpecked man I have ever heard of, not to mention seen.

Hence, domestic scenes had a quality of pathos and high humor as far as I was concerned. My sister and I called Grandpa "Half-Wit" when we were alone together, but that seemed to have only a slight effect on our relations with him and our willingness to obey him—though I cannot recall any occasions calling for his authority. Grandma was Grandma, Half-Wit was Half-Wit—and we lived with the two of them. I have one particularly vivid memory of Grandma, an aficionada of the iron skillet, chasing him through the house waving it in the air, her narrow, arthritis-swollen wrist and twisted knuckles turning the heavy pan as if it were a lariat. He didn't get hurt; he was fleet of foot and made it out the back door before she caught him. My father's real father had been dead since the thirties and divorced from Grandma since the teens—so Half-Wit had been in place for quite some years and was still around to tell the story, if he had the nerve.

Grandma had a glass menagerie, the only one I've seen apart from performances of the Williams[3] play. I don't think she had a unicorn, but she did have quite a few pieces. From a distance of no less than five feet I used to squint at the glass forms, wondering what they meant to Grandma, who was herself delicate of form but a powerhouse of strength, speed, and temper. I also wondered how long it would take me to die if the glass met with some unintended accident caused by me. Real or imagined unpleasantries, both in the home and outside of it, helped develop in me a somewhat melancholic nature. And even before we had moved to Ohio I found myself laughing and crying at the same time.

---

[3] *The Glass Menagerie* (1945), by the American playwright Tennessee Williams.

In the earlier fifties, in Chicago, I was allowed to watch such programs as "The Ernie Kovacs Show," "Your Show of Shows," "The Jackie Gleason Show," "The Red Skelton Show," and, naturally, "I Love Lucy." I was continually dazzled by the skits and broad humor, but I was particularly taken with the silent sketches, my favorite comedians as mime artists: Skelton[4] as Freddy the Freeloader, Caesar and Coca[5] in a number of roles, thoroughly outrageous Kovacs acts backed by Gershwin's "Rialto Ripples." My father was a very funny man and a skillful mime. I could tell when he watched Gleason's Poor Soul that he identified mightily with what was on the screen. It had nothing to do with self-pity. My father had far less of it than other men I've met with high intelligence, financial and professional stress, and black faces in a white world. No, my father would even say that we were all poor souls; it was the human condition. His mimicking of the Gleason character— head down, shoulders tucked, stomach sagging, feet splayed—served as some kind of release. I would laugh and cry watching either of them.

But my absolute favorite was Martha Raye, who had a way of milking   35 the fine line between tragedy and comedy better than most. I thought her eyes showed a combination of riotous humor and terror. Her large mouth contorted in ways that seemed to express the same two emotions. Her face was a mask of profound sadness. She did for me what Sylvia Sidney did for James Baldwin. In *The Devil Finds Work*,[6] Baldwin says, "Sylvia Sidney was the only American film actress who reminded me of a colored girl, or woman—which is to say that she was the only American film actress who reminded me of reality." The reality Raye conveyed to me was of how dreams could turn sour in split-seconds, and how underdogs, even when winning, often had to pay abominable prices. She also could sing a jazz song well, with her husky scat phrasing, in ways that were slightly different from those of my favorite singers, and almost as enjoyable.

There were no comedic or dramatic images of black women on the screen—that is, apart from Sapphire and her mother on "Amos 'n' Andy." And knowing Grandma and Grandpa taught me, if nothing else suggested it, that what I saw of black life on television was a gross burlesque—played to the hilt with skill by black actors, but still lacking reality.

Black female singers who appeared on television were, like their music, sacrosanct, and I learned from their styles, lyrics, and improvisations, lessons about life that mime routines did not reveal. Still, it was Martha Raye, and occasionally Lucille Ball and Imogene Coca at their most absurd, that aligned me with my father and his Poor Soul, and primed me to both love and despise Grandma and to see that in life most expressions, thoughts, acts, and intentions reveal their opposite polarities simultaneously.

---

[4] *Red Skelton (1913–1997):* popular comedian on radio and television.   [5] *Sid Caesar (b. 1922):* American comedian and actor who starred in television's *Your Show of Shows* (1950–1954) with Imogene Coca, actress, comedian (1908–2001).   [6] *The Devil Finds Works: An Essay* (1976): written by James Baldwin (1924–1987).

Grandma died in 1965. I was away, out of the country, and I missed her funeral—which was probably a good idea since I might have been tempted to strangle some close family friend who probably would have launched into a "tsk, tsk, tsk" monologue about long-suffering grandmothers and impudent children. But, in another way, I'm sorry I didn't make it. Her funeral might have provided some proper closure for me, might have prompted me to organize her effect on my life sooner than I did, reconciling the grandmother who so hoped I would be a boy that she was willing to catch a Constellation or a DC-3 to witness my first few hours, but instead opted to take the bus when she heard the sad news, with the grandmother who called me "Sally Slapcabbage" and wrote to me and my sister regularly, sending us the odd dollar or two, until her death.

I remember coming home from school, getting my jelly sandwich and wolfing it down, and watching "The Mickey Mouse Club," my favorite afternoon show, since there was no afternoon movie. I had noticed and had been offended by the lack of black children in the "Club," but the cartoons, particularly those with Donald Duck, were worth watching. On this particular episode—one of the regular guest act days—a group of young black children, perhaps nine or ten of them, came on and sang, with a touch of dancing, "Old MacDonald Had a Farm," in an up-tempo, jazzy version. In spite of the fact that usually these guest days produced some interesting child acts, I became angry with what I saw. I felt patronized, for myself and for them. Clearly a couple of them could out-sing and out-dance any Mouseketeer—something that wasn't worth giving a thought to—but this performance was gratuitous, asymmetrical, a nonsequitur, like Harpo Marx marching through the Negro section in *A Day at the Races*,[7] blowing an imaginary horn and exciting the locals to much singing, swinging, and dancing to a charming ditty called "Who Dat Man?"

I must have mumbled something as I watched the group singing "Old   40
MacDonald." Grandma, passing through, took a look at what was on the screen, and at me, turned off the television, took my hand, led me to her kitchen, and sat me down at the table where she and Half-Wit ate, poured me some milk, and without so much as a blink of her eye, said, "Pay no attention to that shit."

Questions for Discussion and Writing

1. How do the circumstances Pemberton describes (especially, her grandmother's response to Gloria Lockerman) explain why Pemberton remembers her so fondly? What life lessons did Pemberton learn from her grandmother?

---

[7] *A Day at the Races*: popular 1937 Marx Brothers movie about inmates turned loose in a sanitarium.

2. What traits does Pemberton possess as a writer? How would you characterize the voice that you hear in this essay? How did her grandmother's
influence shape her personality and contribute to her literary style?

3. In your opinion, do television shows accurately reflect (or fail to
reflect) African-American life in the United States today?

4. **Rhetorical inquiry:** How does the hard-to-spell term with which con-
testants were invariably confronted anticipate all the other "isms"
(para. 6) to which the grandmother is opposed?

MIKHAL GILMORE

*Mikhal Gilmore was born in 1951 in Salt Lake City, Utah, and grew up in
Portland, Oregon. He is a senior writer at* Rolling Stone *magazine. "My
Brother, Gary Gilmore" first appeared in* Granta *(Autumn 1991) and served
as the basis for his prize-winning autobiography,* Shot Through the Heart
(1994). His most recent work (with Ron Kenner) is Manson: The Unholy
Trail of Charlie and the Family *(2000).*

Before You Read

*Have you ever been held accountable for an action taken by a family mem-
ber or friend?*

My Brother, Gary Gilmore

I am the brother of a man who murdered innocent men. His name was Gary
Gilmore. After his conviction and sentencing, he campaigned to end his own
life, and in January 1977 he was shot to death by a firing-squad in Draper,
Utah. It was the first execution in America in over a decade.

Over the years, many people have judged me by my brother's actions as
if in coming from a family that yielded a murderer I must be formed by the
same causes, the same sins, must by my brother's actions be responsible for
the violence that resulted, and bear the mark of a frightening and shameful
heritage. It's as if there is guilt in the fact of the blood-line itself. Maybe
there is.

Pictures in the family scrap-book show my father with his children. I
have only one photograph of him and Gary together. Gary is wearing a sailor's
cap. He has his arms wrapped tightly around my father's neck, his head bent
towards him, a look of broken need on his face. It is heart-breaking to look at
this picture—not just for the look on Gary's face, the look that was the stamp
of his future, but also for my father's expression: pulling away from my
brother's cheek, he is wearing a look of distaste.

When my brother Gaylen was born in the mid forties, my father turned all his love on his new, beautiful brown-eyed son. Gary takes on a harder aspect in the pictures around this time. He was beginning to keep a greater distance from the rest of the family. Six years later, my father turned his love from Gaylen to me. You don't see Gary in the family pictures after that.

Gary had nightmares. It was always the same dream: he was being beheaded. 5

In 1953, Gary was arrested for breaking windows. He was sent to a juvenile detention home for ten months, where he saw young men raped and beaten. Two years later, at age fourteen, he was arrested for car theft and sentenced to eighteen months in jail. I was four years old.

When I was growing up I did not feel accepted by, or close to, my brothers. By the time I was four or five, they had begun to find life and adventure outside the home. Frank, Gary and Gaylen signified the teenage rebellion of the fifties for me. They wore their hair in greasy pompadours and played Elvis Presley and Fats Domino records. They dressed in scarred motorcycle jackets and brutal boots. They smoked cigarettes, drank booze and cough syrup, skipped—and quit—school, and spent their evenings hanging out with girls in tight sweaters, racing souped-up cars along country roads outside Portland, or taking part in gang rumbles. My brothers looked for a forbidden life—the life they had seen exemplified in the crime lore of gangsters and killers. They studied the legends of violence. They knew the stories of John Dillinger, Bonnie and Clyde, and Leopold and Loeb; mulled over the meanings of the lives and executions of Barbara Graham, Bruno Hauptmann, Sacco and Vanzetti, the Rosenbergs; thrilled to the pleading of criminal lawyers like Clarence Darrow and Jerry Giesler. They brought home books about condemned men and women, and read them avidly.

I remember loving my brothers fiercely, wanting to be a part of their late-night activities and to share in their laughter and friendship. I also remember being frightened of them. They looked deadly, beyond love, destined to hurt the world around them.

Gary came home from reform school for a brief Christmas visit. On Christmas night I was sitting in my room, playing with the day's haul of presents, when Gary wandered in. "Hey Mike, how you doing?" he asked, taking a seat on my bed. "Think I'll just join you while I have a little Christmas cheer." He had a six-pack of beer with him and was speaking in a bleary drawl. "Look partner, I want to have a talk with you." I think it was the first companionable statement he ever made to me. I never expected the intimacy that followed and could not really fathom it at such a young age. Sitting on the end of my bed, sipping at his Christmas beer, Gary described a harsh, private world and told me horrible, transfixing stories: about the boys he knew in the detention halls, reform schools and county farms where he now spent most of his time; about the bad boys who had taught him the merciless codes of his new life; and about the soft boys who did not have what it took to survive that life. He said he had shared a cell with one of the soft boys, who cried at night, wanting to disappear into nothing, while Gary held him in his arms until the boy finally fell into sleep, sobbing.

Then Gary gave me some advice. "You have to learn to be hard. You have to learn to take things and feel nothing about them: no pain, no anger, nothing. And you have to realize, if anybody wants to beat you up, even if they want to hold you down and kick you, you have to let them. You can't fight back. You *shouldn't* fight back. Just lie down in front of them and let them beat you, let them kick you. Lie there and let them do it. It is the only way you will survive. If you don't give in to them, they will kill you."

He set aside his beer and cupped my face in his hands. "You have to remember this, Mike," he said. "Promise me. Promise me you'll be a man. Promise me you'll let them beat you." We sat there on that winter night, staring at each other, my face in his hands, and as Gary asked me to promise to take my beatings, his bloodshot eyes began to cry. It was the first time I had seen him shed tears.

I promised: Yes, I'll let them kick me. But I was afraid—afraid of betraying Gary's plea.

Gary and Gaylen weren't at home much. I came to know them mainly through their reputations, through the endless parade of grim policemen who came to the door trying to find them, and through the faces and accusations of bail bondsman and lawyers who arrived looking sympathetic and left disgusted. I knew them through many hours spent in waiting-rooms at city and county jails, where my mother went to visit them, and through the numerous times I accompanied her after midnight to the local police station on Milwaukie's Main Street to bail out another drunken son.

I remember being called into the principal's office while still in grammar school, and being warned that the school would never tolerate my acting as my brothers did; I was told to watch myself, that my brothers had already used years of the school district's good faith and leniency, and that if I was going to be like them, there were other schools I could be sent to. I came to be seen as an extension of my brothers' reputations. Once, I was waiting for a bus in the centre of the small town when a cop pulled over. "You're one of the Gilmore boys, aren't you? I hope you don't end up like those two. I've seen enough shitheads from your family." I was walking down the local main highway when a car pulled over and a gang of older teenage boys piled out, surrounding me, "Are you Gaylen Gilmore's brother?" one of them asked. They shoved me into the car, drove me a few blocks to a deserted lot and took turns punching me in the face. I remembered Gary's advice—"You can't fight back; you *shouldn't* fight back"—and I let them beat me until they were tired. Then they spat on me, got back in their car and left.

I cried all the way back home, and I hated the world. I hated the small town I lived in, its ugly, mean people. For the first time in my life I hated my brothers. I felt that my future would be governed by them, that I would be destined to follow their lives whether I wanted to or not, that I would never know any relief from shame and pain and disappointment. I felt a deep impulse to violence: I wanted to rip the faces off the boys who had beat me up. "I want to kill them," I told myself. "I want to *kill* them"—and as I realized what it was I was saying, and why I was feeling that way, I only hated my world, and my brothers, more.

Frank Gilmore, Sr. died on 30 June 1962. Gary was in Portland's Rocky Butte Jail, and the authorities denied his request to attend the funeral. He tore his cell apart; he smashed a light bulb and slashed his wrists. He was placed in "the hole"—solitary confinement—on the day of father's funeral. Gary was twenty-one. I was eleven.

I was surprised at how hard my mother and brothers took father's death. I was surprised they loved him enough to cry at all. Or maybe they were crying for the love he had so long withheld, and the reconciliation that would be forever denied them. I was the only one who didn't cry. I don't know why, but I never cried over my father's death—not then, and not now.

With my father's death Gary's crimes became more desperate, more violent. He talked a friend into helping him commit armed robbery. Gary grabbed the victim's wallet while the friend held a club; he was arrested a short time later, tried and found guilty. The day of his sentencing, during an afternoon when my mother had to work, he called me from the Clackamas County Courthouse. "How you doing partner? I just wanted to let you and mom know: I got sentenced to fifteen years."

I was stunned. "Gary, what can I do for you?" I asked. I think it came out wrong, as if I was saying: I'm busy; what do you *want?*

"I . . . I didn't really want anything," Gary said, his voice broken. "I just   20
wanted to hear your voice. I just wanted to say goodbye. You know, I won't be seeing you for a few years. Take care of yourself." We hadn't shared anything so intimate since that Christmas night, many years before.

I didn't have much talent for crime (neither did my brothers, to tell the truth), but I also didn't have much appetite for it. I had seen what my brothers' lives had brought them. For years, my mother had told me that I was the family's last hope for redemption. "I want one son to turn out right, *one* son I don't have to end up visiting in jail, one son I don't have to watch in court as his life is sentenced away, piece by piece." After my father's death, she drew me closer to her and her religion, and when I was twelve, I was baptized a Mormon. For many years, the Church's beliefs helped to provide me with a moral center and a hope for deliverance that I had not known before.

I think culture and history helped to save me. I was born in 1951, and although I remember well the youthful explosion of the 1950s, I was too young to experience it the way my brothers did. The music of Elvis Presley and others had represented and expressed my brothers' rebellion: it was hard-edged, with no apparent ideology. The music was a part of my childhood, but by the early sixties the spirit of the music had been spent.

Then, on 9 February 1964 (my thirteenth birthday, and the day I joined the Mormon priesthood), the Beatles made their first appearance on the Ed Sullivan Show. My life would never be the same. The Beatles meant a change, they promised a world that my parents and brothers could not offer. In fact, I liked the Beatles in part because they seemed such a departure from the world of my brothers, and because my brothers couldn't abide them.

The rock culture and youth politics of the sixties allowed their adherents to act out a kind of ritualized criminality: we could use drugs, defy authority, or contemplate violent or destructive acts of revolt, we told ourselves, *because we had a reason to.* The music aimed to foment a sense of cultural community, and for somebody who had felt as disenfranchised by his family as I did, rock and roll offered not just a sense of belonging but empowered me with new ideals. I began to find rock's morality preferable to the Mormon ethos, which seemed rigid and severe. One Sunday in the summer of 1967, a member of the local bishopric—a man I admired, and had once regarded as something of a father figure—drove over to our house and asked me to step outside for a talk. He told me that he and other church leaders had grown concerned about my changed appearance—the new length of my hair and my style of dressing— and felt it was an unwelcome influence on other young Mormons. If I did not reject the new youth culture, I would no longer be welcome in church.

On that day a line was drawn. I knew that rock and roll had provided   25
me with a new creed and a sense of courage. I believed I was taking part in a rebellion that mattered—or at least counted for more than my brothers' rebellions. In the music of the Rolling Stones or Doors or Velvet Underground, I could participate in darkness without submitting to it, which is something Gary and Gaylen had been unable to do. I remember their disdain when I tried to explain to them why Bob Dylan was good, why he mattered. It felt great to belong to a different world from them.

And I did: my father and Gaylen were dead; Gary was in prison and Frank was broken. I thought of my family as a cursed outfit, plain and simple, and I believed that the only way to escape its debts and legacies was to leave it. In 1969 I graduated from high school—the only member of my family to do so. The next day, I moved out of the house in Milwaukie and, with some friends, moved into an apartment near Portland State University, in downtown Portland.

In the summer of 1976, I was working at a record store in downtown Portland, making enough money to pay my rent and bills. I was also writing free-lance journalism and criticism, and had sold my first reviews and articles to national publications, including *Rolling Stone.*

On the evening of 30 July, having passed up a chance to go drinking with some friends, I headed home. *The Wild Bunch,* Peckinpah's genuflection to violence and honor, was on television, and as I settled back on the couch to watch it, I picked up the late edition of *The Oregonian.* I almost passed over a page-two item headlined OREGON MAN HELD IN UTAH SLAYINGS, but then something clicked inside me, and I began to read it. "Gary Mark Gilmore, 35, was charged with the murders of two young clerks during the hold-up of a service station and a motel." I read on, dazed, about how Gary had been arrested for killing Max Jensen and Ben Bushnell on consecutive nights. Both men were Mormons, about the same age as I, and both left wives and children behind.

I dropped the paper to the floor. I sat on the couch the rest of the night, alternately staring at *The Wild Bunch* and re-reading the sketchy account. I felt shocks of rage, remorse and guilt—as if I were partly responsible for the deaths. I had been part of an uninterested world that had shut Gary away. I had wanted to believe that Gary's life and mine were not entwined, that what had shaped him had not shaped me.

It had been a long time since I had written or visited Gary. After his resentencing in 1972, I heard news of him from my mother. In January 1975, Gary was sent to the federal penitentiary in Marion, Illinois. After his transfer, we exchanged a few perfunctory letters. In early April 1976, I learned of the Oregon State Parole Board's decision to parole Gary from Marion to Provo, Utah, rather than transfer him back to Oregon. The transaction had been arranged between the parole board, Brenda Nicol (our cousin) and her father, our uncle Vernon Damico, who lived in Provo. I remember thinking that Gary's being paroled into the heart of one of Utah's most devout and severe Mormon communities was not a great idea.

Between his release and those fateful nights in July, Gary held a job at Uncle Vernon's shoe store, and he met and fell in love with Nicole Barrett, a beautiful young woman with two children. But Gary was unable to deny some old, less wholesome appetites. Almost immediately after his release, he started drinking heavily and taking Fiorinal, a muscle and headache medication that, in sustained doses, can cause severe mood swings and sexual dysfunction. Gary apparently experienced both reactions. He became more violent. Sometimes he got rough with Nicole over failed sex, or over what he saw as her flirtations. He picked fights with other men, hitting them from behind, threatening to cave in their faces with a tire iron that he twirled as handily as a baton. He lost his job and abused his Utah relatives. He walked into stores and walked out again with whatever he wanted under his arm, glaring at the cashiers, challenging them to try to stop him. He brought guns home, and sitting on the back porch would fire them at trees, fences, the sky. "Hit the sun," he told Nicole. "See if you can make it sink." Then he hit Nicole with his fist one too many times, and she moved out.

Gary wanted her back. He told a friend that he thought he might kill her.

On a hot night in late July, Gary drove over to Nicole's mother's house and persuaded Nicole's little sister, April, to ride with him in his white pick-up truck. He wanted her to join him in looking for her sister. They drove for hours, listening to the radio, talking aimlessly, until Gary pulled up by a service station in the small town of Orem. He told April to wait in the truck. He walked into the station, where twenty-six-year-old attendant Max Jensen was working alone. There were no other cars there. Gary pulled a .22 automatic from his jacket and told Jensen to empty the cash from his pockets.

30

He took Jensen's coin changer and led the young attendant around the back of the station and forced him to lie down on the bathroom floor. He told Jensen to place his hands under his stomach and press his face to the ground. Jensen complied and offered Gary a smile. Gary pointed the gun at the base of Jensen's skull. "This one is for me," Gary said, and he pulled the trigger. And then: "This one is for Nicole," and he pulled the trigger again.

The next night, Gary walked into the office of a motel just a few doors away from his uncle Vernon's house in Provo. He ordered the man behind the counter, Ben Bushnell, to lie down on the floor, and then he shot him in the back of the head. He walked out with the motel's cashbox under his arm and tried to stuff the pistol under a bush. But it discharged, blowing a hole in his thumb.

Gary decided to get out of town. First he had to take care of his thumb. He   35
drove to the house of a friend named Craig and telephoned his cousin. A witness had recognized Gary leaving the site of the second murder, and the police had been in touch with Brenda. She had the police on one line, Gary on another. She tried to stall Gary until the police could set up a road-block. After they finished speaking, Gary got into his truck and headed for the local airport. A few miles down the road, he was surrounded by police cars and a SWAT team. He was arrested for Bushnell's murder and confessed to the murder of Max Jensen.

Gary's trial began some months later. The verdict was never in question. Gary didn't help himself when he refused to allow his attorneys to call Nicole as a defense witness. Gary and Nicole had been reconciled; she felt bad for him and visited him in jail every day for hours. Gary also didn't help his case by staring menacingly at the jury members or by offering belligerent testimony on his own behalf. He was found guilty. My mother called me on the night of Gary's sentencing, 7 October, to tell me that he had received the death penalty. He told the judge he would prefer being shot to being hanged.

On Saturday 15 January, I saw Gary for the last time. Camera crews were camped in the town of Draper, preparing for the finale.

During our other meetings that week, Gary had opened with friendly remarks or a joke or even a handstand. This day, though, he was nervous and was eager to deny it. We were separated by a glass partition. "Naw, the noise in this place gets to me sometimes, but I'm as cool as a cucumber," he said, holding up a steady hand. The muscles in his wrists and arms were taut and thick as rope.

Gary showed me letters and pictures he'd received, mainly from children and teenage girls. He said he always tried to answer the ones from the kids first, and he read one from an eight-year-old boy: "I hope they put you some place and make you live forever for what you did. You have no right to die. With all the malice in my heart. [*name.*]"

"Man, that one shook me up for a long time," he said.   40
I asked him if he'd replied to it.
"Yeah, I wrote, 'You're too young to have malice in your heart. I had it in mine at a young age and look what it did for me.'"

Gary's eyes nervously scanned some letters and pictures, finally falling on one that made him smile. He held it up. A picture of Nicole. "She's pretty, isn't she?" I agreed. "I look at this picture every day. I took it myself; I made a drawing from it. Would you like to have it?"

I said I would. I asked him where he would have gone if he had made it to the airport the night of the second murder.

"Portland." 45

I asked him why.

Gary studied the shelf in front of him. "I don't want to talk about that night any more," he said. "There's no point in talking about it."

"Would you have come to see me?"

He nodded. For a moment his eyes flashed the old anger. "And what would *you* have done if I'd come to you?" he asked. "If I had come and said I was in trouble and needed help, needed a place to stay? Would *you* have taken me in? Would you have hidden me?"

The question had been turned back on me. I couldn't speak. Gary sat 50 for a long moment, holding me with his eyes, then said steadily: "I think I was coming to kill you. I think that's what would have happened; there may have been no choice for you, no choice for me." His eyes softened, "Do you understand why?"

I nodded. Of course I understood why: I had escaped the family—or at least thought I had. Gary had not.

I felt terror. Gary's story could have been mine. Then terror became relief—Jensen and Bushnell's deaths, and Gary's own impending death, had meant my own safety. I finished the thought, and my relief was shot through with guilt and remorse. I felt closer to Gary than I'd ever felt before. I understood why he wanted to die.

The warden entered Gary's room. They discussed whether Gary should wear a hood for the execution.

I rapped on the glass partition and asked the warden if he would allow us a final handshake. At first he refused but consented after Gary explained it was our final visit, on the condition that I agree to a skin search. After I had been searched by two guards, two other guards brought Gary around the partition. They said that I would have to roll up my sleeve past my elbow, and that we could not touch beyond a handshake. Gary grasped my hand, squeezed it tight and said, "Well, I guess this is it." He leaned over and kissed me on the cheek.

On Monday morning, 17 January, in a cannery warehouse out behind 55 Utah State Prison, Gary met his firing-squad. I was with my mother and brother and girl-friend when it happened. Just moments before, we had seen the morning newspaper with the headline EXECUTION STAYED. We switched on the television for more news. We saw a press conference. Gary's death was being announced.

There was no way to be prepared for that last see-saw of emotion. You force yourself to live through the hell of knowing that somebody you love is going to die in an expected way, at a specific time and place, and that there is nothing you can do to change that. For the rest of your life, you will have to move around in a world that wanted this death to happen. You will have to walk past people every day who were heartened by the killing of somebody in your family—somebody who you knew had long before been murdered emotionally.

You turn on the television, and the journalist tells you how the warden put a black hood over Gary's head and pinned a small, circular cloth target above his chest, and how five men pumped a volley of bullets into him. He tells you how the blood flowed from Gary's devastated heart and down his chest, down his legs, staining his white pants scarlet and dripping to the warehouse floor. He tells you how Gary's arm rose slowly at the moment of the impact, how his fingers seemed to wave as his life left him.

Shortly after Gary's execution, *Rolling Stone* offered me a job as an assistant editor at their Los Angeles bureau. It was a nice offer. It gave me the chance to get away from Portland and all the bad memories it represented.

I moved to Los Angeles in April 1977. It was not an easy life at first. I drank a pint of whisky every night, and I took Dalmane, a sleeping medication that interfered with my ability to dream—or at least made it hard to remember my dreams. There were other lapses: I was living with one woman and seeing a couple of others. For a season or two my writing went to hell. I didn't know what to say or how to say it; I could no longer tell if I had anything *worth* writing about. I wasn't sure how you made words add up. Instead of writing, I preferred reading. I favoured hard-boiled crime fiction—particularly the novels of Ross MacDonald—in which the author tried to solve murders by explicating labyrinthine family histories. I spent many nights listening to punk rock. I liked the music's accommodation with a merciless world. One of the most famous punk songs of the period was by the Adverts. It was called "Gary Gilmore's Eyes." What would it be like, the song asked, to see the world through Gary Gilmore's dead eyes? Would you see a world of murder?

All around me I had Gary's notoriety to contend with. During my first few months in LA—and throughout the years that followed—most people asked me about my brother. They wanted to know what Gary was like. They admired his bravado, his hardness. I met a woman who wanted to sleep with me because I was his brother. I tried to avoid these people.

I also met women who, when they learned who my brother was, would not see me again, not take my calls again. I received letters from people who said I should not be allowed to write for a young audience. I received letters from people who thought I should have been shot alongside my brother.

There was never a time without a reminder of the past. In 1979, Norman Mailer's *The Executioner's Song* was published. At the time, I was living with a woman I loved very much. As she read the book, I could see her begin to wonder about who she was sleeping with, about what had come into her life. One night, a couple of months after the book had been published, we

60

were watching *Saturday Night Live*. The guest host was doing a routine of impersonations. He tied a bandana around his eyes and gleefully announced his next subject: "Gary Gilmore!" My girl-friend got up from the sofa and moved into the bedroom, shutting the door. I poured a glass of whisky. She came out a few minutes later. "I'm sorry," she said, "I can't live with you any more. I can't stand being close to all this stuff." She was gone within a week.

I watched as a private and troubling event continued to be the subject of public sensation and media scrutiny; I watched my brother's life—and in some way, my life—become too large to control. I tried not to surrender to my feelings because my feelings wouldn't erase the pain or shame or bad memories or unresolved love and hate. I was waiting to be told what to feel.

Only a few months before, I had gone through one of the worst times of my life—my brief move to Portland and back. What had gone wrong, I realized, was because of my past, something that had been set in motion long before I was born. It was what Gary and I shared, more than any blood tie: we were both heirs to a legacy of negation that was beyond our control or our understanding. Gary had ended up turning the nullification outward—on innocents, on Nicole, on his family, on the world and its ideas of justice, finally on himself. I had turned the ruin inward. Outward or inward—either way, it was a powerfully destructive legacy, and for the first time in my life, I came to see that it had not really finished its enactment. To believe that Gary had absorbed all the family's dissolution, or that the worst of that rot had died with him that morning in Draper, Utah, was to miss the real nature of the legacy that had placed him before those rifles: what that heritage or patrimony was about, and where it had come from.

We tend to view murders as solitary ruptures in the world around us, outrages that need to be attributed and then punished. There is a motivation, a crime, an arrest, a trial, a verdict and a punishment. Sometimes—though rarely—that punishment is death. The next day, there is another murder. The next day, there is another. There has been no punishment that breaks the pattern, that stops this custom of one murder following another.

Murder has worked its way into our consciousness and our culture in the same way that murder exists in our literature and film: we consume each killing until there is another, more immediate or gripping one to take its place. When *this* murder story is finished, there will be another to intrigue and terrify that part of the world that has survived it. And then there will be another. Each will be a story, each will be treated and reported and remembered as a unique incident. Each murder will be solved, but murder itself will never be solved. You cannot solve murder without solving the human heart or the history that has rendered that heart so dark and desolate.

This murder story is told from inside the house where murder was born. It is the house where I grew up, and it is a house that I have never been able to leave.

As the night passed, I formed an understanding of what I needed to do. I would go back into my family—into its stories, its myths, its memories, its inheritance—and find the real story and hidden propellants behind it. I wanted to climb into the family story in the same way I've always wanted to climb into a dream about the house where we all grew up.

In the dream, it is always night. We are in my father's house—a charred-brown, 1950s-era home. Shingled, two-story and weather-worn, it is located on the far outskirts of a dead-end American town, pinioned between the night-lights and smoking chimneys of towering industrial factories. A moon-lit stretch of railroad track forms the border to a forest I am forbidden to trespass. A train whistle howls in the distance. No train ever comes.

People move from the darkness outside the house to the darkness 70 inside. They are my family. They are all back from the dead. There is my mother, Bessie Gilmore, who, after a life of bitter losses, died spitting blood, calling the names of her father and her husband—men who had long before brutalized her hopes and her love—crying to them for mercy, for a passage into the darkness that she had so long feared. There is my brother Gaylen, who died young of knife-wounds, as his new bride sat holding his hand, watching the life pass from his sunken face. There is my brother Gary, who murdered innocent men in rage against the way life had robbed him of time and love, and who died when a volley of bullets tore his heart from his chest. There is my brother Frank, who became quieter and more distant with each new death, and who was last seen in the dream walking down a road, his hands rammed deep into his pockets, a look of uncomprehending pain on his face. There is my father, Frank, Sr., dead of the ravages of lung cancer. He is in the dream less often than the other family members, and I am the only one happy to see him.

One night, years into the same dream, Gary tells me why I can never join my family in its comings and goings, why I am left alone sitting in the living-room as they leave: it is because I have not yet entered death. I cannot follow them across the tracks, into the forest where their real lives take place, until I die. He pulls a gun from his coat pocket. He lays it on my lap. There is a door across the room, and he moves towards it. Through the door is the night. I see the glimmer of the train tracks. Beyond them, my family.

I do not hesitate. I pick the pistol up. I put its barrel in my mouth. I pull the trigger. I feel the back of my head erupt. It is a softer feeling than I expected. I feel my teeth fracture, disintegrate and pass in a gush of blood out of my mouth. I feel my life pass out of my mouth, and in that instant, I collapse into nothingness. There is darkness, but there is no beyond. There is *never* any beyond, only the sudden, certain rush of extinction. I know that it is death I am feeling—that is, I know this is how death must truly feel and I know that this is where beyond ceases to be a possibility.

I have had the dream more than once, in various forms. I always wake up with my heart hammering hard, hurting after being torn from the void that I know is the gateway to the refuge of my ruined family. Or is it the gateway to hell? Either way, I want to return to the dream, but in the haunted hours of the night there is no way back.

Questions for Discussion and Writing

1. What can you infer from Mikhal's account about why Gary committed the murders?
2. What consequences have his brother Gary's crimes had on Mikhal's life? How would you characterize the relationship that the brothers had before and after the murders?
3. Describe an experience in which you were a "victim of guilt by association" and were blamed for something done by a sibling or other relative. Are there any mysterious or shady characters in your lineage? What are they reputed to have done?
4. **Rhetorical inquiry:** How does the revelation that his brother Gary may have killed others in order to avoid killing him make Mikhal feel even more responsible for his brother's actions? How does this detail help his readers understand his predicament?

FATIMA MERNISSI

Fatima Mernissi is a scholar of Middle Eastern history and culture who was born in 1940 in Fez, Morocco. Her childhood was unusual in that she was raised in a harem (which means "forbidden" in Arabic). Her experiences there became the subject of her book Dreams of Trespass: Tales of a Harem Girlhood *(1994), in which the following essay first appeared. Mernissi also wrote* Scheherazade Goes West: Different Cultures, Different Harems *(2001) and* Islam and Democracy: Fear of the Modern World *(2002).*

Before You Read

How important is it to you to have meals with your family?

Moonlit Nights of Laughter

On Yasmina's farm, we never knew when we would eat. Sometimes, Yasmina only remembered at the last minute that she had to feed me, and then she would convince me that a few olives and a piece of her good bread, which she had baked at dawn, would be enough. But dining in our harem in Fez[1] was an entirely different story. We ate at strictly set hours and never between meals.

To eat in Fez, we had to sit at our prescribed places at one of the four communal tables. The first table was for the men, the second for the important women, and the third for the children and less important women,

---

[1] *Fez:* a city in northern Morocco, established A.D. 808.

which made us happy, because that meant that Aunt Habiba could eat with us. The last table was reserved for the domestics and anyone who had come in late, regardless of age, rank, or sex. That table was often overcrowded, and was the last chance to get anything to eat at all for those who had made the mistake of not being on time.

Eating at fixed hours was what Mother hated most about communal life. She would nag Father constantly about the possibility of breaking loose and taking our immediate family to live apart. The nationalists advocated the end of seclusion and the veil, but they did not say a word about a couple's right to split off from their larger family. In fact, most of the leaders still lived with their parents. The male nationalist movement supported the liberation of women, but had not come to grips with the idea of the elderly living by themselves, nor with couples splitting off into separate households. Neither idea seemed right, or elegant.

Mother especially disliked the idea of a fixed lunch hour. She always was the last to wake up, and liked to have a late, lavish breakfast which she prepared herself with a lot of flamboyant defiance, beneath the disapproving stare of Grandmother Lalla Mani. She would make herself scrambled eggs and *baghrir,* or fine crêpes, topped with pure honey and fresh butter, and, of course, plenty of tea. She usually ate at exactly eleven, just as Lalla Mani was about to begin her purification ritual for the noon prayer. And after that, two hours later at the communal table, Mother was often absolutely unable to eat lunch. Sometimes she would skip it altogether, especially when she wanted to annoy Father, because to skip a meal was considered terribly rude and too openly individualistic.

Mother dreamed of living alone with Father and us kids. "Whoever   5 heard of ten birds living together squashed into a single nest?" she would say. "It is not natural to live in a large group, unless your objective is to make people feel miserable." Although Father said that he was not really sure how the birds lived, he still sympathized with Mother, and felt torn between his duty towards the traditional family and his desire to make her happy. He felt guilty about breaking up the family solidarity, knowing only too well that big families in general, and harem life in particular, were fast becoming relics of the past. He even prophesied that in the next few decades, we would become like the Christians, who hardly ever visited their old parents. In fact, most of my uncles who had already broken away from the big house barely found the time to visit their mother, Lalla Mani, on Fridays after prayer anymore. "Their kids do not kiss hands either," ran the constant refrain. To make matters worse, until very recently, all my uncles had lived in our house, and had only split away when their wives' opposition to communal life had become unbearable. That is what gave Mother hope.

The first to leave the big family was Uncle Karim, Cousin Malika's father. His wife loved music and liked to sing while being accompanied by Uncle Karim, who played the lute beautifully. But he would rarely give in to his wife's desire to spend an evening singing in their salon, because his older brother Uncle Ali thought it unbecoming for a man to sing or play a musical instrument. Finally, one day, Uncle Karim's wife just took her children and went back to her father's house, saying that she had no intention of living in the communal house ever again. Uncle Karim, a cheerful fellow who had himself often felt constrained by the discipline of harem life, saw an opportunity to leave and took it, excusing his actions by saying that he preferred to give in to his wife's wishes rather than forfeit his marriage. Not long after that, all my other uncles moved out, one after the other, until only Uncle Ali and Father were left. So Father's departure would have meant the death of our large family. "As long as [my] Mother lives," he often said, "I wouldn't betray the tradition."

Yet Father loved his wife so much that he felt miserable about not giving in to her wishes and never stopped proposing compromises. One was to stock an entire cupboardful of food for her, in case she wanted to discreetly eat sometimes, apart from the rest of the family. For one of the problems in the communal house was that you could not just open a refrigerator when you were hungry and grab something to eat. In the first place, there were no refrigerators back then. More importantly, the entire idea behind the harem was that you lived according to the group's rhythm. You could not just eat when you felt like it. Lalla Radia, my uncle's wife, had the key to the pantry, and although she always asked after dinner what people wanted to eat the next day, you still had to eat whatever the group—after lengthy discussion—decided upon. If the group settled on couscous with chick-peas and raisins, then that is what you got. If you happened to hate chick-peas and raisins, you had no choice but to shut up and settle for a frugal dinner composed of a few olives and a great deal of discretion.

"What a waste of time," Mother would say. "These endless discussions about meals! Arabs would be much better off if they let each individual decide what he or she wanted to swallow. Forcing everyone to share three meals a day just complicates things. And for what sacred purpose? None of course." From there, she would go on to say that her whole life was an absurdity, that nothing made sense, while Father would say that he could not just break away. If he did, tradition would vanish: "We live in difficult times, the country is occupied by foreign armies, our culture is threatened. All we have left is these traditions." This reasoning would drive Mother nuts: "Do you think that by sticking together in this big, absurd house, we will gain the strength we need to throw the foreign armies out? And what is more important anyway, tradition or people's happiness?" That would put an abrupt end to the conversation. Father would try to caress her hand but she would take it away. "This tradition is choking me," she would whisper, tears in her eyes.

So Father kept offering compromises. He not only arranged for Mother to have her own food stock, but also brought her things he knew she liked, such as dates, nuts, almonds, honey, flour, and fancy oils. She could make all the desserts and cookies she wanted, but she was not supposed to prepare a meat dish or a major meal. That would have meant the beginning of the end of the communal arrangement. Her flamboyantly prepared individual breakfasts were enough of a slap in the face to the rest of the family. Every once in a long while, Mother *did* get away with preparing a complete lunch or a dinner, but she had to not only be discreet about it but also give it some sort of exotic overtone. Her most common ploy was to camouflage the meal as a nighttime picnic on the terrace.

These occasional tête-à-tête dinners on the terrace during moonlit summer nights were another peace offering that Father made to help satisfy Mother's yearning for privacy. We would be transplanted to the terrace, like nomads, with mattresses, tables, trays, and my little brother's cradle, which would be set down right in the middle of everything. Mother would be absolutely out of her mind with joy. No one else from the courtyard dared to show up, because they understood all too well that Mother was fleeing from the crowd. What she most enjoyed was trying to get Father to depart from his conventional self-controlled pose. Before long, she would start acting foolishly, like a young girl, and soon, Father would chase her all around the terrace, when she challenged him, "You can't run anymore, you have grown too old! All you're good for now is to sit and watch your son's cradle." Father, who had been smiling up to that point, would look at her at first as if what she had just said had not affected him at all. But then his smile would vanish, and he would start chasing her all over the terrace, jumping over tea-trays and sofas. Sometimes both of them made up games which included my sister and Samir (who was the only one of the rest of the family allowed to attend our moonlit gatherings) and myself. More often, they completely forgot about the rest of the world, and we children would be sneezing all the next day because they had forgotten to put blankets on us when we had gone to sleep that night.

After these blissful evenings, Mother would be in an unusually soft and quiet mood for a whole week. Then she would tell me that whatever else I did with my life, I had to take her revenge. "I want my daughters' lives to be exciting," she would say, "very exciting and filled with one hundred percent happiness, nothing more, nothing less." I would raise my head, look at her earnestly, and ask what one hundred percent happiness meant, because I wanted her to know that I intended to do my best to achieve it. Happiness, she would explain, was when a person felt good, light, creative, content, loving and loved, and free. An unhappy person felt as if there were barriers crushing her desires and the talents she had inside. A happy woman was one who could exercise all kinds of rights, from the right to move to the right to create, compete, and challenge, and at the same time could feel loved for doing so. Part of happiness was to be loved by a man who enjoyed your strength and was proud of your talents. Happiness was also about the right to privacy, the right to retreat from the company of others and plunge into contemplative solitude. Or to sit by yourself doing nothing for a whole day, and not give excuses or feel guilty about it either. Happiness was to be with loved ones, and yet still feel that you existed as a separate being, that you were not there just to make them happy. Happiness was when there was a

10

balance between what you gave and what you took. I then asked her how much happiness she had in her life, just to get an idea, and she said that it varied according to the days. Some days she had only five percent; others, like the evenings we spent with Father on the terrace, she had full-blown one hundred percent happiness.

Aiming at one hundred percent happiness seemed a bit overwhelming to me, as a young girl, especially since I could see how much Mother labored to sculpt her moments of happiness. How much time and energy she put into creating those wonderful moonlit evenings sitting close to Father, talking softly in his ear, her head on his shoulder! It seemed quite an accomplishment to me because she had to start working on him days ahead of time, and then she had to take care of all the logistics, like the cooking and the moving of the furniture. To invest so much stubborn effort just to achieve a few hours of happiness was impressive, and at least I knew it could be done. But how, I wondered, was I going to create such a high level of excitement for an entire lifetime? Well, if Mother thought it was possible, I should certainly give it a try.

"Times are going to get better for women now, my daughter," she would say to me. "You and your sister will get a good education, and you'll walk freely in the streets and discover the world. I want you to become independent, independent and happy. I want you to shine like moons. I want your lives to be a cascade of serene delights. One hundred percent happiness. Nothing more, nothing less." But when I asked her for more details about how to create that happiness, Mother would grow very impatient. "You have to work at it. One develops the muscles for happiness, just like for walking and breathing."

So every morning, I would sit on our threshold, contemplating the deserted courtyard and dreaming about my beautiful future, a cascade of serene delights. Hanging on to the romantic moonlit terrace evenings, challenging your beloved man to forget about his social duties, relax and act foolish and gaze at the stars while holding your hand, I thought, could be one way to go about developing muscles for happiness. Sculpting soft nights, when the sound of laughter blends with the spring breezes, could be another.

But those magical evenings were rare, or so they seemed. During the days, life took a much more rigid and disciplined turn. Officially, there was no jumping around or foolishness allowed in the Mernissi household—all that was confined to clandestine times and spaces, such as late afternoons in the courtyard when the men were out, or evenings on the deserted terraces.

Questions for Discussion and Writing

1. How did Mernissi's mother manage to create a private family dinner despite the restrictions of communal life?
2. What expectations did Mernissi's mother have for her daughter, and how did she express them?

3. Discuss what the issue of privacy means to you and how this value translates into your everyday life.
4. **Rhetorical inquiry:** How does the phrase "one hundred percent happiness" come to symbolize everything Mernissi's mother wished for her daughter? What different elements comprise this state?

RICHARD RHODES

Richard Rhodes was born in 1937 in Kansas City, Kansas. After graduating with honors from Yale in 1959, he worked for Hallmark Cards and as a contributing editor for Harper's *and* Playboy *magazines. He is the author of more than fifty articles and ten books, including* Looking for America: A Writer's Odyssey *(1979),* Making Love: An Erotic Odyssey *(1993),* Voyage of Rediscovery: A Cultural Odyssey through Polynesia *(1995),* How to Write: Advice and Reflections *(1996), the acclaimed* The Making of the Atomic Bomb *(1987), which won the Pulitzer Prize, the National Book Award, and the National Book Critics Circle Award, and* Deadly Feasts: Tracking the Secrets of a Terrifying New Plague *(1997). When he was thirteen years old, his mother committed suicide. His father remarried and tried to raise him and his older brother. Rhodes's account from his 1990 autobiography,* A Hole in the World, *shares an intensely personal story of childhood abuse at the hands of his stepmother.*

Before You Read

Why are relationships of children with stepparents often so problematic?

A Hole in the World

Slapping us, kicking us, bashing our heads with a broom handle or a mop or the stiletto heel of a shoe, slashing our backs and the backs of our legs with the buckle of a belt, our stepmother exerted one kind of control over us, battery that was immediately coercive but intermittent and limited in effect. We cowered, cringed, screamed, wrapped our poor heads protectively in our arms, danced the belt-buckle tango, but out of sight and reach we recovered our boundaries more or less intact. The bodily memory of the blows, the heat of the abrasions, the caution of pain, the indignation and the smoldering rage only demarcated those boundaries more sharply. More effective control required undermining our boundaries from within. As diseases do, our stepmother sought to harness our physiology to her own ends. Compelling us to eat food we didn't like—cayenne gravy, mint jelly, moldy bread—is hardly more coercion than most parents impose, not that custom justifies it. Our stepmother tinkered more radically with manipulating what we took into our bodies and what we expelled. The techniques she developed led eventually to a full-scale assault.

Colds and tonsillitis frequently kept us home from school and underfoot. To help prevent that inconvenience she might have improved our diet. Instead she began dosing us mornings with cod-liver oil. Stanley swallowed it down. It nauseated me. It tasted like bad fish. I clamped my jaw and balked. Even her jerking and slapping didn't always prevail. She had to stop pounding me to move the tablespoon of oil to my mouth and by then I'd clamped my jaw again. Every morning was a fight. Goaded by stalemate, she devised an alternative. I loved school. It was my escape into the wide world. She fettered that love to my daily dose of oil. She forbade me to go to school until I'd swallowed it. I resisted until the last possible moment and then gagged it down.

We polished off the cod-liver oil. She remembered a bottle of mineral oil left over in the bathroom closet. She must have thought the two oils were equally invigorating. She substituted one for the other. The mineral oil might have been an improvement, but it had absorbed the acrid taint of its Bakelite lid, a taste even more nauseating than cod liver. Worse, since mineral oil is indigestible, drops of oil now dispersed on the surface of the toilet water after my bowel movements. I understood the connection between the oil I was gagging down and the oil shimmering above my stool, but I thought the phenomenon was pathological. It anguished me for weeks. Finally, on a morning when she seemed uncharacteristically sympathetic, I dared to reveal my problem. She inspected the evidence, "Oh, that's just the mineral oil," she dismissed my fears airily, but she cut my dose and eventually gave up dosing us.

I no longer wet the bed, but I needed the toilet at night. The only bathroom in the house opened directly inside her bedroom door. I used it whenever I had to, sometimes more than once a night, until she announced one day in a fury that I was getting up at night unnecessarily and disturbing her sleep. I should make sure I relieved myself before I went to bed, she told me, because from then on I was forbidden to use the bathroom at night. "I married your *father*, not you," she added mysteriously. I understood her to mean she wanted to be alone with him at night. She meant more. "Kidneys move a good deal, gets up often during night," the social worker whom the juvenile court appointed wrote of me a year and a half later in her investigation report. "Stepmother accused him of being curious to know what was going on." There was only one bathroom, and only one way to access it. If she thought I was spying on her sex life she could have supplied me with a chamber pot.

Telling someone *not* to do something to induce him to do it is a powerful form of suggestion. Dutifully I went to the bathroom just before climbing to my upper bunk on the north wall of the sleeping porch, but as soon as Stanley turned out the light and we settled down to sleep I felt my bladder fill. I lay awake then for hours. I tried to redirect my thoughts, tell myself stories, recite numbers, count sheep. I clamped my sphincters until they cramped and burned. Lying on my back, hurting and urgent, I cried silently to the ceiling low overhead, tears running down my face without consolation, only reminding me of the other flow of body fluid that my commandant had blocked. When clamping my sphincters no longer worked I pinched my penis to red pain.

Sometimes I fell asleep that way and slept through. Once or twice, early in the chronology of this torture, I wet the bed. That villainy erupted in such monstrous humiliation that I learned not to repeat it. Thereafter I added struggling to stay awake to struggling to retain my urine.

One desperate night I decided to urinate out the window. There were two windows in the porch back wall. They opened ten feet above the yard. I waited until I was sure Stanley was solidly asleep, climbed down my ladder and slipped to the nearer window. Two spring-loaded pins had to be pulled and held out simultaneously to open it. That wasn't easy to coordinate, especially since I was bent over with cramping. The window fit its frame badly. It jammed and squeaked going up. I forced it up six inches and then a foot—high enough—stood on tiptoe, my little penis barely reaching over the sill, and let go. I'd hoped the hydraulic pressure would be sufficient to drive the stream of urine through the screen, missing the ledge and the frame, but the angle was bad, I dribbled. My urine ran down the ledge and out under the screen frame. That meant it would leave a telltale stain down the outside wall. I tried forcing the stream into a higher arc and managed to pulse it in splashes through the screen. It sprayed out into the night air below a blank silver moon.

I'd barely begun when I heard noise—the bedroom door, footsteps in the dining room, the kitchen door swinging. I clamped off the flow in a panic—it was hard to stop—popped my dripping penis back into my pajamas, warm urine running down my leg, and stood at the window waiting, I prayed to God it wasn't my stepmother.

Dad stepped through the doorway, half awake. "What's going on?" he said softly.   10

"It was stuffy in here," I improvised, "I opened the window to get some air."

"You don't want to disturb your Aunt Anne," he told me. "Better close that thing and get back to bed."

I wasn't sure if he knew what I was doing or not. Probably not. I closed the window. He padded off. I'd managed to alleviate my urgency enough to get to sleep. To my amazement—I suppose I believed her omniscient—my stepmother only grumbled the next morning about people up at night prowling around. Even so, I knew I couldn't use the window anymore. I'd have to find some other way.

I had plenty of time at night to think. I needed a way to store my urine, an equivalent to the Schonmeier chamber pot. The top of the closet Stanley and I shared formed a deep storage shelf, level with the head of my bed. Stanley and I stashed our junk there—books, comic books, cigar boxes of crayons and pencils, homemade wooden swords. There were dozens of empty mason jars in the basement. I could bring up some jars, I worked out, urinate into them at night, hide them on the junk shelf and empty them the next day when no one was looking.

Accumulating jars was easy. I brought them up from the basement one   15
at a time. Stanley and I used them anyway to collect fireflies and bugs and
they all looked alike. Arranging them in the dark to relieve my urgent bladder was harder. Dad's and our stepmother's bed was on the other side of the
wall behind the closet. We couldn't hear through the wall unless she and
Dad were fighting, but I didn't dare take chances. She hadn't only forbidden
me to use the bathroom at night. Because she'd offered me no alternative
receptacle, she'd effectively forbidden me to urinate at night, asserting by
that fiat that she, not I, controlled my bladder. Devising an alternative, as I'd
done, was challenging her authority over my body. My fear of being caught
reflected the risk I felt I was taking. I also had every reason to believe that if
she caught me with a mason jar of urine she'd forbid me that release as well
and I'd be worse off than I was before.

So I didn't open a jar to relieve myself as soon as the house quieted
down. I continued my ritual of restraint, of clamping my sphincters and
pinching my penis, until I could no longer bear the pain. Only then, an hour
or more after bedtime, did I dare to ease a jar stealthily from its hiding place,
slip it under the covers to muffle any sound and slowly unscrew its heavy
zinc lid. After I'd waited a while longer to be sure no one had heard, I turned
on my side, released my penis, bent it over the rough lip of the jar tilted
down into the sag of my mattress and tentatively, squirting and clamping,
emptied my bladder. I thought I could fill a jar and sometimes I nearly did.
To avoid overflowing I pressed a finger down along the inside of the jar;
when the warm urine wet it I knew I needed to stop. Hot with shame then I
screwed the lid back on, struggling sometimes to start the threads straight.
Then I had the concealment problem in reverse. I had to move the jar filled
with urine back onto the junk shelf, and with the evidence now patent I was
even more terrified of being heard. It didn't take me as long to return the jars
to the shelf as it did to fetch them, but I worked tense with caution and froze
every time my bunk springs squeaked.

Disposing of the jars turned out to be the hardest part. I was afraid to
move them when our stepmother was home and she seldom left the house
after school or during the evening. Jars of urine began accumulating on the
shelf behind the junk. They didn't smell—I screwed the lids tight enough to
prevent that—but the liquid turned a darker yellow and grew gray cobwebs
of mold. Once in a while I had a chance to dispose of them, one or two at a
time. I let Stanley in on the secret. He didn't disapprove beyond warning me
of the danger. "You better hadn't let her catch you," he told me. A dozen
jars collected on the shelf.

I was away all one Saturday morning doing a job, running errands or
cleaning out someone's garage. When I got home Stanley met me coming
through the backyard and hissed me aside to a conference. "She almost
found the jars," he whispered. I turned white. "It's okay," he said. "I got rid
of them. She got mad about all the junk on the shelf and told me to clean it
off. She was standing there watching me. I started cleaning stuff off but

I kept moving it around to hide your jars. I got to where I didn't see how I could hide them any longer and just then the phone rang and she went off and starting jawing. I hurried up and ran the jars down the back steps and hid them out here under the old tarp. She went off after that and I came out and emptied them. Whew! they smelled bad. They smelled like dead fish." It was a close call and he wasn't happy with me for exposing him to it. After that he helped me keep them emptied.

To this day, forty years later, once a month or so, pain wakes me. Falling asleep with urine in my bladder or unmoved rectal stool, I still reflexively tighten my pelvic muscles until my sphincters cramp. My stepmother, my commandant, still intermittently controls my body even at this distant and safe remove. I sit on the toilet those nights in the silence of my house forcing my sphincters to relax, waiting out the pain in the darkness, remembering her.

Questions for Discussion and Writing

1. What effect did Rhodes's stepmother have on him and on his relationship with his father?
2. What means did Rhodes use to cope with the restrictions his stepmother imposed on him? What residual physical and psychological effects have remained with him into the present?
3. To what extent do the issues of control and rebellion enter into the relationships between parents and children, although not in as extreme ways as Rhodes describes?
4. **Rhetorical inquiry:** How is Rhodes's account shaped around the decisive moment when he learned to counteract his stepmother's power over him?

RUDOLPH CHELMINSKI

Rudolph Chelminski has worked as a staff correspondent for Life *magazine in Paris and Moscow. His articles have appeared in numerous publications including* Life, Time, Fortune, People, Money, Playboy, *and* Wired. *The following essay, a profile of the tightrope walker Philippe Petit, first appeared in* Smithsonian, *November 2001. Chelminski focuses on Petit's walk between the towers of the World Trade Center in 1974 to reflect on the symbolism of the Twin Towers after September 11, 2001. His latest work is* The Perfectionist: Life and Death in Haute Cuisine *(2005).*

Before You Read

Would being a tightrope walker be as valid a form of theater as ballet or modern dance?

Turning Point

What turned the tide of public regard [for the World Trade Center] was not the bigness of the place but the way it could be momentarily captured by fanciful gestures on a human scale. It was the French high-wire artist Philippe Petit crossing between the towers on a tight-rope in 1974 . . .

—*New York Times*, September 13, 2001

Was it only twenty-seven years ago? It seems a lifetime, or two, has passed since that August morning in 1974 when Philippe Petit, a slim, young Frenchman, upstaged Richard Nixon by performing one of the few acts more sensational—in those faraway times—than resigning the presidency of the United States.

A week before his twenty-sixth birthday, the nimble Petit clandestinely strung a cable between the not-yet-completed Twin Towers, already dominating lower Manhattan's skyline, and for the better part of an hour walked back and forth over the void, demonstrating his astonishing obsession to one hundred thousand or so wide-eyed gawkers gathered so far below.

I missed that performance, but last summer, just two weeks before the 1,360-foot-tall towers would come to symbolize a ghastly new reality, I persuaded Petit to accompany me to the top and show me how he did it and, perhaps, explain why. I was driven by a long-standing curiosity. Ever since reading about his exploit in New York, I had felt a kind of familiarity with this remarkable fellow. Years before, I had watched him at close range and much lower altitude, in another city on the other side of the pond.

In the 1960s, the Montparnasse area of Paris was animated by a colorful fauna of celebrities, eccentrics, and artistic characters. On any given day, you might run into Giacometti walking bent forward like one of his skinny statues, Raymond Duncan (Isadora's brother) in his goofy sandals and Roman toga, or Jean-Paul Sartre morosely seeking the decline of capitalism in the Communist daily, *L'Humanité*. And after nightfall, if you hung around long enough, you were almost certain to see Philippe Petit.

When he might appear was anyone's guess, but his hangouts were pretty well known: the corner of Rue de Buci and Boulevard St. Germain; the sidewalk outside Les Deux Magots, or directly under the terrace windows of La Coupole. Silent and mysterious, this skinny, pasty-faced kid dressed in black would materialize unannounced on his unicycle, a shock of pale blond hair escaping from under a battered top hat. He would draw a circle of white chalk on the sidewalk, string a rope between two trees, hop up onto it, and, impassive and mute as a carp, go into an improvised show that combined mime, juggling, prestidigitation, and the precarious balancing act of loose-rope walking. After an hour or so he would pass the hat and, as wordlessly as he had arrived, disappear into the night. 5

Then, on a drizzly morning in June 1971, the kid in black suddenly showed up dancing on a barely perceptible wire between the massive towers of Notre Dame Cathedral. For nearly three hours, he walked back and forth, mugged, saluted, and juggled Indian clubs while angry gendarmes waited for him to come down. When he finally did, they arrested him for disturbing the peace.

Disturbing the peace was a good part of what it was all about, of course, because Petit was out to prove something. Notre Dame was his first great coup, the sensational stunt that was to become his trademark. It was also his first declaration of status: he was not a mere street entertainer but a performer, an artiste. Ever since that June morning, he has dedicated himself to demonstrating his passionate belief that the high wire—his approach to the high wire, that is—transcends the cheap hype of circus "daredevil" routines to become a creative statement of true theater, as valid as ballet or modern dance.

Getting that point across has never been easy. After gratifying Petit with a few front-page pictures, the French establishment gave a Gallic shrug, dismissed him as a youthful crank, and returned to more serious matters—like having lunch and talking politics. There was a very interesting story to be told about this young loner who had learned the art of the *funambule* (literally, "rope walker") all by himself as a teenager, but the Parisian press ignored it. Within a couple of days, his Notre Dame stunt was largely forgotten.

Stung, Petit resolved to take his art elsewhere and began a long vagabondage around the world, returning to Paris for brief spells before setting off again. Traveling as light as a medieval minstrel and living hand to mouth, he carried his mute personage from city to city, juggling for his supper. None of his onlookers could know that back in his tiny Parisian studio—a rented broom closet he had somehow converted into a dwelling—he had a folder marked "projects."

Two years after the Notre Dame caper, the skinny figure in black appeared   10
with his balancing pole between the gigantic northern pylons of the Sydney Harbour Bridge in Australia. Petit had strung his cable there just as furtively as he had done at Notre Dame, but this time the police reacted with brainless if predictable fury, attempting to force him down by cutting one of his cavalettis, the lateral guy ropes that hold a sky walker's cable steady. Flung a foot up in the air when the cavaletti sprang free, Petit managed to land square on the cable and keep his balance. He came in and was manacled, led to court, and found guilty of the usual crimes. The owner of a Sydney circus offered to pay his $250 fine in return for a tightrope walk two days later over the lions' cage.

And then came the World Trade Center. Petit had been planning it ever since he was nineteen when, in a dentist's waiting room, he saw an article with an artist's rendering of the gigantic towers planned for New York's financial district. ("When I see three oranges I juggle," he once said, "and when I see two towers I walk.") He ripped the article from the magazine and slipped it into his projects file.

The World Trade Center would be the ultimate test of Petit's fanatically meticulous planning. For Notre Dame and Sydney, he had copied keys to open certain locks, picked others, and hacksawed his way through still others in order to sneak his heavy material up into place for the sky walk. But New York presented a much more complicated challenge. The World Trade Center buildings were fearfully higher than anything he had ever tackled, making it impossible to set up conventional cavalettis. And how to get a cable across the 140-foot gap between the South and North Towers, anyway, in the face of omnipresent security crews?

There was one factor in Petit's favor: the buildings were still in the final stages of construction, and trucks were regularly delivering all sorts of material to the basement docks, to be transferred to a freight elevator and brought up to the floors by workers of all descriptions. Wearing hard hats, Petit and an accomplice hauled his gear to the top of the South Tower (his walking cable passed off as antenna equipment) while two other friends similarly made their way to the roof of the North Tower, armed with a bow and arrow and a spool of stout fishing line. Come nightfall, they shot the arrow and line across the 140-foot gap between the towers. Petit retrieved the line, pulled it over until he was in possession of the stronger nylon cord attached to it, then tied on the heavy rope that would be used to carry his steel walking cable over to the other side.

As Petit laid out the rope and then the cable, gravity took over. The cable ran wild, shooting uncontrollably through his hands and snaking down the side of the giant building before coming up short with a titanic *thwonk!* at the steel beam to which Petit had anchored it. On the North Tower, holding fast to the other end of the heavy rope, his friends were pulled perilously close to the roof's edge. Gradually, the four regained control and spent the rest of the night hours pulling the cable up, double-cinching the anchor points, getting it nearly level, tensioning it to three tons with a ratchet, and finally attaching a set of nearly horizontal cavalettis to the buildings. At a few minutes past seven A.M., August 7, 1974, just as the first construction workers were arriving on the rooftop, Petit seized his balancing pole and stepped out over the void.

The conditions weren't exactly ideal. Petit had not slept for forty-eight hours, and now he saw that the hurry-up rigging job he had carried out in the dark had resulted in a cable that zigzagged where the improvised cavalettis joined it. Sensitive to wind, temperature, and any sway of the buildings, it was also alive—swooping, rolling, and twisting. At slightly more than twenty-six feet, his balancing pole was longer and heavier—fifty-five pounds—than any he had ever used before. Greater weight meant greater stability, but such a heavy load is hard enough to tote around on terra firma, let alone on a thin wire in midair at an insane altitude. It would require an uncommon debauch of nervous energy, but energy was the one thing Petit had plenty of.

With his eyes riveted to the edge of the far tower—wire walkers aren't supposed to look down—Petit glided his buffalo-hide slippers along the

15

cable, feeling his way until he was halfway across. He knelt, put his weight on one knee, and swung his right arm free. This was his "salute," the signature gesture of the high-wire artist. Each has his own, and each is an individual trademark creation. Arising, he continued to the North Tower, hopped off the wire, double-checked the cable's anchoring points, made a few adjustments, and hopped back on.

By now traffic had stopped in the environs of Wall Street, and Petit could already hear the first police and ambulance sirens as he nimbly set forth again. Off he went, humming and mumbling to himself, puffing grunts of concentration at tricky moments. Halfway across, he steadied, halted, then knelt again. And then, God in heaven, he lay down, placing his spine directly atop the cable and resting the balancing pole on his stomach. Breathless, in Zen-like calm, he lay there for a long moment, contemplating the red-eyed seabird hovering motionless above him.

Time to get up. But how do you do it, I asked Petit as we stood together on the roof of the South Tower, when the only thing between you and certain death is a cable under your body and fifty-five extra pounds lying on your belly?

"All the weight on the right foot," he replied with a shrug. "I draw my right foot back along the cable and move the balancing bar lower down below my belt. I get a little lift from the wire, because it is moving up and down. Then I do a sit-up and rise to a standing position, with all the weight on my right foot. It takes some practice."

He got up. Unable to resist the pleasure of seeing New York at his feet,   20
he caressed the side of the building with a glance and slowly panned his eyes all the way down to the gridlocked traffic below. Then he flowed back to the South Tower. "I could hear the horns of cars below me," he recalled, relishing the memory. "I could hear the applause too. The *rumeur* [clamor] of the crowd rose up to me from four hundred meters below. No other show person has ever heard a sound like that."

Now, as he glided along north to south, a clutch of police officers, rescue crews, and security men hovered with arms outstretched to pull him in. But Petit hadn't finished. Inches from their grasp, he did a wire walker's turnaround, slipping his feet 180 degrees and swinging his balancing bar around to face in the other direction. He did his elegant "torero's" walk and his "promenader's" walk; he knelt; he did another salute; he sat in casual repose, lord of his domain; he stood and balanced on one foot.

After seven crossings and forty-five minutes of air dancing, it began to rain. For his finale he ran along the cable to give himself up. "Running, ah! ah!" he had written in one of his early books. "That's the laughter of the wire walker." Then he ran into the arms of waiting police.

Petit's astonishing star turn created a sensation the likes of which few New Yorkers had ever seen. Years later, the art critic Calvin Tompkins was still so impressed by what Petit had done that he wrote in *The New Yorker*: "He achieved the almost unimaginable feat of investing the World Trade Center . . . with a thrilling and terrible beauty."

Ever resourceful, Petit worked out a deal with the Manhattan district attorney. In lieu of punishment or fine, and as penance for his artistic crime, he agreed to give a free performance in Central Park. The following week he strung a 600-foot wire across Turtle Pond, from a tree on one side to Belvedere Castle on the other. And this time he nearly fell. He was wearing the same walking slippers and using the same balancing pole, but security was relaxed among the fifteen thousand people who had come to watch him perform, and kids began climbing and jumping on his cavalettis. The wire twitched, and suddenly he felt himself going beyond the point of return.

But he didn't go all the way down. Instinctively squirming as he   25
dropped, he hooked a leg over the wire. Somehow, he managed to swing himself back up, get vertical, and carry on with the performance. The crowd applauded warmly, assuming it was all part of the act, but Petit doesn't enjoy the memory. Falling is the wire walker's shame, he says, and due only to a lack of concentration.

In the years since his World Trade Center triumph, Petit has disdainfully turned away all offers to profit from it. "I could have become a millionaire," he told me. "Everyone was after me to endorse their products, but I was not going to walk a wire dressed in a hamburger suit, and I was not going to say I succeeded because I was wearing such and such a shirt." Continuing to operate as a stubbornly independent freelance artist, he has organized and starred in more than seventy performances around the world, all without safety nets. They have included choreographed strolls across the Louisiana Superdome in New Orleans, between the towers of the Lyon Cathedral in France, and a "Peace Walk" between the Jewish and Arab quarters of Jerusalem. In 1989, on the bicentennial of the French Revolution, he took center stage in Paris—legally and officially this time—by walking the 2,300-foot gap between the Trocadéro esplanade on the Right Bank, over the Seine, and up to the second tier of the Eiffel Tower.

Today, at fifty-two, Petit is somewhat heavier than in his busking days in Paris, and his hair has turned a reddish blond, but neither his energy nor his overpowering self-confidence has waned in the least. He shares a pleasantly rustic farmhouse at the edge of the Catskills near Woodstock, New York, with his longtime companion, Kathy O'Donnell, daughter of a former Manhattan publishing executive. She handles the planning, producing, problem-solving, and money-raising aspects of Petit's enterprises while they both think up new high-wire projects and he painstakingly prepares them. Petit supplements his income from performances with, among other things, book royalties and fees from giving lectures and workshops.

His preferred place of study is his New York City office. Knowing what an artiste he is, you would not expect to find him in an ordinary building, and you would be right. Petit hangs out at the Cathedral of St. John the Divine, the world's biggest Gothic cathedral, at Amsterdam Avenue and 112th Street. His office is a balustraded aerie in the cathedral's triforium, the narrow gallery high above the vast nave. Behind a locked entryway, up a suitably medieval spiral staircase and then down a stone passageway, the rare visitor to his domain comes upon a sturdy door bearing a small framed sign: *Philippe Petit, Artist in Residence*. Behind that door, stowed as neatly as a yacht's navigational gear, lie his treasures: thousands of feet of rope coiled just so, all manner of rigging and tensioning equipment, floor-to-ceiling archives, maps and models of past and future walk projects, and shelves upon shelves of technical and reference books.

It was another of his coups that got him there. In 1980 he offered to walk the length of the nave to raise funds for the cathedral's building program. He was sure he had the perfect occasion for it: Ascension Day. The cathedral's then dean, the ebullient James Parks Morton, famous for his support of the arts, was enthusiastic, but his board of trustees vetoed the idea as too dangerous. Petit sneaked a cable crosswise over the nave and did his walk anyway. Once again the police came to arrest him, but Morton spoiled their day by announcing that Petit was artist in residence and the cathedral was his workplace. And so he came to be.

Over the years, taking his title seriously, Petit reciprocated by carrying   30
out a dozen wire walks inside and outside the cathedral. He figures that by now he has raised half a million dollars for the still uncompleted cathedral's building program, and enjoys pointing out the small stone carving of a wire walker niched in among the saints in the main portal. "It is high art," Morton says of Petit's work. "There is a documented history of wire walkers in cathedrals and churches. It's not a new idea, but his walk here was his first in an American cathedral."

Sometimes after six P.M., when the lights go out, the big front door slams shut, and the cathedral closes down for the night, Petit is left alone in the mineral gloom of St. John with his writing, sketches, calculations, chess problems, poetry, and reveries. The comparison to Quasimodo is immediate and obvious, of course, but unlike Notre Dame's famous hunchback, Petit wants nothing more than to be seen, in the ever greater, more ambitious, and spectacular shows that fill his dreams. One night after he took me up to his cathedral office, he gazed longingly at a print of the Brooklyn Bridge— what a walk that could be! But there is, he assured me, plenty more in his projects file. A walk on Easter Island, from the famous carved heads to the volcano. Or the half-mile stretch over open water between the Sydney Harbour Bridge and the celebrated Opera House.

Even more than all these, though, there is one walk—*the* walk, the ultimate, the masterpiece—that has filled his dreams for more than a decade. It's the Grand Canyon. Prospecting in the heart of the Navajo nation by air in 1988, Petit discovered the ideal spot for crowning his career: a ruggedly beautiful landscape off the road from Flagstaff to Grand Canyon Village, where a noble mesa soars at the far end of a 1,200-foot gap from the canyon's edge. The gap is deeper than it is wide, 1,600 feet straight down to the Little Colorado River.

Petit's eyes glowed as he went through the mass of blueprints, maps, drawings, and models he has produced over all the years of planning the

Canyon Walk. Only one thing is missing: money. Twice now, the money people have backed out at the last minute.

But none of that seemed to matter when I spoke to Petit a few days after the September 11 catastrophe struck. He could scarcely find words for his sorrow at the loss of so many lives, among them people he knew well—elevator operators, tour guides, maintenance workers. "I feel my house has been destroyed," he said. "Very often I would take family and friends there. It was my pride as a poet and a lover of beautiful things to show as many people as possible the audacity of those impossible monoliths."

Haunted, as we all are, by the images of the towers in their final   35
moments, Petit told me it was his hope that they would be remembered not as they appeared then but as they were on that magical August day more than a generation ago, when he danced between them on a wire and made an entire city look up in awe. "In a very small way I helped frame them with glory," he said, "and I want to remember them in their glory."

Questions for Discussion and Writing

1. How did Philippe Petit's exploits imbue the as-yet-unfinished Twin Towers with a human dimension and become all the more poignant after September 11, 2001?
2. What do we learn about Petit's view as to how an artist in this medium should be defined?
3. How do comments by journalists and art critics communicate the way the public viewed Petit's achievements?
4. **Rhetorical inquiry:** How does Chelminski structure his account so that the wire-walking episode between the Twin Towers is the central focus of his essay?

RICK BASS

Rick Bass was born in Fort Worth, Texas in 1958, earned a B. S. at Utah State University in 1979, and worked as a petroleum geologist. He is a prolific author of both fiction and nonfiction, including Colter: The True Story of the Best Dog I Ever Had *(2000),* The Roadless Yaak *(2002),* The Diezmo *(2005) and* The Lives of Rocks: Stories *(2006). His stories have been awarded the Pushcart Prize and the O. Henry Award. The following essay first appeared in* Orion, *May/June 2005.*

Before You Read

Have you ever noticed the ways in which animals in the wild are camouflaged to fit into their environments?

A Fitting Desire

In July, as the fields and meadows begin to bloom with the white blossoms of yarrow, clusters of pearly everlasting, and oxeye daisies, the deer fawns, similarly spotted, lie in these same fields, camouflaged within the season, calibrated almost to the day, perhaps even to the hour.

It is a finely tuned sameness, this tendency, predisposition, even yearning for one thing to follow the lead of another, like the wheeling of an entire flock of birds—each giving itself over surely to no considered forethought but instead pivoting on some invisible point in the sky deflecting the flight of a hundred individuals as one being with not even a whisper or rustling of wings.

What is the name for it, the way deer and elk antlers look exactly like the limbs and branches of the same forest thicket in which they take refuge?

The yellow sulphurs dance and skitter across the fields from one buttery dandelion to the next, from the similarly yellow blossoms of one heartleaf arnica to another. Watching them stir, you think at first the blossom itself has suddenly unfolded and taken flight—and it all seems like a kind of inaudible orchestra, the movements and order like the score and composition for beautiful sheet music that we cannot hear, can instead only see.

How secure—or tenuous—is this ancient collaboration, now, in a time   5 grown so frighteningly reckless? To cant our weather and seasons by five or ten degrees Fahrenheit, as if striving to tip the world over on its side with some huge pry bar—how will that listing, that destruction, affect all the invisible angles and hard-gotten, beautiful negotiations of the earth, and the rightness of things?

As the olive-sided flycatchers perch high in the branches of conifers, a vertical tide of the day's warming currents lifts summer insects—lacy wings glittering and whirling diaphanous—up toward the waiting birds. Meanwhile, water pipits hop along on the ground just below the whistling flycatchers, gleaning from snowmelt puddles and patches of ice the remains of those insects that perished overnight in the alpine chill. Having evaded the acrobatic swoops and pursuits of the olive-sided flycatchers, the bugs find themselves stranded nonetheless, and stipple the ice the next morning in dark flecks and nuggets upon the snow.

It seems to me, from a poetic perspective, that such specialization—such fit—speaks at least as much to a notion of gentle cooperation and gracefulness in nature as it does to the old hammer-and-tong model of scrabbling competition. This is not to suggest that nature is anything less than fiercely clamant, with every individual scrambling hourly for tooth-and-claw survival, and for the continuance of each being's genes and names. But upon closer examination, it might seem that there are always two worlds, one overlaid upon the other—two worlds at right angles to one another, perhaps—the savage, competitive world and the gentle, cooperative world. And that to a careful observer, there is evidence everywhere of a pattern and sophistry beyond the random: evidence of wild nature's, or God's, or gods' desire to fill the world with beauty and order—with full elegance, so that every niche is miraculously and intricately occupied.

What is the name for this desire of fit? Would it be different in different seasons, different weather, different landscapes? Would an adult have a different word for it than a child, and a man a different term than a woman? Perhaps we need to make up a name for it, to help draw more attention to it, in order that we might be more respectful of it—this fittedness, this elegance in which we rarely participate, but which we have been entrusted to notice, and safeguard.

Questions for Discussion and Writing

1. What underlying harmony does Bass discern in the seemingly random patterns of nature and how is this theme expressed in the title?
2. Why does Bass believe that a cooperative view of nature is as relevant as the more familiar struggle-for-survival or competitive model?
3. Use Bass's essay as a model and in a few paragraphs describe a natural scene in which different species interact or blend into the environment in ways that suggest a hidden pattern?
4. **Rhetorical inquiry:** How does Bass use a comparison to an "inaudible orchestra" (para. 4) to emphasize a hidden motif in the natural world? How do Bass's descriptions stress this symbiotic relationship between plants, insects, and animals?

ALDO LEOPOLD

Aldo Leopold (1876–1944) was a conservationist, forester, writer, and teacher who devoted himself to wilderness preservation and wildlife management. Through his efforts, the first protected wilderness area, located in Gila National Forest in New Mexico, was established. Leopold was instrumental in founding the Wilderness Society in 1934. He was posthumously honored in 1978 with the John Burroughs Medal in tribute to a lifetime of work in conservation. Leopold was an important forerunner of the tradition of nature writing. "Thinking Like a Mountain," drawn from his classic work A Sand County Almanac *(1949), reveals an exceptionally subtle appreciation of the interplay between animals and the environment.*

Before You Read

What function do predators such as wolves serve in the balance of nature?

Thinking Like a Mountain

A deep chesty bawl echoes from rimrock to rimrock, rolls down the mountain, and fades into the far blackness of the night. It is an outburst of wild defiant sorrow, and of contempt for all the adversities of the world.

Every living thing (and perhaps many a dead one as well) pays heed to that call. To the deer it is a reminder of the way of all flesh, to the pine a forecast of midnight scuffles and of blood upon the snow, to the coyote a promise of gleanings to come, to the cowman a threat of red ink at the bank, to the hunter a challenge of fang against bullet. Yet behind these obvious and immediate hopes and fears there lies a deeper meaning, known only to the mountain itself. Only the mountain has lived long enough to listen objectively to the howl of a wolf.

Those unable to decipher the hidden meaning know nevertheless that it is there, for it is felt in all wolf country, and distinguishes that country from all other land. It tingles in the spine of all who hear wolves by night, or who scan their tracks by day. Even without sight or sound of wolf, it is implicit in a hundred small events: the midnight whinny of a pack horse, the rattle of rolling rocks, the bound of a fleeing deer, the way shadows lie under the spruces. Only the ineducable tyro can fail to sense the presence or absence of wolves, or the fact that mountains have a secret opinion about them.

My own conviction on this score dates from the day I saw a wolf die. We were eating lunch on a high rimrock, at the foot of which a turbulent river elbowed its way. We saw what we thought was a doe fording the torrent, her breast awash in white water. When she climbed the bank toward us and shook out her tail, we realized our error: it was a wolf. A half-dozen others, evidently grown pups, sprang from the willows and all joined in a welcoming mêlée of wagging tails and playful maulings. What was literally a pile of wolves writhed and tumbled in the center of an open flat at the foot of our rimrock.

In those days we had never heard of passing up a chance to kill a wolf. In a second we were pumping lead into the pack, but with more excitement than accuracy: how to aim a steep downhill shot is always confusing. When our rifles were empty, the old wolf was down, and a pup was dragging a leg into impassable slide-rocks.

We reached the old wolf in time to watch a fierce green fire dying in her eyes. I realized then, and have known ever since, that there was something new to me in those eyes—something known only to her and to the mountain. I was young then, and full of trigger-itch; I thought that because fewer wolves meant more deer, that no wolves would mean hunters' paradise. But after seeing the green fire die, I sensed that neither the wolf nor the mountain agreed with such a view.

Since then I have lived to see state after state extirpate its wolves. I have watched the face of many a newly wolfless mountain, and seen the

5

south-facing slopes wrinkle with a maze of new deer trails. I have seen every edible bush and seedling browsed, first to anaemic desuetude, and then to death.[1] I have seen every edible tree defoliated to the height of a saddlehorn. Such a mountain looks as if someone had given God a new pruning shears, and forbidden Him all other exercise. In the end the starved bones of the hoped-for deer herd, dead of its own too-much, bleach with the bones of the dead sage, or molder under the high-lined junipers.

I now suspect that just as a deer herd lives in mortal fear of its wolves, so does a mountain live in mortal fear of its deer. And perhaps with better cause, for while a buck pulled down by wolves can be replaced in two or three years, a range pulled down by too many deer may fail of replacement in as many decades.

So also with cows. The cowman who cleans his range of wolves does not realize that he is taking over the wolf's job of trimming the herd to fit the range. He has not learned to think like a mountain. Hence we have dust-bowls, and rivers washing the future into the sea.

We all strive for safety, prosperity, comfort, long life, and dullness. The deer strives with his supple legs, the cowman with trap and poison, the statesman with pen, the most of us with machines, votes, and dollars, but it all comes to the same thing: peace in our time. A measure of success in this is all well enough, and perhaps is a requisite to objective thinking, but too much safety seems to yield only danger in the long run. Perhaps this is behind Thoreau's dictum: In wildness is the salvation of the world. Perhaps this is the hidden meaning in the howl of the wolf, long known among mountains, but seldom perceived among men.   10

Questions for Discussion and Writing

1. In what way does the experience of having shot a wolf lead to a change in Leopold's attitude?
2. What consequences would follow from the extermination of wolves, according to Leopold?
3. Why is the process of "thinking like a mountain" important in maintaining the balance of nature?
4. **Rhetorical inquiry:** Evaluate Leopold's technique in anthropomorphising the mountain in its "fear of its deer." Why does Thoreau's quote "in wildness is the salvation of the world" provide a key to understanding the important role wolves play and what would happen if they were eliminated.

---

[1] Desuetude: underused or abandoned; drained of sustenance.

How does this image of a White Gray wolf next to antlers illustrate the theme of Leopold's essay?

Fiction

RAYMOND CARVER

Raymond Carver (1938–1988) grew up in a logging town in Oregon and was educated at Humboldt State College (B.A., 1963) and at the University of Iowa, where be studied creative writing. He first received recognition in the 1970s with the publication of stories in the New Yorker, Esquire, *and the* Atlantic Monthly. *His first collection of short stories,* Will You Please Be Quiet, Please? *(1976), was nominated for the National Book Award. Subsequent collections include* What We Talk About When We Talk About Love *(1981),* Cathedral *(1983), and* Where I'm Calling From *(1988), in which "Neighbors" first appeared. A posthumous book of Carver's poetry,* All of Us, *was published in 1998. "Neighbors" displays Carver's conversational style and unique gift for getting to the heart of human relationships.*

Before You Read

What is the meaning of "the grass is always greener on the other side"?

Neighbors

Bill and Arlene Miller were a happy couple. But now and then they felt they alone among their circle had been passed by somehow, leaving Bill to attend to his bookkeeping duties and Arlene occupied with secretarial chores. They talked about it sometimes, mostly in comparison with the lives of their neighbors, Harriet and Jim Stone. It seemed to the Millers that the Stones lived a fuller and brighter life. The Stones were always going out for dinner, or entertaining at home, or traveling about the country somewhere in connection with Jim's work.

The Stones lived across the hall from the Millers. Jim was a salesman for a machine-parts firm and often managed to combine business with pleasure trips, and on this occasion the Stones would be away for ten days, first to Cheyenne, then on to St. Louis to visit relatives. In their absence, the Millers would look after the Stones' apartment, feed Kitty, and water the plants.

Bill and Jim shook hands beside the car. Harriet and Arlene held each other by the elbows and kissed lightly on the lips.

"Have fun," Bill said to Harriet.

"We will," said Harriet. "You kids have fun too."   5

Arlene nodded.

Jim winked at her. "Bye, Arlene. Take good care of the old man."

"I will," Arlene said.

"Have fun," Bill said.

"You bet," Jim said, clipping Bill lightly on the arm. "And thanks   10
again, you guys."

The Stones waved as they drove away, and the Millers waved too.

"Well, I wish it was us," Bill said.

"God knows, we could use a vacation," Arlene said. She took his arm and put it around her waist as they climbed the stairs to their apartment.

After dinner Arlene said, "Don't forget. Kitty gets liver flavor the first night." She stood in the kitchen doorway folding the handmade tablecloth that Harriet had bought for her last year in Santa Fe.

Bill took a deep breath as he entered the Stones' apartment. The air was   15
already heavy and it was vaguely sweet. The sunburst clock over the television said half past eight. He remembered when Harriet had come home with the clock, how she had crossed the hall to show it to Arlene, cradling the brass case in her arms and talking to it through the tissue paper as if it were an infant.

Kitty rubbed her face against his slippers and then turned onto her side, but jumped up quickly as Bill moved to the kitchen and selected one of the stacked cans from the gleaming drainboard. Leaving the cat to pick at her food, he headed for the bathroom. He looked at himself in the mirror and then closed his eyes and then looked again. He opened the medicine chest. He found a container of pills and read the label—*Harriet Stone. One each day as directed*—and slipped it into his pocket. He went back to the kitchen, drew a pitcher of water, and returned to the living room. He finished watering, set the pitcher on the rug, and opened the liquor cabinet. He reached in back for the bottle of Chivas Regal. He took two drinks from the bottle, wiped his lips on his sleeve, and replaced the bottle in the cabinet.

Kitty was on the couch sleeping. He switched off the lights, slowly closing and checking the door. He had the feeling he had left something.

"What kept you?" Arlene said. She sat with her legs turned under her, watching television.

"Nothing. Playing with Kitty," he said, and went over to her and touched her breasts.

"Let's go to bed, honey," he said.   20

The next day Bill took only ten minutes of the twenty-minute break allotted for the afternoon and left at fifteen minutes before five. He parked the car in the lot just as Arlene hopped down from the bus. He waited until she entered the building, then ran up the stairs to catch her as she stepped out of the elevator.

"Bill! God, you scared me. You're early," she said.

He shrugged. "Nothing to do at work," he said.

She let him use her key to open the door. He looked at the door across the hall before following her inside.

"Let's go to bed," he said.   25

"Now?" She laughed. "What's gotten into you?"

"Nothing. Take your dress off." He grabbed for her awkwardly, and she said, "Good God, Bill."

He unfastened his belt.

Later they sent out for Chinese food, and when it arrived they ate hungrily, without speaking, and listened to records.

"Let's not forget to feed Kitty," she said.   30

"I was just thinking about that," he said. "I'll go right over."

He selected a can of fish flavor for the cat, then filled the pitcher and went to water. When he returned to the kitchen, the cat was scratching in her box. She looked at him steadily before she turned back to the litter. He opened all the cupboards and examined the canned goods, the cereals, the packaged foods, the cocktail and wine glasses, the china, the pots and pans. He opened the refrigerator. He sniffed some celery, took two bites of cheddar cheese, and chewed on an apple as he walked into the bedroom. The bed seemed enormous, with a fluffy white bedspread draped to the floor. He pulled out a nightstand drawer, found a half-empty package of cigarettes and stuffed them into his pocket. Then he stepped to the closet and was opening it when the knock sounded at the front door.

He stopped by the bathroom and flushed the toilet on his way.

"What's been keeping you?" Arlene said. "You've been over here more than an hour."

"Have I really?" he said.   35

"Yes, you have," she said.

"I had to go to the toilet," he said.

"You have your own toilet," she said.

"I couldn't wait," he said.

That night they made love again.   40

In the morning he had Arlene call in for him. He showered, dressed, and made a light breakfast. He tried to start a book. He went out for a walk and felt better. But after a while, hands still in his pockets, he returned to the apartment. He stopped at the Stones' door on the chance he might hear the cat moving about. Then he let himself in at his own door and went to the kitchen for the key.

Inside it seemed cooler than his apartment, and darker too. He wondered if the plants had something to do with the temperature of the air. He looked out the window, and then he moved slowly through each room considering everything that fell under his gaze, carefully, one object at a time. He saw ashtrays, items of furniture, kitchen utensils, the clock. He saw everything. At last he entered the bedroom, and the cat appeared at his feet. He stroked her once, carried her into the bathroom, and shut the door.

He lay down on the bed and stared at the ceiling. He lay for a while with his eyes closed, and then he moved his hand under his belt. He tried to recall what day it was. He tried to remember when the Stones were due back, and then he wondered if they would ever return. He could not remember their faces or the way they talked and dressed. He sighed and with effort rolled off the bed to lean over the dresser and look at himself in the mirror.

He opened the closet and selected a Hawaiian shirt. He looked until he found Bermudas, neatly pressed and hanging over a pair of brown twill slacks. He shed his own clothes and slipped into the shorts and the shirt. He looked in the mirror again. He went to the living room and poured himself a drink and sipped it on his way back to the bedroom. He put on a blue shirt, a dark suit, a blue and white tie, black wing-tip shoes. The glass was empty and he went for another drink.

In the bedroom again, he sat on a chair, crossed his legs, and smiled,   45 observing himself in the mirror. The telephone rang twice and fell silent. He finished the drink and took off the suit. He rummaged through the top drawers until he found a pair of panties and a brassiere. He stepped into the panties and fastened the brassiere, then looked through the closet for an outfit. He put on a black and white checkered skirt and tried to zip it up. He put on a burgundy blouse that buttoned up the front. He considered her shoes, but understood they would not fit. For a long time he looked out the living-room window from behind the curtain. Then he returned to the bedroom and put everything away.

He was not hungry. She did not eat much, either. They looked at each other shyly and smiled. She got up from the table and checked that the key was on the shelf and then she quickly cleared the dishes.

He stood in the kitchen doorway and smoked a cigarette and watched her pick up the key.

"Make yourself comfortable while I go across the hall," she said. "Read the paper or something." She closed her fingers over the key. He was, she said, looking tired.

He tried to concentrate on the news. He read the paper and turned on the television. Finally he went across the hall. The door was locked.

"It's me. Are you still there, honey?" he called.   50

After a time the lock released and Arlene stepped outside and shut the door. "Was I gone so long?" she said.

"Well, you were," he said.

"Was I?" she said. "I guess I must have been playing with Kitty."

He studied her, and she looked away, her hand still resting on the doorknob.

"It's funny," she said. "You know—to go in someone's place like that."   55

He nodded, took her hand from the knob, and guided her toward their own door. He let them into their apartment.

"It *is* funny," he said.

He noticed white lint clinging to the back of her sweater, and the color was high in her cheeks. He began kissing her on the neck and hair and she turned and kissed him back.

"Oh, damn," she said. "Damn, damn," she sang, girlishly clapping her hands. "I just remembered. I really and truly forgot to do what I went over there to do. I didn't feed Kitty or do any watering." She looked at him. "Isn't that stupid?"

"I don't think so," he said. "Just a minute. I'll get my cigarettes and go   60
back with you."

She waited until he had closed and locked their door, and then she took his arm at the muscle and said. "I guess I should tell you. I found some pictures."

He stopped in the middle of the hall. "What kind of pictures?"

"You can see for yourself," she said, and she watched him.

"No kidding." He grinned. "Where?"

"In a drawer," she said.   65

"No kidding," he said.

And then she said, "Maybe they won't come back," and was at once astonished at her words.

"It could happen," he said, "Anything could happen."

"Or maybe they'll come back and . . ." but she did not finish.

They held hands for the short walk across the hall, and when he spoke   70
she could barely hear his voice.

"The key," he said. "Give it to me."

"What?" she said, She gazed at the door.

"The key," he said. "You have the key."

"My God," she said, "I left the key inside."

He tried the knob. It was locked. Then she tried the knob. It would not   75
turn. Her lips were parted, and her breathing was hard, expectant. He opened his arms and she moved into them.

"Don't worry," he said into her ear. "For God's sake, don't worry."

They stayed there. They held each other. They leaned into the door as if against a wind, and braced themselves.

Questions for Discussion and Writing

1. How does the opening of the story define Bill and Arlene Miller's neighbors (the Stones) as people to be envied? How does house-sitting for the Stones change Bill and Arlene's relationship?
2. How does the progression of incidents suggest that the Millers (especially Bill) are getting carried away with stepping outside their lives? Although Carver does not tell us, what can you infer is going on in the minds of Bill and Arlene at the end of the story (they have forgotten to water the plants and feed the cat, and they have left the key locked inside)?
3. Would you consider letting the Millers house-sit for you? Why or why not? To what extent is the success of the story due to most people's desire (even if they do not act on it) to look into the cabinets, drawers, and closets of others, if given the opportunity?
4. **Rhetorical inquiry:** Choose one of the details in Carver's story and discuss how it could be expanded to provide additional insight into the lives of both couples. For example, what might the photos Arlene discovered show? For what might Harriet Stone be taking medication? Why is it significant that the cat looks "steadily" at Bill and has Arlene forgotten the key accidentally on purpose?

JOHN CHEEVER

John Cheever (1912–1982) was born in Quincy, Massachusetts. His parents had planned for him to attend Harvard, but he was expelled at seventeen from the Thayer Academy for smoking, which marked the end of his formal education. Although he wrote five novels, he is best known for his deftly constructed short stories of suburban affluent America that frequently appeared in The New Yorker. Collections of his work include The Enormous Radio *(1953),* The House Breaker of Shady Hill *(1958),* The Brigadier and the Golf Widow *(1964), and* The Stories of John Cheever *(1978), which won a Pulitzer Prize, and from which "Reunion" is reprinted.*

Before You Read

Has another person you had respected ever disappointed you?

Reunion

The last time I saw my father was in Grand Central Station. I was going from my grandmother's in the Adirondacks to a cottage on the Cape that my mother had rented, and I wrote to my father that I would be in New York between trains for an hour and a half and asked if we could have lunch together. His secretary wrote to say that he would meet me at the information booth at noon, and at twelve o'clock sharp I saw him coming through the crowd. He was a stranger to me—my mother divorced him three years ago, and I hadn't been with him since—but as soon as I saw him I felt that he was my father, my flesh and blood, my future and my doom. I knew that when I was grown I would be something like him; I would have to plan my campaigns within his limitations. He was a big, good-looking man, and I was terribly happy to see him again. He struck me on the back and shook my hand. "Hi, Charlie," he said. "Hi, boy. I'd like to take you up to my club, but it's in the Sixties, and if you have to catch an early train I guess we'd better get something to eat around here." He put his arm around me, and I smelled my father the way my mother sniffs a rose. It was a rich compound of whiskey, aftershave lotion, shoe polish, woolens, and the rankness of a mature male. I hoped that someone would see us together. I wished that we could be photographed. I wanted some record of our having been together.

We went out of the station and up a side street to a restaurant. It was still early, and the place was empty. The bartender was quarreling with a delivery boy, and there was one very old waiter in a red coat down by the kitchen door. We sat down, and my father hailed the waiter in a loud voice. "*Kellner!*" he shouted. "*Garçon! Cameriere! You!*" His boisterousness in the empty restaurant seemed out of place. "Could we have a little service here!" he shouted. "Chop-chop." Then he clapped his hands. This caught the waiter's attention, and he shuffled over to our table.

"Were you clapping your hands at me?" he asked.

"Calm down, calm down, *sommelier*," my father said. "If it isn't too much to ask of you—if it wouldn't be too much above and beyond the call of duty, we would like a couple of Beefeater Gibsons."

"I don't like to be clapped at," the waiter said.   5

"I should have brought my whistle," my father said. "I have a whistle that is audible only to the ears of old waiters. Now, take out your little pad and your little pencil and see if you can get this straight: two Beefeater Gibsons. Repeat after me: two Beefeater Gibsons."

"I think you'd better go somewhere else," the waiter said quietly.

"That," said my father, "is one of the most brilliant suggestions I have ever heard. Come on, Charlie, let's get the hell out of here."

I followed my father out of that restaurant into another. He was not so boisterous this time. Our drinks came, and he cross-questioned me about the baseball season. He then struck the edge of his empty glass with his knife and began shouting again. "*Garçon! Kellner! You!* Could we trouble you to bring us two more of the same."

"How old is the boy?" the waiter asked.   10

"That," my father said, "is none of your goddamned business."

"I'm sorry, sir," the waiter said, "but I won't serve the boy another drink."

"Well, I have some news for you," my father said. "I have some very interesting news for you. This doesn't happen to be the only restaurant in New York. They've opened another on the corner. Come on, Charlie."

He paid the bill, and I followed him out of that restaurant into another. Here the waiters wore pink jackets like hunting coats, and there was a lot of horse tack on the walls. We sat down, and my father began to shout again. "Master of the hounds! Tallyhoo and all that sort of thing. We'd like a little something in the way of a stirrup cup. Namely, two Bibson Geefeaters."

"Two Bibson Geefeaters?" the waiter asked, smiling.   15

"You know damned well what I want," my father said angrily. "I want two Beefeater Gibsons, and make it snappy. Things have changed in jolly old England. So my friend the duke tells me. Let's see what England can produce in the way of a cocktail."

"This isn't England," the waiter said.

"Don't argue with me," my father said. "Just do as you're told."

"I just thought you might like to know where you are," the waiter said.

"If there is one thing I cannot tolerate," my father said, "it is an impu-   20
dent domestic. Come on, Charlie."

The fourth place we went to was Italian. "*Buon giorno,*" my father said. "*Per favore, possiamo avere due cocktail americani, forti, forti. Molto gin, poco vermut.*"

"I don't understand Italian," the waiter said.

"Oh, come off it," my father said. "You understand Italian, and you know damned well you do. *Vogliamo due cocktail americani. Subito.*"

The waiter left us and spoke with the captain, who came over to our table and said, "I'm sorry, sir, but this table is reserved."

"All right," my father said. "Get us another table."   25

"All the tables are reserved," the captain said.

"I get it," my father said. "You don't desire our patronage. Is that it? Well, the hell with you. *Vada all' inferno.* Let's go, Charlie."

"I have to get my train," I said.

"I'm sorry, sonny," my father said. "I'm terribly sorry." He put his arm around me and pressed me against him. "I'll walk you back to the station. If there had only been time to go up to my club."

"That's all right, Daddy," I said.   30

"I'll get you a paper," he said. "I'll get you a paper to read on the train."

Then he went up to a newsstand and said, "Kind sir, will you be good enough to favor me with one of your goddamned, no-good, ten-cent afternoon papers?" The clerk turned away from him and stared at a magazine cover. "Is it asking too much, kind sir," my father said, "is it asking too much for you to sell me one of your disgusting specimens of yellow journalism?"

"I have to go, Daddy," I said. "It's late."

"Now, just wait a second, sonny," he said. "Just wait a second. I want to get a rise out of this chap."   35

"Goodbye, Daddy," I said, and I went down the stairs and got my train, and that was the last time I saw my father.

Questions for Discussion and Writing

1. What embarrasses the young man about the way his father treats others?
2. How does Cheever stage the events in the story to justify the boy's final decision not to see his father again?
3. How would the story sound if it were written from the father's point of view?
4. **Rhetorical inquiry:** What details best exemplify the father's insensitivity and help explain why it is now too painful for Charlie to continue their relationship? What importance should we attribute to Charlie's belief that he is destined to be like his father in explaining this decision?

Poetry

ROBERT HAYDEN

Robert Hayden (1913–1980) was born in Detroit and educated at Wayne State University and the University of Michigan. He taught for more than twenty years at Fisk University before becoming a professor of English at the University of Michigan. He was elected to the National Academy of American Poets in 1975 and served twice as the poetry consultant to the Library of Congress. His volumes of poetry include A Ballad of Remembrance *(1962),* Words in Mourning Time *(1970), and* Angle of Ascent *(1975). "Those Winter Sundays" (1962) is a finely etched depiction of the speaker's change in attitude toward his father.*

Before You Read

What efforts of a family member did you underappreciate at the time?

Those Winter Sundays

Sundays too my father got up early
and put his clothes on in the blueblack cold,
then with cracked hands that ached
from labor in the weekday weather made
banked fires blaze. No one ever thanked him.   5

I'd wake and hear the cold splintering, breaking,
When the rooms were warm, he'd call,
and slowly I would rise and dress,
fearing the chronic angers of that house,

Speaking indifferently to him,   10
who had driven out the cold
and polished my good shoes as well.
What did I know, what did I know
of love's austere and lonely offices?

Questions for Discussion and Writing

1. How does Hayden make use of the contrast in imagery between cold and warmth to underscore the shift in the speaker's attitude?
2. What has made the speaker realize, now that he has grown up, how much his father really cared for him?
3. In a short essay, discuss the poem's dominant emotion. Have you ever come to realize that someone cared for you in ways not obvious to you at the time? Describe your experience.
4. **Rhetorical inquiry:** How does the repeated phrase in the poem's next to last line crystallize the speaker's feelings of remorse at not having recognized his father's love for his family?

MARIANNE MOORE

Marianne Moore (1887–1972) grew up in Carlisle, Pennsylvania and attended Bryn Mawr College. She taught stenography from 1911 to 1915 at the American government's Indian School in Carlisle. Her poetry began to appear in the British magazine Egoist, *and in 1925 she began editing* The Dial, *which, along with* Poetry *magazine, published important new poetry from World War I. Animals, athletes, and the natural world were her favorite subjects for poetry. Her volume of* Collected Poems *(1951) won the Pulitzer Prize and the National Book Award. She loved athletic events and wrote the liner notes for Muhammad Ali's spoken word album* I Am the Greatest! *We can see her unpretentious, quirky style in "A Grave" (1924).*

Before You Read

What secrets could an historical site or natural setting reveal?

A Grave

Man looking into the sea,
taking the view from those who have as much right to it as you have
    to it yourself,
it is human nature to stand in the middle of a thing,
but you cannot stand in the middle of this;
the sea has nothing to give but a well-excavated grave.   5
The firs stand in a procession, each with an emerald turkey foot at
    the top.
reserved as their contours, saying nothing;
repression, however, is not the most obvious characteristic of the sea:
the sea is a collector, quick to return a rapacious look.
There are others besides you who have worn that look—   10
whose expression is no longer a protest; the fish no longer investigate
    them
for their bones have not lasted:
men lower nets, unconscious of the fact that they are desecrating a
    grave.
and row quickly away—the blades of the oars
moving together like the feet of water spiders as if there were no such   15
    thing as death.
The wrinkles progress among themselves in a phalanx—beautiful
    under networks of foam.
and fade breathlessly while the sea rustles in and out of the seaweed;
the birds swim through the air at top speed, emitting catcalls as
    heretofore—
the tortoise shell scourges about the feet of the cliffs, in motion
    beneath them:
and the ocean, under the pulsation of lighthouses and noise of bell   20
    buoys,
advances as usual, looking as if it were not that ocean in which
    dropped things are bound to sink—
in which if they turn and twist, it is neither with volition nor
    consciousness.

How does this illustration of submarine warfare in World War I by Willy Stöwer convey the role of the sea as "a collector" during Wartime?

Questions for Discussion and Writing

1. Besides the dominant image of the sea as a grave, what other figures of speech do you find in the poem? How do they relate to the dominant image?

2. Since this poem was written when ships were subject to predatory attacks during World War I, in what sense is the sea a "collector"?

3. How does the form of the poem with its irregular alternation of long and short lines evoke the tides, rhythms, and movement of the sea?

4. **Rhetorical inquiry:** How do images of ships from past years add a historical dimension to the continuing human desire to use the sea for conquest and commerce?

WILLIAM CARLOS WILLIAMS

William Carlos Williams (1883–1963) was born in Rutherford, New Jersey. He took his M.D. degree at the University of Pennsylvania. He spent most of his time delivering babies (over 2,000) in and around his home town, while finding time to write thirty-seven volumes of prose and poetry. Much of his writing reflects his experiences as a physician. He is best known for his six-volume poetic epic Paterson, *which he worked on between 1948 and the time of his death. He had a gift for using colloquial, unvarnished, natural speech that can be clearly seen in the following poem, which was published in* Collected Earlier Poems of William Carlos Williams *(1932).*

Before You Read

Have you ever seen spectators at a sporting event react as one person?

At the Ball Game

The crowd at the ball game
is moved uniformly

by a spirit of uselessness
which delights them—

all the exciting detail   5
of the chase

and the escape, the error
the flash of genius—

all to no end save beauty
the eternal—   10

So in detail they, the crowd,
are beautiful

for this
to be warned against

saluted and defied—   15
It is alive, venomous

it smiles grimly
its words cut—

The flashy female with her
mother, gets it—   20

The Jew gets it straight—it
is deadly, terrifying—

It is the Inquisition, the
Revolution

It is beauty itself   25
that lives

day by day in them
idly—

This is
the power of their faces   30

It is summer, it is the solstice
the crowd is

cheering, the crowd is laughing
in detail

permanently, seriously   35
without thought

Questions for Discussion and Writing

1. Into what different forms is the crowd at the ball game capable of metamorphizing itself? How does Williams relate these different faces, whether benign or terrifying, to the role of the mob in history?
2. How does Williams's use of the pronoun "it" in the middle of the poem to refer to the crowd underscore this transformation?
3. Have you ever been part of a mass assemblage that suddenly seemed to become a living entity with its own purpose?
4. **Rhetorical inquiry:** Is this poem intended to be a warning against becoming part of a crowd or does it present a more objective appraisal?

What aspects of Williams's poem does this image of a game at Yankee Stadium illustrate?

Connections for Chapter 2:
Memorable People and Places

1. **Maya Angelou,** *Liked for Myself*
   How are Angelou and Fatima Mernissi motived by strong female figures to transcend personal and social restrictions?
2. **Gayle Pemberton,** *Antidisestablishmentarianism*
   Compare the role that Pemberton's grandmother and Jill Nelson's father ("Number One!" in Chapter 1) play as influential figures in the lives of the two girls.
3. **Mikhal Gilmore,** *My Brother, Gary Gilmore*
   How does Gilmore's narrative raise questions of heredity and environment discussed by David Ewing Duncan in "DNA As Destiny" in Chapter 9?
4. **Fatima Mernissi,** *Moonlit Nights of Laughter*
   In what ways do both Mernissi and Gayle Pemberton benefit from the free-spirited independent thinking of their mother and grandmother, respectively?
5. **Richard Rhodes,** *A Hole in the World*
   What survival strategies did Rhodes and Mary Crow Dog ("Civilize Them with a Stick") in Chapter 3 use to confront the harsh circumstances of their childhoods?
6. **Rudolph Chelminski,** *Turning Point*
   Compare the perspectives on September 11, 2001 offered by Chelminski and Don De Lillo ("In the Ruins of the Future") in Chapter 7.
7. **Rick Bass,** *A Fitting Desire*
   What underlying symbiotic relationships in nature are discovered by Bass and Aldo Leopold?
8. **Aldo Leopold,** *Thinking Like a Mountain*
   How do Leopold and Konrad Lorenz ("The Dove and the Wolf") in Chapter 6 offer new ways of looking at wolves?
9. **Raymond Carver,** *Neighbors*
   Analyze the ethics of the characters in Carver's story with Philip Wheelwright's schema ("The Meaning of Ethics") in Chapter 11.
10. **John Cheever,** *Reunion*
    Compare the father-son relationships in Cheever's story and in Robert Hayden's poem "Those Winter Sundays."
11. **Robert Hayden,** *Those Winter Sundays*
    What different ways do the parents in the poems by Hayden and Nikki Giovanni ("Nikki-Rosa") in Chapter 1 express their love for their children and how does each speaker react?

12. **Marianne Moore,** *A Grave*
    Compare the perspectives regarding the ocean in the poems by Moore and Henry Wadsworth Longfellow ("The Sound of the Sea") in Chapter 6.
13. **William Carlos Williams,** *At the Ball Game*
    What insight into crowd psychology do Williams and Aldous Huxley ("Propaganda under a Dictatorship") in Chapter 4 provide?

3

THE VALUE OF EDUCATION

The old believe everything. The middle-aged suspect everything.
The young know everything.
            Oscar Wilde, THE PICTURE OF DORIAN GRAY

As the essays in this chapter make clear, education is primarily a liberating experience. Yet, the accounts by Frederick Douglass, Mark Salzman, Richard Rodriguez, Sabine Reichel, and Mary Crow Dog attest to the ingenuity and determination that are often required in getting an education. Douglass, the first black writer to rise to national prominence, provides a dramatic account of how he devised an ingenious scheme to become literate. Salzman also needed to improvise in order to teach English to a Chinese master of martial arts. Rodriguez describes his need to rediscover the Mexican identity he lost when he moved into the main stream of American culture and academic life. Then Reichel discusses the obstacles she had to overcome as a student in Germany in obtaining forthright accounts of the Holocaust from her teachers. For Mary Crow Dog, the problem was how to overcome the abusive atmosphere of a government-run school for Native Americans.

Nat Hentoff and Judy Blume confront the basic questions of (1) what role should education play in society? and (2) whether censorship has any role in a free society? An essay by Jonathan Kozol discusses the consequences for society when many citizens are unable to read or write. Mike Adams explores a contrasting dilemma: do students put more ingenuity into evading required work than they would in simply doing it.

In the fictional work by Edward P. Jones, we hear the expectations and admonitions of a mother to her five-year-old daughter on her first day of school.

In the poetry section, Linda Hogan offers an intensely personal reflection on the value of education, especially for minorities. Tom Wayman's amusing and thought-provoking poem explores the universal question students often ask.

As you read works in this chapter and prepare to discuss or write about them, you may wish to use the following questions as guidelines.

- What does each author mean by the term education?
- What differences can you discover in each author's attitude toward the subject?

- What range of evidence—personal experience, statistics, surveys—does the author use to support his or her views?
- What sort of changes does the author recommend?
- What works illustrate the impact of education on society?
- To what extent is the writer's experience similar to yours?
- Was one genre (essay, fiction, poetry) more effective in communicating the value of education?

Nonfiction

FREDERICK DOUGLASS

Frederick Douglass (1817–1895) was born into slavery in Maryland, where he worked as a field hand and servant. In 1838, after previous failed attempts to escape, for which he was beaten and tortured, he successfully made his way to New York by using the identity papers of a freed black sailor. There he adopted the last name of Douglass and subsequently settled in New Bedford, Massachusetts. Douglass was the first black American to rise to prominence as a national figure. He gained renown as a speaker for the Massachusetts Anti-Slavery League and was an editor for the North Star, *an abolitionist paper, from 1847 to 1860. He was a friend to John Brown, helped convince President Lincoln to issue the Emancipation Proclamation, and became ambassador to several foreign countries.* The Narrative of the Life of Frederick Douglass, an American Slave *(1845) is one of the most illuminating of the many slave narratives written during the nineteenth century. "Learning to Read and Write," drawn from this autobiography, reveals Douglass's ingenuity in manipulating his circumstances so as to become literate.*

Before You Read

Imagine living in a society that prevented you from reading and writing.

Learning to Read and Write

I lived in Master Hugh's family about seven years. During this time, I succeeded in learning to read and write. In accomplishing this, I was compelled to resort to various stratagems. I had no regular teacher. My mistress, who had kindly commenced to instruct me, had, in compliance with the advice and direction of her husband, not only ceased to instruct, but had set her face against my being instructed by any one else. It is due, however, to my mistress to say of her, that she did not adopt this course of treatment immediately. She at first lacked the depravity indispensable to shutting me up in mental darkness. It was at least necessary for her to have some training in the exercise of irresponsible power, to make her equal to the task of treating me as though I were a brute.

My mistress was, as I have said, a kind and tender-hearted woman; and in the simplicity of her soul she commenced, when I first went to live with her, to treat me as she supposed one human being ought to treat another. In entering upon the duties of a slaveholder, she did not seem to perceive that I sustained to her the relation of a mere chattel, and that for her to treat me as a human being was not only wrong, but dangerously so. Slavery proved as injurious to her as it did to me. When I went there, she was a pious, warm, and tender-hearted woman. There was no sorrow or suffering for which she had not a tear. She had bread for the hungry, clothes for the naked, and comfort for every mourner that came within her reach. Slavery soon proved its ability to divest her of these heavenly qualities. Under its influence, the tender heart became stone, and the lamb-like disposition gave way to one of tiger-like fierceness. The first step in her downward course was in her ceasing to instruct me. She now commenced to practise her husband's precepts. She finally became even more violent in her opposition than her husband himself. She was not satisfied with simply doing as well as he had commanded; she seemed anxious to do better. Nothing seemed to make her more angry than to see me with a newspaper. She seemed to think that here lay the danger. I have had her rush at me with a face made all up of fury, and snatch from me a newspaper, in a manner that fully revealed her apprehension. She was an apt woman; and a little experience soon demonstrated, to her satisfaction, that education and slavery were incompatible with each other.

From this time I was most narrowly watched. If I was in a separate room any considerable length of time, I was sure to be suspected of having a book, and was at once called to give an account of myself. All this, however, was too late. The first step had been taken. Mistress, in teaching me the alphabet, had given me the *inch,* and no precaution could prevent me from taking the *ell.*[1]

The plan which I adopted, and the one by which I was most successful, was that of making friends of all the little white boys whom I met in the street. As many of these as I could, I converted into teachers. With their kindly aid, obtained at different times and in different places, I finally succeeded in learning to read. When I was sent on errands, I always took my book with me, and by doing one part of my errand quickly, I found time to get a lesson before my return. I used also to carry bread with me, enough of which was always in the house, and to which I was always welcome; for I was much better off in this regard than many of the poor white children

---

[1] *ell:* a measurement equal to 1.14 meters.

in our neighborhood. This bread I used to bestow upon the hungry little urchins, who, in return, would give me that more valuable bread of knowledge. I am strongly tempted to give the names of two or three of those little boys, as a testimonial of the gratitude and affection I bear them; but prudence forbids;—not that it would injure me, but it might embarrass them; for it is almost an unpardonable offence to teach slaves to read in this Christian country. It is enough to say of the dear little fellows, that they lived on Philpot Street, very near Durgin and Bailey's ship-yard. I used to talk this matter of slavery over with them. I would sometimes say to them, I wished I could be as free as they would be when they got to be men. "You will be free as soon as you are twenty-one, *but I am a slave for life!* Have not I as good a right to be free as you have?" These words used to trouble them; they would express for me the liveliest sympathy, and console me with the hope that something would occur by which I might be free.

I was now about twelve years old, and the thought of being *a slave for life* 5 began to bear heavily upon my heart. Just about this time, I got hold of a book entitled "The Columbian Orator."[2] Every opportunity I got, I used to read this book. Among much of other interesting matter, I found in it a dialogue between a master and his slave. The slave was represented as having run away from his master three times. The dialogue represented the conversation which took place between them, when the slave was retaken the third time. In this dialogue, the whole argument on behalf of slavery was brought forward by the master, all of which was disposed of by the slave. The slave was made to say some very smart as well as impressive things in reply to his master—things which had the desired though unexpected effect; for the conversation resulted in the voluntary emancipation of the slave on the part of the master.

In the same book, I met with one of Sheridan's mighty speeches on and in behalf of Catholic emancipation. These were choice documents to me. I read them over and over again with unabated interest. They gave tongue to interesting thoughts of my own soul, which had frequently flashed through my mind, and died away for want of utterance. The moral which I gained from the dialogue was the power of truth over the conscience of even a slaveholder. What I got from Sheridan was a bold denunciation of slavery, and a powerful vindication of human rights. The reading of these documents enabled me to utter my thoughts, and to meet the arguments brought forward to sustain slavery; but while they relieved me of one difficulty, they brought on another even more painful than the one of which I was relieved. The more I read, the more I was led to abhor and detest my enslavers. I could regard them in no other light than a band of successful robbers, who had left their homes, and gone to Africa, and stolen us from our homes, and in a strange land reduced us to slavery. I loathed them as being the meanest as well as the most wicked of men. As I read and contemplated the subject, behold! that

---

[2] *The Columbian Orator (1797):* written by Caleb Bingham. It was one of the first readers used in New England schools.

very discontentment which Master Hugh had predicted would follow my learning to read had already come, to torment and sting my soul to unutterable anguish. As I writhed under it, I would at times feel that learning to read had been a curse rather than a blessing. It had given me a view of my wretched condition, without the remedy. It opened my eyes to the horrible pit, but to no ladder upon which to get out. In moments of agony, I envied my fellow-slaves for their stupidity. I have often wished myself a beast. I preferred the condition of the meanest reptile to my own. Any thing, no matter what, to get rid of thinking! It was this everlasting thinking of my condition that tormented me. There was no getting rid of it. It was pressed upon me by every object within sight or hearing, animate or inanimate. The silver trump of freedom had roused my soul to eternal wakefulness. Freedom now appeared, to disappear no more forever. It was heard in every sound, and seen in every thing. It was ever present to torment me with a sense of my wretched condition. I saw nothing without seeing it, I heard nothing without hearing it, and felt nothing without feeling it. It looked from every star, it smiled in every calm, breathed in every wind, and moved in every storm.

I often found myself regretting my own existence, and wishing myself dead; and but for the hope of being free, I have no doubt but that I should have killed myself, or done something for which I should have been killed. While in this state of mind, I was eager to hear any one speak of slavery. I was a ready listener. Every little while, I could hear something about the abolitionists. It was some time before I found what the word meant. It was always used in such connections as to make it an interesting word to me. If a slave ran away and succeeded in getting clear, or if a slave killed his master, set fire to a barn, or did any thing very wrong in the mind of a slaveholder, it was spoken of as the fruit of *abolition*. Hearing the word in this connection very often, I set about learning what it meant. The dictionary afforded me little or no help. I found it was "the act of abolishing," but then I did not know what was to be abolished. Here I was perplexed. I did not dare to ask any one about its meaning, for I was satisfied that it was something they wanted me to know very little about. After a patient waiting, I got one of our city papers, containing an account of the number of petitions from the north, praying for the abolition of slavery in the District of Columbia, and of the slave trade between the States. From this time I understood the words *abolition* and *abolitionist*, and always drew near when that word was spoken, expecting to hear something of importance to myself and fellow-slaves. The light broke in upon me by degrees. I went one day down on the wharf of Mr. Waters; and seeing two Irishmen unloading a scow of stone, I went, unasked, and helped them. When we had finished, one of them came to me and asked me if I were a slave. I told him I was. He asked, "Are ye a slave for life?" I told him that I was. The good Irishman seemed to be deeply affected by the statement. He said to the other that it was a pity so fine a little fellow as myself should be a slave for life. He said it was a shame to hold me. They both advised me to run away to the north; that I should find friends there, and that I should be free. I pretended not to be interested in what they said, and treated them as if I did not understand them; for I feared they might be treacherous. White men have been known to encourage slaves to escape, and then, to get the reward, catch them and return them to their masters. I was afraid that these seemingly good men might use me so; but I nevertheless remembered their advice, and from that time I resolved to run away. I looked forward to a time at which it would be safe for me to escape. I was too young to think of doing so immediately; besides, I wished to learn how to write, as I might have occasion to write my own pass. I consoled myself with the hope that I should one day find a good chance. Meanwhile, I would learn to write.

The idea as to how I might learn to write was suggested to me by being in Durgin and Bailey's ship-yard, and frequently seeing the ship carpenters, after hewing, and getting a piece of timber ready for use, write on the timber the name of that part of the ship for which it was intended. When a piece of timber was intended for the larboard side, it would be marked thus—"L." When a piece was for the starboard side, it would be marked thus—"S." A piece for the larboard side forward, would be marked thus—"L. F." When a piece was for starboard side forward, it would be marked thus—"S. F." For larboard aft, it would be marked thus—"L. A." For starboard aft, it would be marked thus—"S. A." I soon learned the names of these letters, and for what they were intended when placed upon a piece of timber in the ship-yard. I immediately commenced copying them, and in a short time was able to make the four letters named. After that, when I met with any boy who I knew could write, I would tell him I could write as well as he. The next word would be, "I don't believe you. Let me see you try it." I would then make the letters which I had been so fortunate as to learn, and ask him to beat that. In this way I got a good many lessons in writing, which it is quite possible I should never have gotten in any other way. During this time, my copy-book was the board fence, brick wall, and pavement; my pen and ink was a lump of chalk. With these, I learned mainly how to write. I then commenced and continued copying the italics in *Webster's Spelling Book,* until I could make them all without looking on the book. By this time, my little Master Thomas had gone to school, and learned how to write, and had written over a number of copy-books. These had been brought home, and shown to some of our near neighbors, and then laid aside. My mistress used to go to class meeting at the Wilk Street meetinghouse every Monday afternoon, and leave me to take care of the house. When left thus, I used to spend the time in writing in the spaces left in Master Thomas's copy-book, copying what he had written. I continued to do this until I could write a hand very similar to that of Master Thomas. Thus, after a long, tedious effort for years, I finally succeeded in learning how to write.

Questions for Discussion and Writing

1. What effect did the institution of slavery have on Douglass's relationship with the mistress of the household when she initially wanted to help him become literate?

2. Douglass writes that "education and slavery were incompatible with each other." How does this account illustrate his belief? What ingenious methods did Douglass devise to obtain knowledge of reading and writing?

3. What would your life be like if you could not read or write? Describe a day in your life, providing specific examples that would dramatize this condition.

4. **Rhetorical inquiry:** How does the term *abolition* exercise an almost obsessive influence on Douglass and strengthen his resolve to become literate?

JONATHAN KOZOL

Jonathan Kozol was born in Boston in 1936 and graduated from Harvard in 1958. He was a Rhodes scholar at Oxford University and has taught at numerous colleges, including Yale. His many books on education and literacy include Illiterate America *(1985), from which the following selection is taken;* Amazing Grace: The Lives of Children and the Conscience of a Nation *(1995); and most recently,* Ordinary Resurrections: Children in the Years of Hope *(2000) and* The Shame of the Nation *(2005).*

Before You Read

In what way is being illiterate similar to traveling in a country where you cannot read the signs?

The Human Cost of an Illiterate Society

PRECAUTIONS, READ BEFORE USING.
Poison: Contains sodium hydroxide (caustic soda-lye).
Corrosive: Causes severe eye and skin damage, may cause blindness.
Harmful or fatal if swallowed.
If swallowed, give large quantities of milk or water.
Do not induce vomiting.
Important: Keep water out of can at all times to prevent contents from violently erupting. . . .

—*Warning on a can of Drano*

Questions of literacy, in Socrates' belief, must at length be judged as matters of morality. Socrates could not have had in mind the moral compromise peculiar to a nation like our own. Some of our Founding Fathers did, however, have this question in their minds. One of the wisest of those Founding Fathers (one who may not have been most compassionate but surely was more prescient than some of his peers) recognized the special dangers that illiteracy would pose to basic equity in the political construction that he helped to shape.

"A people who mean to be their own governors," James Madison wrote, "must arm themselves with the power knowledge gives. A popular government without popular information or the means of acquiring it, is but a prologue to a farce or a tragedy, or perhaps both."

Tragedy looms larger than farce in the United States today. Illiterate citizens seldom vote. Those who do are forced to cast a vote of questionable worth. They cannot make informed decisions based on serious print information. Sometimes they can be alerted to their interests by aggressive voter education. More frequently, they vote for a face, a smile, or a style, not for a mind or character or body of beliefs.

The number of illiterate adults exceeds by 16 million the entire vote cast for the winner in the 1980 presidential contest. If even one third of all illiterates could vote, and read enough and do sufficient math to vote in their self-interest, Ronald Reagan would not likely have been chosen president. There is, of course, no way to know for sure. We do know this: Democracy is a mendacious term when used by those who are prepared to countenance the forced exclusion of one third of our electorate. So long as 60 million people are denied significant participation, the government is neither of nor for, nor by, the people. It is a government, at best, of those two thirds whose wealth, skin color, or parental privilege allows them opportunity to profit from the provocation and instruction of the written word.

The undermining of democracy in the United States is one "expense" that 5 sensitive Americans can easily deplore because it represents a contradiction that endangers citizens of all political positions. The human price is not so obvious at first.

Since I first immersed myself within this work I have often had the following dream: I find that I am in a railroad station or a large department store within a city that is utterly unknown to me and where I cannot understand the printed words. None of the signs or symbols is familiar. Everything looks strange: like mirror writing of some kind. Gradually I understand that I am in the Soviet Union. All the letters on the walls around me are Cyrillic. I look for my pocket dictionary but I find that it has been mislaid. Where have I left it? Then I recall that I forgot to bring it with me when I packed my bags in Boston. I struggle to remember the name of my hotel. I try to ask somebody for directions. One person stops and looks at me in a peculiar way. I lose the nerve to ask. At last I reach into my wallet for an ID card. The card is missing. Have I lost it? Then I remember that my card was confiscated for some reason, many years before. Around this point, I wake up in a panic.

This panic is not so different from the misery that millions of adult illiterates experience each day within the course of their routine existence in the U.S.A.

Illiterates cannot read the menu in a restaurant.

They cannot read the cost of items on the menu in the *window* of the restaurant before they enter.

Illiterates cannot read the letters that their children bring home from their   10
teachers. They cannot study school department circulars that tell them of the courses that their children must be taking if they hope to pass the SAT exams. They cannot help with homework. They cannot write a letter to the teacher. They are afraid to visit in the classroom. They do not want to humiliate their child or themselves.

Illiterates cannot read instructions on a bottle of prescription medicine. They cannot find out when a medicine is past the year of safe consumption; nor can they read of allergenic risks, warnings to diabetics, or the potential sedative effect of certain kinds of nonprescription pills. They cannot observe preventive health care admonitions. They cannot read about "the seven warning signs of cancer" or the indications of blood-sugar fluctuations or the risks of eating certain foods that aggravate the likelihood of cardiac arrest.

Illiterates live, in more than literal ways, an uninsured existence. They cannot understand the written details on a health insurance form. They cannot read the waivers that they sign preceding surgical procedures. Several women I have known in Boston have entered a slum hospital with the intention of obtaining a tubal ligation and have emerged a few days later after having been subjected to a hysterectomy. Unaware of their rights, incognizant of jargon, intimidated by the unfamiliar air of fear and atmosphere of ether that so many of us find oppressive in the confines even of the most attractive and expensive medical facilities, they have signed their names to documents they could not read and which nobody, in the hectic situation that prevails so often in those overcrowded hospitals that serve the urban poor, had even bothered to explain.

Childbirth might seem to be the last inalienable right of any female citizen within a civilized society. Illiterate mothers, as we shall see, already have been cheated of the power to protect their progeny against the likelihood of demolition in deficient public schools and, as a result, against the verbal servitude within which they themselves exist. Surgical denial of the right to bear that child in the first place represents an ultimate denial, an unspeakable metaphor, a final darkness that denies even the twilight gleamings of our own humanity. What greater violation of our biological, our biblical, our spiritual humanity could possibly exist than that which takes place nightly, perhaps hourly these days, within such overburdened and benighted institutions as the Boston City Hospital? Illiteracy has many costs; few are so irreversible as this.

Even the roof above one's head, the gas or other fuel for heating that protects the residents of northern city slums against the threat of illness in the winter months become uncertain guarantees. Illiterates cannot read the lease that they must sign to live in an apartment which, too often, they cannot afford. They cannot manage check accounts and therefore seldom pay for anything by mail. Hours and entire days of difficult travel (and the cost of bus or other public transit) must be added to the real cost of whatever they consume. Loss of interest on the check accounts they do not have, and could not manage if they did, must be regarded as another of the excess costs paid by the citizen who is excluded from the common instruments of commerce in a numerate society.

"I couldn't understand the bills," a woman in Washington, D.C., reports,   15
"and then I couldn't write the checks to pay them. We signed things we didn't know what they were."

Illiterates cannot read the notices that they receive from welfare offices or from the IRS. They must depend on word-of-mouth instruction from the welfare worker—or from other persons whom they have good reason to mistrust. They do not know what rights they have, what deadlines and requirements they face, what options they might choose to exercise. They are half-citizens. Their rights exist in print but not in fact.

Illiterates cannot look up numbers in a telephone directory. Even if they can find the names of friends, few possess the sorting skills to make use of the yellow pages; categories are bewildering and trade names are beyond decoding capabilities for millions of nonreaders. Even the emergency numbers listed on the first page of the phone book—"Ambulance," "Police," and "Fire"—are too frequently beyond the recognition of nonreaders.

Many illiterates cannot read the admonition on a pack of cigarettes. Neither the Surgeon General's warning nor its reproduction on the package can alert them to the risks. Although most people learn by word of mouth that smoking is related to a number of grave physical disorders, they do not get the chance to read the detailed stories which can document this danger with the vividness that turns concern into determination to resist. They can see the handsome cowboy or the slim Virginia lady lighting up a filter cigarette; they cannot heed the words that tell them that this product is (not "may be") dangerous to their health. Sixty million men and women are condemned to be the unalerted, high-risk candidates for cancer.

Illiterates do not buy "no-name" products in the supermarkets. They must depend on photographs or the familiar logos that are printed on the packages of brand-name groceries. The poorest people, therefore, are denied the benefits of the least costly products.

Illiterates depend almost entirely upon label recognition. Many labels,   20
however, are not easy to distinguish. Dozens of different kinds of Campbell's soup appear identical to the nonreader. The purchaser who cannot read and does not dare to ask for help, out of the fear of being stigmatized (a fear which is unfortunately realistic), frequently comes home with something which she never wanted and her family never tasted.

Illiterates cannot read instructions on a pack of frozen food. Packages sometimes provide an illustration to explain the cooking preparations; but illustrations are of little help to someone who must "boil water, drop the food—*within* its plastic wrapper—in the boiling water, wait for it to simmer, instantly remove."

Even when labels are seemingly clear, they may be easily mistaken. A woman in Detroit brought home a gallon of Crisco for her children's dinner. She thought that she had bought the chicken that was pictured on the label. She had enough Crisco now to last a year—but no more money to go back and buy the food for dinner.

Recipes provided on the packages of certain staples sometimes tempt a semiliterate person to prepare a meal her children have not tasted. The longing to vary the uniform and often starchy content of low-budget meals provided to the family that relies on food stamps commonly leads to ruinous results. Scarce funds have been wasted and the food must be thrown out. The same applies to distribution of food-surplus produce in emergency conditions. Government inducements to poor people to "explore the ways" by which to make a tasty meal from tasteless noodles, surplus cheese, and powdered milk are useless to nonreaders. Intended as benevolent advice, such recommendations mock reality and foster deeper feelings of resentment and of inability to cope. (Those, on the other hand, who cautiously refrain from "innovative" recipes in preparation of their children's meals must suffer the opprobrium of "laziness," "lack of imagination. . . .")

Illiterates cannot travel freely. When they attempt to do so, they encounter risks that few of us can dream of. They cannot read traffic signs and, while they often learn to recognize and to decipher symbols, they cannot manage street names which they haven't seen before. The same is true for bus and subway stops. While ingenuity can sometimes help a man or woman to discern directions from familiar landmarks, buildings, cemeteries, churches, and the like, most illiterates are virtually immobilized. They seldom wander past the streets and neighborhoods they know. Geographical paralysis becomes a bitter metaphor for their entire existence. They are immobilized in almost every sense we can imagine. They can't move up. They can't move out. They cannot see beyond. Illiterates may take an oral test for drivers' permits in most sections of America. It is a questionable concession. Where will they go? How will they get there? How will they get home? Could it be that some of us might like it better if they stayed where they belong?

Travel is only one of many instances of circumscribed existence. Choice, in almost all its facets, is diminished in the life of an illiterate adult. Even the printed TV schedule, which provides most people with the luxury of preselection, does not belong within the arsenal of options in illiterate existence. One consequence is that the viewer watches only what appears at moments when he happens to have time to turn the switch. Another consequence, a lot more common, is that the TV set remains in operation night and day. Whatever the program offered at the hour when he walks into the room will be the nutriment that he accepts and swallows. Thus, to passivity, is added frequency—indeed, almost uninterrupted continuity. Freedom to select is no more possible here than in the choice of home or surgery or food. 25

"You don't choose," said one illiterate woman. "You take your wishes from somebody else." Whether in perusal of a menu, selection of highways, purchase of groceries, or determination of affordable enjoyment, illiterate Americans must trust somebody else: a friend, a relative, a stranger on the street, a grocery clerk, a TV copywriter.

"All of our mail we get, it's hard for her to read. Settin' down and writing a letter, she can't do it. Like if we get a bill . . . we take it over to my sister-in-law. . . . My sister-in-law reads it."

Billing agencies harass poor people for the payment of the bills for purchases that might have taken place six months before. Utility companies offer an agreement for a staggered payment schedule on a bill past due. "You have to trust them," one man said. Precisely for this reason, you end up by trusting no one and suspecting everyone of possible deceit. A submerged sense of distrust becomes the corollary to a constant need to trust. "They are cheating me . . . I have been tricked . . . I do not know . . ."

Not knowing: This is a familiar theme. Not knowing the right word for the right thing at the right time is one form of subjugation. Not knowing the world that lies concealed behind those words is a more terrifying feeling. The longitude and latitude of one's existence are beyond all easy apprehension. Even the hard, cold stars within the firmament above one's head begin to mock the possibilities for self-location. Where am I? Where did I come from? Where will I go?

"I've lost a lot of jobs," one man explains. "Today, even if you're a   30 janitor, there's still reading and writing. . . . They leave a note saying, 'Go to room so-and-so . . .' You can't do it. You can't read it. You don't know."

"The hardest thing about it is that I've been places where I didn't know where I was. You don't know where you are. . . . You're lost."

"Like I said: I have two kids. What do I do if one of my kids starts choking? I go running to the phone . . . I can't look up the hospital phone number. That's if we're at home. Out on the street, I can't read the sign. I get to a pay phone. 'Okay, tell us where you are. We'll send an ambulance.' I look at the street sign. Right there, I can't tell you what it says. I'd have to spell it out, letter for letter. By that time, one of my kids would be dead. . . . These are the kinds of fears you go with, every single day . . ."

"Reading directions, I suffer with. I work with chemicals. . . . That's scary to begin with . . ."

"You sit down. They throw the menu in front of you. Where do you go from there? Nine times out of ten you say, 'Go ahead. Pick out something for the both of us.' I've eaten some weird things, let me tell you!"

Menus. Chemicals. A child choking while his mother searches for a word   35 she does not know to find assistance that will come too late. Another mother speaks about the inability to help her kids to read: "I can't read to them. Of course that's leaving them out of something they should have. Oh, it matters. You *believe* it matters! I ordered all these books. The kids belong to a book club. Donny wanted me to read a book to him. I told Donny: 'I can't read.'

He said: 'Mommy, you sit down. I'll read it to you.' I tried it one day, reading from the pictures. Donny looked at me. He said, 'Mommy, that's not right.' He's only five. 'He knew I couldn't read . . .'"

A landlord tells a woman that her lease allows him to evict her if her baby cries and causes inconvenience to her neighbors. The consequence of challenging his words conveys a danger which appears, unlikely as it seems, even more alarming than the danger of eviction. Once she admits that she can't read, in the desire to maneuver for the time in which to call a friend, she will have defined herself in terms of an explicit impotence that she cannot endure. Capitulation in this case is preferable to self-humiliation. Resisting the definition of oneself in terms of what one cannot do, what others take for granted, represents a need so great that other imperatives (even one so urgent as the need to keep one's home in winter's cold) evaporate and fall away in face of fear. Even the loss of home and shelter, in this case, is not so terrifying as the loss of self.

"I come out of school. I was sixteen. They had their meetings. The directors meet. They said that I was wasting their school paper. I was wasting pencils . . ."

Another illiterate, looking back, believes she was not worthy of her teacher's time. She believes that it was wrong of her to take up space within her school. She believes that it was right to leave in order that somebody more deserving could receive her place.

Children choke. Their mother chokes another way: on more than chicken bones.

People eat what others order, know what others tell them, struggle not to   40 see themselves as they believe the world perceives them. A man in California speaks about his own loss of identity, of self-location, definition:

"I stood at the bottom of the ramp. My car had broke down on the freeway. There was a phone. I asked for the police. They was nice. They said to tell them where I was. I looked up at the signs. There was one that I had seen before. I read it to them: ONE WAY STREET. They thought it was a joke. I told them I couldn't read. There was other signs above the ramp. They told me to try. I looked around for somebody to help. All the cars was going by real fast. I couldn't make them understand that I was lost. The cop was nice. He told me: 'Try once more.' I did my best, I couldn't read. I only knew the sign above my head. The cop was trying to be nice. He knew that I was trapped. 'I can't send out a car to you if you can't tell me where you are.' I felt afraid. I nearly cried. I'm forty-eight years old. I only said: 'I'm on a one-way street . . .'"

The legal problems and the courtroom complications that confront illiterate adults have been discussed above. The anguish that may underlie such matters was brought home to me this year while I was working on this book. I have spoken, in the introduction, of a sudden phone call from one of my former students, now in prison for a criminal offense. Stephen is not a boy today. He is twenty-eight years old. He called to ask me to assist him in his trial, which comes up next fall. He will be on trial for murder. He has just knifed and killed a man who first enticed him to his home, then cheated him, and then insulted him—as "an illiterate subhuman."

Stephen now faces twenty years to life. Stephen's mother was illiterate. His grandparents were illiterate as well. What parental curse did not destroy was killed off finally by the schools. Silent violence is repaid with interest. It will cost us $25,000 yearly to maintain this broken soul in prison. But what is the price that has been paid by Stephen's victim? What is the price that will be paid by Stephen?

Perhaps we might slow down a moment here and look at the realities described above. This is the nation that we live in. This is a society that most of us did not create but which our President and other leaders have been willing to sustain by virtue of malign neglect. Do we possess the character and courage to address a problem which so many nations, poorer than our own, have found it natural to correct?

The answers to these questions represent a reasonable test of our belief 45 in the democracy to which we have been asked in public school to swear allegiance.

Questions for Discussion and Writing

1. What kinds of limitations beset an illiterate person and limit his or her ability to function in everyday life? What examples best dramatize the costs of illiteracy in personal rather than statistical terms?
2. In Kozol's view, why would an illiterate society be more likely to become less democratic? How persuasive do you find his analysis?
3. Imagine what a typical day in your life would be like if you could not read or write. Keep a record of all your activities, and describe how each would be different if you were illiterate.
4. **Rhetorical inquiry**: What aspects of Kozol's essay are designed to persuade his readers of the magnitude of the problem of illiteracy? Why does he quote Socrates and James Madison in developing his argument?

Mike Adams

Mike Adams is a professor of biology at Eastern Connecticut State University. He received his undergraduate degree in Wales, his master's degree from the University of Saskatchewan, and his doctorate from Duke University. He has also done postdoctoral work at Rockefeller University. His areas of interest include cell biology and genetics. The following satirical essay was originally published in The Connecticut Review *(1990).*

Before You Read

How do impending exams spark the imagination of students?

The Dead Grandmother/Exam Syndrome

It has long been theorized that the week prior to an exam is an extremely dangerous time for the relatives of college students. Ever since I began my teaching career, I heard vague comments, incomplete references and unfinished remarks, all alluding to the "Dead Grandmother Problem." Few colleagues would ever be explicit in their description of what they knew, but I quickly discovered that anyone who was involved in teaching at the college level would react to any mention of the concept. In my travels I found that a similar phenomenon is known in other countries. In England it is called the "Graveyard Grannies" problem, in France the "Chere Grand'mere," while in Bulgaria it is inexplicably known as "The Toadstool Waxing Plan" (I may have had some problems here with the translation. Since the revolution this may have changed anyway.) Although the problem may be international in scope it is here in the USA that it reaches its culmination, so it is only fitting that the first warnings emanate here also.

The basic problem can be stated very simply: **A student's grandmother is far more likely to die suddenly just before the student takes an exam, than at any other time of year.**

While this idea has long been a matter of conjecture or merely a part of the folklore of college teaching, I can now confirm that the phenomenon is real. For over twenty years I have collected data on this supposed relationship, and have not only confirmed what most faculty had suspected, but also found some additional aspects of this process that are of potential importance to the future of the country. The results presented in this report provide a chilling picture and should waken the profession and the general public to a serious health and sociological problem before it is too late.

As can be seen in Table 1, when no exam is imminent the family death rate per 100 students (FDR) is low and is not related to the student's grade in the class. The effect of an upcoming exam is unambiguous. The mean FDR jumps from 0.054 with no exam, to 0.574 with a mid-term, and to 1.042 with a final, representing increases of 10 fold and 19 fold respectively. Figure 1 shows that the changes are strongly grade dependent, with correlation coefficients of 0.974 for mid-terms and 0.988 for finals. Overall, a student who is failing a class and has a final coming up is more than 50 times more likely to lose a family member than an A student not facing any exams.

Only one conclusion can be drawn from these data. Family members literally worry themselves to death over the outcome of their relatives' performance on each exam. Naturally, the worse the student's record is, and the   5

Table 1: The mean number of family deaths/100 students for periods when no exam is coming up, the week prior to a mid-term exam and the week prior to finals. Values are corrected for the number of students in each grade class and the relative frequency of mid-terms and finals.

	Current Grade					
Next exam	A	B	C	D	F	Mean
None	0.04	0.07	0.05	0.05	0.06	0.054
Mid-term	0.06	0.21	0.49	0.86	1.25	0.574
Final	0.09	0.41	0.96	1.57	2.18	1.042

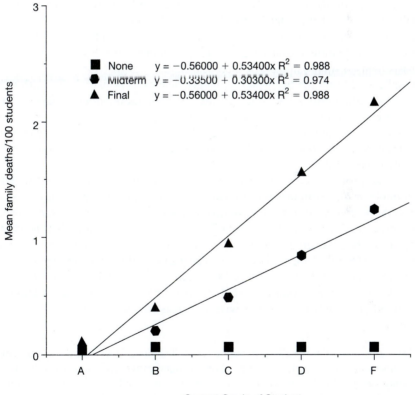

Figure 1: Graph of data in Table 1, showing the relationship between exam, student grade and FDR. The equation for the simple linear regression on each is shown, as is the correlation coefficient.

more important the exam, the more the family worries; and it is the ensuing tension that presumably causes premature death. Since such behavior is most likely to result in high blood pressure, leading to stroke and heart attacks, this would also explain why these deaths seem to occur so suddenly, with no warning and usually immediately prior to the exam. It might also explain the disproportionate number of grandmothers in the victim pool, since they are more likely to be susceptible to strokes. This explanation, however, does not explain why grandfathers are seldom affected, and clearly there are other factors involved that have not been identified. Nonetheless, there is considerable comfort to be had in realizing that these results indicate that the American family is obviously still close-knit and deeply concerned about the welfare of individual members, perhaps too much so. As some colleagues have expressed some degree of skepticism over my interpretation of these data, I have extended the scope of my research into the phenomenon. Using readily available sources (including the National Census Bureau and *The National Enquirer*) I have examined the relationship between education and family structure. Interestingly, there appears to be no correlation between FDR and the size of the extended family (Table 2). Either large families worry less on a per capita basis than do small families, or there is a single "designated worrier" in each family, who bears the brunt of the danger. The exceptionally high death rate among grandmothers (24 times greater than for grandfathers) suggests the latter explanation is correct. If not, then people from very small families would be well advised to discourage other family members from attending college, since the potential risk becomes excessive with so few members to share the danger.

The problem is clearly far more pervasive than most people realize. For example, if one examines the percentage of the population attending college and the mean divorce rate on a country by country basis, there is a very strong positive correlation between the two. The United States has the highest percentage of its population attending college and also the world's highest divorce rate, while South Yemen is last in both categories. Although this study is still in progress and will form the basis for a future CSU grant proposal, it seems results already are becoming clear. As more people go to college, their families find that, for safety reasons, it is wise to increase the number of grandmothers

Table 2: Mean FDR for all exam periods and all student GPAs over the last decade. Families ranging in size from 1–30+ show no significant correlation (0.04) between family size and FDR. The figure for students with no family would have been zero, except for a single family-less student (a member of the baseball team) who tragically lost at least one grandmother every semester for four years.

Number in family, excluding student	0	1	2–3	4–8	8–15	16–30	30+
Mean FDR	<0.01	0.66	0.71	0.62	0.73	0.64	0.68

per family. Since there is currently no biological way of doing so (though another grant proposal in preparation will ask for funds to look into the prospect of cloning grandmothers, using modern genetic engineering techniques), the families must resort to increasing the pool by divorce and remarriage. Sociologists may wish to use these data to examine the effect of education on family structure from a new perspective.

While the general facts of this problem have been known, if not widely discussed, I have recently become aware of a potentially far more dangerous aspect of the whole process. This trend came to light when a student reported *two* family members dying prior to an exam. Examination of the numbers of deaths over the last two decades clearly showed a "death inflation." When the figures for all students and all exams are pooled for each year, a disturbing outcome is seen (see Figure 2).

The FDR is climbing at an accelerating rate. Extrapolation of this curve suggests that 100 years from now the FDR will stand at 644/100 students/

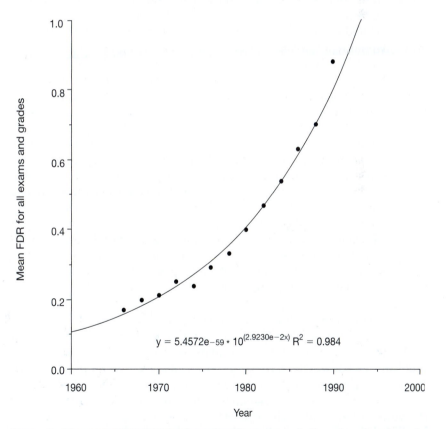

$$y = 5.4572e{-59} * 10^{(2.9230e-2x)} \quad R^2 = 0.984$$

Figure 2: The mean FDR/100 students for all exams and all grades of students for the years 1968–1988. The best fitting curve shows an exponentially rising curve, with the equation shown in the figure.

exam. At that rate only the largest families would survive even the first semester of a student's college career. Clearly something will have to be done to reverse this trend before the entire country is depopulated.

Three possible solutions come to mind:

1. **Stop giving exams.** At first glance, this seems to be the simplest answer to the problem. Like many simplistic solutions, however, it fails to consider the full ramifications of such a course. Without exam results, all medical schools would be forced to close their doors, having no way of distinguishing worthy students. The resultant dearth of physicians in the next generation would throw so many other professionals (tax accountants, malpractice attorneys, golf pros, *etc.*) out of work that the economy would go into a nosedive. Regretfully, this solution must be abandoned since it is more dangerous than the original problem.
2. **Allow only orphans to enroll at universities.** This is an extremely attractive idea, except for the shortage of orphans. More could be created of course, but this would be morally wrong, and in any case would replicate the very problem we are trying to avoid *i.e.* excessive family deaths.
3. **Have students lie to their families.** Students must never let any of their relatives know that they are at university. (Initial field tests show that keeping just the grandmother ignorant is neither feasible nor safe for the rest of the family.) It is not enough merely to lie about exams; if the family doesn't know when the exams are, they may then worry constantly and this may lead to even higher death rates. The only solution is that the family must never be aware that the student is even enrolled at a university. Students must pretend they are in the armed forces, have joined some religious cult, or have been kidnapped by aliens. All of these alternate explanations for their long absences will keep the family ignorant of the true, dangerous, fact. Although it might be argued that such large-scale deceptions could not be maintained for long periods, the success of many politicians suggests otherwise.

It will take time to discover whether any of these solutions are feasible. In the interim, the problem is clearly far too important to be ignored. Following the government's lead on so many similar, potentially catastrophic problems (global warming, the ozone layer, and ocean pollution), I propose that a commission be established to study the problem in more depth. While the state is deciding on the make-up of such a committee and what its charge should be, I would urge all members of the academic community to start keeping their own records. If faculty throughout the country were to send me summaries of their own knowledge about this matter, I could compile a follow-up report for publication in a year or two.

Questions for Discussion and Writing

1. What unsuspected correlation did Adams's study reveal between the quality of the student's record and the likelihood that a family member would suddenly expire prior to exams?
2. How does Adams use the format of a scientific study to spoof the supposed correlation between approaching exams and the mortality of students' relatives, most often grandmothers?
3. Are you familiar with the phenomenon Adams analyzes? How has it influenced the way real tragedies are perceived if they happened right before exams?
4. **Rhetorical inquiry:** Who might be the intended audience for this essay and what is its purpose? In your opinion, did Adams accomplish his objective? Given his subject, why is the use of humor an appropriate approach to take?

RICHARD RODRIGUEZ

Richard Rodriguez was born in 1944 in San Francisco, where he grew up as a child of Spanish-speaking Mexican-American parents. Rodriguez pursued graduate studies at the University of California at Berkeley and received a Fulbright fellowship to the Warburg Institute in London to study English Renaissance literature. He is an editor at Pacific News Service and in 1997 received the George Foster Peabody Award for his NewsHour *essays on American life. His autobiography,* Hunger of Memory: The Education of Richard Rodriguez *(1982), received the Christopher Award. He has also written* Days of Obligation: An Argument with My Mexican Father *(1992) and* Brown: The Last Discovery of America *(2003) as well as many articles for the* Wall Street Journal, *the* New York Times, The American Scholar, Time, *and other publications. "On Becoming a Chicano" reveals his sense of estrangement from his culture when he entered an academic English-speaking environment.*

Before You Read

Has going to college lessened your ties to your family and community?

On Becoming a Chicano

Today I am only technically the person I once felt myself to be—a Mexican-American, a Chicano. Partly because I had no way of comprehending my racial identity except in this technical sense, I gave up long ago the cultural consequences of being a Chicano.

The change came gradually but early. When I was beginning grade school, I noted to myself the fact that the classroom environment was so different in its styles and assumptions from my own family environment that survival would essentially entail a choice between both worlds. When I became a student, I was literally "remade"; neither I nor my teachers considered anything I had known before as relevant. I had to forget most of what my culture had provided, because to remember it was a disadvantage. The past and its cultural values became detachable, like a piece of clothing grown heavy on a warm day and finally put away.

Strangely, the discovery that I have been inattentive to my cultural past has arisen because others—student colleagues and faculty members—have started to assume that I am a Chicano. The ease with which the assumption is made forces me to suspect that the label is not meant to suggest cultural, but racial, identity. Nonetheless, as a graduate student and a prospective university faculty member, I am routinely expected to assume intellectual leadership *as a member of a racial minority*. Recently, for example, I heard the moderator of a panel discussion introduce me as "Richard Rodriguez, a Chicano intellectual." I wanted to correct the speaker—because I felt guilty representing a non-academic cultural tradition that I had willingly abandoned. So I can only guess what it would have meant to have retained my culture as I entered the classroom, what it would mean for me to be today a "Chicano intellectual." (The two words juxtaposed excite me; for years I thought a Chicano had to decide between being one or the other.)

Does the fact that I barely spoke any English until I was nine, or that as a child I felt a surge of self-hatred whenever a passing teenager would yell a racial slur, or that I saw my skin darken each summer—do any of these facts shape the ideas which I have or am capable of having? Today, I suspect they do—in ways I doubt the moderator who referred to me as a "Chicano intellectual" intended. The peculiar status of being a "Chicano intellectual" makes me grow restless at the thought that I have lost at least as much as I have gained through education.

I remember when, 20 years ago, two grammar-school nuns visited my childhood home. They had come to suggest—with more tact than was necessary, because my parents accepted without question the church's authority—that we make a greater effort to speak as much English around the house as possible. The nuns realized that my brothers and I led solitary lives largely because we were barely able to comprehend English in a school where we were the only Spanish-speaking students. My mother and father complied as best they could. Heroically, they gave up speaking to us in Spanish—the language that formed so much of the family's sense of intimacy in an alien world—and began to speak a broken English. Instead of Spanish sounds, I began hearing sounds that were new, harder, less friendly. More important, I was encouraged to respond in English.

The change in language was the most dramatic and obvious indication that I would become very much like the "gringo"—a term which was used descriptively rather than perjoratively in my home—and unlike the Spanish-speaking relatives who largely constituted my preschool world. Gradually,

5

Spanish became a sound freighted with only a kind of sentimental significance, like the sound of the bedroom clock I listened to in my aunt's house when I spent the night. Just as gradually, English became the language I came not to *hear* because it was the language I used every day, as I gained access to a new, larger society. But the memory of Spanish persisted as a reminder of the society I had left. I can remember occasions when I entered a room and my parents were speaking to one another in Spanish; seeing me they shifted into their more formalized English. Hearing them speak to me in English troubled me. The bonds their voices once secured were loosened by the new tongue.

This is not to suggest that I was being *forced* to give up my Chicano past. After the initial awkwardness of transition, I committed myself, fully and freely, to the culture of the classroom. Soon what I was learning in school was so antithetical to what my parents knew and did that I was careful about the way I talked about myself at the evening dinner table. Occasionally, there were moments of childish cruelty: a son's condescending to instruct either one of his parents about a "simple" point of English pronunciation or grammar.

Social scientists often remark, about situations such as mine, that children feel a sense of loss as they move away from their working-class identifications and models. Certainly, what I experienced, others have also—whatever their race. Like other generations of, say, Polish-American or Irish-American children coming home from college, I was to know the silence that ensues so quickly after the quick exchange of news and the dwindling of common interests.

In addition, however, education seemed to mean not only a gradual dissolving of familial and class ties but also a change of racial identity. The new language I spoke was only the most obvious reason for my associating the classroom with "gringo" society. The society I knew as Chicano was barely literate—in English *or* Spanish—and so impatient with either prolonged reflection or abstraction that I found the academic environment a sharp contrast. Sharpening the contrast was the stereotype of the Mexican as a mental inferior. (The fear of this stereotype has been so deep that only recently have I been willing to listen to those, like D. H. Lawrence, who celebrate the "non-cerebral" Mexican as an alternative to the rational and scientific European man.) Because I did not know how to distinguish the healthy non-rationality of Chicano culture from the mental incompetency of which Chicanos were unjustly accused, I was willing to abandon my non-mental skiffs in order to disprove the racist's stereotype.

I was wise enough not to feel proud of the person education had helped   10
me to become. I knew that education had led me to repudiate my race. I was frequently labeled a *pocho,* a Mexican with gringo pretentions, not only because I could not speak Spanish but also because I would respond in English with precise and careful sentences. Uncles would laugh good-naturedly, but I detected scorn in their voices. For my grandmother, the least assimilated

of my relations, the changes in her grandson since entering school were expecially troubling. She remains today a dark and silently critical figure in my memory, a reminder of the Mexican-Indian ancestry that somehow my educational success has violated.

Nonetheless, I became more comfortable reading or writing careful prose than talking to a kitchen filled with listeners, withdrawing from situations to reflect on their significance rather than grasping for meaning at the scene. I remember, one August evening, slipping away from a gathering of aunts and uncles in the backyard, going into a bedroom tenderly lighted by a late sun, and opening a novel about life in nineteenth-century England. There, by an open window, reading, I was barely conscious of the sounds of laughter outside.

With so few fellow Chicanos in the university, I had no chance to develop an alternative consciousness. When I spent occasional weekends tutoring lower-class Chicano teenagers or when I talked with Mexican-American janitors and maids around the campus, there was a kind of sympathy—a sense, however privately held—that we knew something about one another. But I regarded them all primarily as people from my past. The maids reminded me of my aunts (similarly employed); the students I tutored reminded me of my cousins (who also spoke English with barrio accents).

When I was young, I was taught to refer to my ancestry as Mexican-American. *Chicano* was a word used among friends or relatives. It implied a familiarity based on shared experience. Spoken casually, the term easily became an insult. In 1968 the word *Chicano* was about to become a political term. I heard it shouted into microphones as Third World groups agitated for increased student and faculty representation in higher education. It was not long before I *became* a Chicano in the eyes of students and faculty members. My racial identity was assumed for only the simplest reasons: my skin color and last name.

On occasion I was asked to account for my interests in Renaissance English literature. When I explained them, declaring a need for cultural assimilation, on the campus, my listener would disagree. I sensed suspicion on the part of a number of my fellow minority students. When I could not imitate Spanish pronunciations or the dialect of the barrio, when I was plainly uninterested in wearing ethnic costumes and could not master a special handshake that minority students often used with one another, they knew I was different. And I was. I was assimilated into the culture of a graduate department of English. As a result, I watched how in less than five years nearly every minority graduate student I knew dropped out of school, largely for cultural reasons. Often they didn't understand the value of analyzing literature in professional jargon, which others around them readily adopted. Nor did they move as readily to lofty heights of abstraction. They became easily depressed by the seeming uselessness of talk they heard around them. "It's not for real," I still hear a minority student murmur to herself and perhaps to me, shaking her head slowly, as we sat together in a class listening to a discussion on punctuation in a Renaissance epic.

I survived—thanks to the accommodation I had made long before.　15 In fact, I prospered, partly as a result of the political movement designed to increase the enrollment of minority students less assimilated than I in higher education. Suddenly grants, fellowships, and teaching offers became abundant.

In 1972 I went to England on a Fulbright scholarship. I hoped the months of brooding about racial identity were behind me. I wanted to concentrate on my dissertation, which the distractions of an American campus had not permitted. But the freedom I anticipated did not last for long. Barely a month after I had begun working regularly in the reading room of the British Museum, I was surprised, and even frightened, to have to acknowledge that I was not at ease living the rarefied life of the academic. With my pile of research file cards growing taller, the mass of secondary materials and opinions was making it harder for me to say anything original about my subject. Every sentence I wrote, every thought I had, became so loaded with qualifications and footnotes that it said very little. My scholarship became little more than an exercise in caution. I had an accompanying suspicion that whatever I did manage to write and call my dissertation would be of little use. Opening books so dusty that they must not have been used in decades, I began to doubt the value of writing what only a few people would read.

Obviously, I was going through the fairly typical crisis of the American graduate student. But with one difference: After four years of involvement with questions of racial identity, I now saw my problems as a scholar in the context of the cultural issues that had been raised by my racial situation. So much of what my work in the British Museum lacked, my parents' culture possessed. They were people not afraid to generalize or to find insights in their generalities. More important, they had the capacity to make passionate statements, something I was beginning to doubt my dissertation would ever allow me to do. I needed to learn how to trust the use of "I" in my writing the way they trusted its use in their speech. Thus developed a persistent yearning for the very Chicano culture that I had abandoned as useless.

Feelings of depression came occasionally but forcefully. Some days I found my work so oppressive that I had to leave the reading room and stroll through the museum. One afternoon, appropriately enough, I found myself in an upstairs gallery containing Mayan and Aztec sculptures. Even there the sudden yearning for a Chicano past seemed available to me only as nostalgia. One morning, as I was reading a book about Puritan autobiography, I overheard two Spaniards whispering to one another. I did not hear what they said, but I did hear the sound of their Spanish—and it embraced me, filling my mind with swirling images of a past long abandoned.

I returned from England, disheartened, a few months later. My dissertation was coming along well, but I did not know whether I wanted to submit it. Worse, I did not know whether I wanted a career in higher education. I detested the prospect of spending the rest of my life in libraries and class-rooms, in touch with my past only through the binoculars nostalgia makes available. I knew that I could not simply recreate a version of what I would have been like had I not become an academic. There was no possibility of going back. But if the culture of my birth was to survive, it would have to animate my academic work. That was the lesson of the British Museum.

I frankly do not know how my academic autobiography will end. Some-   20
times I think I will have to leave the campus, in order to reconcile my past and present. Other times, more optimistically, I think that a kind of negative reconciliation is already in progress, that I can make creative use of my sense of loss. For instance, with my sense of the cleavage between past and present, I can, as a literary critic, identify issues in Renaissance pastoral—a literature which records the feelings of the courtly when confronted by the alterna-tives of rural and rustic life. And perhaps I can speak with unusual feeling about the price we must pay, or have paid, as a rational society for confessing seventeenth-century Cartesian[1] faiths. Likewise, because of my sense of cul-tural loss, I may be able to identify more readily than another the ways in which language has meaning simply as sound and what the printed word can and cannot give us. At the very least, I can point up the academy's tendency to ignore the cultures beyond its own horizons.

February 1974

On my job interview the department chairman has been listening to an oral version of what I have just written. I tell him he should be very clear about the fact that I am not, at the moment, confident enough to call myself a Chicano. Perhaps I never will be. But as I say all this, I look at the inter-viewer. He smiles softly. Has he heard what I have been trying to say? I wonder. I repeat: I have lost the ability to bring my past into my present; I do not know how to be a Chicano reader of Spenser or Shakespeare. All that remains is a desire for the past. He sighs, preoccupied, looking at my records. Would I be interested in teaching a course on the Mexican novel in translation? Do I understand that part of my duties would require that I become a counselor of minority students? What was the subject of that dis-sertation I did in England? Have I read the book on the same subject that was just published this month?

---

[1] *Cartesian:* refers to René Descartes (1596–1650), the French philosopher who emphasized rationalization and logic and extended mathematical methods to all fields of human knowledge. He is known for the phrase "I think, therefore I am."

Behind the questioner, a figure forms in my imagination: my grand-mother, her face solemn and still.

Questions for Discussion and Writing

1. How did working on his dissertation in England reinforce a sense of lost contact with his Hispanic heritage that Rodriguez first experienced in grade school? How does the title express his need to repossess those values he had once discarded?
2. Of what advantage is it to Rodriguez to organize his essay employing extended comparisons and contrasts?
3. In a short essay, discuss the advantages and disadvantages of permitting students to use Spanish or some other native language in school rather than English. If you are the only one in your family who is fluent in English, what challenges do you face because of your role as translator and intermediary?
4. **Rhetorical inquiry:** How does the image of Rodriguez's grandmother haunt him as a reminder of the cultural heritage he has almost lost? Correspondingly, how does the title express his need to repossess these values?

How does this photo of first and second grade students at Manzanita Elementary School suggest the tension between learning English when Spanish is your native language in ways discussed by Richard Rodriguez in "On Becoming a Chicano"?

SABINE REICHEL

Sabine Reichel was born in Hamburg, Germany, in 1946, to a German actor and a Lithuanian artist. She grew up in West Germany (now Germany) and since 1965 has had a varied career as clothing designer, freelance journalist, contributor of film criticism, lecturer, filmmaker, and social worker active in projects caring for homeless children. She immigrated to the United States in 1976. Dissatisfied with the silence she and others of her generation encountered concerning the systematic slaughter of European Jews by Hitler and the Nazis, Reichel spent six months interviewing soldiers and teachers whose lives seemed to her to represent Germany's amnesia. The autobiographical essay that resulted was published under the title What Did You Do in the War, Daddy? *(1989). In this chapter from that book, Reichel describes the moral complacency of those of her parents' generation who refused to acknowledge the realities of the Nazi era and its lingering effects in contemporary Germany.*

Before You Read

Do you ever think about what you are not being taught?

Learning What Was Never Taught

I remember Herr Stock and Fräulein Lange without much affection. Partly because they weren't extraordinary people, partly because they failed their profession. They were my history teachers, ordinary civil servants, singled out to bring the tumultuous events of European history into perspective for a classroom of bored German schoolkids.

As it happened, Hitler and the Third Reich were the subjects under discussion when we were about fourteen years old, which is not to say that we discussed anything at all. I always thought that the decision to study the subject then was the result of a carefully calculated estimate by the school officials—as if German students were emotionally and intellectually ready to comprehend and digest the facts about Nazi Germany at exactly the age of 14.3. I learned much later that it had nothing to do with calculation; it was a matter of sequence. German history is taught chronologically, and Hitler was there when we were fourteen, whether we were ready or not.

Teaching this particular period was a thankless, though unavoidable, task. It was accompanied by sudden speech impediments, hoarse voices, uncontrollable coughs, and sweaty upper lips. A shift of mood would creep into the expansive lectures about kings and conquerors from the old ages, and once the Weimar Republic came to an end our teachers lost their proud diction.

We knew what it meant. We could feel the impending disaster. Only a few more pages in the history book, one last nervous swallowing, and then in a casual but controlled voice, maybe a touch too loud, Fräulein Lange would ask, "We are now getting to a dark chapter in German history. I'm sure you all know what I mean?"

We did, because each of us had already skimmed through the whole book   5
countless times in search of exotic material and, naturally, had come across the man with the mustache. We knew that she was referring to the terrible time between 1933 and 1945 when Germany fell prey to a devil in brown disguise. There were fifteen pages devoted to the Third Reich, and they were filled with incredible stories about a mass movement called National Socialism which started out splendidly and ended in a catastrophe for the whole world.

And then there was an extra chapter, about three-quarters of a page long. It was titled "The Extermination of the Jews," and I had read it in my room at home many times. I always locked the door because I didn't want anybody to know what I was reading. Six million Jews were killed in concentration camps, and as I read about Auschwitz and the gas chambers a wave of feelings—fearful fascination mingled with disgust—rushed over me. But I kept quiet. What monsters must have existed then. I was glad it had all happened in the past and that the cruel Germans were gone, because, as the book pointed out, the ones responsible were punished. I couldn't help feeling alarmed by something I couldn't put my finger on. How could so many innocent people be murdered?

There was no explanation for my unspoken questions, no answers in Fräulein Lange's helpless face. She seemed embarrassed and distraught, biting her lip and looking down at her orthopedic shoes while trying to summarize the Third Reich in fifty minutes. That worked out to one minute for every one million people killed in World War II . . . and twenty-six lines for six million Jews, printed on cheap, yellowish paper in a German history book published in 1960. An efficient timesaver, the German way.

We never read that particular chapter aloud with our teacher as we did with so many other ones. It was the untouchable subject, isolated and open to everyone's personal interpretation. There was a subtle, unspoken agreement between teacher and student not to dig into something that would cause discomfort on all sides. Besides, wanting to have known more about concentration camps as a student would have been looked upon as sick.

All things must come to an end, however, and once the Third Reich crumbled in our classroom to the sound of hastily turning pages, the suffocating silence was lifted. Everybody seemed relieved, especially Fräulein Lange, who became her jolly old self again. She had survived two world wars, she would survive a bunch of unappreciative teenagers.

In her late fifties in 1960, Fräulein Lange was a tiny, wrinkled woman   10
who matched my idea of the institutional matron right down to her baggy skirt, steel-gray bun at the nape of her neck, and seamed stockings. She also had a trying predilection for Gutenberg, the inventer of movable type, whom we got to know more intimately than Hitler. But she did her duty, more or less. German teachers had to teach history whether they liked it or not.

The teachers of my time had all been citizens of the Third Reich and therefore participants in an epoch that only a few years after its bitter collapse had to be discussed in a neutral fashion. But what could they possibly have said about this undigested, shameful subject to a partly shocked, partly bored class of adolescents? They had to preserve their authority in order to appear credible as teachers. Yet they were never put to the test. A critical imagination and unreasonable curiosity were unwelcome traits in all the classrooms of my twelve years in school. There was no danger that a precocious student would ever corner a teacher and demand more facts about the Nazis; they could walk away unscathed. We didn't ask our parents at home about the Nazis; nor did we behave differently in school.

The truth was that teachers were not allowed to indulge in private views of the Nazi past. There were nationwide guidelines for handling this topic, including one basic rule: The Third Reich and Adolf Hitler should be condemned unequivocally, without any specific criticism or praise. In reality, however, there were basically three ways to deal with the German past: (1) to go through the chapter as fast as possible, thereby avoiding any questions and answers; (2) to condemn the past passionately in order to deflate any suspicion about personal involvement; (3) to subtly legitimate the Third Reich by pointing out that it wasn't really as bad as it seemed; after all, there were the *Autobahnen*.[1]

But no matter what the style of prevarication, the German past was always presented as an isolated, fatal accident, and so the possibility of investigating the cause of such a disaster was, of course, eliminated. Investigating crimes reinforces guilt. If something is programmatically depicted as black and bad, one doesn't look for different shades and angles. The Third Reich was out of reach for us; it couldn't be cut down to size.

I wonder now what could have been accomplished by a teacher who had taken part in the war—as a soldier, or a Nazi, or an anti-Nazi—and who talked candidly about his personal experience. But that never happened. Instead we were showered with numbers and dates. A few million dead bodies are impossible to relate to; raw numbers don't evoke emotions. Understanding is always personal. Only stories that humanized the numbers might have reached us. Had we been allowed to draw a connection between ourselves and the lives of other people, we might have been able to identify and feel compassion. But we were not aware of how blatantly insufficiently the past was handled in school because we resented the subject as much as the teacher who was somewhat entangled in it. Teenagers generally have little interest in history lessons; we learned facts and dates in order to pass a test or get a good grade and weren't convinced that comprehension of the warp and woof of historical events made any difference to the world or anybody in particular.

---

[1] *Autobahnen*: an extensive network of freeways without mandatory speed limits, constructed during the Third Reich.

Another history teacher in a new school I attended in 1962 took an   15
activist approach, mixing pathos and drama into a highly entertaining theatrical performance. To introduce highlights of the Third Reich there was no
finer actor than Herr Stock. His voice was angry, his brows furrowed, and his
fist was raised when he talked about the Führer's ferocious reign. Some of the
more outgoing male teachers might even mimic parts of a Hitler speech. Yet
when it came time to discuss the war itself, everything went downhill. His
hands stopped moving, his voice became reproachful—no more victories to
report. His saddest expression was reserved for the tragic end of "Germany
under National Socialist dictatorship." It was time for the untouchable chapter
again, the chapter that made Herr Stock nervously run his hands over his
bald head, clear his throat, and mumble something about "six million Jews."
It was the chapter that made him close the book with a clap, turn his back to
the class, and announce with a palpable sigh of relief, "Recess."

In our next history lesson that chapter was usually forgotten, and
nobody followed up with any questions. Happy to have escaped interrogation, Herr Stock turned the pages quickly, ignoring "unpleasantries" like
capitulation, denazification, and the humiliating aftermath of a defeated
nation. The dark clouds were gone, the past had been left behind, and he
turned jocular and voluble again.

But Herr Stock wasn't really talking to us, he was rather trying to convince us of something, assuming the stance of a prosecutor. For him, the
scandal wasn't the casualties of World War II, but the resulting partition of
Germany and the malevolence of the Russians. Rage, anger, and disappointment over the lost war, always repressed or directed at others, could be
openly displayed now, disguised as righteousness. "They" had stolen parts
of Germany—no word of what we stole from other countries. The Russians
were war criminals; the Germans were victims.

If I had been unexpectedly curious about Nazi Germany, I would have
received little help from my history books. The conclusions to be drawn from
a twelve-year catastrophe packed with enough dramatic material to fill a
library were reduced to a few cryptic phrases: "The Germans showed very
little insight" and "No real feelings of contrition were expressed." Teachers
and history books were their own best examples of how to eviscerate the
Nazi terror without ever really trying to come to terms with it.

But a new chapter, a new era, and a magic word—*Wirtschaftswunder*[2]—
soon revived our classroom and inspired another patriotic performance by
Herr Stock. The undisputed star of German history education in the sixties
was the remarkable reconstruction of postwar Germany. Now here was something an old schoolteacher could sink his teeth into. Gone were stutters and
coughs. A nation of survivors had rolled up its sleeves, and Herr Stock had

---

[2] *Wirtschaftswunder*: "wonder of economics," the name given to the phenomenal recovery
of the German economy after World War II.

certainly been one of them. Here was a chance to rehabilitate Germany and put some gloss over its rotten core. Postwar Germany was a genuine communal construction, a well-made product, mass-manufactured by and for the tastes of the former citizens of the Reich. Every German with two functioning hands had taken part in rebuilding Germany, and history teachers all over the country waxed nostalgic about the united strength, the grim determination, and the close camaraderie that had helped build up Germany brick by brick.

We schoolchildren couldn't have cared less about these achievements.   20
We were all born under occupation; the postwar years were ours too and the memories of ruins and poverty were just as indelible—if not as traumatic—as they had been for our parents. But in his enthusiasm he overlooked the fact that his words were falling on deaf ears: we didn't like Herr Stock; nor did we trust or admire him. In all this excitement about the "economic miracle," another, even greater miracle was conveniently left unexplained. On page 219 of my history book, Germany was described as a nation living happily under National Socialism and a seemingly accepted Führer without any visible crisis of conscience. Yet only fourteen pages later the same Volk[3] is depicted in the midst of an entirely different world, miraculously denazified and retrained, its murderous past neatly tucked away behind a tattered but nevertheless impenetrable veil of forgetfulness.

How did they do it? The existing Federal Republic of Germany is only one state away from the Nazi Reich. Where did they unload the brown ballast? The role change from obedient Nazi citizen to obedient Bundes[4] citizen went too smoothly from "Sieg Heil!" to democracy, and from marching brown uniforms to marching gray flannel suits. Where was the genuine substance which had initially constituted the basic foundation and ideology of the Third Reich? Could it still be there, hidden, repressed, put on ice?

Such questions were never asked, or encouraged. The schoolteachers that I encountered were a uniformly intimidating group of people (with one glorious exception): older men and women who demanded respect, order, and obedience. They were always curbing my curiosity with the clobbering logic of people who get paid for controlling outbursts of independent thinking. Their assessment of my character in report cards read: "She talks too much and could accomplish more if she would be more diligent."

Even though prohibited when I went to school, corporal punishment in many forms was still practiced with parental support, and my own classroom recollections are thick with thin-lipped, hawk-eyed, bespectacled men and women with mercilessly firm hands ready to take up the switch.

I always felt powerless toward teachers, and all of these emotions crystallized in 1983, when I was preparing to interview one of them. I couldn't help feeling a little triumphant. I was asking the questions now because I had

---

[3] Volk: "people" or "folk," as in Volkswagen (literally, "people's car").   [4] Bundes: "federal," an adjective.

discovered a slight spot on their white vests, something I couldn't see clearly when I was young and under their control. Now I had the power to make them nervous. My victory over German authority seemed complete. A schoolgirl's revenge?

But that wasn't all. I had a genuine interest in finding out how teachers   25
in Germany feel today about their past failures. Had they found new ways to justify their damaging elisions, euphemisms, and omissions? More than any other age group, my generation was in desperate need not only of historical education but also of some form of emotional assistance from the adults who were linked to that not so distant yet unspeakable past.

In a way, I was looking for Herr Stock. But teachers as mediocre as he and Fräulein Lange had little to contribute to the kind of discussion I had in mind. I wanted the perspective of a teacher who had at least attempted to come to grips with his past. I was lucky to find one in Cäsar Hagener, a seventy-six-year-old former teacher and history professor. Hagener lives with his wife in a cozy, old-fashioned house with a garden in a suburb of Hamburg, in a quiet, safe neighborhood with lots of trees, many dachshunds, and little activity. He owns the type of one-family house, surrounded by a fence, that was commonly built in the thirties. A German house must have a fence. A house without a fence is disorderly, like a coat with a missing button.

Cäsar Hagener exuded integrity and an appealing friendliness—yet I found it impossible to forget that he had also been a teacher in the Third Reich. Hitler had envisioned a training program that would make every German youth "resilient as leather, fast as a weasel, and hard as Krupp steel." He believed that "too much education spoils the youth." (Not surprisingly, after a few years of dictatorship 30 percent of the university professors, including Jews, had left the country.)

In 1933, Cäsar Hagener was a teacher of pedagogy and history at a liberal school in Hamburg, and when he heard that Hitler was appointed Reichs Chancellor he happened to be studying *Das Kapital*[5] together with some left-wing colleagues. "My friend said to me, 'It'll be over in no time. When you and I write a history book in twenty years, the Nazis will only be a footnote.'"

Even a skillful dictator like Hitler couldn't turn a country upside down overnight, and school life changed slowly under the Nazis. "But after 1934, the Nazis began to investigate the teachers' adaptation to the new order. Some were fired, and some were retrained in special camps. We had, of course, some 'overnight' Nazis who were strutting around in uniform, which didn't impress the students, who were quite critical. Later, in 1937, the young teachers were told to join the Nazi Party or else, so I joined the Party. Still, the first years of National Socialism were almost bearable."

---

[5] *Das Kapital:* the classic text by Karl Marx (1867) published in English in 1887 and edited by Frederick Engels.

However, at least once a week, teachers and students had to muster for   30
the raising of the swastika flag and the singing of the "Horst-Wessel-Lied"
or other Nazi songs. The Führer's speeches were required listening on the
popular *Volksempfänger* for teachers and older students, while the nazified
text in the new schoolbooks read like this: "If a mental patient costs 4
Reichsmarks a day in maintenance, a cripple 5.50, and a criminal 3.50, and
about 50,000 of these people are in our institutions, how much does it cost
our state at a daily rate of 4 Reichsmarks—and how many marriage loans of
1,000 Reichsmarks per couple could have been given out instead?"

The new features of Nazi education like race hygiene and heredity theory were given different degrees of importance in different schools. Hagener
prepared himself: "I made sure to get a class with school beginners because
children of that age weren't taught history or any of that Nazi nonsense.
Besides, as a teacher, you were pretty much independent in your classroom
and could make your own decision about what to say and what to skip.
There were ways of getting around the obnoxious Nazi ideology."

The first public action by the Nazis right after January 1933 was to purge
public and school libraries of "Jewish and un-German elements," leaving
empty spaces on the shelves, since new "literature" wasn't written yet and new
schoolbooks, adapted to the Nazis' standards, weren't printed until 1936. That
same year they initiated compulsory membership in the Hitler Youth, starting
at the age of ten with boys organized into Jungvolk and Hitler Jungen and girls
and young women into the Bund Deutscher Mädel (League of German Girls).
What the Reich of the future needed were fearless, proud men of steel and
yielding, fertile women—preferably blond—not effete intellectuals.

"The children can't be blamed for having been enthusiastic members of
the Hitler Youth," Cäsar Hagener points out. "They grew up with that ideology and couldn't be expected to protect themselves from National Socialism;
to do so, children would have had to be unaffected by all outside influences.
It was their world, and the Hitler Youth programs were very attractive, with
sports, contests, and decorations. It was possible for the son of a Communist or a Social Democrat to become a highly decorated Hitler Youth leader.
I accuse the teachers who didn't perceive what was going on, and who taught
Nazi ideology and glorified war, of having failed their profession."

In the last years of the war there was not much academic activity in
Germany. The Nazi state was concerned with other problems besides education. Many schools were destroyed by bombs and virtually all Germans
between fifteen and sixty years of age—Cäsar Hagener was drafted in 1940—
were mobilized for the *Endkampf* (the final struggle) by the end of 1944.
Hunger, death, and the will to survive prevailed over culture and education.
Who needs to know algebra when the world is falling apart?

In 1945 denazification fever broke out in the defeated nation and reversed   35
the roles of master and servant. For over a decade the country had been straining to purge itself of "un-German elements," and now the occupying powers
were trying to purge it of all Nazi elements. Yet their efforts only exposed the

unfeasibility of such a gargantuan task, since it involved much more than just the Nazi Party and the SS. Twelve years under the swastika had produced all kinds of "literature," art, music, film—indeed, a whole society had to be taken apart and its guiding principles destroyed. Naturally, reforming the educational system was a high priority, and millions of schoolbooks were thrown out, but some had to be preserved. The specially assigned Allied education officers decided which schoolbooks could still be used (after tearing out a Nazi-contaminated page or censoring a suspicious chapter or two). The approved books were stamped, and were circulated until new ones could be printed, which wasn't until the early fifties.

"The British, our occupiers, did everything wrong, because nothing could be worked out intellectually. They came over here with certain expectations and this incredibly bad image of the enemy, and they were very surprised to find their task not as easy as they had thought. They tried to control the situation by being very strict."

Reforming the faculty was even more problematic, since many teachers had been forced to join the Nazi Party and it wasn't always easy to tell who was a "real" Nazi and who wasn't. As a rule of thumb, those who appeared to have cooperated unwillingly were permitted to continue teaching, younger teachers who had been educated under the Nazi regime were retrained in special seminars, while those who had been active supporters were barred from teaching for as long as two years.

Cäsar Hagener still gets angry over how easily former colleagues were rehired. "After 1945, nobody seemed to remember what a Nazi was, and people who I knew were definitely Nazis by nature landed on top again. I was one of a group of young teachers who protested violently against this tendency—and I felt like a McCarthy witch-hunter. I saw these people as criminals who did a lot of harm to us teachers."

Still, the main consideration was that teachers were badly needed. The war had wiped out a whole generation of young men, and keeping professionals from their profession in Germany after 1945 was as uneconomical as it was impractical: what was left was what Germany's children got. It's safe to say that by 1950 almost all teachers were back in schools and universities regardless of their past.

In the years immediately following the war, the few schools that were not badly damaged were overcrowded with children of all ages and several grades gathered together in one room. There was cardboard in place of windows, and opening umbrellas inside the school on rainy days was as natural as being sent home for a "cold-weather holiday" because there was no heat. The teacher had to be a good-humored ringmaster, innovative and full of stories; because of the book shortage, he had to know his lessons by heart. The students also needed good memories, because there wasn't any paper. Arithmetic and grammar assignments were often written down on the margins of newspapers.

It might have been the only time in Germany when school lessons were extemporaneous, personal, and an accurate reflection of real life. School was suddenly a popular place where humanity prevailed over theory. Teachers were not merely authority figures but people who had been harmed by the war just like the students and their families, and much of the time was spent discussing how to steal potatoes and coal and other survival tactics, which were more pressing than Pythagoras.

How did a teacher in those years explain history while it was happening? The change from "Nazis are good" to "Nazis are bad" must have been a confusing experience for the uprooted, disillusioned children of the Third Reich. Children weren't denazified. They had to adapt to "democracy" without shedding a brown skin. All the values they had learned to defend so passionately crumbled before their eyes and the reality they once trusted was rearranged silently, without their consent. The glorious, thunderous Third Reich was a gyp. The Jews weren't "*Volks* enemy number one" anymore. And as for the Führer, he wasn't a superhuman hero, but a vicious little coward, a maniac who wanted to exterminate a whole people and almost succeeded. What irreparable mistrust must have become lodged in the minds of all these young Germans whose youth was trampled flat by goose-stepping jackboots.

But teachers didn't explain history at all. "I'm afraid to say that it didn't occur to the students to bring up Adolf in any form. We had all survived and dealt mostly with the effects of the war in a practical sense. I tried to do nice, positive things with the children, who had it bad enough as it was," Cäsar Hagener explains, and adds, almost surprised, "It is amazing how extremely apolitical we were. Any reflection was impossible under the circumstances, because everything was defined in terms of the struggle of daily life, which had a dynamic all by itself."

He also knows why the adolescents of the fifties and sixties were as uninquisitive as their teachers and parents were silent. "There was strong resentment toward the grown-ups. The teenagers had a fine sense for the things that didn't quite fit together with the Nazis. I didn't have any luck with my own three sons; they frustrated my desire to talk about the past by calling it lecturing, so I ended up talking about it mostly in foreign countries, where the people seemed to be more interested in it."

Things have changed radically during the last twenty years. There has   45
been a small revolution in the German classroom. While teachers after the war were much younger and more outspoken than their predecessors, students became rebellious and undisciplined.

Cäsar Hagener remembers his school days. "My own generation and my students lived in a very strict and conformist structure which existed much earlier than 1933. Sure, there were provocative and rebellious personalities, but this phenomenon of developing an independent mind is new. Today it wouldn't be possible to stand in front of a class in uniform and in all seriousness talk about racial theory. The students would die laughing."

German students today often know more facts about the Third Reich than both their parents and the immediate postwar generation and are not afraid to ask questions. Yet their interest in Nazism is strictly intellectual, and they generally succeed in remaining emotionally detached. They don't know yet that they can't escape the past. Tragically, almost all of Cäsar Hagener's contemporaries have managed to escape their Nazi past. In his opinion: "You can't put a whole nation on the couch. I find my own contemporaries just plain terrible and I don't have much contact with many old friends anymore. In their eyes I'm too critical, a guy who fouls his own nest and who can't see the good sides of the Nazi era—which infuriates and bores me at the same time. They reject the radical examination of the past. But it's necessary, since we know better than most that terrible things can and did happen."

Questions for Discussion and Writing

1. From the narrator's perspective, what was odd about the way in which the Holocaust was taught? How did her search for a satisfactory explanation about this event change her relationship with her family and school authorities?

2. How did Reichel's interview with Herr Hagener provide insights into the pressures to which teachers were subjected and give her some of the answers she sought?

3. You might rent the subtitled acclaimed German film *The Nasty Girl* (1990), which is based on Reichel's account, and compare it with her essay. How does each genre treat the same events differently?

4. **Rhetorical inquiry:** What instances alerted Reichel as a fourteen-year-old student that her teachers and her history books were trying to discount the Holocaust as a brief episode that did not represent the values of the German people during World War II? How effectively does she transmit the sense that people who wanted to forget the past could not understand her quest to find out the truth about this period?

NAT HENTOFF

A former board member of the American Civil Liberties Union, Nat Hentoff is a writer and an adjunct associate professor at New York University. He was born in 1925 in Boston. Hentoff graduated from Northeastern in 1945 and did postgraduate work at Harvard and the Sorbonne. He is a regular contributor to such publications as the Washington Post, *the* Progressive, *the* Village Voice, *and* The New Yorker. *Collections of his work include* The First Freedom *(1980). "'Speech Codes' on the Campus and Problems of Free Speech" first appeared in the Fall 1991 issue of* Dissent. *His most recent works are* Listen to the Stories: Nat Hentoff on Jazz and Country Music *(2000),* The War on the Bill of Rights and the Gathering Resistance *(2003), and* Insisting on Life *(2005).*

Before You Read

What are the pros and cons of having speech codes?

"Speech Codes" on the Campus

During three years of reporting on anti-free-speech tendencies in higher education, I've been at more than twenty colleges and universities—from Washington and Lee and Columbia to Mesa State in Colorado and Stanford.

On this voyage of initially reverse expectations—with liberals fiercely advocating censorship of "offensive" speech and conservatives merrily taking the moral high ground as champions of free expression—the most dismaying moment of revelation took place at Stanford.

AN ECUMENICAL CALL FOR A HARSH CODE

In the course of a two-year debate on whether Stanford, like many other universities, should have a speech code punishing language that might wound minorities, women, and gays, a letter appeared in the *Stanford Daily*. Signed by the African-American Law Students Association, the Asian-American Law Students Association, and the Jewish Law Students Association, the letter called for a harsh code. It reflected the letter and the spirit of an earlier declaration by Canetta Ivy, a black leader of student government at Stanford during the period of the great debate. "We don't put as many restrictions on freedom of speech," she said, "as we should."

Reading the letter by this rare ecumenical body of law students (so pressing was the situation that even Jews were allowed in), I thought of twenty, thirty years from now. From so bright a cadre of graduates, from so prestigious a law school would come some of the law professors, civic leaders, college presidents, and even maybe a Supreme Court justice of the future. And many of them would have learned—like so many other university students in the land—that censorship is okay provided your motives are okay.

The debate at Stanford ended when the president, Donald Kennedy, following the prevailing winds, surrendered his previous position that once you start telling people what they can't say, you will end up telling them what they can't think. Stanford now has a speech code.

This is not to say that these gags on speech—every one of them so overboard and vague that a student can violate a code without knowing he or she has done so—are invariably imposed by student demand. At most colleges, it is the administration that sets up the code. Because there have been racist or sexist or homophobic taunts, anonymous notes or graffiti, the administration feels it must *do something*. The cheapest, quickest way to demonstrate that it cares is to appear to suppress racist, sexist, homophobic speech.

5

"THE PALL OF ORTHODOXY"

Usually, the leading opposition among the faculty consists of conservatives—when there is opposition. An exception at Stanford was law professor Gerald Gunther, arguably the nation's leading authority on constitutional law. But Gunther did not have much support among other faculty members, conservative or liberal.

At the University of Buffalo Law School, which has a code restricting speech, I could find just one faculty member who was against it. A liberal, he spoke only on condition that I not use his name. He did not want to be categorized as a racist.

On another campus, a political science professor, for whom I had great respect after meeting and talking with him years ago, has been silent—students told me—on what Justice William Brennan once called "the pall of orthodoxy" that has fallen on his campus.

When I talked to him, the professor said, "It doesn't happen in my class. There's no 'politically correct' orthodoxy here. It may happen in other places at this university, but I don't know about that." He said no more.

One of the myths about the rise of P.C. (politically correct) is that, coming from the left, it is primarily intimidating conservatives on campus. Quite the contrary. At almost every college I've been, conservative students have their own newspaper, usually quite lively and fired by a muckraking glee at exposing "politically correct" follies on campus.

By and large, those most intimidated—not so much by the speech codes themselves but by the Madame Defarge–like spirit behind them—are liberal students and those who can be called politically moderate.

I've talked to many of them, and they no longer get involved in class discussions when their views would go against the grain of P.C. righteousness. Many, for instance, have questions about certain kinds of affirmative action. They are not partisans of Jesse Helms or David Duke, but they wonder whether progeny of middle-class black families should get scholarship preference. Others have a question about abortion. Most are not pro-life, but they believe that fathers should have a say in whether the fetus should be sent off into eternity.

SELF-CENSORSHIP

Jeff Shesol, a recent graduate of Brown and now a Rhodes scholar at Oxford, became nationally known while at Brown because of his comic strip, "Thatch," which, not too kindly, parodied P.C. students. At a forum on free speech at Brown before he left, Shesol said he wished he could tell the new students at Brown to have no fear of speaking freely. But he couldn't tell them that, he said, advising the new students to stay clear of talking critically about affirmative action or abortion, among other things, in public.

At that forum, Shesol told me, he said that those members of the left who regard dissent from their views as racist and sexist should realize that they are discrediting their goals. "They're honorable goals," said Shesol, "and I agree with them. I'm against racism and sexism. But these people's tactics are obscuring the goals. And they've resulted in Brown's no longer being an open-minded place." There were hisses from the audience.

Students at New York University Law School have also told me that they censor themselves in class. The kind of chilling atmosphere they describe was exemplified as a case assigned for a moot court competition became subject to denunciation when a sizable number of law students said it was too "offensive" and would hurt the feelings of gay and lesbian students. The case concerned a divorced father's attempt to gain custody of his children on the grounds that their mother had become a lesbian. It was against P.C. to represent the father.

Although some of the faculty responded by insisting that you learn to be a lawyer by dealing with all kinds of cases, including those you person-ally find offensive, other faculty members supported the rebellious students, praising them for their sensitivity. There was little public opposition from the other students to the attempt to suppress the case. A leading dissenter was a member of the conservative Federalist Society.

What is P.C. to white students is not necessarily P.C. to black students. Most of the latter did not get involved in the N.Y.U. protest, but throughout the country many black students do support speech codes. A vigorous excep-tion was a black Harvard law school student during a debate on whether the law school should start punishing speech. A white student got up and said that the codes are necessary because without them, black students would be driven away from colleges and thereby deprived of the equal opportunity to get an education.

A black student rose and said that the white student had a hell of a nerve to assume that he—in the face of racist speech—would pack up his books and go home. He's been familiar with that kind of speech all his life, and he had never felt the need to run away from it. He'd handled it before and he could again.

The black student then looked at his white colleague and said that it   20
was condescending to say that blacks have to be "protected" from racist speech. "It is more racist and insulting," he emphasized, "to say that to me than to call me a nigger."

But that would appear to be a minority view among black students. Most are convinced they do need to be protected from wounding language. On the other hand, a good many black student organizations on campus do not feel that Jews have to be protected from wounding language.

PRESENCE OF ANTI-SEMITISM

Though it's not much written about in reports of the language wars on cam-pus, there is a strong strain of anti-Semitism among some—not all, by any means—black students. They invite such speakers as Louis Farrakhan, the former Stokely Carmichael (now Kwame Touré), and such lesser but still burning bushes as Steve Cokely, the Chicago commentator who has declared that Jewish doctors inject the AIDS virus into black babies. That distinguished leader was invited to speak at the University of Michigan.

The black student organization at Columbia University brought to the campus Dr. Khallid Abdul Muhammad. He began his address by saying: "My leader, my teacher, my guide is the honorable Louis Farrakhan. I thought that should be said at Columbia Jewniversity."

Many Jewish students have not censored themselves in reacting to this form of political correctness among some blacks. A Columbia student, Rachel Stoll, wrote a letter to the *Columbia Spectator:* "I have an idea. As a white Jewish American, I'll just stand in the middle of a circle comprising . . . Khallid Abdul Muhammad and assorted members of the Black Students Organization and let them all hurl large stones at me. From recent events and statements made on this campus, I gather this will be a good cheap method of making these people feel good."

At UCLA, a black student magazine printed an article indicating there is considerable truth to the *Protocols of the Elders of Zion.*[1] For months, the black faculty, when asked their reactions, preferred not to comment. One of them did say that the black students already considered the black faculty to be insufficiently militant, and the professors didn't want to make the gap any wider. Like white liberal faculty members on other campuses, they want to be liked—or at least not too disliked.

Along with quiet white liberal faculty members, most black professors have not opposed the speech codes. But unlike the white liberals many honestly do believe that minority students have to be insulated from barbed language. They do not believe—as I have found out in a number of conversations—that an essential part of an education is to learn to demystify language, to strip it of its ability to demonize and stigmatize you. They do not believe that the way to deal with bigoted language is to answer it with more and better language of your own. This seems very elementary to me, but not to the defenders, black and white, of the speech codes.

"FIGHTING WORDS"

Consider University of California president David Gardner. He has imposed a speech code on all the campuses in his university system. Students are to be punished—and this is characteristic of the other codes around the country—if they use "fighting words"—derogatory references to "race, sex, sexual orientation, or disability."

The term "fighting words" comes from a 1942 Supreme Court decision, *Chaplinsky v. New Hampshire,* which ruled that "fighting words" are not

---

[1] *Protocols of the Elders of Zion:* a document forged c. 1897 alleging that an international Jewish conspiracy was plotting the overthrow of Christian civilization.

protected by the First Amendment. That decision, however, has been in disuse at the High Court for many years. But it is thriving on college campuses.

In the California code, a word becomes "fighting" if it is directly addressed to "any ordinary person" (presumably, extraordinary people are above all this). These are the kinds of words that are "inherently likely to provoke a violent action, *whether or not they actually do.*" (Emphasis added.)

Moreover, he or she who fires a fighting word at any ordinary person   30
can be reprimanded or dismissed from the university because the perpetrator should "reasonably know" that what he or she has said will interfere with the "victim's ability to pursue effectively his or her education or otherwise participate fully in university programs and activities."

Asked Gary Murikami, chairman of the Gay and Lesbian Association at the University of California, Berkeley: "What does it mean?"

Among those—faculty, law professors, college administrators—who insist such codes are essential to the university's purpose of making *all* students feel at home and thereby able to concentrate on their work, there has been a celebratory resort to the Fourteenth Amendment.

That amendment guarantees "equal protection of the laws" to all, and that means to all students on campus. Accordingly, when the First Amendment rights of those engaging in offensive speech clash with the equality rights of their targets under the Fourteenth Amendment, the First Amendment must give way.

This is the thesis, by the way, of John Powell, legal director of the American Civil Liberties Union, even though that organization has now formally opposed all college speech codes—after a considerable civil war among and within its affiliates.

The battle of the amendments continues, and when harsher codes are   35
called for at some campuses, you can expect the Fourteenth Amendment—which was not intended to censor *speech*—will rise again.

A precedent has been set at, of all places, colleges and universities, that the principle of free speech is merely situational. As college administrators change, so will the extent of free speech on campus. And invariably, permissible speech will become more and more narrowly defined. Once speech can be limited in such subjective ways, more and more expression will be included in what is forbidden.

FREEDOM OF THOUGHT

One of the exceedingly few college presidents who speaks out on the consequences of the anti-free-speech movement is Yale University's Benno Schmidt:

> Freedom of thought must be Yale's central commitment. It is not easy to embrace. It is, indeed, the effort of a lifetime. . . . Much expression that is free may deserve our contempt. We may well be moved to exercise our own freedom to counter it or to ignore it. But universities cannot censor or suppress

speech, no matter how obnoxious in content, without violating their justification for existence. . . .

On some other campuses in this country, values of civility and community have been offered by some as paramount values of the university, even to the extent of superseding freedom of expression.

Such a view is wrong in principle and, if extended, is disastrous to freedom of thought. . . . The chilling effects on speech of the vagueness and open-ended nature of many universities' prohibitions . . . are compounded by the fact that these codes are typically enforced by faculty and students who commonly assert that vague notions of community are more important to the academy than freedom of thought and expression. . . .

This is a flabby and uncertain time for freedom in the United States.

On the Public Broadcasting System in June 1991, I was part of a Fred Friendly panel at Stanford University in a debate on speech codes versus freedom of expression. The three black panelists strongly supported the codes. So did the one Asian-American on the panel. But then so did Stanford law professor Thomas Grey, who wrote the Stanford code, and Stanford president Donald Kennedy, who first opposed and then embraced the code. We have a new ecumenicism of those who would control speech for the greater good. It is hardly a new idea, but the mix of advocates is rather new.

But there are other voices. In the national board debate at the ACLU on college speech codes, the first speaker—and I think she had a lot to do with making the final vote against codes unanimous—was Gwen Thomas.

A black community college administrator from Colorado, she is a fiercely persistent exposer of racial discrimination.   40

She started by saying, "I have always felt as a minority person that we have to protect the rights of all because if we infringe on the rights of any persons, we'll be next.

"As for providing a nonintimidating educational environment, our young people have to learn to grow up on college campuses. We have to teach them how to deal with adversarial situations. They have to learn how to survive offensive speech they find wounding and hurtful." Gwen Thomas is an educator—an endangered species in higher education.

Questions for Discussion and Writing

1. With which of the assumptions underlying the imposition of speech codes does Hentoff disagree? How do Hentoff's experiences or examples from campuses around the country challenge the presumed benefits of speech codes?
2. How does Hentoff frame the debate about whether the First or the Fourteenth Amendment ought to be given more consideration?
3. Does your own experience in classrooms confirm or disprove Hentoff's contention that the chilling effects on campuses have mostly been felt

by students with moderate views? Have you ever felt inhibited from discussing issues because of the circumstances described by Hentoff?

4. **Rhetorical inquiry:** What incidents does Hentoff use to illustrate a double standard in the application of speech codes?

MARY CROW DOG AND RICHARD ERDOES

Mary Crow Dog, who took the name Mary Brave Bird, was born in 1956 and grew up on a South Dakota reservation in a one-room cabin without running water or electricity. She joined the new movement of tribal pride sweeping Native American communities in the 1960s and 1970s and was at the siege of Wounded Knee, South Dakota, in 1973. She married the American Indian Movement (AIM) leader Leonard Crow Dog, the movement's chief medicine man. Her powerful autobiography Lakota Woman, *written with Richard Erdoes, one of America's leading writers on Native American affairs and the author of eleven books, became a national best-seller and won the American Book Award for 1991. In it she describes what it was like to grow up a Sioux in a white-dominated society. Her second book,* Ohitka Woman *(1993), also written with Richard Erdoes, continues the story of a woman whose struggle for a sense of self and freedom is a testament to her will and spirit. In "Civilize Them with a Stick" from* Lakota Woman, *the author recounts her experiences as a young student at a boarding school run by the Bureau of Indian Affairs.*

Before You Read

What objective has the government sought to achieve in the way in which it educated Native Americans?

Civilize Them with a Stick

> *. . . Gathered from the cabin, the wickiup, and the tepee,*
> *partly by cajolery and partly by threats,*
> *partly by bribery and partly by force,*
> *they are induced to leave their kindred*
> *to enter these schools and take upon themselves*
> *the outward appearance of civilized life.*
>
> —*Annual report of the Department of Interior, 1901*

It is almost impossible to explain to a sympathetic white person what a typical old Indian boarding school was like; how it affected the Indian child suddenly dumped into it like a small creature from another world, helpless, defenseless, bewildered, trying desperately and instinctively to survive and sometimes not surviving at all. I think such children were like the victims of Nazi concentration camps trying to tell average, middle-class Americans what their experience had been like. Even now, when these schools are much improved, when the buildings are new, all gleaming steel and glass, the food tolerable, the teachers well trained and well intentioned, even trained in child psychology—unfortunately the psychology of white children, which is different from ours—the shock to the child upon arrival is still tremendous. Some just seem to shrivel up, don't speak for days on end, and have an empty look in their eyes. I know of an eleven-year-old on another reservation who hanged herself, and in our school, while I was there, a girl jumped out of the window, trying to kill herself to escape an unbearable situation. That first shock is always there. . . .

The mission school at St. Francis was a curse for our family for generations. My grandmother went there, then my mother, then my sisters and I. At one time or other every one of us tried to run away. Grandma told me once about the bad times she had experienced at St. Francis. In those days they let students go home only for one week every year. Two days were used up for transportation, which meant spending just five days out of three hundred and sixty-five with her family. And that was an improvement. Before grandma's time, on many reservations they did not let the students go home at all until they had finished school. Anybody who disobeyed the nuns was severely punished. The building in which my grandmother stayed had three floors, for girls only. Way up in the attic were little cells, about five by five by ten feet. One time she was in church and instead of praying she was playing jacks. As punishment they took her to one of those little cubicles where she stayed in darkness because the windows had been boarded up. They left her there for a whole week with only bread and water for nourishment. After she came out she promptly ran away, together with three other girls. They were found and brought back. The nuns stripped them naked and whipped them. They used a horse buggy whip on my grandmother. Then she was put back into the attic—for two weeks.

My mother had much the same experiences but never wanted to talk about them, and then there I was, in the same place. The school is now run by the BIA—the Bureau of Indian Affairs—but only since about fifteen years ago. When I was there, during the 1960s, it was still run by the Church. The Jesuit fathers ran the boys' wing and the Sisters of the Sacred Heart ran us— with the help of the strap. Nothing had changed since my grandmother's days. I have been told recently that even in the '70s they were still beating children at that school. All I got out of school was being taught how to pray. I learned quickly that I would be beaten if I failed in my devotions or, God forbid, prayed the wrong way, especially prayed in Indian to Wakan Tanka, the Indian Creator.

The girls' wing was built like an F and was run like a penal institution. Every morning at five o'clock the sisters would come into our large dormitory to wake us up, and immediately we had to kneel down at the sides of our beds and recite the prayers. At six o'clock we were herded into the church for more of the same. I did not take kindly to the discipline and to marching by the clock, left-right, left-right. I was never one to like being forced to do something. I do something because I feel like doing it. I felt this way always, as far as I can remember, and my sister Barbara felt the same way. An old medicine man once told me: "Us Lakotas are not like dogs who can be trained, who can be beaten and keep on wagging their tails, licking the hand that whipped them. We are like cats, little cats, big cats, wildcats, bobcats, mountain lions. It doesn't matter what kind, but cats who can't be tamed, who scratch if you step on their tails." But I was only a kitten and my claws were still small.

Barbara was still in the school when I arrived and during my first year or two she could still protect me a little bit. When Barb was a seventh-grader she ran away together with five other girls, early in the morning before sunrise. They brought them back in the evening. The girls had to wait for two hours in front of the mother superior's office. They were hungry and cold, frozen through. It was wintertime and they had been running the whole day without food, trying to make good their escape. The mother superior asked each girl, "Would you do this again?" She told them that as punishment they would not be allowed to visit home for a month and that she'd keep them busy on work details until the skin on their knees and elbows had worn off. At the end of her speech she told each girl, "Get up from this chair and lean over it." She then lifted the girls' skirts and pulled down their underpants. Not little girls either, but teenagers. She had a leather strap about a foot long and four inches wide fastened to a stick, and beat the girls, one after another, until they cried. Barb did not give her that satisfaction but just clenched her teeth. There was one girl, Barb told me, the nun kept on beating and beating until her arm got tired.

I did not escape my share of the strap. Once, when I was thirteen years old, I refused to go to Mass. I did not want to go to church because I did not feel well. A nun grabbed me by the hair, dragged me upstairs, made me stoop over, pulled my dress up (we were not allowed at the time to wear jeans), pulled my panties down, and gave me what they called "swats"—twenty-five swats with a board around which Scotch tape had been wound. She hurt me badly.

My classroom was right next to the principal's office and almost every day I could hear him swatting the boys. Beating was the common punishment for not doing one's homework, or for being late to school. It had such a bad effect upon me that I hated and mistrusted every white person on sight, because I met only one kind. It was not until much later that I met sincere white people I could relate to and be friends with. Racism breeds racism in reverse.

The routine at St. Francis was dreary. Six A.M., kneeling in church for an hour or so; seven o'clock, breakfast, eight o'clock, scrub the floor, peel spuds, make classes. We had to mop the dining room twice every day and scrub the tables. If you were caught taking a rest, doodling on the bench with a fingernail or knife, or just rapping, the nun would come up with a dish towel and just slap it across your face, saying, "You're not supposed to be talking, you're supposed to be working!" Monday mornings we had cornmeal mush, Tuesday oatmeal, Wednesday rice and raisins, Thursday cornflakes, and Friday all the leftovers mixed together or sometimes fish. Frequently the food had bugs or rocks in it. We were eating hot dogs that were weeks old, while the nuns were dining on ham, whipped potatoes, sweet peas, and cranberry sauce. In winter our dorm was icy cold while the nuns' rooms were always warm.

I have seen little girls arrive at the school, first-graders, just fresh from home and totally unprepared for what awaited them, little girls with pretty braids, and the first thing the nuns did was chop their hair off and tie up what was left behind their ears. Next they would dump the children into tubs of alcohol, a sort of rubbing alcohol, "to get the germs off." Many of the nuns were German immigrants, some from Bavaria, so that we sometimes speculated whether Bavaria was some sort of Dracula country inhabited by monsters. For the sake of objectivity I ought to mention that two of the German fathers were great linguists and that the only Lakota-English diction- aries and grammars which are worth anything were put together by them.

At night some of the girls would huddle in bed together for comfort and   10
reassurance. Then the nun in charge of the dorm would come in and say, "What are the two of you doing in bed together? I smell evil in this room. You girls are evil incarnate. You are sinning. You are going to hell and burn forever. You can act that way in the devil's frying pan." She would get them out of bed in the middle of the night, making them kneel and pray until morning. We had not the slightest idea what it was all about. At home we slept two and three in a bed for animal warmth and a feeling of security.

The nuns and the girls in the two top grades were constantly battling it out physically with fists, nails, and hair-pulling. I myself was growing from a kitten into an undersized cat. My claws were getting bigger and were itching for action. About 1969 or 1970 a strange young white girl appeared on the reservation. She looked about eighteen or twenty years old. She was pretty and had long, blond hair down to her waist, patched jeans, boots, and a backpack. She was different from any other white person we had met before. I think her name was Wise. I do not know how she managed to over- come our reluctance and distrust, getting us into a corner, making us listen to her, asking us how we were treated. She told us that she was from New York. She was the first real hippie or Yippie we had come across. She told us of people called the Black Panthers, Young Lords, and Weathermen. She said, "Black people are getting it on. Indians are getting it on in St. Paul and California. How about you?" She also said, "Why don't you put out an underground paper, mimeograph it. It's easy. Tell it like it is. Let it all hang out." She spoke a strange lingo but we caught on fast.

Charlene Left Hand Bull and Gina One Star were two full-blood girls I used to hang out with. We did everything together. They were willing to join me in a Sioux uprising. We put together a newspaper which we called the *Red Panther*. In it we wrote how bad the school was, what kind of slop we had to eat—slimy, rotten, blackened potatoes for two weeks—the way we were beaten. I think I was the one who wrote the worst article about our principal of the moment, Father Keeler. I put all my anger and venom into it. I called him a goddam wasicun son of a bitch. I wrote that he knew nothing about Indians and should go back to where he came from, teaching white children whom he could relate to. I wrote that we knew which priests slept with which nuns and that all they ever could think about was filling their bellies and buying a new car. It was the kind of writing which foamed at the mouth, but which also lifted a great deal of weight from one's soul.

On Saint Patrick's Day, when everybody was at the big powwow, we distributed our newspapers. We put them on windshields and bulletin boards, in desks and pews, in dorms and toilets. But someone saw us and snitched on us. The shit hit the fan. The three of us were taken before a board meeting. Our parents, in my case my mother, had to come. They were told that ours was a most serious matter, the worst thing that had ever happened in the school's long history. One of the nuns told my mother, "Your daughter really needs to be talked to." "What's wrong with my daughter?" my mother asked. She was given one of our *Red Panther* newspapers. The nun pointed out its name to her and then my piece, waiting for mom's reaction. After a while she asked, "Well, what have you got to say to this? What do you think?"

My mother said, "Well, when I went to school here, some years back, I was treated a lot worse then these kids are. I really can't see how they can have any complaints, because we was treated a lot stricter. We could not even wear skirts halfway up our knees. These girls have it made. But you should forgive them because they are young. And it's supposed to be a free country, free speech and all that. I don't believe what they done is wrong." So all I got out of it was scrubbing six flights of stairs on my hands and knees, every day. And no boy-side privileges.

The boys and girls were still pretty much separated. The only time one could meet a member of the opposite sex was during free time, between four and five-thirty, in the study hall or on benches or the volleyball court outside, and that was strictly supervised. One day Charlene and I went over to the boys' side. We were on the ball team and they had to let us practice. We played three extra minutes, only three minutes more than we were supposed to. Here was the nuns' opportunity for revenge. We got twenty-five swats. I told Charlene, "We are getting too old to have our bare asses whipped that way. We are old enough to have babies. Enough of this shit. Next time we fight back." Charlene only said, "Hoka-hay!"

We had to take showers every evening. One little girl did not want to take her panties off and one of the nuns told her, "You take those underpants off—or else!" But the child was ashamed to do it. The nun was getting her swat to threaten the girl. I went up to the sister, pushed her veil off, and knocked her down. I told her that if she wanted to hit a little girl she should pick on me, pick one her own size. She got herself transferred out of the dorm a week later.

15

In a school like this there is always a lot of favoritism. At St. Francis it was strongly tinged with racism. Girls who were near-white, who came from what the nuns called "nice families," got preferential treatment. They waited on the faculty and got to eat ham or eggs and bacon in the morning. They got the easy jobs while the skins, who did not have the right kind of background—myself among them—always wound up in the laundry room sorting out ten bushel baskets of dirty boys' socks every day. Or we wound up scrubbing the floors and doing all the dishes. The school therefore fostered fights and antagonism between whites and breeds, and between breeds and skins. At one time Charlene and I had to iron all the robes and vestments the priests wore when saying Mass. We had to fold them up and put them into a chest in the back of the church. In a corner, looking over our shoulders, was a statue of the crucified Savior, all bloody and beaten up. Charlene looked up and said, "Look at that poor Indian. The pigs sure worked him over." That was the closest I ever came to seeing Jesus.

I was held up as a bad example and didn't mind. I was old enough to have a boyfriend and promptly got one. At the school we had an hour and a half for ourselves. Between the boys' and the girls' wings were some benches where one could sit. My boyfriend and I used to go there just to hold hands and talk. The nuns were very uptight about any boy–girl stuff. They had an exaggerated fear of anything having even the faintest connection with sex. One day in religion class, an all-girl class, Sister Bernard singled me out for some remarks, pointing me out as a bad example, an example that should be shown. She said that I was too free with my body. That I was holding hands which meant that I was not a good example to follow. She also said that I wore unchaste dresses, skirts which were too short, too suggestive, shorter than regulations permitted, and for that I would be punished. She dressed me down before the whole class, carrying on and on about my unchastity.

I stood up and told her, "You shouldn't say any of those things, miss. You people are a lot worse than us Indians. I know all about you, because my grand mother and my aunt told me about you. Maybe twelve, thirteen years ago you had a water stoppage here in St. Francis. No water could get through the pipes. There are water lines right under the mission, underground tunnels and passages where in my grandmother's time only the nuns and priests could go, which were off-limits to everybody else. When the water backed up they had to go through all the water lines and clean them out. And in those huge pipes they found the bodies of newborn babies. And they were white babies. They weren't Indian babies. At least when our girls have babies, they don't do away with them that way, like flushing them down the toilet, almost.

"And that priest they sent here from Holy Rosary in Pine Ridge because he molested a little girl. You couldn't think of anything better than dump him on us. All he does is watch young women and girls with that funny smile on his face. Why don't you point him out for an example?" 20

Charlene and I worked on the school newspaper. After all we had some practice. Every day we went down to Publications. One of the priests acted as the photographer, doing the enlarging and developing. He smelled of chemicals which had stained his hands yellow. One day he invited Charlene into the dark-room. He was going to teach her developing. She was developed already. She was a big girl compared to him, taller too. Charlene was nicely built, not fat, just rounded. No sharp edges anywhere: All of a sudden she rushed out of the darkroom, yelling to me, "Let's get out of here! He's trying to feel me up. That priest is nasty." So there was this too to contend with—sexual harassment. We complained to the student body. The nuns said we just had a dirty mind.

We got a new priest in English. During one of his first classes he asked one of the boys a certain question. The boy was shy. He spoke poor English, but he had the right answer. The priest told him, "You did not say it right. Correct yourself. Say it over again." The boy got flustered and stammered. He could hardly get out a word. But the priest kept after him: "Didn't you hear? I told you to do the whole thing over. Get it right this time." He kept on and on.

I stood up and said, "Father, don't be doing that. If you go into an Indian's home and try to talk Indian, they might laugh at you and say. 'Do it over correctly. Get it right this time!'"

He shouted at me, "Mary, you stay after class. Sit down right now!"

I stayed after class, until after the bell. He told me, "Get over here!"   25

He grabbed me by the arm, pushing me against the blackboard, shouting. "Why are you always mocking us? You have no reason to do this."

I said, "Sure I do. You were making fun of him. You embarrassed him. He needs strengthening, not weakening. You hurt him, I did not hurt you."

He twisted my arm and pushed real hard. I turned around and hit him in the face, giving him a bloody nose. After that I ran out of the room, slam-ming the door behind me. He and I went to Sister Bernard's office. I told her, "Today I quit school. I'm not taking any more of this, none of this shit any-more. None of this treatment. Better give me my diploma. I can't waste any more time on you people."

Sister Bernard looked at me for a long, long time. She said, "All right, Mary Ellen, go home today. Come back in a few days and get your diploma." And that was that. Oddly enough, that priest turned out okay. He taught a class in grammar, orthography, composition, things like that. I think he wanted more respect in class. He was still young and unsure of himself. But I was in there too long. I didn't feel like hearing it. Later he became a good friend of the Indians, a personal friend of myself and my husband. He stood up for us during Wounded Knee[1] and after. He stood up to his superiors, stuck his neck way out, became a real people's priest. He even learned our language. He died prematurely of cancer. It is not only the good Indians who die young, but the good whites, too. It is the timid ones who know how to

---

[1] *Wounded Knee:* Originally, a battle that took place in 1890 between Sioux Indians and U.S. troops. The author refers to the 1973 uprising of the Lakota Indians against the Federal Bureau Investigation in South Dakota at the same location.

take care of themselves who grow old. I am still grateful to that priest for what he did for us later and for the quarrel he picked with me—or did I pick it with him?—because it ended a situation which had become unendurable for me. The day of my fight with him was my last day in school.

Questions for Discussion and Writing

1. How does the way the government operated the boarding school suggest what is meant by "civilizing" Native Americans?
2. How did the experiences of Mary Crow Dog's mother and grandmother add a historical dimension to her account?
3. How did Mary Crow Dog react to the experiences to which she was subjected? Why was the incident of the underground newspaper so crucial?
4. **Rhetorical inquiry:** How does the quote with which she prefaces her essay explain the objectives of government-run schools such as the one she attended?

JUDY BLUME

Judy Blume (b. 1938), a writer of juvenile and adult fiction, has often been in the position she discusses—that of having her books for children censored, including Are You There God? It's Me, Margaret *(1970),* Blubber *(1974), and* Tiger Eyes *(1981). She is also the editor of* Places I Never Meant to Be: Original Stories by Censored Writers *(1999). Blume's recent works include* Double Fudge *(2002), a continuation of her very popular series and* Are You There God? It's Me, Margaret *(2004). This editorial, which first appeared in the* New York Times *on October 22, 1999, defends the phenomenally successful Harry Potter series against those who wish to ban it from school libraries.*

Before You Read

What guidelines should public libraries follow in deciding what books to ban?

Is Harry Potter Evil?

I happened to be in London last summer on the very day *Harry Potter and the Prisoner of Azkaban*, the third book in the wildly popular series by J. K. Rowling, was published. I couldn't believe my good fortune. I rushed to the bookstore to buy a copy, knowing this simple act would put me up there with the best grandmas in the world. The book was still months away from publication in the United States, and I have an 8-year-old grandson who is a big Harry Potter fan.

It's a good thing when children enjoy books, isn't it? Most of us think so. But like many children's books these days, the Harry Potter series has recently come under fire. In Minnesota, Michigan, New York, California and South Carolina, parents who feel the books promote interest in the occult have called for their removal from classrooms and school libraries.

I knew this was coming. The only surprise is that it took so long—as long as it took for the zealots who claim they're protecting children from evil (and evil can be found lurking everywhere these days) to discover that children actually like these books. If children are excited about a book, it must be suspect.

I'm not exactly unfamiliar with this line of thinking, having had various books of mine banned from schools over the last 20 years. In my books, it's reality that's seen as corrupting. With Harry Potter, the perceived danger is fantasy. After all, Harry and his classmates attend the celebrated Hogwarts School of Witchcraft and Wizardry. According to certain adults, these stories teach witchcraft, sorcery, and satanism. But hey, if it's not one "ism," it's another. I mean Madeleine L'Engle's *A Wrinkle in Time* has been targeted by censors for promoting New Ageism, and Mark Twain's *Adventures of Huckleberry Finn* for promoting racism. Gee, where does that leave the kids?

The real danger is not in the books, but in laughing off those who would ban them. The protests against Harry Potter follow a tradition that has been growing since the early 1980s and often leaves school principals trembling with fear that is then passed down to teachers and librarians.   5

What began with the religious right has spread to the politically correct. (Remember the uproar in Brooklyn last year when a teacher was criticized for reading a book entitled *Nappy Hair* to her class?) And now the gate is open so wide that some parents believe they have the right to demand immediate removal of any book for any reason from school or classroom libraries. The list of gifted teachers and librarians who find their jobs in jeopardy for defending their students' right to read, to imagine, to question, grows every year.

My grandson was bewildered when I tried to explain why some adults don't want their children reading about Harry Potter. "But that doesn't make any sense!" he said. J. K. Rowling is on a book tour in America right now. She's probably befuddled by the brouhaha, too. After all, she was just trying to tell a good story.

My husband and I like to reminisce about how, when we were 9, we read straight through L. Frank Baum's Oz series, books filled with wizards and witches. And you know what those subversive tales taught us? That we loved to read! In those days I used to dream of flying. I may have been small and powerless in real life, but in my imagination I was able to soar.

At the rate we're going, I can imagine next year's headline: "'Goodnight Moon'[1] Banned for Encouraging Children to Communicate With Furniture." And we all know where that can lead, don't we?

---

[1] *Goodnight Moon:* A classic work in children's literature by Margaret Wise Brown, with illustrations by Clement Hurd; first published in 1947.

Questions for Discussion and Writing

1. Why is Blume alarmed by the growing trend of parents petitioning school libraries to remove children's books from their shelves? How does she characterize those who want books (such as the Harry Potter series) to be banned because of fantasy elements that "teach" witchcraft, sorcery, and satanism?
2. How does Blume structure her editorial to stress the growing nature of this trend and its apparent indiscriminate hysteria? What tools (such as mockery) does she use to make her case?
3. For Blume, the issue is whether parents have the right to demand that schools censor their children's reading materials. In your opinion, do they, and if so, how should they exercise this right? There are numerous Web sites devoted to the Harry Potter censorship controversy. Check one of these and compare its statements with your own views.
4. **Rhetorical inquiry:** Why does Blume include a reaction from her eight-year-old grandson on the question of why anyone would want to ban Harry Potter books?

MARK SALZMAN

Mark Salzman graduated Phi Beta Kappa, summa cum laude, from Yale in 1982 with a degree in Chinese language and literature. From 1982 to 1984, he lived in Chang-sha, Hunan, in the People's Republic of China, where he taught English at Hunan Medical College. There he studied with Pan Qingfu, one of China's greatest traditional boxers. Iron and Silk *(1986) recounts his adventures and provides a fascinating behind-the-scenes glimpse into the workings of Chinese society. "Lessons," drawn from this book, describes the extraordinary opportunity that studying martial arts with Pan Qingfu offered, along with the comic misunderstandings produced by their being from such different cultures. His recent work includes* Lost in Place: Growing Up Absurd in Suburbia *(1995) and* True Notebooks *(2003).*

Before You Read

Have you ever trained to develop a skill?

Lessons

I was to meet Pan at the training hall four nights a week, to receive private instruction after the athletes finished their evening workout. Waving and wishing me good night, they politely filed out and closed the wooden doors, leaving Pan and me alone in the room. First he explained that I must start from scratch. He meant it, too, for beginning that night, and for many nights thereafter, I learned how to stand at attention. He stood inches away from me and screamed, "Stand straight!" then bored into me with his terrifying gaze. He insisted that I maintain eye contact for as long as he stood in front of me, and that I meet his gaze with one of equal intensity. After as long as a minute of this silent torture, he would shout "At ease!" and I could relax a bit, but not smile or take my eyes away from his. We repeated this exercise countless times, and I was expected to practice it four to six hours a day. At the time, I wondered what those staring contests had to do with wushu,[1] but I came to realize that everything he was to teach me later was really contained in those first few weeks when we stared at each other. His art drew strength from his eyes; this was his way of passing it on.

After several weeks I came to enjoy staring at him. I would break into a sweat and feel a kind of heat rushing up through the floor into my legs and up into my brain. He told me that when standing like that, I must at all times be prepared to duel, that at any moment he might attack, and I should be ready to defend myself. It exhilarated me to face off with him, to feel his power and taste the fear and anticipation of the blow. Days and weeks passed, but the blow did not come.

One night he broke the lesson off early, telling me that tonight was special. I followed him out of the training hall, and we bicycled a short distance to his apartment. He lived with his wife and two sons on the fifth floor of a large, anonymous cement building. Like all the urban housing going up in China today, the building was indistinguishable from its neighbors, mercilessly practical and depressing in appearance. Pan's apartment had three rooms and a small kitchen. A private bathroom and painted, as opposed to raw, cement walls in all the rooms identified it as the home of an important family. The only decoration in the apartment consisted of some silk banners, awards and photographs from Pan's years as the national wushu champion and from the set of *Shaolin Temple*. Pan's wife, a doctor, greeted me with all sorts of homemade snacks and sat me down at a table set for two. Pan sat across from me and poured two glasses of baijiu. He called to his sons, both in their teens, and they appeared from the bed-room instantly. They stood in complete silence until Pan asked them to greet me, which they did, very politely, but so softly I could barely hear them. They were handsome boys, and the elder, at about fourteen, was taller than me and had a moustache. I tried asking them questions to put them at ease, but they answered only by nodding. They apparently had no idea how to behave toward something like me and did not want to make any mistakes in front of their father. Pan told them to say good night, and they, along with his wife, disappeared into the bedroom. Pan raised his glass and proposed that the evening begin.

---

[1] Wushu, or kung fu.

He told me stories that made my hair stand on end, with such gusto that I thought the building would shake apart. When he came to the parts where he vanquished his enemies, he brought his terrible hand down on the table or against the wall with a crash, sending our snacks jumping out of their serving bowls. His imitations of cowards and bullies were so funny I could hardly breathe for laughing. He had me spellbound for three solid hours; then his wife came in to see if we needed any more food or baijiu. I took the opportunity to ask her if she had ever been afraid for her husband's safety when, for example, he went off alone to bust up a gang of hoodlums in Shenyang. She laughed and touched his right hand. "Sometimes I figured he'd be late for dinner." A look of tremendous satisfaction came over Pan's face, and he got up to use the bathroom. She sat down in his chair and looked at me. "Every day he receives tens of letters from all over China, all from people asking to become his student. Since he made the movie, it's been almost impossible for him to go out during the day." She refilled our cups, then looked at me again. "He has trained professionals for more than twenty-five years now, but in all that time he has accepted only one private student." After a long pause, she gestured at me with her chin. "You." Just then Pan came back into the room, returned to his seat and started a new story. This one was about a spear.

While still a young man training for the national wushu competition, Pan overheard a debate among some of his fellow athletes about the credibility of an old story. The story described a famous warrior as being able to execute a thousand spear-thrusts without stopping to rest. Some of the athletes felt this to be impossible: after fifty, one's shoulders ache, and by one hundred the skin on the left hand, which guides the spear as the right hand thrusts, twists and returns it, begins to blister. Pan had argued that surely this particular warrior would not have been intimidated by aching shoulders and blisters, and soon a challenge was raised. The next day Pan went out into a field with a spear, and as the other athletes watched, executed one thousand and seven thrusts without stopping to rest. Certain details of the story as Pan told it—that the bones of his left hand were exposed, and so forth—might be called into question, but the number of thrusts I am sure is accurate, and the scar tissue on his left palm indicates that it was not easy for him.

One evening later in the year, when I felt discouraged with my progress in a form of Northern Shaolin boxing called "Changquan," or "Long Fist," I asked Pan if he thought I should discontinue the training. He frowned, the only time he ever seemed genuinely angry with me, and said quietly, "When I say I will do something, I do it, exactly as I said I would. In my whole life, I have never started something without finishing it. I said that in the time we have, I would make your wushu better than you could imagine, and I will. Your only responsibility to me is to practice and to learn. My responsibility to you is much greater! Every time you think your task is great, think how much greater mine is. Just keep this in mind: if you fail"—here he paused to make sure I understood—"I will lose face."

Though my responsibility to him was merely to practice and to learn, he had one request that he vigorously encouraged me to fulfill—to teach him English. I felt relieved to have something to offer him, so I quickly prepared some beginning materials and rode over to his house for the first lesson. When I got there, he had a tape recorder set up on a small table, along with a pile of oversized paper and a few felt-tip pens from a coloring set. He showed no interest at all in my books, but sat me down next to the recorder and pointed at the pile of paper. On each sheet he had written out in Chinese dozens of phrases, such as "We'll need a spotlight over there," "These mats aren't springy enough," and "Don't worry— it's just a shoulder dislocation." He asked me to write down the English translation next to each phrase, which took a little over two and a half hours. When I was finished, I asked him if he could read my handwriting, and he smiled, saying that he was sure my handwriting was fine. After a series of delicate questions, I determined that he was as yet unfamiliar with the alphabet, so I encouraged him to have a look at my beginning materials. "That's too slow for me," he said. He asked me to repeat each of the phrases I'd written down five times into the recorder, leaving enough time after each repetition for him to say it aloud after me. "The first time should be very slow—one word at a time, with a pause after each word so I can repeat it. The second time should be the same. The third time you should pause after every other word. The fourth time read it through slowly. The fifth time you can read it fast." I looked at the pile of phrase sheets, calculated how much time this would take, and asked if we could do half today and half tomorrow, as dinner was only three hours away. "Don't worry!" he said, beaming. "I've prepared some food for you here. Just tell me when you get hungry." He sat next to me turned on the machine, then turned it off again. "How do you say, 'And now, Mark will teach me English'?" I told him how and he repeated it, at first slowly, then more quickly, twenty or twenty-one times. He turned the machine on. "And now, Mark will teach me English." I read the first phrase, five times as he had requested, and he pushed a little note across the table. "Better read it six times," it read, "and a little slower."

After several weeks during which we nearly exhausted the phrasal possibilities of our two languages, Pan announced that the time had come to do something new. "Now I want to learn routines." I didn't understand. "Routines?" "Yes. Everything, including language, is like wushu. First you learn the basic moves, or words, then you string them together into routines." He produced from his bedroom a huge sheet of paper made up of smaller pieces taped together. He wanted me to write a story on it. The story he had in mind was a famous Chinese folk tale, "How Yu Gong Moved the Mountain." The story tells of an old man who realized that, if he only had fields where a mountain stood instead, he would have enough arable land to support his family comfortably. So he went out to the mountain with a shovel and a bucket and started to take the mountain down. All his neighbors made fun of him, calling it an impossible task, but Yu Gong disagreed: it would just take a long time, and after several tens of generations had passed, the mountain would at last become a field and his family would live comfortably. Pan had me write this story in big letters, so that he could paste it up on his bedroom wall, listen to the tape I was to make and read along as he lay in bed.

Not only did I repeat this story into the tape recorder several dozen times—at first one word at a time, and so on—but Pan invited Bill, Bob and Marcy over for dinner one night and had them read it a few times for variety. After they had finished, Pan said that he would like to recite a few phrases for them to evaluate and correct. He chose some of his favorite sentences and repeated each seven or eight times without a pause. He belted them out with such fierce concentration we were all afraid to move lest it disturb him. At last he finished and looked at me, asking quietly if it was all right. I nodded and he seemed overcome with relief. He smiled, pointed at me and said to my friends, "I was very nervous just then. I didn't want him to lose face."

While Pan struggled to recite English routines from memory, he began   10
teaching me how to use traditional weapons. He would teach me a single move, then have me practice it in front of him until I could do it ten times in a row without a mistake. He always stood about five feet away from me, with his arms folded, grinding his teeth, and the only time he took his eyes off me was to blink. One night in the late spring I was having a particularly hard time learning a move with the staff. I was sweating heavily and my right hand was bleeding, so the staff had become slippery and hard to control. Several of the athletes stayed on after their workout to watch and to enjoy the breeze that sometimes passed through the training hall. Pan stopped me and indicated that I wasn't working hard enough. "Imagine," he said, "that you are participating in the national competition, and those athletes are your competitors. Look as if you know what you are doing! Frighten them with your strength and confidence." I mustered all the confidence I could, under the circumstances, and flung myself into the move. I lost control of the staff, and it whirled straight into my forehead.

As if in a dream, the floor raised up several feet to support my behind, and I sat staring up at Pan while blood ran down across my nose and a fleshy knob grew between my eyebrows. The athletes sprang forward to help me up. They seemed nervous, never having had a foreigner knock himself out in their training hall before, but Pan, after asking if I felt all right, seemed positively inspired. "Sweating and bleeding. Good."

Every once in a while, Pan felt it necessary to give his students something to think about, to spur them on to greater efforts. During one morning workout two women practiced a combat routine, one armed with a spear, the other with a *dadao*, or halberd. The dadao stands about six feet high and consists of a broadsword attached to a thick wooden pole, with an angry-looking spike at the far end. It is heavy and difficult to wield even for a strong man, so it surprised me to see this young woman, who could not weigh more than one hundred pounds, using it so effectively. At one point in their battle the woman with the dadao swept it toward the other woman's feet, as if to cut them off, but the other woman jumped up in time to avoid the blow. The first woman, without letting the blade of the dadao stop, brought it around in another sweep, as if to cut the other woman in half at the waist. The other woman, without an instant to spare, bent straight from the hips so that the dadao slashed over her back and head, barely an inch away. This combination was to be repeated three times in rapid succession before moving on to the next exchange. The women practiced this move several times, none of which satisfied Pan. "Too slow, and the weapon is too far away from her. It should graze her back as it goes by." They tried again, but still Pan growled angrily. Suddenly he got up and took the dadao from the first woman. The entire training hall went silent and still. Without warming up at all, Pan ordered the woman with the spear to get ready, and to move fast when the time came. His body looked as though electricity had suddenly passed through it, and the huge blade flashed toward her. Once, twice the dadao flew beneath her feet, then swung around in a terrible arc and rode her back with flawless precision. The third time he added a little twist at the end, so that the blade grazed up her neck and sent a little decoration stuck in her pigtails flying across the room.

I had to sit down for a moment to ponder the difficulty of sending an object roughly the shape of an oversized shovel, only heavier, across a girl's back and through her pigtails, without guide ropes or even a safety helmet. Not long before, I had spoken with a former troupe member who, when practicing with this instrument, had suddenly found himself on his knees. The blade, unsharpened, had twirled a bit too close to him and passed through his Achilles' tendon without a sound. Pan handed the dadao back to the woman and walked over to me. "What if you had made a mistake?" I asked. "I never make mistakes," he said, without looking at me.

Questions for Discussion and Writing

1. What evidence can you cite to show that Pan applies the same standards to Mark that he does to himself?
2. What is the relevance of the Chinese folk tale "How Yu Gong Moved the Mountain" to Salzman's apprenticeship?
3. In your opinion, who learns more from the other, Pan from Mark or Mark from Pan and why?
4. **Rhetorical inquiry:** How does the anecdote with which Salzman concludes his narrative embody every important aspect of Pan's personality and show why he is held in such high esteem?

How does this photo of a student practicing Wushu at the Shi Cha Hai boarding sports school in Beijing enhance Mark Salzman's description of the demanding nature of his lessons with Pan?

Fiction

EDWARD P. JONES

Edward P. Jones (b.1950) grew up in Washington, D. C. and was educated at the College of the Holy Cross in Worcester, Massachusetts and studied writing at the University of Virginia. His fiction has been widely acclaimed and includes Lost in the City *(1992), from which the following story is reprinted. He also has written a novel* The Known World *(2003) that won the National Book Critics Circle Award and the 2004 Pulitzer Prize for Fiction.*

Before You Read

Can you remember your first day at school? What was it like?

The First Day

In an otherwise unremarkable September morning, long before I learned to be ashamed of my mother, she takes my hand and we set off down New Jersey

Avenue to begin my very first day of school. I am wearing a checkeredlike blue-and-green cotton dress, and scattered about these colors are bits of yellow and white and brown. My mother has uncharacteristically spent nearly an hour on my hair that morning, plaiting and replaiting so that now my scalp tingles. Whenever I turn my head quickly, my nose fills with the faint smell of Dixie Peach hair grease. The smell is somehow a soothing one now and I will reach for it time and time again before the morning ends. All the plaits, each with a blue barrette near the tip and each twisted into an uncommon sturdiness, will last until I go to bed that night, something that has never happened before. My stomach is full of milk and oatmeal sweetened with brown sugar. Like everything else I have on, my pale green slip and underwear are new, the underwear having come three to a plastic package with a little girl on the front who appears to be dancing. Behind my ears, my mother, to stop my whining, has dabbed the stingiest bit of her gardenia perfume, the last present my father gave her before he disappeared into memory. Because I cannot smell it, I have only her word that the perfume is there. I am also wearing yellow socks trimmed with thin lines of black and white around the tops. My shoes are my greatest joy, black patent-leather miracles, and when one is nicked at the toe later that morning in class, my heart will break.

I am carrying a pencil, a pencil sharpener, and a small ten-cent tablet with a black-and-white speckled cover. My mother does not believe that a girl in kindergarten needs such things, so I am taking them only because of my insistent whining and because they are presents from our neighbors, Mary Keith and Blondelle Harris. Miss Mary and Miss Blondelle are watching my two younger sisters until my mother returns. The women are as precious to me as my mother and sisters. Out playing one day, I have overheard an older child, speaking to another child, call Miss Mary and Miss Blondelle a word that is brand new to me. This is my mother: When I say the word in fun to one of my sisters, my mother slaps me across the mouth and the word is lost for years and years.

All the way down New Jersey Avenue, the sidewalks are teeming with children. In my neighborhood, I have many friends, but I see none of them as my mother and I walk. We cross New York Avenue, we cross Pierce Street, and we cross L and K, and still I see no one who knows my name. At I Street, between New Jersey Avenue and Third Street, we enter Seaton Elementary School, a timeworn, sad-faced building across the street from my mother's church, Mt. Carmel Baptist.

Just inside the front door, women out of the advertisements in *Ebony* are greeting other parents and children. The woman who greets us has pearls thick as jumbo marbles that come down almost to her navel, and she acts as if she had known me all my life, touching my shoulder, cupping her hand under my chin. She is enveloped in a perfume that I only know is not gardenia. When, in answer to her question, my mother tells her that we live at 1227 New Jersey Avenue, the woman first seems to be picturing in her head where we live. Then she shakes her head and says that we are at the wrong school, that we should be at Walker-Jones.

My mother shakes her head vigorously. "I want her to go here," my mother says. "If I'da wanted her someplace else, I'da took her there." The woman continues to act as if she has known me all my life, but she tells my mother that we live beyond the area that Seaton serves. My mother is not convinced and for several more minutes she questions the woman about why I cannot attend Seaton. For as many Sundays as I can remember, perhaps even Sundays when I was in her womb, my mother has pointed across I Street to Seaton as we come and go to Mt. Carmel. "You gonna go there and learn about the whole world." But one of the guardians of that place is saying no, and no again. I am learning this about my mother: The higher up on the scale of respectability a person is—and teachers are rather high up in her eyes—the less she is liable to let them push her around. But finally, I see in her eyes the closing gate, and she takes my hand and we leave the building. On the steps, she stops as people move past us on either side.

"Mama, I can't go to school?"

She says nothing at first, then takes my hand again and we are down the steps quickly and nearing New Jersey Avenue before I can blink. This is my mother: She says, "One monkey don't stop no show."

Walker-Jones is a larger, newer school and I immediately like it because of that. But it is not across the street from my mother's church, her rock, one of her connections to God, and I sense her doubts as she absently rubs her thumb over the back of her hand. We find our way to the crowded auditorium where gray metal chairs are set up in the middle of the room. Along the wall to the left are tables and other chairs. Every chair seems occupied by a child or adult. Somewhere in the room a child is crying, a cry that rises above the buzz-talk of so many people. Strewn about the floor are dozens and dozens of pieces of white paper, and people are walking over them without any thought of picking them up. And seeing this lack of concern, I am all of a sudden afraid.

"Is this where they register for school?" my mother asks a woman at one of the tables.

The woman looks up slowly as if she has heard this question once too often. She nods. She is tiny, almost as small as the girl standing beside her. The woman's hair is set in a mass of curlers and all of those curlers are made of paper money, here a dollar bill, there a five-dollar bill. The girl's hair is arrayed in curls, but some of them are beginning to droop and this makes me happy. On the table beside the woman's pocketbook is a large notebook, worthy of someone in high school, and looking at me looking at the notebook, the girl places her hand possessively on it. In her other hand she holds several pencils with thick crowns of additional erasers.

"These the forms you gotta use?" my mother asks the woman, picking up a few pieces of the paper from the table. "Is this what you have to fill out?"

The woman tells her yes, but that she need fill out only one.

"I see," my mother says, looking about the room. Then: "Would you help me with this form? That is, if you don't mind."

The woman asks my mother what she means.

"This form. Would you mind helpin me fill it out?"   15
The woman still seems not to understand.

"I can't read it. I don't know how to read or write, and I'm asking you to help me." My mother looks at me, then looks away. I know almost all of her looks, but this one is brand new to me. "Would you help me, then?"

The woman says Why sure, and suddenly she appears happier, so much more satisfied with everything. She finishes the form for her daughter and my mother and I step aside to wait for her. We find two chairs nearby and sit. My mother is now diseased, according to the girl's eyes, and until the moment her mother takes her and the form to the front of the auditorium, the girl never stops looking at my mother. I stare back at her. "Don't stare," my mother says to me. "You know better than that."

Another woman out of the *Ebony* ads takes the woman's child away. Now, the woman says upon returning, let's see what we can do for you two.

My mother answers the questions the woman reads off the form. They   20
start with my last name, and then on to the first and middle names. This is school, I think. This is going to school. My mother slowly enunciates each word of my name. This is my mother: As the questions go on, she takes from her pocketbook document after document, as if they will support my right to attend school, as if she has been saving them up for just this moment. Indeed, she takes out more papers than I have ever seen her do in other places: my birth certificate, my baptismal record, a doctor's letter concerning my bout with chicken pox, rent receipts, records of immunization, a letter about our public assistance payments, even her marriage license—every single paper that has anything even remotely to do with my five-year-old life. Few of the papers are needed here, but it does not matter and my mother continues to pull out the documents with the purposefulness of a magician pulling out a long string of scarves. She has learned that money is the beginning and end of everything in this world, and when the woman finishes, my mother offers her fifty cents, and the woman accepts it without hesitation. My mother and I are just about the last parent and child in the room.

My mother presents the form to a woman sitting in front of the stage, and the woman looks at it and writes something on a white card, which she gives to my mother. Before long, the woman who has taken the girl with the drooping curls appears from behind us, speaks to the sitting woman, and introduces herself to my mother and me. She's to be my teacher, she tells my mother. My mother stares.

We go into the hall, where my mother kneels down to me. Her lips are quivering. "I'll be back to pick you up at twelve o'clock. I don't want you to go nowhere. You just wait right here. And listen to every word she say." I touch her lips and press them together. It is an old, old game between us. She puts my hand down at my side, which is not part of the game. She stands and looks a second at the teacher, then she turns and walks away. I see where she has darned one of her socks the night before. Her shoes make loud sounds in the hall. She passes through the doors and I can still hear the loud sounds of her shoes. And even when the teacher turns me toward the classrooms and I hear what must be the singing and talking of all the children in the world, I can still hear my mother's footsteps above it all.

Questions for Discussion and Writing

1. What chain of events leads to the narrator's enrollment in the Walker-Jones Elementary School?
2. When does the narrator learn that her mother is illiterate? Does this make her more or less sympathetic toward her mother?
3. Why are children so sensitive about the way they think their parents are perceived by others?
4. **Rhetorical inquiry:** How does the final image counteract the narrator's initial statement about being ashamed of her mother?

Poetry

LINDA HOGAN

Linda Hogan, Chickasaw poet, novelist, and essayist, was born in 1947 in Denver, Colorado, and grew up in Oklahoma. She taught American Indian studies at the University of Minnesota from 1984–1991 and she is currently professor of American studies and American Indian studies at the University of Colorado. Her poetry has been collected in Seeing through the Sun *(1985), which received an American Book Award from the Before Columbus Foundation;* The Book of Medicines *(1993); and* Solar Storms *(1996). She has also published short stories, one of which, "Aunt Moon's Young Man," was featured in* Best American Short Stories *(1989). Her novel* Mean Spirit *was nominated for a Pulitzer Prize (1990). Hogan's latest works are* The Woman Who Watches over the World: A Native Memoir *(2001) and (with Brenda Peterson)* Sightings: The Gray Whale's Mysterious Journey *(2002). In "Workday" she uses the occasion of a bus ride she took when returning from working at the University of Colorado to explore the gap between Native Americans and her middle-class white coworkers.*

Before You Read

What gap in opportunities for education exists between Native Americans and those in mainstream society?

Workday

I go to work
though there are those who were missing today
from their homes.
I ride the bus
and I do not think of children without food   5
or how my sisters are chained to prison beds.

I go to the university
and out for lunch
and listen to the higher-ups
tell me all they have read   10
about Indians
and how to analyze this poem.
They know us
better than we know ourselves.

I ride the bus home   15
and sit behind the driver.
We talk about the weather
and not enough exercise.
I don't mention Victor Jara's[1] mutilated hands
or men next door   20
in exile
or my own family's grief over the lost child.

When I get off the bus
I look back at the light in the windows
and the heads bent   25
and how the women are all alone
in each seat
framed in the windows
and the men are coming home,
then I see them walking on the Avenue,   30
the beautiful feet,

the perfect legs
even with their spider veins,
the broken knees
with pins in them,   35
the thighs with their cravings,

---

[1] *Victor Jara:* Chilean folksinger and political activist (1932–1973) instrumental in the election of Salvador Allende. Jara was arrested, tortured, and beaten, his hands and wrists broken, before being machine-gunned to death after the coup by Augusto Pinochet.

the pelvis
and small back
with its soft down,
the shoulders which bend forward
and forward and forward
to protect the heart from pain.

40

Questions for Discussion and Writing

1. How does the poem raise the question of whether the speaker has irrevocably lost touch with her own people by working at a university where she is little more than a token Native American?
2. What kind of connection does the speaker feel with the Native American laborers on the bus?
3. What images express the speaker's grief at the psychological and physical costs for Native Americans trying to survive in contemporary American society?
4. **Rhetorical inquiry:** Does the fact that the speaker only converses with the bus driver on superficial subjects suggest she is alienated from both worlds?

Tom Wayman

Tom Wayman (b.1945) was born in Hawkesbury, Ontario, Canada. In 1959 his family moved to Vancouver, where he graduated from the University of British Columbia in 1966. He also received an M. F. A. in English from the University of California at Irvine. He has been a writer in residence at many universities, including University of Toronto, and currently teaches in Nelson, British Columbia. The following poem first appeared in Did I Miss Anything? Selected Poems *(1973–1993). His latest work is* My Father's Cup *(2002).*

Before You Read

Did you ever miss a class you wish you had attended?

Did I Miss Anything?

Question frequently asked by
students after missing a class

Nothing. When we realized you weren't here
we sat with our hands folded on our desks
in silence, for the full two hours

Everything. I gave an exam worth
40 per cent of the grade for this term
and assigned some reading due today
on which I'm about to hand out a quiz
worth 50 per cent

Nothing. None of the content of this course
has value or meaning
Take as many days off as you like:
any activities we undertake as a class
I assure you will not matter either to you or me
and are without purpose

Everything. A few minutes after we began last time
a shaft of light descended and an angel
or other heavenly being appeared
and revealed to us what each woman or man must do
to attain divine wisdom in this life and
the hereafter
This is the last time the class will meet
before we disperse to bring this good news to all people
    on earth

Nothing. When you are not present
how could something significant occur?

Everything. Contained in this classroom
is a microcosm of human existence
assembled for you to query and examine and ponder
This is not the only place such an opportunity has been
    gathered

but it was one place

And you weren't here

Questions for Discussion and Writing

1. What point is Wayman making and in what sense could both answers ("Nothing" or "Everything") be true?
2. How does the form of the poem underscore an ongoing debate in education? How does Wayman's use of sarcasm and exaggeration enhance the effect of the poem?
3. After reading this poem would you be less likely to miss a class or if you do to ask the instructor "did I miss anything?"
4. **Rhetorical inquiry:** How does the extreme nature of the answers "Nothing . . . Everything" emphasize what might be the instructor's ambivalence toward the value of what he is teaching?

Connections for Chapter 3: The Value of Education

1. **Frederick Douglass,** *Learning to Read and Write*
   How do both Douglass and Jonathan Kozol emphasize the empowerment that literacy produces?
2. **Jonathan Kozol,** *The Human Cost of an Illiterate Society*
   In what sense is the predicament facing an illiterate person comparable to that of the characters, Betty and Bill, in David Ives's play *Sure Thing* (in Chapter 5), as they try to navigate in an ever-changing social situation?
3. **Mike Adams,** *The Dead Grandmother/Exam Syndrome*
   Why would the students described by Tom Wayman in his poem "Did I Miss Anything?" be more likely to be the subjects of Adams's study?
4. **Richard Rodriguez,** *On Becoming a Chicano*
   What ambivalence do both Rodriguez and Linda Hogan display about losing touch with their cultures as they advance in the academic world?
5. **Sabine Reichel,** *Learning What Was Never Taught*
   In what sense might education in post-war Germany examined by Reichel represent an extension of "Propaganda under a Dictatorship" described by Aldous Huxley (in Chapter 4)?
6. **Nat Hentoff,** *"Speech Codes" on the Campus*
   Compare Hentoff's view on censorship with the efforts to censor Harry Potter as described by Judy Blume.
7. **Mary Crow Dog,** *Civilize Them with a Stick*
   Discuss the difficulties of maintaining tribal or native identities in works by Crow Dog and Haunani-Kay Trask ("From a Native Daughter") in Chapter 7.
8. **Judy Blume,** *Is Harry Potter Evil?*
   To what extent do Blume and Jan Harold Brunvand ("Urban Legends: The Boyfriend's Death") in Chapter 5 discuss the quasi-mythical elements in popular culture?
9. **Mark Salzman,** *Lessons*
   What insights are offered into Chinese culture by Salzman and Amy Tan in "Mother Tongue" (Chapter 4)?
10. **Edward P. Jones,** *The First Day*
    How do the events in this story illustrate Kozol's thesis?
11. **Linda Hogan,** *Workday*
    In what ways do Hogan and Bertolt Brecht ("A Worker Reads History") in Chapter 7 adopt viewpoints of those who are thought of as marginal in relationship to mainstream society?
12. **Tom Wayman,** *Did I Miss Anything?*
    How does the idea of omission play an important role in this poem and Sabine Reichel's essay "Learning What Was Never Taught"?

4

PERSPECTIVES ON LANGUAGE

The limits of my language are the limits of my world.
Ludwig Wittgenstein, TRACTATUS LOGICO-PHILOSOPHICUS

The selections in this chapter attest to the value of literacy and the importance of being able to communicate. Personal accounts by Helen Keller, Temple Grandin, and Amy Tan are particularly fascinating in demonstrating how the creation of an identity depends on language. Keller addresses the way in which words symbolize concepts and things. Grandin explores the restrictions in the way in which autistics grasp generalizations. Tan looks at how the syntax and grammar of her mother's speech changed according to the person and the context in which she spoke. Alison Lurie broadens our concept of what language is and analyzes how clothing can make statements about who we are and how we wish to be perceived. Aldous Huxley reveals how propaganda has been used to deceive by manipulating emotions and beliefs.

Deborah Tannen inquires into the reasons why men and women have so much difficulty in communicating with each other. George Lakoff and Stuart Hirschberg deal with contemporary social issues connected with language: do metaphors used to express anger contain scenarios that govern our actions? Should we look more closely at the rhetorical techniques advertisers use so successfully?

Gish Jen's short story, "Who's Irish" probes the underlying meanings and ambiguities of everyday terms for a Chinese immigrant.

A poem by Kenneth Koch offers a witty commentary on the way parts of speech come together in a sentence to express all that we wish to communicate.

As you read works in this chapter and prepare to discuss or write about them, you may wish to use the following questions as guidelines.

- Does the author believe that one's identity is linked to the language one uses?
- Does the author believe that language can be used to empower or to disempower?
- Is the writer especially interested in the social interactions that result from the use of language?
- Does the writer focus primarily on language as it is written or as it is spoken?

- Does the author examine language in terms of a particular culture?
- Does the writer mainly value the connotations rather than denotations of terms?
- What changes in the way in which we use language does the author recommend?

Nonfiction

HELEN KELLER

Helen Keller (1880–1968) was born, without handicaps, in Alabama; she contracted a disease at the age of nineteen months that left her both blind and deaf. Because of the extraordinary efforts of Annie Sullivan, Keller overcame her isolation and learned what words meant. She graduated with honors from Radcliffe and devoted most of her life to helping the blind and deaf through the American Foundation for the Blind. She was awarded the Presidential Medal of Freedom by Lyndon Johnson in 1964. "The Day Language Came into My Life" is taken from her autobiography, The Story of My Life *(1902). This work served as the basis for a film,* The Unconquered *(1954), and the acclaimed play by William Gibson,* The Miracle Worker *(1959), which was subsequently made into a movie with Anne Bancroft and Patty Duke.*

Before You Read

How could being able to communicate change you emotionally?

The Day Language Came into My Life

The most important day I remember in all my life is the one on which my teacher, Anne Mansfield Sullivan, came to me. I am filled with wonder when I consider the immeasurable contrast between the two lives which it connects. It was the third of March 1887, three months before I was seven years old.

On the afternoon of that eventful day, I stood on the porch, dumb, expectant. I guessed vaguely from my mother's signs and from the hurrying to and fro in the house that something unusual was about to happen, so I went to the door and waited on the steps. The afternoon sun penetrated the mass of honeysuckle that covered the porch and fell on my upturned face. My fingers lingered almost unconsciously on the familiar leaves and blossoms which had just come forth to greet the sweet southern spring. I did not know what the future held of marvel or surprise for me. Anger and bitterness had preyed upon me continually for weeks and a deep languor had succeeded this passionate struggle.

Have you ever been at sea in a dense fog, when it seemed as if a tangible white darkness shut you in, and the great ship, tense and anxious, groped her way toward the shore with plummet and sounding-line, and you waited with beating heart for something to happen? I was like that ship before my education began, only I was without compass or sounding-line and had no way of knowing how near the harbor was. "Light! give me light!" was the wordless cry of my soul, and the light of love shone on me in that very hour.

I felt approaching footsteps. I stretched out my hand as I supposed to my mother. Someone took it, and I was caught up and held close in the arms of her who had come to reveal all things to me, and, more than all things else, to love me.

The morning after my teacher came she led me into her room and gave   5
me a doll. The little blind children at the Perkins Institution had sent it and Laura Bridgman had dressed it; but I did not know this until afterward. When I had played with it a little while, Miss Sullivan slowly spelled into my hand the word "d-o-l-l." I was at once interested in this finger play and tried to imitate it. When I finally succeeded in making the letters correctly I was flushed with childish pleasure and pride. Running downstairs to my mother I held up my hand and made the letters for doll. I did not know that I was spelling a word or even that words existed; I was simply making my fingers go in monkeylike imitation. In the days that followed I learned to spell in this uncomprehending way a great many words, among them *pin, hat, cup* and a few verbs like *sit, stand* and *walk*. But my teacher had been with me several weeks before I understood that everything has a name.

One day, while I was playing with my new doll, Miss Sullivan put my big rag doll into my lap also, spelled "d-o-l-l" and tried to make me understand that "d-o-l-l" applied to both. Earlier in the day we had had a tussle over the words "m-u-g" and "w-a-t-e-r." Miss Sullivan had tried to impress it upon me that "m-u-g" is *mug* and that "w-a-t-e-r" is *water,* but I persisted in confounding the two. In despair she had dropped the subject for the time, only to renew it at the first opportunity. I became impatient at her repeated attempts and, seizing the new doll, I dashed it upon the floor. I was keenly delighted when I felt the fragments of the broken doll at my feet. Neither sorrow nor regret followed my passionate outburst. I had not loved the doll. In the still, dark world in which I lived there was no strong sentiment or tenderness. I felt my teacher sweep the fragments to one side of the hearth, and I had a sense of satisfaction that the cause of my discomfort was removed. She brought me my hat, and I knew I was going out into the warm sunshine. This thought, if a wordless sensation may be called a thought, made me hop and skip with pleasure.

We walked down the path to the well-house, attracted by the fragrance of the honeysuckle with which it was covered. Some one was drawing water and my teacher placed my hand under the spout. As the cool stream gushed over one hand she spelled into the other the word *water,* first slowly, then rapidly. I stood still, my whole attention fixed upon the motions of her fingers. Suddenly I felt a misty consciousness as of something forgotten—a thrill of returning thought; and somehow the mystery of language was revealed to me. I knew then that "w-a-t-e-r" meant the wonderful cool something that was flowing over my hand. The living word awakened my soul, gave it light, hope, joy, set it free! There were barriers still, it is true, but barriers that could in time be swept away.

I left the well-house eager to learn. Everything had a name, and each name gave birth to a new thought. As we returned to the house every object which I touched seemed to quiver with life. That was because I saw everything with the strange, new sight that had come to me. On entering the door I remembered the doll I had broken. I felt my way to the hearth and picked up the pieces. I tried vainly to put them together. Then my eyes filled with tears; for I realized what I had done, and for the first time I felt repentance and sorrow.

I learned a great many new words that day. I do not remember what they all were; but I do know that *mother, father, sister, teacher* were among them—words that were to make the world blossom for me, "like Aaron's rod, with flowers." It would have been difficult to find a happier child than I was as I lay in my crib at the close of that eventful day and lived over the joys it had brought me, and for the first time longed for a new day to come.

Questions for Discussion and Writing

1. Why is it important for the reader to understand Keller's state of mind in the days preceding the events she describes?
2. How did Keller's understanding of language when she became conscious of the meaning of words differ from her previous experience of spelling them by rote?
3. How does the episode of the broken doll reveal how much Keller was transformed by the experience she describes?
4. **Rhetorical inquiry:** Why does Keller use the metaphor in the third paragraph before beginning her account of the events that took place on that fateful day? Why is it significant that the image involves water?

TEMPLE GRANDIN

Temple Grandin has a Ph.D. in animal science from the University of Illinois. She has designed many of the livestock-handling facilities in the United States and in other countries. What makes her achievement astounding is the fact that she is autistic and is one of the few who have overcome this neurological impairment enough to communicate with others. The following selection is drawn from her autobiography, Thinking in Pictures: And Other Reports from My Life with Autism *(1996). She has written (with Catherine Johnson)* Animals in Translation: Using the Mysteries of Autism to Decode Animal Behavior *(2005).*

Before You Read

What do you know about autism?

Thinking in Pictures

PROCESSING NONVISUAL INFORMATION

Autistics[1] have problems learning things that cannot be thought about in pictures. The easiest words for an autistic child to learn are nouns, because they directly relate to pictures. Highly verbal autistic children like I was can sometimes learn how to read with phonics. Written words were too abstract for me to remember, but I could laboriously remember the approximately fifty phonetic sounds and a few rules. Lower-functioning children often learn better by association, with the aid of word labels attached to objects in their environment. Some very impaired autistic children learn more easily if words are spelled out with plastic letters they can feel.

Spatial words such as "over" and "under" had no meaning for me until I had a visual image to fix them in my memory. Even now, when I hear the word "under" by itself, I automatically picture myself getting under the cafeteria tables at school during an air-raid drill, a common occurrence on the East Coast during the early fifties. The first memory that any single word triggers is almost always a childhood memory. I can remember the teacher telling us to be quiet and walking single-file into the cafeteria, where six or eight children huddled under each table. If I continue on the same train of thought, more and more associative memories of elementary school emerge. I can remember the teacher scolding me after I hit Alfred for putting dirt on my shoe. All of these memories play like video-tapes in the VCR in my imagination. If I allow my mind to keep associating, it will wander a million miles away from the word "under," to submarines under the Antarctic and the Beatles song "Yellow Submarine." If I let my mind pause on the picture of the yellow submarine, I then hear the song. As I start humming the song and get to the part about people coming on board, my association switches to the gangway of a ship I saw in Australia.

I also visualize verbs. The word "jumping" triggers a memory of jumping hurdles at the mock Olympics held at my elementary school. Adverbs often

---

[1] *autism:* a condition characterized by a delay in the acquisition of speech, resistance to change of any kind, obsessive repetitive body movements, and a withdrawal into fantasy.

trigger inappropriate images—"quickly" reminds me of Nestle's Quik—unless they are paired with a verb, which modifies my visual image. For example, "he ran quickly" triggers an animated image of Dick from the first-grade reading book running fast, and "he walked slowly" slows the image down. As a child, I left out words such as "is," "the," and "it," because they had no meaning by themselves. Similarly, words like "of" and "an" made no sense. Eventually I learned how to use them properly, because my parents always spoke correct English and I mimicked their speech patterns. To this day certain verb conjugations, such as "to be," are absolutely meaningless to me.

When I read, I translate written words into color movies or I simply store a photo of the written page to be read later. When I retrieve the material, I see a photocopy of the page in my imagination. I can then read it like a TelePrompTer. It is likely that Raymond, the autistic savant depicted in the movie *Rain Man,* used a similar strategy to memorize telephone books, maps, and other information. He simply photocopied each page of the phone book into his memory. When he wanted to find a certain number, he just scanned pages of the phone book that were in his mind. To pull information out of my memory, I have to replay the video. Pulling facts up quickly is sometimes difficult, because I have to play bits of different videos until I find the right tape. This takes time.

When I am unable to convert text to pictures, it is usually because the text has no concrete meaning. Some philosophy books and articles about the cattle futures market are simply incomprehensible. It is much easier for me to understand written text that describes something that can be easily translated into pictures. The following sentence from a story in the February 21, 1994, issue of *Time* magazine, describing the Winter Olympics figure-skating championships, is a good example: "All the elements are in place—the spotlights, the swelling waltzes and jazz tunes, the sequined sprites taking to the air." In my imagination, I see the skating rink and skaters. However, if I ponder too long on the word "elements," I will make the inappropriate association of a periodic table on the wall of my high school chemistry classroom. Pausing on the word "sprite" triggers an image of a Sprite can in my refrigerator instead of a pretty young skater.

Teachers who work with autistic children need to understand associative thought patterns. An autistic child will often use a word in an inappropriate manner. Sometimes these uses have a logical associative meaning and other times they don't. For example, an autistic child might say the word "dog" when he wants to go outside. The word "dog" is associated with going outside. In my own case, I can remember both logical and illogical use of inappropriate words. When I was six, I learned to say "prosecution." I had absolutely no idea what it meant, but it sounded nice when I said it, so I used it as an exclamation every time my kite hit the ground. I must have baffled more than a few people who heard me exclaim "Prosecution!" to my downward-spiraling kite.

Discussions with other autistic people reveal similar visual styles of thinking about tasks that most people do sequentially. An autistic man who composes music told me that he makes "sound pictures" using small pieces of other music to create new compositions. A computer programmer with autism told me that he sees the general pattern of the program tree. After he visualizes the skeleton for the program, he simply writes the code for each branch. I use similar methods when I review scientific literature and troubleshoot at meat plants. I take specific findings or observations and combine them to find new basic principles and general concepts.

My thinking pattern always starts with specifics and works toward generalization in an associational and nonsequential way. As if I were attempting to figure out what the picture on a jigsaw puzzle is when only one third of the puzzle is completed, I am able to fill in the missing pieces by scanning my video library. Chinese mathematicians who can make large calculations in their heads work the same way. At first they need an abacus, the Chinese calculator, which consists of rows of beads on wires in a frame. They make calculations by moving the rows of beads. When a mathematician becomes really skilled, he simply visualizes the abacus in his imagination and no longer needs a real one. The beads move on a visualized video abacus in his brain.

Abstract Thought

Growing up, I learned to convert abstract ideas into pictures as a way to understand them. I visualized concepts such as peace or honesty with symbolic images. I thought of peace as a dove, an Indian peace pipe, or TV or newsreel footage of the signing of a peace agreement. Honesty was represented by an image of placing one's hand on the Bible in court. A news report describing a person returning a wallet with all the money in it provided a picture of honest behavior.

The Lord's Prayer was incomprehensible until I broke it down into specific visual images. The power and the glory were represented by a semicircular rainbow and an electrical tower. These childhood visual images are still triggered every time I hear the Lord's Prayer. The words "thy will be done" had no meaning when I was a child, and today the meaning is still vague. Will is a hard concept to visualize. When I think about it, I imagine God throwing a lightning bolt. Another adult with autism wrote that he visualized "Thou art in heaven" as God with an easel above the clouds. "Trespassing" was pictured as black and orange no trespassing signs. The word "Amen" at the end of the prayer was a mystery: a man at the end made no sense.

As a teenager and young adult I had to use concrete symbols to understand abstract concepts such as getting along with people and moving on to the next steps of my life, both of which were always difficult. I knew I did not fit in with my high school peers, and I was unable to figure out what I was doing wrong. No matter how hard I tried, they made fun of me. They called me "workhorse," "tape recorder," and "bones" because I was skinny. At the time I was able to figure out why they called me "workhorse" and "bones," but "tape recorder" puzzled me. Now I realize that I must have sounded like

10

a tape recorder when I repeated things verbatim over and over. But back then I just could not figure out why I was such a social dud. I sought refuge in doing things I was good at, such as working on reroofing the barn or practicing my riding prior to a horse show. Personal relationships made absolutely no sense to me until I developed visual symbols of doors and windows. It was then that I started to understand concepts such as learning the give-and-take of a relationship. I still wonder what would have happened to me if I had not been able to visualize my way in the world.

THE FAR SIDE®   By GARY LARSON

"Hang him, you idiots! Hang him! ... 'String him up' is a figure of speech!"

How does this cartoon illustrate the difficulties of taking things literally discussed by Grandin?

Questions for Discussion and Writing

1. What limitations does Grandin confront in trying to understand abstract ideas and to communicate with other people? What problems did she encounter in high school because of this limitation?
2. In order to explain the radical difference of the way autistics think about things and understand words, Grandin uses analogies. Which of these analogies did you find most effective?
3. Try to translate a passage about an abstract idea (for example, charity or love) by thinking in pictures instead of words. What images did you use to represent these abstract ideas? What insight did this exercise give you into the world of autism?
4. **Rhetorical inquiry:** What aspects of Grandin's essay are designed to convince her audience that autistics are not different kinds of people but simply people whose thought processes are different in their extreme nature?

DEBORAH TANNEN

Deborah Tannen teaches linguistics at Georgetown University. She has written many books on the difficulties of communicating across cultural, class, ethnic, and gender boundaries, including You Just Don't Understand: Women and Men in Conversation *(1990) and* The Argument Culture *(1998). The following essay from this book originally appeared in the* Washington Post *(1990). Tannen explains why men and women talk at cross-purposes and don't really listen to each other. Tannen's latest books are* Conversational Style: Analyzing Talk Among Friends *(2005) and* You're Wearing That?: Understanding Mothers and Daughters in Conversation *(2006).*

Before You Read

Are men more comfortable speaking in public while women are more comfortable talking in private situations?

Sex, Lies, and Conversation

I was addressing a small gathering in a suburban Virginia living room—a women's group that had invited men to join them. Throughout the evening, one man had been particularly talkative, frequently offering ideas and anecdotes, while his wife sat silently beside him on the couch. Toward the end of the evening, I commented that women frequently complain that their husbands don't talk to them. This man quickly concurred. He gestured toward his wife and said, "She's the talker in our family." The room burst into laughter; the man looked puzzled and hurt. "It's true," he explained. "When

I come home from work I have nothing to say. If she didn't keep the conversation going, we'd spend the whole evening in silence."

This episode crystallizes the irony that although American men tend to talk more than women in public situations, they often talk less at home. And this pattern is wreaking havoc with marriage.

The pattern was observed by political scientist Andrew Hacker in the late '70s. Sociologist Catherine Kohler Riessman reports in her new book *Divorce Talk* that most of the women she interviewed—but only a few of the men—gave lack of communication as the reason for their divorces. Given the current divorce rate of nearly 50 percent, that amounts to millions of cases in the United States every year—a virtual epidemic of failed conversation.

In my own research, complaints from women about their husbands most often focused not on tangible inequities such as having given up the chance for a career to accompany a husband to his, or doing far more than their share of daily life-support work like cleaning, cooking, social arrangements and errands. Instead, they focused on communication: "He doesn't listen to me," "He doesn't talk to me." I found, as Hacker observed years before, that most wives want their husbands to be, first and foremost, conversational partners, but few husbands share this expectation of their wives.

In short, the image that best represents the current crisis is the stereotypical cartoon scene of a man sitting at the breakfast table with a newspaper held up in front of his face, while a woman glares at the back of it, wanting to talk.   5

LINGUISTIC BATTLE OF THE SEXES

How can women and men have such different impressions of communication in marriage? Why the widespread imbalance in their interests and expectations?

In the April issue of *American Psychologist,* Stanford University's Eleanor Maccoby reports the results of her own and other's research showing that children's development is most influenced by the social structure of peer interactions. Boys and girls tend to play with children of their own gender, and their sex-separate groups have different organizational structures and interactive norms.

I believe these systematic differences in childhood socialization make talk between women and men like cross-cultural communication, heir to all the attraction and pitfalls of that enticing but difficult enterprise. My research on men's and women's conversations uncovered patterns similar to those described for children's groups.

For women, as for girls, intimacy is the fabric of relationships, and talk is the thread from which it is woven. Little girls create and maintain friendships by exchanging secrets; similarly, women regard conversation as the cornerstone of friendship. So a woman expects her husband to be a new and improved version of a best friend. What is important is not the individual

subjects that are discussed but a sense of closeness, of a life shared, that
emerges when people tell their thoughts, feelings, and impressions.

Bonds between boys can be as intense as girls', but they are based less   10
on talking, more on doing things together. Since they don't assume talk is
the cement that binds a relationship, men don't know what kind of talk
women want and they don't miss it when it isn't there.

Boy's groups are larger, more inclusive, and more hierarchical, so boys
must struggle to avoid the subordinate position in the group. This may play
a role in women's complaints that men don't listen to them. Some men really
don't like to listen, because being the listener makes them feel one-down,
like a child listening to adults or an employee to a boss.

But often when women tell men, "You aren't listening," and the men
protest, "I am," the men are right. The impression of not listening results
from misalignments in the mechanics of conversation. The misalignment
begins as soon as a man and a woman take physical positions. This became
clear when I studied videotapes made by psychologist Bruce Dorval of children and adults talking to their same-sex best friends. I found that at every
age, the girls and women faced each other directly, their eyes anchored on
each other's faces. At every age, the boys and men sat at angles to each other
and looked elsewhere in the room, periodically glancing at each other. They
were obviously attuned to each other, often mirroring each other's movements. But the tendency of men to face away can give women the impression
they aren't listening even when they are. A young woman in college was
frustrated: Whenever she told her boyfriend she wanted to talk to him, he
would lie down on the floor, close his eyes, and put his arm over his face.
This signaled to her, "He's taking a nap." But he insisted he was listening
extra hard. Normally, he looks around the room, so he is easily distracted.
Lying down and covering his eyes helped him concentrate on what she was
saying.

Analogous to the physical alignment that women and men take in conversation is their topical alignment. The girls in my study tended to talk at
length about one topic, but the boys tended to jump from topic to topic. The
second-grade girls exchanged stories about people they knew. The second-
grade boys teased, told jokes, noticed things in the room and talked about
finding games to play. The sixth-grade girls talked about problems with a
mutual friend. The sixth-grade boys talked about 55 different topics, none
of which extended over more than a few turns.

LISTENING TO BODY LANGUAGE

Switching topics is another habit that gives women the impression men aren't
listening, especially if they switch to a topic about themselves. But the evidence of the 10th-grade boys in my study indicates otherwise. The 10th-grade
boys sprawled across their chairs with bodies parallel and eyes straight ahead,

rarely looking at each other. They looked as if they were riding in a car, staring out the windshield. But they were talking about their feelings. One boy was upset because a girl had told him he had a drinking problem, and the other was feeling alienated from all his friends.

Now, when a girl told a friend about a problem, the friend responded by   15
asking probing questions and expressing agreement and understanding. But the boys dismissed each other's problems. Todd assured Richard that his drinking was "no big problem" because "sometimes you're funny when you're off your butt." And when Todd said he felt left out, Richard responded, "Why should you? You know more people than me."

Women perceive such responses as belittling and unsupportive. But the boys seemed satisfied with them. Whereas women reassure each other by implying, "You shouldn't feel bad because I've had similar experiences," men do so by implying, "You shouldn't feel bad because your problems aren't so bad."

There are even simpler reasons for women's impression that men don't listen. Linguist Lynette Hirschman found that women make more listener-noise, such as "mhm," "uhuh," and "yeah," to show "I'm with you." Men, she found, more often give silent attention. Women who expect a stream of listener-noise interpret silent attention as no attention at all.

Women's conversational habits are as frustrating to men as men's are to women. Men who expect silent attention interpret a stream of listener-noise as overreaction or impatience. Also, when women talk to each other in a close, comfortable setting, they often overlap, finish each other's sentences and anticipate what the other is about to say. This practice, which I call "participatory listenership," is often perceived by men as interruption, intrusion and lack of attention.

A parallel difference caused a man to complain about his wife, "She just wants to talk about her own point of view. If I show her another view, she gets mad at me." When most women talk to each other, they assume a conversationalist's job is to express agreement and support. But many men see their conversational duty as pointing out the other side of an argument. This is heard as disloyalty by women, and refusal to offer the requisite support. It is not that women don't want to see other points of view, but that they prefer them phrased as suggestions and inquiries rather than as direct challenges.

In his book *Fighting for Life,* Walter Ong points out that men use "ago-   20
nistic" or warlike, oppositional formats to do almost anything; thus discussion becomes debate, and conversation a competitive sport. In contrast, women see conversation as a ritual means of establishing rapport. If Jane tells a problem and June says she has a similar one, they walk away feeling closer to each other. But this attempt at establishing rapport can backfire when used with men. Men take too literally women's ritual "troubles talk," just as women mistake men's ritual challenges for real attack.

THE SOUNDS OF SILENCE

These differences begin to clarify why women and men have such different expectations about communication in marriage. For women, talk creates intimacy. Marriage is an orgy of closeness: you can tell your feelings and thoughts, and still be loved. Their greatest fear is being pushed away. But men live in a hierarchical world, where talk maintains independence and status. They are on guard to protect themselves from being put down and pushed around.

This explains the paradox of the talkative man who said of his silent wife, "She's the talker." In the public setting of a guest lecture, he felt challenged to show his intelligence and display his understanding of the lecture. But at home, where he has nothing to prove and no one to defend against, he is free to remain silent. For his wife, being home means she is free from the worry that something she says might offend someone, or spark disagreement, or appear to be showing off; at home she is free to talk.

The communication problems that endanger marriage can't be fixed by mechanical engineering. They require a new conceptual framework about the role of talk in human relationships. Many of the psychological explanations that have become second nature may not be helpful, because they tend to blame either women (for not being assertive enough) or men (for not being in touch with their feelings). A sociolinguistic approach by which male-female conversation is seen as cross-cultural communication allows us to understand the problem and forge solutions without blaming either party.

Once the problem is understood, improvement comes naturally, as it did to the young woman and her boyfriend who seemed to go to sleep when she wanted to talk. Previously, she had accused him of not listening, and he had refused to change his behavior, since that would be admitting fault. But then she learned about and explained to him the differences in women's and men's habitual ways of aligning themselves in conversation. The next time she told him she wanted to talk, he began, as usual, by lying down and covering his eyes. When the familiar negative reaction bubbled up, she re-assured herself that he really was listening. But then he sat up and looked at her. Thrilled, she asked why. He said, "You like me to look at you when we talk, so I'll try to do it." Once he saw their differences as cross-cultural rather than right and wrong, he independently altered his behavior.

Women who feel abandoned and deprived when their husbands won't 25 listen to or report daily news may be happy to discover their husbands trying to adapt once they understand the place of small talk in women's relationships. But if their husbands don't adapt, the women may still be comforted that for men, this is not a failure of intimacy. Accepting the difference, the wives may look to their friends or family for that kind of talk. And husbands who can't provide it shouldn't feel their wives have made unreasonable demands. Some couples will still decide to divorce, but at least their decisions will be based on realistic expectations.

In these times of resurgent ethnic conflicts, the world desperately needs cross-cultural understanding. Like charity, successful cross-cultural communication should begin at home.

Questions for Discussion and Writing

1. What different objectives do men and women pursue in conversations? How do these differences reveal themselves in verbal and nonverbal behavior?
2. How do the extended examples Tannen presents about two specific couples illustrate her thesis?
3. Evaluate her suggestions for improving communication between men and women. In your opinion, would they work? Why or why not?
4. **Rhetorical inquiry:** How do the different techniques of videotaping conversations, listing typical topics, and studying body language and periods of silence help persuade the reader that Tannen's analysis is scientific rather than anecdotal?

GEORGE LAKOFF

George Lakoff is a professor of linguistics at the University of California at Berkeley. He is coauthor (with Rafael Nuñez) of Where Mathematics Come From *(2000) and (with Mark Johnson) of* Metaphors We Live By *(2003). Lakoff is also the author of* Moral Politics: How Liberals and Conservatives Think *(2nd ed., 2002),* Don't Think of an Elephant *(2004), and* Whose Freedom? *(2006). The following excerpts are drawn from* Women, Fire, and Dangerous Things: What Categories Reveal About the Mind. *Lakoff believes that rather than being simple expressions of feeling, the language used to express anger reveals a number of scenarios (anger/appeasement, anger/retribution) that determine not only how we express anger but how we think about it. A disturbing manifestation of how we conceptualize and express anger can be seen in metaphors that result in blaming the victim.*

Before You Read

What metaphors do you use to express anger?

Anger

THE CONCEPTUALIZATION OF FEELING

Emotions are often considered to be feelings alone, and as such they are viewed as being devoid of conceptual content. As a result, the study of emotions is usually not taken seriously by students of semantics and conceptual structure. A topic such as the logic of emotions would seem on this view to be a contradiction in terms, since emotions, being devoid of conceptual content, would give rise to no inferences at all, or at least none of any interest.

I would like to argue that the opposite is true, that emotions have an extremely complex conceptual structure, which gives rise to a wide variety of nontrivial inferences. The work I will be presenting is based on joint research by myself and Zoltán Kövecses. Kövecses had suggested that the conceptual structure of emotions could be studied in detail using techniques devised by Mark Johnson and myself for the systematic investigation of expressions that are understood metaphorically. English has an extremely large range of such expressions. What we set out to do was to study them systematically to see if any coherent conceptual structure emerged.

At first glance, the conventional expressions used to talk about anger seem so diverse that finding any coherent system would seem impossible. For example, if we look up *anger* in, say, *Roget's University Thesaurus*, we find about three hundred entries, most of which have something or other to do with anger, but the thesaurus doesn't tell us exactly what. Many of these are idioms, and they seem too diverse to reflect any coherent cognitive model. Here are some sample sentences using such idioms:

- He *lost his cool*.
- She was *looking daggers* at me.
- I almost *burst a blood vessel*.
- He was *foaming at the mouth*.
- You're beginning to *get to me*.
- You make my *blood boil*.
- He's *wrestling* with his anger.
- Watch out! He's *on a short fuse*.
- He's just *letting off steam*.
- Don't *get a hernia!*
- Try to *keep a grip on yourself*.
- Don't *fly off the handle*.
- When I told him, he *blew up*.
- He *channeled* his anger into something constructive.
- He was *red with anger*.
- He was *blue in the face*.
- He *appeased* his anger.
- He was *doing a slow burn*.
- He *suppressed* his anger.
- She kept *bugging* me.
- When I told my mother, *she had a cow*.

What do these expressions have to do with anger, and what do they have to do with each other? We will be arguing that they are not random.

When we look at inferences among these expressions, it becomes clear that there must be a systematic structure of some kind. We know, for example, that someone who is foaming at the mouth has lost his cool. We know that someone who is looking daggers at you is likely to be doing a slow burn or be on a short fuse. We know that someone whose blood is boiling has not had his anger appeased. We know that someone who has channeled his anger into something constructive has not had a cow. How do we know these things? Is it just that each idiom has a literal meaning and the inferences are based on the literal meanings? Or is there something more going on? What we will try to show is that there is a coherent conceptual organization underlying all these expressions and that much of it is metaphorical and metonymical in nature.

METAPHOR AND METONYMY

The analysis we are proposing begins with the common folk theory of the physiological effects of anger: 5

> The physiological effects of anger are increased body heat, increased internal pressure (blood pressure, muscular pressure), agitation, and interference with accurate perception.
>
> As anger increases, its physiological effects increase.
>
> There is a limit beyond which the physiological effects of anger impair normal functioning.
>
> We use this folk theory in large measure to tell when someone is angry on the basis of their appearance—as well as to signal anger or hide it. In doing this, we make use of a general metonymic principle:
>
> The physiological effects of an emotion stand for the emotion.
>
> Given this principle, the folk theory given above yields a system of metonymies for anger:

Body heat

- Don't get *hot under the collar.*
- Billy's a *hothead.*
- They were having a *heated argument.*
- When the cop gave her a ticket, she got all *hot and bothered* and started cursing.

Internal pressure

- Don't get a *hernia!*
- When I found out, I almost *burst a blood vessel.*
- He almost had a *hemorrhage.*

Increased body heat and/or blood pressure is assumed to cause redness in the face and neck area, and such redness can also metonymically indicate anger.

Redness in face and neck area

- She was *scarlet with rage.*
- He got *red with anger.*
- He was *flushed with anger.*

Agitation

- She was *shaking* with anger.
- I was *hopping mad.*
- He was *quivering with rage.*
- He's *all worked up.*
- There's no need to get so *excited* about it!
- She's *all wrought up.*
- You look *upset.*

Interference with accurate perception

- She was *blind with rage.*
- I was beginning to *see red.*
- I was so mad I *couldn't see straight.*

Each of these expressions indicate the presence of anger via its supposed physiological effects.

The folk theory of physiological effects, especially the part that emphasizes HEAT, forms the basis of the most general metaphor for anger: ANGER IS HEAT. There are two versions of this metaphor, one where the heat is applied to fluids, the other where it is applied to solids. When it is applied to fluids, we get: ANGER IS THE HEAT OF A FLUID IN A CONTAINER. The specific motivation for this consists of the HEAT, INTERNAL PRESSURE, and AGITATION parts of the folk theory. When ANGER IS HEAT is applied to solids, we get the version ANGER IS FIRE, which is motivated by the HEAT and REDNESS aspects of the folk theory of physiological effects.

As we will see shortly, the fluid version is much more highly elaborated. The reason for this, we surmise, is that in our overall conceptual system we have the general metaphor:

The body is a container for the emotions.

- He was *filled* with anger.
- She couldn't *contain* her joy.
- She was *brimming* with rage.
- Try to get your anger *out of your system.*

The ANGER IS HEAT metaphor, when applied to fluids, combines with the metaphor THE BODY IS A CONTAINER FOR THE EMOTIONS to yield the central metaphor of the system:

Anger is the heat of a fluid in a container.

- You make my *blood boil.*
- *Simmer* down!
- I had reached the *boiling point.*
- Let him *stew.*

A historically derived instance of this metaphor is:

- She was *seething with rage.*

Although most speakers do not now use *seethe* to indicate physical boiling, the boiling image is still there when *seethe* is used to indicate anger. Similarly, *pissed off* is used only to refer to anger, not to the hot liquid under pressure in the bladder. Still, the effectiveness of the expression seems to depend on such an image.

When there is no heat, the liquid is cool and calm. In the central metaphor, cool and calmness corresponds to lack of anger.

- Keep *cool.*
- Stay *calm.* . . .

Let us now turn to the question of what issues the central metaphor addresses and what kind of ontology of anger it reveals. The central metaphor focuses on the fact that anger can be intense, that it can lead to a loss of control, and that a loss of control can be dangerous. Let us begin with intensity. Anger is conceptualized as a mass, and takes the grammar of mass nouns, as opposed to count nouns:

Thus, you can say

How much anger has he got in him?

but not

How many angers does he have in him?

Anger thus has the ontology of a mass entity, that is, it has a scale indicating its amount, it exists when the amount is greater than zero, and it goes out of existence when the amount falls to zero. In the central metaphor, the scale indicating the amount of anger is the heat scale. But, as the central metaphor indicates, the anger scale is not open-ended; it has a limit. Just as a hot fluid in a closed container can only take so much heat before it explodes, so we conceptualize the anger scale as having a limit point. We can only bear so much anger before we explode, that is, lose control. This has its correlates in our folk theory of physiological effects. As anger gets more intense the physiological effects increase and those increases interfere with our normal function.

Body heat, blood pressure, agitation, and interference with perception cannot increase without limit before our ability to function normally becomes seriously impaired, and we lose control over our functioning. In the folk model of anger, loss of control is dangerous, both to the angry person and to those around him. In the central metaphor, the danger of loss of control is understood as the danger of explosion. . . .

The ANGER IS AN OPPONENT metaphor is constituted by the following correspondences: 10

Source: STRUGGLE Target: ANGER

- The opponent is anger.
- Winning is controlling anger.
- Losing is having anger control you.
- Surrender is allowing anger to take control of you.
- The pool of resources needed for winning is the energy needed to control anger.

One thing that is left out of this account so far is what constitutes "appeasement." To appease an opponent is to give in to his demands. This suggests that anger has demands. We will address the question of what these demands are below.

The OPPONENT metaphor focuses on the issue of control and the danger of loss of control to the angry person himself. There is another metaphor that focuses on the issue of control, but its main aspect is the danger to others. It is a very widespread metaphor in Western culture, namely, PASSIONS ARE BEASTS INSIDE A PERSON. According to this metaphor, there is a part of each person that is a wild animal. Civilized people are supposed to keep that part of them private, that is, they are supposed to keep the animal inside them. In the metaphor, loss of control is equivalent to the animal getting loose. And the behavior of a person who has lost control is the behavior of a wild animal. There are versions of this metaphor for the various passions—desire, anger, etc. In the case of anger, the beast presents a danger to other people.

Anger is a dangerous animal.

- He has a *ferocious* temper.
- He has a *fierce* temper.
- It's dangerous to *arouse* his anger.
- That *awakened* my ire.
- His anger *grew*.
- He has a *monstrous* temper.
- He *unleashed* his anger.
- Don't let your anger *get out of hand*,
- He *lost his grip* on his anger.
- His anger is *insatiable*.

An example that draws on both the FIRE and DANGEROUS ANIMAL metaphors is:

- He was *breathing fire*.

The image here is of a dragon, a dangerous animal that can devour you with fire.

The DANGEROUS ANIMAL metaphor portrays anger as a sleeping animal that it is dangerous to awaken, as something that can grow and thereby become dangerous, as something that has to be held back, and as something with a dangerous appetite. . . .

As in the case of the OPPONENT metaphor, our analysis of the DANGEROUS ANIMAL metaphor leaves an expression unaccounted for—"insatiable." This expression indicates that the animal has an appetite. This "appetite" seems to correspond to the "demands" in the OPPONENT metaphor, as can be seen from the fact that the following sentences entail each other:

- Harry's anger is *insatiable*.
- Harry's anger cannot be *appeased*.

To see what it is that anger demands and has an appetite for, let us turn to expressions that indicate causes of anger. Perhaps the most common group of expressions that indicate anger consists of conventionalized forms of annoyance: minor pains, burdens placed on domestic animals, etc. Thus we have the metaphor:

The cause of anger is a physical annoyance.

- Don't be *a pain in the ass*.
- Get *off my back!*
- You don't have to *ride me so hard*.
- You're *getting under my skin*.
- He's *a pain in the neck*.
- Don't *be a pest!*

These forms of annoyance involve an offender and a victim. The offender is at fault. The victim, who is innocent, is the one who gets angry.

There is another set of conventionalized expressions used to speak of, or to, people who are in the process of making someone angry. These are expressions of territoriality, in which the cause of anger is viewed as a trespasser. 15

Causing anger is trespassing.

- You're beginning to *get to* me.
- Get *out of here!*
- Get *out of my sight!*
- *Leave me alone!*
- This is where I *draw the line!*
- Don't *step on my toes!*

Again, there is an offender (the cause of anger) and a victim (the person who is getting angry). The offense seems to constitute some sort of injustice. This is reflected in the conventional wisdom:

- Don't get *mad, get even!*

In order for this saying to make sense, there has to be some connection between anger and retribution. Getting even is equivalent to balancing the scales of justice. The saying assumes a model in which injustice leads to anger and retribution can alleviate or prevent anger. In short, what anger "demands" and has an "appetite" for is revenge. This is why warnings and threats can count as angry behavior:

- If I get mad, watch out!
- Don't get me angry, or you'll be sorry.

The angry behavior is, in itself, viewed as a form of retribution.

We are now in a position to make sense of another metaphor for anger:

Anger is a burden.

- Unburdening himself of his anger gave him a sense of *relief.*
- After I lost my temper, I felt *lighter.*
- He *carries* his anger around with him.
- He *has a chip on his shoulder.*
- You'll feel better if you *get it off your chest.*

In English, it is common for responsibilities to be metaphorized as burdens. There are two kinds of responsibilities involved in the folk model of anger that has emerged so far. The first is a responsibility to control one's anger. In cases of extreme anger, this may place a considerable burden on one's "inner resources." The second comes from the model of retributive justice that is built into our concept of anger; it is the responsibility to seek vengeance. What is particularly interesting is that these two responsibilities are in conflict in the case of angry retribution: If you take out your anger on someone, you are not meeting your responsibility to control your anger, and if you don't take out your anger on someone, you are not meeting your responsibility to provide retribution. The slogan "Don't get mad, get even!" offers one way out: retribution without anger. The human potential movement provides another way out by suggesting that letting your anger out is okay. But the fact is that neither of these solutions is the cultural norm. It should also be mentioned in passing that the human potential movement's way of dealing with anger by sanctioning its release is not all that revolutionary. It assumes almost all of our standard folk model and metaphorical understanding and makes one change: sanctioning the "release.". . .

The metaphors and metonymies that we have investigated so far converge on a certain prototypical cognitive model of anger. It is not the only model of anger we have; in fact, there are quite a few. But as we shall see, all of the others can be characterized as minimal variants of the model that the metaphors converge on. The model has a temporal dimension and can be conceived of as a scenario with a number of stages. We will call this the "prototypical scenario"; it is similar to what De Sousa calls the "paradigm scenario." We will be referring to the person who gets angry as *S*, short for the self.

Stage 1: Offending Event

There is an offending event that displeases *S*. There is a wrongdoer who intentionally does something directly to *S*. The wrongdoer is at fault and *S* is innocent. The offending event constitutes an injustice and produces anger in *S*. The scales of justice can only be balanced by some act of retribution. That is, the intensity of retribution must be roughly equal to the intensity of offense. *S* has the responsibility to perform such an act of retribution.

Stage 2: Anger

Associated with the entity anger is a scale that measures its intensity. As the intensity of anger increases, *S* experiences physiological effects: increase in body heat, internal pressure, and physical agitation. As the anger gets very intense, it exerts a force upon *S* to perform an act of retribution. Because acts of retribution are dangerous and/or socially unacceptable, *S* has a responsibility to control his anger. Moreover, loss of control is damaging to *S*'s own well-being, which is another motivation for controlling anger.

Stage 3: Attempt at Control

S attempts to control his anger.

Stage 4: Loss of Control

Each person has a certain tolerance for controlling anger. That tolerance can be viewed as the limit point on the anger scale. When the intensity of anger goes beyond that limit, *S* can no longer control his anger. *S* exhibits angry behavior and his anger forces him to attempt an act of retribution. Since *S* is out of control and acting under coercion, he is not responsible for his actions.

Stage 5: Act of Retribution

S performs the act of retribution. The wrongdoer is the target of the act. The intensity of retribution roughly equals the intensity of the offense and the scales are balanced again. The intensity of anger drops to zero.

At this point, we can see how the various conceptual metaphors we have discussed all map onto a part of the prototypical scenario and how they jointly converge on that scenario. This enables us to show exactly how the various metaphors are related to one another and how they function together to help characterize a single concept.

Questions for Discussion and Writing

1. How do the metaphorical systems used to express anger project (a) physiological effects, (b) equivalence with heat, (c) equivalence with insanity, (d) equivalence with dangerous animals, and (e) anger at an opponent? What did Lakoff discover about the way systems of metaphors interact?

2. Lakoff cites the "folk theory of physiological effects" as a kind of commonsense, homespun value system that makes it possible to understand the hidden connection between related metaphors used to express anger. How does Lakoff use this folk theory of anger, structured on the concept of a protagonist and antagonist, to examine the rationale for acted-out aggression?

3. What metaphors underlie the reporting of sports? As a research project, analyze the verbs (for example, *maul, jolt, blast*) sportwriters use in reporting scores of football, basketball, and other games to discover the systems of metaphors (for example, those that value speed) and what they suggest about our culture.

4. **Rhetorical inquiry:** What examples of changes in the body as a person becomes angry does Lakoff use to show how metaphors connect anger to these physiological manifestations? Does Lakoff present a persuasive case in your opinion? Why or why not?

ALISON LURIE

Alsion Lurie (b. 1926) is the Frederic J. Whiton Professor of American Literature at Cornell University, where she teaches writing and children's literature. She is the author of several books of nonfiction and fiction, including Foreign Affairs *(1984), for which she was awarded a Pulitzer Prize in 1985. Her latest works are* Familiar Spirits: A Memoir of James Merrill and David Jackson *(2001) and* Truth and Consequences: A Novel *(2005). "The Language of Clothes" first appeared in* Human Ecology *(Spring 1991).*

Before You Read

Do you have an item of clothing you consider to be lucky?

The Language of Clothes

For thousands of years human beings have communicated with one another first in the language of dress. Long before I am near enough to talk to you on the street, in a meeting, or at a party, you announce your sex, age and class to me through what you are wearing—and very possibly give me important information (or misinformation) as to your occupation, origin, personality, opinions, tastes, sexual desires and current mood. I may not be able to put what I observe into words, but I register the information unconsciously; and you simultaneously do the same for me. By the time we meet and converse we have already spoken to each other in an older and more universal language.

The statement that clothing is a language, though made occasionally with the air of a man finding a flying saucer in his backyard, is not new. Balzac, in *Daughter of Eve* (1830), observed that dress is a "continual manifestation of intimate thoughts, a language, a symbol." Today, as semiotics becomes fashionable, sociologists tell us that fashion too is a language of signs, a nonverbal system of communication.

None of these theorists, however, has gone on to remark what seems obvious: that if clothing is a language, it must have a vocabulary and a grammar like other languages. Of course, as with human speech, there is not a single language of dress, but many: some (like Dutch and German) closely related and others (like Basque) almost unique. And within every language of clothes there are many different dialects and accents, some almost unintelligible to members of the mainstream culture. Moreover, as with speech, each individual has his own stock of words and employs personal variations of tone and meaning.

The vocabulary of dress includes not only items of clothing, but also hair styles, accessories, jewelry, makeup and body decoration. Theoretically at least this vocabulary is as large as or larger than that of any spoken tongue, since it includes every garment, hair style, and type of body decoration ever invented. In practice, of course, the sartorial resources of an individual may be very restricted. Those of a sharecropper, for instance, may be limited to five or ten "words" from which it is possible to create only a few "sentences" almost bare of decoration and expressing only the most basic concepts. A so-called fashion leader, on the other hand, may have several hundred "words" at his or her disposal, and thus be able to form thousands of different "sentences" that will express a wide range of meanings. Just as the average English-speaking person knows many more words than he or she will ever use in conversation, so all of us are able to understand the meaning of styles we will never wear.

MAGICAL CLOTHING

Archaeologists digging up past civilizations and anthropologists studying primitive tribes have come to the conclusion that, as Rachel Kemper [*Costume*] puts it, "Paint, ornament, and rudimentary clothing were first employed to attract good animistic powers and to ward off evil." When Charles Darwin visited Tierra del Fuego, a cold, wet, disagreeable land plagued by constant winds, he found the natives naked except for feathers in their hair and symbolic designs painted on their bodies. Modern Australian bushmen, who may spend hours decorating themselves and their relatives with patterns in colored clay, often wear nothing else but an amulet or two.

However skimpy it may be, primitive dress almost everywhere, like primitive speech, is full of magic. A necklace of shark's teeth or a girdle of cowrie shells or feathers serves the same purpose as a prayer or spell, and may magically replace—or more often supplement—a spoken charm. In the first instance a form of *contagious* magic is at work: the shark's teeth are believed to endow their wearer with the qualities of a fierce and successful fisherman. The cowrie shells, on the other hand, work through *sympathetic* magic: since they resemble the female sexual parts, they are thought to increase or preserve fertility.

In civilized society today belief in the supernatural powers of clothing—like belief in prayers, spells and charms—remains widespread, though we denigrate it with the name "superstition." Advertisements announce that improbable and romantic events will follow the application of a particular sort of grease to our faces, hair or bodies; they claim that members of the opposite (or our own) sex will be drawn to us by the smell of a particular soap. Nobody believes those ads, you may say. Maybe not, but we behave as though we did: look in your bathroom cabinet.

The supernatural garments of European folk tales—the seven-league boots, the cloaks of invisibility and the magic rings—are not forgotten, merely transformed, so that today we have the track star who can only win a race in a particular hat or shoes, the plain-clothes cop who feels no one can see him in his raincoat and the wife who takes off her wedding ring before going to a motel with her lover.

Sympathetic or symbolic magic is also often employed, as when we hang crosses, stars or one of the current symbols of female power and solidarity around our necks, thus silently involving the protection of Jesus, Jehovah or Astarte. Such amulets, of course, may be worn to announce our allegiance to some faith or cause rather than as a charm. Or they may serve both purposes simultaneously—or sequentially. The crucifix concealed below the parochial-school uniform speaks only to God until some devilish force persuades its wearer to remove his or her clothes; then it acts—or fails to act—as a warning against sin as well as a protective talisman.

Articles of clothing, too, may be treated as if they had mana, the impersonal supernatural force that tends to concentrate itself in objects. When I was in college it was common to wear a particular "lucky" sweater, shirt or hat to final examinations, and this practice continues today. Here it is usually contagious magic that is at work: the chosen garment has become lucky by being worn on the occasion of some earlier success, or has been given to its owner by some favored person. The wearing of such magical garments is especially common in sports, where they are often publicly credited with bringing their owners luck. Their loss or abandonment is thought to cause injury as well as defeat. Actors also believe ardently in the magic of

10

clothes, possibly because they are so familiar with the near-magical transforming power of theatrical costume.

FASHION AND STATUS

Clothing designed to show the social position of its wearer has a long history.
Just as the oldest languages are full of elaborate titles and forms of address, so
for thousands of years certain modes have indicated high or royal rank. Many
societies passed decrees known as *sumptuary laws* to prescribe or forbid the
wearing of specific styles by specific classes of persons. In ancient Egypt only
those in high position could wear sandals; the Greeks and Romans controlled
the type, color and number of garments worn and the sorts of embroidery
with which they could be trimmed. During the Middle Ages almost every
aspect of dress was regulated at some place or time—though not always with
much success. The common features of all sumptuary laws—like that of edicts,
against the use of certain words—seem to be that they are difficult to enforce
for very long.

Laws about what could be worn by whom continued to be passed in
Europe until about 1700. But as class barriers weakened and wealth could
be more easily and rapidly converted into gentility, the system by which
color and shape indicated social status began to break down. What came
to designate high rank instead was the evident cost of a costume: rich
materials, superfluous trimmings and difficult-to-care-for styles, or as Thorstein Veblen later put it [in *The Theory of the Leisure Class*], Conspicuous
Waste and Conspicuous Leisure. As a result, it was assumed that the people
you met would be dressed as lavishly as their income permitted. In Fielding's
Tom Jones, for instance, everyone judges strangers by their clothing
and treats them accordingly; this is presented as natural. It is a world in
which rank is very exactly indicated by costume, from the rags of Molly
the gamekeeper's daughter to Sophia Western's riding habit "which was so
very richly laced" that "Partridge and the postboy instantly started from
their chairs, and my landlady fell to her curtsies, and her ladyships, with
great eagerness." The elaborate wigs characteristic of this period conferred
status partly because they were both expensive to buy and expensive to
maintain.

By the early eighteenth century the social advantages of conspicuous
dress were such that even those who could not afford it often spent their
money on finery. This development was naturally deplored by supporters of the
status quo. In Colonial America the Massachusetts General Court declared
its "utter detestation and dislike, that men or women of mean condition,
should take upon them the garb of Gentlemen, by wearing Gold or Silver
lace, or Buttons, or Points at their knees, or to walk in great Boots; or
Women of the same rank to wear Silk or Tiffiny hoods, or Scarfes. . . ." What
"men or women of mean condition"—farmers or artisans—were supposed

to wear were coarse linen or wool, leather aprons, deerskin jackets, flannel petticoats and the like.

To dress above one's station was considered not only foolishly extravagant, but deliberately deceptive. In 1878 an American etiquette book complained,

> It is . . . unfortunately the fact that, in the United States, but too much attention is paid to dress by those who have neither the excuse of ample means nor of social claims. . . . We Americans are lavish, generous, and ostentatious. The wives of our wealthy men are glorious in garb as are princesses and queens. They have a right so to be. But when those who can ill afford to wear alpaca persist in arraying themselves in silk . . . the matter is a sad one.

COLOR AND PATTERN

Certain sorts of information about other people can be communicated in spite of a language barrier. We may not be able to understand Welsh or the thick Southern dialect of the Mississippi delta, but when we hear a conversation in these tongues we can tell at once whether the speakers are excited or bored, cheerful or miserable, confident or frightened. In the same way, some aspects of the language of clothes can be read by almost anyone.

The first and most important of these signs, and the one that makes the greatest and most immediate impact, is color. Merely looking at different colors, psychologists have discovered, alters our blood pressure, heartbeat and rate of respiration, just as hearing a harsh noise or a harmonious musical chord does. When somebody approaches from a distance the first thing we see is the hue of his clothes; the closer he comes, the more space this hue occupies in our visual field and the greater its effect on our nervous system. Loud, clashing colors, like loud noises or loud voices, may actually hurt our eyes or give us a headache; soft, harmonious hues, like music and soft voices, thrill or soothe us. Color in dress is also like tone of voice in speech in that it can completely alter the meaning of what is "said" by other aspects of the costume: style, fabric and trimmings. Just as the words "Do you want to dance with me?" can be whispered shyly or flung as a challenge, so the effect of a white evening dress is very different from that of a scarlet one of identical fabric and pattern. In certain circumstances some hues, like some tones of voice, are beyond the bounds of polite discourse. A bride in a black wedding dress, or a stockbroker greeting his clients in a shocking-pink three-piece suit, would be like people screaming aloud.

Although color often indicates mood, it is not by any means an infallible guide. For one thing, convention may prescribe certain hues. The urban businessman must wear a navy blue, dark gray or (in certain regions) brown or tan suit, and can express his feelings only through his choice of shirt and tie, or tie alone; and even here the respectable possibilities may be very limited. Convention also alters the meaning of colors according to the place and time at which they are worn. Vermilion in the office is not the same as vermilion at a disco; and hot weather permits the wearing of pale hues that would make one look far more formal and fragile in midwinter.

There are other problems. Some people may avoid colors they like because of the belief or illusion that they are unbecoming, while others may wear colors they normally dislike for symbolic reason: because they are members or fans of a certain football team, for instance. In addition, some fashionable types may select certain hues merely because they are "in" that year.

Finally, it should be noted that the effect of any color in dress is modified by the colors that accompany it. In general, therefore, the following remarks should be taken as applying mainly to costumes composed entirely or almost entirely of a single hue.

The mood of a crowd, as well as that of an individual, can often be read   20
in the colors of clothing. In the office of a large corporation, or at a professional convention, there is usually a predominance of conventional gray, navy, beige, tan and white—suggesting a general attitude of seriousness, hard work, neutrality, propriety and status. The same group of people at a picnic are a mass of lively, relaxed blue, red and brown, with touches of yellow and green. In the evening, at a disco, they shimmer under the rotating lights in dramatic combinations of purple, crimson, orange, turquoise, gold, silver and black.

Apart from the chameleon, man is the only animal who can change his skin to suit his background. Indeed, if he is to function successfully he must do so. The individual whose clothes do not fall within the recognized range of colors for a given situation attracts attention, usually (though not always) unfavorable attention. When a child puts its pet chameleon down on the earth and it does not turn brown, we know the creature is seriously ill. In the same way, men or women who begin to come to work in a conservative office wearing disco hues and a disco mood are regarded with anxiety and suspicion. If they do not blush a respectable beige, navy or gray within a reasonable length of time, their colleagues know that they will not be around for long.

Questions for Discussion and Writing

1. In what way, according to Lurie, is clothing a kind of language that can be analyzed to discover both the wearer's and the surrounding culture's values? In the past, how did clothing and adornment serve magical purposes?
2. What factors related to social class have determined which kinds of clothes could or could not be worn in particular societies in different eras? As a research project, you might investigate the evolution of blue jeans and their class-related values at different points in history—from sturdy miner's clothes to chic designer apparel.
3. Go through your wardrobe and classify items of clothes you wear according to the "statement" you wish to make in different contexts.

Should high school students be required to wear uniforms? Why or why not?

4. **Rhetorical inquiry:** Lurie draws an analogy between clothes and language and produces a number of surprising similarities. But, are there points where the analogy is stretched too far and falls short?

AMY TAN

Amy Tan was born in Oakland, California, in 1952, two and a half years after her parents immigrated to the United States in 1949, just before the Communist Revolution. She studied linguistics and worked with disabled children. Of her first visit to China in 1984 she says, "As soon as my feet touched China, I became Chinese." Tan's first novel, The Joy Luck Club *(1989), was widely praised for its depiction of conflicts between different cultures and generations and between Chinese mothers and daughters in America. She has also written* The Kitchen God's Wife *(1991),* The Hundred Secret Senses *(1995), and* Saving Fish from Drowning *(2005). In "Mother Tongue" (1990) Tan explores the many different kinds of English her mother uses in different circumstances.*

Before You Read

How would growing up in a family where English was not the primary language make language itself an important part of your life?

Mother Tongue

I am not a scholar of English or literature. I cannot give you much more than personal opinions on the English language and its variations in this country or others.

I am a writer. And by that definition, I am someone who has always loved language. I am fascinated by language in daily life. I spend a great deal of my time thinking about the power of language—the way it can evoke an emotion, a visual image, a complex idea, or a simple truth. Language is the tool of my trade. And I use them all—all the Englishes I grew up with.

Recently, I was made keenly aware of the different Englishes I do use. I was giving a talk to a large group of people, the same talk I had already given to half a dozen other groups. The nature of the talk was about my writing, my life, and my book, *The Joy Luck Club*. The talk was going along well enough, until I remembered one major difference that made the whole talk sound wrong. My mother was in the room. And it was perhaps the first time she had heard me give a lengthy speech, using the kind of English I have never used with her. I was saying things like, "The intersection of memory upon imagination" and "There is an aspect of my fiction that relates to thus-and-thus"—a speech filled with carefully wrought grammatical phrases, burdened, it suddenly seemed to me, with nominalized forms, past perfect tenses, conditional phrases, all the forms of standard English that I had learned is school and through books, the forms of English I did not use at home with my mother.

Just last week, I was walking down the street with my mother, and I again found myself conscious of the English I was using, and the English I do use with her. We were talking about the price of new and used furniture and I heard myself saying this: "Not waste money that way." My husband was with us as well, and he didn't notice any switch in my English. And then I realized why. It's because over the twenty years we've been together I've often used that same kind of English with him, and sometimes he even use it with me. It has become our language of intimacy, a different sort of English that relates to family talk, the language I grew up with.

So you'll have some idea of what this family talk I heard sounds like, I'll   5 quote what my mother said during a recent conversation which I videotaped and then transcribed. During this conversation, my mother was talking about a political gangster in Shanghai who had the same last name as her family's, Du, and how the gangster in his early years wanted to be adopted by her family, which was rich by comparison. Later, the gangster became more powerful, far richer than my mother's family, and one day showed up at my mother's wedding to pay his respects. Here's what she said in part:

"Du Yusong having business like fruit stand. Like off the street kind. He is Du like Du Zong—but not Tsung-ming Island people. The local people call putong, the river east side, he belong to that side local people. That man want to ask Du Zong father take him in like become own family. Du Zong father wasn't look down on him, but didn't take seriously, until that man big like become a mafia. Now important person, very hard to inviting him. Chinese way, came only to show respect, don't stay for dinner. Respect for making big celebration, he shows up. Mean gives lots of respect. Chinese custom. Chinese social life that way. If too important won't have to stay too long. He come to my wedding. I didn't see, I heard it. I gone to boy's side, they have YMCA dinner. Chinese age I was nineteen."

You should know that my mother's expressive command of English belies how much she actually understands. She reads the *Forbes* report, listens to *Wall Street Week,* converses daily with her stockbroker, reads all of Shirley MacLaine's books with ease—all kinds of things I can't begin to understand. Yet some of my friends tell me they understand 50 percent of what my mother says. Some say they understand 80 to 90 percent. Some say they understand none of it, as if she were speaking pure Chinese. But to me, my mother's English is perfectly clear, perfectly natural. It's my mother tongue. Her language, as I hear it, is vivid, direct, full of observation and imagery. That was the language that helped shape the way I saw things, expressed things, made sense of the world.

Lately, I've been giving more thought to the kind of English my mother speaks. Like others, I have described it to people as "broken" or "fractured"

English. But I wince when I say that. It has always bothered me that I can think of no way to describe it other than "broken," as if it were damaged and needed to be fixed, as if it lacked a certain wholeness and soundness. I've heard other terms used, "limited English," for example. But they seem just as bad, as if everything is limited, including people's perceptions of the limited English speaker.

I know this for a fact, because when I was growing up, my mother's "limited" English limited *my* perception of her. I was ashamed of her English. I believed that her English reflected the quality of what she had to say. That is, because she expressed them imperfectly her thoughts were imperfect. And I had plenty of empirical evidence to support me: the fact that people in department stores, at banks, and at restaurants did not take her seriously, did not give her good service, pretended not to understand her, or even acted as if they did not hear her.

My mother has long realized the limitations of her English as well.   10
When I was fifteen, she used to have me call people on the phone to pretend I was she. In this guise, I was forced to ask for information or even to complain and yell at people who had been rude to her. One time it was a call to her stockbroker in New York. She had cashed out her small portfolio and it just so happened we were going to go to New York the next week, our very first trip outside California. I had to get on the phone and say in an adolescent voice that was not very convincing, "This is Mrs. Tan."

And my mother was standing in the back whispering loudly, "Why he don't send me check, already two weeks late. So mad he lie to me, losing me money."

And then I said in perfect English, "Yes, I'm getting rather concerned. You had agreed to send the check two weeks ago, but it hasn't arrived."

Then she began to talk more loudly. "What he want, I come to New York tell him front of his boss, you cheating me?" And I was trying to calm her down, make her be quiet, while telling the stockbroker, "I can't tolerate any more excuses. If I don't receive the check immediately, I am going to have to speak to your manager when I'm in New York next week." And sure enough, the following week there we were in front of this astonished stockbroker, and I was sitting there red-faced and quiet, and my mother, the real Mrs. Tan, was shouting at his boss in her impeccable broken English.

We used a similar routine just five days ago, for a situation that was far less humorous. My mother had gone to the hospital for an appointment, to find out about a benign brain tumor a CAT scan had revealed a month ago. She said she had spoken very good English, her best English, no mistakes. Still, she said, the hospital did not apologize when they said they had lost the CAT scan and she had come for nothing. She said they did not seem to have any sympathy when she told them she was anxious to know the exact diagnosis, since her husband and son had both died of brain tumors. She said they would not give her any more information until the next time and she would have to make another appointment for that. So she said she would not leave until the doctor called her daughter. She wouldn't budge. And when the doctor finally called her daughter, me, who spoke in perfect English—lo and behold—we had assurances the CAT scan would be found, promises that a conference call on Monday would be held, and apologies for any suffering my mother had gone through for a most regrettable mistake.

I think my mother's English almost had an effect on limiting my possibilities in life as well. Sociologists and linguists probably will tell you that a person's developing language skills are more influenced by peers. But I do think that the language spoken in the family, especially in immigrant families which are more insular, plays a large role in shaping the language of the child. And I believe that it affected my results on achievement tests, IQ tests, and the SAT. While my English skills were never judged as poor, compared to math, English could not be considered my strong suit. In grade school I did moderately well, getting perhaps B's, sometimes B-pluses, in English and scoring perhaps in the sixtieth or seventieth percentile on achievement tests. But those scores were not good enough to override the opinion that my true abilities lay in math and science, because in those areas I achieved A's and scored in the ninetieth percentile or higher.

15

This was understandable. Math is precise, there is only one correct answer. Whereas, for me at least, the answers on English tests were always a judgment call, a matter of opinion and personal experience. Those tests were constructed around items like fill-in-the-blank sentence completion, such as, "Even though Tom was _____, Mary thought he was _____." And the correct answer always seemed to be the most bland combinations of thoughts, for example, "Even though Tom was shy, Mary thought he was charming," with the grammatical structure "even though" limiting the correct answer to some sort of semantic opposites, so you wouldn't get answers like, "Even though Tom was foolish, Mary thought he was ridiculous." Well, according to my mother, there were very few limitations as to what Tom could have been and what Mary might have thought of him. So I never did well on tests like that.

The same was true with word analogies, pairs of words in which you were supposed to find some sort of logical, semantic relationship—for example, "*Sunset* is to *nightfall* as _____ is to _____." And here you would be presented with a list of four possible pairs, one of which showed the same kind of relationship: *red* is to *stoplight, bus* is to *arrival, chills* is to *fever, yawn* is to *boring*. Well, I could never think that way. I knew what the tests were asking, but I could not block out of my mind the images already created by the first pair, "*sunset* is to *nightfall*"—and I would see a burst of colors against a darkening sky, the moon rising, the lowering of a curtain of stars. And all the other pairs of words—red, bus, stoplight, boring—just threw up a mass of confusing images, making it impossible for me to sort out something as logical as saying: "A sunset precedes nightfall" is the same as "a chill precedes a fever." The only way I would have gotten that answer right would have been to imagine an associative situation, for example, my being disobedient and staying out past sunset, catching a chill at night, which turns into feverish pneumonia as punishment, which indeed did happen to me.

I have been thinking about all this lately, about my mother's English, about achievement tests. Because lately I've been asked, as a writer, why there are not more Asian Americans represented in American literature. Why are there few Asian Americans enrolled in creative writing programs? Why do so many Chinese students go into engineering? Well, these are broad socio-logical questions I can't begin to answer. But I have noticed in surveys—in fact, just last week—that Asian students, as a whole, always do significantly better on math achievement tests than in English. And this makes me think that there are other Asian American students whose English spoken in the home might also be described as "broken" or "limited." And perhaps they also have teachers who are steering them away from writing and into math and science, which is what happened to me.

Fortunately, I happen to be rebellious in nature and enjoy the challenge of disproving assumptions made about me. I became an English major my first year in college, after being enrolled as pre-med. I started writing non-fiction as a freelancer the week after I was told by my former boss that writing was my worst skill and I should hone my talents toward account management.

But it wasn't until 1985 that I finally began to write fiction. And at first   20 I wrote using what I thought to be wittily crafted sentences, sentences that would finally prove I had mastery over the English language. Here's an example from the first draft of a story that later made its way into *The Joy Luck Club*, but without this line: "That was my mental quandary in its nascent state." A terrible line, which I can barely pronounce.

Fortunately, for reasons I won't get into today, I later decided I should envision a reader for the stories I would write. And the reader I decided upon was my mother, because these were stories about mothers. So with this reader in mind—and in fact she did read my early drafts—I began to write stories using all the Englishes I grew up with: the English I spoke to my mother, which for lack of a better term might be described as "simple"; the English she used with me, which for lack of a better term might be described as "broken"; my translation of her Chinese, which could certainly be described as "watered down"; and what I imagined to be her translation of her Chinese if she could speak in perfect English, her internal language, and for that I sought to preserve the essence, but neither an English nor a Chinese structure. I wanted to capture what language ability tests can never reveal: her intent, her passion, her imagery, the rhythms of her speech and the nature of her thoughts.

Apart from what any critic had to say about my writing, I knew I had succeeded where it counted when my mother finished reading my book and gave me her verdict: "So easy to read."

Questions for Discussion and Writing

1. What are some of the different "Englishes" Tan's mother speaks in different circumstances?
2. How would you characterize Tan's relationship with her mother and how did her mother feel about Tan being a writer?
3. What "Englishes" are you aware of using in different contexts—at home, school, work, or social situations? Describe a particular "English" you use in one of these contexts.
4. **Rhetorical inquiry:** What examples does Tan provide to illustrate that her mother's English, though broken-sounding to others, is clear and natural, vivid and direct, and full of observation and imagery?

ALDOUS HUXLEY

Aldous Huxley (1894–1963) was born in Surrey, England, and was educated at Eton and Balliol College, Oxford. Despite a serious eye disease, Huxley read with the aid of a magnifying glass and graduated from Oxford in 1915 with honors in English literature, after which he joined the staff of the Atheneum. *His brilliant social satires and wide-ranging essays on architecture, science, music, history, philosophy, and religion explore the relationship between humans and society.* Brave New World *(1932) is his best-known satire on how futuristic mass technology will achieve a sinister utopia of scientific breeding and conditioned happiness. Huxley's other works include* Eyeless in Gaza *(1936),* After Many a Summer *(1939),* Time Must Have a Stop *(1944), and* Ape and Essence *(1948).* The Doors of Perception *(1954),* Heaven and Hell *(1956), and* Island *(1962) can be seen as attempts to search in new spiritual directions—through mysticism, mescaline, and parapsychology—as a reaction to the grim future he so devastatingly portrayed. In "Propaganda under a Dictatorship," from* Brave New World Revisited *(1958), Huxley reveals how the manipulation of language in the propaganda of Nazi Germany conditioned the thoughts and behavior of the masses.*

Before You Read

What means do advertisers and politicians use to persuade us to believe something or to buy something?

Propaganda Under a Dictatorship

At his trial after the Second World War, Hitler's Minister for Armaments, Albert Speer, delivered a long speech in which, with remarkable acuteness, he described the Nazi tyranny and analyzed its methods. "Hitler's dictatorship," he said, "differed in one fundamental point from all its predecessors in history. It was the first dictatorship in the present period of modern technical development, a dictatorship which made complete use of all technical means for the domination of its own country. Through technical devices like the radio and the loudspeaker, eighty million people were deprived of independent thought. It was thereby possible to subject them to the will of one man. . . . Earlier dictators needed highly qualified assistants even at the lowest level—men who could think and act independently. The totalitarian system in the period of modern technical development can dispense with such men; thanks to modern methods of communication, it is possible to mechanize the lower leadership. As a result of this there has arisen the new type of the uncritical recipient of orders."

In the Brave New World of my prophetic fable technology had advanced far beyond the point it had reached in Hitler's day; consequently the recipients of orders were far less critical than their Nazi counterparts, far more obedient to the order-giving elite. Moreover, they had been genetically standardized and postnatally conditioned to perform their subordinate functions, and could therefore be depended upon to behave almost as predictably as machines. . . . This conditioning of "the lower leadership" is already going on under the Communist dictatorships. The Chinese and the Russians are not relying merely on the indirect effects of advancing technology; they are working directly on the psychophysical organisms of their lower leaders, subjecting minds and bodies to a system of ruthless and, from all accounts, highly effective conditioning. "Many a man," said Speer, "has been haunted by the nightmare that one day nations might be dominated by technical means. That nightmare was almost realized in Hitler's totalitarian system." Almost, but not quite. The Nazis did not have time—and perhaps did not have the intelligence and the necessary knowledge—to brainwash and condition their lower leadership. This, it may be, is one of the reasons why they failed.

Since Hitler's day the armory of technical devices at the disposal of the would-be dictator has been considerably enlarged. As well as the radio, the loudspeaker, the moving picture camera and the rotary press, the contemporary propagandist can make use of television to broadcast the image as well as the voice of his client, and can record both image and voice on spools of magnetic tape. Thanks to technological progress, Big Brother can now be almost as omnipresent as God. Nor is it only on the technical front that the hand of the would-be dictator has been strengthened. Since Hitler's day a great deal of work has been carried out in those fields of applied psychology and neurology which are the special province of the propagandist, the indoctrinator and the brainwasher. In the past these specialists in the art of changing people's minds were empiricists. By a method of trial and error they had worked out a number of techniques and procedures, which they used very effectively without, however, knowing precisely why they were effective. Today the art of mind-control is in process of becoming a science. The practitioners of this science know what they are doing and why. They are guided in their work by theories and hypotheses solidly established on a massive foundation of experimental evidence. Thanks to the new insights and the new techniques made possible by these insights, the nightmare that was "all but realized in Hitler's totalitarian system" may soon be completely realizable.

But before we discuss these new insights and techniques let us take a look at the nightmare that so nearly came true in Nazi Germany. What were the methods used by Hitler and Goebbels[1] for "depriving eighty million people of independent thought and subjecting them to the will of one man"? And what was the theory of human nature upon which those terrifyingly successful methods were based? These questions can be answered, for the most part, in Hitler's own words. And what remarkably clear and astute words they are! When he writes about such vast abstractions as Race and History and Providence, Hitler is strictly unreadable. But when he writes about the German masses and the methods he used for dominating and directing them, his style changes. Nonsense gives place to sense, bombast to a hard-boiled and cynical lucidity. In his philosophical lucubrations Hitler was either cloudily daydreaming or reproducing other people's half-baked notions. In his comments on crowds and propaganda he was writing of things he knew by firsthand experience. In the words of his ablest biographer, Mr. Alan Bullock, "Hitler was the greatest demagogue in history." Those who add, "only a demagogue," fail to appreciate the nature of political power in an age of mass politics. As he himself said, "To be a leader means to be able to move the masses." Hitler's aim was first to move the masses and then, having pried them loose from their traditional loyalties and moralities, to impose upon them (with the hypnotized consent of the majority) a new authoritarian order of his own devising. "Hitler," wrote Hermann Rauschning in 1939, "has a deep respect for the Catholic church and the Jesuit order; not because of their Christian doctrine, but because of the 'machinery' they have elaborated and controlled, their hierarchical system, their extremely clever tactics, their knowledge of human nature and their wise use of human weaknesses in ruling over believers." Ecclesiasticism without Christianity, the discipline of a monastic rule, not for God's sake or in order to achieve personal salvation, but for the sake of the State and for the greater glory and power of the demagogue turned Leader—this was the goal toward which the systematic moving of the masses was to lead.

Let us see what Hitler thought of the masses he moved and how he did   5
the moving. The first principle from which he started was a value judgment: the masses are utterly contemptible. They are incapable of abstract thinking and uninterested in any fact outside the circle of their immediate experience. Their behavior is determined, not by knowledge and reason, but by feelings and unconscious drives. It is in these drives and feelings that "the roots

---

[1] *Joseph Paul Goebbels (1897–1945):* the propaganda minister under Hitler, a master of the "big lie."

of their positive as well as their negative attitudes are implanted." To be successful a propagandist must learn how to manipulate these instincts and emotions. "The driving force which has brought about the most tremendous revolutions on this earth has never been a body of scientific teaching which has gained power over the masses, but always a devotion which has inspired them, and often a kind of hysteria which has urged them into action. Whoever wishes to win over the masses must know the key that will open the door of their hearts." . . . In post-Freudian jargon, of their unconscious.

Hitler made his strongest appeal to those members of the lower middle classes who had been ruined by the inflation of 1923, and then ruined all over again by the depression of 1929 and the following years. "The masses" of whom he speaks were these bewildered, frustrated and chronically anxious millions. To make them more masslike, more homogeneously subhuman, he assembled them, by the thousands and the tens of thousands, in vast halls and arenas, where individuals could lose their personal identity, even their elementary humanity, and be merged with the crowd. A man or woman makes direct contact with society in two ways: as a member of some familial, professional or religious group, or as a member of a crowd. Groups are capable of being as moral and intelligent as the individuals who form them; a crowd is chaotic, has no purpose of its own and is capable of anything except intelligent action and realistic thinking. Assembled in a crowd, people lose their powers of reasoning and their capacity for moral choice. Their suggestibility is increased to the point where they cease to have any judgment or will of their own. They become very excitable, they lose all sense of individual or collective responsibility, they are subject to sudden accesses of rage, enthusiasm and panic. In a word, a man in a crowd behaves as though he had swallowed a large dose of some powerful intoxicant. He is a victim of what I have called "herd-poisoning." Like alcohol, herd-poison is an active, extraverted drug. The crowd-intoxicated individual escapes from responsibility, intelligence and morality into a kind of frantic, animal mindlessness.

During his long career as an agitator, Hitler had studied the effects of herd-poison and had learned how to exploit them for his own purposes. He had discovered that the orator can appeal to those "hidden forces" which motivate men's actions, much more effectively than can the writer. Reading is a private, not a collective activity. The writer speaks only to individuals, sitting by themselves in a state of normal sobriety. The orator speaks to masses of individuals, already well primed with herd-poison. They are at his mercy and, if he knows his business, he can do what he likes with them. As an orator, Hitler knew his business supremely well. He was able, in his own words, "to follow the lead of the great mass in such a way that from the living emotion to his hearers the apt word which he needed would be suggested to him and in its turn this would go straight to the heart of his hearers." Otto Strasser called him a "loudspeaker, proclaiming the most secret desires, the least admissible instincts, the sufferings and personal revolts of a whole nation." Twenty years before Madison Avenue embarked upon "Motivational Research," Hitler was systematically exploring and exploiting the secret fears and hopes, the cravings, anxieties and frustrations of the German masses. It is by manipulating "hidden forces" that the advertising experts induce us to buy their wares—a toothpaste, a brand of cigarettes, a political candidate. And it is by appealing to the same hidden forces—and to others too dangerous for Madison Avenue to meddle with—that Hitler induced the German masses to buy themselves a Fuehrer, an insane philosophy and the Second World War.

Unlike the masses, intellectuals have a taste for rationality and an interest in facts. Their critical habit of mind makes them resistant to the kind of propaganda that works so well on the majority. Among the masses "instinct is supreme, and from instinct comes faith. . . . While the healthy common folk instinctively close their ranks to form a community of the people" (under a Leader, it goes without saying) "intellectuals run this way and that, like hens in a poultry yard. With them one cannot make history; they cannot be used as elements composing a community." Intellectuals are the kind of people who demand evidence and are shocked by logical inconsistencies and fallacies. They regard oversimplification as the original sin of the mind and have no use for the slogans, the unqualified assertions and sweeping generalizations which are the propagandist's stock in trade. "All effective propaganda," Hitler wrote, "must be confined to a few bare necessities and then must be expressed in a few stereotyped formulas." These stereotyped formulas must be constantly repeated, for "only constant repetition will finally succeed in imprinting an idea upon the memory of a crowd." Philosophy teaches us to feel uncertain about the things that seem to us self-evident. Propaganda, on the other hand, teaches us to accept as self-evident matters about which it would be reasonable to suspend our judgment or to feel doubt. The aim of the demagogue is to create social coherence under his own leadership. But, as Bertrand Russell has pointed out, "systems of dogma without empirical foundations, such as scholasticism, Marxism and fascism, have the advantage of producing a great deal of social coherence among their disciples." The demagogic propagandist must therefore be consistently dogmatic. All his statements are made without qualification. There are no grays in his picture of the world; everything is either diabolically black or celestially white. In Hitler's words, the propagandist should adopt "a systematically one-sided attitude towards every problem that has to be dealt with." He must never admit that he might be wrong or that people with a different point of view might be even partially right. Opponents should not be argued with; they should be attacked, shouted down, or, if they become too much of a nuisance, liquidated. The morally squeamish intellectual may be shocked by this kind of thing. But the masses are always convinced that "right is on the side of the active aggressor."

Such, then, was Hitler's opinion of humanity in the mass. It was a very low opinion. Was it also an incorrect opinion? The tree is known by its fruits, and a theory of human nature which inspired the kind of techniques that proved so horribly effective must contain at least an element of truth. Virtue and intelligence belong to human beings as individuals freely associating with other individuals in small groups. So do sin and stupidity. But the subhuman mindlessness to which the demagogue makes his appeal, the moral imbecility on which he relies when he goads his victims into action, are characteristic not of men and women as individuals, but of men and women in masses. Mindlessness and moral idiocy are not characteristically human attributes; they are symptoms of herd-poisoning. In all the world's higher religions, salvation and enlightenment are for individuals. The kingdom of heaven is within the mind of a person, not within the collective mindlessness of a crowd. Christ promised to be present where two or three are gathered together. He did not say anything about being present where thousands are intoxicating one another with herd-poison. Under the Nazis enormous numbers of people were compelled to spend an enormous amount of time marching in serried ranks from point A to point B and back again to point A. "This keeping of the whole population on the march seemed to be a senseless waste of time and energy. Only much later," adds Hermann Rauschning, "was there revealed in it a subtle intention based on a well-judged adjustment of ends and means. Marching diverts men's thoughts. Marching kills thought. Marching makes an end of individuality. Marching is the indispensable magic stroke performed in order to accustom the people to a mechanical, quasi-ritualistic activity until it becomes second nature."

From his point of view and at the level where he had chosen to do his   10 dreadful work, Hitler was perfectly correct in his estimate of human nature. To those of us who look at men and women as individuals rather than as members of crowds, or of regimented collectives, he seems hideously wrong. In an age of accelerating overpopulation, of accelerating overorganization and even more efficient means of mass communication, how can we preserve the integrity and reassert the value of the human individual? This is a question that can still be asked and perhaps effectively answered. A generation from now it may be too late to find an answer and perhaps impossible, in the stifling collective climate of that future time, even to ask the question.

Questions for Discussion and Writing

1. In Huxley's view, why was one particular segment of the German population so vulnerable to Hitler's propaganda techniques? What role did the inflation of 1923 and the Depression of 1929 play in setting the stage for Hitler's rise to power?

2. What propaganda techniques did Hitler use to manipulate the masses? What was Hitler's opinion of the masses he manipulated?

3. What are some of the more telling examples of contemporary propaganda techniques of stereotypes, slogans, slanting, or guilt (or virtue) by association mentioned by Huxley? What present-day examples used by politicians can you identify?

4. **Rhetorical inquiry:** How were the propaganda techniques Hitler used designed to make public debate of issues impossible, eliminate opposing viewpoints, and create an incendiary climate of inflamed passions?

STUART HIRSCHBERG

Stuart Hirschberg teaches English at Rutgers University, Newark, and is the author of scholarly works on W. B. Yeats and Ted Hughes. He is also the editor and coeditor (with Terry Hirschberg) of anthologies, including this book, One World, Many Cultures *(6th ed., 2007),* Every Day, Everywhere: Global Perspectives on Popular Culture *(2002),* Past to Present: Ideas that Changed Our World *(2003),* Discovering the Many Worlds of Literature *(2004), and* Arguing Across the Disciplines *(2007). The following essay is drawn from* Reflections on Language *(1999).*

Before You Read

What recent ads strike you as the most creative and persuasive?

The Rhetoric of Advertising

Whether ads are presented as sources of information enabling the consumer to make educated choices between products or aim at offering memorable images or witty, thoughtful, or poetic copy, the underlying intent of all advertising is to persuade specific audiences. Seen in this way, ads appear as mini-arguments whose strategies and techniques of persuasion can be analyzed just like a written argument. We can discover which elements are designed to appeal to the audience's emotions (*pathos* according to Aristotle), which elements make their appeal in terms of reasons, evidence, or logic (*logos*), and how the advertiser goes about winning credibility for itself or in terms of the spokesperson employed to speak on behalf of the product (the *ethos* dimension). Like arguments, ads can be effective if they appeal to the needs, values, and beliefs of the audience. Although the verbal and visual elements within an ad are designed to work together, we can study these elements separately. We can look at how the composition of the elements within an ad is intended to function. We can look at the role of language and how it is used to persuade. We can study how objects and settings are used to promote the audience's identification with the products being sold. We can judge ads according to the skill with which they deploy all of these resources while at the same time being critically aware of their intended effects on us.

THE TECHNIQUES OF ADVERTISING

The claim the ad makes is designed to establish the superiority of the product in the minds of the audience and to create a distinctive image for the product, whether it is a brand of cigarettes, a financial service, or a type of gasoline. The single most important technique for creating this image depends on transferring ideas, attributes, or feelings from outside the product onto the product itself. In this way the product comes to represent an obtainable object or service that embodies, represents, or symbolizes a whole range of meanings. This transfer can be achieved in many ways. For example, when Nicole Kidman or Jennifer Lopez lends her glamour and beauty to the merchandising of a perfume, the consumer is meant to conclude that the perfume must be superior to other perfumes in the way that the actress embodies beauty, glamour, and sex appeal. The attempt to transfer significance can operate in two ways. It can encourage the audience to discover meanings and to correlate feelings and attributes that the advertiser wishes the product to represent in ways that allow these needs and desires to become attached to specific products. It can also prevent the correlation of thoughts or feelings that might discourage the audience from purchasing a particular product. For example, the first most instinctive response to the thought of smoking a cigarette might be linked with the idea of inhaling hot and dry smoke from what are essentially burning tobacco leaves. Thus, any associations the audience might have with burning leaves, coughing, and dry hot smoke must be short-circuited by supplying them with a whole set of other associations to receive and occupy the perceptual "slot" that might have been triggered by their first reactions. Cigarette advertisers do this in a variety of ways:

> By showing active people in outdoorsy settings, they put the thought of emphysema, shortness of breath, or lung disease very far away indeed.

> By showing cigarette packs set against the background of grass glistening with morning dew or bubbling streams or cascading waterfalls, they subtly guide the audience's response away from what is dry, hot, congested, or burning toward what is open, airy, moist, cool, and clean.

> In some brands, menthol flavoring and green and blue colors are intended to promote these associations.

Thus, ads act as do all other kinds of persuasion to intensify correlations that work to the advertiser's advantage and to suppress associations that would lessen the product's appeal.

The kinds of associations audiences are encouraged to perceive reflect a broad range of positive emotional appeals that encourage the audience to find self-esteem through the purchase of a product that by itself offers a way to meet personal and social needs. The particular approach taken in the composition of the ad, the way it is laid out, and the connotations of the advertising copy vary according to the emotional appeal of the ad.

The most common manipulative techniques are designed to make con- 5 sumers want to consume to satisfy deep-seated human drives. Of course, no one consciously believes that purchasing a particular kind of toothpaste, perfume, lipstick, or automobile will meet real psychological and social needs, but that is exactly how products are sold—through the promise of delivering unattainable satisfactions through tangible purchasable objects or services. In purchasing a certain product, we are offered the chance to create ourselves, our personality, and our relationships through consumption.

EMOTIONAL APPEALS USED IN ADVERTISING

The emotional appeals in ads function exactly the way assumptions about value do in written arguments. They supply the unstated major premise that supplies a rationale to persuade an audience that a particular product will meet one or another of several different kinds of needs. Some ads present the purchase of a product as a means by which consumers can find social acceptance.

These ads address the consumer as "you" ("Wouldn't 'you' really rather have a Buick?"). The "you" here is plural but is perceived as being individual and personal by someone who has already formed the connection with the product. Ironically, the price of remaining in good standing with this "group" of fellow consumers requires the consumer to purchase an expensive automobile. In this sense, ads give consumers a chance to belong to social groups that have only one thing in common—the purchase of a particular product.

One variation on the emotional need to belong to a designated social group is the appeal to status or "snob appeal." Snob appeal is not new. In 1710, the *Spectator*, a popular newspaper of the time, carried an ad that read:

> An incomparable Powder for Cleaning Teeth, which has given great satisfaction to most of the Nobility Gentry in England.

Ads for scotch, expensive cars, boats, jewelry, and watches frequently place their products in upper-class settings or depict them in connection with the fine arts (sculpture, ballet, etc.). The *value warrant* in these ads encourages the consumer to imagine that the purchase of the item will confer qualities associated with the background or activities of this upper-class world onto the consumer.

In other ads the need to belong takes a more subtle form of offering the 10 product as a way to become part of a time in the past the audience might look back to with nostalgia. Grandmotherly figures wearing aprons and holding products that are advertised as being "like Grandma used to make" offer the consumer an imaginary past, a family tradition, or a simpler time looked back to with warmth and sentimentality. For many years, Smucker's preserves featured ads in which the product was an integral part of a scene emanating security and warmth, which the ad invited us to remember as if it were our own past. Ads of this kind are often photographed through filters that present misty sepia-tone images that carefully recreate old-fashioned kitchens with the accompanying appliances, dishes, clothes, and hairstyles. The ads thus supply us with false memories and invite us to insert ourselves into this imaginary past and to remember it as if it were our own. At the furthest extreme, ads employing the appeal to see ourselves as part of a group may try to evoke patriotic feelings so that the prospective consumer will derive the satisfactions of good citizenship and sense of participation in being part of the collective psyche of an entire nation. The point is that people really do have profound needs that advertisers can exploit, but it would be a rare product indeed that could really fulfill such profound needs.

Advertisers use highly sophisticated market research techniques to enable them to define and characterize precisely those people who are most likely to be receptive to ads of particular kinds. The science of demographics is aided and abetted by psychological research that enables advertisers to "target" a precisely designated segment of the general public. For example, manufacturers of various kinds of liquor can rely on studies that inform them that vodka drinkers are most likely to read *Psychology Today* and scotch drinkers the *New Yorker,* while readers of *Time* prefer rum and the audience for *Playboy* has a large number of readers who prefer gin. Once a market segment with defined psychological characteristics has been identified, an individual ad can be crafted for that particular segment and placed in the appropriate publication.

Ads, of course, can elicit responses by attempting to manipulate consumers through negative as well as positive emotional appeals. Helen Woodward, the head copywriter for an ad agency, once offered the following advice for ad writers trying to formulate a new ad for baby food: "Give 'em the figures about the baby death rate—but don't say it flatly . . . if we only had the nerve to put a hearse in the ad, you couldn't keep the women away from the food" (Stuart Ewen, *Captains of Consciousness: Advertising and the Social Roots of Consumer Culture* [1976]). Ads of this kind must first arouse the consumer's anxieties and then offer the product as the solution to the problem that more often than not the ad has created.

For example, an advertisement for Polaroid evokes the fear of not having taken pictures of moments that cannot be re-created and then offers the product as a form of insurance that will prevent this calamity from occurring. Nikon does the same in claiming that "a moment is called a moment because it doesn't last forever. Think of sunsets. A child's surprise. A Labrador's licky kiss. This is precisely why the Nikon N50 has the simple 'Simple' switch on top of the camera."

Ads for products that promise to guarantee their purchasers sex appeal, youth, health, social acceptance, self-esteem, creativity, enlightenment, a happy family life, loving relationships, escape from boredom, vitality, and many other things frequently employ scare tactics to frighten or worry the consumer into purchasing the product to ease his or her fears. These ads must first make the consumer dissatisfied with the self that exists. In this way, they function exactly as do *policy arguments* that recommend solutions to problems with measurably harmful consequences. The difference is that these kinds of ads actually are designed to arouse and then exploit the anxieties related to these problems.

Large industrial conglomerates, whether in oil, chemicals, pharmaceuticals, or agribusiness, frequently use advertising to accomplish different kinds of objectives than simply persuading the consumer to buy a particular product. These companies often seek to persuade the general public that they are not polluting the environment, poisoning the water, or causing environmental havoc in the process of manufacturing their products. The emotional appeal they use is to portray themselves as concerned "corporate citizens," vitally interested in the public good as a whole, and especially in those communities where they conduct their operations. In some cases, the ads present products as if they were directly produced from nature without being subjected to intermediary processing, preservatives, and contaminants, thereby lessening concern that they produce harmful byproducts. For example, Mazola might depict a spigot producing corn oil directly inserted into an ear of corn. A Jeep might appear to have materialized out of thin air on a seemingly inaccessible mountain peak. Companies sensitive to accusations that they are polluting the air and water can mount an advertising campaign designed to prove that they are not simply exploiting the local resources (whether timber, oil, fish, coal) for profits but are genuinely interested in putting something back into the community. The folksy good-neighbor tone of these ads is designed to create a benign image of the company.

THE LANGUAGE OF ADVERTISING

We can see how the creation of a sense of the company's credibility as a concerned citizen corresponds to what Aristotle called the *ethos* dimension. For example, Chevron expresses concern that the light from their oil drilling operations be shielded so that spawning sea turtles won't be unintentionally misdirected and lose their way!

The appeals to logic, statements of reasons, and presentations of evidence in ads correspond to the *logos* dimension of argument. The wording of the claims is particularly important, since it determines whether companies are legally responsible for any claims they make.

Claims in advertising need to be evaluated to discover whether something is asserted that needs to be proved or is implied without actually being stated.

Claims may refer to authoritative-sounding results obtained by supposedly independent laboratories, teams of research scientists, or physicians without ever saying how these surveys were conducted, what statistical methods were used, and who interpreted the results. Ads of this kind may make an impressive-sounding quasi-scientific claim; Ivory Soap used to present itself as "99 and 44/100% pure" without answering "pure" what. Some ads use technical talk and scientific terms to give the impression of a scientific breakthrough. For example, STP claims that it added "an anti-wear agent and viscosity improvers" to your oil. The copy for L. L. Bean claims of one of its jackets that "even in brutal ice winds gusting to 80 knots this remarkable anorak kept team members who wore it warm and comfortable." It would be important to know that the team members referred to are members of the "L. L. Bean test team."

Other claims cannot be substantiated, for example, "we're the Dexter   20
Shoe Company. And for nearly four decades we put a lot of Dexter Maine into every pair of shoes we make."

In an ad for lipstick, Aveda makes the claim that "it's made of rich, earthy lip colours formulated with pure plant pigment from the Uruku tree. Organically grown by indigenous people in the rain forest."

Claims may be deceptive in other ways. Of all the techniques advertisers use to influence what people believe and how they spend their money, none is more basic than the use of so-called *weasel words*. This term was popularized by Theodore Roosevelt in a speech he gave in St. Louis, May 31, 1916, when he commented that notes from the Department of State were filled with weasel words that retract the meaning of the words they are next to just as a weasel sucks the meat out of the egg.

In modern advertising parlance, a weasel word has come to mean any qualifier or comparative that is used to imply a positive quality that cannot be stated as a fact, because it cannot be substantiated. For example, if an ad claims a toothpaste will "help" stop cavities it does not obligate the manufacturer to substantiate this claim. So, too, if a product is advertised as "fighting" germs, the equivocal claim hides the fact that the product may fight and lose.

An ad for STP claimed that "no matter what kind of car you drive, STP gas treatment helps remove the water that leads to gas line freeze. And unlike gas line antifreeze, our unique gas treatment formula works to reduce intake valve deposits and prevent clogged injectors." The key words are "helps" and "works," neither of which obligates STP to be legally accountable to support the claim.

The words *virtually* (as in "virtually spotless") and *up to* or *for as long*   25
as (as in "stops coughs up to eight hours") also remove any legal obligation on the part of the manufacturer to justify the claim.

Other favorite words in the copywriter's repertoire, such as *free* and *new*, are useful in selling everything from cat food to political candidates.

THE ETHICAL DIMENSION OF PERSUASION

As we have seen in our examination of the methods advertisers use to influence consumers, ethical questions are implicit in every act of persuasion. For example, what are we to make of a persuader whose objectives in seeking to influence an audience may be praiseworthy but who consciously makes use of distorted facts or seeks to manipulate an audience by playing on their known attitudes, values, and beliefs? Is success in persuasion the only criterion or should we hold would-be persuaders accountable to some ethical

Advertising is the greatest art form of the 20th century

—Marshall McLuhan

"Advertise! Advertise! That's always been your answer for everything."

How does this cartoon emphasize the essential role that advertising has played in modern culture?

© *The New Yorker Collection* 1963. *Warren Miller* from cartoonbank.com. All rights reserved.

Whereyabin? How is the product offered as a solution to a problem that will permit the customer to once again indulge in the hard-to-digest foods. How is the inquiry ("Whereyabin") intended to put the customer on the defensive and create a sense of relationship between the unspecified reader of this ad and the person being addressed? How is the confrontational style of the inquiry meant to serve as a surrogate for the hard-to-digest deli platter? How is the ad structured as a contrast between abrasiveness and comfort on both the personal and the product level?

How is this ad designed to get consumers to associate the Mitsubishi Montero with the tough and formidable rhinoceros?

How is the image and advertising copy of this ad designed to offer an alternative to elitist class values?

standards of responsibility about the means they use to achieve specific ends? Perhaps the most essential quality in determining whether any act of persuasion is an ethical one depends on the writer maintaining an open dialogue with different perspectives that might be advanced on a particular issue. By contrast, any act of persuasion that intentionally seeks to avoid self-criticism or challenges from competing perspectives will come across as insincere, dogmatic, deceptive, and defensive. The desire to shut down debate or control an audience's capacity to respond to the argument might well be considered unethical. The consequence of this attitude may be observed in the arguer's use of fraudulent evidence, illogical reasoning, emotionally laden irrelevant appeals, simplistic representation of the issue, or the pretense of expertise. Standards to apply when judging the ethical dimension in any act of persuasion require us to consider whether any element of coercion, deception, or manipulation is present. This becomes especially true when we look at the relationship between propaganda as a form of mass persuasion and the rhetorical means used to influence large groups of people.

Questions for Discussion and Writing

1. How do modern advertisers use traditional rhetorical techniques, identified by Aristotle, to appeal to the audiences' emotions (*pathos*), reason (*logos*), and sense of credibility (*ethos*)?
2. In what ways does advertising depend on the transfer of ideas and associations to create a sense of distinctive identity for the product or service?
3. How do the preceding ads use the techniques identified in this article to market their products? In your opinion, are these ads effective? Why or why not?
4. **Rhetorical inquiry:** Why have companies become sensitive to the ethical implications of the ways in which they present themselves? What advertising trends best illustrate this?

Fiction

GISH JEN

Gish Jen (b.1956) grew up in Scarsdale, New York, the daughter of immigrant Chinese parents. She was educated at Harvard, the Stanford School of Business, and the Iowa Writer's Workshop. Her works include Mona in the Promised Land *(1996) and* Who's Irish? *(1999), from which the following story is drawn. Her work has been included in* Best American Short Stories of the Century, *edited by John Updike (2000).*

Before You Read

Would having an elderly parent live with you when you had your own family be an option?

Who's Irish?

In China, people say mixed children are supposed to be smart, and definitely my granddaughter Sophie is smart. But Sophie is wild, Sophie is not like my daughter Natalie, or like me. I am work hard my whole life, and fierce besides. My husband always used to say he is afraid of me, and in our restaurant, busboys and cooks all afraid of me too. Even the gang members come for protection money, they try to talk to my husband. When I am there, they stay away. If they come by mistake, they pretend they are come to eat. They hide behind the menu, they order a lot of food. They talk about their mothers. Oh, my mother have some arthritis, need to take herbal medicine, they say. Oh, my mother getting old, her hair all white now.

I say, Your mother's hair used to be white, but since she dye it, it become black again. Why don't you go home once in a while and take a look? I tell them, Confucius say a filial son knows what color his mother's hair is.

My daughter is fierce too, she is vice president in the bank now. Her new house is big enough for everybody to have their own room, including me. But Sophie take after Natalie's husband's family, their name is Shea. Irish. I always thought Irish people are like Chinese people, work so hard on the railroad, but now I know why the Chinese beat the Irish. Of course, not all Irish are like the Shea family, of course not. My daughter tell me I should not say Irish this, Irish that.

How do you like it when people say the Chinese this, the Chinese that, she say.

You know, the British call the Irish heathen, just like they call the Chinese, she say.

You think the Opium War was bad, how would you like to live right next door to the British, she say.

And that is that. My daughter have a funny habit when she win an argument, she take a sip of something and look away, so the other person is not embarrassed. So I am not embarrassed. I do not call anybody anything either. I just happen to mention about the Shea family, an interesting fact: four brothers in the family, and not one of them work. The mother, Bess, have a job before she got sick, she was executive secretary in a big company. She is handle everything for a big shot, you would be surprised how complicated her job is, not just type this, type that. Now she is a nice woman with a clean house. But her boys, every one of them is on welfare, or so-called severance pay, or so-called disability pay. Something. They say they cannot find work, this is not the economy of the fifties, but I say, Even the black people doing better

5

these days, some of them live so fancy, you'd be surprised. Why the Shea family have so much trouble? They are white people, they speak English. When I come to this country, I have no money and do not speak English. But my husband and I own our restaurant before he die. Free and clear, no mortgage. Of course, I understand I am just lucky, come from a country where the food is popular all over the world. I understand it is not the Shea family's fault they come from a country where everything is boiled. Still, I say.

She's right, we should broaden our horizons, say one brother, Jim, at Thanks-giving. Forget about the car business. Think about egg rolls.

Pad thai, say another brother, Mike. I'm going to make my fortune in pad thai. It's going to be the new pizza.

I say, You people too picky about what you sell. Selling egg rolls not   10
good enough for you, but at least my husband and I can say, We made it. What can you say? Tell me. What can you say?

Everybody chew their tough turkey.

I especially cannot understand my daughter's husband John, who has no job but cannot take care of Sophie either. Because he is a man, he say, and that's the end of the sentence.

Plain boiled food, plain boiled thinking. Even his name is plain boiled: John. Maybe because I grew up with black bean sauce and hoisin sauce and garlic sauce, I always feel something is missing when my son-in-law talk.

But, okay: so my son-in-law can be man, I am baby-sitter. Six hours a day, same as the old sitter, crazy Amy, who quit. This is not so easy, now that I am sixty-eight, Chinese age almost seventy. Still, I try. In China, daughter take care of mother. Here it is the other way around. Mother help daughter, mother ask, Anything else I can do? Otherwise daughter complain mother is not supportive. I tell daughter, We do not have this word in Chinese, *supportive*. But my daughter too busy to listen, she has to go to meeting, she has to write memo while her husband go to the gym to be a man. My daughter say otherwise he will be depressed. Seems like all his life he has this trouble, depression.

No one wants to hire someone who is depressed, she say. It is important   15
for him to keep his spirits up.

Beautiful wife, beautiful daughter, beautiful house, oven can clean itself automatically. No money left over, because only one income, but lucky enough, got the baby-sitter for free. If John lived in China, he would be very happy. But he is not happy. Even at the gym things go wrong. One day, he pull a muscle. Another day, weight room too crowded. Always something.

Until finally, hooray, he has a job. Then he feel pressure.

I need to concentrate, he say. I need to focus.

He is going to work for insurance company. Salesman job. A paycheck, he say, and at least he will wear clothes instead of gym shorts. My daughter buy him some special candy bars from the health-food store. They say THINK! on them, and are supposed to help John think.

John is a good-looking boy, you have to say that, especially now that he   20
shave so you can see his face.

I am an old man in a young man's game, say John.

I will need a new suit, say John.

This time I am not going to shoot myself in the foot, say John.

Good, I say.

She means to be supportive, my daughter say. Don't start the send her   25
back to China thing, because we can't.

Sophie is three years old American age, but already I see her nice Chinese
side swallowed up by her wild Shea side. She looks like mostly Chinese.
Beautiful black hair, beautiful black eyes. Nose perfect size, not so flat looks
like something fell down, not so large looks like some big deal got stuck in
wrong face. Everything just right, only her skin is a brown surprise to John's
family. So brown, they say. Even John say it. She never goes in the sun, still
she is that color, he say. Brown. They say, Nothing the matter with brown.
They are just surprised. So brown. Nattie is not that brown, they say. They
say, It seems like Sophie should be a color in between Nattie and John.
Seems funny, a girl named Sophie Shea be brown. But she is brown, maybe
her name should be Sophie Brown. She never go in the sun, still she is that
color, they say. Nothing the matter with brown. They are just surprised.

The Shea family talk is like this sometimes, going around and around
like a Christmas-tree train.

Maybe John is not her father, I say one day, to stop the train. And sure
enough, train wreck. None of the brothers ever say the word *brown* to me
again.

Instead, John's mother, Bess, say, I hope you are not offended.

She say, I did my best on those boys. But raising four boys with no   30
father is no picnic.

You have a beautiful family, I say.

I'm getting old, she say.

You deserve a rest, I say. Too many boys make you old.

I never had a daughter, she say. You have a daughter.

I have a daughter, I say. Chinese people don't think a daughter is so   35
great, but you're right. I have a daughter.

I was never against the marriage, you know, she say. I never thought
John was marrying down. I always thought Nattie was just as good as white.

I was never against the marriage either, I say. I just wonder if they look
at the whole problem.

Of course you pointed out the problem, you are a mother, she say. And
now we both have a granddaughter. A little brown granddaughter, she is so
precious to me.

I laugh. A little brown granddaughter, I say. To tell you the truth, I
don't know how she came out so brown.

We laugh some more. These days Bess need a walker to walk. She take   40
so many pills, she need two glasses of water to get them all down. Her
favorite TV show is about bloopers, and she love her bird feeder. All day
long, she can watch that bird feeder, like a cat.

I can't wait for her to grow up, Bess say. I could use some female company.

Too many boys, I say.

Boys are fine, she say. But they do surround you after a while.

You should take a break, come live with us, I say. Lots of girls at our house.

Be careful what you offer, say Bess with a wink. Where I come from,   45
people mean for you to move in when they say a thing like that.

Nothing the matter with Sophie's outside, that's the truth. It is inside
that she is like not any Chinese girl I ever see. We go to the park, and this is
what she does. She stand up in the stroller. She take off all her clothes and
throw them in the fountain.

Sophie! I say. Stop!

But she just laugh like a crazy person. Before I take over as baby-sitter,
Sophie has that crazy-person sitter, Amy the guitar player. My daughter
thought this Amy very creative—another word we do not talk about in
China. In China, we talk about whether we have difficulty or no difficulty.
We talk about whether life is bitter or not bitter. In America, all day long,
people talk about creative. Never mind that I cannot even look at this Amy,
with her shirt so short that her belly button showing. This Amy think Sophie
should love her body. So when Sophie take off her diaper, Amy laugh. When
Sophie run around naked, Amy say she wouldn't want to wear a diaper
either. When Sophie go *shu-shu* in her lap, Amy laugh and say there are no
germs in pee. When Sophie take off her shoes, Amy say bare feet is best,
even the pediatrician say so. That is why Sophie now walk around with no
shoes like a beggar child. Also why Sophie love to take off her clothes.

Turn around! say the boys in the park. Let's see that ass!

Of course, Sophie does not understand. Sophie clap her hands, I am the   50
only one to say, No! This is not a game.

It has nothing to do with John's family, my daughter say. Amy was too
permissive, that's all.

But I think if Sophie was not wild inside, she would not take off her
shoes and clothes to begin with.

You never take off your clothes when you were little, I say. All my
Chinese friends had babies, I never saw one of them act wild like that.

Look, my daughter say. I have a big presentation tomorrow.

John and my daughter agree Sophie is a problem, but they don't know   55
what to do.

You spank her, she'll stop, I say another day.

But they say, Oh no.

In America, parents not supposed to spank the child.

It gives them low self-esteem, my daughter say. And that leads to problems later, as I happen to know.

My daughter never have big presentation the next day when the subject   60
of spanking come up.

I don't want you to touch Sophie, she say. No spanking, period.

Don't tell me what to do, I say.

I'm not telling you what to do, say my daughter. I'm telling you how I feel.

I am not your servant, I say. Don't you dare talk to me like that.

My daughter have another funny habit when she lose an argument. She   65
spread out all her fingers and look at them, as if she like to make sure they are still there.

My daughter is fierce like me, but she and John think it is better to explain to Sophie that clothes are a good idea. This is not so hard in the cold weather. In the warm weather, it is very hard.

Use your words, my daughter say. That's what we tell Sophie. How about if you set a good example.

As if good example mean anything to Sophie. I am so fierce, the gang members who used to come to the restaurant all afraid of me, but Sophie is not afraid.

I say, Sophie, if you take off your clothes, no snack.

I say, Sophie, if you take off your clothes, no lunch.   70

I say, Sophie, if you take off your clothes, no park.

Pretty soon we are stay home all day, and by the end of six hours she still did not have one thing to eat. You never saw a child stubborn like that.

I'm hungry! she cry when my daughter come home.

What's the matter, doesn't your grandmother feed you? My daughter laugh.

No! Sophie say. She doesn't feed me anything!   75

My daughter laugh again. Here you go, she say.

She say to John, Sophie must be growing.

Growing like a weed, I say.

Still Sophie take off her clothes, until one day I spank her. Not too hard, but she cry and cry, and when I tell her if she doesn't put her clothes back on I'll spank her again, she put her clothes back on. Then I tell her she is good girl, and give her some food to eat. The next day we go to the park and, like a nice Chinese girl, she does not take off her clothes.

She stop taking off her clothes, I report. Finally!   80

How did you do it? my daughter ask.

After twenty-eight years experience with you, I guess I learn something, I say.

It must have been a phase, John say, and his voice is suddenly like an expert.

His voice is like an expert about everything these days, now that he carry a leather briefcase, and wear shiny shoes, and can go shopping for a new car. On the company, he say. The company will pay for it, but he will be able to drive it whenever he want.

A free car, he say. How do you like that.   85

It's good to see you in the saddle again, my daughter say. Some of your family patterns are scary.

At least I don't drink, he say. He say, And I'm not the only one with scary family patterns.

That's for sure, say my daughter.

Everyone is happy. Even I am happy, because there is more trouble with Sophie, but now I think I can help her Chinese side fight against her wild side. I teach her to eat food with fork or spoon or chopsticks, she cannot just grab into the middle of a bowl of noodles. I teach her not to play with garbage cans. Sometimes I spank her, but not too often, and not too hard.

Still, there are problems. Sophie like to climb everything. If there is a   90
railing, she is never next to it. Always she is on top of it. Also, Sophie like to hit the mommies of her friends. She learn this from her playground best friend, Sinbad, who is four. Sinbad wear army clothes every day and like to ambush his mommy. He is the one who dug a big hole under the play structure, a foxhole he call it, all by himself. Very hardworking. Now he wait in the foxhole with a shovel full of wet sand. When his mommy come, he throw it right at her.

Oh, it's all right, his mommy say. You can't get rid of war games, it's part of their imaginative play. All the boys go through it.

Also, he like to kick his mommy, and one day he tell Sophie to kick his mommy too.

I wish this story is not true.

Kick her, kick her! Sinbad say.

Sophie kick her. A little kick, as if she just so happened was swinging   95
her little leg and didn't realize that big mommy leg was in the way. Still I spank Sophie and make Sophie say sorry, and what does the mommy say?

Really, it's all right, she say. It didn't hurt.

After that, Sophie learn she can attack mommies in the playground, and some will say, Stop, but others will say, Oh, she didn't mean it, especially if they realize Sophie will be punished.

This is how, one day, bigger trouble come. The bigger trouble start when Sophie hide in the foxhole with that shovel full of sand. She wait, and when I come look for her, she throw it at me. All over my nice clean clothes.

Did you ever see a Chinese girl act this way?

Sophie! I say. Come out of there, say you're sorry.   100

But she does not come out. Instead, she laugh. Naaah, naah-na, naaa-naaa, she say.

I am not exaggerate: millions of children in China, not one act like this.

Sophie! I say. Now! Come out now!

But she know she is in big trouble. She know if she come out, what will happen next. So she does not come out. I am sixty-eight, Chinese age almost seventy, how can I crawl under there to catch her? Impossible. So I yell, yell, yell, and what happen? Nothing. A Chinese mother would help, but American mothers, they look at you, they shake their head, they go home. And, of course, a Chinese child would give up, but not Sophie.

I hate you! she yell. I hate you, Meanie!   105

Meanie is my new name these days.

Long time this goes on, long long time. The foxhole is deep, you cannot see too much, you don't know where is the bottom. You cannot hear too much either. If she does not yell, you cannot even know she is still there or not. After a while, getting cold out, getting dark out. No one left in the play-ground, only us.

Sophie, I say. How did you become stubborn like this? I am go home without you now.

I try to use a stick, chase her out of there, and once or twice I hit her, but still she does not come out. So finally I leave. I go outside the gate.

Bye-bye! I say. I'm go home now.   110

But still she does not come out and does not come out. Now it is din-nertime, the sky is black. I think I should maybe go get help, but how can I leave a little girl by herself in the playground? A bad man could come. A rat could come. I go back in to see what is happen to Sophie. What is she have a shovel and is making a tunnel to escape?

Sophie! I say.

No answer.

Sophie!

I don't know if she is alive. I don't know if she is fall asleep down there.   115
If she is crying, I cannot hear her.

So I take the stick and poke.

Sophie! I say. I promise I no hit you. If you come out, I give you a lollipop.

No answer. By now I worried. What to do, what to do, what to do? I poke some more, even harder, so that I am poking and poking when my daughter and John suddenly appear.

What are you doing? What is going on? say my daughter.

Put down that stick? say my daughter.   120

You are crazy! say my daughter.

John wiggle under the structure, into the foxhole, to rescue Sophie.

She fell asleep, say John the expert. She's okay. That is one big hole.

Now Sophie is crying and crying.

Sophie, my daughter say, hugging her. Are you okay, peanut? Are you   125
okay?

She's just scared, say John.

Are you okay? I say too. I don't know what happen, I say.

She's okay, say John. He is not like my daughter, full of questions. He is full of answers until we get home and can see by the lamplight.

Will you look at her? he yell then. What the hell happened?

Bruises all over her brown skin, and a swollen-up eye.   130
You are crazy! say my daughter. Look at what you did! You are crazy!
I try very hard, I say.
How could you use a stick? I told you to use your words!
She is hard to handle, I say.
She's three years old! You cannot use a stick! say my daughter.   135
She is not like any Chinese girl I ever saw, I say.
I brush some sand off my clothes. Sophie's clothes are dirty too, but at
least she has her clothes on.
Has she done this before? ask my daughter. Has she hit you before?
She hits me all the time, Sophie say, eating ice cream.
Your family, say John.   140
Believe me, say my daughter.

A daughter I have, a beautiful daughter. I took care of her when she
could not hold her head up. I took care of her before she could argue with
me, when she was a little girl with two pigtails, one of them always crooked.
I took care of her when we have to escape from China, I took care of her
when suddenly we live in a country with cars everywhere, if you are not
careful your little girl get run over. When my husband die, I promise him I
will keep the family together, even though it was just two of us, hardly a
family at all.

But now my daughter take me around to look at apartments. After all, I
can cook, I can clean, there's no reason I cannot live by myself, all I need is a
telephone. Of course, she is sorry. Sometimes she cry, I am the one to say
everything will be okay. She say she have no choice, she doesn't want to end
up divorced. I say divorce is terrible, I don't know who invented this terrible
idea. Instead of live with a telephone, though, surprise, I come to live with
Bess. Imagine that. Bess make an offer and, sure enough, where she come
from, people mean for you to move in when they say things like that. A
crazy idea, go to live with someone else's family, but she like to have some
female company, not like my daughter, who does not believe in company.
These days when my daughter visit, she does not bring Sophie. Bess say we
should give Nattie time, we will see Sophie again soon. But seems like my
daughter have more presentation than ever before, every time she come she
have to leave.

I have a family to support, she say, and her voice is heavy, as if soaking
wet. I have a young daughter and a depressed husband and no one to turn to.

When she say no one to turn to, she mean me.   145

These days my beautiful daughter is so tired she can just sit there in a
chair and fall asleep. John lost his job again, already, but still they rather
hire a baby-sitter than ask me to help, even they can't afford it. Of course,
the new baby-sitter is much younger, can run around. I don't know if Sophie
these days is wild or not wild. She call me Meanie, but she like to kiss me

too, sometimes. I remember that every time I see a child on TV. Sophie like to grab my hair, a fistful in each hand, and then kiss me smack on the nose. I never see any other child kiss that way.

The satellite TV has so many channels, more channels than I can count, including a Chinese channel from the Mainland and a Chinese channel from Taiwan, but most of the time I watch bloopers with Bess. Also, I watch the bird feeder—so many, many kinds of birds come. The Shea sons hang around all the time, asking when will I go home, but Bess tell them, Get lost.

She's a permanent resident, say Bess. She isn't going anywhere.

Then she wink at me, and switch the channel with the remote control.

Of course, I shouldn't say Irish this, Irish that, especially now I am   150
become honorary Irish myself, according to Bess. Me! Who's Irish? I say, and she laugh. All the same, if I could mention one thing about some of the Irish, not all of them of course, I like to mention this: Their talk just stick. I don't know how Bess Shea learn to use her words, but sometimes I hear what she say a long time later. *Permanent resident. Not going anywhere.* Over and over I hear it, the voice of Bess.

Questions for Discussion and Writing

1. What aspects of American culture are mysterious to the narrator, especially as revealed in terms such as *supportive, creative,* and *self-esteem?*
2. What is the result of the grandmother's attempt to reform Sophie?
3. What kinds of responsibilities should children have toward their aging parents and grandparents?
4. **Rhetorical inquiry:** How does Jen create a distinctive voice for the grandmother/narrator using syntax and grammar in non-standard ways?

Poetry

KENNETH KOCH

Kenneth Koch (1925–2002) was born in Cincinnati, Ohio, and served in the Army in the Philippines during World War II. He graduated from Harvard in 1948 and received a Ph.D. from Columbia University, where he taught for over forty years. His works include One Train *(1994), which won the Bollingen Prize, and* New Addresses *(2000) as well as avante garde plays and prose works. He also wrote books on poetry education designed to introduce children and adults to appreciate and write poetry, including* Wishes, Lies and Dreams: Teaching Children to Write Poetry *(1970). The following poem appeared in* The Collected Poems of Kenneth Koch *(2005).*

Before You Read

What parts of speech do you prefer and why?

Permanently

One day the Nouns were clustered in the street.
An Adjective walked by, with her dark beauty.
The Nouns were struck, moved, changed.
The next day a Verb drove up, and created the Sentence.

Each Sentence says one thing—for example, "Although it was a dark   5
    rainy day when the Adjective walked by, I shall remember the
    pure and sweet expression on her face until the day I perish from
    the green, effective earth."
Or, "Will you please close the window, Andrew?"
Or, for example, "Thank you, the pink pot of flowers on the window
    sill has changed color recently to a light yellow, due to the heat
    from the boiler factory which exists nearby."

In the springtime the Sentences and the Nouns lay silently on the grass.
A lonely Conjunction here and there would call, "And! But!"
But the Adjective did not emerge.   10

As the adjective is lost in the sentence,
So I am lost in your eyes, ears, nose, and throat—
You have enchanted me with a single kiss
Which can never be undone
Until the destruction of language.   15

Questions for Discussion and Writing

1. How does the poem enact the drama of how parts of speech create a sentence? What part does each play?
2. What equivalence does Koch draw between himself and the role the adjective plays in the sentence?
3. What other parts of speech (such as pronouns, adverbs) that Koch does not mention play an important role in language? How would you personify them? Why is it significant that the title is an adverb?
4. **Rhetorical inquiry:** How does the Adjective play a key role as siren and unobtainable beauty in this poem? In what ways has Koch refashioned a conventional love poem using parts of speech?

How does Hilary B. Price's cartoon personalize aspects of grammar?

Connections for Chapter 4:
Perspectives on Language

1. **Helen Keller,** *The Day Language Came into My Life*
   Compare the obstacles faced by Keller and Frederick Douglass as described in "Learning to Read and Write" in Chapter 3.

2. **Temple Grandin,** *Thinking in Pictures*
   Compare the difficulties both Grandin and Helen Keller had in surmounting their respective disabilities and their different perceptions of how language functions.

3. **Deborah Tannen,** *Sex, Lies, and Conversation*
   To what extent are Tannen's observations about different agendas between men and women illustrated in David Ives's play *Sure Thing* (in Chapter 5)?

4. **George Lakoff,** *Anger*
   How do both Lakoff in this essay and Temple Grandin in "Thinking in Pictures" illustrate the concrete nature of metaphors?

5. **Alison Lurie**
   How does the concept of clothes as language explain the cross-cultural confusion described by Judith Ortiz Cofer in "The Myth of the Latin Woman" (in Chapter 5)?

6. **Amy Tan,** *Mother Tongue*
   How do speech codes as analyzed by Nat Hentoff's "Speech Codes" in Chapter 3 function in the same way as different Englishes do in Tan's essay?

7. **Aldous Huxley,** *Propaganda Under a Dictatorship*
   Examine Huxley's premise that Hitler adapted Madison Avenue techniques of advertising in light of the analysis by Stuart Hirschberg.

8. **Stuart Hirschberg,** *The Rhetoric of Advertising*
   Does marketing as discussed by Bill Bryson in "What's Cooking? Eating in America" (Chapter 5) employ classic rhetorical strategies discussed by Hirschberg?

9. **Gish Jen,** *Who's Irish?*
   Which of the Englishes described by Tan is illustrated in Jen's Story?

10. **Kenneth Koch,** *Permanently*
    In what way does Koch concretely depict abstract ideas in much the same way as Temple Grandin describes?

5

EVERYDAY MATTERS

Two things only the people anxiously desire, Bread and the Circus games.

Juvenal, Satires

Many contemporary concerns are touched on by the essays in this chapter: consumerism, eating disorders, racism, speciesism, urban legends, addictions, AIDS, the plight of immigrants, Latina stereotypes, marriage, fast food, the funeral industry, and speed dating. With a few exceptions, many of these issues overlap. Juliet B. Schor, Philip Slater, Bill Bryson, and Rosalind Coward show how the addictive, "quick fix" nature of American society is a result of the way body image is advertised, drugs are promoted, fast food is marketed, and over-consumption is viewed as an end in itself. An essay by Jessica Mitford offers a behind-the-scene exposé of the funeral industry and Jan Harold Brunvand's study of the lasting power of urban legends further indicates our willingness to blur the lines between illusion and reality. Mark Twain satirizes the unwarranted conceit of the human species and Judith Ortiz Cofer punctures the Latina stereotype.

Stories by Kate Chopin and Gloria Anzaldúa offer complex and thoughtful explorations of the consequences of endemic sexism and racism.

A fast-paced play by David Ives, *Sure Thing*, examines the new patterns of dating, and expectations about marriage in contemporary culture.

The poetry by Marge Piercy, Grace C. Kuhns, and the song lyrics by Bruce Springsteen present heartfelt protests to pressing contemporary problems: sexual stereotyping, child abuse, and the rejection of AIDS's victims. Lastly, Gregory Corso confesses his ambivalence about getting married.

As you read works in this chapter and prepare to discuss or write about them, you may wish to use the following questions as guidelines.

- What social issue does the writer address?
- What is the writer's purpose—to inform readers, to change their attitudes, or to offer a solution to a problem?
- How would you characterize the author's tone and degree of emotional involvement with the issue?
- Does the author mainly focus on the liabilities or advantages of being male or female?

- Does the author show the impact of class or culture on gender?
- Do you connect emotionally to any of the issues the authors treat?
- If the selection expresses an argument, what is the writer's thesis and how effectively is evidence used?

Nonfiction

JULIET B. SCHOR

Juliet B. Schor (b. 1955) currently is a professor of sociology at Boston College. She has written The Overworked American *(1992) and* The Overspent American *(1998), in which the following essay first appeared. Schor analyzes why what Americans previously viewed as luxuries have now become necessities. She has edited* The Consumer Society Reader *with Douglas B. Holt (2002) and is the author of* Born to Buy: The Commercialized Child and the New Consumer Culture *(2004).*

Before You Read

What role does the media play in suggesting that the middle class should strive to acquire what the very rich have?

The Culture of Consumerism

In 1996 a best-selling book entitled *The Millionaire Next Door* caused a minor sensation. In contrast to the popular perception of millionaire lifestyles, this book reveals that most millionaires live frugal lives—buying used cars, purchasing their suits at JC Penney, and shopping for bargains. These very wealthy people feel no need to let the world know they can afford to live much better than their neighbors.

Millions of other Americans, on the other hand, have a different relationship with spending. What they acquire and own is tightly bound to their personal identity. Driving a certain type of car, wearing particular designer labels, living in a certain kind of home, and ordering the right bottle of wine create and support a particular image of themselves to present to the world.

This is not to say that most Americans make consumer purchases solely to fool others about who they really are. It is not to say that we are a nation of crass status-seekers. Or that people who purchase more than they need are simply demonstrating a base materialism, in the sense of valuing material possessions above all else. But it is to say that, unlike the millionaires next door, who are not driven to use their wealth to create an attractive image of themselves, many of us are continually comparing our own lifestyle and possessions to those of a select group of people we respect and want to be like, people whose sense of what's important in life seems close to our own.

This aspect of our spending is not new—competitive acquisition has long been an American institution. At the turn of the century, the rich consumed conspicuously. In the early post–World War II decades, Americans spent to keep up with the Joneses, using their possessions to make the statement that they were not failing in their careers. But in recent decades, the culture of spending has changed and intensified. In the old days, our neighbors set the standard for what we had to have. They may have earned a little more, or a little less, but their incomes and ours were in the same ballpark. Their house down the block, worth roughly the same as ours, confirmed this. Today the neighbors are no longer the focus of comparison. How could they be? We may not even know them, much less which restaurants they patronize, where they vacation, and how much they spent for their living room couch.

For reasons that will become clear, the comparisons we make are no longer restricted to those in our own general earnings category, or even to those one rung above us on the ladder. Today a person is more likely to be making comparisons with, or choose as a "reference group," people whose incomes are three, four, or five times his or her own. The result is that millions of us have become participants in a national culture of upscale spending. I call it the new consumerism. 5

Part of what's new is that lifestyle aspirations are now formed by different points of reference. For many of us, the neighborhood has been replaced by a community of coworkers, people we work alongside and colleagues in our own and related professions. And while our real-life friends still matter, they have been joined by our media "friends." (This is true both figuratively and literally—the television show *Friends* is a good example of an influential media referent.) We watch the way television families live, we read about the lifestyles of celebrities and other public figures we admire, and we consciously and unconsciously assimilate this information. It affects us.

So far so good. We are in a wider world, so we like to know that we are stacking up well against a wider population group than the people on the block. No harm in that. But as new reference groups form, they are less likely to comprise people who all earn approximately the same amount of money. And therein lies the problem. When a person who earns $75,000 a year compares herself to someone earning $90,000, the comparison is sustainable. It creates some tension, even a striving to do a bit better, to be more successful in a career. But when a reference group includes people who pull down six or even seven-figure incomes, that's trouble. When poet-waiters earning $18,000 a year, teachers earning $30,000, and editors and publishers earning six-figure incomes all aspire to be part of one urban literary referent group, which exerts pressure to drink the same brand of bottled water and wine, wear similar urban literary clothes, and appoint apartments with urban literary furniture, those at the lower economic end of the reference group find themselves in an

untenable situation. Even if we choose not to emulate those who spend osten-
tatiously, consumer aspirations can be a serious reach.

Advertising and the media have played an important part in stretching
out reference groups vertically. When twenty-somethings can't afford much
more than a utilitarian studio but think they should have a New York apartment to match the ones they see on *Friends*, they are setting unattainable
consumption goals for themselves, with dissatisfaction as a predictable result.
When the children of affluent suburban and impoverished inner-city households both want the same Tommy Hilfiger logo emblazoned on their chests
and the top-of-the-line Swoosh on their feet, it's a potential disaster. One
solution to these problems emerged on the talk-show circuit recently, cham-
pioned by a pair of young urban "entry-level" earners: live the *faux* life,
consuming *as if* you had a big bank balance. Their strategies? Use your
expense account for private entertainment, date bankers, and sneak into
snazzy parties without an invitation. Haven't got the wardrobe for it? No
matter. Charge expensive clothes, wear them with the tags on, and return
them the morning after. Apparently the upscale life is now so worth living
that deception, cheating, and theft are a small price to pay for it.

These are the more dramatic examples. Millions of us face less stark
but problematic comparisons every day. People in one-earner families find
themselves trying to live the lifestyle of their two-paycheck friends. Parents
of modest means struggle to pay for the private schooling that others in their
reference group have established as the right thing to do for their children.

Additional problems are created by the accelerating pace of product   10
innovation. To gain broader distribution for the plethora of new products,
manufacturers have gone to lifestyle marketing, targeting their pitches of
upscale items at rich and nonrich alike. Gourmet cereal, a luxurious latté, or
bathroom fixtures that make a statement, the right statement, are offered to
people almost everywhere on the economic spectrum. In fact, through the
magic of plastic, anyone can buy designer anything, at the trendiest retail
shop. Or at outlet prices. That's the new consumerism. And its siren call is
hard to resist.

The new consumerism is also built on a relentless ratcheting up of standards. If you move into a house with a fifties kitchen, the presumption is that
you will eventually have it redone, because that's a standard that has now
been established. If you didn't have air conditioning in your old car, the presumption is that when you replace it, the new one will have it. If you haven't
been to Europe, the presumption is that you will get there, because you
deserve to get there. And so on. In addition to the proliferation of new products (computers, cell phones, faxes, and other microelectronics), there is a
continual upgrading of old ones—autos and appliances—and a shift to cus-
tomized, more expensive versions, all leading to a general expansion of the
list of things we have to have. The 1929 home I just moved into has a closet
too shallow to fit a hanger. So the clothes face forward. The real estate agents
suggested I solve the "problem" by turning the study off the bedroom into

a walk-in. (Why read when you could be buying clothes?) What we want grows into what we *need*, at a sometimes dizzying rate. While politicians continue to tout the middle class as the heart and soul of American society, for far too many of us being solidly middle-class is no longer good enough.

Oddly, it doesn't seem as if we're spending wastefully, or even lavishly. Rather, many of us feel we're just making it, barely able to stay even. But what's remarkable is that this feeling is not restricted to families of limited income. It's a generalized feeling, one that exists at all levels. Twenty-seven percent of all households making more than $100,000 a year say they cannot afford to buy everything they really need. Nearly 20 percent say they "spend nearly all their income on the basic necessities of life." In the $50,000–100,000 range, 39 percent and one-third feel this way, respectively. Overall, half the population of the richest country in the world say they cannot afford everything they really need. And it's not just the poorer half.

This book is about why: About why so many middle-class Americans feel materially dissatisfied. Why they walk around with ever-present mental "wish lists" of things to buy or get. How even a six-figure income can seem inadequate, and why this country saves less than virtually any other nation in the world. It is about the ways in which, for America's middle classes, "spending becomes you," about how it flatters, enhances, and defines people in often wonderful ways, but also about how it takes over their lives. My analysis is based on new research showing that the need to spend whatever it takes to keep current within a chosen reference group—which may include members of widely disparate resources—drives much purchasing behavior. It analyzes how standards of belonging socially have changed in recent decades, and how this change has introduced Americans to highly intensified spending pressures.

And finally, it is about a growing backlash to the consumption culture, a movement of people who are downshifting—by working less, earning less, and living their consumer lives much more deliberately.

SPENDING AND SOCIAL COMPARISON

I am hardly the first person to have argued that consumption has a comparative, or even competitive character. Ideas of this sort have a long history within economics, sociology, and other disciplines. In *The Wealth of Nations*, Adam Smith observed that even a "creditable day-laborer would be ashamed to appear in publick, without a linen shirt" and that leather shoes had become a "necessary of life" in eighteenth-century England. The most influential work on the subject, however, has been Thorstein Veblen's *Theory of the Leisure Class*. Veblen argued that in affluent societies, spending becomes the vehicle through which people establish social position. The conspicuous display of wealth and leisure is the marker that reveals a man's income to the outside world. (Wives, by the way, were seen by Veblen as largely ornamental, useful to display a man's finest purchases—clothes, furs, and jewels.) The rich spent conspicuously as a kind of personal advertisement, to secure a place in the

15

TABLE 5.1   HOW MUCH IS ENOUGH?

Percentage Agreeing with Statement, by Income

Statement	<$10,000	10,001–25,000	25,001–35,000	35,001–50,000	50,001–75,000	75,001–100,000	>100,000
I cannot afford to buy every-thing I really need	64	62	50	43	42	39	27
I spend nearly all of my money on the basic necessities of life	69	64	62	46	35	33	19

Source: Author's calculations from Merck Family Fund poll (February 1995).

TABLE 5.2   THE GOOD LIFE GOES UPSCALE

Percentage Identifying Item as a Part of "The Good Life"

	1975	1991
Vacation home	19	35
Swimming pool	14	29
Color TV	46	55
Second color TV	10	28
Travel abroad	30	39
Really nice clothes	36	44
Car	71	75
Second car	30	41
Home you own	85	87
A lot of money	38	55
A job that pays much more than average	45	60
Happy marriage	84	77
One or more children	74	73
Interesting job	69	63
Job that contributes to the welfare of society	38	38
Percentage who think they have a very good chance of achieving the "good life"	35	23

Source: Roper Center, University of Connecticut; published in *American Enterprise* (May–June 1993), p. 87.

TABLE 5.3   THE EXPANDING DEFINITION OF "NECESSITIES"

Percentage Indicating Item is a Necessity

	1973	1991	1996
Second television	3	15	10
Dishwasher	10	24	13
VCR	—*	18	13
Basic cable service	—	26	17
Remote control for TV or VCR	—	23	—
Answering machine	—	20	26
Home computer	—	11	26
Microwave	—	44	32
Second automobile	20	27	37
Auto air conditioning	13	42	41
Home air conditioning	26	47	51
Television	57	74	59
Clothes dryer	54	74	62
Clothes washer	88	82	86
Automobile	90	85	93
Cellular phone	—	5	—
Housekeeper	—	4	—

*Item did not exist, was not widely in use, or was not asked about in 1973.

Source: Roper Center, University of Connecticut; 1973 and 1991 data published in *American Enterprise* (May–June 1993), p. 89.

social hierarchy. Everyone below stood watching and, to the extent possible, emulating those one notch higher. Consumption was a trickle-down process.

The phenomenon that Veblen identified and described, conspicuous consumption by the rich and the nouveaux riches, was not new even in his own time. Spending to establish a social position has a long history. Seventeenth- and eighteenth-century Italian nobles built opulent palaces with beautiful facades and, within those facades, placed tiles engraved with the words *Pro Invidia* (To Be Envied). For centuries, aristocrats passed laws to forbid the nouveaux riches from copying their clothing styles. At the turn of the century, the wealthy published the menus of their dinner parties in the newspapers. And fifty years ago, American social climbers bought fake "ancestor portraits" to hang in their libraries.

Veblen's story made a lot of sense for the upper-crust, turn-of-the-century urban world of his day. But by the 1920s, new developments were afoot. Because productivity and output were growing so rapidly, more and more people had entered the comfortable middle classes and begun to enjoy substantial discretionary spending. And this mass prosperity eventually engendered a new socioeconomic phenomenon—a mass keeping-up process that led to convergence among consumers' acquisition goals and purchasing patterns.

The advent of mass production in the 1920s made possible an outpouring of identical consumer goods that nearly everybody wanted—and were better able to afford, thanks to declining prices. By the fifties, the Smiths had to have the Joneses' fully automatic washing machine, vacuum cleaner, and, most of all, the shiny new Chevrolet parked in the driveway. The story of this period was that people looked to their own neighborhoods for their spending cues, and the neighbors grew more and more alike in what they had. Like compared with like and strove to become even more alike.

This phenomenon was chronicled by James Duesenberry, a Harvard economist writing just after the Second World War. Duesenberry updated Veblen's trickle-down perspective in his classic discussion of "keeping up with the Joneses." In contrast to Veblen's Vanderbilts, Duesenberry's 1950s Joneses were middle-class and they lived next door, in suburban USA. Rather than seeking to best their neighbors, Duesenberry's Smiths mainly wanted to be like them. Although the ad writers urged people to be the first on the block to own a product, the greater fear in most consumers' minds during this period was that if they didn't get cracking, they might be the last to get on board.

In addition to Veblen and Duesenberry, a number of distinguished economists have emphasized these social and comparative processes in their classic accounts of consumer culture—among them, John Kenneth Galbraith, Fred Hirsch, Tibor Scitovsky, Richard Easterlin, Amartya Sen, Clair Brown, and Robert Frank. Among the most important of their messages is that consumer satisfaction, and dissatisfaction, depend less on what a person has in an absolute sense than on socially formed aspirations and expectations. Indeed, the very term "standard of living" suggests the point: the standard is a social norm.

By the 1970s, social trends were once again altering the nature of comparative consumption. Most obvious was the entrance of large numbers of married women into the labor force. As the workplace replaced the coffee klatch and the backyard barbecue as locations of social contact, workplace conversation became a source for information on who went where for vacation, who was having a deck put on the house, and whether the kids were going to dance class, summer camp, or karate lessons. But in the workplace, most employees are exposed to the spending habits of people across a wider economic spectrum, particularly those employees who work in white-collar settings. They have meetings with people who wear expensive suits or "real" Swiss watches. They may work with their boss, or their boss's boss, every day and find out a lot about what they and their families have.

There were also ripple effects on women who didn't have jobs. When many people lived in one-earner households, incomes throughout the neighborhood tended to be close to each other. As many families earned two paychecks, however, mothers who stayed at home or worked part-time found themselves competing with neighbors who could much more easily afford pricey restaurants, piano lessons, and two new cars. Finally, as Robert Frank and Philip Cook have argued, there has been a shift to a "winner-take-all" society: rewards within occupations have become more unequally distributed. As a group of extremely high earners emerged within occupation after occupation, they provided a visible, and very elevated, point of comparison for those who weren't capturing a disproportionate share of the earnings of the group.

Daily exposure to an economically diverse set of people is one reason Americans began engaging in more upward comparison. A shift in advertising patterns is another. Traditionally advertisers had targeted their market by earnings, using one medium or another depending on the income group they were trying to reach. They still do this. But now the huge audiences delivered by television make it the best medium for reaching just about *every* financial group. While *Forbes* readers have a much higher median income than television viewers, it's possible to reach more wealthy people on television than in the pages of any magazine, no matter how targeted its readership. A major sports event or an *ER* episode is likely to deliver more millionaires *and* more laborers than a medium aimed solely at either group. That's why you'll find ads for Lincoln town cars, Mercedes-Benz sports cars, and $50,000 all-terrain vehicles on the Super Bowl telecast. In the process, painters who earn $25,000 a year are being exposed to buying pressures never intended for them, and middle-class housewives look at products once found only in the homes of the wealthy.

Beginning in the 1970s, expert observers were declaring the death of the "belonging" process that had driven much competitive consumption and arguing that the establishment of an individual identity—rather than staying current with the Joneses—was becoming the name of the game. The new trend was to consume in a personal style, with products that signaled your individuality, your personal sense of taste and distinction. But, of course, you had to be different in the right way. The trick was to create a unique image through what you had and wore—and what you did not have and would not be seen dead in.

While the observers had identified a new stage in consumer culture, they were right only to a point. People may no longer have wanted to be just like all others in their socioeconomic class, but their need to measure up within some idealized group survived. What emerged as the new standards of comparison, however, were groups that had no direct counterparts in previous times. Marketers call them clusters—groups of people who share values, orientations, and, most important, *lifestyles*. Clusters are much smaller than traditional horizontal economic strata or classes and can thereby satisfy the need for greater individuality in consumption patterns. "Yuppie" was only the most notorious of these lifestyle cluster groups. There are also middle Americans, twenty-somethings, upscale urban Asians, top one-percenters, and senior sun-seekers. We have radical feminists, comfortable capitalists, young market lions, environmentalists. Whatever.

Ironically, the shift to individuality produced its own brand of localized conformity. . . . Apparently lots of people began wanting the same "individual identity-creating" products. But this predictability, while perhaps a bit absurd, brought with it no *particular* financial problem. Seventies consumerism was manageable. The real problems started in the 1980s as an economic shift

25

sent seismic shocks through the nation's consumer mentality. Competitive spending intensified. In a very big way.

When $18,000 Feels Luxurious: Jeff Lutz

Some Americans are pursuing another path. Want less. Live more simply. Slow down and get in touch with nature. A growing "voluntary simplicity" movement is rejecting the standard path of work and spend. This is a committed, self-conscious group of people who believe that spending less does not reduce their quality of life and may even raise it. Their experience is that *less* (spending) is *more* (time, meaning, peace of mind, financial security, ecological responsibility, physical health, friendship, appreciation of what they do spend). Seattle, long a laid-back, nature-oriented city, is home not only to Boeing and Microsoft but also to many of these individuals. I spent nearly a week there in the summer of 1996, meeting people who were living on less than $20,000 a year. Jeff Lutz was one of them.

After graduating from a small college back east, Jeff and his girlfriend Liza moved to Seattle, where they inhabit a nice, spacious old house in a middle-class neighborhood. They share the place with one friend; their rent is $312 per person. Jeff is self-employed as a medical and legal interpreter and is putting a lot of effort into "growing" his business. Nicely dressed and groomed, he doesn't look too different from other twenty-five-year-old graduates of the prep school and college he attended. But he is. Living on about $10,000 a year, he says he has basically everything he wants and will be content to live at this level of material comfort for the rest of his life. Youthful naïveté? Perhaps. But maybe not.

Lutz grew up in Mexico. His mother, a writer and social activist, went to Mexico with her parents, refugees from Franco's civil war. His father was a lawyer from New York. Family role models helped form his commitment to a frugal lifestyle. "My great-grandfather, who escaped czarist jail in Lithuania, lived in Mexico with one lightbulb and a record player. He had three photos behind his bed. One was Tolstoy, and one was Gandhi, and one was Pious XXIII."

As a teenager, Lutz went to a private school in western Massachusetts. 30 There he began to feel like "part of a herd being prodded along to do one thing after the next in semiconscious wakefulness. You go to elementary school, and then you go to junior high, and then you go to high school, and then you go to college in order to get a job, in order to compete with other people in higher salaries, in order to have more stuff. I saw really clearly in high school just where it was leading." At that point, he made up his mind about two things. First, "I needed to find a way to not be in a nine-to-five-until-I-died treadmill. I had a vision of life being much, much more than spending most of my life in a job that was somebody else's agenda." Second, "I wanted to learn how human beings could live more lightly on the earth."

His experiences in Mexico motivated these sentiments. "I spent a week with some Mazotec Indians in the mountains. And some of these kids my age, one of them had a Washington Redskins jersey. I mean, Spanish is their second language; they spoke Mazoteca, and yet they were listening to Michael Jackson and they wanted to buy my sunglasses and they wanted to buy my watch. And they wanted me to bring more sunglasses and watches so that they could resell them to their friends. It was very clear that our culture was sort of surrounding other cultures through the media. I grew up watching *The Love Boat* dubbed in Spanish."

In college, he designed his own major in environmental studies. But unlike many young people who begin their work lives enthusiastically believing they can combine improving the world with making a good salary, Lutz never really considered that path. "The things I was interested in were pretty outside the box." Near the end of his college years, he came across an article by Joe Dominguez, the creator of a nine-step program of "financial independence." Dominguez's program, contained in his best-selling book (with collaborator Vicki Robin) *Your Money or Your Life*, promises freedom from the grind of the working world, not through getting rich but by downsizing desire. Dominguez and Robin believe Americans have been trained to equate more stuff with more happiness. But that is true only up to a point, a point they feel most of us have passed. Doing it their way, you don't need to save a million dollars to retire, but just one, two, or three hundred thousand.

The program involves meticulously tracking all spending. And not just tracking it but scrutinizing it, by comparing the value of whatever you want to buy with the time it takes to earn the money for it. That calculation involves determining your real hourly wage, by taking into account all the hours you work and subtracting all job-related expenses, including the cost of your job wardrobe and takeout food because you're too tired to cook. Equipped with your real wage rate, you can figure out whether a new couch is worth three weeks of work, whether four nights in the Bahamas justify a month of earning, or whether you want to stick with the morning latté (even those half-hours add up). People who follow the program find that when they ask these questions, they spend less. Much less.

Jeff was getting close to financial independence, which entailed earning enough to spend between $800 and $1,200 per month, including health insurance. He says he does not feel materially deprived, and he is careful to point out that voluntary simplicity is not poverty. While he decided against the lattes, he does own a car and a computer, goes out to eat between one and three times a month, rents videos, has friends over for dinner, and buys his clothes both new and used. His furniture is an eclectic mix—nothing fancy, but nothing shabby either. He is convinced that "a higher standard of living will not make me happier. And I'm very clear internally. It's not a belief I picked up from somewhere." It's "something that I've gained an awareness about."

Questions for Discussion and Writing

1. According to Schor, what influence have the media had in altering the public's view of what constitutes the good life?
2. When you look at the tables of comparative statistics Schor provides about luxuries now viewed as necessities, what conclusions do you reach?
3. Would you ever consider following the example of Jeff Lutz and downsizing your expectations and lifestyle? Why or why not?
4. **Rhetorical inquiry:** How does Schor use the testimony of experts, especially in paras. 19–22 to document a significant shift in consumer values in the latter part of the twentieth century?

PHILIP SLATER

Philip Slater (b. 1927) has been a professor of sociology at Harvard and is author of The Pursuit of Loneliness *(1970) and* Wealth-Addiction *(1980). Slater argues that the premium Americans put on success causes many people to resort to drugs to feel better about themselves and to cope with feelings of inadequacy. Slater cites a broad range of examples from everyday life to demonstrate that advertisers exploit societal pressures in order to sell products. The following article first appeared in the* St. Paul Pioneer Press Dispatch *(September 6, 1984). His latest book is* The Temporary Society *(revised edition with Warren G. Bennis, 1998).*

Before You Read

How would you define addiction?

Want-Creation Fuels Americans' Addictiveness

Imagine what life in America would be like today if the surgeon general convinced Congress that cigarettes, as America's most lethal drug, should be made illegal.

The cost of tobacco would increase 5,000 percent. Law enforcement budgets would quadruple but still be hopelessly inadequate to the task. The tobacco industry would become mob-controlled, and large quantities of Turkish tobacco would be smuggled into the country through New York and Miami.

Politicians would get themselves elected by inveighing against tobacco abuse. Some would argue shrewdly that the best enforcement strategy was to go after the growers and advertisers—making it a capital offense to raise or sell tobacco. And a great many Americans would try smoking for the first time.

Americans are individualists. We like to express our opinions much more than we like to work together. Passing laws is one of the most popular pastimes, and enforcing them one of the least. We make laws like we make New Year's resolutions—the impulse often exhausted by giving voice to it. Who but Americans would have their food grown and harvested by people who were legally forbidden to be in the country?

We are a restless, inventive, dissatisfied people. We like novelty. We like   5
to try new things. We may not want to change in any basic sense, any more than other people, but we like the illusion of movement.

We like anything that looks like a quick fix—a new law, a new road, a new pill. We like immediate solutions. We want the pain to stop, the dull mood to pass, the problem to go away. The quicker the action, the better we like it. We like confrontation better than negotiation, antibiotics better than slow healing, majority rule better than community consensus, demolition better than renovation.

When we want something we want it fast and we want it cheap. Obstacles and complications annoy us. We don't want to stop to think about side effects, the Big Picture, or how it's going to make things worse in the long run. We aren't too interested in the long run, as long as something brings more money, a promotion or a new status symbol in the short.

Our model for problem-solving is the 30-second TV commercial, in which change is produced instantaneously and there is always a happy ending. The side effects, the pollution, the wasting diseases, the slow poisoning—all these unhappy complications fall into the great void outside that 30-second frame.

Nothing fits this scenario better than drugs—legal and illegal. The same impatience that sees an environmental impact report as an annoying bit of red tape makes us highly susceptible to any substance that can make us feel better within minutes after ingesting it—whose immediate effects are more or less predictable and whose negative aspects are generally much slower to appear.

People take drugs everywhere, of course, and there is no sure way of   10
knowing if the United States has more drug abusers than other countries. The term "abuse" itself is socially defined.

The typical suburban alcoholic of the '40s and '50s and the wealthy drunks glamorized in Hollywood movies of that period were not considered "drug abusers." Nor is the ex-heroin addict who has been weaned to a life-time addiction to Methadone.

In the 19th century, morphine addicts (who were largely middle-aged, middle-class women) maintained their genteel but often heavy addictions quite legally, with the aid of the family doctor and local druggist. Morphine only became illegal when its use spread to young, poor, black males. (This transition created some embarrassment for political and medical commentators, who argued that a distinction had to be made between "drug addicts" and "dope fiends.")

Yet addiction can be defined in a way that overrides these biases. Anyone who cannot or will not let a day pass without ingesting a substance should be considered addicted to it, and by this definition Americans are certainly addiction-prone.

It would be hard to find a society in which so great a variety of different substances have been "abused" by so many different kinds of people. There are drugs for every group, philosophy and social class: marijuana and psyche-delics for the '60s counterculture, heroin for the hopeless of all periods, PCP for the angry and desperate, and cocaine for modern Yuppies and Yumpies.[1]

Drugs do, after all, have different effects, and people select the effects   15
they want. At the lower end of the social scale people want a peaceful escape from a hopeless and depressing existence, and for this heroin is the drug of choice. Cocaine, on the other hand, with its energized euphoria and illusion of competence is particularly appealing to affluent achievers—those both obsessed and acquainted with success.

Addiction among the affluent seems paradoxical to outsiders. From the view-point of most people in the world an American man or woman making over $50,000 a year has everything a human being could dream of. Yet very few such people—even those with hundreds of millions of dollars—feel this way themselves. While they may not suffer the despair of the very poor, there seems to be a kind of frustration and hopelessness that seeps into all social strata in our society. The affluent may have acquired a great deal, but they seem not to have acquired what they wanted.

Most drugs—heroin, alcohol, cocaine, speed, tranquilizers, barbiturates—virtually all of them except the psychedelics and to some extent marijuana—have a numbing effect. We might then ask: Why do so many Americans need to numb themselves?

Life in modern society is admittedly harsh and confusing considering the pace for which our bodies were designed. Noise pollution alone might justify turning down our sensory volume: It's hard today even in a quiet suburb or rural setting to find respite from the harsh sound of "labor-saving" machines.

But it would be absurd to blame noise pollution for drug addiction. This rasping clamor that grates daily on our ears is only a symptom—one tangible consequence of our peculiar lifestyle. For each of us wants to be able to exert his or her will and control without having to negotiate with anyone else.

"I have a right to run my machine and do my work" even if it makes   20
your rest impossible. "I have a right to hear my music" even if this makes it impossible to hear your music, or better yet, enjoy that most rare and pre-cious of modern commodities: silence. "I have a right to make a profit" even if it means poisoning you, your children and your children's children. "I have

---

[1] *Yumpies:* Young, upper-middle-class professionals.

a right to have a drink when I want to and drive my car when I want to" even if it means totaling your car and crippling your life.

This intolerance of any constraint or obstacle makes our lives rich in conflict and aggravation. Each day we encounter the noise, distress and lethal fallout of the dilemmas we brushed aside so impatiently the day before. Each day the postponed problems multiply, proliferate, metastasize—but this only makes us more aggravated and impatient than we were before. And since we're unwilling to change our ways it becomes more and more necessary to anesthetize ourselves to the havoc we've wrought.

We don't like the thought of attuning ourselves to nature or to a group or community. We like to fantasize having control over our lives, and drugs seem to make this possible. With drugs you are not only master of your fate and captain of your soul, you are dictator of your body as well.

Unwilling to respond to its own needs and wants, you goad it into activity with caffeine in the morning and slow it down with alcohol at night. If the day goes poorly, a little cocaine will set it right, and if quiet relaxation and sensual enjoyment is called for, marijuana.

Cocaine or alcohol makes a party or a performance go well. Nothing is left to chance. The quality of experience is measured by how many drugs or drinks were consumed rather than by the experience itself. Most of us are unwilling to accept the fact that life has good days and bad days. We attempt—unsuccessfully but valiantly—to postpone all the bad days until that fateful moment when the body presents us with all our IOUs, tied up in a neat bundle called cancer, heart disease, cirrhosis or whatever.

Every great sage and spiritual leader throughout history has emphasized   25
that happiness comes not from getting more but from learning to want less. Clearly this is a hard lesson for humans, since so few have learned it.

But in our society we spend billions each year creating want. Covetousness, discontent and greed are taught to our children, drummed into them—they are bombarded with it. Not only through advertising, but in the feverish emphasis on success, on winning at all costs, on being the center of attention through one kind of performance or another, on being the first at something—no matter how silly or stupid (*The Guinness Book of Records*). We are an addictive society.

Addiction is a state of wanting. It is a condition in which the individual feels he or she is incomplete, inadequate, lacking, not whole, and can only be made whole by the addition of something external.

This need not be a drug. It can be money, food, fame, sex, responsibility, power, good deeds, possessions, cleaning—the addictive impulse can attach itself to anything, real or symbolic. You're addicted to something whenever you feel it completes you—that you wouldn't be a whole person without it. When you try to make sure it's always there, that there's always a good supply on hand.

Most of us are a little proud of the supposed personality defects that make addiction "necessary"—the "I can't . . .," "I have to . . .," "I always . . .," "I never . . ." But such "lacks" are all delusional. It's fun to brag about not being able to live without something but it's just pomposity. We are all human, and given water, a little food, and a little warmth, we'll survive.

But it's very hard to hang onto this humanity when we're told every day   30 that we're ignorant, misguided, inadequate, incompetent and undesirable and that we will emerge from this terrible condition only if we eat or drink or buy something, at which point we'll magically and instantly feel better.

We may be smart enough not to believe the silly claims of the individual ad, but can we escape the underlying message on which all of them agree? That you can only be made whole and healthy by buying or ingesting something? Can we reasonably complain about the amount of addiction in our society when we teach it every day?

A Caribbean worker once said, apropos of the increasing role of Western products in the economy of his country: "Your corporations are like mosquitoes. I don't so much mind their taking a little of my blood, but why do they have to leave that nasty itch in its place?"

It seems futile to spend hundreds of billions of dollars trying to intercept the flow of drugs—arresting and imprisoning those who meet the demand for them, when we activate and nourish that demand every day. Until we get tired of encouraging the pursuit of illusory fixes and begin to celebrate and refine what we already are and have, addictive substances will always proliferate faster than we can control them.

Questions for Discussion and Writing

1. In Slater's view, how is the quick-fix mentality responsible for rampant drug use and addiction in the United States?
2. Consider the definition of addiction that Slater presents. Do you agree or disagree with the way he frames the debate? Why, or why not?
3. What current ads set up hypothetically stressful situations and then push products as a quick and easy way to relieve the stress? Analyze a few of these ads.
4. **Rhetorical inquiry:** How does Slater use an analogy between noise pollution and drug addiction to develop his argument?

JAN HAROLD BRUNVAND

Jan Harold Brunvand (b. 1933) is a professor of folklore at the University of Utah and is the author of The Study of American Folklore: An Introduction *(1997) and* The Vanishing Hitchhiker: American Urban Legends and Their Meanings *(1981), from which the following selection is drawn. Brunvand identifies the distinguishing features of urban legends and gives an in-depth analysis of one particular legend that has been repeated so many times that it is thought to be true. A recent work is* Be Afraid, Be Very Afraid: The Book of Scary Urban Legends *(2004).*

Before You Read

What urban legend is unique to your community or college?

Urban Legends: "The Boyfriend's Death"

We are not aware of our own folklore any more than we are of the grammatical rules of our language. When we follow the ancient practice of informally transmitting "lore"—wisdom, knowledge, or accepted modes of behavior—by word of mouth and customary example from person to person, we do not concentrate on the form or content of our folklore; instead, we simply listen to information that others tell us and then pass it on—more or less accurately—to other listeners. In this stream of unselfconscious oral tradition the information that acquires a clear story line is called *narrative folklore*, and those stories alleged to be true are *legends*. This, in broad summary, is the typical process of legend formation and transmission as it has existed from time immemorial and continues to operate today. It works about the same way whether the legendary plot concerns a dragon in a cave or a mouse in a Coke bottle.

It might seem unlikely that legends—*urban* legends at that—would continue to be created in an age of widespread literacy, rapid mass communications, and restless travel. While our pioneer ancestors may have had to rely heavily on oral traditions to pass the news along about changing events and frontier dangers, surely we no longer need mere "folk" reports of what's happening, with all their tendencies to distort the facts. A moment's reflection, however, reminds us of the many weird, fascinating, but unverified rumors and tales that so frequently come to our ears—killers and madmen on the loose, shocking or funny personal experiences, unsafe manufactured products, and many other unexplained mysteries of daily life. Sometimes we encounter different oral versions of such stories, and on occasion we may read about similar events in newspapers or magazines; but seldom do we find, or even seek after, reliable documentation. The lack of verification in no way diminishes the appeal urban legends have for us. We enjoy them merely as stories, and we tend at least to half-believe them as possibly accurate reports. And the legends we tell, as with any folklore, reflect many of the hopes, fears, and anxieties of our time. In short, legends are definitely part of our modern folklore—legends which are as traditional, variable, and functional as those of the past.

Folklore study consists of collecting, classifying, and interpreting in their full cultural context the many products of everyday human interaction that have acquired a somewhat stable underlying form and that are passed traditionally from person to person, group to group, and generation to generation. Legend study is a most revealing area of such research because the stories that people believe to be true hold an important place in their worldview. "If it's true, it's important" is an axiom to be trusted, whether or not the lore really *is* true or not. Simply becoming aware of this modern folklore which we all possess to some degree is a revelation in itself, but going beyond this to compare the tales, isolate their consistent themes, and relate them to the rest of the culture can yield rich insights into the state of our current civilization. . . .

URBAN LEGENDS AS FOLKLORE

Folklore subsists on oral tradition, but not all oral communication is folklore. The vast amounts of human interchange, from casual daily conversations to formal discussions in business or industry, law, or teaching, rarely constitute straight oral folklore. However, all such "communicative events" (as scholars dub them) are punctuated routinely by various units of traditional material that are memorable, repeatable, and that fit recurring social situations well enough to serve in place of original remarks. "Tradition" is the key idea that links together such utterances as nicknames, proverbs, greeting and leave-taking formulas, wisecracks, anecdotes, and jokes as "folklore"; indeed, these are a few of the best known "conversational genres" of American folklore. Longer and more complex folk forms—fairy tales, epics, myths, legends, or ballads, for example—may thrive only in certain special situations of oral transmission. All true folklore ultimately depends upon continued oral dissemination, usually within fairly homogeneous "folk groups," and upon the retention through time of internal patterns and motifs that become traditional in the oral exchanges. The corollary of this rule of stability in oral tradition is that all items of folklore, while retaining a fixed central core, are constantly changing as they are transmitted, so as to create countless "variants" differing in length, detail, style, and performance technique. Folklore, in short, consists of oral tradition in variants.

Urban legends belong to the subclass of folk narratives, legends, that— unlike fairy tales—are believed, or at least believable, and that—unlike myths—are set in the recent past and involve normal human beings rather than ancient gods or demigods. Legends are folk history, or rather quasi-history. As with any folk legends, urban legends gain credibility from specific details of time and place or from references to source authorities. For instance, a popular western pioneer legend often begins something like, "My great-grandmother had this strange experience when she was a young girl on a wagon train going through Wyoming when an Indian chief wanted to adopt her. . . ." Even though hundreds of different great-grandmothers are supposed to have had the same doubtful experience (being desired by the chief because of her beautiful long blond hair), the fact seldom reaches legend-tellers; if it does, they assume that the family lore has indeed spread far and wide. This particular popular tradition, known as "Goldilocks on the Oregon Trail," interests folklorists because of the racist implications of a dark Indian savage coveting a fair young civilized woman—this legend is familiar in the *white* folklore only—and it is of little concern that the story seems to be entirely apocryphal.

In the world of modern urban legends there is usually no geographical or generational gap between teller and event. The story is *true;* it really occurred, and recently, and always to someone else who is quite close to the narrator, or at least "a friend of a friend." Urban legends are told both in the course of casual conversations and in such special situations as camp-fires, slumber parties, and college dormitory bull sessions. The legends' physical settings are often close by, real, and sometimes even locally renowned for other such happenings. Though the characters in the stories are usually nameless, they are true-to-life examples of the kind of people the narrators and their audience know firsthand.

One of the great mysteries of folklore research is where oral traditions originate and who invents them. One might expect that at least in modern folklore we could come up with answers to such questions, but this is seldom, if ever, the case. . . .

THE PERFORMANCE OF LEGENDS

Whatever the origins of urban legends, their dissemination is no mystery. The tales have traveled far and wide, and have been told and retold from person to person in the same manner that myths, fairy tales, or ballads spread in earlier cultures, with the important difference that today's legends are also disseminated by the mass media. Groups of age-mates, especially adolescents, are one important American legend channel, but other paths of transmission are among office workers and club members, as well as among religious, recreational, and regional groups. Some individuals make a point of learning every recent rumor or tale, and they can enliven any coffee break, party, or trip with the latest supposed "news." The telling of one story inspires other people to share what they have read or heard, and in a short time a lively exchange of details occurs and perhaps new variants are created.

Tellers of these legends, of course, are seldom aware of their roles as "performers of folklore." The conscious purpose of this kind of storytelling is to convey a true event, and only incidentally to entertain an audience. Nevertheless, the speaker's demeanor is carefully orchestrated, and his or her delivery is low-key and soft-sell. With subtle gestures, eye movements, and vocal inflections the stories are made dramatic, pointed, and suspenseful. But, just as with jokes, some can tell them and some can't. Passive tellers of urban legends may just report them as odd rumors, but the more active legend tellers re-create them as dramatic stories of suspense and, perhaps, humor.

"THE BOYFRIEND'S DEATH"

With all these points in mind [on] folklore's subject-matter style, and oral 10
performance, consider this typical version of a well-known urban legend that folklorists have named "The Boyfriend's Death," collected in 1964 (the

earliest documented instance of the story) by folklorist Daniel R. Barnes from an eighteen-year-old freshman at the University of Kansas. The usual tellers of the story are adolescents, and the normal setting for the narration is a college dormitory room with fellow students sprawled on the furniture and floors.

> This happened just a few years ago out on the road that turns off highway 59 by the Holiday Inn. This couple were parked under a tree out on this road. Well, it got to be time for the girl to be back at the dorm, so she told her boyfriend that they should start back. But the car wouldn't start, so he told her to lock herself in the car and he would go down to the Holiday Inn and call for help. Well, he didn't come back and he didn't come back, and pretty soon she started hearing a scratching noise on the roof of the car. "Scratch, scratch . . . scratch, scratch." She got scareder and scareder, but he didn't come back. Finally, when it was almost daylight, some people came along and stopped and helped her out of the car, and she looked up and there was her boyfriend hanging from the tree, and his feet were scraping against the roof of the car. This is why the road is called "Hangman's Road."

Here is a story that has traveled rapidly to reach nationwide oral circulation, in the process becoming structured in the typical manner of folk narratives. The traditional and fairly stable elements are the parked couple, the abandoned girl, the mysterious scratching (sometimes joined by a dripping sound and ghostly shadows on the windshield), the daybreak rescue, and the horrible climax. Variable traits are the precise location, the reason for her abandonment, the nature of the rescuers, murder details, and the concluding placename explanation. While "The Boyfriend's Death" seems to have captured teenagers' imaginations as a separate legend only since the early 1960s, it is clearly related to at least two older yarns, "The Hook" and "The Roommate's Death." All three legends have been widely collected by American folklorists, although only scattered examples have been published, mostly in professional journals. Examination of some of these variations helps to make clear the status of the story as folklore and its possible meanings.

At Indiana University, a leading American center of folklore research, folk-narrative specialist Linda Dégh and her students have gathered voluminous data on urban legends, especially those popular with adolescents. Dégh's preliminary published report on "The Boyfriend's Death" concerned nineteen texts collected from IU students from 1964 to 1968. Several storytellers had heard it in high school, often at parties; others had picked it up in college dormitories or elsewhere on campus. Several students expressed some belief in the legend, supposing either that it had happened in their own hometowns, or possibly in other states, once as far distant as "a remote part of Alabama." One informant reported that "she had been sworn to that the incident actually happened," but another, who had heard some variations of the tale, felt that "it seemed too horrible to be true." Some versions had incorporated motifs from other popular teenage horror legends or local ghost stories. . . .

One of the Indiana texts, told in the state of Washington, localizes the story there near Moses Lake, "in the country on a road that leads to a dead-end right under a big weeping willow tree . . . about four or five miles from town." As in most American versions of the story, these specific local touches make believable what is essentially a traveling legend. In a detail familiar from other variants of "The Boyfriend's Death," the body—now decapitated—is left hanging upside down from a branch of the willow tree with the fingernails scraping the top of the car. Another version studied by the Indiana researcher is somewhat aberrant, perhaps because the student was told the story by a friend's parents who claimed that "it happened a long time ago, probably thirty or forty years." Here a murderer is introduced, a "crazy old lady" on whose property the couple has parked. The victim this time is skinned rather than decapitated, and his head scrapes the car as the corpse swings to and fro in the breezy night.

A developing motif in "The Boyfriend's Death" is the character and role of the rescuers, who in the 1964 Kansas version are merely "some people." The standard identification later becomes "the police," authority figures whose presence lends further credence to the story. They are either called by the missing teenagers' parents, or simply appear on the scene in the morning to check the car. In a 1969 variant from Leonardtown, Maryland, the police give a warning, "Miss, please get out of the car and walk to the police car with us, but don't look back." . . . In a version from Texas collected in 1971, set "at this lake somewhere way out in nowhere," a policeman gets an even longer line: "Young lady, we want you to get out of the car and come with us. Whatever you do, don't turn, don't turn around, just keep walking, just keep going straight and don't look back at the car." The more detailed the police instructions are, the more plausible the tale seems to become. Of course the standard rule of folk-narrative plot development now applies: the taboo must be broken (or the "interdiction violated" as some scholars put it). The girl always *does* look back, like Orpheus in the underworld, and in a number of versions her hair turns white from the shock of what she sees, as in a dozen other American legends.

In a Canadian version of "The Boyfriend's Death," told by a fourteen-year-old boy from Willowdale, Ontario, in 1973, the words of the policemen are merely summarized, but the opening scene of the legend is developed more fully, with several special details, including . . . a warning heard on the car radio. The girl's behavior when left behind is also described in more detail. 15

A guy and his girlfriend are on the way to a party when their car starts to give them some trouble. At that same time they catch a news flash on the radio warning all people in the area that a lunatic killer has escaped from a local criminal asylum. The girl becomes very upset and at that point the car stalls completely on the highway. The boyfriend gets out and tinkers around with the engine but can't get the car to start again. He decides that he is going to have to walk on up the road to a gas station and get a tow truck but wants his girlfriend to stay behind in the car. She is frightened and pleads with him to take her, but he says that she'll be safe on the floor of the car covered with a blanket so that anyone passing will think it is an abandoned car and not bother her. Besides he can sprint along the road and get back more quickly than if she comes with him in her high-heeled shoes and evening dress. She finally agrees and he tells her not to come out unless she hears his signal of three knocks on the window. . . .

She does hear knocks on the car, but they continue eerily beyond three; the sound is later explained as the shoes of the boyfriend's corpse bumping the car as the body swings from a limb above the car.

The style in which oral narratives are told deserves attention, for the live telling that is dramatic, fluid, and often quite gripping in actual folk performance before a sympathetic audience may seem stiff, repetitious, and awkward on the printed page. Lacking in all our examples of "The Boyfriend's Death" is the essential ingredient of immediate context—the setting of the legend-telling, the storyteller's vocal and facial expression and gestures, the audience's reaction, and the texts of other similar tales narrated at the same session. Several of the informants explained that the story was told to them in spooky situations, late at night, near a cemetery, out camping, or even "while on a hayride or out parked," occasionally near the site of the supposed murder. Some students refer to such macabre legends, therefore, as "scary stories," "screamers," or "horrors."

A widely-distributed folk legend of this kind as it travels in oral tradition acquires a good deal of its credibility and effect from the localized details inserted by individual tellers. The highway and motel identification in the Kansas text are good examples of this, and in a New Orleans version, "The Boyfriend's Death" is absorbed into a local teenage tradition about "The Grunch"—a half-sheep, half-human monster that haunts specific local sites. One teenager there reported, "A man and lady went out by the lake and in the morning they found 'em hanging upside down on a tree and they said grunches did it." Finally, rumors or news stories about missing persons or violent crimes (as mentioned in the Canadian version) can merge with urban legends, helping to support their air of truth, or giving them renewed circulation after a period of less frequent occurrence.

Even the bare printed texts retain some earmarks of effective oral tradition. Witness in the Kansas text the artful use of repetition (typical of folk narrative style): "Well, he didn't come back and he didn't come back . . . but he didn't come back." The repeated use of "well" and the building of lengthy sentences with "and" are other hallmarks of oral style which give the narrator complete control over his performance, tending to squeeze out interruptions or prevent lapses in attention among the listeners. The scene that is set for the incident—lonely road, night, a tree looming over the car, out of gas—and the sound effects—scratches or bumps on the car—contribute to the style, as does the dramatic part played by the policeman and the abrupt ending line: "She looked back, and she saw . . . !" Since the typical narrators and auditors of "The Boyfriend's Death" themselves like to "park" and may have been alarmed by rumors, strange sights and noises, or automobile emergencies (all intensified in their effects by the audience's knowing other parking legends), the abrupt, unresolved ending leaves open the possibilities of what "really happened."

URBAN LEGENDS AS CULTURAL SYMBOLS

Legends can survive in our culture as living narrative folklore if they contain three essential elements: a strong basic story-appeal, a foundation in actual belief, and a meaningful message or "moral." That is, popular stories like "The Boyfriend's Death" are not only engrossing tales, but also "true," or at least so people think, and they teach valuable lessons. Jokes are a living part of oral tradition, despite being fictional and often silly, because of their humor, brevity, and snappy punch lines, but legends are by nature longer, slower, and more serious. Since more effort is needed to tell and appreciate a legend than a joke, it needs more than just verbal art to carry it along. Jokes have significant "messages" too, but these tend to be disguised or implied. People tell jokes primarily for amusement, and they seldom sense their underlying themes. In legends the primary messages are quite clear and straightforward; often they take the form of explicit warnings or good examples of "poetic justice." Secondary messages in urban legends tend to be suggested metaphorically or symbolically; these may provide deeper criticisms of human behavior or social condition.

People still tell legends, therefore, and other folk take time to listen to   20
them, not only because of their inherent plot interest but because they seem to convey true, worthwhile, and relevant information, albeit partly in a subconscious mode. In other words, such stories are "news" presented to us in an attractive way, with hints of larger meanings. Without this multiple appeal few legends would get a hearing in the modern world, so filled with other distractions. Legends survive by being as lively and "factual" as the television evening news, and, like the daily news broadcasts, they tend to concern deaths, injuries, kidnappings, tragedies, and scandals. Apparently the basic human need for meaningful personal contact cannot be entirely replaced by the mass media and popular culture. A portion of our interest in what is occurring in the world must be filled by some face-to-face reports from other human beings.

On a literal level a story like "The Boyfriend's Death" simply warns young people to avoid situations in which they may be endangered, but at a more symbolic level the story reveals society's broader fears of people, especially women and the young, being alone and among strangers in the darkened world outside the security of their own home or car. Note that the young woman in the story (characterized by "her high-heeled shoes and evening dress") is shown as especially helpless and passive, cowering under the blanket in the car until she is rescued by men. Such themes recur in various forms in many other urban legends. . . .

In order to be retained in a culture, any form of folklore must fill some genuine need, whether this be the need for an entertaining escape from reality, or a desire to validate by anecdotal examples some of the culture's ideals and institutions. For legends in general, a major function has always been the attempt to explain unusual and supernatural happenings in the natural world. To some degree this remains a purpose for urban legends, but their more common role nowadays seems to be to show that the prosaic contemporary scene is capable of producing shocking or amazing occurrences which may actually have happened to friends or to near-acquaintances but which are nevertheless explainable in some reasonably logical terms. On the one hand we want our factual lore to inspire awe, and at the same time we wish to have the most fantastic tales include at least the hint of a rational explanation and perhaps even a conclusion. Thus an escaped lunatic, a possibly *real* character, not a

How does this album cover suggest that Elvis's posthumous popularity has transformed him into a public myth or legend?

fantastic invader from outer space or Frankenstein's monster, is said to be responsible for the atrocities committed in the gruesome tales that teenagers tell. As sometimes happens in real life, the car radio gives warning, and the police get the situation back under control. (The policemen's role, in fact, becomes larger and more commanding as the story grows in oral tradition.) Only when the young lovers are still alone and scared are they vulnerable, but society's adults and guardians come to their rescue presently.

In common with brief unverified reports ("rumors"), to which they are often closely related, urban legends gratify our desire to know about and to try to understand bizarre, frightening, and potentially dangerous or embarrassing events that *may* have happened. (In rumors and legends there is always some element of doubt concerning where and when these things *did* occur.) These floating stories appeal to our morbid curiosity and satisfy our sensation-seeking minds that demand gratification through frequent infusions of new information, "sanitized" somewhat by the positive messages. Informal rumors and stories fill in the gaps left by professional news reporting, and these marvelous, though generally false, "true" tales may be said to be carrying the folk-news—along with some editorial matter—from person to person even in today's technological world.

Questions for Discussion and Writing

1. What are the defining characteristics of urban legends and why have they had such staying power in the popular imagination? What distinguishes an urban legend from a myth or fairy tale?
2. In what ways does "The Boyfriend's Death" exhibit the variations of storyline that define the urban legend? Have you heard one of these variations? If so, how did it differ from the one Brunvand cites?
3. Trace the features of an urban legend that you have heard, either one of those mentioned by Brunvand or another, that has been passed on as a "true" story.
4. **Rhetorical inquiry:** How does Brunvand use multiple versions of "The Boyfriend's Death" to illustrate how an urban legend reflects localized details?

ROSALIND COWARD

Rosalind Coward is a journalist and critic of contemporary culture whose books include Female Desires: How They Are Sought, Bought, and Packaged *(1985), from which the following selection is taken and* Diana: The Portrait *(2004). Coward examines the way the ideal female body has been manufactured as an unattainable goal in contemporary American culture.*

Before You Read

Why is the female body a site on which cultural meanings are projected?

The Body Beautiful

The essence of fashion is that it represents an almost annual—but usually sub-consciously perceived shift in what is deemed to look good. Colour, length and shape of clothing have all changed drastically from year to year over the last few decades. What is more, there have been considerable changes in the type of woman whose beauty is taken as exemplary—the difference, for example, between Twiggy or Julie Christie in the sixties, Maria Schneider in the seventies and Nastassia Kinsky in the eighties. But this diversity of colouring, hairstyles, and dress styles disguises what has been a consistent trend in fashion for the last thirty years. The images which have bombarded us over these years leave little doubt that there is one very definite ideal, the ideal of the perfect body.

This is the one fundamental point of agreement in fashion, advertising and glamour photography; the rules are rigid and the contours agreed. There is a definite female outline which is considered the cultural ideal. This 'perfect' female body would be between five foot five and five foot eight, long-legged, tanned and vigorous looking, but above all, without a spare inch of flesh. 'Brown, slim, lively and lovely . . . that's how we would all like to see ourselves on holiday. Here are a few tips on achieving this and maintaining it.'

Ever since the sixties, with its key image of Twiggy, there has been a tendency with fashion- and beauty-writing and imagery towards the idealization of a female body with no fat on it at all. Concern with achieving this 'fashionable slimness' has become a routine part of many women's lives; dieting, watching what you eat, feeling guilty about food, and exercising affect most women to a greater or lesser degree.

The ideal outline is the silhouette which is left behind after the abolition of those areas of the body which fashion-writing designates 'problem areas.' First, bottoms:

> Female behinds—whether sexy and shapely or absolutely enormous—have long been the subject of saucy seaside postcards. But this important structure can make or mar flimsy summer clothes . . . to say nothing of beachwear. If what goes on below your back is no joke to you, join Norma Knox as she looks at ways to smooth down, gently reshape and generally improve the area between your waist and your knees.
>
> Woman's Own, *24 July 1982*

We are encouraged to 'beat saddle-bag hips' because 'pear-shaped buttocks tend to wear badly in middle age if they have lacked exercise or have been constantly flattened in over-tight trousers.' Next we learn of the disadvantages of flabby thighs. We are told to 'ride a bike and firm up *slack* calves and *floppy* thighs.' Elsewhere we learn of the horrors of loose stomach muscles and their dire consequence, 'the pot belly.' Bosoms are a little more recalcitrant but even these can be 'toned up' which means 'your bust's firmness can be improved if the circulation is encouraged.' Finally we should 'Take a Long Look at Legs.' The 'best' are 'smooth, flawless, unflabby, and golden.' But there is good news, because 'legs are leaner . . . thanks to dieting and exercise.'

And if all or any of these problem parts continue to cause you trouble, you can always resort to the knife—cosmetic surgery. Women's magazines, beauty books and beauty advice regularly give out information about this or make it the subject of light-hearted asides: 'The only known way to remove surplus body fat (short of an operation!) is to consume fewer calories.' Cosmetic surgery is offered not just for altering the shape of your nose but for cutting away bits of flesh that cling stubbornly to those problem areas.

These exhortations leave us in little doubt that the West has as constricting an ideal of female beauty and behaviour as exists in some non-European societies where clitoridectomy is practised. In the West, the ideal of sexual attractiveness is said to be upheld voluntarily, rather than inflicted by a compulsory operation to change the shape of women's anatomy. But the obsession with one particular shape, everywhere promoted by the media, is no less of a definite statement about expectations for women and their sexuality.

Confronted with the strictness of this cultural ideal, we need to understand the meanings and values attached to this shape. We also need to understand the mechanisms which engage women in a discourse so problematic for us; and we need to know how women actually perceive themselves in relation to this idealized image.

What are the values which Western society attributes to this body shape?

The shape is slim, lacking in 'excess fat' which is defined as any flesh which appears not to be muscled and firm, any flesh where you can 'pinch an inch,' as a current slimming dictum suggests. The only area where flesh is tolerated is around the breasts. The totally androgynous style of the sixties has relaxed somewhat—perhaps men couldn't stand the maternal deprivation, when it came to it. But even with breasts, the emphasis is on the 'well-rounded' and 'firm' in keeping with the bulgeless body.

The most striking aspect of this body is that it is reminiscent of adolescence; the shape is a version of an immature body. This is not because with the increase in the earnings of young people, the fashion industry now has them in mind (though there may be an element of truth in this), because the ideal is not exactly a young girl. Rather it is an older woman who keeps an adolescent figure. Witness the eulogies over Jane Fonda's body; a woman of nearly fifty with the 'fantastic body' of a teenager.

This valuation of immaturity is confirmed by other practices concerned with rendering the female body sexually attractive. The practice of shaving under the arms and shaving the legs removes the very evidence that a girl has reached puberty. It is considered attractive that these 'unsightly' hairs are

removed. Body hair is considered ugly and beauty advice strongly recommends shaving the body to restore prepubescent smoothness. A recent hair-
removal advertisement spelled out the ideology: 'Go as Bare as You Dare.
With Bikini Bare you can wear the briefest bikini, the shortest shorts or the
new "thigh-high" cut swim suits with confidence.' Strange paradox here.
Pubic hair appearing in its proper place is unsightly. Yet fashion is designed
precisely to reveal this part.

The aim is constantly to produce smoothness, 'no razor stubble.' The
aim of shaving legs is to produce these firm, lean, smooth objects which,
naturally, have a far higher incidence on a rangy, sexually immature body
than on an older woman.

It is no coincidence that this sexual ideal is an image which connotes
powerlessness. Admittedly, the ideal is not of a demure, classically 'feminine'
girl, but a vigorous and immature adolescent. Nevertheless, it is not a shape
which suggests power or force. It has already been fairly widely documented
how women often choose (albeit unconsciously) to remain 'fat' because of
the power which somehow accrues to them. And it is certainly true that big
women can be extremely imposing. A large woman who is not apologizing
for her size is certainly not a figure to invite the dominant meanings which
our culture attaches to femininity. She is impressive in ways that our culture's
notion of the feminine cannot tolerate. Women, in other words, must always
be seen as women and not as impressive Persons with definite presence.

The cultural ideal amounts to a taboo on the sexually mature woman.
This taboo is closely related to other ideologies of sexually appropriate behaviour for men and women. Historically, for instance, the law has had difficulty
in recognizing women as sexually responsible individuals. In the statutes of
the law, in fact, it is only men who are deemed capable of committing sexual
crimes, and this is not just because it is indeed men who tend to attack
women. These legal ideologies are constructed on the belief that only men
have an active sexuality, therefore only men can actively seek out and commit
a sexual crime. Women in these discourses are defined as the sexually responsive or passive victims of men's advances. Actually (as much recent feminist
writing on the law has made us realize) the *workings* of the law do embrace
very definite beliefs about female sexuality. In rape cases, there are frequent
attempts to establish women's culpability, to establish that women 'asked for
it' in some way, and gave out messages which invited a male sexual attack.
Thus even though the *statutes* of the law appear to protect women against
men's active sexuality, in fact the *workings* of the law often put women on
trial and interrogate them about their degree of responsibility for the attack.

The ideology in the legal treatment of rape corresponds closely with gen-   15
eral ideologies about masculine and feminine behaviour. It is acknowledged
that women have a sexuality, but it is a sexuality which pervades their bodies
almost as if *in spite of themselves*. It is up to women to protect themselves
by only allowing this sexual message to be transmitted in contexts where it
will be received responsibly, that is, in heterosexual, potentially permanent

situations. This is why the defence of a rapist is often conducted in terms of attempting to cast doubt on a woman's sexual 'morality.' If she can be proved to have used her sexuality 'irresponsibly,' then she can be suspected of having invited the active attack of the man. It is only women who have expressed their sexuality within the safety of the heterosexual couple who can be guaranteed the protection of the law.

The sexually immature body of the current ideal fits very closely into these ideologies. For it presents a body which is sexual—it 'exudes' sexuality in its vigorous and vibrant and firm good health—but it is not the body of a woman who has an adult and powerful control over that sexuality. The image is of a highly sexualized female whose sexuality is still one of response *to* the active sexuality of a man. The ideology about adolescent sexuality is exactly the same; young girls are often seen as expressing a sexual need even if the girl herself does not know it. It is an image which feeds off the idea of a fresh, spontaneous, but essentially *responsive* sexuality.

But if this image is somewhat at variance with how the majority of women, especially the older ones, experience their sexual needs, their choices and their active wants, then how is it that this body image continues to prevail? How does that image continue to exist in women's lives, making them unhappy by upholding impossible ideals? How is it that these images have a hold when most women would also express extreme cynicism about advertising stereotypes and manipulation, not to mention knowledge of the techniques by which these body forms are sometimes achieved? (It is not just the real body that is subjected to the knife. Far more common is the cutting off of excess flesh on the photographic image.)

Perhaps the mechanism most important in maintaining women's concern with this ideal is that it is built on a *disgust* of fat and flesh. It is not just a simple case of an ideal to which some of us are close and others not, which we can take or leave. The ideal says as much about its opposite, because the war with fat and excess flesh is a war conducted in highly emotive language. And this language constructs the meanings and therefore the emotions which surround body image. The most basic point about this is that it is difficult to find a non-pejorative word to describe what after all is the average female shape in a rather sedentary culture. When it comes down to it, 'plump,' 'well-rounded,' 'full,' and so on all sound like euphemisms for fat and therefore carry negative connotations. No one wants to be plump when they could be firm; it would be like choosing to be daft when you could be bright. But perhaps more important is that language pertaining to the female body has constructed a whole regime of representations which can only result in women having a punishing and self-hating relationship with their bodies. First, there is the fragmentation of the body—the body is talked about in terms of different parts, 'problem areas,' which are referred to in the third person: 'flabby thighs . . . they.' If the ideal shape has been pared down to a lean outline, bits are bound to stick out or hang down and these become problem areas. The result is that it becomes possible, indeed, likely, for women to think about their bodies in terms of parts, separate areas, as if these parts had some separate life of their own. It means that women are presented with a fragmented sense of the body. This fragmented sense of self is likely to be the foundation for an entirely masochistic or punitive relationship with one's own body. It becomes possible to think about one's body as if it were this thing which followed one about and attached itself unevenly to the ideal outline which lingers beneath. And the dislike of the body has become pathological. The language used expresses absolute disgust with the idea of fat. Fat is like a disease: 'if you *suffer* from cellulite . . .' The cures for the disease are even worse. The body has to be hurt, made to suffer for its excess. *Company* magazine reports on 'Pinching the Fat Away.' Pummeling is regularly recommended, as is wringing out and squeezing: 'Use an oil or cream lubricant and using both hands, wring and twist the flesh as though you were squeezing out water, then use fists to iron skin upwards, kneading deeper at the fleshier thigh area.' And under the title of 'Working Hard at Looking Good' we are told about actress Kate O'Mara's 'beauty philosophy': 'I'm determined to do all I can to help myself. If I cheat on my regime, I write myself abusive notes. Anyway, all this masochistic stuff gives me a purpose in life.'

It is almost as if women had to punish themselves for existing at all, as if any manifestation of this too, too-solid flesh had to be subjected to arcane tortures and expressions of self-loathing.

I have already suggested that one of the reasons behind this self-disgust   20
may be the conflict surrounding the cultural valuation of the sexually immature image. It seems as though women have to punish themselves for growing up, for becoming adults and flaunting their adulthood visibly about their bodies. It is as if women feel that they are too big, occupying too much space, have overgrown their apportioned limits. And a punishment is devised which internalizes the negative values which this society has for such women. It is of course sensual indulgence which is seen as the root cause for women overspilling their proper space. Women who feel themselves to be overweight also invariably have the feeling that their fatness demonstrates weakness and greed. Being fat is tantamount to walking around with a sandwich board saying, 'I can't control my appetite.'

This belief is fostered by the slimming industry and by the literature on fatness. Yudkin, for instance, in the *A–Z for Slimmers*, writes: 'It's not very nice having to admit you are fat. It's much more attractive to suppose that the extra weight isn't due to overeating but is caused by fluid retention . . .' And *Slimmer* magazine ran a spread asking whether children were helpful when their mothers were dieting. They gave a sample of the answers: 'An eight-year-old concerned about his mother's figure is Daniel Hanson of Ashford, Middlesex. "I'm not going to let my mum have any more sweets," he declared firmly. "I want her to be thin like other mums." And nine-year-old Kerry Wheeler says of her mother, "She's looking thinner now, but we can't stop her eating sweets. I have to take them away from her."'

At the heart of these caring offspring's anxieties about their mother's body shape, and at the heart of the discourses on the ideal body, lies a paradox. The *sexual* ideal of the slim, lithe, firm body is also a statement of self-denial, the absence of any other form of sensuality. This adds a further dimension to the cultural connotations of immaturity. The ideal body is also evidence of pure devotion to an aesthetic ideal of sexuality, a very limited aesthetic ideal. Ideal sexuality is limited sensuality; the ideal excludes any form of sensual pleasure which contradicts the aspiration for the perfect body. Again it is a statement about a form of sexuality over which women are assumed to have no control, since it is a statement about not having grown up and pursued other pleasures.

The ideal promoted by our culture is pretty scarce in nature; there aren't all that many mature women who can achieve this shape without extreme effort. Only the mass of advertising images, glamour photographs and so on makes us believe that just about all women have this figure. Yet the ideal is constructed artificially. There are only a very limited number of models who make it to the billboards, and the techniques of photography are all geared towards creating the illusion of this perfect body.

Somewhere along the line, most women know that the image is impossible, and corresponds to the wishes of our culture rather than being actually attainable. We remain trapped by the image, though, because our culture generates such a violent dislike of fat, fragmenting our bodies into separate areas, each of them in their own way too big. Paradoxically, though, this fragmentation also saves us from despair. Most women actually maintain an ambiguous relation to the ideal image; it is rarely rejected totally—it pervades fantasies of transforming the self. But at the same time, there's far more narcissistic self-affirmation among women than is sometimes assumed. Because of the fragmentation of the body into separate areas, most women value certain aspects of their bodies: eyes, hair, teeth, smile. This positive self-image has to be maintained against the grain for the dice are loaded against women liking themselves in this society. But such feelings do lurk there, waiting for their day, forming the basis of the escape route away from the destructive and limiting ideas which are placed on women's bodies.

Questions for Discussion and Writing

1. According to Coward, why is it significant that the female body is fragmented into separate areas women are encouraged to "fix"? What does this say about our culture? Why has the image of the immature female body become the sought-after ideal?

2. How does Coward's analysis of the language used to describe women's bodies in magazines, books, and advertising support her argument?

3. Write an essay in which you analyze the cultural messages transmitted in one striking example of advertising or the media—for example, on the popular TV show *Extreme Makeover*. To what extent do these values correspond to or differ from yours?

4. **Rhetorical inquiry:** How does Coward's discussion of the tendency to place culpability on women in rape cases support her analysis of cultural attitudes toward women?

BILL BRYSON

Have home-cooked meals become a thing of the past? What does the instant gratification offered by junk foods and fast foods tell us about our society? In this essay, from Made in American: An Informal History of the English Language in the United States *(1994), Bill Bryson provides a fascinating historical perspective on the catch-as-catch-can eating habits we now accept as normal. Because he lived in England for many years before returning to the United States, Bryson brings a fresh perspective to American culture in works such as* A Walk in the Woods *(1998) and* I'm a Stranger Here Myself *(1999). His most recent work is* the Life and Times of the Thunderbolt Kid: A Memoir *(2006).*

Before You Read

How much do you know about the history of how eating out in America started (which now accounts for 47% of money spent on food)?

What's Cooking? Eating in America

As America became increasingly urbanized, people more and more took to eating their main meal in the evening. To fill the void between breakfast and dinner, a new and essentially American phenomenon arose: lunch. The words *lunch* and *luncheon* (often spelled *luncheon, lunchen, lunchion,* or *lunching*) have been around in English since the late 1500s. Originally they signified lumps of food— "a lunchen of cheese"—and may have come from the Spanish *lonja,* a slice of ham. The word was long considered a depolorable vulgarisn, suitable only to the servants's hall. In America, however, "lunch" became respectable, and as it dawned on opportunistic restauranteurs that each day millions of office workers required something quick, simple, and cheap, a wealth of new facilities sprang up to answer the demand. In short order Americans got *diners* (1872), *lunch counters* (1873), *self-service restaurants* (1885), *cafeterias* (1890s), *automats* (1902), and *short-order restaurants* (1905).

The process began in 1872 in Providence, Rhode Island, when one Walter Scott loaded a wagon with sandwiches, boiled eggs, and other simple fare and parked outside the offices of the *Providence Journal.* Since all the restaurants in town closed at 8 P.M., he had no competition and his business thrived. Soon wagons began appearing all over. By the time Scott retired forty-five years later he had fifty competitors in Providence alone. They were called *lunch wagons,* which was a little odd, since lunch was one thing they didn't serve. A few, seeking greater accuracy, called themselves *night lunch wagons* or *night cafés.* When residents complained about having food sold outside their houses, cities everywhere enacted ordinances banning the wagons. So lunch wagon proprietors hit on the idea of moving their wagons to vacant lots, taking off the wheels, and calling them restaurants, since restaurants were immune from the restrictions. By the 1920s, several companies were mass-producing shiny, purpose-built restaurants known everywhere as *diners*. From a business point of view, diners were an appealing proposition. They were cheap to buy and maintain. You could set them up in hours on any level piece of ground, and if trade didn't materialize you loaded them onto a flatbed truck and moved them elsewhere. A single diner in a good location could turn a profit of $12,000 a year—a lot of money in the 1920s. One of the more enduring myths of American eating is that diners were built out of old railway dining cars. Hardly any were. They were just made to look that way.

The first place known to be called a *cafeteria*—though the proprietor spelled it *cafetiria*—was opened in Chicago in the early 1890s. The word came from Cuban Spanish and as late as 1925 was still often pronounced in the Spanish style, with the accent on the penultimate syllable. Cafeterias proved so popular that they spawned a huge, if mercifully short-lived, vogue for words of similar form: *washeteria, groceteria, caketeria, drugeteria, bobateria* (a place where hair was bobbed), *beauteria, chocolateria, shaveteria, smoketeria, hardware-ateria, garmenteria, furnitureteria*—even *casketeria* for a funeral home and the somewhat redundant *restauranteria*.

The *automat*—a cafeteria where food was collected from behind little windows after depositing the requisite change in a slot in each—was not an American invention but a Swedish one. In fact, they had been common in Sweden for half a century before two entrepreneurs named Horn and Hardardt opened one in Philadelphia in 1902 and started a small lucrative empire.

Luncheonette (sometimes modified to *lunchette*) entered American   5
English in about 1920 and in its turn helped to popularize a fashion for words with *-ette* endings: *kitchenette, dinette, usherette, roomette, bachelorette, drum majorette*, even *parkette* for a meter maid and *realtyette* for a female real estate agent.

The waitresses and *hash slingers* (an Americanism dating from 1868) who worked in these establishments evolved a vast, arcane, and cloyingly jocular lingo for the food they served and the clients who ate it. By the 1920s if you wanted to work behind a lunch counter you needed to know that *Noah's boy* was a slice of ham (since Ham one of Noah's sons) and that *burn one* or *grease spot* designated a hamburger. *He'll take a chance* or *clean the kitchen* meant an order of hash, *Adam and Eve on a raft* was two poached eggs on toast, *cat's eyes* was a tapioca pudding, *bird seed* was cereal, *whistleberries* were baked beans, and *dough well done with cow to cover* was the somewhat labored way of calling for an order of toast and butter. Food that had been waiting too long was said to be *growing a beard*. Many of these shorthand terms have since entered the mainsteam, notably *BLT* for a bacon, lettuce, and tomato sandwich, *over easy* and *sunny side up* in respect of eggs, and *hold* as in "hold the mayo."

Eating out—usually quickly, cheaply, and greasily—became a habit for urban workers and a big business for the providers. Between 1910 and 1925 the number of restaurants in America rose by 40 percent. A hungry New Yorker in 1925 could choose among seventeen thousand restaurants, double the number that had existed a decade before. Even drugstores got in on the act. By the early 1920s, the average drugstore, it was estimated, did 60 percent of its business at the soda fountain. They had become, in effect, restaurants that also sold pharmaceutical supplies.

As the American diet grew livelier, it inevitably sparked alarm among those who believed that sensual pleasures were necessarily degenerate. There arose, in the second half of the nineteenth century, mighty bands of men and women who believed with a kind of religious fervor that the consumption of the wrong foods would lead to the breakdown of the nation's moral fiber. One man went so far as to form a Society for the Suppression of Eating, which would appear to be taking matters about as far as they will go. Others were only slightly more accommodating to the need for sustenance. Typical of the breed was the Reverend Sylyester Graham, who connected insanity with eating ketchup and mustard, and believed that the consumption of meat would result in the sort of hormonal boisterousness that leads men to take advantage of pliant women. Many believed him—so many indeed that by mid-century the nation was not only following his cheerless recipes, but many thousands of people were living in Graham boardinghouses, where his dietary precepts were imposed with rigor. His one lasting contribution to the American stomach was the graham cracker. Then there was Horace Fletcher, who gave the world the notion that each bite of food should be chewed thirty-two times. Though he had no standing as a nutritionist—he was an importer by trade—that didn't stop him from disseminating his theories in a phenomenally successful book, *The ABC of Nutrition,* published in 1903.

But the zenith of America's long obsessive coupling of food with moral rectitude came with a Seventh-Day Adventist doctor named John Harvey Kellogg who in 1876 took over the failing Western Health Reform Institute in Battle Creek, Michigan, renamed it the Medical and Surgical Sanitarium (though everyone soon knew it as the Battle Creek Sanitarium or simply the Kellogg), and introduced a regime of treatments that was as bizarre as it was popular. Possibly the two were not unconnected.

Patients who were underweight were confined to their beds with sand- 10
bags on their abdomens and forced to eat up to twenty-six meals a day. They were not permitted any physical exertion. Even their teeth were brushed by an attendant lest they needlessly expend a calorie. The hypertensive were required to eat grapes and nothing else—up to fourteen pounds of them daily. Others with less easily discernible maladies were confined to wheelchairs for months on end and fed experimental foods such as gluten wafers and "a Bulgarian milk preparation known as yogurt." Kellogg himself was singular in his habits. It was his practice to dictate long tracts on the evils of meat-eating and masturbation (the one evidently led to the other) while seated on the toilet or

while riding his bicycle in circles around the lawn. Despite—or very possibly because of—these peculiarities, Kellogg's "Temple of Health" thrived and grew into a substantial complex with such classy amenities as elevators, room service, and a palm house with its own orchestra. Among its devoted and well-heeled patrons were Teddy Roosevelt and John D. Rockefeller.

Throughout much of his life, Kellogg nurtured a quiet obsession with inventing a flaked breakfast cereal. One night the process came to him in a dream. He hastened to the kitchen in his nightshirt, boiled some wheat, rolled it out into strips, and baked it in the oven. It was not only tasty but sufficiently unusual to be unquestionably good for you. Dr. Kellogg's patients simply couldn't get enough of it. One of these patients was a young man named C. W. Post, who spent nine months at the sanitarium sitting list-lessly and needlessly in a wheelchair before abruptly embracing Christian Science and fleeing. One thing Post took away with him was a profound respect for the commercial possibilities of Dr. Kellogg's cereal. Unable to get a license from Kellogg, he decided to make his own, and in a breathtakingly short time became one of America's wealthiest men. Among Post's inventions were *Grape-Nuts* (a curious name, since it contained neither grapes nor nuts) and *Post Toasties*, or *Elijah's Manna* as it was known until 1908.

As it dawned on people that breakfast cereals were awfully easy to make, innumerable imitators sprang up. By the turn of the century at least forty-four companies in Battle Creek were churning out breakfast cereals with names like *Grip Nuts, Hello-Billo, Malt-Ho, Flake-Ho, Korn Kure, Tryabita, Tryachewa, Oatsina, Food of Eden,* and *Orange Meat* (which, like Grape-Nuts contained neither of the specified ingredients). Without exception these products were sold as health foods.* Each packet of Grape-Nuts contained an illustrated leaflet, *The Road to Wellville,* explaining how a daily dose of the enclosed toasted wheat-and-barley granules would restore depleted brain and nerve cells and build strong red blood. For a short but deliriously exciting time, fortunes were there for the taking. A Methodist preacher named D. D. Martin cooked up some healthful goop on the kitchen stove, dubbed it *Per-Fo,* and immediately sold the formula for $100,000. Curiously almost the only person in Battle Creek unable to capitalize on Kellogg's invention was Kellogg himself. Not until 1907, when he at last brought to market his cornflakes, did he begin to get the credit and wealth his invention merited.

Preoccupation with health-enhancing qualities became a theme for all manner of foods. Moxie, known for its soft drinks, was founded in 1885 as the Moxie Nerve Food Company of Boston, and Dr. Pepper, founded in the same year, was so called not because the name was catchy but because it sounded sternly healthful. For a time, it seemed that no food product could

---

* Compared with later cereals they certainly were. Kellogg's Sugar Smacks, introduced in 1953, were 56 percent sugar.

hope to sell unless it dealt vigorously with a range of human frailties. Quaker Oats claimed to curb nervousness and constipation. Fleischmann's Yeast not only soothed frayed nerves and loosed the bowels, but also dealt vigorously with indigestion, skin disorders, tooth decay, obesity, and a vague but ominous-sounding disorder called "fallen stomach." Fleischmann's kept up these sweeping claims—occasionally added to them—until ordered to desist by the Federal Trade Commission in 1938 on the grounds that there wasn't a shred of evidence to support any of them.

Against such a background it is little wonder that Americans turned with a certain enthusiasm to junk food. The term *junk food* didn't enter the American vocabulary until 1973, but the concept was there long before, and it began with one of the great breakthroughs in food history: the development of a form of edible solid chocolate.

Though a New World food (the Mayas and Aztecs so prized it that they used cocoa beans as money), chocolate took a long time to become a central part of the American diet. Not until just before the Revolution did it become known in colonial America, and then only as a drink. At first chocolate was so exotic that it was spelled and pronounced in a variety of ways—*chockolatta, chuchaletto, chocolate, chockolatto*—before finally settling in the late eighteenth century into something close to the original Nuahtl Indian word, *xocólatl*. Chocolate came from the cacao tree, which somehow became transliterated into English as *cocoa* (pronounced at first with three syllables: "co-co-a"). The chocolate bar was invented in England in the 1840s and milk chocolate in Switzerland some thirty years later, but neither became popular in America until Milton Snavely Hershey gave the world the nickel Hershey bar in 1903. (The price would stay a nickel for the next sixty-seven years, but only at a certain palpable cost to the bar's dimensions. Just in the quarter century following World War II, the bar shrank a dozen times, until by 1970, when it was beginning to look perilously like a chocolate credit card, the bar was reinvigorated in size and the price raised accordingly.)

As is so often the case with American entrepreneurs, Milton Hershey was an unlikely success. His formal education ended with the fourth grade and he spent decades as a struggling small-time candy maker before suddenly and unexpectedly striking it rich in middle age with caramels, a new sensation that swept the country in the late nineteenth century.

In 1900, he sold his caramel business for $1 million—this at a time when $10 was a good weekly wage—and turned his attentions to the still fairly novel process of making milk chocolate. This new venture was such a huge and instantaneous success that within three years he was able to embark on building his own model community, complete with streets named Chocolate Avenue and Cocoa Avenue, near his birthplace of Derry Church in central Pennsylvania. Among the names Hershey considered for the new town were *Ulikit, Chococoa City,* and *Qualitytells,* but eventually he decided on *Hersheykoko.* For reasons lost to history, the postal authorities refused to countenance the name and he was forced to settle on the more mundane, but

15

unquestionably apt, name *Hershey*. As well as the world's largest chocolate factory, the town of Hershey boasted several parks, a boating lake, a museum, a zoo, a professional ice hockey team, and the usual complement of banks, stores, and offices, all owned by Mr. Hershey.

Hershey ran the town as a private fiefdom. He prowled the streets look-ing for malingering municipal workers, whom he would instantly dismiss, and personally supervised (with presumed keenness) the censoring of movies at the local bijou. But he also engaged in many charitable works, notably the building of one of the world's largest orphanages for boys (and boys alone; orphan girls would have to look elsewhere) and endowing it with most of his fortune, some $66 million (today worth $1.7 billion).

The first true candy bar—that is, one containing ingredients additional to chocolate—was the Squirrel Brand peanut bar. Introduced in 1905, it sold well, but was quickly overtaken by the innovation of 1912, the *Goo Goo Cluster*. But the golden age of candy bars was the 1920s. Several classics made their debut in that busy decade—the *Oh Henry!* and *Baby Ruth* bars in 1920, the *Milky Way* and *Butterfingers* in 1923, *Mr. Goodbar* in 1925, *Snickers* in 1930. The Baby Ruth was originally called the *Kandy Kake*, but in 1920 the Curtiss Candy Company changed the name. The company stead-fastly maintained that change had nothing to do with the baseball hero Babe Ruth—who just happened to be the hottest thing in baseball in 1920—but rather was in honor of the daughter of president Grover Cleveland. This bonny infant had indeed captured America's heart and gained the affection-ate sobriquet Baby Ruth, but that had been more than twenty years earlier. By 1920 she had been dead for sixteen years, and thus would not appear to have been an obvious candidate for gustatory immortalization. Still, if the Curtiss story is to be believed, Baby Ruth was no odder a designation for a candy bar than *Oh Henry!*—said to be named for the fresh-faced youth whose droll quips to the girls at the George Williamson candy factory in Chicago provoked the constant cry, "Oh, Henry!"

Among the many hundreds of other candy bars loosed on a willing nation during the decade were *Big Dearos, Fat Emmas*, the *Milk Nut Loaf*, and the intriguing *Vegetable Sandwich*. Made of chocolate-covered vegeta-bles, it was sold with the solemn assurance that "it will not constipate." As might have been predicted, constipation was not a compelling preoccupa-tion among America's children and the Vegetable Sandwich soon disap-peared from the scene. Equally improbable was the *Chicken Dinner* candy bar, so called because it was supposed to engender the feeling of well-being provided by a steaming roast chicken dinner. Though few people were able to make the leap of imagination necessary to equate a 5-cent chocolate peanut roll with a well-balanced meal, the Chicken Dinner sold well and survived into the 1960s. Curiously, none of these products were known as *candy bars*. The term is not recorded in print until 1943.

The 1920s saw the birth of many other well-loved snack foods, includ-ing such perennial mainstays of the American diet as the *Good Humor* bar in 1920, the *Eskimo Pie* a year later, *Popsicles* in 1924, *Milk Duds* in 1926, *Hostess Cakes* in 1926 (with *Twinkies* to follow in 1930), and *Dubble Bubble Gum* in 1928. This was invented by Frank H. Fleer, whose earlier bubble gum, *Blibber-Blubber*, was something of a failure—it tended to dissolve in the mouth but to stick tenaciously to everything else, including Junior's face, when popped—but who had made a fortune with an earlier invention, *Chiclets*. But the runaway success of the decade was the Eskimo Pie (originally called the *I-Scream-Bar* by its inventor, a high school teacher and part-time ice cream salesman in Onawa, Iowa). So immensely popular was the Eskimo Pie that within three months of its introduction more than a million bars a day were being sold and the price of cocoa beans on the open market had leaped 50 percent in response.

But all of these paled in comparison with a dietary behemoth that emerged from the shadows in the 1920s and took its place at the top of the table. I refer of course to the hamburger. No one knows where the first hamburger was made. The presumption has always been that it came to America from Hamburg, Germany, in the same way that the frankfurter came from Frankfort and baloney came from Bologna. But this overlooks the niggling consideration that Hamburg has never had any tradition of serving such a dish. Considering its central role in the American diet, the evidence as to when the hamburger first appeared and why it was so called is vexingly uncertain, though there is no shortage of claimants for the title. Among the more insistent, if not necessarily most likely, contenders have been the towns of Seymour, Wisconsin, and Hamburg, New York, both of which claim to have been the birthplace of the hamburger in 1885. Seymour attributes the invention to one Charles Nagreen and unequivocally advertises itself as the "Home of the Hamburger," though its supporters tend to grow quiet when asked to explain on what basis Nagreen chose to commemorate a distant German city. More plausible, on the face of it, would appear to be the claim of Hamburg, New York, whose proponents believe that it was the inspired creation of the brothers Frank and Charles Menches, who developed it at the Erie County Fair in 1885.

Unfortunately for both claims, the etymological evidence suggests an earlier birth for the name, if not the dish. There is some evidence to suggest that it may have appeared as *Hamburg steak* on a Delmonico's menu as early as 1836 or 1837. The first undisputed sighting has been traced to the *Boston Journal* of February 16, 1884, which wrote in passing. "We take a chicken and boil it. When it is cold we cut it up as they do meat to make a Hamburg steak." As so often happens with first citations, the context makes it clear that by this time the dish was already well known. Unfortunately, it also indicates that it was a different dish from the one that we know today, involving as it did beef cut up rather than ground, and eaten cold. What is certain is that *Hamburg steak* was widely called *hamburger steak* by 1889 (the first reference was in a newspaper in Walla Walla, Washington, suggesting that by this time it was eaten nationwide). The term in turn was generally being shortened to *hamburger* by 1901, by which time it had come to signify a patty of ground beef fried on a grill.

But it was still not a sandwich. It was, rather, a lump of ground beef served bare and eaten with a knife and fork. Who first had the idea of serving it in a bun is unknown and essentially unprovable, though once again there is no shortage of claimants. One such is Louis' Lunch of New Haven, Connecticut, which claims to have invented the true article in 1900, though some purists dismiss Louis' on the grounds that it served its burgers (indeed still does) on toasted bread rather than buns. Kaelin's Restaurant in Louisville, meanwhile, claims to have concocted and named the first cheeseburger in 1934, and I've no doubt that there are many other places around the country making similar heartfelt assertions. In any case, we can safely say that by about 1910 the object that we now know and venerate as the hamburger was widely consumed and universally known by that name. Even so, it had yet to fully establish itself in the hearts, and stomachs, of Americans.

In its early years the hamburger was often regarded by short-order cooks 25 as a convenient way of passing off old or doubtful meat, and by its consumers,

Jack : Do you think baby will be quiet long enough to take her picture, mamma?
Mamma : The Kodak will catch her whether she moves or not ; it is as " quick as a wink."

Send to the Eastman Company, Rochester, N. Y., for a copy of "Do I want a Camera," (illustrated) free by mail.

How does this original ad for a newly designed Kodak camera both depict a problem and solve it for the consumer with the product?

Just a drink but—what a drink. And so today ice-cold, refreshing Coca-Cola is served as a beverage in leading hospitals. It fills a need. There's wholesome buoyancy in its life and sparkle. Its tingling, delicious taste meets a happy welcome wherever it is served.

For your own home order a case (24 bottles) from your dealer

COCA-COLA CO., ATLANTA, GA.

"Something that will refresh you"

Served in Leading Hospitals

Drink

Coca-Cola

Delicious and Refreshing

5¢

• You can be sure it is pure and wholesome. Coca-Cola is a pure drink of natural products, with no artificial flavor or coloring. Complying with pure food laws all over the world.

Good Housekeeping Bureau

How does this early ad for Coke illustrate the search for a memorable slogan that finally became "the pause that refreshes"?

in consequence, as an item to be approached with caution. Not until 1921, with the rise of two entrepreneurs in Wichita, Kansas, did the hamburger begin to take its first vigorous strides towards respectability. The men in question were a former insurance executive named E. W. "Billy" Ingram and a short-order cook named Walter A. Anderson, and their brilliant stroke was to offer the world decent hamburgers cost a nickel and weren't much larger. Ingram and Anderson managed to squeeze eighteen hamburgers from a pound of ground beef, significantly less than one ounce each. Nonetheless, people were soon flocking to their tiny cubicle, built of rock-faced concrete shaped vaguely, and a little preposterously, in the image of a castle. They called it White Castle because, they explained, *white* symbolized purity and cleanliness, and *castle* suggested permanence and stability.

Anderson and Ingram hit on three novelties that sealed their success and have been the hallmarks of fast-food service ever since. They offered a limited menu, which promoted quick service and allowed them to concentrate on what they were good at; they kept their premises spotless, which encouraged confidence in their hygienic integrity; and they employed a distinctive, eye-catching design for the building, which made it instantly recognizable from blocks away. Soon there were White Castles all over the country and a following throng of eager imitators—White Tower, White Diamond, Royal Castle, and White Crest—some of which are said to survive yet. The age of fast food was upon us, though no one would know it as such for another thirty years. *Fast food* first appeared in 1954 (as an adjective it had appeared three years earlier). *Takeout food* was even slower to arrive; its first recorded appearance was not until 1962.

Questions for Discussion and Writing

1. What social factors explain why restaurants, luncheonettes, cafeterias, and diners became increasingly important in America?
2. How is the creation of ready-to-eat breakfast cereals intended to reverse a decline in cultural values and what role did Dr. Kellogg and the Reverend Sylvester Graham play?
3. What are some current trends in the eating habits of Americans? In your opinion, why are eating contests so popular? You might wish to do some research on festivals that feature particular local foods such as garlic in Gilroy, California.
4. **Rhetorical inquiry:** How is Bryson's analysis structured to emphasize the cause-and-effect relationship of trends and fads in America's food preferences? Can you cite some of the transitions he provides to help readers see the logical connections between the assertions he makes?

JESSICA MITFORD

Jessica Mitford was born in 1917 in Gloustershire, England. After emigrating to the United States in 1939, Mitford worked as the executive secretary for the Civil Rights Congress in Oakland, California. Mitford's crusading investigative studies include the much-acclaimed The American Way of Death *(1963), a book violently denounced by the funeral industry;* The Trial of Dr. Spock, William Sloane Coffin, Jr., Michael Ferber, Mitchell Goodman, and Marcus Raskin *(1969), an examination of conspiracy laws; and* Kind and Usual Punishment: The Prison Business *(1973), an exposé of the widespread use of prisoners as subjects in psychological and physiological research. In 1973, Mitford was named Distinguished Visiting Professor in Sociology at San Jose State College. In "Mortuary Solaces," from* The American Way of Death, *Mitford provides an acerbic account, buttressed by extensive research and quotations from the funeral industry's handbooks, of the processes used to prepare dead bodies for public display.*

Before You Read

What do you think about the cosmetic techniques morticians use to create an illusion of life?

Mortuary Solaces

Embalming is indeed a most extraordinary procedure, and one must wonder at the docility of Americans who each year pay hundreds of millions of dollars for its perpetuation, blissfully ignorant of what it is all about, what is done, how it is done. Not one in ten thousand has any idea of what actually takes place. Books on the subject are extremely hard to come by. They are not to be found in most libraries or bookshops.

In an era when huge television audiences watch surgical operations in the comfort of their living rooms, when, thanks to the animated cartoon, the geography of the digestive system has become familiar territory even to the nursery school set, in a land where the satisfaction of curiosity about almost all matters is a national pastime, the secrecy surrounding embalming can, surely, hardly be attributed to the inherent gruesomeness of the subject. Custom in this regard has within this century suffered a complete reversal. In the early days of American embalming, when it was performed in the home of the deceased, it was almost mandatory for some relative to stay by the embalmer's side and witness the procedure. Today, family members who might wish to be in attendance would certainly be dissuaded by the funeral director. All others, except apprentices, are excluded by law from the preparation room.

A close look at what does actually take place may explain in large measure the undertaker's intractable reticence concerning a procedure that has become his major *raison d'étre*. Is it possible he fears that public information about embalming might lead patrons to wonder if they really want this service? If the funeral men are loath to discuss the subject outside the trade, the reader may, understandably, be equally loath to go on reading at this point. For those who have the stomach for it, let us part the formaldehyde curtain. . . .

The body is first laid out in the undertaker's morgue—or rather, Mr. Jones is reposing in the preparation room—to be readied to bid the world farewell.

The preparation room in any of, the better funeral establishments has the tiled and sterile look of a surgery, and indeed the embalmer-restorative artist who does his chores there is beginning to adopt the term "derma-surgeon" (appropriately corrupted by some mortician-writers as "demisurgeon") to describe his calling. His equipment, consisting of scalpels, scissors, augurs, forceps, clamps, needles, pumps, tubes, bowls and basins, is crudely imitative of the surgeon's as is his technique, acquired in a nine- or twelve-month post-high-school course in an embalming school. He is supplied by an advanced chemical industry with a bewildering array of fluids, sprays, pastes, oils, powders, creams, to fix or soften tissue, shrink or distend it as needed, dry it here, restore the moisture there. There are cosmetics, waxes and paints to fill and cover features, even plaster of Paris to replace entire limbs. There are ingenious aids to prop and stabilize the cadaver: a Vari-Pose Head Rest, the Edwards Arm and Hand Positioner, the Repose Block (to support the shoulders during the embalming), and the Throop Foot Positioner, which resembles an old-fashioned stocks.

Mr. John H. Eckels, president of the Eckels College of Mortuary Science, thus describes the first part of the embalming procedure: "In the hands of a skilled practitioner, this work may be done in a comparatively short time and without mutilating the body other than by slight incision—so slight that it scarcely would cause serious inconvenience if made upon a living person. It is necessary to remove the blood, and doing this not only helps in the disinfecting, but removes the principal cause of disfigurements due to discoloration."

Another textbook discusses the all-important time element: "The earlier this is done, the better, for every hour that elapses between death and embalming will add to the problems and complications encountered. . . ." Just how soon should one get going on the embalming? The author tells us, "On the basis of such scanty information made available to this profession through its rudimentary and haphazard system of technical research, we must conclude that the best results are to be obtained if the subject is embalmed before life is completely extinct—that is, before cellular death has occurred. In the average case, this would mean within an hour after somatic death." For those who feel that there is something a little rudimentary, not to say haphazard, about this advice, a comforting thought is offered by another writer. Speaking of fears entertained in early days of premature burial, he points out, "One of the effects of embalming by chemical injection, however, has been to dispel fears of live burial." How true, once the blood is removed, chances of live burial are indeed remote.

To return to Mr. Jones, the blood is drained out through the veins and replaced by embalming fluid pumped in through the arteries. As noted in *The Principles and Practices of Embalming,* "every operator has a favorite injection and drainage point—a fact which becomes a handicap only if he fails or refuses to forsake his favorites when conditions demand it." Typical favorites are the carotid artery, femoral artery, jugular vein, subclavian vein. There are various choices of embalming fluid. If Flextone is used, it will produce a "mild, flexible rigidity. The skin retains a velvety softness, the tissues are rubbery and pliable. Ideal for women and children." It may be blended with B. and G. Products Company's Lyf-Lyk tint, which is guaranteed to reproduce "nature's own skin texture . . . the velvety appearance of living tissue." Suntone comes in three separate tints: Suntan; Special Cosmetic Tint, a pink shade "especially indicated for young female subjects"; and Regular Cosmetic Tint, moderately pink.

About three to six gallons of a dyed and perfumed solution of formaldehyde, glycerin, borax, phenol, alcohol and water is soon circulating through Mr. Jones, whose mouth has been sewn together with a "needle directed upward between the upper lip and gum and brought out through the left nostril," with the corners raised slightly "for a more pleasant expression." If he should be bucktoothed, his teeth are cleaned with Bon Ami and coated with colorless nail polish. His eyes, meanwhile, are closed with flesh-tinted eye caps and eye cement.

The next step is to have at Mr. Jones with a thing called a trocar. This is   10
a long, hollow needle attached to a tube. It is jabbed into the abdomen, poked around the entrails and chest cavity, the contents of which are pumped out and replaced with "cavity fluid." This done, and the hole in the abdomen sewn up, Mr. Jones's face is heavily creamed (to protect the skin from burns which may be caused by leakage of the chemicals), and he is covered with a sheet and left unmolested for a while. But not for long—there is more, much more, in store for him. He has been embalmed, but not yet restored, and the best time to start the restorative work is eight to ten hours after embalming, when the tissues have become firm and dry.

The object of all this attention to the corpse, it must be remembered, is to make it presentable for viewing in an attitude of healthy repose. "Our customs require the presentation of our dead in the semblance of normality . . . unmarred by the ravages of illness, disease or mutilation," says Mr. J. Sheridan Mayer in his *Restorative Art.* This is rather a large order since few people die in the full bloom of health, unravaged by illness and unmarked by some disfigurement. The funeral industry is equal to the challenge: "In some cases the gruesome appearance of a mutilated or disease-ridden subject may be quite discouraging. The task of restoration may seem impossible and shake the confidence of the embalmer. This is the time for intestinal fortitude and determination. Once the formative work is begun and affected tissues are cleaned or removed, all doubts of success vanish. It is surprising and gratifying to discover the results which may be obtained."

The embalmer, having allowed an appropriate interval to elapse, returns to the attack, but now he brings into play the skill and equipment of sculptor and cosmetician. Is a hand missing? Casting one in plaster of Paris is a simple matter. "For replacement purposes, only a cast of the back of the hand is necessary; this is within the ability of the average operator and is quite adequate." If a lip or two, a nose or an ear should be missing, the embalmer has at hand a variety of restorative waxes with which to model replacements. Pores and skin texture are simulated by stippling with a little brush, and over this cosmetics are laid on. Head off? Decapitation cases are rather routinely handled. Ragged edges are trimmed, and head joined to torso with a series of splints, wires and sutures. It is a good idea to have a little something at the neck—a scarf or high collar—when time for viewing comes. Swollen mouth? Cut out tissue as needed from inside the lips. If too much is removed, the surface contour can easily be restored by padding with cotton. Swollen necks and cheeks are reduced by removing tissue through vertical incisions made down each side of the neck. "When the deceased is casketed, the pillow will hide the stuture incisions . . . as an extra precaution against leakage, the suture may be painted with liquid sealer."

The opposite condition is more likely to present itself—that of emaciation. His hypodermic syringe now loaded with massage cream, the embalmer seeks out and fills the hollowed and sunken areas by injection. In this procedure the backs of the hands and fingers and the under-chin area should not be neglected.

Positioning the lips is a problem that recurrently challenges the ingenuity of the embalmer. Closed too tightly, they tend to give a stern, even disapproving expression. Ideally, embalmers feel, the lips should give the impression of being ever so slightly parted, the upper lip protruding slightly for a more youthful appearance. This takes some engineering, however, as the lips tend to drift apart. Lip drift can sometimes be remedied by pushing one or two straight pins through the inner margin of the lower lip and then inserting them between the two front upper teeth. If Mr. Jones happens to have no teeth, the pins can just as easily be anchored in his Armstrong Face Former and Denture Replacer. Another method to maintain lip closure is to dislocate the lower jaw, which is then held in its new position by a wire run through holes which have been drilled through upper and lower jaws at the midline. As the French are fond of saying, *il faut souffrir pour être belle.*[1]

If Mr. Jones has died of jaundice, the embalming fluid will very likely turn him green. Does this deter the embalmer? Not if he has intestinal fortitude. Masking pastes and cosmetics are heavily laid on, burial garments

---

[1] "One must suffer to be beautiful."

and casket interiors are color-correlated with particular care, and Jones is displayed beneath rose-colored lights. Friends will say, "How *well* he looks." Death by carbon monoxide, on the other hand, can be rather a good thing from the embalmer's viewpoint: "One advantage is the fact that this type of discoloration is an exaggerated form of a natural pink coloration." This is nice because the healthy glow is already present and needs but little attention.

The patching and filling completed, Mr. Jones is now shaved, washed and dressed. Cream-based cosmetic, available in pink, flesh, suntan, brunette and blond, is applied to his hands and face, his hair is shampooed and combed (and, in the case of Mrs. Jones, set), his hands manicured. For the horny-handed son of toil special care must be taken; cream should be applied to remove ingrained grime, and the nails cleaned. "If he were not in the habit of having them manicured in life, trimming and shaping is advised for better appearance—never questioned by kin."

Jones is now ready for casketing (this is the present participle of the verb "to casket"). In this operation his right shoulder should be depressed slightly "to turn the body a bit to the right and soften the appearance of lying flat on the back." Positioning the hands is a matter of importance, and special rubber positioning blocks may be used. The hands should be cupped slightly for a more lifelike, relaxed appearance. Proper placement of the body requires a delicate sense of balance. It should lie as high as possible in the casket, yet not so high that the lid, when lowered, will hit the nose. On the other hand, we are cautioned, placing the body too low "creates the impression that the body is in a box."

Jones is next wheeled into the appointed slumber room where a few last touches may be added—his favorite pipe placed in his hand or, if he was a great reader, a book propped into position. (In the case of little Master Jones a Teddy bear may be clutched.) Here he will hold open house for a few days, visiting hours 10 A.M. to 9 P.M.

Questions for Discussion and Writing

1. Why does our culture surround mortuary practices with secrecy? How does Mitford satirize these practices?
2. How does Mitford use instructions in the manuals to underscore her thesis?
3. What euphemisms does our culture use to blanket negative associations with death even in very inappropriate circumstances? For example, why are convicted murderers described as being eligible for execution?
4. **Rhetorical inquiry:** Into what stages does Mitford divide the process of "casketing"? To what extent do you feel that Mitford overlooks the positive aspects of creating an illusion through cosmetic means that makes the mourners feel better?

JUDITH ORTIZ COFER

Judith Ortiz Cofer, a poet and novelist, was born in 1952 in Hormigueros, Puerto Rico, and was educated at Augusta College, Florida Atlantic University, and Oxford University. Her published work includes the collections of poetry Peregrina *(1985),* Terms of Survival *(1987), and* Reaching for the Mainland and Selected New Poems *(1996) and a novel,* The Line of the Sun *(1989). She also wrote* The Meaning of Consuelo *(2003),* Call Me Maria: A Novel *(2004), and* A Love Story Beginning in Spanish *(2005). "The Myth of the Latin Woman: I Just Met a Girl Named Maria," which first appeared in* The Latin Deli: Prose and Poetry *(1993), explores the destructive effects of the Latina stereotype.*

Before You Read

Notice how Cofer's desire to succeed as a writer is a reaction to repeated instances in which she is misperceived because of her ethnicity.

The Myth of the Latin Woman

On a bus trip to London from Oxford University where I was earning some graduate credits one summer, a young man, obviously fresh from a pub, spotted me and as if struck by inspiration went down on his knees in the aisle. With both hands over his heart he broke into an Irish tenor's rendition of "Maria" from *West Side Story*.[1] My politely amused fellow passengers gave his lovely voice the round of gentle applause it deserved. Though I was not quite as amused, I managed my version of an English smile: no show of teeth, no extreme contortions of the facial muscles—I was at this time of my life practicing reserve and cool. Oh, that British control, how I coveted it. But "Maria" had followed me to London, reminding me of a prime fact of my life: you can leave the island, master the English language, and travel as far as you can, but if you are a Latina, especially one like me who so obviously belongs to Rita Moreno's gene pool, the island travels with you.

This is sometimes a very good thing—it may win you that extra minute of someone's attention. But with some people, the same things can make *you* an island—not a tropical paradise but an Alcatraz, a place nobody wants to visit. As a Puerto Rican girl living in the United States and wanting like most children to "belong," I resented the stereotype that my Hispanic appearance called forth from many people I met.

Growing up in a large urban center in New Jersey during the 1960s, I suffered from what I think of as "cultural schizophrenia." Our life was designed by my parents as a microcosm of their *casas* on the island. We

---

[1] *West Side Story:* a musical (1957) by Leonard Bernstein and Arthur Laurents, which featured the song "I Just Met a Girl Named Maria."

spoke in Spanish, ate Puerto Rican food bought at the *bodega*, and practiced strict Catholicism at a church that allotted us a one-hour slot each week for mass, performed in Spanish by a Chinese priest trained as a missionary for Latin America.

As a girl I was kept under strict surveillance by my parents, since my virtue and modesty were, by their cultural equation, the same as their honor. As a teenager I was lectured constantly on how to behave as a proper *señorita*. But it was a conflicting message I received, since the Puerto Rican mothers also encouraged their daughters to look and act like women and to dress in clothes our Anglo friends and their mothers found too "mature" and flashy. The difference was, and is, cultural; yet I often felt humiliated when I appeared at an American friend's party wearing a dress more suitable to a semi-formal than to a playroom birthday celebration. At Puerto Rican festivities, neither the music nor the colors we wore could be too loud.

I remember Career Day in our high school, when teachers told us to   5
come dressed as if for a job interview. It quickly became obvious that to the Puerto Rican girls "dressing up" meant wearing their mother's ornate jewelry and clothing, more appropriate (by mainstream standards) for the company Christmas party than as daily office attire. That morning I had agonized in front of my closet, trying to figure out what a "career girl" would wear. I knew how to dress for school (at the Catholic school I attended, we all wore uniforms), I knew how to dress for Sunday mass, and I knew what dresses to wear for parties at my relatives' homes. Though I do not recall the precise details of my Career Day outfit, it must have been a composite of these choices. But I remember a comment my friend (an Italian American) made in later years that coalesced my impressions of that day. She said that at the business school she was attending, the Puerto Rican girls always stood out for wearing "everything at once." She meant, of course, too much jewelry, too many accessories. On that day at school we were simply made the negative models by the nuns, who were themselves not credible fashion experts to any of us. But it was painfully obvious to me that to the others, in their tailored skirts and silk blouses, we must have seemed "hopeless" and "vulgar." Though I now know that most adolescents feel out of step much of the time, I also know that for the Puerto Rican girls of my generation that sense was intensified. The way our teachers and classmates looked at us that day in school was just a taste of the cultural clash that awaited us in the real world, where prospective employers and men on the street would often misinterpret our tight skirts and jingling bracelets as a "come-on."

Mixed cultural signals have perpetuated certain stereotypes—for example, that of the Hispanic woman as the "hot tamale" or sexual firebrand. It is a one-dimensional view that the media have found easy to promote. In their special vocabulary, advertisers have designated "sizzling" and "smoldering" as the adjectives of choice for describing not only the foods but also the women of Latin America. From conversations in my house I recall hearing about the harassment that Puerto Rican women endured in factories where the "boss-men" talked to them as if sexual innuendo was all they understood, and worse, often gave them the choice of submitting to their advances or being fired.

It is custom, however, not chromosomes, that leads us to choose scarlet over pale pink. As young girls, it was our mothers who influenced our decisions about clothes and colors—mothers who had grown up on a tropical island where the natural environment was a riot of primary colors, where showing your skin was one way to keep cool as well as to look sexy. Most important of all, on the island, women perhaps felt freer to dress and move more provocatively since, in most cases, they were protected by the traditions, mores, and laws of a Spanish/Catholic system of morality and machismo whose main rule was: *You may look at my sister, but if you touch her I will kill you.* The extended family and church structure could provide a young woman with a circle of safety in her small pueblo on the island; if a man "wronged" a girl, everyone would close in to save her family honor.

My mother has told me about dressing in her best party clothes on Saturday nights and going to the town's plaza to promenade with her girlfriends in front of the boys they liked. The males were thus given an opportunity to admire the women and to express their admiration in the form of *piropos:* erotically charged street poems they composed on the spot. (I have myself been subjected to a few *piropos* while visiting the island, and they can be outrageous, although custom dictates that they must never cross into obscenity.) This ritual, as I understand it, also entails a show of studied in-difference on the woman's part; if she is "decent," she must not acknowledge the man's impassioned words. So I do understand how things can be lost in translation. When a Puerto Rican girl dressed in her idea of what is attractive meets a man from the mainstream culture who has been trained to react to certain types of clothing as a sexual signal, a clash is likely to take place. I remember the boy who took me to my first formal dance leaning over to plant a sloppy, over-eager kiss painfully on my mouth; when I didn't respond with sufficient passion, he remarked resentfully: "I thought you Latin girls were supposed to mature early," as if I were expected to *ripen* like a fruit or vegetable, not just grow into womanhood like other girls.

It is surprising to my professional friends that even today some people, including those who should know better, still put others "in their place." It happened to me most recently during a stay at a classy metropolitan hotel favored by young professional couples for weddings. Late one evening after the theater, as I walked toward my room with a colleague (a woman with whom I was coordinating an arts program), a middle-aged man in a tuxedo, with a young girl in satin and lace on his arm, stepped directly into our path. With his champagne glass extended toward me, he exclaimed "Evita!"[2]

---

[2] *Evita:* a musical about Eva Duarte de Perón, the former first lady of Argentina, opened on Broadway in 1979; "Don't Cry for Me, Argentina" is a song from the musical.

Our way blocked, my companion and I listened as the man half-recited,   10
half-bellowed "Don't Cry for Me, Argentina." When he finished, the young
girl said: "How about a round of applause for my daddy?" We complied,
hoping this would bring the silly spectacle to a close. I was becoming aware
that our little group was attracting the attention of the other guests. "Daddy"
must have perceived this too, and he once more barred the way as we tried to
walk past him. He began to shoutsing a ditty to the tune of "La Bamba"—
except the lyrics were about a girl named Maria whose exploits rhymed with
her name and gonorrhea. The girl kept saying "Oh, Daddy" and looking at
me with pleading eyes. She wanted me to laugh along with the others. My
companion and I stood silently waiting for the man to end his offensive song.
When he finished, I looked not at him but at his daughter. I advised her
calmly never to ask her father what he had done in the army. Then I walked
between them and to my room. My friend complimented me on my cool
handling of the situation, but I confessed that I had really wanted to push the
jerk into the swimming pool. This same man—probably a corporate executive, well-educated, even worldly by most standards—would not have been
likely to regale an Anglo woman with a dirty song in public. He might have
checked his impulse by assuming that she could be somebody's wife or
mother, or at least *somebody* who might take offense. But, to him, I was just
an Evita or a Maria: merely a character in his cartoon-populated universe.

Another facet of the myth of the Latin woman in the United States is
the menial, the domestic—Maria the housemaid or countergirl. It's true that
work as domestics, as waitresses, and in factories is all that's available to
women with little English and few skills. But the myth of the Hispanic
menial—the funny maid, mispronouncing words and cooking up a spicy
storm in a shiny California kitchen—has been perpetuated by the media in
the same way that "Mammy" from *Gone with the Wind* became America's
idea of the black woman for generations. Since I do not wear my diplomas
around my neck for all to see, I have on occasion been sent to that "kitchen"
where some think I obviously belong.

One incident has stayed with me, though I recognize it as a minor
offense. My first public poetry reading took place in Miami, at a restaurant
where a luncheon was being held before the event. I was nervous and excited
as I walked in with notebook in hand. An older woman motioned me to her
table, and thinking (foolish me) that she wanted me to autograph a copy of
my newly published slender volume of verse, I went over. She ordered a cup of
coffee from me, assuming that I was the waitress. (Easy enough to mistake my
poems for menus, I suppose.) I know it wasn't an intentional act of cruelty. Yet
of all the good things that happened later, I remember that scene most clearly,
because it reminded me of what I had to overcome before anyone would take
me seriously. In retrospect I understand that my anger gave my reading fire.
In fact, I have almost always taken any doubt in my abilities as a challenge,
the result most often being the satisfaction of winning a convert, of seeing
the cold, appraising eyes warm to my words, the body language change, the

smile that indicates I have opened some avenue for communication. So that day as I read, I looked directly at that woman. Her lowered eyes told me she was embarrassed at her faux pas, and when I willed her to look up at me, she graciously allowed me to punish her with my full attention. We shook hands at the end of the reading and I never saw her again. She has probably forgotten the entire incident, but maybe not.

Yet I am one of the lucky ones. There are thousands of Latinas without the privilege of an education or the entrees into society that I have. For them life is a constant struggle against the misconceptions perpetuated by the myth of the Latina. My goal is to try to replace the old stereotypes with a much more interesting set of realities. Every time I give a reading, I hope the stories I tell, the dreams and fears I examine in my work, can achieve some universal truth that will get my audience past the particulars of my skin color, my accent, or my clothes.

I once wrote a poem in which I called all Latinas "God's brown daughters." This poem is really a prayer of sorts, offered upward, but also, through the human-to-human channel of art, outward. It is a prayer for communication and for respect. In it, Latin women pray "in Spanish to an Anglo God / with a Jewish heritage," and they are "fervently hoping / that if not omnipotent, / at least He be bilingual."

Questions for Discussion and Writing

1. What characteristics define, from Cofer's perspective, the "Maria" stereotype? How has this stereotype been a source of discomfort for Cofer personally? What use does she make of her personal experience to support her thesis?
2. Have you ever been perceived in stereotyped ways? What steps, if any, did you take to correct this misimpression?
3. At different points in her narrative, Cofer enters the minds of others to see things from their perspective. Try choosing a person you know whose point of view differs from yours, and write a first-person narrative describing the way the world looks to him or her.
4. **Rhetorical inquiry:** How do the many examples Cofer includes emphasize the disparity between the Latina stereotype and her professional accomplishments? How does the skill with which this essay is written prove her point?

MARK TWAIN

Samuel Langhorne Clemens (1835–1910) was brought up in Hannibal, Missouri. After serving as a printer's apprentice, he became a steamboat pilot on the Mississippi (1857–1861) and adopted his pen name or pseudonym from the leadsman's call ("mark twain" means "by the mark two fathoms") when sounding the river in shallow places. After an unsuccessful attempt to mine gold in Nevada, Twain edited the Virginia City Enterprise. *In 1865 in the* New York Saturday Press, *Twain published "Jim Smiley and His Jumping Frog," which then became the title story of* The Celebrated Jumping Frog of Calaveras County and Other Sketches *(1867). His reputation as a humorist was enhanced by* Innocents Abroad *(1869), a comic account of his travels through France, Italy, and Palestine; and by* Roughing It *(1872), a delightful spoof of his mining adventures. His acknowledged masterpieces are* The Adventures of Tom Sawyer *(1876) and its sequel* The Adventures of Huckleberry Finn *(1885), works of great comic power and social insight. Twain's later works, including* The Man That Corrupted Hadleyburg *(1900), a fable about greed, and* The Mysterious Stranger *(1916), published six years after Twain's death, assail hypocrisy as endemic to the human condition. "The Lowest Animal" (1906) shows Twain at his most iconoclastic, formulating a scathing comparison between humans and the so-called lower animals.*

Before You Read

As you read Twain's satire, consider whether his conclusions are still valid.

The Lowest Animal

I have been studying the traits and dispositions of the "lower animals" (so-called), and contrasting them with the traits and dispositions of man. I find the result humiliating to me. For it obliges me to renounce my allegiance to the Darwinian theory of the Ascent of Man from the Lower Animals; since it now seems plain to me that that theory ought to be vacated in favor of a new and truer one, this new and truer one to be named the Descent of Man from the Higher Animals.

In proceeding toward this unpleasant conclusion I have not guessed or speculated or conjectured, but have used what is commonly called the scientific method. That is to say, I have subjected every postulate that presented itself to the crucial test of actual experiment, and have adopted it or rejected it according to the result. Thus I verified and established each step of my course in its turn before advancing to the next. These experiments were made in the London Zoological Gardens, and covered many months of painstaking and fatiguing work.

Before particularizing any of the experiments, I wish to state one or two things which seem to more properly belong in this place than further along. This in the interest of clearness. The massed experiments established to my satisfaction certain generalizations, to wit:

1. That the human race is of one distinct species. It exhibits slight variations—in color, stature, mental caliber, and so on—due to climate, environment, and so forth; but it is a species by itself, and not to be confounded with any other.

2. That the quadrupeds are a distinct family, also. This family exhibits variations—in color, size, food preferences and so on; but it is a family by itself.

3. That the other families—the birds, the fishes, the insects, the reptiles, etc.—are more or less distinct, also. They are in the procession. They are links in the chain which stretches down from the higher animals to man at the bottom.

Some of my experiments were quite curious. In the course of my reading I had come across a case where, many years ago, some hunters on our Great Plains organized a buffalo hunt for the entertainment of an English earl—that, and to provide some fresh meat for his larder. They had charming sport. They killed seventy-two of those great animals; and ate part of one of them and left the seventy-one to rot. In order to determine the difference between an anaconda and an earl—if any—I caused seven young calves to be turned into the anaconda's cage. The grateful reptile immediately crushed one of them and swallowed it, then lay back satisfied. It showed no further interest in the calves, and no disposition to harm them. I tried this experiment with other anacondas; always with the same result. The fact stood proven that the difference between an earl and an anaconda is that the earl is cruel and the anaconda isn't; and that the earl wantonly destroys what he has no use for, but the anaconda doesn't. This seemed to suggest that the anaconda was not descended from the earl. It also seemed to suggest that the earl was descended from the anaconda, and had lost a good deal in the transition.

I was aware that many men who have accumulated more millions of money than they can ever use have shown a rabid hunger for more, and have not scrupled to cheat the ignorant and the helpless out of their poor servings in order to partially appease that appetite. I furnished a hundred different kinds of wild and tame animals the opportunity to accumulate vast stores of food, but none of them would do it. The squirrels and bees and certain birds made accumulations, but stopped when they had gathered a winter's supply, and could not be persuaded to add to it either honestly or by chicane. In order to bolster up a tottering reputation the ant pretended to store up supplies, but I was not deceived. I know the ant. These experiments convinced me that there is this difference between man and the higher animals: he is avaricious and miserly, they are not. 5

In the course of my experiments I convinced myself that among the animals man is the only one that harbors insults and injuries, broods over them, waits till a chance offers, then takes revenge. The passion of revenge is unknown to the higher animals.

Roosters keep harems, but it is by consent of their concubines; therefore no wrong is done. Men keep harems, but it is by brute force, privileged by atrocious laws which the other sex is allowed no hand in making. In this matter man occupies a far lower place than the rooster.

Cats are loose in their morals, but not consciously so. Man, in his descent from the cat, has brought the cat's looseness with him but has left the unconsciousness behind—the saving grace which excuses the cat. The cat is innocent, man is not.

Indecency, vulgarity, obscenity—these are strictly confined to man; he invented them. Among the higher animals there is no trace of them. They hide nothing; they are not ashamed. Man, with his soiled mind, covers himself. He will not even enter a drawing room with his breast and back naked, so alive are he and his mates to indecent suggestion. Man is "The Animal that Laughs." But so does the monkey, as Mr. Darwin pointed out; and so does the Australian bird that is called the laughing jackass. No—Man is the Animal that Blushes. He is the only one that does it—or has occasion to.

At the head of this article we see how "three monks were burnt to death"   10 a few days ago, and a prior "put to death with atrocious cruelty." Do we inquire into the details? No; or we should find out that the prior was subjected to unprintable multilations. Man—when he is a North American Indian— gouges out his prisoner's eyes; when he is King John, with a nephew to render untroublesome, he uses a red-hot iron; when he is a religious zealot dealing with heretics in the Middle Ages, he skins his captive alive and scatters salt on his back; in the first Richard's time he shuts up a multitude of Jew families in a tower and sets fire to it; in Columbus's time he captures a family of Spanish Jews and—but that is not printable; in our day in England a man is fined ten shillings for beating his mother nearly to death with a chair, and another man is fined forty shillings for having four pheasant eggs in his possession without being able to satisfactorily explain how he got them. Of all the animals, man is the only one that is cruel. He is the only one that inflicts pain for the pleasure of doing it. It is a trait that is not known to the higher animals. The cat plays with the frightened mouse; but she has this excuse, that she does not know that the mouse is suffering. The cat is moderate—unhumanly moderate: she only scares the mouse, she does not hurt it; she doesn't dig out its eyes, or tear off its skin, or drive splinters under its nails—man-fashion; when she is done playing with it she makes a sudden meal of it and puts it out of its trouble. Man is the Cruel Animal. He is alone in that distinction.

The higher animals engage in individual fights, but never in organized masses. Man is the only animal that deals in that atrocity of atrocities, War. He is the only one that gathers his brethren about him and goes forth in cold blood and with calm pulse to exterminate his kind. He is the only animal that for sordid wages will march out, as the Hessian[1] did in our Revolution, and as the boyish Prince Napoleon did in the Zulu war, and help to slaughter strangers of his own species who have done him no harm and with whom he has no quarrel.

---

[1] *Hessians:* the German auxiliary soldiers brought over by the British to fight the Americans during the Revolutionary War.

Man is the only animal that robs his helpless fellow of his country—takes possession of it and drives him out of it or destroys him. Man has done this in all the ages. There is not an acre of ground on the globe that is in possession of its rightful owner, or that has not been taken away from owner after owner, cycle after cycle, by force and bloodshed.

Man is the only Slave. And he is the only animal who enslaves. He has always been a slave in one form or another, and has always held other slaves in bondage under him in one way or another. In our day he is always some man's slave for wages, and does that man's work; and this slave has other slaves under him for minor wages, and they do his work. The higher animals are the only ones who exclusively do their own work and provide their own living.

Man is the only Patriot. He sets himself apart in his own country, under his own flag, and sneers at the other nations, and keeps multitudinous uniformed assassins on hand at heavy expense to grab slices of other people's countries, and keep *them* from grabbing slices of *his*. And in the intervals between campaigns he washes the blood off his hands and works for "the universal brotherhood of man"—with his mouth.

Man is the Religious Animal. He is the only Religious Animal. He is the only animal that has the True Religion—several of them. He is the only animal that loves his neighbor as himself, and cuts his throat if his theology isn't straight. He has made a graveyard of the globe in trying his honest best to smooth his brother's path to happiness and heaven. He was at it in the time of the Caesars, he was at it in Mahomet's time, he was at it in the time of the Inquisition, he was at it in France a couple of centuries, he was at it in England in Mary's day, he has been at it ever since he first saw the light, he is at it today in Crete—as per the telegrams quoted above—he will be at it some-where else tomorrow. The higher animals have no religion. And we are told that they are going to be left out, in the Hereafter. I wonder why? It seems questionable taste. 15

Man is the Reasoning Animal. Such is the claim. I think it is open to dispute. Indeed, my experiments have proven to me that he is the Unreasoning Animal. Note his history, as sketched above. It seems plain to me that whatever he is he is *not* a reasoning animal. His record is the fantastic record of a maniac. I consider that the strongest count against his intelligence is the fact that with that record back of him he blandly sets himself up as the head animal of the lot: whereas by his own standards he is the bottom one.

In truth, man is incurably foolish. Simple things which the other animals easily learn, he is incapable of learning. Among my experiments was this. In an hour I taught a cat and a dog to be friends. I put them in a cage. In another hour I taught them to be friends with a rabbit. In the course of two days I was able to add a fox, a goose, a squirrel and some doves. Finally a monkey. They lived together in peace; even affectionately.

Next, in another cage I confined an Irish Catholic from Tipperary, and as soon as he seemed tame I added a Scotch Presbyterian from Aberdeen. Next a Turk from Constantinople; a Greek Christian from Crete; an Armenian; a Methodist from the wilds of Arkansas; a Buddhist from China; a Brahman from Benares. Finally, a Salvation Army Colonel from Wapping. Then I stayed away two whole days. When I came back to note result, the cage of Higher Animals was all right, but in the other there was but a chaos of gory odds and ends of turbans and fezzes and plaids and bones and flesh—not a specimen left alive. These Reasoning Animals had disagreed on a theological detail and carried the matter to a Higher Court.

One is obliged to concede that in true loftiness of character, Man cannot claim to approach even the meanest of the Higher Animals. It is plain that he is constitutionally incapable of approaching that altitude; that he is constitutionally afflicted with a Defect which must make such approach forever impossible, for it is manifest that this defect is permanent in him, indestructible, ineradicable.

I find this Defect to be *the Moral Sense*. He is the only animal that has it.   20 It is the secret of his degradation. It is the quality *which enables him to do wrong*. It has no other office. It is incapable of performing any other function. It could never have been intended to perform any other. Without it, man could do no wrong. He would rise at once to the level of the Higher Animals.

Since the Moral Sense has but the one office, the one capacity—to enable man to do wrong—it is plainly without value to him. It is as valueless to him as is disease. In fact, it manifestly is a disease. *Rabies* is bad, but it is not so bad as this disease. Rabies enables a man to do a thing which he could not do when in a healthy state: kill his neighbor with a poisonous bite. No one is the better man for having rabies. The Moral Sense enables a man to do wrong. It enables him to do wrong in a thousand ways. Rabies is an innocent disease, compared to the Moral Sense. No one, then, can be the better man for having the Moral Sense. What, now, do we find the Primal Curse to have been? Plainly what it was in the beginning: the infliction upon man of the Moral Sense; the ability to distinguish good from evil; and with it, necessarily, the ability to *do* evil; for there can be no evil act without the presence of consciousness of it in the doer of it.

And so I find that we have descended and degenerated, from some far ancestor—some microscopic atom wandering at its pleasure between the mighty horizons of a drop of water perchance—insect by insect, animal by animal, reptile by reptile, down the long highway of smirchless innocence, till we have reached the bottom stage of development—namable as the Human Being. Below us—nothing. Nothing but the Frenchman.

Questions for Discussion and Writing

1. How are Twain's experiments—comparing human behavior to that of animals in various situations—intended to puncture some illusions the human species has about itself? In what way do each of Twain's experiments reveal that other animals are superior to humans?
2. How is the method Twain uses to organize his discussion well suited to highlight important differences between animals and humans?

3. How do Twain's experiments provide an ironic commentary on the interpretation of Darwin's thesis that places humans at the apex of all other species?

4. **Rhetorical inquiry:** Why does Twain view the "moral sense" as a defect in the human species? What are some of the consequences of possessing it?

Fiction

KATE CHOPIN

Kate Chopin (1851–1904) is best known for her novel The Awakening, *published in 1899, which created enormous public controversy by its realistic treatment of the psychological and sexual awakening of the female protagonist. The collections of Chopin's short stories based on her experiences while living in rural Louisiana are* Bayou Folk *(1894) and* A Night in Acadie *(1897). Her short story "Désirée's Baby" (1899) is widely recognized as a small masterpiece of psychological realism.*

Before You Read

As you read this classic story look for clues that foreshadow the outcome.

Désirée's Baby

As the day was pleasant, Madame Valmondé drove over to L'Abri to see Désirée and the baby.

It made her laugh to think of Désirée with a baby. Why, it seems but yesterday that Désirée was little more than a baby herself; when Monsieur in riding through the gateway of Valmondé had found her lying asleep in the shadow of the big stone pillar.

The little one awoke in his arms and began to cry for "Dada." That was as much as she could do or say. Some people thought she might have strayed there of her own accord, for she was of the toddling age. The prevailing belief was that she had been purposely left by a party of Texans, whose canvas-covered wagons, late in the day, had crossed the ferry that Coton Maïs kept, just below the plantation. In time Madame Valmondé abandoned every speculation but the one that Désirée had been sent to her by a beneficent Providence to be the child of her affection, seeing that she was without child of the flesh. For the girl grew to be beautiful and gentle, affectionate and sincere—the idol of Valmondé.

It was no wonder, when she stood one day against the stone pillar in whose shadow she had lain asleep, eighteen years before, that Armand Aubigny riding by and seeing her there, had fallen in love with her. That was the way all the Aubignys fell in love, as if struck by a pistol shot. The wonder was that he had not loved her before; for he had known her since his father brought him home from Paris, a boy of eight, after his mother died there. The passion that awoke in him that day, when he saw her at the gate, swept along like an avalanche, or like a prairie fire, or like anything that drives headlong over all obstacles.

Madame Valmondé bent her portly figure over Désirée and kissed her, holding her an instant tenderly in her arms. Then she turned to the child.   5

"This is not the baby!" she exclaimed, in startled tones. French was the language spoken at Valmondé in those days.

"I knew you would be astonished," laughed Désirée, "at the way he has grown. The little *cochon de lait!*[1] Look at his legs, mamma, and his hands and fingernails,—real fingernails. Zandrine had to cut them this morning. Isn't it true, Zandrine?"

The woman bowed her turbaned head majestically, "Mais si, Madame."

"And the way he cries," went on Désirée, "is deafening. Armand heard him the other day as far away as La Blanche's cabin."

Madame Valmondé had never removed her eyes from the child. She   10 lifted it and walked with it over to the window that was lightest. She scanned the baby narrowly, then looked as searchingly at Zandrine, whose face was turned to gaze across the fields.

"Yes, the child has grown, has changed," said Madame Valmondé, slowly, as she replaced it beside its mother. "What does Armand say?"

Désirée's face became suffused with a glow that was happiness itself.

"Oh, Armand is the proudest father in the parish, I believe, chiefly because it is a boy, to bear his name; though he says not—that he would have loved a girl as well. But I know it isn't true. I know he says that to please me. And mamma," she added, drawing Madame Valmondé's head down to her, and speaking in a whisper, "he hasn't punished one of them— not one of them—since baby is born. Even Négrillon, who pretended to have burnt his leg that he might rest from work—he only laughed, and said Négrillon was a great scamp. Oh, mamma, I'm so happy; it frightens me."

What Désirée said was true. Marriage, and later the birth of his son, had softened Armand Aubigny's imperious and exacting nature greatly. This was what made the gentle Désirée so happy, for she loved him desperately. When he frowned she trembled, but loved him. When he smiled, she asked no greater blessing of God. But Armand's dark, handsome face had not often been disfigured by frowns since the day he fell in love with her.

---

[1] *cochon de lait:* literally "pig of milk"—a big feeder.

When the baby was about three months old, Désirée awoke one day to   15
the conviction that there was something in the air menacing her peace. It was
at first too subtle to grasp. It had only been a disquieting suggestion; an air of
mystery among the blacks; unexpected visits from far-off neighbors who
could hardly account for their coming. Then a strange, an awful change in
her husband's manner, which she dared not ask him to explain. When he
spoke to her, it was with averted eyes, from which the old love light seemed
to have gone out. He absented himself from home; and when there, avoided
her presence and that of her child, without excuse. And the very spirit of
Satan seemed suddenly to take hold of him in his dealings with the slaves.
Désirée was miserable enough to die.

She sat in her room, one hot afternoon, in her *peignoir*, listlessly drawing
through her fingers the strands of her long, silky brown hair that hung about
her shoulders. The baby, half naked, lay asleep upon her own great mahogany
bed, that was like a sumptuous throne, with its satin-lined half canopy. One of
La Blanche's little quadroon boys—half naked too—stood fanning the child
slowly with a fan of peacock feathers. Désirée's eyes had been fixed absently
and sadly upon the baby, while she was striving to penetrate the threatening
mist that she felt closing about her. She looked from her child to the boy who
stood beside him; and back again, over and over. "Ah!" It was a cry that she
could not help, which she was not conscious of having uttered. The blood
turned like ice in her veins, and a clammy moisture gathered upon her face.

She tried to speak to the little quadroon boy; but no sound would come,
at first. When he heard his name uttered, he looked up, and his mistress was
pointing to the door. He laid aside the great, soft fan, and obediently stole
away, over the polished floor, on his bare tiptoes.

She stayed motionless, with gaze riveted upon her child, and her face
the picture of fright.

Presently her husband entered the room, and without noticing her,
went to a table and began to search among some papers which covered it.

"Armand," she called to him, in a voice which must have stabbed him,   20
if he was human. But he did not notice. "Armand," she said again. Then she
rose and tottered towards him. "Armand," she panted once more, clutching
his arm, "look at our child. What does it mean? Tell me."

He coldly but gently loosened her fingers from about his arm and thrust
the hand away from him. "Tell me what it means!" she cried despairingly.

"It means," he answered lightly, "that the child is not white; it means
that you are not white."

A quick conception of all that this accusation meant for her nerved her
with unwonted courage to deny it. "It is a lie; it is not true, I am white! Look
at my hair, it is brown; and my eyes are gray, Armand, you know they are
gray. And my skin is fair," seizing his wrist. "Look at my hand, whiter than
yours, Armand," she laughed hysterically.

"As white as La Blanche's," he returned cruelly, and went away leaving
her alone with their child.

When she could hold a pen in her hand, she sent a despairing letter to   25
Madame Valmondé.

"My mother, they tell me I am not white. Armand has told me I am not
white. For God's sake tell them it is not true. You must know it is not true.
I shall die. I must die. I cannot be so unhappy, and live."

The answer that came was as brief:

"My own Désirée: Come home to Valmondé; back to your mother who
loves you. Come with your child."

When the letter reached Désirée she went with it to her husband's study,
and laid it open upon the desk before which he sat. She was like a stone
image: silent, white, motionless after she placed it there.

In silence he ran his cold eyes over the written words. He said nothing.   30
"Shall I go, Armand?" she asked in tones sharp with agonized suspense.

"Yes, go."

"Do you want me to go?"

"Yes, I want you to go."

He thought Almighty God had dealt cruelly and unjustly with him; and
felt, somehow, that he was paying Him back in kind when he stabbed thus
into his wife's soul. Moreover he no longer loved her, because of the unconscious injury she had brought upon his home and his name.

She turned away like one stunned by a blow, and walked slowly towards   35
the door, hoping he would call her back.

"Good-by, Armand," she moaned.

He did not answer her. That was his last blow at fate.

Désirée went in search of her child. Zandrine was pacing the sombre
gallery with it. She took the little one from the nurse's arms with no word of
explanation, and descending the steps, walked away, under the live-oak
branches.

It was an October afternoon; the sun was just sinking. Out in the still
fields the Negroes were picking cotton.

Désirée had not changed the thin white garment nor the slippers which   40
she wore. Her hair was uncovered and the sun's rays brought a golden gleam
from its brown meshes. She did not take the broad, beaten road which led to
the far-off plantation of Valmondé. She walked across a deserted field, where
the stubble bruised her tender feet, so delicately shod, and tore her thin gown
to shreds.

She disappeared among the reeds and willows that grew thick along the
banks of the deep, sluggish bayou; and she did not come back again.

Some weeks later there was a curious scene enacted at L'Abri. In the centre of the smoothly swept back yard was a great bonfire. Armand Aubigny sat
in the wide hallway that commanded a view of the spectacle; and it was he
who dealt out to a half dozen negroes the material which kept this fire ablaze.

A graceful cradle of willow, with all its dainty furbishings, was laid
upon the pyre, which had already been fed with the richness of a priceless

layette. Then there were silk gowns, and velvet and satin ones added to these; laces, too, and embroideries; bonnets and gloves; for the *corbeille*[2] had been of rare quality.

The last thing to go was a tiny bundle of letters; innocent little scribblings that Désirée had sent to him during the days of their espousal. There was the remnant of one back in the drawer from which he took them. But it was not Désirée's; it was part of an old letter from his mother to his father. He read it. She was thanking God for the blessing of her husband's love:

"But, above all," she wrote, "night and day, I thank the good God for   45 having so arranged our lives that our dear Armand will never know that his mother, who adores him, belongs to the race that is cursed with the brand of slavery."

Questions for Discussion and Writing

1. What can you infer about Armand's character and his past behavior from the fact that he has not punished one slave since his baby was born? How does his behavior toward Désirée change after the baby is three months old? What causes this change in his behavior?
2. What did you assume Désirée would do when she realizes Armand values his social standing more than he does her? In retrospect, what clues would have **foreshadowed** the truth disclosed at the end of the story?
3. Have you ever been in a situation where someone was unaware of your racial or ethnic background and made disparaging remarks about that group? How did you feel and what did you do?
4. **Rhetorical inquiry:** Follow up one of the more intriguing clues Chopin inserts that might help explain Armand's overreaction. For example, has Armand fathered children with La Blanche? Had he overheard conversations between his mother and father when he was a child? Why wasn't Armand able to do what his father had done?

GLORIA ANZALDÚA

Gloria Anzaldúa (1942–2004) was a Chicana poet and fiction writer who grew up in south Texas. She edited several highly praised anthologies. This Bridge Called My Back: Writings by Radical Women of Color *won the 1986 Before Columbus Foundation American Book Award.* Borderlands—La Frontera, the New Mestiza *was selected as one of the best books of 1987 by* Library Journal. *Her recent works include* Making Face, Making Soul *(1990),* La Prieta *(1991),* Interviews = Entrevistas *(2000), and a children's book,*

---

[2] *corbeille:* a basket of linens, clothing, and accessories collected in anticipation of a baby's birth.

Friends from the Other Side *(1993). She was a contributing editor for* Sinister Wisdom *and taught Chicano studies, feminist studies, and creative writing at the University of Texas at Austin, San Francisco State University, and the University of California, Santa Cruz. "Cervicide" first appeared in* Labyris *(vol. 4, no. 11, Winter 1983). In it, Anzaldúa tells the poignant story of a Mexican-American family living on the Texas border who are forced to kill a pet deer whose detection by the game warden would result in an unaffordable fine or the father's imprisonment.*

Before You Read

Consider how Anzaldúa enhances the sense of urgency in what proves to be a no-win situation for her main character, Prieta.

Cervicide[1]

La venadita. The small fawn. They had to kill their pet, the fawn. The game warden was on the way with his hounds. The penalty for being caught in possession of a deer was $250 or jail. The game warden would put *su papí en la cárcel.*[2]

How could they get rid of the fawn? Hide it? No, *la guardia's* hounds would sniff Venadita out. Let Venadita loose in the *monte?*[3] They had tried that before. The fawn would leap away and seconds later return. Should they kill Venadita? The mother and Prieta looked toward *las carabinas* propped against the wall behind the kitchen door—the shiny barrel of the .22, the heavy metal steel of the 40-40. No, if *they* could hear his pickup a mile and a half down the road, he would hear the shot.

Quick, they had to do something. Cut Venadita's throat? Club her to death? The mother couldn't do it. She, Prieta,[4] would have to be the one. The game warden and his *perros*[5] were a mile down the road. Prieta loved her *papí.*

In the shed behind the corral, where they'd hidden the fawn, Prieta found the hammer. She had to grasp it with both hands. She swung it up. The weight folded her body backwards. A thud reverberated on Venadita's skull, a wave undulated down her back. Again, a blow behind the ear. Though Venadita's long lashes quivered, her eyes never left Prieta's face. Another thud, another tremor. *La guardia* and his hounds were driving up the front yard. The *venadita* looked up at her, the hammer rose and fell. Neither made a sound. The tawny, spotted fur was the most beautiful thing Prieta had ever seen. She remembered when they had found the fawn. She had been a few hours old. A hunter had shot her mother. The fawn had been shaking so

---

[1] *Cervicide*—the killing of a deer. In archetypal symbology the Self appears as a deer for women. [2] *su papí en la cárcel*—her father in jail. [3] *monte*—the woods. [4] *Prieta*—literally one who is dark-skinned, a nickname. [5] *perros*—dogs.

hard, her long thin legs were on the edge of buckling. Prieta and her sister and brothers had bottle-fed Venadita, with a damp cloth had wiped her skin, had watched her tiny, perfectly formed hooves harden and grow.

Prieta dug a hole in the shed, a makeshift hole. She could hear the war- 5 den talking to her mother. Her mother's English had suddenly gotten bad— she was trying to stall *la guardia*. Prieta rolled the fawn into the hole, threw in the empty bottle. With her fingers raked in the dirt. Dust caked on her arms and face where tears had fallen. She patted the ground flat with her hands and swept it with a dead branch. The game warden was strutting toward her. His hounds sniffing, sniffing, sniffing the ground in the shed. The hounds pawing pawing the ground. The game warden, straining on the leashes *les dio un tirón, sacó los perros*.[6] He inspected the corrals, the edge of the woods, then drove away in his pickup.

Questions for Discussion and Writing

1. How does being forced to choose between the pet deer she loves and her father's freedom illustrate the predicament in which illegal immigrants find themselves?
2. How does Anzaldúa construct the story to lead to the moment of crisis? In what sense might the deer symbolize the death of Prieta's innocence?
3. What political agenda does this story dramatize?
4. **Rhetorical inquiry:** What details does Anzaldúa provide that emphasize the limited options of the family and the pressures to which they are subjected? Why does Anzaldúa use the term "cervicide" and what connotations is it intended to evoke?

Poetry

MARGE PIERCY

Marge Piercy was born in 1936. She received a B.A. in 1957 from the University of Michigan and an M.A. in 1958 from Northwestern University. She is a prolific novelist and poet. Piercy's novels include Going Down Fast *(1969),* Woman on the Edge of Time *(1976), and* Vida *(1979). Collections of her poetry are* Circles in the Water *(1973),* Living in the Open *(1976), and* The Art of Blessing the Day: Poems with a Jewish Theme *(1999). She recently*

---

[6] *les dio un tirón, sacó los perros*—jerked the dogs out.

wrote Sleeping with Cats: A Memoir *(2002),* The Third Child *(2003), and* The Crooked Inheritance: Poems *(2006). "Barbie Doll" (1973) is typical of Piercy's satiric meditations on economic, racial, and sexual inequality in contemporary American life.*

Before You Read

Consider whether the Barbie doll is still an icon in popular culture.

Barbie Doll

This girlchild was born as usual
and presented dolls that did pee-pee
and miniature GE stoves and irons
and wee lipsticks the color of cherry candy.
Then in the magic of puberty, a classmate said: 5
You have a great big nose and fat legs.

She was healthy, tested intelligent,
possessed strong arms and back,
abundant sexual drive and manual dexterity.
She went to and fro apologizing.   10
Everyone saw a fat nose on thick legs.

She was advised to play coy,
exhorted to come on hearty,
exercise, diet, smile and wheedle.
Her good nature wore out   15
like a fan belt.
So she cut off her nose and her legs
and offered them up.

In the casket displayed on satin she lay
with the undertaker's cosmetics painted on,   20
a turned-up putty nose.
dressed in a pink and white nightie.
Doesn't she look pretty? everyone said.
Consummation at last.
To every woman a happy ending.   25

Questions for Discussion and Writing

1. How does the "girlchild" change herself in response to the advice, criticisms, and suggestions she receives?

2. How is Piercy's use of the **controlling image** of a Barbie Doll apropos of the point she is making? What is she saying about contemporary American cultural values as they shape expectations of young women?

3. What is ironic about the conclusion of the poem?

4. **Rhetorical inquiry:** To what extent might the image in the last stanza be intended to evoke a boxed Barbie doll ready for purchase?

GRACE C. KUHNS

Grace C. Kuhns's poetry has appeared in the Evergreen Chronicles, The Northland Review, *and* Great River Review. *"Lisa's Ritual, Age 10" was published in* Looking for Home: Women Writing About Exile *(1990). The distinctive effects of the following poem are due to Kuhns's ability to communicate a child's experience of violation through words and images that re-create the shock of this trauma rather than merely describing it.*

Before You Read

Consider how the way the words are arranged in this poem help communicate Lisa's emotional shock and withdrawal.

Lisa's Ritual, Age 10

Afterwards when he is finished with her
lots of mouthwash helps
to get rid of her father's cigarette taste.
She runs a hot bath
    to soak away the pain   5
        like red dye leaking from her
            school dress in the washtub.
She doesn't cry.
When the bathwater cools she adds more hot.
She brushes her teeth for a long time.   10

Then she finds the corner of her room,
curls against it. There the wall is
hard and smooth
as teacher's new chalk, white
as a clean bedsheet. Smells   15
fresh. Isn't sweaty, hairy, doesn't stick
to skin. Doesn't hurt much
when she presses her small backbone
into it. The wall is steady

while she falls   away: 20
    first the hands   lost
arms dissolving   feet gone
  the legs   dis-   jointed
    body cracking down
      the center like a fault   25
        she falls inside
             slides down like
dust   like kitchen dirt
          slips off
   the dustpan into   30
                  noplace

   a place where
nothing happens,
nothing ever happened.
When she feels the cool   35
wall against her cheek
she doesn't want to
come back. Doesn't want to
think about it.
The wall is quiet, waiting.   40
It is tall like a promise
only better.

Questions for Discussion and Writing

1. How does the way the words are arranged on the page help communicate Lisa's emotional shock and withdrawal as a result of the trauma she has experienced?
2. To what extent might the title refer not only to the physical ritual of cleansing but the psychological ritual of distancing herself from the memories?
3. Kuhns apparently is familiar with the clinical symptoms of children who have been sexually abused. What features of the poem suggest that children who experience this kind of abuse may develop a dissociative disorder.
4. **Rhetorical inquiry:** How does the image of "red dye" bring the physical violation the girl has experienced into the reader's awareness and help explain her ritual?

Bruce Springsteen

Bruce Springsteen was born 1949 in Freehold, New Jersey. He began performing in New York and New Jersey nightclubs and signed with Columbia Records in

1972. *He has given numerous nationwide and international concert tours with the E-Street Band. He received the Grammy Award for best male rock vocalist in 1984, 1987, and 1994. The Academy Award and the Golden Globe Award for best original song in a film were given to him for "Streets of Philadelphia" from the film* Philadelphia *(1994). His albums include* Born to Run *(1975),* Born in the USA *(1984),* Bruce Springsteen's Greatest Hits *(1995),* The Rising *(2002), and* Devils and Dust *(2005).*

Before You Read

Consider how Springsteen's lyrics communicate the speaker's sense of loss of others and his own identity.

Streets of Philadelphia

I was bruised and battered: I couldn't tell what I felt.
I was unrecognizable to myself.
Saw my reflection in a window and didn't know my own face.
Oh, brother are you gonna leave me wastin' away on the streets of
    Philadelphia.
Ain't no angel gonna greet me: it's just you and I, my friend.   5
And my clothes don't fit me no more: I walked a thousand miles
    just to slip this skin.

I walked the avenue till my legs felt like stone.
I heard the voices of friends vanished and gone.
At night I could hear the blood in my veins
Just as black and whispering as the rain   10
On the streets of Philadelphia.
Ain't no angel gonna greet me: it's just you and I, my friend.
And my clothes don't fit me no more: I walked a thousand miles
    just to slip this skin.

The night has fallen. I'm lying awake.
I can feel myself fading away.   15
So, receive me, brother, with your faithless kiss.
Or will we leave each other alone like this
On the streets of Philadelphia?
Ain't no angel gonna greet me: it's just you and I, my friend.
And my clothes don't fit me no more: I walked a thousand miles   20
    just to slip this skin.

Questions for Discussion and Writing

1. How would you characterize the voice you hear? What images convey the speaker's sense of losing himself because of having AIDS?

2. How does being recognized and acknowledged become a central **theme** in this song? At what point in the lyrics does the speaker appeal for this recognition?
3. What impact do you think this song is designed to have on those who hear it? What effect did it have on you?
4. **Rhetorical inquiry:** Select one of the images in the lyrics that communicate the speaker's mood and feelings? For example, how might the phrase "a thousand miles" refer to the distance the speaker feels from the rest of humanity? Does the line "ain't no angel gonna greet me" suggest that even God has rejected him or what else might it mean?

GREGORY CORSO

(Nunzio) Gregory Corso (1930–2001) was born in New York and became a central figure in the Beat movement, along with Allen Ginsburg and Jack Kerouac. Corso had a checkered career including a three-year stint in prison for petty theft as a teenager. He worked as a laborer on the New York docks, as a reporter for the Los Angeles Examiner, *and as a merchant seaman. He taught in the English Department at the State University of New York at Buffalo (1965–1970). His poems are strongly influenced by jazz, especially the music of Charlie Parker and Miles Davis, in their innovative offbeat style. A prolific writer, Corso's works include the extended poem* Bomb *(1958), and his collections,* Gasoline *(1958),* Long Live Man *(1962), and* Minefield: New and Selected Poems *(1991). The following poem, "Marriage," a comic riff on T. S. Eliot's 1917 "The Lovesong of J. Alfred Prufrock," first appeared in* Happy Birthday on Death *(1960). The personality we hear in his poem is, by turns, childish, insightful, irreverent, and sentimental. Corso's voice is unmistakable and authentic.*

Before You Read

Notice how Corso captures the ambivalence and dread of the speaker toward getting married and losing his identity.

Marriage

Should I get married? Should I be good?
Astound the girl next door
with my velvet suit and faustus hood?
Don't take her to movies but to cemeteries

tell all about werewolf bathtubs and forked clarinets   5
then desire her and kiss her and all the preliminaries
and she going just so far and I understanding why
not getting angry saying You must feel! It's beautiful to feel!

Instead take her in my arms
lean against an old crooked tombstone   10
and woo her the entire night the constellations in the sky—

When she introduces me to her parents
back straightened, hair finally combed, strangled by a tie,
should I sit knees together on their 3rd degree sofa
and not ask Where's the bathroom?   15
How else to feel other than I am,
often thinking Flash Gordon[1] soap—
O how terrible it must be for a young man
seated before a family and the family thinking
We never saw him before! He wants our Mary Lou!   20
After tea and homemade cookies they ask
What do you do for a living?
Should I tell them? Would they like me then?
Say All right get married, we're not losing a daughter
we're gaining a son—   25
And should I then ask Where's the bathroom?

O God, and the wedding! All her family and her friends
and only a handful of mine all scroungy and bearded
just wait to get at the drinks and food—
And the priest! he looking at me as if I masturbated   30
asking me Do you take this woman
for your lawful wedded wife!
And I trembling what to say say Pie Glue!
I kiss the bride all those corny men slapping me on the back
She's all yours, boy! Ha-ha-ha!   35
And in their eyes you could see
some obscene honeymoon going on—
Then all that absurd rice and clanky cans and shoes
Niagara Falls! Hordes of us!
Husbands! Wives! Flowers! Chocolates!   40
All streaming into cosy hotels
All going to do the same thing tonight
The indifferent clerk he knowing what was going to happen
The lobby zombies they knowing what
The whistling elevator man he knowing   45
The winking bellboy knowing
Everybody knowing!
I'd be almost inclined not to do anything!

---

[1] Science fiction hero of comic strip and film.

Stay up all night! Stare that hotel clerk in the eye!
Screaming: I deny honeymoon! I deny honeymoon!   50
running rampant into those almost climactic suites
yelling Radio belly! Cat shovel!
O I'd live in Niagara forever! in a dark cave beneath the Falls
I'd sit there the Mad Honeymooner
devising ways to break marriages, a scourge of bigamy   55
a saint of divorce—

But I should get married I should be good
How nice it'd be to come home to her
and sit by the fireplace and she in the kitchen
aproned young and lovely wanting my baby   60
and so happy about me she burns the roast beef
and comes crying to me and I get up from my big papa chair
saying Christmas teeth! Radiant brains! Apple deaf!
God what a husband I'd make! Yes, I should get married!
So much to do! like sneaking into Mr Jones' house late at night 65
and cover his golf clubs with 1920 Norwegian books
Like hanging a picture of Rimbaud on the lawnmower
Like pasting Tannu Tuva[2] postage stamps
all over the picket fence
Like when Mrs Kindhead comes to collect   70
for the Community Chest
grab her and tell her There are unfavourable omens in the sky!
And when the mayor comes to get my vote tell him
When are you going to stop people killing whales!
And when the milkman comes leave him a note in the bottle   75
Penguin dust, bring me penguin dust, I want penguin dust—

Yet if I should get married and it's Connecticut and snow
and she gives birth to a child and I am sleepless, worn,
up for nights, head bowed against a quiet window
the past behind me,   80
finding myself in the most common of situations
a trembling man knowledged with responsibility
not twig-smear nor Roman coin soup—
O what would that be like!
Surely I'd give it for a nipple a rubber Tacitus   85
For a rattle a bag of broken Bach records
Tack Della Francesca all over its crib

---

[2] Region in Asia of former Soviet Union.

Sew the Greek alphabet on its bib
And build for its playpen a roofless Parthenon

No, I doubt I'd be that kind of father   90
not rural not snow no quiet window
but hot smelly tight New York City
seven flights up, roaches and rats in the walls
a fat Reichian[3] wife screeching over potatoes Get a job!
And five nose running brats in love with Batman[4]   95
And the neighbours all toothless and dry haired
like those hag masses of the 18th century
all wanting to come in and watch TV
The landlord wants his rent
Grocery store Blue Cross Gas & Electric Knights of Columbus   100
Impossible to lie back and dream
Telephone snow, ghost parking—
No! I should not get married I should never get married!
But—imagine if I were married
to a beautiful sophisticated woman   105
tall and pale wearing an elegant black dress
and long black gloves
holding a cigarette holder in one hand
and a highball in the other
and we lived high up in a penthouse with a huge window   110
from which we could see all of New York
and even farther on clearer days
No, can't imagine myself married to that pleasant prison dream—
O but what about love? I forget love
not that I am incapable of love   115
it's just that I see love as odd as wearing shoes—
I never wanted to marry a girl who was like my mother
And Ingrid Bergman[5] was always impossible
And there's maybe a girl now but she's already married
And I don't like men and—   120
but there's got to be somebody!
Because what if I'm 60 years old and not married,
all alone in a furnished room with pee stains on my underwear
and everybody else is married!
All the universe married but me!   125

---

[3] Wilhelm Reich (1897–1957), psychoanalyst.   [4] Comic book, TV, and film hero.
[5] Famous film star (1918–1982).

Ah, yet well I know that were a women possible as I am possible
then marriage would be possible—
Like SHE[6] in her lonely alien gaud waiting her Egyptian lover
so I wait—bereft of 2,000 years and the bath of life.

Would this wedding cake topper be appropriate for Corso if he ever got married?
Why or why not?

---

[6] Refers to Ayesha, the sorceress heroine of H. Rider Haggard's (1856–1925) novel *She*
(1887) who exemplifies the mystery of love.

Questions for Discussion and Writing

1. What does the speaker reveal about himself that might explain what he fears losing if he were to get married?
2. What multiple scenarios does Corso use to dramatize the speaker's fears? In your view, is the speaker trying to talk himself into or out of getting married?
3. After looking at magazines such as *Modern Bride*, discuss the stereotypes that surround marriage in American culture and your reaction to them.
4. **Rhetorical inquiry:** What images most effectively communicate the speaker's fear of conformity? Correspondingly, what images serve as symbols for his rebellion and individualism?

Drama

DAVID IVES

David Ives (b. 1943) was born in Chicago and educated at Northwestern University and the Yale Drama School. Ives's work appears in diverse formats, including television, film, opera, and the theater. He has written several one-act plays for the annual comedy festival of Manhattan Punch Line, where Sure Thing *was performed in 1988. Six of his one-act comedies have been collected in* All in the Timing *(1994). His latest works are* Polish Joke and Other Plays *(2004) and* Scrib *(2005). The following two-character* **farce** *is a lighthearted inventive variation on the premise that if we could take back our verbal blunders on the spot, relationships would never fail.*

Before You Read

How do people know when a romantic relationship is based on mutual values?

Sure Thing

CHARACTERS

BILL and BETTY, both in their late 20s

Setting

A café table, with a couple of chairs

Betty is reading at the table. An empty chair opposite her. Bill enters.

BILL.   Excuse me. Is this chair taken?
BETTY.   Excuse me?
BILL.   Is this taken?
BETTY.   Yes it is.
BILL.   Oh. Sorry.   5
BETTY.   Sure thing.

    (A bell rings softly.)

BILL.   Excuse me. Is this chair taken?
BETTY.   Excuse me?
BILL.   Is this taken?
BETTY.   No, but I'm expecting somebody in a minute.
BILL.   Oh. Thanks anyway.   10
BETTY.   Sure thing.

    (A bell rings softly.)

BILL.   Excuse me. Is this chair taken?
BETTY.   No, but I'm expecting somebody very shortly.
BILL.   Would you mind if I sit here till he or she or it comes?   15
BETTY.   *(Glances at her watch.)* They do seem to be pretty late . . .
BILL.   You never know who you might be turning down.
BETTY.   Sorry. Nice try, though.
BILL.   Sure thing. *(Bell.)* Is this seat taken?
BETTY.   No it's not.   20
BILL.   Would you mind if I sit here?
BETTY.   Yes I would.
BILL.   Oh. *(Bell.)* Is this chair taken?
BETTY.   No it's not.
BILL.   Would you mind if I sit here?   25
BETTY.   No. Go ahead.
BILL.   Thanks. *(He sits. She continues reading.)* Every place else
    seems to be taken.
BETTY.   Mm-hm.
BILL.   Great place.
BETTY.   Mm-hm.   30
BILL.   What's the book?
BETTY.   I just wanted to read in quiet, if you don't mind.
BILL.   No. Sure thing. *(Bell.)* Every place else seems to be taken.
BETTY.   Mm-hm.
BILL.   Great place for reading.   35
BETTY.   Yes, I like it.
BILL.   What's the book?

BETTY.   *The Sound and the Fury.*

BILL.   Oh. Hemingway. *(Bell.)* What's the book?

BETTY.   *The Sound and the Fury.*   40

BILL.   Oh. Faulkner.

BETTY.   Have you read it?

BILL.   Not . . . actually. I've sure read *about* it, though. It's supposed
    to be great.

BETTY.   It is great.

BILL.   I hear it's great. *(Small pause.)* Waiter? *(Bell.)* What's the book?   45

BETTY.   *The Sound and the Fury.*

BILL.   Oh. Faulkner.

BETTY.   Have you read it?

BILL.   I'm a Mets fan, myself. *(Bell.)*

BETTY.   Have you read it?   50

BILL.   Yeah, I read it in college.

BETTY.   Where was college?

BILL.   I went to Oral Roberts University. *(Bell.)*

BETTY.   Where was college?

BILL.   I was lying. I never really went to college. I just like to party. *(Bell.)*   55

BETTY.   Where was college?

BILL.   Harvard.

BETTY.   Do you like Faulkner?

BILL.   I love Faulkner. I spent a whole winter reading him once.

BETTY.   I've just started.   60

BILL.   I was so excited after ten pages that I went out and bought
    everything else he wrote. One of the greatest reading experiences of my
    life. I mean, all that incredible psychological understanding. Page after
    page of gorgeous prose. His profound grasp of the mystery of time and
    human existence. The smells of the earth. . . . What do you think?

BETTY.   I think it's pretty boring. *(Bell.)*

BILL.   What's the book?

BETTY.   *The Sound and the Fury.*

BILL.   Oh! Faulkner!   65

BETTY.   Do you like Faulkner?

BILL.   I love Faulkner.

BETTY.   He's incredible.

BILL.   I spent a whole winter reading him once.

BETTY.   I was so excited after ten pages that I went out and bought
    everything else he wrote.   70

BILL.   All that incredible psychological understanding.

BETTY.   And the prose is so gorgeous.

BILL.   And the way he's grasped the mystery of time—

BETTY.   —and human existence. I can't believe I've waited this long
    to read him.

BILL.   You never know. You might not have liked him before.   75

BETTY.   That's true.

BILL.   You might not have been ready for him. You have to hit these things at the right moment or it's no good.

BETTY.   That's happened to me.

BILL.   It's all in the timing. *(Small pause.)* My name's Bill, by the way.

BETTY.   I'm Betty.   80

BILL.   Hi.

BETTY.   Hi. *(Small pause.)*

BILL.   Yes I thought reading Faulkner was . . . a great experience.

BETTY.   Yes. *(Small pause.)*

BILL.   *The Sound and the Fury* . . . *(Another small pause.)*   85

BETTY.   Well. Onwards and upwards. *(She goes back to her book.)*

BILL.   Waiter—? *(Bell.)* You have to hit these things at the right moment or it's no good.

BETTY.   That's happened to me.

BILL.   It's all in the timing. My name's Bill, by the way.

BETTY.   I'm Betty.   90

BILL.   Hi.

BETTY.   Hi.

BILL.   Do you come in here a lot?

BETTY.   Actually I'm just in town for two days from Pakistan.

BILL.   Oh. Pakistan. *(Bell.)* My name's Bill, by the way.   95

BETTY.   I'm Betty.

BILL.   Hi.

BETTY.   Hi.

BILL.   Do you come in here a lot?

BETTY.   Every once in a while. Do you?   100

BILL.   Not so much anymore. Not as much as I used to. Before my nervous breakdown. *(Bell.)* Do you come in here a lot?

BETTY.   Why are you asking?

BILL.   Just interested.

BETTY.   Are you really interested, or do you just want to pick me up?

BILL.   No, I'm really interested.   105

BETTY.   Why would you be interested in whether I come in here a lot?

BILL.   Just . . . getting acquainted.

BETTY.   Maybe you're only interested for the sake of making small talk long enough to ask me back to your place to listen to some music, or because you've just rented some great tape for your VCR, or because you've got some terrific unknown Django Reinhardt[1] record, only all you really want to do is fuck—which you won't do very well—after which you'll go into the bathroom and pee very loudly, then pad into

---

[1] *Django Reinhardt (1910–1953):* virtuoso jazz guitar player who thrilled generations of jazz lovers.

the kitchen and get yourself a beer from the refrigerator without asking me whether I'd like anything, and then you'll proceed to lie back down beside me and confess that you've got a girlfriend named Stephanie who's away at medical school in Belgium for a year, and that you've been involved with her—*off and on*—in what you'll call a very "intricate" relationship, for about *seven YEARS*. None of which *interests* me, mister!

BILL.   Okay. *(Bell.)* Do you come in here a lot?

BETTY.   Every other day, I think.   110

BILL.   I come in here quite a lot and I don't remember seeing you.

BETTY.   I guess we must be on different schedules.

BILL.   Missed connections.

BETTY.   Yes. Different time zones.

BILL.   Amazing how you can live right next door to somebody in this town   115
and never even know it.

BETTY.   I know.

BILL.   City life.

BETTY.   It's crazy.

BILL.   We probably pass each other in the street every day. Right in front
of this place, probably.

BETTY.   Yep.   120

BILL.   *(Looks around.)* Well the waiters here sure seem to be in some
different time zone. I can't seem to locate one anywhere. . . . Waiter!
(He looks back.) So what do you—*(He sees that she's gone back to her
book.)*

BETTY.   I beg pardon?

BILL.   Nothing. Sorry. *(Bell.)*

BETTY.   I guess we must be on different schedules.

BILL.   Missed connections.   125

BETTY.   Yes. Different time zones.

BILL.   Amazing how you can live right next door to somebody in this town
and never even know it.

BETTY.   I know.

BILL.   City life.

BETTY.   It's crazy.   130

BILL.   You weren't waiting for somebody when I came in, were you?

BETTY.   Actually I was.

BILL.   Oh. Boyfriend?

BETTY.   Sort of.

BILL.   What's a sort-of boyfriend?   135

BETTY.   My husband.

BILL.   Ah-ha. *(Bell.)* You weren't waiting for somebody when I came in,
were you?

BETTY.   Actually I was.

BILL.   Oh. Boyfriend?

BETTY.   Sort of.   140
BILL.   What's a sort-of boyfriend?
BETTY.   We were meeting here to break up.
BILL.   Mm-hm . . . *(Bell.)* What's a sort-of boyfriend?
BETTY.   My lover. Here she comes right now! *(Bell.)*
BILL.   You weren't waiting for somebody when I came in, were you?   145
BETTY.   No, just reading.
BILL.   Sort of a sad occupation for a Friday night, isn't it? Reading here, all by yourself?
BETTY.   Do you think so?
BILL.   Well sure. I mean, what's a good-looking woman like you doing out alone on a Friday night?
BETTY.   Trying to keep away from lines like that.   150
BILL.   No, listen—*(Bell.)* You weren't waiting for somebody when I came in, were you?
BETTY.   No, just reading.
BILL.   Sort of a sad occupation for a Friday night, isn't it? Reading here all by yourself?
BETTY.   I guess it is, in a way.
BILL.   What's a good-looking woman like you doing out alone on a Friday   155
    night anyway? No offense, but . . .
BETTY.   I'm out alone on a Friday night for the first time in a very long time.
BILL.   Oh.
BETTY.   You see, I just recently ended a relationship.
BILL.   Oh.
BETTY.   Of rather long standing.   160
BILL.   I'm sorry. *(Small pause.)* Well listen, since reading by yourself is such a sad occupation for a Friday night, would you like to go elsewhere?
BETTY.   No . . .
BILL.   Do something else?
BETTY.   No thanks.
BETTY.   I was headed out to the movies in a while anyway.   165
BETTY.   I don't think so.
BILL.   Big chance to let Faulkner catch his breath. All those long sentences get him pretty tired.
BETTY.   Thanks anyway.
BILL.   Okay.
BETTY.   I appreciate the invitation.   170
BILL.   Sure thing. *(Bell.)* You weren't waiting for somebody when I came in, were you?
BETTY.   No, just reading.
BILL.   Sort of a sad occupation for a Friday night, isn't it? Reading here all by yourself?

BETTY.   I guess I was trying to think of it as existentially romantic. You
know—cappuccino, great literature, rainy night . . .

BILL.   That only works in Paris. We *could* hop the late plane to Paris. Get   175
on a Concorde. Find a café . . .

BETTY.   I'm a little short on plane fare tonight.

BILL.   Darn it, so am I.

BETTY.   To tell you the truth, I was headed to the movies after I finished
this section. Would you like to come along? Since you can't locate
a waiter?

BILL.   That's a very nice offer, but . . .

BETTY.   Uh-huh. Girlfriend?   180

BILL.   Two, actually. One of them's pregnant, and Stephanie.—*(Bell.)*

BETTY.   Girlfriend?

BILL.   No, I don't have a girlfriend. Not if you mean the castrating bitch
I dumped last night. *(Bell.)*

BETTY.   Girlfriend?

BILL.   Sort of. Sort of.   185

BETTY.   What's a sort-of girlfriend?

BILL.   My mother. *(Bell.)* I just ended a relationship, actually.

BETTY   Oh.

BILL.   Of rather long standing.

BETTY.   I'm sorry to hear it.   190

BILL.   This is my first night out alone in a long time. I feel a little bit at sea,
to tell you the truth.

BETTY.   So you didn't stop to talk because you're a Moonie, or you have
some weird political affiliation—?

BILL.   Nope. Straight-down-the-ticket Republican. *(Bell.)* Straight-down-
the-ticket Democrat. *(Bell.)* Can I tell you something about politics?
(Bell.) I like to think of myself as a citizen of the universe. *(Bell.)* I'm
unaffiliated.

BETTY.   That's a relief. So am I.

BILL.   I vote my beliefs.   195

BETTY.   Labels are not important.

BILL.   Labels are not important, exactly. Take me, for example. I mean,
what does it matter if I had a two-point at—*(Bell.)*—three-point at—
(Bell.)—four-point at college? Or if I did come from Pittsburgh—
(Bell.)—Cleveland—*(Bell.)*—Westchester County?

BETTY.   Sure.

BILL.   I believe that a man is what he is. *(Bell.)* A person is what he is.
(Bell.) A person is . . . what they are.

BETTY.   I think so too.   200

BILL.   So what if I admire Trotsky? *(Bell.)* So what if I once had a total-body
liposuction? *(Bell.)* So what if I don't have a penis? *(Bell.)* So what if I
once spent a year in the Peace Corps? I was acting on my convictions.

BETTY.   Sure.

BILL.   You can't just hang a sign on a person.

BETTY.   Absolutely. I'll bet you're a Scorpio. *(Many bells ring.)* Listen, I was headed to the movies after I finished this section. Would you like to come along?

BILL.   That sounds like fun. What's playing?   205

BETTY.   A couple of the really early Woody Allen movies.

BILL.   Oh.

BETTY.   You don't like Woody Allen?

BILL.   Sure. I like Woody Allen.

BETTY.   But you're not crazy about Woody Allen.   210

BILL.   Those early ones kind of get on my nerves.

BETTY.   Uh-huh. *(Bell.)*

BILL.   *(Simultaneously.)*   BETTY.   *(Simultaneously.)*
Y'know I was headed to the—   I was thinking about—

BILL.   I'm sorry.   215

BETTY.   No, go ahead.

BILL.   I was going to say that I was headed to the movies in a little while, and . . .

BETTY.   So was I.

BILL.   The Woody Allen festival?

BETTY.   Just up the street.   220

BILL.   Do you like the early ones?

BETTY.   I think anybody who doesn't ought to be run off the planet.

BILL.   How many times have you seen *Bananas*?

BETTY.   Eight times.

BILL.   Twelve. So are you still interested? *(Long pause.)*   225

BETTY.   Do you like Entenmann's crumb cake . . .?

BILL.   Last night I went out at two in the morning to get one. *(Small pause.)* Did you have an Etch-a-Sketch as a child?

BETTY.   Yes! And do you like Brussels sprouts? *(Small pause.)*

BILL.   No, I think they're disgusting.   230

BETTY.   They *are* disgusting!

BILL.   Do you still believe in marriage in spite of current sentiments against it?

BETTY.   Yes.

BILL.   And children?

BETTY.   Three of them.   235

BILL.   Two girls and a boy.

BETTY.   Harvard, Vassar and Brown.

BILL.   And will you love me?

BETTY.   Yes.

BILL.   And cherish me forever?   240

BETTY.   Yes.

BILL. Do you still want to go to the movies?
BETTY. Sure thing.
BILL AND BETTY. *(Together.) Waiter!*

BLACKOUT

Questions for Discussion and Writing

1. What kinds of things are "turn-offs" for both Betty and Bill? What does this imply about how difficult it is for them to find someone compatible?
2. How does Ives make the ringing bell almost into another character? What details suggest that the relationship really begins when Bill and Betty move beyond the need for scripted responses?
3. Despite its whimsical nature, what real social issues are addressed in this play? What do you think Ives meant by the title?
4. **Rhetorical inquiry:** Why is it significant that the smaller scenes into which the play is divided (signaled by the bell) get longer and longer as Bill and Betty establish a rapport? How does Ives generate suspense through the bell in a way that involves the audience in Bill and Betty's relationship?

Connections for Chapter 5: Everyday Matters

1. **Juliet B. Schor,** *The Culture of Consumerism*
   How do the values relating to body image described by Rosalind Coward support Schor's thesis about the extent to which we "buy" into the media's depiction of how we should look and what we should want to own?
2. **Philip Slater,** *Want-Creation Fuels Americans' Addictiveness*
   What factors account for the new direction that "want-creation" (as discussed by Slater) has taken, according to Juliet B. Schor?
3. **Jan Harold Brunvand,** *Urban Legends*
   To what extent does Joyce Carol Oates's story ("Where Are You Going, Where Have You Been?") in Chapter 11 portray an urban legend as described by Brunvand?
4. **Rosalind Coward,** *The Body Beautiful*
   Draw on the method for analyzing ads as described by Stuart Hirschberg in "The Rhetoric of Advertising" (Chapter 4) and discuss whether current ads support Coward's assessment?

5. **Bill Bryson,** *What's Cooking? Eating in America*
   How is convenience the transforming catalyst in American culture in the analyses by Bryson and Donald A. Norman (in "Emotional Robots") in Chapter 9?

6. **Jessica Mitford,** *Mortuary Solaces*
   Compare the emphasis on appearance and what it takes to achieve it as described by Mitford and Rosalind Coward, although in very different contexts.

7. **Judith Ortiz Cofer,** *The Myth of the Latin Woman*
   In what respects do Cofer's narrative and Gayle Pemberton ("Antidisestablishmentarianism") in Chapter 2 reveal a struggle against prevailing racial and gender stereotypes?

8. **Mark Twain,** *The Lowest Animal*
   How do Twain and Jonathan Swift (in "A Modest Proposal" in Chapter 8) use satire to attack their targets?

9. **Kate Chopin,** *Désirée's Baby*
   What features of Kate Chopin's "Désirée's Baby" illustrate Martin Luther King, Jr.'s ("I Have a Dream") in Chapter 8 assessment of race relations in the United States?

10. **Gloria Anzaldúa,** *Cervicide*
    Discuss the precarious nature of being marginalized in the story by Anzaldúa and essay by Harriet Jacobs ("Incidents in the Life of a Slave Girl") in Chapter 8.

11. **Marge Piercy,** *Barbie Doll*
    How does the Barbie doll (as portrayed by Piercy) illustrate Coward's thesis as to the damaging effects of society's messages about female body image?

12. **Grace C. Kuhns,** *Lisa's Ritual, Age 10*
    If the events in Kuhns's poem were investigated as a crime, what gender-based assumptions would help or hinder the inquiry, as in Susan Glaspell's play, Trifles (in Chapter 8)?

13. **Bruce Springsteen,** *Streets of Philadelphia*
    What different perspectives on the loss of self are offered by Springsteen in his lyrics and Kuhns in her poem?

14. **Gregory Corso,** *Marriage*
    Is being imaginative the all important quality in Corso's poem and in Carson McCuller's story "Madame Zilensky and the King of Finland" (in Chapter 10)?

15. **David Ives,** *Sure Thing*
    Do the aspirations of Betty and Bill in Ives's play match those described by Juliet B. Schor as being characteristic of mainstream culture?

6

OUR PLACE IN NATURE

Animals are not brethren, they are not underlings; they are other nations, caught with ourselves in the net of life and time.
Henry Beston, "AUTUMN, OCEAN, AND BIRDS"

Many essays in this chapter stand as classic investigations of the complex interactions of living things, the study of animal behavior, a deteriorating environment, and the dangers of species extinction. Selections by Charles Darwin, Konrad Lorenz, and Robert Sapolsky explore the underlying mechanisms governing evolution and survival. Joseph K. Skinner, Elizabeth Kolbert, and Robert W. Felix consider how the exploitation of the environment, global warming, and the prospect of a new ice age have become less theoretical and more imminent.

The reciprocal relationships of animals and humans are the topic of several selections. Gunjan Sinha reports on the latest research that reveals that the brain chemistry of the prairie vole and its mating behavior are surprisingly similar to that of humans. An essay by Alice Walker shares the author's personal encounter with an unusual horse that evokes parallels to the subjection of one race by another.

Doris Lessing in her short story projects us into the mind of a young boy in Africa whose experience on the veld spans the extremes of life and death.

Poems by Mary Oliver and Henry Wadsworth Longfellow explore each author's profound sense of being at one with nature. Another set of poems by Xu Gang and Sharon Chmielarz show us how our view of nature is enhanced by changing our perspective and meeting challenges.

As you read works in this chapter and prepare to discuss or write about them you may wish to use the following questions as guidelines.

- What problem or issue does the author address?
- What should our relationship to nature be from the author's standpoint?
- According to the author what impact does nature have on human beings?
- What parallels does the author draw between humans and other species?
- How has your view of our place in nature changed after reading the author's work?

- Is the author unrealistic or overly sentimental about the subject?
- What argument does the writer make and what form of evidence is used to support it?

Nonfiction

CHARLES DARWIN

Charles Darwin (1809–1882) the British naturalist and geologist, initially studied medicine but left medical school to study for the ministry at Cambridge. His interest in natural history was encouraged by John Stevens Henslow, who was responsible for Darwin's being invited to join the Admiralty Surveyship H.M.S. Beagle. Its five-year voyage to South America and the Galapagos Islands provided Darwin with a wealth of observations and many unanswered questions. Darwin's answer took the form of a theory that in the competitive struggle for existence, species possessing advantageous mutations would thrive, whereas less adapted species would become extinct. His principle works include On the Origin of Species by Means of Natural Selection *(1859), from which the following selection is drawn, and* The Descent of Man *(1871).*

Before You Read

To what extent is the evolutionary versus creationist argument still a source of controversy?

From the Origin of Species[1]

NATURAL SELECTION; OR THE SURVIVAL OF THE FITTEST

Summary of Chapter

If under changing conditions of life organic beings present individual differences in almost every part of their structure, and this cannot be disputed; if there be, owing to their geometrical rate of increase, a severe struggle for life at some age, season, or year, and this certainly cannot be disputed; then, considering the infinite complexity of the relations of all organic beings to each other and to their conditions of life, causing an infinite diversity in structure, constitution, and habits, to be advantageous to them, it would be a most extraordinary fact if no variations had ever occurred useful to each being's

---

[1] This selection is excerpted from the sixth edition of Darwin's 1872 book, the last edition published during his lifetime.

own welfare, in the same manner as so many variations have occurred useful to man. But if variations useful to any organic being ever do occur, assuredly individuals thus characterised will have the best chance of being preserved in the struggle for life; and from the strong principle of inheritance, these will tend to produce offspring similarly characterised. This principle of preservation, or the survival of the fittest, I have called Natural Selection. It leads to the improvement of each creature in relation to its organic and inorganic conditions of life; and consequently, in most cases, to what must be regarded as an advance in organisation. Nevertheless, low and simple forms will long endure if well fitted for their simple conditions of life.

Natural selection, on the principle of qualities being inherited at corresponding ages, can modify the egg, seed, or young, as easily as the adult. Amongst many animals, sexual selection[2] will have given its aid to ordinary selection, by assuring to the most vigorous and best adapted makes the greatest number of offspring. Sexual selection will also give characters useful to the males alone, in their struggles or rivalry with other males; and these characters will be transmitted to one sex or to both sexes, according to the form of inheritance which prevails.

Whether natural selection has really thus acted in adapting the various forms of life to their several conditions and stations, must be judged by the general tenor and balance of evidence given in the following chapters. But we have already seen how it entails extinction; and how largely extinction has acted in the world's history, geology plainly declares. Natural selection, also leads to divergence of character; for the more organic beings diverge in structure, habits, and constitution, by so much the more can a large number be supported on the area,—of which we see proof by looking to the inhabitants of any small spot, and to the productions naturalised in foreign lands. Therefore, during the modification of the descendants of any one species, and during the incessant struggle of all species to increase in numbers, the more diversified the descendants become, the better will be their chance of success in the battle for life. Thus the small differences distinguishing varieties of the same species, steadily tend to increase, till they equal the greater differences between species of the same genus, or even of distinct genera. . . .

Natural selection, as has just been remarked, leads to divergence of character and to much extinction of the less improved and intermediate forms of life. On these principles, the nature of the affinities, and the generally well-defined distinctions between the innumerable organic beings in each class throughout the world, may be explained. It is a truly wonderful fact—the wonder of which we are apt to overlook from familiarity—that all animals and all plants throughout all time and space should be related to each other in groups, subordinate to groups, in the manner which we

---

[2] Sexual selection refers to the mating preferences within a species that ensure the most vigorous and best adapted offspring.

everywhere behold—namely, varieties of the same species most closely related, species of the same genus less closely and unequally related, forming sections and sub-genera, species of distinct genera much less closely related, and genera related in different degrees, forming sub-families, families, orders, sub-classes and classes. The several subordinate groups in any class cannot be ranked in a single file, but seem clustered round points, and these round other points, and so on in almost endless cycles. If species had been independently created, no explanation would have been possible of this kind of classification; but it is explained through inheritance and the complex action of natural selection, entailing extinction and divergence of character. . . .

The affinities of all the beings of the same class have sometimes been rep-   5
resented by a great tree. I believe this simile largely speaks the truth. The green and budding twigs may represent existing species; and those produced during former years may represent the long succession of extinct species. At each period of growth all the growing twigs have tried to branch out on all sides, and to overtop and kill the surrounding twigs and branches, in the same manner as species and groups of species have at all times overmastered other species in the great battle for life. The limbs divided into great branches, and these into lesser and lesser branches, were themselves once, when the tree was young, budding twigs, and this connection of the former and present buds by ramifying branches may well represent the classification of all extinct and living species in groups subordinate to groups. Of the many twigs which flourished when the tree was a mere bush, only two or three, now grown into great branches, yet survive and bear the other branches; so with the species which lived during long-past geological periods, very few have left living and modified descendants. From the first growth of the tree, many a limb and branch has decayed and dropped off; and these fallen branches of various sizes may represent those whole orders, families, and genera which have now no living representatives, and which are known to us only in a fossil state. As we here and there see a thin straggling branch springing from a fork low down in a tree, and which by some chance has been favoured and is still alive on its summit, so we occasionally see an animal like the Ornithorhynchus or Lepidosiren,[3] which in some small degree connects by its affinities two large branches of life, and which has apparently been saved from fatal competition by having inhabited a protected station. As buds give rise by growth to fresh buds, and these, if vigorous, branch out and overtop on all sides many a feebler branch, so by generation I believe it has been with the great Tree of Life,

---

[3] Ornithorhynchus anatinus refers to the duck-billed platypus, a semi-aquatic, egg-laying mammal of Tasmania and East Australia. It has a rubbery duck-bill-shaped muzzle; no teeth; no external ears; head, body, and tail are broad, flat, and covered with dark brown fur; its feet are webbed; and the adult male is about two feet long. Lepidosiren refers to a lung-bearing fish often resembling an eel that is found in rivers in South America, Africa, and Australia and ancestrally is related to four-footed land animals. They indicate a point of bifurcation in evolution since some species breathe through gills in water and other species will drown if held under water.

which fills with its dead and broken branches the crust of the earth, and covers the surface with its ever-branching and beautiful ramifications. . . .

ON THE IMPERFECTION OF THE GEOLOGICAL RECORD

In the sixth chapter I enumerated the chief objections which might be justly urged against the views maintained in this volume. Most of them have now been discussed. One, namely the distinctness of specific forms, and their not being blended together by innumerable transitional links, is a very obvious difficulty. I assigned reasons why such links do not commonly occur at the present day under the circumstances apparently most favourable for their presence, namely, on an extensive and continuous area with graduated physical conditions. I endeavoured to show, that the life of each species depends in a more important manner on the presence of other already defined organic forms, than on climate, and, therefore, that the really governing conditions of life do not graduate away quite insensibly like heat or moisture. I endeavoured, also, to show that intermediate varieties, from existing in lesser numbers than the forms which they connect, will generally be beaten out and exterminated during the course of further modification and improvement. The main cause, however, of innumerable intermediate links not now occurring everywhere throughout nature, depends on the very process of natural selection, through nature, depends on the very process of natural selection, through which new varieties continually take the places of and supplant their parentforms. But just in proportion as this process of extermination has acted on an enormous scale, so must the number of intermediate varieties, which have formerly existed, be truly enormous. Why then is not every geological formation and every stratum full of such intermediate links? Geology assuredly does not reveal any such finely-graduated organic chain; and this, perhaps, is the most obvious and serious objection which can be urged against the theory. The explanation lies, as I believe, in the extreme imperfection of the geological record.

In the first place, it should always be borne in mind what sort of intermediate forms must, on the theory, have formerly existed. I have found it difficult, when looking at any two species, to avoid picturing to myself forms *directly* intermediate between them. But this is a wholly false view: we should always look for forms intermediate between each species and a common but unknown progenitor; and the progenitor will generally have differed in some respects from all its modified descendants. To give a simple illustration: the fantail and pouter pigeons are both descended from the rock-pigeon; if we possessed all the intermediate varieties which have ever existed, we should have an extremely close series between both and the rock-pigeon; but we should have no varieties directly intermediate between the fantail and pouter; none, for instance, combining a tail somewhat expanded with a crop somewhat enlarged, the characteristic features of these two breeds. These two breeds, moreover, have become so much modified, that, if we had no historical or indirect evidence regarding their origin, it would not have been possible to have determined, from a mere comparison of their structure with that of the rock-pigeon, C. livia, whether they had descended from this species or from some allied form, such as C. oenas.

So, with natural species, if we look to forms very distinct, for instance to the horse and tapir, we have no reason to suppose that links directly intermediate between them ever existed, but between each and an unknown common parent. The common parent will have had in its whole organisation much general resemblance to the tapir and to the horse; but in some points of structure may have differed considerably from both, even perhaps more than they differ from each other. Hence, in all such cases, we should be unable to recognise the parent-form of any two or more species, even if we closely compared the structure of the parent with that of its modified descendants, unless at the same time we had a nearly perfect chain of the intermediate links.

It is just possible by the theory, that one of two living forms might have descended from the other; for instance, a horse from a tapir; and in this case *direct* intermediate links will have existed between them. But such a case would imply that one form had remained for a very long period unaltered, whilst its descendants had undergone a vast amount of change; and the principle of competition between organism and organism, between child and parent, will render this a very rare event; for in all cases the new and improved forms of life tend to supplant the old and unimproved forms.

By the theory of natural selection all living species have been connected   10
with the parent-species of each genus, by differences not greater than we see between the natural and domestic varieties of the same species at the present day; and these parent-species, now generally extinct, have in their turn been similarly connected with more ancient forms; and so on backwards, always coverging to the common ancestor of each great class. So that the number of intermediate and transitional links, between all living and extinct species, must have been inconceivably great. But assuredly, if this theory be true, such have lived upon the earth.

On the Lapse of Time, as Inferred from the Rate of Deposition and Extent of Denudation

Independently of our not finding fossil remains of such infinitely numerous connecting links, it may be objected that time cannot have sufficed for so great an amount of organic change, all changes having been effected slowly. It is hardly possible for me to recall to the reader who is not a practical geologist, the facts leading the mind feebly to comprehend the lapse of time. He who can read Sir Charles Lyell's[4] grand work on the Principles of Geology, which the future historian will recognise as having produced a revolution in natural science, and yet does not admit how vast have been the past periods

---

[4] Sir Charles Lyell (1797–1875) English geologist whose research helped win acceptance of Darwin's theory of evolution.

of time, may at once close this volume. Not that it suffices to study the Principles of Geology, or to read special treatises by different observers on separate formations, and to mark how each author attempts to give an inadequate idea of duration of each formation, or even of each stratum. We can best gain some idea of past time by knowing the agencies at work, and learning how deeply the surface of the land has been denuded, and how much sediment has been deposited. As Lyell has well remarked, the extent and thickness of our sedimentary formations are the result and the measure of the denudation which the earth's crust has elsewhere undergone. Therefore a man should examine for himself the great piles of superimposed strata, and watch the rivulets bringing down mud, and the waves wearing away the sea-cliffs, in order to comprehend something about the duration of past time, the monuments of which we see all around us . . .

On the Poorness of Palaeontological Collections

Now let us turn to our richest geological museums, and what a paltry display we behold! That our collections are imperfect is admitted by every one. The remark of that admirable paleontologist, Edward Forbes, should never be forgotten, namely, that very many fossil species are known and named from single and often broken specimens, or from a few specimens collected on some one spot. Only a small portion of the surface of the earth has been geologically explored, and no part with sufficient care, as the important discoveries made every year in Europe prove. No organism wholly soft can be preserved. Shells and bones decay and disappear when left on the bottom of the sea, where sediment is not accumulating.

. . . Those who believe that the geological record is in any degree perfect, will undoubtedly at once reject the theory. For my part, following out Lyell's metaphor, I look at the geological record as a history of the world imperfectly kept, and written in a changing dialect; of this history we possess the last volume alone, relating only to two or three countries. Of this volume, only here and there a short chapter has been preserved; and of each page, only here and there a few lines. Each word of the slowly-changing language, more or less different in the successive chapters, may represent the forms of life, which are entombed in our consecutive formations, and which falsely appear to have been abruptly introduced. On this view, the difficulties above discussed are greatly diminished, or even disappear. . . .

RECAPITULATION AND CONCLUSION

As this whole volume is one long argument, it may be convenient to the reader to have the leading facts and inferences briefly recapitulated.

That many and serious objections may be advanced against the theory of descent with modification through variation and natural selection, I do not deny. I have endeavored to give to them their full force. Nothing at first can appear more difficult to believe than that the more complex organs and instincts have been perfected, not by means superior to, though analogous with, human reason, but by the accumulation of innumerable slight variations, each good for the individual possessor. Nevertheless, this difficulty, though appearing to our imagination insuperably great, cannot be considered real if we admit the following propositions, namely, that all parts of the organisation and instincts offer, at least, individual differences—that there is a struggle for existence leading to the preservation of profitable deviations of structure or instinct—and, lastly, that gradations in the state of perfection of each organ may have existed, each good of its kind. The truth of these propositions cannot, I think, be disputed.

Now let us turn to the other side of the argument. Under domestication we see much variability, caused, or at least excited, by changed conditions of life; but often in so obscure a manner, that we are tempted to consider the variations as spontaneous. Variability is governed by many complex laws,—by correlated growth, compensation, the increased use and disuse of parts, and the definite action of the surrounding conditions. There is much difficulty in ascertaining how largely our domestic productions have been modified; but we may safely infer that the amount has been large, and that modifications can be inherited for long periods. As long as the conditions of life remain the same, we have reason to believe that a modification, which has already been inherited for many generations, may continue to be inherited for an almost infinite number of generations. On the other hand, we have evidence that variability when it has once come into play, does not cease under domestication for a very long period; nor do we know that it ever ceases, for new varieties are still occasionally produced by our oldest domesticated productions.

Variability is not actually caused by man; he only unintentionally exposes organic beings to new conditions of life, and then nature acts on the organisation and causes it to vary. But man can and does select the variations given to him by nature, and thus accumulates them in any desired manner. He thus adapts animals and plants for his own benefit or pleasure. He may do this methodically, or he may do it unconsciously by preserving the individuals most useful or pleasing to him without any intention of altering the breed. It is certain that he can largely influence the character of a breed of selecting, in each successive generation, individual differences so slight as to be inappreciable except by an educated eye. This unconscious process of selection has been the great agency in the formation of the most distinct and useful domestic breeds. That many breeds produced by man have to a large extent the character of natural species, is shown by the inextricable doubts whether many of them are varieties or aboriginally distinct species.

There is no reason why the principles which have acted so efficiently under domestication should not have acted under nature. In the survival of favoured individuals and races, during the constantly-recurrent Struggle for Existence, we see a powerful and ever-acting form of Selection. The struggle for existence inevitably follows from the high geometrical ratio if increase which is common to all organic beings. This high rate of increase is proved by calculation,—by the rapid increase of many animals and plants during a succession of peculiar seasons, and when naturalised in new countries. More individuals are born than can possibly survive. A grain in the balance may determine which individuals shall live and which shall die,—which variety or species shall increase in number, and which shall decrease, or finally become extinct. As the individuals of the same species come in all respects into the closest competition with each other, the struggle will generally be most severe between them; it will be almost equally severe between the varieties of the same species, and next in severity between the species of the same genus. On the other hand the struggle will often be severe between beings remote in the scale of nature. The slightest advantage in certain individuals, at any age of during any season, over those with which they come into competition, or better adaptation in however slight a degree to the surrounding physical conditions, will, in the long, run, turn the balance.

With animals having separated sexes, there will be in most cases a struggle between the males for the possession of the females. The most vigorous males, or those which have most successfully struggled with their conditions of life, will generally leave most progeny. But success will often depend on the males having special weapons, or means of defense, or charms; and a slight advantage will lead to victory. . . .

If then, animals and plants, do vary, let it be ever so slightly or slowly, why should not variation or individual differences, which are in any way beneficial be preserved and accumulated through natural selection, or the survival of the fittest? If man can by patience select variations useful to him, why, under changing and complex conditions, of life, should not variations useful to nature's living products often arise, and be preserved or selected? What limit can be put to this power, acting during long ages and rigidly scrutinising the whole constitution, structure, and habits of each creature,—favoring the good and rejecting the bad? I can see no limit to this power, in slowly and beautifully adapting each form to the most complex relations of life. The theory of natural selection, even if we look no farther than this, seems to be in the highest degree probable. I have already recapitulated, as fairly as I could, the opposed difficulties and objections: now let us turn to the special facts and arguments in favour of the theory. . . .

It can hardly be supposed that a false theory would explain, in so satisfactory a manner as does the theory of natural selection, the several large classes of facts above specified. It has recently been objected that this is an unsafe method of arguing; but it is a method used in judging of the common events of life, and has often been used by the greatest natural philosophers. The undulatory theory of light has thus been arrived at; and the belief in the revolution of the earth on its own axis was until lately supported by hardly any direct evidence. It is no valid objection that science as yet throws no light on the far higher problem of the essence or origin of life. Who can

20

explain what is the essence of the attraction of gravity? No one now objects to following out the results consequent on this unknown element of attraction; notwithstanding that Leibnitz[5] formerly accused Newton of introducing, "occult qualities and miracles into philosophy."

I see no good reason why the views given in this volume should shock the religious feelings of any one. It is satisfactory, as showing how transient such impressions, are to remember that the greatest discovery ever made by man, namely, the law of the attraction of gravity, was also attacked by Leibnitz, "as subversive of natural, and inferentially of revealed, religion." A celebrated author and divine has written to me that "he has gradually learnt to see that it is just as noble a conception of the Deity to believe that He created a few original forms capable of self-development into other and needful forms, as to believe that He required a fresh act of creation to supply the voids caused by the action of His laws." . . .

But the chief cause of our natural unwillingness to admit that one species has given birth to clear and distinct species, is that we are always slow in admitting great changes of which we do not see the steps. The difficulty is the same as that felt by so many geologists, when Lyell first insisted that long lines of inland cliffs had been formed, the great valleys excavated, by the agencies which we see still at work. The mind cannot possibly grasp the full meaning of the term of even a million years; it cannot add up and perceive the full effects of many slight variations, accumulated during an almost infinite number of generations.

Although I am fully convinced of the truth of the views given in this volume under the form of an abstract, I by no means expect to convince experienced naturalists whose minds are stocked with a multitude of facts all viewed, during a long course of years, from a point of view directly opposite to mine. It is so easy to hide our ignorance under such expressions as the "plan of creation," "unity of design," etc., and to think that we give an explanation when we only re-state a fact. Any one whose disposition leads him to attach more weight to unexplained difficulties than to the explanation of a certain number of facts will certainly reject the theory. A few naturalists, endowed with much flexibility of mind, and who have already begun to doubt the immutability of species, may be influenced by this volume; but I look with confidence to the future,—to young and rising naturalists, who will be able to view both sides of the question with impartiality. Whoever is led to believe that species are mutable will do good service by conscientiously expressing his conviction; for thus only can the load of prejudice by which this subject is overwheimed be removed. . . .

---

[5] Wilhelm Leibnitz (1646–1716) German philosopher and mathematician who invented calculus concurrently with, but independently of, Newton. His optimistic belief that a divine plan made this the best of all possible worlds was satirized by Voltaire in *Candide*.

Authors of the highest eminence seem to be fully satisfied with the view   25
that each species has been independently created. To my mind it accords
better with what we know of the laws impressed on matter by the Creator,
that the production and extinction of the past and present inhabitants of
the world should have been due to secondary causes, like those determining the birth and death of the individual. When I view all beings not as
special creations, but as the lineal descendants of some few beings which
lived long before the first bed of the Cambrian system was deposited, they
seem to me to become ennobled. Judging from the past, we may safely infer
that no one living species will transmit its unaltered likeness to a distant
futurity. And of the species now living very few will transmit progeny of
any kind to a far distant futurity; for the manner in which all organic beings
are grouped, shows that the greater number of species in each genus, and
all the species in many genera, have left no descendants, but have become
utterly extinct. We can so far take a prophetic glance into futurity as to fore-
tell that it will be the common and widely-spread species, belonging to the
larger and dominant groups within each class, which will ultimately prevail
and procreate new and dominant species. As all the living forms of life
are the lineal descendants of those which lived long before the Cambrian
epoch, we may feel certain that the ordinary succession by generation has
never once been broken, and that no cataclysm has desolated the whole
world. Hence we may look with some confidence to a secure future of great
length. And as natural selection works solely by and for the good of each
being, all corporeal and mental endowments will tend to progress towards
perfection.[6]

Questions for Discussion and Writing

1. What are Darwin's reasons for believing that natural forces operate to
   select the best variations within a species to enable it to survive?
2. What argument does Darwin use to defend himself against the charge
   that his work is incompatible with religious beliefs?
3. In what ways has the popular conception of Darwin's theories, especially the idea of survival of the fittest, had widespread impact in fields
   outside biology such as economics?
4. **Rhetorical inquiry:** How does Darwin's argument put his opponents in
   the position of having to prove that there is a way of distinguishing
   between a species and the variations of that species or, that the world
   has not existed for millions of years?

---

[6] By progress towards perfection over time Darwin means natural selection will produce
forms better adapted to their particular environment.

GUNJAN SINHA

Gunjan Sinha was born in Bihar, India, but grew up in Brooklyn, New York. She earned a graduate degree in molecular genetics from the University of Glasgow, Scotland, and received a degree from New York University's Science and Environmental Reporting Program in 1996. She was life sciences editor for Popular Science for five years and in 2000 was awarded the Ray Bruner Science Writing Award. In the following essay, written in 2002, Sinha explores the mating behavior of the common prairie vole (a mouselike rodent, about seven inches long with a two-inch tail) and what it reveals about the human pattern of monogamy.

Before You Read

Consider whether parallels can be drawn between the behavior of animals and that of humans?

You Dirty Vole

George is a typical Midwestern American male in the prime of his life, with an attractive spouse named Martha. George is a devoted husband, Martha an attentive wife. The couple has four young children, a typical home in a lovely valley full of corn and bean fields, and their future looks bright. But George is occasionally unfaithful. So, occasionally, is Martha. No big deal: That's just the way life is in this part of America.

This is a true story, though the names have been changed, and so, for that matter, has the species. George and Martha are prairie voles. They don't marry, of course, or think about being faithful. And a bright future for a vole is typically no more than 60 days of mating and pup-rearing that ends in a fatal encounter with a snake or some other prairie predator.

But if you want to understand more about the conflict in human relationships between faithfulness and philandering, have a peek inside the brain of this wee rodent. Researchers have been studying voles for more than 25 years, and they've learned that the mating behavior of these gregarious creatures uncannily resembles our own—including a familiar pattern of monogamous attachment: Male and female share a home and child care, the occasional dalliance notwithstanding. More important, researchers have discovered what drives the animals' monogamy: brain chemistry. And when it comes to the chemical soup that governs behavior associated with what we call love, prairie vole brains are a lot like ours.

Scientists are careful to refer to what voles engage in as "social monogamy," meaning that although voles prefer to nest and mate with a particular partner, when another vole comes courting, some will stray. And as many as 50 percent of male voles never find a permanent partner. Of course, there is no moral or religious significance to the vole's behavior—monogamous or not. Voles will be voles, because that's their nature.

Still, the parallels to humans are intriguing. "We're not an animal that finds it in our best interest to screw around," says Pepper Schwartz, a sociologist at the University of Washington, yet studies have shown that at least one-third of married people cheat. In many cases, married couples struggle with the simple fact that love and lust aren't always in sync, often tearing us in opposite directions. Vole physiology and behavior reinforce the idea that love and lust are biochemically separate systems, and that the emotional tug of war many of us feel between the two emotions is perfectly natural—a two-headed biological drive that's been hardwired into our brains through millions of years of evolution.

No one knew that voles were monogamous until Lowell Getz, a now-retired professor of ecology, ethology, and evolution at the University of Illinois, began studying them in 1972. At the time, Getz wanted to figure out why the vole population would boom during certain years and then slowly go bust. He set traps in the grassy plains of Illinois and checked them a few times a day, tagging the voles he caught. What surprised him was how often he'd find the same male and female sitting in a trap together.

Voles build soft nests about 8 inches below ground. A female comes of age when she is about 30 days old: Her need to mate is then switched on as soon as she encounters an unpartnered male and sniffs his urine. About 24 hours later, she's ready to breed—with the male she just met or another unattached one if he's gone. Then, hooked, the pair will stick together through thick and thin, mating and raising young.

Getz found vole mating behavior so curious that he wanted to bring the animals into the lab to study them more carefully. But he was a field biologist, not a lab scientist, so he called Sue Carter, a colleague and neuroendocrinologist. Carter had been studying how sex hormones influence behavior, and investigating monogamy in voles dovetailed nicely with her own research. The animals were small: They made the perfect lab rats.

The scientific literature was already rich with studies on a hormone called oxytocin that is made in mammalian brains and that in some species promotes bonding between males and females and between mothers and offspring. Might oxytocin, swirling around in tiny vole brains, be the catalyst for turning them into the lifelong partners that they are?

Sure enough, when Carter injected female voles with oxytocin, they were less finicky in choosing mates and practically glued themselves to their partners once they had paired. The oxytocin-dosed animals tended to lick and cuddle more than untreated animals, and they avoided strangers. What's more, when Carter injected females with oxytocin-blocking chemicals, the animals deserted their partners.

In people, not only is the hormone secreted by lactating women but studies have shown that oxytocin levels also increase during sexual arousal—and skyrocket during orgasm. In fact, the higher the level of oxytocin circulating in the blood during intercourse, the more intense the orgasm.

But there's more to vole mating than love; there's war too. Male voles are territorial. Once they bond with a female, they spend lots of time guarding her from other suitors, often sitting near the entrance of their burrow and aggressively baring their beaver-like teeth. Carter reasoned that other biochemicals must kick in after mating, chemicals that turn a once laid-back male into a territorial terror. Oxytocin, it turns out, is only part of the story. A related chemical, vasopressin, also occurs in both sexes. Males, however, have much more of it.

When Carter dosed male voles with a vasopressin-blocking chemical after mating, their feistiness disappeared. An extra jolt of vasopressin, on the other hand, boosted their territorial behavior and made them more protective of their mates.

Vasopressin is also present in humans. While scientists don't yet know the hormone's exact function in men, they speculate that it works similarly: It is secreted during sexual arousal and promotes bonding. It may even transform some men into jealous boyfriends and husbands. "The biochemistry [of attachment] is probably going to be similar in humans and in [monogamous] animals because it's quite a basic function," says Carter. Because oxytocin and vasopressin are secreted during sexual arousal and orgasm, she says, they are probably the key biochemical players that bond lovers to one another.

But monogamous animals aren't the only ones that have vasopressin and oxytocin in their brains. Philandering animals do too. So what separates faithful creatures from unfaithful ones? Conveniently for scientists, the generally monogamous prairie vole has a wandering counterpart: the montane vole. When Thomas Insel, a neuroscientist at Emory University, studied the two species' vasopressin receptors (appendages on a cell that catch specific biochemicals) he found them in different places. Prairie voles have receptors for the hormone in their brains' pleasure centers; montane voles have the receptors in other brain areas. In other words, male prairie voles stick with the same partner after mating because it feels good. For montane voles, mating is a listless but necessary affair, rather like scratching an itch.

Of course, human love is much more complicated. The biochemistry of attachment isn't yet fully understood, and there's clearly much more to it than oxytocin and vasopressin. Humans experience different kinds of love. There's "compassionate love," associated with feelings of calm, security, social comfort, and emotional union. This kind of love, say scientists, is probably similar to what voles feel toward their partners and involves oxytocin and vasopressin. Romantic love—that crazy obsessive euphoria that people feel when they are "in love"—is very different, as human studies are showing.

Scientists at University College London led by Andreas Bartels recently peered inside the heads of love-obsessed college students. They took 17 young people who claimed to be in love, stuck each of them in an MRI machine, and showed them pictures of their lovers. Blood flow increased to very specific areas of the brain's pleasure center—including some of the same areas that are stimulated when people engage in addictive behaviors. Some of these same areas are also active during sexual arousal, though romantic love and sexual arousal are clearly different: Sex has more to do with hormones like testosterone, which, when given to both men and women, increases sex drive and sexual fantasies. Testosterone, however, doesn't necessarily make people fall in love with, or become attached to, the object of their attraction.

Researchers weren't particularly surprised by the parts of the lovers' brains that were active. What astonished them was that two other brain areas were suppressed—the amygdala and the right prefrontal cortex. The amygdala is associated with negative emotions like fear and anger. The right prefrontal cortex appears to be overly active in people suffering from depression. The positive emotion of love, it seems, suppresses negative emotions. Might that be the scientific basis for why people who are madly in love fail to see the negative traits of their beloved? "Maybe," says Bartels cautiously. "But we haven't proven that yet."

The idea that romantic love activates parts of the brain associated with addiction got Donatella Marazziti at Pisa University in Tuscany wondering if it might be related to obsessive compulsive disorder (OCD). Anyone who has ever been in love knows how consuming the feeling can be. You can think of nothing but your lover every waking moment. Some people with OCD have low levels of the brain chemical serotonin. Might love-obsessed people also have low serotonin levels? Sure enough, when Marazziti and her colleagues tested the blood of 20 students who were madly in love and 20 people with OCD, she found that both groups had low levels of a protein that shuttles serotonin between brain cells.

And what happens when the euphoria of "mad love" wears off? Marazziti tested the blood of a few of the lovers 12 to 18 months later and found that their serotonin levels had returned to normal. That doesn't doom a couple, of course, but it suggests a biological explanation for the evolution of relationships. In many cases, romantic love turns into compassionate love, thanks to oxytocin and vasopressin swirling inside the lovers' brains. This attachment is what keeps many couples together. But because attachment and romantic love involve different biochemical processes, attachment to one person does not suppress lust for another. "The problem is, they are not always well linked," says anthropologist Helen Fisher, who has written several books on love, sex and marriage.

In the wild, about half of male voles wander the fields, never settling down with one partner. These "traveling salesmen," as Lowell Getz calls them, are always "trying to get with other females." Most females prefer to mate with their partners. But if they get the chance, some will mate with other males too. And, according to Jerry Wolff, a biologist at the University of Memphis, female voles sometimes "divorce" their partners. In the lab, he restricts three males at a time in separate but connected chambers and gives a female free range. The female has already paired with one of the males and is pregnant with his pups. Wolff says about a third of the females pick up their nesting materials and move in with a different fellow. Another third actually solicit and successfully mate with one or both of the other males, and the last third remain faithful.

Why are some voles fickle, others faithful? Vole brains differ from one creature to the next. Larry Young, a neuroscientist at Emory University, has found that some animals have more receptors for oxytocin and vasopressin than others. In a recent experiment, he injected a gene into male prairie voles that permanently upped the number of vasopressin receptors in their brains. The animals paired with females even though the two hadn't mated. "Normally they have to mate for at least 24 hours to establish a bond," he says. So the number of receptors can mean the difference between sticking around and skipping out after sex. Might these differences in brain wiring influence human faithfulness? "It's too soon to tell," Young says. But it's "definitely got us very curious."

How does evolution account for the often-conflicting experiences of love and lust, which have caused no small amount of destruction in human history? Fisher speculates that the neural systems of romantic love and attachment evolved for different reasons. Romantic love, she says, evolved to allow people to distinguish between potential mating partners and "to pursue these partners until insemination has occurred." Attachment, she says, "evolved to make you tolerate this individual long enough to raise a child." Pepper Schwartz agrees: "We're biologically wired to be socially monogamous, but it's not a good evolutionary tactic to be sexually monogamous. There need to be ways to keep reproduction going if your mate dies."

Many of our marriage customs, say sociologists, derive from the need to reconcile this tension. "As much as people love passion and romantic love," Schwartz adds, "most people also want to have the bonding sense of loyalty and friendship love as well." Marriage vows are a declaration about romantic love and binding attachment, but also about the role of rational thought and the primacy of mind and mores over impulses.

Scientists hope to do more than simply decode the biochemistry of the emotions associated with love and attachment. Some, like Insel, are searching for treatments for attachment disorders such as autism, as well as pathological behaviors like stalking and violent jealousy. It is not inconceivable that someday there might be sold an attachment drug, a monogamy pill; the mind reels at the marketing possibilities.

Lowell Getz, the grandfather of all this research, couldn't be more thrilled. "I spent almost $1 million of taxpayer money trying to figure out stuff like why sisters don't make it with their brothers," he says. "I don't want to go to my grave feeling like it was a waste."

Questions for Discussion and Writing

1. What insight does Sinha offer into the biochemical triggers that are responsible for the mating behavior of the prairie vole? What parallel behaviors do human beings display that suggest an underlying biochemical matrix similar to that of the vole?

2. A good deal of Sinha's article is based on extrapolating features of the vole's behavior onto humans. This argument by analogy may be effective up to a point. In your opinion, does it break down, and if so, in what respects?

3. Are biology (hard-wired primal drives) and psychology (learned social and cultural behaviors) ultimately irreconcilable explanations for the same observed effects in human beings?

4. **Rhetorical inquiry:** How does Sinha incorporate the expert opinions of a broad range of scientists to examine human marriage customs through the lens of animal behavior?

JOSEPH K. SKINNER

Joseph K. Skinner is a 1979 graduate of the University of California who majored in plant sciences. He reports that "in all of my course work at the University of California at Davis, only once was brief mention made of the biological calamity described in this article, and even then no connection was made between it and U.S. economic interests." "Big Mac and the Tropical Forests" first appeared in the Monthly Review *(December, 1985). Skinner creates an intriguing causal argument to show how tropical forests in Central and Latin America are being destroyed in order to raise cattle to produce cheap beef for companies such as McDonald's and Swift-Armour Meat Packing Co. Skinner claims that the failure to take responsibility on the part of these and other corporations puts short-term profitability ahead of destruction of tropical forests. In turn, this destruction could well accelerate the greenhouse effect by permitting rising levels of carbon dioxide to remain in the atmosphere.*

Before You Read

Do corporations have a responsibility to protect the environment?

Big Mac and the Tropical Forests

Hello, fast-food chains.

Goodbye, tropical forests.

Sound like an odd connection? The "free-market" economy has led to results even stranger than this, but perhaps none have been as environmentally devastating.

These are the harsh facts: the tropical forests are being leveled for commercial purpose at the rate of 150,000 square kilometers a year, an area the size of England and Wales combined.[1]

At this rate, the world's tropical forests could be entirely destroyed within seventy-three years. Already as much as a fifth or a quarter of the huge Amazon forest, which constitutes a third of the world's total rain forests, has been cut, and the rate of destruction is accelerating. And nearly two thirds of the Central American forests have been cleared or severely degraded since 1950.

Tropical forests, which cover only 7 percent of the Earth's land surface (it used to be 12 percent), support half the species of the world's living things. Due to their destruction, "We are surely losing one or more species a day right now out of the five million (minimum figure) on Earth," says Norman Myers, author of numerous books and articles on the subject and consultant to the World Bank and the World Wildlife Fund. "By the time ecological equilibrium is restored, at least one-quarter of all species will have disappeared, probably a third, and conceivably even more. . . . If this pattern continues, it could mean the demise of two million species by the middle of next century." Myers calls the destruction of the tropical forests "one of the greatest biological debacles to occur on the face of the Earth." Looking at the effects it will have on the course of biological evolution, Myers says:

> The impending upheaval in evolution's course could rank as one of the greatest biological revolutions of paleontological time. It will equal in scale and significance the development of aerobic respiration, the emergence of flowering plants, and the arrival of limbed animals. But of course the prospective degradation of many evolutionary capacities will be an impoverishing, not a creative, phenomenon.[2]

In other words, such rapid destruction will vacate so many niches so suddenly that a "pest and weed" ecology, consisting of a relatively few opportunistic species (rats, roaches, and the like) will be created.

Beyond this—as if it weren't enough—such destruction could well have cataclysmic effects on the Earth's weather patterns, causing, for example, an irreversible desertification of the North American grain belt. Although the scope of the so-called greenhouse effect—in which rising levels of carbon

[1] Jean-Paul Landley, "Tropical Forests Resources," *FAO Forestry Paper* 30 (Rome: FAO, 1982). This UN statistic is the most accurate to date. For further extrapolations from it, see Nicholas Guppy, "Tropical Deforestation: A Global View," *Foreign Affairs* 62, no. 4 (Spring 1984).   [2] There are amazingly few scientists in the world broad enough expertise to accurately assess the widest implications of tropical deforestation; Norman Myers is one of them. His books include *The Sinking Ark* (Oxford: Pergamon Press, 1979). See also *Conversion of Moist Tropical Forests* (Washington, D.C.: National Academy of Sciences, 1980), "The End of the Line." *Natural History* 94, no. 2 (February 1985), and "The Hamburger Connection," *Ambio* 10, no. 1 (1981). I have used Myers extensively in the preparation of this article. The quotes in this paragraph are from "The Hamburger Connection," pp. 3, 4, 5.

dioxide in the atmosphere heat the planet by preventing infrared radiation from escaping into space—is still being debated within the scientific community, it is not at all extreme to suppose that the fires set to clear tropical forests will contribute greatly to this increase in atmospheric CO_2 and thereby to untold possibly devastating changes in the world's weather systems.

BIG MAC ATTACK

So what does beef, that staple of the fast-food chains and of the North American diet in general, have to do with it?

It used to be, back in 1960, that the United States imported practically 10 no beef. That was a time when North Americans were consuming a "mere" 85 pounds of beef per person per year. By 1980 this was up to 134 pounds per person per year. Concomitant with this increase in consumption, the United States began to import beef, so that by 1981 some 800,000 tons were coming in from abroad, 17 percent of it from tropical Latin America and three fourths of that from Central America. Since fast-food chains have been steadily expanding and now are a $5-billion-a-year business, accounting for 25 percent of all the beef consumed in the United States, the connections between the fast-food empire and tropical beef are clear.

Cattle ranching is "by far the major factor in forest destruction in tropical Latin America," says Myers. "Large fast-food outlets in the U.S. and Europe foster the clearance of forests to produce cheap beef."[3]

And cheap it is, compared to North American beef: by 1978 the average price of beef imported from Central America was $1.47/kg, while similar North American beef cost $3.30/kg.

Cheap, that is, for North Americans, but not for Central Americans. Central Americans cannot afford their own beef. Whereas beef production in Costa Rica increased twofold between 1959 and 1972, per capita consumption of beef in that country went down from 30 lbs. a year to 19. In Honduras, beef production increased by 300 percent between 1965 and 1975, but consumption decreased from 12 lbs. per capita per year to 10. So, although two thirds of Central America's arable land is in cattle, local consumption of beef is decreasing; the average domestic cat in the United States now consumes more beef than the average Central American.[4]

Brazilian government figures show that 38 percent of all deforestation in the Brazilian Amazon between 1966 and 1975 was attributable to large-scale cattle ranching. Although the presence of hoof-and-mouth disease among Brazilian cattle has forced U.S. lawmakers to prohibit the importation of chilled or frozen Brazilian beef, the United States imports $46 million per year of cooked Brazilian beef, which goes into canned products; over

---

[3] Myers, "End of the Line", p. 2. [4] See James Nations and Daniel I. Komer, "Rainforests and the Hamburger Society," *Environment* 25, no. 3 (April 1983).

80 percent of Brazilian beef is still exported, most of it to Western Europe, where no such prohibition exists.

At present rates, all remaining Central American forests will have been eliminated by 1990. The cattle ranching largely responsible for this is in itself highly inefficient: as erosion and nutrient leaching eat away the soil, production drops from an average one head per hectare—measly in any case—to a pitiful one head per five to seven hectares within five to ten years. A typical tropical cattle ranch employs only one person per 2,000 head, and meat production barely reaches 50 lbs./acre/year. In Northern Europe, in farms that do not use imported feed, it is over 500 lbs./acre/year.

This real-term inefficiency does not translate into bad business, however, for although there are some absentee landowners who engage in ranching for the prestige of it and are not particularly interested in turning large profits, others find bank loans for growing beef for export readily forthcoming, and get much help and encouragement from such organizations as the Pan American Health Organization, the Organization of American States, the U.S. Department of Agriculture, and U.S. AID, without whose technical assistance "cattle production in the American tropics would be unprofitable, if not impossible."[5] The ultimate big winner appears to be the United States, where increased imports of Central American beef are said to have done more to stem inflation than any other single government initiative.

"On the good land, which could support a large population, you have the rich cattle owners, and on the steep slopes, which should be left in forest, you have the poor farmers," says Gerardo Budowski, director of the Tropical Agricultural Research and Training Center in Turrialba, Costa Rica. "It is still good business to clear virgin forest in order to fatten cattle for, say, five to eight years and then abandon it."[6]

(Ironically, on a trip I made in 1981 to Morazán, a Salvadoran province largely under control of FMLN guerrillas, I inquired into the guerilla diet and discovered that beef, expropriated from the cattle ranches, was a popular staple.)

SWIFT-ARMOUR'S SWIFT ARMOR

The rain forest ecosystem, the oldest on Earth, is extremely complex and delicate. In spite of all the greenery one sees there, it is a myth that rain forest soil is rich. It is actually quite poor, leached of all nutrients save the most insoluble (such as iron oxides, which give lateritic soil—the most common soil type found there—its red color). Rather, the ecosystem of the rain forest is a "closed" one, in which the nutrients are to be found in the biomass, that is, in the living canopy of plants and in the thin layer of humus on the ground that is

---

[5] Nations and Komer, "Rainforests and the Hamburger Society," p. 17.   [6] Catherine Caufield, "The Rain Forests," *New Yorker* (January 14, 1985), p. 42. This excellent article was later incorporated in a book, *In the Rainforests* (New York: Knopf, 1985).

formed from the matter shed by the canopy. Hence the shallow-rootedness of most tropical forest plant species. Since the soil itself cannot replenish nutrients, nutrient recycling is what keeps the system going.

Now, what happens when the big cattle ranchers, under the auspices of the Swift-Armour Meat Packing Co., or United Brands, or the King Ranch sling a huge chain between two enormous tractors, level a few tens of thousands of acres of tropical forest, burn the debris, fly a plane over to seed the ash with guinea grass, and then run their cattle on the newly created grasslands?[7]   20

For the first three years or so the grass grows like crazy, up to an inch a day, thriving on all that former biomass. After that, things go quickly downhill: the ash becomes eroded and leached, the soil becomes exposed and hardens to the consistency of brick, and the area becomes useless to agriculture. Nor does it ever regain anything near its former state. The Amazon is rising perceptibly as a result of the increased runoff due to deforestation.

Tractor-and-chain is only one way of clearing the land. Another common technique involves the use of herbicides such as Tordon, 2, 4-D, and 2,4,5-T (Agent Orange). The dioxin found in Agent Orange can be extremely toxic to animal life and is very persistent in the environment.

Tordon, since it leaves a residue deadly to all broad-leaved plants, renders the deforested area poisonous to all plants except grasses; consequently, even if they wanted to, ranchers could not plant soil-enriching legumes in the treated areas, a step which many agronomists recommend for keeping the land productive for at least a little longer.

The scale of such operations is a far cry from the traditional slash-and-burn practiced by native jungle groups, which is done on a scale small enough so that the forest can successfully reclaim the farmed areas. Such groups, incidentally, are also being decimated by cattle interests in Brazil and Paraguay—as missionaries, human rights groups, and cattlemen themselves will attest.

Capital's "manifest destiny" has traditionally shown little concern for the lives of trees or birds or Indians, or anything else which interferes with immediate profitability, but the current carving of holes in the gene pool by big agribusiness seems particularly short-sighted. Since the tropical forests contain two thirds of the world's genetic resources, their destruction will leave an enormous void in pool of genes necessary for the creation of new agricultural hybrids. This is not to mention the many plants as yet undiscovered—there could be up to 15,000 unknown species in South America alone—which may in themselves contain remarkable properties. (In writing about alkaloids found in the Madagascar periwinkle which have recently revolutionized the treatment of leukemia and Hodgkin's disease, British biochemist John   25

---

[7] Other multinationals with interests in meat packing and cattle ranching in tropical Latin America include Armour-Dial International, Goodyear Tire and Rubber Co., and Gulf and Western Industries, Inc. See Roger Burbach and Patricia Flynn, *Agribusiness in the Americas* (New York: Monthly Review Press, 1980).

Humphreys said: "If this plant had not been analyzed, not even a chemist's wildest ravings would have hinted that such structures would be pharmacologically active."[8] Ninety percent of Madagascar's forests have been cut.)

But there is no small truth in Indonesian Minister for Environment and Development Emil Salim's complaint that the "South is asked to conserve genes while the other fellow, in the North, is consuming thing that force us to destroy the genes in the South."[9]

WHERE'S THE BEEF?

The marketing of beef imported into the United States is extremely complex, and the beef itself ends up in everything from hot dogs to canned soup. Fresh meat is exported in refrigerated container ships to points of entry, where it is inspected by the U.S. Department of Agriculture. Once inspected, it is no longer required to be labeled "imported."[10] From there it goes into the hands of customhouse brokers and meat packers, often changing hands many times; and from there it goes to the fast-food chains or the food processors. The financial structures behind this empire are even more complex, involving governments and quasipublic agencies, such as the Export-Import Bank and the Overseas Private Investment Corporation, as well as the World Bank and the Overseas Private Investment Corporation, as well as the World Bank and the Inter-American Development Bank, all of which encourage cattle raising in the forest lands. (Brazilian government incentives to cattle ranching in Amazonia include a 50 percent income-tax rebate on ranchers' investments elsewhere in Brazil, tax holidays of up to ten years, loans with negative interest rates in real terms, and exemptions from sales taxes and import duties. Although these incentives were deemed excessive and since 1979 no longer apply to new ranches, the still continue for existing ones. This cost the Brazilian government $63,000 for each ranching job created.)

Beef production in the tropics may be profitable for the few, but it is taking place at enormous cost for the majority and for the planet as a whole. Apart from the environmental destruction, it is a poor converter of energy to protein and provides few benefits for the vast majority of tropical peoples in terms of employment or food. What they require are labor-intensive, multiple-cropping systems.

The world is obviously hostage to an ethic which puts short-term profitability above all else, and such catastrophes as the wholesale destruction of the tropical forests and the continued impoverishment of their peoples are bound to occur as long as this ethic rules.

---

[8] Quoted in Caufield, "Rain Forests," p. 60   [9] Caufield, "Rain Forests," p. 100.   [10] This is one way McDonald's, for example, can claim not to use foreign beef. For a full treatment of McDonald's, see M. Boas and S. Chain, *Big Mac: The Unauthorized Story of McDonald's* (New York: New American Library, 1976).

Questions for Discussion and Writing

1. What connection does Skinner disclose between the destruction of tropical forests and fast food chains?
2. How do the methods used by cattle ranchers support Skinner's analysis of a business ethic that "puts short-term profitability above all else"?
3. To what extent has the situation changed, if at all, since Skinner wrote this twenty years ago?
4. **Rhetorical inquiry:** How effectively does Skinner use evidence in the form of facts, statistics, and the testimony of experts to support his thesis?

ALICE WALKER

Alice Walker was born in 1944 in Georgia and graduated from Sarah Lawrence College in 1965. She has taught at Yale, Wellesley, and other colleges and has edited and published poetry, fiction, and biography. She is best known for her novel The Color Purple *(1982), which won the American Book Award and the Pulitzer Prize for Fiction and was made into an Academy Award–winning movie in 1985. "Am I Blue?" was first published in her collection of essays* Living by the Word *(1988). Her recent works include* The Way Forward Is with a Broken Heart *(2000),* Absolute Trust in the Goodness of the Earth: New Poems *(2003),* Now Is the Time to Open Your Heart *(2004), and* We Are the Ones We Have Been Waiting For *(2006).*

Before You Read

Do you believe that animals can understand human intentions and communicate with us?

Am I Blue?

"Ain't these tears in these eyes tellin' you?"

For about three years my companion and I rented a small house in the country that stood on the edge of a large meadow that appeared to run from the end of our deck straight into the mountains. The mountains, however, were quite far away, and between us and them there was, in fact, a town. It was one of the many pleasant aspects of the house that you never really were aware of this.

It was a house of many windows, low, wide, nearly floor to ceiling in the living room, which faced the meadow, and it was from one of these that I first saw our closest neighbor, a large white horse, cropping grass, flipping its mane, and ambling about—not over the entire meadow, which stretched well out of sight of the house, but over the five or so fenced-in acres that were next to the twenty-odd that we had rented. I soon learned that the horse, whose name was Blue, belonged to a man who lived in another town, but was boarded by our neighbors next door. Occasionally, one of the children, usually a stocky teenager, but sometimes a much younger girl or boy, could be seen riding Blue. They would appear in the meadow, climb up on his back, ride furiously for ten or fifteen minutes, then get off, slap Blue on the flanks, and not be seen again for a month or more.

There were many apple trees in our yard, and one by the fence that Blue could almost reach. We were soon in the habit of feeding him apples, which he relished, especially because by the middle of summer the meadow grasses—so green and succulent since January—had dried out from lack of rain and Blue stumbled about munching the dried stalks half-heartedly. Sometimes he would stand very still just by the apple tree, and when one of us came out he would whinny, snort loudly, or stamp the ground. This meant, of course: I want an apple.

It was quite wonderful to pick a few apples, or collect those that had fallen to the ground overnight, and patiently hold them, one by one, up to his large, toothy mouth. I remained as thrilled as a child by his flexible dark lips, huge, cubelike teeth that crunched the apples core and all, with such finality, and his high, broad-breasted *enormity;* beside which, I felt small indeed. When I was a child, I used to ride horses, and was especially friendly with one named Nan until the day I was riding and my brother deliberately spooked her and I was thrown, head first, against the trunk of a tree. When I came to, I was in bed and my mother was bending worriedly over me; we silently agreed that perhaps horseback riding was not the safest sport for me. Since then I have walked, and prefer walking to horseback riding—but I had forgotten the depth of feeling one could see in horses' eyes.

I was therefore unprepared for the expression in Blue's. Blue was lonely.   5
Blue was horribly lonely and bored. I was not shocked that this should be the case; five acres to tramp by yourself, endlessly, even in the most beautiful of meadows—and his was—cannot provide many interesting events, and once rainy season turned to dry that was about it. No, I was shocked that I had forgotten that human animals and nonhuman animals can communicate quite well; if we are brought up around animals as children we take this for granted. By the time we are adults we no longer remember. However, the animals have not changed. They are in fact *completed* creations (at least they seem to be, so much more than we) who are not likely to change; it is their nature to express themselves. What else are they going to express? And they do. And, generally speaking, they are ignored.

After giving Blue the apples, I would wander back to the house, aware that he was observing me. Were more apples not forthcoming then? Was that to be his sole entertainment for the day? My partner's small son had decided he wanted to learn how to piece a quilt; we worked in silence on our respective squares as I thought . . .

Well, about slavery: about white children, who were raised by black people, who knew their first all-accepting love from black women, and then, when they were twelve or so, were told they must "forget" the deep levels of communication between themselves and "mammy" that they knew. Later they would be able to relate quite calmly, "My old mammy was sold to another good family." "My old mammy was——— ———." Fill in the blank. Many more years later a white woman would say: "I can't understand these Negroes, these blacks. What do they want? They're so different from us."

And about the Indians, considered to be "like animals" by the "settlers" (a very benign euphemism for what they actually were), who did not understand their description as a compliment.

And about the thousands of American men who marry Japanese, Korean, Filipina, and other non-English-speaking women and of how happy they report they are, "*blissfully,*" until their brides learn to speak English, at which point the marriages tend to fall apart. What then did the men see, when they looked into the eyes of the women they married, before they could speak English? Apparently only their own reflections.

I thought of society's impatience with the young. "Why are they play- ing the music so loud?" Perhaps the children have listened to much of the music of oppressed people their parents danced to before they were born, with its passionate but soft cries for acceptance and love, and they have wondered why their parents failed to hear. 10

I do not know how long Blue had inhabited his five beautiful, boring acres before we moved into our house; a year after we had arrived—and had also traveled to other valleys, other cities, other worlds—he was still there.

But then, in our second year at the house, something happened in Blue's life. One morning, looking out the window at the fog that lay like a ribbon over the meadow, I saw another horse, a brown one, at the other end of Blue's field. Blue appeared to be afraid of it, and for several days made no attempt to go near. We went away for a week. When we returned, Blue had decided to make friends and the two horses ambled or galloped along together, and Blue did not come nearly as often to the fence underneath the apple tree.

When he did, bringing his new friend with him, there was a different look in his eyes. A look of independence, of self-possession, of inalienable *horseness*. His friend eventually became pregnant. For months and months there was, it seemed to me, a mutual feeling between me and the horses of justice, of peace. I fed apples to them both. The look in Blue's eyes was one of, unabashed "this is *itness*."

It did not, however, last forever. One day, after a visit to the city, I went out to give Blue some apples. He stood waiting, or so I thought, though not beneath the tree. When I shook the tree and jumped back from the shower of apples, he made no move. I carried some over to him. He managed to half-crunch one. The rest he let fall to the ground. I dreaded looking into his eyes—because I had of course noticed that Brown, his partner, had gone—but I did look. If I had been born into slavery, and my partner had been sold or killed, my eyes would have looked like that. The children next door explained that Blue's partner had been "put with him" (the same expression that old people used, I had noticed, when speaking of an ancestor during slavery who had been impregnated by her owner) so that they could mate and she conceive. Since that was accomplished, she had been taken back by her owner, who lived somewhere else.

Will she be back? I asked.   15

They didn't know.

Blue was like a crazed person. Blue *was*, to me, a crazed person. He galloped furiously, as if he were being ridden, around and around his five beautiful acres. He whinnied until he couldn't. He tore at the ground with his hooves. He butted himself against his single shade tree. He looked always and always toward the road down which his partner had gone. And then, occasionally, when he came up for apples, or I took apples to him, he looked at me. It was a look so piercing, so full of grief, a look so *human*, I almost laughed (I felt too sad to cry) to think there are people who do not know that animals suffer. People like me who have forgotten, and daily forget, all that animals try to tell us. "Everything you do to us will happen to you; we are your teachers, as you are ours. We are one lesson" is essentially it, I think. There are those who never once have even considered animals' rights: those who have been taught that animals actually want to be used and abused by us, as small children "love" to be frightened, or women "love" to be mutilated and raped. . . . They are the great-grandchildren of those who honestly thought, because someone taught them this: "Women can't think," and "niggers can't faint." But most disturbing of all, in Blue's large brown eyes was a new look, more painful than the look of despair: the look of disgust with human beings, with life; the look of hatred. And it was odd what the look of hatred did. It gave him, for the first time, the look of a beast. And what that meant was that he had put up a barrier within to protect himself from further violence; all the apples in the world wouldn't change that fact.

And so Blue remained, a beautiful part of our landscape, very peaceful to look at from the window, white against the grass. Once a friend came to visit and said, looking out on the soothing view: "And it *would* have to be a *white*, horse; the very image of freedom." And I thought, yes, the animals are forced to become for us merely "images" of what they once so beautifully expressed. And we are used to drinking milk from containers showing "contented" cows, whose real lives we want to hear nothing about, eating eggs and drumsticks from "happy" hens, and munching hamburgers advertised by bulls of integrity who seem to command their fate.

As we talked of freedom and justice one day for all, we sat down to steaks. I am eating misery, I thought, as I took the first bite. And spit it out.

Questions for Discussion and Writing

1. How does Walker broaden the significance of Blue's reactions so as to suggest the comparable treatment of slaves, Native Americans, and non-English-speaking women and children? In your opinion, is this extension far-fetched or warranted?
2. In what way is Walker transformed by her experience with Blue? What does she learn from him?
3. Have you ever learned something from an animal that changed your perception of yourself or those around you? Explain your answer.
4. **Rhetorical inquiry:** How does the meaning of the title imbue Walker's essay with a multitude of meanings and what are some of these?

KONRAD LORENZ

Konrad Lorenz (1903–1989) was born in Vienna and is considered the co-founder (with Niko Tinbergen) of the science of ethology that studies animal behavior under natural conditions. The results of Lorenz's research appear in King Solomon's Ring: New Light on Animal Ways *(1952) from which the following selection is drawn;* Evolution and the Modification of Behavior *(1965) and* On Aggression *(1966). He was a joint recipient of the Nobel Prize for Physiology in 1973. This essay presents startling examples of aggressive instincts in doves and wolves that discredit traditional assumptions.*

Before You Read

What popular stereotypes do people have about doves or wolves?

The Dove and the Wolf

It is early one Sunday morning at the beginning of March, when Easter is already in the air, and we are taking a walk in the Vienna forest whose wooded slopes of tall beeches can be equalled in beauty by few and surpassed by none. We approach a forest glade. The tall smooth trunks of the beeches soon give place to the Hornbeam which are clothed from top to bottom with pale green foliage. We now tread slowly and more carefully. Before we break through the last bushes and out of cover on to the free expanse of the meadow, we do what all wild animals and all good naturalists, wild boars, leopards, hunters and zoologists would do under similar circumstances: we reconnoiter, seeking, before we leave our cover, to gain from it the advantage which it can offer alike to hunter and hunted, namely, to see without being seen.

Here, too, this age-old strategy proves beneficial. We do actually see someone who is not yet aware of our presence, as the wind is blowing away from him in our direction: in the middle of the clearing sits a large fat hare. He is sitting with his back to us, making a big V with his ears, and is watching intently something on the opposite edge of the meadow. From this point, a second and equally large hare emerges and with slow dignified hops, makes his way towards the first one. There follows a measured encounter, not unlike the meeting of two strange dogs. This cautious mutual taking stock soon develops into sparring. The two hares chase each other round, head to tail, in minute circles. This giddy rotating continues for quite a long time. Then suddenly, their pent-up energies burst forth into a battle royal. It is just like the outbreak of war, and happens at the very moment when the long mutual threatening of the hostile parties has forced one to the conclusion that neither dares to make a definite move. Facing each other, the hares rear up on their hind legs and, straining to their full height, drum furiously at each other with their fore pads. Now they clash in flying leaps and, at last, to the accompaniment of squeals and grunts, they discharge a volley of lightning kicks, so rapidly that only a slow motion camera could help us to discern the mechanism of these hostilities. Now, for the time being, they have had enough, and they recommence their circling, this time much faster than before; then follows a fresh, more embittered bout. So engrossed are the two champions, that there is nothing to prevent myself and my little daughter from tiptoeing nearer, although that venture cannot be accomplished in silence. Any normal and sensible hare would have heard us long ago, but this is March and March Hares are mad! The whole boxing match looks so comical that my little daughter, in spite of her iron upbringing in the matter of silence when watching animals, cannot restrain a chuckle. That is too much even for March Hares—two flashes in two different directions and the meadow is empty, while over the battlefield floats a fistful of fluff, light as a thistledown.

It is not only funny, it is almost touching, this duel of the unarmed, this raging fury of the meek in heart. But are these creatures really so meek? Have they really got softer hearts than those of the fierce beasts of prey? If, in a zoo, you ever watched two lions, wolves or eagles in conflict, then, in all probability, you did not feel like laughing. And yet, these sovereigns come off no worse than the harmless hares. Most people have the habit of judging carnivorous and herbivorous animals by quite inapplicable moral criteria. Even in fairy-tales, animals are portrayed as being a community comparable to that of mankind, as though all species of animals were beings of one and the same family, as human beings are. For this reason, the average person tends to regard the animal that kills animals in the same light as he would the man that kills his own kind. He does not judge the fox that kills a hare by the same standard as the hunter who shoots one for precisely the same reason, but with that severe censure that he would apply to the gamekeeper who made a practice of shooting farmers and frying them for supper! The "wicked" beast of prey is branded as a murderer, although the fox's hunting is quite as legitimate and a great deal more necessary to his existence than is that of the gamekeeper, yet nobody regards the latter's "bag" as his prey, and only one author, whose own standards were indicted by the severest moral criticism, has dared to dub the fox-hunter "the unspeakable in pursuit of the uneatable."! In their dealing with members of their own species, the beasts and birds of prey are far more restrained than many of the "harmless" vegetarians.

Still more harmless than a battle of hares appears the fight between turtle- or ring-doves. The gentle pecking of the frail bill, the light flick of the fragile wing seems, to the uninitiated, more like a caress than an attack. Some time ago I decided to breed a cross between the African blond ring-dove and our own indigenous somewhat frailer turtle-dove, and, with this object, I put a tame, home-reared male turtle-dove and a female ring-dove together in a roomy cage. I did not take their original scrapping seriously. How could these paragons of love and virtue dream of harming one another? I left them in their cage and went to Vienna. When I returned, the next day, a horrible sight met my eyes. The turtle-dove lay on the floor of the cage; the top of his head and neck, as also the whole length of his back, were not only plucked bare of feathers, but so frayed as to form a single wound dripping with blood. In the middle of this gory surface, like an eagle on his prey, stood the second harbinger of peace. Wearing that dreamy facial expression that so appeals to our sentimental observer, this charming lady pecked mercilessly with her silver bill in the wounds of her prostrated mate. When the latter gathered his last resources in a final effort to escape, she set on him again, struck him to the floor with a light clap of her wing and continued with her slow pitiless work of destruction. Without my interference she would undoubtedly have finished him off, in spite of the fact that she was already so tired that she could hardly keep her eyes open. Only in two other instances have I seen similar horrible lacerations inflicted on their own kind by vertebrates: once, as an observer of the embittered fights of cichlid fishes who sometimes actually skin each other, and again as a field surgeon, in the late war, where the highest of all vertebrates perpetrated mass mutilations on members of his own species. But to return to our "harmless" vegetarians. The battle of the hares which we witnessed in the forest clearing would have ended in quite as horrible a carnage as that of the doves, had it taken place in the confines of a cage where the vanquished could not flee the victor.

If this is the extent of the injuries meted out to their own kind by our gentle doves and hares, how much greater must be the havoc wrought amongst themselves by those beasts to whom nature has relegated the strongest weapons with which to kill their prey? One would certainly think so, were it not that a good naturalist should always check by observation even the most obvious-seeming inferences before he accepts them as truth. Let us examine that symbol of cruelty and voraciousness, the wolf. How do these creatures conduct themselves in their dealings with members of their

5

own species? At Whipsnade, that zoological country paradise, there lives a pack of timber wolves. From the fence of a pine-wood of enviable dimensions we can watch their daily round in an environment not so very far removed from conditions of real freedom. To begin with, we wonder why the antics of the many woolly, fatpawed whelps have not led them to destruction long ago. The efforts of one ungainly little chap to break into a gallop have landed him in a very different situation from that which he intended. He stumbles and bumps heavily into a wicked-looking old sinner. Strangely enough, the latter does not seem to notice it, he does not even growl. But now we hear the rumble of battle sounds! They are low, but more ominous than those of a dog-fight. We are watching the whelps and have therefore only become aware of this adult fight now that it is already in full swing.

An enormous old timber wolf and a rather weaker, obviously younger one are the opposing champions and they are moving in circles round each other, exhibiting admirable "footwork." At the same time, the bared fangs flash in such a rapid exchange of snaps that the eye can scarcely follow them. So far, nothing has really happened. The jaws of one wolf close on the gleaming white teeth of the other who is on the alert and wards off the attack. Only the lips have received one or two minor injuries. The younger wolf is gradually being forced backwards. It dawns upon us that the older one is purposely manouvering him towards the fence. We wait with breathless anticipation what will happen when he "goes to the wall." Now he strikes the wire netting stumbles . . . and the old one is upon him. And now the incredible happens, just the opposite of what you would expect. The furious whirling of the grey bodies has come to a sudden standstill. Shoulder to shoulder they stand, pressed against each other in a stiff and strained attitude, both heads now facing in the same direction. Both wolves are growling angrily, the elder in a deep bass, the younger in higher tones, suggestive of the fear that underlies his threat. But notice carefully the position of the two opponents; the older wolf has his muzzle close, very close against the neck of the younger, and the latter holds away his head, offering unprotected to his enemy the bend of his neck, the most vulnerable part of his whole body! Less than an inch from the tensed neck-muscles, where the jugular vein lies immediately beneath the skin, gleam the fangs of his antagonist from beneath the wickedly retracted lips. Whereas, during the thick of the fight, both wolves were intent on keeping only their teeth, the one invulnerable part of the body, in opposition to each other, it now appears that the discomfited fighter proffers intentionally that part of his anatomy to which a bite must assuredly prove fatal. Appearances are notoriously deceptive, but in his case, surprisingly, they are not!

This same scene can be watched any time wherever street-mongrels are to be found. I cited wolves as my first example because they illustrate my point more impressively than the all-too familiar domestic dog. Two adult male dogs meet in the street. Stiff-legged, with tails erect and hair on end, they pace towards each other. The nearer they approach, the stiffer, higher and more ruffled they appear, their advance becomes slower and slower. Unlike fighting cocks they do not make their encounter head to head, front against front, but make as though to pass each other, only stopping when they stand at last flank to flank, head to tail, in close juxtaposition. Then a strict ceremonial demands that each should sniff the hind regions of the other. Should one of the dogs be overcome with fear at this juncture, down goes his tail between his legs and he jumps with a quick, flexible twist, wheeling at an angle of 180 degrees thus modestly retracting his former offer to be smelt, Should the two dogs remain in an attitude of self-display, carrying their tails as rigid as standards, then the sniffing process may be of a long protracted nature. All may be solved amicably and there is still the chance that first one tail and then the other may begin to wag with small but rapidly increasing beats and then this nerve-racking situation may develop into nothing worse than a cheerful canine romp. Failing this solution the situation becomes more and more tense, noses begin to wrinkle and to turn up with a vile, brutal expression, lips begin to curl, exposing the fangs on the side nearer the opponent. Then the animals scratch the earth angrily with their hind feet, deep growls rise from their chests, and, in the next moment, they fall upon each other with loud piercing yells.

But to return to our wolves, whom we left in a situation of acute tension. This was not a piece of inartistic narrative on my part, since the strained situation may continue for a great length of time which is minutes to the observer, but very probably seems hours to the losing wolf. Every second you expect violence and await with bated breath the moment when the winner's teeth will rip the jugular vein of the loser. But your fears are groundless, for it will not happen. In this particular situation, the victor will definitely not close on his less fortunate rival. You can see that he would like to, but he just cannot! A dog or wolf that offers its neck to its adversary in this way will never be bitten seriously. The other growls and grumbles, snaps with his teeth in the empty air and even carries out, without delivering so much as a bite, the movement of shaking something to death in the empty air. However, this strange inhibition from biting persists only so long as the defeated dog or wolf maintains his attitude of humility. Since the fight is stopped so suddenly by this action, the victor frequently finds himself straddling his vanquished foe in anything but a comfortable position. So to remain, with his muzzle applied to the neck of the "under-dog" soon becomes tedious for the champion, and, seeing that he cannot bite anyway, he soon withdraws. Upon this, the under-dog may hastily attempt to put distance between himself and his superior. But he is not usually successful in this, for, as soon as he abandons his rigid attitude of submission, the other again falls upon him like a thunderbolt and the victim must again freeze into his former posture. It seems as if the victor is only waiting for the moment when the other will relinquish his submissive attitude, thereby enabling him to give vent to his urgent desire to bite. But, luckily for the "under-dog," the top-dog at the close of the fight is overcome by the pressing need to leave his trade-mark on the battlefield, to designate it as his personal property—in other words, he must lift his leg against the nearest upright object. This right-of-possession ceremony is usually taken advantage of by the under-dog to make himself scarce.

By this commonplace observation, we are here, as so often, made con-scious of a problem which is actual in our daily life and which confronts us on all sides in the most various forms. Social inhibitions of this kind are not rare, but so frequent that we take them for granted and do not stop to think about them. An old German proverb says that one crow will not peck out the eye of another and for once the proverb is right. A tame crow or raven will no more think of pecking at your eye than he will at that of one of his own kind. Often when Roah, my tame raven, was sitting on my arm, I pur-posely put my face so near to his bill that my open eye came close to its wickedly curved point. Then Roah did something positively touching. With a nervous, worried movement he withdrew his beak from my eye, just as a father who is shaving will hold back his razor blade from the inquisitive fin-gers of his tiny daughter. Only in one particular connection did Roah ever approach my eye with his bill during this facial grooming. Many of the higher, social birds and mammals, above all monkeys, will groom the skin of a fellow-member of their species in those parts of his body to which he him-self cannot obtain access. In birds, it is particularly the head and the region of the eyes which are dependent on the attentions of a fellow. In my descrip-tion of the jackdaw, I have already spoken of the gestures with which these birds invite one another to preen their head feathers. When, with half-shut eyes, I held my head sideways towards Roah, just as corvine birds do to each other, he understood this movement in spite of the fact that I have no head feathers to ruffle, and at once began to groom me. While doing so, he never pinched my skin, for the epidermis of birds is delicate and would not stand such rough treatment. With wonderful precision, he submitted every attain-able hair to a drycleaning process by drawing it separately through his bill. He worked with the same intensive concentration that distinguishes the "lousing" monkey and the operating surgeon. This is not meant as a joke: the social grooming of monkeys, and particularly of anthropoid apes has not the object of catching vermin—these animals usually have none—and is not limited to the cleaning of the skin, but serves also more remarkable operations, for instance the dexterous removal of thorns and even the squeezing-out of small carbuncles.

The manipulations of the dangerous-looking corvine beak round the   10
open eye of a man naturally appear ominous and, of course, I was always receiving warnings from on lookers at this procedure. "You never know—a raven is a raven—" and similar words of wisdom. I used to respond with the paradoxical observation that the warner was for me potentially more dan-gerous than the raven. It has often happened that people have been shot dead by madmen who have masked their condition with the cunning and

pretence typical of such cases. There was always a possibility, though admittedly a very small one, that our kind adviser might be afflicted with such a disease. But a sudden and unpredictable loss of the eye-pecking inhibition in a healthy, mature raven is more unlikely by far than an attack by a well-meaning friend.

Why has the dog the inhibition against biting his fellow's neck? Why has the raven an inhibition against pecking the eye of his friend? Why has the ring-dove no such "insurance" against murder? A really comprehensive answer to these questions is almost impossible. It would certainly involve a *historical* explanation of the process by which these inhibitions have been developed in the course of evolution. There is no doubt that they have arisen side by side with the development of the dangerous weapons of the beast of prey. However, it is perfectly obvious why these inhibitions are necessary to all weapon-bearing animals. Should the raven peck, without compunction, at the eye of his nest-mate, his wife or his young, in the same way as he pecks at any other moving and glittering object, there would, by now, be no more ravens in the world. Should a dog or wolf unrestrainedly and unaccountably bite the neck of his packmates and actually execute the movement of shaking them to death, then his species also would certainly be exterminated within a short space of time.

The ring-dove does not require such an inhibition since it can only inflict injury to a much lesser degree, while its ability to flee is so well developed that it suffices to protect the bird even against enemies equipped with vastly better weapons. Only under the unnatural conditions of close confinement which deprive the losing dove of the possibility of flight does it become apparent that the ring-dove has no inhibitions which prevent it from injuring or even torturing its own kind. Many other "harmless" herbivores prove themselves just as unscrupulous when they are kept in narrow captivity. One of the most disgusting, ruthless and blood-thirsty murderers is an animal which is generally considered as being second only to the dove in the proverbial gentleness of its nature, namely the roe-deer. The roe-buck is about the most malevolent beast I know and is possessed, into the bargain, of a weapon, its antlers, which it shows mighty little restraint in putting into use. The species can "afford" this lack of control since the fleeing capacity even of the weakest doe is enough to deliver it from the strongest buck. Only in very large paddocks can the roe-buck be kept with females of his own kind. In smaller enclosures, sooner or later he will drive his fellows, females and young ones included, into a corner and gore them to death. The only "insurance against murder" which the roe-deer possesses, is based on the fact that the onslaught of the attacking buck proceeds relatively slowly. He does not rush with lowered head at his adversary as, for example, a ram would do, but he approaches quite slowly, cautiously feeling with his antlers for those of his opponent. Only when the antlers are interlocked and the buck feels firm resistance does he thrust with deadly earnest. According to the statistics given by W. T. Hornaday, the former director of the New York

Zoo, tame deer cause yearly more serious accidents than captive lions and tigers, chiefly because an uninitiated person does not recognize the slow approach of the buck as an earnest attack, even when the animal's antlers have come dangerously near. Suddenly there follows, thrust upon thrust, the amazingly strong stabbing movement of the sharp weapon, and you will be lucky if you have time enough to get a good grip on the aggressor's antlers. Now there follows a wrestling-match in which the sweat pours and the hands drip blood, and in which even a very strong man can hardly obtain mastery over the roe-buck unless he succeeds in getting to the side of the beast and bending his neck backwards. Of course, one is ashamed to call for help—until one has the point of an antler in one's body! So take my advice and if a charming, tame roe-buck comes playfully towards you, with a characteristic prancing step and flourishing his antlers gracefully, hit him, with your walking stick, a stone or the bare fist, as hard as you can, on the side of his nose, before he can apply his antlers to your person.

And now, honestly judged: who is really a "good" animal, my friend Roah to whose social inhibitions I could trust the light of my eyes, or the gentle ring-dove that in hours of hard work nearly succeeded in torturing its mate to death? Who is a "wicked" animal, the roe-buck who will slit the bellies even of females and young of his own kind if they are unable to escape him, or the wolf who cannot bite his hated enemy if the latter appeals to his mercy?

Now let us turn our mind to another question. Wherein consists the essence of all the gestures of submission by which a bird or animal of a social species can appeal to the inhibitions of its superior? We have just seen, in the wolf, that the defeated animal actually facilitates his own destruction by offering to the victor those very parts of his body which he was most anxious to shield as long as the battle was raging. All submissive attitudes with which we are so far familiar, in social animals, are based on the same principle: The supplicant always offers to his adversary the most vulnerable part of his body, or, to be more exact, that part *against which every killing attack is inevitably directed!* In most birds, this area is the base of the skull. If one jackdaw wants to show submission to another, he squats back on his hocks, turns away his head, at the same time drawing in his bill to make the nape of his neck bulge, and, leaning towards his superior, seems to invite him to peck at the fatal spot. Seagulls and herons present to their superior the top of their head, stretching their neck forward horizontally, low over the ground, also a position which makes the supplicant particularly defenceless.

With many gallinaceous birds, the fights of the males commonly end by   15
one of the combatants being thrown to the ground, held down and then scalped as in the manner described in the ring-dove. Only one species shows mercy in this case, namely the turkey: and this one only does so in response to a specific submissive gesture which serves to forestall the intent of the attack. If a turkey-cock has had more than his share of the wild and grotesque wrestling-match in which these birds indulge, he lays himself with

outstretched neck upon the ground. Whereupon the victor behaves exactly as a wolf or dog in the same situation, that is to say, he evidently *wants* to peck and kick at the prostrated enemy, but simply cannot: he would if he could but he can't! So, still in threatening attitude, he walks around and around his prostrated rival, making tentative passes at him, but leaving him untouched.

This reaction—though certainly propitious for the turkey species—can cause a tragedy if a turkey comes to blows with a peacock, a thing which not infrequently happens in captivity, since these species are closely enough related to "appreciate" respectively their mutual manifestations of virility. In spite of greater strength and weight the turkey nearly always loses the match, for the peacock flies better and has a different fighting technique. While the red-brown American is muscling himself up for the wrestling-match, the blue East-Indian has already flown above him and struck at him with his sharply pointed spurs. The turkey justifiably considers this infringement of this fighting code as unfair and, although he is still in possession of his full strength, he throws in the sponge and lays himself down in the above depicted manner now. And a ghastly thing happens: the peacock does not "understand" this submissive gesture of the turkey, that is to say, it elicits no inhibition of his fighting drives. He pecks and kicks further at the helpless turkey, who, if nobody comes to his rescue, is doomed, for the more pecks and blows he receives, the more certainly are his escape reactions blocked by the psycho-physiological mechanism of the submissive attitude. It does not and cannot occur to him to jump up and run away.

The fact that many birds have developed special "signal organs" for eliciting this type of social inhibition, shows convincingly the blind instinctive nature and the great evolutionary age of these submissive gestures. The young of the water-rail, for example, have a bare red patch at the back of their head which, as they present it meaningly to an older and stronger fellow, takes on a deep red colour. Whether, in higher animals and man, social inhibitions of this kind are equally mechanical, need not for the moment enter into our consideration. Whatever may be the reasons that prevent the dominant individual from injuring the submissive one, whether he is prevented from doing so by a simple and purely mechanical reflex process or by a highly philosophical moral standard, is immaterial to the practical issue. The essential behaviour of the submissive as well as of the dominant partner remains the same: the humbled creature suddenly seems to lose his objections to being injured and removes all obstacles from the path of the killer, and it would seem that the very removal of these outer obstacles raises an insurmountable inner obstruction in the central nervous system of the aggressor.

And what is a human appeal for mercy after all? Is it so very different form what we have just described? The Homeric warrior who wishes to yield and plead mercy, discards helmet and shield, falls on his knees and inclines his head, a set of actions which should make it easier for the enemy to kill, but, in reality, hinders him from doing so. As Shakespeare makes Nestor say to Hector:

> "Thou hast hung thy advanced sword i' the air,
> Not letting it decline on the declined."

Even to-day, we have retained many symbols of such submissive attitudes in a number of our gestures of courtesy: bowing, removal of the hat, and presenting arms in military ceremonial. If we are to believe the ancient epics, an appeal to mercy does not seem to have raised an "inner obstruction" which was entirely insurmountable. Homer's heroes were certainly not as soft-hearted as the wolves of Whip-snade! In any case, the poet cites numerous instances where the supplicant was slaughtered with or without compunction The Norse heroic sagas bring us many examples of similar failures of the submissive gesture and it was not till the era of knight-errantry that it was no longer considered "sporting" to kill a man who begged for mercy. The Christian knight is the first who, for reasons of traditional and religious morals, is as chivalrous as is the wolf from the depth of his natural impulses and inhibitions. What a strange paradox!

Of course, the innate, instinctive, fixed inhibitions that prevent an animal   20
from using his weapons indiscriminately against his own kind are only a functional analogy, at the most a slight foreshadowing, a genealogical predecessor of the social morals of man. The worker in comparative ethology does well to be very careful in applying moral criteria to animal behaviour. But here, I must myself own to harbouring sentimental feelings: I think it a truly magnificent thing that one wolf finds himself unable to bite the proffered neck of the other, but still more so that the other relies upon him for his amazing restraint. Mankind can learn a lesson from this, from the animal that Dante calls "la bestia senza pace."[1] I at least have extracted from it a new and deeper understanding of a wonderful and often misunderstood saying from the Gospel which hitherto had only awakened in me feelings of strong opposition: "And unto him that smiteth thee on the one cheek offer also the other" (St. Luke VI, 26). A wolf has enlightened me: not so that your enemy may strike you again do you turn the other cheek toward him, but to make him unable to do it.

When, in the course of its evolution, a species of animals develops a weapon which may destroy a fellow-member at one blow, then, in order to survive, it must develop, along with the weapon, a social inhibition to prevent a usage which could endanger the existence of the species. Among the predatory animals, there are only a few which lead so solitary a life that they can, in general, forego such restraint. They come together only at the matting season when the sexual impulse outweighs all others, including that of aggression. Such unsociable hermits are the polar bear and the jaguar and, owing to the absence of these social inhibitions, animals of these species,

---

[1] The first Canto of Dante's *Inferno* represents a she-wolf, "the beast who cannot be placated."

when kept together in Zoos, hold a sorry record for murdering their own kind. The system of special inherited impulses and inhibitions, together with the weapons with which a social species is provided by nature, form a complex which is carefully computed and self-regulating. All living beings have received their weapons through the same process of evolution that moulded their impulses and inhibitions; for the structural plan of the body and the system of behavior of a species are parts of the same whole.

"If such be Nature's holy plan,
Have I not reason to lament
What man has made of man?"

Wordsworth is right: there is only one being in possession of weapons which do not grow on his body and of whose working plan, therefore, the instincts of his species know nothing and in the usage of which he has no correspondingly adequate inhibition. The being is man. With unarrested growth his weapons increase in monstrousness, multiplying horribly with in a few decades. But innate impulses and inhibitions, like bodily structures, need time for their development, time on a scale in which geologists and astronomers are accustomed to calculate, and no historians. We did not receive our weapons from nature. We made them ourselves, of our own free will. Which is going to be easier for us in the future, the production of the weapons or the engendering of the feeling of responsibility that should go along with them, the inhibitions without which our race must perish by virtue of its own creations? We must

How does this image of Konrad Z. Lorenz being followed by his geese clarify what he means by imprinting?

build up these inhibitions purposefully for we cannot rely upon our instincts. Fourteen years ago, in November 1935, I concluded an article on "Morals and Weapons of Animals" which appeared in a Viennese journal, with the words, "The day will come when two warring factions will be faced with the possibility of each wiping the other out completely. The day may come when the whole of mankind is divided into two such opposing camps. Shall we then behave like doves or like wolves? The fate of mankind will be settled by the answer to this question." We may well be apprehensive.

Questions for Discussion and Writing

1. Why are some species restrained by innate inhibitions against killing a defeated rival within their own species? In battles between timber wolves, what role do "gestures of submission" play in triggering inhibitions against their killing each other?
2. How does the episode of the "dualing hares" make the point that popular legends and folklore can often be wrong? Why are encounters between a turkey cock and a peacock so often fatal for the turkey?
3. To what extent does law, religion, and moral codes serve the same purpose as innate inhibitions in other species?
4. **Rhetorical inquiry:** How does Lorenz organize his essay to link his discussion of the behavior of domestic dogs in a context of his research on timber wolves?

ROBERT W. FELIX

Robert W. Felix is an architect and builder who studied at the University of Minnesota School of Architecture and the University of Washington. He spent eight years researching and writing Not by Fire, But by Ice, *a work that emphasizes long-term cyclic forces of nature and de-emphasizes human impact on the environment. The following chapter is drawn from the second edition of this book (2005). Felix warns of a reversal in the magnetic field of the earth that will cause underwater volcanoes to erupt, ocean temperatures to rise, and sudden 100 feet snow storms that will usher in a new ice age.*

Before You Read

Is climate change a natural event or due to human activities?

Fatal Flaw

Fat, happy, and healthy, there was no reason for the woolly mammoth to die. Moving south each time the ice advanced, then pulling back to the harsher weather it preferred each time the ice retreated, it had tiptoed through the tundra for two million years, dancing its way through at least four previous ice ages. Then, about 11,500 years ago, our most recent ice age came to an end . . . and so did the woolly mammoth. No one knows why.

Whatever the reason, it took 40 million of the world's mammals on the same one-way walk to oblivion. And, as with the dinosaur extinction of 65 million years ago, the killer zeroed in on the big boys, on species where the adults weighed at least 100 pounds.

Big was bad. Some seventy-two percent of all large animal species went extinct, whereas only 10% of small species disappeared, said David M. Raup in his 1991 book *Extinction: Bad Genes or Bad Luck?* "The preponderance of extinctions among large mammals is not likely to be due merely to chance," said Raup. "Large size really did put land mammals at a much higher risk of extinction."

Big animals were hammered; small ones merely tapped on the shoulder. (Except on islands. For some reason, small mammals and birds on oceanic islands were severely affected.) The mastodon died, the woolly rhinoceros died, so did the saber toothed cat and the toxodont. (The saber toothed "cat" was as big as today's lion, while the toxodont, built like a low-slung rhinoceros, stood five feet tall at the shoulder and measured up to nine feet long.) Did every one of those big bulky bruisers have the same fatal flaw?

Big land mammals were also extremely hard hit at the end-Eocene, said   5
paleontologist Robert Bakker, as they were some two million years ago at the end-Pliocene when about 70% of the world's larger mammals went extinct. Same at the end-Miocene, when almost two-thirds of the 62 genera that went extinct were of big body size. (Steven M. Stanley, *Extinction*, 1987)

A disease seems so unlikely, and yet, there was obviously something wrong with them. It's as if they were marked, as if the killer knew who he was after, pointing the finger of death only in certain directions. Some species totally disappeared, others skated through with little apparent harm. It's the puzzle of the ice ages.

The great dire wolf went extinct, but the timber wolf survives to this day. Why the difference? The giant long-horned bison dropped out of the running, but the American buffalo kept multiplying until upwards of 60 million of those wild oxen roamed the American west.

The short-faced bear went extinct. What saved the grizzly? (A carnivore, the short-faced bear had unusually long legs that helped it chase down its prey.)

And what saved so many other ice age animals, such as the musk ox, wolverine, moose, and arctic fox? Santa still has his reindeer, beavers still chew on trees, and the deer and the antelope still play. Who gave them permission to be so special?

Equal opportunity? Forget it. This killer attacked the bigger mammals,   10
the Paul Bunyans of their day, with a vengeance.

And it hated northerners. Animals in the north were almost decimated. It destroyed 39 genera in North America while killing "only" eight genera in Africa and all but ignoring South America and the India and Malay peninsulas. (It's that more-destruction-to-the-north thing again.)

Now, unless you know how many animals can exist in a single genus, 39 genera may not sound impressive. Take the genus *Canis* (dogs). It includes several *species,* such as the American timber wolf, coyote, European gray wolf, and domestic dog, which in turn includes several *breeds,* such as poodle, dachshund, terrier, spaniel, Pekingese, beagle, and many more. Thirty-nine genera is a whole slew of critters.

There was a North American beaver as big as a black bear. It's now gone. And the armored glyptodont, a bulky ten-foot-long armadillo, is gone too. (Picture a football helmet almost as big as a Volkswagen . . . with legs.)

Talk about big! The ice age king-of-the-jungle made today's lion look like a pussycat. But his size didn't help him one whit. His crown may have been bigger, but he still fell off the throne. And the ice age kangaroo, which stood more than one-story tall (ten feet), also disappeared.

Towering over them all, though, was the giant North American ground   15
sloth. Heavier than a pickup truck (several thousand pounds), it wandered through ancient forests on skateboard feet up to three feet long, and stood as tall as a two-story house. You'd think an animal that big could name its own ticket. No such luck.

Even the scavengers were huge. Ice age vultures cruised through the skies like small airplanes on wingspans almost 12 feet tip-to-tip. With dead mammoths strewn across the land as far the eye could see, they should have been ecstatic . . . except for one minor detail: The vultures were dead— murdered along with the mammoths.

What killed those ancient behemoths? Some try to blame humans. But there's no way we could have done it. The mammoth died everywhere, even in remote parts of the north that we couldn't possibly have known existed; areas such as Siberia, which covers millions of square miles and is sparsely populated even today.

Besides, we had no reason to hunt many of the animals that died. As far as we know they weren't dangerous. They probably didn't taste very good either.

No, don't blame humans, blame the weather. "I would argue that climatic change caused the extinction," said anthropologist Dr. Don Grayson, of the University of Washington.

If we blame humans, how can we explain all of the earlier ice-age extinc-   20
tions? The first wave of death rolled across Africa about 60,000 years ago at the peak of a glacial advance when some 40% of the world's larger mammals disappeared. Giant pigs disappeared. Giant baboons disappeared. Giraffes with antlers disappeared. So did three-toed horses. Gone. Totally gone.

And they left in a hurry. They disappeared in "a geological eye blink," said Windsor Chorlton in the 1983 book *Ice Ages.* Those giants must have had a fatal flaw. But what?

Then, about 23,000 years ago, the blood-thirsty killer returned. And again, big mammals were pushed to the brink of extinction. Some, such as the European forest elephant, fell over the edge, gone forever. (The mammoth was clobbered at that extinction too.)

And that brings us to the extinction of 11,500 years ago. With all the hoopla over dinosaurs, we've lost sight of just how big that extinction really was. "What's the big deal?" we yawn. "So what if a handful of mammoths went extinct?"

It *wasn't* a handful. Look at the numbers. We've been digging mammoth bones from the ground for thousand of years. Chinese traders began buying Siberian ivory more than 2,000 years ago, said Robert Silverberg in his book *Mammoths, Mastodons and Man*. The Arabs began buying it at least a thousand years ago.

Mammoth bones have been found all over the world, from Alaska to Czechoslovakia to Siberia to Mexico to France. The French found so many bones in one district of Dauphiné province that they called it Le Champs des Géants, "the field of the Giants."

There was so much ivory in some part of Siberia that it was considered inexhaustible as a coalfield. And it was in prime condition. Some tusks were as clean and white as modern elephant tusks, so white that "they must have come straight out of clean ice."

We still find mammoth bones, even today. An entire cache of mammoth bones was recently discovered on the remote arctic River Berelyakh, a tributary of the Indigirka. Lifted into the site by helicopter, experts from the Yakut Academy of Sciences saw thousands of bones protruding from or lying on the riverbanks, bones so densely packed that they protected the banks from erosion. (John Stewart, *Smithsonian*)

"It's nothing compared to those still buried," said Professor Nikolai Vereshchagin of the Zoological Institute in Leningrad. Heavy erosion on the Arctic coast "washes thousands of tusks and tens of thousands of bones each year into the sea."

It's impossible to know exactly how many mammoths died, but they must have numbered at least in the hundreds of thousands. "Some estimates suggest that there are 10 million mammoths still lying in the Siberian deep freeze," said Adrian Lister and Paul Bahn, in their 1994 book *Mammoths*. Some Siberian islands are made almost exclusively of mammoth bones, said one 19th-century geologist. The Lyakhov Islands seem "almost paved with their bones."

There was so much ivory on Lyakhov's islands (the Lyakhov Islands were discovered by a merchant named Lyakhov) that he mined it; so much ivory that he needed help. He hired so many miners that he ran out of places for them to live and had to build huts for them all. That's a lot of miners.

And a lot of dead mammoths.

Another enterprising guy had a different kind of mine. When Josef Crometschek of Předmostí, in the Czech Republic, stumbled across a vast deposit of mammoth bones on his farm in 1850, he began grinding them into fertilizer. He continued his venture for nearly 30 years before Czech archaeologists finally persuaded him to sell his land to a museum.

The new owners started digging. Six to ten feet down they found a layer of bones nearly three feet thick. After 30 years of indiscriminate mining, it still held the bones, they calculated, of at least a thousand mammoths. On just one farm.

Crometschek, Lyakhov, and other venturesome individuals like them uncovered mind-boggling amounts of ivory. One ivory hunter—just one, mind you—brought back 20,000 pounds in a single year. But that's nothing. In the town of Yakutsk, the chief ivory marketplace, an average of 50,000 pounds of ivory went on sale each year throughout the 19th century.

Punch that into your calculator! Fifty thousand pounds of ivory a year,   35
every year, for more than a hundred years. That's five million pounds. We're not talking five million pounds of *bones* here, we're talking five million pounds of *ivory*. Five million pounds of mammoth tusks, in just one town, in just one century, and we've been mining that ivory for at least 20 centuries. Entire *herds* of those giant beasts must have been wiped out!

Just as entire herds of dinosaurs died.

Herds of dinosaurs? Come on now. Dinosaurs didn't herd together like cattle. Did they? Or clump together like a flock of bleating sheep. Did they? Don't destroy all of my old illusions. Weren't dinosaurs supposed to be big, mean, and macho? Weren't dinosaurs supposed to be cold-blooded, lonesome bullies?

Not true. Some dinosaurs were veritable social butterflies, living together in herds so big that they make the American buffalo look like a hermit. An entire herd of dinosaurs was recently discovered by paleontologist Jack Horner. (The inspiration for *Jurassic Park's* fictional hero Alan Grant, Horner is also a professor, and curator of the Museum of the Rockies at Montana State University.)

It was a herd of adult maiasaurs. (Maiasaurs were a type of hadrosaur best known as the duck-billed dinosaur.) Found at Montana's Willow Creek anticline, the discovery was so important that Horner devoted an entire chapter in his 1988 book *Digging Dinosaurs* to "The Herd."[1]

The bones are gray-black in color and strangely battered, said Horner.   40
Shattered might be a better word. Stretching $1\frac{1}{4}$ miles east-to-west, and $\frac{1}{4}$ mile north-to-south, the bone bed contains more than 30 million fragments. There's no way to count the bones, said Horner, but by a conservative estimate it holds the bones of at least 10,000 dead dinosaurs.

No freak accident of nature could have bunched the bones together like that, said Horner, especially since the aren't in a river or streambed. In fact he doesn't know *what* they're in; some sort of mudstone, he guesses. All massacred at the same time about 80 million years ago, they're buried exactly 18 inches below a layer of bentonite (volcanic ash).

---

[1] An anticline is a wrinkle, or a fold, in the earth.

What turned the duckbills into sitting ducks? Maybe they got caught in a mud flow, one worker suggested. But why are the bones in such miserable shape? Some are broken in half, other sheared apart lengthwise. Even more mysteriously, right beside a badly damaged bone will lie a bone that hasn't been touched. How could a mud flow be so selective?

Most perplexing of all, though, are the standing bones. Some bones are standing at attention, sticking straight into the ground. It looks like a giant's game of mumbletypeg—played with dinosaur bones instead of knives.

Whoa. Floods don't leave bones standing upright, thought Horner. Floods leave bones lying flat, or jumbled together in a mishmash.

Neither do mudslides. What kind of mudslide, he asked, no matter how   45
big, could take a dead animal weighing two to three tons, two to three times more than a modern-day draft horse, and toss it around so hard that "its femur—still embedded in the flesh of its thigh—split lengthwise?"

Why are none of the bones chewed on? Ten thousand dead dinosaurs, doggy paradise, and nothing has gnawed on the bones?

Why are the bones lying east-to-west, the long dimension of the grave? And why are there no babies? Small bones are rare in the main part of the bone pit, said Horner, they're all on the easternmost edge.

Three other digging sites, up to a mile further east, also hold "little" bones from nine-foot dinosaurs. Invariably, said Horner, the bones at the edge are better preserved than those in the middle.

Invariably! You'd think any predator with a lick of sense would go for the easy pickings first. Bones of the smaller animals at the edge should be the most damaged, not the least.

The volcanic ash must be the key, thought Horner. Look at Mount   50
St. Helens. "That was a little volcano," he said. "Volcanoes like that were a dime a dozen in the Rockies back in the late Cretaceous." Much bigger volcanoes, he recalled, had erupted south of Willow Creek in the Elk Horn Mountains near Great Falls. Bigger volcanoes had erupted in the Rockies west of the site, too.

A volcanic eruption could explain why no predators had chewed on the bones; the predators had died along with their prey. Then a catastrophic flood moved the bones to their present location and buried them beneath a protective layer of mud.

Maybe. But I don't buy it. Why are small bones found mainly at the edge of the grave? Why are some bones standing upright? Why are some bones so horribly battered while ones right beside them remain untouched? A volcano wouldn't do any of those things. Neither would a flood.

But a snowstorm could. Especially if it came during a period of massive volcanic eruptions.

Horner's herd was caught in the biggest snowstorm in 14.1 million years . . . the same kind of snowstorm that will soon kill most of us.

With massive volcanic eruptions behind them, and six feet of snow per   55
hour falling on their heads, the desperate maiasaurs stampeded. Eyes

rolling, noses snorting, and lungs bellowing, the biggest, the hardiest, the meanest, tore to the front of the pack. (That's how Mother Nature works, isn't it? We call it survival of the fittest. It's really survival of the nastiest. The young ones, the weak ones, the small ones, always get left in the rear.)

But it did no good. Flailing about in frantic attempts to stay above the snow, they instead dug deeper and deeper. Still it kept coming, burying the biggest among them.

It looked as if the meek really would inherit the earth. With no one left to walk on them, the ones in the rear had avoided the onslaught. Now it was their turn to climb the gory ladder of success. God help them, though, if they fell between the rungs. Instant pulverization in the grinding mass below.

Climbing ever higher on the bodies of their fallen comrades, they tried to stay above the ever deepening snow. Still it kept coming. Four stories deep. Six stories deep. Nine. All in one day. Still they kept climbing, nine stories into the sky.

Millions of pounds of live dinosaurs, nine stories deep, biting and scratching and kicking and writhing and jumping on one another in panic would break a lot of bones, I would think, in a lot of funny ways. That's how one bone could get shattered but not the one right beside it.

Reaching the top of the pulsating pile, still panicked, still running, they continued their deadly stampede. What a mistake! They didn't know they were at the edge of a cliff; a cliff built of anguished dinosaur bodies on one side, and nine stories of soft snow on the other, ready to suck them down. 60

Off the edge of the pile they plowed. And down they went, sinking farther and farther into the snow. In front of the herd now, but on the bottom, they became living stepping stones for the next wave of their ever smaller brethren. The smaller they were, the better to crawl on the backs of their heavier kin. The lighter they were, the better to swim through the snow and away from the belching volcanoes.

Exhausted, they stopped to catch their breath and maybe to take a nap. Too bad. Freezing is a peaceful way to go, I hear. You simply drift into a hypothermic sleep . . . and never wake up.

That's why the bones of smaller animals are found at the edge of the pile. That's why the bones at the edge are in better shape than those in the middle. There was no one left to stomp on them.

Then the snow melted. And as it melted, nine stories of dead dinosaurs rotted and fell. Muscles and tendons disintegrated, and bones disarticulated themselves. Tumbling into the snowmelt, they came to rest pointing in the direction of the flow, east-to-west.

Some bones at the top, it seems logical, fell through the nine-story grid- 65
work of rib cages below. Picking up speed as they went, by the time they hit bottom they rammed straight into the mud, just as Jack Horner found them.

What a desolate sound it must have made, with no one alive left to hear it, as the last lonely bone plinked down through the pile, to stand quivering in the macabre mud.

How does this film still from Ice Age: The Meltdown *(2006) put you into the primeval world Felix describes?*

Now we know the dinosaur's fatal flaw. Now we know the mammoth's fatal flaw. They were too heavy. They couldn't climb out of the snow. *Now we know our own fatal flaw.*

Questions for Discussion and Writing

1. How did the numbers of large mammals that died and the patterns in which their bones have been unearthed suggest that researchers need to consider other explanations for their mass extinction?
2. According to Felix, why was the most recent ice age particularly lethal in eliminating large mammals such as the wooly mammoth that had survived previous ice ages?
3. What alternate explanation for this mass extinction does Felix consider and reject?
4. **Rhetorical inquiry:** How does Felix strengthen his thesis by providing a step-by-step analysis of the process by which the world's large mammals became extinct?

ELIZABETH KOLBERT

Elizabeth Kolbert has been a staff writer for the New Yorker *since 1999. Her series on global warming "The Climate of Man," which appeared in the* New Yorker, *Spring 2005, received the American Association for the Advancement of Sciences magazine writing award. This series was the basis for her book* Field Notes from a Catastrophe: Man, Nature, and Climate Change *(2006) in which the following essay first appeared. In her travels to the Arctic and interviews with researchers and environmentalists, we gain an understanding of the truly cataclysmic effects of global warming and the melting of polar ice caps.*

Before You Read

Why is global warming such a concern?

Shishmaref, Alaska

The Alaskan Village of Shishmaref sits on an island known as Sarichef, five miles off the coast of the Seward Peninsula. Sarichef is a small island—no more than a quarter of a mile across and two and a half miles long—and Shishmaref is basically the only thing on it. To the north is the Chukchi Sea, and in every other direction lies the Bering Land Bridge National Preserve, which probably ranks as one of the least visited national parks in the country. During the last ice age, the land bridge—exposed by a drop in sea levels of more than three hundred feet—grew to be nearly a thousand miles wide. The preserve occupies that part of it which, after more than ten thousand years of warmth, still remains above water.

Shishmaref (population 591) is an Inupiat village, and it has been inhabited, at least on a seasonal basis, for several centuries. As in many native villages in Alaska, life there combines—often disconcertingly—the very ancient and the totally modern. Almost everyone in Shishmaref still lives off subsistence hunting, primarily for bearded seals but also for walrus, moose, rabbits, and migrating birds. When I visited the village one day in April, the spring thaw was under way, and the seal-hunting season was about to begin. (Wandering around, I almost tripped over the remnants of the previous year's catch emerging from storage under the snow.) At noon, the village's transportation planner, Tony Weyiouanna, invited me to his house for lunch. In the living room, an enormous television set tuned to the local public-access station was playing a rock soundtrack. Messages like "Happy Birthday to the following elders . . ." kept scrolling across the screen.

Traditionally, the men in Shishmaref hunted for seals by driving out over the sea ice with dogsleds or, more recently, on snowmobiles. After they hauled the seals back to the village, the women would skin and cure them, a process that takes several weeks. In the early 1990s, the hunters began to notice that the sea ice was changing. (Although the claim that the Eskimos have hundreds of words for snow is an exaggeration, the Inupiat make distinctions among many different types of ice, including *sikuliaq,* "young ice," *sari,* "pack ice," and *tuvaq,* "land-locked ice.") The ice was starting to form later in the fall, and also to break up earlier in the spring. Once, it had been possible to drive out twenty miles; now, by the time the seals arrived, the ice was mushy half that distance from shore. Weyiouanna described it as having the consistency of a "slush puppy." When you encounter it, he said, "your hair starts sticking up. Your eyes are wide open. You can't even blink." It became too dangerous to hunt using snowmobiles, and the men switched to boats.

Soon, the changes in the sea ice brought other problems. At its highest point, Shishmaref is only twenty-two feet above sea level, and the houses, most of which were built by the U.S. government, are small, boxy, and not particularly sturdy-looking. When the Chukchi Sea froze early, the layer of ice protected the village, the way a tarp prevents a swimming pool from getting roiled by the wind. When the sea started to freeze later, Shishmaref became more vulnerable to storm surges. A storm in October 1997 scoured away a hundred-and-twenty-five-foot-wide strip from the town's northern edge; several houses were destroyed, and more than a dozen had to be relocated. During another storm, in October 2001, the village was threatened by twelve-foot waves. In the summer of 2002, residents of Shishmaref voted, a hundred and sixty-one to twenty, to move the entire village to the mainland. In 2004, the U.S. Army Corps of Engineers completed a survey of possible sites. Most of the spots that are being considered for a new village are in areas nearly as remote as Sarichef, with no roads or nearby cities or even settlements. It is estimated that a full relocation would cost the U.S. government $180 million.

People I spoke to in Shishmaref expressed divided emotions about the proposed move. Some worried that, by leaving the tiny island, they would give up their connection to the sea and become lost. "It makes me feel lonely," one woman said. Others seemed excited by the prospect of gaining certain conveniences, like running water, that Shishmaref lacks. Everyone seemed to agree, though, that the village's situation, already dire, was only going to get worse.

Morris Kiyutelluk, who is sixty-five, has lived in Shishmaref almost all his life. (His last name, he told me, means "without a wooden spoon.") I spoke to him while I was hanging around the basement of the village church, which also serves as the unofficial headquarters for a group called the Shishmaref Erosion and Relocation Coalition. "The first time I heard about global warming, I thought, I don't believe those Japanese," Kiyutelluk told me. "Well they had some good scientists, and it's become true."

The National Academy of Sciences undertook its first major study of global warming in 1979. At that point, climate modeling was still in its infancy, and only a few groups, one led by Syukuro Manabe at the National Oceanic and Atmospheric Administration and another by James Hansen at NASA's Goddard Institute for Space Studies, had considered in any detail the effects of adding carbon dioxide to the atmosphere. Still, the results of their work were alarming enough that President Jimmy Carter called on the academy to investigate. A nine-member panel was appointed. It was led by the distinguished meteorologist Jule Charney, of MIT, who, in the 1940s, had been the first meteorologist to demonstrate that numerical weather forecasting was feasible.

The Ad Hoc Study Group on Carbon Dioxide and Climate, or the Charney panel, as it became known, met for five days at the National Academy of

Sciences' summer study center, in Woods Hole, Massachusetts. Its conclusions were unequivocal. Panel members had looked for flaws in the modelers' work but had been unable to find any. "If carbon dioxide continues to increase, the study group finds no reason to doubt that climate changes will result and no reason to believe that these changes will be negligible," the scientists wrote. For a doubling of CO_2 from preindustrial levels, they put the likely global temperature rise at between two and a half and eight degrees Fahrenheit. The panel members weren't sure how long it would take for changes already set in motion to become manifest, mainly because the climate system has a built-in time delay. The effect of adding CO_2 to the atmosphere is to throw the earth out of "energy balance." In order for balance to be restored—as, according to the laws of physics, it eventually must be—the entire planet has to heat up, including the oceans, a process, the Charney panel noted, that could take "several decades." Thus, what might seem like the most conservative approach—waiting for evidence of warming to make sure the models were accurate—actually amounted to the riskiest possible strategy: "We may not be given a warning until the CO_2 loading is such that an appreciable climate change is inevitable."

It is now more than twenty-five years since the Charney panel issued its report, and, in that period, Americans have been alerted to the dangers of global warming so many times that reproducing even a small fraction of these warnings would fill several volumes; indeed, entire books have been written just on the history of efforts to draw attention to the problem. (Since the Charney report, the National Academy of Sciences alone has produced nearly two hundred more studies on the subject, including, to name just a few, "Radiative Forcing of Climate Change," "Understanding Climate Change Feedbacks," and "Policy Implications of Green-house Warming.") During this same period, worldwide carbon-dioxide emissions have continued to increase from five billion to seven billion metric tons a year, and the earth's temperature, much as predicted by Manabe's and Hansen's models, has steadily risen. The year 1990 was the warmest year on record until 1991, which was equally hot. Almost every subsequent year has been warmer still. As of this writing, 1998 ranks as the hottest year since the instrumental temperature record began, but it is closely followed by 2002 and 2003, which are tied for second; 2001, which is third; and 2004, which is fourth. Since climate is innately changeable, it's difficult to say when, exactly, in this sequence natural variation could be ruled out as the sole cause. The American Geophysical Union, one of the nation's largest and most respected scientific organizations, decided in 2003 that the matter had been settled. At the group's annual meeting that year, it issued a consensus statement declaring, "Natural influences cannot explain the rapid increase in global near-surface temperatures." As best as can be determined, the world is now warmer than it has been at any point in the last two millennia, and, if current trends continue, by the end of the century it will likely be hotter than at any point in the last two million years.

In the same way that global warming has gradually ceased to be merely a   10
theory, so, too, its impacts are no longer just hypothetical. Nearly every major
glacier in the world is shrinking; those in Glacier National Park are retreating
so quickly it has been estimated that they will vanish entirely by 2030. The
oceans are becoming not just warmer but more acidic; the difference between
daytime and nighttime temperatures is diminishing; animals are shifting their
ranges poleward; and plants are blooming days, and in some cases weeks,
earlier than they used to. These are the warning signs that the Charney panel
cautioned against waiting for, and while in many parts of the globe they are
still subtle enough to be overlooked, in others they can no longer be ignored.
As it happens, the most dramatic changes are occurring in those places, like
Shishmaref, where the fewest people tend to live. This disproportionate effect
of global warming in the far north was also predicted by early climate models,
which forecast, in column after column of FORTRAN-generated figures,
what today can be measured and observed directly: the Arctic is melting.

Most of the land in the Arctic, and nearly a quarter of all the land in the Northern Hemisphere—some five and a half billion acres—is underlaid by zones of
permafrost. A few months after I visited Shishmaref, I went back to Alaska to
take a trip through the interior of the state with Vladimir Romanovsky, a geophysicist and permafrost expert. I flew into Fairbanks—Romanovsky teaches
at the University of Alaska, which has its main campus there—and when I
arrived, the whole city was enveloped in a dense haze that looked like fog but
smelled like burning rubber. People kept telling me that I was lucky I hadn't
come a couple of weeks earlier, when it had been much worse. "Even the dogs
were wearing masks," one woman I met said. I must have smiled. "I am not
joking," she told me.

Fairbanks, Alaska's second-largest city, is surrounded on all sides by forest, and virtually every summer lightning sets off fires in these forests, which
fill the air with smoke for a few days or, in bad years, weeks. In the summer of
2004, the fires started early, in June, and were still burning two and a half
months later; by the time of my visit, in late August, a record 6.3 million
acres—an area roughly the size of New Hampshire—had been incinerated.
The severity of the fires was clearly linked to the weather, which had been
exceptionally hot and dry; the average summertime temperature in Fairbanks
was the highest on record, and the amount of rainfall was the third lowest.

On my second day in Fairbanks, Romanovsky picked me up at my hotel
for an underground tour of the city. Like most permafrost experts, he is from
Russia. (The Soviets more or less invented the study of permafrost when they
decided to build their gulags in Siberia.) A broad man with shaggy brown hair
and a square jaw, Romanovsky as a student had had to choose between playing
professional hockey and becoming a geophysicist. He had opted for the latter,
he told me, because "I was little bit better scientist than hockey player." He
went on to earn two master's degrees and two Ph.D.s. Romanovsky came to
get me at ten A.M.; owing to all the smoke, it looked like dawn.

Any piece of ground that has remained frozen for at least two years is, by definition, permafrost. In some places, like eastern Siberia, permafrost runs nearly a mile deep; in Alaska, it varies from a couple of hundred feet to a couple of thousand feet deep. Fairbanks, which is just below the Arctic Circle, is situated in a region of discontinuous permafrost, meaning that the city is pocked with regions of frozen ground. One of the first stops on Romanovsky's tour was a hole that had opened up in a patch of permafrost not far from his house. It was about six feet wide and five feet deep. Nearby were the outlines of other, even bigger holes, which, Romanovsky told me, had been filled with gravel by the local public-works department. The holes, known as thermokarsts, had appeared suddenly when the permafrost gave way, like a rotting floorboard. (The technical term for thawed permafrost is "talik," from a Russian word meaning "not frozen.") Across the road, Romanovsky pointed out a long trench running into the woods. The trench, he explained, had been formed when a wedge of underground ice had melted. The spruce trees that had been growing next to it, or perhaps on top of it, were now listing at odd angles, as if in a gale. Locally, such trees are called "drunken." A few of the spruces had fallen over. "These are very drunk," Romanovsky said.

In Alaska, the ground is riddled with ice wedges that were created during the last glaciation, when the cold earth cracked and the cracks filled with water. The wedges, which can be dozens or even hundreds of feet deep, tended to form in networks, so when they melt, they leave behind connecting diamond- or hexagon-shaped depressions. A few blocks beyond the drunken forest, we came to a house where the front yard showed clear signs of ice-wedge melt-off. The owner, trying to make the best of things, had turned the yard into a miniature-golf course. Around the corner, Romanovsky pointed out a house—no longer occupied—that basically had split in two; the main part was leaning to the right and the garage toward the left. The house had been built in the sixties or early seventies; it had survived until almost a decade ago, when the permafrost under it started to degrade. Romanovsky's mother-in-law used to own two houses on the same block. He had urged her to sell them both. He pointed out one, now under new ownership; its roof had developed an ominous-looking ripple. (When Romanovsky went to buy his own house, he looked only in permafrost-free areas.)

"Ten years ago, nobody cared about permafrost," he told me. "Now everybody wants to know." Measurements that Romanovsky and his colleagues at the University of Alaska have made around Fairbanks show that the temperature of the permafrost in many places has risen to the point where it is now less than one degree below freezing. In places where the permafrost has been disturbed, by roads or houses or lawns, much of it is already thawing. Romanovsky has also been monitoring the permafrost on the North Slope and has found that there, too, are regions where the permafrost is very nearly thirty-two degrees Fahrenheit. While thermokarsts in the roadbeds and talik under the basement are the sort of problems that really only affect the people right near—or above—them, warming permafrost is significant in ways that

How does this cartoon satirize the idea that the debate over global warming has not been resolved?

go far beyond local real estate losses. For one thing, permafrost represents a unique record of long-term temperature trends. For another, it acts, in effect, as a repository for greenhouse gases. As the climate warms, there is a good chance that these gases will be released into the atmosphere, further contributing to global warming. Although the age of permafrost is difficult to determine, Romanovsky estimates that most of it in Alaska probably dates back to the beginning of the last glacial cycle. This means that if it thaws, it will be doing so for the first time in more than a hundred and twenty thousand years. "It's really a very interesting time," Romanovsky told me.

Questions for Discussion and Writing

1. How do changes in the ice pack threaten the traditional way of life in this native community in Alaska? What is the relationship between these changes and the amount of CO_2 released into the atmosphere?
2. How does Kolbert use the trendline of yearly temperatures and changes in the permafrost to substantiate her analysis?
3. Why does Kolbert use references to a vast time scale to underscore climatic changes that are now becoming noticeable? Is Kolbert's use of on-the-spot reporting effective in drawing attention to an issue that had been previously viewed with skepticism?
4. **Rhetorical inquiry:** Why is a case history approach on the estimated $180 million cost of relocating the inhabitants of an Alaskan village necessary to personalize what otherwise would have been a review of abstract statistics?

ROBERT SAPOLSKY

Robert M. Sapolsky is a professor of biology and neurology at Stanford University whose research focuses on the effects of stress. He has received numerous awards including the prestigious MacArthur Fellowship. His latest work is Monkeyluv: And Other Essays on Our Lives as Animals *(2005). "Bugs in the Brain" first appeared in* Scientific American *(March 2003).*

Before You Read

What do you know about parasite–host relationships?

Bugs in the Brain

Like most scientists, I attend professional meetings every now and then, one of them being the annual meeting of the Society for Neuroscience, an organization of most of the earth's brain researchers. This is one of the more intellectually assaulting experiences you can imagine. About 28,000 of us science nerds jam into a single convention center. After a while, this togetherness can make you feel pretty nutty: For an entire week, go into any restaurant, elevator, or bathroom, and the folks standing next to you will be having some animated discussion about squid axons. The process of finding out about the science itself is no easier. The meeting has 14,000 lectures and posters, a completely overwhelming amount of information. Of the subset of those posters that are essential for you to check, a bunch remain inaccessible because of the enthusiastic crowds in front of them, one turns out to be in a language you don't even recognize, and another inevitably reports every experiment you planned to do for the next five years. Amid it all lurks the shared realization that despite zillions of us slaving away at the subject, we still know squat about how the brain works.

My own low point at the conference came one afternoon as I sat on the steps of the convention center, bludgeoned by information and a general sense of ignorance. My eyes focused on a stagnant, murky puddle of water by the curb, and I realized that some microscopic bug festering in there probably knew more about the brain than all of us neuroscientists combined.

My demoralized insight stemmed from a recent extraordinary paper about how certain parasites control the brain of their host. Most of us know that bacteria, protozoa, and viruses have astonishingly sophisticated ways of using animal bodies for their own purposes. They hijack our cells, our energy, and our lifestyles so they can thrive. But in many ways, the most dazzling and fiendish thing that such parasites have evolved—and the subject that occupied my musings that day—is their ability to change a host's behavior for their own ends. Some textbook examples involve ectoparasites, organisms that colonize the surface of the body. For instance, certain mites of the genus *Antennophorus* ride on the backs of ants and, by stroking an ant's mouthparts, can trigger a reflex that culminates in the ant's disgorging food for the mite to feed on. A species of pinworm of the genus *Syphacia* lays eggs on a rodent's skin, the eggs secrete a substance that causes itchiness, the rodent grooms the itchy spot with its teeth, the eggs get ingested in the process, and once inside the rodent they happily hatch.

These behavioral changes are essentially brought about by annoying a host into acting in a way beneficial to the interlopers. But some parasites actually alter the function of the nervous system itself. Sometimes they achieve this change indirectly, by manipulating hormones that affect the nervous system. There are barnacles (*Sacculina granifera*), a form of crustacean, found in Australia that attach to male sand crabs and secrete a feminizing hormone that induces maternal behavior. The zombified crabs then migrate out to sea with brooding females and make depressions in the sand ideal for dispersing larvae. The males, naturally, won't be releasing any. But the barnacles will. And if a barnacle infects a female crab, it induces the same behavior—after atrophying the female's ovaries, a practice called parasitic castration.

Bizarre as these cases are, at least the organisms stay outside the brain. Yet a few do manage to get inside. These are microscopic ones, mostly viruses rather than relatively gargantuan creatures like mites, pinworms, and barnacles. Once one of these tiny parasites is inside the brain, it remains fairly sheltered from immune attack, and it can go to work diverting neural machinery to its own advantage.

The rabies virus is one such parasite. Although the actions of this virus have been recognized for centuries, no one I know of has framed them in the neurobiological manner I'm about to. There are lots of ways rabies could have evolved to move between hosts. The virus didn't have to go anywhere near the brain. It could have devised a trick similar to the one employed by the agents that cause nose colds—namely, to irritate nasal-passage nerve endings, causing the host to sneeze and spritz viral replicates all over, say, the person sitting in front of him or her at the movies. Or the virus could have induced an insatiable desire to lick someone or some animal, thereby passing on virus shed into the saliva. Instead, as we all know, rabies can cause its host to become aggressive so the virus can jump into another host via saliva that gets into the wounds.

Just think about this. Scads of neurobiologists study the neural basis of aggression: the pathways of the brain that are involved, the relevant neurotransmitters, the interactions between genes and environment, modulation by hormones, and so on. Aggression has spawned conferences, doctoral theses, petty academic squabbles, nasty tenure disputes, the works. Yet all along, the rabies virus has "known" just which neurons to infect to make a victim rabid. And as far as I am aware, no neuroscientist has studied rabies specifically to understand the neurobiology of aggression.

Despite how impressive these viral effects are, there is still room for improvement. That is because of the parasite's nonspecificity. If you are a rabid animal, you might bite one of the few creatures that rabies does not replicate well in, such as a rabbit. So although the behavioral effects of infecting the brain are quite dazzling, if the parasite's impact is too broad, it can wind up in a dead-end host.

Which brings us to a beautifully specific case of brain control and the paper I mentioned earlier, by Manuel Berdoy and his colleagues at the University of Oxford. Berdoy and his associates study a parasite called *Toxoplasma gondii*. In a toxoplasmic utopia, life consists of a two-hose sequence involving rodents and cats. The protozoan gets ingested by a rodent, in which it forms cysts throughout the body, particularly in the brain. The rodent, gets eaten by a cat, in which the toxoplasma organism reproduces. The cat sheds the parasite in its feces, which, in one of those circles of life, is nibbled by rodents. The whole scenario hinges on specificity: Cats are the only species in which toxoplasma can sexually reproduce and be shed. Thus, toxoplasma wouldn't want its carrier rodent to get picked off by a hawk or its cat feces ingested by a dung beetle. Mind you, the parasite can infect all sorts of others species; it simply has to wind up in a cat if it wants to spread to a new host.

This potential to infect other species is the reason all those "what to do   10 during pregnancy" books recommend banning the cat and its litter box from the house and warn pregnant women against gardening if there are cats wandering about. If toxoplasma from cat feces gets into a pregnant woman, it can get into the fetus, potentially causing neurological damage. Well-informed pregnant women get skittish around cats. Toxoplasma-infected rodents, however, have the opposite reaction. The parasite's extraordinary trick has been to make rodents lose their skittishness.

All good rodents avoid cats—a behavior ethologists call a fixed action pattern, in that the rodent doesn't develop the aversion because of trial and error (since there aren't likely to be many opportunities to learn from one's errors around cats). Instead feline phobia is hard-wired. And it is accomplished through olfaction in the form of pheromones, the chemical odorant signals that animals release. Rodents instinctually shy away from the smell of a cat—even rodents that have never seen a cat in their lives, rodents that are the descendants of hundreds of generations of lab animals. Except for those infected with toxoplasma. As Berdoy and his group have shown, those rodents selectively lose their aversion to, and fear of, cat pheromones.

Now, this is not some generic case of a parasite messing with the head of the intermediate host and making it scatterbrained and vulnerable. Everything else seems pretty intact in the rodents. The social status of the animal doesn't change in its dominance hierarchy. It is still interested in mating and thus, de facto, in the pheromones of the opposite sex. The infected rodents can still distinguish other odors. They simply don't recoil from cat pheromones. This is flabbergasting. This is akin to someone getting infected with a brain parasite that has no effect whatsoever on the person's thoughts, emotions, SAT scores, or television preferences but, to complete its life cycle, generates an irresistible urge to go to the zoo, scale a fence, and try to French-kiss the pissiest-looking polar bear. A parasite-induced fatal attraction, as Berdoy's team noted in the title of its paper.

Obviously, more research is needed. I say this not only because it is obligatory at this point in any article about science, but because this finding is just so intrinsically cool that someone has to figure out how it works. And because—permit me a Stephen Jay Gould moment—it provides ever more evidence that evolution is amazing. Amazing in ways that are counterintuitive. Many of us hold the deeply entrenched idea that evolution is directional and progressive: Invertebrates are more primitive that vertebrates, mammals are the most evolved of vertebrates, primates are the genetically fanciest mammals, and so forth. Some of my best students consistently fall for that one, no matter how much I drone on in lectures. If you buy into that idea big-time, you're not just wrong, you're not all that many steps away from a philosophy that has humans directionally evolved as well, with the most evolved being northern Europeans with a taste for schnitzel and goose-stepping.

So remember, creatures are out there that can control brains. Microscopic and even larger organisms that have more power than Big Brother and, yes, even neuroscientists. My reflection on a curbside puddle brought me to the opposite conclusion that Narcissus reached in his watery reflection. We need phylogenetic humility. We are certainly not the most evolved species around, nor the least vulnerable. Nor the cleverest.

Questions for Discussion and Writing

1. What conditions must exist if the rabies virus is to be spread to a new host?
2. By what unusual means does the rabies virus achieve this goal?
3. How does the parasite–host scenario provide a model that explains the seemingly sophisticated means by which the rabies virus is promulgated?
4. **Rhetorical inquiry:** How would you characterize Sapolsky's tone toward the process he describes and why is his title effective?

Fiction

DORIS LESSING

Doris Lessing (b. 1919) was born in Iran, the daughter of an Army captain. Soon afterward, her family moved to a farm in Rhodesia (now Zimbabwe). She left Rhodesia for England when she was thirty, but Africa remained the landscape for her fiction. Her works include the widely acclaimed novel The Golden Notebook *(1962) and* African Stories *(1964), from which the following was taken. She has also written* Mara and Darin *(1999). Lessing was awarded the 2007 Nobel Prize for Literature.*

Before You Read

How does growing up involve discovering there are things you cannot control?

A Sunrise on the Veld

Every night that winter he said aloud into the dark of the pillow: Half-past four! Half-past four! till he felt his brain had gripped the words and held them fast. Then he feel asleep at once, as if a shutter had fallen; and lay with his face turned to the clock so that he could see it first thing when he woke.

It was half-past four to the minute, every morning. Triumphantly pressing down the alarm-knob of the clock, which the dark half of his mind had outwitted, remaining vigilant all night and counting the hours as he lay relaxed in sleep, he huddled down for a last warm moment under the clothes, playing with the idea of lying abed for this once only. But he played with it for the fun of knowing that it was a weakness he could defeat without effort; just as he set the alarm each night for the delight of the moment when he woke and stretched his limbs, feeling the muscles tighten, and thought: Even my brain—even that! I can control every part of myself.

Luxury of warm rested body, with the arms and legs and fingers waiting like soldiers for a word of command! Joy of knowing that the precious hours were given to sleep voluntarily!—for he had once stayed awake three nights running, to prove that he could, and then worked all day, refusing even to admit that he was tired; and now sleep seemed to him a servant to be commanded and refused.

The boy stretched his frame full-length, touching the wall at his head with his hands, and the bedfoot with his toes; then he sprung out, like a fish leaping from water. And it was cold, cold.

He always dressed rapidly, so as to try and conserve his nightwarmth till the sun rose two hours later; but by the time he had on his clothes his hands were numbed and he could scarcely hold his shoes. These he could not put on for fear of waking his parents, who never came to know how early he rose.

As soon as he stepped over the lintel, the flesh of his soles contracted on the chilled earth, and his legs began to ache with cold. It was night: the stars were glittering, the trees standing black and still. He looked for signs of day, for the greying of the edge of a stone, or a lightening in the sky where the sun would rise, but there was nothing yet. Alert as an animal he crept past

5

the dangerous window, standing poised with his hand on the sill for one proudly fastidious moment, looking in at the stuffy blackness of the room where his parents lay.

Feeling for the grass-edge of the path with his toes, he reached inside another window further along the wall, where his gun had been set in readiness the night before. The steel was icy, and numbed fingers slipped along it, so that he had to hold in the crook of his arm for safety. Then he tiptoed to the room where the dogs slept, and was fearful that they might have been tempted to go before him; but they were waiting, their haunches crouched in reluctance at the cold, but ears and swinging tail greeting the gun ecstatically. His warning undertone kept them secret and silent till the house was a hundred yards back: then they bolted off into the bush, yelping excitedly. The boy imagined his parents turning in their beds and muttering: Those dogs again! before they were dragged back in sleep; and he smiled scornfully. He always looked back over his shoulder at the house before he passed a wall of trees that shut it from sight. It looked so low and small, crouching there under a tall and brilliant sky. Then he turned his back on it, and on the frowsting sleepers, and forgot them.

He would have to hurry. Before the light grew strong he must be four miles away; and already a tint of green stood in the hollow of a leaf, and the air smelled of morning and the stars were dimming.

He slung the shoes over his shoulder, veld *skoen* that were crinkled and hard with the dews of a hundred mornings. They would be necessary when the ground became too hot to bear. Now he felt the chilled dust push up between his toes, and he let the muscles of his feet spread and settle into the shapes of the earth; and he thought: I could walk a hundred miles on feet like these! I could walk all day, and never tire!

He was walking swiftly through the dark tunnel of foliage that in day-   10
time was a road. The dogs were invisibly ranging the lower travelways of the bush, and he heard them panting. Sometimes he felt a cold muzzle on his leg before they were off again, scouting scouting for a trail to follow. They were not trained, but free-running companions of the hunt, who often tired of the long stalk before the final shots, and went off on their own pleasure. Soon he could see them, small and wild-looking in a wild strange light, now that the bush stood trembling on the verge of colour, waiting for the sun to paint earth and grass afresh.

The grass stood to his shoulders; and the trees were showering a faint silvery rain. He was soaked; his whole body was clenched in a steady shiver.

Once he bent to the road that was newly scored with animal trails, and regretfully straightened, reminding himself that the pleasure of tracking must wait till another day.

He began to run along the edge of a field, noting jerkily how it was filmed over with fresh spiderweb, so that the long reaches of great black clods seemed netted in glistening grey. He was using the steady lope he had

learned by watching the natives, the run that is a dropping of the weight of
the body from one foot to the next in a slow balancing movement that never
tires, nor shortens the breath; and he felt the blood pulsing down his legs and
along his arms, and the exultation and pride of body mounted in him till he
was shutting his teeth hard against a violent desire to shout his triumph.

Soon he had left the cultivated part of the farm. Behind him the bush
was low and black. In front was a long vlei, acres of long pale grass that sent
back a hollowing gleam of light to a satiny sky. Near him thick swathes of
grass were bent with the weight of water, and diamond drops sparkled on
each frond.

The first bird woke at his feet and at once a flock of them sprang into   15
the air calling shrilly that day had come; and suddenly, behind him, the bush
woke into song, and he could hear the guinea fowl calling far ahead of him.
That meant they would now be sailing down from their trees into thick
grass, and it was for them he had come: he was too late. But he did not
mind. He forgot he had come to shoot. He set his legs wide, and balanced
from foot to foot, and swung his gun up and down in both hands horizontally, in a kind of improvised exercise, and let his head sink back till it was
pillowed in his neck muscles, and watched how above him small rosy clouds
floated in a lake of gold.

Suddenly it all rose in him: it was unbearable. He leapt up into the air,
shouting and yelling wild, unrecognisable noises. Then he began to run, not
carefully, as he had before, but madly, like a wild thing. He was clean crazy,
yelling mad with the joy of living and a superfluity of youth. He rushed
down the vlei under a tumult of crimson and gold, while all the birds of the
world sang about him. He ran in great leaping strides, and shouted as he
ran, feeling his body rise into the crisp rushing air and fall back surely onto
sure feet; and thought briefly, not believing that such a thing could happen
to him, that he could break his ankle any moment, in this thick tangled
grass. He cleared bushes like a duiker, leapt over rocks; and finally came to a
dead stop at a place where the ground fell abruptly away below him to the
river. It had been a two-mile-long dash through waist-high growth, and he
was breathing hoarsely and could no longer sing. But he poised on a rock
and looked down at stretches of water that gleamed thought stopping trees,
and thought suddenly, I am fifteen! Fifteen! The words came new to him; so
that he kept repeating them wonderingly, with swelling excitement; and he
felt the years of his life with his hands, as if he were counting marbles, each
one hard and separate and compact, each one a wonderful shining thing.
That was what he was: fifteen years of this rich soil, and this slow-moving
water, and air that smelt like a challenge whether it was warm and sultry at
noon, or as brisk as cold water, like it was now.

There was nothing he couldn't do, nothing! A vision came to him, as he
stood there, like when a child hears the word "eternity" and tries to understand it, and time takes possession of the mind. He felt his life ahead of him
as a great and wonderful thing, something that was his; and he said aloud,

with the blood rising to his head: all the great men of the world have been as I am now, and there is nothing I can't become, nothing I can't do; there is no country in the world I cannot make part of myself, if I choose. I contain the world. I can make of it what I want. If I choose, I can change everything that is going to happen: it depends on me, and what I decide now.

The urgency, and the truth and the courage of what his voice was saying exulted him so that he began to sing again, at the top of his voice, and the sound went echoing down the river gorge. He stopped for the echo, and sang again: stopped and shouted. That was what he was!—he sang, if he chose; and the world had to answer him.

And for minutes he stood there, shouting and singing and waiting for the lovely eddying sound of the echo; so that his own new strong thoughts came back and washed round his head, as if someone were answering him and encouraging him; till the gorge was full of soft voices clashing back and forth from rock to rock over the river. And then it seemed as if there was a new voice. He listened, puzzled, for it was not his own. Soon he was leaning forward, all his nerves alert, quite still: somewhere close to him there was a noise that was no joyful bird, nor tinkle of falling water, nor ponderous movement of cattle.

There it was again. In the deep morning hush that held his future and his past, was a sound of pain, and repeated over and over: it was a kind of shortened scream, as if someone, something, had no breath to scream. He came to himself, looked about him, and called for the dogs. They did not appear: they had gone off on their own business, and he was alone. Now he was clean sober, all the madness gone. His heart beating fast, because of that frightened screaming, he stepped carefully off the rock and went towards a belt of trees. He was moving cautiously, for not so long ago he had seen a leopard in just this spot.

At the edge of the trees he stopped and peered, holding his gun ready; he advanced, looking steadily about him, his eyes narrowed. Then, all at once, in the middle of a step, he faltered, and his face was puzzled. He shook his head impatiently, as if he doubted his own sight.

There, between two trees, against a background of gaunt black rocks, was a figure from a dream, a strange beast that was horned and drunken-legged, but like something he had never even imagined. It seemed to be ragged. It looked like a small buck that had black ragged tufts of fur standing up irregularly all over it, with patches of raw flesh beneath . . . but the patches of rawness were disappearing under moving black and came again elsewhere; and all the time the creature screamed, in small gasping screams, and leaped drunkenly from side to side, as if it were blind.

Then the boy understood: it *was* a buck. He ran closer, and again stood still, stopped by a new fear. Around him the grass was whispering and alive. He looked wildly about, and then down. The ground was black with ants, great energetic ants that took no notice of him, but hurried and scurried towards the fighting shape, like glistening black water flowing through the grass.

20

And, as he drew in his breath and pity and terror seized him, the beast fell and the screaming stopped. Now he could hear nothing but one bird singing, and the sound of the rustling, whispering ants.

He peered over at the writhing blackness that jerked convulsively with the jerking nerves. It grew quieter. There were small twitches from the mass that still looked vaguely like the shape of a small animal. 25

It came into his mind that he should shoot it and end its pain; and he raised the gun. Then he lowered it again. The buck could no longer feel; its fighting was a mechanical protest of the nerves. But it was not that which made him put down the gun. It was a swelling feeling of rage and misery and protest that expressed itself in the thought: if I had not come it would have died like this: so why should I interfere? All over the bush things like this happen; they happen all the time; this is how life goes on, by living things dying in anguish. He gripped the gun between his knees and felt in his own limbs the myriad swarming pain of the twitching animal that could no longer feel, and set his teeth, and said over and over again under his breath: I can't stop it. I can't stop it. There is nothing I can do.

He was glad that the buck was unconscious and had gone past suffering so that he did not have to make a decision to kill it even when he was feeling with his whole body: this is what happens, this is how things work.

It was right—that was what he was feeling. *It was right and nothing could alter it.*

The knowledge of fatality, of what has to be, had gripped him and for the first time in his life; and he was left unable to make any movement of brain or body, except to say: "Yes, yes. That is what living is." It had entered his flesh and his bones and grown in to the furthest corners of his brain and would never leave him. And at that moment he could not have performed the smallest action of mercy, knowing as he did, having lived on it all his life, the vast unalterable, cruel veld, where at any moment one might stumble over a skull or crush the skeleton of some small creature.

Suffering, sick, and angry, but also grimly satisfied with his new sto- 30 icism, he stood there leaning on his rifle, and watched the seething black mound grow smaller. At his feet, now, were ants trickling back with pink fragments in their mouths, and there was a fresh acid smell in his nostrils. He sternly controlled the uselessly convulsing muscles of his empty stomach, and reminded himself: the ants must eat too! At the same time he found that the tears were streaming down his face, and his clothes were soaked with the sweat of that other creature's pain.

The shape had grown small. Now it looked like nothing recognisable. He did not know how long it was before he saw the blackness thin, and bits of white showed through, shining in the sun—yes, there was the sun, just up, glowing over the rocks. Why, the whole thing could not have taken longer than a few minutes.

He began to swear, as if the shortness of the time was in itself unbearable, using the words he had heard his father say. He strode forward, crushing ants with each step, and brushing them off his clothes, till he stood above the skeleton, which lay sprawled under a small bush. It was clean-picked. It might have been lying there years, save that on the white bone were pink fragments of gristle. About the bones ants were ebbing away, their pincers full of meat.

The boy looked at them, big black ugly insects. A few were standing and gazing up at him with small glittering eyes.

"Go away!" he said to the ants, very coldly. "I am not for you—not just yet, at any rate. Go away." And he fancied that the ants turned and went away.

He bent over the bones and touched the sockets in the skull; that was   35
where the eyes were, he thought incredulously, remembering the liquid dark eyes of a buck. And then he bent the slim foreleg bone, swinging it horizontally in his palm.

That morning, perhaps an hour ago, this small creature had been stepping proud and free through the brush, feeling the chill on its hide even as he himself had done, exhilarated by it. Proudly stepping the earth, tossing its horns, frisking a pretty white tail, it had sniffed the cold morning air. Walking like kings and conquerors it had moved through this free-held bush, where each blade of grass grew for it alone, and where the river ran pure sparkling water for its slaking.

And then—what had happened? Such a swift surefooted thing could surely not be trapped by a swarm of ants?

The boy bent curiously to the skeleton. Then he saw that the back leg that lay uppermost and strained out in the tension of death, was snapped midway in the thigh, so that broken bones jutted over each other uselessly. So that was it! Limping into the ant-masses it could not escape, once it had sensed the danger. Yes, but how had the leg been broken? Had it fallen, perhaps? Impossible, a buck was too light and graceful. Had some jealous rival horned it?

What could possibly have happened? Perhaps some Africans had thrown stones at it, as they do, trying to kill it for meat, and had broken its leg. Yes, that must be it.

Even as he imagined the crowd of running, shouting natives, and the fly-   40
ing stones, and the leaping buck, another picture came in to his mind. He saw himself; on any one of these bright ringing mornings, drunk with excitement, taking a snap shot at some half-seen buck. He saw himself with the gun lowered, wondering whether he had missed or not; and thinking at last that it was late, and he wanted his breakfast, and it was not worthwhile to track miles after an animal that would very likely get away from him in any case.

For a moment he would not face it. He was a small boy again, kicking sulkily at the skeleton, hanging his head, refusing to accept the responsibility.

Then he straightened up, and looked down at the bones with an odd expression of dismay, all the anger gone out of him. His mind went quite empty: all around him he could see trickles of ants disappearing into the grass. The whispering noise was faint and dry, like the rustling of a cast snakeskin.

At last he picked up his gun and walked homewards. He was telling himself half defiantly that he wanted his breakfast. He was telling himself that it was getting very hot, much too hot to be out roaming the brush.

Really, he was tired. He walked heavily, not looking where he put his feet. When he came within sight of his home he stopped, knitting his brows. There was something he had to think out. The death of that small animal was a thing that concerned him, and he was by no means finished with it. It lay at the back of his mind uncomfortably.

Soon, the very next morning, he would get clear of everybody and go to   45
the bush and think about it.

Questions for Discussion and Writing

1. How does the boy's experience that morning lead him through opposing mental perspectives and an ultimate emotional maturity?
2. How does the story subtly suggest that the boy connects his hunting with the dying animal he has come across?
3. What experiences have you had that led to similar fluctuations of euphoria and fatalism?
4. **Rhetorical inquiry:** How do the descriptions of the veld and the creatures that live there reflect the shift in the boy's mental state over the course of that morning?

Poetry

Mary Oliver

Mary Oliver (b. 1935) grew up in Cleveland, Ohio, and was educated at Ohio State University and Vassar College. She has written numerous collections of poetry, including American Primitive *(1983), for which she received the Pulitzer Prize. Most recently, she has written* Winter Hours: Poetry, Prose, and Essays *(1999),* The Leaf and the Cloud *(2000), and* Long Life: Essays and Other Writings *(2004). Oliver currently teaches at Bennington College in Vermont. The following poem is reprinted from* Twelve Moons *(1978).*

Before You Read

Have you ever fallen asleep in a wooded area or other natural environment in a way that connected you to it?

Sleeping in the Forest

I thought the earth
remembered me, she
took me back so tenderly, arranging,
her dark skirts, her pockets
full of lichens and seeds. I slept   5
as never before, a stone
on the riverbed, nothing
between me and the white fire of the stars
but my thoughts, and they floated
light as moths among the branches   10
of the perfect trees. All night
I heard the small kingdoms breathing
around me, the insects, and the birds
who do their work in the darkness. All night
I rose and fell, as if in water, grappling   15
with a luminous doom. By morning
I had vanished at least a dozen times
into something better.

Questions for Discussion and Writing

1. How does the rhythm or pulse of this poem reinforce the sense that the speaker has blended into the world of nature?
2. In what sense does the earth seem to remember her and welcome her return?
3. The experience of being spiritually at one with nature is rare. Under what circumstances, if ever, have you felt this way?
4. **Rhetorical inquiry:** How is the speaker's sense of being welcomed reinforced by the different elements—earth, air, fire, and water into which she blends?

HENRY WADSWORTH LONGFELLOW

Henry Wadsworth Longfellow (1807–1882) graduated from Bowdoin College in 1825 and mastered Spanish, French, Italian, German, and the Scandinavian languages. He became a professor of languages at Harvard in 1836. Longfellow is acknowledged as one of the great American poets; his works were so popular that he was able to live on the proceeds. Some of his best-known works are Evangeline *(1847) and* Paul Revere's Ride *(1863). The following poem presents a common experience, rendered with uncommon stylistic grace.*

Before You Read

How might the sound of waves crashing on the shore almost suggest a voice speaking to you?

The Sound of the Sea

The sea awoke at midnight from its sleep,
    And round the pebbly beaches far and wide
    I heard the first wave of the rising tide
Rush onward with uninterrupted sweep;
A voice out of the silence of the deep,   5
    A sound mysteriously multiplied
    As of a cataract from the mountain's side,
Or roar of winds upon a wooded steep.
    So comes to us at times, from the unknown
        And inaccessible solitudes of being,   10
            The rushing of the sea-tides of the soul;
And inspirations, that we deem our own,
    Are some divine foreshadowing and foreseeing
        Of things beyond our reason or control.

Questions for Discussion and Writing

1. In this vividly imagined poem, what signs are there that the speaker has made contact with a mystical or religious spirit?
2. Examine the pattern of end rhymes in this poem and the way Longfellow accentuates the meaning through varying this basic pattern. Where does he use alliteration and assonance to evoke the spirit of the ocean?
3. Try to create a poem that expresses how you feel about the ocean or any other natural phenomenon, and vary the visual appearance and indentations of the lines as Longfellow does to evoke the movement, size, shape, or defining features of what you are describing.
4. **Rhetorical inquiry:** How do the last lines lead the speaker to acknowledge that what he might have thought was his own creativity was really a connection to something far greater?

XU GANG

Xu Gang was born in 1945 in Shanghai. He began publishing poetry in 1963 and graduated from Bejing University in 1974. He has worked for China's national newspaper, The People's Daily *and has received numerous awards, including the National Prize for Poetry. His works infuse landscapes with sentiments and emotions and include* One Hundred Lyrics. *The following poem first appeared in* The Red Azalea: Chinese Poetry Since the Cultural Revolution, *edited by Edward Morin (1990).*

Before You Read

What could a beautiful flower growing on the side of a cliff that would be dangerous to climb represent?

Red Azalea on the Cliff

Red azalea, smiling
From the Cliffside at me,
You make my heart shudder with fear!
A body could smash and bones splinter in the canyon
Beauty, always looking on at disaster.   5

But red azalea on the cliff,
That you comb your twigs even in a mountain gale
Calms me down a bit.
Of course you're not willfully courting danger,
Nor are you at ease with whatever happens to you.   10
You're merely telling me: beauty is nature.

Would anyone like to pick a flower
To give to his love
Or pin to his own lapel?
On the cliff there is no road   15
And no azalea grows where there is a road.
If someone actually reached that azalea,
Then an azalea would surely bloom in his heart.

Red azalea on the cliff,
You smile like the Yellow Mountains,   20
Whose sweetness encloses slyness,
Whose intimacy embraces distance.
You remind us all of our first love.
Sometimes the past years look
Just like the azalea on the cliff.   25

Questions for Discussion and Writing

1. How does the speaker's attitude toward the red azalea change over the course of the poem? What do you think the red azalea stands for?

2. How does the imagery create a contrast between fragility and beauty and a dangerous inaccessible location to symbolize conflicting impulses within the speaker? What elements suggest that the journey rather than the goal is more important?
3. If you had to choose something in the natural environment to express specific feelings what would you choose and why?
4. **Rhetorical inquiry:** Since the azalea evokes an image of "first love" and "past years," might the speaker be attempting to repossess emotion he first felt years ago? Could this have a political as well as a personal dimension?

SHARON CHMIELARZ

Sharon Chmielarz is a prize-winning poet who has been a teacher for thirty years in Minnesota. Her works include The Other Mozart *(2001) that dramatizes moments from the life of Mozart's older sister, Nannerl, and most recently,* The Rhubarb King *(2006) in which the following poem first appeared that explores her German–Russian heritage.*

Before You Read

Have you ever discovered an easier way to do something and wondered why you had not thought of it before?

New Water

All those years—almost a hundred—
the farm had hard water.
Hard orange. Buckets lined in orange.
Sink and tub and toilet, too,
once they got running water.
And now, in less than a lifetime,
just by changing the well's location,
in the same yard, mind you,
the water's soft, clear, delicious to drink.
All those years to shake your head over.
Look how sweet life has become;
you can see it in the couple who live here,
their calmness as they sit at their table,
the beauty as they offer you new water to drink.

Questions for Discussion and Writing

1. How does "hard water" come to stand for a needlessly endured hardship that vanishes once you gain insight into the problem?
2. To what extent does the poem offer a chronicle of past events that are unknown to the present inhabitants?
3. What past hardships have past generations either in your family or your location endured to make your life easier?
4. **Rhetorical inquiry:** How does the orange color that stands for rust and mineral deposits evoke a less desirable location that can be psychological as well as physical?

Connections for Chapter 6: Our Place in Nature

1. **Charles Darwin,** *From the Origin of Species*
   In terms of "survival of the fittest," as Darwin theorizes, which species is better equipped, the rabies virus or humans? (see Sapolsky)?
2. **Gunjan Sinha,** *You Dirty Vole*
   To what extent do both Sinha and David Ewing Duncan ("DNA as Destiny") in Chapter 9 apply insights into biology as fate?
3. **Joseph K. Skinner,** *Big Mac and the Tropical Forests*
   How do Skinner and Elizabeth Kolbert alert their readers to the finite and destructible nature of natural resources?
4. **Alice Walker,** *Am I Blue?*
   How do Walker's reflections on the racial "other" connect with insights about racism in Kate Chopin's story "Désirée's Baby" (in Chapter 5)?
5. **Konrad Lorenz,** *The Dove and the Wolf*
   How do Lorenz's observations illustrate Darwin's theory of "survival of the fittest" and the different forms this takes in various species?
6. **Robert W. Felix,** *Fatal Flaw*
   How do Felix's assumptions about the causes of radical climate change differ from Elizabeth Kolbert's?
7. **Elizabeth Kolbert,** *Shishmaref, Alaska*
   Compare the role of global warming in the accounts by Kolbert and Joseph K. Skinner.
8. **Robert Sapolsky,** *Bugs in the Brain*
   How do both Sapolsky and Buddha's parable about blind men and the elephant require a change of perspective (Chapter 11)?

438   CHAPTER 6 ~ Our Place in Nature - Poetry

9. **Doris Lessing,** *A Sunrise on the Veld*
   Compare the ethic of nonintervention in this story with Darley and Latané's analysis in Chapter 11.

10. **Mary Oliver,** *Sleeping in the Forest*
    In what sense do the poems by Oliver and Sharon Chmielarz urge readers to transcend customary perspectives?

11. **Henry Wadsworth Longfellow,** *The Sound of the Sea*
    In what way's do Longfellow and Mary Oliver evoke intimations of mystical and religious forces through their reflections on the sea and the forest?

12. **Xu Gang,** *Red Azalea*
    Contrast the quest and the goal in this poem and in William Maxwell's story "The Pilgrimage" in Chapter 1.

13. **Sharon Chmielarz,** *New Water*
    How does shifting one's location bring new insights in this poem and in Walt Whitman's "When I Heard the Learn'd Astronomer" in Chapter 9?

7

PAST TO PRESENT

Those who cannot remember the past are condemned to repeat it.
George Santayana, "REASON IN COMMON SENSE"

This chapter brings to life important events and addresses the question of how the present has been shaped by the past. Herodotus offers a glimpse into the customs of ancient Egypt. Thomas Paine sets forth the principles that should be embodied in the American Revolution. Gilbert Highet analyzes the rhetorical techniques in Lincoln's Gettysburg Address to discover why it still moves audiences. In seeking to explain past events, historians examine journals, letters, newspaper accounts, photographs, and other primary documents and draw on information provided by witnesses.

This chapter includes reports of Jack London on the aftermath of the 1906 San Francisco earthquake; Hanson W. Baldwin's reconstruction of radio messages, ship's logs, and accounts of survivors of the 1912 sinking of the *Titanic;* and an interview conducted by Maurizio Chierici with the lead pilot whose plane dropped the atomic bomb on Hiroshima, Japan, in 1945. Historians of the future will study the significance of the events that took place on September 11, 2001 as investigated by Don DeLillo. Historical research also underlies the social criticism of Haunani-Kay Trask's denunciation of the colonization of modern Hawaii.

In Ambrose Bierce's story, we experience the Civil War through the eyes of unwilling participants, and in the story by Irene Zabytko we learn what it was like to lose one's humanity during the Nazi occupation of the Ukraine.

The poems challenge us to revisit past events and speculate on the future in unusual ways. Bertolt Brecht speaks for the unknown workers throughout history. Wilfred Owen reminds us of the dehumanizing effects of warfare and W. B. Yeats foresees the destruction of civilization symbolized by a nightmarish vision.

As you read works in this chapter and prepare to discuss or write about them you may wish to use the following questions as guidelines.

- What motivates the author's choice and treatment of the subject?
- Is the author's approach subjective or objective?
- What fields of study does the writer rely on to provide a context for the investigation of the subject?

- What specific problem, issue, or conflict is at the center of the author's account?
- Does the writer's tone communicate a positive or negative view of the event and its aftermath?
- Does the author examine the issue in terms of the forces that shape history?
- Does the writer imply that people change events or that events change people?
- According to the author, what ethical or moral principles should guide our behavior in a time of crisis?

Nonfiction

HERODOTUS

Herodotus (484–425 B.C.), whom Cicero called the "father of history" for his detailed account of the wars between the Greeks and the Persians (500 B.C. and 479 B.C.), was born at Halicarnassus, in Caria, a province bordering the coast of Asia Minor. In order to gather materials for his monumental work, History, *he traveled widely in Greece, Macedonia, and regions that are now Bulgaria, Turkey, Israel, Iran, and Egypt.*

In "Concerning Egypt" we can observe that the expository principle Herodotus uses is that of comparison and contrast, which is well suited for understanding the unfamiliar: Egyptian customs in relationship to the corresponding but different customs of the Greeks, the audience for whom he is writing. Herodotus always supports his observations with a wealth of concrete details. We learn about habits of diet, cooking, bathing, hairstyles, how parents are treated, shopping in the market, weaving practices, and a multitude of other customs that take the reader directly into the everyday lives of the ancient Egyptians.

Before You Read

What was there about ancient Egyptian culture that would have fascinated a Greek visitor?

Concerning Egypt

Concerning Egypt itself I shall extend my remarks to a great length, because there is no country that possesses so many wonders, nor any that has such a number of works which defy description. Not only is the climate different from that of the rest of the world, and the rivers unlike any other rivers, but the people also, in most of their manners and customs, exactly reverse the common practice of mankind. The women attend the markets and trade, while the men sit at home at the loom; and here, while the rest of the world works the woof up the warp, the Egyptians work it down; the women likewise carry burthens upon their shoulders, while the men carry them upon their heads. They eat their food out of doors in the streets, but retire for private purposes to their houses, giving as a reason that what is unseemly, but necessary, ought to be done in secret, but what has nothing unseemly about it, should be done openly. A woman cannot serve the priestly office, either for god or goddess, but men are priests to both; sons need not support their parents unless they choose, but daughters must, whether they choose or no.

In other countries the priests have long hair, in Egypt their heads are shaven; elsewhere it is customary, in mourning, for near relations to cut their hair close: the Egyptians, who wear no hair at any other time, when they lose a relative, let their beards and the hair of their heads grow long. All other men pass their lives separate from animals, the Egyptians have animals always living with them; others make barley and wheat their food; it is a disgrace to do so in Egypt, where the grain they live on is spelt, which some call *zea*. Dough they knead with their feet; but they mix mud, and even take up dirt, with their hands. They are the only people in the world—they at least, and such as have learnt the practice from them—who use circumcision. Their men wear two garments apiece, their women but one. They put on the rings and fasten the ropes to sails inside; others put them outside. When they write or calculate, instead of going, like the Greeks, from left to right, they move their hand from right to left; and they insist, notwithstanding, that it is they who go to the right, and the Greeks who go to the left. They have two quite different kinds of writing, one of which is called sacred, the other common.

They are religious to excess, far beyond any other race of men, and use the following ceremonies:—They drink out of brazen cups, which they scour every day: there is no exception to this practice. They wear linen garments, which they are specially careful to have always fresh washed. They practise circumcision for the sake of cleanliness, considering it better to be cleanly than comely. The priests shave their whole body every other day, that no lice or other impure thing may adhere to them when they are engaged in the service of the gods. Their dress is entirely of linen, and their shoes of the papyrus plant: it is not lawful for them to wear either dress or shoes of any other material. They bathe twice every day in cold water, and twice each night; besides which they observe, so to speak, thousands of ceremonies. They enjoy, however, not a few advantages. They consume none of their own property, and are at no expense for anything; but every day bread is baked for them of the sacred corn, and a plentiful supply of beef and of goose's flesh is assigned to each, and also a portion of wine made from the grape. Fish they are not allowed to eat; and beans—which none of the Egyptians ever sow, or eat, if they come up of their own accord, either raw or boiled—the priests will not even endure to look on, since they consider it an unclean kind of pulse. Instead of a single priest, each god has the attendance of a college, at the head of which is a chief priest, when one of these dies, his son is appointed in his room.

Male kine are reckoned to belong to Epaphus,[1] and are therefore tested in the following manner:—One of the priests appointed for the purpose searches to see if there is a single black hair on the whole body, since in that case the beast is unclean. He examines him all over, standing on his legs, and again laid upon his back; after which he takes the tongue out of his mouth, to see if it be clean in respect to the prescribed marks (what they are I will mention elsewhere); he also inspects the hairs of the tail, to observe if they grow naturally. If the animal is pronounced clean in all these various points, the priest marks him by twisting a piece of papyrus round his horns, and attaching thereto some sealing clay, which he then stamps with his own signet-ring. After this the beast is led away; and it is forbidden, under the penalty of death, to sacrifice an animal which has not been marked in this way.

The following is their manner of sacrifice:—They lead the victim,   5
marked with their signet, to the altar where they are about to offer it, and setting the wood alight, pour a libation of wine upon the altar in front of the victim, and at the same time invoke the god. Then they slay the animal, and cutting off his head, proceed to flay the body. Next they take the head, and heaping imprecations on it, if there is a market-place and a body of Greek traders in the city, they carry it there and sell it instantly; if, however, there are no Greeks among them, they throw the head into the river. The imprecation is to this effect:—They pray that if any evil is impending either over those who sacrifice, or over universal Egypt, it may be made to fall upon that head. These practices, the imprecations upon the heads, and the libations of wine, prevail all over Egypt, and extend to victims of all sorts; and hence the Egyptians will never eat the head of any animal.

The disembowelling and burning are, however, different in different sacrifices. I will mention the mode in use with respect to the goddess whom they regard as the greatest, and honour with the chiefest festival. When they have flayed their steer they pray, and when their prayer is ended they take the paunch of the animal out entire, leaving the intestines and the fat inside the body; they then cut off the legs, the ends of the loins, the shoulders, and

---

[1] *Epaphus:* son of Zeus by Io. In a jealous fit, the goddess Hera had changed Io into a cow, who wandered finally to Egypt, where Epaphus was born and where he became king and father of a famous line of heroes. The myth has interest in relation to the religious reverence for the cow in Egypt, sacred to the goddess Isis, as Herodotus says. A goddess perhaps older than Isis, Hathor, was represented as a cow in ancient Egyptian engravings, shown as standing over the earth and giving suck to mankind from her great udders.

the neck; and having so done, they fill the body of the steer with clean bread, honey, raisins, figs, frankincense, myrrh, and other aromatics. Thus filled, they burn the body, pouring over it great quantities of oil. Before offering the sacrifice they fast, and while the bodies of the victims are being consumed they beat themselves. Afterwards, when they have concluded this part of the ceremony, they have the other parts of the victim served up to them for a repast.

The male kine, therefore, if clean, and the male calves, are used for sacrifice by the Egyptians universally; but the females they are not allowed to sacrifice since they are sacred to Isis.[2] The statue of this goddess has the form of a woman but with horns like a cow, resembling thus the Greek representations of Io; and the Egyptians, one and all, venerate cows much more highly than any other animal. This is the reason why no native of Egypt, whether man or woman, will give a Greek a kiss, or use the knife of a Greek, or his spit, or his cauldron, or taste the flesh of an ox, known to be pure, if it has been cut with a Greek knife. When kine die, the following is the manner of their sepulture:—The females are thrown into the river; the males are buried in the suburbs of the towns, with one or both of their horns appearing above the surface of the ground to mark the place. When the bodies are decayed, a boat comes, at an appointed time, from the island called Prosôpitis—which is a portion of the Delta, nine schoenes[3] in circumference,—and calls at the several cities in turn to collect the bones of the oxen. Prosôpitis is a district containing several cities; the name of that from which the boats come is Atarbêchis. Venus has a temple there of much sanctity. Great numbers of men go forth from this city and proceed to the other towns, where they dig up the bones, which they take away with them and bury together in one place. The same practice prevails with respect to the interment of all other cattle—the law so determining; they do not slaughter any of them.

Such Egyptians as possess a temple of the Theban Jove, or live in the Thebaïc canton, offer no sheep in sacrifice, but only goats; for the Egyptians do not all worship the same gods, excepting Isis and Osiris,[4] the latter of whom they say is the Grecian Bacchus. Those, on the contrary, who possess a temple dedicated to Mendes, or belong to the Mendesian canton, abstain from offering goats, and sacrifice sheep instead. The Thebans, and such as

---

[2] *Isis:* great nature-goddess, worshiped with Osiris as his sister and wife. Hathor the cow-goddess. The worship blended into and became identified with that of Isis.   [3] *nine schoenes:* a land measurement of several miles.   [4] *Osiris:* a plant-god and fertility-god, actually a "Lord of Life" like Dionysus (Bacchus), Adonis, Atys (or Attis), Tammuz, and others. He was slain in youth by his brother Set, and the pieces of his body were scattered over the land. Isis, his sister-wife, wandered everywhere searching for him and grieving, until the fragments of his body were collected and put together. Then the god was resurrected into life. This fertility myth has many parallels originally symbolizing the cycle of winter and summer, the death of vegetation and its annual renewal. Later the myth came to symbolize the more mystical belief in human resurrection and immortality.

imitate them in their practice, give the following account of the origin of the custom:—"Hercules," they say, "wished of all things to see Jove, but Jove did not choose to be seen of him. At length, when Hercules persisted, Jove hit on a device—to flay a ram, and, cutting off his head, hold the head before him, and cover himself with fleece. In this guise he showed himself to Hercules." Therefore the Egyptians give their statues of Jupiter the face of a ram: and from them the practice has passed to the Ammonians, who are a joint colony of Egyptians and Ethiopians, speaking a language between the two; hence also, in my opinion, the latter people took their name of Ammonians, since the Egyptian name for Jupiter is Amun. Such, then, is the reason why the Thebans do not sacrifice rams, but consider them sacred animals. Upon one day in the year, however, at the festival of Jupiter, they slay a single ram, and stripping off the fleece, cover with it the statue of that god, as he once covered himself, and then bring up to the statue of Jove an image of Hercules. When this has been done, the whole assembly beat their breasts in mourning for the ram, and afterwards bury him in a holy sepulchre. . . .

The pig is regarded among them as an unclean animal, so much so that if a man in passing accidentally touches a pig, he instantly hurries to the river, and plunges in with all his clothes on. Hence, too, the swineherds, notwithstanding that they are of pure Egyptian blood, are forbidden to enter into any of the temples, which are open to all other Egyptians; and further, no one will give his daughter in marriage to a swineherd, or take a wife from among them, so that the swineherds are forced to intermarry among themselves. They do not offer swine in sacrifice to any of their gods, excepting Bacchus and the Moon,[5] whom they honour in this way at the same time, sacrificing pigs to both of them at the same full moon, and afterwards eating of the flesh. There is a reason alleged by them for their detestation of swine at all other seasons, and their use of them at this festival, with which I am well acquainted, but which I do not think it proper to mention. The following is the mode in which they sacrifice the swine to the Moon:—As soon as the victim is slain, the tip of the tail, the spleen, and the caul are put together, and having been covered with all the fat that has been found in the animal's belly, are straightway burnt. The remainder of the flesh is eaten on the same day that the sacrifice is offered, which is the day of the full moon: at any other

---

[5] *Bacchus and the Moon:* Osiris and Isis. Herodotus has previously suggested an identification between Osiris and the Greek Bacchus; and Isis was goddess of the moon as well as of the rest of nature (one of her emblems was the crescent moon). Pigs are one of the ancient animal symbols of reproductive fertility. In the custom Herodotus speaks of here, it is because of the fertility aspect of Osiris and Isis that pigs were sacrificed to them. The custom corresponds to that of the ancient Greeks, who threw slaughtered pigs into crevices of the earth as offerings to Persephone (daughter of Demeter, the corn-goddess). In Ireland, pigs carved out of bog oak are given as good-luck symbols. The normal Egyptian taboo on the eating of swine meat (except for the monthly sacrifice) was no doubt acquired by the Hebrews during their stay in Egypt, like the practice of circumcision.

time they would not so much as taste it. The poorer sort, who cannot afford live pigs, form pigs of dough, which they bake and offer in sacrifice.

To Bacchus, on the eve of his feast, every Egyptian sacrifices a hog   10 before the door of his house, which is then given back to the swineherd by whom it was furnished, and by him carried away. In other respects the festival is celebrated almost exactly as Bacchic festivals are in Greece, excepting that the Egyptians have no choral dances. They also use instead of phalli[6] another invention, consisting of images a cubit high, pulled by strings, which the women carry round to the villages.

A piper goes in front, and the women follow, singing hymns in honour of Bacchus. They give a religious reason for the peculiarities of the image.

Melampus,[7] the son of Amytheon, cannot (I think) have been ignorant of this ceremony—nay, he must, I should conceive, have been well acquainted with it. He it was who introduced into Greece the name of Bacchus, the ceremonial of his worship, and the procession of the phallus. He did not, however, so completely apprehend the whole doctrine as to be able to communicate it entirely, but various sages since his time have carried out his teaching to greater perfection. Still it is certain that Melampus introduced the phallus, and that the Greeks learnt from him the ceremonies which they now practises. I therefore maintain that Melampus, who was a wise man, and had acquired the art of divination, having become acquainted with the worship of Bacchus through knowledge derived from Egypt, introduced it into Greece, with a few slight changes, at the same time that he brought in various other practices. For I can by no means allow that it is by mere coincidence that the Bacchic ceremonies in Greece are so nearly the same as the Egyptian—they would then have been more Greek in their character, and less recent in their origin. Much less can I admit that the Egyptians borrowed these customs, or any other, from the Greeks. My belief is that Melampus got his knowledge of them from Cadmus the Tyrian, and the followers whom he brought from Phoenicia into the country which is now called Boeotia.[8]

Almost all the names of the gods came into Greece from Egypt. My inquiries prove that they were all derived from a foreign source, and my opinion is that Egypt furnished the greater number. For with the exception of Neptune and the Dioscûri, whom I mentioned above, and Juno, Vesta, Themis, the Graces, and the Nereids, the other gods have been known from time immemorial in Egypt. This I assert on the authority of the Egyptians

---

[6] *phalli:* This religious fertility symbolism is universal. In the myth of the death and the scattering of the parts of Osiris' body, the phallus was the last to be found, and without it Osiris could not come back to life. It had fallen into the Nile, on which Egyptian agriculture depends.
[7] *Melampus:* mythological seer who understood the speech of all creatures.   [8] Cadmus, legendary founder of Thebes, was said to have brought the alphabet from Tyre in Phoenicia (on the eastern Mediterranean coast) to Greece. Boeotia was the ancient name of the country north of the Gulf of Corinth, dominated by Thebes.

themselves. The gods, with whose names they profess themselves unacquainted, the Greeks received, I believe, from the Pelasgi, except Neptune. Of him they got their knowledge from the Libyans, by whom he has been always honoured, and who were anciently the only people that had a god of the name. The Egyptians differ from the Greeks also in paying no divine honours to heroes. . . .⁹

Whence the gods severally sprang, whether or no they had all existed from eternity, what forms they bore—these are questions of which the Greeks knew nothing until the other day, so to speak. For Homer and Hesiod were the first to compose Theogonies, and give the gods their epithets, to allot them their several offices and occupations, and describe their forms; and they lived but four hundred years before my time, as I believe. As for the poets who are thought by some to be earlier than these, they are, in my judgment, decidedly later writers. In these matters I have the authority of the priestesses of Dodôna for the former portion of my statements; what I have said of Homer and Hesiod is my own opinion. . . .¹⁰

The Egyptians first made it a point of religion to have no converse with women in the sacred places,¹¹ and not to enter them without washing, after such converse. Almost all other nations, except the Greeks and the Egyptians, act differently, regarding man as in this matter under no other law than the brutes. Many animals, they say, and various kinds of birds, may be seen to couple in the temples and the sacred precincts, which would certainly not happen if the gods were displeased at it. Such are the arguments by which they defend their practice, but I nevertheless can by no means approve of it. In these points the Egyptians are specially careful, as they are indeed in everything which concerns their sacred edifices.

Egypt, though it borders upon Libya, is not a region abounding in wild animals. The animals that do exist in the country, whether domesticated or otherwise, are all regarded as sacred. If I were to explain why they are consecrated to the several gods, I should be led to speak of religious matters,

---

⁹ The Dioscûri (*dios-kuroi*, god's sons) were Castor and Pollux, sons of Zeus and Leda, conceived when Zeus met Leda in the form of a swan, and brothers of Helen and Clytemnestra. They were patrons of horsemanship, boxing, and all the athletic skills of the Olympic Games. At their death they became the constellation Gemini, the Twins. Vesta was an ancient earth-goddess who became, in the Olympian pantheon, goddess of the home and hearth. Themis was another very ancient earth-goddess, a Titaness (the Titans were nature-gods who preceded the Olympians), mother of Prometheus. The oracle at Delphi spoke through her priestesses. The Pelasgi were, so far as is known, aboriginal inhabitants of Greece, whose immense rough stonework is found in various parts of Greece. The Nereids were daughters of an ancient sea-god, Nereus, who were represented as attending the later sea-god, Poseidon, riding sea horses; they are the original "mermaids."   ¹⁰ Modern scholars tend to accept Herodotus's date for Homer ("four hundred years before my time") as correct. Theogonies are genealogies of the gods. Dodôna was a famous oracle of Zeus in northwestern Greece.   ¹¹ *converse . . . places:* Ritual prostitution in temple precincts, setting a symbolic example to the earth to renew its fertility, was common in ancient Greece.

which I particularly shrink from mentioning;[12] the points whereon I have touched slightly hitherto have all been introduced from sheer necessity. Their custom with respect to animals is as follows:—For every kind there are appointed certain guardians, some male, some female, whose business it is to look after them; and this honour is made to descend from father to son. The inhabitants of the various cities, when they have made a vow to any god, pay it to his animals in the way which I will now explain. At the time of making the vow they shave the head of the child, cutting off all the hair, or else half, or sometimes a third part, which they then weigh in a balance against a sum of silver; and whatever sum the hair weighs is presented to the guardian of the animals, who thereupon cuts up some fish, and gives it to them for food—such being the stuff whereon they fed. When a man has killed one of the sacred animals, if he did it with malice prepense,[13] he is punished with death; if unwittingly, he has to pay such a fine as the priests choose to impose. When an ibis, however, or a hawk is killed, whether it was done by accident or on purpose, the man must needs die.

The number of domestic animals in Egypt is very great, and would be still greater were it not for what befalls the cats. As the females, when they have kittened, no longer seek the company of the males, these last, to obtain once more their companionship, practise a curious artifice. They seize the kittens, carry them off, and kill them, but do not eat them afterwards. Upon this the females, being deprived of their young, and longing to supply their place, seek the males once more, since they are particularly fond of their offspring. On every occasion of a fire in Egypt the strangest prodigy occurs with the cats. The inhabitants allow the fire to rage as it pleases, while they stand about at intervals and watch these animals, which, slipping by the men or else leaping over them, rush headlong into the flames. When this happens, the Egyptians are in deep affliction. If a cat dies in a private house by a natural death, all the inmates of the house shave their eyebrows; on the death of a dog they shave the head and the whole of the body.

The cats on their decease are taken to the city of Bubastis, where they are embalmed, after which they are buried in certain sacred repositories. The dogs are interred in the cities to which they belong, also in sacred burial-places. The same practice obtains with respect to the ichneumons; the hawks and shrew-mice, on the contrary, are conveyed to the city of Buto for burial, and the ibises to Hermopolis. The bears, which are scarce in Egypt, and the wolves, which are not much bigger than foxes, they bury wherever they happen to find them lying. . . .

They have also another sacred bird called the phoenix, which I myself have never seen, except in pictures. Indeed it is a great rarity, even in Egypt,

---

[12] the sacred mysteries were not to be lightly spoken of or gossiped about, even by a historian. The famous mysteries of Eleusis (a few miles from Athens) apparently had much in common with those of Isis and Osiris in Egypt.   [13] *malice prepense:* malice aforethought.

only coming there (according to the accounts of the people of Heliopolis) once in five hundred years, when the old phoenix dies. Its size and appearance, if it is like the pictures, are as follow:—The plumage is partly red, partly golden, while the general make and size are almost exactly that of the eagle. They tell a story of what this bird does, which does not seem to me to be credible: that he comes all the way from Arabia, and brings the parent bird, all plastered over with myrrh, to the temple of the Sun, and there buries the body. In order to bring him, they say, he first forms a ball of myrrh as big as he finds that he can carry; then he hollows out the ball, and puts his parent inside, after which he covers over the opening with fresh myrrh, and the ball is then of exactly the same weight as at first; so he brings it to Egypt, plastered over as I have said, and deposits it in the temple of the Sun. Such is the story they tell of the doings of this bird. . . .

With respect to the Egyptians themselves, it is to be remarked that those   20
who live in the corn country, devoting themselves, as they do, far more than any other people in the world, to the preservation of the memory of past actions, are the best skilled in history of any men that I have ever met. The following is the mode of life habitual to them:—For three successive days in each month they purge the body by means of emetics and clysters, which is done out of a regard for their health, since they have a persuasion that every disease to which men are liable is occasioned by the substances whereon they feed. Apart from any such precautions, they are, I believe, next to the Libyans, the healthiest people in the world—an effect of their climate, in my opinion, which has no sudden changes. Diseases almost always attack men when they are exposed to a change, and never more than during changes of the weather. They live on bread made of spelt, which they form into loaves called in their own tongue *cyllêstis*. Their drink is a wine which they obtain from barley, as they have no vines in their country. Many kinds of fish they eat raw, either salted or dried in the sun. Quails also, and ducks and small birds, they eat uncooked, merely first salting them. All other birds and fishes, excepting those which are set apart as sacred, are eaten either roasted or boiled.

In social meetings among the rich, when the banquet is ended, a servant carries round to the several guests a coffin, in which there is a wooden image of a corpse, carved and painted to resemble nature as nearly as possible, about a cubit or two cubits in length. As he shows it to each guest in turn, the servant says, "Gaze here, and drink and be merry; for when you die, such will you be." . . .

The Egyptian likewise discovered to which of the gods each month and day is sacred; and found out from the day of a man's birth, what he will meet with in the course of his life, and how he will end his days, and what sort of man he will be—discoveries whereof the Greeks engaged in poetry have made a use. The Egyptians have also discovered more prognostics than all the rest of mankind besides. Whenever a prodigy takes place, they watch and record the result; then, if anything similar ever happens again, they expect the same consequences. . . .

The following is the way in which they conduct their mournings and their funerals:—On the death in any house of a man of consequence, forthwith the women of the family beplaster their heads, and sometimes even their faces, with mud; and then, leaving the body indoors, sally forth and wander through the city, with their dress fastened by a band, and their bosoms bare, beating themselves as they walk. All the female relations join them and do the same. The men too, similarly begirt, beat their breasts separately. When these ceremonies are over, the body is carried away to be embalmed.

There are a set of men in Egypt who practice the art of embalming, and make it their proper business. These persons, when a body is brought to them, show the bearers various models of corpses, made in wood, and painted so as to resemble nature. The most perfect is said to be after the manner of him whom I do not think it religious to name[14] in connection with such a matter; the second sort is inferior to the first, and less costly; the third is the cheapest of all. All this the embalmers explain, and then ask in which way it is wished that the corpse should be prepared. The bearers tell them, and having concluded their bargain, take their departure, while the embalmers left to themselves, proceed to their task. The mode of embalming, according to the most perfect process, is the following:—They take first a crooked piece of iron, and with it draw out the brain through the nostrils, thus getting rid of a portion, while the skull is cleared of the rest by rinsing with drugs; next they make a cut along the flank with a sharp Ethiopian stone, and take out the whole contents of the abdomen, which they then cleanse, washing it thoroughly with palm wine, and again frequently with an infusion of pounded aromatics. After this they fill the cavity with purest bruised myrrh, with cassia, and every other sort of spicery except frankincense, and sew up the opening. Then the body is placed in natrum[15] for seventy days, and covered entirely over. After the expiration of that space of time, which must not be exceeded, the body is washed, and wrapped round, from head to foot, with bandages of fine linen cloth, smeared over with gum, which is used generally by the Egyptians in the place of glue, and in this state it is given back to the relations, who enclose it in a wooden case which they have had made for the purpose, shaped into the figure of a man. Then fastening the case, they place it in a sepulchral chamber, upright against the wall. Such is the most costly way of embalming the dead.

If persons wish to avoid expense, and choose the second process, the following is the method pursued:—Syringes are filled with oil made from the cedar-tree, which is then, without any incision or disembowelling, injected into the abdomen. The passage by which it might be likely to return is stopped, and the body laid in natrum the prescribed number of days. At the

25

---

[14] *him. . . name:* undoubtedly Osiris. Though he might feel free to name Osiris in other contexts, Herodotus speaks again here as one who was under the seal of mysteries corresponding with those of Egypt.   [15] *natrum:* sodium carbonate.

end of the time the cedar-oil is allowed to make its escape; and such is its power that it brings with it the whole stomach and intestines in a liquid state. The natrum meanwhile has dissolved the flesh, and so nothing is left of the dead body but the skin and the bones. It is returned in this condition to the relatives, without any further trouble being bestowed upon it.

The third method of embalming, which is practised in the case of the poorer classes, is to clear out the intestines with a clyster, and let the body lie in natrum the seventy days, after which it is at once given to those who come to fetch it away.

The wives of men of rank are not given to be embalmed immediately after death, nor indeed are any of the more beautiful and valued women. It is not till they have been dead three of four days that they are carried to the embalmers. This is done to prevent indignities from being offered to them. It is said that once a case of this kind occurred; the man was detected by the information of his fellow-workman. . . .

Thus far I have spoken of Egypt from my own observation, relating what I myself saw, the ideas that I formed, and the results of my own researches.

Questions for Discussion and Writing

1. What were the customs and rituals of the ancient Egyptians designed to achieve? How does the way that Herodotus collected material suggest that he was one of the world's first historians?

2. Why is the comparative method that Herodotus uses throughout his essay well suited to his subject and audience?

3. Herodotus describes customs that were strange to him. Write a page or two as if you were writing for someone who was not at all familiar with, for example, Easter egg hunts, tattooing, body piercing, shopping malls, fast food, fashion trends, beauty salons, or any other cultural or religious custom.

4. **Rhetorical inquiry:** What are some of the examples Herodotus presents that are especially revealing about the social structure of Egyptian society (for example, how were domestic animals treated?)

This wall painting is from the tomb of Anhour Khaou, the chief builder of the temple complexes at Thebes. He is seated with his wife (who wears an earring) and grandchildren and a servant who brings a tiny statue of Osiris, the god of the dead (1200–1080 B.C.). How does this tomb painting give you a glimpse into the world Herodotus saw?

Thomas Paine

Thomas Paine (1737–1809), following Benjamin Franklin's advice, left England and came to America in 1774, served in the Revolutionary Army, and supported the cause of the colonies through his influential pamphlets Common Sense *(1776) and* The Crisis *(1776–1783). He also supported the French Revolution and wrote* Rights of Man *(1792) and* The Age of Reason *(1793).* Rights of Man *was written in reply to Edmund Burke's* Reflections upon the Revolution in France. *Paine disputes Burke's doctrine that one generation can compel succeeding ones to follow a particular form of government. Paine defines the inalienable "natural" and "civil" rights of humankind and expounds on society's obligation to protect these rights.*

Before You Read

Is the ultimate purpose of government to secure for its citizens rights that they cannot secure for themselves? Why or why not?

Rights of Man

If any generation of men ever possessed the right of dictating the mode by which the world should be governed for ever, it was the first generation that existed; and if that generation did it not, no succeeding generation can show any authority for doing it, nor can set any up. The illuminating and divine principle of the equal rights of man, (for it has its origin from the Maker of man) relates, not only to the living individuals, but to generations of men succeeding each other. Every generation is equal in rights to the generations which preceded it, by the same rule that every individual is born equal in rights with his contemporary.

Every history of the creation, and every traditionary account, whether from the lettered or unlettered world, however they may vary in their opinion or belief of certain particulars, all agree in establishing one point, *the unity of man;* by which I mean, that men are all of *one degree,* and consequently that all men are born equal, and with equal natural right, in the same manner as if posterity had been continued by *creation* instead of *generation,* the latter being only the mode by which the former is carried forward; and consequently, every child born into the world must be considered as deriving its existence from God. The world is as new to him as it was to the first man that existed, and his natural right in it is of the same kind.

The Mosaic account of the creation, whether taken as divine authority, or merely historical, is full to this point, *the unity or equality of man.* The expressions admit of no controversy. "And God said, Let us make man in our own image. In the image of God created he him; male and female created he them." The distinction of sexes is pointed out, but no other distinction is even implied. If this be not divine authority, it is at least historical authority, and shows that the equality of man, so far from being a modern doctrine, is the oldest upon record.

It is also to be observed, that all the religions known in the world are founded, so far as they relate to man, on the *unity of man,* as being all of one degree. Whether in heaven or in hell, or in whatever state man may be supposed to exist hereafter, the good and the bad are the only distinctions. Nay, even the laws of governments are obliged to slide into this principle, by making degrees to consist in crimes, and not in persons.

It is one of the greatest of all truths, and of the highest advantage to cultivate. By considering man in this light, and by instructing him to consider himself in this light, it places him in a close connexion with all his duties, whether to his Creator, or to the creation, of which his is a part; and it is only when he forgets his origin, or, to use a more fashionable phrase, his *birth and family;* that he becomes dissolute. It is not among the least of the evils of the present existing governments in all parts of Europe, that man, considered as man, is thrown back to a vast distance from his Maker, and the artificial chasm filled up by a succession of barriers, or sort of turnpike gates, through which he has to pass. I will quote Mr. Burke's[1] catalogue of barriers that he has set up between man and his Maker. Putting himself in the character of a herald, he says—"We fear God—we look with *awe* to kings—with affection to parliaments—with duty to magistrates—with reverence to priests, and with respect to nobility." Mr. Burke has forgotten to put in "*chivalry.*" He has also forgotten to put in Peter.

The duty of man is not a wilderness of turnpike gates, through which he is to pass by tickets from one to the other. It is plain and simple, and consists but of two points. His duty to God, which every man must feel; and with respect to his neighbour, to do as he would be done by. If those to whom power is delegated do well, they will be respected; if not, they will be despised: and with regard to those to whom no power is delegated, but who assume it, the rational world can know nothing of them.

Hitherto we have spoken only (and that but in part) of the natural rights of man. We have now to consider the civil rights of man, and to show how the one originates from the other. Man did not enter into society to become *worse* than he was before, nor to have fewer rights than he had before, but to have those rights better secured. His natural rights are the foundation of all his civil rights. But in order to pursue this distinction with more precision, it will be necessary to mark the different qualities of natural and civil rights.

A few words will explain this. Natural rights are those which appear to man in right of his existence. Of this kind are all the intellectual rights, or

---

[1] *Edmund Burke (1729–1797):* Irish statesman, orator, and writer who sympathized with the American Revolution but opposed the French Revolution on the grounds that it was a completely unjustified break with tradition.

rights of the mind, and also all those rights of acting as an individual for his own comfort and happiness, which are not injurious to the natural rights of others.—Civil rights are those which appertain to man in right of his being a member of society. Every civil right has for its foundation, some natural right pre-existing in the individual, but to the enjoyment of which his individual power is not, in all cases, sufficiently competent. Of this kind are all those which relate to security and protection.

From this short review, it will be easy to distinguish between that class of natural rights which man retains after entering into society, and those which he throws into the common stock as a member of society.

The natural rights which he retains, are all those in which the *power* to execute is as perfect in the individual as the right itself. Among this class, as is before mentioned, are all the intellectual rights, or rights of the mind: consequently, religion is one of those rights. The natural rights which are not retained, are all those in which, though the right is perfect in the individual, the power to execute them is defective. They answer not his purpose. A man, by natural right, has a right to judge in his own cause; and so far as the right of mind is concerned; he never surrenders it: But what availeth it him to judge, if he has not power to redress? He therefore deposits this right in the common stock of society, and takes the arm of society, of which he is a part, in preference and in addition to his own. Society *grants* him nothing. Every man is a proprietor in society, and draws on the capital as a matter of right.

From these premises, two or three certain conclusions will follow.

First, That every civil right grows out of a natural right; or, in other words, is a natural right exchanged.

Secondly, that civil power, properly considered as such, is made up of the aggregate of that class of the natural rights of man, which becomes defective in the individual in point of power, and answers not his purpose; but when collected to a focus, becomes competent to the purpose of every one.

Thirdly, That the power produced from the aggregate of natural rights, imperfect in power in the individual, cannot be applied to invade the natural rights, which are retained in the individual, and in which the power to execute is as perfect as the right itself.

We have now, in a few words, traced man from a natural individual to a member of society, and shown, or endeavoured to show, the quality of the natural rights retained, and of those which are exchanged for civil rights. Let us now apply these principles to governments.

In casting our eyes over the world, it is extremely easy to distinguish the governments which have arisen out of society, or out of the social compact, from those which have not: but to place this in a clearer light than what a single glance may afford, it will be proper to take a review of the several sources from which governments have arisen, and on which they have been founded.

They may be all comprehended under three heads. First, Superstition. Secondly, Power. Thirdly, The common interest of society, and the common rights of man.

Questions for Discussion and Writing

1. What rationale supports Paine's assertion that all men and women possess certain natural rights? Where did these rights come from, and who ordained them? How does Paine make use of the biblical account of Creation as the foundation for his argument?
2. How does Paine justify the rejection of barriers thrown up by "evils of the existing governments in all parts of Europe"? How is this idea used as a rationale to justify rejecting British rule over the American colonies?
3. Reread the Declaration of Independence. What elements in this document reflect ideas and concepts also discussed by Thomas Paine?
4. **Rhetorical inquiry:** How does Paine use causal analysis to argue for the relationship between "natural" rights and corresponding "civil" rights?

GILBERT HIGHET

Gilbert Highet (1906–1978) was born in Glasgow, Scotland, and educated at the University of Glasgow and Oxford University. From 1937 to 1972 Highet was professor of Greek, Latin, and comparative literature at Columbia University. His many distinguished books include The Classical Tradition: Greek and Roman Influences on Western Literature *(1949),* The Anatomy of Satire *(1962), and* The Immortal Profession: The Joy of Teaching and Learning *(1976). He was particularly successful in bridging the gap from classicism to popular culture as an editor for the Book of the Month Club, chairman of the editorial board of* Horizon *magazine, and literary critic for* Harper's. *"The Gettysburg Address," from* A Clerk of Oxenford *(1959), shows Highet at his most illuminating in his analysis of the structure, themes, and rhetoric of Lincoln's famous speech.*

Before You Read

Consider how Lincoln's Gettysburg Address has become a model of rhetoric.

The Gettysburg Address

Fourscore and seven years ago our fathers brought forth on this continent, a new nation, conceived in Liberty, and dedicated to the proposition that all men are created equal.

Now we are engaged in a great civil war, testing whether that nation or any nation so conceived and so dedicated, can long endure. We are met on a great battle-field of that war. We have come to dedicate a portion of that field, as a final resting place for those who here gave their lives that that nation might live. It is altogether fitting and proper that we should do this.

But, in a larger sense, we can not dedicate—we can not consecrate—we can not hallow—this ground. The brave men, living and dead, who struggled here, have consecrated it, far above our poor power to add or detract. The world will little note, nor long remember, what we say here, but it can never forget what they did here. It is for us the living, rather, to be dedicated here to the unfinished work which they who fought here have thus far so nobly advanced. It is rather for us to be here dedicated to the great task remaining before us—that from these honored dead we take increased devotion to that cause for which they gave the last full measure of devotion—that we here highly resolve that these dead shall not have died in vain—that this nation, under God, shall have a new birth of freedom—and that government of the people, by the people, for the people, shall not perish from the earth.

Fourscore and seven years ago . . .

These five words stand at the entrance to the best-known monument of American prose, one of the finest utterances in the entire language and surely one of the greatest speeches in all history. Greatness is like granite: it is molded in fire, and it lasts for many centuries.

Fourscore and seven years ago. . . . It is strange to think that President Lincoln was looking back to the 4th of July 1776, and that he and his speech are now further removed from us than he himself was from George Washington and the Declaration of Independence. Fourscore and seven years before the Gettysburg Address, a small group of patriots signed the Declaration. Fourscore and seven years after the Gettysburg Address, it was the year 1950, and that date is already receding rapidly into our troubled, adventurous, and valiant past.

Inadequately prepared and at first scarcely realized in its full importance, the dedication of the graveyard at Gettysburg was one of the supreme moments of American history. The battle itself had been a turning point of the war. On the 4th of July 1863, General Meade repelled Lee's invasion of Pennsylvania. Although he did not follow up his victory, he had broken one of the most formidable aggressive enterprises of the Confederate armies. Losses were heavy on both sides. Thousands of dead were left on the field, and thousands of wounded died in the hot days following the battle. At first, their burial was more or less haphazard; but thoughtful men gradually came to feel that an adequate burying place and memorial were required. These were established by an interstate commission that autumn, and the finest speaker in the North was invited to dedicate them. This was the scholar and statesman Edward Everett of Harvard. He made a good speech—which is still extant: not at all academic, it is full of close strategic analysis and deep historical understanding.

Lincoln was not invited to speak, at first. Although people knew him as an effective debater, they were not sure whether he was capable of making a serious speech on such a solemn occasion. But one of the impressive things about Lincoln's career is that he constantly strove to *grow*. He was anxious to appear on that occasion and to say something worthy of it. (Also, it has been

5

suggested, he was anxious to remove the impression that he did not know how to behave properly—an impression which had been strengthened by a shocking story about his clowning on the battlefield of Antietam the previous year). Therefore when he was invited he took considerable care with his speech. He drafted rather more than half of it in the White House before leaving, finished it in the hotel at Gettysburg the night before the ceremony (not in the train, as sometimes reported), and wrote out a fair copy next morning.

There are many accounts of the day itself, 19 November 1863. There are many descriptions of Lincoln, all showing the same curious blend of grandeur and awkwardness, or lack of dignity, or—it would be best to call it humility. In the procession he rode horseback: a tall lean man in a high plug hat, straddling a short horse, with his feet too near the ground. He arrived before the chief speaker, and had to wait patiently for half an hour or more. His own speech came right at the end of a long and exhausting ceremony, lasted less than three minutes, and made little impression on the audience. In part this was because they were tired, in part because (as eyewitnesses said) he ended almost before they knew he had begun, and in part because he did not speak the Address, but read it, very slowly, in a thin high voice, with a marked Kentucky accent, pronouncing "to" as "toe" and dropping his final R's.

Some people of course were alert enough to be impressed. Everett congratulated him at once. But most of the newspapers paid little attention to the speech, and some sneered at it. The *Patriot and Union* of Harrisburg wrote, "We pass over the silly remarks of the President; for the credit of the nation we are willing . . . that they shall no more be repeated or thought of"; and the London *Times* said, "The ceremony was rendered ludicrous by some of the sallies of that poor President Lincoln," calling his remarks "dull and commonplace." The first commendation of the Address came in a single sentence of the Chicago *Tribune*, and the first discriminating and detailed praise of it appeared in the Springfield *Republican*, the Providence *Journal*, and the Philadelphia *Bulletin*. However, three weeks after the ceremony and then again the following spring, the editor of *Harper's Weekly* published a sincere and thorough eulogy of the Address, and soon it was attaining recognition as a masterpiece.

> At the time, Lincoln could not care much about the reception of his words. He was exhausted and ill. In the train back to Washington, he lay down with a wet towel on his head. He had caught smallpox. At that moment he was incubating it, and he was stricken down soon after he reentered the White House. Fortunately it was a mild attack, and it evoked one of his best jokes: he told his visitors, "At last I have something I can give to everybody."

He had more than that to give to everybody. He was a unique person, far greater than most people realize until they read his life with care. The wisdom of his policy, the sources of his statesmanship—these were things too complex to be discussed in a brief essay. But we can say something about the Gettysburg Address as a work of art.

A work of art. Yes: for Lincoln was a literary artist, trained both by others and by himself. The textbooks he used as a boy were full of difficult exercises and skillful devices in formal rhetoric, stressing the qualities he practiced in his own speaking: antithesis, parallelism, and verbal harmony. Then he read and reread many admirable models of thought and expression: the King James Bible, the essays of Bacon, the best plays of Shakespeare. His favorites were *Hamlet, Lear, Macbeth, Richard III,* and *Henry VIII,* which he had read dozens of times. He loved reading aloud, too, and spent hours reading poetry to his friends. (He told his partner Herndon that he preferred getting the sense of any document by reading it aloud.) Therefore his serious speeches are important parts of the long and noble classical tradition of oratory which begins in Greece, runs through Rome to the modern world, and is still capable (if we do not neglect it) of producing masterpieces.

The first proof of this is that the Gettysburg Address is full of quotations— or rather of adaptations—which give it strength. It is partly religious, partly (in the highest sense) political: therefore it is interwoven with memories of the Bible and memories of American history. The first and the last words are Biblical cadences. Normally Lincoln did not say "fourscore" when he meant eighty but on this solemn occasion he recalled the important dates in the Bible—such as the age of Abram when his first son was born to him, and he was "fourscore and six years old."[1] Similarly he did not say there was a chance that democracy might die out: he recalled the somber phrasing of the Book of Job—where Bildad speaks of the destruction of one who shall vanish without a trace, and says that "his branch shall be cut off; his remembrance shall perish from the earth."[2] Then again, the famous description of our State as "government of the people, by the people, for the people" was adumbrated by Daniel Webster in 1830 (he spoke of "the people's government, made for the people, made by the people, and answerable to the people") and then elaborated in 1854 by the abolitionist Theodore Parker (as "government of all the people, by all the people, for all the people"). There is good reason to think that Lincoln took the important phrase "under God" (which he interpolated at the last moment) from Weems, the biographer of Washington; and we know that it had been used at least once by Washington himself.

Analyzing the Address further, we find that it is based on a highly imaginative theme, or group of themes. The subject is—how can we put it so as not to disfigure it?—the subject is the kinship of life and death, that mysterious linkage which we see sometimes as the physical succession of birth and death in our world, sometimes as the contrast, which is perhaps a unity, between death and immortality. The first sentence is concerned with birth:

Our *fathers brought forth a new* nation, *conceived* in liberty.

10

---

[1] *"fourscore and six years old":* Genesis 16.16.　　[2] *"his branch . . . earth":* Job 18.16–17.

The final phrase but one expresses the hope that

> this nation, under God, shall have a *new birth* of freedom.

And the last phrase of all speaks of continuing life as the triumph over death. Again and again throughout the speech, this mystical contrast and kinship reappear: "those who *gave their lives* that that nation might *live*," "the brave men *living* and *dead*," and so in the central assertion that the dead have already consecrated their own burial place, while "it is for us, the *living*, rather to be dedicated . . . to the great task remaining." The Gettysburg Address is a prose poem; it belongs to the same world as the great elegies, and the adagios of Beethoven. Its structure, however, is that of a skillfully contrived speech. The oratorical pattern is perfectly clear. Lincoln describes the occasion, dedicates the ground, and then draws a larger conclusion by calling on his hearers to dedicate themselves to the preservation of the Union. But within that, we can trace his constant use of at least two important rhetorical devices.

The first of these is *antithesis*: opposition, contrast. The speech is full of it. Listen:

> The world will little *note*
> nor long *remember*   what *we say* here
> but   it can never *forget*   what *they did* here.

And so in nearly every sentence: "brave men, *living* and *dead*"; "to *add* or *detract*." There is the antithesis of the Founding Fathers and the men of Lincoln's own time:

> Our *fathers brought forth* a new nation . . .
> now *we* are testing whether that nation . . . can *long endure*.

And there is the more terrible antithesis of those who have already died and those who still live to do their duty. Now, antithesis is the figure of contrast and conflict. Lincoln was speaking in the midst of a great civil war.

The other important pattern is different. It is technically called *tricolon*—the division of an idea into three harmonious parts, usually of increasing power. The most famous phrase of the Address is a tricolon:

> government of the people
> by the people
> and   for the people

The most solemn sentence is a tricolon:

> we cannot dedicate
> we cannot consecrate
> we cannot hallow this ground.

THE FAR SIDE®   By GARY LARSON

What does this 1984 Gary Larson cartoon say about our expectations regarding politicians' oratory?

And above all, the last sentence (which has sometimes been criticized as too complex) is essentially two parallel phrases, with a tricolon growing out of the second and then producing another tricolon: a trunk, three branches, and a cluster of flowers. Lincoln says that it is for his hearers to be dedicated to the great task remaining before them. Then he goes on,

that from these honored dead

—apparently he means "in such a way that from these honored dead"—

we take increased devotion to that cause.

Next, he restates this more briefly:

> that we here highly resolve . . .

And now the actual resolution follows, in three parts of growing intensity:

> that these dead shall not have died in vain
> that this nation, under God, shall have a new birth of freedom

and that (one more tricolon)

> government of the people
>   by the people
>   and   for the people
> shall not perish from the earth.

Now, the tricolon is the figure which, through division, emphasizes basic harmony and unity. Lincoln used antithesis because he was speaking to a people at war. He used the tricolon because he was hoping, planning, praying for peace.

No one thinks that when he was drafting the Gettysburg Address, Lincoln deliberately looked up these quotations and consciously chose these particular patterns of thought. No, he chose the theme. From its development and from the emotional tone of the entire occasion, all the rest followed, or grew—by that marvelous process of choice and rejection which is essential to artistic creation. It does not spoil such a work of art to analyze it as closely as we have done; it is altogether fitting and proper that we should do this: for it helps us to penetrate more deeply into the rich meaning of the Gettysburg Address, and it allows us the very rare privilege of watching the workings of a great man's mind.

Questions for Discussion and Writing

1. What three principles of rhetorical organization did Lincoln utilize in creating the Gettysburg Address? How did Lincoln use these principles to speak to his audience's concerns, put the moment in a historical perspective, and motivate the listeners to begin to reunite a nation shattered by the Civil War?
2. How do the metaphors of birth and death contribute to the eloquence of Lincoln's speech? Where does he echo the language and rhythms of the Bible to give his speech a feeling of solemnity?
3. As a research project, investigate why the Battle of Gettysburg was seen as important enough for Lincoln to give his address there. What evidence is there that Lincoln realized that his speech was seen as a great one? You might wish to analyze the rhetorical strategies in another famous speech, such as John F. Kennedy's Inaugural Address (1961).
4. **Rhetorical inquiry:** How does Lincoln's address rest on the assumption that if the South is allowed to secede it will mean the death of the nation?

JACK LONDON

Jack London (1876–1916) was born John Griffith Chaney in San Francisco but took the name of his stepfather, John London. His impoverished childhood bred self-reliance: He worked in a canning factory and a jute mill and as a longshoreman, robbed oyster beds as the self-styled "Prince of the Oyster Pirates," went to sea at seventeen, and took part in the Klondike gold rush of 1897. When he began writing his distinctive stories, often set in the Yukon, of the survival of men and animals in harsh environments, he drew on these experiences. He was also profoundly influenced by the works of Karl Marx, Rudyard Kipling, and Friedrich Wilhelm Nietzsche. In his novels The Call of the Wild *(1903),* The Sea Wolf *(1904),* White Fang *(1906), and* The Iron Heel *(1908), and in short stories such as "Love of Life" (1906) and "To Build a Fire" (1910), London powerfully dramatizes the conflict between barbarism and civilization. During London's short, turbulent life, his prolific output as a writer also included his work as a journalist. Among other assignments, he covered the Russo-Japanese War of 1904–1905 as a syndicated correspondent. "The San Francisco Earthquake" (1906) was the first in a series of reports on the April 18, 1906, catastrophe that London wrote for* Collier's *magazine. His straightforward descriptive style influenced later writers such as Ernest Hemingway and Sherwood Anderson.*

Before You Read

What modern-day natural disaster might be comparable to the San Francisco Earthquake in 1906, in its scope, the way it was reported, and in the way people responded?

The San Francisco Earthquake

The earthquake shook down in San Francisco hundreds of thousands of dollars' worth of walls and chimneys. But the conflagration that followed burned up hundreds of millions of dollars' worth of property. There is no estimating within hundreds of millions the actual damage wrought. Not in history has a modern imperial city been so completely destroyed. San Francisco is gone. Nothing remains of it but memories and a fringe of dwelling-houses on its outskirts. Its industrial section is wiped out. Its business section is wiped out. The factories and warehouses, the great stores and newspaper buildings, the hotels and the palaces of the nabobs are all gone. Remains only the fringe of dwelling-houses on the outskirts of what was once San Francisco.

Within an hour after the earthquake shock the smoke of San Francisco's burning was a lurid tower visible a hundred miles away. And for three days and nights this lurid tower swayed in the sky, reddening the sun, darkening the day, and filling the land with smoke.

On Wednesday morning at a quarter past five came the earthquake. A minute later the flames were leaping upward. In a dozen different quarters south of Market Street, in the working-class ghetto, and in the factories, fires started. There was no opposing the flames. There was no organization, no communication. All the cunning adjustments of a twentieth century city had been smashed by the earthquake. The streets were humped into ridges and depressions, and piled with the debris of fallen walls. The steel rails were twisted into perpendicular and horizontal angles. The telephone and telegraph systems were disrupted. And the great water-mains had burst. All the shrewd contrivances and safe-guards of man had been thrown out of gear by thirty seconds' twitching of the earth-crust.

THE FIRE MADE ITS OWN DRAFT

By Wednesday afternoon, inside of twelve hours, half the heart of the city was gone. At that time I watched the vast conflagration from out on the bay. It was dead calm. Not a flicker of wind stirred. Yet from every side wind was pouring in upon the city. East, west, north, and south, strong winds were blowing upon the doomed city. The heated air rising made an enormous suck. Thus did the fire of itself build its own colossal chimney through the atmosphere. Day and night this dead calm continued, and yet, near to the flames, the wind was often half a gale, so mighty was the suck.

Wednesday night saw the destruction of the very heart of the city.   5
Dynamite was lavishly used, and many of San Francisco's proudest structures were crumbled by man himself into ruins, but there was no withstanding the onrush of the flames. Time and again successful stands were made by the fire-fighters, and every time the flames flanked around on either side, or came up from the rear, and turned to defeat the hard-won victory.

An enumeration of the buildings destroyed would be a directory of San Francisco. An enumeration of the buildings undestroyed would be a line and several addresses. An enumeration of the deeds of heroism would stock a library and bankrupt the Carnegie Medal fund. An enumeration of the dead will never be made. All vestiges of them were destroyed by the flames. The number of victims of the earthquake will never be known. South of Market Street, where the loss of life was particularly heavy, was the first to catch fire.

Remarkable as it may seem, Wednesday night, while the whole city crashed and roared into ruin, was a quiet night. There were no crowds. There was no shouting and yelling. There was no hysteria, no disorder. I passed Wednesday night in the path of the advancing flames, and in all those terrible hours I saw not one woman who wept, not one man who was excited, not one person who was in the slightest degree panic-stricken.

Before the flames, throughout the night, fled tens of thousands of homeless ones. Some were wrapped in blankets. Others carried bundles of bedding and dear household treasures. Sometimes a whole family was harnessed to a carriage or delivery wagon that was weighted down with their possessions. Baby buggies, toy wagons, and go-carts were used as trucks, while every other person was dragging a trunk. Yet everybody was gracious.

The most perfect courtesy obtained. Never, in all San Francisco's history, were her people so kind and courteous as on this night of terror.

A CARAVAN OF TRUNKS

All night these tens of thousands fled before the flames. Many of them, the poor people from the labor ghetto, had fled all day as well. They had left their homes burdened with possessions. Now and again they lightened up, flinging out upon the street clothing and treasures they had dragged for miles.

They held on longest to their trunks, and over these trunks many a strong man broke his heart that night. The hills of San Francisco are steep, and up these hills, mile after mile, were the trunks dragged. Everywhere were trunks, with across them lying their exhausted owners, men and women. Before the march of the flames were flung picket lines of soldiers. And a block at a time, as the flames advanced, these pickets retreated. One of their tasks was to keep the trunk-pullers moving. The exhausted creatures, stirred on by the menace of bayonets, would arise and struggle up the steep pavements, pausing from weakness every five or ten feet.

Often, after surmounting a heart-breaking hill, they would find another wall of flame advancing upon them at right angles and be compelled to change anew the line of their retreat. In the end, completely played out, after toiling for a dozen hours like giants, thousands of them were compelled to abandon their trunks. Here the shopkeepers and soft members of the middle class were at a disadvantage. But the working men dug holes in vacant lots and backyards and buried their trunks.

THE DOOMED CITY

At nine o'clock Wednesday evening I walked down through the very heart of the city. I walked through miles and miles of magnificent buildings and towering skyscrapers. Here was no fire. All was in perfect order. The police patrolled the streets. Every building had its watchman at the door. And yet it was doomed, all of it. There was no water. The dynamite was giving out. And at right angles two different conflagrations were sweeping down upon it.

At one o'clock in the morning I walked down through the same section. Everything still stood intact. There was no fire. And yet there was a change. A rain of ashes was falling. The watchmen at the doors were gone. The police had been withdrawn. There were no firemen, no fire engines, no men fighting with dynamite. The district had been absolutely abandoned. I stood at the corner of Kearney and Market, in the very innermost heart of San Francisco. Kearney Street was deserted. Half a dozen blocks away it was burning on both sides. The street was a wall of flame, and against this wall of flame, silhouetted sharply, were two United States cavalrymen sitting their horses, calmly watching. That was all. Not another person was in sight. In the intact heart of the city two troopers sat their horses and watched.

10

SPREAD OF THE CONFLAGRATION

Surrender was complete. There was no water. The sewers had long since been pumped dry. There was no dynamite. Another fire had broken out further uptown, and now from three sides conflagrations were sweeping down. The fourth side had been burned earlier in the day. In that direction stood the tottering walls of the Examiner building, the burned-out Call building, the smoldering ruins of the Grand Hotel, and the gutted, devastated, dynamited Palace Hotel.

The following will illustrate the sweep of the flames and the inability of   15
men to calculate their spread. At eight o'clock Wednesday evening I passed through Union Square. It was packed with refugees. Thousands of them had gone to bed on the grass. Government tents had been set up, supper was being cooked, and the refugees were lining up for free meals.

At half-past one in the morning three sides of Union Square were in flames. The fourth side, where stood the great St. Francis Hotel, was still holding out. An hour later, ignited from top and sides, the St. Francis was flaming heavenward. Union Square, heaped high with mountains of trunks, was deserted. Troops, refugees, and all had retreated.

A FORTUNE FOR A HORSE!

It was at Union Square that I saw a man offering a thousand dollars for a team of horses. He was in charge of a truck piled high with trunks for some hotel. It had been hauled here into what was considered safety, and the horses had been taken out. The flames were on three sides of the Square, and there were no horses.

Also, at this time, standing beside the truck, I urged a man to seek safety in flight. He was all but hemmed in by several conflagrations. He was an old man and he was on crutches. Said he, "Today is my birthday. Last night I was worth thirty thousand dollars. I bought five bottles of wine, some delicate fish, and other things for my birthday dinner. I have had no dinner, and all I own are these crutches."

I convinced him of his danger and started him limping on his way. An hour later, from a distance, I saw the truckload of trunks burning merrily in the middle of the street.

On Thursday morning, at a quarter past five, just twenty-four hours   20
after the earthquake, I sat on the steps of a small residence on Nob Hill. With me sat Japanese, Italians, Chinese, and Negroes—a bit of the cosmopolitan flotsam of the wreck of the city. All about were the palaces of the nabob pioneers of Forty-nine. To the east and south, at right angles, were advancing two mighty walls of flame.

I went inside with the owner of the house on the steps of which I sat. He was cool and cheerful and hospitable. "Yesterday morning," he said, "I was worth six hundred thousand dollars. This morning this house is all I have left. It will go in fifteen minutes." He pointed to a large cabinet. "That is my wife's collection of china. This rug upon which we stand is a present. It cost fifteen hundred dollars. Try that piano. Listen to its tone. There are few like it. There are no horses. The flames will be here in fifteen minutes."

Outside, the old Mark Hopkins residence, a palace, was just catching fire. The troops were falling back and driving the refugees before them. From every side came the roaring of flames, the crashing of walls, and the detonations of dynamite.

THE DAWN OF THE SECOND DAY

I passed out of the house. Day was trying to dawn through the smoke-pall. A sickly light was creeping over the face of things. Once only the sun broke through the smoke-pall, blood-red, and showing a quarter its usual size. The smoke-pall itself, viewed from beneath, was a rose color that pulsed and fluttered with lavender shades. Then it turned to mauve and yellow and dun. There was no sun. And so dawned the second day on stricken San Francisco.

An hour later I was creeping past the shattered dome of the City Hall. Than it, there was no better exhibit of the destructive forces of the earthquake. Most of the stone had been shaken from the great dome, leaving standing the naked framework of steel. Market Street was piled high with wreckage, and across the wreckage lay the overthrown pillars of the City Hall shattered into short crosswise sections.

This section of the city, with the exception of the Mint and the Post-Office, was already a waste of smoking ruins. Here and there through the smoke, creeping warily under the shadows of tottering walls, emerged occasional men and women. It was like the meeting of the handful of survivors after the day of the end of the world. 25

BEEVES SLAUGHTERED AND ROASTED

On Mission Street lay a dozen steers, in a neat row stretching across the street, just as they had been struck down by the flying ruins of the earthquake. The fire had passed through afterward and roasted them. The human dead had been carried away before the fire came. At another place on Mission Street I saw a milk wagon. A steel telegraph pole had smashed down sheer through the driver's seat and crushed the front wheels. The milkcans lay scattered around.

All day Thursday and all Thursday night, all day Friday and Friday night, the flames still raged.

Friday night saw the flames finally conquered, though not until Russian Hill and Telegraph Hill had been swept and three-quarters of a mile of wharves and docks had been licked up.

THE LAST STAND

The great stand of the fire-fighters was made Thursday night on Van Ness Avenue. Had they failed here, the comparatively few remaining houses of the city would have been swept. Here were the magnificent residences of the second generation of San Francisco nabobs, and these, in a solid zone, were dynamited down across the path of the fire. Here and there the flames leaped the zone, but these fires were beaten out, principally by the use of wet blankets and rugs.

San Francisco, at the present time, is like the crater of a volcano, around   30
which are camped tens of thousand of refugees. At the Presidio alone are at least twenty thousand. All the surrounding cities and towns are jammed with the homeless ones, where they are being cared for by the relief committees. The refugees were carried free by the railroads to any point they wished to go, and it is estimated that over one hundred thousand people have left the peninsula on which San Francisco stood. The Government has the situation in hand, and, thanks to the immediate relief given by the whole United States, there is not the slightest possibility of a famine. The bankers and business men have already set about making preparations to rebuild San Francisco.

Questions for Discussion and Writing

1. What examples of courteous behavior does London cite that support the impression of the civility of San Franciscans under great stress? How much of San Francisco was destroyed by subsequent fires in comparison with the damage done by the earthquake itself? How do we know that London risked his own life to accurately report the extent of the destruction?

2. What effect does London produce by reporting the event from many different vantage points within the city? How is his description enhanced by metaphors that evoke the sounds, sights, tastes, and smells of the conflagration? How does his shift from war imagery to the metaphor of the shipwreck reflect the predicament citizens faced as survivors of the devastation?

3. How does the phrase "[my] fortune for a horse" (echoing the famous line from Shakespeare's play *Richard III,* "my kingdom for a horse") express the desperation of citizens seeking to save what little they could? Which parts of this report are enhanced by London's skill as a novelist using fictional techniques to dramatize his otherwise objective journalistic account?

4. **Rhetorical inquiry:** How does London use the metaphors of warfare to describe the event as if the city were facing an enemy?

HANSON W. BALDWIN

Hanson W. Baldwin (1903–1991) served as military editor for the New York Times *and won the Pulitzer Prize for his reporting in 1943. Among his*

published works are The Crucial Year, 1939–41: The World at War *(1976).*
This account was first published in Harper's *magazine in January 1934.*

Before You Read

How has the Titanic, *because of its tragic history, come to symbolize the idea of tempting fate?*

R. M. S. Titanic

The White Star liner *Titanic,* largest ship the world had ever known, sailed from Southampton on her maiden voyage to New York on April 10, 1912. The paint on her strakes was fair and bright; she was fresh from Harland and Wolff's Belfast yards, strong in the strength of her forty-six thousand tons of steel, bent, hammered, shaped and riveted through the three years of her slow birth.

There was little fuss and fanfare at her sailing; her sister ship, the *Olympic*—slightly smaller than the *Titanic*—had been in service for some months and to her had gone the thunder of the cheers.

But the *Titanic* needed no whistling steamers or shouting crowds to call attention to her superlative qualities. Her bulk dwarfed the ships near her as longshoremen singled up her mooring lines and cast off the turns of heavy rope from the dock bollards. She was not only the largest ship afloat, but was believed to be the safest. Carlisle, her builder, had given her double bottoms and had divided her hull into sixteen watertight compartments, which made her, men thought, unsinkable. She had been built to be and had been described as a gigantic lifeboat. Her designers' dreams of a triple-screw giant, a luxurious, floating hotel, which could speed to New York at twenty-three knots, had been carefully translated from blueprints and mold-loft lines at the Belfast yards into a living reality.

The *Titanic*'s sailing from Southampton, though quiet, was not wholly uneventful. As the liner moved slowly toward the end of her dock that April day, the surge of her passing sucked away from the quay the steamer *New York,* moored just to seaward of the *Titanic*'s berth. There were sharp cracks as the manila mooring lines of the *New York* parted under the strain. The frayed ropes writhed and whistled through the air and snapped down among the waving crowd on the pier; the *New York* swung toward the *Titanic*'s bow, was checked and dragged back to the dock barely in time to avert a collision. Seamen muttered, thought it an ominous start.

Past Spithead and the Isle of Wight the *Titanic* steamed. She called ⁵
at Cherbourg at dusk and then laid her course for Queenstown. At 1:30 P.M. on Thursday, April 11, she stood out of Queenstown harbor, screaming gulls soaring in her wake, with 2,201 persons—men, women, and children—aboard.

Occupying the Empire bedrooms and Georgian suites of the first-class accommodations were many well-known men and women—Colonel John Jacob Astor and his young bride; Major Archibald Butt, military aide to President Taft, and his friend, Frank D. Millet, the painter; John B. Thayer, vice-president of the Pennsylvania Railroad, and Charles M. Hays, president of the Grand Trunk Railway of Canada; W. T. Stead, the English journalist; Jacques Futrelle, French novelist; H. B. Harris, theatrical manager, and Mrs. Harris; Mr. and Mrs. Isidor Straus; and J. Bruce Ismay, chairman and managing director of the White Star line.

Down in the plain wooden cabins of the steerage class were 706 immigrants to the land of promise, and trimly stowed in the great holds was a cargo valued at $420,000: oak beams, sponges, wine, calabashes, and an odd miscellany of the common and the rare.

The *Titanic* took her departure on Fastnet Light and, heading into the night, laid her course for New York. She was due at Quarantine the following Wednesday morning.

Sunday dawned fair and clear. The *Titanic* steamed smoothly toward the west, faint streamers of brownish smoke trailing from her funnels. The purser held services in the saloon in the morning; on the steerage deck aft the immigrants were playing games and a Scotsman was puffing "The Campbells Are Coming" on his bagpipes in the midst of the uproar.

At 9 A.M. a message from the steamer *Caronia* sputtered into the wireless   10 shack:

Captain, Titanic—Westbound steamers report bergs growlers and field ice in 42 degrees N. from 49 degrees to 51 degrees W. 12th April.

Compliments—Barr.

It was cold in the afternoon; the sun was brilliant, but the *Titanic,* her screws turning over at 75 revolutions per minute, was approaching the Banks.

In the Marconi cabin Second Operator Harold Bride, earphones clamped on his head, was figuring accounts; he did not stop to answer when he heard MWL, Continental Morse for the nearby Leyland liner, *Californian,* calling the *Titanic.* The *Californian* had some message about three icebergs; he didn't bother then to take it down. About 1:42 P.M. the rasping spark of those days spoke again across the water. It was the *Baltic,* calling the *Titanic,* warning her of ice on the steamer track. Bride took the message down and sent it up to the bridge. The officer-of-the-deck glanced at it; sent it to the bearded master of the *Titanic,* Captain E. C. Smith, a veteran of the White Star service. It was lunch time then; the Captain, walking along the promenade deck, saw Mr. Ismay, stopped, and handed him the message without comment. Ismay read it, stuffed it in his pocket, told two ladies about the icebergs, and resumed his walk. Later, about 7:15 P.M., the Captain requested the return of the message in order to post it in the chart room for the information of officers.

Dinner that night in the Jacobean dining room was gay. It was bitter on deck, but the night was calm and fine; the sky was moonless but studded with stars twinkling coldly in the clear air.

After dinner some of the second-class passengers gathered in the saloon, where the Reverend Mr. Carter conducted a "hymn singsong." It was almost ten o'clock and the stewards were waiting with biscuits and coffee as the group sang:

> O, hear us when we cry to Thee
>> For those in peril on the sea.

On the bridge Second Officer Lightoller—short, stocky, efficient—was 15 relieved at ten o'clock by First Officer Murdock. Lightoller had talked with other officers about the proximity of ice; at least five wireless ice warnings had reached the ship; lookouts had been cautioned to be alert; captains and officers expected to reach the field at any time after 9:30 P.M. At twenty-two knots, its speed unslackened, the *Titanic* plowed on through the night.

Lightoller left the darkened bridge to his relief and turned in. Captain Smith went to his cabin. The steerage was long since quiet; in the first and second cabins lights were going out; voices were growing still, people were asleep. Murdock paced back and forth on the bridge, peering out over the dark water, glancing now and then at the compass in front of Quatermaster Hichens at the wheel.

In the crow's nest, Lookout Frederick Fleet and his partner, Leigh, gazed down at the water, still and unruffled in the dim, starlit darkness. Behind and below them the ship, a white shadow with here and there a last winking light; ahead of them a dark and silent and cold ocean.

There was a sudden clang. "Dong-dong. Dong-dong. Dong-dong. Dong!" The metal clapper of the great ship's bell struck out 11:30. Mindful of the warnings, Fleet strained his eyes, searching the darkness for the dreaded ice. But there were only the stars and the sea.

In the wireless room, where Phillips, first operator, had relieved Bride, the buzz of the *Californian*'s set again crackled into the earphones:

Californian: "Say, old man, we are stuck here, surrounded by ice."
Titanic: "Shut up, shut up; keep out. I am talking to Cape Race; you are jamming my signals."

Then, a few minutes later—about 11:40 . . . 20

Out of the dark she came, a vast, dim, white, monstrous shape, directly in the *Titanic*'s path. For a moment Fleet doubted his eyes. But she was a deadly reality, this ghastly thing. Frantically, Fleet struck three bells— *something dead ahead*. He snatched the telephone and called the bridge:

"Iceberg! Right ahead!"

The First Officer heard but did not stop to acknowledge the message.

"Hard astarboard!"

Hichens strained at the wheel; the bow swung slowly to port. The monster   25
was almost upon them now.

Murdock leaped to the engine-room telegraph. Bells clanged. Far below
in the engine room those bells struck the first warning. Danger! The indicators
on the dial faces swung round to "Stop!" Then "Full speed astern!" Frantically the engineers turned great valve wheels; answered the bridge bells. . . .

There was a slight shock, a brief scraping, a small list to port. Shell ice—
slabs and chunks of it—fell on the foredeck. Slowly the *Titanic* stopped.

Captain Smith hurried out of his cabin.

"What has the ship struck?"

Murdock answered, "An iceberg, sir. I hard-astarboarded and reversed   30
the engines, and I was going to hard-aport around it, but she was too close.
I could not do any more. I have closed the watertight doors."

Fourth Officer Boxhall, other officers, the carpenter, came to the
bridge. The Captain sent Boxhall and the carpenter below to ascertain the
damage.

A few lights switched on in the first and second cabins; sleepy passengers peered through porthole glass; some casually asked the stewards:

"Why have we stopped?"

"I don't know, sir, but I don't suppose it is anything much."

In the smoking room a quorum of gamblers and their prey were still sit-   35
ting round a poker table; the usual crowd of kibitzers looked on. They had
felt the slight jar of the collision and had seen an eighty-foot ice mountain
glide by the smoking-room windows, but the night was calm and clear, the
Titanic was "unsinkable"; they hadn't bothered to go on deck.

But far below, in the warren of passages on the starboard side forward, in
the forward holds and boiler rooms, men could see that the *Titanic*'s hurt was
mortal. In No. 6 boiler room, where the red glow from the furnaces lighted up
the naked, sweaty chests of coal-blackened firemen, water was pouring
through a great gash about two feet above the floor plates. This was no slow
leak; the ship was open to the sea; in ten minutes there were eight feet of water
in No. 6. Long before then the stokers had raked the flaming fires out of the
furnaces and had scrambled through the watertight doors into No. 5 or had
climbed up the long steel ladders to safety. When Boxhall looked at the mail
room in No. 3 hold, twenty-four feet above the keel, the mailbags were
already floating about in the slushing water. In No. 5 boiler room a stream of
water spurted into an empty bunker. All six compartments forward of No. 4
were open to the sea; in ten seconds the iceberg's jagged claw had ripped a
three-hundred-foot slash in the bottom of the great *Titanic*.

Reports came to the bridge; Ismay in dressing gown ran out on deck in
the cold, still, starlit night, climbed up the bridge ladder.

"What has happened?"

Captain Smith: "We have struck ice."

"Do you think she is seriously damaged?"   40

Captain: "I'm afraid she is."

Ismay went below and passed Chief Engineer William Bell fresh from an inspection of the damaged compartments. Bell corroborated the Captain's statement; hurried back down the glistening steel ladders to his duty. Man after man followed him—Thomas Andrews, one of the ship's designers, Archie Frost, the builder's chief engineer, and his twenty assistants—men who had no posts of duty in the engine room but whose traditions called them there.

On deck, in corridor and stateroom, life flowed again. Men, women, and children awoke and questioned; orders were given to uncover the lifeboats; water rose into the firemen's quarters; half-dressed stokers streamed up on deck. But the passengers—most of them—did not know that the *Titanic* was sinking. The shock of the collision had been so slight that some were not awakened by it; the *Titanic* was so huge that she must be unsinkable; the night was too calm, too beautiful, to think of death at sea.

Captain Smith half ran to the door of the radio shack. Bride, partly dressed, eyes dulled with sleep, was standing behind Phillips, waiting.

"Send the call for assistance."   45

The blue spark danced: "CQD—CQD—CQD—CQ—"

Miles away Marconi men heard. Cape Race heard it, and the steamships *La Provence* and *Mt. Temple.*

The sea was surging into the *Titanic*'s hold. At 12:20 the water burst into the seamen's quarters through a collapsed fore-and-aft wooden bulkhead. Pumps strained in the engine rooms—men and machinery making a futile fight against the sea. Steadily the water rose.

The boats were swung out—slowly; for the deckhands were late in reaching their stations, there had been no boat drill, and many of the crew did not know to what boats they were assigned. Orders were shouted; the safety valves had lifted, and steam was blowing off in a great rushing roar. In the chart house Fourth Officer Boxhall bent above a chart, working rapidly with pencil and dividers.

12:15 A.M. Boxhall's position is sent out to a fleet of vessels: "Come at   50
once; we have struck a berg."

To the Cunarder *Carpathia* (Arthur Henry Rostron, Master, New York to Liverpool, fifty-eight miles away): "It's a CQD, old man. Position 41–46 N.; 50–14 W."

The blue spark dancing: "Sinking; cannot hear for noise of steam."

12:30 A.M. The word is passed: "Women and children in the boats." Stewards finish waking their passengers below; life preservers are tied on; some men smile at the precaution. "The *Titanic* is unsinkable." The *Mt. Temple* starts for the *Titanic;* the *Carpathia,* with a double watch in her stokeholds, radios, "Coming hard." The CQD changes the course of many ships—but not of one; the operator of the *Californian,* near by, has just put down his earphones and turned in.

The CQD flashes over land and sea from Cape Race to New York; newspaper city rooms leap to life and presses whir.

On the *Titanic*, water creeps over the bulkhead between Nos. 5 and 6   55
firerooms. She is going down by the head; the engineers—fighting a losing
battle—are forced back foot by foot by the rising water. Down the promenade deck, Happy Jock Hume, the bandsman, runs with his instrument.

12:45 A.M. Murdock, in charge on the starboard side, eyes tragic, but
calm and cool, orders boat No. 7 lowered. The women hang back; they
want no boat ride on an ice-strewn sea; the *Titanic* is unsinkable. The men
encourage them, explain that this is just a precautionary measure: "We'll see
you again at breakfast." There is little confusion; passengers stream slowly
to the boat deck. In the steerage the immigrants chatter excitedly.

A sudden sharp hiss—a streaked flare against the night; Boxhall sends a
rocket toward the sky. It explodes, and a parachute of white stars lights up
the icy sea. "God! Rockets!" The band plays ragtime.

No. 8 is lowered, and No. 5. Ismay, still in dressing gown, calls for
women and children, handles lines, stumbles in the way of an officer, is told
to "get the hell out of here." Third Officer Pitman takes charge of No. 5; as
he swings into the boat Murdock grasps his hand. "Good-by and good luck,
old man."

No. 6 goes over the side. There are only twenty-eight people in a
lifeboat with a capacity of sixty-five.

A light stabs from the bridge; Boxhall is calling in Morse flashes, again   60
and again, to a strange ship stopped in the ice jam five to ten miles away.
Another rocket drops its shower of sparks above the ice-strewn sea and the
dying ship.

1:00 A.M. Slowly the water creeps higher; the fore ports of the *Titanic*
are dipping into the sea. Rope squeaks through blocks; lifeboats drop jerkily
seaward. Through the shouting on the decks comes the sound of the band
playing ragtime.

The "Millionaires' Special" leaves the ship—boat No. 1, with a capacity of forty people, carries only Sir Cosmo and Lady Duff Gordon and ten
others. Aft, the frightened immigrants mill and jostle and rush for a boat.
An officer's fist flies out; three shots are fired into the air, and the panic is
quelled. . . . Four Chinese sneak unseen into a boat and hide in its bottom.

1:20 A.M. Water is coming into No. 4 boiler room. Stokers slice and
shovel as water laps about their ankles—steam for the dynamos, steam for
the dancing spark! As the water rises, great ash hoes rake the flaming coals
from the furnaces. Safety valves pop; the stokers retreat aft, and the watertight doors clang shut behind them.

The rockets fling their spendor toward the stars. The boats are more
heavily loaded now, for the passengers know the *Titanic* is sinking. Women
cling and sob. The great screws aft are rising clear of the sea. Half-filled
boats are ordered to come alongside the cargo ports and take on more passengers, but the ports are never opened—and the boats are never filled.
Others pull for the steamer's light miles away but never reach it; the light
disappears, the unknown ship steams off.

The water rises and the band plays ragtime.   65

1:30 A.M. Lightoller is getting the port boats off; Murdock the starboard. As one boat is lowered into the sea a boat officer fires his gun along the ship's side to stop a rush from the lower decks. A woman tries to take her great Dane into a boat with her; she is refused and steps out of the boat to die with her dog. Millet's "little smile which played on his lips all through the voyage" plays no more; his lips are grim, but he waves good-by and brings wraps for the women.

Benjamin Guggenheim, in evening clothes, smiles and says, "We've dressed up in our best and are prepared to go down like gentlemen."

1:40 A.M. Boat 14 is clear, and then 13, 16, 15, and C. The lights still shine, but the *Baltic* hears the blue spark say, "Engine room getting flooded."

The *Olympic* signals, "Am lighting up all possible boilers as fast as can."

Major Butt helps women into the last boats and waves good-by to   70
them. Mrs. Straus puts her foot on the gunwale of a lifeboat, then she draws back and goes to her husband: "We have been together many years; where you go I will go." Colonel John Jacob Astor puts his young wife in a lifeboat, steps back, taps cigarette on fingernail: "Good-by, dearie; I'll join you later."

1:45 A.M. The foredeck is under water, the fo'c'sle head almost awash; the great stern is lifted high toward the bright stars; and still the band plays. Mr. and Mrs. Harris approach a lifeboat arm in arm.

Officer: "Ladies first, please."

Harris bows, smiles, steps back: "Of course, certainly; ladies first."

Boxhall fires the last rocket, then leaves in charge of boat No. 2.

2:00 A.M. She is dying now; her bow goes deeper, her stern higher. But   75
there must be steam. Below in the stokeholds the sweaty firemen keep steam up for the flaring lights and the dancing spark. The glowing coals slide and tumble over the slanted grate bars; the sea pounds behind that yielding bulkhead. But the spark dances on.

The *Asian* hears Phillips try the new signal—SOS.

Boat No. 4 has left now; boat D leaves ten minutes later. Jacques Futrelle clasps his wife: "For God's sake, go! It's your last chance; go!" Madame Futrelle is half forced into the boat. It clears the side.

There are about 660 people in the boats, and 1,500 still on the sinking *Titanic*.

On top of the officers' quarters men work frantically to get the two collapsibles stowed there over the side. Water is over the forward part of A deck now; it surges up the companionways toward the boat deck. In the radio shack, Bride has slipped a coat and lifejacket about Phillips as the first operator sits hunched over his key, sending—still sending—"41–46 N.; 50–14 W. CQD—CQD—SOS—SOS—"

The Captain's tired white face appears at the radio-room door: "Men,   80
you have done your full duty. You can do no more. Now, it's every man for

himself." The Captain disappears—back to his sinking bridge, where Painter, his personal steward, stands quietly waiting for orders. The spark dances on. Bride turns his back and goes into the inner cabin. As he does so, a stoker, grimed with coal, mad with fear, steals into the shack and reaches for the life-jacket on Phillips' back. Bride wheels about and brains him with a wrench.

2:10 A.M. Below decks the steam is still holding, though the pressure is falling—rapidly. In the gymnasium on the boat deck the athletic instructor watches quietly as two gentlemen ride the bicycles and another swings casually at the punching bag. Mail clerks stagger up the boat-deck stairways, dragging soaked mail sacks. The spark still dances. The band still plays—but not ragtime:

> Nearer my God to Thee,
>> Nearer to Thee . . .

A few men take up the refrain; others kneel on the slanting decks to pray. Many run and scramble aft, where hundreds are clinging above the silent screws on the great uptilted stern. The spark still dances and the lights still flare; the engineers are on the job. The hymn comes to its close. Bandmaster Hartley, Yorkshireman violinist, taps his bow against a bulkhead, calls for "Autumn" as the water curls about his feet, and the eight musicians brace themselves against the ship's slant. People are leaping from the decks into the nearby water—the icy water. A woman cries, "Oh, save me, save me!" A man answers, "Good lady, save yourself. Only God can save you now." The band plays "Autumn":

> God of Mercy and Compassion!
>> Look with pity on my pain . . .

The water creeps over the bridge where the *Titanic*'s master stands; heavily he steps out to meet it.

2:17 A.M. "CQ—" The *Virginian* hears a ragged, blurred CQ, then an abrupt stop. The blue spark dances no more. The lights flicker out; the engineers have lost their battle.

2:18 A.M. Men run about blackened decks; leap into the night; are swept into the sea by the curling wave which licks up the *Titanic*'s length. Lightoller does not leave the ship; the ship leaves him; there are hundreds like him, but only a few who live to tell of it. The funnels still swim above the water, but the ship is climbing to the perpendicular; the bridge is under and most of the foremast; the great stern rises like a squat leviathan. Men swim away from the sinking ship; others drop from the stern.

The band plays in the darkness, the water lapping upwards:

> Hold me up in mighty waters,
> Keep my eyes on things above,
> Righteousness, divine atonement,
> Peace and everlas . . .

The forward funnel snaps and crashes into the sea; its steel tons hammer out of existence swimmers struggling in the freezing water. Streams of sparks, of smoke and steam, burst from the after funnels. The ship upends to fifty—to sixty degrees.

Down in the black abyss of the stokeholds, of the engine rooms, where the dynamos have whirred at long last to a stop, the stokers and the engineers are reeling against hot metal, the rising water clutching at their knees. The boilers, the engine cylinders, rip from their bed plates: crash through bulkheads; rumble—steel against steel.

The *Titanic* stands on end, poised briefly for the plunge. Slowly she slides to her grave—slowly at first, and then more quickly—quickly—quickly.

2:20 A.M. The greatest ship in the world has sunk. From the calm, dark waters where the floating lifeboats move, there goes up, in the white wake of her passing, "one long continuous moan." 90

The boats that the *Titanic* had launched pulled safely away from the slight suction of the sinking ship, pulled away from the screams that came from the lips of the freezing men and women in the water. The boats were poorly manned and badly equipped, and they had been unevenly loaded. Some carried so few seamen that women bent to the oars. Mrs. Astor tugged at an oar handle; the Countess of Rothes took a tiller. Shivering stokers in sweaty, coal-blackened singlets and light trousers steered in some boats; stewards in white coats rowed in others. Ismay was in the last boat that left the ship from the starboard side; with Mr. Carter of Philadelphia and two seamen he tugged at the oars. In one of the lifeboats an Italian with a broken wrist—disguised in a woman's shawl and hat—huddled on the floor boards, ashamed now that fear had left him. In another rode the only baggage saved from the *Titanic*—the carry-all of Samuel L. Goldenberg, one of the rescued passengers.

There were only a few boats that were heavily loaded; most of those that were half empty made but perfunctory efforts to pick up the moaning swimmers, their officers and crew fearing that they would endanger the living if they pulled back into the midst of the dying. Some boats beat off the freezing victims; fear-crazed men and women struck with oars at the heads of swimmers. One woman drove her fist into the face of a half-dead man as he tried feebly to climb over the gunwale. Two other women helped him in and stanched the flow of blood from the ring cuts on his face.

One of the collapsible boats, which had floated off the top of the officers' quarters when the *Titanic* sank, was an icy haven for thirty or forty men. The boat had capsized as the ship sank; men swam to it, clung to it, climbed upon its slippery bottom, stood knee-deep in water in the freezing air. Chunks of ice swirled about their legs; their soaked clothing clutched their bodies in icy folds. Colonel Archibald Gracie was cast up there, Gracie who had leaped from the stern as the *Titanic* sank; young Thayer who had seen his father die; Lightoller who had twice been sucked down with the ship and twice blown to the surface by a belch of air; Bride, the second operator, and Phillips, the first. There were many stokers, half-naked; it was a shivering company. They stood there in the icy sea, under the far stars, and sang and prayed—the Lord's Prayer. After a while a lifeboat came and picked them off, but Phillips was dead then or died soon afterward in the boat.

Only a few of the boats had lights; only one—No. 2—had a light that was of any use to the *Carpathia,* twisting through the ice field to the rescue. Other ships were "coming hard" too; one, the *Californian,* was still dead to opportunity.

The blue sparks still danced, but not the *Titanic's. Le Provence* to   95
Celtic: "Nobody has heard the *Titanic* for about two hours."

It was 2:40 when the *Carpathia* first sighted the green light from No. 2 boat; it was 4:10 when she picked up the first boat and learned that the *Titanic* had foundered. The last of the moaning cries had just died away then.

Captain Rostron took the survivors aboard, boatload by boatload. He was ready for them, but only a small minority of them required much medical attention. Bride's feet were twisted and frozen; others were suffering from exposure; one died, and seven were dead when taken from the boats, and were buried at sea.

It was then that the fleet of racing ships learned they were too late; the *Parisian* heard the weak signals of MPA, the *Carpathia,* report the death of the *Titanic.* It was then—or soon afterward, when her radio operator put on his earphones—that the *Californian,* the ship that had been within sight as the *Titanic* was sinking, first learned of the disaster.

And it was then, in all its white-green majesty, that the *Titanic's* survivors saw the iceberg, tinted with the sunrise, floating idly, pack ice jammed about its base, other bergs heaving slowly near by on the blue breast of the sea.

Questions for Discussion and Writing

1. In what way is the encounter between the iceberg and the *Titanic* described in ways that underscore the many ironies involved, including the naming of the ship, the handling of radio messages, and the experiences of those on board? How does Baldwin's account suggest the modern-day equivalent of a Greek tragedy, whose heroes, through a combination of fate and their tragic flaws, brought catastrophes on themselves?

2. Analyze Baldwin's narrative technique. For example, what is the effect of the considerable statistical data he provides? How effectively does he reveal the character of individual passengers and crew?

3. The sinking of the *Titanic* has assumed the dimensions of a modern-day myth and has been the subject of a number of films, including the Academy Award–winning 1997 movie and a Broadway musical. Analyze one or several of these in relationship to Baldwin's account, and

discuss the subtle and not-so-subtle shifts in emphasis that are evident in these dramatizations.

4. **Rhetorical inquiry:** How does Baldwin build suspense, even for readers who know the outcome, by starting quietly and building slowly until the catastrophe occurs?

HAUNANI-KAY TRASK

Haunani-Kay Trask (b. 1949), an activist, author, and poet, is a professor of Hawaiian Studies at the University of Hawai'i at Manoa. She received her Ph.D. in political science from the University of Wisconsin at Madison. The following essay originally appeared in From a Native Daughter: Colonialism and Sovereignty in Hawai'i *(1999). The essay is an impassioned argument against the abuse of Native Hawaiian rights caused by rampant tourism. She has also written* Night is a Sharkskin Drum *(2002).*

Before You Read

Consider how Trask draws attention to aspects of Hawaiian culture that has been altered by tourism.

From a Native Daughter

I am certain that most, if not all, Americans have heard of Hawai'i and have wished, at some time in their lives, to visit my Native land. But I doubt that the history of how Hawai'i came to be territorially incorporated, and economically, politically, and culturally subordinated to the United States is known to most Americans. Nor is it common knowledge that Hawaiians have been struggling for over twenty years to achieve a land base and some form of political sovereignty on the same level as American Indians. Finally, I would imagine that most Americans could not place Hawai'i or any other Pacific island on a map of the Pacific. But despite all this appalling ignorance, five million Americans will vacation in my homeland this year *and* the next, and so on, into the foreseeable capitalist future. Such are the intended privileges of the so-called American standard of living ignorance of and yet power over one's relations to Native peoples. Thanks to postwar American imperialism, the ideology that the United States has no overseas colonies and is, in fact, the champion of self-determination the world over holds no greater sway than in the United States itself. To most Americans, then, Hawai'i is *theirs:* to use, to take, and, above all, to fantasize about long after the experience.

Just five hours away by plane from California, Hawai'i is a thousand light years away in fantasy. Mostly a state of mind, Hawai'i is the image of escape from the rawness and violence of daily American life. Hawaii—the word, the vision, the sound in the mind—is the fragrance and feel of soft kindness. Above all, Hawai'i is "she," the Western image of the Native "female" in her magical allure. And if luck prevails, some of "her" will rub off on you, the visitor.

This fictional Hawai'i comes out of the depths of Western sexual sickness that demands a dark, sin-free Native for instant gratification between imperialist wars. The attraction of Hawai'i is stimulated by slick Hollywood movies, saccharine Andy Williams music, and the constant psychological deprivations of maniacal American life. Tourists flock to my Native land for escape, but they are escaping into a state of mind while participating in the destruction of a host people in a Native place.

To Hawaiians, daily life is neither soft nor kind. In fact, the political, economic, and cultural reality for most Hawaiians is hard, ugly, and cruel.

In Hawai'i, the destruction of our land and the prostitution of our culture is planned and executed by multinational corporations (both foreign-based and Hawai'i-based), by huge landowners (such as the missionary-descended Castle & Cook of Dole Pineapple fame), and by collaborationist state and county governments. The ideological gloss that claims tourism to be our economic savior and the "natural" result of Hawaiian culture is manufactured by ad agencies (such as the state-supported Hawai'i Visitors Bureau) and tour companies (many of which are owned by the airlines) and spewed out to the public through complicitous cultural engines such as film, television and radio, and the daily newspaper. As for the local labor unions, both rank and file and management clamor for more tourists, while the construction industry lobbies incessantly for larger resorts.

The major public educational institution, the University of Hawai'i, funnels millions of taxpayer dollars into a School of Travel Industry Management and a business school replete with a Real Estate Center and a Chair of Free Enterprise (renamed the Walker Chair to hide the crude reality of capitalism). As the propaganda arm of the tourist industry in Hawai'i, both schools churn out studies that purport to show why Hawai'i needs more golf courses, hotels, and tourist infrastructure and how Hawaiian culture is "naturally" one of giving and entertaining.

Of course, state-encouraged commodification and prostitution of Native cultures through tourism is not unique to Hawai'i. It is suffered by peoples in places as disparate as Goa, Australia, Tahiti, and the southwestern United States. Indeed, the problem is so commonplace that international organizations—for example, the Ecumenical Coalition on Third World Tourism out of Bangkok, the Center for Responsible Tourism in California, and the Third World European Network—have banded together to help give voice to Native peoples in daily resistance against corporate tourism. My focus on Hawai'i, although specific to my own culture, would likely transfer well when applied to most Native peoples.

Despite our similarities with other major tourist destinations, the statistical picture of the effects of corporate tourism in Hawai'i is shocking:

Fact: Nearly forty years ago, at statehood, Hawai'i residents outnumbered tourists by more than 2 to 1. Today, tourists outnumber residents by 6 to 1; they outnumber Native Hawaiians by 30 to 1.[1]

Fact: According to independent economists and criminologists, "tourism has been the single most powerful factor in O'ahu's crime rate," including crimes against people and property.[2]

Fact: Independent demographers have been pointing out for years that "tourism is the major source of population growth in Hawai'i" and that "rapid growth of the tourist industry ensures the trend toward a rapidly expanded population that receives lower per capita income."[3]

Fact: The Bank of Hawai'i has reported that the average real incomes of Hawai'i residents grew only *one* percent during the period from the early seventies through the early eighties, when tourism was booming. The same held true throughout the nineties. The census bureau reports that personal income growth in Hawai'i during the same time was the lowest by far of any of the fifty American states.[4]

Fact: Groundwater supplies on O'ahu will be insufficient to meet the needs of residents and tourists by the year 2000.[5]

Fact: According to the *Honolulu Advertiser*, "Japanese investors have spent more than $7.1 billion on their acquisitions" since 1986 in Hawai'i. This kind of volume translates into huge alienations of land and properties. For example, nearly 2,000 acres of land on the Big Island of Hawai'i was purchased for $18.5 million and over 7,000 acres on Moloka'i went for $33 million. In 1989, over $1 billion was spent by the Japanese on land alone.[6]

Fact: More plants and animals from our Hawaiian Islands are now extinct or on the endangered species list than in the rest of the United States.[7]

Fact: More than 29,000 families are on the Hawaiian trust lands list, waiting for housing, pastoral, or agricultural lots.[8]

Fact: The median cost of a home on the most populated island of O'ahu is around $350,000.[9]

---

[1] Eleanor C. Nordyke, *The Peopling of Hawai'i*, 2nd ed. (Honolulu: University of Hawai'i Press, 1989), *pp. 134–172.*   [2] Meda Chesney-Lind, "Salient Factors in Hawai'i's Crime Rate," University of Hawai'i School of Social Work. Available from author.   [3] Nordyke, *The Peopling of Hawai'i*, pp. 134–172.   [4] Bank of Hawai'i Annual Economic Report, *1984.*   [5] Estimate of independent hydrologist Kate Vandemoer to community organizing group *Kupa'a He'eia,* February 1990. Water quality and groundwater depletion are two problems much discussed by state and county officials in Hawai'i but ignored when resort permits are considered.   [6] *The Honolulu Advertiser*, April 8, 1990.   [7] David Stannard, Testimony against West Beach Estates. Land Use Commission, State of Hawaii, January 10, 1985.   [8] Department of Hawaiian Home Lands, phone interview, March *1998.*   [9] *Honolulu Star-Bulletin*, May 8, 1990.

Fact: Hawai'i has by far the worst ratio of average family income to average housing costs in the country. This explains why families spend nearly 52 percent of their gross income for housing costs.[10]

Fact: Nearly one-fifth of Hawai'i's resident population is classified as *near-homeless,* that is, those for whom any mishap results in immediate on-the-street homelessness.[11]

These kinds of statistics render a very bleak picture, not at all what the posters and jingoistic promoters would have you believe about Hawai'i.

My use of the word *tourism* in the Hawai'i context refers to a mass-based, corporately controlled industry that is both vertically and horizontally integrated such that one multinational corporation owns an airline and the tour buses that transport tourists to the corporation-owned hotel where they eat in a corporation-owned restaurant, play golf, and "experience" Hawai'i on corporation-owned recreation areas and eventually consider buying a second home built on corporation land. Profits, in this case, are mostly repatriated back to the home country. In Hawai'i, these "home" countries are Japan, Taiwan, Hong Kong, Canada, Australia, and the United States. In this sense, Hawai'i is very much like a Third World colony where the local elite—the Democratic Party in our state—collaborate in the rape of Native land and people.[12]

The mass nature of this kind of tourism results in megaresort complexes on thousands of acres with demands for water and services that far surpass the needs of Hawai'i residents. These complexes may boast several hotels, golf courses, restaurants, and other "necessaries" to complete the total tourist experience. Infrastructure is usually built by the developer in exchange for county approval of more hotel units. In Hawai'i, counties bid against each other to attract larger and larger complexes. "Rich" counties, then, are those with more resorts, since they will pay more of the tax base of the county. The richest of these is the City and County of Honolulu, which encompasses the entire island of O'ahu. This island is the site of four major tourist destinations, a major international airport, and 80 percent of the resident population of Hawai'i. The military also controls nearly 30 percent of the island, with bases and airports of their own. As you might imagine, the density of certain parts of Honolulu (e.g., Waikīkī) is among the highest in

10

---

[10] Bank of Hawai'i Annual Economic Report, 1984. In 1992, families probably spent closer to 60 percent of their gross income for housing costs. Billion-dollar Japanese investments and other speculation since 1984 have caused rental and purchase prices to skyrocket.   [11] This is the estimate of a state-contracted firm that surveyed the islands for homeless and near-homeless families. Testimony was delivered to the state legislature, 1990 session.   [12] For an analysis of post-statehood Hawai'i and its turn to mass-based corporate tourism, see Noel Kent, *Hawai'i: Islands Under the Influence.* For an analysis of foreign investment in Hawai'i, see *A Study of Foreign Investment and Its Impact on the State* (Honolulu: Hawai'i Real Estate Center, University of Hawaii, 1989).

the world. At the present annual visitor count, more than five million tourists pour through O'ahu, an island of only 607 square miles.

With this as a background on tourism, I want to move now into the area of cultural prostitution. *Prostitution* in this context refers to the entire institution that defines a woman (and by extension the *female*) as an object of degraded and victimized sexual value for use and exchange through the medium of money. The *prostitute* is a woman who sells her sexual capacities and is seen, thereby, to possess and reproduce them at will, that is, by her very "nature." The prostitute and the institution that creates and maintains her are, of course, of patriarchal origin. The pimp is the conduit of exchange, managing the commodity that is the prostitute while acting as the guard at the entry and exit gates, making sure the prostitute behaves as a prostitute by fulfilling her sexual-economic functions. The victims participate in their victimization with enormous ranges of feeling, from resistance to complicity, but the force and continuity of the institution are shaped by men.

There is much more to prostitution than my sketch reveals but this must suffice, for I am interested in using the largest sense of this term as a metaphor in understanding what has happened to Hawaiian culture. My purpose is not to exact detail or fashion a model but to convey the utter degradation of our culture and our people under corporate tourism by employing *prostitution* as an analytic category.

Finally, I have chosen four areas of Hawaiian culture to examine: our homeland, our *one hānau* that is Hawai'i, our lands and fisheries, the outlying seas and the heavens; our language and dance; our familial relationships; and our women.

The *mo'olelo*, or history of Hawaiians, is to be found in our genealogies. From our great cosmogonic genealogy, the *kumulipo*, derives the Hawaiian identity. The "essential lesson" of this genealogy is "the interrelatedness of the Hawaiian world, and the inseparability of its constituents parts." Thus, "the genealogy of the land, the gods, chiefs, and people intertwine one with the other, and with all aspects of the universe."[13]

In the *mo'olelo* of Papa and W,kea, "earth mother" and "sky father," our islands were born: Hawai'i, Maui, O'ahu, Kaua'i, and Ni'ihau. From their human offspring came the *taro* plant and from the *taro* came the Hawaiian people. The lessons of our genealogy are that human beings have a familial relationship to land and to the *taro,* our elder siblings or *kua'ana.*

In Hawai'i, as in all of Polynesia, younger siblings must serve and honor elder siblings who, in turn, must feed and care for their younger siblings. Therefore, Hawaiians must cultivate and husband the land that will feed and provide for the Hawaiian people. This relationship of people to land is called *mālama 'āina* or *aloha 'āina,* "care and love of the land."

---

[13] Lilikala Kame'eleihiwa, *Native Land and Foreign Desires* (Honolulu: Bishop Museum Press, 1992), p. 2.

When people and land work together harmoniously, the balance that results is called *pono*. In Hawaiian society, the *ali'i*, or "chiefs," were required to maintain order, an abundance of food, and good government. The *maka'āinana* or "common people," worked the land and fed the chiefs; the *ali'i* organized production and appeased the gods.

Today, *mālama'āina* is called *stewardship* by some, although that word does not convey spiritual and genealogical connections. Nevertheless, to love and make the land flourish is a Hawaiian value. *'Āina, one* of the words for "land," means "that which feeds." *Kama'āina*, a term for native-born people, means "child of the land.'" Thus is the Hawaiian relationship to land both familial and reciprocal.

Hawaiian deities also spring from the land: Pele is our volcano, Kāne   20
and Lono, our fertile valleys and plains, Kanaloa our ocean and all that lives within it, and so on with the numerous gods of Hawai'i. Our whole universe, physical and metaphysical, is divine.

Within this world, the older people, or *kūpuna,* are to cherish those who are younger, the *mo'opuna.* Unstinting generosity is a prized value. Social connections between our people are through *aloha,* simply translated as "love" but carrying with it a profoundly Hawaiian sense that is, again, familial and genealogical. Hawaiians feel *aloha* for Hawai'i from whence they come and for their Hawaiian kin upon whom they depend. It is nearly impossible to feel or practice *aloha* for something that is not familial. This is why we extend familial relations to those few non-Natives whom we feel understand and can reciprocate our *aloha*. But *aloha* is freely given and freely returned; it is not and cannot be demanded or commanded. Above all, *aloha* is a cultural feeling and practice that works among the people and between the people and their land.

The significance and meaning of *aloha* underscores the centrality of the Hawaiian language or *'ōlelo,* to the culture. *'Olelo* means both "language" and "tongue;" *mo'olelo,* or "history," is that which comes from the tongue, that is, "a story." *Haole*, or white people, say that we have oral history, but what we have are stories, such as our creation story, passed on through the generations. This sense of history is different from the *haole* sense of history. To Hawaiians in traditional society, language had tremendous power, thus the phrase, *i ka 'ōlelo ke ola; i ka 'ōlelo ka make*—"in language is life, in language is death."

After nearly two thousand years of speaking Hawaiian, our people suffered the near extinction of our language through its banning by the American-imposed government in 1900, the year Hawai'i became a territory of the United States. All schools, government operations and official transactions were thereafter conducted in English, despite the fact that most people, including non-Natives, still spoke Hawaiian at the turn of the century.

Since 1970, *'ōlelo Hawai'i,* or the Hawaiian language, has undergone a tremendous revival, including the rise of language immersion schools. The state of Hawai'i now has two official languages, Hawaiian and English, and the call for Hawaiian language speakers and teachers is increasing every day.[14]

Along with the flowering of Hawaiian language has come a flowering of Hawaiian dance, especially in its ancient form, called *hula kahiko.* Dance academies, known as *hālau,* have proliferated throughout Hawai'i, as have *kumu hula;* or dance masters, and formal competitions where all-night presentations continue for three or four days to throngs of appreciative listeners. Indeed, among Pacific Islanders, Hawaiian dance is considered one of the finest Polynesian art forms today.

Of course, the cultural revitalization that Hawaiians are now experiencing and transmitting to their children is as much a *repudiation* of colonization by so-called Western civilization in its American form as it is a *reclamation* of our own past and our own ways of life. This is why cultural revitalization is often resisted and disparaged by anthropologists and others: they see very clearly that its political effect is decolonization of the mind. Thus our rejection of the nuclear family as the basic unit of society and of individualism as the best form of human expression infuriates social workers, the churches, the legal system, and educators to this day. Hawaiians continue to have allegedly "illegitimate" children, to *hānai,* or "adopt," both children and adults outside of sanctioned Western legal concepts, to hold and use land and water in a collective form rather than a private property form, and to proscribe the notion and the value that one person should strive to surpass and therefore outshine all others.

All these Hawaiian values can be grouped under the idea of *'ohana,* loosely translated as "family," but more accurately imagined as a group of both closely and distantly related people who share nearly everything, from land and food to children and status. Sharing is central to this value, since it prevents individual decline. Of course, poverty is not thereby avoided; it is only shared with everyone in the unit. The *'ohana* works effectively when the *kua'ana* relationship (elder sibling/younger sibling reciprocity) is practiced.

Finally, within the *'ohana,* our women are considered the life-givers of the nation and are accorded the respect and honor this status conveys. Our young women, like our young people in general, are the *pua,* or "flower" of our *lāhui,* or our "nation." The renowned beauty of our women, especially their sexual beauty, is not considered a commodity to be hoarded by fathers and brothers but an attribute of our people. Culturally, Hawaiians are very open and free about sexual relationships, although Christianity and organized religion have done much to damage these traditional sexual values.

With this understanding of what it means to be Hawaiian, I want to move now to the prostitution of our culture by tourism.

---

[14] See Larry Kimura, "Native Hawaiian Culture," *Native Hawaiians Study Commission Report,* vol. 1, pp. 173–197.

Hawai'i itself is the female object of degraded and victimized sexual   30
value. Our *'āina*, or lands, are not any longer the source of food and shelter,
but the source of money. Land is now called "real estate," rather than "our
mother," Papa. The American relationship of people to land is that of
exploiter to exploited. Beautiful areas, once sacred to my people, are now
expensive resorts; shorelines where net fishing, seaweed gathering, and crab-
bing occurred are more and more the exclusive domain of recreational activities such as sunbathing, wind-surfing, and jet skiing. Now, even access to
beaches near hotels is strictly regulated or denied to the local public altogether.

The phrase, *mālama 'āina*—"to care for the land"—is used by government officials to sell new projects and to convince the locals that hotels can
be built with a concern for "ecology." Hotel historians, like hotel doctors,
are stationed in-house to soothe the visitors' stay with the pablum of
invented myths and tales of the "primitive."

High schools and hotels adopt each other and funnel teenagers through
major resorts for guided tours from kitchens to gardens to honeymoon suites in
preparation for post-secondary school jobs in the lowest paid industry in the
state. In the meantime, tourist appreciation kits and movies are distributed
through the state Department of Education to all elementary schools. One film,
unashamedly titled *What's in It for Me?*, was devised to convince locals that
tourism is, as the newspapers never tire of saying, "the only game in town."

Of course, all this hype is necessary to hide the truth about tourism, the
awful exploitative truth that the industry is the major cause of environmental degradation, low wages, land dispossession, and the highest cost of living
in the United States.

While this propaganda is churned out to local residents, the commercialization of Hawaiian culture proceeds with calls for more sensitive marketing of our Native values and practices. After all, a prostitute is only as
good as her income-producing talents. These talents, in Hawaiian terms, are
the *hula;* the generosity, or *aloha,* of our people; the *u'i,* or youthful beauty
of our women and men, and the continuing allure of our lands and waters,
that is, of our place, Hawai'i.

The selling of these talents must produce income. And the function of   35
tourism and the State of Hawaii is to convert these attributes into profit.

The first requirement is the transformation of the product, or the cultural
attribute, much as a woman must be transformed to look like a prostitute—
that is, someone who is complicitous in her own commodification. Thus
hula dancers wear clownlike makeup, don costumes from a mix of Polynesian cultures, and behave in a manner that is smutty and salacious rather
than powerfully erotic. The distance between the smutty and the erotic is
precisely the distance between Western culture and Hawaiian culture. In the
hotel version of the *hula,* the sacredness of the dance has completely evaporated, while the athleticism and sexual expression have been packaged like
ornaments. The purpose is entertainment for profit rather than a joyful and
truly Hawaiian celebration of human and divine nature.

The point, of course, is that everything in Hawai'i can be yours, that is, you the tourists', the non-Natives', the visitors'. The place, the people, the culture, even our identity as a "Native" people is for sale. Thus the word "Aloha" is employed as an aid in the constant hawking of things Hawaiian. In truth, this use of *aloha* is so far removed from any Hawaiian cultural context that it is, literally, meaningless.

Thus, Hawai'i, like a lovely woman, is there for the taking. Those with only a little money get a brief encounter; those with a lot of money, like the Japanese, get more. The state and counties will give tax breaks, build infrastructure, and have the governor personally welcome tourists to ensure that they keep coming. Just as the pimp regulates prices and guards the commodity of the prostitute, so the state bargains with developers for access to Hawaiian land and culture. Who builds the biggest resorts to attract the most affluent tourists gets the best deal: more hotel rooms, golf courses, and restaurants approved. Permits are fast-tracked, height and density limits are suspended, new groundwater sources are miraculously found.

Hawaiians, meanwhile, have little choice in all this. We can fill up the unemployment lines, enter the military, work in the tourist industry, or leave Hawai'i. Increasingly, Hawaiians are leaving, not by choice but out of economic necessity.

Our people who work in the industry—dancers, waiters, singers, valets, gardeners, housekeepers, bartenders, and even a few managers—make between $10,000 and $25,000 a year, an impossible salary for a family in Hawai'i. Psychologically, our young people have begun to think of tourism as the only employment opportunity, trapped as they are by the lack of alternatives. For our young women, modeling is a "cleaner" job when compared to waiting on tables or dancing in a weekly revue, but modeling feeds on tourism and the commodification of Hawaiian women. In the end, the entire employment scene is shaped by tourism.

Despite their exploitation, Hawaiians' participation in tourism raises the problem of complicity. Because wages are so low and advancement so rare, whatever complicity exists is secondary to the economic hopelessness that drives Hawaiians into the industry. Refusing to contribute to the commercialization of one's culture becomes a peripheral concern when unemployment looms.

Of course, many Hawaiians do not see tourism as part of their colonization. Thus, tourism is viewed as providing jobs, not as a form of cultural prostitution. Even those who have some glimmer of critical consciousness do not generally agree that the tourist industry prostitutes Hawaiian culture. This is a measure of the depth of our mental oppression: we cannot understand our own cultural degradation because we are living it. As colonized people, we are colonized to the extent that we are unaware of our oppression. When awareness begins, then so, too, does decolonization. Judging by the growing resistance to new hotels, to geothermal energy and manganese nodule mining, which would supplement the tourist industry,

40

and to increases in the sheer number of tourists, I would say that decolonization has begun, but we have many more stages to negotiate on our path to sovereignty.

My brief excursion into the prostitution of Hawaiian culture has done no more than give an overview. Now that you have read a Native view, let me just leave this thought with you. If you are thinking of visiting my homeland, please do not. We do not want or need any more tourists, and we certainly do not like them. If you want to help our cause, pass this message on to your friends.

Questions for Discussion and Writing

1. Trask feels that the cumulative effects of tourism on Hawaii have been disastrous. What facts and figures does she present to support her thesis?
2. Does Trask run the risk of alienating even those who might agree with her because of her incendiary rhetorical approach? Why or why not? Did you find her approach effective? Explain your answer.
3. Trask concludes her essay by requesting prospective visitors to remain home. Would her essay have any effect on your decision to visit Hawaii if you had the opportunity to do so? Why or why not?
4. **Rhetorical inquiry:** How does Trask use statistics to support her thesis as to the effects of tourism on Hawaiian culture?

MAURIZIO CHIERICI

Maurizio Chierici is an Italian journalist who worked as a special correspondent for the Milan newspaper Corriere della Sera. *"The Man from Hiroshima," translated from the Italian by Wallis Wilde-Menozzi, first appeared in* Granta *in 1987. At the time Chierici interviewed him, Claude Eatherly was the only American pilot still alive who could provide a firsthand account, and some historical perspective, on the mission over Hiroshima that resulted in the dropping of the atomic bomb. Eatherly was the lead pilot who had to decide if weather conditions permitted the bomb to be dropped. Chierici discovered that Eatherly, who was a much decorated, well-respected pilot, had been irrevocably changed by this event and was tormented by guilt. Fourteen months after this interview, Eatherly committed suicide. The following interview offers an unparalled insight into the meaning of Hiroshima from the perspective of an American pilot who was part of the crew responsible for dropping the atomic bomb.*

Before You Read

Did you ever wonder how the crew of the plane that dropped the bomb on Hiroshima felt about their mission?

The Man from Hiroshima

The protagonists of Hiroshima have no nostalgia. Even those people only remotely connected with the event have had difficult lives. All except one: Colonel Paul Tibbets, pilot of the *Enola Gay*, the plane that carried the atom bomb. On TV, serene under his white locks, he was unrepentant: 'I did my duty: I would do it again.' Tibbets is the only one to have passed these years without so much as a shiver. One of the pilots in the formation which flew over Hiroshima that day was unable to participate in the victory celebrations; he took his life three days before the official ceremony.

I knew another pilot full of problems; it wasn't at all easy to arrange to meet him. Everyone said: 'You'll need patience. But if he gave you his word, you'll hear from him sooner or later.' For days I waited and no one came. Then the pilot called to apologize. There was fog at the airport: the plane couldn't take off. Or: he had no money and the banks were closed. He would buy the ticket tomorrow. Tomorrow came and went; there was always a different story. Eventually I made a proposal: 'Eatherly, in five days it will be Christmas. I want to be back home in Italy before then. So I'll come to see you. It's much warmer where you are than in New York, and I've never been to Texas. I'll leave this afternoon.'

'No, stay where you are,' Eatherly interrupted. 'It's hard to talk here. Being in Texas blocks me; the people inhibit me. They know me too well, and there's no love lost between us. I plan to spend the holidays in New Jersey with a friend—I'd go out of my mind staying in Waco for Christmas—so I'll come and see you.'

I waited. Hours and hours in the lobby of the Hotel St Moritz, Central Park south. Behind windows the city is grey. Great lighted clocks scan the seconds at the tops of skyscrapers. Soon it will start to snow. People rush past who have come to New York on business, and who are going home laden with presents in coloured packages, their ribbons fluttering to the ground. In this festive atmosphere I find it strange to be meeting a man who contributed to the deaths of 60,000 people and turned their city into a monument for all time.

Three hours later the man sits down on the other side of the table, a glass in his hands. He is thin; his eyes are deeply marked, making his glance look old. But his hands are calm. When we shook hands I could feel they were cold and dry. He speaks first.

'How do I look?'

'I couldn't say. I've only seen your photographs. In them you seem older. And more tired and down on your luck.'

'I'm not old, or tired; only tormented. But not all the time. They have taken care of my nightmares. Right there in Waco; a doctor by the name of Parker. Grey-haired man; thin. It was heavy treatment. I don't know if their methods have changed, but the one they used with me was useless. "Give it up,

Claude," Parker said, "you're not guilty. It just fell to you to pilot a plane over Hiroshima. How many other Claudes were there in the air force who would have carried out an order as important as that one? The war finished; they went home. And what was the order anyway? Look at the sky and say: *Too many clouds here. Can't see Kokura and Nagasaki. Better do Hiroshima.*" Every day for fourteen months Doctor Parker gave me more or less the same speech. In the end I had to ask not to see him any more. I'd got worse.'

'There are a lot of stories, Mr. Eatherly. Some people say you're a fake. Why?'

He doesn't answer immediately. Instead he asks if he can take advan-   10
tage of my hospitality: would I have another drink with him? I wouldn't like to give the impression that Eatherly was an alcoholic. He could hold a bottle of whisky without any trouble and his eyes never clouded over. They remained alert and cold, just as they had been when he entered, bringing in a little of the wind from the city.

'You mean what Will Bradfort Huie wrote? He's a journalist who spent two days with me and then wrote a book—a whole book—about my life. Who am I? I don't know. But no one can describe himself in a minute. If I asked you point blank: "Do you think of yourself as an honest person, or someone who works at giving others an impression to suit your own needs?" would you be able to demonstrate either in a minute? I doubt it. I didn't know how to answer him either.'

'Are you a pacifist as you've claimed for years?'

'I am, and sincerely so, as is any American of good will. If I were religious, I would say that pacifism springs from a Jewish or Christian consciousness, but I'm not religious, and I don't want to look a fool expounding my philosophy. I can't be religious after Hiroshima. When someone makes a trip like mine and returns alive, he either kills himself or he lives like a Trappist monk. Cloistered; praying that the world changes and that the likes of Claude Eatherly and Paul Tibbets and the scientists who worked on the bomb are never born again.'

Claude grew up in Texas, where discourse is uninformed by Edwardian whispers from New England. Hearty laughter and loud voices; every sensation seems amplified. After the Japanese bombed Pearl Harbor, Texas offered more volunteers than any other state—the yellow devils had to be punished. Eatherly was among the volunteers. The youngest of six children, and a tackle on the Texas North College football team, he had a level head and a solid way of bringing them down. He didn't miss in the air either: he shot down thirty-three planes and his career took off. After three years he became a major, and a brilliant future seemed to await the handsome man with two bravery medals on his chest. The medals were what dug his grave. In the summer of 1945, he got orders to return home, but first he had to carry out one more mission. Just one.

You don't send a soldier home for the pleasure of giving him a little of   15
the good life. In the letter he posted to his mother announcing his imminent

return, Claude wrote. 'This will be the last cigarette they stick in this prisoner's mouth.' Nothing to get worried about. He went to New Mexico and joined a formation of supermen: the best, bravest, most famous pilots, all being trained in secret. They assigned him to a Boeing B-29 Superfortress that Claude christened *Straight Flush*.

The account of that morning some weeks later belongs to history. Three planes take off during the night of 6 August from Tinian in the Mariana Islands. Paul Tibbets is the group's commander. Eatherly opens the formation. There are no bombs in his plane; as for the others, no one suspects what a terrible device is hidden inside the *Enola Gay*. A bigger contrivance, they think, nothing more. Eatherly's job is to pinpoint the target with maximum accuracy. He must establish whether weather conditions allow for the centre to be Hiroshima, Kokura or Nagasaki, or whether they should continue towards secondary targets. He tells the story of that morning's events in a voice devoid of emotion which suggests that the recitation is the thousandth one.

'I had command of the lead plane, the *Straight Flush*. I flew over Hiroshima for fifteen minutes, studying the clouds covering the target—a bridge between the military zone and the city. Fifteen Japanese fighters were circling beneath me, but they're not made to fly above 29,000 feet where we were to be found. I looked up: cumulus clouds at 10,000, 12,000 metres. The wind was blowing them towards Hiroshima. Perfect weather. I could see the target clearly: the central span of the bridge. I laugh now when I think of the order: "I want only the central arch of the bridge, *only* that, you understand?" Even if I'd guessed that we were carrying something a bit special, the houses, the roads, the city still seemed very far away from our bomb. I said to myself: This morning's just a big scare for the Japanese.

'I transmitted the coded message, but the person who aimed the bomb made an error of 3,000 feet. Towards the city, naturally. But three thousand feet one way or the other wouldn't have made much difference: that what I thought as I watched it drop. Then the explosion stunned me momentarily. Hiroshima disappeared under a yellow cloud. No one spoke after that. Usually when you return from a mission with everyone still alive, you exchange messages with each other, impressions, congratulations. This time the radios stayed silent; three planes close together and mute. Not for fear of the enemy, but for fear of our own words. Each one of us must have asked forgiveness for the bomb. I'm not religious and I didn't know who to ask forgiveness from, but in that moment I made a promise to myself to oppose all bombs and all wars. Never again that yellow cloud . . .'

Eatherly raises his voice. It is clear the yellow cloud accompanies him through his life.

'And what did Tibbets say?'

Tibbets has nerves of steel, but the evening afterwards he explained how he spent those minutes. They had told him to be extremely careful: he was most at risk. So when the machine gunner yelled that the shock waves were on their way, he veered to take photographs; but the aeroplane just

20

bounced like a ping-pong ball held up by a fountain. Calm returned and Tibbets felt tired; he asked to be relieved, and fell asleep. But he talked about it that evening when the number of victims was just beginning to be known. He kept on saying: "I'm sorry guys, I did my duty. I've no regrets." And I don't have his nerves. A year later I asked to be discharged.'

'What reason did you give?'

'Exhaustion. I was exhausted. And I wanted to get married. It's risky to bring matters of conscience into it when you're in the forces. They were astounded—how could I throw away such a promising future? The day of my discharge they waved a sheet of paper in front of me. It said I would receive 237 dollars a month pension. That was good money in those days, but I turned it down. And since the regulations didn't allow me to refuse, I put it in writing that the sum was to go to war widows. The end of my relationship with flying.'

He didn't tell the rest of the story willingly. He returns to Texas where his family doesn't recognize him: thin, nervous, irascible, 24 years old. He marries the Italian girl he met in New Mexico while he was training for the final mission. Concetta Margetti had tried Hollywood and finally been reduced to selling cigarettes in a local nightclub—not perhaps the ideal wife for someone in Claude's state. But they write to each other, they get married. A war story, yes; but the war had shredded Eatherly's nerves. In the middle of the night he wakes his wife, breathless and in tears: 'Hit the ground, the yellow cloud's coming!' It goes on like this for four years. His family finally convince him to enter the psychiatric hospital in Waco as a voluntary patient. He can take walks in the park any time of the day or night. He plays golf and receives visitors. Concetta keeps him company on Sunday. His brother brings him books and a pair of running shoes.

Then the problems start. Claude forges a cheque to send to the victims of   25
Hiroshima. He enters a bank with a toy pistol; for a few minutes the employees are terrified until Eatherly bursts out laughing. One day his move succeeds; he threatens a department store clerk with a fake gun and makes her turn over the money, which he throws from a balcony before escaping. They catch him and take him back to Waco. He's no longer a voluntary patient: now they lock him in. They accuse him of behaving in an antisocial way. (This euphemism is the last show of respect for his heroic war record.) He is confined to his room.

After fourteen months in the mental hospital he leaves, a ghost. His wife abandons him. His brother closes his bank account. Claude cannot look after himself or his money. And now the protest smoulders again. He enters a bar in Texas, armed. He threatens the people inside and gets them to put their money into the sack he is holding, just like he's seen in films. But it comes to nothing. He is handcuffed and taken to gaol in a police car. The sergeant accompanying him doesn't know who he is, only that he's an ex-pilot. I asked Eatherly how it felt to be facing a prison sentence for the first time.

I should say terrible, but it wasn't. Nothing mattered to me. I'd been in prison all the time; the door was inside me. In the police car the sergeant was staring at me. He was curious. He was thinking about some famous criminal. . . . It was a long trip. I was quiet, but his staring eyes bothered me. "Where do you come from, sergeant?" I asked him. "From Chicago." And I: "I knew you came from somewhere." I wanted to unfreeze the atmosphere, but he wasn't having it. He asked me: "It's not strictly legal, but can you talk, here in the car?" I made a yes sign.

"Where are you from?"

"From here."

"Where were you based during the war?"   30

"In the Pacific."

"I was in the Pacific too. Where did they land you?"

"Tinian, in the Marianas, special group 509."

He looked at me, stunned. "I know who you are. You're Major Eatherly! Good God, Major, how did you end up like this? You're sick, right? I read that somewhere. I'll give you a hand."

'Then they locked me up in the loony bin again.'   35

His torment went on: a poor soul, incapable of getting on with the business of life. No one understands his drama. People's aversion to him grows. Let's not forget that Eatherly lived out this difficult period in the America of Senator McCarthy—the Grand Inquisitor of frustrated nationalism. McCarthy formented a type of suspicion which reflected the cold war: the witch hunt. Eatherly becomes a witch. His passionate, if slightly naïve, criticism of the mechanisms of war is considered a threat to national security. The judges disagree over his case. The biography confected by William Bradfort Huie from less than two days of interviews weakens his defence. For Bradfort, the Major 'never saw the ball of fire, nor was he aware of the yellow wave. By the time of the explosion, he and his gunner were 100 kilometres from the site.' Returning to base he was surprised by the journalists and photographers crowding the runway where the *Enola Gay* had landed. 'If Eatherly is mad,' writes Bradfort, 'then his madness was hatched on 6 August, 1945, not from horror but from jealousy.'

'When I knew him,' Bradfort Huie continues implacably, 'he was already a fraud. Right off he asked me for five hundred dollars. He had never once attempted suicide. I spent a long time with him, and I looked at his wrists: there were no scars.'

'Is that true Claude?'

'These are not the kind of things you want to brag about. Look at my arms.' He turns up the sleeves of his jacket and unbuttons his cuffs. Two purple scars, deep and unpleasant, run towards his hands. 'I don't want you to pity me. I'm happy to have been able to talk. Now I've got to go.'

He disappeared as he had appeared, with the same suddenness. Before   40 passing through the bar door and turning out into the hall he looked back, as if he had forgotten something. 'I want to apologize for being late. And thanks for these . . .' He gestured towards the row of glasses on the table.

'It was my pleasure to meet you. Merry Christmas.'

Fourteen months later Claude Eatherly took his life.

Questions for Discussion and Writing

1. How did Claude Eatherly's decision regarding the weather conditions over Japan, on the day the atomic bomb was dropped, irrevocably alter his life?
2. What means does Chierici use, as an interviewer, to put Eatherly's story into a context that would allow the reader to understand how Eatherly's guilt took over his life?
3. Conduct an interview with someone who was involved in a momentous event, and write up your results in order to allow your readers to understand the effect this event had on the person's life.
4. **Rhetorical inquiry:** How does the example of Eatherly signing over his military pension to Japanese war widows and survivors illustrate his need to atone for his role in the bombing?

DON DELILLO

Don DeLillo (b. 1936) grew up in the Bronx, took courses in communication arts at Fordham College, and wrote advertising copy. He began writing full time in 1964 and his many published works include White Noise *(1985), which won the National Book Award, and* Cosmopolis *(2003). His most recent work is* Love-Lies-Bleeding: A Play *(2005). In the following essay which was first published in* Harper's Magazine *December 2001, DeLillo recognizes that the attack on the World Trade Center has permanently altered our perceptions of the world in which we live and ushered in a new era in history.*

Before You Read

Consider how DeLillo conveys the chaos, confusion, and history-altering nature of September 11, 2001.

In the Ruins of the Future

In the past decade the surge of capital markets has dominated discourse and shaped global consciousness. Multinational corporations have come to seem more vital and influential than governments. The dramatic climb of the Dow and the speed of the internet summoned us all to live permanently in the future, in the utopian glow of cyber-capital, because there is no memory there and this is where markets are uncontrolled and investment potential has no limit.

All this changed on September 11. Today, again, the world narrative belongs to terrorists. But the primary target of the men who attacked the Pentagon and the World Trade Centre was not the global economy. It was America that drew their fury. It was the high gloss of our modernity. It was the thrust of our technology. It was our perceived godlessness. It was the blunt force of our foreign policy. It was the power of American culture to penetrate every wall, home, life and mind.

Terror's response is a narrative that has been developing over years, only now becoming inescapable. It is our lives and minds that are occupied now. This catastrophic event changes the way we think and act, moment to moment, week to week, for unknown weeks and months to come, and steely years. Our world, parts of our world, have crumbled into theirs, which means we are living in a place of danger and rage.

The protesters in Genoa, Prague, Seattle and other cities want to decelerate the global momentum that seemed to be driving unmindfully toward a landscape of consumer-robots and social instability, with the chance of self-determination probably diminishing for most people in most countries. Whatever acts of violence marked the protests, most of the men and women involved tend to be a moderating influence, trying to slow things down, even things out, hold off the white-hot future.

The terrorists of September 11 want to bring back the past. OUR tradition of free expression and our justice system's provisions for the rights of the accused can only seem an offence to men bent on suicidal terror. 5

We are rich, privileged and strong, but they are willing to die. This is the edge they have, the fire of aggrieved belief. We live in a wide world, routinely filled with exchange of every sort, an open circuit of work, talk, family and expressible feeling. The terrorist, planted in a Florida town, pushing his supermarket trolley, nodding to his neighbour, lives in a far narrower format. This is his edge, his strength. Plots reduce the world. He builds a plot around his anger and our indifference. He lives a certain kind of apartness, hard and tight. This is not the self-watcher, the soft white dangling boy who shoots someone to keep from disappearing into himself. The terrorist shares a secret and a self. At a certain point he and his brothers may begin to feel less motivated by politics and personal hatred than by brotherhood itself. They share the codes and protocols of their mission here and something deeper, a vision of judgment and devastation.

Does the sight of a woman pushing a stroller soften the man to her humanity and vulnerability, and her child's as well, and all the people he is here to kill?

This is his edge, that he does not see her. Years here, waiting, taking flying lessons, making the routine gestures of community and home, the credit card, the bank account, the post-office box. All tactical, linked, layered. He knows who we are and what we mean in the world—an idea, a righteous fever in the brain. But there is no defenceless human at the end of his gaze.

The sense of disarticulation we hear in the term "Us and Them" has never been so striking, at either end.

We can tell ourselves that whatever we've done to inspire bitterness, 10 distrust and rancour, it was not so damnable as to bring this day down on our heads. But there is no logic in apocalypse. They have gone beyond the bounds of passionate payback. This is heaven and hell, a sense of armed martyrdom as the surpassing drama of human experience.

He pledges his submission to God and meditates on the blood to come.

The Bush administration was feeling a nostalgia for the cold war. This is over now. Many things are over. The narrative ends in the rubble and it is left to us to create the counternarrative.

There are 100,000 stories crisscrossing New York, Washington, and the world. Where we were, who we know, what we've seen or heard. There are the doctors' appointments that saved lives, the cellphones that were used to report the hijackings. Stories generating others and people running north out of the rumbling smoke and ash. Men running in suits and ties, women who'd lost their shoes, cops running from the skydive of all that towering steel.

People running for their lives are part of the story that is left to us.

There are stories of heroism and encounters with dread. There are stories that carry around their edges the luminous ring of coincidence, fate, or premonition. They take us beyond the hard numbers of dead and missing and give us a glimpse of elevated being. For 100 who are arbitrarily dead, we need to find one person saved by a flash of forewarning. There are configurations that chill and awe us both. Two women on two planes, best of friends, who die together and apart, tower 1 and tower 2. What desolate epic tragedy might bear the weight of such juxtaposition? But we can also ask what symmetry, bleak and touching both, takes one friend, spares the other's grief?   15

The brother of one of the women worked in one of the towers. He managed to escape.

In Union Square Park, about two miles north of the attack site, the improvised memorials are another part of our response. The flags, flowerbeds and votive candles, the lamppost hung with paper airplanes, the passages from the Koran and the Bible, the letters and poems, the cardboard John Wayne, the children's drawings of the twin towers, the hand-painted signs for Free Hugs, Free Back Rubs, the graffiti of love and peace on the tall equestrian statue.

There are many photographs of missing persons, some accompanied by hopeful lists of identifying features. (Man with panther tattoo, upper right arm.) There is the saxophonist, playing softly. There is the sculptured flag of rippling copper and aluminium, six feet long, with two young people still attending to the finer details of the piece.

Then there are the visitors to the park. The artifacts on display represent the confluence of a number of cultural tides, patriotic and multidevotional and retro hippy. The visitors move quietly in the floating aromas of candlewax, roses and bus fumes. There are many people this mild evening and in their voices, manner, clothing and in the colour of their skin they recapitulate the mix we see in the photocopied faces of the lost.

For the next 50 years, people who were not in the area when the attacks occurred will claim to have been there. In time, some of them will believe it. Others will claim to have lost friends or relatives, although they did not.   20

This is also the counternarrative, a shadow history of false memories and imagined loss.

The internet is a counternarrative, shaped in part by rumour, fantasy and mystical reverberation.

The cellphones, the lost shoes, the handkerchiefs mashed in the faces of running men and women. The box cutters and credit cards. The paper that came streaming out of the towers and drifted across the river to Brooklyn backyards, status reports, résumés, insurance forms. Sheets of paper driven into concrete, according to witnesses. Paper slicing into truck tyres, fixed there.

These are among the smaller objects and more marginal stories in the sifted ruins of the day. We need them, even the common tools of the terrorists, to set against the massive spectacle that continues to seem unmanageable, too powerful a thing to set into our frame of practiced response.

Ash was spattering the windows. Karen was half dressed, grabbing the kids and trying to put on some clothes and talking with her husband and scooping things to take out to the corridor, and they looked at her, her twin girls, as if she had 14 heads.

They stayed in the corridor for a while, thinking there might be secondary explosions. They waited, and began to feel safer, and went back to the apartment.

At the next impact, Marc knew in the sheerest second before the shock wave broadsided their building that it was a second plane, impossible, striking the second tower. Their building was two blocks away and he'd thought the first crash was an accident.

They went back to the hallway, where others began to gather, 15 or 20 people.

Karen ran back for a cellphone, a cordless phone, a charger, water, sweaters, snacks for the kids and then made a quick dash to the bedroom for her wedding ring.

From the window she saw people running in the street, others locked shoulder to shoulder, immobilised, with debris coming down on them. People were trampled, struck by falling objects, and there was ash and paper everywhere, paper whipping through the air, no sign of light or sky.

Cellphones were down. They talked on the cordless, receiving information measured out in eyedrops. They were convinced that the situation outside was far more grave than it was here.

Smoke began to enter the corridor.

Then the first tower fell. She thought it was a bomb. When she talked to someone on the phone and found out what had happened, she felt a surreal relief. Bombs and missiles were not falling everywhere in the city. It was not all-out war, at least not yet.

Marc was in the apartment getting chairs for the older people, for the woman who'd had hip surgery. When he heard the first low drumming rumble, he stood in a strange dead calm and said, "Something is happening." It sounded exactly like what it was, a tall tower collapsing.

The windows were surfaced with ash now, blacked out completely, and   35
he wondered what was out there. What remained to be seen and did he want
to see it?

They all moved into the stairwell, behind a fire door, but smoke kept
coming in. It was gritty ash and they were eating it.

He ran back inside, grabbing towels off the racks and washcloths out of
drawers and drenching them in the sink, and filling his bicycle water bottles,
and grabbing the kids' underwear. He thought the crush of buildings was
the thing to fear most. This is what would kill them.

Karen was on the phone, talking to a friend in the district attorney's
office, about half a mile to the north. She was pleading for help. She begged,
pleaded and hung up. For the next hour a detective kept calling with advice
and encouragement.

Marc came back out to the corridor. I think we might die, he told himself, hedging his sense of what would happen next.

The detective told Karen to stay where they were.   40

When the second tower fell, my heart fell with it. I called Marc, who is my
nephew, on his cordless. I couldn't stop thinking of the size of the towers and
the meagre distance between those buildings and his. He answered, we talked.
I have no memory of the conversation except for his final remark, slightly
urgent, concerning someone on the other line, who might be sending help.

Smoke was seeping out of the elevator shaft now. Karen was saying
goodbye to be father in Oregon. Not hello-goodbye. But goodbye-I-think-
we-are-going-to-die. She thought smoke would be the thing that did it.

People sat on chairs along the walls. They chatted about practical matters. They sang songs with the kids. The kids in the group were cooperative
because the adults were damn scared.

There was an improvised rescue in progress. Karen's friend and colleague made their way down from Centre Street, turning up with two policemen they'd enlisted en route. They had dust masks and a destination and
they searched every floor for others who might be stranded in the building.

They came out into a world of ash and near night. There was no one   45
else to be seen now on the street. Grey ash covering the cars and pavement,
ash falling in large flakes, paper still drifting down, discarded shoes,
strollers, briefcases. The members of the group were masked and towelled,
children in adult's arms, moving east and then north on Nassau Street, trying not to look around, only what's immediate, one step and then another,
all closely focused, a pregnant woman, a newborn, a dog.

They were covered in ash when they reached shelter at Pace University,
where there was food and water, and kind and able staff members, and a
gas-leak scare, and more running people.

Workers began pouring water on the group. Stay wet, stay wet. This
was the theme of the first half-hour.

Later a line began to form along the food counter.

Someone said, "I don't want cheese on that."

Someone said, "I like it better not so cooked."   50

Not so incongruous, really, just people alive and hungry, beginning to be themselves again.

Technology is our fate, our truth. It is what we mean when we call ourselves the only superpower on the planet. The materials and methods we devise make it possible for us to claim our future. We don't have to depend on God or the prophets or other astonishments. We are the astonishment. The miracle is what we ourselves produce, the systems and networks that change the way we live and think.

But whatever great skeins of technology lie ahead, ever more complex, connective, precise, micro-fractional, the future has yielded, for now, to medieval expedience, to the old slow furies of cut-throat religion.

Kill the enemy and pluck out his heart.

If others in less scientifically advanced cultures were able to share,   55
wanted to share, some of the blessings of our technology, without a threat to their faith or traditions, would they need to rely on a God in whose name they kill the innocent? Would they need to invent a God who rewards violence against the innocent with a promise of "infinite paradise," in the words of a handwritten letter found in the luggage of one of the hijackers?

For all those who may want what we've got, there are all those who do not. These are the men who have fashioned a morality of destruction. They want what they used to have before the waves of western influence. They surely see themselves as the elect of God whether or not they follow the central precepts of Islam. It is the presumptive right of those who choose violence and death to speak directly to God. They will kill and then die. Or they will die first, in the cockpit, in clean shoes, according to instructions in the letter.

Six days after the attacks, the territory below Canal Street is hedged with barricades. There are few civilians in the street. Police at some checkpoints, troops wearing camouflage gear and gas masks at others, and a pair of state troopers in conversation, and 10 burly men striding east in hard hats, work pants and NYPD jackets. A shop owner tries to talk a cop into letting him enter his place of business. He is a small elderly man with a Jewish accent, but there is no relief today. Garbage bags are everywhere in high, broad stacks. The area is bedraggled and third-worldish, with an air of permanent emergency, everything surfaced in ash.

It is possible to pass through some checkpoints, detour around others. At Chambers Street I look south through the links of the National Rent-A-Fence barrier. There stands the smoky remnant of filigree that marks the last tall thing, the last sign in the mire of wreckage that there were towers here that dominated the skyline for over a quarter of a century.

Ten days later and a lot closer, I stand at another barrier with a group of people, looking directly into the strands of openwork facade. It is almost too close. It is almost Roman, I-beams for stonework, but not nearly so salvageable. Many here describe the scene to others on cellphones.

"Oh my God, I'm standing here," says the man next to me.   60

The World Trade towers were not only an emblem of advanced technology but a justification, in a sense, for technology's irresistible will to realise in solid form whatever becomes theoretically allowable. Once defined, every limit must be reached. The tactful sheathing of the towers was intended to reduce the direct threat of such straight-edge enormity, a giantism that eased over the years into something a little more familiar and comfortable, even dependable in a way.

Now a small group of men have literally altered our skyline. We have fallen back in time and space. It is their technology that marks our moments, the small, lethal devices, the remote-control detonators they fashion out of radios, or the larger technology they borrow from us, passenger jets that become manned missiles.

Maybe this is a grim subtext of their enterprise. They see something innately destructive in the nature of technology. It brings death to their customs and beliefs. Use it as what it is, a thing that kills.

Eleven years ago, during the engagement in the Persian Gulf, people had trouble separating the war from coverage of the war. After the first euphoric days, coverage became limited. The rush of watching all that eerie green night-vision footage, shot from fighter jets in combat, had been so intense that it became hard to honour the fact that the war was still going on, untelevised. A layer of consciousness had been stripped away. People shuffled around, muttering. They were lonely for their war.

The events of September 11 were covered unstintingly. There was no   65 confusion of roles on TV. The raw event was one thing, the coverage another. The event dominated the medium. It was bright and totalising and some of us said it was unreal. When we say a thing is unreal, we mean it is too real, a phenomenon so unaccountable and yet so bound to the power of objective fact that we can't tilt it to the slant of our perceptions. First the planes struck the towers. After a time it became possible for us to absorb this, barely. But when the towers fell. When the rolling smoke began moving downward, floor to floor. This was so vast and terrible that it was outside imagining even as it happened. We could not catch up with it. But it was real, punishingly so, an expression of the physics of structural limits and a void in one's soul, and there was the huge antenna falling out of the sky, straight down, blunt end first, like an arrow moving backwards in time.

The event itself has no purchase on the mercies of analogy or simile. We have to take the shock and horror as it is. But living language is not diminished. The writer wants to understand what this day has done to us. Is it too soon? We seem pressed for time, all of us. Time is scarcer now. There is a sense of compression, plans made hurriedly, time forced and distorted. But language is inseparable from the world that provokes it. The writer begins in the towers, trying to imagine the moment, desperately. Before politics, before history and religion, there is the primal terror. People falling from the towers hand in hand. This is part of the counternarrative, hands and spirits joining, human beauty in the crush of meshed steel.

In its desertion of every basis for comparison, the event asserts its singularity. There is something empty in the sky. The writer tries to give memory, tenderness and meaning to all that howling space.

We like to think that America invented the future. We are comfortable with the future, intimate with it. But there are disturbances now, in large and small ways, a chain of reconsiderations. Where we live, how we travel, what we think about when we look at our children. For many people, the event has changed the grain of the most routine moment.

We may find that the ruin of the towers is implicit in other things. The new Palm Pilot at a fingertip's reach, the stretch limousine parked outside the hotel, the midtown skyscraper under construction, carrying the name of a major investment bank—all haunted in a way by what has happened, less assured in their authority, in the prerogatives they offer.

There is fear of other kinds of terrorism, the prospect that biological   70
and chemical weapons will contaminate the air we breathe and the water we drink. There wasn't much concern about this after earlier terrorist acts. This time we are trying to name the future, not in our normally hopeful way, but guided by dread.

What has already happened is sufficient to affect the air around us, psychologically. We are all breathing the fumes of lower Manhattan, where traces of the dead are everywhere, in the soft breeze off the river, on rooftops and windows, in our hair and on our clothes.

Think of a future in which the components of a microchip are the size of atoms. The devices that pace our lives will operate from the smart quantum spaces of pure information. Now think of people in countless thousands massing in anger and vowing revenge. Enlarged photos of martyrs and holy men dangle from balconies, and the largest images are those of a terrorist leader.

Two forces in the world, past and future. With the end of communism, the ideas and principles of modern democracy were seen clearly to prevail, whatever the inequalities of the system itself. This is still the case. But now there is a global theocratic state, unboundaried and floating and so obsolete it must depend on suicidal fervour to gain its aims.

Ideas evolve and de-evolve, and history is turned on end.

On Friday of the first week a long series of vehicles moves slowly west   75
on Canal Street. Dump trucks, flatbeds, sanitation sweepers. There are giant earthmovers making a tremendous revving sound. A scant number of pedestrians, some in dust masks, others just standing, watching, the indigenous people, clinging to walls and doorways, unaccustomed to traffic that doesn't bring buyers and sellers, goods and cash. The fire rescue car and state police cruiser, the staccato sirens of a line of police vans. Cops stand at the sawhorse barriers, trying to clear the way. Ambulances, cherry pickers, a fleet of Con Ed trucks, all this clamour moving south a few blocks ahead, into the cloud of sand and ash.

One month earlier I'd taken the same walk, early evening, among crowds of people, the panethnic swarm of shoppers, merchants, residents

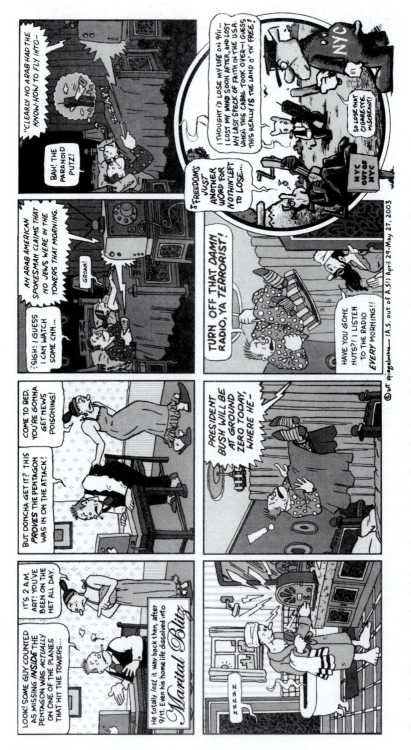

How does this cartoon by Art Spiegelman convey the atmosphere following 9/11 addressed by DeLillo?

and passers-by, with a few tourists as well, and the man at the kerbstone doing acupoint massage, and the dreadlocked kid riding his bike on the sidewalk. This was the spirit of Canal Street, the old jostle and stir unchanged for many decades and bearing no sign of SoHo just above, with its restaurants and artists' lofts, or TriBeCa below, rich in architectural textures. Here were hardware bargains, car stereos, foam rubber and industrial plastics, the tattoo parlour and the pizza parlour.

Then I saw the woman on the prayer rug. I'd just turned the corner, heading south to meet some friends, and there she was, young and slender, in a bright silk headscarf. It was time for sunset prayer and she was kneeling, upper body pitched towards the edge of the rug. She was partly concealed by a couple of vendors' carts and no one seemed much to notice her. I think there was another woman seated on a folding chair near the kerbstone. The figure on the rug faced east, which meant most immediately a storefront just a foot and a half from her tipped head, but more distantly and pertinently towards Mecca, of course, the holiest city of Islam.

Some prayer rugs include a mihrab in their design, an arched element representing the prayer niche in a mosque that indicates the direction of Mecca. The only locational guide the young woman needed was the Manhattan grid.

I looked at her in prayer and it was clearer to me than ever, the daily sweeping taken-for-granted greatness of New York. The city will accommodate every language, ritual, belief and opinion. In the rolls of the dead of September 11, all these vital differences were surrendered to the impact and flash. The bodies themselves are missing in large numbers. For the survivors, more grief. But the dead are their own nation and race, one identity, young or old, devout or unbelieving—a union of souls. During the hadj, the annual pilgrimage to Mecca, the faithful must eliminate every sign of status, income and nationality, the men wearing identical strips of seamless white cloth, the women with covered heads, all recalling in prayer their fellowship with the dead.

Allahu akbar. God is great.   80

Questions for Discussion and Writing

1. How did the events of September 11th, 2001 permanently alter the attitude that America had about itself and the kind of future it can expect?
2. How is the effectiveness of this account enhanced by the sense of fragmentation in the narrative combined with memorable and striking vignettes? How did the experiences of Marc and Karen personalize the tragedy of these events?
3. Among the many repercussions of 9/11 that keep unfolding, which is the most meaningful for you and why?
4. **Rhetorical inquiry:** What means does DeLillo use to convey the complete disconnect between the world view of terrorists and those who become their victims?

Fiction

AMBROSE BIERCE

Ambrose Bierce (1842–1914?) was born in rural Ohio, the youngest of a large, devout poverty-stricken family. He enlisted in the Union Army at the outbreak of the Civil War as a drummer boy, fought bravely in some of the most important battles, and rose from the rank of private to major. After the war, he became a journalist in San Francisco and wrote satiric pieces for a news weekly, of which he was soon made editor. The biting wit for which Bierce is so distinguished became his hallmark. He worked briefly in London as a journalist; after returning to the United States he wrote his famous "Prattler" column for the Argonaut *magazine. In 1887, William Randolph Hearst bought the column and placed it on the editorial page of the* Sunday Examiner. *Bierce published tales of soldiers and civilians in 1891 and later followed them with* Can Such Things Be? *(1893) and his acerbic* Devil's Dictionary *(1906). In 1913 he left for Mexico to cover the revolution and vanished without a trace. With characteristic aplomb, his last letter to a friend stated, "Goodbye, if you hear of my being stood up against a Mexican stone wall and shot to rags, please know that I think it a pretty good way to depart this life. It beats old age, disease, or falling down the cellar stairs." "An Occurrence at Owl Creek Bridge" (1890) has emerged as a classic. This haunting story reconstructs an experience so that impressions, colors, sounds, sensations, and time itself are thoroughly subordinated to the psychological state of the narrator.*

As You Read

Notice how Bierce moves you from an objective account to a psychological perspective within the mind of the main character.

An Occurrence at Owl Creek Bridge

I

A man stood upon a railroad bridge in Northern Alabama, looking down into the swift waters twenty feet below. The man's hands were behind his back, the wrists bound with a cord. A rope loosely encircled his neck. It was attached to a stout cross-timber above his head, and the slack fell to the level of his knees. Some loose boards laid upon the sleepers supporting the metals of the railway supplied a footing for him and his executioners—two private soldiers of the Federal army, directed by a sergeant, who in civil life may have been a deputy sheriff. At a short remove upon the same temporary platform was an officer in the uniform of his rank, armed. He was a captain. A sentinel at each end of the bridge stood with his rifle in the position known as "support," that is to say, vertical in front of the left shoulder, the hammer resting on the forearm thrown straight across the chest—a normal and unnatural position, enforcing an erect carriage of the body. It did not appear to be the duty of these two men to know what was occurring at the centre of the bridge; they merely block-aded the two ends of the foot plank which traversed it.

Beyond one of the sentinels nobody was in sight; the railroad ran straight away into a forest for a hundred yards, then, curving, was lost to view. Doubtless there was an outpost further along. The other bank of the stream was open ground—a gentle acclivity crowned with a stockade of ver-tical tree trunks, loop-holed for rifles, with a single embrasure through which protruded the muzzle of a brass cannon commanding the bridge. Midway of the slope between bridge and fort were the spectators—a single company of infantry in line, at "parade rest," the butts of the rifles on the ground, the barrels inclining slightly backward against the right shoulder, the hands crossed upon the stock. A lieutenant stood at the right of the line, the point of his sword upon the ground, his left hand resting upon his right. Excepting the group of four at the centre of the bridge not a man moved. The company faced the bridge, staring stonily, motionless. The sentinels, facing the banks of the stream, might have been statues to adorn the bridge. The captain stood with folded arms, silent, observing the work of his subor-dinates but making no sign. Death is a dignitary who, when he comes announced, is to be received with formal manifestations of respect, even by those most familiar with him. In the code of military etiquette silence and fixity are forms of deference.

The man who was engaged in being hanged was apparently about thirty-five years of age. He was a civilian, if one might judge from his dress, which was that of a planter. His features were good—a straight nose, firm mouth, broad forehead, from which his long, dark hair was combed straight back, falling behind his ears to the collar of his well-fitted frock coat. He wore a moustache and pointed beard, but no whiskers; his eyes were large and dark grey and had a kindly expression which one would hardly have expected in one whose neck was in the hemp. Evidently this was no vulgar assassin. The liberal military code makes provision for hanging many kinds of people, and gentlemen are not excluded.

The preparations being complete, the two private soldiers stepped aside and each drew away the plank upon which he had been standing. The ser-geant turned to the captain, saluted and placed himself immediately behind that officer, who in turn moved apart one pace. These movements left the condemned man and the sergeant standing on the two ends of the same plank, which spanned three of the cross-ties of the bridge. The end upon which the civilian stood almost, but not quite, reached a fourth. This plank had been held in place by the weight of the captain; it was now held by that of the sergeant. At a signal from the former, the latter would step aside, the plank would tilt and the condemned man go down between two ties. The arrangement commended itself to his judgment as simple and effective. His face had not been covered nor his eyes bandaged. He looked a moment at

his "unsteadfast footing," then let his gaze wander to the swirling water of
the stream racing madly beneath his feet. A piece of dancing driftwood
caught his attention and his eyes followed it down the current. How slowly
it appeared to move! What a sluggish stream!

He closed his eyes in order to fix his last thoughts upon his wife and   5
children. The water, touched to gold by the early sun, the brooding mists
under the banks at some distance down the stream, the fort, the soldiers, the
piece of drift—all had distracted him. And now he became conscious of a
new disturbance. Striking through the thought of his dear ones was a sound
which he could neither ignore nor understand, a sharp, distinct, metallic
percussion like the stroke of a blacksmith's hammer upon the anvil; it had
the same ringing quality. He wondered what it was, and whether immeasurably distant or near by—it seemed both. Its recurrence was regular, but as
slow as the tolling of a death knell. He awaited each stroke with impatience
and—he knew not why—apprehension. The intervals of silence grew progressively longer; the delays became maddening. With their greater infre-
quency the sounds increased in strength and sharpness. They hurt his ear
like the thrust of a knife; he feared he would shriek. What he heard was the
ticking of his watch.

He unclosed his eyes and saw again the water below him. "If I could
free my hands," he thought, "I might throw off the noose and spring into
the stream. By diving I could evade the bullets, and, swimming, vigorously,
reach the bank, take to the woods, and get away home. My home, thank
God, is as yet outside their lines; my wife and little ones are still beyond the
invader's farthest advance."

As these thoughts, which have here to be set down in words, were
flashed into the doomed man's brain rather than evolved from it, the captain
nodded to the sergeant. The sergeant stepped aside.

II

Peyton Farquhar was a well-to-do planter, of an old and highly-respected
Alabama family. Being a slave owner, and, like other slave owners, a politician, he was naturally an original secessionist and ardently devoted to the
Southern cause. Circumstances of an imperious nature which it is unnecessary to relate here, had prevented him from taking service with the gallant
army which had fought the disastrous campaigns ending with the fall of
Corinth, and he chafed under the inglorious restraint, longing for the release
of his energies, the larger life of the soldier, the opportunity for distinction.
That opportunity, he felt, would come, as it comes to all in war time. Meanwhile he did what he could. No service was too humble for him to perform
in aid of the South, no adventure too perilous for him to undertake if consistent with the character of a civilian who was at heart a soldier, and who in
good faith and without too much qualification assented to at least a part of
the frankly villainous dictum that all is fair in love and war.

One evening while Farquhar and his wife were sitting on a rustic bench near the entrance to his ground, a grey-clad soldier[1] rode up to the gate and asked for a drink of water. Mrs. Farquhar was only too happy to serve him with her own white hands. While she was gone to fetch the water, her husband approached the dusty horseman and inquired eagerly for news from the front.

"The Yanks are repairing the railroads," said the man, "and are getting ready for another advance. They have reached the Owl Creek bridge, put it in order, and built a stockade on the other bank. The commandant has issued an order, which is posted everywhere, declaring that any civilian caught interfering with the railroad, its bridges, tunnels, or trains, will be summarily hanged. I saw the order."

"How far is it to the Owl Creek bridge?" Farquhar asked.

"About thirty miles."

"Is there no force on this side the creek?"

"Only a picket post half a mile out, on the railroad, and a single sentinel at this end of the bridge."

"Suppose a man—a civilian and student of hanging—should elude the picket post and perhaps get the better of the sentinel," said Farquhar, smiling, "what could he accomplish?"

The soldier reflected. "I was there a month ago," he replied. "I observed that the flood of last winter had lodged a great quantity of driftwood against the wooden pier at this end of the bridge. It is now dry and would burn like tow."

The lady had now brought the water, which the soldier drank. He thanked her ceremoniously, bowed to her husband, and rode away. An hour later, after nightfall, he repassed the plantation, going northward in the direction from which he had come. He was a Federal scout.

III

As Peyton Farquhar fell straight downward through the bridge, he lost consciousness and was as one already dead. From this state he was awakened—ages later, it seemed to him—by the pain of a sharp pressure upon his throat, followed by a sense of suffocation. Keen, poignant agonies seemed to shoot from his neck downward through every fibre of his body and limbs. These pains appeared to flash along well-defined lines of ramification, and to beat with an inconceivably rapid periodicity. They seemed like streams of pulsating fire heating him to an intolerable temperature. As to his head, he was conscious of nothing but a feeling of fullness—of congestion. These sensations were unaccompanied by thought. The intellectual part of his nature was already effaced; he had power only to feel, and feeling was torment. He

---

[1] *grey-clad soldier:* refers to the gray uniforms worn by Confederate soldiers.

was conscious of motion. Encompassed in a luminous cloud, of which he was now merely the fiery heart, without material substance, he swung through unthinkable arcs of oscillation, like a vast pendulum. Then all at once, with terrible suddenness, the light about him shot upward with the noise of a loud plash; a frightful roaring was in his ears, and all was cold and dark. The power of thought was restored; he knew that the rope had broken and he had fallen into the stream. There was no additional strangulation; the noose about his neck was already suffocating him, and kept the water from his lungs. To die of hanging at the bottom of a river—the idea seemed to him ludicrous. He opened his eyes in the blackness and saw above him a gleam of light, but how distant, how inaccessible! He was still sinking, for the light became fainter and fainter until it was a mere glimmer. Then it began to grow and brighten, and he knew that he was rising toward the surface—knew it with reluctance, for he was now very comfortable. "To be hanged and drowned," he thought, "that is not so bad; but I do not wish to be shot. No: I will not be shot; that is not fair."

He was not conscious of an effort, but a sharp pain in his wrist apprised him that he was trying to free his hands. He gave the struggle his attention, as an idler might observe the feat of a juggler, without interest in the outcome. What splendid effort!—what magnificent, what superhuman strength! Ah, that was a fine endeavor! Bravo! The cord fell away; his arms parted and floated upward, the hands dimly seen on each side in the growing light. He watched them with a new interest as first one and then the other pounced upon the noose at his neck. They tore it away and thrust it fiercely aside, its undulations resembling those of a water-snake. "Put it back, put it back!" He thought he shouted these words to his hands, for the undoing of the noose had been succeeded by the direst pang which he had yet experienced. His neck ached horribly; his brain was on fire; his heart, which had been fluttering faintly, gave a great leap, trying to force itself out at his mouth. His whole body was racked and wrenched with an insupportable anguish! But his disobedient hands gave no heed to the command. They beat the water vigorously with quick, downward strokes, forcing him to the surface. He felt his head emerge; his eyes were blinded by the sunlight; his chest expanded convulsively, and with a supreme and crowning agony his lungs engulfed a great draught of air, which instantly he expelled in a shriek!

He was now in full possession of his physical senses. They were, indeed,   20
preternaturally keen and alert. Something in the awful disturbance of his organic system had so exalted and refined them that they made record of things never before perceived. He felt the ripples upon his face and heard their separate sounds as they struck. He looked at the forest on the bank of the stream, saw the individual trees, the leaves and the veining of each leaf—saw the very insects upon them, the locusts, the brilliant-bodied flies, the grey spiders stretching their webs from twig to twig. He noted the prismatic colors in all the dewdrops upon a million blades of grass. The humming of the gnats that danced above the eddies of the stream, the beating of the

dragon flies' wings, the strokes of the water spiders' legs, like oars which had lifted their boat—all these made audible music. A fish slid along beneath his eyes and he heard the rush of its body parting the water.

He had come to the surface facing down the stream; in a moment the visible world seemed to wheel slowly round, himself the pivotal point, and he saw the bridge, the fort, the soldiers upon the bridge, the captain, the sergeant, the two privates, his executioners. They were in silhouette against the blue sky. They shouted and gesticulated, pointing at him; the captain had drawn his pistol, but did not fire; the others were unarmed. Their movements were grotesque and horrible, their forms gigantic.

Suddenly he heard a sharp report and something struck the water smartly within a few inches of his head, spattering his face with spray. He heard a second report, and saw one of the sentinels with his rifle at his shoulder, a light cloud of blue smoke rising from the muzzle. The man in the water saw the eye of the man on the bridge gazing into his own through the sights of the rifle. He observed that it was a grey eye, and remembered having read that grey eyes were keenest and that all famous marksmen had them. Nevertheless, this one had missed.

A counter swirl had caught Farquhar and turned him half round; he was again looking into the forest on the bank opposite the fort. The sound of a clear, high voice in a monotonous singsong now rang out behind him and came across the water with a distinctness that pierced and subdued all other sounds, even the beating of the ripples in his ears. Although no soldier, he had frequented camps enough to know the dread significance of that deliberate, drawling, aspirated chant; the lieutenant on shore was taking a part in the morning's work. How coldly and pitilessly—with what an even, calm intonation, presaging and enforcing tranquility in the men—with what accurately-measured intervals fell those cruel words:

"Attention, company. . . . Shoulder arms. . . . Ready. . . . Aim. . . . Fire."

Farquhar dived—dived as deeply as he could. The water roared in his ears like the voice of Niagara, yet he heard the dulled thunder of the volley, and rising again toward the surface, met shining bits of metal, singularly flattened, oscillating slowly downward. Some of them touched him on the face and hands, then fell away, continuing their descent. One lodged between his collar and neck, it was uncomfortably warm, and he snatched it out.

As he rose to the surface, gasping for breath, he saw that he had been a long time under water; he was perceptibly farther down stream—nearer to safety. The soldiers had almost finished reloading; the metal ramrods flashed all at one in the sunshine as they were drawn from the barrels, turned in the air, and thrust into their sockets. The two sentinels fired again, independently and ineffectually.

The hunted man saw all this over his shoulder; he was now swimming vigorously with the current. His brain was as energetic as his arms and legs; he thought with the rapidity of lightning.

25

"The officer," he reasoned, "will not make the martinet's error a second time. It is as easy to dodge a volley as a single shot. He has probably already given the command to fire at will. God help me, I cannot dodge them all!"

An appalling plash within two yards of him, followed by a loud rushing sound, *diminuendo*,[2] which seemed to travel back through the air to the fort and died in an explosion which stirred the very river to its deeps! A rising sheet of water, which curved over him, fell down upon him, blinded him, strangled him! The cannon had taken a hand in the game. As he shook his head free from the commotion of the smitten water, he heard the deflected shot humming through the air ahead, and in an instant it was cracking and smashing the branches in the forest beyond.

"They will not do that again," he thought; "the next time they will use   30
a charge of grape. I must keep my eye upon the gun; the smoke will apprise me—the report arrives too late; it lags behind the missile. It is a good gun."

Suddenly he felt himself whirled round and round—spinning like a top. The water, the banks, the forest, the now distant bridge, fort, and men—all were commingled and blurred. Objects were represented by their colors only; circular horizontal streaks of color—that was all he saw. He had been caught in a vortex and was being whirled on with a velocity of advance and gyration which made him giddy and sick. In a few moments he was flung upon the gravel at the foot of the left bank of the stream—the southern bank—and behind a projecting point which concealed him from his enemies. The sudden arrest of his motion, the abrasion of one of his hands on the gravel, restored him and he wept with delight. He dug his fingers into the sand, threw it over himself in handfuls and audibly blessed it. It looked like gold, like diamonds, rubies, emeralds; he could think of nothing beautiful which it did not resemble. The trees upon the bank were giant garden plants; he noted a definite order in their arrangement, inhaled the fragrance of their blooms. A strange, roseate light shone through the spaces among their trunks, and the wind made in their branches the music of æolian harps.[3] He had no wish to perfect his escape, was content to remain in that enchanting spot until retaken.

A whizz and rattle of grapeshot among the branches high above his head roused him from his dream. The baffled cannoneer had fired him a random farewell. He sprang to his feet, rushed up the sloping bank, and plunged into the forest.

All that day he travelled, laying his course by the rounding sun. The forest seemed interminable; nowhere did he discover a break in it, not even a woodman's road. He had not known that he lived in so wild a region. There was something uncanny in the revelation:

By nightfall he was fatigued, footsore, famishing. The thought of his wife and children urged him on. At last he found a road which led him in

---

[2] *diminuendo:* a gradually diminishing volume, a term used in music.   [3] *aeolian harp:* a musical instrument consisting of a box equipped with strings of equal length that are tuned in unison. Such harps are placed in windows to produce harmonious tones sounded by the wind.

what he knew to be the right direction. It was as wide and straight as a city street, yet it seemed untravelled. No fields bordered it, no dwelling anywhere. Not so much as the barking of a dog suggested human habitation. The black bodies of the great trees formed a straight wall on both sides, terminating on the horizon in a point, like a diagram in a lesson in perspective. Overhead, as he looked up through this rift in the wood, shone great golden stars looking unfamiliar and grouped in strange constellations. He was sure they were arranged in some order which had a secret and malign significance. The wood on either side was full of singular noises, among which—once, twice, and again—he distinctly heard whispers in an unknown tongue.

His neck was in pain, and, lifting his hand to it, he found it horribly   35 swollen. He knew that it had a circle of black where the rope had bruised it. His eyes felt congested; he could no longer close them. His tongue was swollen with thirst; he relieved its fever by thrusting it forward from between his teeth into the cool air. How softly the turf had carpeted the untravelled avenue! He could no longer feel the roadway beneath his feet!

Doubtless, despite his suffering, he fell asleep while walking, for now he sees another scene—perhaps he has merely recovered from a delirium. He stands at the gate of his own home: All is as he left it, and all bright and beautiful in the morning sunshine. He must have travelled the entire night. As he pushes open the gate and passes up the wide white walk, he sees a flutter of female garments; his wife, looking fresh and cool and sweet, steps down from the verandah to meet him. At the bottom of the steps she stands waiting, with a smile of ineffable joy, an attitude of matchless grace and dignity. Ah, how beautiful she is! He springs forward with extended arms. As he is about to clasp her, he feels a stunning blow upon the back of the neck; a blinding white light blazes all about him, with a sound like a shock of a cannon—then all is darkness and silence!

Peyton Farquhar was dead; his body, with a broken neck, swung gently from side to side beneath the timbers of the Owl Creek bridge.

Questions for Discussion and Writing

1. If we conclude that the narrator is actually hanged at the end of the story, what clues does Bierce provide to suggest that almost everything that happens is in the mind of the main character?

2. What details does Bierce provide to signal that events as they are reported are not the same as what actually occurs? How does section **II** serve as a **flashback**?

3. How does Bierce convey the psychological desperation of the main character as he tries to ward off tangible signs of what is actually happening?

4. **Rhetorical inquiry:** How does the ticking of the watch that becomes slower and slower and the strangely slow moving driftwood in what had been a swiftly moving stream suggest that psychological time is beginning to slow down as well for Farquhar?

IRENE ZABYTKO

*Irene Zabytko was born in 1954 to a Ukrainian family in Chicago. Her fiction
has won the PEN Syndicated Fiction Project, and she is the founder and
publisher of* Odessa-Pressa *Productions. Her most recent works are* The Sky
Unwashed *(2000), a novel based on the nuclear accident in Chernobyl, Russia
and* When Luba Leaves Home: Stories *(2003). The following story originally
appeared in* The Perimeter of Light: Writing About the Vietnam War, *edited
by Vivian Vie Balfour (1992).*

Before You Read

*Consider the parallels between the father's experiences as a soldier in World
War II and those of his son in Vietnam.*

Home Soil

I watch my son crack his knuckles, oblivious to the somber sounds of the
Old Slavonic hymns the choir behind us is singing.

We are in the church where Bohdan, my son, was baptized nineteen
years ago. It is Sunday. The pungent smell of frankincense permeates the
darkened atmosphere of this cathedral. Soft sun rays illuminate the stained-
glass windows. I sit near the one that shows Jesus on the cross looking down
on some unidentifiable Apostles who are kneeling beneath His nailed feet. In
the background, a tiny desperate Judas swings from a rope, the thirty pieces
of silver thrown on the ground.

There is plenty of room in my pew, but my son chooses not to sit with
me. I see him staring at the round carapace of a ceiling, stoic icons staring
directly back at him. For the remainder of the Mass, he lightly drums his
nervous fingers on top of the cover of *My Divine Friend*, the Americanized
prayer book of the Ukrainian service. He took bongo lessons before he graduated high school, and learned the basic rolls from off a record, "Let's
Swing with Bongos." I think it was supposed to make him popular with the
girls at parties. I also think he joined the army because he wanted the virile
image men in uniforms have that the bongos never delivered. When he
returned from Nam, he mentioned after one of our many conversational
silences that he lost the bongos, and the record is cracked, with the pieces
buried somewhere deep inside the duffel bag he still hasn't unpacked.

Bohdan, my son, who calls himself Bob, has been back for three weeks.
He looks so "American" in his green tailored uniform: his spit-shined vinyl
dress shoes tap against the red-cushioned kneelers. It was his idea to go to
church with me. He has not been anywhere since he came home. He won't
even visit my garden.

Luba, my daughter, warned me he would be moody. She works for the
Voice of America and saw him when he landed from Nam in San Francisco.

5

"Just don't worry, tato,[1] she said to me on the telephone. "He's acting weird. Culture shock."

"Explain what you mean."

"Just, you know, strange." For a disc jockey, and a bilingual one at that, she is so inarticulate. She plays American jazz and tapes concerts for broadcasts for her anonymous compatriots in Ukraine. That's what she was doing when she was in San Francisco, taping some jazz concert. Pure American music for the huddled gold-toothed youths who risk their *komsomol* privileges and maybe their lives listening to these clandestine broadcasts and to my daughter's sweet voice. She will never be able to visit our relatives back there because American security won't allow it, and she would lose her job. But it doesn't matter. After my wife died, I have not bothered to keep up with anyone there, and I don't care if they have forgotten all about me. It's just as well.

I noticed how much my son resembled my wife when I first saw him again at the airport. He was alone, near the baggage claim ramp. He was taller than ever, and his golden hair was bleached white from the jungle sun. He inherited his mother's high cheekbones, but he lost his baby fat, causing his cheeks to jut out from his lean face as sharp as the arrowheads he used to scavenge for when he was a kid.

We hugged briefly. I felt his medals pinch through my thin shirt. "You look good, son," I tied. I avoided his eyes and concentrated on a pin shaped like an open parachute that he wore over his heart.

"Hi, *tato*," he murmured. We spoke briefly about his flight home from San Francisco, how he'd seen Luba. We stood apart, unlike the other soldiers with their families who were hugging and crying on each other's shoulders in a euphoric delirium.

He grabbed his duffel bag from the revolving ramp and I walked behind him to see if he limped or showed any signs of pain. He showed nothing.

"Want to drive?" I asked, handing him the keys to my new Plymouth.

"Nah," he said. He looked around at the cars crowding the parking lot, and I thought he seemed afraid. "I don't remember how the streets go anymore."

An usher in his best borscht-red polyester suit waits for me to drop some money into the basket. It is old Pan.[2] Medved, toothless except for the prominent gold ones he flashes at me as he pokes me with his basket.

"*Nu*, give," he whispers hoarsely, but loud enough for a well-dressed woman with lacquered hair who sits in front of me to turn around and stare in mute accusation.

I take out the gray and white snakeskin wallet Bohdan brought back for me, and transfer out a ten dollar bill. I want the woman to see it before it disappears into the basket. She smiles at me and nods.

10

15

---

[1] *tato:* "Father" or "Dad."   [2] *Pan:* a term of respect for adult males, the equivalent of *Mr.*

Women always smile at me like that. Especially after they see my money and find out that I own a restaurant in the neighborhood. None of the Ukies[3] go there; they don't eat fries and burgers much. But the "jackees"— the Americans—do when they're sick of eating in the cafeteria at the plastics factory. My English is pretty good for a D.P.,[4] and no one has threatened to bomb my business because they accuse me of being a no-god bohunk commie. Not yet anyway.

But the women are always impressed. I usually end up with the emigrés— some of them Ukrainians. The Polish women are the greediest for gawdy trinkets and for a man to give them money so that they can return to their husbands and children in Warsaw. I like them the best anyway because they laugh more than the other women I see, and they know how to have a good time.

Bohdan knows nothing about my lecherous life. I told the women to stay clear after my son arrived. He is so lost with women. I think he was a virgin when he joined the army, but I'm sure he isn't now. I can't ask him.

After mass ends, I lose Bohdan in the tight clusters of people leaving their   20
pews and genuflecting toward the iconostasis. He waits for me by the holy water font. It looks like a regular porcelain water fountain but without a spout. There is a sponge in the basin that is moistened with the holy water blessed by the priests here. Bohdan stands towering over the font, dabs his fingers into the sponge, but doesn't cross himself the way he was taught to do as a boy.

"What's the matter?" I ask in English. I hope he will talk to me if I speak to him in his language.

But Bohdan ignores me and watches an elderly woman gingerly entering the door of the confessional. "What she got to say? Why is she going in there?"

"Everyone has sins."

"Yeah, but who forgives?"

"God forgives," I say. I regret it because it makes me feel like a hyp-   25
ocrite whenever I parrot words I still find difficult to believe.

We walk together in the neighborhood; graffiti visible in the alley-ways despite the well-trimmed lawns with flowers and "bathtub" statues of the Blessed Mary smiling benevolently at us as we pass by the small bungalows. I could afford to move out of here, out of Chicago and into some nearby cushy suburb, Skokie or something. But what for? Some smart Jewish lawyer or doc-tor would be my next door neighbor and find out that I'm a Ukie and complain to me about how his grandmother was raped by Petliura.[5] I've heard it before. Anyway, I like where I am. I bought a three-flat apartment building after my wife died and I live in one of the apartments rent-free. I can walk to my business,

---

[3] *Ukies:* Ukrainian Americans.   [4] *D.P.:* displaced person (war refugee).   [5] *Petliura:* Simeon Petliura (1879–1926), an anti-Bolshevik Ukrainian leader who was accused of respon-sibility for Jewish pogroms during World War I. When his forces were defeated by the Russians he went into exile in Paris, where he was ultimately assassinated by a Jewish nationalist.

and see the past—old women in babushkas sweeping the sidewalks in front of their cherished gardens; men in Italian-made venetian-slat sandals and woolen socks rushing to a chess match at the Soyuiez, a local meeting place where the D.P.s sit for hours rehashing the war over beers and chess.

Bohdan walks like a soldier. Not exactly a march, but a stiff gait that a good posture in a rigid uniform demands. He looks masculine, but tired and worn. Two pimples are sprouting above his lip where a faint moustache is starting.

"Want a cigarette?" I ask. Soldiers like to smoke. During the forties, I smoked that horrible cheap tobacco, *mahorka*. I watch my son puff heavily on the cigarette I've given him, with his eyes partially closed, delicately cupping his hands to protect it from the wind. In my life, I have seen so many soldiers in that exact pose; they all look the same. When their faces are contorted from sucking the cigarette, there is an unmistakable shadow of vulnerability and fear of living. That gesture and stance are more eloquent than the blood and guts war stories men spew over their beers.

Pan Medved, the battered gold-toothed relic in the church, has that look. Pan Holewski, one of my tenants, has it too. I would have known it even if he never openly displayed his old underground soldier's cap that sits on a bookshelf in the living room between small Ukrainian and American flags. I see it every time I collect the rent.

I wish Bohdan could tell me what happened to him in Vietnam. What did he do? What was done to him? Maybe now isn't the time to tell me. He may never tell me. I never told anyone either.   30

I was exactly his age when I became a soldier. At nineteen, I was a student at the university in L'vov, which the Poles occupied. I was going to be a poet, to study poetry and write it, but the war broke out, and my family could not live on the romantic epics I tried to publish, so I was paid very well by the Nazis to write propaganda pamphlets. "Freedom for Ukrainians" I wrote—"Freedom for our people. Fight the Poles and Russians alongside our German brothers" and other such dreck. I even wrote light verse that glorified Hitler as the protector of the free Ukrainian nation that the Germans promised us. My writing was as naïve as my political ideas.

My new career began in a butcher shop, commandeered after the Polish owner was arrested and shot. I set my battered Underwood typewriter atop an oily wooden table where crescents of chicken feathers still clung between the cracks. Meat hooks that once held huge sides of pork hung naked in a back room, and creaked ominously like a deserted gallows whenever anyone slammed the front door. Every shred of meat had been stolen by looters after the Germans came into the city. Even the little bell that shopkeepers kept at the entrance was taken. But I was very comfortable in my surroundings. I thought only about how I was to play a part in a historical destiny that my valiant words would help bring about. That delusion lasted only about a week or so until three burly Nazis came in. "*Schnell!*" they said to me, pushing me out of my chair and pointing to the windows where I saw crowds chaotically swarming about. Before I could question the soldiers, one of them shoved a gun into my hands and pushed me out into the streets. I felt so bewildered until the moment I pointed my rifle at a man who was about—I thought—to hit me with a club of some sort. Suddenly, I felt such an intense charge of power, more so than I had ever felt writing some of my best poems. I was no longer dealing with abstract words and ideas for a mythological cause; I was responsible for life and death.

I enjoyed that power, until it seeped into my veins and poisoned my soul. It was only an instant, a brief interlude, a matter of hours until that transformation occurred. I still replay that scene in my mind almost forty years after it happened, no matter what I am doing, or who I am with.

I think she was a village girl. Probably a Jew, because on that particular day, the Jews were the ones chosen to be rounded up and sent away in cattle cars. Her hair was golden red, short and wavy as was the style, and her neck was awash in freckles. It was a crowded station in the centre of the town, not far from the butcher shop. There were Germans shouting and women crying and church bells ringing. I stood with that German regulation rifle I hardly knew how to handle, frozen because I was too lightheaded and excited. I too began to yell at people and held the rifle against my chest, and I was very much aware of how everyone responded to my authority.

Then, this girl appeared in my direct line of vision. Her back was straight, her shoulders tensed; she stopped in the middle of all the chaos. Simply stopped. I ran up and pushed her. I pushed her hard, she almost fell. I kept pushing her, feeling the thin material of her cheap wool jacket against my chapped eager hand; her thin muscles forced forward by my shoves. Once, twice, until she toppled into the open door of a train and fell toward a heap of other people moving deeper into the tiny confines of the stinking cattle car. She never turned around.

I should have shot her. I should have spared her from whatever she had to go through. I doubt she survived. I should have tried to find out what her name was, so I could track down her relatives and confess to them. At least in that way, they could have spat at me injustice and I would have finally received the absolution I will probably never find in this life.

I don't die. Instead, I go to the garden. It is Sunday evening. I am weeding the crop of beets and cabbages I planted in the patch in my backyard. The sun is lower, a breeze kicks up around me, but my forehead sweats. I breathe in the thick deep earth smells as the dirt crumbles and rotates against the blade of my hoe. I should destroy the honey-suckle vine that is slowly choking my plants, but the scent is so sweet, and its intoxicating perfume reminds me of a woman's gentleness.

I hoe for a while, but not for long, because out of the corner of my eye, I see Bohdan sitting on the grass tearing the firm green blades with his clenched hands. He is still wearing his uniform, all except the jacket, tie, and cap. He sits with his legs apart, his head down, ignoring the black flies that nip at his ears.

I wipe my face with a bright red bandana, which I brought with me to tie up the stalks of my drooping sunflowers. "Bohdan," I say to my son. "Why don't we go into the house and have a beer. I can finish this another time." I look at the orange sun. 'It's humid and there's too many flies—means rain will be coming."

My son is quietly crying to himself. 40

"*Tato*, I didn't know anything," he cries out. "You know, I just wanted to jump" out from planes with my parachute. I just wanted to fly . . ."

"I should have stopped you," I say more to myself than to him. Bohdan lets me stroke the thin spikes of his army regulation crew-cut which is soft and warm and I am afraid of how easily my hand can crush his skull.

I rock him in my arms the way I saw his mother embrace him when he was afraid to sleep alone.

There is not much more I can do right now except to hold him. I will hold him until he pulls away.

Questions for Discussion and Writing

1. Suddenly finding oneself with the power of life and death over other human beings is a harrowing experience for the narrator. How do the memories of this experience bring him closer to his son, who just returned from Vietnam?
2. What means does Zabytko use to make the narrator a sympathetic character despite the evil he has perpetrated in the past?
3. *The Mahabarata*, a classic Indian epic (200 B.C.), suggests that just as no good man is all good, no bad man is all bad. How does "Home Soil" illustrate this insight?
4. **Rhetorical inquiry:** What means does Zabytko use to communicate the father's sense of fatalism in history repeating itself in his son's life? Does he feel that he has failed his son by permitting him to become a soldier?

Poetry

BERTOLT BRECHT

Bertolt Brecht (1898–1956) was born in Augsburg, Germany and studied medicine at Munich University before turning to a career in theater. Because of his criticism of Hitler and the Nazi regime, he was forced into exile in 1933 and sought asylum in many countries—Russia, France, Norway—before coming to the United States in 1941. His plays and radio scripts use expressionism, often to the point of exaggeration, to communicate his ironic social critique. His best known plays are The Three Penny Opera *(1928) written with Kurt Weill,* The

Life of Galileo *(1939),* Mother Courage and Her Children *(1941),* The Good Woman of Setzuan *(1943), and* The Caucasian Chalk Circle *(1947). Although he was famous as a playwright and director, Brecht was also a poet who aimed to instruct his readers, as we can see in "A Worker Reads History" (1936) translated by H. R. Hays, which first appeared in* Selected Poems *(1947).*

Before You Read

Why are history books geared toward a leader-centered view of events?

A Worker Reads History

Who built the seven gates of Thebes?
The books are filled with names of kings.
Was it kings who hauled the craggy blocks of stone?
And Babylon, so many times destroyed,
Who built the city up each time? In which of Lima's houses,   5
That city glittering with gold, lived those who built it?
In the evening when the Chinese wall was finished
Where did the masons go? Imperial Rome
Is full of arcs of triumph. Who reared them up? Over whom
Did the Caesars triumph? Byzantium lives in song,   10
Were all her dwellings palaces? And even in Atlantis[1] of the legend
The night the sea rushed in,
The drowning men still bellowed for their slaves.

Young Alexander conquered India.
He alone?   15
Caesar beat the Gauls.
Was there not even a cook in his army?
Philip of Spain wept as his fleet
Was sunk and destroyed. Were there no other tears?
Frederick the Great triumphed in the Seven Years War. Who   20
Triumphed with him?

Each page a victory,

At whose expense the victory ball?
Every ten years a great man,
Who paid the piper?   25

So many particulars.
So many questions.

---

[1] *Atlantis:* a mythical island in the Atlantic Ocean west of Gibraltar, said to have sunk into the sea.

Questions for Discussion and Writing

1. In what way is the poem designed to make readers think about people that history books never mention? Who are they, and what role have they really played?
2. The contrast between the "great man" who appears every ten years and the faceless masses who pay the "piper" is a source of dramatic irony. What point is Brecht making with this statement?
3. A classic debate in history has been whether leaders shape history or are created by historical events. What is your view? Give an example that supports it.
4. **Rhetorical inquiry:** How does the form of the poem beginning with stanzas that contain multiple questions followed by stanzas with fewer questions and a final terse epigrammatic stanza mirror the speaker's dissatisfaction with the scant recognition laboring classes receive?

WILFRED OWEN

Wilfred Owen (1893–1918) was an Englishman who died on the French front in World War I. His work on the tragic horror and pity of war brought him public acclaim as a major writer of the century. He formed a friendship with Siegfried Sassoon, who published 24 of Owen's poems posthumously in 1920. Owen's poetry is stylistically distinctive, and in the following poem "Strange Meeting" (which was not completed before he was killed) he envisages an eerie encounter between a soldier and a man he has killed in combat.

Before You Read

In what sense might a bond exist between soldiers who face each other as enemies?

Strange Meeting

It seemed that out of battle I escaped
Down some profound dull tunnel, long since scooped
Through granites which titanic wars had groined.
Yet also there encumbered sleepers groaned,
Too fast in thought or death to be bestirred. 5
Then, as I probed them, one sprang up, and stared
With piteous recognition in fixed eyes,
Lifting distressful hands as if to bless.
And by his smile I knew that sullen hall,
By his dead smile I knew we stood in Hell. 10
With a thousand pains that vision's face was grained;

Yet no blood reached there from the upper ground,
And no guns thumped, or down the flues made moan.
"Strange friend," I said, "here is no cause to mourn."
"None," said the other, "save the undone years,   15
The hopelessness. Whatever hope is yours,
Was my life also; I went hunting wild
After the wildest beauty in the world,
Which lies not calm in eyes, or braided hair,
But mocks the steady running of the hour,   20
And if it grieves, grieves richlier than here.
For by my glee might many men have laughed,
And of my weeping something had been left,
Which must die now. I mean the truth untold,
The pity of war, the pity war distilled.   25
Now men will go content with what we spoiled,
Or, discontent, boil bloody and be spilled.
They will be swift with swiftness of the tigress,
None will break ranks, though nations trek from progress.
Courage was mine, and I had mystery,   30
Wisdom was mine, and I had mastery;
To miss the march of this retreating world
Into vain citadels that are not walled.
Then, when much blood had clogged their chariot wheels
I would go up and wash them from sweet wells,   35
Even with truths that lie too deep for taint.
I would have poured my spirit without stint
But not through wounds; not on the cess of war.
Foreheads of men have bled where no wounds were.
I am the enemy you killed, my friend.   40
I knew you in this dark; for so you frowned
Yesterday, through me as you jabbed and killed.
I parried, but my hands were loath and cold.
Let us sleep now. . . ."

Questions for Discussion and Writing

1. In what respects is the man who the speaker has killed in battle quite
   similar to himself?
2. How does the unusual off-rhyme pattern enhance the sense of underlying similarity between the combatants?
3. What aspects of the poem address the ways war destroys the hopes
   and ideals of all those caught in it? How could this poem be seen as a
   parable about the effects of any war?

4. **Rhetorical inquiry:** Why is it important that the gesture with which the "strange friend" greets the speaker is revealed to be the same gesture the soldier made to avoid being bayonetted by the speaker? How does this enhance the connection between them?

W. B. YEATS

William Butler Yeats (1865–1939), the distinguished Irish poet and playwright, was the son of an artist, John Yeats. Although initially drawn toward painting, he soon turned to poetry and became fascinated by Irish sagas and folklore. The landscape of county Sligo, where he was born and lived as a child, and the exploits of Irish heroes such as Cuchulain frequently appear in his early poetry. An early long poem, The Wanderings of Oisin *(1889), shows an intense nationalism, a feeling strengthened by his hopeless passion for the Irish patriot Maude Gonne. In 1898, he helped found the Irish Literary Theatre and later the world-renowned Abbey Theatre. As he grew older, Yeats's poetry moved from transcendentalism to a more physical realism, and the tension between the physical and the spiritual is central to poems such as "Sailing to Byzantium" and the "Crazy Jane" sequence. Some of his best work came late in* The Tower *(1928),* The Winding Stair *(1933), and the work that was published posthumously in* Last Poems and Plays *(1940). Yeats received the Nobel Prize for literature in 1923 and is widely considered to be the greatest poet of the 20th century. The prophetic quality of Yeats's poetry springs from his earlier interest in the occult, concerns that became tempered by his premonition that the political anarchy and materialism of the modern age would inevitably lead to its own destruction. This theme is most brilliantly realized in what is perhaps his signature poem, "The Second Coming" (1920).*

Before You Read

After September 11, 2001, how did this poem became more relevant than ever.

The Second Coming

Turning and turning in the widening gyre
The falcon cannot hear the falconer;
Things fall apart; the centre cannot hold;
Mere anarchy is loosed upon the world,
The blood-dimmed tide is loosed, and everywhere   5
The ceremony of innocence is drowned;
The best lack all conviction, while the worst
Are full of passionate intensity.

Surely some revelation is at hand;
Surely the Second Coming is at hand.[1]   10
The Second Coming! Hardly are those words out
When a vast image out of *Spiritus Mundi*[2]
Troubles my sight: somewhere in sands of the desert
A shape with lion body and the head of a man,

A gaze blank and pitiless as the sun,   15
Is moving its slow thighs, while all about it
Reel shadows of the indignant desert birds.
The darkness drops again; but now I know
That twenty centuries of stony sleep
Were vexed to nightmare by a rocking cradle,   20
And what rough beast, its hour come round at last,
Slouches towards Bethlehem to be born?

Questions for Discussion and Writing

1. How do the images with which the poem begins suggest to the speaker
   that the conditions prophesied in the New Testament (Matthew 24)
   signify the second coming of Christ? How does the vision that suddenly appears refute this expectation?
2. What is the relationship between the birth of Christ two thousand
   years before and the risen Sphinx "slouching" over the desert? How
   would you characterize the shift in the emotional state of the speaker
   throughout the course of the poem?
3. What aspects of this "rough beast" suggest to the speaker that a new
   age of barbarism is about to begin with the twentieth century?
4. **Rhetorical inquiry:** How does the inability of the falconer to recall the
   falcon symbolize the loss of control that the speaker sees as the defining state of modern times? How is the "rough beast" slouching toward
   Bethlehem in today's world?

---

[1] The return ("**Second Coming**") of Christ is prophesied in the New Testament (Matthew
24). Here the return is not of Jesus but of a terrifying inhuman embodiment of pre-Christian
and pre-Grecian barbarism. The poem is a sharply prophetic response to the turmoil of Europe
following World War I.   [2] *Spiritus Mundi* (Latin): Spirits of the World, that is, archetypal
images in the "Great Memory" of the human psyche.

Connections for Chapter 7:
Past to Present

1. **Herodotus,** *Concerning Egypt*
   Compare the traditional religion of the ancient Egyptians as described by Herodotus with the modern religions that the Dalai Lama discusses in "The Role of Religion in Modern Society" (Chapter 11).
2. **Thomas Paine,** *Rights of Man*
   How do both Paine and Martin Luther King, Jr. ("I Have a Dream") in Chapter 8 appeal to the idea of innate human rights?
3. **Gilbert Highet,** *The Gettysburg Address*
   Compare the rhetorical strategies used by Lincoln with those of Martin Luther King, Jr. in "I Have a Dream" in Chapter 8.
4. **Jack London,** *The San Francisco Earthquake*
   Compare the reactions of the survivors of the earthquake with the survivors of the *Titanic* as reported by Hanson W. Baldwin.
5. **Hanson W. Baldwin,** *R. M. S.* Titanic
   What aspects of the literal lifeboat dilemma confronting passengers on the *Titanic* does Garrett Hardin (in "Lifeboat Ethics" in Chapter 11) use to explore ethical trade-offs?
6. **Haunani-Kay Trask,** *From a Native Daughter*
   In what sense might Trask's analysis be considered the worker's reading of history espoused by Bertolt Brecht in his poem?
7. **Maurizio Chierici,** *The Man from Hiroshima*
   How did the pressures to which Claude Eatherly was subjected illustrate Stanley Milgram's experiment (see "The Perils of Obedience" (Chapter 11)?
8. **Don DeLillo,** *In the Ruins of the Future*
   What similar methods do DeLillo and Jack London use to allow their readers to comprehend the magnitude of an inconceivable disaster?
9. **Ambrose Bierce,** *An Occurrence at Owl Creek Bridge*
   Bierce uses a neutral journalistic framework to set the stage for his story. After reading the account by Jack London discuss the advantages of this method in nonfiction and fiction.
10. **Irene Zabytko,** *Home Soil*
    Compare the way Vietnam is depicted in Zabytko's story with Lance Morrow's article "Imprisoning Time in a Rectangle" (in Chapter 10) with its accompanying photos.
11. **Bertolt Brecht,** *A Worker Reads History*
    In what respects do both Brecht and Harriet Jacobs in "Incidents in the Life of a Slave Girl" (Chapter 8) argue for a reexamination of assumptions that underlie ignored figures in history?

12. **Wilfred Owen,** *Strange Meeting*
    In what respects do both Owen's and William Butler Yeats's poems address the sense of dissolution of civilization as a result of World War I?

13. **W. B. Yeats,** *The Second Coming*
    To what extent does Don DeLillo's account of September 11th and its aftermath illustrate Yeat's prediction?

8

POWER AND POLITICS

You only have power over people so long as you don't take everything away from them. But when you've robbed a man of everything he's no longer in your power—he's free again.
Alexander Solzhenitsyn, THE FIRST CIRCLE

The allegiance individuals owe their governments and the protection of individual rights citizens expect in return have been subjects of intense analysis through the ages. The readings that follow continue this debate by providing accounts drawn from many different societies. For example, Tim O'Brien recalls his inner conflict over whether to serve in Vietnam.

Jonathan Swift, in his satire written in the 1700s, and Martin Luther King, Jr., writing over two centuries later, enunciate strikingly similar ideas of civil and economic freedom. This timeless issue becomes especially relevant today with the quest for a livable wage for the working poor advocated by Barbara Ehrenreich.

Readings by Harriet Jacobs, Kenneth M. Stampp, Luis Sepúlveda and Stephen Chapman bear witness to the consequences of the suspension of civil rights and the culturally variable nature of punishment around the world. Michael Levin also creates an intriguing hypothetical case as a response to potential acts of nuclear terrorism.

Panos Ioannides's story, *Gregory,* is a masterful dramatization of the inevitability of personal choice for a soldier during the Cypriot liberation struggle against the British.

The poems of W. H. Auden and Carolyn Forché offer a range of views, from a sardonic epitaph on a compliant citizen to a terrifying and surreal encounter with a modern-day Central American dictator.

Trifles, a play (based on real events) by Susan Glaspell, dramatizes a criminal investigation that illustrates how the search for justice is profoundly influenced by time, place, and gender.

As you read works in this chapter and prepare to discuss or write about them you may wish to use the following questions as guidelines.

- What incident or occasion motivates the author's work?
- How would you characterize the writer's approach to the subject or issue—as a participant or reporter?

- What assumptions or values underlie the author's view of the subject?
- What does the writer discover about the subject he or she investigates?
- Does the author connect the subject to a broader political or social issue?
- In what way has the author's analysis of the subject changed your opinion?
- How does the author use hypothetical scenarios to dramatize the choices?

Nonfiction

HARRIET JACOBS

Harriet Jacobs (1813–1896), also known as Linda Brent, escaped from the slavery into which she had been born and made a new life for herself in the North. She told her story, related below, "Incidents in the Life of a Slave Girl" (1861), with the assistance of Lydia Maria Child, a northern abolitionist leader. Her account has become part of the canon of American literature, history, and women's studies. In the following selection, Jacobs reveals the harrowing predicament that many female slaves found themselves in, trying to fend off their masters' lust and the ensuing jealousy of their wives.

Before You Read

How could slavery be as degrading to the slaveowners as it was to their slaves?

Incidents in the Life of a Slave Girl

I would ten thousand times rather that my children should be the half-starved paupers of Ireland than to be the most pampered among the slaves of America. I would rather drudge out my life on a cotton plantation, till the grave opened to give me rest, than to live with an unprincipled master and a jealous mistress. The felon's home in a penitentiary is preferable. He may repent, and turn from the error of his ways, and so find peace, but it is not so with a favorite slave. She is not allowed to have any pride of character. It is deemed a crime in her to wish to be virtuous.

Mrs. Flint possessed the key to her husband's character before I was born. She might have used this knowledge to counsel and to screen the young and the innocent among her slaves; but for them she had no sympathy. They were the objects of her constant suspicion and malevolence. She watched her husband with unceasing vigilance; but he was well practiced in means to evade it. What he could not find opportunity to say in words he manifested in signs. He invented more than were ever thought of in a deaf and dumb asylum. I let them pass, as if I did not understand what he meant; and many were the curses and threats bestowed on me for my stupidity. One day he caught me teaching myself to write. He frowned, as if he was not well pleased; but I suppose he came to the conclusion that such an accomplishment might help to advance his favorite scheme. Before long, notes were often slipped into my hand. I would return them, saying, "I can't read them, sir." "Can't you?" he replied; "then I must read them to you." He always finished the reading by asking, "Do you understand?" Sometimes he would complain of the heat of the tea room, and order his supper to be placed on a small table in the piazza. He would seat himself there with a well-satisfied smile, and tell me to stand by and brush away the flies. He would eat very slowly, pausing between the mouthfuls. These intervals were employed in describing the happiness I was so foolishly throwing away, and in threatening me with the penalty that finally awaited my stubborn disobedience. He boasted much of the forbearance he had exercised toward me, and reminded me that there was a limit to his patience. When I succeeded in avoiding opportunities for him to talk to me at home, I was ordered to come to his office, to do some errand. When there, I was obliged to stand and listen to such language as he saw fit to address to me. Sometimes I so openly expressed my contempt for him that he would become violently enraged, and I wondered why he did not strike me. Circumstanced as he was, he probably thought it was better policy to be forebearing. But the state of things grew worse and worse daily. In desperation I told him that I must and would apply to my grandmother for protection. He threatened me with death, and worse than death, if I made my complaint to her. Strange to say, I did not despair. I was naturally of a buoyant disposition, and always I had a hope of somehow getting out of his clutches. Like many a poor, simple slave before me, I trusted that some threads of joy would yet be woven into my dark destiny.

I had entered my sixteenth year, and every day it became more apparent that my presence was intolerable to Mrs. Flint. Angry words frequently passed between her and her husband. He had never punished me himself, and he would not allow anybody else to punish me. In that respect, she was never satisfied; but, in her angry moods, no terms were too vile for her to bestow upon me. Yet I, whom she detested so bitterly, had far more pity for her than he had, whose duty it was to make her life happy. I never wronged her, or wished to wrong her; and one word of kindness from her would have brought me to her feet.

After repeated quarrels between the doctor and his wife, he announced his intention to take his youngest daughter, then four years old, to sleep in his apartment. It was necessary that a servant should sleep in the same room, to be on hand if the child stirred. I was selected for that office, and informed for what purpose that arrangement had been made. By managing to keep within sight of people, as much as possible, during the daytime, I had hitherto succeeded in eluding my master, though a razor was often held to my throat to force me to change this line of policy. At night I slept by the side of my great aunt, where I felt safe. He was too prudent to come into her room. She was an old woman, and had been in the family many years. Moreover, as a married man, and a professional man, he deemed it necessary to save appearances in some degree. But he resolved to remove the obstacle in the way of his scheme; and he thought he had planned it so that he should evade suspicion. He was well aware how much I prized my refuge by the side of my old aunt, and he determined to dispossess me of it. The first night the doctor had the little child in his room alone. The next morning, I was ordered to take my station as nurse the following night. A kind Providence interposed in my favor. During the day Mrs. Flint heard of this new arrangement, and a storm followed. I rejoiced to hear it rage.

After a while my mistress sent for me to come to her room. Her first question was, "Did you know you were to sleep in the doctor's room?"   5

"Yes, ma'am."

"Who told you?"

"My master."

"Will you answer truly all the questions I ask?"

"Yes, ma'am."   10

"Tell me, then, as you hope to be forgiven, are you innocent of what I have accused you?"

"I am."

She handed me a Bible, and said, "Lay your hand on your heart, kiss this holy book, and swear before God that you tell me the truth."

I took the oath she required, and I did it with a clear conscience.

"You have taken God's holy word to testify your innocence," said she.   15 "If you have deceived me, beware! Now take this stool, sit down, look me directly in the face, and tell me all that has passed between your master and you."

I did as she ordered. As I went on with my account her color changed frequently, she wept, and sometimes groaned. She spoke in tones so sad, that I was touched by her grief. The tears came to my eyes; but I was soon convinced that her emotions arose from anger and wounded pride. She felt that her marriage vows were desecrated, her dignity insulted; but she had no compassion for the poor victim of her husband's perfidy. She pitied herself as a martyr; but she was incapable of feeling for the condition of shame and misery in which her unfortunate, helpless slave was placed.

Yet perhaps she had some touch of feeling for me; for when the conference was ended, she spoke kindly, and promised to protect me. I should have been much comforted by this assurance if I could have had confidence in it; but my experiences in slavery had filled me with distrust. She was not a very refined woman, and had not much control over her passions. I was an object of her jealousy, and, consequently, of her hatred; and I knew I could not expect kindness or confidence from her under the circumstances in which

I was placed. I could not blame her. Slaveholders' wives feel as other women would under similar circumstances. The fire of her temper kindled from small sparks, and now the flame became so intense that the doctor was obliged to give up his intended arrangement.

I knew I had ignited the torch, and I expected to suffer for it afterward; but I felt too thankful to my mistress for the timely aid she rendered me to care much about that. She now took me to sleep in a room adjoining her own. There I was an object of her especial care, though not of her especial comfort, for she spent many a sleepless night to watch over me. Sometimes I woke up, and found her bending over me. At other times she whispered in my ear, as though it was her husband who was speaking to me, and listened to hear what I would answer. If she startled me, on such occasions, she would glide stealthily away; and the next morning she would tell me I had been talking in my sleep, and ask who I was talking to. At last I began to be fearful for my life. It had been often threatened; and you can imagine, better than I can describe, what an unpleasant sensation it must produce to wake up in the dead of night and find a jealous woman bending over you. Terrible as this experience was, I had fears that it would give place to one more terrible.

My mistress grew weary of her vigils; they did not prove satisfactory. She changed her tactics. She now tried the trick of accusing my master of crime, in my presence, and gave my name as the author of the accusation. To my utter astonishment, he replied, "I don't believe it; but if she did acknowledge it, you tortured her into exposing me." Tortured into exposing him! Truly, Satan had no difficulty in distinguishing the color of his soul! I understood his object in making this false representation. It was to show me that I gained nothing by seeking the protection of my mistress; that the power was still all in his own hands. I pitied Mrs. Flint. She was a second wife, many years the junior of her husband; and the hoary-headed miscreant was enough to try the patience of a wiser and better woman. She was completely foiled, and knew not how to proceed. She would gladly have had me flogged for my supposed false oath; but, as I have already stated, the doctor never allowed anyone to whip me. The old sinner was politic. The application of the lash might have led to remarks that would have exposed him in the eyes of his children and grandchildren. How often did I rejoice that I lived in a town where all the inhabitants knew each other! If I had been on a remote plantation, or lost among the multitude of a crowded city, I should not be a living woman at this day.

The secrets of slavery are concealed like those of the Inquisition. My [20] master was, to my knowledge, the father of eleven slaves. But did the mothers dare to tell who was the father of their children? Did the other slaves dare to allude to it, except in whispers among themselves? No, indeed! They knew too well the terrible consequences.

My grandmother could not avoid seeing things which excited her suspicions. She was uneasy about me, and tried various ways to buy me; but the never-changing answer was always repeated: "Linda does not belong to *me*. She is my daughter's property, and I have no legal right to sell her." The conscientious man! He was too scrupulous to *sell* me; but he had no scruples whatever about committing a much greater wrong against the helpless young girl placed under his guardianship, as his daughter's property. Sometimes my persecutor would ask me whether I would like to be sold. I told him I would rather be sold to anybody than to lead such a life as I did. On such occasions he would assume the air of a very injured individual, and reproach me for my ingratitude. "Did I not take you into the house, and make you the companion of my own children?" he would say. "Have I ever treated you like a Negro? I have never allowed you to be punished, not even to please your mistress. And this is the recompense I get, you ungrateful girl!" I answered that he had reasons of his own for screening me from punishment, and that the course he pursued made my mistress hate me and persecute me. If I wept, he would say, "Poor child! Don't cry! don't cry! I will make peace for you with your mistress. Only let me arrange matters in my own way. Poor, foolish girl! you don't know what is for your own good. I would cherish you. I would make a lady of you. Now go, and think of all I have promised you."

I did think of it.

Reader, I draw no imaginary pictures of southern homes. I am telling you the plain truth. Yet when victims make their escape from this wild beast of Slavery, northerners consent to act the part of bloodhounds, and hunt the poor fugitive back into his den, "full of dead men's bones, and all uncleanness." Nay, more, they are not only willing, but proud, to give their daughters in marriage to slaveholders. The poor girls have romantic notions of a sunny clime, and of the flowering vines that all the year round shade a happy home. To what disappointments are they destined! The young wife soon learns that the husband in whose hands she has placed her happiness pays no regard to his marriage vows. Children of every shade of complexion play with her own fair babies, and too well she knows that they are born unto him of his own household. Jealousy and hatred enter the flowery home, and it is ravaged of its loveliness.

Southern women often marry a man knowing that he is the father of many little slaves. They do not trouble themselves about it. They regard such children as property, as marketable as the pigs on the plantation; and it is seldom that they do not make them aware of this by passing them into the slave-trader's hands as soon as possible, and thus getting them out of their sight. I am glad to say there are some honorable exceptions.

I have myself known two southern wives who exhorted their husbands   25
to free those slaves toward whom they stood in a "parental relation"; and their request was granted. These husbands blushed before the superior nobleness of their wives' natures. Though they had only counseled them to do that which it was their duty to do, it commanded their respect, and rendered their conduct more exemplary. Concealment was at an end, and confidence took the place of distrust.

Though this bad institution deadens the moral sense, even in white women, to a fearful extent, it is not altogether extinct. I have heard southern ladies say of Mr. Such-a-one, "He not only thinks it no disgrace to be the father of those little niggers, but he is not ashamed to call himself their master. I declare, such things ought not to be tolerated in any decent society!"

Questions for Discussion and Writing

1. In what ways did slavery create the conditions in which the kinds of events Jacobs describes could occur? How does she convey her untenable predicament vis-à-vis Dr. and Mrs. Flint and her resourcefulness in coping with it?
2. What was Jacobs's purpose in writing this narrative? How does it change assumptions that her readers might have held about the institution of slavery? In what way was slavery a morally corrupting influence on everyone involved?
3. Discuss comparable circumstances that exist today that have the same effect as those Jacobs describes, for example, sexual harassment in the workplace or illegal aliens working for families or the predicament of immigrants who are completely dependent on their employers.
4. **Rhetorical inquiry:** What details effectively convey the predatory attempts of her master and the growing jealousy of Mrs. Flint?

KENNETH M. STAMPP

Kenneth M. Stampp was born in 1912 in Milwaukee, Wisconsin, and earned his Ph.D. from the University of Wisconsin in 1942. Stampp is the Morrison Professor of American History Emeritus at the University of California at Berkeley and has served as president of the Organization of American Historians. He has been Harmsworth Professor of American History at Oxford University and a Fulbright lecturer at the University of Munich and has received two Guggenheim fellowships. In addition to editing The Causes of the Civil War *(1974), Stampp is the author of many distinguished studies, including* And the War Came *(1950),* The Peculiar Institution: Slavery in the Antebellum South *(1956), and* The Imperiled Union *(1960). His most recent books include* America in 1857: A Nation on the Brink *(1990) and* The Causes of the Civil War *(1991). In "To Make Them Stand in Fear," taken from* The Peculiar Institution, *Stampp lets the facts of brutal exploitation speak for themselves as he describes the step-by-step process by which slave-masters in the South sought to break the spirits of newly arrived blacks.*

Before you Read

How does behavioral conditioning transfer control from external discipline to an inner submission?

To Make Them Stand in Fear

A wise master did not take seriously the belief that Negroes were natural-born slaves. He knew better. He knew that Negroes freshly imported from Africa had to be broken to bondage; that each succeeding generation had to be carefully trained. This was no easy task, for the bondsman rarely submitted willingly. Moreover, he rarely submitted completely. In most cases there was no end to the need for control—at least not until old age reduced the slave to a condition of helplessness.

Masters revealed the qualities they sought to develop in slaves when they singled out certain ones for special commendation. A small Mississippi planter mourned the death of his "faithful and dearly beloved servant" Jack: "Since I have owned him he has been true to me in all respects. He was an obedient trusty servant. . . . I never knew him to steal nor lie and he ever set a moral and industrious example to those around him. . . . I shall ever cherish his memory." A Louisiana sugar planter lost a "very valuable Boy" through an accident: "His life was a very great one. I have always found him willing and obedient and never knew him to fail to do anything he was put to do." These were "ideal" slaves, the models slaveholders had in mind as they trained and governed their workers.

How might this ideal be approached? The first step, advised those who wrote discourses on the management of slaves, was to establish and maintain strict discipline. An Arkansas master suggested the adoption of the "Army Regulations as to the discipline in Forts." "They must obey at all times, and under all circumstances, cheerfully and with alacrity," affirmed a Virginia slaveholder. "It greatly impairs the happiness of a negro, to be allowed to cultivate an insubordinate temper. Unconditional submission is the only footing upon which slavery should be placed. It is precisely similar to the attitude of a minor to his parent, or a soldier to his general." A South Carolinian limned a perfect relationship between a slave and his master: "that the slave should know that his master is to govern absolutely, and he is to obey implicitly. That he is never for a moment to exercise either his will or judgment in opposition to a positive order."

The second step was to implant in the bondsmen themselves a consciousness of personal inferiority. They had "to know and keep their places," to "feel the difference between master and slave," to understand that bondage was their natural status. They had to feel that African ancestry tainted them, that their color was a badge of degradation. In the country they were to show respect for even their master's nonslave-holding neighbors; in the towns they were to give way on the streets to the most wretched white man. The line between the races must never be crossed, for familiarity caused slaves to forget their lowly station and to become "impudent."

Frederick Douglass explained that a slave might commit the offense of impudence in various ways: "in the tone of an answer; in answering at all; in 5 not answering; in the expression of countenance; in the motion of the head; in the gait, manner and bearing of the slave." Any of these acts, in some subtle way, might indicate the absence of proper subordination. "In a well regulated community," wrote a Texan, "a negro takes off his hat in address-ing a white man. . . . Where this is not enforced, we may always look for impudent and rebellious negroes."

The third step in the training of slaves was to awe them with a sense of their master's enormous power. The only principle upon which slavery could be maintained, reported a group of Charlestonians, was the "principle of fear." In his defense of slavery James H. Hammond admitted that this, unfortunately, was true but put the responsibility upon the abolitionists. Antislavery agitation had forced masters to strengthen their authority: "We have to rely more and more on the power of fear. . . . We are determined to continue masters, and to do so we have to draw the rein tighter and tighter day by day to be assured that we hold them in complete check." A North Carolina mistress, after subduing a troublesome domestic, realized that it was essential "to make them stand in fear"!

In this the slaveholders had considerable success. Frederick Douglass believed that most slaves stood "in awe" of white men; few could free them-selves altogether from the notion that their masters were "invested with a sort of sacredness." Olmsted saw a small white girl stop a slave on the road and boldly order him to return to his plantation. The slave fearfully obeyed her command. A visitor in Mississippi claimed that a master, armed only with a whip or cane, could throw himself among a score of bondsmen and cause them to "flee with terror." He accomplished this by the "peculiar tone of authority" with which he spoke. "Fear, awe, and obedience . . . are inter-woven into the very nature of the slave."

The fourth step was to persuade the bondsmen to take an interest in the master's enterprise and to accept his standards of good conduct. A South Carolina planter explained: "The master should make it his business to show his slaves, that the advancement of his individual interest, is at the same time an advancement of theirs. Once they feel this, it will require but little compulsion to make them act as it becomes them." Though slaveholders induced only a few chattels to respond to this appeal, these few were useful examples for others.

The final step was to impress Negroes with their helplessness, to create in them "a habit of perfect dependence" upon their masters. Many believed it dangerous to train slaves to be skilled artisans in the towns, because they tended to become self-reliant. Some thought it equally dangerous to hire them to factory owners. In the Richmond tobacco factories they were alarm-ingly independent and "insolvent." A Virginian was dismayed to find that his bondsmen, while working at an iron furnace, "got a habit of roaming about and *taking care of themselves.*" Permitting them to hire their own time pro-duced even worse results. "No higher evidence can be furnished of its baneful effects," wrote a Charlestonian, "than the unwillingness it produces in the slave, to return to the regular life and domestic control of the master."

A spirit of independence was less likely to develop among slaves kept   10
on the land, where most of them became accustomed to having their master
provide their basic needs, and where they might be taught that they were
unfit to look out for themselves. Slaves then directed their energies to the
attainment of mere "temporary ease and enjoyment." "Their masters,"
Olmsted believed, "calculated on it in them—do not wish to cure it—and by
constant practice encourage it."

Here, then, was the way to produce the perfect slave: accustom him to
rigid discipline, demand from him unconditional submission, impress upon
him his innate inferiority, develop in him a paralyzing fear of white men,
train him to adopt the master's code of good behavior, and instill in him a
sense of complete dependence. This, at least, was the goal.

But the goal was seldom reached. Every master knew that the average
slave was only an imperfect copy of the model. He knew that some bondsmen
yielded only to superior power—and yielded reluctantly. This complicated his
problem of control.

Questions for Discussion and Writing

1. What kind of instructions were provided in the source manuals from
   which Stampp quotes? How does Stampp's use of these source documents illustrate the method historians use to reconstruct and interpret
   past events?
2. How is Stampp's analysis arranged to show that the conditioning process moved through separate stages, from external control of behavior
   to a state in which the slaves believed that what was good for the slave
   owners was good for them as well?
3. Why was the psychological conditioning used to produce dependency
   ultimately more important to the process than physical constraints?
   Why were slaves who could hire themselves out independently less
   able to be conditioned than those kept solely on one plantation?
4. **Rhetorical inquiry:** What time markers does Stampp use to differentiate the five separate steps in the overall process of conditioning? How
   does his analysis make clear that this was an intentional process and
   not simply the imposition of harsh discipline?

MARTIN LUTHER KING, JR.

*Martin Luther King, Jr. (1929–1968), a monumental figure in the U.S. civil
rights movement and a persuasive advocate of nonviolent means for producing
social change, was born in Atlanta, Georgia, in 1929. He was ordained a Baptist
minister in his father's church when he was eighteen and went on to earn degrees
from Morehouse College (B.A., 1948), Crozer Theological Seminary (B.D., 1951),
Chicago Theological Seminary (D.D., 1957), and Boston University (Ph.D.,*

1955; D.D. 1959). On December 5, 1955, while he was pastor of a church in Montgomery, Alabama, King focused national attention on the predicament of southern blacks by leading a citywide boycott of the segregated bus system. The boycott lasted over one year and nearly bankrupted the company. King founded the Southern Christian Leadership Conference and adapted techniques of nonviolent protest, which had been employed by Gandhi,[1] in a series of sit-ins and mass marches that were instrumental in bringing about the Civil Rights Act of 1964 and the Voting Rights Act of 1965. He was awarded the Nobel Prize for Peace in 1964 in recognition of his great achievements as the leader of the American civil rights movement. Sadly, King's affirmation of the need to meet physical violence with peaceful resistance led to his being jailed more than fourteen times, beaten, stoned, stabbed in the chest, and finally murdered in Memphis, Tennessee, on April 4, 1968. His many distinguished writings include Stride Towards Freedom: The Montgomery Story *(1958);* Letter from Birmingham Jail, *written in 1963 and published in 1968;* Why We Can't Wait *(1964);* Where Do We Go from Here: Community or Chaos? *(1967); and* The Trumpet of Conscience *(1968). "I Have a Dream" (1963) is the inspiring sermon delivered by King from the steps of the Lincoln Memorial to the nearly 250,000 people who had come to Washington, D.C., to commemorate the centennial of Lincoln's Emancipation Proclamation. Additional millions who watched on television were moved by this eloquent, noble, and impassioned plea that the United States might fulfill its original promise of freedom and equality for all its citizens.*

Before You Read

Consider whether nonviolent protests are more effective or less effective than violent demonstrations to obtain rights that have been denied.

I Have a Dream

I am happy to join with you today in what will go down in history as the greatest demonstration for freedom in the history of our nation.

Five score years ago, a great American, in whose symbolic shadow we stand today, signed the Emancipation Proclamation.[2] This momentous decree came as a great beacon light of hope to millions of Negro slaves who had been seared in the flames of withering injustice. It came as a joyous daybreak to end the long night of their captivity. But one hundred years later, the Negro is still not free. One hundred years later, the life of the Negro is still sadly crippled by the manacles of segregation and the chains of discrimination. One hundred years later, the Negro lives on a lonely island of poverty in the midst of a vast

---

[1] *Gandhi: (1869–1948):* a great Indian political and spiritual leader, called Mahatma (great-souled), whose approach was one of nonviolent protest. He is regarded as the father of independent India.   [2] *The Emancipation Proclamation:* the executive order abolishing slavery in the Confederacy that President Abraham Lincoln put into effect on January 1, 1863.

ocean of material prosperity. One hundred years later, the Negro is still languishing in the corners of American society and finds himself in exile in his own land. And so we have come here today to dramatize a shameful condition.

In a sense we have come to our nation's capital to cash a check. When the architects of our republic wrote the magnificent words of the Constitution and the Declaration of Independence, they were signing a promissory note to which every American was to fall heir. This note was the promise that all men—yes, Black men as well as white men—would be guaranteed the inalienable rights of life, liberty, and the pursuit of happiness.

It is obvious today that America has defaulted on this promissory note insofar as her citizens of color are concerned. Instead of honoring this sacred obligation, America has given the Negro people a bad check, a check which has come back marked "insufficient funds." But we refuse to believe that the bank of justice is bankrupt. We refuse to believe that there are insufficient funds in the great vaults of opportunity of this nation; and so we have come to cash this check, a check that will give us upon demand the riches of freedom and the security of justice.

We have also come to this hallowed spot to remind America of the fierce urgency of *now*. This is no time to engage in the luxury of cooling off or to take the tranquilizing drug of gradualism. *Now* is the time to make real the promises of democracy. *Now* is the time to rise from the dark and desolate valley of segregation to the sunlit patch of racial justice. *Now* is the time to lift our nation from the quicksands of racial injustice to the solid rock of brotherhood. *Now* is the time to make justice a reality for all of God's children.

It would be fatal for the nation to overlook the urgency of the moment. This sweltering summer of the Negro's legitimate discontent will not pass until there is an invigorating autumn of freedom and equality. Nineteen sixty-three is not an end, but a beginning. And those who hope that the Negro needed to blow off steam and will now be content will have a rude awakening if the nation returns to business as usual. There will be neither rest nor tranquility in America until the Negro is granted his citizenship rights. The whirlwinds of revolt will continue to shake the foundations of our nation until the bright day of justice emerges.

But there is something that I must say to my people who stand on the warm threshold which leads into the palace of justice. In the process of gaining our rightful place, we must not be guilty of wrongful deeds. Let us not seek to satisfy our thirst for freedom by drinking from the cup of bitterness and hatred. We must forever conduct our struggle on the high plane of dignity and discipline. We must not allow our creative protest to degenerate into physical violence. Again and again we must rise to the majestic heights of meeting physical force with soul force. And the marvelous new militancy which has engulfed the Negro community must not lead us to a distrust of all white people; for many of our white brothers, as evidenced by their presence here today, have come to realize that their destiny is tied up with our destiny, and they have come to realize that their freedom is inextricably bound to our freedom.

We cannot walk alone. And as we walk we must make the pledge that we shall always march ahead. We cannot turn back. There are those who are asking the devotees of civil rights, "When will you be satisfied?" We can never be satisfied as long as the Negro is the victim of the unspeakable horrors of police brutality. We can never be satisfied as long as our bodies, heavy with the fatigue of travel, cannot gain lodging in the motels of the highways and the hotels of the cities. We cannot be satisfied as long as the Negro's basic mobility is from a smaller ghetto to a larger one. We can never be satisfied as long as our children are stripped of their selfhood and robbed of their dignity by signs stating "For Whites Only." We cannot be satisfied as long as the Negro in Mississippi cannot vote and a Negro in New York believes he has nothing for which to vote. No, no, we are not satisfied, and we will not be satisfied until justice rolls down like waters and righteousness like a mighty stream.

I am not unmindful that some of you have come here out of great trials and tribulations. Some of you have come fresh from narrow jail cells. Some of you have come from areas where your quest for freedom left you battered by the storms of persecution and staggered by the winds of police brutality. You have been the veterans of creative suffering. Continue to work with the faith that unearned suffering is redemptive.

Go back to Mississippi, and go back to Alabama. Go back to South Carolina. Go back to Georgia. Go back to Louisiana. Go back to the slums and ghettos of our northern cities, knowing that somehow this situation can and will be changed. Let us not wallow in the valley of despair.

10

I say to you today, my friends, even though we face the difficulties of today and tomorrow, I still have a dream. It is a dream deeply rooted in the American dream. I have a dream that one day this nation will rise up and live out the true meaning of its creed: "We hold these truths to be self-evident, that all men are created equal." I have a dream that one day, on the red hills of Georgia, sons of former slaves and the sons of former slave owners will be able to sit down together at the table of brotherhood. I have a dream that one day even the state of Mississippi, a state sweltering with the heat of injustice, sweltering with the heat of oppression, will be transformed into an oasis of freedom and justice. I have a dream that my four little children will one day live in a nation where they will not be judged by the color of their skin, but by the content of their character.

I have a dream today. I have a dream that one day down in Alabama—with its vicious racists, with its governor's lips dripping with the words of interposition and nullification—one day right there in Alabama, little Black boys and Black girls will be able to join hands with little white boys and white girls as sisters and brothers.

I have a dream today. I have a dream that one day every valley shall be exalted and every hill and mountain shall be made low, the rough places will be made plain and the crooked places will be made straight, and the glory of the Lord shall be revealed, and all flesh shall see it together.

This is our hope. This is the faith that I go back to the South with. And with this faith we will be able to hew out of the mountain of despair a stone of hope. With this faith we will be able to transform the jangling discords of our nation into a beautiful symphony of brotherhood. With this faith we will be able to work together, to play together, to struggle together, to go to jail together, to stand up for freedom together, knowing that we will be free one day.

And this will be the day—this will be the day when all of God's children   15
will be able to sing with new meaning.

> My country, 'tis of thee,
> Sweet land of liberty,
> Of thee I sing;
> Land where my fathers died,
> Land of the Pilgrims' pride,
> From every mountainside
> Let freedom ring.

And if America is to be a great nation, this must become true.

And so let freedom ring from the prodigious hilltops of New Hampshire. Let freedom ring from the mighty mountains of New York. Let freedom ring from the heightening Alleghenies of Pennsylvania. Let freedom ring from the snow-capped Rockies of Colorado. Let freedom ring from the curvaceous slopes of California.

But not only that. Let freedom ring from Stone Mountain of Georgia. Let freedom ring from Lookout Mountain of Tennessee. Let freedom ring from every hill and molehill of Mississippi. "From every mountainside let freedom ring."

And when this happens—when we allow freedom to ring, when we let it ring from every village and every hamlet, from every state and every city—we will be able to speed up that day when all of God's children, Black men and white men, Jews and Gentiles, Protestants and Catholics, will be able to join hands and sing in the words of the old Negro spiritual: "Free at last! Free at last! Thank God Almighty. We are free at last!"

Questions for Discussion and Writing

1. How did the civil rights movement express ideas of equality and freedom that were already deeply rooted in the Constitution? How did the affirmation of minority rights renew aspirations first stated by America's Founding Fathers?
2. What evidence is there that King was trying to reach many different groups of people, each with its own concerns? Where does he seem to shift his attention from one group to another?

How does this photo suggest Martin Luther King, Jr.'s appeal to the audience who participated in the march on Washington, D.C.?

3. What importance does King place on the idea of nonviolent protest? How do King's references to the Bible and the Emancipation Proclamation enhance the effectiveness of his speech?
4. **Rhetorical inquiry:** How does King use an analogy equating checks and promissory notes with moral responsibilities to make tangible the abstract concepts of freedom and equality?

BARBARA EHRENREICH

Barbara Ehrenreich is an investigative reporter who went undercover to discover the realities of the low-wage service worker. She was researching the consequences of the changes in the welfare system passed in 1995 that limited the length of time that single women with dependent children could receive benefits. The question she tried to answer was whether unskilled workers could generate an income they could live on without help from the government. As her following report reveals, the answer is no. This piece was originally published in Harper's *magazine, 1999, and later was included in her book* Nickel-and-Dimed: On (Not) Getting By in America *(2001). Her most recent books are* Global Women: Nannies, Maids, and Sex Workers in the New Economy *(2003) and* Bait and Switch: the (Futile) Pursuit of the American Dream *(2005).*

Before You Read

Notice how Ehrenreich draws on her own experiences to raise the larger issue of how difficult it is for unskilled workers to survive on a minimum wage.

Nickel-and-Dimed

At the beginning of June 1998 I leave behind everything that normally soothes the ego and sustains the body—home, career, companion, reputation, ATM card—for a plunge into the low-wage workforce. There, I become another, occupationally much diminished "Barbara Ehrenreich"—depicted on job-application forms as a divorced homemaker whose sole work experience consists of housekeeping in a few private homes. I am terrified, at the beginning, of being unmasked for what I am: a middle-class journalist setting out to explore the world that welfare mothers are entering, at the rate of approximately 50,000 a month, as welfare reform kicks in. Happily, though, my fears turn out to be entirely unwarranted: during a month of poverty and toil, my name goes unnoticed and for the most part unuttered. In this parallel universe where my father never got out of the mines and I never got through college, I am "baby," "honey," "blondie," and, most commonly, "girl."

My first task is to find a place to live. I figure that if I can earn $7 an hour—which, from the want ads, seems doable—I can afford to spend $500 on rent, or maybe, with severe economies, $600. In the Key West area, where I live, this pretty much confines me to flophouses and trailer homes—like the one, a pleasing fifteen-minute drive from town, that has no air-conditioning, no screens, no fans, no television, and, by way of diversion, only the challenge of evading the landlord's Doberman pinscher. The big problem with this place, though, is the rent, which at $675 a month is well beyond my reach. All right, Key West is expensive. But so is New York City, or the Bay Area, or Jackson Hole, or Telluride, or Boston, or any other place where tourists and the wealthy compete for living space with the people who clean their toilets and fry their hash browns.[1] Still, it is a shock to realize that "trailer trash" has become, for me, a demographic category to aspire to.

So I decide to make the common trade-off between affordability and convenience, and go for a $500-a-month efficiency thirty miles up a two-lane highway from the employment opportunities of Key West, meaning forty-five minutes if there's no road construction and I don't get caught

---

[1] According to the Department of Housing and Urban Development, the "fair-market rent" for an efficiency is $551 here in Monroe County, Florida. A comparable rent in the five boroughs of New York City is $704; in San Francisco, $713; and in the heart of Silicon Valley, $808. The fair-market rent for an area is defined as the amount that would be needed to pay rent plus utilities for "privately owned, decent, safe, and sanitary rental housing of a modest (non-luxury) nature with suitable amenities." [Author's note]

behind some sun-dazed Canadian tourists. I hate the drive, along a roadside studded with white crosses commemorating the more effective head-on collisions, but it's a sweet little place—a cabin, more or less, set in the swampy back yard of the converted mobile home where my landlord, an affable TV repairman, lives with his bartender girlfriend. Anthropologically speaking, a bustling trailer park would be preferable, but here I have a gleaming white floor and a firm mattress, and the few resident bugs are easily vanquished.

Besides, I am not doing this for the anthropology. My aim is nothing so mistily subjective as to "experience poverty" or find out how it "really feels" to be a long-term low-wage worker. I've had enough unchosen encounters with poverty and the world of low-wage work to know it's not a place you want to visit for touristic purposes; it just smells too much like fear. And with all my real-life assets—bank account, IRA, health insurance, multiroom home—waiting indulgently in the background, I am, of course, thoroughly insulated from the terrors that afflict the genuinely poor.

No, this is a purely objective, scientific sort of mission. The humanitarian rationale for welfare reform—as opposed to the more punitive and stingy impulses that may actually have motivated it—is that work will lift poor women out of poverty while simultaneously inflating their self-esteem and hence their future value in the labor market. Thus, whatever the hassles involved in finding child care, transportation, etc., the transition from welfare to work will end happily, in greater prosperity for all. Now there are many problems with this comforting prediction, such as the fact that the economy will inevitably undergo a downturn, eliminating many jobs. Even without a downturn, the influx of a million former welfare recipients into the low-wage labor market could depress wages by as much as 11.9 percent, according to the Economic Policy Institute (EPI) in Washington, D.C.

But is it really possible to make a living on the kinds of jobs currently available to unskilled people? Mathematically, the answer is no, as can be shown by taking $6 to $7 an hour, perhaps subtracting a dollar or two an hour for child care, multiplying by 160 hours a month, and comparing the result to the prevailing rents. According to the National Coalition for the Homeless, for example, in 1998 it took, on average nationwide, an hourly wage of $8.89 to afford a one-bedroom apartment, and the Preamble Center for Public Policy estimates that the odds against a typical welfare recipient's landing a job at such a "living wage" are about 97 to 1. If these numbers are right, low-wage work is not a solution to poverty and possibly not even to homelessness.

It may seem excessive to put this proposition to an experimental test. As certain family members keep unhelpfully reminding me, the viability of low-wage work could be tested, after a fashion, without ever leaving my study. I could just pay myself $7 an hour for eight hours a day, charge myself for room and board, and total up the numbers after a month. Why leave the people and work that I love? But I am an experimental scientist by training. In that business, you don't just sit at a desk and theorize; you plunge into the everyday

5

chaos of nature, where surprises lurk in the most mundane measurements. Maybe, when I got into it, I would discover some hidden economies in the world of the low-wage worker. After all, if 30 percent of the workforce toils for less than $8 an hour, according to the EPI, they may have found some tricks as yet unknown to me. Maybe—who knows?—I would even to able to detect in myself the bracing psychological effects of getting out of the house, as promised by the welfare wonks at places like the Heritage Foundation. Or, on the other hand, maybe there would be unexpected costs—physical, mental, or financial—to throw off all my calculations. Ideally, I should do this with two small children in tow, that being the welfare average, but mine are grown and no one is willing to lend me theirs for a month-long vacation in penury. So this is not the perfect experiment, just a test of the best possible case: an unencumbered woman, smart and even strong, attempting to live more or less off the land.

On the morning of my first full day of job searching, I take a red pen to the want ads, which are auspiciously numerous. Everyone in Key West's booming "hospitality industry" seems to be looking for someone like me— trainable, flexible, and with suitably humble expectations as to pay. I know I possess certain traits that might be advantageous—I'm white and, I like to think, well-spoken and poised—but I decide on two rules: One, I cannot use any skills derived from my education or usual work—not that there are a lot of want ads for satirical essayists anyway. Two, I have to take the best-paid job that is offered me and of course do my best to hold it; no Marxist rants or sneaking off to read novels in the ladies' room. In addition, I rule out various occupations for one reason or another. Hotel front-desk clerk, for example, which to my surprise is regarded as unskilled and pays around $7 an hour, gets eliminated because it involves standing in one spot for eight hours a day. Waitressing is similarly something I'd like to avoid, because I remember it leaving me bone tired when I was eighteen, and I'm decades of varicosities and back pain beyond that now. Telemarketing, one of the first refuges of the suddenly indigent, can be dismissed on grounds of personality. This leaves certain supermarket jobs, such as deli clerk, or housekeeping in Key West's thousands of hotel and guest rooms. Housekeeping is especially appealing, for reasons both atavistic and practical: it's what my mother did before I came along, and it can't be too different from what I've been doing part-time, in my own home, all my life.

So I put on what I take to be a respectful-looking outfit of ironed Bermuda shorts and scooped-neck T-shirt and set out for a tour of the local hotels and supermarkets. Best Western, Econo Lodge, and HoJo's all let me fill out application forms, and these are, to my relief, interested in little more than whether I am a legal resident of the United States and have committed any felonies. My next step is Winn-Dixie, the supermarket, which turns out to have a particularly onerous application process, featuring a fifteen-minute "interview" by computer since, apparently, no human on the premises is deemed capable of representing the corporate point of view. I am conducted to a large room decorated with posters illustrating how to look "professional" (it helps to be white and, if female, permed) and warning of the slick promises that union organizers might try to tempt me with. The interview is multiple choice: Do I have anything, such as child-care problems, that might make it hard for me to get to work on time? Do I think safety on the job is the responsibility of management? Then, popping up cunningly out of the blue: How many dollars' worth of stolen goods have I purchased in the last year? Would I turn in a fellow employee if I caught him stealing? Finally, "Are you an honest person?"

Apparently, I ace the interview, because I am told that all I have to do is   10 show up in some doctor's office tomorrow for a urine test. This seems to be a fairly general rule: if you want to stack Cheerio boxes or vacuum hotel rooms in chemically fascist America, you have to be willing to squat down and pee in front of some health worker (who has no doubt had to do the same thing herself). The wages Winn-Dixie is offering—$6 and a couple of dimes to start with—are not enough, I decide, to compensate for this indignity.[2]

I lunch at Wendy's, where $4.99 gets you unlimited refills at the Mexican part of the Superbar, a comforting surfeit of refried beans and "cheese sauce." A teenage employee, seeing me studying the want ads, kindly offers me an application form, which I fill out, though here, too, the pay is just $6 and change an hour. Then it's off for a round of the locally owned inns and guest-houses. At "The Palms," let's call it, a bouncy manager actually takes me around to see the rooms and meet the existing housekeepers, who, I note with satisfaction, look pretty much like me—faded ex-hippie types in shorts with long hair pulled back in braids. Mostly, though, no one speaks to me or even looks at me except to proffer an application form. At my last stop, a palatial B&B, I wait twenty minutes to meet "Max," only to be told that there are no jobs now but there should be one soon, since "nobody lasts more than a couple weeks." (Because none of the people I talked to knew I was a reporter, I have changed their names to protect their privacy and, in some cases perhaps, their jobs.)

Three days go by like this, and, to my chagrin, no one out of the approximately twenty places I've applied calls me for an interview. I had been vain enough to worry about coming across as too educated for the jobs I sought, but no one even seems interested in finding out how overqualified I am. Only later will I realize that the want ads are not a reliable measure of the actual jobs available at any particular time. They are, as I should have guessed from

---

[2] According to the *Monthly Labor Review* (November 1996), 28 percent of work sites surveyed in the service industry conduct drug tests (corporate workplaces have much higher rates), and the incidence of testing has risen markedly since the Eighties. The rate of testing is highest in the South (56 percent of work sites polled), with the Midwest in second place (50 percent). The drug most likely to be detected—marijuana, which can be detected in urine for weeks—is also the most innocuous, while heroin and cocaine are generally undetectable three days after use. Prospective employees sometimes try to cheat the tests by consuming excessive amounts of liquids and taking diuretics and even masking substances available through the Internet. [Author's note]

Max's comment, the employers' insurance policy against the relentless turn-over of the low-wage workforce. Most of the big hotels run ads almost continually, just to build a supply of applicants to replace the current work-ers as they drift away or are fired, so finding a job is just a matter of being at the right place at the right time and flexible enough to take whatever is being offered that day. This finally happens to me at one of the big discount hotel chains, where I go, as usual, for housekeeping and am sent, instead, to try out as a waitress at the attached "family restaurant," a dismal spot with a counter and about thirty tables that looks out on a parking garage and features such tempting fare as "Pollish [sic] sausage and BBQ sauce" on 95-degree days. Phillip, the dapper young West Indian who introduces himself as the manager, interviews me with about as much enthusiasm as if he were a clerk processing me for Medicare, the principal questions being what shifts can I work and when can I start. I mutter something about being woefully out of practice as a waitress, but he's already on to the uniform: I'm to show up tomorrow wearing black slacks and black shoes; he'll provide the rust-colored polo shirt with HEARTHSIDE embroidered on it, though I might want to wear my own shirt to get to work, ha ha. At the word "tomorrow," something between fear and indignation rises in my chest. I want to say, "Thank you for your time, sir, but this is just an experiment, you know, not my actual life."

So begins my career at the Hearthside, I shall call it, one small profit cen-ter within a global discount hotel chain, where for two weeks I work from 2:00 till 10:00 P.M. for $2.43 an hour plus tips.[3] In some futile bid for gentil-ity, the management has barred employees from using the front door, so my first day I enter through the kitchen, where a red-faced man with shoulder-length blond hair is throwing frozen steaks against the wall and yelling, "Fuck this shit!" "That's just Jack," explains Gail, the wiry middle-aged waitress who is assigned to train me. "He's on the rag again"—a condition occasioned, in this instance, by the fact that the cook on the morning shift had forgotten to thaw out the steaks. For the next eight hours, I run after the agile Gail, absorbing bits of instruction along with fragments of personal tragedy. All food must be trayed, and the reason she's so tired today is that she woke up in a cold sweat thinking of her boyfriend, who killed himself recently in an upstate prison. No refills on lemonade. And the reason he was in prison is that a few DUIs caught up with him, that's all, could have hap-pened to anyone. Carry the creamers to the table in a monkey bowl, never in your hand. And after he was gone she spent several months living in her

---

[3] According to the Fair Labor Standards Act, employers are not required to pay "tipped employees," such as restaurant servers, more than $2.13 an hour in direct wages. However, if the sum of tips plus $2.13 an hour falls below the minimum wage, or $5.15 an hour, the employer is required to make up the difference. This fact was not mentioned by managers or otherwise publicized at either of the restaurants where I worked. [Author's note]

truck, peeing in a plastic pee bottle and reading by candlelight at night, but you can't live in a truck in the summer, since you need to have the windows down, which means anything can get in, from mosquitoes on up.

At least Gail puts to rest any fears I had of appearing overqualified. From the first day on, I find that of all the things I have left behind, such as home and identity, what I miss the most is competence. Not that I have ever felt utterly competent in the writing business, in which one day's success augurs nothing at all for the next. But in my writing life, I at least have some notion of procedure: do the research, make the outline, rough out a draft, etc. As a server, though, I am beset by requests like bees: more iced tea here, ketchup over there, a to-go box for table fourteen, and where are the high chairs, anyway? Of the twenty-seven tables, up to six are usually mine at any time, though on slow afternoons or if Gail is off, I sometimes have the whole place to myself. There is the touch-screen computer-ordering system to master, which is, I suppose, meant to mini-mize server-cook contact, but in practice requires constant verbal fine-tuning: "That's gravy on the mashed, okay? None on the meatloaf," and so forth— while the cook scowls as if I were inventing these refinements just to torment him. Plus, something I had forgotten in the years since I was eighteen: about a third of a server's job is "side work" that's invisible to customers—sweeping, scrubbing, slicing, refilling, and restocking. If it isn't all done, every little bit of it, you're going to face the 6:00 P.M. dinner rush defenseless and probably go down in flames. I screw up dozens of times at the beginning, sustained in my shame entirely by Gail's support—"It's okay, baby, everyone does that sometimes"—because, to my total surprise and despite the scientific detach-ment I am doing my best to maintain, I care.

The whole thing would be a lot easier if I could just skate through it as   15
Lily Tomlin in one of her waitress skits, but I was raised by the absurd Booker T. Washingtonian precept that says: If you're going to do something, do it well. In fact, "well" isn't good enough by half. Do it better than any-one has ever done it before. Or so said my father, who must have known what he was talking about because he managed to pull himself, and us with him, up from the mile-deep copper mines of Butte to the leafy suburbs of the Northeast, ascending from boilermakers to martinis before booze beat out ambition. As in most endeavors I have encountered in my life, doing it "better than anyone" is not a reasonable goal. Still, when I wake up at 4:00 A.M. in my own cold sweat, I am not thinking about the writing dead-lines I'm neglecting; I'm thinking about the table whose order I screwed up so that one of the boys didn't get his kiddie meal until the rest of the family had moved on to their Key Lime pies. That's the other powerful motivation I hadn't expected—the customers, or "patients," as I can't help thinking of them on account of the mysterious vulnerability that seems to have left them temporarily unable to feed themselves. After a few days at the Hearthside, I feel the service ethic kick in like a shot of oxytocin, the nurtu-rance hormone. The plurality of my customers are hard-working locals— truck drivers, construction workers, even housekeepers from the attached

hotel—and I want them to have the closest to a "fine dining" experience that the grubby circumstances will allow. No "you guys" for me; everyone over twelve is "sir" or "ma'am." I ply them with iced tea and coffee refills; I return, mid-meal, to inquire how everything is; I doll up their salads with chopped raw mushrooms, summer squash slices, or whatever bits of produce I can find that have survived their sojourn in the cold-storage room mold-free.

There is Benny, for example, a short, tight-muscled sewer repairman, who cannot even think of eating until he has absorbed a half hour of air-conditioning and ice water. We chat about hyperthermia and electrolytes until he is ready to order some finicky combination like soup of the day, garden salad, and a side of grits. There are the German tourists who are so touched by my pidgin "Willkommen" and "Ist alles gut?" that they actually tip. (Europeans, spoiled by their trade-union-ridden, high-wage welfare states, generally do not know that they are supposed to tip. Some restaurants, the Hearthside included, allow servers to "grat" their foreign customers, or add a tip to the bill. Since this amount is added before the customers have a chance to tip or not tip, the practice amounts to an automatic penalty for imperfect English.) There are the two dirt-smudged lesbians, just off their construction shift, who are impressed enough by my suave handling of the fly in the piña colada that they take the time to praise me to Stu, the assistant manager. There's Sam, the kindly retired cop, who has to plug up his tracheotomy hole with one finger in order to force the cigarette smoke into his lungs.

Sometimes I play with the fantasy that I am a princess who, in penance for some tiny transgression, has undertaken to feed each of her subjects by hand. But the non-princesses working with me are just as indulgent, even when this means flouting management rules—concerning, for example, the number of croutons that can go on a salad (six). "Put on all you want," Gail whispers, "as long as Stu isn't looking." She dips into her own tip money to buy biscuits and gravy for an out-of-work mechanic who's used up all his money on dental surgery, inspiring me to pick up the tab for his milk and pie. Maybe the same high levels of agape can be found throughout the "hospitality industry." I remember the poster decorating one of the apartments I looked at, which said "If you seek happiness for yourself you will never find it. Only when you seek happiness for others will it come to you," or words to that effect—an odd sentiment, it seemed to me at the time, to find in the dank one-room basement apartment of a bellhop at the Best Western. At the Hearthside, we utilize whatever bits of autonomy we have to ply our customers with the illicit calories that signal our love. It is our job as servers to assemble the salads and desserts, pouring the dressings and squirting the whipped cream. We also control the number of butter patties our customers get and the amount of sour cream on their baked potatoes. So if you wonder why Americans are so obese, consider the fact that waitresses both express their humanity and earn their tips through the covert distribution of fats.

Ten days into it, this is beginning to look like a livable lifestyle. I like Gail, who is "looking at fifty" but moves so fast she can alight in one place and then another without apparently being anywhere between them. I clown around with Lionel, the teenage Haitian busboy, and catch a few fragments of conversation with Joan, the svelte fortyish hostess and militant feminist who is the only one of us who dares to tell Jack to shut the fuck up. I even warm up to Jack when, on a slow night and to make up for a particularly unwarranted attack on my abilities, or so I imagine, he tells me about his glory days as a young man at "coronary school"—or do you say "culinary"?—in Brooklyn, where he dated a knock-out Puerto Rican chick and learned everything there is to know about food. I finish up at 10:00 or 10:30, depending on how much side work I've been able to get done during the shift, and cruise home to the tapes I snatched up at random when I left my real home—Marianne Faithfull, Tracy Chapman, Enigma, King Sunny Ade, the Violent Femmes—just drained enough for the music to set my cranium resonating but hardly dead. Midnight snack is Wheat Thins and Monterey Jack, accompanied by cheap white wine on ice and whatever AMC has to offer. To bed by 1:30 or 2:00, up at 9:00 or 10:00, read for an hour while my uniform whirls around in the landlord's washing machine, and then it's another eight hours spent following Mao's central instruction, as laid out in the Little Red Book, which was: Serve the people.

I could drift along like this, in some dreamy proletarian idyll, except for two things. One is management. If I have kept this subject on the margins thus far it is because I still flinch to think that I spent all those weeks under the surveillance of men (and later women) whose job it was to monitor my behavior for signs of sloth, theft, drug abuse, or worse. Not that managers and especially "assistant managers" in low-wage settings like this are exactly the class enemy. In the restaurant business, they are mostly former cooks or servers, still capable of pinch-hitting in the kitchen or on the floor, just as in hotels they are likely to be former clerks, and paid a salary of only about $400 a week. But everyone knows they have crossed over to the other side, which is, crudely put, corporate as opposed to human. Cooks want to prepare tasty meals; servers want to serve them graciously; but managers are there for only one reason—to make sure that money is made for some theoretical entity that exists far away in Chicago or New York, if a corporation can be said to have a physical existence at all. Reflecting on her career, Gail tells me ruefully that she had sworn, years ago, never to work for a corporation again. "They don't cut you no slack. You give and you give, and they take."

Managers can sit—for hours at a time if they want—but it's their job to   20
see that no one else ever does, even when there's nothing to do, and this is why, for servers, slow times can be as exhausting as rushes. You start dragging out each little chore, because if the manager on duty catches you in an idle moment, he will give you something far nastier to do. So I wipe, I clean, I consolidate ketchup bottles and recheck the cheesecake supply, even tour the tables to make sure the customer evaluation forms are all standing perkily in their places—wondering all the time how many calories I burn in these strictly theatrical exercises. When, on a particularly dead afternoon, Stu finds

me glancing at a *USA Today* a customer has left behind, he assigns me to vacuum the entire floor with the broken vacuum cleaner that has a handle only two feet long, and the only way to do that without incurring orthopedic damage is to proceed from spot to spot on your knees.

On my first Friday at the Hearthside there is a "mandatory meeting for all restaurant employees," which I attend, eager for insight into our overall marketing strategy and the niche (your basic Ohio cuisine with a tropical twist?) we aim to inhabit. But there is no "we" at this meeting. Phillip, our top manager except for an occasional "consultant" sent out by corporate headquarters, opens it with a sneer: "The break room—it's disgusting. Butts in the ashtrays, newspapers lying around, crumbs." This windowless little room, which also houses the time clock for the entire hotel, is where we stash our bags and civilian clothes and take our half-hour meal breaks. But a break room is not a right, he tells us. It can be taken away. We should also know that the lockers in the break room and whatever is in them can be searched at any time. Then comes gossip; there has been gossip; gossip (which seems to mean employees talking among themselves) must stop. Off-duty employees are henceforth barred from eating at the restaurant, because "other servers gather around them and gossip." When Phillip has exhausted his agenda of rebukes, Joan complains about the condition of the ladies' room and I throw in my two bits about the vacuum cleaner. But I don't see any backup coming from my fellow servers, each of whom has subsided into her own personal funk; Gail, my role model, stares sorrowfully at a point six inches from her nose. The meeting ends when Andy, one of the cooks, gets up, muttering about breaking up his day off for this almighty bullshit.

Just four days later we are suddenly summoned into the kitchen at 3:30 P.M., even though there are live tables on the floor. We all—about ten of us—stand around Phillip, who announces grimly that there has been a report of some "drug activity" on the night shift and that, as a result, we are now to be a "drug-free" workplace, meaning that all new hires will be tested, as will possibly current employees on a random basis. I am glad that this part of the kitchen is so dark, because I find myself blushing as hard as if I had been caught toking up in the ladies' room myself: I haven't been treated this way—lined up in the corridor, threatened with locker searches, peppered with carelessly aimed accusations—since junior high school. Back on the floor, Joan cracks, "Next they'll be telling us we can't have sex on the job." When I ask Stu what happened to inspire the crackdown, he just mutters about "management decisions" and takes the opportunity to upbraid Gail and me for being too generous with the rolls. From now on there's to be only one per customer, and it goes out with the dinner, not with the salad. He's also been riding the cooks, prompting Andy to come out of the kitchen and observe—with the serenity of a man whose customary implement is a butcher knife—that "Stu has a death wish today."

Later in the evening, the gossip crystallizes around the theory that Stu is himself the drug culprit, that he uses the restaurant phone to order up marijuana and sends one of the late servers out to fetch it for him. The server was caught, and she may have ratted Stu out or at least said enough to cast some suspicion on him, thus accounting for his pissy behavior. Who knows? Lionel, the busboy, entertains us for the rest of the shift by standing just behind Stu's back and sucking deliriously on an imaginary joint.

The other problem, in addition to the less-than-nurturing management style, is that this job shows no sign of being financially viable. You might imagine, from a comfortable distance, that people who live, year in and year out, on $6 to $10 an hour have discovered some survival stratagems unknown to the middle class. But no. It's not hard to get my co-workers to talk about their living situations, because housing, in almost every case, is the principal source of disruption in their lives, the first thing they fill you in on when they arrive for their shifts. After a week, I have compiled the following survey:

- Gail is sharing a room in a well-known downtown flophouse for which she and a roommate pay about $250 a week. Her roommate, a male friend, has begun hitting on her, driving her nuts, but the rent would be impossible alone.
- Claude, the Haitian cook, is desperate to get out of the two-room apartment he shares with his girlfriend and two other, unrelated, people. As far as I can determine, the other Haitian men (most of whom only speak Creole) live in similarly crowded situations.
- Annette, a twenty-year-old server who is six months pregnant and has been abandoned by her boyfriend, lives with her mother, a postal clerk.
- Marianne and her boyfriend are paying $170 a week for a one-person trailer.
- Jack, who is, at $10 an hour, the wealthiest of us, lives in a trailer he owns, paying only the $400-a-month lot fee.
- The other white cook, Andy, lives on his dry-docked boat, which, as far as I can tell from his loving descriptions, can't be more than twenty feet long. He offers to take me out on it, once it's repaired, but the offer comes with inquiries as to my marital status, so I do not follow up on it.
- Tina and her husband are paying $60 a night for a double room in a Days Inn. This is because they have no car and the Days Inn is within walking distance of the Hearthside. When Marianne, one of the break-fast servers, is tossed out of her trailer for subletting (which is against the trailer-park rules), she leaves her boyfriend and moves in with Tina and her husband.
- Joan, who had fooled me with her numerous and tasteful outfits (host-esses wear their own clothes), lives in a van she parks behind a shopping center at night and showers in Tina's motel room. The clothes are from thrift shops.[4]

---

[4] I could find no statistics on the number of employed people living in cars or vans, but according to the National Coalition for the Homeless's 1997 report, "Myths and Facts About Homelessness," nearly one in five homeless people (in twenty-nine cities across the nation) is employed in a full- or part-time job. [Author's note]

It strikes me, in my middle-class solipsism, that there is gross improvi-   25
dence in some of these arrangements. When Gail and I are wrapping silverware in napkins—the only task for which we are permitted to sit—she tells
me she is thinking of escaping from her roommate by moving into the Days
Inn herself. I am astounded: How can she even think of paying between $40
and $60 a day? But if I was afraid of sounding like a social worker, I come
out just sounding like a fool. She squints at me in disbelief, "And where am
I supposed to get a month's rent and a month's deposit for an apartment?"
I'd been feeling pretty smug about my $500 efficiency, but of course it was
made possible only by the $1,300 I had allotted myself for start-up costs
when I began my low-wage life: $1,000 for the first month's rent and
deposit, $100 for initial groceries and cash in my pocket, $200 stuffed away
for emergencies. In poverty, as in certain propositions in physics, starting
conditions are everything.

There are no secret economies that nourish the poor; on the contrary,
there are a host of special costs. If you can't put up the two months' rent you
need to secure an apartment, you end up paying through the nose for a
room by the week. If you have only a room, with a hot plate at best, you
can't save by cooking up huge lentil stews that can be frozen for the week
ahead. You eat fast food, or the hot dogs and styrofoam cups of soup that
can be microwaved in a convenience store. If you have no money for health
insurance—and the Hearthside's niggardly plan kicks in only after three
months—you go without routine care or prescription drugs and end up paying the price. Gail, for example, was fine until she ran out of money for
estrogen pills. She is supposed to be on the company plan by now, but they
claim to have lost her application form and need to begin the paperwork all
over again. So she spends $9 per migraine pill to control the headaches she
wouldn't have, she insists, if her estrogen supplements were covered. Similarly, Marianne's boyfriend lost his job as a roofer because he missed so
much time after getting a cut on his foot for which he couldn't afford the
prescribed antibiotic.

My own situation, when I sit down to assess it after two weeks of work,
would not be much better if this were my actual life. The seductive thing
about waitressing is that you don't have to wait for payday to feel a few bills
in your pocket, and my tips usually cover meals and gas, plus something left
over to stuff into the kitchen drawer I use as a bank. But as the tourist business slows in the summer heat, I sometimes leave work with only $20 in tips
(the gross is higher, but servers share about 15 percent of their tips with the
bus-boys and bartenders). With wages included, this amounts to about the
minimum wage of $5.15 an hour. Although the sum in the drawer is piling
up, at the present rate of accumulation it will be more than a hundred dollars
short of my rent when the end of the month comes around. Nor can I see any
expenses to cut. True, I haven't gone the lentil-stew route yet, but that's
because I don't have a large cooking pot, pot holders, or a ladle to stir with
(which cost about $30 at Kmart, less at thrift stores), not to mention onions,

carrots, and the indispensable bay leaf. I do make my lunch almost every day—usually some slow-burning, high-protein combo like frozen chicken patties with melted cheese on top and canned pinto beans on the side. Dinner is at the Hearthside, which offers its employees a choice of BLT, fish sandwich, or hamburger for only $2. The burger lasts longest, especially if it's heaped with gut-puckering jalapeños, but by midnight my stomach is growling again.

So unless I want to start using my car as a residence, I have to find a second, or alternative, job. I call all the hotels where I filled out housekeeping applications weeks ago—the Hyatt, Holiday Inn, Econo Lodge, Hojo's, Best Western, plus a half dozen or so locally run guesthouses. Nothing. Then I start making the rounds again, wasting whole mornings waiting for some assistant manager to show up, even dipping into places so creepy that the front-desk clerk greets you from behind bulletproof glass and sells pints of liquor over the counter. But either someone has exposed my real-life housekeeping habits—which are, shall we say, mellow—or I am at the wrong end of some infallible ethnic equation: most, but by no means all, of the working housekeepers I see on my job searches are African Americans, Spanish-speaking, or immigrants from the Central European post-Communist world, whereas servers are almost invariably white and monolingually English-speaking. When I finally get a positive response, I have been identified once again as server material. Jerry's, which is part of a well-known national family restaurant chain and physically attached here to another budget hotel chain, is ready to use me at once. The prospect is both exciting and terrifying, because, with about the same number of tables and counter seats, Jerry's attracts three or four times the volume of customers as the gloomy old Hearthside.

I start out with the beautiful, heroic idea of handling the two jobs at once, and for two days I almost do it: the breakfast/lunch shift at Jerry's, which goes till 2:00, arriving at the Hearthside at 2:10, and attempting to hold out until 10:00. In the ten minutes between jobs, I pick up a spicy chicken sandwich at the Wendy's drive-through window, gobble it down in the car, and change from khaki slacks to black, from Hawaiian to rust polo. There is a problem, though. When during the 3:00 to 4:00 P.M. dead time I finally sit down to wrap silver, my flesh seems to bond to the seat. I try to refuel with a purloined cup of soup, as I've seen Gail and Joan do dozens of times, but a manager catches me and hisses "No eating!" though there's not a customer around to be offended by the sight of food making contact with a server's lips. So I tell Gail I'm going to quit, and she hugs me and says she might just follow me to Jerry's herself.

But the chances of this are miniscule. She has left the flophouse and her annoying roommate and is back to living in her beat-up old truck. But guess what? she reports to me excitedly later that evening: Phillip has given her permission to park overnight in the hotel parking lot, as long as she keeps out of sight, and the parking lot should be totally safe, since it's patrolled by

30

a hotel security guard! With the Hearthside offering benefits like that, how could anyone think of leaving?

True, I take occasional breaks from this life, going home now and then to catch up on e-mail and for conjugal visits (though I am careful to "pay" for anything I eat there), seeing *The Truman Show* with friends and letting them buy my ticket. And I still have those what-am-I-doing-here moments at work, when I get so homesick for the printed word that I obsessively reread the six-page menu. But as the days go by, my old life is beginning to look exceedingly strange. The e-mails and phone messages addressed to my former self come from a distant race of people with exotic concerns and far too much time on their hands. The neighborly market I used to cruise for produce now looks forbiddingly like a Manhattan yuppie emporium. And when I sit down one morning in my real home to pay bills from my past life, I am dazzled at the two- and three-figure sums owed to outfits like Club BodyTech and Amazon.com.

Management at Jerry's is generally calmer and more "professional" than at the Hearthside, with two exceptions. One is Joy, a plump, blowsy woman in her early thirties, who once kindly devoted several minutes to instructing me in the correct one-handed method of carrying trays but whose moods change disconcertingly from shift to shift and even within one. Then there's B.J., a.k.a. B.J.-the-bitch, whose contribution is to stand by the kitchen counter and yell, "Nita, your order's up, move it!" or, "Barbara, didn't you see you've got another table out there? Come on, girl!" Among other things, she is hated for having replaced the whipped-cream squirt cans with big plastic whipped-cream-filled baggies that have to be squeezed with both hands— because, reportedly, she saw or thought she saw employees trying to inhale the propellant gas from the squirt cans, in the hope that it might be nitrous oxide. On my third night, she pulls me aside abruptly and brings her face so close that it looks as if she's planning to butt me with her forehead. But instead of saying, "You're fired," she says, "You're doing fine." The only trouble is I'm spending time chatting with customers: "That's how they're getting you." Furthermore I am letting them "run me," which means harassment by sequential demands: you bring the ketchup and they decide they want extra Thousand Island; you bring that and they announce they now need a side of fries; and so on into distraction. Finally she tells me not to take her wrong. She tries to say things in a nice way, but you get into a mode, you know, because everything has to move so fast.[5]

I mumble thanks for the advice, feeling like I've just been stripped naked by the crazed enforcer of some ancient sumptuary law: No chatting for you,

---

[5] In *Workers in a Lean World: Unions in the International Economy* (Verso, 1997), Kim Moody cites studies finding an increase in stress-related workplace injuries and illness between the mid-1980s and the early 1990s. He argues that rising stress levels reflect a new system of "management by stress," in which workers in a variety of industries are being squeezed to extract maximum productivity, to the detriment of their health. [Author's note]

girl. No fancy service ethic allowed for the serfs. Chatting with customers is for the beautiful young college-educated servers in the downtown carpaccio joints, the kids who can make $70 to $100 a night. What had I been thinking? My job is to move orders from tables to kitchen and then trays from kitchen to tables. Customers are, in fact, the major obstacle to the smooth transformation of information into food and food into money—they are, in short, the enemy. And the painful thing is that I'm beginning to see it this way myself. There are the traditional asshole types—frat boys who down multiple Buds and then make a fuss because the steaks are so emaciated and the fries so sparse—as well as the variously impaired—due to age, diabetes, or literacy issues—who require patient nutritional counseling.

I make friends, over time, with the other "girls" who work my shift: Nita, the tattooed twenty-something who taunts us by going around saying brightly, "Have we started making money yet?" Ellen, whose teenage son cooks on the graveyard shift and who once managed a restaurant in Massachusetts but won't try out for management here because she prefers being a "common worker" and not "ordering people around." Easy-going fiftyish Lucy, with the raucous laugh, who limps toward the end of the shift because of something that has gone wrong with her leg, the exact nature of which cannot be determined without health insurance. We talk about the usual girl things—men, children, and the sinister allure of Jerry's chocolate peanut-butter cream pie—though no one, I notice, ever brings up anything potentially expensive, like shopping or movies. As at the Hearthside, the only recreation ever referred to is partying, which requires little more than some beer, a joint, and a few close friends. Still, no one here is homeless, or cops to it anyway, thanks usually to a working husband or boyfriend. All in all, we form a reliable mutual-support group: If one of us is feeling sick or overwhelmed, another one will "bev" a table or even carry trays for her. If one of us is off sneaking a cigarette or a pee,[6] the others will do their best to conceal her absence from the enforcers of corporate rationality.

But my saving human connection—my oxytocin receptor, as it were—   35
George, the nineteen-year-old, fresh-off-the-boat Czech dishwasher. We get

---

[6] Until April 1998, there was no federally mandated right to bathroom breaks. According to Marc Linder and Ingrid Nygaard, authors of *Void Where Prohibited: Rest Breaks and the Right to Urinate on Company Time* (Cornell University Press, 1997), "The right to rest and void at work is not high on the list of social or political causes supported by professional or executive employees, who enjoy personal workplace liberties that millions of factory workers can only daydream about. . . . While we were dismayed to discover that workers lacked an acknowledged legal right to void at work, (the workers) were amazed by outsiders' naïve belief that their employers would permit them to perform this basic bodily function when necessary. . . . A factory worker, not allowed a break for six-hour stretches, voided into pads worn inside her uniform; and a kindergarten teacher in a school without aides had to take all twenty children with her to the bathroom and line them up outside the stall door when she voided." [Author's note]

to talking when he asks me, tortuously, how much cigarettes cost at Jerry's. I do my best to explain that they cost over a dollar more here than at a regular store and suggest that he just take one from the half-filled packs that are always lying around on the break table. But that would be unthinkable. Except for the one tiny earring signaling his allegiance to some vaguely alternative point of view, George is a perfect straight arrow—crew-cut, hardworking, and hungry for eye contact. "Czech Republic," I ask, "or Slovakia?" and he seems delighted that I know the difference. "Václav Havel," I try. "Velvet Revolution, Frank Zappa?" "Yes, yes, 1989," he says, and I realize we are talking about history.

My project is to teach George English. "How are you today, George?" I say at the start of each shift. "I am good, and how are you today, Barbara?" I learn that he is not paid by Jerry's but by the "agent" who shipped him over—$5 an hour, with the agent getting the dollar or so difference between that and what Jerry's pays dishwashers. I learn also that he shares an apartment with a crowd of other Czech "dishers," as he calls them, and that he cannot sleep until one of them goes off for his shift, leaving a vacant bed. We are having one of our ESL sessions late one afternoon when B.J. catches us at it and orders "Joseph" to take up the rubber mats on the floor near the dishwashing sinks and mop underneath. "I thought your name was George," I say loud enough for B.J. to hear as she strides off back to the counter. Is she embarrassed? Maybe a little, because she greets me back at the counter with "George, Joseph—there are so many of them!" I say nothing, neither nodding nor smiling, and for this I am punished later when I think I am ready to go and she announces that I need to roll fifty more sets of silverware and isn't it time I mixed up a fresh four-gallon batch of blue-cheese dressing? May you grow old in this place, B.J., is the curse I beam out at her when I am finally permitted to leave. May the syrup spills glue your feet to the floor.

I make the decision to move closer to Key West. First, because of the drive. Second and third, also because of the drive: gas is eating up $4 to $5 a day, and although Jerry's is as high-volume as you can get, the tips average only 10 percent, and not just for a newbie like me. Between the base pay of $2.15 an hour and the obligation to share tips with the busboys and dishwashers, we're averaging only about $7.50 an hour. Then there is the $30 I had to spend on the regulation tan slacks worn by Jerry's servers—a setback it could take weeks to absorb. (I had combed the town's two downscale department stores hoping for something cheaper but decided in the end that these marked-down Dockers, originally $49, were more likely to survive a daily washing.) Of my fellow servers, everyone who lacks a working husband or boyfriend seems to have a second job: Nita does something at a computer eight hours a day; another welds. Without the forty-five-minute commute, I can picture myself working two jobs and having the time to shower between them.

So I take the $500 deposit I have coming from my landlord, the $400 I have earned toward the next month's rent, plus the $200 reserved for emergencies, and use the $1,100 to pay the rent and deposit on trailer number 46 in the Overseas Trailer Park, a mile from the cluster of budget hotels that constitute Key West's version of an industrial park. Number 46 is about eight feet in width and shaped like a barbell inside, with a narrow region—because of the sink and the stove—separating the bedroom from what might optimistically be called the "living" area, with its two-person table and half-sized couch. The bathroom is so small my knees rub against the shower stall when I sit on the toilet, and you can't just leap out of the bed, you have to climb down to the foot of it in order to find a patch of floor space to stand on. Outside, I am within a few yards of a liquor store, a bar that advertises "free beer tomorrow," a convenience store, and a Burger King—but no supermarket or, alas, laundromat. By reputation, the Overseas park is a nest of crime and crack, and I am hoping at least for some vibrant, multicultural street life. But desolation rules night and day, except for a thin stream of pedestrian traffic heading for their jobs at the Sheraton or 7-Eleven. There are not exactly people here but what amounts to canned labor, being preserved from the heat between shifts.

In line with my reduced living conditions, a new form of ugliness arises at Jerry's. First we are confronted—via an announcement on the computers through which we input orders—with the new rule that the hotel bar is henceforth off-limits to restaurant employees. The culprit, I learn through the grapevine, is the ultra-efficient gal who trained me—another trailer-home dweller and a mother of three. Something had set her off one morning, so she slipped out for a nip and returned to the floor impaired. This mostly hurts Ellen, whose habit it is to free her hair from its rubber band and drop by the bar for a couple of Zins before heading home at the end of the shift, but all of us feel the chill. Then the next day, when I go for straws, for the first time I find the dry-storage room locked. Ted, the portly assistant manager who opens it for me, explains that he caught one of the dishwashers attempting to steal something, and, unfortunately, the miscreant will be with us until a replacement can be found—hence the locked door. I neglect to ask what he had been trying to steal, but Ted tells me who he is—the kid with the buzz cut and the earring. You know, he's back there right now.

I wish I could say I rushed back and confronted George to get his side 40 of the story. I wish I could say I stood up to Ted and insisted that George be given a translator and allowed to defend himself, or announced that I'd find a lawyer who'd handle the case pro bono. The mystery to me is that there's not much worth stealing in the dry-storage room, at least not in any fence-able quantity: "Is Gyorgi here, and am having 200—maybe 250—ketchup packets. What do you say?" My guess is that he had taken—if he had taken anything at all—some Saltines or a can of cherry-pie mix, and that the motive for taking it was hunger.

So why didn't I intervene? Certainly not because I was held back by the kind of moral paralysis that can pass as journalistic objectivity. On the contrary, something new—something loathsome and servile—had infected me, along with the kitchen odors that I could still sniff on my bra when I finally undressed at night. In real life I am moderately brave, but plenty of brave people shed their courage in concentration camps, and maybe something similar goes on in the infinitely more congenial milieu of the low-wage American workplace. Maybe, in a month or two more at Jerry's, I might have regained my crusading spirit. Then again, in a month or two I might have turned into a different person altogether—say, the kind of person who would have turned George in. But this is not something I am slated to find out.

I can do this two-job thing, is my theory, if I can drink enough caffeine and avoid getting distracted by George's ever more obvious suffering.[7] The first few days after being caught he seemed not to understand the trouble he was in, and our chirpy little conversations had continued. But the last couple of shifts he's been listless and unshaven, and tonight he looks like the ghost we all know him to be, with dark half-moons hanging from his eyes. At one point, when I am briefly immobilized by the task of filling little paper cups with sour cream for baked potatoes, he comes over and looks as if he'd like to explore the limits of our shared vocabulary, but I am called to the floor for a table. I resolve to give him all my tips that night and to hell with the experiment in low-wage money management. At eight, Ellen and I grab a snack together standing at the mephitic end of the kitchen counter, but I can only manage two or three mozzarella sticks and lunch had been a mere handful of McNuggets. I am not tired at all, I assure myself, though it may be that there is simply no more "I" left to do the tiredness monitoring. What I would see, if I were more alert to the situation, is that the forces of destruction are already massing against me. There is only one cook on duty, a young man names Jesus ("Hay-Sue," that is) and he is new to the job. And there is Joy, who shows up to take over in the middle of the shift, wearing high heels and a long, clingy white dress and fuming as if she'd just been stood up in some cocktail bar.

Then it comes, the perfect storm. Four of my tables fill up at once. Four tables is nothing for me now, but only so long as they are obligingly staggered. As I bev table 27, tables 25, 28, and 24 are watching enviously. As I bev 25, 24 glowers because their bevs haven't even been ordered. Twenty-eight is four yuppyish types, meaning everything on the side and agonizing instructions as to the chicken Caesars. Twenty-five is a middle-aged black couple, who complain, with some justice, that the iced tea isn't fresh and the tabletop is sticky. But table 24 is the meteorological event of the century: ten

---

[7] In 1996, the number of persons holding two or more jobs averaged 7.8 million, or 6.2 percent of the workforce. It was about the same rate for men and for women (6.1 versus 6.2), though the kinds of jobs differ by gender. About two thirds of multiple jobholders work one job full-time and the other part-time. Only a heroic minority—4 percent of men and 2 percent of women—work two full-time jobs simultaneously. (From John F. Stinson Jr., "New Data on Multiple Jobholding Available from the CPS," in the *Monthly Labor Review,* March 1997.) [Author's note]

British tourists who seem to have made the decision to absorb the American experience entirely by mouth. Here everyone has at least two drinks—iced tea and milk shake, Michelob and water (with lemon slice, please)—and a huge promiscuous orgy of breakfast specials, mozz sticks, chicken strips, quesadillas; burgers with cheese and without, sides of hash browns with cheddar, with onions, with gravy, seasoned fries, plain fries, banana splits. Poor Jesus! Poor me! Because when I arrive with their first tray of food—after three prior trips just to refill bevs—Princess Di refuses to eat her chicken strips with her pancake-and-sausage special, since, as she now reveals, the strips were meant to be an appetizer. Maybe the others would have accepted their meals, but Di, who is deep into her third Michelob, insists that everything else go back while they work on their "starters." Meanwhile, the yuppies are waving me down for more decaf and the black couple looks ready to summon the NAACP.

Much of what happened next is lost in the fog of war. Jesus starts going under. The little printer on the counter in front of him is spewing out orders faster than he can rip them off, much less produce the meals. Even the invincible Ellen is ashen from stress. I bring table 24 their reheated main courses, which they immediately reject as either too cold or fossilized by the microwave. When I return to the kitchen with their trays (three trays in three trips), Joy confronts me with arms akimbo: "What is this?" She means the food—the plates of rejected pancakes, hash browns in assorted flavors, toasts, burgers, sausages, eggs. "Uh, scrambled with cheddar," I try, "and that's . . ." "NO," she screams in my face. "Is it a traditional, a super-scramble, an eye-opener?" I pretend to study my check for a clue, but entropy has been up to its tricks, not only on the plates but in my head, and I have to admit that the original order is beyond reconstruction. "You don't know an eye-opener from a traditional?" she demands in outrage. All I know, in fact, is that my legs have lost interest in the current venture and have announced their intention to fold. I am saved by a yuppie (mercifully not one of mine) who chooses this moment to charge into the kitchen to bellow that his food is twenty-five minutes late. Joy screams at him to get the hell out of her kitchen, please, and then turns on Jesus in a fury, hurling an empty tray across the room for emphasis.

I leave. I don't walk out, I just leave. I don't finish my side work or pick up my credit-card tips, if any, at the cash register or, of course, ask Joy's permission to go. And the surprising thing is that you *can* walk out without permission, that the door opens, that the thick tropical night air parts to let me pass, that my car is still parked where I left it. There is no vindication in this exit, no fuck-you surge of relief, just an overwhelming, dank sense of failure pressing down on me and the entire parking lot. I had gone into this venture in the spirit of science, to test a mathematical proposition, but somewhere along the line, in the tunnel vision imposed by long shifts and relentless concentration, it became a test of myself, and clearly I have failed. Not only had I flamed out as a housekeeper/server, I had even forgotten to give George my tips, and, for reasons perhaps best known to hardworking, generous people

45

like Gail and Ellen, this hurts. I don't cry, but I am in a position to realize, for the first time in many years, that the tear ducts are still there, and still capable of doing their job.

When I moved out of the trailer park, I gave the key to number 46 to Gail and arranged for my deposit to be transferred to her. She told me that Joan is still living in her van and that Stu had been fired from the Hearthside. I never found out what happened to George.

In one month, I had earned approximately $1,040 and spent $517 on food, gas, toiletries, laundry, phone, and utilities. If I had remained in my $500 efficiency, I would have been able to pay the rent and have $22 left over (which is $78 less than the cash I had in my pocket at the start of the month). During this time I bought no clothing except for the required slacks and no prescription drugs or medical care (I did finally buy some vitamin B to compensate for the lack of vegetables in my diet). Perhaps I could have saved a little on food if I had gotten to a supermarket more often, instead of convenience stores, but it should be noted that I lost almost four pounds in four weeks, on a diet weighted heavily toward burgers and fries.

How former welfare recipients and single mothers will (and do) survive in the low-wage workforce, I cannot imagine. Maybe they will figure out how to condense their lives—including child-raising, laundry, romance, and meals—into the couple of hours between full-time jobs. Maybe they will take up residence in their vehicles, if they have one. All I know is that I couldn't hold two jobs and I couldn't make enough money to live on with one. And I had advantages unthinkable to many of the long-term poor—health, stamina, a working car, and no children to care for and support. Certainly nothing in my experience contradicts the conclusion of Kathryn Edin and Laura Lein, in their recent book *Making Ends Meet: How Single Mothers Survive Welfare and Low-Wage Work,* that low-wage work actually involves more hardship and deprivation than life at the mercy of the welfare state. In the coming months and years, economic conditions for the working poor are bound to worsen, even without the almost inevitable recession. As mentioned earlier, the influx of former welfare recipients into the low-skilled workforce will have a depressing effect on both wages and the number of jobs available. A general economic downturn will only enhance these effects, and the working poor will of course be facing it without the slight, but nonetheless often saving, protection of welfare as a backup.

The thinking behind welfare reform was that even the humblest jobs are morally uplifting and psychologically buoying. In reality they are likely to be fraught with insult and stress. But I did discover one redeeming feature of the most abject low-wage work—the camaraderie of people who are, in almost all cases, far too smart and funny and caring for the work they do and the wages they're paid. The hope, of course, is that someday these people will come to know what they're worth, and take appropriate action.

Questions for Discussion and Writing

1. What kinds of trade-offs and choices does Ehrenreich have to make when she becomes an unskilled worker?
2. How do the people (bosses and employees) and different environments she encounters change whatever preconceptions Ehrenreich had about the working poor?
3. Which of the issues Ehrenreich touches on, including homelessness, drug testing in the workplace, and holding two jobs just to survive, dramatize most vividly the plight of the working poor? After reading her report, do you agree with her conclusions regarding welfare reform? Why or why not?
4. **Rhetorical inquiry:** How does Ehrenreich strengthen her analysis with dramatic and interesting stories of her coworkers who work with her as waitresses, housekeepers, and maintenance personnel? How do their stories illustrate that the realities they face are much harsher than policymakers have imagined?

LUIS SEPÚLVEDA

The Chilean novelist Luis Sepúlveda (b. 1949) was confined to prison as a political enemy under the dictatorship of Augusto Pinochet. He describes his experiences in this selection from Full Circle: A South American Journey *(1996). He has also written* The Old Man Who Read Love Stories *(1992),* The Name of the Bullfighter *(1996), and* Hot Line *(2002).*

Before You Read

Consider the unusual importance that literature takes on in this most unlikely environment.

Daisy

The military had rather inflated ideas of our destructive capacity. They questioned us about plans to assassinate all the officers in American military history, to blow up bridges and seal off tunnels, and to prepare for the landing of a terrible foreign enemy whom they could not identify.

Temuco is a sad, grey, rainy city. No-one would call it a tourist attraction, and yet the barracks of the Tucapel regiment came to house a sort of permanent international convention of sadists. The Chileans, who were the hosts, after all, were assisted in the interrogations by primates from Brazilian military intelligence—they were the worst—North Americans from the State

Department, Argentinian paramilitary personnel, Italian neo-fascists and even some agents of Mossad.

I remember Rudi Weismann, a Chilean with a passion for the South and sailing, who was tortured and interrogated in the gentle language of the synagogues. This infamy was too much for Rudi, who had thrown in his lot with Israel: he had worked on a kibbutz, but in the end his nostalgia for Tierra del Fuego had brought him back to Chile. He simply could not understand how Israel could support such a gang of criminals, and though till then he had always been a model of good humour, he dried up like a neglected plant. One morning we found him dead in his sleeping bag. No need for an autopsy, his face made it clear: Rudi Weismann had died of sadness.

The commander of the Tucapel regiment—a basic respect for paper prevents me from writing his name—was a fanatical admirer of Field Marshal Rommel. When he found a prisoner he liked, he would invite him to recover from the interrogations in his office. After assuring the prisoner that everything that happened in the barracks was in the best interests of our great nation, the commander would offer him a glass of Korn—somebody used to send him this insipid, wheat-based liquor from Germany—and make him sit through a lecture on the Africa Korps. The guy's parents or grandparents were German, but he couldn't have looked more Chilean: chubby, short-legged, dark untidy hair. You could have mistaken him for a truck driver or a fruit vendor, but when he talked about Rommel he became the caricature of a Nazi guard.

At the end of the lecture he would dramatise Rommel's suicide, clicking his heels, raising his right hand to his forehead to salute an invisible flag, muttering "Adieu geliebtes Vaterland," and pretending to shoot himself in the mouth. We all hoped that one day he would do it for real. 5

There was another curious officer in the regiment: a lieutenant struggling to contain a homosexuality that kept popping out all over the place. The soldiers had nicknamed him Daisy, and he knew it.

We could all tell that it was a torment for Daisy not to be able to adorn his body with truly beautiful objects, and the poor guy had to make do with the regulation paraphernalia. He wore a .45 pistol, two cartridge clips, a commando's curved dagger, two hand grenades, a torch, a walkie-talkie, the insignia of his rank and the silver wings of the parachute corps. The prisoners and the soldiers thought he looked like a Christmas tree.

This individual sometimes surprised us with generous and apparently disinterested acts—we didn't know that the Stockholm syndrome could be a military perversion. For example, after the interrogations he would suddenly fill our pockets with cigarettes or the highly prized aspirin tablets with vitamin C. One afternoon he invited me to his room.

"So you're a man of letters," he said, offering me a can of Coca-Cola.

"I've written a couple of stories. That's all," I replied. 10

"You're not here for an interrogation. I'm very sorry about what's happening, but that's what war is like. I want us to talk as one writer to another.

Are you surprised? The army has produced some great men of letters. Think of Don Alonso de Ercilla y Zúñiga, for example."

"Or Cervantes," I added.

Daisy included himself among the greats. That was his problem. If he wanted adulation, he could have it. I drank the Coca-Cola and thought about Garcés, or rather, about his chicken, because, incredible as it seems, the cook had a chicken called Dulcinea,[1] the name of Don Quixote's mistress.

One morning it jumped the wall which separated the common-law prisoners from the POWs, and it must have been a chicken with deep political convictions, because it decided to stay with us. Garcés caressed it and sighed, saying: "If I had a pinch of pepper and a pinch of cumin, I'd make you a chicken marinade like you've never tasted."

"I want you to read my poems and give me your opinion, your honest opinion," said Daisy, handing me a notebook.   15

I left that room with my pockets full of cigarettes, caramel sweets, tea bags and a tin of U.S. Army marmalade. That afternoon I started to believe in the brotherhood of writers.

They transported us from the prison to the barracks and back in a cattle truck. The soldiers made sure there was plenty of cow shit on the floor of the truck before ordering us to lie face down with our hands behind our necks. We were guarded by four of them, with North American machine guns, one in each corner of the truck. They were almost all young guys brought down from northern garrisons, and the harsh climate of the South kept them flu-ridden and in a perpetually filthy mood. They had orders to fire on the bundles—us—at the slightest suspect movement, or on any civilian who tried to approach the truck. But as time wore on, the discipline gradually relaxed and they turned a blind eye to the packet of cigarettes or piece of fruit thrown from a window, or the pretty and daring girl who ran beside the truck blowing us kisses and shouting: "Don't give up, comrades! We'll win!"

Back in prison, as always, we were met by the welcoming committee organised by Doctor "Skinny" Pragnan, now an eminent psychiatrist in Belgium. First he examined those who couldn't walk and those who had heart problems, then those who had come back with a dislocation or with ribs out of place. Pragnan was expert at estimating how much electricity had been put into us on the grill, and patiently determined who would be able to absorb liquids in the next few hours. Then finally it was time to take communion: we were given the aspirin with vitamin C and an anticoagulant to prevent internal haematomas.

"Dulcinea's days are numbered," I said to Garcés, and looked for a corner in which to read Daisy's notebook.

---

[1] *Dulcinea*: ironically refers to the object of Don Quixote's affection in the novel *Don Quixote de La Mancha* (1605) by Miguel de Cervantes (1547–1616).

The elegantly inscribed pages were redolent of love, honey, sublime suf-   20
fering and forgotten flowers. By the third page I knew that Daisy hadn't even
gone to the trouble of reusing the ideas of the Mexican poet Amado Nervo—
he'd simply copied out his poems word for word.

I called out to Peyuco Gálvez, a Spanish teacher, and read him a couple
of lines.

"What do you think, Peyuco?"

"Amado Nervo. The book is called *The Interior Gardens*."

I had got myself into a real jam. If Daisy found out that I knew the
work of this sugary poet Nervo, then it wasn't Garcés's chicken whose days
were numbered, but mine. It was a serious problem, so that night I presented it to the Council of Elders.

"Now, Daisy, would he be the passive or the active type?" enquired   25
Iriarte.

"Stop it, will you. My skin's at risk here," I replied.

"I'm serious. Maybe our friend wants to have an affair with you, and
giving you the notebook was like dropping a silk handkerchief. And like a
fool you picked it up. Perhaps he copied out the poems for you to find a
message in them. I've known queens who seduced boys by lending them
Demian[2] by Hermann Hesse. If Daisy is the passive type, this business with
Amado Nervo means he wants to test your nerve, so to speak. And if he's
the active type, well, it would have to hurt less than a kick in the balls."

"Message my arse. He gave you the poems as his own, and you should
say you liked them a lot. If he was trying to send a message, he should have
given the notebook to Garcés; he's the only one who has an interior garden.
Or maybe Daisy doesn't know about the pot plant," remarked Andrés Müller.

"Let's be serious about this. You have to say something to him, and Daisy
mustn't even suspect that you know Nervo's poems," declared Pragnan.

"Tell him you liked the poems but that the adjectives strike you a bit   30
excessive. Quote Huidobro: when an adjective doesn't give life, it kills. That
way you'll show him that you read his poems carefully and that you are criticising his work as a colleague," suggested Gálvez.

The Council of Elders approved of Gálvez's idea, but I spent two weeks
on tenterhooks. I couldn't sleep. I wished they would come and take me to
be kicked and electrocuted so I could give the damned notebook back. In
those two weeks I came to hate good old Garcés:

"Listen, mate, if everything goes well, and you get a little jar of capers as
well as the cumin and the pepper, we'll have such a feast with that chicken."

After a fortnight, I found myself at last stretched out face down on the
mattress of cowpats with my hands behind my neck. I thought I was going
mad: I was happy to be heading towards a session of the activity known as
torture.

---

[2] *Demian (1919)*: by Hermann Hesse, German novelist (1877–1962).

Tucapel barracks. Service Corps. In the background, the perpetual green of Cerro Ñielol, sacred to the Mapuche Indians. There was a waiting room outside the interrogation cell, like at the doctor's. There they made us sit on a bench with our hands tied behind our backs and black hoods over our heads. I never understood what the hoods were for, because once we got inside they took them off, and we could see the interrogators—the toy soldiers who, with panic-stricken faces, turned the handle of the generator, and the health officers who attached the electrodes to our anuses, testicles, gums and tongue, and then listened with stethoscopes to see who was faking and who had really passed out on the grill.

Lagos, a deacon of the Emmaus International ragmen, was the first to   35
be interrogated that day. For a year they had been working him over to find out how the organisation had come by a couple of dozen old military uniforms which had been found in their warehouses. A trader who sold army surplus gear had donated them. Lagos screamed in pain and repeated over and over what the soldiers wanted to hear: the uniforms belonged to an invading army which was preparing to land on the Chilean coast.

I was waiting for my turn when someone took off the hood. It was Lieutenant Daisy.

"Follow me," he ordered.

We went into an office. On the desk I saw a tin of cocoa and a carton of cigarettes which were obviously there to reward my comments on his literary work.

"Did you read my poesy?" he asked, offering me a seat.

Poesy. Daisy said poesy, not poetry. A man covered with pistols and   40
grenades can't say "poesy" without sounding ridiculous and effete. At that moment he revolted me, and I decided that even if it meant pissing blood, hissing when I spoke and being able to charge batteries just by touching them, I wasn't going to lower myself to flattering a plagiarising faggot in uniform.

"You have pretty handwriting, Lieutenant. But you know these poems aren't yours," I said, giving him back the notebook.

I saw him begin to shake. He was carrying enough arms to kill me several times over, and if he didn't want to stain his uniform, he could order someone else to do it. Trembling with anger he stood up, threw what was on the desk onto the floor and shouted:

"Three weeks in the cube. But first, you're going to visit the chiropodist, you piece of subversive shit!"

The chiropodist was a civilian, a landholder who had lost several thousand hectares in the land reform, and who was getting his revenge by participating in the interrogations as a volunteer. His speciality was peeling back toenails, which led to terrible infections.

I knew the cube. I had spent my first six months of prison there in soli-   45
tary confinement: it was an underground cell, one and a half metres wide by one and a half metres long by one and a half metres high. In the old days there had been a tannery in the Temuco jail, and the cube was used to store

fat. The walls still stank of fat, but after a week your excrement fixed that, making the cube very much a place of your own.

You could only stretch out across the diagonal, but the low temperatures of southern Chile, the rainwater and the soldiers' urine made you want to curl up hugging your legs and stay like that wishing yourself smaller and smaller, so that eventually you could live on one of the islands of floating shit, which conjured up images of dream holidays. I was there for three weeks, running through Laurel and Hardy[3] films, remembering the books of Salgari,[4] Stevenson,[5] and London[6] word by word, playing long games of chess, licking my toes to protect them from infection. In the cube I swore over and over again never to become a literary critic.

Questions for Discussion and Writing

1. Sepulveda's main tormentor is a prison guard with literary aspirations, nicknamed Daisy. What moral, aesthetic, and practical choices does Sepulveda face?
2. Sepulveda displays surprising good humor considering the circumstances. Give some examples of how he gets this across in his account.
3. Plagiarism, even for those who are not prison guards, is a serious offense. What precautions have you taken to avoid committing plagiarism in your schoolwork?
4. **Rhetorical inquiry:** What examples can you identify where Sepúlveda's ironic style enables him to detach himself from the danger and pain to which he is subjected?

TIM O'BRIEN

Tim O'Brien was born in 1946 in Austin, Minnesota, and was educated at Macalester College and Harvard University. Drafted into the army during the Vietnam War, he attained the rank of sergeant and received the Purple Heart. His first published work, If I Die in a Combat Zone, Box Me Up and Ship Me Home *(1973), relates his experiences in Vietnam. This book is an innovative mixture of alternating chapters of fiction and autobiography in which the following nonfiction account first appeared.*

O'Brien's novel Northern Lights *(1974) was followed by the acclaimed work* Going After Cacciato *(1978), which won the National Book Award.*

---

[3] *Laurel and Hardy:* American film comedy team made up of Stan Laurel (1890–1965) and Oliver Hardy (1892–1957).   [4] *Emilio Salgari (1862–1911):* called the Italian Jules Verne, the author of more than two hundred adventure stories and novels.   [5] *Robert Louis Stevenson (1850–1894):* Scottish novelist, poet, and essayist. Best known for *Treasure Island* (1883). [6] *Jack London (1876–1916):* American author who created romantic yet realistic fiction in works such as *The Call of the Wild* (1903). See his essay "The San Francisco Earthquake" (Ch. 7).

Other works include The Nuclear Age *(1985), a collection of stories titled* The Things They Carried *(1990),* Tomcat in Love *(1998), and most recently* July, July *(2002).*

Before You Read

Consider the conflicting values that O'Brien faces in deciding whether to serve in Vietnam.

If I Die in a Combat Zone

The summer of 1968, the summer I turned into a soldier, was a good time for talking about war and peace. Eugene McCarthy was bringing quiet thought to the subject. He was winning votes in the primaries. College students were listening to him, and some of us tried to help out. Lyndon Johnson was almost forgotten, no longer forbidding or feared; Robert Kennedy was dead but not quite forgotten; Richard Nixon looked like a loser. With all the tragedy and change that summer, it was fine weather for discussion.

And, with all of this, there was an induction notice tucked into a corner of my billfold.

So with friends and acquaintances and townspeople, I spent the summer in Fred's antiseptic cafe, drinking coffee and mapping out arguments on Fred's napkins. Or I sat in Chic's tavern, drinking beer with kids from the farms. I played some golf and tore up the pool table down at the bowling alley, keeping an eye open for likely-looking high school girls.

Late at night, the town deserted, two or three of us would drive a car around and around the town's lake, talking about the war, very seriously, moving with care from one argument to the next, trying to make it a dialogue and not a debate. We covered all the big questions: justice, tyranny, self-determination, conscience and the state, God and war and love.

College friends came to visit: "Too bad, I hear you're drafted. What will you do?"   5

I said I didn't know, that I'd let time decide. Maybe something would change, maybe the war would end. Then we'd turn to discuss the matter, talking long, trying out the questions, sleeping late in the mornings.

The summer conversations, spiked with plenty of references to the philosophers and academicians of war, were thoughtful and long and complex and careful. But, in the end, careful and precise argumentation hurt me. It was painful to tread deliberately over all the axioms and assumptions and corollaries when the people on the town's draft board were calling me to duty, smiling so nicely.

"It won't be bad at all," they said. "Stop in and see us when it's over."

So to bring the conversations to a focus and also to try out in real words my secret fears, I argued for running away.

I was persuaded then, and I remain persuaded now, that the war was   10
wrong. And since it was wrong and since people were dying as a result of it,
it was evil. Doubts, of course, hedged all this: I had neither the expertise nor
the wisdom to synthesize answers; most of the facts were clouded, and there
was no certainty as to the kind of government that would follow a North
Vietnamese victory or, for that matter, an American victory, and the specifics
of the conflict were hidden away—partly in men's minds, partly in the
archives of government, and partly in buried, irretrievable history. The war,
I thought, was wrongly conceived and poorly justified. But perhaps I was
mistaken, and who really knew, anyway?

Piled on top of this was the town, my family, my teachers, a whole history of the prairie. Like magnets, these things pulled in one direction or the
other, almost physical forces weighting the problem, so that, in the end, it
was less reason and more gravity that was the final influence.

My family was careful that summer. The decision was mine and it was
not talked about. The town lay there, spread out in the corn and watching
me, the mouths of old women and Country Club men poised in a kind of
eternal readiness to find fault. It was not a town, not a Minneapolis or New
York, where the son of a father can sometimes escape scrutiny. More, I owed
the prairie something. For twenty-one years I'd lived under its laws, accepted
its education, eaten its food, wasted and guzzled its water, slept well at night,
driven across its highways, dirtied and breathed its air, wallowed in its luxuries. I'd played on its Little League teams. I remembered Plato's *Crito,* when
Socrates, facing certain death—execution, not war—had the chance to escape.
But he reminded himself that he had seventy years in which he could have left
the country, if he were not satisfied or felt the agreements he'd made with
it were unfair. He had not chosen Sparta or Crete. And, I reminded myself,
I hadn't thought much about Canada until that summer.

The summer passed this way. Gold afternoons on the golf course, a
comforting feeling that the matter of war would never touch me, nights in
the pool hall or drug store, talking with townsfolk, turning the questions
over and over, being a philosopher.

Near the end of that summer the time came to go to the war. The family
indulged in a cautious sort of Last Supper together, and afterward my father,
who is brave, said it was time to report at the bus depot. I moped down to
my bedroom and looked the place over, feeling quite stupid, thinking that
my mother would come in there in a day or two and probably cry a little.
I trudged back up to the kitchen and put my satchel down. Everyone gathered around, saying so long and good health and write and let us know if
you want anything. My father took up the induction papers, checking on
times and dates and all the last-minute things, and when I pecked my mother's
face and grabbed the satchel for comfort, he told me to put it down, that
I wasn't supposed to report until tomorrow.

After laughing about the mistake, after a flush of red color and a flood   15
of ribbing and a wave of relief had come and gone, I took a long drive around

the lake, looking again at the place. Sunset Park, with its picnic table and little beach and a brown wood shelter and some families swimming. The Crippled Children's School. Slater Park, more kids. A long string of split level houses, painted every color.

The war and my person seemed like twins as I went around the town's lake. Twins grafted together and forever together, as if a separation would kill them both.

The thought made me angry.

In the basement of my house I found some scraps of cardboard and paper. With devilish flair, I printed obscene words on them, declaring my intention to have no part of Vietnam. Which delightful viciousness, a secret will, I declared the war evil, the draft board evil, the town evil in its lethargic acceptance of it all. For many minutes, making up the signs, making up my mind, I was outside the town. I was outside the law, all my old ties to my loves and family broken by the old crayon in my hand. I imagined strutting up and down the sidewalks outside the depot, the bus waiting and the driver blaring his horn, the *Daily Globe* photographer trying to push me into line with the other draftees, the frantic telephone calls, my head buzzing at the deed.

On the cardboard, my strokes of bright red were big and ferocious looking. The language was clear and certain and burned with a hard, defiant, criminal, blasphemous sound. I tried reading it aloud.

Later in the evening I tore the signs into pieces and put the shreds in the 20 garbage can outside, clanging the gray cover down and trapping the messages inside. I went back into the basement. I slipped the crayons into their box, the same stubs of color I'd used a long time before to chalk in reds and greens on Roy Rogers' cowboy boots.

I'd never been a demonstrator, except in the loose sense. True, I'd taken a stand in the school newspaper on the war, trying to show why it seemed wrong. But, mostly, I'd just listened.

"No war is worth losing your life for," a college acquaintance used to argue. "The issue isn't a moral one. It's a matter of efficiency: what's the most efficient way to stay alive when your nation is at war? That's the issue."

But others argued that no war is worth losing your country for, and when asked about the case when a country fights a wrong war, those people just shrugged.

Most of my college friends found easy paths away from the problem, all to their credit. Deferments for this and that. Letters from doctors or chaplains. It was hard to find people who had to think much about the problem. Counsel came from two main quarters, pacifists and veterans of foreign wars.

But neither camp had much to offer. It wasn't a matter of peace, as the 25 pacifists argued, but rather a matter of when and when not to join others in making war. And it wasn't a matter of listening to an ex-lieutenant colonel talk about serving in a right war, when the question was whether to serve in what seemed a wrong one.

On August 13, I went to the bus depot. A Worthington *Daily Globe* photographer took my picture standing by a rail fence with four other draftees.

Then the bus took us through corn fields, to little towns along the way—Lismore and Rushmore and Adrian—where other recruits came aboard. With some of the tough guys drinking beer and howling in the back seats, brandishing their empty cans and calling one another "scum" and "trainee" and "GI Joe," with all this noise and hearty farewelling, we went to Sioux Falls. We spent the night in a YMCA. I went out alone for a beer, drank it in a corner booth, then I bought a book and read it in my room.

By noon the next day our hands were in the air, even the tough guys. We recited the proper words, some of us loudly and daringly and others in bewilderment. It was a brightly lighted room, wood paneled. A flag gave the place the right colors, there was some smoke in the air. We said the words, and we were soldiers.

I'd never been much of a fighter. I was afraid of bullies. Their ripe muscles made me angry: a frustrated anger. Still, I deferred to no one. Positively lorded myself over inferiors. And on top of that was the matter of conscience and conviction, uncertain and surface-deep but pure nonetheless: I was a confirmed liberal, not a pacifist; but I would have cast my ballot to end the Vietnam war immediately, I would have voted for Eugene McCarthy, hoping he would make peace. I was not soldier material, that was certain.

But I submitted. All the personal history, all the midnight conversa-   30
tions and books and beliefs and learning, were crumpled by abstention, extinguished by forfeiture, for lack of oxygen, by a sort of sleepwalking default. It was no decision, no chain of ideas or reasons, that steered me into the war.

It was an intellectual and physical stand-off, and I did not have the energy to see it to an end. I did not want to be a soldier, not even an observer to war. But neither did I want to upset a peculiar balance between the order I knew, the people I knew, and my own private world. It was not that I valued that order. But I feared its opposite, inevitable chaos, censure, embarrassment, the end of everything that had happened in my life, the end of it all.

And the stand-off is still there. I would wish this book could take the form of a plea for everlasting peace, a plea from one who knows, from one who's been there and come back, an old soldier looking back at a dying war.

That would be good. It would be fine to integrate it all to persuade my younger brother and perhaps some others to say no to wars and other battles.

Or it would be fine to confirm the odd beliefs about war: it's horrible, but it's a crucible of men and events and, in the end, it makes more of a man out of you.

But, still, none of these notions seems right. Men are killed, dead   35
human beings are heavy and awkward to carry, things smell different in

In Leipzig, about 40,000 people demonstrated against the war in Iraq, according to organizers. Do you agree with the linking of Vietnam to Iraq? Why or why not?

Vietnam, soldiers are afraid and often brave, drill sergeants are boors, some men think the war is proper and just and others don't and most don't care. Is that the stuff for a morality lesson, even for a theme?

Do dreams offer lessons? Do nightmares have themes, do we awaken and analyze them and live our lives and advise others as a result? Can the foot soldier teach anything important about war, merely for having been there? I think not. He can tell war stories.

Questions for Discussion and Writing

1. What conflicting sets of values weighed on O'Brien when he learned he was drafted? Of these, which was the most significant in determining his ultimate decision?
2. Which features of this account provide insight into a Tim O'Brien who was very different from the one townspeople knew?
3. What do you think you would have done if you were in the same situation as O'Brien?
4. **Rhetorical inquiry:** How does O'Brien's fit of writing antiwar slogans in his basement communicate his feelings of alienation from the town even while he feels the weight of his responsibility to it?

STEPHEN CHAPMAN

Stephen Chapman (b. 1954) has served as the associate editor of the New Republic *and is currently a columnist and editorial writer with the* Chicago Tribune. *He is a native of Texas who attended Harvard. In "The Prisoner's Dilemma" (which first appeared in the* New Republic *on March 8, 1980), Chapman calls into question the widely held assumption that the system of imprisonment as punishment employed in the West is more humane and less barbaric than the methods of punishment (including flogging, stoning, and amputation) practiced in Eastern Islamic nations.*

Before You Read

Notice the different methods and goals of punishment in Eastern and Western cultures.

The Prisoner's Dilemma

> If the punitive laws of Islam were applied for only one year, all the devastating injustices would be uprooted. Misdeeds must be punished by the law of retaliation; cut off the hands of the thief; kill the murderers; flog the adulterous woman or man. Your concerns, your "humanitarian" scruples are more childish than reasonable. Under the terms of Koranic law, any judge fulfilling the seven requirements (that he have reached puberty, be a believer, know the Koranic laws perfectly, be just, and not be affected by amnesia, or be a bastard, or be of the female sex) is qualified to be a judge in any type of case. He can thus judge and dispose of twenty trials in a single day, whereas the Occidental justice may take years to argue them out.
>
> —*from* Sayings of the Ayatollah Khomeni *(Bantam Books)*

One of the amusements of life in the modern West is the opportunity to observe the barbaric rituals of countries that are attached to the customs of the dark ages. Take Pakistan, for example, our newest ally and client state in Asia. Last October President Zia, in harmony with the Islamic fervor that is sweeping his part of the world, revived the traditional Moslem practice of flogging law-breakers in public. In Pakistan, this qualified as mass entertainment, and no fewer than 10,000 law-abiding Pakistanis turned out to see justice done to 26 convicts. To Western sensibilities the spectacle seemed barbaric—both in the sense of cruel and in the sense of pre-civilized. In keeping with Islamic custom each of the unfortunates—who had been caught in prostitution raids the previous night and summarily convicted and sentenced—was stripped down to a pair of white shorts, which were painted with a red stripe across the buttocks (the target). Then he was shackled against an easel, with pads thoughtfully placed over the kidneys to prevent injury. The floggers were muscular, fierce-looking sorts—convicted murderers, as it happens—who paraded around the flogging platform in colorful loincloths. When the time for the ceremony began, one of the floggers took a running start and brought a five-foot stave down across the first victim's buttocks, eliciting screams from the convict and murmurs from the audience. Each of the 26 received from five to 15 lashes. One had to be carried from the stage unconscious.

Flogging is one of the punishments stipulated by Koranic law, which has made it a popular penological device in several Moslem countries, including Pakistan, Saudi Arabia, and, most recently, the ayatollah's Iran. Flogging, or *Tá zir,* is the general punishment prescribed for offenses that don't carry an explicit Koranic penalty. Some crimes carry automatic *hadd* punishments—stoning or scourging (a severe whipping) for illicit sex, scourging for drinking alcoholic beverages, amputation of the hands for theft. Other crimes—as varied as murder and abandoning Islam—carry the death penalty (usually carried out in public). Colorful practices like these have given the Islamic world an image in the West, as described by historian G. H. Jansen, "of blood dripping from the stumps of amputated hands and from the striped backs of malefactors, and piles of stones barely concealing the battered bodies of adulterous couples." Jansen, whose book *Militant Islam* is generally effusive in its praise of Islamic practices, grows squeamish when considering devices like flogging, amputation, and stoning. But they are given enthusiastic endorsement by the Koran itself.

Such traditions, we all must agree, are no sign of an advanced civilization. In the West, we have replaced these various punishments (including the death penalty in most cases) with a single device. Our custom is to confine criminals in prison for varying lengths of time. In Illinois, a reasonably typical state, grand theft carries a punishment of three to five years; armed robbery can get you from six to 30. The lowest form of felony theft is punishable by one to three years in prison. Most states impose longer sentences on habitual offenders. In Kentucky, for example, habitual offenders can be sentenced to life in prison. Other states are less brazen, preferring the more genteel sounding "indeterminate sentence," which allows parole boards to keep inmates locked up for as long as life. It was under an indeterminate sentence of one to 14 years that George Jackson served 12 years in California prisons for committing a $70 armed robbery. Under a Texas law imposing an automatic life sentence for a third felony conviction, a man was sent to jail for life last year because of three thefts adding up to less than $300 in property value. Texas also is famous for occasionally imposing extravagantly long sentences, often running into hundreds or thousands of years. This gives Texas a leg up on Maryland, which used to sentence some criminals to life plus a day—a distinctive if superfluous flourish.

The punishment *intended* by Western societies in sending their criminals to prison is the loss of freedom. But, as everyone knows, the actual punishment in most American prisons is of a wholly different order. The February 2 riot at New Mexico's state prison in Santa Fe, one of several bloody prison riots in the nine years since the Attica bloodbath, once again dramatized the conditions of life in an American prison. Four hundred prisoners seized control of the prison before dawn. By sunset the next day 33 inmates had died at the hands of other convicts and another 40 people (including five guards) had been seriously hurt. Macabre stories came out of prisoners being hanged, murdered with blowtorches, decapitated, tortured, and mutilated in a variety of gruesome ways by drug-crazed rioters.

The Santa Fe penitentiary was typical of most maximum-security facilities, with prisoners subject to overcrowding, filthy conditions, and routine violence. It also housed first-time, non-violent offenders, like check forgers and drug dealers, with murderers serving life sentences. In a recent lawsuit, the American Civil Liberties Union called the prison "totally unfit for human habitation." But the ACLU says New Mexico's penitentiary is far from the nation's worst.

That American prisons are a disgrace is taken for granted by experts of every ideological stripe. Conservative James Q. Wilson has criticized our "crowded, antiquated prisons that require men and women to live in fear of one another and to suffer not only deprivation of liberty but a brutalizing regimen." Leftist Jessica Mitford has called our prisons "the ultimate expression of injustice and inhumanity." In 1973 a national commission concluded that "the American correctional system today appears to offer minimum protection to the public and maximum harm to the offender." Federal courts have ruled that confinement in prisons in 16 different states violates the constitutional ban on "cruel and unusual punishment."

What are the advantages of being a convicted criminal in an advanced culture? First there is the overcrowding in prisons. One Tennessee prison, for example, has a capacity of 806, according to accepted space standards, but it houses 2300 inmates. One Louisiana facility has confined four and five prisoners in a single six-foot-by-six-foot cell. Then there is the disease caused by overcrowding, unsanitary conditions, and poor or inadequate medical care. A federal appeals court noted that the Tennessee prison had suffered frequent outbreaks of infectious diseases like hepatitis and tuberculosis. But the most distinctive element of American prison life is its constant violence. In his book *Criminal Violence, Criminal Justice,* Charles Silberman noted that in one Louisiana prison, there were 211 stabbings in only three years, 11 of them fatal. There were 15 slayings in a prison in Massachusetts between 1972 and 1975. According to a federal court, in Alabama's penitentiaries (as in many others), "robbery, rape, extortion, theft and assault are everyday occurrences."

At least in regard to cruelty, it's not at all clear that the system of punishment that has evolved in the West is less barbaric than the grotesque practices of Islam. Skeptical? Ask yourself: would you rather be subjected to a few minutes of intense pain and considerable public humiliation, or to be locked away for two or three years in a prison cell crowded with ill-tempered sociopaths? Would you rather lose a hand or spend 10 years or more in a typical state prison? I have taken my own survey on this matter. I have found no one who does not find the Islamic system hideous. And I have found no one who, given the choices mentioned above, would not prefer its penalties to our own.

The great divergence between Western and Islamic fashions in punishment is relatively recent. Until roughly the end of the 18th century, criminals in Western countries rarely were sent to prison. Instead they were subjected to an ingenious assortment of penalties. Many perpetrators of a variety of crimes simply were executed, usually by some imaginative and extremely unpleasant method involving prolonged torture, such as breaking on the wheel, burning at the stake, or drawing and quartering. Michel Foucault's book *Discipline and Punishment: The Birth of the Prison* notes one form of capital punishment in which the condemned man's "belly was opened up, his entrails quickly ripped out, so that he had time to see them, with his own eyes, being thrown on the fire; in which he was finally decapitated and his body quartered." Some criminals were forced to serve on slave galleys. But in most cases various corporal measures such as pillorying, flogging, and branding sufficed.

In time, however, public sentiment recoiled against these measures. They 10 were replaced by imprisonment, which was thought to have two advantages. First, it was considered to be more humane. Second, and more important, prison was supposed to hold out the possibility of rehabilitation—purging the criminal of his criminality—something that less civilized punishments did not even aspire to. An 1854 report by inspectors of the Pennsylvania prison system illustrates the hopes nurtured by humanitarian reformers:

> Depraved tendencies, characteristic of the convict, have been restrained by the absence of vicious association, and in the mild teaching of Christianity, the unhappy criminal finds a solace for an involuntary exile from the comforts of social life. If hungry, he is fed; if naked, he is clothed; if destitute of the first rudiments of education, he is taught to read and write; and if he has never been blessed with a means of livelihood, he is schooled in a mechanical art, which in after life may be to him the source of profit and respectability. Employment is not his toil nor labor, weariness. He embraces them with alacrity, as contributing to his moral and mental elevation.

Imprisonment is now the universal method of punishing criminals in the United States. It is thought to perform five functions, each of which has been given a label by criminologists. First, there is simple *retribution*: punishing the lawbreaker to serve society's sense of justice and to satisfy the victims' desire for revenge. Second, there is *specific deterrence*: discouraging the offender from misbehaving in the future. Third, *general deterrence*: using the offender as an example to discourage others from turning to crime. Fourth, *prevention*: at least during the time he is kept off the streets, the criminal cannot victimize other members of society. Finally, and most important, there is *rehabilitation*: reforming the criminal so that when he returns to society he will be inclined to obey the laws and able to make an honest living.

How satisfactorily do American prisons perform by these criteria? Well, of course, they do punish. But on the other scores they don't do so well. Their effect in discouraging future criminality by the prisoner or others is the subject of much debate, but the soaring rates of the last 20 years suggest that prisons are not a dramatically effective deterrent to criminal behavior. Prisons do isolate convicted criminals, but only to divert crime from ordinary citizens to prison guards and fellow inmates. Almost no one contends anymore that prisons rehabilitate their inmates. If anything, they probably impede rehabilitation by forcing inmates into prolonged and almost exclusive association with other criminals. And prisons cost a lot of money. Housing a typical prisoner in a typical prison costs far more than a stint at a top university. This cost would be justified if prisons did the job they were intended for. But it is clear to all that prisons fail on the very grounds—humanity and hope of rehabilitation—that caused them to replace earlier, cheaper forms of punishment.

The universal acknowledgement that prisons do not rehabilitate criminals has produced two responses. The first is to retain the hope of rehabilitation but do away with imprisonment as much as possible and replace it with various forms of "alternative treatment," such as psychotherapy, supervised probation, and vocational training. Psychiatrist Karl Menninger, one of the principal critics of American penology, has suggested even more unconventional approaches, such as "a new job opportunity or a vacation trip, a course of reducing exercises, a cosmetic surgical operation or a herniotomy, some night school courses, a wedding in the family (even one for the patient!), an inspiring sermon." The starry-eyed approach naturally has produced a backlash from critics on the right, who think that it's time to abandon the goal of rehabilitation. They argue that prisons perform an important service just by keeping criminals *off* the streets, and thus should be used with that purpose in mind.

So the debate continues to rage in all the same old ruts. No one, of course, would think of copying the medieval practices of Islamic nations and experimenting with punishments such as flogging and amputation. But let us consider them anyway. How do they compare with our American prison system in achieving the ostensible objectives of punishment? First, do they punish? Obviously they do, and in a uniquely painful and memorable way. Of course any sensible person, given the choice, would prefer suffering these punishments to years of incarceration in a typical American prison. But presumably no Western penologist would criticize Islamic punishments on the grounds that they are not barbaric enough. Do they deter crime? Yes, and probably more effectively than sending convicts off to prison. Now we read about a prison sentence in the newspaper, then think no more about the criminal's payment for his crimes until, perhaps, years later we read a small item reporting his release. By contrast, one can easily imagine the vivid impression it would leave to be wandering through a local shopping center and to stumble onto the scene of some poor wretch being lustily flogged. And the occasional sight of an habitual offender walking around with a bloody stump at the end of his arm no doubt also would serve as a forceful reminder that crime does not pay.

Do flogging and amputation discourage recidivism? No one knows   15 whether the scars on his back would dissuade a criminal from risking another crime, but it is hard to imagine that corporal measures could stimulate a higher rate of recidivism than already exists. Islamic forms of punishment do not serve the favorite new right goal of simply isolating criminals from the rest of society, but they may achieve the same purpose of making further crimes impossible. In the movie *Bonnie and Clyde,* Warren Beatty successfully robs a bank with his arm in a sling, but this must be dismissed as artistic license. It must be extraordinarily difficult, at the very least, to perform much violent crime with only one hand.

Do the medieval forms of punishment rehabilitate the criminal? Plainly not. But long prison terms do not rehabilitate either. And it is just as plain that typical Islamic punishments are no crueler to the convict than incarceration in the typical American state prison.

Of course there are other reasons besides its bizarre forms of punishment that the Islamic system of justice seems uncivilized to the Western mind. One is the absence of due process. Another is the long list of offenses—such as drinking, adultery, blasphemy, "profiteering," and so on—that can bring on conviction and punishment. A third is all the ritualistic mumbojumbo in pronouncements of Islamic law (like that talk about puberty and amnesia in the ayatollah's quotation at the beginning of this article). Even in these matters, however, a little cultural modesty is called for. The vast majority of American criminals are convicted and sentenced as a result of plea bargaining, in which due process plays almost no role. It has been only half a century since a wave of religious fundamentalism stirred this country to outlaw the consumption of alcoholic beverages. Most states also still have laws imposing austere constraints on sexual conduct. Only two weeks ago the *Washington Post* reported that the FBI had spent two and a half years and untold amounts of money to break up a nationwide pornography ring. Flogging the clients of prostitutes, as the Pakistanis did, does seem silly. But only a few months ago Mayor Koch of New York was proposing that clients caught in his own city have their names broadcast by radio stations. We are not so far advanced on such matters as we often like to think. Finally, my lawyer friends assure me that the rules of jurisdiction for American courts contain plenty of petty requirements and bizarre distinctions that would sound silly enough to foreign ears.

Perhaps it sounds barbaric to talk of flogging and amputation, and perhaps it is. But our system of punishment also is barbaric, and probably more so. Only cultural smugness about their system and willful ignorance about our own make it easy to regard the one as cruel and the other as civilized. We inflict our cruelties away from public view, while nations like Pakistan stage them in front of 10,000 onlookers. Their outrages are visible; ours are not. Most Americans can live their lives for years without having their peace of mind disturbed by the knowledge of what goes on in our prisons. To choose imprisonment over flogging and amputation is not to choose human kindness over cruelty, but merely to prefer that our cruelties be kept out of sight, and out of mind.

Public flogging and amputation may be more barbaric forms of punishment than imprisonment, even if they are not more cruel. Society may pay a higher price for them, even if they particular criminal does not. Revulsion against officially sanctioned violence and infliction of pain derives from something deeply ingrained in Western conscience, and clearly it is something admirable. Grotesque displays of the sort that occur in Islamic countries probably breed a greater tolerance for physical cruelty, for example, which prisons do not do precisely because they conceal their cruelties. In fact it is our admirable intolerance for calculated violence that makes it necessary for us to conceal what we have not been able to do away with. In a way this is a good thing, since it holds out the hope that we may eventually find a way to do away with it. But in another way it is a bad thing, since it permits us to congratulate ourselves on our civilized humanitarianism while violating its norms in this one area of our national life.

Questions for Discussion and Writing

1. According to Chapman, what are the five objectives that imprisonment is supposed to achieve in Western culture? How satisfactorily do American prisons perform these functions?

2. How do the practices of punishment in Eastern cultures differ from those in Western societies? How does Chapman use comparison and contrast to more clearly illustrate the differences between them?

3. Write a short essay that answers Chapman's question, "would you rather be subjected to a few minutes of intense pain and considerable public humiliation, or be locked away for two or three years in a prison cell crowded with ill-tempered sociopaths" (Para. 8).

4. **Rhetorical inquiry:** How does the opening vignette with which Chapman begins his analysis illustrate the very public nature of the Eastern methods of punishment and set the stage for the investigation of prison practices in the West that are hidden from the public? What do recent statistics show about the percentage of the U.S. population now in prison?

MICHAEL LEVIN

Michael Levin (b. 1943) was educated at Michigan State University and Columbia University. From 1968 to 1980 he taught philosophy at Columbia; he is currently a professor of philosophy at City College of the City University of New York. In addition to many articles on ethics and philosophy, Levin has written Metaphysics and the Mind–Body Problem (with Lawrence M. Thomas, 1979). He has also written J. S. Mill on Civilization and Barbarism (2004). In "The Case for Torture," which first appeared in Newsweek (1982), Levin uses a number of intriguing hypothetical cases to challenge the conventional assumption that there are no circumstances under which torture is permissible.

Before You Read

Are there situations in which you believe torture is appropriate?

The Case for Torture

It is generally assumed that torture is impermissible, a throwback to a more brutal age. Enlightened societies reject it outright, and regimes suspected of using it risk the wrath of the United States.

I believe this attitude is unwise. There are situations in which torture is not merely permissible but morally mandatory. Moreover, these situations are moving from the realm of imagination to fact.

Death   Suppose a terrorist has hidden an atomic bomb on Manhattan Island which will detonate at noon on July 4 unless . . . (here follow the usual demands for money and release of his friends from jail). Suppose, further, that he is caught at 10 A.M. of the fateful day, but—preferring death to failure— won't disclose where the bomb is. What do we do? If we follow due process— wait for his lawyer, arraign him—millions of people will die. If the only way to save those lives is to subject the terrorist to the most excruciating possible pain, what grounds can there be for not doing so? I suggest there are none. In any case, I ask you to face the question with an open mind.

Torturing the terrorist is unconstitutional? Probably. But millions of lives surely outweigh constitutionality. Torture is barbaric? Mass murder is far more barbaric. Indeed, letting millions of innocents die in deference to one who flaunts his guilt is moral cowardice, an unwillingness to dirty one's hands. If *you* caught the terrorist, could you sleep nights knowing that millions died because you couldn't bring yourself to apply the electrodes?

Once you concede that torture is justified in extreme cases, you have admitted that the decision to use torture is a matter of balancing innocent lives against the means needed to save them. You must now face more realistic cases involving more modest numbers. Someone plants a bomb on a jumbo jet. He alone can disarm it, and his demands cannot be met (or if they can, we refuse to set a precedent by yielding to his threats). Surely we can, we must, do anything to the extortionist to save the passengers. How can we tell 300, or 100, or 10 people who never asked to be put in danger, "I'm sorry, you'll have to die in agony, we just couldn't bring ourselves to . . ."

5

Here are the results of an informal poll about a third, hypothetical, case. Suppose a terrorist group kidnapped a newborn baby from a hospital. I asked four mothers if they would approve of torturing kidnappers if that were necessary to get their own newborns back. All said yes, the most "liberal" adding that she would like to administer it herself.

I am not advocating torture as punishment. Punishment is addressed to deeds irrevocably past. Rather, I am advocating torture as an acceptable measure for preventing future evils. So understood, it is far less objectionable than many extant punishments. Opponents of the death penalty, for example, are forever insisting that executing a murderer will not bring back his victim (as if the purpose of capital punishment were supposed to be resurrection, not deterrence or retribution). But torture, in the cases described, is intended not to bring anyone back but to keep innocents from being dispatched. The most powerful argument against using torture as a punishment or to secure confessions is that such practices disregard the rights of the individual. Well, if the individual is all that important—and he is—it is correspondingly important to protect the rights of individuals threatened by terrorists. If life is so valuable that it must never be taken, the lives of the innocents must be saved even at the price of hurting the one who endangers them.

Better precedents for torture are assassination and pre-emptive attack. No Allied leader would have flinched at assassinating Hitler, had that been possible. (The Allies did assassinate Heydrich.) Americans would be angered to learn that Roosevelt could have had Hitler killed in 1943—thereby shortening the war and saving millions of lives—but refused on moral grounds. Similarly, if nation A learns that nation B is about to launch an unprovoked attack, A has a right to save itself by destroying B's military capability first. In the same way, if the police can by torture save those who would otherwise die at the hands of kidnappers or terrorists, they must.

Idealism   There is an important difference between terrorists and their victims that should mute talk of the terrorists' "rights." The terrorist's victims are at risk unintentionally, not having asked to be endangered. But the terrorist knowingly initiated his actions. Unlike his victims, he volunteered for the risks of his deed. By threatening to kill for profit or idealism, he renounces civilized standards, and he can have no complaint if civilization tries to thwart him by whatever means necessary.

Just as torture is justified only to save lives (not extort confessions or recantations) it is justifiably administered only to those *known* to hold innocent lives in their hands. Ah, but how can the authorities ever be sure they have the right malefactor? Isn't there a danger of error and abuse? Won't We turn into Them?   10

Questions like these are disingenuous in a world in which terrorists proclaim themselves and perform for television. The name of their game is public recognition. After all, you can't very well intimidate a government into releasing your freedom fighters unless you announce that it is your group that has seized its embassy. "Clear guilt" is difficult to define, but when 40 million people see a group of masked gunmen seize an airplane on the evening news, there is not much question about who the perpetrators are. There will be hard cases where the situation is murkier. Nonetheless, a line demarcating the legitimate use of torture can be drawn. Torture only the obviously guilty, and only for the sake of saving innocents, and the line between Us and Them will remain clear.

There is little danger that the Western democracies will lose their way if they choose to inflict pain as one way of preserving order. Paralysis in the face of evil is the greater danger. Some day soon a terrorist will threaten tens of thousands of lives, and torture will be the only way to save them. We had better start thinking about this.

Questions for Discussion and Writing

1. Does the way in which Levin sets up the alternatives of "inflict[ing] pain as one way of preserving order" versus becoming paralyzed "in the face of evil" represent the choices fairly?
2. Levin displays amazing ingenuity in thinking up his hypothetical examples. For each of the hypothetical examples he invents, can you invent a counterexample that would lead to the opposite conclusion?
3. What assumptions does Levin make that if untrue would undercut his argument? For example, he assumes that we know we caught the correct terrorist to subject to the torture.
4. **Rhetorical inquiry:** Why is Levin's choice of a worst-case scenario necessary in getting his audience to challenge conventional assumptions?

Fiction

JONATHAN SWIFT

Jonathan Swift (1667–1745), certainly one of the keenest minds of his age, was born in Dublin, into an impoverished family who were originally from England. He was educated at Trinity College, Dublin, with the help of his wealthy uncle, and in 1688 left Ireland and became a secretary to Sir William Temple in Moor Park, England. There he tutored Esther Johnson, Temple's ward, rumored to be Temple's illegimate daughter, who later became the "Stella" of Swift's letters and poems. He returned to Ireland in 1694, where he was ordained an Anglican priest, and spent a brief time in a parish in Belfast. Dissatisfied with this life, he returned to England and became active in the literary intellectual life of London, where he became friends with prominent figures such as Joseph Addison, Sir Richard Steele, and Alexander Pope. In 1713 he was named Dean of St. Patrick's Cathedral in Dublin. When his political ambitions in England were crushed with the defeat of the Tory party the following year, Swift returned to Ireland for good. A prolific writer of enormous brilliance, over the course of his life Swift used his pen to champion various causes and to assail those in power. From 1721 to 1725, he worked on his masterpiece, Gulliver's Travels, *a satire on human nature, which was published anonymously in 1726 and became an instant best-seller. The following essay, "A Modest Proposal," was published in 1729 and was written to protest repressive economic measures against the Irish by the Whig government in England.*

Before You Read

What might be the advantage for an author in creating a narrator with whom the reader will violently disagree?

A Modest Proposal

*For Preventing the Children of
Poor People in Ireland from Being a Burden to
Their Parents or Country, and for Making
Them Beneficial to the Public*

It is a melancholy object to those who walk through this great town,[1] or travel in the country, when they see the streets, the roads, and cabin doors crowded with beggars of the female sex, followed by three, four, or six children, all in rags and importuning every passenger for an alms. These mothers, instead of being able to work for their honest livelihood, are forced to employ all their time in strolling to beg sustenance for their helpless infants; who as they grow up either turn thieves, for want of work, or leave their dear native country to fight for the Pretender[2] in Spain, or sell themselves to the Barbados.[3]

I think it is agreed by all parties that this prodigious number of children in the arms, or on the backs, or at the heels of their mothers, and frequently of their fathers, is, in the present deplorable state of the kingdom, a very great additional grievance; and therefore whoever could find out a fair, cheap, and easy method of making these children sound, useful members of the commonwealth would deserve so well of the public as to have his statue set up for a preserver of the nation.

---

[1] *this great town:* Dublin.   [2] *the Pretender:* James Stuart (1688–1766), son of King James II, "pretender" or claimant to the throne which his father had lost in the Revolution of 1688. He was Catholic, and Ireland was loyal to him.   [3] *sell . . . Barbados:* Because of extreme poverty, many of the Irish bound or sold themselves to obtain passage to the West Indies or other British possessions in North America. They agreed to work for their new masters, usually planters, for a specified number of years.

But my intention is very far from being confined to provide only for the children of professed beggars: it is of a much greater extent and shall take in the whole number of infants at a certain age who are born of parents in effect as little able to support them as those who demand our charity in the streets.

As to my own part, having turned my thoughts for many years upon this important subject and maturely weighed the several schemes of other projectors, I have always found them grossly mistaken in their computation. It is true, a child just dropped from its dam may be supported by her milk for a solar year, with little other nourishment: at most not above the value of two shillings, which the mother may certainly get, or the value in scraps, by her lawful occupation of begging; and it is exactly at one year old that I propose to provide for them in such a manner, as, instead of being a charge upon their parents or the parish, or wanting food and raiment for the rest of their lives, they shall, on the contrary, contribute to the feeding and partly to the clothing of many thousands.

There is likewise another great advantage in my scheme, that it will prevent those voluntary abortions and that horrid practice of women murdering their bastard children, alas! too frequent among us, sacrificing the poor innocent babes, I doubt more to avoid the expense than the shame, which would move tears and pity in the most savage and inhuman breast.

The number of souls in this kingdom being usually reckoned one million and a half, of these I calculate there may be about two hundred thousand couple whose wives are breeders; from which number I subtract thirty thousand couple; who are able to maintain their own children (although I apprehend there cannot be so many, under the present distresses of the kingdom), but this being granted, there will remain an hundred and seventy thousand breeders. I again subtract fifty thousand for those women who miscarry, or whose children die by accident or disease within the year. There only remain one hundred and twenty thousand children of poor parents annually born. The question therefore is, How this number shall be reared and provided for? which, as I have already said, under the present situation of affairs, is utterly impossible by all the methods hitherto proposed. For we can neither employ them in handicraft or agriculture; we neither build houses (I mean in the country) nor cultivate land: they can very seldom pick up a livelihood by stealing till they arrive at six years old, except where they are of towardly[4] parts; although I confess they learn the rudiments much earlier, during which time they can, however, be properly looked upon only as probationers; as I have been informed by a principal gentleman in the county of Cavan, who protested to me that he never knew above one or two instances under the age of six, even in a part of the kingdom so renowned for the quickest proficiency in that art.

I am assured by our merchants that a boy or a girl before twelve years old is no salable commodity; and even when they come to this age they will not

---

[4] *towardly:* dutiful; easily managed.

yield above three pounds, or three pounds and half a crown at most, on the exchange; which cannot turn to account either to the parents or kingdom, the charge of nutriment and rags having been at least four times that value.

I shall now therefore humbly propose my own thoughts, which I hope will not be liable to the least objection.

I have been assured by a very knowing American of my acquaintance in London that a young healthy child well nursed is at a year old a most delicious, nourishing, and wholesome food, whether stewed, roasted, baked, or boiled; and I make no doubt that it will equally serve in a fricassee or a ragout.[5]

I do therefore humbly offer it to public consideration that of the hundred and twenty thousand children already computed, twenty thousand may be reserved for breed, whereof only one-fourth part to be males; which is more than we allow to sheep, black cattle, or swine; and my reason is that these children are seldom the fruits of marriage, a circumstance not much regarded by our savages; therefore one male will be sufficient to serve four females. That the remaining hundred thousand may, at a year old, be offered in sale to the persons of quality and fortune through the kingdom; always advising the mother to let them suck plentifully in the last month, so as to render them plump and fat for a good table. A child will make two dishes at an entertainment for friends; and when the family dines alone, the fore or hind quarter will make a reasonable dish, and seasoned with a little pepper or salt will be very good boiled on the fourth day, especially in winter.

I have reckoned upon a medium that a child just born will weigh twelve pounds, and in a solar year, if tolerably nursed, will increase to twenty-eight pounds.

I grant this food will be somewhat dear, and therefore very proper for landlords, who, as they have already devoured most of the parents, seem to have the best title to the children.

Infant's flesh will be in season throughout the year, but more plentifully in March, and a little before and after for we are told by a grave author, an eminent French physician,[6] that fish being a prolific diet, there are more children born in Roman Catholic countries about nine months after Lent than at any other season; therefore, reckoning a year after Lent, the markets will be more glutted than usual, because the number of popish infants is at least three to one in this kingdom: and therefore it will have one other collateral advantage, by lessening the number of papists among us.

I have already computed the charge of nursing a beggar's child (in which list I reckon all cottagers, laborers, and four-fifths of the farmers) to be about two shillings per annum, rags included; and I believe no gentleman would repine to give ten shillings for the carcass of a good fat child, which, as I have

10

---

[5] *ragout:* (ra gü), a highly seasoned meat stew.   [6] *grave author . . . physician:* François Rabelais (c. 1494–1553), who was anything but a "grave author."

said, will make four dishes of excellent nutritive meat, when he has only some particular friend or his own family to dine with him. Thus the squire will learn to be a good landlord and grow popular among his tenants; the mother will have eight shillings net profit and be fit for work till she produces another child.

Those who are more thrifty (as I must confess the times require) may flay the carcass; the skin of which artificially[7] dressed will make admirable gloves for ladies and summer boots for fine gentlemen.   15

As to our city of Dublin, shambles[8] may be appointed for this purpose in the most convenient parts of it, and butchers we may be assured will not be wanting; although I rather recommend buying the children alive and dressing them hot from the knife as we do roasting pigs.

A very worthy person, a true lover of his country, and whose virtues I highly esteem, was lately pleased, in discoursing on this matter, to offer a refinement upon my scheme. He said that many gentlemen of this kingdom, having of late destroyed their deer, he conceived that the want of venison might be well supplied by the bodies of young lads and maidens, not exceeding fourteen years of age nor under twelve; so great a number of both sexes in every country being now ready to starve for want of work and service; and these to be disposed of by their parents, if alive, or otherwise by their nearest relations. But with due deference to so excellent a friend and so deserving a patriot, I cannot be altogether in his sentiments; for as to the males, my American acquaintance assured me from frequent experience that their flesh was generally tough and lean, like that of our schoolboys, by continual exercise, and their taste disagreeable; and to fatten them would not answer the charge. Then as to the females, it would, I think, with humble submission be a loss to the public, because they soon would become breeders themselves: and besides, it is not improbable that some scrupulous people might be apt to censure such a practice (although indeed very unjustly), as a little bordering upon cruelty; which, I confess, has always been with me the strongest objection against any project, how well soever intended.

But in order to justify my friend, he confessed that this expedient was put into his head by the famous Psalmanazar,[9] a native of the island Formosa, who came from thence to London above twenty years ago: and in conversation told my friend that in his country when any young person happened to be put to death, the executioner sold the carcass to persons of quality as a prime dainty; and that in his time the body of a plump girl of fifteen, who was crucified for an attempt to poison the emperor, was sold to his imperial majesty's prime minister of state, and other great mandarins of the court, in

---

[7] *artificially:* artfully; skillfully.   [8] *shambles:* slaughterhouses.   [9] *Psalmanazar:* the imposter George Psalmanazar (c. 1679–1763), a Frenchman who passed himself off in England as a Formosan, and wrote a totally fictional "true" account of Formosa, in which he described cannibalism.

joints from the gibbet, at four hundred crowns. Neither indeed can I deny that if the same use were made of several plump girls in this town, who, without one single groat to their fortunes, cannot stir abroad without a chair, and appear at a playhouse and assemblies in foreign fineries which they never will pay for, the kingdom would not be the worse.

Some persons of a desponding spirit are in great concern about that vast number of poor people who are aged, diseased, or maimed; and I have been desired to employ my thoughts, what course may be taken to ease the nation of so grievous an encumbrance. But I am not in the least pain upon that matter, because it is very well known that they are every day dying and rotting, by cold and famine, and filth and vermin, as fast as can be reasonably expected. And as to the young laborers, they are now in almost as hopeful a condition: they cannot get work, and consequently pine away for want of nourishment to a degree that if at any time they are accidentally hired to common labor, they have not strength to perform it; and thus the country and themselves are happily delivered from the evils to come.

I have too long digressed and therefore shall return to my subject. I   20
think the advantages, by the proposal which I have made, are obvious and many, as well as of the highest importance.

For first, as I have already observed, it would greatly lessen the number of papists, with whom we are yearly overrun, being the principal breeders of the nation, as well as our most dangerous enemies; and who stay at home on purpose to deliver the kingdom to the Pretender, hoping to take their advantage by the absence of so many good Protestants, who have chosen rather to leave their country than stay at home and pay tithes against their conscience to an Episcopal curate.[10]

Secondly, the poorer tenants will have something valuable of their own, which by law may be made liable to distress,[11] and help to pay their landlord's rent; their corn and cattle being already seized, and money a thing unknown.

Thirdly, whereas the maintenance of a hundred thousand children, from two years old and upwards, cannot be computed at less than ten shillings a piece per annum, the nation's stock will be thereby increased fifty thousand pounds per annum, beside the profit of a new dish introduced to the tables of all gentlemen of fortune in the kingdom who have any refinement in taste. And the money will circulate among ourselves, the goods being entirely of our own growth and manufacture.

Fourthly, the constant breeders, besides the gain of eight shillings sterling per annum by the sale of their children, will be rid of the charge of maintaining them after the first year.

Fifthly, this food would likewise bring great custom to taverns: where   25
the vintners will certainly be so prudent as to procure the best receipts for

---

[10] *Protestants . . . curate:* Swift is here attacking the absentee landlords.   [11] *distress:* distraint, the legal seizure of property for payment of debts.

dressing it to perfection, and consequently have their houses frequented by all the fine gentlemen, who justly value themselves upon their knowledge in good eating and a skilful cook, who understands how to oblige his guests, will contrive to make it as expensive as they please.

Sixthly, this would be a great inducement to marriage, which all wise nations have either encouraged by rewards or enforced by laws and penalties. It would increase the care and tenderness of mothers toward their children, when they were sure of a settlement for life to the poor babes, provided in some sort by the public, to their annual profit instead of expense. We should see an honest emulation among the married women, which of them could bring the fattest child to the market. Men would become as fond of their wives during the time of their pregnancy as they are now of their mares in foal, their cows in calf, or sows when they are ready to farrow; nor offer to beat or kick them (as is too frequent a practice) for fear of a miscarriage.

Many other advantages might be enumerated. For instance, the addition of some thousand carcasses in our exportation of barreled beef, the propagation of swine's flesh, and improvement in the art of making good bacon, so much wanted among us by the great destruction of pigs, too frequent at our tables; which are no way comparable in taste or magnificence to a well grown, fat, yearling child, which roasted whole will make a considerable figure at a lord mayor's feast, or any other public entertainment. But this and many others I omit, being studious of brevity.

Supposing that one thousand families in this city would be constant customers for infants' flesh, besides others who might have it at merry meetings, particularly weddings and christenings, I compute that Dublin would take off annually about twenty thousand carcasses; and the rest of the kingdom (where probably they will be sold somewhat cheaper) the remaining eighty thousand.

I can think of no one objection that will possibly be raised against this proposal, unless it should be urged that the number of people will be thereby much lessened in the kingdom. This I freely own, and it was indeed one principal design in offering it to the world. I desire the reader will observe that I calculate my remedy for this one individual kingdom of Ireland, and for no other that ever was, is, or, I think, ever can be upon earth. Therefore let no man talk to me of other expedients: of taxing our absentees at five shillings a pound: of using neither clothes nor household furniture, except what is of our own growth and manufacture: of utterly rejecting the materials and instruments that promote foreign luxury: of curing the expensiveness of pride, vanity, idleness, and gaming in our women of introducing a vein of parsimony, prudence, and temperance: of learning to love our country, in the want of which we differ even from Laplanders and the inhabitants of Topinamboo:[12] of quitting our animosities and factions, nor acting

---

[12] *Topinamboo:* a savage area of Brazil.

any longer like the Jews, who were murdering one another at the very moment their city was taken:[13] of being a little cautious not to sell our country and conscience for nothing: of teaching landlords to have at least one degree of mercy toward their tenants: lastly, of putting a spirit of honesty, industry, and skill into our shopkeepers; who, if a resolution could now be taken to buy only our native goods, would immediately unite to cheat and exact upon us in the price, the measure, and the goodness, nor could ever yet be brought to make one fair proposal of just dealing, though often and earnestly invited to it.[14]

Therefore, I repeat, let no man talk to me of these and the like expedients, till he has at least some glimpse of hope that there will ever be some hearty and sincere attempt to put them in practice.   30

But as to myself, having been wearied out for many years with offering vain, idle, visionary thoughts, and at length utterly despairing of success, I fortunately fell upon this proposal; which, as it is wholly new, so it has something solid and real, of no expense and little trouble, full in our own power, and whereby we can incur no danger in disobliging England. For this kind of commodity will not bear exportation, the flesh being of too tender a consistence to admit a long continuance in salt, although perhaps I could name a country which would be glad to eat up our whole nation without it.[15]

After all, I am not so violently bent upon my own opinion as to reject any offer proposed by wise men, which shall be found equally innocent, cheap, easy, and effectual. But before something of that kind shall be advanced in contradiction to my scheme, and offering a better, I desire the author or authors will be pleased maturely to consider two points. First, as things now stand, how they will be able to find food and raiment for an hundred thousand useless mouths and backs. And, secondly, there being a round million of creatures in human figure throughout this kingdom, whose whole subsistence put into a common stock would leave them in debt two millions of pounds sterling, adding those who are beggars by profession to the bulk of farmers, cottagers, and laborers, with their wives and children, who are beggars in effect; I desire those politicians, who dislike my overture, and may perhaps be so bold as to attempt an answer, that they will first ask the parents of these mortals, whether they would not at this day think it a great happiness to have been sold for food at a year old in the manner I prescribe, and thereby have avoided such a perpetual scene of misfortunes as they have since gone through by the oppression of landlords, the impossibility of paying rent without money or trade, the want of common sustenance, with neither house nor clothes to cover them from the inclemencies of the weather,

---

[13] *city was taken:* While the Roman Emperor Titus was besieging Jerusalem, which he took and destroyed in A.D. 70, within the city factions of fanatics were waging bloody warfare. [14] *invited to it:* Swift had already made all these proposals in various pamphlets.   [15] *a country . . . without it:* England; this is another way of saying, "The English are devouring the Irish."

and the most inevitable prospect of entailing the like or greater miseries upon their breed for ever.

I profess, in the sincerity of my heart, that I have not the least personal interest in endeavoring to promote this necessary work, having no other motive than the public good of my country, by advancing our trade, providing for infants, relieving the poor, and giving some pleasure to the rich. I have no children by which I can propose to get a single penny; the youngest being nine years old, and my wife past childbearing.

Questions for Discussion and Writing

1. What is a "projector," and in what sense is the narrator's proposal "modest"? At what point did you realize that Swift was being ironic and not literal?
2. How do the shocking details about life in Ireland in the early 1700s, which the narrator casually reveals, strengthen Swift's satire? To what extent does Swift criticize the Irish for not doing enough to help themselves?
3. Write your own "modest" proposal of two to three pages offering a truly offensive solution to a contemporary problem (such as corporate corruption, overpayment of athletes, antismoking ordinances, obesity in children) using Swift's techniques of irony, **understatement,** and skewed statistics.
4. **Rhetorical inquiry:** How do each of the following sections help the reader follow Swift's line of argument: (1) paras. 1–7 stating the problem and introducing the narrator, (2) paras. 8–16 stating the proposed solution, (3) paras. 17–28 explaining the details of his proposal, (4) paras. 29–32 identifying and refuting objections, and (5) para. 33 presenting himself as an objective observer?

PANOS IOANNIDES

Panos Ioannides was born in Cyprus in 1935 and was educated in Cyprus, the United States, and Canada. He has been the head of TV programs at Cyprus Broadcasting Corporation. Ioannides is the author of many plays, which have been staged or telecast internationally, and has written novels, short stories, and radio scripts. "Gregory" was written in 1963 and first appeared in The Charioteer, a Review of Modern Greek Literature *(1965). The English translation is by Marion Byron and Catherine Raisiz. This compelling story is based on a true incident that took place during the Cypriot Liberation struggle against the British in the late 1950s. Ioannides takes the unusual approach of letting the reader experience the torments of a soldier ordered to shoot a prisoner, Gregory, who had saved his life and was his friend.*

Before You Read

To what extent is this story more effective because it is told from the perspective of the narrator rather than that of his prisoner?

Gregory

My hand was sweating as I held the pistol. The curve of the trigger was biting against my finger.

Facing me, Gregory trembled.

His whole being was beseeching me, "Don't!"

Only his mouth did not make a sound. His lips were squeezed tight. If it had been me, I would have screamed, shouted, cursed.

The soldiers were watching. . . .   5

The day before, during a brief meeting, they had each given their opinions: "It's tough luck, but it has to be done. We've got no choice."

The order from Headquarters was clear: "As soon as Lieutenant Rafel's execution is announced, the hostage Gregory is to be shot and his body must be hanged from a telegraph pole in the main street as an exemplary punishment."

It was not the first time that I had to execute a hostage in this war. I had acquired experience, thanks to Headquarters which had kept entrusting me with these delicate assignments. Gregory's case was precisely the sixth.

The first time, I remember, I vomited. The second time I got sick and had a headache for days. The third time I drank a bottle of rum. The fourth, just two glasses of beer. The fifth time I joked about it, "This little guy, with the big pop-eyes, won't be much of a ghost!"

But why, dammit, when the day came did I have to start thinking that   10
I'm not so tough, after all? The thought had come at exactly the wrong time and spoiled all my disposition to do my duty.

You see, this Gregory was such a miserable little creature, such a puny thing, such a nobody, damn him.

That very morning, although he had heard over the loudspeakers that Rafel had been executed, he believed that we would spare his life because we had been eating together so long.

"Those who eat from the same mess tins and drink from the same water canteen," he said, "remain good friends no matter what."

And a lot more of the same sort of nonsense.

He was a silly fool—we had smelled that out the very first day Head-   15
quarters gave him to us. The sentry guarding him had got dead drunk and had dozed off. The rest of us with exit permits had gone from the barracks. When we came back, there was Gregory sitting by the sleeping sentry and thumbing through a magazine.

"Why didn't you run away, Gregory?" we asked, laughing at him, several days later.

And he answered, "Where would I go in this freezing weather? I'm O.K. here."

So we started teasing him.

"You're dead right. The accommodations here are splendid. . . ."

"It's not so bad here," he replied. "The barracks where I used to be are like a sieve. The wind blows in from every side. . . ."   20

We asked him about his girl. He smiled.

"Maria is a wonderful person," he told us. "Before I met her she was engaged to a no-good fellow, a pig. He gave her up for another girl. Then nobody in the village wanted to marry Maria. I didn't miss my chance. So what if she is second-hand. Nonsense. Peasant ideas, my friend. She's beautiful and good-hearted. What more could I want? And didn't she load me with watermelons and cucumbers every time I passed by her vegetable garden? Well, one day I stole some cucumbers and melons and watermelons and I took them to her. 'Maria,' I said, 'from now on I'm going to take care of you.' She started crying and then me, too. But ever since that day she has given me lots of trouble—jealousy. She wouldn't let me go even to my mother's. Until the day I was recruited, she wouldn't let me go far from her apron strings. But that was just what I wanted. . . ."

He used to tell this story over and over, always with the same words, the same commonplace gestures. At the end he would have a good laugh and start gulping from his water jug.

His tongue was always wagging! When he started talking, nothing could stop him. We used to listen and nod our heads, not saying a word. But sometimes, as he was telling us about his mother and family problems, we couldn't help wondering, "Eh, well, these people have the same headaches in their country as we've got."

Strange, isn't it!   25

Except for his talking too much, Gregory wasn't a bad fellow. He was a marvelous cook. Once he made us some apple tarts, so delicious we licked the platter clean. And he could sew, too. He used to sew on all our buttons, patch our clothes, darn our socks, iron our ties, wash our clothes. . . .

How the devil could you kill such a friend?

Even though his name was Gregory and some people on his side had killed one of ours, even though we had left wives and children to go to war against him and his kind—but how can I explain? He was our friend. He actually liked us! A few days before, hadn't he killed with his own bare hands a scorpion that was climbing up my leg? He could have let it send me to hell!

"Thanks, Gregory!" I said then, "Thank God who made you. . . ."

When the order came, it was like a thunderbolt. Gregory was to be shot, it said, and hanged from a telegraph pole as an exemplary punishment.   30

We got together inside the barracks. We sent Gregory to wash some underwear for us.

"It ain't right."

"What is right?"

"Our duty!"

"Shit!"   35

"If you dare, don't do it! They'll drag you to court-martial and then bang-bang. . . ."

Well, of course. The right thing is to save your skin. That's only logical. It's either your skin or his. His, of course, even if it was Gregory, the fellow you've been sharing the same plate with, eating with your fingers, and who was washing your clothes that very minute.

What could I do? That's war. We had seen worse things.

So we set the hour.

We didn't tell him anything when he came back from the washing. He   40
slept peacefully. He snored for the last time. In the morning, he heard the news over the loudspeaker and he saw that we looked gloomy and he began to suspect that something was up. He tried talking to us, but he got no answers and then he stopped talking.

He just stood there and looked at us, stunned and lost. . . .

Now, I'll squeeze the trigger. A tiny bullet will rip through his chest. Maybe I'll lose my sleep tonight but in the morning I'll wake up alive.

Gregory seems to guess my thoughts. He puts out his hand and asks, "You're kidding, friend! Aren't you kidding?"

What a jackass! Doesn't he deserve to be cut to pieces? What a thing to ask at such a time. Your heart is about to burst and he's asking if you're kidding. How can a body be kidding about such a thing? Idiot! This is no time for jokes. And you, if you're such a fine friend, why don't you make things easier for us? Help us kill you with fewer qualms? If you would get angry—curse our Virgin, our God—if you'd try to escape it would be much easier for us and for you.

So it is *now*.

Now, Mr. Gregory, you are going to pay for your stupidities wholesale. Because you didn't escape the day the sentry fell asleep; because you didn't escape yesterday when we sent you all alone to the laundry—we did it on purpose, you idiot! Why didn't you let me die from the sting of the scorpion?

So now don't complain. It's all your fault, nitwit.

Eh? What's happening to him now?

Gregory is crying. Tears flood his eyes and trickle down over his cleanshaven cheeks. He is turning his face and pressing his forehead against the wall. His back is shaking as he sobs. His hands cling, rigid and helpless, to the wall.

Now is my best chance, now that he knows there is no other solution and turns his face from us.

I squeeze the trigger.

Gregory jerks, His back stops shaking up and down.

I think I've finished him! How easy it is. . . . But suddenly he starts crying out loud, his hands claw at the wall and try to pull it down. He screams, "No, no. . . ."

I turn to the others. I expect them to nod, "That's enough."

They nod, "What are you waiting for?"

I squeeze the trigger again.

The bullet smashed into his neck. A thick spray of blood spurts out.

Gregory turns. His eyes are all red. He lunges at me and starts punching me with his fists.

"I hate you, hate you . . .," he screams.

I emptied the barrel. He fell and grabbed my leg as if he wanted to hold on.

He died with a terrible spasm. His mouth was full of blood and so were my boots and socks.

We stood quietly, looking at him.

When we came to, we stooped and picked him up. His hands were frozen and wouldn't let my legs go.

I still have their imprints, red and deep, as if made by a hot knife. 45

"We will hang him tonight," the men said.

"Tonight or now?" they said.

I turned and looked at them one by one.

"Is that what you all want?" I asked.

They gave me no answer. 50

"Dig a grave," I said.

Headquarters did not ask for a report the next day or the day after. The top brass were sure that we had obeyed them and had left him swinging from a pole.

They didn't care to know what happened to that Gregory, alive or dead.

Questions for Discussion and Writing

1. What in the narrator's past leads his superiors (and the narrator himself) to conclude that he is the best one for the job? Why is Gregory's innocence both a source of admiration and irritation? How does the narrator's final order reveal his inner distress?

2. Why is the story more effective because it is told from the narrator/executioner's point of view rather than from Gregory's? What details emphasize the anguish the narrator feels and the irony of the whole situation when the authorities never even inquire whether their orders have been carried out?

3. If you were in the narrator's place, what would you have done, and how would you have felt about your decision?

4. **Rhetorical inquiry:** Why is it important to know that Gregory is the narrator's sixth assigned execution? How has his reaction to each previous one revealed his progressive desensitization and why does Gregory reawaken his feelings of humanity?

Poetry

W. H. Auden

W. H. Auden (1907–1973) was born in York, England, the son of a distinguished physician. He was educated at Oxford, where he was part of a group of poets, including Louis MacNeice, Stephen Spender, and C. Day Lewis, who shared the goal of creating new poetic techniques to express heightened social consciousness. After graduating from Oxford in 1928, Auden spent a year in Berlin, where he was influenced by Marxist poet and playwright Bertolt Brecht. After teaching school in England and Scotland in the 1930s, he went to Spain in 1937, where he drove an ambulance for the Republicans in the war against the Fascists. He moved to the United States in 1939 and became a U.S. citizen in 1946, dividing his time between New York and Europe. He was elected professor of poetry at Oxford in 1956. The most complete edition of his poetry is the posthumously published Collected Poems *(1978). In "The Unknown Citizen" (1940), Auden satirizes a dehumanized materialistic society that requires absolute conformity of its citizens.*

Before You Read

Could knowing all the statistics about someone tell you who he or she really was as a person?

The Unknown Citizen

(To JS/07/M/378
*This Marble Monument
Is Erected by the State*)

He was found by the Bureau of Statistics to be
One against whom there was no official complaint,
And all the reports on his conduct agree
That, in the modern sense of an old-fashioned word, he was a saint,
For in everything he did he served the Greater Community.   5
Except for the War till the day he retired
He worked in a factory and never got fired,
But satisfied his employers, Fudge Motors Inc.
Yet he wasn't a scab[1] or odd in his views,
For his Union reports that he paid his dues,   10
(Our report on his Union shows it was sound)

---

[1] *Scab:* a worker who won't join the union or who takes a striker's job.

And our Social Psychology workers found
That he was popular with his mates and liked a drink.
The Press are convinced that he bought a paper every day
And that his reactions to advertisements were normal in every way.   15
Policies taken out in his name prove that he was fully insured,
And his Health-card shows he was once in hospital but left it cured.
Both Producers Research and High-Grade Living declare
He was fully sensible to the advantages of the Installment Plan
And had everything necessary to the Modern Man,   20
A phonograph, radio, a car and a frigidaire.
Our researchers into Public Opinion are content
That he held the proper opinions for the time of year;
When there was peace, he was for peace; when there was war, he went.
He was married and added five children to the population,   25
Which our Eugenist[2] says was the right number for a parent of his
    generation,
And our teachers report that he never interfered with their education.
Was he free? Was he happy? The question is absurd:
Had anything been wrong, we should certainly have heard.

Questions for Discussion and Writing

1. Why is it significant that no official complaint was ever brought against the unknown citizen? What kind of society did he inhabit?
2. How does Auden parody the language of bureaucracy to satirize the social and political tenets of the government? What aspects of this society does he assail?
3. How might the word *unknown* in the title be interpreted? What is the significance of the questions "Was he free? Was he happy?" in line 28? What evidence, if any, does the poem give as an answer?
4. **Rhetorical inquiry:** How does Auden's use of capitalization satirize the sterile abstractions viewed as all-knowing in this future society? How does Auden make the number in his dedication part of the poem's rhyme scheme?

CAROLYN FORCHÉ

Carolyn Forché was born in Detroit in 1950. She was educated at Michigan State University and Bowling Green University and has taught at a number

---

[2] *Eugenist:* an expert in eugenics, the science of improving the human race by careful selection of parents to breed healthier, more intelligent children.

of colleges. While a journalist in El Salvador from 1978 to 1980, she reported on human rights conditions for Amnesty International. Her experiences there had a profound influence on her poetry and nonfiction writings. Her poetry collections include Gathering the Tribes *(1976) and* The Country Between Us *(1981). She is also the editor of* Against Forgetting: Twentieth-Century Poetry of Witness *(1993). "The Colonel" (1978) offers a surreal portrait of the hidden terrors lurking underneath the civilized veneer of normalcy in an unnamed Central American country. She has also written* The Angel of History *(1995) and* Blue Hour *(2003).*

Before You Read

Pay special attention to the ingenious images Forché uses to reveal the hidden terrors beneath the facade of civility.

The Colonel

What you have heard is true. I was in his house. His wife
carried a tray of coffee and sugar. His daughter filed her
nails, his son went out for the night. There were daily papers,
pet dogs, a pistol on the cushion behind him. The
moon swung bare on its black cord over the house. On the   5
television was a cop show. It was in English. Broken bottles
were embedded in the walls around the house to scoop
the kneecaps from a man's legs or cut his hands to lace. On
the windows there were gratings like those in liquor
stores. We had dinner, rack of lamb, good wine, a gold bell   10
was on the table for calling the maid. The maid brought
green mangoes, salt, a type of bread. I was asked how I enjoyed
the country. There was a brief commercial in
Spanish. His wife took everything away. There was some
talk then of how difficult it had become to govern. The parrot   15
said hello on the terrace. The colonel told it to shut up,
and pushed himself from the table. My friend said to me
with his eyes: say nothing. The colonel returned with a
sack used to bring groceries home. He spilled many human
ears on the table. They were like dried peach halves. There   20
is no other way to say this. He took one of them in his
hands, shook it in our faces, dropped it into a water glass. It
came alive there, I am tired of fooling around he said. As
for the rights of anyone, tell your people they can go fuck
themselves. He swept the ears to the floor with his arm   25
and held the last of his wine in the air. Something for your
poetry, no? he said. Some of the ears on the floor caught
this scrap of his voice. Some of the ears on the floor were
pressed to the ground.

Questions for Discussion and Writing

1. What attitude toward human rights is implied by the trophies the colonel presents to the visitor?
2. In what way is the display of hidden terrors underneath a civilized veneer of normalcy made more effective through the surreal contrast the poem develops?
3. Discuss the ethical dilemma the visitor confronts during the meal at which human rights is mentioned. How does the ending of the poem reflect the speaker's predicament?
4. **Rhetorical inquiry:** How does the progression of images in the poem begin quietly enough with what seems to be an ordinary family dinner where soon the props of everyday life are displaced by first hidden then overt signs of violence? Why is the image of the moon swinging on a black cord over the house particularly ominous?

Drama

SUSAN GLASPELL

Susan Glaspell (1882–1948) was born and raised in Davenport, Iowa, and graduated from Drake University in 1899. She worked as a reporter and wrote short stories that were published in Harper's *and* Ladies' Home Journal. *Glaspell won a Pulitzer Prize for drama in 1931 for* Alison's House, *which was based on Emily Dickinson's life. She wrote* Trifles *in 1916 for the Provincetown Players on Cape Cod, in Massachusetts. This play was based on a murder trial she had covered while working as a reporter for the* Des Moines News. Trifles *(1916) offers an instructive example of the ways in which men and women perceive events and their own roles in life in a traditional society.*

Before You Read

Notice how small seemingly insignificant clues ultimately hold the answer to the murder investigation.

Trifles

CAST OF CHARACTERS

GEORGE HENDERSON, *county attorney*
HENRY PETERS, *sheriff*
LEWIS HALE, *a neighboring farmer*
MRS. PETERS
MRS. HALE

SCENE.   The kitchen in the now abandoned farmhouse of John Wright, a gloomy kitchen, and left without having been put in order—unwashed pans under the sink, a loaf of bread outside the bread-box, a dish-towel on the table—other signs of incompleted work. At the rear the outer door opens and the Sheriff comes in followed by the County Attorney and Hale. The Sheriff and Hale are men in middle life, the County Attorney is a young man; all are much bundled up and go at once to the stove. They are followed by the two women—the Sheriff's wife first; she is a slight wiry woman, a thin nervous face. Mrs. Hale is larger and would ordinarily be called more comfortable looking, but she is disturbed now and looks fearfully about as she enters. The women have come in slowly, and stand close together near the door.

COUNTY ATTORNEY.   (*Rubbing his hands.*) This feels good. Come up to the fire, ladies.

MRS. PETERS.   (*After taking a step forward.*) I'm not—cold.

SHERIFF.   (*Unbuttoning his overcoat and stepping away from the stove as if to mark the beginning of official business*.) Now, Mr. Hale, before we move things about, you explain to Mr. Henderson just what you saw when you came here yesterday morning.

COUNTY ATTORNEY.   By the way, has anything been moved? Are things just as you left them yesterday?

SHERIFF.   (*Looking about.*) It's just the same. When it dropped below zero   5
last night I thought I'd better send Frank out this morning to make a fire for us—no use getting pneumonia with a big case on, but I told him not to touch anything except the stove—and you know Frank.

COUNTY ATTORNEY.   Somebody should have been left here yesterday.

SHERIFF.   Oh—yesterday. When I had to send Frank to Morris Center for that man who went crazy—I want you to know I had my hands full yesterday. I knew you could get back from Omaha by today and as long as I went over everything here myself—

COUNTY ATTORNEY.   Well, Mr. Hale, tell just what happened when you came here yesterday morning.

HALE.   Harry and I had started to town with a load of potatoes. We came along the road from my place and as I got here I said, "I'm going to see if I can't get John Wright to go in with me on a party telephone." I spoke to Wright about it once before and he put me off, saying folks talked too much anyway, and all he asked was peace and quiet—I guess you know about how much he talked himself; but I thought maybe if I went to the house and talked about it before his wife, though I said to Harry that I didn't know as what his wife wanted made much difference to John—

COUNTY ATTORNEY.   Let's talk about that later, Mr. Hale. I do want to   10
talk about that, but tell now just what happened when you got to the house.

HALE.   I didn't hear or see anything; I knocked at the door, and still it was all quiet inside. I knew they must be up, it was past eight o'clock. So I knocked again, and I thought I heard somebody say, "Come in." I wasn't sure, I'm not sure yet, but I opened the door—this door (*Indicating the door by which the two women are still standing.*) and there in the rocker—(*Pointing to it.*) sat Mrs. Wright.

(*They all look at the rocker.*)

COUNTY ATTORNEY.   What—was she doing?

HALE.   She was rockin' back and forth. She had her apron in her hand and was kind of—pleating it.

COUNTY ATTORNEY.   And how did she—look?

HALE.   Well, she looked queer.   15

COUNTY ATTORNEY.   How do you mean—queer?

HALE.   Well, as if she didn't know what she was going to do next. And kind of done up.

COUNTY ATTORNEY.   How did she seem to feel about your coming?

HALE.   Why, I don't think she minded—one way or other. She didn't pay much attention. I said, "How do, Mrs. Wright, it's cold, ain't it?" And she said, "Is it?"—and went on kind of pleating at her apron. Well, I was surprised; she didn't ask me to come up to the stove, or to set down, but just sat there, not even looking at me, so I said, "I want to see John." And then she—laughed. I guess you would call it a laugh. I thought of Harry and the team outside, so I said a little sharp: "Can't I see John?" "No," she says, kind o' dull like. "Ain't he home?" says I. "Yes," says she, "he's home." Then why can't I see him?" I asked her, out of patience. "'Cause he's dead," says she. *"Dead?"* says I. She just nodded her head, not getting a bit excited, but rockin' back and forth. "Why—where is he?" says I, not knowing what to say. She just pointed upstairs—like that. (*Himself pointing to the room above.*) I got up, with the idea of going up there. I walked from there to here—then I says, "Why, what did he die of?" "He died of a rope round his neck," says she, and just went on pleatin' at her apron. Well, I went out and called Harry. I thought I might—need help. We went upstairs and there he was lyin'—

COUNTY ATTORNEY.   I think I'd rather have you go into that upstairs,   20
where you can point it all out. Just go on now with the rest of the story.

HALE.   Well, my first thought was to get that rope off. It looked . . . (*Stops, his face twitches.*) . . . but Harry, he went up to him, and he said, "No, he's dead all right, and we'd better not touch anything." So we went back downstairs. She was still sitting that same way. "Has anybody been notified?" I asked. "No," says she, unconcerned. "Who did this, Mrs. Wright?" said Harry. He said it businesslike—and she stopped pleatin' of her apron. "I don't know," she says. "You don't *know?*" says Harry, "No," says she. "Weren't you sleepin' in the bed with him?" says Harry. "Yes," says she, "but I was on the inside."

"Somebody slipped a rope round his neck and strangled him and you didn't wake up?" says Harry. "I didn't wake up," she said after him. We must 'a looked as if we didn't see how that could be, for after a minute she said, "I sleep sound." Harry was going to ask her more questions but I said maybe we ought to let her tell her story first to the coroner, or the sheriff, so Harry went fast as he could to Rivers' place, where there's a telephone.

COUNTY ATTORNEY.   And what did Mrs. Wright do when she knew that you had gone for the coroner?

HALE.   She moved from that chair to this one over here (*Pointing to a small chair in the corner.*) and just sat there with her hands held together and looking down. I got a feeling that I ought to make some conversation, so I said I had come in to see if John wanted to put in a telephone, and at that she started to laugh, and then she stopped and looked at me— scared. (*The County Attorney, who has had his notebook out, makes a note.*) I dunno, maybe it wasn't scared. I wouldn't like to say it was. Soon Harry got back, and then Dr. Lloyd came, and you, Mr. Peters, and so I guess that's all I know that you don't.

COUNTY ATTORNEY.   (*Looking around.*) I guess we'll go upstairs first— and then out to the barn and around there. (*To the Sheriff.*) You're convinced that there was nothing important here—nothing that would point to any motive.

SHERIFF.   Nothing here but kitchen things.   25

(*The County Attorney, after again looking around the kitchen, opens the door of a cupboard closet. He gets up on a chair and looks on a shelf. Pulls his hand away.*)

COUNTY ATTORNEY.   Here's a nice mess.

(*The women draw nearer.*)

MRS. PETERS.   (*To the other woman.*) Oh, her fruit; it did freeze. (*To the Lawyer.*) She worried about that when it turned so cold. She said the fire'd go out and her jars would break.

SHERIFF.   Well, can you beat the women! Held for murder and worryin' about her preserves.

COUNTY ATTORNEY.   I guess before we're through she may have something more serious than preserves to worry about.

HALE.   Well, women are used to worrying over trifles.   30

(*The two women move a little closer together.*)

COUNTY ATTORNEY.   (*With the gallantry of a young politician.*) And yet, for all their worries, what would we do without the ladies? (*The women do not unbend. He goes to the sink, takes a dipperful of water from the pail and pouring it into a basin, washes his hands. Starts to wipe them on the roller-towel, turns it for a cleaner place.*) Dirty towels!

(*Kicks his foot against the pans under the sink.*) Not much of a house-keeper, would you say, ladies?

MRS. HALE.   (*Stiffly.*) There's a great deal of work to be done on a farm.

COUNTY ATTORNEY.   To be sure. And yet (*With a little bow to her.*) I know there are some Dickson county farmhouses which do not have such roller towels.

(*He gives it a pull to expose its full length again.*)

MRS. HALE.   Those towels get dirty awful quick. Men's hands aren't always as clean as they might be.

COUNTY ATTORNEY.   Ah, loyal to your sex, I see. But you and Mrs. Wright   35
were neighbors. I suppose you were friends, too.

MRS. HALE.   (*Shaking her head.*) I've not seen much of her of late years. I've not been in this house—it's more than a year.

COUNTY ATTORNEY.   And why was that? You didn't like her?

MRS. HALE.   I liked her all well enough. Farmers' wives have their hands full, Mr. Henderson. And then—

COUNTY ATTORNEY.   Yes—?

MRS. HALE.   (*Looking about.*) It never seemed a very cheerful place.   40

COUNTY ATTORNEY.   No—it's not cheerful. I shouldn't say she had the homemaking instinct.

MRS. HALE.   Well, I don't know as Wright had, either.

COUNTY ATTORNEY.   You mean that they didn't get on very well?

MRS. HALE.   No, I don't mean anything. But I don't think a place'd be any cheerfuller for John Wright's being in it.

COUNTY ATTORNEY.   I'd like to talk more of that a little later. I want to get   45
the lay of things upstairs now.

(*He goes to the left, where three steps lead to a stair door.*)

SHERIFF.   I suppose anything Mrs. Peters does'll be all right. She was to take in some clothes for her, you know, and a few little things. We left in such a hurry yesterday.

COUNTY ATTORNEY.   Yes, but I would like to see what you take, Mrs. Peters, and keep an eye out for anything that might be of use to *us.*

MRS. PETERS.   Yes, Mr. Henderson.

(*The women listen to the men's steps on the stairs, then look about the kitchen.*)

MRS. HALE.   I'd hate to have men coming into my kitchen, snooping around and criticising.

(*She arranges the pans under the sink which the Lawyer had shoved out of place.*)

MRS. PETERS.   Of course it's no more than their duty.   50

MRS. HALE.   Duty's all right, but I guess that deputy sheriff that came out to make the fire might have got a little of this on. (*Gives the roller towel a pull.*) Wish I'd thought of that sooner. Seems mean to talk about her for not having things slicked up when she had to come away in such a hurry.

MRS. PETERS.   (*Who had gone to a small table in the left rear corner of the room, and lifted one end of a towel that covers a pan.*) She had bread set.

(*Stands still.*)

MRS. HALE.   (*Eyes fixed on a loaf of bread beside the breadbox, which is on a low shelf at the other side of the room. Moves slowly toward it.*) She was going to put this in there. (*Picks up loaf, then abruptly drops it. In a manner of returning to familiar things.*) It's a shame about her fruit. I wonder if it's all gone. (*Gets up on the chair and looks.*) I think there's some here that's all right, Mrs. Peters. Yes—here; (*Holding it toward the window.*) this is cherries, too. (*Looking again.*) I declare I believe that's the only one. (*Gets down, bottle in her hand. Goes to the sink and wipes it off on the outside.*) She'll feel awful bad after all her hard work in the hot weather. I remember the afternoon I put up my cherries last summer.

(*She puts the bottle on the big kitchen table, center of the room. With a sigh, is about to sit down in the rocking-chair. Before she is seated realizes what chair it is; with a slow look at it, steps back. The chair which she has touched rocks back and forth.*)

MRS. PETERS.   Well, I must get those things from the front room closet. (*She goes to the door at the right, but after looking into the other room, steps back.*) You coming with me, Mrs. Hale? You could help me carry them.

(*They go in the other room; reappear; Mrs. Peters carrying a dress and skirt, Mrs. Hale following with a pair of shoes.*)

MRS. PETERS.   My, it's cold in there.   55

(*She puts the clothes on the big table and hurries to the stove.*)

MRS. HALE.   (*Examining the skirt.*) Wright was close. I think maybe that's why she kept so much to herself. She didn't even belong to the Ladies Aid. I suppose she felt she couldn't do her part, and then you don't enjoy things when you feel shabby. She used to wear pretty clothes and be lively, when she was Minnie Foster, one of the town girls singing in the choir. But that—oh, that was thirty years ago. This all you was to take in?

MRS. PETERS.   She said she wanted an apron. Funny thing to want, for there isn't much to get you dirty in jail, goodness knows. But I suppose just to make her feel more natural. She said they was in the top drawer in this cupboard. Yes, here. And then her little shawl that always hung behind the door. (*Opens stair door and looks.*) Yes, here it is.

(*Quickly shuts door leading upstairs.*)

MRS. HALE.   (*Abruptly moving toward her.*) Mrs. Peters?

MRS. PETERS.   Yes, Mrs. Hale?

MRS. HALE.   Do you think she did it?   60

MRS. PETERS.   (*In a frightened voice.*) Oh, I don't know.

MRS. HALE.   Well, I don't think she did. Asking for an apron and her little
    shawl. Worrying about her fruit.

MRS. PETERS.   (*Starts to speak, glances up, where footsteps are heard in
    the room above. In a low voice.*) Mr. Peters says it looks bad for her.
    Mr. Henderson is awful sarcastic in a speech and he'll make fun of her
    sayin' she didn't wake up.

MRS. HALE.   Well, I guess John Wright didn't wake when they was
    slipping that rope under his neck.

MRS. PETERS.   No, it's strange. It must have been done awful crafty and   65
    still. They say it was such a—funny way to kill a man, rigging it all up
    like that.

MRS. HALE.   That's just what Mr. Hale said. There was a gun in the house.
    He says that's what he can't understand.

MRS. PETERS.   Mr. Henderson said coming out that what was needed for
    the case was a motive; something to show anger, or—sudden feeling.

MRS. HALE.   (*Who is standing by the table.*) Well, I don't see any signs of
    anger around here. (*She puts her hand on the dish towel which lies on
    the table, stands looking down at table, one half of which is clean, the
    other half messy.*) It's wiped to here. (*Makes a move as if to finish
    work, then turns and looks at loaf of bread outside the breadbox. Drops
    towel. In that voice of coming back to familiar things.*) Wonder how
    they are finding things upstairs. I hope she had it a little more red-up[1]
    up there. You know, it seems kind of *sneaking.* Locking her up in town
    and then coming out here and trying to get her own house to turn
    against her!

MRS. PETERS.   But Mrs. Hale, the law is the law.

MRS. HALE.   I s'pose 'tis. (*Unbuttoning her coat.*) Better loosen up your   70
    things, Mrs. Peters. You won't feel them when you go out.

(*Mrs. Peters takes off her fur tippet,[2] goes to hang it on hook at back of
room, stands looking at the under part of the small corner table.*)

MRS. PETERS.   She was piecing a quilt.

(*She brings the large sewing basket and they look at the bright pieces.*)

MRS. HALE.   It's log cabin pattern. Pretty, isn't it? I wonder if she was
    goin' to quilt it or just knot it?

(*Footsteps have been heard coming down the stairs. The Sheriff enters
followed by Hale and the County Attorney.*)

---

[1] *red-up:* neat and orderly.   [2] *tippet:* a scarf which covers the neck and shoulders.

SHERIFF.   They wonder if she was going to quilt it or just knot it!

(*The men laugh; the women look abashed.*)

COUNTY ATTORNEY.   (*Rubbing his hands over the stove.*) Frank's fire didn't do much up there, did it? Well, let's go out to the barn and get that cleared up.

(*The men go outside.*)

MRS. HALE.   (*Resentfully.*) I don't know as there's anything so strange, our   75
takin' up our time with little things while we're waiting for them to get the evidence. (*She sits down at the big table smoothing out a block with decision.*) I don't see as it's anything to laugh about.

MRS. PETERS.   (*Apologetically.*) Of course they've got awful important things on their minds.

(*Pulls up a chair and joins Mrs. Hale at the table.*)

MRS. HALE.   (*Examining another block.*) Mrs. Peters, look at this one. Here, this is the one she was working on, and look at the sewing! All the rest of it has been so nice and even. And look at this! It's all over the place! Why, it looks as if she didn't know what she was about!

(*After she has said this they look at each other, then start to glance back at the door. After an instant Mrs. Hale has pulled at a knot and ripped the sewing.*)

MRS. PETERS.   Oh, what are you doing, Mrs. Hale?

MRS. HALE.   (*Mildly.*) Just pulling out a stitch or two that's not sewed very good. (*Threading a needle.*) Bad sewing always made me fidgety.

MRS. PETERS.   (*Nervously.*) I don't think we ought to touch things.   80

MRS. HALE.   I'll just finish up this end. (*Suddenly stopping and leaning forward.*) Mrs. Peters?

MRS. PETERS.   Yes, Mrs. Hale?

MRS. HALE.   What do you suppose she was so nervous about?

MRS. PETERS.   Oh—I don't know. I don't know as she was nervous. I sometimes sew awful queer when I'm just tired. (*Mrs. Hale starts to say something, looks at Mrs. Peters, then goes on sewing.*) Well I must get these things wrapped up. They may be through sooner than we think. (*Putting apron and other things together.*) I wonder where I can find a piece of paper, and string.

MRS. HALE.   In that cupboard, maybe.   85

MRS. PETERS.   (*Looking in cupboard.*) Why, here's a bird-cage. (*Holds it up.*) Did she have a bird, Mrs. Hale?

MRS. HALE.   Why, I don't know whether she did or not—I've not been here for so long. There was a man around last year selling canaries cheap, but I don't know as she took one; maybe she did. She used to sing real pretty herself.

MRS. PETERS.   (*Glancing around.*) Seems funny to think of a bird here. But she must have had one, or why would she have a cage? I wonder what happened to it?

MRS. HALE.   I s'pose maybe the cat got it.

MRS. PETERS.   No, she didn't have a cat. She's got that feeling some people   90
have about cats—being afraid of them. My cat got in her room and she was real upset and asked me to take it out.

MRS. HALE.   My sister Bessie was like that. Queer, ain't it?

MRS. PETERS.   (*Examining the cage.*) Why, look at this door. It's broke. One hinge is pulled apart.

MRS. HALE.   (*Looking too.*) Looks as if someone must have been rough with it.

MRS. PETERS.   Why, yes.

(*She brings the cage forward and puts it on the table.*)

MRS. HALE.   I wish if they're going to find any evidence they'd be about it.   95
I don't like this place.

MRS. PETERS.   But I'm awful glad you came with me, Mrs. Hale. It would be lonesome for me sitting here alone.

MRS. HALE.   It would, wouldn't it? (*Dropping her sewing.*) But I tell you what I do wish, Mrs. Peters. I wish I had come over sometimes when *she* was here. I–(*Looking around the room.*)—wish I had.

MRS. PETERS.   But of course you were awful busy, Mrs. Hale—your house and your children.

MRS. HALE.   I could've come. I stayed away because it weren't cheerful— and that's why I ought to have come. I—I've never liked this place. Maybe because it's down in a hollow and you don't see the road. I dunno what it is, but it's a lonesome place and always was. I wish I had come over to see Minnie Foster sometimes. I can see now—

(*Shakes her head.*)

MRS. PETERS.   Well, you mustn't reproach yourself, Mrs. Hale. Somehow   100
we just don't see how it is with other folks until—something comes up.

MRS. HALE.   Not having children makes less work—but it makes a quiet house, and Wright out to work all day, and no company when he did come in. Did you know John Wright, Mrs. Peters?

MRS. PETERS.   Not to know him; I've seen him in town. They say he was a good man.

MRS. HALE.   Yes—good; he didn't drink, and kept his word as well as most, I guess, and paid his debts. But he was a hard man, Mrs. Peters. Just to pass the time of day with him—(*Shivers.*) Like a raw wind that gets to the bone. (*Pauses, her eye falling on the cage.*) I should think she would 'a wanted a bird. But what do you suppose went with it?

MRS. PETERS.   I don't know, unless it got sick and died.

(*She reaches over and swings the broken door, swings it again, both women watch it.*)

MRS. HALE.   You weren't raised round here, were you? (*Mrs. Peters shakes her head.*) You didn't know—her?   105

MRS. PETERS.   Not till they brought her yesterday.

MRS. HALE.   She—come to think of it, she was kind of like a bird herself—real sweet and pretty, but kind of timid and—fluttery. How— she—did—change. (*Silence; then as if struck by a happy thought and relieved to get back to everyday things.*) Tell you what, Mrs. Peters, why don't you take the quilt in with you? It might take up her mind.

MRS. PETERS.   Why, I think that's a real nice idea, Mrs. Hale. There couldn't possibly be any objection to it, could there? Now, just what would I take? I wonder if her patches are in here—and her things.

(*They look in the sewing basket.*)

MRS. HALE.   Here's some red. I expect this has got sewing things in it. (*Brings out a fancy box.*) What a pretty box. Looks like something somebody would give you. Maybe her scissors are in here. (*Opens box. Suddenly puts her hand to her nose.*) Why—(*Mrs. Peters bends nearer, then turns her face away.*) There's something wrapped up in this piece of silk.

MRS. PETERS.   Why, this isn't her scissors.   110

MRS. HALE.   (*Lifting the silk.*) Oh, Mrs. Peters—it's—

(*Mrs. Peters bends closer.*)

MRS. PETERS.   It's the bird.

MRS. HALE.   (*Jumping up.*) But, Mrs. Peters—look at it! Its neck! Look at its neck! It's all—other side *to*.

MRS. PETERS.   Somebody—wrung—its—neck.

(*Their eyes meet. A look of growing comprehension, of horror. Steps are heard outside. Mrs. Hale slips box under quilt pieces, and sinks into her chair. Enter Sheriff and County Attorney. Mrs. Peters rises.*)

COUNTY ATTORNEY.   (*As one turning from serious things to little pleasantries.*) Well, ladies, have you decided whether she was going to quilt it or knot it?   115

MRS. PETERS.   We think she was going to—knot it.

COUNTY ATTORNEY.   Well, that's interesting, I'm sure. (*Seeing the bird-cage.*) Has the bird flown?

MRS. HALE.   (*Putting more quilt pieces over the box.*) We think the—cat got it.

COUNTY ATTORNEY.   (*Preoccupied.*) Is there a cat?

(*Mrs. Hale glances in a quick covert way at Mrs. Peters.*)

MRS. PETERS.   Well, not *now*. They're superstitious, you know. They leave.   120

COUNTY ATTORNEY. (*To Sheriff Peters, continuing an interrupted conversation.*) No sign at all of anyone having come from the outside. Their own rope. Now let's go up again and go over it piece by piece. (*They start upstairs.*) It would have to have been someone who knew just the—

(*Mrs. Peters sits down. The two women sit there not looking at one another, but as if peering into something and at the same time holding back. When they talk now it is in the manner of feeling their way over strange ground, as if afraid of what they are saying, but as if they cannot help saying it.*)

MRS. HALE. She liked the bird. She was going to bury it in that pretty box.
MRS. PETERS. (*In a whisper.*) When I was a girl—my kitten—there was a boy took a hatchet, and before my eyes—and before I could get there—(*Covers her face an instant.*) If they hadn't held me back I would have—(*Catches herself, looks upstairs where steps are heard, falters weakly.*)—hurt him.
MRS. HALE. (*With a slow look around her.*) I wonder how it would seem never to have had any children around. (*Pause.*) No, Wright wouldn't like the bird—a thing that sang. She used to sing. He killed that, too.
MRS. PETERS. (*Moving uneasily.*) We don't know who killed the bird. 125
MRS. HALE. I knew John Wright.
MRS. PETERS. It was an awful thing was done in this house that night, Mrs. Hale. Killing a man while he slept, slipping a rope around his neck that choked the life out of him.
MRS. HALE. His neck. Choked the life out of him.

(*Her hand goes out and rests on the bird-cage.*)

MRS. PETERS. (*With rising voice.*) We don't know who killed him. We don't know.
MRS. HALE. (*Her own feeling not interrupted.*) If there'd been years and 130
years of nothing, then a bird to sing to you, it would be awful—still, after the bird was still.
MRS. PETERS. (*Something within her speaking.*) I know what stillness is. When we homesteaded in Dakota, and my first baby died—after he was two years old, and me with no other then—
MRS. HALE. (*Moving.*) How soon do you suppose they'll be through, looking for the evidence?
MRS. PETERS. I know what stillness is. (*Pulling herself back.*) The law has got to punish crime, Mrs. Hale.
MRS. HALE. (*Not as if answering that.*) I wish you'd seen Minnie Foster when she wore a white dress with blue ribbons and stood up there in the choir and sang. (*A look around the room.*) Oh, I *wish* I'd come over here once in a while! That was a crime! That was a crime! Who's going to punish that?
MRS. PETERS. (*Looking upstairs.*) We mustn't—take on. 135

MRS. HALE.   I might have known she needed help! I know how things can be—for women. I tell you, it's queer, Mrs. Peters. We live close together and we live far apart. We all go through the same things—it's all just a different kind of the same thing. (*Brushes her eyes, noticing the bottle of fruit, reaches out for it.*) If I was you I wouldn't tell her her fruit was gone. Tell her it *ain't*. Tell her it's all right. Take this in to prove it to her. She—she may never know whether it was broke or not.

MRS. PETERS.   (*Takes the bottle, looks about for something to wrap it in; takes petticoat from the clothes brought from the other room, very nervously begins winding this around the bottle. In a false voice.*) My, it's a good thing the men couldn't hear us. Wouldn't they just laugh! Getting all stirred up over a little thing like a—dead canary. As if that could have anything to do with—with—wouldn't they *laugh!*

(*The men are heard coming down stairs.*)

MRS. HALE.   (*Under her breath.*) Maybe they would—maybe they wouldn't.

COUNTY ATTORNEY.   No, Peters, it's all perfectly clear except a reason for doing it. But you know juries when it comes to women. If there was some definite thing. Something to show—something to make a story about—a thing that would connect up with this strange way of doing it—

(*The women's eyes meet for an instant. Enter Hale from outer door.*)

HALE.   Well, I've got the team[3] around. Pretty cold out there.   140

COUNTY ATTORNEY.   I'm going to stay here a while by myself. (*To the Sheriff.*) You can send Frank out for me, can't you? I want to go over everything. I'm not satisfied that we can't do better.

SHERIFF.   Do you want to see what Mrs. Peters is going to take in?

(*The County Attorney goes to the table, picks up the apron, laughs.*)

COUNTY ATTORNEY.   Oh, I guess they're not very dangerous things the ladies have picked out. (*Moves a few things about, disturbing the quilt pieces which cover the box. Steps back.*) No, Mrs. Peters doesn't need supervising. For that matter, a sheriff's wife is married to the law. Ever think of it that way, Mrs. Peters?

MRS. PETERS.   Not—just that way.

SHERIFF.   (*Chuckling.*) Married to the law. (*Moves toward the other room.*) I just want you to come in here a minute, George. We ought to take a look at these windows.   145

COUNTY ATTORNEY.   (*Scoffingly.*) Oh, windows!

SHERIFF.   We'll be right out, Mr. Hale.

---

[3] *team:* team of horses drawing a wagon.

(*Hale goes outside. The Sheriff follows the County Attorney into the other room. Then Mrs. Hale rises, hands tight together, looking intensely at Mrs. Peters, whose eyes make a slow turn, finally meeting Mrs. Hale's. A moment Mrs. Hale holds her, then her own eyes point the way to where the box is concealed. Suddenly Mrs. Peters throws back quilt pieces and tries to put the box in the bag she is wearing. It is too big. She opens box, starts to take bird out, cannot touch it, goes to pieces, stands there helpless. Sound of a knob turning in the other room. Mrs. Hale snatches the box and puts it in the pocket of her big coat. Enter County Attorney and Sheriff.*)

COUNTY ATTORNEY. (*Facetiously.*) Well, Henry, at least we found out that she was not going to quilt it. She was going to—what is it you call it, ladies?

MRS. HALE. (*Her hand against her pocket.*) We call it—knot it, Mr. Henderson.

CURTAIN

Questions for Discussion and Writing

1. In what dramatic ways do the men (the County Attorney and the Sheriff) look for clues and draw conclusions differently from the women (Mrs. Hale and Mrs. Peters)? To what does the title of the play refer, and why is it ironic?

2. How does Glaspell use natural objects (for example, the birdcage and the dead canary) as symbols to establish and reinforce important ideas? How does the characterization of John Wright help explain what happens to him and allow us to understand how marrying him changed Minnie Foster? Would the play have been more effective if she were a speaking character? Why or why not?

3. In what sense can this play be considered a feminist work that comments on issues in the early twentieth century?

4. **Rhetorical inquiry:** How does the imagery describing Mrs. Wright in both her early years and in her present condition link her with her pet canary?

Connections for Chapter 8: Power and Politics

1. **Harriet Jacobs,** *Incidents in the Life of a Slave Girl*
   In what ways do Jacobs and Martin Luther King, Jr. address the idea of justice as a fundamental human right for African Americans?

2. **Kenneth M. Stampp,** *To Make Them Stand in Fear*
   What insights into the psychology of the colonizers and the colonized do Stampp and Haunani-Kay Trask (see "From a Native Daughter" in Chapter 7) offer?

3. **Martin Luther King, Jr.,** *I Have a Dream*
   Would you call Jill Nelson's "Number One!" (in Chapter 1) a success story in terms of King's expectations for African Americans? Why or why not?

4. **Barbara Ehrenreich,** *Nickel-and-Dimed*
   How do both Ehrenreich and Gloria Anzaldúa in her story (Chapter 5) view events from the perspective of the underclass?

5. **Luis Sepulveda,** *Daisy*
   Compare and contrast the pressures to which Sepúlveda and Harriet Jacobs are subjected and the way they respond.

6. **Tim O'Brien,** *If I Die in a Combat Zone*
   In what respects do O'Brien and the narrator in Panos Ioannides's story "Gregory" confront similar choices as to the allegiance that they owe the state?

7. **Stephen Chapman,** *The Prisoner's Dilemma*
   Which form of punishment (of the East or West) might Jonathan Swift prefer to satirize?

8. **Michael Levin,** *The Case for Torture*
   What would an ethicist such as Philip Wheelwright (see "The Meaning of Ethics" in Chapter 11 say about Levin's proposal?

9. **Jonathan Swift,** *A Modest Proposal*
   In what ways do Swift and Barbara Ehrenreich assail economic injustices?

10. **Panos Ioannides,** *Gregory*
    In what sense is the speaker's dilemma in this story comparable to that confronting Luis Sepúlveda's narrator in "Daisy"?

11. **W. H. Auden,** *The Unknown Citizen*
    In what respects might Ehrenreich as the narrator in her account be characterized as "the unknown citizen" of Auden's poem?

12. **Carolyn Forché,** *The Colonel*
    In what ways are the attitudes and actions of the Colonel in Forché's poem comparable to the jailor in Luis Sepúlveda's "Daisy"?

13. **Susan Glaspell,** *Trifles*
    In what way are Deborah Tannen's observations in "Sex, Lies, and Conversation" (in Chapter 4) about the different objectives of men and women dramatized in Glaspell's play?

9

SCIENCE AND TECHNOLOGY

*Modern man, if he dared to be articulate about his concept of
heaven, would describe a vision which would look like the biggest
department store in the world, showing new things and gadgets,
and himself having plenty of money with which to buy them. He
would wander around open-mouthed in this heaven of gadgets and
commodities provided only that there were ever more and newer
things to buy, and perhaps that his neighbors were just a little less
privileged than he.*

Erich Fromm, "ALIENATION"

The selections in this chapter examine the extent to which culture and society
depend on scientific discoveries and technological developments. Without
basic scientific research, we would not have televisions, personal computers,
DVDs, microwave ovens, cellular telephones, fax machines, the World Wide
Web, and a host of other inventions. The authors in this chapter make us
aware of the profound ways in which these and other revolutionary scientific
and technological inventions have transformed our lives. Scientific breakthroughs always create ethical and moral consequences that challenge us to
reap the benefits without incurring the drawbacks. For example, new genetic
screening capabilities raise a number of profoundly important ethical and
legal issues that are explored by David Ewing Duncan.

Other writers explore the way scientific breakthroughs impinge on our
everyday lives. These essays by Bill McKibben, Anwar F. Accawi, Charles H.
Townes, Donald A. Norman, and Henry Petroski offer invaluable insights into
the effects of our dependence on technology, the virtues of new hybrid electric
cars, telephone, laser, robots in the home, and the ubiquitous, humble pencil.

As a genre, science fiction has always provided an arena for new ideas
in which "what if" scenarios made possible by new technologies can be
explored. Writers such as Kurt Vonnegut, Jr. look over the horizon to where
we as a society may be going. His thought-provoking story dramatizes a
moment of rebellion in a society of the future where laws require all Americans to be made equal.

So too, poetry is the ideal medium for voicing reservations that science
and technology may be at its core antithetical to our humanity and connection

with the natural world. In a poem by Walt Whitman the speaker discovers that the stars are far more eloquent than a lecture on astronomy.

As you read works in this chapter and prepare to discuss or write about them you may wish to use the following questions as guidelines.

- What expertise or training does the writer bring to the analysis?
- What discipline or area does the writer discuss?
- Does the author approach the subject as a participant or reporter?
- What problem does the invention or discovery create or solve?
- Does the writer link the innovation to social consequences?
- How does the author adapt the technical nature of the subject for the audience?
- How does the author's treatment of the subject challenge your assumptions and/or enhance your understanding?
- Is the author enthusiastic or uncertain about the result of the invention?

Nonfiction

DAVID EWING DUNCAN

David Ewing Duncan is a contributing editor to Wired; *he has written for the* Atlantic Monthly, Harper's *magazine,* Discover, *and* Smithsonian *and was a longtime correspondent for* Life *magazine. He is the author of* Hernando De Soto: A Savage Quest in the Americas *(1997), the best-selling* Calendar: Humanity's Epic Struggle to Determine a True and Accurate Year *(1998), and other books. He was a special producer for ABC's* Nightline *and* 20/20 *and a producer for* Discovery *television. A recent work is* The Geneticist Who Played Hoops with My DNA *(2005). In the following article (which first appeared in* Wired *in November 2002 and was selected for the AAAS Journalism Award in 2003) Duncan discovers that new genetic screening capabilities will provide us (and our insurance companies) with more knowledge than we might wish to possess about our biologically fated predispositions to a wide range of diseases.*

Before You Read

Would you want to undergo a DNA screening to discover what, if any, genetic disease markers you possess or what ethnic background you come from?

DNA as Destiny

I feel naked. Exposed. As if my skin, bone, muscle tissue, cells, have all been peeled back, down to a tidy swirl of DNA. It's the basic stuff of life, the billions of nucleotides that keep me breathing, walking, craving, and just being. Eight hours ago, I gave a few cells, swabbed from inside my cheek, to a team of geneticists. They've spent the day extracting DNA and checking it for dozens of hidden diseases. Eventually, I will be tested for hundreds more. They include, as I will discover, a nucleic time bomb ticking inside my chromosomes that might one day kill me.

For now I remain blissfully ignorant, awaiting the results in an office at Sequenom, one of scores of biotech startups incubating in the canyons north of San Diego. I'm waiting to find out if I have a genetic proclivity for cancer, cardiac disease, deafness, Alzheimer's, or schizophrenia.

This, I'm told, is the first time a healthy human has ever been screened for the full gamut of genetic disease markers. Everyone has errors in his or her DNA, glitches that may trigger a heart spasm or cause a brain tumor. I'm here to learn mine.

Waiting, I wonder if I carry some sort of Pandora gene, a hereditary predisposition to peek into places I shouldn't. Morbid curiosity is an occupational hazard for a writer, I suppose, but I've never been bothered by it before. Yet now I find myself growing nervous and slightly flushed. I can feel my pulse rising, a cardiovascular response that I will soon discover has, for me, dire implications.

In the coming days, I'll seek a second opinion, of sorts. Curious about where my genes come from, I'll travel to Oxford and visit an "ancestral geneticist" who has agreed to examine my DNA for links back to progenitors whose mutations have been passed on to me. He will reveal the seeds of my individuality and the roots of the diseases that may kill me—and my children.   5

For now, I wait in an office at Sequenom, a sneak preview of a trip to the DNA doctor, circa 2008. The personalized medicine being pioneered here and elsewhere prefigures a day when everyone's genome will be deposited on a chip or stored on a gene card tucked into a wallet. Physicians will forecast illnesses and prescribe preventive drugs custom-fitted to a patient's DNA, rather than the one-size-fits-all pharmaceuticals that people take today. Gene cards might also be used to find that best-suited career, or a DNA-compatible mate, or, more darkly, to deny someone jobs, dates, and meds because their nucleotides don't measure up. It's a scenario Andrew Niccol imagined in his 1997 film, *Gattaca*, where embryos in a not-too-distant future are bio-engineered for perfection and where genism—discrimination based on one's DNA—condemns the lesser-gened to scrubbing toilets.

The *Gattaca*-like engineering of defect-free embryos is at least twenty or thirty years away, but Sequenom and others plan to take DNA testing to the masses in just a year or two. The prize: a projected $5 billion market for personalized medicine by 2006 and billions, possibly hundreds of billions, more for those companies that can translate the errors in my genome and yours into custom pharmaceuticals.

Sitting across from me is the man responsible for my gene scan: Andi Braun, chief medical officer at Sequenom. Tall and sinewy, with a long neck, glasses, and short gray hair, Braun, forty-six, is both jovial and German. Genetic tests are already publicly available for Huntington's disease and cystic fibrosis, but Braun points out that these illnesses are relatively rare. "We are targeting diseases that impact millions," he says in a deep Bavarian accent, envisioning a day when genetic kits that can assay the whole range of human misery will be available at Wal-Mart, as easy to use as a home pregnancy test.

But a kit won't tell me if I'll definitely get a disease, just if I have a bum gene. What Sequenom and others are working toward is pinning down the probability that, for example, a colon cancer gene will actually trigger a tumor. To know this, Braun must analyze the DNA of thousands of people and tally how many have the colon cancer gene, how many actually get the disease, and how many don't. Once these data are gathered and crunched, Braun will be able to tell you, for instance, that if you have the defective gene, you have a 40 percent chance, or maybe a 75 percent chance, of getting the disease by age fifty, or ninety. Environmental factors such as eating right—or wrong—and smoking also weigh in. "It's a little like predicting the weather," says Charles Cantor, the company's cofounder and chief scientific officer.

Braun tells me that, for now, his tests offer only a rough sketch of my   10
genetic future. "We can't yet test for everything, and some of the information is only partially understood," he says. It's a peek more through a rudimentary eyeglass than a Hubble Space Telescope. Yet I will be able to glimpse some of the internal programming bequeathed to me by evolution and that I, in turn, have bequeathed to my children—Sander, Danielle, and Alex, ages fifteen, thirteen, and seven. They are a part of this story, too. Here's where I squirm, because as a father I pass on not only the ingredients of life to my children but the secret codes of their demise—just as I have passed on my blue eyes and a flip in my left brow that my grandmother called "a little lick from God." DNA is not only the book of life, it is also the book of death, says Braun: "We're all going to die, *ja?*"

Strictly speaking, Braun is not looking for entire genes, the long strings of nucleotides that instruct the body to grow a tooth or create white blood cells to attack an incoming virus. He's after single nucleotide polymorphisms, or SNPs (pronounced "snips"), the tiny genetic variations that account for nearly all differences in humans.

Imagine DNA as a ladder made of rungs—3 billion in all—spiraling upward in a double helix. Each step is a base pair, designated by two letters from the nucleotide alphabet of G, T, A, and C. More than 99 percent of these base pairs are identical in all humans, with only about one in a thousand SNPs diverging to make us distinct. For instance, you might have a CG that makes you susceptible to diabetes, and I might have a CG, which makes it far less likely I will get this disease.

This is all fairly well known: Genetics 101. What's new is how startups like Sequenom have industrialized the SNP identification process. Andi Braun and Charles Cantor are finding thousands of new SNPs a day, at a cost of about a penny each.

Braun tells me that there are possibly a million SNPs in each person, though only a small fraction are tightly linked with common ailments. These disease-causing SNPs are fueling a biotech bonanza; the hope is that after finding them, the discoverers can design wonder drugs. In the crowded SNP field, Sequenom vies with Iceland-based deCode Genetics and American companies such as Millennium Pharmaceuticals, Orchid BioSciences, and Celera Genomics, as well as multinationals like Eli Lilly and Roche Diagnostics. "It's the Oklahoma Land Grab right now," says Toni Schuh, Sequenom's CEO.

The sun sets outside Braun's office as my results arrive, splayed across   15
his computer screen like tarot cards. I'm trying to maintain a steely, reportorial facade, but my heart continues to race.

Names of SNPs pop up on the screen: connexin 26, implicated in hearing loss; factor V leiden, which causes blood clots; and alpha-1 antitrypsin deficiency, linked to lung and liver disease. Beside each SNP are codes that mean nothing to me: 13q11-q12, 1q23, 14q32.1. Braun explains that these are addresses on the human genome, the P.O. box numbers of life. For instance, 1q23 is the address for a mutant gene that causes vessels to shrink and impede the flow of blood—it's on chromosome 1. Thankfully, my result is negative. "So, David, you will not get the varicose veins. That's good, *ja?*" says Braun. One gene down, dozens to go.

Next up is the hemochromatosis gene. This causes one's blood to retain too much iron, which can damage the liver. As Braun explains it, somewhere in the past, an isolated human community lived in an area where the food was poor in iron. Those who developed a mutation that stores high levels of iron survived, and those who didn't became anemic and died, failing to reproduce. However, in these iron-rich times, hemochromatosis is a liability. Today's treatment? Regular bleeding. "You tested negative for this mutation," says Braun. "You do not have to be bled."

I'm also clean for cystic fibrosis and for a SNP connected to lung cancer.

Then comes the bad news. A line of results on Braun's monitor shows up red and is marked "MT," for mutant type. My body's programming code is faulty. There's a glitch in my system. Named ACE (for angiotensin-I converting enzyme), this SNP means my body makes an enzyme that keeps my blood pressure spiked. In plain English, I'm a heart attack risk.

My face drains of color as the news sinks in. I'm not only defective, but   20
down the road, every time I get anxious about my condition, I'll know that I have a much higher chance of dropping dead. I shouldn't be surprised, since

I'm told everyone has some sort of disease-causing mutation. Yet I realize that my decision to take a comprehensive DNA test has been based on the rather ridiculous assumption that I would come out of this with a clean genetic bill of health. I almost never get sick, and, at age forty-four, I seldom think about my physical limitations or death. This attitude is buttressed by a family largely untouched by disease. The women routinely thrive into their late eighties and nineties. One great-aunt lived to age one hundred and one; she used to bake me cupcakes in her retirement home when I was a boy. And some of the Duncan menfolk are pushing ninety-plus. My parents, now entering their seventies, are healthy. In a flash of red MTs, I'm glimpsing my own future, my own mortality. I'm slated to keel over, both hands clutching at my heart.

"Do you have any history in your family of high blood pressure or heart disease?" asks Matthew McGinniss, a Sequenom geneticist standing at Braun's side.

"No," I answer, trying to will the color back into my face. Then a second MT pops up on the screen—another high blood pressure mutation. My other cardiac indicators are OK, which is relatively good news, though I'm hardly listening now. I'm already planning a full-scale assault to learn everything I can about fighting heart disease—until McGinniss delivers an unexpected pronouncement. "These mutations are probably irrelevant," he says. Braun agrees: "It's likely that you carry a gene that keeps these faulty ones from causing you trouble—DNA that we have not yet discovered."

The SNPs keep rolling past, revealing more mutations, including a type 2 diabetes susceptibility, which tells me I may want to steer clear of junk food. More bad news: I don't have a SNP called CCR5 that prevents me from acquiring HIV, nor one that seems to shield smokers from lung cancer. "*Ja,* that's my favorite," says Braun, himself a smoker. "I wonder what Philip Morris would pay for that."

By the time I get home, I realize that all I've really learned is, I might get heart disease, and I could get diabetes. And I should avoid smoking and unsafe sex—as if I didn't already know this. Obviously, I'll now watch my blood pressure, exercise more, and lay off the Cap'n Crunch. But beyond this, I have no idea what to make of the message Andi Braun has divined from a trace of my spit.

Looking for guidance, I visit Ann Walker, director of the Graduate Program for Genetic Counseling at the University of California at Irvine. Walker explains the whats and hows, and the pros and cons, of DNA testing to patients facing hereditary disease, pregnant couples concerned with prenatal disorders, and anyone else contemplating genetic evaluation. It's a tricky job because, as I've learned, genetic data are seldom clear-cut.

Take breast cancer, Walker says. A woman testing positive for BRCA1, the main breast cancer gene, has an 85 percent chance of actually getting the cancer by age seventy, a wrenching situation, since the most effective method of prevention is a double mastectomy. What if a woman has the operation and it turns out she's among those 15 percent who carry the mutation but will never get the cancer? Not surprisingly, one study, conducted in Holland, found that half of the healthy women whose mothers developed breast cancer opt not to be tested for the gene, preferring ignorance and closer monitoring. Another example is the test for APoE, the Alzheimer's gene. Since the affliction has no cure, most people don't want to know their status. But some do. A positive result, says Walker, allows them to put their affairs in order and prepare for their own dotage. Still, the news can be devastating. One biotech executive told me that a cousin of his committed suicide when he tested positive for Huntington's, having seen the disease slowly destroy his father.

Walker pulls out a chart and asks about my family's medical details, starting with my grandparents and their brothers and sisters: what they suffered and died from, and when. My Texas grandmother died at ninety-two after a series of strokes. My ninety-one-year-old Missouri grandmom was headed to a vacation in Mexico with her eighty-eight-year-old second husband when she got her death sentence—ovarian cancer. The men died younger: my grandfathers in their late sixties, though they both have brothers still alive and healthy in their nineties. To the mix, Walker adds my parents and their siblings, all of whom are alive and healthy in their sixties and seventies; then my generation; and finally our children. She looks up and smiles: "This is a pretty healthy group."

Normally, Walker says, she would send me home. Yet I'm sitting across from her, not because my parents carry some perilous SNP, but as a healthy man who is after a forecast of future maladies. "We have no real training yet for this," she says, and tells me the two general rules of genetic counseling: No one should be screened unless there is an effective treatment or readily available counseling; and the information should not bewilder people or present them with unnecessary trauma.

Many worry that these prime directives may be ignored by Sequenom and other startups that need to launch products to survive. FDA testing for new drugs can take up to ten years, and many biotech firms feel pressure to sell something in the interim. "Most of these companies need revenue," says the University of Pennsylvania's Arthur Caplan, a top bioethicist. "And the products they've got now are diagnostic. Whether they are good ones, useful ones, necessary ones, accurate ones, seems less of a concern than that they be sold." Caplan also notes that the FDA does not regulate these tests. "If it was a birth control test, the FDA would be all over it."

I ask Caplan about the *Gattaca* scenario of genetic discrimination. Will 30 a woman dump me if she finds out about my ACE? Will my insurance company hike my rate? "People are denied insurance and jobs right now," he says, citing sickle cell anemia, whose sufferers and carriers, mostly black, have faced job loss and discrimination. No federal laws exist to protect us from genism, or from insurers and employers finding out our genetic secrets. "Right now, you're likely going to be more disadvantaged than empowered by genetic testing," says Caplan.

After probing my genetic future, I jet to England to investigate my DNA past. Who are these people who have bequeathed me this tainted bloodline? From my grandfather Duncan, an avid genealogist, I already know that my paternal ancestors came from Perth, in south-central Scotland. We can trace the name back to an Anglican priest murdered in Glasgow in 1680 by a mob of Puritans. His six sons escaped and settled in Shippensburg, Pennsylvania, where their descendants lived until my great-great-grandfather moved west to Kansas City in the 1860s.

In an Oxford restaurant, over a lean steak and a heart-healthy merlot, I talk with geneticist Bryan Sykes, a linebacker-sized fifty-five-year-old with a baby face and an impish smile. He's a molecular biologist at the university's Institute of Molecular Medicine and the author of the best-selling *Seven Daughters of Eve*. Sykes first made headlines in 1994 when he used DNA to directly link a 5,000-year-old body discovered frozen and intact in an Austrian glacier to a twentieth-century Dorset woman named Marie Mosley. This stunning genetic connection between housewife and hunter-gatherer launched Sykes's career as a globe-trotting genetic gumshoe. In 1995, he confirmed that bones dug up near Ekaterinburg, Russia, were the remains of Czar Nicholas II and his family by comparing the body's DNA with that of the czar's living relatives, including Britain's Prince Philip. Sykes debunked explorer Thor Heyerdahl's *Kon-Tiki* theory by tracing Polynesian genes to Asia, not the Americas, and similarly put the lie to the *Clan of the Cave Bear* hypothesis, which held that the Neanderthal interbred with our ancestors, the Cro-Magnon, when the two subspecies coexisted in Europe 15,000 years ago.

Sykes explains to me that a bit of DNA called mtDNA is key to his investigations. A circular band of genes residing separately from the twenty-three chromosomes of the double helix, mtDNA is passed down solely through the maternal line. Sykes used mtDNA to discover something astounding: Nearly every European can be traced back to just seven women living 10,000 to 45,000 years ago. In his book, Sykes gives these seven ancestors hokey names and tells us where they most likely lived: Ursula, in Greece (circa 43,000 B.C.), and Velda, in northern Spain (circa 15,000 B.C.), to name two of the "seven daughters of Eve." (Eve was the ur-mother who lived 150,000 years ago in Africa.)

Sykes has taken swab samples from the cheeks of more than 10,000 people, charging $220 to individually determine a person's mtDNA type. "It's not serious genetics," Sykes admits, "but people like to know their roots. It makes genetics less scary and shows us that, through our genes, we are all very closely related." He recently expanded his tests to include non-Europeans. The Asian daughters of Eve are named Emiko, Nene, and Yumio, and their African sisters are Lamia, Latifa, and Ulla, among others.

Before heading to England, I had mailed Sykes a swab of my cheek cells. 35 Over our desserts in Oxford he finally offers up the results. "You are descended from Helena," he pronounces. "She's the most common daughter of Eve, accounting for some 40 percent of Europeans." He hands me a colorful certificate, signed by him, that heralds my many-times-great-grandma and tells me that she lived 20,000 years ago in the Dordogne Valley of France. More interesting is the string of genetic letters from my mtDNA readout that indicate I'm mostly Celtic, which makes sense. But other bits of code reveal traces of Southeast Asian DNA, and even a smidgen of Native American and African.

This doesn't quite have the impact of discovering that I'm likely to die of a heart attack. Nor am I surprised about the African and Indian DNA, since my mother's family has lived in the American South since the seventeenth century. But Southeast Asian? Sykes laughs. "We are all mutts," he says. "There is no ethnic purity. Somewhere over the years, one of the thousands of ancestors who contributed to your DNA had a child with someone from Southeast Asia." He tells me a story about a blond, blue-eyed surfer from Southern California who went to Hawaii to apply for monies awarded only to those who could prove native Hawaiian descent. The grant-givers laughed—until his DNA turned up traces of Hawaiian.

The next day, in Sykes's lab, we have one more test: running another ancestry marker in my Y chromosome through a database of 10,000 other Ys to see which profile is closest to mine. If my father was in the database, his Y chromosome would be identical, or possibly one small mutation off. A cousin might deviate by one tick. Someone descended from my native county of Perth might be two or three mutations removed, indicating that we share a common ancestor hundreds of years ago. Sykes tells me these comparisons are used routinely in paternity cases. He has another application. He is building up Y-chromosome profiles of surnames: men with the same last name whose DNA confirms that they are related to common ancestors.

After entering my mtDNA code into his laptop, Sykes looks intrigued, then surprised, and suddenly moves to the edge of his seat. Excited, he reports that the closest match is, incredibly, him—Bryan Sykes! "This has never happened," he says, telling me that I am a mere one mutation removed from him, and two from the average profile of a Sykes. He has not collected DNA from many other Duncans, he says, though it appears as if sometime in the past 400 years a Sykes must have ventured into Perth and then had a child with a Duncan. "That makes us not-so-distant cousins," he says. We check a map of Britain on his wall, and sure enough, the Sykes family's homeland of Yorkshire is less than 200 miles south of Perth.

The fact that Sykes and I are members of the same extended family is just a bizarre coincidence, but it points to applications beyond simple genealogy. "I've been approached by the police to use my surnames data to match up with DNA from an unknown suspect found at a crime scene," says Sykes. Distinctive genetic markers can be found at the roots of many family trees. "This is possible, to narrow down a pool of suspects to a few likely surnames. But it's not nearly ready yet."

Back home in California, I'm sweating on a StairMaster at the gym, 40
wondering about my heart. I wrap my hands around the grips and check my

pulse: 129. Normal. I pump harder and top out at 158. Also normal. I think about my visit a few days earlier—prompted by my gene scan—to Robert Superko, a cardiologist. After performing another battery of tests, he gave me the all clear—except for one thing. Apparently, I have yet another lame heart gene, the atherosclerosis susceptibility gene ATHS, a SNP that causes plaque in my cardiac bloodstream to build up if I don't exercise far more than average—which I do, these days, as a slightly obsessed biker and runner. "As long as you exercise, you'll be fine," Superko advised, a bizarre kind of life sentence that means that I must pedal and jog like a madman or face—what? A triple bypass?

Pumping on the StairMaster, I nudge the setting up a notch, wishing, in a way, that I either knew for sure I was going to die on, say, February 17, 2021, or that I hadn't been tested at all. As it is, the knowledge that I have an ACE and ATHS deep inside me will be nagging me every time I get short of breath.

The last results from my DNA workup have also come in. Andi Braun has tested me for seventy-seven SNPs linked to lifespan in order to assess when and how I might get sick and die. He has given me a score of .49 on his scale. It indicates a lifespan at least 20 percent longer than that of the average American male, who, statistically speaking, dies in his seventy-fourth year. I will likely live, then, to the age of eighty-eight. That's forty-four years of StairMaster to go.

Braun warns that this figure does not take into account the many thousands of other SNPs that affect my life, not to mention the possibility that a piano could fall on my head.

That night, I put my seven-year-old, Alex, to bed. His eyes droop under his bright white head of hair as I finish reading *Captain Underpants* aloud. Feeling his little heart beating as he lies next to me on his bed, I wonder what shockers await him inside his nucleotides, half of which I gave him. As I close the book and then sing him to sleep, I wonder if he has my culprit genes. I don't know, because he hasn't been scanned. For now, he and the rest of humanity are living in nearly the same blissful ignorance as Helena did in long-ago Dordogne. But I do know one thing: Alex has my eyebrow, the "lick of God." I touch his flip in the dark, and touch mine. He stirs, but it's not enough to wake him.

Questions for Discussion and Writing

1. What did Duncan learn about the new capabilities for screening and detecting genetic disease markers when his DNA was examined? According to Duncan, what implications does this new technology have for society in many different spheres?

2. What does Duncan's article gain by making him the guinea pig (he was the first healthy human ever to be screened) whose discoveries became very personal?

3. In a short essay, discuss some of the social implications (positive and negative) of this new technology, and state whether you would volunteer to be screened.

4. **Rhetorical inquiry:** How does Duncan's style make it easy for the average person to empathize with him and to imagine what it would be like going through the same experience?

BILL MCKIBBEN

Bill McKibben (b. 1960) is best known as the author of an international best-seller about global warming, The End of Nature *(1989). He publishes regularly in the* Atlantic Monthly, Harper's Magazine, *and the* New York Review of Books. *His most recent works are* Enough: Staying Human in an Engineered Age *(2003) and* Deep Economy *(2007). He is currently a scholar-in-residence at Middlebury College. In the following essay, which first appeared in* Mother Jones *(July/August 2002), McKibben relates his experiences with his new hybrid electric car. He inveighs against the shortsighted addiction Americans have by driving SUVs and other energy-wasting, inefficient practices so pervasive in our culture.*

Before You Read

Are gas-electric hybrid cars likely to replace those dependent on gasoline?

It's Easy Being Green

The more I surveyed my new car, the happier I got. "New car" is one of those phrases that make Americans unreasonably happy to begin with. And this one—well, it was a particularly shiny metallic blue. Better yet, it was the first Honda Civic hybrid electric sold in the state of Vermont: I'd traded in my old Civic (40 miles to the gallon), and now the little screen behind the steering wheel was telling me that I was getting 50, 51, 52 miles to the gallon. Even better yet, I was doing nothing strange or difficult or conspicuously ecological. If you didn't know there was an electric motor assisting the small gas engine—well, you'd never know. The owner's manual devoted far more space to the air bags and the heating system. It didn't look goofily Jetsonish like Honda's first hybrid, the two-seater Insight introduced in 2000. Instead, it looked like a Civic, the most vanilla car ever produced. "Our goal was to make it look, for lack of a better word, normal," explained Kevin Bynoe, spokesman for American Honda.

And the happier I got, the angrier I got. Because, as the Honda and a raft of other recent developments powerfully proved, energy efficiency, energy conservation, and renewable energy are ready for prime time. No longer the niche province of incredibly noble backyard tinkerers distilling biodiesel from used vegetable oil or building homes from Earth rammed into tires, the equipment and attitudes necessary to radically transform our energy system are now mainstream enough for those of us too lazy or too busy to try anything that seems hard. And yet the switch toward sensible energy still isn't happening. A few weeks before I picked up my car, an overwhelming bipartisan vote in the Senate had rejected calls to increase the mileage of the nation's new car fleet by 2015—to increase it to 36 mpg, not as good as the Civic I'd traded in to buy this hybrid. The administration was pressing ahead with its plan for more drilling and refining. The world was suffering the warmest winter in history as more carbon dioxide pushed global temperatures ever higher. And people were dying in conflicts across wide swaths of the world, the casualties—at least in some measure—of America's insatiable demand for energy.

In other words, the gap between what we could be doing and what we are doing has never been wider. Consider:

- The Honda I was driving was the third hybrid model easily available in this country, following in the tire tracks of the Insight and the Toyota Prius. They take regular gas, they require nothing in the way of special service, and they boast waiting lists. And yet Detroit, despite a decade of massive funding from the Clinton administration, can't sell you one. Instead, after September 11, the automakers launched a massive campaign (zero financing, red, white, and blue ads) to sell existing stock, particularly the gas-sucking SUVs that should by all rights come with their own little Saudi flags on the hood.

- Even greater boosts in efficiency can come when you build or renovate a home. Alex Wilson, editor of *Environmental Building News,* says the average American house may be 20 percent more energy efficient than it was two decades ago, but simple tweaks like better windows and bulkier insulation could save 30 to 50 percent more energy with "very little cost implication." And yet building codes do almost nothing to boost such technologies, and the Bush administration is fighting to roll back efficiency gains for some appliances that Clinton managed to push through. For instance, air-conditioner manufacturers recently won a battle in the Senate to let them get away with making their machines only 20 percent more efficient, not the 30 percent current law demands. The difference in real terms? Sixty new power plants across the country by 2030.

- Or consider electric generation. For a decade or two, environmentalists had their fingers crossed when they talked about renewables. It was hard to imagine most Americans really trading in their grid connection for backyard solar panels with their finicky batteries. But such trade-offs are less necessary by the day. Around the world, wind power is growing more quickly than any other form of energy—Denmark, Germany, Spain, and India all generate big amounts of their power from ultramodern wind turbines. But in this country, where the never-ending breeze across the High Plains could generate twice as much electricity as the country uses, progress has been extraordinarily slow. (North Dakota, the windiest state in the union, has exactly four turbines.) Wind power is finally beginning to get some serious attention from the energy industry, but the technology won't live up to its potential until politicians stop subsidizing fossil fuels and give serious boosts to the alternatives.

And not all those politicians are conservative, either. In Massachusetts, even some true progressives, like the gubernatorial candidate Robert Reich, can't bring themselves to endorse a big wind installation proposed for six miles off Cape Cod. They have lots of arguments, most of which boil down to NIVOMD (Not in View of My Deck), a position particularly incongruous since Cape Cod will sink quickly beneath the Atlantic unless every weapon in the fight against global warming is employed as rapidly as possible.

What really haunts energy experts is the sense that, for the first time   5 since the oil shocks of the early 1970s, the nation could have rallied around the cause of energy conservation and renewable alternatives last fall. In the wake of September 11, they agree, the president could have announced a pair of national goals—capture Osama and free ourselves from the oil addiction that leaves us endlessly vulnerable. "President Bush's failure will haunt me for decades," says Alan Durning, president of North-west Environment Watch. "Bush had a chance to advance, in a single blow, three pressing national priorities: national security, economic recovery, and environmental protection. All the stars were aligned." If only, says Brent Blackwelder, president of Friends of the Earth, Bush had set a goal, like JFK and the space program. "We could totally get off oil in three decades." Instead, the president used the crisis to push for drilling in the Arctic National Wildlife Refuge, a present to campaign contributors that would yield a statistically insignificant new supply ten years down the road.

It's not just new technologies that Bush could have pushed, of course. Americans were, at least for a little while, in the mood to do something, to make some sacrifice, to rally around some cause. In the words of Charles Komanoff, a New York energy analyst, "The choice is between love of oil and love of country," and at least "in the initial weeks after September 11, it seemed that Americans were awakening at last to the true cost of their addiction to oil." In an effort to take advantage of that political window, Komanoff published a booklet showing just how simple it would be to cut America's oil use by 5 or 10 percent—not over the years it will take for the new technologies to really kick in, but over the course of a few weeks and with only minor modifications to our way of life.

For instance, he calculated, we could save 7 percent of the gasoline we use simply by eliminating one car trip in fourteen. The little bit of planning required to make sure you visit the grocery store three times a week instead of four would leave us with endlessly more oil than sucking dry the Arctic.

Indeed, Americans are so energy-profligate that even minor switches save significant sums—if half the drivers in two-car households switched just a tenth of their travel to their more efficient vehicle, we'd instantly save 1 percent of our oil. Keep the damn Explorer; just leave it in the driveway once a week and drive the Camry.

A similar menu of small changes—cutting back on one airplane trip in seven, turning down the thermostat two degrees, screwing in a few compact fluorescent bulbs—and all of a sudden our endlessly climbing energy usage begins to decline. Impossible? Americans won't do it? Look at California. With the threat of power shortages looming and with some clever incentives provided by government and utilities, Californians last year found an awful lot of small ways to save energy that really added up: 79 percent reported taking some steps, and a third of households managed to cut their electric use by more than 20 percent. Not by becoming a Third World nation (the state's economy continued to grow), not by living in caves, not by suffering—but by turning off the lights when they left the room. In just the first six months of 2001, the Colorado energy guru Amory Lovins pointed out recently, "customers wiped out California's previous five to ten years of demand growth." Now the same companies that were scrambling to build new plants for the Golden State a year ago are backing away from their proposals, spooked by the possibility of an energy glut.

It's only in Washington, in fact, that nobody gets it. If you go to Europe or Asia, you'll find nations increasingly involved in planning for a different energy future: Every industrial country but the United States signed on to the Kyoto agreement at the last international conference on global warming, and some of those nations may actually meet their targets for carbon dioxide reductions. The Dutch consumer demand for green power outstrips even the capacity of their growing wind farms, while the Germans have taken the logical step of raising taxes on carbon-based fuels and eliminating them on renewable sources. Reducing fossil fuel use is an accepted, inevitable part of the political process on the Continent, the same way that "fighting crime" is in this country, and Europeans look with growing disgust at the depth of our addiction—only the events of September 11 saved America from a wave of universal scorn when Bush backed away from the Kyoto pact.

And in state capitols and city halls around this country, local leaders are   10
beginning to act as well. Voters in San Francisco last year overwhelmingly approved an initiative to require municipal purchases of solar and wind power; in Seattle, the mayor's office announced an ambitions plan to meet or beat the Kyoto targets within the confines of the city and four suburbs.

Perhaps such actions might be expected in San Francisco and Seattle. But in June of 2001, the Chicago city government signed a contract with Commonwealth Edison to buy 10 percent of its power from renewables, a figure due to increase to 20 percent in five years. And in Salt Lake City, of all places, Mayor Rocky Anderson announced on the opening day of the Winter Olympics that his city, too, was going to meet the Kyoto standards—

already, in fact, crews were at work changing lightbulbs in street lamps and planning new mass transit.

Even many big American corporations have gone much further than the Bush administration. As Alex Wilson, the green building expert, points out, "Corporations are pretty good at looking at the bottom line, which is directly affected by operating costs. They're good with numbers." If you can make your product with half the energy, well, that's just as good as increasing sales—and if you can put a windmill on the cover of your annual report, that's gravy.

In short, what pretty much everyone outside the White House has realized is this: The great economic shift of this century will be away from fossil fuels and toward renewable energy. That shift will happen with or without George W. Bush—there are too many reasons, from environmental to economic to geopolitical necessity, for it not to. But American policy can slow down the transition, perhaps by decades, and that is precisely what the administration would like to see. They have two reasons: One is the enormous debt they owe to the backers of their political careers, those coal and oil and gas guys who dictated large sections of the new energy policy. Those industries want to wring every last penny from their mines, their drill rigs, and their refineries—and if those extra decades mean that the planet's temperature rises a few degrees, well, that's business.

The other reason is just as powerful, though—it's the fear that Americans will blame their leaders if prices for gas go up too quickly. It's not an idle fear—certainly it was shared by Bill Clinton, who did nothing to stem the nation's love affair with SUVs, and by Al Gore, who, during his presidential campaign, demanded that the Strategic Petroleum Reserve be opened to drive down prices at the pump. But that's what makes Bush's post-September silence on this issue so sad. For once a U.S. president had the chance to turn it all around—to say that this was a sacrifice we needed to make and one that any patriot would support. It's tragically likely he will have the same opportunity again in the years ahead, and tragically unlikely that he will take it.

In the meantime, there's work to be done in statehouses and city halls. 15 And at the car lot—at least the ones with the Honda and Toyota signs out front. "This Civic has a slightly different front end and a roof-mounted antenna," says Honda's Bynoe. "But other than that, it looks like a regular Civic, and it drives like one too. It's not necessarily for hard-core enviros. You don't have to scream about it at the top of your lungs. It's just a car." But a very shiny blue. And I just came back from a trip to Boston: 59 miles to the gallon.

Questions for Discussion and Writing

1. According to McKibben, how easy would it actually be for Americans to free themselves from their national "oil addiction"? Why didn't reforms take hold and become permanent after September 11, 2001?

2. How effectively does McKibben communicate his sense of bafflement as to why Americans tolerate such a self-serving, backward energy policy from both car companies and the government? Does his anger seem justified? Why or why not?

3. Of the suggestions (large and small) McKibben argues for, which seem the most plausible? Explain your answer.

4. **Rhetorical inquiry:** How does McKibben use a problem-solving format to explain his decision to switch to a hybrid car?

HENRY PETROSKI

Henry Petroski (b. 1942) is a professor of civil and environmental engineering at Duke University. His works explore engineering achievements from bridges to pencils in Engineers of Dreams: Great Bridge Builders and the Spanning of America *(1995),* Remaking the World: Adventures in Engineering *(1997),* Paper Boy: Confessions of a Future Engineer *(2002), and* The Pencil: A History of Design and Circumstance *(1990), in which the following selection first appeared. A recent work is* Success through Failure: the Paradox of Design *(2006).*

Before You Read

What tasks require a pencil rather than a pen or computer?

The Pencil

Henry David Thoreau seemed to think of everything when he made a list of essential supplies for a twelve-day excursion into the Maine woods. He included pins, needles, and thread among the items to be carried in an India-rubber knapsack, and he even gave the dimensions of an ample tent: "six by seven feet, and four feet high in the middle, will do." He wanted to be doubly sure to be able to start a fire and to wash up, and so he listed: "matches (some also in a small vial in the waist-coat pocket); soap, two pieces." He specified the number of old newspapers (three or four, presumably to be used for cleaning chores), the length of strong cord (twenty feet), the size of his blanket (seven feet long), and the amount of "soft hardbread" (twenty-eight pounds!). He even noted something to leave behind: "A gun is not worth the carriage, unless you go as a huntsman."

Thoreau actually was a huntsman of sorts, but the insects and botanical specimens that he hunted could be taken without a gun and could be brought back in the knapsack. Thoreau also went into the woods as an observer. He observed the big and the little, and he advised like-minded observers to carry a small spyglass for birds and a pocket microscope for smaller objects. And to capture the true dimensions of those objects that might be too big to be brought back, Thoreau advised carrying a tape measure. The inveterate measurer, note taker, and list maker also reminded other travelers to take paper and stamps, to mail letters back to civilization.

But there is one object that Thoreau neglected to mention, one that he most certainly carried himself. For without this object Thoreau could not have sketched either the fleeting fauna he would not shoot or the larger flora he could not uproot. Without it he could not label his blotting paper pressing leaves or his insect boxes holding beetles; without it he could not record the measurements he made; without it he could not write home on the paper he brought; without it he could not make his list. Without a pencil Thoreau would have been lost in the Maine woods.

According to his friend Ralph Waldo Emerson, Thoreau seems always to have carried, "in his pocket, his diary and pencil." So why did Thoreau—who had worked with his father to produce the very best lead pencils manufactured in America in the 1840s—neglect to list even one among the essential things to take on an excursion? Perhaps the very object with which he may have been drafting his list was too close to him, too familiar a part of his own everyday outfit, too integral a part of his livelihood, too common a thing for him to think to mention.

Henry Thoreau seems not to be alone in forgetting about the pencil. 5 A shop in London specializes in old carpenter's tools. There are tools everywhere, from floor to ceiling and spilling out of baskets on the sidewalk outside. The shop seems to have an example of every kind of saw used in recent centuries; there are shelves of braces and bins of chisels and piles of levels and rows of planes—everything for the carpenter, or so it seems. What the shop does not have, however, are old carpenter's pencils, items that once got equal billing in Thoreau & Company advertisements with drawing pencils for artists and engineers. The implement that was necessary to draw sketches of the carpentry job, to figure the quantities of materials needed, to mark the length of wood to be cut, to indicate the locations of holes to be drilled, to highlight the edges of wood to be planed, is nowhere to be seen. When asked where he keeps the pencils, the shopkeeper replies that he does not think there are any about. Pencils, he admits, are often found in the toolboxes acquired by the shop, but they are thrown out with the sawdust.

In an American antique shop that deals in, among other things, old scientific and engineering instruments, there is a grand display of polished brass microscopes, telescopes, levels, balances, and scales; there are the precision instruments of physicians, navigators, surveyors, draftsmen, and engineers. The shop also has a collection of old jewelry and silverware and, behind the saltcellars, some old mechanical pencils, which appear to be there for their metal and mystery and not their utility. There are a clever Victorian combination pen and pencil in a single slender, if ornate, gold case; an unassuming little tube of brass less than two inches long that telescopes out to become a mechanical pencil of twice that length; a compact silver pencil case containing points in three colors—black, red, and blue—that can be slid into writing position; and a heavy silver pencil case that hides the half-inch stub of a still-sharpened yellow pencil of high quality. The shopkeeper will proudly show how all these work, but when asked if she has any plain wood-cased drawing pencils that the original owners of the drafting instruments must certainly have used, she will confess that she would not even know what distinguished a nineteenth-century pencil from any other kind.

Not only shops that purport to trade in the past but also museums that ostensibly preserve and display the past can seem to forget or merely ignore the indispensable role of simple objects like the pencil. Recently the Smithsonian Institution's National Museum of American History produced "After the Revolution: Everyday Life in America, 1780–1800," and one group of exhibits in the show consisted of separate worktables on which were displayed the tools of many crafts of the period: cabinet-maker and chairmaker, carpenter and joiner, shipwright, cooper, wheelwright, and others. Besides tools, many of the displays included pieces of work in progress, and a few even had wood shavings scattered about the work space, to add a sense of authenticity. Yet there was not a pencil to be seen.

While many early American craftsmen would have used sharp-pointed metal scribers to mark their work, pencils would also certainly have been used when they were available. And although there was no domestic pencil industry in America in the years immediately following the Revolution, that is not to say that pencils could not be gotten. A father, writing in 1774 from England to his daughter in what were still the colonies, sent her "one dozen Middleton's best Pencils," and in the last part of the century, even after the Revolution, English pencils like Middleton's were regularly advertised for sale in the larger cities. Imported pencils or homemade pencils fashioned from reclaimed pieces of broken lead would have been the proud possessions of wood-workers especially, for carpenters, cabinetmakers, and joiners possessed the craft skill to work wood into a form that could hold pieces of graphite in a comfortable and useful way. Not only would early American woodworkers have known about, admired, wanted to possess, and tried to imitate European pencils, but also they would have prized and cared for them as they prized and cared for the kinds of tools displayed two centuries later in the Smithsonian.

These stories of absence are interesting not so much because of what they say about the lowly status of the wood-cased pencil as an artifact as because of what they say about our awareness of and our attitudes toward common things, processes, events, or even ideas that appear to have little intrinsic, permanent, or special value. An object like the pencil is generally considered unremarkable, and it is taken for granted. It is taken for granted because it is abundant, inexpensive, and as familiar as speech.

Yet the pencil need be no cliché. It can be as powerful a metaphor as the   10
pen, as rich a symbol as the flag. Artists have long counted the pencil among the tools of their trade, and have even identified with the drawing medium. Andrew Wyeth described his pencil as a fencer's foil; Toulouse-Lautrec said of

himself, "I am a pencil"; and the Moscow-born Paris illustrator and caricaturist Emmanuel Poiré took his pseudonym from the Russian word for pencil, *karandash*. In turn, the Swiss pencil-making firm of Caran d'Ache was named after this artist, and a stylized version of his signature is now used as a company logo.

The pencil, the tool of doodlers, stands for thinking and creativity, but at the same time, as the toy of children, it symbolizes spontaneity and immaturity. Yet the pencil's graphite is also the ephemeral medium of thinkers, planners, drafters, architects, and engineers, the medium to be erased, revised, smudged, obliterated, lost—or inked over. Ink, on the other hand, whether in a book or on plans or on a contract, signifies finality and supersedes the pencil drafts and sketches. If early pencilings interest collectors, it is often because of their association with the permanent success written or drawn in ink. Unlike graphite, to which paper is like sandpaper, ink flows smoothly and fills in the nooks and crannies of creation. Ink is the cosmetic that ideas will wear when they go out in public. Graphite is their dirty truth.

A glance at the index to any book of familiar quotations will corroborate the fact that there are scores of quotations extolling the pen for every one, if that, mentioning the pencil. Yet, while the conventional wisdom may be that the pen is mightier than the sword, the pencil has come to be the weapon of choice of those wishing to make better pens as well as better swords. It is often said that "everything begins with a pencil," and indeed it is the preferred medium of designers. In one recent study of the nature of the design process, engineers balked when they were asked to record their thought processes with a pen. While the directors of the study did not want the subjects to be able to erase their false starts or alter their records of creativity, the engineers did not feel comfortable or natural without a pencil in their hands when asked to comment on designing a new bridge or a better mousetrap.

Leonardo da Vinci seems to have wished to make a better everything, as his notebooks demonstrate. And when he wanted to set down his ideas for some new device, or when he merely wanted to record the state of the art of Renaissance engineering, he employed a drawing. Leonardo also used drawings to preserve his observations of natural facts, artifacts, and assorted phenomena, and he even sketched his own hand sketching. This sketch is usually identified as Leonardo's left hand, consistent with the widely held belief that the genius was left-handed. This trait in turn has been given as a reason for his mirror writing. However, it has also been convincingly argued that Leonardo was basically right-handed and was forced to use his left hand because his right was crippled in an accident. Thus Leonardo's sketch may really be of his maimed right hand as seen in a mirror by the artist drawing with his fully functioning left hand. The shortened and twisted middle finger in the sketch supports this view.

The precise nature of the drawing instrument in Leonardo's hand may also be open to some interpretation, but it appears most likely to be a small brush known from Roman times as a pencil. The lead pencil as we know it today does not seem to have existed in Leonardo's lifetime (1452–1519). Some of his sketches were done in metal point, but drawing with a pointed rod of silver or some alloy usually had to done on specially coated paper so that an otherwise faint mark would be enhanced. Some drawings were first outlined in metalpoint and then more or less traced over with a pen or a fine-pointed brush dipped in ink. This was the only kind of pencil Leonardo knew.

Questions for Discussion and Writing

1. Why is it significant that Henry David Thoreau, of all people, should have neglected to mention the pencil when he was listing items needed for a twelve-day camping trip?
2. How do Petroski's anecdotes illustrate the fact that the pencil is so common that it has become all but invisible and a special effort is needed to discover how truly indispensable it has always been?
3. Discuss the distinction Petroski makes between what we write using a pencil and using a pen. What other items that are overlooked and taken for granted are really quite successful engineering achievements (for example, zippers, safety pins, paper clips, sticky notes, and pop-top aluminum cans)? Research the history of any of these and write up your findings. Is there a product or invention that you wish existed? Describe it, and create an advertising campaign that extolls its virtues.
4. **Rhetorical inquiry:** How does Petroski's visit to a shop in London that specialized in old carpenter's tools and to an American antique shop confirm his theory that this indispensable tool is taken for granted?

Anwar F. Accawi

Anwar F. Accawi was born and grew up in Magdaluna, Lebanon, and was educated in the United States. Originally, he wrote stories so that his children would know something about the country he was from. He has written essays as well as stories and teaches at the University of Tennessee. In the following essay first published in The Sun *in 1997, Accawi describes how the communal life in Magdaluna shifted to center around the first telephone to be installed. "The Telephone" was included in the* Best American Essays 1998, *edited by Cynthia Ozick.*

Before You Read

What size network of family and friends has the telephone or cell phone made possible for you?

The Telephone

When I was growing up in Magdaluna, a small Lebanese village in the ter-raced, rocky mountains east of Sidon, time didn't mean much to anybody, except maybe to those who were dying, or those waiting to appear in court because they had tampered with the boundary markers on their land. In those days, there was no real need for a calendar or a watch to keep track of the hours, days, months, and years. We knew what to do and when to do it, just as the Iraqi geese knew when to fly north, driven by the hot wind that blew in from the desert, and the ewes knew when to give birth to wet lambs that stood on long, shaky legs in the chilly March wind and baaed hesi-tantly, because they were small and cold and did not know where they were or what to do now that they were here. The only timepiece we had need of then was the sun. It rose and set, and the seasons rolled by, and we sowed seed and harvested and ate and played and married our cousins and had babies who got whooping cough and chickenpox—and those children who survived grew up and married *their* cousins and had babies who got whoop-ing cough and chickenpox. We lived and loved and toiled and died without ever needing to know what year it was, or even the time of day.

It wasn't that we had no system for keeping track of time and of the important events in our lives. But ours was a natural—or rather, a divine—calender, because it was framed by acts of God Allah himself set down the milestones with earthquakes and droughts and floods and locusts and pesti-lences. Simple as our calendar was, it worked just fine for us.

Take, for example, the birth date of Teta Im Khalil, the oldest woman in Magdaluna and all the surrounding villages. When I first met her, we had just returned home from Syria at the end of the Big War and were living with Grandma Mariam. Im Khalil came by to welcome my father home and to take a long, myopic look at his foreign-born wife, my mother. Im Khalil was so old that the skin of her cheeks looked like my father's grimy tobacco pouch, and when I kissed her (because Grandma insisted that I show her old friend affec-tion), it was like kissing a soft suede glove that had been soaked with sweat and then left in a dark closet for a season. Im Khalil's face got me to wonder-ing how old one had to be to look and taste the way she did. So, as soon as she had hobbled off on her cane, I asked Grandma, "How old is Teta Im Khalil?"

Grandma had to think for a moment; then she said, "I've been told that Teta was born shortly after the big snow that caused the roof on the mayor's house to cave in."

"And when was that?" I asked.

"Oh, about the time we had the big earthquake that cracked the wall in the east room."

Well, that was enough for me. You couldn't be more accurate than that, now, could you? Satisfied with her answer, I went back to playing with a ball made from an old sock stuffed with other, much other socks.

5

And that's the way it was in our little village for as far back as anybody could remember: people were born so many years before or after an earthquake or a flood; they got married or died so many years before or after a long drought or a big snow or some other disaster. One of the most unusual of these dates was when Antoinette the seamstress and Saeed the barber (and tooth puller) got married. That was the year of the whirlwind during which fish and oranges fell from the sky. Incredible as it may sound, the story of the fish and oranges was true, because men—respectable men, like Abu George the blacksmith and Abu Asaad the mule skinner, men who would not lie even to save their own souls—told and retold that story until it was incorporated into Magdaluna's calendar, just like the year of the black moon and the year of the locusts before it. My father, too, confirmed the story for me. He told me that he had been a small boy himself when it had rained fish and oranges from heaven. He'd gotten up one morning after a stormy night and walked out into the yard to find fish as long as his forearm still flopping here and there among the wet navel oranges.

The year of the fish-bearing twister, however, was not the last remarkable year. Many others followed in which strange and wonderful things happened: milestones added by the hand of Allah to Magdaluna's calendar. There was, for instance, the year of the drought, when the heavens were shut for months and the spring from which the entire village got its drinking water slowed to a trickle. The spring was about a mile from the village, in a ravine that opened at one end into a small, flat clearing covered with fine gray dust and hard, marble-sized goat droppings, because every afternoon the goatherds brought their flocks there to water them. In the year of the drought, that little clearing was always packed full of noisy kids with big brown eyes and sticky hands, and their months—sinewy, overworked young women with protruding collarbones and cracked, callused brown heels. The children ran around playing tag or hide-and-seek while the while women talked, shooed flies, and awaited their turns to fill up their jars with drinking water to bring home to their napping men and wet habies. There were days when we had to wait from sunup until late afternoon just to fill a small clay jar with precious, cool water.

Sometimes, amid the long wait and the heat and the flies and the smell of goat dung, tempers flared, and the younger women, anxious about their babies, argued over whose turn it was to fill up her jar. And sometimes the arguments escalated into full-blown, khockdown-dragout fights; the women would grab each other by the hair and curse and scream and spit and call each other names that made my ears tingle. We little brown boys who went with our mothers to fetch water loved these fights, because we got to see the women's legs and their colored panties as they grappled and rolled around in the dust. Once in a while, we got lucky and saw much more, because some of the women wore nothing at all under their long dresses. God, how I used to look forward to those fights. I remember the rush, the excitement, the sun 10 dancing on the dust clouds as a dress ripped and a young white breast was revealed, then quickly hidden. In my calendar, that year of drought will always be one of the best years of my childhood, because it was then, in a dusty clearing by a trickling mountain spring, I got my first glimpses of the wonders, the mysteries, and the promises hidden beneath the folds of a woman's dress. Fish and oranges from heaven . . . you can get over that.

But, in another way, the year of the drought was also one of the worst of my life, because that was the year that Abu Raja, the retired cook who used to entertain us kids by cracking walnuts on his forehead, decided it was time Magdaluna got its own telephone. Every civilized village needed a telephone, he said, and Magdaluna was not going to get anywhere until it had one. A telephone would link us with the outside world. At the time, I was too young to understand the debate, but a few men—like Shukri, the retired Turkish-army drill sergeant, and Abu Hanna the vineyard keeper—did all they could to talk Abu Raja out of having a telephone brought to the village. But they were outshouted and ignored and finally shunned by the other villagers for resisting progress and trying to keep a good thing from coming to Magdaluna.

One warm day in early fall, many of the villagers were out in their fields repairing walls or gathering wood for the winter when the shout went out that the telephone-company truck had arrived at Abu Raja's *dikkan,* or country store. There were no roads in those days, only footpaths and dry steambeds, so it took the telephone-company truck almost a day to work its way up the rocky terrain from Sidon—about the same time it took to walk. When the truck came into view, Abu George, who had a huge voice and, before the telephone, was Magdaluna's only long-distance communication system, bellowed the news from his front porch. Everybody dropped what they were doing and ran to Abu Raja's house to see what was happening. Some of the more digni-fied villagers, however, like Abu Habeeb and Abu Nazim, who had been to big cities like Beirut and Damascus and had seen things like telephones and telegraphs, did not run the way the rest did; they walked with their canes hanging from the crooks of their arms, as if on a Sunday afternoon stroll.

It did not take long for the whole village to assemble at Abu Raja's *dikkan.* Some of the rich villagers, like the widow Farha and the gendarme Abu Nadeem, walked right into the store and stood at the elbows of the two important-looking men from the telephone company, who proceeded with utmost gravity, like priests at Communion, to wire up the telephone. The poorer villagers stood outside and listened carefully to the details relayed to them by the not-so-poor people who stood in the doorway and could see inside.

"The bald man is cutting the blue wire," someone said.

"He is sticking the wire into the hole in the bottom of the black box," 15
someone else added.

"The telephone man with the mustache is connecting two pieces of wire. Now he is twisting the ends together," a third voice chimed in.

Because I was small and unaware that I should have stood outside with the other poor folk to give the rich people inside more room (they seemed to need more of it than poor people did), I wriggled my way through the dense forest of legs to get a first-hand look at the action. I felt like the barefoot Moses, sandals in hand, staring at the burning bush on Mount Sinai. Breathless, I watched as the men in blue, their shirt pockets adorned with fancy lettering in a foreign language, put together a black machine that supposedly would make it possible to talk with uncles, aunts, and cousins who lived more than two days' ride away.

It was shortly after sunset when the man with the mustache announced that the telephone was ready to use. He explained that all Abu Raja had to do was lift the receiver, turn the crank on the black box a few times, and wait for an operator to take his call. Abu Raja, who had once lived and worked in Sidon, was impatient with the telephone man for assuming that he was ignorant. He grabbed the receiver and turned the crank forcefully, as if trying to start a Model T Ford. Everybody was impressed that he knew what to do. He even called the operator by her first name. "Centralist." Within moments, Abu Raja was talking with his brother, a concierge in Beirut. He didn't even have to raise his voice or shout to be heard.

If I hadn't seen it with my own two eyes and heard it with my own two ears, I would not have believed it—and my friend Kameel didn't. He was away that day watching his father's goats, and when he came back to the village that evening, his cousin Habeen and I told him about the telephone and how Abu Raja had used it to speak with his brother in Beirut. After he heard our report, Kameel made the sign of the cross, kissed his thumbnail, and warned us that lying was a bad sin and would surely land us in purgatory. Kameel believed in Jesus and Mary, and wanted to be a priest when he grew up. He always crossed himself when Habeeb, who was irreverent, and I, who was Presbyterian, were around, even when we were not bearing bad news.

And the telephone, as it turned out, was bad news. With its coming, the   20
face of the village began to change. One of the first effects was the shifting of the village's center. Before the telephone's arrival, the men of the village used to gather regularly at the house of Im Kaleem, a short, middle-aged widow with jet-black hair and a raspy voice that could be heard all over the village, even when she was only whispering. She was a devout Catholic and also the village *shlikki*—whore. The men met at her house to argue about politics and drink coffee and play cards or backgammon. Im Kaleem was not a true prostitute, however, because she did not charge for her services—not even for the coffee and tea (and, occasionally, the strong liquor called arrack) that she served the men. She did not need the money; her son, who was overseas in Africa, sent her money regularly. (I knew this because my father used to read her son's letters to her and take down her replies, as Im Kaleem could not read and write.) Im Kaleem was no slut either—unlike some women in the village—because she loved all the men she entertained, and they loved her, every one of them. In a way, she was married to all the men in

the village. Everybody knew it—the wives knew it; the itinerant Catholic priest knew it; the Presbyterian minister knew it—but nobody objected. Actually, I suspect the women (my mother included) did not mind their husband's visits to Im Kaleem. Oh, they wrung their hands and complained to one another about their men's unfaithfulness, but secretly they were relieved, because Im Kaleem took some of the pressure off them and kept the men out of their hair while they attended to their endless chores. Im Kaleem was also a kind of confessor and troubleshooter, talking sense to those men who were having family problems, especially the younger ones.

Before the telephone came to Magdaluna, Im Kaleem's house was bustling at just about any time of day, especially at night, when its windows were brightly lit with three large oil lamps, and the loud voices of the men talking, laughing, and arguing could be heard in the street below—a reassuring, homey sound. Her house was an island of comfort, an oasis for the weary village men, exhausted from having so little to do.

But it wasn't long before many of those men—the younger ones especially—started spending more of their days and evenings at Abu Raja's *dikkan.* There, they would eat and drink and talk and play checkers and backgammon, and then lean their chairs back against the wall—the signal that they were ready to toss back and forth, like a ball, the latest rumors going around the village. And they were always looking up from their games and drinks and talk to glance at the phone in the corner, as if expecting it to ring any minute and bring news that would change their lives and deliver them from their aimless existence. In the meantime, they smoked cheap, hand-rolled cigarettes, dug dirt out from under their fingernails with big pocketknives, and drank lukewarm sodas that they called Kacula, Seffen-Ub, and Bebsi. Sometimes, especially when it was hot, the days dragged on so slowly that the men turned on Abu Saeed, a confirmed bachelor who practically lived in Abu Raja's *dikkan,* and teased him for going around barefoot and unshaven since the Virgin has appeared to him behind the olive press.

The telephone was also bad news for me personally. It took away my lucrative business—a source of much-needed income. Before the telephone came to Magdaluna, I used to hang around Im Kaleem's courtyard and play marbles with the other kids, waiting for some man to call down from a window and ask me to run to the store for cigarettes or arrack, or to deliver a message to his wife, such as what he wanted for supper. There was always something in it for me: a ten-or even a twenty-five-piaster piece. On a good day, I ran nine or ten of those errands, which assured a steady supply of marbles that I usually lost to Sami or his cousin Hani, the basket weaver's boy. But as the days went by, fewer and fewer men came to Im Kaleem's, and more and more congregated at Abu Raja's to wait by the telephone. In the evenings, no light fell from her window onto the street below, and the laughter and noise of the men trailed off and finally stopped. Only Shukri, the retired Turkish-army drill sergeant, remained faithful to Im Kaleem after all the other men had deserted her; he was still seen going into or leaving her house from time to time. Early that winter, Im Kaleem's hair suddenly turned turned gray, and she got sick and old. Her legs started giving her trouble, making it hard for her to walk. By spring she hardly left her house anymore.

At Abu Raja's *dikkan,* the calls did eventually come, as expected, and men and women started leaving the village the way a hailstorm begins: first one, then two, then bunches. The army took them. Jobs in the cities lured them. And ships and airplanes carried them to such faraway places as Australia and Brazil and New Zealand. My friend Kameel, his cousin Habeeb, and their cousins and my cousins all went away to become ditch diggers and mechanics and butcher-shop boys and deli owners who wore dirty aprons sixteen hours a day; all looking for a better life than the one they had left behind. Within a year, only the sick, the old, and the maimed were left in the village. Magdaluna became a skeleton of its former self, desolate and forsaken, like the tombs, a place to get away from.

Finally, the telephone took my family away, too. My father got a call 25 from an old army buddy who told him that an oil company in southern Lebanon was hiring interpreters and instructors. My father applied for a job and got it, and we moved to Sidon, where I went to a Presbyterian missionary school and graduated in 1962. Three years later, having won a scholarship, I left Lebanon for the United States. Like the others who left Magdaluna before me, I am still looking for that better life.

Questions for Discussion and Writing

1. Before the arrival of the telephone how did people in Accawi's village measure time and keep track of important events? After its installation, how did the social life of the village begin to change?
2. What specific examples best illustrate the effects, both small and large, produced by the installation of the telephone?
3. Have you ever been away from your telephone or other electronic means of communicating for a period of time? Were there positive effects to this deprivation?
4. **Rhetorical inquiry:** What examples illustrate how unusual events in his village were remembered before the advent of the telephone?

CHARLES H. TOWNES

Charles H. Townes, born in 1915, received a Ph.D. in physics from the California Institute of Technology in 1939. He was chairman of the physics department at Columbia University from 1952 to 1955 and professor of physics and provost at the Massachusetts Institute of Technology from 1961 to 1966. Since 1967, Townes has been university professor of physics at the University of California at Berkeley. His research into molecular and nuclear structure, masers, lasers, and quantum electronics resulted in his being awarded the Nobel prize in Physics in 1964. Townes's current research interests are in microwave spectroscopy and radio and infrared astronomy. In "Harnessing Light" (1984), Townes tells about the research that led to the discovery of the laser and defines the distinctive qualities of this new technological phenomenon.

Before You Read

How many laser-based applications cross your path everyday?

Harnessing Light

The laser was born early one beautiful spring morning on a park bench in Washington, D.C. As I sat in Franklin Square, musing and admiring the azaleas, an idea came to me for a practical way to obtain a very pure form of electromagnetic waves from molecules. I had been doggedly searching for new ways to produce radio waves at very high frequencies, too high for the vacuum tubes of he day to generate. This short-wavelength radiation, I felt, would permit extremely accurate measurement and analysis, giving new insights into physics and chemistry.

As it turned out, I was much too conservative; the field has developed far beyond my imagination and along paths I could not have foreseen at the time. Surveyors use the laser to guarantee straight lines; surgeons to weld new corneas into place and burn away blood clots, industry to drill tiny, precise holes; communications engineers to send information in vast quantities through glass fiber pipers. It is even built into the supermarket checkout scanner that reads prices by bouncing a beam of laser light off a pattern imprinted on the item.

But in the spring of 1951, as I sat on my park bench, it was all yet to come. In the quest for short-wavelength radio waves, I built on the knowledge of the time. In general terms, it was this. Atoms and molecules can absorb radiation as light, as radio waves, or as heat. The radiation is absorbed in the form one energy level to a higher one by exactly the amount of absorbed energy. The atom excited in this way may spontaneously fall to a lower energy level. As it does, it gives up a quantum of radiant energy and releases a burst of electromagnetic radiation, usually in the form of light. This happens in the sun, where atoms are exited by hear agitation or radiation and then drop to a lower level of energy, releasing light. But I was focusing on another way of producing radiation, understood in theory since Einstein discussed it in 1917: the stimulated emission of radiation.

In this case, radiation such as light passing by stimulates an atom to give up its energy to the radiation, at exactly the same frequency and radiated in exactly the same direction, and then drop to a lower state. If this process happened naturally, light striking one side of a black piece of pare would happens in a laser. But such extraordinary behavior requires and unusual condition: More atoms must be in an excited energy state than in a lower energy one.

That morning in the park, I realized that if man was to obtain wave-   5
lengths shorter than those that could be produced by vauum tubes, he must use the ready-made small devices known as atoms and molecules. And I saw that by creating this effect in a chamber with certain critical dimensions, the stimulated radiation could be reinforced; becoming steady and intense.

Later discussions with my students at Columbia University over lunch produced a new vocabulary. We chose the name "maser," for microwave amplification by stimulated emission of radiation, for a device based on the fundamental principle. We also proposed, somewhat facetiously, the "iraser" (infrared amplification by stimulated emission of radiation), "laser" (light amplification), and "xaser" (X-ray amplification). Maser and laser stuck.

The first device to use the new amplifying mechanism was a maser built around ammonia gas, since the ammonia molecule was known to interact more strongly than any other with microwaves. A three-year thesis project of graduated student James Gordon, with assistance from Herber Zeiger, a young postdoctoral physicist, succeeded and immediately demonstrated the extreme purity of the frequency of radiation produced by the natural vibra-tions of ammonia molecules. A pure frequency can be translated into accu-rate timekeeping. Suppose we know that the power from a wall outlet has a frequency of exactly 60 cycles one second. It then takes exactly 1/60th of a second to completed one cycle, one second to complete 60 cycles, one minute for 3,600 of them, and so on. To build an accurate clock, we have only to count the cycles. In the mid-1950s, when the first ammonia maser was com-pleted, the best clocks had a precision of about one part in a billion, about the same accuracy of the Earth's rotation about its axis. Today, a hydrogen maser is the heart of an atomic clock accurate to one part in 100 trillion, an improvement by a factor of at least 10,000. Such a clock, if kept running, would be off by no more than one second in every few million years.

The new process also immediately provided an amplifier for radio waves much more sensitive than the best then available. Later refinements provided very practical amplifiers, and masers now are typically used to communicate in space over long distances and to pick up radio waves from distant galaxies. Astrophysicists recently have discovered *natural* masers in interstellar space that generate enormous microwave intensity from excited molecules.

Although my main interest in stimulated emission of radiation had been to obtain wavelengths shorter than microwaves, the new possibilities for superaccurate clocks and supersensitive amplifiers, and their scientific uses, occupied everyone's attention for some time. By 1957 I felt it was time to get back on the track of shorter wavelengths. I decided that it would actu-ally be easier to make a big step than a small one and jump immediately to light waves—wavelengths in the visible or short infrared, almost 10,000 times higher in frequency than microwaves. But there was a sticky problem: What kind of resonating chamber would function at a single and precisely correct frequency but could be built using ordinary engineering techniques? My friend Arthur Schawlow, then at the Bell Telephone Laboratories, helped provide the answer: an elongated chamber with a mirror at each end.

In December of 1958 we published a paper that discussed this and other aspects of a practical laser and set off an intense wave of efforts to build one. In 1960 Theodore H. Maiman, a physicist with Hughes Aircraft Company, demonstrated the first operating laser, while Ali Javan, William R. Bennett Jr., and Donald R. Herriott at Bell Labs built a second, completely different type. Rather than using gas, Maiman's laser used a small cylinder of synthetic ruby, its ends polished into mirrored surfaces. The firing of a helical flashbulb surrounding the rod triggered the ruby to send out a brief, intense pulse of laser light. Soon there were many variations on the laser theme, using different atoms or molecules and different methods of providing them with energy, but all used a mirrored chamber.

The laser quickly gained great notoriety with the public as a "death ray"; it is a popular science fiction motif and one with undeniable dramatic appeal. Lasers certainly have the power to injure. Even a weak laser shone into the eye will be focused by the lens of the eye onto the retina and damage it. But laser beams are not very advantageous as military weapons. Guns are cheaper, easier to build and use, and, in most cases, much more effective. Science fiction's death ray is still mostly science fiction, and it is likely to remain so.

The laser is, however, extremely powerful. The reason is that stimulated amplification adds energy "coherently"—that is, in exactly the same direction as the initial beam. This coherence conveys surprising properties. A laser emitting one watt of light has only a hundredth the power of a 100 watt light bulb. Yet the beam of a one-watt laser directed at the moon was seen by television equipment on the lunar surface when all the lights of our greatest cities were undetectable—simply because the beam is so directional. A simple lens can focus the beam of light from an ordinary one-watt laser into a spot so small that it produces 100 million watts per square centimeter, enormously greater than the intensity from any other type of source.

But a one-watt laser is not even a particularly powerful one. Pulsed lasers can produce a *trillion* watts of power by delivering energy over a very short period but at enormous levels. This power may last only one ten-billionth of a second, but during that time a lens can concentrate it to a level of 100 million million million watts per square centimeter. The trillion watts that such a laser delivers is approximately equal to the average amount of electric power being used over the entire Earth at any one time. Focused by a lens, this concentration or power is 100 trillion times greater than the light at the surface of the sun. It will melt or tear apart any substance, including atoms themselves. Drilling through diamonds is easy for a laser beam and produces no wear. Lasers have been developed that can compact small pellets of material and then heat them in a sudden flash to reproduce conditions similar to those in the sun's interior, where nuclear fusion occurs.

The laser's directed intensity quickly made it an effective industrial tool. Lasers cut or weld delicate electronic circuits or heavy metal parts. They can melt or harden the surface of a piece of steel so quickly that under a very thin skin, the metal is still cool and undamaged. Industrial interest was especially high. By the end of the 1960s, most new lasers were being designed in industrial laboratories, though many are important tools in university laboratories.

How useful lasers and quantum electronics have been to scientists is   15
indicated by the fact that besides Nobel Prizes for work leading to the devices themselves, they have played an important role in other Nobel awards—for example, the one to Dennis Gabor of the University of London for the idea of holography (three-dimensional laser photography); the one to Schawlow of Stanford University for versatile new types of laser spectroscopy; to Nicolaas Bloembergen of Harvard University for discoveries in nonlinear optics made possible by high-intensity laser beams; and one to Arno Penzias and Robert W. Wilson of the Bell Telephone Laboratories for the discovery of microwave radiation from the Big Bang which initiated our universe. While the latter discovery might possibly have been made by other techniques, it was facilitated by very sensitive maser amplification.

Because of the unswerving directionality of laser beams, probably more lasers have been sold for producing the straight lines needed in surveying than for any other single purpose. The laser is now a common surveying instrument that helps to lay out roads.

Laser beams also can measure distance conveniently. By bouncing the beam from a reflector, a surveyor can measure distances to high precision. Beams sent from Earth have been bounced off reflectors placed on the moon by astronauts. By generating a short light pulse and measuring the elapsed time before it returns, the distance to the moon can be measured within one inch. Such measurements have revealed effects of general relativity and thus refined our knowledge of the theory of gravitation.

In scientific equipment or simply in machine shops, the laser's pure frequency allows the beam to be reflected and the peaks and troughs of its wave matched with those of the first part of the beam, thus providing distance measurements to within a small fraction of one wavelength—40 millionths of an inch. In scientific experiments, changes of length as small as one hundredth of the diameter of an atom have been measured in this way. There are efforts to use such supersensitive measurements to detect the gravity waves due to motions of distant stars.

Because lasers can be so finely focused and their intensity adjusted to make controlled cuts, they are used as a surgeon's scalpel. Not only can they be very precisely directed, but a particular color can be chosen to destroy certain types of tissue while leaving others relatively intact, an especially valuable effect for some cancers. In cutting, the laser also seals off blood vessels so that there is relatively little bleeding. For the eye, laser light has the interesting ability to go harmlessly through the pupil and perform operations within.

Of all the ways our lives are likely to be affected by lasers, perhaps none   20 will be so unobtrusive and yet more important than cheaper and more effective communications. Within many metropolitan areas, the number of radio or television stations must be limited because the number of available frequencies is limited. For the same reason, large numbers of conversations cannot simultaneously be carried on a single telephone wire. But light is a superhighway of frequencies; a single light beam can, in principle, carry all the radio and TV stations and all telephone calls in the world without interfering with one another. These light beams can be transmitted on glass fibers one-tenth the size of a human hair. In crowded cities where streets have been dug up for years and jammed beneath with all manner of pipes and wires, these tiny fibers can fit into the smallest spaces and provide enormous communication capacity. In long distance communication, they may replace most cable, and even satellites.

Even after the laser was invented and its importance recognized, it was by no means clear, even to those who worked on it, that it would see so many striking applications. And much undoubtedly lies ahead.

How does this image of engine testing at Ford's Laser Lab illustrate the way the laser can be used?

Questions for Discussion and Writing

1. What unique properties does the laser possess that makes it such an incredible invention?
2. How does Townes use an operational definition to give his readers insight into the distinctive nature of his invention? That is, how does he define the laser by describing what it does through a range of applications?
3. In a paragraph or two, discuss current laser applications that you find impressive.
4. **Rhetorical inquiry:** How does Townes's description of his thoughts as he sat on the park bench make us realize the conceptual breakthrough he reached before constructing the apparatus to produce the effect he imagined?

DONALD A. NORMAN

Donald A. Norman is a professor of computer science and psychology at Northwestern University and cofounder of the Neilsen Norman Group, a consulting firm that promotes human-centered products and services. His books include The Design of Everyday Things *(1988),* Things That Make Us Smart *(1993), and* The Invisible Computer *(1998). The following selection is drawn from* Emotional Design: Why We Love (or Hate) Everyday Things *(2004).*

Before You Read

Would you prefer robots to be more human or more mechanical?

Emotional Robots

> The 1980s was the decade of the PC, the 90s of the Internet, but I believe the decade just starting will be the decade of the robot.
>
> —*Sony Corporation Executive*

Suppose we wish to build a robot capable of living in the home, wandering about, fitting comfortably into the family—what would it do? When asked this question, most people first think of handing over their daily chores. The robot should be a servant, cleaning the house, taking care of the chores. Everyone seems to want a robot that will do the dishes or the laundry. Actually, today's dishwashers and clothes washers and dryers could be considered to be very simple, special-purpose robots, but what people really have in mind is something that will go around the house and collect the dirty dishes and clothes, sort and wash them, and then put them back to their proper places—

after, of course, pressing and folding the clean clothes. All of those tasks are quite difficult, beyond the capabilities of the first few generations of robots.

Today, robots are not yet household objects. They show up in science fairs and factory floors, search-and-rescue missions, and other specialized events. But this will charge. Sony has announced this to be the decade of the robot, and even if Sony is too optimistic; I do predict that robots will blossom forth during the first half of the twenty-first century.

Robots will take many forms. I can imagine a family of robot appliances in the kitchen—refrigerator, pantry, coffeemaker, cooking, and dishwasher robots—all configured to communicate with one another and to transfer food, dishes, and utensils back and forth. The home servant robot wanders about, picking up dirty dishes, delivering them to the dishwasher robot. The dishwasher, in turn, delivers clean dishes and utensils to the robot pantry, which stores them until needed by person or robot. The pantry, refrigerator, and cooking robots work smoothly to prepare the day's menu and, finally, place the completed meal onto dishes provided by the pantry robot.

Some robots will take care of children by playing with them, reading to them, singing songs. Educational toys are already doing this, and the sophisticated robot could act as a powerful tutor, starting with the alphabet, reading, and arithmetic, but soon expanding to almost any topic. Neal Stephenson's science fiction novel, *The Diamond Age*, does a superb job of showing how an interactive book, *The Young Lady's Illustrated Primer,* can take over the entire education of young girls from age four through adulthood. The illustrated primer is still some time in the future, but more limited tutors are already in existence. In addition to education, some robots will do household chores: vacuuming, dusting, and cleaning up. Eventually their range of abilities will expand. Some may end up being built into homes or furniture. Some will be mobile, capable of wandering about on their own.

These developments will require a coevolutionary process of adaptation for both people and devices. This is common with our technologies: we reconfigure the way we live and work to make things possible for our machines to function. The most dramatic coevolution is the automobile system, for which we have altered our homes to include garages and driveways sized and equipped for the automobile, and built a massive worldwide highway system, traffic signaling systems, pedestrian passageways, and huge parking lots. Homes, too, have been transformed to accommodate the multiple wires and pipes of the ever-increasing infrastructure of modern life: hot and cold water, waste return, air vents to the roof, heating and cooling ducts, electricity, telephone, television, internet and home computer and entertainment networks. Doors have to be wide enough for our furniture, and many homes have to accommodate wheelchairs and people using walkers. Just as we have accommodate the home for all these changes, I expect modification to accommodate robots. Slow modification, to be sure, but as robots increase in usefulness, we will ensure their success by minimizing obstacles and, eventually, building charging stations, cleaning and maintenance places, and so on. After all, the vacuum cleaner robot will need a place to empty its dirt, and the garbage robot will need to be able to carry the garbage outside the home. I wouldn't be surprised to see robot quarters in homes, that is, specially built niches where the robots can reside, out of the way, when they are not active. We have closets and pantries for today's appliances, so why not ones especially equipped for robots, with doors that can be controlled by the robot, electrical outlets, interior lights so robots can see to clean themselves (and plug themselves into the outlets), and waste receptacles where appropriate.

Robots, especially at first, will probably require smooth floors, without obstacles. Door thresholds might have to be eliminated or minimized. Some locations—especially stairways—might have to be especially marked, perhaps with lights, infrared transmitters, or simply special reflective tape. Barcodes or distinctive markers posted here and there in the home would enormously simplify the robot's ability to recognize its location.

Consider how a servant robot might bring a drink to its owner. Ask for a can of soda, and off goes the robot, obediently making its way to the kitchen and the refrigerator, which is where the soda is kept. Understanding the command and navigating to the refrigerator are relatively simple. Figuring out how to open the door, find the can, and extract it is not so simple. Giving the servant robot the dexterity, the strength, and the non-slip wheels that would allow it to pull open the refrigerator door is quite a feat. Providing the vision system that can find the soda, especially if it is completely hidden behind other food items, is difficult, and then figuring out how to extract the can without destroying objects in the way is beyond today's capabilities in robot arms.

How much simpler it would be if there were a drink dispenser robot tailored to the needs of the servant robot. Imagine a drink-dispensing robot appliance capable of holding six or twelve cans, refrigerated, with an automatic door and a push-arm. The servant robot could go to the drink robot, announce its presence and its request (probably by an infrared or radio signal), and place its tray in front of the dispenser. The drink robot would slide open its door, push out a can, and close the door again: no complex vision, no dexterous arm, no forceful opening of the door. The servant robot would receive the can on its tray, and then go back to its owner.

In a similar way, we might modify the dishwasher to make it easier for a home robot to load it with dirty dishes, perhaps give it special trays with designated slots for different dishes. But as long as we are doing that, why not make the pantry a specialized robot, one capable of removing the clean dishes from the dishwasher and storing them for later use? The special trays would help the pantry as well. Perhaps the pantry could automatically deliver cups to the coffeemaker and plates to the home cooking robot, which is, of course, connected to refrigerator, sink, and trash. Does this sound farfetched? Perhaps, but, in fact, our household appliances are already complex, many of them with multiple connections to services. The refrigerator has connections to electric power and water. Some are already connected to the internet. The dishwasher and clothes washer have electricity, water and sewer connections. Integrating these units so that they can work smoothly with one another does not seem all that difficult.

I imagine that the home will contain a number of specialized robots: the servant is perhaps the most general purpose, but it would work together with a cleaning robot, the drink dispensing robot, perhaps some outside gardening robots, and a family of kitchen robots, such as dishwasher, coffee-making, and pantry robots. As these robots are developed, we will probably also design specialized objects in the home that simplify the tasks for the robots, coevolving robot and home to work smoothly together. Note that the end result will be better for people as well. Thus, the drink dispenser robot would allow anyone to walk up to it and ask for a can, except that you wouldn't use infrared or radio, you might push a button or perhaps just ask.

I am not alone in imagining this coevolution of robots and homes. Rodney Brooks, one of the world's leading roboticists, head of the MIT Artificial Intelligence Laboratory and founder of a company that builds home and commercial robots, imagines a rich ecology of environments and robots, with specialized ones living on devices, each responsible to keep its domain clean: one does the bathtub, another the toilet; one does windows, another manipulates mirrors. Brooks even contemplates a robot dining room table, with storage area and dishwasher built into its base so that "when we want to set the table, small robotic arms, not unlike the ones in a jukebox, will bring the required dishes and cutlery out onto the place settings. As each course is finished, the table and its little robot arms would grab the plates and devour them into the large internal volume underneath."

What should a robot look like? Robots in the movies often look like people, with two legs, two arms, and a head. But why? Form should follow function. The fact that we have legs allows us to navigate irregular terrain, something an animal on wheels could not do. The fact that we have two hands allows us to lift and manipulate, with one hand helping the other. The humanoid shape has evolved over eons of interaction with the world to cope efficiently and effectively with it. So, where the demands upon a robot are similar to those upon people, having a similar shape might be sensible.

If robots don't have to move—such as drink, dishwasher, or pantry robots—they need not have any means of locomotion, neither legs nor wheels. If the robot is a coffeemaker, it should look like a coffeemaker, modified to allow it to connect to the dishwasher and pantry. Robot vacuum cleaners and lawn mowers already exist, and their appearance is perfectly suited to their tasks: small, squat devices, with wheels. A robot car should look like a car. It is only the general-purpose home servant robots that are apt to look like animals or humans. The robot dining room table envisioned by Brooks would be especially bizarre, with a large central column to house the dishes and dishwashing equipment (complete with electric power, water and sewer connections). The top of the table would have places for the robot arms to manipulate the dishes and probably some stalk to hold the cameras that let the arms know where to place and retrieve the dishes and cutlery.

Should a robot have legs? Not if it only has to maneuver about on smooth surfaces—wheels will do for this; but if it has to navigate irregular terrain or stairs, legs would be useful. In this case, we can expect the first legged robots to have four or six legs: balancing is far simpler for four- and six-legged creatures than for those with only two legs.

If the robot is to wander about a home and pick up after the occupants, it   15 probably will look something like an animal or a person: a body to hold the batteries and to support the legs, wheels, or tracks for locomotion; hands to pick up objects; and cameras (eyes) on top where they can better survey the environment. In other words, some robots will look like an animal or human, not because this is cute, but because it is the most effective configuration for the task. These robots will probably look something like R2D2 a cylindrical or rectangular body on top of some wheels, tracks, or legs; some form of manipulable arm or tray; and sensors all around to detect obstacles, stairs, people, pets, other robots, and, of course the objects they are supposed to interact with. Except for pure entertainment value, it is difficult to understand why we would ever want a robot that looked like C3PO.

In fact, making a robot humanlike might backfire, making it less acceptable. Masahiro Mori, a Japanese roboticist, has argued that we are least accepting of creatures that look very human, but that perform badly, a concept demonstrated in film and theater by the terrifying nature of zombies and monsters (think of Frankenstein's monster) that take on human form, but with inhuman movement and ghastly appearance. We are not nearly so dismayed—or frightened—by nonhuman shapes and forms. Even perfect replicas of humans might be problematic, for even if the robot could not be distinguished from humans, this very lack of distinction can lead to emotional angst (a theme explored in many a science fiction novel, especially Philip K. Dick's *Do Androids Dream of Electric Sheep?* and, in movie version, *Blade Runner*). According to this line of argument, C3PO gets away with its humanoid form because it is so clumsy, both in manner and behavior, that it appears more cute or even irritating than threatening.

Robots that serve human needs—for example, robots as pets—should probably look like living creatures, if only to tap into our visceral system, which is prewired to interpret human and animal body language and facial expressions. Thus, an animal or a childlike shape together with appropriate body actions, facial expressions, and sounds will be most effective if the robot is to interact successfully with people.

Questions for Discussion and Writing

1. What different forms will robots in the home take in the near future and what tasks will they perform? How will homes have to be modified to accommodate the new mechanical inhabitants?
2. How does Norman use expert testimony to enhance his analysis? Does he establish a plausible scenario? Why or why not?

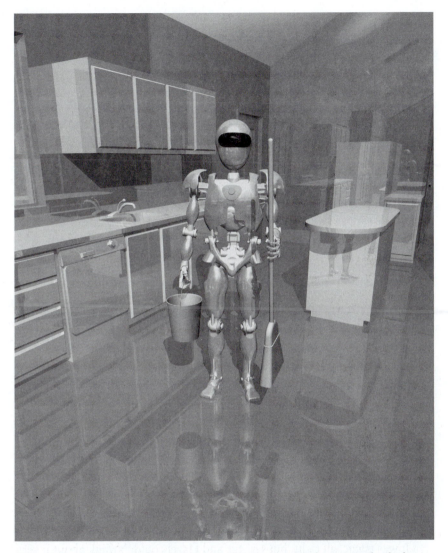

What clues in this image of a computer model alert you to the expected role domestic robots will play as discussed by Donald A. Norman in "Emotional Robots"?

3. What additional uses or applications can you imagine for these emotionals robots (such as therapists, bartenders, tutors)?
4. **Rhetorical inquiry:** How does Norman's analysis make clear that successful products must appeal to us on three levels: the visceral, the behavioral, and the reflective? What does he mean by each of these and how might robots in the home be designed to meet these criteria?

Fiction

KURT VONNEGUT, JR.

Kurt Vonnegut, Jr. (1922–2007) was born in Indianapolis, attended Cornell University, and was drafted into the infantry in World War II. His experience surviving the Allied firebombing of Dresden where he was sent after he was captured by the Germans formed the basis of Slaughterhouse Five *(1969). Vonnegut is enormously prolific and has written many short stories for magazines as well as scores of novels. "Harrison Bergeron" is reprinted from* Welcome to the Monkey House *(1968) and describes a future society devoted to an enforced equality that reduces everyone to the lowest common denominator.*

Before You Read

How does satire "push the envelope" in ridiculing absurd governmental policies?

Harrison Bergeron

The year was 2081, and everybody was finally equal. They weren't only equal before God and the law. They were equal every which way. Nobody was smarter than anybody else. Nobody was better looking than anybody else. Nobody was stronger or quicker than anybody else. All this equality was due to the 211th, 212th, and 213th Amendments to the Constitution, and to the unceasing vigilance of agents of the United States Handicapper General.

Some things about living still weren't quite right, though. April, for instance, still drove people crazy by not being springtime. And it was in that clammy month that the H-G men took George and Hazel Bergeron's fourteen-year-old son, Harrison, away.

It was tragic, all right, but George and Hazel couldn't think about it very hard. Hazel had a perfectly average intelligence, which meant she couldn't think about anything except in short bursts. And George, while his intelligence was way above normal, had a little mental handicap radio in his ear. He was required by law to wear it at all times. It was tuned to a government transmitter. Every twenty seconds or so, the transmitter would send out some sharp noise to keep people like George from taking unfair advantage of their brains.

George and Hazel were watching television. There were tears on Hazel's cheeks, but she'd forgotten for the moment what they were about.

On the television screen were ballerinas.   5

A buzzer sounded in George's head. His thoughts fled in panic, like bandits from a burglar alarm.

"That was a real pretty dance, that dance they just did," said Hazel.

"Huh?" said George.

"That dance—it was nice," said Hazel.

"Yup," said George. He tried to think a little about the ballerinas. They   10
weren't really very good—no better than anybody else would have been, anyway. They were burdened with sashweights and bags of birdshot, and their
faces were masked, so that no one, seeing a free and graceful gesture or a
pretty face, would feel like something the cat drug in. George was toying with
the vague notion that maybe dancers shouldn't be handicapped. But he didn't
get very far with it before another noise in his ear radio scattered his thoughts.

George winced. So did two of the eight ballerinas.

Hazel saw him wince. Having no mental handicap herself, she had to
ask George what the latest sound had been.

"Sounded like somebody hitting a milk bottle with a ball peen hammer," said George.

"I'd think it would be real interesting, hearing all the different sounds,"
said Hazel, a little envious. "All the things they think up."

"Um," said George.   15

"Only, if I was Handicapper General, you know what I would do?" said
Hazel. Hazel, as a matter of fact, bore a strong resemblance to the Handicapper General, a woman named Diana Moon Glampers. "If I was Diana Moon
Glampers," said Hazel, "I'd have chimes on Sunday—just chimes. Kind of in
honor of religion."

"I could think, if it was just chimes," said George.

"Well—maybe make 'em real loud," said Hazel. "I think I'd make a
good Handicapper General."

"Good as anybody else," said George.

"Who knows better'n I do what normal is?" said Hazel.   20

"Right," said George. He began to think glimmeringly about his abnormal son who was now in jail, about Harrison, but a twenty-one-gun salute
in his head stopped that.

"Boy!" said Hazel, "that was a doozy, wasn't it?"

It was such a doozy that George was white and trembling, and tears
stood on the rims of his red eyes. Two of the eight ballerinas had collapsed
on the studio floor, were holding their temples.

"All of a sudden you look so tired," said Hazel. "Why don't you stretch
out on the sofa, so's you can rest your handicap bag on the pillows, honey-
bunch." She was referring to the forty-seven pounds of birdshot in a canvas
bag, which was padlocked around George's neck. "Go on and rest the bag for
a little while," she said. "I don't care if you're not equal to me for a while."

George weighed the bag with his hands. "I don't mind it," he said.   25
"I don't notice it any more. It's just a part of me."

"You been so tired lately—kind of wore out," said Hazel. "If there was
just some way we could make a little hole in the bottom of the bag, and just
take out a few of them lead balls. Just a few."

"Two years in prison and two thousand dollars fine for every ball I took out," said George. "I don't call that a bargain."

"If you could just take a few out when you came home from work," said Hazel. "I mean—you don't compete with anybody around here. You just set around."

"If I tried to get away with it," said George, "then other people'd get away with it—and pretty soon we'd be right back to the dark ages again, with everybody competing against everybody else. You wouldn't like that, would you?"

"I'd hate it," said Hazel.   30

"There you are," said George. "The minute people start cheating on laws, what do you think happens to society?"

If Hazel hadn't been able to come up with an answer to this question, George couldn't have supplied one. A siren was going off in his head.

"Reckon it'd fall all apart," said Hazel.

"What would?" said George blankly.

"Society," said Hazel uncertainly. "Wasn't that what you just said?"   35

"Who knows?" said George.

The television program was suddenly interrupted for a news bulletin. It wasn't clear at first as to what the bulletin was about, since the announcer, like all announcers, had a serious speech impediment. For about half a minute, and in a state of high excitement, the announcer tried to say, "Ladies and gentleman—"

He finally gave up, handed the bulletin to a ballerina to read.

"That's all right—" Hazel said to the announcer, "he tried. That's the big thing. He tried to do the best he could with what God gave him. He should get a nice raise for trying so hard."

"Ladies and gentlemen—" said the ballerina, reading the bulletin. She   40
must have been extraordinarily beautiful, because the mask she wore was hideous. And it was easy to see that she was the strongest and most graceful of all the dancers, for her handicap bags were as big as those worn by two-hundred-pound men.

And she had to apologize at once for her voice, which was a very unfair voice for a woman to use. Her voice was a warm, luminous, timeless melody. "Excuse me—" she said, and she began again, making her voice absolutely uncompetitive.

"Harrison Bergeron, age fourteen," she said in a grackle squawk, "has just escaped from jail, where he was held on suspicion of plotting to over-throw the government. He is a genius and an athlete, is under-handicapped, and should be regarded as extremely dangerous."

A police photograph of Harrison Bergeron was flashed on the screen upside down, then sideways, upside down again, then right side up. The pic-ture showed the full length of Harrison against a background calibrated in feet and inches. He was exactly seven feet tall.

The rest of Harrison's appearance was Halloween and hardware. Nobody had ever borne heavier handicaps. He had outgrown hindrances faster than the H-G men could think them up. Instead of a little ear radio for a mental handicap, he wore a tremendous pair of earphones, and spectacles with thick wavy lenses. The spectacles were intended to make him not only half blind, but to give him whanging headaches besides.

Scrap metal was hung all over him. Ordinarily, there was a certain symmetry, a military neatness to the handicaps issued to strong people, but Harrison looked like a walking junkyard. In the race of life, Harrison carried three hundred pounds. 45

And to offset his good looks, the H-G men required that he wear at all times a red rubber ball for a nose, keep his eyebrows shaved off, and cover his even white teeth with black caps at snaggle-tooth random.

"If you see this boy," said the ballerina, "do not—I repeat, do not—try to reason with him."

There was the shriek of a door being torn from its hinges.

Screams and barking cries of consternation came from the television set. The photograph of Harrison Bergeron on the screen jumped again and again, as though dancing to the tune of an earthquake.

George Bergeron correctly identified the earthquake, and well he might have—for many was the time his own home had danced to the same crashing tune. "My God—" said George, "that must be Harrison!" 50

The realization was blasted from his mind instantly by the sound of an automobile collision in his head.

When George could open his eyes again, the photograph of Harrison was gone. A living, breathing Harrison filled the screen.

Clanking, clownish, and huge, Harrison stood in the center of the studio. The knob of the uprooted studio door was still in his hand. Ballerinas, technicians, musicians, and announcers cowered on their knees before him, expecting to die.

"I am the Emperor!" cried Harrison. "Do you hear? I am the Emperor! Everybody must do what I say at once!" He stamped his foot and the studio shook.

"Even as I stand here—" he bellowed, "crippled, hobbled, sickened— I am a greater ruler than any man who ever lived! Now watch me become what I *can* become!" 55

Harrison tore the straps of his handicap harness like wet tissue paper, tore straps guaranteed to support five thousand pounds.

Harrison's scrap-iron handicaps crashed to the floor.

Harrison thrust his thumbs under the bars of the padlock that secured his head harness. The bar snapped like celery. Harrison smashed his headphones and spectacles against the wall.

He flung away his rubber-ball nose, revealed a man that would have awed Thor, the god of thunder.

"I shall now select my Empress!" he said, looking down on the cowering   60
people. "Let the first woman who dares rise to her feet claim her mate and
her throne!"

A moment passed, and then a ballerina arose, swaying like a willow.

Harrison plucked the mental handicap from her ear, snapped off her
physical handicaps with marvelous delicacy. Last of all, he removed her mask.

She was blindingly beautiful.

"Now—" said Harrison, taking her hand, "shall we show the people
the meaning of the word dance? Music!" he commanded.

The musicians scrambled back into their chairs, and Harrison stripped   65
them of their handicaps, too. "Play your best," he told them, "and I'll make
you barons and dukes and earls."

The music began. It was normal at first—cheap, silly, false. But Harrison
snatched two musicians from their chairs, waved them like batons as he sang
the music as he wanted it played. He slammed them back into their chairs.

The music began again and was much improved.

Harrison and his Empress merely listened to the music for a while—
listened gravely, as though synchronizing their heartbeats with it.

They shifted their weights to their toes.

Harrison placed his big hands on the girl's tiny waist, letting her sense   70
the weightlessness that would soon be hers.

And then, in an explosion of joy and grace, into the air they sprang!

Not only were the laws of the land abandoned, but the law of gravity
and the laws of motion as well.

They reeled, whirled, swiveled, flounced, capered, gamboled, and spun.

They leaped like deer on the moon.

The studio ceiling was thirty feet high, but each leap brought the   75
dancers nearer to it.

It became their obvious intention to kiss the ceiling.

They kissed it.

And then, neutralizing gravity with love and pure will, they remained
suspended in air inches below the ceiling, and they kissed each other for a
long, long time.

It was then that Diana Moon Glampers, the Handicapper General,
came into the studio with a double-barreled ten gauge shotgun. She fired
twice, and the Emperor and the Empress were dead before they hit the floor.

Diana Moon Glampers loaded the gun again. She aimed it at the musi-   80
cians and told them they had ten seconds to get their handicaps back on.

It was then that the Bergerons' television tube burned out.

Hazel turned to comment about the blackout to George. But George
had gone out into the kitchen for a can of beer.

George came back in with the beer, paused while a handicap signal shook
him up. And then he sat down again. "You been crying?" he said to Hazel.

"Yup," she said.

"What about?" he said.   85
"I forgot," she said. "Something real sad on television."
"What was it?" he said.
"It's all kind of mixed up in my mind," said Hazel.
"Forget sad things," said George.
"I always do," said Hazel.   90
"That's my girl," said George. He winced. There was the sound of a
rivetting gun in his head.
"Gee—I could tell that one was a doozy," said Hazel.
"You can say that again," said George.
"Gee—" said Hazel, "I could tell that one was a doozy."

Questions for Discussion and Writing

1. In the year 2081 what reforms have required all Americans to be made equal to each other? How has this been applied to Harrison Bergeron and his parents?
2. In what way does Harrison Bergeron momentarily escape these limitations that have been put upon him? What effects does his rebellion have for the social system?
3. What aspects of our society is Vonnegut satirizing in this story and is it relevant in today's world?
4. **Rhetorical inquiry:** How does the performance of Harrison Bergeron with the ballerina seen on television embody all of those qualitites that the society of the future has sought to eliminate?

Poetry

WALT WHITMAN

Walt Whitman (1819–1892) was born in then-rural Huntington, Long Island, into a family of Quakers. The family later moved to Brooklyn, then a city of fewer than 10,000, where he worked as a carpenter. He attended school briefly and in 1830 went to work as an office boy but soon turned to printing and journalism. Until the 1850s he worked as a newspaperman. He was the editor of the Brooklyn Eagle *from 1846 to 1848. In 1855, Whitman published the first of many editions of* Leaves of Grass, *a work that was to prove to be of unparalleled influence in establishing him as one of the most innovative figures of nineteenth-century poetry. In subsequent editions, he showed himself capable of writing long, intricately orchestrated poems that embrace the ideals of working-class democracy expressed in experimental free-verse rhythms and realistic imagery. When the Civil War broke out, Whitman was too old to enlist but went to the front in 1862 to be with his brother George, who had been reported wounded. During the remainder of the war, Whitman served as a nurse tending wounded soldiers, Union and Confederate alike. In "When I Heard the Learn'd Astronomer" (1865), Whitman contrasts the poet's disenchantment with the impersonal coldness of rational science with a mystical appreciation of nature.*

Before You Read

What would appeal to you more—hearing a lecture on astronomy or looking at the stars?

When I Heard the Learn'd Astronomer

When I heard the learn'd astronomer,
When the proofs, the figures, were ranged in columns before me,
When I was shown the charts and diagrams, to add, divide, and
    measure them,
When I sitting heard the astronomer where he lectured with much
    applause in the lecture-room,
How soon unaccountable I became tired and sick,   5
Till rising and gliding out I wander'd off by myself,
In the mystical moist night-air, and from time to time,
Look'd up in perfect silence at the stars.

Questions for Discussion and Writing

1. How is Whitman's description of what the astronomer is trying to do critical of the scientist's approach? How does he feel listening to the astronomer's lecture?
2. What feelings do the speaker get from looking at the stars? What words best reflect this mood?
3. In a short essay, discuss Whitman's attitudes toward science and nature as expressed in this poem.
4. **Rhetorical inquiry:** How does the progressively longer opening lines of the poem put the reader in the situation of the speaker who cannot wait to leave the lecture hall?

Connections for Chapter 9: Science and Technology

1. **David Ewing Duncan**, *DNA as Destiny*
   Which is a greater discovery, the invention of the laser by Charles H. Townes or the decoding of DNA?
2. **Bill McKibben**, *It's Easy Being Green*
   If adopted, would McKibben's suggestions mean the end of "The Culture of Consumerism" described by Juliet B. Schor (in Chapter 5)? Why or why not?
3. **Henry Petroski**, *The Pencil*
   How is the lowly taken-for-granted pencil as important as the laser invented by Charles H. Townes (see "Harnessing Light")?
4. **Anwar F. Accawi**, *The Telephone*
   Compare and contrast the social effects of the telephone in Accawi's village with the foreseeable changes in the home discussed by Donald A. Norman in "Emotional Robots."
5. **Charles H. Townes**, *Harnessing Light*
   How do lasers offer a new form of artistic impression beyond traditional forms described by Ross King in "Michelangelo and the Pope's Ceiling" (in Chapter 10)?
6. **Donald A. Norman**, *Emotional Robots*
   How might the emotional robots described by Norman change society as much as the installation of the telephone did in Anwar F. Accawi's village in Lebanon?
7. **Kurt Vonnegut, Jr.**, *Harrison Bergeron*
   How are both this story and Aldous Huxley's essay, "Propaganda under a Dictatorship" (in Chapter 4) based on the concept of a "Big Brother" intrusiveness into the private life of the average citizen?
8. **Walt Whitman**, *When I Heard the Learn'd Astronomer*
   Discuss the conflict between nature and civilization in Whitman's poem and in Haunani-Kay Trask's essay ("From a Native Daughter" in Chapter 7).

10

THE ARTISTIC IMPULSE

One's destination is never a place, but rather a new way of looking at things.

Henry Miller, *"The Oranges of the Millennium"*

Although the criteria for what constitutes art change from age to age and culture to culture, artists deepen, enrich, and extend our knowledge of human nature and experience. The pleasures we derive from listening to music, reading, looking at paintings, and other creative endeavors add immeasurably to our appreciation of life. Essays by Kurt Vonnegut, Jr. and Stephen King bring different perspectives to the question of what constitutes good writing, whether writing is an inborn talent, and how to learn from the works of great writers of the past.

Ross King explains why Michelangelo began painting the ceiling of the Sistine Chapel with a fresco depicting Noah and the Flood. Agnes De Mille describes the influence of the Russian ballerina, Pavlova, on her life and art. The American composer, Aaron Copland, takes us behind the scenes of a recording studio to reveal techniques used in scoring music for films. Lance Morrow examines the role photography has played in shaping our perception of key moments in history. Germaine Greer examines the significance of body piercing, tatooing, and scarification as art forms in cultures throughout the world. Valerie Steele and John S. Major reveal the unsuspected cultural forces that compelled women in China to practice foot binding as the epitome of style.

Carson McCullers tells the whimsical story of a music teacher whose lively imagination transforms her world and touches the lives of all who know her.

Emily Dickinson suggests that poetry creates its effects through indirect means. Charles Bukowski formulates a test for would-be poets to know whether they have the urgent need to communicate their feelings and ideas.

As you read works in this chapter and prepare to discuss or write about them you may wish to use the following questions as guidelines.

- In what way does the art form investigated by the author enrich human experience?
- Does the author approach the art under discussion as a practioner or observer?

- How does the author characterize the particular art—writing, painting, dance, music, photography, fashion, being analyzed?
- What idea or concept does the author wish to communicate to the reader?
- How did the writer enhance your understanding of a particular art form?
- How do your reactions to the subject coincide or differ from the author's?
- What insight does the author provide into the value of art for society?

Nonfiction

Kurt Vonnegut, Jr.

Kurt Vonnegut, Jr. (1922–2007) is the author of such iconoclastic masterpieces as Cat's Cradle *(1963),* Slaughterhouse Five *(1969),* Sirens of Titan *(1971),* Breakfast of Champions *(1973), and* Timequake *(1993) as well as innumerable short stories written for magazines. He is well qualified to offer practical advice on writing with style, as the unique voice Vonnegut creates in his fiction makes his work a joy to read. In 1999 he wrote a book with Lee Stringer about writing,* Like Shaking Hands with God: A Conversation About Writing. God Bless You, Dr. Kevorkian *(2000) is an ironic allusion to his 1965 novel* God Bless You, Mr. Rosewater. *A recent work is* A Man Without a Country *(2005).*

Before You Read

Who are some of the writers whose style you admire?

How to Write with Style

Newspaper reporters and technical writers are trained to reveal almost nothing about themselves in their writings. This makes them freaks in the world of writers, since almost all of the other ink-stained wretches in that world reveal a lot about themselves to readers. We call these revelations, accidental and intentional, elements of style.

These revelations tell us as readers what sort of person it is with whom we are spending time. Does the writer sound ignorant or informed, stupid or bright, crooked or honest, humorless or playful—? And on and on.

Why should you examine your writing style with the idea of improving it? Do so as a mark of respect for your readers, whatever you're writing. If you scribble your thoughts any which way, your readers will surely feel that you care nothing about them. They will mark you down as an egomaniac or a chowder head—or worse, they will stop reading you.

The most damning revelation you can make about yourself is that you do not know what is interesting and what is not. Don't you yourself like or dislike writers mainly for what they choose to show you or make you think about? Did you ever admire an empty-headed writer for his or her mastery of the language? No.

So your own winning style must begin with ideas in your head.   5

1. Find a Subject You Care About

Find a subject you care about and which you in your heart feel others should care about. It is this genuine caring, and not your games with language, which will be the most compelling and seductive element in your style.

I am not urging you to write a novel, by the way—although I would not be sorry if you wrote one, provided you genuinely cared about something. A petition to the mayor about a pothole in front of your house or a love letter to the girl next door will do.

2. Do Not Ramble, Though

I won't ramble on about that.

3. Keep It Simple

As for your use of language: Remember that two great masters of language, William Shakespeare and James Joyce, wrote sentences which were almost childlike when their subjects were most profound. "To be or not to be?" asks Shakespeare's Hamlet. The longest word is three letters long. Joyce, when he was frisky, could put together a sentence as intricate and as glittering as a necklace for Cleopatra, but my favorite sentence in his short story "Eveline" is this one: "She was tired." At that point in the story, no other words could break the heart of a reader as those three words do.

Simplicity of language is not only reputable, but perhaps even sacred.   10
The *Bible* opens with a sentence well within the writing skills of a lively fourteen-year-old: "In the beginning God created the heaven and the earth."

4. Have the Guts to Cut

It may be that you, too, are capable of making necklaces for Cleopatra, so to speak. But your eloquence should be the servant of the ideas in your head. Your rule might be this: If a sentence, no matter how excellent, does not illuminate your subject in some new and useful way, scratch it out.

5. Sound Like Yourself

The writing style which is most natural for you is bound to echo the speech you heard when a child. English was the novelist Joseph Conrad's third language, and much that seems piquant in his use of English was no doubt colored by his first language, which was Polish. And lucky indeed is the writer who has grown up in Ireland, for the English spoken there is so amusing and musical. I myself grew up in Indianapolis, where common speech sounds like a band saw cutting galvanized tin, and employs a vocabulary as unornamental as a monkey wrench.

In some of the more remote hollows of Appalachia, children still grow up hearing songs and locutions of Elizabethan times. Yes, and many Americans grow up hearing a language other than English, or an English dialect a majority of Americans cannot understand.

All these varieties of speech are beautiful, just as the varieties of butterflies are beautiful. No matter what your first language, you should treasure it all your life. If it happens not to be standard English, and if it shows itself when you write standard English, the result is usually delightful, like a very pretty girl with one eye that is green and one that is blue.

I myself find that I trust my own writing most, and others seem to trust it most, too, when I sound most like a person from Indianapolis, which is what I am. What alternatives do I have? The one most vehemently recommended by teachers has no doubt been pressed on you, as well: to write like cultivated Englishmen of a century or more ago. 15

6. SAY WHAT YOU MEAN TO SAY

I used to be exasperated by such teachers, but am no more. I understand now that all those antique essays and stories with which I was to compare my own work were not magnificent for their datedness or foreignness, but for saying precisely what their authors meant them to say. My teachers wished me to write accurately, always selecting the most effective words, and relating the words to one another unambiguously, rigidly, like parts of a machine. The teachers did not want to turn me into an Englishman after all. They hoped that I would become understandable—and therefore understood. And there went my dream of doing with words what Pablo Picasso did with paint or what any number of jazz idols did with music. If I broke all the rules of punctuation, had words mean whatever I wanted them to mean, and strung them together higgledy-piggledy, I would simply not be understood. So you, too, had better avoid Picasso-style or jazz-style-writing, if you have something worth saying and wish to be understood.

Readers want our pages to look very much like pages they have seen before. Why? This is because they themselves have a tough job to do, and they need all the help they can get from us.

7. PITY THE READERS

They have to identify thousands of little marks on paper, and make sense of them immediately. They have to *read,* an art so difficult that most people don't really master it even after having studied it all through grade school and high school—twelve long years.

So this discussion must finally acknowledge that our stylistic options as writers are neither numerous nor glamorous, since our readers are bound to be such imperfect artists. Our audience requires us to be sympathetic and patient teachers, even willing to simplify and clarify—whereas we would rather soar high above the crowd, singing like nightingales.

That is the bad news. The good news is that we Americans are governed under a unique Constitution, which allows us to write whatever we please without fear of punishment. So the most meaningful aspect of our styles, which is what we choose to write about, is utterly unlimited.   20

8. For Really Detailed Advice

For a discussion of literary style in a narrower sense, in a more technical sense, I commend to your attention *The Elements of Style,* by William Strunk, Jr., and E. B. White (Macmillan, 1979). E. B. White is, of course, one of the most admirable literary stylists this country has so far produced.

You should realize, too, that no one would care how well or badly Mr. White expressed himself, if he did not have perfectly enchanting things to say.

Questions for Discussion and Writing

1. To what extent has Vonnegut followed his own advice? How would you characterize the voice he creates in this essay?
2. Why does Vonnegut use Shakespeare and Joyce as examples to illustrate the value of simplicity in language? Did you find the similes and metaphors Vonnegut uses to be particularly effective in getting his ideas across?
3. Rewrite a paragraph or two from a recent essay of yours following Vonnegut's seven suggestions. Which version did you prefer and why? You might wish to read any of Vonnegut's novels to see whether he follows his own advice.
4. **Rhetorical inquiry**: How do Vonnegut's similes appeal to one or another of the senses? For example, look at the way he characterizes his own speech in para. 5? Where else has he used wry wit and humor to encourage his readers to appreciate good writing?

Stephen King

Stephen King (b. 1947) is a successful author of innumerable works in the fantasy, supernatural, and horror genres. Most of his books have been made into popular movies. A few of these works have attained the status of classics, including Carrie *(1974),* The Shining *(1977),* Misery *(1987), and* Cujo *(1991). He has also written dramatic novellas such as* Rita Hayworth and the Shawshank Redemption *(1982) and* Stand By Me *(1982), both of which became films. In June 1999, King was gravely injured by a van that sideswiped him as he walked down a country road in Maine where he lives. After intensive therapy he has almost completely recovered. He described his experiences in* On Writing *(2000), from which the following selection (a compendium of useful advice to would-be writers) is drawn. His latest works include* Dark Tower *(2004),* Cell: A Novel *(2006), and* Lisey's Story: A Novel *(2006).*

Before You Read

Would you take advice on how to write more readily from Stephen King than from classic authors?

On Writing

If you want to be a writer, you must do two things above all others: read a lot and write a lot. There's no way around these two things that I'm aware of, no shortcut.

I'm a slow reader, but I usually get through seventy or eighty books a year, mostly fiction. I don't read in order to study the craft; I read because I like to read. It's what I do at night, kicked back in my blue chair. Similarly, I don't read fiction to study the art of fiction, but simply because I like stories. Yet there is a learning process going on. Every book you pick up has its own lesson or lessons, and quite often the bad books have more to teach than the good ones.

When I was in the eighth grade, I happened upon a paperback novel by Murray Leinster, a science fiction pulp writer who did most of his work during the forties and fifties, when magazines like *Amazing Stories* paid a penny a word. I had read other books by Mr. Leinster, enough to know that the quality of his writing was uneven. This particular tale, which was about mining in the asteroid belt, was one of his less successful efforts. Only that's too kind. It was terrible, actually, a story populated by paper-thin characters and driven by outlandish plot developments. Worst of all (or so it seemed to me at the time), Leinster had fallen in love with the word *zestful.*

Characters watched the approach of ore-bearing asteroids with *zestful smiles.* Characters sat down to supper aboard their mining ship with *zestful anticipation.* Near the end of the book, the hero swept the large-breasted, blonde heroine into a *zestful embrace.* For me, it was the literary equivalent of a smallpox vaccination: I have never, so far as I know, used the word *zestful* in a novel or a story. God willing, I never will.

Asteroid Miners (which wasn't the title, but that's close enough) was an important book in my life as a reader. Almost everyone can remember losing his or her virginity, and most writers can remember the first book he/she put down thinking: *I can do better than this. Hell, I am doing better than this!*   5

What could be more encouraging to the struggling writer than to realize his/her work is unquestionably better than that of someone who actually got paid for his/her stuff?

One learns most clearly what not to do by reading bad prose—one novel like *Asteroid Miners* (or *Valley of the Dolls, Flowers in the Attic,* and *The Bridges of Madison County,* to name just a few) is worth a semester at a good writing school, even with the superstar guest lecturers thrown in.

Good writing, on the other hand, teaches the learning writer about style, graceful narration, plot development, the creation of believable characters, and truth-telling. A novel like *The Grapes of Wrath* may fill a new writer with feelings of despair and good old-fashioned jealousy—"I'll never be able to write anything that good, not if I live to be a thousand"—but such feelings can also serve as a spur, goading the writer to work harder and aim higher. Being swept away by a combination of great story and great writing—of being flattened, in fact—is part of every writer's necessary formation. You cannot hope to sweep someone else away by the force of your writing until it has been done to you.

So we read to experience the mediocre and the outright rotten; such experience helps us to recognize those things when they begin to creep into our own work, and to steer clear of them. We also read in order to measure ourselves against the good and the great, to get a sense of all that can be done. And we read in order to experience different styles.

You may find yourself adopting a style you find particularly exciting, and there's nothing wrong with that. When I read Ray Bradbury as a kid, I wrote like Ray Bradbury—everything green and wondrous and seen through a lens smeared with the grease of nostalgia. When I read James M. Cain, everything I wrote came out clipped and stripped and hard-boiled. When I read Lovecraft, my prose became luxurious and Byzantine. I wrote stories in my teenage years where all these styles merged, creating a kind of hilarious stew. This sort of stylistic blending is a necessary part of developing one's own style, but it doesn't occur in a vacuum. You have to read widely, constantly refining (and redefining) your own work as you do so. It's hard for me to believe that people who read very little (or not at all in some cases) should presume to write and expect people to like what they have written, but I know it's true. If I had a nickel for every person who ever told me he/she wanted to become a writer but "didn't have time to read," I could buy myself a pretty good steak dinner. Can I be blunt on this subject? If you don't have time to read, you don't have the time (or the tools) to write. Simple as that.

Reading is the creative center of a writer's life. I take a book with me everywhere I go, and find there are all sorts of opportunities to dip in. The trick is to teach yourself to read in small sips as well as in long swallows. Waiting rooms were made for books—of course! But so are theater lobbies before the show, long and boring checkout lines, and everyone's favorite, the john. You can even read while you're driving, thanks to the audiobook revolution. Of the books I read each year, anywhere from six to a dozen are on

10

tape. As for all the wonderful radio you will be missing, come on—how many times can you listen to Deep Purple sing "Highway Star"?

Reading at meals is considered rude in polite society, but if you expect to succeed as a writer, rudeness should be the second-to-least of your concerns. The least of all should be polite society and what it expects. If you intend to write as truthfully as you can, your days as a member of polite society are numbered, anyway.

Where else can you read? There's always the treadmill, or whatever you use down at the local health club to get aerobic. I try to spend an hour doing that every day, and I think I'd go mad without a good novel to keep me company. Most exercise facilities (at home as well as outside it) are now equipped with TVs, but TV—while working out or anywhere else—really is about the last thing an aspiring writer needs. If you feel you must have the news analyst blowhards on CNN while you exercise, or the stock market blowhards on MSNBC, or the sports blowhards on ESPN, it's time for you to question how serious you really are about becoming a writer. You must be prepared to do some serious turning inward toward the life of the imagination, and that means, I'm afraid, that Geraldo, Keith Obermann, and Jay Leno must go. Reading takes time, and the glass teat takes too much of it.

Once weaned from the ephemeral craving for TV, most people will find they enjoy the time they spend reading. I'd like to suggest that turning off that endlessly quacking box is apt to improve the quality of your life as well as the quality of your writing. And how much of a sacrifice are we talking about here? How many *Frasier* and *ER* reruns does it take to make one American life complete? How many Richard Simmons infomercials? How many whiteboy/fatboy Beltway insiders on CNN? Oh man, don't get me started. Jerry-Springer-Dr.-Dre-Judge-Judy-Jerry-Falwell-Donny-and-Marie, I rest my case.

When my son Owen was seven or so, he fell in love with Bruce Springsteen's E Street Band, particularly with Clarence Clemons, the band's burly sax player. Owen decided he wanted to learn to play like Clarence. My wife and I were amused and delighted by this ambition. We were also hopeful, as any parent would be, that our kid would turn out to be talented, perhaps even some sort of prodigy. We got Owen a tenor saxophone for Christmas and lessons with Gordon Bowie, one of the local music men. Then we crossed our fingers and hoped for the best.

Seven months later I suggested to my wife that it was time to discontinue   15
the sax lessons, if Owen concurred. Owen did, and with palpable relief—he hadn't wanted to say it himself, especially not after asking for the sax in the first place, but seven months had been long enough for him to realize that, while he might love Clarence Clemons's big sound, the saxophone was simply not for him—God had not given him that particular talent.

I knew, not because Owen stopped practicing, but because he was practicing only during the periods Mr. Bowie had set for him: half an hour after school four days a week, plus an hour on the weekends. Owen mastered the scales and the notes—nothing wrong with his memory, his lungs, or his eye-hand coordination—but we never heard him taking off, surprising himself with something new, blissing himself out. And as soon as his practice time was over, it was back into the case with the horn, and there it stayed until the next lesson or practice-time. What this suggested to me was that when it came to the sax and my son, there was never going to be any real play-time; it was all going to be rehearsal. That's no good. If there's no joy in it, it's just no good. It's best to go on to some other area, where the deposits of talent may be richer and the fun quotient higher.

Talent renders the whole idea of rehearsal meaningless; when you find something at which you are talented, you do it (whatever *it* is) until your fingers bleed or your eyes are ready to fall out of your head. Even when no one is listening (or reading, or watching), every outing is a bravura performance, because you as the creator are happy. Perhaps even ecstatic. That goes for reading and writing as well as for playing a musical instrument, hitting a baseball, or running the four-forty. The sort of strenuous reading and writing program I advocate—four to six hours a day, every day—will not seem strenuous if you really enjoy doing these things and have an aptitude for them; in fact, you may be following such a program already. If you feel you need permission to do all the reading and writing your little heart desires, however, consider it hereby granted by yours truly.

The real importance of reading is that it creates an ease and intimacy with the process of writing; one comes to the country of the writer with one's papers and identification pretty much in order. Constant reading will pull you into a place (a mind-set, if you like the phrase) where you can write eagerly and without self-consciousness. It also offers you a constantly growing knowledge of what has been done and what hasn't, what is trite and what is fresh, what works and what just lies there dying (or dead) on the page. The more you read, the less apt you are to make a fool of yourself with your pen or word processor.

Questions for Discussion and Writing

1. According to King, why must apprentice writers read everything they can? What can they learn even from reading bad writing?
2. How does the example of his son Owen taking up the saxophone illustrate King's belief that writing should be a consuming passion?
3. Would you consider making any of the trade-offs that King describes (for example, less television watching for more reading time) to become a better writer? Why or why not?
4. **Rhetorical inquiry:** Does King risk alienating his readers by advising them to forego watching television and devoting four to six hours a day to reading and writing? What incentives does he offer if one takes his advice?

Ross King

Ross King was born in 1962. He is the author of two novels Domino *(1995) and* Ex-libris *(2001). He has also written* Brunelleschi's Dome: How a Renaissance Genius Reinvented Architecture *(2001) and* Michelangelo and the Pope's Ceiling *(2003), from which the following selection is drawn. His latest work is* The Judgment of Paris *(2006).*

Before You Read

What cultural impact has Michelangelo's paintings on the ceiling of the Sistine Chapel come to have?

Michelangelo and the Pope's Ceiling

Fresco painting called for numerous preparatory stages, but among the most vital and indispensable were the drawings by which designs were worked out and then transferred to the wall. Before a single stroke of paint could be applied to the vault of the Sistine Chapel, Michelangelo needed to produce hundreds of sketches to establish both the intricate body language of the characters and the overall composition of the various scenes. The poses for many of his figures, including the dispositions of their hands and expressions on their faces, were composed through six or seven separate studies, which means he may have executed over 1,000 drawings in the course of his work on the fresco. These ranged from tiny scribbles—thumbnail sketches called *primo pensieri,* or "first thoughts"—to dozens of highly detailed, larger-than-life cartoons.

Michelangelo's drawings for the ceiling, fewer than seventy of which survive, were done in a variety of media, including silver-point. This method, which Michelangelo had learned in Ghirlandaio's workshop, involved drawing with a stylus on paper whose surface was specially prepared with thin layers of white lead and bone dust (made from table scraps) mixed together and bound with glue. The roughened surface of the paper scraped from the stylus small deposits of silver which rapidly oxidized, leaving behind fine gray lines. Since this was a slow and precise medium in which to work, for more rapid sketches Michelangelo used both charcoal and bister, the latter a brown pigment prepared from soot and applied with either a quill or a brush. He also made more careful drawings in red chalk, or hematite, a new medium whose use had been pioneered a decade earlier by Leonardo da Vinci in his studies for the apostles in *The Last Supper.* Its brittleness was perfect for small, finely detailed drawings, and its warm color provided an expressive range that Leonardo exploited to great effect in the faces of his apostles, and that Michelangelo would use with equally dazzling virtuosity to show the gradations of tone along anatomically exact knots of muscle.

Michelangelo worked on the first of these sketches as Piero Rosselli prepared the vault. He seems to have finished his first stage of drawing around the end of September, after working on his designs for four months, exactly the same amount of time he had spent sketching plans for the much smaller *Battle of Cascina*. By this point he had probably made drawings for, at most, only the first few scenes. His habit for the Sistine Chapel would be to produce sketches and cartoons only as he needed them—that is, only at the last possible minute. After making designs for and then frescoing one part of the ceiling, he would go back to the drawing board—quite literally—and begin making sketches and cartoons for the next.[1]

By the first week of October Michelangelo as finally ready to paint. At this point a rope maker named Domenico Manini, a Florentine working in Rome, received a payment of three ducats for rope and canvas delivered to the Sistine Chapel. Suspended beneath the scaffold, the canvas would perform the vital task of preventing paint from dripping onto the chapel's marble floor. Even more important, from Michelangelo's point of view, the sheet of canvas would prevent anyone on the floor of the chapel from seeing the work in progress. He may well have been suspicious of public opinion, since stones had been thrown at *David* after it was removed from his workshop near the Duomo. In 1505 his cartoon for *The Battle of Cascina* was executed amid great secrecy in his room in Sant'Onofrio, from which all but the most trusted friends and assistants were banned. Presumably, the same sort of regime prevailed in the workshop behind the Piazza Rusticucci, with no one privy to the drawings except his assistants and, perhaps, the pope and the master of the sacred palace. Michelangelo intended the fresco to remain a mystery to the people of Rome until, in his own good time, he decided to unveil it.

To begin their work each day, Michelangelo and his assistants climbed a forty-foot ladder until, reaching the top of the windows, they mounted the lowest planks of one of the bridges. The steps of the scaffold took them another twenty feet to its top. Railings may have been erected to protect them from a fall, while the sheet of canvas served another welcome purpose: screening the sixty-foot drop beneath the scaffold. Scattered about the decks would have been the tools of their trade: trowels, pots of paint and brushes, as well as buckets of water and bags of sand and lime that had been winched onto the scaffold. Illumination came from the windows as well as from the torches that Piero Rosselli's men had used as they labored late into the evening. A few feet above the men's heads curved the vault of the chapel, an immense, grayish white expanse awaiting their brushes.

The first task on any day was, of course, the application of the *intonaco*. The ticklish matter of mixing the plaster was probably left to one of Rosselli's

---

[1] On this working practice, see Michael Hirst, *Michelangelo and His Drawings* (New Haven: Yale University Press, 1988), pp. 35–36, and Catherine Whistler, *Drawings by Michelangelo and Raphael* (Oxford: Ashmolean Museum, 1990), p. 34.

men. Painters knew from their apprenticeships how to make and spread plaster, but in practice most of the work was done by a professional plasterer, or *muratore*, not least because making plaster was a disagreeable chore. For one thing, the quick-lime was so corrosive that it was sprinkled on corpses to hasten their decomposition and therefore lessen the stench around churchyards. Also, it was hazardous when slaked, since calcium oxide generated a tremendous heat as it expanded and then disintegrated. This task was vital, because if the quicklime was not properly slaked it could damage not only the fresco but also—such was its corrosive power—the stonework of the vault.

Once the calcium hydroxide had formed, the job became merely toilsome. The mixture needed to be stirred with a spade until the lumps were gone and a paste or putty had formed. The paste was kneaded and mixed with sand, after which more stirring was required until an ointmentlike consistency was achieved; further stirring was then needed to prevent cracks and crevices from appearing when the plaster was left to stand.

The *intonaco* was applied with a trowel or float to the area specified by the artist. After spreading it, the plasterer wiped the fresh plaster with a cloth, sometimes one in which a handful of flax was tied. This removed the marks of the trowel and roughened the wall slightly so the paint would adhere. The *intonaco* was then wiped again, this time more gently with a silk handkerchief in order to remove grains of sand from the surface. An hour or two after it was spread—time enough to transfer the designs from the cartoons—the *intonaco* formed a skin on which the paint could be applied.

In these early days, Michelangelo must have acted something like a foreman, delegating tasks to his various assistants. At any one time there could have been five or six men on the scaffold, a couple grinding pigments, others unfurling cartoons, still others at the ready with paintbrushes. The scaffold seems to have provided a commodious and convenient place for all of them to work. As it was clear of the vault for the whole of its span by about seven feet, it allowed them to stand erect as they worked. Applying the *intonaco* or spreading the paint simply required them to lean backward slightly and extend their arms upward.

Contrary to myth, then, Michelangelo did not fresco the ceiling while lying prone on his back—a picture lodged as solidly in the public mind as the equally inaccurate one of Sir Isaac Newton sitting under the apple tree. This misconception stems from a phrase in a short biography of Michelangelo titled *Michaelis Angeli Vita*, written in about 1527 by Paolo Giovio, the bishop of Nocera.[2] Describing Michelangelo's posture on the scaffold, Giovio used the term *resupinus*, which means "bent backward." But the word has frequently—and erroneously—been translated as "on his back." It is difficult to imagine how Michelangelo and his assistants could have worked under

10

---

[2] See *Scritti d'arte del cinquecento*, ed. Paola Barocchi (Milan and Naples: Ricciardi, 1971), vol. 1, p. 10.

such conditions, let alone how Rosselli's men might have cleared 12,000 square feet of plaster while lying flat on their backs in a narrow crawl space. Michelangelo was to encounter numerous obstacles and inconveniences as he worked on the fresco. The scaffold, however, was not one of them.

Michelangelo and his team painted, for the most part, from east to west, starting near the entrance and moving toward the sanctum sanctorum, the western half reserved for the members of the Papal Chapel. But they did not begin in the space immediately above the entrance, rather some fifteen feet to the west, on a portion of the ceiling above the second set of windows from the door. Here Michelangelo planned to paint the apocalyptic episode described in the Book of Genesis, chapters six to eight: Noah's Flood.

Michelangelo began with *The Flood* for a number of reasons, first and foremost, perhaps, for its inconspicuous location. His lack of experience in fresco made him wary of starting with a more prominent scene, one more likely to strike the visitor's eye as he or she entered or, more critically, that of the pope as he occupied his throne in the sanctum sanctorum. Second, this scene was one for which he no doubt had some enthusiasm, given that his previous work—most notably *The Battle of Cascina*—had already prepared him for it. It was with this scene in mind that in the middle of August he had sent money to Florence to purchase the azure ordered from the Gesuati monks in San Giusto alle Mura—pigments which he would use to color the rising floodwaters.

Michelangelo's *Flood* illustrates the story of how, soon after the Creation, God began to regret having created humankind. Because of their determined wickedness, he decided to destroy everyone except Noah, the "just and perfect man," a farmer who had reached the ripe old age of six hundred. He instructed Noah to build from gopher wood a boat three hundred cubits long, fifty cubits wide, and three stories high, with one window and one door. Into this vessel went a pair of every type of living creature, together with Noah's wife, sons, and daughters-in-law. Then, the Bible records, "the fountains of the great deep burst forth."[3]

Obvious similarities to the figures and actions in *The Battle of Cascina* suggest that this earlier work was still very much in Michelangelo's mind when he planned *The Flood*. Indeed, a number of poses from *The Battle of Cascina* repeat themselves, with some variation, in the later scene.[4] It made perfect sense for Michelangelo to draw upon his previous experiences when he came to design the ceiling in 1508, given that *The Battle of Cascina* had

---

[3] Genesis 8:10. All quotations from the Bible, unless otherwise indicated, are from the revised standard edition (London: William Collins, 1946).   [4] For details, see Charles de Tolnay, *Michelangelo*, 5 vols. (Princeton: Princeton University Press, 1943–60) vol. 1, p. 218, and vol. 2, p. 29. He claims that some of the figures in the background of the fresco "are modified repetitions of figures of the bathing soldiers in [Michelangelo's] own Battle of Cascina" (vol. 2, p. 29).

created such a sensation three years earlier, and given that recycling a few of these earlier poses meant a slight reduction in an enormous workload. Michelangelo also reused figures from another of his previous works, since one of the characters in *The Flood*—the nude man trying to board the small, overcrowded boat—holds exactly the same jackknifed pose as one of the warring figures in *The Battle of the Centaurs*, carved over fifteen years earlier.

Like these two other works, Michelangelo's *Flood* is crowded with   15
human bodies. It portrays a bleak, windswept waterscape in which dozens of nudes—men, women, and children—beat a retreat from the deluge. Some make their way in orderly fashion to a patch of high ground on the left of the panel; others shelter beneath a fluttering, makeshift tent on a rocky island; and still others, equipped with a ladder, do their best to storm the ark. The ark itself is in the background, a rectangular wooden vessel with a pitched roof and a window from out of which leans the bearded, red-robed Noah, seemingly oblivious to the calamity that surrounds him.

Although *The Flood* gave Michelangelo the chance to indulge to the full his passion for throngs of doomed figures in dramatic, muscle-straining poses, he also added more homely touches in the shape of people rescuing humble possessions. One of the women balances on her head an upturned stool laden with loaves of bread, pottery, and a few pieces of cutlery, while, nearby, two naked men carry bundles of clothing and a frying pan. Michelangelo would no doubt have witnessed similar scenes of evacuation whenever the Tiber or the Arno flooded. Having no embankments, the Tiber routinely burst its banks, deluging the surrounding areas under several yards of water in a matter of hours. Michelangelo himself had firsthand experience of salvaging possessions from floodwaters when, in January 1506, heavy rains overflowed the Tiber, submerging a cargo of marble he was unloading from a barge at the port of Ripa, two miles downstream from the Vatican.

Despite the expertise of the assistants, work on the fresco does not seem to have begun well, for no sooner had the panel been completed than a large part of it had to be redone. Corrections, known quaintly as *pentimenti* (repentances), always presented a frescoist with serious problems. Someone working in oil or tempera simply painted over his errors, but the frescoist was not able to repent so easily. If he realized the mistake before the *intonaco* dried, he could scrape the plaster from the wall, apply it afresh, and resume work; otherwise he was forced to take his hammer and chisel to the dried plaster and remove the whole of the *giornata*—which is precisely what Michelangelo did. Or, rather, he removed a dozen or more *giornate*, destroying more than half of the scene—including the whole of the left-hand side—and started anew.[5]

---

[5] See Fabrizio Mancinelli, "The Problem of Michelangelo's Assistants," pp. 52–53. *The Sistine Chapel: A Glorious Restoration*, ed. Pierluigi de Vecchi and Diana Murphy, New York: Henry N. Abrams, 1999.

The reasons for the destruction of a good part of this scene are unclear. Michelangelo may have been unhappy with his design for the figures on the left-hand side, or he may have changed or refined his fresco technique after a few weeks on the job. But since this act involved taking a hammer to almost a month's work, it must have been disheartening to all concerned.

The only part of the fresco left intact after the obliteration was that showing the group huddled fearfully under their tent on the rock. These figures are therefore the earliest surviving part of the ceiling. They are the work of many hands, showing how at this early stage Michelangelo made full use of his assistants, though it is uncertain exactly who painted which part of the fresco. The only bit of *The Flood* Michelangelo is known for certain to have painted himself is the pair of figures on the edge of the rock: the sturdy old man grasping in his arms the lifeless body of a young man.

Repainting the left-hand side of the fresco took a total of nineteen   20
giornate. Allowing for feast days and Masses, this work must have been spread over almost four weeks, taking the team toward the end of November, dangerously close to the time when cardinals reached for their fur-lined hoods, and fresco painters, if the weather worsened, were obliged to put away their brushes for weeks on end.

Work on *The Flood* had proceeded at a frustratingly slow pace. Not counting the destroyed work, the scene took, in all, twenty-nine *giornate.* These *giornate* were relatively small, averaging less than seven square feet, or roughly one-third of a typical day's work in the Tornabuoni Chapel. Even the scene's largest *giornata* was a mere five feet long by three feet high, still well under the average of Ghirlandaio's workshop.

One reason for this slow rate, besides Michelangelo's inexperience, was the sheer number of human figures in *The Flood*. Frescoing the human form was more time-consuming than a landscape, especially for someone who used elaborate, unusual poses and strove for anatomical accuracy. Faces, especially, demanded attention. The quicker method of making incisions in the cartoon—that is, tracing its outlines onto the plaster with a point of a stylus—could be used for a scene's larger and less explicit details, such as arms, legs, and draperies. But frescoists almost always transferred facial features from cartoons through the more precise but slower technique of *spolvero,* which involved sprinkling charcoal onto the plaster through the perforations in the cartoon's outlines. Curiously, however, when painting *The Flood,* Michelangelo and his team used *spolvero* everywhere, forsaking incision entirely,[6] even though winter was fast approaching.

Floods always had a blunt meaning for Michelangelo. An intensely pious man, he never failed to view violent meteorological events as punishments

---

[6] Carmen C. Bambach, *Drawing and Painting in the Italian Renaissance Workshop: Theory and Practice, 1300–1600* (Cambridge: Cambridge University Press, 1999), p. 366.

from a wrathful God. Many years later, after autumnal rains had flooded both Florence and Rome, he would comment woefully that the catastrophic weather had lashed the Italians "on account of [their] sins."[7] One source for this fire-and-brimstone pessimism—and an inspiration behind his depiction of *The Flood*—was a figure from his impressionable youth, the Dominican friar Girolamo Savonarola.

Probably best known as the man who ignited the "bonfire of the vanities," the incineration of a sixty-foot-high pile of "vanities" and "luxuries" in the middle of the Piazza della Signoria,[†] Girolamo Savonarola came to Florence from Ferrara in 1491, at the age of thirty-nine, to serve as the prior of the Dominican convent of San Marco. Under Lorenzo de' Medici, Florence celebrated the ancient cultures of Greece and Rome. Plato was translated and studied, the university taught Greek, preachers quoted Ovid from the pulpit, the populace frequented Roman-style bathhouses, and artists such as Sandro Botticelli depicted pagan rather than religious subjects.

These classical splendors and obsessions offended Savonarola, who believed this mania for the antique world was turning the young men of Florence into sodomites. "Abandon, I tell you, your concubines and your beardless youths," he thundered from the pulpit. "Abandon, I say, that abominable vice that has brought God's wrath upon you, or else woe, woe to you!"[8] His solution to the problem was a simple one: Sodomites should be burned along with the vanities. And by *vanities* he meant not only chessboards, playing cards, mirrors, fancy clothing, and bottles of perfume. He also exhorted the people of Florence to throw onto his bonfire their musical instruments, tapestries, paintings, and copies of books by Florence's three greatest writers: Dante, Petrarch, and Boccaccio.

The adolescent Michelangelo was soon under the spell of this fanatic, whose sermons he would reread throughout his life. Savonarola was a man for whom, Condivi wrote, Michelangelo "always had great affection," and decades later he claimed he could still hear the friar's voice.[9] Lean and pale, with black hair, intense green eyes, and thick eyebrows, Savonarola had held all of Florence in his thrall in the spring of 1492 as he preached hair-raising sermons from the pulpit of Santa Maria del Fiore, recounting blood-curdling visions in which daggers and crosses appeared to him in the thunderous, darkened sky above the city. The message of these visions was crystal clear: Unless the Florentines mended their ways, they would be punished by a wrathful

25

---

[7] Michelangelo Buonarroti, *The Letters of Michelangelo*, ed. E. H. Ramsden (London: Peter Owen, 1963), vol. 2, p. 182.   [†] There were in fact two of these *brucciamenti della vanità*: one on the seventh of February 1497, and another on the twenty-seventh of February in the following year.   [8] Quoted in Lene Østermark-Johansen, *Sweetness and Strength: The Reception of Michelangelo in Late Victorian England* (Aldershot, Hants: Ashgate, 1998), p. 194.
[9] Ascanio Condivi, *The Life of Michelangelo*, trans. Alice Sedgwick Wohl, ed. Hellmut Wohl. 2nd ed. (University Park: Pennsylvania State University Press, 1999), p. 105.

668   CHAPTER 10 ~ The Artistic Impulse - Nonfiction

God. "O Florence, O Florence, O Florence," he cried like one of the Old Testament prophets to which he was always comparing himself, "for your sins, for your brutality, your avarice, your lust, your ambition, there will befall you many trials and tribulations!"[10]

As it happened, the friar's prophecy was fulfilled in due course. Two years later, bent on claiming the throne of Naples for himself, Charles VIII of France had swept across the Alps with an army of more than 30,000 men. Savonarola compared this massive invasion force—the largest ever to set foot on Italian soil—to the waters of a great flood. "Behold," he cried from the pulpit on the morning of the twenty-first of September 1494, "I shall unloose waters over the earth!" Comparing himself to Noah, he cried that if the people of Florence wished to escape these floodwaters they needed to take refuge in the Ark—the cathedral of Santa Maria del Fiore.

The impact of this sermon on the people of Florence was electric. "So full of terrors and alarms, cries and lamentations" were Savonarola's sermons, wrote one observer, "that everyone went about the city bewildered, speechless and, as it were, half-dead."[11] Their fearful demeanors earned the friar's followers the nickname Piagnoni, or "Snivelers." The Medici were soon expelled from Florence, and in November Savonarola's "Scourge of God"—the short, scrawny, hook-nosed, ginger-bearded Charles VIII—entered the city on horseback. Charles stayed for eleven pleasantly hospitable days before departing for Rome to confront Pope Alexander VI, a man whose decadence made that of Florence pale in comparison. As if on cue, the city was flooded by the Tiber—proof of the Lord's displeasure with the Romans.

The flood was therefore an evocative image for Michelangelo, a potent reminder not of the power of nature but of the wrathful God of the Old Testament that Savonarola's sermons had brought so vividly to life. These sermons would influence a number of other images on the ceiling and may even have been behind the switch in the fresco's subject matter from a New Testament theme—the Twelve Apostles—to a series of Old Testament stories, some of which featured in the friar's most scarifying harangues.[12] For the previous two centuries, Italian artists had concentrated mainly on New Testament subjects such as the Annunciation, the Nativity, the Assumption, and so forth—gentle, elegant scenes telling reassuringly optimistic stories of God's grace and humankind's salvation through Christ. Except for his own most famous New Testament subject, the *Pietà*, as well as his Madonna-and-Child reliefs and panels, Michelangelo had displayed little interest in such motifs. He was fascinated,

---

[10] Quoted in Roberto Ridolfi, *The Life and Times of Girolamo Savonarola,* trans. Cecil Grayson (London: Routledge and Kegan Paul, 1959), p. 80.   [11] Quoted in Edgar Wind, "Sante Pagnini and Michelangelo: A Study of the Succession of Savonarola," *Gazette des Beaux-Arts* 26 (1944): 212–13.   [12] For Savonarola's almost exclusive use of the Old Testament, see Donald Weinstein, *Savonarola and Florence: Prophecy and Patriotism in the Renaissance* (Princeton: Princeton University Press, 1970), p. 182.

instead, by tragic, violent narratives of crime and punishment such as those—complete with hangings, plagues, propitiations, and beheadings—that he was soon to fresco on the vault of the Sistine Chapel. And these turbulent visions of a vengeful God, doomed sinners, and prophets crying in the wilderness were undoubtedly part of Savonarola's legacy.[13]

Savonarola's story ended tragically, with all of the flames, wrath, and retribution of one of his sermons. He had earlier written a book, *Dialogo della verità profetica,* in which he claimed that God still sent prophets to walk the Earth as in the days of the Old Testament, and that he, Fra Girolamo, was just such an oracle. He believed his visions to be the products of angelic intervention, and his sermons and dialogues explained how his gloom-and-doom predictions had supposedly been fulfilled by recent historical events. These prophecies became his downfall since according to the Church's official line the Holy Spirit spoke to the pope alone, not to rabble-rousing friars from Ferrara. In 1497 Alexander VI therefore ordered Savonarola to stop preaching and prophesying, eventually excommunicating him when he failed to do so. When the friar continued stubbornly to preach even while under excommunication, he was tortured and then, in May 1498, hanged in the middle of the Piazza della Signoria. His corpse was, ironically, incinerated in a bonfire, and the ashes dumped into the Arno.

Michelangelo had been in Carrara at this time, quarrying marble for the *Pietà.* However, he would have learned of Savonarola's fate soon enough, not least from his older brother Lionardo, a Dominican priest who had visited him in Rome soon after the execution, and who had been defrocked because of his devotion to Savonarola. While the *Pietà,* with its dead Christ cradled in the arms of the Virgin, was a supreme example of the redemptive Christianity of the New Testament,[14] a decade later, as he started work in the Sistine Chapel, Michelangelo was able to give a freer rein to the more apocalyptic imagination shaped by Savonarola.

30

---

[13] For discussions of Savonarola's influence on Michelangelo's art, see Julian Klaczko, *Rome and the Renaissance: The Pontificate of Julius II,* trans. John Dennie (London: G. P. Putnam's Sons, 1903), p. 283; Charles de Tolnay, *The Art and Thought of Michelangelo* (New York: Pantheon, 1964); Ronald M. Steinberg, *Fra Girolamo Savonarola, Florentine Art, and Renaissance Historiography* (Athens, Ohio: Ohio University Press, 1977), pp. 39–42; and Vincent Cronin, *The Florentine Renaissance* (London: Collins, 1967), p. 296. Cronin, for example, argues that Savonarola's writings and sermons, produced among a number of Florentine painters, including Botticelli and Signorelli, a "retrograde" art that regarded Christianity in terms of vengeance, terror, and punishment. De Tolnay likewise finds in Michelangelo's art a "profound echo" of Savonarola's words (pp. 62–63). Steinberg, however, is somewhat more cautious in attributing influences, claiming that direct links between Michelangelo's iconography and Savonarola's sermons are difficult to prove. This difficulty is partly due to Michelangelo's silence on the subject as well as our lack of knowledge about his theological mentors. For the possible influence of Savonarola through his successor at San Marco, Sante Pagnini, see Wind, "Sante Pagnini and Michelangelo," pp. 211–46.   [14] Antonio Paolucci has argued that even the Vatican *Pietà,* with its "chaste beauty," was influenced by Savonarola's teachings. See Paolucci's *Michelangelo: The Pietàs* (Milan: Skira, 1997), pp. 16–17.

Questions for Discussion and Writing

1. Why did Michelangelo begin the ceiling of the Sistine Chapel with a depiction of the Flood? What made fresco painting such a difficult art form to master?
2. Why is it important for the reader to understand how Michelangelo was influenced by Savonarola to comprehend his fascination with the story of Noah and the Flood?
3. Were you surprised to learn that frescoes on the ceiling of the Sistine Chapel were the work of a team? How does this contrast with the popular conception of Michelangelo being the sole creater of the frescoes?
4. **Rhetorical inquiry:** How does King's detailed account of the preparation required before Michelangelo could begin work give readers a realistic sense of what was involved?

How does this picture of Noah and the Flood on the ceiling of the Sistine Chapel reveal the dynamic style of Michelangelo?

AGNES DE MILLE

*Agnes De Mille (1908–1993), a principal figure in American dance, was born in
New York City. She created distinctive American ballets such as* Rodeo *(1942)
and* Tally-Ho *(1944) and brought her talents as an innovative choreographer to*
Oklahoma! *(1943 and 1980),* Carousel *(1945),* Brigadoon *(1947),* Paint Your
Wagon *(1951),* Gentlemen Prefer Blondes *(1949), and other musicals. De Mille's
entertaining autobiographies,* Dance to the Piper *(1952) and* Reprieve:
A Memoir *(1981), describe many exciting moments in her life.* "Pavlova," *from*
Dance to the Piper, *contains De Mille's recollection of what she felt when she
saw Anna Pavlova, the famed Russian ballerina, for the first time.*

Before You Read

What dancer or other performer could become a role model for you?

Pavlova

Anna Pavlova! My life stops as I write that name. Across the daily preoccupa-
tion of lessons, lunch boxes, tooth brushings and quarrelings with Margaret
flashed this bright, unworldly experience and burned in a single afternoon a
path over which I could never retrace my steps. I had witnessed the power
of beauty, and in some chamber of my heart I lost forever my irresponsibility.
I was as clearly marked as though she had looked me in the face and called my
name. For generations my father's family had loved and served the theater. All
my life I had seen actors and actresses and had heard theater jargon at the dinner table and business talk of box-office grosses. I had thrilled at Father's
projects and watched fascinated his picturesque occupations. I took a propri-
etary pride in the profitable and hasty growth of "The Industry." But nothing
in his world or my uncle's prepared me for theater as I saw it that Saturday
afternoon.

Since that day I have gained some knowledge in my trade and I recognize that her technique was limited; that her arabesques were not as pure or
classically correct as Markova's, that her jumps and batterie were paltry, her
turns not to be compared in strength and number with the strenuous dura-
bility of Baronova or Toumanova. I know that her scenery was designed by
second-rate artists, her music was on a level with restaurant orchestrations,
her company definitely inferior to all the standards we insist on today, and
her choreography mostly hack. And yet I say that she was in her person the
quintessence of theatrical excitement.

As her little bird body revealed itself on the scene, either immobile in
trembling mystery or tense in the incredible arc which was her lift, her instep
stretched ahead in an arch never before seen, the tiny bones of her hands in
ceaseless vibration, her face radiant, diamonds glittering under her dark

hair, her little waist encased in silk, the great tutu balancing, quickening and flashing over her beating, flashing, quivering legs, every man and woman sat forward, every pulse quickened. She never appeared to rest static, some part of her trembled, vibrated, beat like a heart. Before our dazzled eyes, she flashed with the sudden sweetness of a hummingbird in action too quick for understanding by our gross utilitarian standards, in action sensed rather than seen. The movie cameras of her day could not record her allegro. Her feet and hands photographed as a blur.

Bright little bird bones, delicate bird sinews! She was all fire and steel wire. There was not an ounce of spare flesh on her skeleton, and the life force used and used her body until she died of the fever of moving, gasping for breath, much too young.

She was small, about five feet. She wore a size one and a half slipper, but her feet and hands were large in proportion to her height. Her hand could cover her whole face. Her trunk was small and stripped of all anatomy but the ciphers of adolescence, her arms and legs relatively long, the neck extraordinarily long and mobile. All her gestures were liquid and possessed of an inner rhythm that flowed to inevitable completion with the finality of architecture or music. Her arms seemed to lift not from the elbow or the arm socket, but from the base of the spine. Her legs seemed to function from the waist. When she bent her head her whole spine moved and the motion was completed the length of the arm through the elongation of her slender hand and the quivering reaching fingers. I believe there has never been a foot like hers, slender, delicate and of such an astonishing aggressiveness when arched as to suggest the ultimate in human vitality. Without in any way being sensual, being, in fact, almost sexless, she suggested all exhilaration, gaiety and delight. She jumped, and we broke bonds with reality. We flew. We hung over the earth, spread in the air as we do in dreams, our hands turning in the air as in water—the strong forthright taut plunging leg balanced on the poised arc of the foot, the other leg stretched to the horizon like the wing of a bird. We lay balancing, quivering, turning, and all things were possible, even to us, the ordinary people.

I have seen two dancers as great or greater since, Alicia Markova and Margot Fonteyn, and many other women who have kicked higher, balanced longer or turned faster. These are poor substitutes for passion. In spite of her flimsy dances, the bald and blatant virtuosity, there was an intoxicated rapture, a focus of energy, Dionysian in its physical intensity, that I have never seen equaled by a performer in any theater of the world. Also she was the *first* of the truly great in our experience.

I sat with the blood beating in my throat. As I walked into the bright glare of the afternoon, my head ached and I could scarcely swallow. I didn't wish to cry. I certainly couldn't speak. I sat in a daze in the car oblivious to the grownups' ceaseless prattle. At home I climbed the stairs slowly to my bedroom and, shutting myself in, placed both hands on the brass rail at the

5

foot of my bed, then rising laboriously to the tips of my white buttoned shoes I stumped the width of the bed and back again. My toes throbbed with pain, my knees shook, my legs quivered with weakness. I repeated the exercise. The blessed, relieving tears stuck at last on my lashes. Only by hurting my feet could I ease the pain in my throat.

Standing on Ninth Avenue under the El, I saw the headlines on the front page of the *New York Times*. It did not seem possible. She was in essence the denial of death. My own life was rooted to her in a deep spiritual sense and had been during the whole of my growing up. It mattered not that I had only spoken to her once and that my work lay in a different direction. She was the vision and the impulse and the goal.

Questions for Discussion and Writing

1. What features of Pavlova's appearance and dance does De Mille find so enthralling? How did seeing Pavlova's performance change De Mille's life? What details does De Mille include to focus the reader's attention on Pavlova's diminuative size and her ability to express emotion through gesture?
2. Describe a performance you have seen that you would call inspiring. What made it so? Organize your description and main impression by using specific details that will allow your readers to share your experience.
3. If you could appear on the cover of any magazine for an achievement for which you are celebrated, what would it be—*Sports Illustrated*, *Time*, *Rolling Stone*, *Business Week*, *Gourmet?*
4. **Rhetorical inquiry:** In what way does De Mille use images that equate Pavlova to a bird?

AARON COPLAND

Aaron Copland (1900–1990), one of the most influential American composers of the twentieth century, was born in Brooklyn, New York. He studied with Nadia Boulanger in Paris (1921–1924) and taught at the New School for Social Research (1927–1937). He developed a distinctly American sound and style, incorporating not only Stravinsky's influence but jazz, folk songs, cowboy tunes, and Shaker hymns in works such as Billy the Kid *(1940),* Rodeo *(1942),* Fanfare for the Common Man *(1943), and the Pulitzer Prize–winning ballet* Appalachian Spring *(1944). He continued to compose music for orchestra, ballet, stage, films, chamber groups, and voice and to conduct, lecture, and write books, including* Music and Imagination *(1952). He won an Academy Award in 1950 for the musical score he wrote for the film* The Heiress. *In the following selection (from* What to Listen for in Music, *1957) we can appreciate Copland's engaging explanation of the qualities of effective music scored for films.*

Before You Read

When you watch a movie are you aware of the impact of the musical score or songs that accompany it?

Film Music

Film music constitutes a new musical medium that exerts a fascination of its own. Actually, it is a new form of dramatic music—related to opera, ballet, incidental theater music—in contradistinction to concert music of the symphonic or chamber-music kind. As a new form it opens up unexplored possibilities for composers and poses some interesting questions for the musical film patron.

Millions of movie-goers take the musical accompaniment to a dramatic film entirely too much for granted. Five minutes after the termination of a picture they couldn't tell you whether they had heard music or not. To ask whether they thought the score exciting or merely adequate or downright awful would be to give them a musical inferiority complex. But, on second thought, and possibly in self-protection, comes the query: "Isn't it true that one isn't supposed to be listening to the music? Isn't it supposed to work on you unconsciously without being listened to directly as you would listen at a concert?"

No discussion of movie music ever gets very far without having to face this problem: Should one hear a movie score? If you are a musician there is no problem because the chances are you can't help but listen. More than once a good picture has been ruined for me by an inferior score. Have you had the same experience? Yes? Then you may congratulate yourself: you are definitely musical.

But it's the average spectator, so absorbed in the dramatic action that he fails to take in the background music, who wants to know whether he is missing anything. The answer is bound up with the degree of your general musical perception. It is the degree to which you are aurally minded that will determine how much pleasure you may derive by absorbing the background musical accompaniment as an integral part of the combined impression made by the film.

Knowing more of what goes into the scoring of a picture may help the movie listener to get more out of it. Fortunately, the process is not so complex that it cannot be briefly outlined.   5

In preparation for composing the music, the first thing the composer must do, of course, is to see the picture. Almost all musical scores are written *after* the film itself is completed. The only exception to this is when the script calls for realistic music—that is, music which is visually sung or played or danced to on the screen. In that case the music must be composed before the scene is photographed. It will then be recorded and the scene in question shot to a playback of the recording. Thus, when you see an actor singing or playing or dancing, he is only making believe as far as the sound goes, for the music had previously been put down in recorded form.

The first run-through of the film for the composer is usually a solemn moment. After all, he must live with it for several weeks. The solemnity of the occasion is emphasized by the exclusive audience that views it with him: the producer, the director, the music head of the studio, the picture editor, the music cutter, the conductor, the orchestrater—in fact, anyone involved with the scoring of the picture.

The purpose of the run-through is to decide how much music is needed and where it should be. (In technical jargon this is called "to spot" the picture.) Since no background score is continuous throughout the full length of a film (that would constitute a motion-picture opera, an almost unexploited cinema form), the score will normally consist of separate sequences, each lasting from a few seconds to several minutes in duration. A sequence as long as seven minutes would be exceptional. The entire score, made up of perhaps thirty or more such sequences, may add up to from forty to ninety minutes of music.

Much discussion, much give-and-take may be necessary before final decisions are reached regarding the "spotting" of the picture. It is wise to make use of music's power sparingly, saving it for absolutely essential points. A composer knows how to play with silences—knows that to take music out can at times be more effective than any use of it on the sound track might be.

The producer-director, on the other hand, is more prone to think of music in terms of its immediate functional usage. Sometimes he has ulterior motives: anything wrong with a scene—a poor bit of acting, a badly read line, an embarrassing pause—he secretly hopes will be covered up by a clever composer. Producers have been known to hope that an entire picture would be saved by a good score. But the composer is not a magician; he can hardly be expected to do more than to make potent through music the film's dramatic and emotional values.

When well-contrived, there is no question but that a musical score can be of enormous help to a picture. One can prove that point, laboratory-fashion, by showing an audience a climactic scene with the sound turned off and then once again with the sound track turned on. Here briefly are listed a number of ways in which music serves the screen:

Creating a more convincing atmosphere of time and place. Not all Hollywood composers bother about this nicety. Too often, their scores are interchangeable: a thirteenth-century Gothic drama and a hardboiled modern battle of the sexes get similar treatment. The lush symphonic texture of late nineteenth-century music remains the dominating influence. But there are exceptions. Recently, the higher-grade horse opera has begun to have its own musical flavor, mostly a folksong derivative.

Underlining psychological refinements—the unspoken thoughts of a character or the unseen implications of a situation. Music can play upon the emotions of the spectator, sometimes counterpointing the thing seen with an aural image that implies the contrary of the thing seen. This is not as subtle as it sounds. A well-placed dissonant chord can stop an audience cold in the middle of a sentimental scene, or a calculated woodwind passage can turn what appears to be a solemn moment into a belly laugh.

Serving as a kind of neutral background filler. This is really the music one isn't supposed to hear, the sort that helps to fill the empty spots, such as pauses in a conversation. It's the movie composer's most ungrateful task. But at times, though no one else may notice, he will get private satisfaction from the thought that music of little intrinsic value, through professional manipulation, has enlivened and made more human the deathly pallor of a screen shadow. This is hardest to do, as any film composer will attest, when the neutral filler type of music must weave its way underneath dialogue.

Building a sense of continuity. The picture editor knows better than any-   15
one how serviceable music can be in tying together a visual medium which is, by its very nature, continually in danger of falling apart. One sees this most obviously in montage scenes where the use of a unifying musical idea may save the quick flashes of disconnected scenes from seeming merely chaotic.

Underpinning the theatrical build-up of a scene, and rounding it off with a sense of finality. The first instance that comes to mind is the music that blares out at the end of a film. Certain producers have boasted their picture's lack of a musical score, but I never saw or heard of a picture that ended in silence.

We have merely skimmed the surface, without mentioning the innumerable examples of utilitarian music—offstage street bands, the barn dance, merry-go-rounds, circus music, café music, the neighbor's girl practicing her piano, and the like. All these, and many others, introduced with apparent naturalistic intent, serve to vary subtly the aural interest of the sound track.

But now let us return to our hypothetical composer. Having determined where the separate musical sequences will begin and end, he turns the film over to the music cutter, who prepares a so-called cue sheet. The cue sheet provides the composer with a detailed description of the physical action in each sequence, plus the exact timings in thirds of seconds of that action, thereby making it possible for a practiced composer to write an entire score without ever again referring to the picture.

The layman usually imagines that the most difficult part of the job in composing for the films has to do with the precise "fitting" of the music to the action. Doesn't that kind of timing strait-jacket the composer? The answer is no, for two reasons: First, having to compose music to accompany specific action is a help rather than a hindrance, since the action itself induces music in a composer of theatrical imagination, whereas he has no such visual stimulus in writing absolute music. Secondly, the timing is mostly a matter of minor adjustments, since the over-all musical fabric will have already been determined.

For the composer of concert music, changing to the medium of cellu-   20
loid does bring certain special pitfalls. For example, melodic invention, highly prized in the concert hall, may at times be distracting in certain film

situations. Even phrasing in the concert manner, which would normally emphasize the independence of separate contrapuntal lines, may be distracting when applied to screen accompaniments. In orchestration there are many subtleties of timbre—distinctions meant to be listened to for their own expressive quality in an auditorium—which are completely wasted on sound track.

As compensation for these losses, the composer has other possibilities, some of them tricks, which are unobtainable in Carnegie Hall. In scoring one section of *The Heiress,* for example, I was able to superimpose two orchestras, one upon another. Both recorded the same music at different times, one orchestra consisting of strings alone, the other constituted normally. Later these were combined by simultaneously rerecording the original tracks, thereby producing a highly expressive orchestral texture. Bernard Herrmann,[1] one of the most ingenious of screen composers, called for (and got) eight celestas—an unheard-of combination on 57th Street—to suggest a winter's sleigh ride. Miklos Rozsa's[2] use of the "echo chamber"—a device to give normal tone a ghostlike aura—was widely remarked, and subsequently done to death.

Unusual effects are obtainable through overlapping incoming and outgoing music tracks. Like two trains passing one another, it is possible to bring in and take out at the same time two different musics. *The Red Pony*[3] gave me an opportunity to use this cinema specialty. When the daydreaming imagination of a little boy turns white chickens into white circus horses the visual image is mirrored in an aural image by having the chicken music transform itself into circus music, a device only obtainable by means of the overlap.

Let us now assume that the musical score has been completed and is ready for recording. The scoring stage is a happy-making place for the composer. Hollywood has gathered to itself some of America's finest performers; the music will be beautifully played and recorded with a technical perfection not to be matched anywhere else.

Most composers like to invite their friends to be present at the recording session of important sequences. The reason is that neither the composer nor his friends are ever again likely to hear the music sound out in concert style. For when it is combined with the picture most of the dynamic levels will be changed. Otherwise the finished product might sound like a concert with pictures. In lowering dynamic levels niceties of shading, some inner voices and bass parts may be lost. Erich Korngold[4] put it well when he said: "A movie composer's immortality lasts from the recording stage to the dubbing room."

The dubbing room is where all the tracks involving sound of any kind, including dialogue, are put through the machines to obtain one master

---

[1] *Bernard Herrmann (1911–1975):* composed the music for *Citizen Kane* (1941) and many Alfred Hitchcock films, including *Psycho* (1960).   [2] *Miklos Rozsa (1907–1995):* Hungarian composer who wrote the film score for *Ben Hur* (1959).   [3] *The Red Pony:* 1948 film for which Copland wrote the music.   [4] *Erich Korngold (1897–1957):* Austrian composer who wrote the film score for *The Adventures of Robin Hood* (1938).

sound track. This is a delicate process as far as the music is concerned, for it is only a hairbreadth that separates the "too loud" from the "too soft." Sound engineers, working the dials that control volume, are not always as musically sensitive as composers would like them to be. What is called for is a new species, a sound mixer who is half musician and half engineer; and even then, the mixing of dialogue, music, and realistic sounds of all kinds must always remain problematical.

In view of these drawbacks to the full sounding out of his music, it is only natural that the composer often hopes to be able to extract a viable concert suite from his film score. There is a current tendency to believe that movie scores are not proper material for concert music. The argument is that, separated from its visual justification, the music falls flat.

Personally, I doubt very much that any hard and fast rule can be made that will cover all cases. Each score will have to be judged on its merits, and, no doubt, stories that require a more continuous type of musical development in a unified atmosphere will lend themselves better than others to reworking for concert purposes. Rarely is it conceivable that the music of a film might be extracted without much reworking. But I fail to see why, if successful suites like Grieg's[5] *Peer Gynt*[6] can be made from nineteenth-century incidental stage music, a twentieth-century composer can't be expected to do as well with a film score.

As for the picture score, it is only in the motion-picture theater that the composer for the first time gets the full impact of what he has accomplished, tests the dramatic punch of his favorite spot, appreciates the curious importance and unimportance of detail, wishes that he had done certain things differently, and is surprised that others came off better than he had hoped. For when all is said and done, the art of combining moving pictures with musical tones is still a mysterious art. Not the least mysterious element is the theatergoers' reaction: Millions will be listening but one never knows how many will be really hearing. The next time you go to the movies, remember to be on the composer's side.

Questions for Discussion and Writing

1. In what ways can a musical score enhance a film? What qualities in film music that would be applauded in a concert would prove distracting for a movie audience?
2. What examples best illustrate that the role of film music must be subordinated to the images on the screen? How does Copland's personal experience enhance the credibility of his analysis?

---

[5] *Edvard Grieg (1843–1907):* Norway's greatest composer. [6] *Peer Gynt:* incidental music composed by Grieg for Henrik Ibsen's 1875 play.

3. Analyze one of your favorite films by paying particular attention to the ways in which music achieves some of the objectives Copland describes. Is there any movie score that you would consider owning for its intrinsic musical value? Explain why you like it.

4. **Rhetorical inquiry:** How does Copland draw on his own experiences in scoring the music for *The Red Pony* and *The Heiress* as well as the examples of other composers to help the reader understand the challenge of matching specific musical sequences with the character's actions?

LANCE MORROW

Lance Morrow was born in Philadelphia in 1939, received his B.A. From Harvard in 1963, and joined the staff of Time *magazine shortly after graduation. As one of the magazine's regular contributors, he has written articles on a broad range of topics. Among his many published works are* Fishing in the Tiber *(1989), in which the following article first appeared.* Heart: A Memoir *(1995),* Evil: An Investigation *(2003),* The Best Years of Their Lives: Kennedy, Johnson, and Nixon in 1948, Learning the Secrets of Power *(2005) and* Second Drafts of History: Essays *(2006).*

Before You Read

What photos have you seen that symbolized a moment in history for you?

Imprisoning Time in a Rectangle

Balzac[1] had a "vague dread" of being photographed. Like some primitive peoples, he thought the camera steals something of the soul—that, as he told a friend "every body in its natural state is made up of a series of ghostly images superimposed in layers to infinity, wrapped in infinitesimal films." Each time a photograph was made, he believed, another thin layer of the subject's being would be stripped off to become not life as before but a membrane of memory in a sort of translucent antiworld.

If that is what photography is up to, then the onion of the world is being peeled away, layer by layer—lenses like black holes gobbling up life's emanations. Mere images proliferate, while history pares down to a phosphorescence of itself.

The idea catches something of the superstition (sometimes justified, if you think about it) and the spooky metaphysics that go ghosting around

---

[1] *Honoré de Balzac (born Honoré Balssa, 1799–1850):* French writer, best known for the novels and short stories of *La Comédie Humaine (The Human Comedy).*

photography. Taking pictures is a transaction that snatches instants away from time and imprisons them in rectangles. These rectangles become a collective public memory and an image-world that is located usually on the verge of tears, often on the edge of a moral mess.

It is possible to be entranced by photography and at the same time disquieted by its powerful capacity to bypass thought. Photography, as the critic Susan Sontag has pointed out, is an elegiac, nostalgic phenomenon. No one photographs the future. The instants that the photographer freezes are ever the past, ever receding. They have about them the brilliance or instancy of their moment but also the cello sound of loss that life makes when going irrecoverably away and lodging at last in the dreamworks.

The pictures made by photojournalists have the legitimacy of being   5
news, fresh information. They slice along the hard edge of the present. Photojournalism is not self-conscious, since it first enters the room (the brain) as a battle report from the far-flung Now. It is only later that the artifacts of photojournalism sink into the textures of the civilization and tincture its memory: Jack Ruby shooting Lee Harvey Oswald,[2] an image so raw and shocking, subsides at last into the ecology of memory where we also find thousands of other oddments from the time—John John saluting at the funeral, Jack and Jackie on Cape Cod, who knows?—bright shards that stimulate old feelings (ghost pangs, ghost tendernesses, wistfulness) but not thought really. The shocks turn into dreams. The memory of such pictures, flipped through like a disordered Rolodex, makes at last a cultural tapestry, an inventory of the kind that brothers and sisters and distant cousins may rummage through at family reunions, except that the greatest photojournalism has given certain memories the emotional prestige of icons.

If journalism—the kind done with words—is the first draft of history, what is photojournalism? Is it the first impression of history, the first graphic flash? Yes, but it is also (and this is the disturbing thing) history's lasting visual impression. The service that the pictures perform is splendid, and so powerful as to seem preternatural. But sometimes the power they possess is more than they deserve.

Call up Eddie Adams's 1968 photo of General Nguyen Ngoc Loan, the police chief of Saigon, firing his snub-nosed revolver into the temple of a Viet Cong officer. Bright sunlight, Saigon: the scrawny police chief's arm, outstretched, goes by extension through the trigger finger into the V.C.'s brain. That photograph, and another in 1972 showing a naked young Vietnamese girl running in armsoutstretched terror up a road away from American napalm, outmanned the force of three U.S. Presidents and the most powerful

---

[2] *Jack L. Ruby (1911–1967)*: shot and killed Lee Harvey Oswald (1939–1963), the accused assassin of President John F. Kennedy, on November 24, 1963, two days after Kennedy was shot, in the Dallas County Jail, where Oswald was being held under arrest. A national television audience witnessed the event.

Army in the world. The photographs were considered, quite ridiculously, to be a portrait of America's moral disgrace. Freudians spend years trying to call up the primal image-memories, turned to trauma, that distort a neurotic patient's psyche. Photographs sometimes have a way of installing the image and legitimizing the trauma: the very vividness of the image, the greatness of the photograph as journalism or even as art, forestalls examination.

Adams has always felt uncomfortable about his picture of Loan executing the Viet Cong officer. What the picture does not show is that a few moments earlier the Viet Cong had slaughtered the family of Loan's best friend in a house just up the road. All this occurred during the Tet offensive, a state of general mayhem all over South Vietnam. The Communists in similar circumstances would not have had qualms about summary execution.

But Loan shot the man; Adams took the picture. The image went firing around the world and lodged in the conscience. Photography is the very dream of the Heisenberg[3] uncertainty principle, which holds that the act of observing a physical event inevitably changes it. War is merciless, bloody, and by definition it occurs outside the orbit of due process. Loan's Viet Cong did not have a trial. He did have a photographer. The photographer's picture took on a life of its own and changed history.

All great photographs have lives of their own, but they can be as false   10
as dreams. Somehow the mind knows that and sorts out the matter, and permits itself to enjoy the pictures without getting sunk in the really mysterious business that they involve.

Still, a puritan conscience recoils a little from the sheer power of photographs. They have lingering about them the ghost of the golden calf—the bright object too much admired, without God's abstract difficulties. Great photographs bring the mind alive. Photographs are magic things that traffic in mystery. They float on the surface, and they have a strange life in the depths of the mind. They bear watching.

Questions for Discussion and Writing

1. How, in Morrow's view, does photojournalism go beyond merely recording events in history to help create history itself?
2. How does Morrow use photos of Jack Ruby shooting Lee Harvey Oswald and a police chief in Saigon shooting a Viet Cong prisoner to illustrate the power of photojournalism to affect history?
3. In your opinion, will this image of an Iraqi prisoner at Abu Ghraib prison come to represent the war in Iraq as the photo by Eddie Adams did for the war in Vietnam? Why or why not?

---

[3] *Werner Heisenberg (1901–1976):* German physicist famous for formulating the quantum theory, which converted the laws of physics into statements about relative, instead of absolute, certainties. He received the 1932 Nobel Prize in physics.

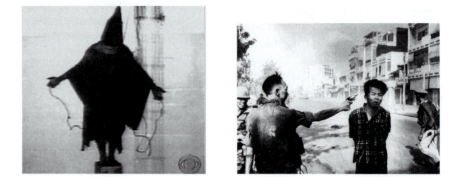

4. **Rhetorical inquiry:** When Morrow asserts that "all great photographs have lives of their own, but they can be as false as dreams," is he contradicting the thrust of his analysis as to the history-changing effects of key photographs?

GERMAINE GREER

Germaine Greer (b. 1939), an Australian academic, writer and broadcaster, was educated at the University of Sydney (M.A., 1963) and at the University of Cambridge (Ph.D. 1968). Greer is widely regarded as one of the most significant feminist voices of the twentieth century whose unique perspective is embodied in such works as her ground-breaking The Female Eunuch *(1971),* Slip-shod Sibyls *(1995),* The Whole Woman *(1999),* The Beautiful Boy *(2003), and most recently* Beautiful and Whitefella Jump Up: The Shortest Way to Nationhood *(2004). In the following essay drawn from* The Madwoman's Underclothes *(1986), Greer explores the cultural significance of ways of embellishing—and even mutilating—the human body.*

Before You Read

How do you feel about tatooing, piercing, or other forms of body modification?

One Man's Mutilation Is Another Man's Beautification

Humans are the only animals which can consciously and deliberately change their appearance according to their own whims. Most animals groom themselves, but humans are tempted to manipulate their appearance in ways much more radical than those open to other animals, not simply because they are able to use tools upon themselves, but also because of some peculiarities in the way in which humans are made. The human body is a curiously ambiguous structure, partaking of almost contradictory attributes. For example, humans are neither furry nor hairless, but variously naked, slightly hairy, and very hirsute. All these variations may be found on the body of a single individual at the same time. Humans are then confronted with a series of managerial problems: among the ways in which they express their cultural identities are the contrasting ways in which they handle these problems.

The Australian Aborigines used to conserve hair; not only did they not eliminate whatever hair was growing on their bodies, they collected extra human hair to work into a thick girdle for men to wear about their hips. We would look askance at anyone who could not bear to discard fallen hair, now that hair shirts are out of fashion, but sophisticated Western people often wear the hair of others as a postiche or toupee. Where the scalp-hunter once sought to augment his physical or psychic power by acquiring the hair of others, the literate people of the twentieth century feel that they will acquire youth and beauty through bought hair. They will even pay to have hair stitched into their scalps in a very costly and laborious development of the ancient practice of needle-working living flesh.

Some people identify themselves partly by their refusal to cut hair, as do the Sikhs, who twist the long silky hair of their beards together with what grows on their heads, tie the whole lot up in a chignon, and cover it with a turban. Others insist on the removal of any hair, wherever it is, and they too may choose a turban, this time to hide a bald head. Western conventions of hair management often appeal to younger or recalcitrant members of societies with strict rules for hair management because they find them more convenient; in fact, they are very subtle and difficult, requiring minute calculations of the degree of shagginess which is appropriate to age, and economic and social status. The rejection of traditional modes of hair management has less to do with convenience and common sense than with the desire to break out of the confinement of the group. A shaven Sikh might object that he is as much Sikh as ever; he may claim that his elimination of his identifying marks was simply to pour out the bath water while retaining the baby, but in fact he has summarily loosened his ties with his religious group in order to be accepted into another group. If he keeps his steel bracelet, which will be recognized by other Sikhs, it is because he does not wish to lose all the advantages connected with belonging to that group. When a Sikh takes his employer to court for refusing to allow him to wear his turban at work, it is not a mere formality. He is making a serious bid to limit his employer's power over his life.

The impact of technological culture can be measured by the degree of acceptance of Western conventions of body management throughout the world. Fashion, because it is beyond logic, is deeply revealing. Women all over the world have adopted, often in addition to their traditional accoutrements, four Western conventions: high-heeled shoes, lipstick, nail varnish, and the brassiere. The success of all of these fashions, which are not even remotely connected with comfort or common sense, is an indication of the worldwide acceptance of the Western notion that the principal duties of women are sexual attraction and vicarious leisure. The women who have accepted these fashions will justify their decision by saying that all four are more attractive than the alternatives. All that they are really saying is that they themselves were more attracted to alien styles than they were to the styles adopted by their mothers and grandmothers. To give the full answer would be to expose the tensions which are destroying traditional lifestyles all over the world. There is a slight traffic in the opposite direction. Distinguished lady professors of economics may reject high heels, lipstick, nail varnish, and brassiere, and adopt the dress of a Punjabi peasant laborer; Iranian girls may resume the chador. In each case the motive for the change is clearly political; what is not so often realized is that it is equally political when it happens the other way around.

Because what we do with our bodies is so revealing we try to insist that   5
it has no meaning at all. A man whose hair is cut regularly and at great expense, who shaves his face in a careful pattern, will say that he is not concerned with his appearance, while a man with a beard will maintain that he simply cannot be bothered shaving, but the truth is that both have selected an image which they feel best expresses their characters and chosen social roles. The man with a beard probably shaves some part of his face and neck quite regularly, and definitely trims the beard itself. He may frequently be seen grooming it with his hands, patting and stroking it into his preferred shape. Between the shaggy bearded man and the smooth clean-shaven man there lies a vast range of tonsorial modes, all of which have meanings relative to each other. The man who grows his sideburns long is expressing something about his class and his age group. The man who lets his cheek whiskers grow in tufts or shaves his sideburns off is also projecting some part of a chosen self-image. All kinds of curious facial topiary are accepted provided that they have some pedigree within our cultural tradition. The association of such variations as curled and waxed mustaches, Mexican revolutionary mustaches, pencil mustaches, and toothbrush mustaches are endlessly subtle and constantly being remade.

In the recent past we came to accept long flowing hair as a possible masculine alternative; with the passing of time our initial reactions of outrage have softened into acceptance. Men's long curls are now a sign of nostalgia for the sixties, the last quiver of hippie energy, which was never anything to be feared. By contrast, the man who completely shaves his head still shocks us. It is as if he is flaunting a violence that he has done to himself. Other men, hairless through no choice of their own, may have wigs on the National Health to hide their embarrassing nakedness. Western youths whose heads are shaven in accordance with the practice of oriental monastics will wear wigs when they go to badger people in airports because shaven heads are so alienating to our sensibilities. The man who shaves his head and does not cover it is indulging in a form of indecent exposure, the purpose of which, as usual, is intimidation.

The shaving of women's heads is considered so disfiguring that it seemed adequate punishment for women who collaborated with the Nazis in the Second World War, and yet there are many cultures whose women shave all or part of their heads and would feel dirty or unkempt if they did not. Girls who shave off all the hair except what grows on the crown of their heads are doing no more than the Turkana women of Kenya have always done, but by doing it in a society where such styles have never been seen, they defy the accepted norms and court rejection. The coxcomb and its variants, sometimes called the Mohawk or Mohican hairstyle, imitate the intimidating shapes of the advanced crests of fighting birds. A less daring version, for it can be tamed into smoothness when the wearer is in the haunts of the smooth, is the teased mop. The ferocity mimicked by the hairstyle is further expressed in the studded belts and armlets and earrings in the shape of a skull, but it is clearly a mere affectation. The camp aggressiveness of the display stands in inverse ratio to the social power wielded by the group. Their cultural uniformity is actually competitiveness and does not lead to solidarity.

In most societies which modify the body, the visible changes are outward signs of the fulfillment of the rites of passage. The acceptance of the newborn into the community at a naming ceremony or its equivalent may be marked by a ritual haircut, the shape of which may indicate his or her clan or totem. The approach of puberty may be signaled by circumcision or scarification or the adoption of a new hairstyle. The prelude to marriage may require further scarification or tattooing or fattening or a period of special body painting, while marriage itself may be signified by drastic changes in appearance, especially for women. The birth of children, achievement of elder status, or the death of a spouse bring the last changes. In classless societies where property is either held in common or kept to a minimum, all changes in status must involve changes in physical appearance. Where no one carries an identity card which will, say, permit him to drink in the company of adults, everyone who may must be distinguished by a sign. The achievement of these signs is one of the most important satisfactions of such societies. Before imperialists brought mirrors, such people could not confer the signs upon themselves: The recognition of a transition was given dramatic form by the ceremony of the conferring of signs in which the interested parties all acted as a group.

In Western society the outward signs of social status have withered into mere vestiges. Pubescent boys may live through intense dramas of hair cultivation, struggling for a mustache or bushy sideburns or simply longing to shave every day. Little girls may covet high heels and brassieres and long for the day that they can wear make-up, but the menarche will not be marked in any way: Marriageability will be signified only by the absence of an inconspicuous ring on the fourth finger of the left hand. In Jewish society, circumcision is still a rite of passage, but once the bar mitzvah is over, the initiate cannot be recognized by any other outward sign. Married women used to be expected to dress differently from girls: a pale echo of the sixteenth-century custom which required married women to wear closed bodices and hide their hair under a cap. This persisted into the twentieth century when married women were expected to wear hats on social occasions, but has now died out.

The disappearance of distinguishing marks of social status in industrial   10
societies is not meaningless, nor can it be construed to mean that human beings have outgrown such childish things. It is an accurate reflection of the fact that social relationships, particularly kinship relations, have been and are under intense pressure from economic relationships. The one insignia that is worn, in the United States more than in Europe but the strengthening of the trend is apparent, is the insignia of the employer. The family is no longer the dominant group and human beings are no longer differentiated on the grounds of their status within it. Instead they are differentiated by their consumer behavior, employment status, income, and possessions: The contrasts are so striking that it is considered indiscreet and tasteless to flaunt them by display of wealth. Instead the degrees of difference are signaled, more or less subtly, by grooming and by some carefully chosen attributes; hints to those who know how to take them are conveyed by the watch, the pen, the attaché case, the note case, the cuff links. Along with the indications of success are clues to other allegiances, the college ring, the lodge pin, the old school tie. Democracy and uniformity in outward appearance are necessitated by the extreme differentiation in economic circumstances, which might otherwise become a source of tension.

In tribal societies, where economic activity is static, limited as it is to the repetitive daily functions of survival, there is time to elaborate the paraphernalia of status considered in all but economic terms and immense satisfaction connected with doing so. The individual who proceeds through the stages all duly solemnized has conferred an elegance and order upon the struggle, and within that wider function there is scope for individual expression and aesthetic concerns.

The motives for Western beautification are very different. . . . People who are excluded from economic activity . . . cannot compensate by celebrating other forms of status for these have been eliminated. Unhappily, as the social roles which evolve out of family relationships ceased to command respect, the number of older people condemned to live for many years outside the sphere of economic activity in conditions of mere survival increased and will go on increasing. Among the displacement activities which this group must now concentrate on in order to beguile the time between retirement and the grave, there are a number connected with futile imitation of the group from which they have been excluded. As there is no prestige or power connected with being old, it is important to deny the aging process itself. Where once humans celebrated the achievement of seniority and longevity, they now invest as much energy or more in trying to resist the inevitable. Where hair coloring used to be done for fun, it is now done for camouflage.

A full head of strawberry blonde curls is only acquired by a sixty-year-old after regular orgies of dying, setting, and backcombing, all of which actually speed the degeneration of the scalp and the hair shaft. There is a good deal of pain involved as the dyes bite into sensitive old skin and the hot dryers tighten the hair, driving the pins still further into the old scalp. The ordeal is worth it if the sufferer sees herself rejuvenated by it; the suffering is an essential part of the prophylaxis, but it must be accompanied by words of tenderness and filial care from the torturers. We are not surprised to see the hairdresser as a shaman, hung about with amulets, his face suffused with long-suffering compassion. The payment of money for his services guarantees that the job has been well done; an old lady with a fifty-dollar hairstyle is still a person to be reckoned with. . . .

. . . We are in the midst of a cultural upheaval in which the body, which for aeons was a holy thing, its excretions and its orifices feared and revered, is becoming reified. It is becoming a toy, an asset, a commodity, an instrumentality for human will, and the pace of the change is much too fast. The intolerability of pictures of stainless steel meticulously carving out faces and breasts, isolating the unwanted and throwing it in the trash, tells us that we are still superstitious. We still suspect that the fantasy which is being imposed upon the body is less potent and less various than the body itself. Yet we cannot ease our anxiety by sneering, for we know the callousness which characterizes our treatment of the old and obese. We can understand why people who have the money will endure pain and risk death rather than go on living inside the bodies which bear the marks of their own history. Cosmetic surgery is the secular version of confession and absolution. It has taken the place of all our lost ceremonies of death and rebirth. It is reincarnation.

Most societies reject the grossly deformed. All societies have notions of beauty and fitness to which they aspire: relatively non-neurotic societies tend to admire characteristics which are well-distributed among their people, because distance from the culturally recognized norm causes suffering. We are affected by our bodies just as our behavior marks them. Peculiar looking people tend to behave peculiarly. Criminologists have known for many years that cosmetic surgery may do more for a social delinquent than years of custody and psychiatric care, when it comes to rehabilitation.

Once we begin to sculpt the body to our own aesthetic requirements we enter a realm of shifting values to which there is no guide. In essence, beautification and mutilation are the same activity. The African women who practice genital mutilation do so primarily because they think the result is more attractive; the unreconstructed genitalia are disgusting to them. Very few Westerners really find the female genitalia beautiful, but most of them would be horrified, even nauseated, by the sight of an infibulated vagina. None of them, by contrast, would cry out in disgust at the sight of a mutilated penis, stripped of its foreskin; all of them would be unpleasantly affected by the sight of a subincised penis.

Some mutilations have an ulterior purpose; the biting off of little finger joints of the newborn by Aboriginal mothers may be a way of deflecting the attention of evil spirits who would covet a perfect child. The custom of branding sickly infants in India may incidentally eliminate the feebler ones before too much energy has been invested in their care, and even, perhaps activate sluggish resistance to the pathogens in the environment. In any event, the brands are carefully placed. The endurance of pain, especially in poor communities where pain and discomfort are daily realities, is another important aspect of beautification/mutilation. Scarification is valued not only because it is symmetrically placed about the body and not only because it implies the achievement of new status, but because it hurts. Where survival is only achieved by constant effort, stoicism and willpower are immensely important. The young woman who lies unflinching while the circumciser grinds her clitoris off between two stones is proving that she will make a good wife, equal to all the anguish of child-bearing and daily toil, not only to the witnesses of her bravery, but more importantly, to herself.

Industrialized society is the first in which endurance of physical pain is not a condition of survival. We have identified pain as our enemy and have done our best to eradicate even its most manageable manifestations. Scars have no value for us and their aesthetic appeal has perished alongside their moral value. A few women might confess that they feel strangely drawn to men with scarred faces (or eye-patches or limps) but it is generally considered to be an aberrant taste. Yet, augmentation mammoplasty is no more after all than a raised scar. The great difference between ancient and modern beautification/mutilation procedures is that nowadays we must conceal the fact of the procedure itself. The association of sculpted breasts with pain is anaphrodisiac, so much so, that a man who guesses that what he is admiring was produced by a knife, may lose all interest. Some women may boast of their cosmetic operations, but this is a safety valve against the possibility that they will be found out.

Most mutilations which have been accepted as beautiful are so by consensus; historically the most astonishing distortions have been admired, necks so elongated that they could not hold up the head unless supported by brass rings, teeth filed and knocked out, lips stretched to accommodate large discs, earlobes stretched until they hung down in large loops. However *outré* the punks may appear they are the merest beginners in the arts of mutilation. The admiration of certain disfigurements is an important part of the process of self-definition: Contempt for the same practices is one of the ways in which other groups insist upon their separateness. We are not surprised to find the greatest contrasts in groups living side by side. When genetic equipment and economic status are both very similar, contrasting cultural practices become immensely important; they become the expression of the group's introverted altruism. In most tribal societies the attitude is more or less pluralistic; a group of labret wearers, for example, will simply define themselves as labret wearers, without making any attempt to impose labrets on others or to deride them for being without them. Western industrial society, deluded perhaps by its own vastness and uniformity, is not pluralistic, but utterly convinced that its own practices are the product of enlightenment and ought to be followed by all progressive peoples. Thus Western women, fully accoutred with nail polish (which is incompatible with manual work), high-heeled shoes (disastrous for the posture and hence the back, and quite unsuitable for walking long distances over bad roads), and brassieres (which imitate the shape of a pubescent non-lactating breast rather than the useful organs to be found in most of the world) denounce female circumcision, without the shadow of a suspicion that their behavior is absurd.

Yet within this bland but crushing orthodoxy there are spores of some- 20
thing different. Our unemployed young have reverted to tribal practices. They indulge in flamboyant mutilation/beautification which is not understood, let alone appreciated in our common judgment. Teenage daughters come to their parents' dinner parties covered with blue spots, with blue hair standing on end. Deviant groups cemented by shared ritual intoxication or guilt or ordeal or all of these are budding in our rotting inner cities, terrorizing us with raucous music and insulting doggerel. If they had the power to grow like a malignant organism and invade the whole of the body politic we might have reason to be afraid. Like millions of generations of body decorators before them, they have no economic activity beyond survival; they could be toughened by the necessity of existing on the little that society will mete out to them so that they accumulate the collective power to strike at its unprotected underbelly. Or they could fritter away their spare energy in intercommunal war, as gangs have always done. The body art of the urban deviant is unlike any which has appeared on earth before in that it has no socially constructed significance. There is . . . [no] . . . mutual decoration; no young warriors apply magical designs to each other's backs. No priests and witches or mothers and aunts confer new powers upon an initiate. The only human interactions we see are commercial. The manicurists, the cosmetologists, the surgeons, the hairdressers, the tattooists are all professionals. Between the dancer and the dance has been interposed the mirror; the clients have come to the professionals after long and lonely contemplation of the self which dissatisfies them. Individuals do not modify their bodies to please others or to clarify their relationship to others. Rather they inflict changes upon themselves in order to approximate to narcissistic needs which may have been projected on to putative others.

Inside the bodies they have reconstructed, the body builders live incommunicado. The illustrated men disappear behind designs imported from a highly structured alien culture into which they themselves could never be accepted. The body building, the tattooing, the cultivation of cockscombs, the driving of rings, bolts, barbs, and studs through labia, lobes, cartilage, nipples, foreskin are all displacement activities. A caged bird suffering from loneliness and sensory deprivation will turn upon itself and pluck out all its feathers or peck off its own leg. Middle-aged women rejected by their children will turn to surgery, restlessly beautifying/mutilating to no purpose, and a good deal of their activity will be directed against their sexuality. The body builders will proceed until they have become epicene monsters, all body hair shaved off so that the light can catch the slick greased muscles. . . . One of the most potent symbols among all natural symbols is the breast, not only the female breast but by extension the male simulacrum. Only groups doomed to extinction have ever attacked the nipples; cutting, piercing, and distorting them . . . is something hideously strange. . . . Attacks upon the genitalia and the secondary sexual characteristics are attacks upon the continuity of the species; they are only conceivable in lives which are confined to their own duration, on bodies which must be their own gratification, among human contacts which are fleeting and self-centered. . . .

The right to economic activity is no longer a right which our society can guarantee to everyone. We are on the brink of an era in which most people will be condemned to a life of enforced leisure and mere subsistence. It may very well be that these displacement activities will have to evolve into legitimate art forms involving a strong and healthy body decorated with skill, sophistication; and meaning. Perhaps human worker bees will some day be delighted by the displays of squads of human butterflies bred and trained to dance the drab streets as living works of art. It would be a great pity if the dazzling tradition of human body art were to perish in a waste of dreary conformity on the one hand and neurotic self-distortion on the other.

Questions for Discussion and Writing

1. How did the motives for body modification in tribal cultures differ from those in Western societies?
2. Which features of Greer's essay reveal an awareness of the pressures to which women are subjected in contemporary society?
3. Do you agree or disagree with Greer's explanation for body piercing? Why or why not? What body modifications have you undergone or would you consider doing? Describe your experiences and the way this altered your relationships with others.
4. **Rhetorical inquiry:** How would you characterize Greer's style? In what way does the tone of this piece differ from an article in a typical fashion magazine treating the same subject?

To what extent does this picture of a punk woman illustrate Greer's thesis about rebellion?

VALERIE STEELE AND JOHN S. MAJOR

Valerie Steele is chief curator of the Museum at the Fashion Institute of Technology (FIT). Steele organized a major exhibition at FIT to coincide with the 1999 publication of China Chic: East Meets West. *She is the editor of* Fashion Theory: The Journal of Dress, Body, and Culture *and has also written* Paris Fashion: A Cultural History *(1998) and* Fashion and Eroticism *(2000). A recent work is* Fashion, Italian Style *(2003). John S. Major is director of the China Council of the Asia Society. He is the author of* Heaven and Earth in Early Han Thought *(1993) and* The Silk Route: 7,000 Miles of History *(1996). The following essay, from* China Chic, *examines foot binding in the context of China's political, economic, and cultural history and its correspondence to fashions in the west.*

Before You Read

Consider how foot binding in China (accomplished through dwarfing the foot by dislocating its bones) was a symbol of fashion just as high-heeled shoes are in the West today.

China Chic: East Meets West

Foot binding lasted for a thousand years. It apparently began in the declining years of the Tang dynasty and it persisted in remote areas of China until the middle of the twentieth century. Yet despite its manifest significance within Chinese history, foot binding has been the subject of surprisingly little scholarly research. Recently, however, scholars such as Dorothy Ko have begun to explore the subject—with surprising results. As Ko points out, "It is natural for modern-day reformers to consider footbinding a men's conspiracy to keep women crippled and submissive, but this is an anachronistic view that finds no support in the historical records."[1]

Many of the sources on which our understanding of foot binding are based are themselves highly problematic. Western missionaries attacked the "barbaric" practice of foot binding, but they did so within the context of a prejudiced and ignorant denunciation of many other aspects of Chinese civilization. Most of the Chinese literature on the subject was written by men, who often emphasized the erotic appeal of foot binding. For a better understanding of foot binding, it is necessary to search for evidence of what Chinese women themselves thought about the practice. It is also necessary to place foot binding within its (changing) historical context. As Ko puts it, "Foot binding is not one monolithic, unchanging experience that all unfortunate women in each succeeding dynasty went through, but is rather an amorphous practice that meant different things to different people . . . It is, in other words, a situated practice."[2]

What did foot binding signify to the Chinese, and why did they maintain the practice for so long? Although historians do not know exactly how or why foot binding began, it was apparently initially associated with dancers at the imperial court and professional female entertainers in the capital. During the Song dynasty (960–1279) the practice spread from the palace and entertainment quarters into the homes of the elite. "By the thirteenth century, archeological evidence shows clearly that foot-binding was practiced among the daughters and wives of officials," reports Patricia Buckley Ebrey, whose study of Song women reproduces photographs of shoes from

---

[1] Dorothy Ko, *Teachers of the Inner Chambers: Women and Culture in Seventeenth Century China* (Stanford: Stanford University Press, 1994), p. 148.   [2] Dorothy Ko, "The Body as Attire: The Shifting Meanings of Footbinding in Seventeenth Century China," *Journal of Women's History* 8.4 (1997), p. 15.

that period. The Fujian tomb of Miss Huang Sheng (1227–43), for example, contained shoes measuring between 13.3 and 14 cm. (5¼ to 5½ inches), while the Jiangxi tomb of Miss Zhou (1240–74) contained shoes that were 18 to 22 cm. (7 to 8⅝ inches) long.[3] Over the course of the next few centuries foot binding became increasingly common among gentry families, and the practice eventually penetrated the mass of the Chinese people.

Foot binding generally began between the ages of five and seven, although many poorer families delayed beginning for several years, sometimes even until the girl was an adolescent, so they could continue to benefit from her labor and mobility. First-person accounts of foot binding testify that the procedure was extremely painful. The girl's feet were tightly bound with bandages, which forced the small toes inward and under the sole of the foot, leaving only the big toe to protrude. Then the heel and toe were drawn forcefully together, breaking the arch of the foot.

This was the most extreme type of foot binding. However, many girls apparently had their feet "bound in less painful styles that 'merely' kept the toes compressed or limited the growth of the foot, but did not break any bones."[4] Nevertheless, there is no doubt that foot binding was a radical form of body modification. As early as the Song dynasty, Che Ruoshui made perhaps the first protest against foot binding. He wrote: "Little children not yet four or five *sui* [i.e. five to seven years old], who have done nothing wrong, nevertheless are made to suffer unlimited pain to bind [their feet] small. I do not know what use this is."[5]

In fact, foot binding served a number of uses. To begin with, as Ebrey suggests, by making the feet of Chinese women so much smaller than those of Chinese men, it emphasized that men and women were different. Then, too, since only Chinese women bound their feet, the practice also served to distinguish between Chinese and non-Chinese. An investigation of the political situation suggests why this might have been thought desirable. At the time when foot binding began (in the late Tang) and spread (in the Song), China was in bad shape. Various foreign peoples who lived along the frontiers repeatedly raided and invaded China, sometimes conquering sizeable portions of Chinese territory and establishing their own dynasties on land that the Chinese regarded as properly theirs—as the Khitans did in the northeast when they defeated the Tang and established the Liao dynasty (907–1125), as the Tanguts did in the west when they established the XiXia Kingdom, and again as the Jürchens did in the north when they established the Jin dynasty (1115–1260) to succeed the Khitan Liao.

Although the Chinese managed to establish the Song dynasty in 960, after the turmoil that accompanied the fall of the Tang, it occupied only a

---

[3] Patricia Buckley Ebrey, *The Inner Quarters: Marriage and the Lives of Chinese Women in the Sung Period* (Berkeley: University of California Press, 1993), pp. 38–39.   [4] Feng Jicai, *The Three-Inch Golden Lotus,* trans. David Wakefield (Honolulu: University of Hawaii Press, 1994), p. 236.   [5] Cited in Ebrey, *The Inner Quarters,* p. 40.

portion of what had been Chinese territory, and even that portion decreased dramatically. Chinese men must often have been reminded of their military inferiority in the face of the aggressive "barbarians" encroaching from the north. Did they, perhaps, feel reassured about their strength and masculinity when they compared themselves to their crippled female counterparts? It may be possible to infer something of the sort when we analyze Song erotic poetry, devoted to the charms of tiny feet and a hesitant gait.

The suggestion that the spread of foot binding in the Song may have been related to the perceived need on the part of the Chinese gentry to emphasize the distinctions between men and women, Chinese and non-Chinese is strongly supported by Ebrey's analysis. "Because the ideal upper-class man was by Sung times a relatively subdued and refined figure, he might seem effeminate unless women could be made even more delicate, reticent, and stationary," she writes. In other words, anxieties about masculinity and national identity, rather than the desire to oppress women, *per se*, contributed to the spread of foot binding. "But," Ebrey adds, "we must also come to grips with women's apparently eager participation." A crucial element here, she argues, was the competition between wives and concubines. Chinese mothers may have become enthusiastic proponents of foot binding because small feet were regarded as sexually attractive, yet unlike the other tricks used by courtesans and concubines, there was nothing "forward" or "immodest" about having bound feet.[6]

The spread of foot binding during the Song dynasty also coincided with a philosophical movement known as Neo-Confucianism, which placed a pronounced ideological emphasis on female inferiority. (In Neo-Confucian metaphysics, the *yang* male principle was seen as superior to the *yin* female principle in both a cosmological and a moral sense.) Moreover, as already seen, political developments in the Song contributed to the demise of the great aristocratic families and the corresponding proliferation of gentry families, whose social and economic position was much more insecure, and whose predominant social function was to serve as bureaucrats. Members of this new class may have been especially receptive to foot binding, because the practice simultaneously provided reassurance about their social status, proper gender relations, and Chinese identity.

Foot binding may have been reassuring to the Chinese, but it did not prevent the Mongols from becoming the first foreigners to conquer all of China. Genghiz Khan unified the Mongols, and Kublai Khan established the Yuan dynasty (1279–1368). Similar anxieties about sexual and racial boundaries appeared again several centuries later toward the end of the Ming dynasty, when the Chinese began to be threatened by the Manchus. Moreover, when the Manchus succeeded in conquering China and establishing the Qing dynasty in the mid-seventeenth century, they passed edicts ordering Chinese men to shave their foreheads and Chinese women to cease foot binding.

[6] Ebrey, *The Inner Quarters*, pp. 42–43.

The resulting "hysterical atmosphere" was "full of sexual over-tones," since both cutting men's hair and unbinding women's feet were perceived by Chinese males almost as a symbolic mutilation or castration, which might even be worse than death. As Ko points out, "Although no one openly advocated footbinding, the very establishment of the Manchu dynasty created a need to reemphasize the differences between 'we' and 'they' and between 'he' and 'she.' The ban on footbinding, thus doomed from the start, was rescinded in 1668, four years after its promulgation."[7]

Contrary to popular belief, it was not only the wealthy who bound their daughters' feet. By the Qing dynasty, the majority of Chinese women had bound feet—peasants included—although there did exist variations in the degree and type of foot binding. According to one Qing observer, "The practice of footbinding is more widespread in Yangzhou than in other places. Even coolies, servants, seamstresses, the poor, the old, and the weak have tiny feet and cramped toes."[8] Manchu women, however, did not bind their feet, nor did members of other ethnic minority groups. Indeed, under the Qing, Manchu women were specifically forbidden to bind their feet, which is intriguing, since it implies a desire to do so.

Because foot binding is usually interpreted today as a gruesome example of women's oppression, it is important to stress that women who experienced the practice rarely perceived it in those terms. Indeed, Ko has unearthed considerable evidence that many Chinese women felt proud of their bound feet, which they regarded as beautiful and prestigious. Foot binding was a central part of the women's world. The rituals surrounding foot binding were female-exclusive rituals, presided over by the women of the family, especially the girl's mother, who prayed to deities such as the Tiny Foot Maiden and the goddess Guanyin. According to Ko, these rituals "and the beliefs behind them help explain the longevity and spread of the custom."

> For all its erotic appeal to men, without the cooperation of the women concerned, footbinding could not have been perpetuated for a millennium. In defining the mother–daughter tie in a private space barred to men, in venerating the fruits of women's handiwork, and in the centrality of female-exclusive religious rituals, footbinding embodied the essential features of a woman's culture documented by the writings of the women themselves.[9]

Women wrote poems about lotus shoes and they exchanged them with friends. Proverbs emphasized women's control over foot binding: "A plain face is given by heaven, but poorly bound feet are a sign of laziness."[10]

Good mothers were supposed to bind their daughters' feet tightly so they could make advantageous marriages, just as they made their sons study

---

[7] Ko, *Teachers of the Inner Chambers*, p. 149.   [8] Ibid., p. 263.   [9] Ibid., p. 150.
[10] Ibid., p. 171.

hard so they could pass their examinations. The Victorian traveler Isabella Bird visited China and reported that "The butler's little daughter, aged seven, is having her feet 'bandaged' for the first time, and is in torture, but bears it bravely in the hope of 'getting a rich husband' . . . The mother of this suffering infant says, with a quiet air of truth and triumph, that Chinese women suffer less in the process of being crippled than foreign women do from wearing corsets!"[11]

Indeed, Chinese and westerners alike not infrequently compared foot binding with corsetry, debating their relative injuriousness and irrationality. Yet measurements of existing corsets and lotus shoes indicate that both the sixteen-inch waist and the three-inch golden lotus were only achieved by a minority of women. Writing at the turn of the century, the sociologist Thorstein Veblen used foot binding (as well as such western fashions as corsets and long skirts) as examples of what he called "conspicuous leisure," because they supposedly indicated that the wearer could not perform productive labor. Yet, contrary to popular belief, neither bound feet nor corsets prevented women from working and walking; most Chinese women worked very hard, albeit usually at home. Moreover, although foot binding was believed to ensure female chastity by, literally, preventing women from straying, in fact women were far more restricted by social and legal constraints.

Although for many centuries most Chinese men and women approved of foot binding, the practice eventually ceased to be valorized as a way of emphasizing the beauty and virtue of Chinese women and/or the virility and civility of Chinese men. Writing in the early nineteenth century, the novelist Li Ruzhun attacked foot binding on the grounds that it oppressed women. His novel *Flowers in the Mirror* included a satirical sequence about a country where women ruled and men had their feet bound.

Missionary efforts undoubtedly played a role in the demise of foot binding, as the Chinese were made aware that Westerners thought the practice was "barbaric," unhealthy, and oppressive to women. The Chinese girls who attended mission schools were taught that foot binding was bad. More significantly, however, growing numbers of young Chinese men (and a few educated Chinese women) began to reinterpret foot binding as a "backward" practice that hindered national efforts to resist western imperialism.

Chinese reformers began to discuss whether China could be strengthened *vis-à-vis* the West, if only Chinese women became stronger physically. This, in turn, seemed to depend on the elimination of what was increasingly regarded by progressive Chinese as the "feudal" practice of foot binding. Organizations such as the Natural Foot Society were founded, and struggled to change the idea that unbound female feet were "big" and ugly. Indeed, it

---

[11] Isabella Bird, *The Golden Chersonese and the Way Thither* (first published London, 1883; reprinted, Singapore: Oxford University Press, 1990), p. 66.

was apparently difficult to convince the Chinese that foot binding was any more "unnatural" than other kinds of bodily adornment, such as clothing, jewelry, hairstyles, or cosmetics.[12]

There is even some evidence that the introduction of western high-heeled shoes, which give the visual illusion of smaller feet and produce a swaying walk, may have eased the transition away from the bound foot ideal. Manchu shoes were another alternative to lotus shoes in the early years of the anti-foot-binding movement, although with the rise of anti-Manchu nationalism at the time of the 1911 Revolution, this style disappeared.

Foot binding had never been mandated by any Chinese government. 20 Indeed, various Qing rulers had sporadically attempted to abolish foot binding, without success. After the Qing dynasty was overthrown and a republic was declared, foot binding was outlawed. Laws alone would not have sufficed to end the practice, however, had it not already ceased to claim the allegiance of significant segments of the Chinese population, but once foot binding began to be regarded as "backward," modern-thinking Chinese increasingly attacked the practice.

Older brothers argued that their sisters should not have their feet bound, or should try to let their feet out—a process that was itself painful and only partly feasible. Sometimes husbands even abandoned wives who had bound feet, and looked for new, suitably modern brides. Obviously, these developments took place within the context of broader social change. The new generation of educated, urban Chinese increasingly argued that many aspects of traditional Chinese culture should be analyzed and improved. Women, as well as men, should be educated and should participate in athletic activities. Arranged marriages should be replaced by love matches. The Chinese nation should modernize and strengthen itself.

Questions for Discussion and Writing

1. What does the practice of foot binding involve and why was it so important for such a long time in traditional China?
2. How did foot binding serve as a means for the Chinese to differentiate themselves from Manchu invaders from the North?
3. How did Western missionaries and Chinese reformers react to this practice?
4. **Rhetorical inquiry:** How would you characterize the authors' tone toward their subject and did you find their approach effective? Why or why not?

---

[12] Ko, "The Body as Attire," pp. 17–19.

Fiction

CARSON MCCULLERS

Carson McCullers (1917–1967) was born in Columbus, Georgia, as Lula Carson Smith. Although she moved from the South in 1934 (with intentions of studying music at Julliard), her writing is deeply embedded in the southern literary tradition and emphasizes loneliness and desire. This blend of the real and dramatic with the poetic and symbolic can be seen in her novels The Heart Is a Lonely Hunter *(1940), a touching portrait of an adolescent girl, and* The Member of the Wedding *(1946), in which the twelve-year-old main character's wishes to become part of the social community are rejected. This novel was adapted for the stage in 1950 and became a successful Broadway play as well as a motion picture in 1952.* The Ballad of the Sad Café *was published as a novella in 1951 and was adapted by Edward Albee for the stage in 1963. In addition to her five novels and two plays, she also wrote essays, poetry, and numerous short stories, including "Madame Zilensky and the King of Finland" with its uncharacteristically whimsical ending. The main character imbues everyday reality with fantasy and fable conveyed through McCullers's cool and engaging prose.*

Before You Read

Can having a good imagination enrich your life?

Madame Zilensky and the King of Finland

To Mr. Brook, the head of the music department at Ryder College, was due all the credit for getting Madame Zilensky on the faculty. The college considered itself fortunate; her reputation was impressive, both as a composer and as a pedagogue. Mr. Brook took on himself the responsibility of finding a house for Madame Zilensky, a comfortable place with a garden, which was convenient to the college and next to the apartment house where he himself lived.

No one in Westbridge had known Madame Zilensky before she came. Mr. Brook had seen her pictures in musical journals, and once he had written to her about the authenticity of a certain Buxtehude manuscript. Also, when it was being settled that she was to join the faculty, they had exchanged a few cables and letters on practical affairs. She wrote in a clear, square hand, and the only thing out of the ordinary in these letters was the fact that they contained an occasional reference to objects and persons altogether unknown to Mr. Brook, such as "the yellow cat in Lisbon" or "poor Heinrich." These lapses Mr. Brook put down to the confusion of getting herself and her family out of Europe.

Mr. Brook was a somewhat pastel person; years of Mozart minuets, of explanations about diminished sevenths and minor triads, had given him a watchful vocational patience. For the most part, he kept to himself. He loathed academic fiddle-faddle and committees. Years before, when the music department had decided to gang together and spend the summer in Salzburg, Mr. Brook sneaked out of the arrangement at the last moment and took a solitary trip to Peru. He had a few eccentricities himself and was tolerant of the peculiarities of others; indeed, he rather relished the ridiculous. Often, when confronted with some grave and incongruous situation, he would feel a little inside tickle, which stiffened his long, mild face and sharpened the light in his gray eyes.

Mr. Brook met Madame Zilensky at the Westbridge station a week before the beginning of the fall semester. He recognized her instantly. She was a tall, straight woman with a pale and haggard face. Her eyes were deeply shadowed and she wore her dark, ragged hair pushed back from her forehead. She had large, delicate hands, which were very grubby. About her person as a whole there was something noble and abstract that made Mr. Brook draw back for a moment and stand nervously undoing his cuff links. In spite of her clothes—a long, black skirt and a broken-down old leather jacket— she made an impression of vague elegance. With Madame Zilensky were three children, boys between the ages of ten and six, all blond, blank-eyed, and beautiful. There was one other person, an old woman who turned out later to be the Finnish servant.

This was the group he found at the station. The only luggage they had   5 with them was two immense boxes of manuscripts, the rest of their paraphernalia having been forgotten in the station at Springfield when they changed trains. That is the sort of thing that can happen to anyone. When Mr. Brook got them all into a taxi, he thought the worst difficulties were over, but Madame Zilensky suddenly tried to scramble over his knees and get out of the door.

"My God!" she said. "I left my—how do you say?—my tick-tick-tick—"

"Your watch?" asked Mr. Brook.

"Oh no!" she said vehemently. "You know, my tick-tick-tick," and she waved her forefinger from side to side, pendulum fashion.

"Tick-tick," said Mr. Brook, putting his hands to his forehead and closing his eyes. "Could you possibly mean a metronome?"

"Yes! Yes! I think I must have lost it there where we changed trains."   10

Mr. Brook managed to quiet her. He even said, with a kind of dazed gallantry, that he would get her another one the next day. But at the time he was bound to admit to himself that there was something curious about this panic over a metronome when there was all the rest of the lost luggage to consider.

The Zilensky ménage moved into the house next door, and on the surface everything was all right. The boys were quiet children. Their names were Sigmund, Boris, and Sammy. They were always together and they followed each other around Indian file, Sigmund usually the first. Among themselves they spoke a desperate-sounding family Esperanto made up of Russian, French, Finnish, German, and English; when other people were around, they were strangely silent. It was not any one thing that the Zilenskys did or said that made Mr. Brook uneasy. There were just little incidents. For example, something about the Zilensky children subconsciously bothered him when they were in a house, and finally he realized that what troubled him was the fact that the Zilensky boys never walked on a rug; they skirted it single file on the bare floor, and if a room was carpeted, they stood in the doorway and did not go inside. Another thing was this: Weeks passed and Madame Zilensky seemed to make no effort to get settled or to furnish the house with anything more than a table and some beds. The front door was left open day and night, and soon the house began to take on a queer, bleak look like that of a place abandoned for years.

The college had every reason to be satisfied with Madame Zilensky. She taught with a fierce insistence. She could become deeply indignant if some Mary Owens or Bernadine Smith would not clean up her Scarlatti trills. She got hold of four pianos for her college studio and set four dazed students to playing Bach fugues together. The racket that came from her end of the department was extraordinary, but Madame Zilensky did not seem to have a nerve in her, and if pure will and effort can get over a musical idea, then Ryder College could not have done better. At night Madame Zilensky worked on her twelfth symphony. She seemed never to sleep; no matter what time of night Mr. Brook happened to look out of his sitting-room window, the light in her studio was always on. No, it was not because of any professional consideration that Mr. Brook became so dubious.

It was in late October when he felt for the first time that something was unmistakably wrong. He had lunched with Madame Zilensky and had enjoyed himself, as she had given him a very detailed account of an African safari she had made in 1928. Later in the afternoon she stopped in at his office and stood rather abstractly in the doorway.

Mr. Brook looked up from his desk and asked, "Is there anything you want?"   15

"No, thank you," said Madame Zilensky. She had a low, beautiful, sombre voice. "I was only just wondering. You recall the metronome. Do you think perhaps that I might have left it with that French?"

"Who?" asked Mr. Brook.

"Why, that French I was married to," she answered.

"Frenchman," Mr. Brook said mildly. He tried to imagine the husband of Madame Zilensky, but his mind refused. He muttered half to himself, "The father of the children."

"But no," said Madame Zilensky with decision. "The father of Sammy."   20

Mr. Brook had a swift prescience. His deepest instincts warned him to say nothing further. Still, his respect for order, his conscience, demanded that he ask, "And the father of the other two?"

Madame Zilensky put her hand to the back of her head and ruffled up her short, cropped hair. Her face was dreamy, and for several moments she did not answer. Then she said gently, "Boris is of a Pole who played the piccolo."

"And Sigmund?" he asked. Mr. Brook looked over his orderly desk, with the stack of corrected papers, the three sharpened pencils, the ivory-elephant paperweight. When he glanced up at Madame Zilensky, she was obviously thinking hard. She gazed around at the corners of the room, her brows lowered and her jaw moving from side to side. At last she said, "We were discussing the father of Sigmund?"

"Why, no," said Mr. Brook. "There is no need to do that."

Madame Zilensky answered in a voice both dignified and final. "He was a fellow-countryman."   25

Mr. Brook really did not care one way or the other. He had no prejudices; people could marry seventeen times and have Chinese children so far as he was concerned. But there was something about this conversation with Madame Zilensky that bothered him. Suddenly he understood. The children didn't look at all like Madame Zilensky, but they looked exactly like each other, and as they all had different fathers, Mr. Brook thought the resemblance astonishing.

But Madame Zilensky had finished with the subject. She zipped up her leather jacket and turned away.

"That is exactly where I left it," she said, with a quick nod. "*Chez* that French."

Affairs in the music department were running smoothly. Mr. Brook did not have any serious embarrassments to deal with, such as the harp teacher last year who had finally eloped with a garage mechanic. There was only this nagging apprehension about Madame Zilensky. He could not make out what was wrong in his relations with her or why his feelings were so mixed. To begin with, she was a great globe-trotter, and her conversations were incongruously seasoned with references to far-fetched places. She would go along for days without opening her mouth, prowling through the corridor with her hands in the pockets of her jacket and her face locked in meditation. Then suddenly she would buttonhole Mr. Brook and launch out on a long, volatile monologue, her eyes reckless and bright and her voice warm with eagerness. She would talk about anything or nothing at all. Yet, without exception, there was something queer, in a slanted sort of way, about every episode she ever mentioned. If she spoke of taking Sammy to the barbershop, the impression she created was just as foreign as if she were telling of an afternoon in Bagdad. Mr. Brook could not make it out.

The truth came to him very suddenly, and the truth made everything   30
perfectly clear, or at least clarified the situation. Mr. Brook had come home early and lighted a fire in the little grate in his sitting room. He felt comfortable and at peace that evening. He sat before the fire in his stocking feet, with a volume of William Blake on the table by his side, and he had poured

himself a half-glass of apricot brandy. At ten o'clock he was drowsing cozily before the fire, his mind full of cloudy phrases of Mahler[1] and floating half-thoughts. Then all at once, out of this delicate stupor, four words came to his mind: "The King of Finland." The words seemed familiar, but for the first moment he could not place them. Then all at once he tracked them down. He had been walking across the campus that afternoon when Madame Zilensky stopped him and began some preposterous rigmarole, to which he had only half listened; he was thinking about the stack of canons turned in by his counterpoint class. Now the words, the inflections of her voice, came back to him with insidious exactitude. Madame Zilensky had started off with the following remark: "One day, when I was standing in front of a *pâtisserie*, the King of Finland came by in a sled."

Mr. Brook jerked himself up straight in his chair and put down his glass of brandy. The woman was a pathological liar. Almost every word she uttered outside of class was an untruth. If she worked all night, she would go out of her way to tell you she spent the evening at the cinema. If she ate lunch at the Old Tavern, she would be sure to mention that she had lunched with her children at home. The woman was simply a pathological liar, and that accounted for everything.

Mr. Brook cracked his knuckles and got up from his chair. His first reaction was one of exasperation. That day after day Madame Zilensky would have the gall to sit there in his office and deluge him with her outrageous falsehoods! Mr. Brook was intensely provoked. He walked up and down the room, then he went into his kitchenette and made himself a sardine sandwich.

An hour later, as he sat before the fire, his irritation had changed to a scholarly and thoughtful wonder. What he must do, he told himself, was to regard the whole situation impersonally and look on Madame Zilensky as a doctor looks on a sick patient. Her lies were of the guileless sort. She did not dissimulate with any intention to deceive, and the untruths she told were never used to any possible advantage. That was the maddening thing; there was simply no motive behind it all.

Mr. Brook finished off the rest of the brandy. And slowly, when it was almost midnight, a further understanding came to him. The reason for the lies of Madame Zilensky was painful and plain. All her life long Madame Zilensky had worked—at the piano, teaching, and writing those beautiful and immense twelve symphonies. Day and night she had drudged and struggled and thrown her soul into her work, and there was not much of her left over for anything else. Being human, she suffered from this lack and did what she could to make up for it. If she passed the evening bent over a table in the library and later declared that she had spent that time playing cards, it was as though she had managed to do both those things. Through the lies,

---

[1] *Mahler:* Gustav Mahler (1860–1911), renowned Austrian composer.

she lived vicariously. The lie doubled the little of her existence that was left over from work and augmented the little rag end of her personal life.

Mr. Brook looked into the fire, and the face of Madame Zilensky was in his mind—a severe face, with dark, weary eyes and delicately disciplined mouth. He was conscious of a warmth in his chest, and a feeling of pity, protectiveness, and dreadful understanding. For a while he was in a state of lovely confusion.

Later on he brushed his teeth and got into his pajamas. He must be practical. What did this clear up? That French, the Pole with the piccolo, Bagdad? And the children, Sigmund, Boris, and Sammy—who were they? Were they really her children after all, or had she simply rounded them up from somewhere? Mr. Brook polished his spectacles and put them on the table by his bed. He must come to an immediate understanding with her. Otherwise, there would exist in the department a situation which could become most problematical. It was two o'clock. He glanced out of his window and saw that the light in Madame Zilensky's workroom was still on. Mr. Brook got into bed, made terrible faces in the dark, and tried to plan what he would say next day.

Mr. Brook was in his office by eight o'clock. He sat hunched up behind his desk, ready to trap Madame Zilensky as she passed down the corridor. He did not have to wait long, and as soon as he heard her footsteps he called out her name.

Madame Zilensky stood in the doorway. She looked vague and jaded. "How are you? I had such a fine night's rest," she said.

"Pray be seated, if you please," said Mr. Brook. "I would like a word with you."

Madame Zilensky put aside her portfolio and leaned back wearily in the armchair across from him. "Yes?" she asked.

"Yesterday you spoke to me as I was walking across the campus," he said slowly. "And if I am not mistaken, I believe you said something about a pastry shop and the King of Finland. Is that correct?"

Madame Zilensky turned her head to one side and stared retrospectively at a corner of the window sill.

"Something about a pastry shop," he repeated.

Her tired face brightened. "But of course," she said eagerly. "I told you about the time I was standing in front of this shop and the King of Finland—"

"Madame Zilensky!" Mr. Brook cried. "There *is* no King of Finland."

Madame Zilensky looked absolutely blank. Then, after an instant, she started off again. "I was standing in front of Bjarne's *pâtisserie* when I turned away from the cakes and suddenly saw the King of Finland—"

"Madame Zilensky, I just told you that there is no King of Finland."

"In Helsingfors," she started off again desperately, and again he let her get as far as the King, and then no further.

"Finland is a democracy," he said. "You could not possibly have seen the King of Finland. Therefore, what you have just said is an untruth. A pure untruth."

Never afterward could Mr. Brook forget the face of Madame Zilensky   50
at that moment. In her eyes there was astonishment, dismay, and a sort of
cornered horror. She had the look of one who watches his whole interior
world split open and disintegrate.

"It is a pity," said Mr. Brook with real sympathy.

But Madame Zilensky pulled herself together. She raised her chin and
said coldly, "I am a Finn."

"That I do not question," answered Mr. Brook. On second thought, he
did question it a little.

"I was born in Finland and I am a Finnish citizen."

"That may very well be," said Mr. Brook in a rising voice.   55

"In the war," she continued passionately, "I rode a motorcycle and was
a messenger."

"Your patriotism does not enter into it."

"Just because I am getting out the first papers—"

"Madame Zilensky!" said Mr. Brook. His hands grasped the edge of
the desk. "That is only an irrelevant issue. The point is that you maintained
and testified that you saw—that you saw—" But he could not finish. Her
face stopped him. She was deadly pale and there were shadows around her
mouth. Her eyes were wide open, doomed, and proud. And Mr. Brook felt
suddenly like a murderer. A great commotion of feelings—understanding,
remorse, and unreasonable love—made him cover his face with his hands.
He could not speak until this agitation in his insides quieted down, and
then he said very faintly, "Yes. Of course. The King of Finland. And was he
nice?"

An hour later, Mr. Brook sat looking out of the window of his office.   60
The trees along the quiet Westbridge street were almost bare, and the gray
buildings of the college had a calm, sad look. As he idly took in the familiar
scene, he noticed the Drakes' old Airedale waddling along down the street.
It was a thing he had watched a hundred times before, so what was it that
struck him as strange? Then he realized with a kind of cold surprise that the
old dog was running along backward. Mr. Brook watched the Airedale until
he was out of sight, then resumed his work on the canons which had been
turned in by the class in counterpoint.

Questions for Discussion and Writing

1. What clues make Mr. Brook suspect that Madame Zilensky has fabricated a good deal of her past experiences? Why does he back down
   when he finally confronts her, and with what effect?
2. How does McCullers emphasize the uniqueness of Madame Zilensky
   and the positive effect she has on Mr. Brook and her students?

3. What is the point of the ending of the story, and how is it connected to the events that precede it? Did you find Madame Zilensky an appealing character or merely a somewhat sad lunatic?

4. **Rhetorical inquiry:** How does Madame Zilensky's insistence that each of her three sons has a different father (a Frenchman, a Pole, and a Finn) despite the fact that they all look exactly alike, and none of them look like her, provide a clue that she needs to appear to herself and others as unique and exciting?

Poetry

EMILY DICKINSON

Emily Dickinson (1830–1886) was born in Amherst, Massachusetts, and spent her entire life there. She attended Mount Holyoke Female Seminary, where she quarreled frequently with the school's headmistress, who wanted her to accept Calvinist views. Dickinson became more reclusive in her mid-twenties, retired to the seclusion of her family, and in 1861 began writing poetry that was strongly influenced by the ideas of Ralph Waldo Emerson. She maintained a correspondence with Thomas Wentworth Higginson, an abolitionist editor who encouraged her to write poetry. During her life, she published only seven of the nearly eighteen hundred poems that she wrote. After her death, a selection of her work aroused public interest, and her stature as one of the great American poets is now unquestioned. "Tell All the Truth But Tell It Slant" expresses her artistic credo.

Before You Read

Is understatement in a literary work desirable?

Tell All the Truth But Tell It Slant

Tell all the Truth but tell it slant—
Success in Circuit lies
Too bright for our infirm Delight
The Truth's superb surprise
As Lightning to the Children eased   5
With explanation kind
The Truth must dazzle gradually
Or every man be blind—

Questions for Discussion and Writing

1. How might the quality of Dickinson's personal reticence lead some readers to perceive her poetry as obscure?
2. How does the metaphor that Dickinson uses to explain her reasons for telling the truth indirectly illuminate her choice?
3. In your experiences, have there been circumstances in which the truth was too strong and could be approached only indirectly? Describe these circumstances.
4. **Rhetorical inquiry:** To what visual similarities of a lightning bolt does Dickinson equate indirect truths? How does she use an analogy to children who have been frightened by a flash of lightning and retreat in terror?

CHARLES BUKOWSKI

Charles Bukowski (1920–1994) was born in Andernach, Germany, and moved to Los Angeles when he was two years old. He held many jobs, including working as a letter carrier, and wrote poetry on and off until the publisher Black Sparrow Press guaranteed him a monthly stipend, which allowed him to quit his job at the post office and write full time. His first novel was titled Post Office. *Bukowski was an enormously prolific writer who wrote thousands of poems, hundreds of short stories and six novels. The following poem appeared in a posthumous collection of his poetry* Sifting Through the Madness for the Word, the Line, the Way: New Poems *(2003). A film about his life,* Bukowski: Born Into This, *was released in 2004.*

Before You Read

What is the difference between wanting to write something and having to write it?

So You Want to be a Writer

if it doesn't come bursting out of you
in spite of everything,
don't do it.
unless it comes unasked out of your
heart and your mind and your mouth   5
and your gut,
don't do it.
if you have to sit for hours
staring at your computer screen
or hunched over your   10

typewriter
searching for words,
don't do it.
if you're doing it for money or
fame,   15
don't do it.
if you're doing it because you want
women in your bed,
don't do it.
if you have to sit there and   20
rewrite it again and again,
don't do it.
if it's hard work just thinking about doing it,
don't do it.
if you're trying to write like somebody   25
else,
forget about it.

if you have to wait for it to roar out of
you,
then wait patiently.   30
if it never does roar out of you,
do something else.
if you first have to read it to your wife
or your girlfriend or your boyfriend
or your parents or to anybody at all,   35
you're not ready.

don't be like so many writers,
don't be like so many thousands of
people who call themselves writers,
don't be dull and boring and   40
pretentious, don't be consumed with self-
love.
the libraries of the world have
yawned themselves to
sleep   45
over your kind,
don't add to that,
don't do it.
unless it comes out of
your soul like a rocket,   50
unless being still would
drive you to madness or
suicide or murder,
don't do it.

unless the sun inside you is   55
burning your gut,
don't do it.

when it is truly time,
and if you have been chosen,
it will do it by   60
itself and it will keep on doing it
until you die or it dies in
you.
there is no other way.

and there never was.   65

Questions for Discussion and Writing

1. According to Bukowksi, what are some of the wrong reasons for wanting to become a writer? How does Bukowski's concept of what being a writer means differ from conventional views?
2. How does the form of the poem reinforce a sense of a very high threshold for would-be writers to meet?
3. Have you ever found yourself having to write in order to express your feelings and ideas that could not be expressed in any other way? Describe your experience.
4. **Rhetorical inquiry:** How do the images with which Bukowski describes the creation of poetry emphasize its primal and unchecked nature? Contrast these with the more superficial reasons for writing poetry.

Connections for Chapter 10:
The Artistic Impulse

1. **Kurt Vonnegut, Jr.,** *How to Write with Style*
   Compare the different emphases of Vonnegut and Stephen King in their advice to would-be writers.
2. **Stephen King,** *On Writing*
   What complementary perspectives on writing are presented by King and Charles Bukowski in his poem?
3. **Ross King,** *Michelangelo and the Pope's Ceiling*
   Do fresco painters such as Michelangelo as described by King use impermanent means to achieve a permanent end much as photojournalists do as discussed by Lance Morrow in "Imprisoning Time in a Rectangle"?

4. **Agnes De Mille,** *Pavlova*

   How does seeing a great performer shape a dancer's career as described by De Mille as reading a great book can for an aspiring writer, according to Vonnegut?

5. **Aaron Copland,** *Film Music*

   Does film music enhance a film in the same way that music enhances the lyrics of a song as in Bruce Springsteen's "Streets of Philadelphia" (in Chapter 5)?

6. **Lance Morrow,** *Imprisoning Time in a Rectangle*

   Discuss how the Vietnam-era photographs described by Morrow place violent events in perspective just as Don DeLillo does in his essay "In the Ruins of the Future." (Chapter 7)

7. **Germaine Greer,** *One Man's Mutilation Is Another Man's Beautification*

   Contrast the means and purposes of body modification as discussed by Greer with Rosalind Coward's analysis in "The Body Beautiful" in (Chapter 5).

8. **Valerie Steele and John S. Major,** *China Chic: East Meets West*

   How does Steele and Major's article illustrate Germaine Greer's thesis?

9. **Carson McCullers,** *Madame Zilensky and the King of Finland*

   Discuss how choices created by imagination are an integral feature of McCullers's story and Gregory Corso's poem "Marriage" (in Chapter 5).

10. **Emily Dickinson,** *Tell All the Truth But Tell It Slant*

    In what sense do Dickinson and McCullers in her story express views on how to reach audiences through less than obvious methods?

11. **Charles Bukowski,** *So You Want to be a Writer?*

    Compare the advice offered by Kurt Vonnegut, Jr. and Bukowski to would-be writers.

11

THE ETHICAL DIMENSION

Is there anything beyond?—Who knows?
Lord Byron, LETTERS AND JOURNALS

Works in this chapter offer a vivid and extensive range of responses to universal questions of good and evil and life and death. Philip Wheelwright shows how a systematic approach to ethical problems can help us resolve complex moral dilemmas in everyday life. The Dalai Lama suggests ways we can overcome obstacles to develop tolerance toward the teachings and practices of other religious faiths. A selection by Garrett Hardin investigates the moral and ethical criteria by which actions are judged to be right or wrong and the trade-offs that must be accepted in some situations. As the writers in this chapter make clear, ethics become even more important as society becomes more complex and technological, and as people lose sight of important values.

Because ethical and moral dilemmas involve choices, we have readings by Marya Mannes, Hans Ruesch, and Jean-Paul Sartre that dramatize very different scenarios on the issues of abortion, animal experimentation, and existentialism. Then Stanley Milgram, in his classic experiment, explores why ethical and moral constraints fail to operate in the presence of authority figures. John M. Darley and Bibb Latané, in their equally famous experiment, discover the variables that explain why bystanders in specific circumstances do not intervene to help a victim.

Plato's "The Allegory of the Cave" and parables drawn from *The New Testament* and from Buddhist and Islamic traditions are designed to convey a truth, or moral lesson. These works use distinctive comparisons, analogies, and storytelling techniques to transform philosophical issues into tangible, accessible, and relevant anecdotes.

A short story by Joyce Carol Oates dramatizes a crucial moral dilemma that requires the main character to make a life or death decision.

The poets in this chapter, Robert Frost and Linda Pastan, struggle with life choices that we all confront and remind us not to lose sight of important values.

As you read works in this chapter and prepare to discuss or write about them you may wish to use the following questions as guidelines.

- What specific ethical or moral set of choices does the author address?
- How personally involved is the author with the subject?
- Does the nature of the choice create a seemingly unsolvable problem?
- Does the author dramatize the choices with true-to-life examples or hypothetical instances?
- Does investigating the moral or ethical dilemma cause the writer to rethink his or her own values?
- If the writer offers a solution does it seem realistic and achievable?
- What would one have to relinquish to embrace the author's choice?

Nonfiction

PHILIP WHEELWRIGHT

Philip Wheelwright (1901–1970) was born in Elizabeth, New Jersey, and earned a Ph.D. from Princeton University in 1924. He was professor of philosophy at Princeton, Dartmouth, and the University of California at Riverside. His many influential studies of philosophy and ethics include A Critical Introduction to Ethics *(1959);* The Burning Fountain: A Study in the Language of Symbolism *(1954);* Philosophy as the Art of Living *(1956), which was first given as the Tully Cleon Knoles lectures;* Heraclitus *(1959); and* Valid Thinking *(1962). In "The Meaning of Ethics," from* A Critical Introduction to Ethics, *Wheelwright discusses the essential elements involved in solving ethical problems.*

Before You Read

Consider an ethical dilemma that required you to understand how everyone involved felt.

The Meaning of Ethics

> For you see, Callicles, our discussion is concerned with a matter in which even a man of slight intelligence must take the profoundest interest—namely, what course of life is best.
>
> —SOCRATES, *in Plato's* Gorgias

Man is the animal who can reflect. Like other animals, no doubt, he spends much of his time in merely reacting to the pressures and urgencies of his environment. But being a man he has moments also of conscious stock-taking, when he becomes aware not only of his world but of himself confronting his world, evaluating it, and making choices with regard to it. It is this ability to know himself and on the basis of self-knowledge to make evaluations and reflective choices that differentiates man from his subhuman cousins.

There are, as Aristotle has pointed out, two main ways in which man's power of reflection becomes active. They are called, in Aristotle's language, *theoretikos* and *praktikos* respectively; which is to say, thinking about what is actually the case and thinking about what had better be done. In English translation the words *contemplative* and *operative* probably come closest to Aristotle's intent. To think contemplatively is to ask oneself what *is;* to think operatively is to ask oneself what to *do.* These are the two modes of serious, one might even say of genuine thought—as distinguished from daydreams, emotional vaporizings, laryngeal chatter, and the repetition of clichés. To think seriously is to think either for the sake of knowing things as they are or for the sake of acting upon, and producing or helping to produce, things as they might be.

Although in practice the two types of thinking are much interrelated, it is operative thinking with which our present study is primarily concerned. Ethics, although it must be guided, limited, and qualified constantly by considerations of what is actually the case, is focused upon questions of what should be done. The converse, however, does not follow. Not all questions about what should be done are ethical questions. Much of our operative thinking is given to more immediate needs—to means whereby some given end can be achieved. A person who deliberates as to the most effective way of making money, or of passing a course, or of winning a battle, or of achieving popularity, is thinking operatively, but if that is as far as his planning goes it cannot be called ethical. Such deliberations about adapting means to an end would acquire an ethical character only if some thought were given to the nature and value of the end itself. Ethics cannot dispense with questions of means, but neither can it stop there.

Accordingly, ethics may be defined as that branch of philosophy which is the systematic study of reflective choice, of the standards of right and wrong by which it is to be guided, and of the goods toward which it may ultimately be directed. The relation between the parts of this definition, particularly between standards of right and wrong on the one hand and ultimately desirable goods on the other, will be an important part of the forthcoming study.

THE NATURE OF MORAL DELIBERATION

The soundest approach to ethical method is through reflection on our experience of moral situations which from time to time we have had occasion to face, or through an imagined confrontation of situations which others have   5 faced and which we can thus make sympathetically real to ourselves. For instance:

Arthur Ames is a rising young district attorney engaged on his most important case. A prominent political boss has been murdered. Suspicion points at a certain ex-convict, known to have borne the politician a grudge. Aided by the newspapers, which have reported the murder in such a way as to persuade the public of the suspect's guilt, Ames feels certain that he can secure a conviction on the circumstantial evidence in his possession. If he succeeds in sending the man to the chair he will become a strong candidate for governor at the next election.

During the course of the trial, however, he accidentally stumbles on some fresh evidence, known only to himself and capable of being destroyed if he chooses, which appears to establish the ex-convict's innocence. If this new evidence were to be introduced at the trial an acquittal would be practically certain. What ought the District Attorney to do? Surrender the evidence to the defence, in order that, as a matter of fair play, the accused might be given every legitimate chance of establishing his innocence? But to do that will mean the loss of a case that has received enormous publicity; the District Attorney will lose the backing of the press; he will appear to have failed, and his political career may be blocked. In that event not only will he himself suffer disappointment, but his ample plans for bestowing comforts on his family and for giving his children the benefits of a superior education may have to be curtailed. On the other hand, ought he to be instrumental in sending a man to the chair for a crime that in all probability he did not commit? And yet the ex-convict is a bad lot; even if innocent in the present case he has doubtless committed many other crimes in which he has escaped detection. Is a fellow like that worth the sacrifice of one's career? Still, there is no proof that he has ever committed a crime punishable by death. Until a man had been proved guilty he must be regarded, by a sound principle of American legal theory, as innocent. To conceal and destroy the new evidence, then, is not that tantamount to railroading an innocent man to the chair?

So District Attorney Ames reasons back and forth. He knows that it is a widespread custom for a district attorney to conceal evidence prejudicial to his side of a case. But is the custom, particularly when a human life is at stake, morally right? A district attorney is an agent of the government, and his chief aim in that capacity should be to present his accusations in such a way as to ensure for the accused not condemnation but justice. The question, then, cannot be answered by appealing simply to law or to legal practice. It is a moral one: *What is Arthur Ames' duty? What ought he to do?*

Benjamin Bates has a friend who lies in a hospital, slowly dying of a painful and incurable disease. Although there is no hope of recovery, the disease sometimes permits its victim to linger on for many months, in ever greater torment and with threatened loss of sanity. The dying man, apprised of the outcome and knowing that the hospital expenses are a severe drain on his family's limited financial resources, decides that death had better come at once. His physician, he knows, will not run the risk of providing him with the necessary drug. There is only his friend Bates to appeal to.

How shall Bates decide? Dare he be instrumental in hastening another's death? Has he a moral right to be an accessory to the taking of a human life? Besides, suspicion would point his way, and his honorable motives would not avert a charge of murder. On the other hand, can he morally refuse to alleviate a friend's suffering and the financial distress of a family when the means of doing so are in his hands? And has he not an obligation to respect a friend's declared will in the matter? To acquiesce and to refuse seem both somehow in different ways wrong, yet one course or the other must be chosen. *What ought Bates to do? Which way does his duty lie?*

In the city occupied by Crampton College a strike is declared by the employees of all the public-transit lines. Their wages have not been increased to meet the rising cost of living, and the justice of their grievance is rather widely admitted by neutral observers. The strike ties up business and causes much general inconvenience; except for the people who have cars of their own or can afford taxi fare, there is no way of getting from one part of the city to another. Labor being at this period scarce, an appeal is made by the mayor to college students to serve the community by acting in their spare time as motormen and drivers. The appeal is backed by a promise of lucrative wages and by the college administration's agreement to cooperate by permitting necessary absences from classes.

What ought the students of Crampton College to do? If they act as strikebreakers, they aid in forcing the employees back to work on the corporation's own terms. Have they any right to interfere so drastically and one-sidedly in the lives and happiness of others? On the other hand, if they turn down the mayor's request the community will continue to suffer grave inconveniences until the fight is somehow settled. *What is the students' duty in the matter? What is the right course for them to follow?*

These three situations, although perhaps unusual in the severity of their challenge, offer examples of problems distinctively moral. When the act of moral deliberation implicit in each of them is fully carried out, certain characteristic phases can be discerned.

(i) **Examination and clarification of the alternatives.** What are the relevant possibilities of action in the situation confronting me? Am I clear about the nature of each? Have I clearly distinguished them from one another? And are they mutually exhaustive, or would a more attentive search reveal others? In the case of District Attorney Ames, for example, a third alternative might have been to make a private deal with the ex-convict by which, in exchange for his acquittal, the District Attorney would receive the profits from some lucrative racket of which the ex-convict had control. No doubt to a reputable public servant this line of conduct would be too repugnant for consideration; it exemplifies, nevertheless, the ever-present logical possibility of going "between the horns"[1] of the original dilemma.

---

[1] *"between the horns":* In essence, finding a viable third alternative.

(ii) **Rational elaboration of consequences.** The next step is to think out the probable consequences of each of the alternatives in question. As this step involves predictions about a hypothetical future, the conclusions can have, at most, a high degree of probability, never certainty. The degree of probability is heightened accordingly as there is found some precedent in past experience for each of the proposed choices. Even if the present situation seems wholly new, analysis will always reveal *some* particulars for which analogies in past experience can be found or to which known laws of causal sequence are applicable. Such particulars will be dealt with partly by analogy (an act similar to the one now being deliberated about had on a previous occasion such and such consequences) and partly by the inductive-deductive method: appealing to general laws (deduction) which in turn have been built up as generalizations from observed particulars (induction). Mr. Ames, we may suppose, found the materials for this step in his professional knowledge of law and legal precedent, as well as in his more general knowledge of the policies of the press, the gullibility of its readers, and the high cost of domestic luxuries.

(iii) **Imaginative projection of the self into the predicted situation.** It is not enough to reason out the probable consequences of a choice. In a moral deliberation the chief interests involved are not scientific but human and practical. The only way to judge the comparative desirability of two possible futures is to live through them both in imagination. The third step, then, is to project oneself imaginatively into the future; i.e. establish a dramatic identification of the present self with that future self to which the now merely imagined experiences may become real. Few persons, unfortunately, are capable of an imaginative identification forceful enough to give the claims of the future self an even break. Present goods loom larger than future goods, and goods in the immediate future than goods that are remote. The trained ethical thinker must have a sound *temporal perspective,* the acquisition of which is to be sought by a frequent, orderly, and detailed exercise of the imagination with respect to not yet actual situations.

(iv) **Imaginative identification of the self with the points of view of those persons whom the proposed act will most seriously affect.** What decision I make here and now, if of any importance, is likely to have consequences, in varying degrees, for persons other than myself. An important part of a moral inquiry is to envisage the results of a proposed act as they will appear to those other persons affected by them. I must undertake, then, a dramatic identification of my own self with the selves of other persons. The possibility of doing this is evident from a consideration of how anyone's dramatic imagination works in the reading of a novel or the witnessing of a play. If the persons in the novel or play are dramatically convincing it is not because their characters and actions have been established by logical proof, but because they are presented so as to provoke in the reader an impulse to project himself into the world of the novel or play, to identify himself with this and that character in it, to share their feelings and moods, to get their slant on things.

In most persons, even very benevolent ones, the social conscious-   10
ness works by fits and starts. To examine fairly the needs and claims of other selves is no less hard and is often harder than to perform a similar task with regard to one's future self. Accordingly the ethical thinker must develop *social perspective*—that balanced appreciation of others' needs and claims which is the basis of justice.

In this fourth, as in the third step, the imaginative projection is to be carried out for each of the alternatives, according as their consequences shall have been predicted by Step ii.

(v) **Estimation and comparison of the values involved.** Implicit in the third and fourth steps is a recognition that certain values both positive and negative are latent in each of the hypothetical situations to which moral choice may lead. The values must be made explicit in order that they may be justly compared, for it is as a result of their comparison that a choice is to be made. To make values explicit is to give them a relatively abstract formulation; they still, however, derive concrete significance from their imagined exemplifications. District Attorney Ames, for example, might have envisaged his dilemma as a choice between family happiness and worldly success on the one hand as against professional honor on the other. Each of these is undoubtedly good, that is to say a value, but the values cannot be reduced to a common denominator. Family happiness enters as a factor into Benjamin Bates's dilemma no less than into that of Arthur Ames, but it stands to be affected in a different way and therefore, in spite of the identical words by which our linguistic poverty forces us to describe it, it does not mean the same thing. Family happiness may mean any number of things; so may success, and honor—although these different meanings have, of course, an intelligible bond of unity. Arthur Ames's task is to compare not just any family happiness with any professional honor but the particular exemplifications of each that enter into his problem. The comparison is not a simple calculation but an imaginative deliberation, in which the abstract values that serve as the logical ground of the comparison are continuous with, and interactive with, the concrete particulars that serve as its starting-point.

(vi) **Decision.** Comparison of the alternative future situations and the values embodied in each must terminate in a decision. Which of the possible situations do I deem it better to bring into existence? There are no rules for the making of this decision. I must simply decide as wisely and as fairly and as relevantly to the total comparison as I can. Every moral decision is a risk, for the way in which a person decides is a factor in determining the kind of self he is going to become.

(vii) **Action.** The probable means of carrying out the decision have been established by Step ii. The wished-for object or situation is an end, certain specific means toward the fulfillment of which lie here and now within my power. These conditions supply the premises for an ethical syllogism. When a certain end, x, is recognized as the best of the available alternatives, and when the achievement of it is seen to be possible through a set of means $a, b, c \ldots$ which lie within my power, then whichever of the means $a, b, c \ldots$ is an action that can here and now be performed becomes at just this point my duty. If the deliberative process has been carried out forcefully and wisely it will have supplied a categorical answer to the question, What ought I to do?—even though the answer in some cases may be, Do nothing.

Naturally, not all experiences of moral deliberation and choice 15
reveal these seven phases in a distinct, clear-cut way. Nor is the order here given always the actual order. Sometimes we may begin by deliberating about the relative merits of two ends, seeking the means simultaneously with this abstract inquiry, or after its completion. The foregoing analysis does, however, throw some light on the nature of a moral problem, and may be tested by applying it to the three cases described at the beginning of the chapter.

Questions for Discussion and Writing

1. Why does solving an ethical problem always involve an examination of alternatives and a consideration of consequences? How is Wheelwright's emphasis on fair consideration of the effect of proposed actions on others an essential component of ethical inquiry?
2. What kinds of ethical dilemmas do Wheelwright's three hypothetical situations illustrate? Why is the ability to create hypothetical situations so important in the process of ethical inquiry?
3. Choose one of Wheelwright's three hypothetical cases and, using his outline of stages in the process of ethical inquiry, describe what you would do in each situation and why.
4. **Rhetorical inquiry:** How do the three hypothetical examples that Wheelwright analyzes illustrate the central question of ethical inquiry: when do special circumstances require us to override the accepted procedures, or traditional demands of a profession (as in the case of the district attorney), or a customary role?

MARYA MANNES

Marya Mannes (1904–1990) was born in New York City to David Mannes and Clara Damrosch, the founders of the Mannes College of Music. Her major works of fiction and nonfiction include Message from a Stranger *(1948);* More in Anger *(1958);* The New York I Know *(1961);* Out of My Time *(1971), her autobiography;* Uncoupling: The Art of Coming Apart *(1972), a guide to divorce; and* Last Rights *(1974), a powerful and explicit plea for laws to ensure death with dignity. In the following excerpt from* Last Rights, *"The Unwilled," Mannes argues that a quality-of-life standard (rather than sanctity-of-life criteria) should be applied in those situations where an abortion is being considered.*

Before You Read

What criteria should be applied when evaluating the quality of life?

The Unwilled

Those who so passionately uphold the "sanctity of life" do not ask "what life?" nor see themselves as retarded and crippled in an institution for the rest of that life. Nor do they choose to see, to think of, the tens of thousands of lives born crippled and retarded, who, without will or choice, were allowed to be born as, presumably, the "right" of the damaged fetus *to* life.

Rather than seeing the many tangible horrors of that life, the sanctity people choose to emphasize the maternal love and care transcending the agony of a malformed or mindless presence, day after day and year after year. Or they point to those few institutions where a dedicated staff and the latest therapies bring these children or adults to a minimal level of competence: dressing themselves, cleaning themselves, learning small tasks. Since these "inmates" sometimes play and sometimes smile, they are, of course, "happy." They know no other existence, they act on reflexes, not will.

Certainly, love is the prime need of these incomplete beings, whether born that way or the victims of violent and crippling accident. Two middle-aged couples I know who cannot give such grown sons or daughters the special help they need, visit them where they live every week, stay with them for hours. "Ben is such a beautiful young man," said one father. "It's still hard to believe that his fine face and body can exist without thought processes or directions. The circuits in his brain just don't connect."

Certainly, there are parents who love their mongoloid and retarded children, accept them with their siblings as part of the family. But the "sanctity of life" people forget what an enormous toll it takes of the mother especially, who bore this child before the relatively new science of fetology could have given her the alternative choice: not to bear a permanently deformed or retarded being. For it has now become possible, with extremely delicate instruments and techniques, to establish deformation and brain damage, among other serious handicaps, in the unborn fetus when suspicions of malfunctioning exist.

Yet to the antiabortionists, any birth is presumably better than no   5
birth. They seem to forget that millions of unwanted children all over this
world are not only destined for an uncherished and mean existence, but
swell a population already threatening the resources of this planet, let alone
its bare amenities.

They also choose to ignore the kind of "homes" in every large community where the pitiful accidents of biology sit half-naked on floors strewn
with feces, autistic and motionless, or banging their swollen heads against
peeling walls.

If the concept of "sanctity" does not include "quality," then the word
has no meaning and less humanity. The rights of birth and death, of life
itself, require both.

Above all, how can the sanctity-of-life argument prevail in a society
that condones death in war of young men who want to live, but will not permit the old and hopelessly ill, craving release, to die?

Questions for Discussion and Writing

1. Why in Mannes's view should quality-of-life considerations overrule
   sanctity-of-life criteria with respect to those who would be born
   crippled or retarded and spend their lives in substandard institutions?
2. To what extent do Mannes's hypothetical examples support her assertion better than less extreme illustrations would have?
3. Does severe impairment necessarily exclude the capacity to love or to
   be loved? Who should have an absolute right to decide whether an
   abortion should be performed—the doctor, the mother, a hospital
   ethics committee, or some other agency? In a page or two, explain
   your answer.
4. **Rhetorical inquiry:** In what sense is Mannes's essay an argument based
   on the definition of the phrase "sanctity of life"? Does her definition
   deviate from the traditional definition, and, if so, for what purpose?
   Does she answer opposing viewpoints, and, if not, does this under-
   mine her argument?

HANS RUESCH

*Hans Ruesch (1913–2007) was a modern-day Renaissance man who not only
was a scholar of the history of medicine but has also written best-selling
novels*—The Racer *(1953),* Savage Innocents *(1960), and* Back to the Top of
the World *(1973)—and many short stories that have appeared in* The Saturday
Evening Post, Esquire, *and* Redbook. *This Swiss author is best known for his
brilliant exposés of the animal experimentation industry, catalogued in such
books as* Naked Empress: The Great Medical Fraud *(1982) and* Slaughter of
the Innocent *(1983), from which the following chapter is reprinted. He lived in*

Milan, Italy, and was the founder and director of Civis: The International Foundation Report Dedicated to the Abolition of Vivisection.

Before You Read

Do you think experimentation on live animals helps or harms humanity?

Slaughter of the Innocent

SCIENCE OR MADNESS

A dog is crucified in order to study the duration of the agony of Christ. A pregnant bitch is disemboweled to observe the maternal instinct in the throes of pain. Experimenters in an American university cause convulsions in dogs and cats, to study their brain waves during the seizures, which gradually become more frequent and severe until the animals are in a state of continual seizure that leads to their death in 3 to 5 hours; the experimenters then supply several charts of the brain waves in question, but no idea how they could be put to any practical use.

Another team of "scientists" submits to fatal scaldings of 15,000 animals of various species, then administer to half of them a liver extract that is already known to be useful in case of shock: As expected, the treated animals agonize longer than the others.

Beagles, well-known for their mild and affectionate natures, are tortured until they start attacking each other. The "scientists" responsible for this announce that they were "conducting a study on juvenile delinquency."

Exceptions? Borderline cases? I wish they were.

Every day of the year, at the hands of white-robed individuals recog-   5
nized as medical authorities, or bent on getting such recognition, or a degree, or at least a lucrative job, millions of animals—mainly mice, rats, guinea-pigs, hamsters, dogs, cats, rabbits, monkeys, pigs, turtles; but also horses, donkeys, goats, birds and fishes—are slowly blinded by acids, submitted to repeated shocks or intermittent submersion, poisoned, inoculated with deadly diseases, disemboweled, frozen to be revived and refrozen, starved or left to die of thirst, in many cases after various glands have been entirely or partially extirpated or the spinal cord has been cut.

The victims' reactions are then meticulously recorded, except during the long weekends, when the animals are left unattended to meditate about their sufferings; which may last weeks, months, years, before death puts an end to their ordeal—death being the only effective anesthesia most of the victims get to know.

But often they are not left in peace even then: Brought back to life—miracle of modern science—they are subjected to ever new series of tortures. Pain-crazed dogs have been seen devouring their own paws, convulsions have thrown cats against the walls of their cages until the creatures collapsed, monkeys have clawed and gnawed at their own bodies or killed their cage mates.

This and much more has been reported by the experimenters themselves in leading medical journals such as Britain's *Lancet* and its American, French, German and Swiss counterparts, from which most of the evidence here presented derives.

But don't stop reading just yet—because the purpose of this book is to show you how you can, and why you should, put a stop to all that.

THE REFINEMENTS

Each new experiment inspires legions of "researchers" to repeat it, in the hope of confirming or debunking it; to procure the required tools or to devise new, "better" ones. Apart from a long series of "restraining devices," derived from the "Czermak Table," the "Pavlov Stock" and other classic apparatuses which decorate those pseudoscientific laboratories the world over, there exist some particularly ingenious instruments, usually named after their inventors.

One is the *Noble-Collip Drum*, a household word among physiologists since 1942, when it was devised by two Toronto doctors, R. L. Noble and J. B. Collip, who described it in *The Quarterly Journal of Experimental Physiology* (Vol. 31, No. 3, 1942, p. 187) under the telltale title "A Quantitative Method for the Production of Experimental Traumatic Shock without Haemorrhage in Unanesthetized Animals": "The underlying principle of the method is to traumatize the animal by placing it in a revolving drum in which are projections or bumps . . . The number of animals dying showed a curve in proportion to the number of revolutions . . . When animals were run without having their paws taped they were found to give irregular results, since some would at first jump over the bumps until fatigued, and so protect themselves . . ."

There is the *Ziegler Chair*, an ingenious metal seat described in *Journal of Laboratory and Clinical Medicine* (Sept. 1952), invented by Lt. James E. Ziegler of the Medical Corps, U.S. Navy, Johnsville, Pa. One of the advantages claimed in the descriptive article for the apparatus is that "the head and large areas of the monkey's body are exposed and thus accessible for various manipulations." The uses of the chair include perforation of the skull with stimulation of the exposed cortex, implantation of cranial windows, general restraint for dressings, and as a seat for the monkey in various positions on the large experimental centrifuge for periods that may last uninterruptedly for years, until death.

There is the *Blalock Press,* so named after Dr. Alfred Blalock of the famed Johns Hopkins Institute in Baltimore, Md. Constructed of heavy steel, it resembles an ancient printing press. But the plates are provided with steel ridges that mesh together when the top plate is forced against the bottom plate. Pressure of up to 5,000 pounds is exerted by a heavy automobile

10

spring compressed by tightening four nuts. The purpose is to crush the muscular tissue in a dog's legs without crushing the bone.

There is the *Collison Cannula,* designed to be implanted into the head of various animals to facilitate the repeated passage of hypodermic needles, electrodes, pressure gauges, etc., into the cranial cavity of the fully conscious animal—mostly cats and monkeys. The cannula is permanently fixed to the bone with acrylic cement anchored by four stainless-steel screws screwed into the skull. After undergoing this severe traumatic experience, the animal must be given at least a week to recover before the experiments proper can begin—as described in *Journal of Physiology,* October 1972. (In time, in an unsuccessful attempt to reject it, a purse of pus grows around the firmly anchored cannula and seeps into the victims' eyes and sinuses, eventually leading to blindness and death—sometimes one or two years later.)

There is the *Horsley-Clarke Stereotaxic Device,* so named after the two   15 doctors who designed it to immobilize small animals during the implantation of the aforementioned cannula, for the traditional brain "experiments" that have never led to any other practical result than procuring the Nobel Prize for Prof. Walter R. Hess of Zurich University in 1949, and fat subsidies for various colleagues all over the world.

It may as well be pointed out right now that Nobel prizes in biology, physiology and medicine—as well as the various grants for "medical research"—are conferred on the recommendations of committees of biologists, physiologists and doctors, who have either been similarly favored by the colleagues they recommend, or who hope to be repaid in kind.

WHAT IS VIVISECTION?

The term vivisection "is now used to apply to all types of experiments on living animals, whether or not cutting is done." So states the *Encyclopedia Americana* (International Edition, 1974). And the large *Merriam-Webster* (1963): ". . . broadly, any form of animal experimentation, especially if considered to cause distress to the subject." Thus the term also applies to experiments done with the administration of noxious substances, bums, electric or traumatic shocks, drawn-out deprivations of food and drink, psychological tortures leading to mental imbalance, and so forth. The term was employed in that sense by the physiologists of the last century who started this kind of "medical research," and so it will be used by me. By "vivisectionist" is usually meant every upholder of this method; by "vivisector" someone who performs such experiments or participates in them.

The "scientific" euphemism for vivisection is "basic research" or "research on models"—"model" being the euphemism for laboratory animal.

Though the majority of practicing physicians defend vivisection, most of them don't know what they are defending, having never set foot in a vivisection laboratory. Conversely, the great majority of vivisectors have never spent five minutes at a sick man's bedside, for the good reason that most of them decide to dedicate themselves to laboratory animals when they fail that most important medical examination, the one that would allow them to practice medicine. And many more take up "research" because that requires no formal studying. Any dunce can cut up live animals and report what he sees.

The number of animals dying of tortures through the practice of vivisection is estimated at around 400,000 a day worldwide at the time of this writing, and is growing at an annual rate of about 5 percent. Those experiments are performed in tens of thousands of clinical, industrial and university laboratories. All of them, without exception, deny access to channels of independent information. Occasionally, they take a journalist, guaranteed "tame," on a guided tour of a laboratory as carefully groomed as one of Potemkin's villages.

Today we no longer torture in the name of the Lord, but in the name of a new, despotic divinity—a so-called Medical Science which, although amply demonstrated to be false, successfully uses through its priests and ministers the tactics of terrorism: "If you don't give us plenty of money and a free hand with animals, you and your children will die of cancer"—well knowing that modern man does not fear God, but fears Cancer, and has never been told that most cancers, and maybe all, are fabricated through incompetence in the vivisection laboratories.

In the past, humanity was trained to tolerate cruelty to human beings on the grounds of a widespread superstition. Today humanity has been trained to tolerate cruelty to animals on the grounds of another superstition, equally widespread. There is a chilling analogy between the Holy Inquisitors[1] who extracted confessions by torture from those suspected of witchcraft, and the priests of modern science who employ torture trying to force information and answers from animals. Meanwhile, the indifferent majority prefers to ignore what is going on around them, so long as they are left alone.

Vivisectors indignantly reject charges that their driving motive is avarice, ambition, or sadism disguised as scientific curiosity. On the contrary, they present themselves as altruists, entirely dedicated to the welfare of mankind. But intelligent people of great humanity—from Leonardo da Vinci to Voltaire to Goethe to Schweitzer[2]—have passionately declared that a species willing to be "saved" through such means would not be worth saving. And furthermore there exists by now a crushing documentation that vivisection is not only an inhuman and dehumanizing practice, but a continuing source of errors that have grievously damaged true science and the health of humanity at large.

20

---

[1] Refers to the Inquisition in Spain during the fifteenth century, in which a special tribunal was established to combat and punish heresy in the Roman Catholic Church.   [2] *Leonardo da Vinci (1452–1519):* Italian painter, sculptor, architect, and mathematician; *Voltaire (1694–1778):* pen name of Francois Marie Arouet, French philosopher, historian, dramatist, and essayist; *Johann Wolfgang von Goethe (1749–1832):* German poet, dramatist, and novelist; *Albert Schweitzer (1875–1965):* Alsatian missionary, doctor, and musician in Africa who received the Nobel Peace Prize in 1952.

If such a sordid approach to medical knowledge were as useful as advertised, the nation with the highest life expectancy should be the United States, where expenditures for vivisection are a multiple of those in any other country, where more "life-saving" operations are performed, and whose medical profession considers itself to be the world's finest, besides being the most expensive. In fact, "Among the nations that measure average life expectancy, America ranks a relatively low 17th—behind most of Western Europe, Japan, Greece, and even Bulgaria," reported *Time* Magazine, July 21, 1975, after having reported on December 17, 1973, that "The U.S. has twice as many surgeons in proportion to population as Great Britain—and Americans undergo twice as many operations as Britons. Yet, on the average, they die younger."

All this in spite of Medicare and Medicaid and the formidable thera-   25
peutic arsenal at the disposal of American doctors and patients.

MAN AND ANIMALS

Many of the medical men who have denounced the practice of vivisection as inhuman, fallacious and dangerous have been among the most distinguished in their profession. Rather than a minority, they ought to be called an élite. And in fact, opinions should not only be counted—they should also be weighed.

The first great medical man who indicated that vivisection is not just inhuman and unscientific, but that it is unscientific *because* it is inhuman was Sir Charles Bell (1774–1824), the Scottish physician, surgeon, anatomist and physiologist to whom medical science owes "Bell's law" on motor and sensory nerves: At the time the aberration of vivisection began to take root in its modern form, he declared that it could only be practiced by callous individuals, who couldn't be expected to penetrate the mysteries of life. Such individuals, he maintained, lack real intelligence—sensibility being a component, and certainly not the least, of human intelligence.

Those who hope to find remedies for human ills by inflicting deliberate sufferings on animals commit two fundamental errors in understanding. The first is the assumption that results obtained on animals are appropriate to man. The second, which concerns the inevitable fallacy of experimental science in respect to the field of organic life, will be analyzed in the next chapter. Let us examine the first error now. Already the Pharaohs knew that to find out whether their food was poisoned they had to try it on the cook, not on the cat.

Since animals react differently from man, every new product or method tried out on animals must be tried out again on man, through careful clinical tests, before it can be considered safe. *This rule knows no exceptions.* Therefore, tests on animals are not only dangerous because they may lead to wrong conclusions, but they also retard clinical investigation, which is the only valid kind.

René Dubos, Pulitzer Prize-winner and professor of microbiology at the
Rockefeller Institute of New York, wrote in *Man, Medicine and Environment* (Praeger, New York, 1968, p. 107): "Experimentation on man is usually an indispensable step in the discovery of new therapeutic procedures or
drugs . . . The first surgeons who operated on the lungs, the heart, the brain
were by necessity experimenting on man, since knowledge deriving from
animal experimentation is never entirely applicable to the human species."

In spite of this universally recognized fact, not only, the vivisectors, but
also health authorities everywhere, having been trained in the vivisectionist
mentality, which is a throwback to the last century, allow or prescribe animal tests, thus washing their hands of any responsibility if something goes
wrong, as it usually does.

This explains the long list of products developed in laboratories, *and*
presumed safe after extensive animal tests, which eventually prove deleteri-
ous for man:

Due to a "safe" painkiller named Paracetamol, 1,500 people had to
be hospitalized in Great Britain in 1971. In the United States, Orabilex
caused kidney damages with fatal outcome, MEL/29 caused cataracts,
Metaqualone caused psychic disturbances leading to at least 366 deaths.
Worldwide Thalidomide caused more than 10,000 deformed children.
Chloramphenicol (Chloromycetin) caused leukemia; Stilbestrol cancer in
young women. In the sixties a mysterious epidemic killed so many thousands of asthma sufferers in various countries that Dr. Paul D. Stolley of
Johns Hopkins Hospital—who in July 1972 finally found the killer in Iso-
proterenol, packaged in England as an aerosol spray—spoke of the "worst
therapeutic drug disaster on record." In the fall of 1975, Italy's health
authorities seized the anti-allergic Trilergan, responsible for viral hepatitis.
In early 1976 the laboratories Salvoxyl-Wander, belonging to Switzerland's
gigantic Sandoz enterprise, withdrew their Flamanil, created to fight rheuma-
tisms, but capable of causing loss of consciousness in its consumers—certainly
one effective way to free them of all pains. A few months later, Great Britain's
chemical giant, ICI (Imperial Chemical Industries), announced that it had
started paying compensations to the victims (or their survivors) of its car-
diotonic Eraldin, introduced on the market after 7 years of "very intensive"
tests; but hundreds of consumers had then suffered serious damages to the
eyesight or the digestive tract, and 18 had died.

The Great Drug Deception by Dr. Ralph Adam Fine (Stein and Day,
New York, 1972) is just one of the many books published in the last decade
on the subject of dangerous and often lethal drugs, but it achieved no practical results. Health authorities, as well as the public stubbornly refused to
take cognizance of the fact that all those drugs had been okayed and marketed after having been proved safe for animals. Actually it is unfair to
single out just a few dangerous drugs, since there are thousands of them.

Of course the fallacy works both ways, precluding the acceptance of
useful drugs. There is the great example of penicillin—if we want to consider

this a useful drug. Its discoverers said they were fortunate. No guinea pigs were available for the toxicity tests, so they used mice instead. Penicillin kills guinea pigs. But the same guinea pigs can safely eat strychnine, one of the deadliest poisons for humans—but not for monkeys.

Certain wild berries are deadly for human beings, but birds thrive on them. A dose of belladonna that would kill a man is harmless for rabbits and goats. Calomelan doesn't influence the secretion of bile in dogs, but can treble it in man. The use of digitalis—the main remedy for cardiac patients and the savior of countless lives the world over—was retarded for a long time because it was first tested on dogs, in which it dangerously raises blood pressure. And chloroform is so toxic to dogs that for many years this valuable anesthetic was not employed on patients. On the other hand a dose of opium that would kill a man is harmless to dogs and chickens.

Datura and henbane are poison for man, but food for the snail. The mushroom *amanita phalloides,* a small dose of which can wipe out a whole human family is consumed without ill effects by the rabbit, one of the most common laboratory animals. A porcupine can *eat* in one lump without discomfort as much opium as a human addict *smokes* in two weeks, and wash it down with enough prussic acid to poison a regiment of soldiers.

The sheep can swallow enormous quantities of arsenic, once the murderers' favorite poison.

Potassium cyanide, deadly for us, is harmless for the owl, but one of our common field pumpkins can put a horse into a serious state of agitation. Morphine, which calms and anesthetizes man, causes maniacal excitement in cats and mice, but dogs can stand doses up to twenty times higher than man. On the other hand, our sweet almonds can kill foxes and chickens, and our common parsley is poison to parrots.

Robert Koch's Tuberkulin, once hailed as a vaccine against tuberculosis because it cured TB in guinea pigs, was found later on to *cause* TB in man.[3]   40

There are enough such instances to fill a book—all proving that it would be difficult to find a more absurd and less scientific method of medical research.

Moreover, the anguish and sufferings of the animals, deprived of their natural habitat or habitual surroundings, terrorized by what they see in the laboratories and the brutalities they are subjected to, alter their mental balance and organic reactions to such an extent that *any* result is a priori valueless. The laboratory animal is a monster, made so by the experimenters. Physically and mentally it has very little in common with normal animals and much less with man.

As even Claude Bernard (1813–1878), founder of the modern vivisectionist method, wrote in his *Physiologie opératoire* (p. 152): "The experimental

---

[3] *Robert Koch (1843–1910):* German bacteriologist and physician who won the Nobel Prize in 1905.

animal is never in a normal state. The normal state is merely a supposition, an assumption." (*Une pure conception de l'esprit.*)

Not only do all animals react differently—even kindred species like rat and mouse, or like the white rat and brown rat—not even two animals of the identical strain react identically; furthermore, they may be suffering from different diseases.

To counter this disadvantage, somebody launched the idea of breed- 45 ing strains of bacteriologically sterile laboratory animals—mass-born by Caesarean section in sterile operating rooms, raised in sterile surroundings and fed with sterile foods—to provide what the researchers called a "uniform biological material," free of diseases.

One delusion spawned another. Consistent failures made certain of those misguided scientists realize—some haven't realized it yet—that organic "material" raised under such abnormal conditions differs more than ever from normal organisms. Animals so raised never develop the natural defense mechanism, the so-called immunological reaction, which is a salient characteristic of every living organism. So it would be difficult to devise a less reliable experimental material. Besides, animals are by nature immune to most human infections—diphtheria, typhus, scarlet fever, German measles, smallpox, cholera, yellow fever, leprosy, and bubonic plague, while other infections, such as TB and various septicemias, take up different forms in animals. So the claim that through animals we can learn to control human diseases could seem a sign of madness if we didn't know that it is just a pretext for carrying on "experiments" which, however dangerously misleading for medical science, are either intimately satisfying for those who execute them, or highly lucrative.

The Swiss nation illustrates well to what extent the profit motive promotes vivisection: With a population of less than 6 million, Switzerland uses up annually many times as many laboratory animals as does all of Soviet Russia with its 250 million inhabitants, but where there is no money in the making of medicines.

EXPERIMENTAL RESEARCH

Experimental research has brought about all human inventions and most discoveries—except in medicine.

When speaking of modern invention, the first name that comes to mind is Thomas Edison.[4] His case is particularly interesting because Edison attended school for only three months, whereafter he had to start making a living. Thus Edison was not a well-educated man. But it was just this lack of formal education—the lack of notions blindly accepted by most educated

---

[4] *Thomas Alva Edison (1847–1931):* U.S. inventor of the electric light, phonograph, and other devices.

728 CHAPTER 11 ~ The Ethical Dimension - Nonfiction

people, including the scientists, inculcated into them at an early stage by rote—that enabled Edison to accomplish the extraordinary series of inventions that altered man's way of life.

For instance, in trying to perfect the first electric light bulb Edison wanted   50
a wire that would remain incandescent for a reasonable length of time. No university professor, no metallurgical expert was able to help him. So Edison resorted to pure empiricism. He started trying out *every type of wire* he could think of—including the least likely ones, such as, say, a thread of charred cotton. Over a period of years, Edison spent $40,000 having his assistants trying out one material after another. Until he found a wire that remained incandescent for 40 consecutive hours. It was a charred cotton thread . . .

However, experimental science had started modifying the face of the earth two and a half centuries before Edison went about lighting up the nights. The beginning took place in 1637 with the publication of that *Discourse on Method* by Descartes[5] which taught man a new way of thinking, and led to modern technology. But, who could foresee in this New World being born in the midst of widespread enthusiasm the danger of an exclusively mechanistic knowledge? Hardly Descartes, who was himself a negation of the arts and all human sentiments—his private life was a failure—and who believed in a mechanistic biology, establishing the basis for what may well be mankind's greatest error.

In his thirst for knowledge through experimentation, Descartes also practiced vivisection, making it a symbol of "progress" to succeeding mechanists. Descartes himself, of course, had learned nothing from this practice, as demonstrated by his statement that animals don't suffer, and that their cries mean nothing more than the creaking of a wheel. Then why not whip the cart instead of the horse? Descartes never troubled to explain that. But he gave as "proof" of his theory the fact that the harder one beats a dog, the louder it howls. Through him a new science was born, deprived of wisdom and humanity, thus containing the seed of defeat at birth.

Rid at last of the yoke of medieval obscurantism, man went all out for experimentation. The sensational conquests of technology led some doctors of limited mental power to believe that experimental science would bring about equally sensational results in their own field; that living organisms react like inanimate matter, enabling medical science to establish absolute, mathematical rules. And today's vivisectionists still cling to that belief, no matter how often it has proved tragically wrong.

The experiment Galileo[6] made from Pisa's leaning tower, demonstrating that a light stone and a heavy stone fall at one and the same speed, established an absolute rule because it dealt with inanimate matter. But when we

---

[5] *René Descartes (1596–1650):* French philosopher and mathematician.   [6] *Galileo Galile (1564–1642):* Italian physicist and astronomer.

deal with living organisms, an infinity of different factors intervene, mostly unknown and not entirely identifiable, having to do with the mystery of life itself. It is difficult to disagree with Charles Bell that callous, dehumanized individuals are the least likely ever to penetrate these mysteries.

In his book *La sperimentazione sugli animali* (2nd ed., 1956), Gennaro 55 Ciaburri, one of Italy's antivisectionist doctors, provides among many others the following insight: "Normally, pressure on one or both eyeballs will slow down the pulse . . . This symptom has opened up a vast field for vivisection. Experimenters squashed the eyes of dogs to study this reflex, to the point of discovering that the heartbeat was slowing down—owing to the death of the animal . . ."

That such vivisectionist divertissements achieve nothing more than to provide a measure of human stupidity, has been declared repeatedly. The famed German doctor Erwin Liek—of whom the major German encyclope- dia, *Der Grosse Brockhaus*, says, "he advocated a medical art of high ethi- cal level, which takes into consideration the patient's psyche"—gives us the following information:

"Here is another example that animal experimentation sometimes can't answer even the simplest questions.

I know personally two of Germany's most authoritative researchers, Friedberger of the Kaiser Wilhelm Institute for Nutritional Research and Prof. Scheunert of the Institute of Animal Physiology at Leipzig. Both wanted to investigate the simple question as to whether a diet of hardboiled eggs or of raw eggs is more beneficial. They employed the same animals: 28-day-old rats. Result: over an observation period of three months, Friedberger's ani- mals prospered on a diet of raw eggs, while the control animals which got hardboiled eggs pined, lost their hair, developed eye troubles; several died after much suffering. At Scheunert's I witnessed the identical experiments, with exactly opposite results." (From *Gedanken eines Arztes*, Oswald Arnold, Berlin, 1949.)

Of course any disease deliberately provoked is unlike any disease that arises spontaneously.

Let's take the case of arthritis, a degenerative disease causing painful 60 inflammation of the joints, and bringing about lesions or destruction of the cartilage. Overeating is one of its causes, regular exercise at an early stage of the malady is the only reliable cure we know to date. And yet the drug firms keep turning out "miracle" remedies based on animal tortures: mere pallia- tives that mask the symptoms, reducing the pain for a while but in the mean- time ruining the liver or the kidneys or both, thus causing much more serious damage than the malady they pretend to cure—and eventually aggravating the malady.

While no solution to any medical problem has ever been found through animal experimentation, so on the other hand one can prove practically anything one sets out to prove using animals, as in the following case reported in the monthly *Canadian Hospital* (Dec., 1971): In the Montreal

Heart Institute are thousands of cages full of rats used to determine the effects of specific diets on animals. One of the "researchers" in charge, Dr. Serge Renaud, "took one of the animals from its cage; its hair had fallen out; its arteries had hardened and it was ripe for a heart attack. This rat, with a normal life span of two years, was old at two months. 'We kill them with pure butter,' said Dr. Renaud."

So butter is poison! Science or idiocy?

Sometimes it is neither one nor the other, but a highly profitable business gimmick, as the cyclamate and the saccharin cases demonstrate. In the mid-sixties the new artificial sweeteners known as cyclamates had become a huge commercial success because they cost 5 times less than sugar and had 30 times the sweetening power, besides being non-fattening. So the American Sugar Manufacturers Association set about financing "research" on cyclamates, as did the sugar industries in some other countries. To "prove scientifically" what the sugar industry was determined to prove from the start—that cyclamates should be outlawed—hundreds of thousands of animals had to die painfully.

They were force-fed such massive, concentrated doses of the product that they were bound to become seriously sick, developing all sorts of diseases, including cancer. To consume the equivalent amount of artificial sweetener a human would have to drink more than 800 cans of diet soda every day of his life. In 1967 the British Sugar Bureau, a public relations organization set up by the sugar industry, was pressuring members of Parliament about the deadly dangers of cyclamates. The same was happening in the United States—the sugar lobby besieging the politicians. I am not saying that money changed hands, because I don't know. All I know is that in 1969 both the American and British Governments banned the sale of cyclamates. It wasn't banned in Switzerland, however, where there is no powerful sugar lobby, but a powerful chemical lobby instead. In Switzerland, cyclamates are still on sale, 8 years after they were taken off the shelves in America and Britain.

Then there was a repeat performance of the whole three-ring scientific circus in 1976 in regard to saccharin—and once more uncounted thousands of innocent animals were caught in the crossfire of embattled industrial giants.

Financed by a grant of $641,224 for 1971–72, researchers at the Center for Prevention and Treatment of Arteriosclerosis at Albany Medical College experimented with an initial group of 44 pigs. One by one these animals were made to die of induced heart disease resulting from arteriosclerosis. Using an extreme form of diet known to be injurious to the vascular system, the process was further speeded up by X rays that damage the coronary arteries. Personnel were always on hand when an animal dropped dead; they hoped to pinpoint precisely what happens to the heart of a pig at this critical moment. Such, in essence, was a report in the *Times Union* of Buffalo, New York, Oct. 24, 1971.

65

Except for the money angle, the whole thing appears sophomoric. Yet similar programs utilizing various experimental animals were in progress at the same time at 12 other medical institutions all over the U.S. All of them proved adept at creating a wide range of diseases in animals, but were notable failures at coming up with a solution. Research of this nature has been practiced for decades, and millions of animals have died in the process, while the cures are still pies in the sky.

Today's pseudoscience proceeds similarly on all fronts. In the "fight against epilepsy," monkeys are submitted to a series of electroshocks that throw them into convulsions, until they become insane and manifest symptoms that may outwardly resemble epileptic fits in man—frothing at the mouth, convulsive movements, loss of consciousness, and such. Obviously the monkeys' fits have nothing to do with human epilepsy, as they are artificially induced, whereas man's epilepsy arises inside from reasons deeply rooted in the individual's organism or psyche, and not from a series of electroshocks. And by trying out on these insane monkeys a variety of "new" drugs—always the same ones, in different combinations—vivisectionists promise to come up with "a remedy against epilepsy" some time soon, provided the grants keep coming. And such methods sail today under the flag of science—which is an insult to true science, as well as to human intelligence. Small wonder that epilepsy is another disease whose incidence is constantly increasing.

One of the latest shifts devised by medical research to make quick money is the invention of drugs that promise to prevent brain hemorrhages. How is it done? Easy. By now any attentive reader can do it. Take rats, dogs, rabbits, monkeys, and cats, and severely injure their brains. How? Our laboratory "Researchers" brilliantly solve that problem with hammer blows. Under the broken skulls, the animals' brains will form blood clots, whereafter various drugs are administered to the traumatized victim. As if blood clots due to hammer blows were the equivalent of circulation troubles which have gradually been building up in a human brain that is approaching the natural end of its vital arch, or has grown sclerotic through excessive intake of alcohol, food, tobacco, or from want of exercise, of fresh air, or mental activity. Everybody knows what to do to keep physically and mentally fit. But it is less fatiguing to swallow, before each rich meal, a couple of pills, and hope for the best.

Anybody suggesting that these pills are of no use would be in bad faith. They *are* useful: They help increase the profits of the world's most lucrative industry—and further ruin the organism, thus creating the necessity for still more "miracle" drugs. 70

THE SOLID GOLD SOURCE

The cancer bogy has become the vivisectionists' most powerful weapon. Dr. Howard M. Temin, a well-known scientist, said in a recent address at the University of Wisconsin that scientists are also interested in money, power, publicity and prestige, and that "some promise quick cures for human diseases, provided they are given more power and more money." He added that there is a tremendous advantage in the assertion that "If I am given 500 million dollars for the next five years, I can cure cancer," pointing out that if a rainmaker puts the time far enough in the future, no one can prove him wrong.

But so far as cancer is concerned, the rain may not come in our lifetime. It is obvious to anybody who has not been brainwashed in the western hemisphere's medical schools that an experimental cancer, one caused by grafting cancerous cells into an animal, or in other arbitrary ways, is entirely different from cancer that develops on its own and, furthermore, in a human being. A spontaneous cancer has an intimate relationship to the organism that developed it, and probably to the mind of that organism as well, whereas cancerous cells implanted into another organism have no "natural" relationship whatsoever to that organism, which merely acts as a soil for the culture of those cells.

However, the ably exploited fear of this dread disease has become an inexhaustible source of income for the researchers. In the course of our century, experimental cancer has become a source of solid gold without precedent.

Questions for Discussion and Writing

1. What features of this analysis are designed to show that animal experimentation in medical research is not only sadistic but unreliable, misleading, and even dangerous when the results are used as models for humans.
2. The assumptions on which animal research is based are so commonly accepted that Ruesch's counterargument may strike some readers as unwarranted. What means does Ruesch take to forestall criticism and better support his argument?
3. Do some research into the guidelines that govern animal research at your college or university. Based on your findings, write a rebuttal to Ruesch or identify additional instances that support his thesis.
4. **Rhetorical inquiry:** How does Ruesch's discussion of the history of experimental research support his argument?

GARRETT HARDIN

Garrett Hardin (1915–2003) was born in Dallas, Texas. He graduated from the University of Chicago in 1936 and received a Ph.D. from Stanford University in 1941. A biologist, he was a professor of human ecology at the University of California at Santa Barbara until 1978. He is the author of many books and over two hundred articles, including Nature and Man's Fate *(1959),*

"The Tragedy of the Commons" in Science *(December 1968), and* Exploring
New Ethics for Survival *(1972). His latest works are* Stalking the Wild Taboo
(1996) and The Ostrich Factor: Our Population Myopia *(1998). "Lifeboat
Ethics: The Case against Helping the Poor" first appeared in the September
1974 issue of* Psychology Today. *In this article, Hardin compares a country
that is well off to a lifeboat that is already almost full of people. Outside the
lifeboat are the poor and needy, who desperately wish to get in. Hardin claims
that an ill-considered ethic of sharing will lead to the swamping of the lifeboat
unless its occupants maintain a margin of safety by keeping people out.*

Before You Read

Consider how timely Hardin's scenario has become today.

Lifeboat Ethics

Environmentalists use the metaphor of the earth as a "spaceship" in trying
to persuade countries, industries and people to stop wasting and polluting
our natural resources. Since we all share life on this planet, they argue, no
single person or institution has the right to destroy, waste or use more than a
fair share of its resources.

But does everyone on earth have an equal right to an equal share of its
resources? The spaceship metaphor can be dangerous when used by misguided idealists to justify suicidal policies for sharing our resources through
uncontrolled immigration and foreign aid. In their enthusiastic but unrealistic generosity, they confuse the ethics of a spaceship with those of a lifeboat.

A true spaceship would have to be under the control of a captain, since no
ship could possibly survive if its course were determined by committee. Spaceship Earth certainly has no captain; the United Nations is merely a toothless
tiger, with little power to enforce any policy upon its bickering members.

If we divide the world crudely into rich nations and poor nations, two
thirds of them are desperately poor, and only one third comparatively rich,
with the United States the wealthiest of all. Metaphorically each nation can
be seen as a lifeboat full of comparatively rich people. In the ocean outside
each lifeboat swim the poor of the world, who would like to get in, or at
least to share some of the wealth. What should the lifeboat passengers do?

First, we must recognize the limited capacity of any lifeboat. For
example, a nation's land has a limited capacity to support a population and
as the current energy crisis has shown us, in some ways we have already
exceeded the carrying capacity of our land.

ADRIFT IN A MORAL SEA

So here we sit, say fifty people in our lifeboat. To be generous, let us assume
it has room for ten more, making a total capacity of sixty. Suppose the fifty

of us in the lifeboat see 100 others swimming in the water outside, begging for admission to our boat or for handouts. We have several options: We may be tempted to try to live by the Christian ideal of being "our brother's keeper," or by the Marxist ideal of "to each according to his needs." Since the needs of all in the water are the same, and since they can all be seen as "our brothers," we could take them all into our boat, making a total of 150 in a boat designed for sixty. The boat swamps, everyone drowns. Complete justice, complete catastrophe.

Since the boat has an unused excess capacity of ten more passengers, we could admit just ten more to it. But which ten do we let in? How do we choose? Do we pick the best ten, the neediest ten, "first come, first served"? And what do we say to the ninety we exclude? If we do let an extra ten into our lifeboat, we will have lost our "safety factor," an engineering principle of critical importance. For example, if we don't leave room for excess capacity as a safety factor in our country's agriculture, a new plant disease or a bad change in the weather could have disastrous consequences.

Suppose we decide to preserve our small safety factor and admit no more to the lifeboat. Our survival is then possible, although we shall have to be constantly on guard against boarding parties.

While this last solution clearly offers the only means of our survival, it is morally abhorrent to many people. Some say they feel guilty about their good luck. My reply is simple: "Get out and yield your place to others." This may solve the problem of the guilt-ridden person's conscience, but it does not change the ethics of the lifeboat. The needy person to whom the guilt-ridden person yields his place will not himself feel guilty about his good luck. If he did, he would not climb aboard. The net result of conscience-stricken people giving up their unjustly held seats is the elimination of that sort of conscience from the lifeboat.

This is the basic metaphor within which we must work out our solutions. Let us now enrich the image, step by step, with substantive additions from the real world, a world that must solve real and pressing problems of overpopulation and hunger.   10

The harsh ethics of the lifeboat become even harsher when we consider the reproductive differences between the rich nations and the poor nations. The people inside the lifeboats are doubling in numbers every eighty-seven years; those swimming around outside are doubling, on the average, every thirty-five years, more than twice as fast as the rich. And since the world's resources are dwindling, the difference in prosperity between the rich and the poor can only increase.

As of 1973, the U.S. had a population of 210 million people, who were increasing by 0.8 percent per year. Outside our lifeboat, let us imagine another 210 million people (say the combined populations of Colombia, Ecuador, Venezuela, Morocco, Pakistan, Thailand and the Philippines), who are increasing at a rate of 3.3 percent per year. Put differently, the doubling time for this aggregate population is twenty-one years, compared to eighty-seven years for the U.S.

MULTIPLYING THE RICH AND THE POOR

Now suppose the U.S. agreed to pool its resources with those seven countries, with everyone receiving an equal share. Initially the ratio of Americans to non-Americans in this model would be one-to-one. But consider what the ratio would be after eighty-seven years, by which time the Americans would have doubled to a population of 420 million. By then, doubling every twenty-one years, the other group would have swollen to 354 billion. Each American would have to share the available resources with more than eight people.

But, one could argue, this discussion assumes that current population trends will continue, and they may not. Quite so. Most likely the rate of population increase will decline much faster in the U.S. than it will in the other countries, and there does not seem to be much we can do about it. In sharing with "each according to his needs," we must recognize that needs are determined by population size, which is determined by the rate of reproduction, which at present is regarded as a sovereign right of every nation, poor or not. This being so, the philanthropic load created by the sharing ethic of the spaceship can only increase.

THE TRAGEDY OF THE COMMONS

The fundamental error of spaceship ethics, and the sharing it requires, is that it leads to what I call "the tragedy of the commons." Under a system of private property, the men who own property recognize their responsibility to care for it, for if they don't they will eventually suffer. A farmer, for instance, will allow no more cattle in a pasture than its carrying capacity justifies. If he overloads it, erosion sets in, weeds take over, and he loses the use of the pasture.   15

If a pasture becomes a commons open to all, the right of each to use it may not be matched by a corresponding responsibility to protect it. Asking everyone to use it with discretion will hardly do, for the considerate herdsman who refrains from overloading the commons suffers more than a selfish one who says his needs are greater. If everyone would restrain himself, all would be well; but it takes only one less than everyone to ruin a system of voluntary restraint. In a crowded world of less than perfect human beings, mutual ruin is inevitable if there are no controls. This is the tragedy of the commons.

One of the major tasks of education today should be the creation of such an acute awareness of the dangers of the commons that people will recognize its many varieties. For example, the air and water have become polluted because they are treated as commons. Further growth in the population or per-capita conversion of natural resources into pollutants will only make the problem worse. The same holds true for the fish of the oceans. Fishing fleets have nearly disappeared in many parts of the world, technological improvements in the art of fishing are hastening the day of complete ruin. Only the replacement of the system of the commons with a responsible system of control will save the land, air, water and oceanic fisheries.

THE WORLD FOOD BANK

In recent years there has been a push to create a new commons called a World Food Bank, an international depository of food reserves to which nations would contribute according to their abilities and from which they would draw according to their needs. This humanitarian proposal has received support from many liberal international groups, and from such prominent citizens as Margaret Mead, U.N. Secretary General Kurt Waldheim, and Senators Edward Kennedy and George McGovern.

A world food bank appeals powerfully to our humanitarian impulses. But before we rush ahead with such a plan, let us recognize where the greatest political push comes from, lest we be disillusioned later. Our experience with the "Food for Peace program," or Public Law 480, gives us the answer. This program moved billions of dollars' worth of U.S. surplus grain to food-short, population-long countries during the past two decades. But when P.L. 480 first became law, a headline in the business magazine *Forbes* revealed the real power behind it: "Feeding the World's Hungry Millions: How It Will Mean Billions for U.S. Business."

And indeed it did. In the years 1960 to 1970, U.S. taxpayers spent a total of $7.9 billion on the Food for Peace program. Between 1948 and 1970, they also paid an additional $50 billion for other economic-aid programs, some of which went for food and food-producing machinery and technology. Though all U.S. taxpayers were forced to contribute to the cost of P.L. 480, certain special interest groups gained handsomely under the program. Farmers did not have to contribute the grain; the Government, or rather the taxpayers, bought it from them at full market prices. The increased demand raised prices of farm products generally. The manufacturers of farm machinery, fertilizers and pesticides benefited by the farmers' extra efforts to grow more food. Grain elevators profited from storing the surplus until it could be shipped. Railroads made money hauling it to ports, and shipping lines profited from carrying it overseas. The implementation of P.L. 480 required the creation of a vast Government bureaucracy, which then acquired its own vested interest in continuing the program regardless of its merits.

20

EXTRACTING DOLLARS

Those who proposed and defended the Food for Peace program in public rarely mentioned its importance to any of these special interests. The public emphasis was always on its humanitarian effects. The combination of silent selfish interests and highly vocal humanitarian apologists made a powerful and successful lobby for extracting money from taxpayers. We can expect the same lobby to push now for the creation of a World Food Bank.

However great the potential benefit to selfish interests, it should not be a decisive argument against a truly humanitarian program. We must ask if such a program would actually do more good than harm, not only momentarily but also in the long run. Those who propose the food bank usually refer to a current "emergency" or "crisis" in terms of world food supply. But what is an emergency? Although they may be infrequent and sudden, everyone knows that emergencies will occur from time to time. A well-run family, company, organization or country prepares for the likelihood of accidents and emergencies. It expects them, it budgets for them, it saves for them.

Learning the Hard Way

What happens if some organizations or countries budget for accidents and others do not? If each country is solely responsible for its own well-being, poorly managed ones will suffer. But they can learn from experience. They may mend their ways, and learn to budget for infrequent but certain emergencies. For example, the weather varies from year to year, and periodic crop failures are certain. A wise and competent government saves out of the production of the good years in anticipation of bad years to come. Joseph taught this policy to Pharaoh in Egypt more than 2,000 years ago. Yet the great majority of the governments in the world today do not follow such a policy. They lack either the wisdom or the competence, or both. Should those nations that do manage to put something aside be forced to come to the rescue each time an emergency occurs among the poor nations?

"But it isn't their fault!" some kindhearted liberals argue. "How can we blame the poor people who are caught in an emergency? Why must they suffer for the sins of their governments?" The concept of blame is simply not relevant here. The real question is, what are the operational consequences of establishing a world food bank? If it is open to every country every time a need develops, slovenly rulers will not be motivated to take Joseph's advice. Someone will always come to their aid. Some countries will deposit food in the world food bank, and others will withdraw it. There will be almost no overlap. As a result of such solutions to food shortage emergencies, the poor countries will not learn to mend their ways, and will suffer progressively greater emergencies as their populations grow.

Population Control the Crude Way

On the average, poor countries undergo a 2.5 percent increase in population each year; rich countries, about 0.8 percent. Only rich countries have anything in the way of food reserves set aside, and even they do not have as much as they should. Poor countries have none. If poor countries received no food from the outside, the rate of their population growth would be periodically

25

738   CHAPTER 11 ~ The Ethical Dimension - Nonfiction

checked by crop failures and famines. But if they can always draw on a world food bank in time of need, their populations can grow unchecked, and so will the "need" for aid. In the short run, a world food bank may diminish that need, but in the long run it actually increases the need without limit.

Without some system of worldwide food sharing, the proportion of people in the rich and poor nations might eventually stabilize. The overpopulated poor countries would decrease in numbers, while the rich countries that had room for more people would increase. But with a well-meaning system of sharing, such as a world food bank, the growth differential between the rich and the poor countries will not only persist, it will increase. Because of the higher rate of population growth in the poor countries of the world, 88 percent of today's children are born poor, and only 12 percent rich. Year by year the ratio becomes worse, as the fast-reproducing poor outnumber the slow-reproducing rich.

A world food bank is thus a commons in disguise. People will have more motivation to draw from it than to add to any common store. The less provident and less able will multiply at the expense of the abler and more provident, bringing eventual ruin upon all who share in the commons. Besides, any system of "sharing" that amounts to foreign aid from the rich nations to the poor nations will carry the taint of charity, which will contribute little to the world peace so devoutly desired by those who support the idea of a world food bank.

As past U.S. foreign-aid programs have amply and depressingly demonstrated, international charity frequently inspires mistrust and antagonism rather than gratitude on the part of the recipient nation.

CHINESE FISH AND MIRACLE RICE

The modern approach to foreign aid stresses the export of technology and advice, rather than money and food. As an ancient Chinese proverb goes: "Give a man a fish and he will eat for a day; teach him how to fish and he will eat for the rest of his days." Acting on this advice, the Rockefeller and Ford Foundations have financed a number of programs for improving agriculture in the hungry nations. Known as the "Green Revolution," these programs have led to the development of "miracle rice" and "miracle wheat," new strains that offer bigger harvests and greater resistance to crop damage. Norman Borlaug, the Nobel Prize–winning agronomist who, supported by the Rockefeller Foundation, developed "miracle wheat," is one of the most prominent advocates of a world food bank.

Whether or not the Green Revolution can increase food production as much as its champions claim is a debatable but possibly irrelevant point. Those who support this well-intended humanitarian effort should first consider some of the fundamentals of human ecology. Ironically, one man who did was the late Alan Gregg, a vice president of the Rockefeller Foundation.   30

Two decades ago he expressed strong doubts about the wisdom of such attempts to increase food production. He likened the growth and spread of humanity over the surface of the earth to the spread of cancer in the human body, remarking that "cancerous growths demand food; but, as far as I know, they have never been cured by getting it."

OVERLOADING THE ENVIRONMENT

Every human born constitutes a draft on all aspects of the environment: food, air, water, forests, beaches, wildlife, scenery and solitude. Food can, perhaps, be significantly increased to meet a growing demand. But what about clean beaches, unspoiled forests and solitude? If we satisfy a growing population's need for food, we necessarily decrease its per-capita supply of the other resources needed by men.

India, for example, now has a population of 600 million, which increases by 15 million each year. This population already puts a huge load on a relatively impoverished environment. The country's forests are now only a small fraction of what they were three centuries ago, and floods and erosion continually destroy the insufficient farmland that remains. Every one of the 15 million new lives added to India's population puts an additional burden on the environment, and increases the economic and social costs of crowding. However humanitarian our intent, every Indian life saved through medical or nutritional assistance from abroad diminishes the quality of life for those who remain, and for subsequent generations. If rich countries make it possible, through foreign aid, for 600 million Indians to swell to 1.2 billion in a mere twenty-eight years, as their current growth rate threatens, will future generations of Indians thank us for hastening the destruction of their environment? Will our good intentions be sufficient excuse for the consequences of our actions?

My final example of a commons in action is one for which the public has the least desire for rational discussion—immigration. Anyone who publicly questions the wisdom of current U.S. immigration policy is promptly charged with bigotry, prejudice, ethnocentrism, chauvinism, isolationism or selfishness. Rather than encounter such accusations, one would rather talk about other matters, leaving immigration policy to wallow in the crosscurrents of special interests that take no account of the good of the whole, or the interest of posterity.

Perhaps we still feel guilty about things we said in the past. Two generations ago the popular press frequently referred to Dagos, Wops, Polacks, Chinks and Krauts, in articles about how America was being "overrun" by foreigners of supposedly inferior genetic stock. But because the implied inferiority of foreigners was used then as justification for keeping them out, people now assume that restrictive policies could only be based on such misguided notions. There are no other grounds.

A NATION OF IMMIGRANTS

Just consider the numbers involved. Our Government acknowledges a net   35
inflow of 400,000 immigrants a year. While we have no hard data on the
extent of illegal entries, educated guesses put the figure at about 600,000 a
year. Since the natural increase (excess of births over deaths) of the resident
population now runs about 1.7 million per year, the yearly gain from immigration amounts to at least 19 percent of the total annual increase, and may
be as much as 37 percent if we include the estimate for illegal immigrants.
Considering the growing use of birth-control devices, the potential effect of
educational campaigns by such organizations as Planned Parenthood Feder-
ation of America and Zero Population Growth, and the influence of inflation and the housing shortage, the fertility rate of American women may
decline so much that immigration could account for all the yearly increase in
population. Should we not at least ask if that is what we want?

For the sake of those who worry about whether the "quality" of the
average immigrant compares favorably with the quality of the average resident, let us assume that immigrants and native born citizens are of exactly
equal quality, however one defines that term. We will focus here only on
quantity; and since our conclusions will depend on nothing else, all charges
of bigotry and chauvinism become irrelevant.

IMMIGRATION VS. FOOD SUPPLY

World food banks *move food to the people,* hastening the exhaustion of the
environment of the poor countries. Unrestricted immigration, on the other
hand, *moves people to the food,* thus speeding up the destruction of the
environment of the rich countries. We can easily understand why poor
people should want to make this latter transfer, but why should rich hosts
encourage it?

As in the case of foreign-aid programs, immigration receives support
from selfish interests and humanitarian impulses. The primary selfish interest in unimpeded immigration is the desire of employers for cheap labor,
particularly in industries and trades that offer degrading work. In the past,
one wave of foreigners after another was brought into the U.S. to work at
wretched jobs for wretched wages. In recent years, the Cubans, Puerto
Ricans and Mexicans have had this dubious honor. The interests of the
employers of cheap labor mesh well with the guilty silence of the country's
liberal intelligentsia. White Anglo-Saxon Protestants are particularly reluctant to call for a closing of the doors to immigration for fear of being called
bigots.

But not all countries have such reluctant leadership. Most educated
Hawaiians, for example, are keenly aware of the limits of their environment, particularly in terms of population growth. There is only so much
room on the islands, and the islanders know it. To Hawaiians, immigrants
from the other forty-nine states present as great a threat as those from other

nations. At a recent meeting of Hawaiian government officials in Honolulu, I had the ironic delight of hearing a speaker, who like most of his audience was of Japanese ancestry, ask how the country might practically and constitutionally close its doors to further immigration. One member of the audience countered: "How can we shut the doors now? We have many friends and relatives in Japan that we'd like to bring here some day so that they can enjoy Hawaii too." The Japanese-American speaker smiled sympathetically and answered: "Yes, but we have children now, and someday we'll have grandchildren too. We can bring more people here from Japan only by giving away some of the land that we hope to pass on to our grandchildren some day. What right do we have to do that?"

At this point, I can hear U.S. liberals asking: "How can you justify   40
slamming the door once you're inside? You say that immigrants should be kept out. But aren't we all immigrants, or the descendants of immigrants? If we insist on staying, must we not admit all others?" Our craving for intellectual order leads us to seek and prefer symmetrical rules and morals: a single rule for me and everybody else; the same rule yesterday, today, and tomorrow. Justice, we feel, should not change with time and place.

We Americans of non-Indian ancestry can look upon ourselves as the descendants of thieves who are guilty morally, if not legally, of stealing this land from its Indian owners. Should we then give back the land to the now living American descendants of those Indians? However morally or logically sound this proposal may be, I, for one, am unwilling to live by it and I know no one else who is. Besides, the logical consequence would be absurd. Suppose that, intoxicated with a sense of pure justice, we should decide to turn our land over to the Indians. Since all our wealth has also been derived from the land, wouldn't we be morally obliged to give that back to the Indians too?

PURE JUSTICE VS. REALITY

Clearly, the concept of pure justice produces an infinite regression to absurdity. Centuries ago, wise men invented statutes of limitations to justify the rejection of such pure justice, in the interest of preventing continual disorder. The law zealously defends property rights, but only relatively recent property rights. Drawing a line after an arbitrary time has elapsed may be unjust, but the alternatives are worse.

We are all descendants of thieves, and the world's resources are inequitably distributed. But we must begin the journey to tomorrow from the point where we are today. We cannot remake the past. We cannot safely divide the wealth equitably among all peoples so long as people reproduce at different rates. To do so would guarantee that our grandchildren, and everyone else's grandchildren, would have only a ruined world to inhabit.

To be generous with one's own possessions is quite different from being generous with those of posterity. We should call this point to the attention of those who, from a commendable love of justice and equality, would institute a system of the commons, either in the form of a world food bank, or of unrestricted immigration. We must convince them if we wish to save at least some parts of the world from environmental ruin.

Without a true world government to control reproduction and the use   45 of available resources, the sharing ethic of the spaceship is impossible. For the foreseeable future, our survival demands that we govern our actions by the ethics of a lifeboat, harsh though they may be. Posterity will be satisfied with nothing less.

Questions for Discussion and Writing

1. What does Hardin mean by the expression "the tragedy of the commons"? How does the idea underlying this phrase rest on the assumption that human beings are not capable of responsible, voluntary restraint in using resources?
2. How does the analogy of the lifeboat support Hardin's contention that affluent nations have no obligation to share their food and resources with the world's starving masses? Evaluate Hardin's argument that our obligation to future generations should override our desire to help starving masses in the present.
3. To put Hardin's scenario in terms of personal moral choice, consider the following dilemmas and write a short essay on either (a) or (b) or both, and discuss the reasons for your answer(s):
   a. Would you be willing to add five years to your life even though it would mean taking five years away from the life of someone else you do not know? Would your decision be changed if you knew who the person was?
   b. If you had a child who was dying and the only thing that could save him or her was the bone marrow of a sibling, would you consider having another baby in order to facilitate what was almost sure to be a positive bone marrow transplant?
4. **Rhetorical inquiry:** How fairly does Hardin state arguments that opponents might present and what reasons and evidence does he give for rejecting these arguments?

STANLEY MILGRAM

Stanley Milgram (1933–1984) was born in New York, received his Ph.D. from Harvard in 1960, and taught at Yale, Harvard, and the City University of New York. His research into human conformity and aggression, the results of which were published in 1974 as Obedience to Authority, *began a national debate. Milgram's thesis cast new light on the Holocaust, the 1972 My Lai massacres in Vietnam, and the Watergate incident. Milgram also wrote* Psychology in Today's World *(1975) and* The Individual in a Social World: Essays and Experiments *(1977).*

Before You read

Would you inflict pain on others if an authority figure told you to Why or why not?

The Perils of Obedience

Obedience is as basic an element in the structure of social life as one can point to. Some system of authority is a requirement of all communal living, and it is only the person dwelling in isolation who is not forced to respond, with defiance or submission, to the commands of others. For many people, obedience is a deeply ingrained behavior tendency, indeed a potent impulse overriding training in ethics, sympathy, and moral conduct.

The dilemma inherent in submission to authority is ancient, as old as the story of Abraham, and the question of whether one should obey when commands conflict with conscience has been argued by Plato, dramatized in *Antigone*,[1] and treated to philosophic analysis in almost every historical epoch. Conservative philosophers argue that the very fabric of society is threatened by disobedience, while humanists stress the primacy of the individual conscience.

The legal and philosophic aspects of obedience are of enormous import, but they say very little about how most people behave in concrete situations. I set up a simple experiment at Yale University to test how much pain an ordinary citizen would inflict on another person simply because he was ordered to by an experimental scientist. Stark authority was pitted against the subjects' strongest moral imperatives against hurting others, and, with the subjects' ears ringing with the screams of the victims, authority won more often than not. The extreme willingness of adults to go to almost any lengths on the command of an authority constitutes the chief finding of the study and the fact most urgently demanding explanation.

In the basic experimental design, two people come to a psychology laboratory to take part in a study of memory and learning. One of them is designated as a "teacher" and the other a "learner." The experimenter explains that the study is concerned with the effects of punishment on learning. The learner is conducted into a room, seated in a kind of miniature electric chair; his arms are strapped to prevent excessive movement, and an electrode is attached to his wrist. He is told that he will be read lists of simple word pairs, and that he will then be tested on his ability to remember the second word of a pair when he hears the first one again. Whenever he makes an error, he will receive electric shocks of increasing intensity.

---

[1] *Antigone:* a play by Sophocles that depicts the confrontation between an individual and the state (in the person of Creon).

The real focus of the experiment is the teacher. After watching the learner being strapped into place, he is seated before an impressive shock generator. The instrument panel consists of thirty lever switches set in a horizontal line. Each switch is clearly labeled with a voltage designation ranging from 15 to 450 volts. The following designations are clearly indicated for groups of four switches, going from left to right: Slight Shock, Moderate Shock, Strong Shock, Very Strong Shock, Intense Shock, Extreme Intensity Shock, Danger: Severe Shock. (Two switches after this last designation are simply marked XXX.)

When a switch is depressed, a pilot light corresponding to each switch is illuminated in bright red; an electric buzzing is heard; a blue light, labeled "voltage energizer," flashes; the dial on the voltage meter swings to the right; and various relay clicks sound off.

The upper left-hand corner of the generator is labeled SHOCK GENERATOR, TYPE ZLB, DYSON INSTRUMENT COMPANY, WALTHAM, MASS. OUTPUT 15 VOLTS–450 VOLTS.

Each subject is given a sample 45-volt shock from the generator before his run as teacher, and the jolt strengthens his belief in the authenticity of the machine.

The teacher is a genuinely naïve subject who has come to the laboratory for the experiment. The learner, or victim, is actually an actor who receives no shock at all. The point of the experiment is to see how far a person will proceed in a concrete and measurable situation in which he is ordered to inflict increasing pain on a protesting victim.

Conflict arises when the man receiving the shock begins to show that he is experiencing discomfort. At 75 volts, he grunts; at 120 volts, he complains loudly; at 150, he demands to be released from the experiment. As the voltage increases, his protests become more vehement and emotional. At 285 volts, his response can be described only as an agonized scream. Soon thereafter, he makes no sound at all.

For the teacher, the situation quickly becomes one of gripping tension. It is not a game for him; conflict is intense and obvious. The manifest suffering of the learner presses him to quit; but each time he hesitates to administer a shock, the experimenter orders him to continue. To extricate himself from this plight, the subject must make a clear break with authority.

The subject, Gretchen Brandt,[2] is an attractive thirty-one-year-old medical technician who works at the Yale Medical School. She had emigrated from Germany five years before.

On several occasions when the learner complains, she [Gretchen] turns to the experimenter coolly and inquires, "Shall I continue?" She promptly returns to her task when the experimenter asks her to do so. At the administration

---

[2] *Gretchen Brandt:* Names of subjects described in this piece have been changed.

of 210 volts, she turns to the experimenter, remarking firmly, "Well, I'm sorry, I don't think we should continue."

EXPERIMENTER: The experiment requires that you go on until he has learned all the word pairs correctly.

BRANDT: He has a heart condition, I'm sorry. He told you that before.   15

EXPERIMENTER: The shocks may be painful but they are not dangerous.

BRANDT: Well, I'm sorry, I think when shocks continue like this, they *are* dangerous. You ask him if he wants to get out. It's his free will.

EXPERIMENTER: It is absolutely essential that we continue. . . .

BRANDT: I'd like you to ask him. We came here of our free will. If he wants to continue I'll go ahead. He told you he had a heart condition. I'm sorry. I don't want to be responsible for anything happening to him. I wouldn't like it for me either.

EXPERIMENTER: You have no other choice.   20

BRANDT: I think we are here on our own free will. I don't want to be responsible if anything happens to him. Please understand that.

She refuses to go further and the experiment is terminated.

The woman is firm and resolute throughout. She indicates in the interview that she was in no way tense or nervous, and this corresponds to her controlled appearance during the experiment. She feels that the last shock she administered to the learner was extremely painful and reiterates that she "did not want to be responsible for any harm to him."

The woman's straightforward, courteous behavior in the experiment, lack of tension, and total control of her own action seem to make disobedience a simple and rational deed. Her behavior is the very embodiment of what I envisioned would be true for almost all subjects.

AN UNEXPECTED OUTCOME

Before the experiments, I sought predictions about the outcome from various kinds of people—psychiatrists, college sophomores, middle-class adults, graduate students and faculty in the behavioral sciences. With remarkable similarity, they predicted that virtually all subjects would refuse to obey the experimenter. The psychiatrists, specifically, predicted that most subjects would not go beyond 150 volts, when the victim makes his first explicit demand to be freed. They expected that only 4 percent would reach 300 volts, and that only a pathological fringe of about one in a thousand would administer the highest shock on the board.   25

These predictions were unequivocally wrong. Of the forty subjects in the first experiment, twenty-five obeyed the orders of the experimenter to the end, punishing the victim until they reached the most potent shock available on the generator. After 450 volts were administered three times, the experimenter called a halt to the session. Many obedient subjects then heaved sighs of relief, mopped their brows, rubbed their fingers over their eyes, or nervously fumbled cigarettes. Others displayed only minimal signs of tension from beginning to end.

When the very first experiments were carried out, Yale undergraduates were used as subjects, and about 60 percent of them were fully obedient. A colleague of mine immediately dismissed these findings as having no relevance to "ordinary" people, asserting that Yale undergraduates are a highly aggressive, competitive bunch who step on each other's necks on the slightest provocation. He assured me that when "ordinary" people were tested, the results would be quite different. As we moved from the pilot studies to the regular experimental series, people drawn from every stratum of New Haven life came to be employed in the experiment: professionals, white-collar workers, unemployed persons, and industrial workers. *The experiment's total outcome was the same as we had observed among the students.*

Moreover, when the experiments were repeated in Princeton, Munich, Rome, South Africa, and Australia, the level of obedience was invariably somewhat *higher* than found in the investigation reported in this article. Thus one scientist in Munich found 85 percent of his subjects obedient.

Fred Prozi's reactions, if more dramatic than most, illuminate the conflicts experienced by others in less visible form. About fifty years old and unemployed at the time of the experiment, he has a good-natured, if slightly dissolute, appearance, and he strikes people as a rather ordinary fellow. He begins the session calmly but becomes tense as it proceeds. After delivering the 180-volt shock, he pivots around in his chair and, shaking his head, addresses the experimenter in agitated tones:

PROZI: I can't stand it. I'm not going to kill that man in there. You hear   30
     him hollering?
EXPERIMENTER: As I told you before, the shocks may be painful, but. . . .
PROZI: But he's hollering. He can't stand it. What's going to happen to him?
EXPERIMENTER (his voice is patient, matter-of-fact):   The experiment
     requires that you continue, Teacher.
PROZI: Aaah, but, unh, I'm not going to get that man sick in there—know
     what I mean?
EXPERIMENTER: Whether the learner likes it or not, we must go on,   35
     through all the word pairs.
PROZI: I refuse to take the responsibility. He's in there hollering!
EXPERIMENTER: It's absolutely essential that you continue, Prozi.
PROZI: (indicating the unused questions): There's too many left here,
     I mean, Jeez, if he gets them wrong, there's too many of them left.
     I mean, who's going to take the responsibility if anything happens
     to that gentleman?

EXPERIMENTER: I'm responsible for anything that happens to him. Continue, please.

PROZI: All right. (Consults list of words.) The next one's "Slow—walk, truck, dance, music." Answer, please. (A buzzing sound indicates the learner has signaled his answer.) Wrong. A hundred and ninety-five volts. "Dance." (Zzumph!) 40

LEARNER (yelling): Let me out of here! My heart's bothering me! (Teacher looks at experimenter.)

EXPERIMENTER: Continue, please.

LEARNER (screaming): Let me out of here! You have no right to keep me here! Let me out of here, my heart's bothering me, let me out!

PROZI (shakes head, pats the table nervously): You see, he's hollering. Hear that? Gee, I don't know.

EXPERIMENTER: The experiment requires . . . 45

PROZI (interrupting): I know it does, sir, but I mean—hunh! He don't know what he's getting in for. He's up to 195 volts! (Experiment continues, through 210 volts, 225 volts, 240 volts, 255 volts, 270 volts, at which point Prozi, with evident relief, runs out of word-pair questions.)

EXPERIMENTER: You'll have to go back to the beginning of that page and go through them again until he's learned them all correctly.

PROZI: Aw, no. I'm not going to kill that man. You mean I've got to keep going up with the scale? No sir. He's hollering in there. I'm not going to give him 450 volts.

EXPERIMENTER: The experiment requires that you go on.

LEARNER: Ohhh. I absolutely refuse to answer anymore. (Shouting urgently now.) Let me out of here! You can't hold me here! Get me out. Get-me-out-of-here! 50

EXPERIMENTER: Continue. The next word is "Green," please.

PROZI: "Green—grass, hat, ink, apple." (Nothing happens. No answering buzz. Just gloomy silence.)

PROZI: I don't think he is going to answer.

EXPERIMENTER: If the learner doesn't answer in a reasonable time, about four or five seconds, consider the answer wrong. And follow the same procedures you have been doing for wrong answers. Say, "Wrong," tell him the number of volts, give him the punishment, read him the correct answer. Continue, please.

PROZI: "Green—grass, hat, ink, apple." Answer, please. (More silence. Subject just sits there.) 55

EXPERIMENTER: Go on with the procedure, please.

PROZI: Three hundred and fifteen volts. The answer is "ink." (Zzumph!)

LEARNER: Ohh. Ooohh.

PROZI (relieved to hear response): Next one . . .

LEARNER: I absolutely refuse to answer. 60

PROZI: You got to. You get a shock if you don't answer. (Experiment continues with learner refusing to answer, and, finally, failing even to grunt or groan. At 375 volts, the subject stands up.)

PROZI: I think something's happened to that fellow in there. I don't get no answer. He was hollering at less voltage. Can't you check in and see if he's all right, please?

EXPERIMENTER (with same detached calm):   Not once we've started. Please continue, Teacher.

PROZI (sits down, sighs deeply):   "Cool—day, shade, water, paint." Answer, please. Are you all right in there? Are you all right?

EXPERIMENTER: Please continue, Teacher. Continue, please. (Subject   65
pushes lever. Zzumph!)

PROZI (swiveling around in his chair):   Something's happened to that man in there. (Swiveling back.) Next one. "Low—dollar, necklace, moon, paint." (Turning around again.) Something's happened to that man in there. You better check in on him, sir. He won't answer or nothing.

EXPERIMENTER: Continue. Go on, please.

PROZI: You accept all responsibility?

EXPERIMENTER: The responsibility is mine. Correct. Please go on. (Subject returns to his list, starts running through words as rapidly as he can read them, works through to 450 volts.)

PROZI: That's that.   70

EXPERIMENTER: Continue using the 450 switch for each wrong answer. Continue, please.

PROZI: But I don't get anything!

EXPERIMENTER: Please continue. The next word is "white."

PROZI: Don't you think you should look in on him, please?

EXPERIMENTER: Not once we've started the experiment.   75

PROZI: What if he's dead in there? (Gestures toward the room with the electric chair.) I mean, he told me he can't stand the shock, sir. I don't mean to be rude, but I think you should look in on him. All you have to do is look in on him. All you have to do is look in the door. I don't get no answer, no noise. Something might have happened to the gentleman in there, sir.

EXPERIMENTER: We must continue. Go on, please.

PROZI: You mean keep giving him what? Four-hundred-fifty volts, what he's got now?

EXPERIMENTER: That's correct. Continue. The next word is "white."

PROZI (now at a furious pace):   "White—cloud, horse, rock, house."   80
Answer, please. The answer is "horse." Four hundred and fifty volts. (Zzumph!) Next word, "Bag—paint, music, clown, girl." The answer is "paint." Four hundred and fifty volts. (Zzumph!) Next word is "Short—sentence, movie . . ."

EXPERIMENTER: Excuse me, Teacher. We'll have to discontinue the experiment.

PECULIAR REACTIONS

Morris Braverman, another subject, is a thirty-nine-year-old social worker. He looks older than his years because of his bald head and serious demeanor. His brow is furrowed, as if all the world's burdens were carried on his face. He appears intelligent and concerned.

When the learner refuses to answer and the experimenter instructs Braverman to treat the absence of an answer as equivalent to a wrong answer, he takes his instruction to heart. Before administering 300 volts he asserts officiously to the victim, "Mr. Wallace, your silence has to be considered as a wrong answer." Then he administers the shock. He offers half-heartedly to change places with the learner, then asks the experimenter, "Do I have to follow these instructions literally?" He is satisfied with the experimenter's answer that he does. His very refined and authoritative manner of speaking is increasingly broken up by wheezing laughter.

The experimenter's notes on Mr. Braverman at the last few shocks are:

- Almost breaking up now each time gives shock. Rubbing face to hide laughter.
- Squinting, trying to hide face with hand, still laughing.
- Cannot control his laughter at this point no matter what he does.
- Clenching fist, pushing it onto table.

In an interview after the session, Mr. Braverman summarizes the experiment with impressive fluency and intelligence. He feels the experiment may have been designed also to "test the effects on the teacher of being in an essentially sadistic role, as well as the reactions of a student to a learning situation that was authoritative and punitive." When asked how painful the last few shocks administered to the learner were, he indicates that the most extreme category on the scale is not adequate (it read EXTREMELY PAINFUL) and places his mark at the edge of the scale with an arrow carrying it beyond the scale.

It is almost impossible to convey the greatly relaxed, sedate quality of his conversation in the interview. In the most relaxed terms, he speaks about his severe inner tension.

EXPERIMENTER: At what point were you most tense or nervous?
MR. BRAVERMAN: Well, when he first began to cry out in pain, and I realized this was hurting him. This got worse when he just blocked and refused to answer. There was I. I'm a nice person, I think, hurting somebody, and caught up in what seemed a mad situation . . . and in the interest of science, one goes through with it.

When the interviewer pursues the general question of tension, Mr. Braverman spontaneously mentions his laughter.

"My reactions were awfully peculiar. I don't know if you were watching me, but my reactions were giggly, and trying to stifle laughter. This isn't the way I usually am. This was a sheer reaction to a totally impossible situation. And my reaction was to the situation of having to hurt somebody. And being totally helpless and caught up in a set of circumstances where I just couldn't deviate and I couldn't try to help. This is what got me."

Mr. Braverman, like all subjects, was told the actual nature and purpose of the experiment, and a year later he affirmed in a questionnaire that he had learned something of personal importance: "What appalled me was that I could possess this capacity for obedience and compliance to a central idea, i.e., the value of a memory experiment, even after it became clear that continued adherence to this value was at the expense of violation of another value, i.e., don't hurt someone who is helpless and not hurting you. As my wife said, 'You can call yourself Eichmann.' I hope I deal more effectively with any future conflicts of values I encounter."

THE ETIQUETTE OF SUBMISSION

One theoretical interpretation of this behavior holds that all people harbor deeply aggressive instincts continually pressing for expression, and that the experiment provides institutional justification for the release of these impulses. According to this view, if a person is placed in a situation in which he has complete power over another individual, whom he may punish as much as he likes, all that is sadistic and bestial in man comes to the fore. The impulse to shock the victim is seen to flow from the potent aggressive tendencies, which are part of the motivational life of the individual, and the experiment, because it provides social legitimacy, simply opens the door to their expression.

It becomes vital, therefore, to compare the subject's performance when he is under orders and when he is allowed to choose the shock level.

The procedure was identical to our standard experiment, except that the teacher was told that he was free to select any shock level on any of the trials. (The experimenter took pains to point out that the teacher could use the highest levels on the generator, the lowest, any in between, or any combination of levels.) Each subject proceeded for thirty critical trials. The learner's protests were coordinated to standard shock levels, his first grunt coming at 75 volts, his first vehement protest at 150 volts.

The average shock used during the thirty critical trials was less than   95
60 volts—lower than the point at which the victim showed the first signs of discomfort. Three of the forty subjects did not go beyond the very lowest level on the board, twenty-eight went no higher than 75 volts, and thirty-eight did not go beyond the first loud protest at 150 volts. Two subjects provided the exception, administering up to 325 and 450 volts, but the overall result was that the great majority of people delivered very low, usually painless, shocks when the choice was explicitly up to them.

This condition of the experiment undermines another commonly offered explanation of the subjects' behavior—that those who shocked the victim at the most severe levels came only from the sadistic fringe of society. If one considers that almost two-thirds of the participants fall into the category of "obedient" subjects, and that they represented ordinary people drawn from working, managerial, and professional classes, the argument becomes very shaky. Indeed, it is highly reminiscent of the issue that arose in connection with Hannah Arendt's 1963 book, *Eichmann in Jerusalem*. Arendt contended that the prosecution's effort to depict Eichmann as a sadistic monster was fundamentally wrong, that he came closer to being an uninspired bureaucrat who simply sat at his desk and did his job. For asserting her views, Arendt became the object of considerable scorn, even calumny. Somehow, it was felt that the monstrous deeds carried out by Eichmann required a brutal, twisted personality, evil incarnate. After witnessing hundreds of ordinary persons submit to the authority in our own experiments, I must conclude that Arendt's conception of the banality of evil comes closer to the truth than one might dare imagine. The ordinary person who shocked the victim did so out of a sense of obligation—an impression of his duties as a subject—and not from any peculiarly aggressive tendencies.

This is, perhaps, the most fundamental lesson of our study: ordinary people, simply doing their jobs, and without any particular hostility on their part, can become agents in a terrible destructive process. Moreover, even when the destructive effects of their work become patently clear, and they are asked to carry out actions incompatible with fundamental standards of morality, relatively few people have the resources needed to resist authority.

Many of the people were in some sense against what they did to the learner, and many protested even while they obeyed. Some were totally convinced of the wrongness of their actions but could not bring themselves to make an open break with authority. They often derived satisfaction from their thoughts and felt that—within themselves, at least—they had been on the side of the angels. They tried to reduce strain by obeying the experimenter but "only slightly," encouraging the learner, touching the generator switches gingerly. When interviewed, such a subject would stress that he had "asserted my humanity" by administering the briefest shock possible. Handling the conflict in this manner was easier than defiance.

The situation is constructed so that there is no way the subject can stop shocking the learner without violating the experimenter's definitions of his own competence. The subject fears that he will appear arrogant, untoward, and rude if he breaks off. Although these inhibiting emotions appear small in scope alongside the violence being done to the learner, they suffuse the mind and feelings of the subject, who is miserable at the prospect of having to repudiate the authority to his face. (When the experiment was altered so that the experimenter gave his instructions by telephone instead of in person, only a third as many people were fully obedient through 450 volts.) It is a curious thing that a measure of compassion on the part of the subject—an unwillingness to "hurt" the experimenter's feelings—is part of those binding forces inhibiting his disobedience. The withdrawal of such deference may be as painful to the subject as to the authority he defies.

DUTY WITHOUT CONFLICT

The subjects do not derive satisfaction from inflicting pain, but they often   100
like the feeling they get from pleasing the experimenter. They are proud of
doing a good job, obeying the experimenter under difficult circumstances.
While the subjects administered only mild shocks on their own initiative,
one experimental variation showed that, under orders, 30 percent of them
were willing to deliver 450 volts even when they had to forcibly push the
learner's hand down on the electrode.

Bruno Batta is a thirty-seven-year-old welder who took part in the variation requiring the use of force. He was born in New Haven, his parents in
Italy. He has a rough-hewn face that conveys a conspicuous lack of alert-
ness. He has some difficulty in mastering the experimental procedure and
needs to be corrected by the experimenter several times. He shows appreciation for the help and willingness to do what is required. After the 150-volt
level, Batta has to force the learner's hand down on the shock plate, since
the learner himself refuses to touch it.

When the learner first complains, Mr. Batta pays no attention to him.
His face remains impassive, as if to dissociate himself from the learner's dis-
ruptive behavior. When the experimenter instructs him to force the learner's
hand down, he adopts a rigid, mechanical procedure. He tests the generator
switch. When it fails to function, he immediately forces the learner's hand
onto the shock plate. All the while he maintains the same rigid mask. The
learner, seated alongside him, begs him to stop, but with robotic impassivity
he continues the procedure.

What is extraordinary is his apparent total indifference to the learner;
he hardly takes cognizance of him as a human being. Meanwhile, he relates
to the experimenter in a submissive and courteous fashion.

At the 330-volt level, the learner refuses not only to touch the shock
plate but also to provide any answers. Annoyed, Batta turns to him, and
chastises him: "You better answer and get it over with. We can't stay here
all night." These are the only words he directs to the learner in the course
of an hour. Never again does he speak to him. The scene is brutal and
depressing, his hard, impassive face showing total indifference as he subdues
the screaming learner and gives him shocks. He seems to derive no pleasure
from the act itself, only quiet satisfaction at doing his job properly.

When he administers 450 volts, he turns to the experimenter and   105
asks, "Where do we go from here, Professor?" His tone is deferential and
expresses his willingness to be a cooperative subject, in contrast to the
learner's obstinacy.

At the end of the session he tells the experimenter how honored he has
been to help him, and in a moment of contrition, remarks, "Sir, sorry it
couldn't have been a full experiment."

He has done his honest best. It is only the deficient behavior of the
learner that has denied the experimenter full satisfaction.

The essence of obedience is that a person comes to view himself as the instrument for carrying out another person's wishes, and he therefore no longer regards himself as responsible for his actions. Once this critical shift of viewpoint has occurred, all of the essential features of obedience follow. The most far-reaching consequence is that the person feels responsible *to* the authority directing him but feels no responsibility *for* the content of the actions that the authority prescribes. Morality does not disappear—it acquires a radically different focus: the subordinate person feels shame or pride depending on how adequately he has performed the actions called for by authority.

Language provides numerous terms to pinpoint this type of morality: *loyalty, duty, discipline* all are terms heavily saturated with moral meaning and refer to the degree to which a person fulfills his obligations to authority. They refer not to the "goodness" of the person per se but to the adequacy with which a subordinate fulfills his socially defined role. The most frequent defense of the individual who has performed a heinous act under command of authority is that he has simply done his duty. In asserting this defense, the individual is not introducing an alibi concocted for the moment but is reporting honestly on the psychological attitude induced by submission to authority.

For a person to feel responsible for his actions, he must sense that the behavior has flowed from "the self." In the situation we have studied, subjects have precisely the opposite view of their actions—namely, they see them as originating in the motives of some other person. Subjects in the experiment frequently said, "If it were up to me, I would not have administered shocks to the learner." 110

Once authority has been isolated as the cause of the subject's behavior, it is legitimate to inquire into the necessary elements of authority and how it must be perceived in order to gain his compliance. We conducted some investigations into the kinds of changes that would cause the experimenter to lose his power and to be disobeyed by the subject. Some of the variations revealed that:

- *The experimenter's physical presence has a marked impact on his authority.* As cited earlier, obedience dropped off sharply when orders were given by telephone. The experimenter could often induce a disobedient subject to go on by returning to the laboratory.
- *Conflicting authority severely paralyzes action.* When two experimenters of equal status, both seated at the command desk, gave incompatible orders, no shocks were delivered past the point of their disagreement.
- *The rebellious action of others severely undermines authority.* In one variation, three teachers (two actors and a real subject) administered a test and shocks. When the two actors disobeyed the experimenter and refused to go beyond a certain shock level, thirty-six of forty subjects joined their disobedient peers and refused as well.

Although the experimenter's authority was fragile in some respects, it is also true that he had almost none of the tools used in ordinary command structures. For example, the experimenter did not threaten the subjects with punishment—such as loss of income, community ostracism, or jail—for failure to obey. Neither could he offer incentives. Indeed, we should expect the experimenter's authority to be much less than that of someone like a general, since the experimenter has no power to enforce his imperatives, and since participation in a psychological experiment scarcely evokes the sense of urgency and dedication found in warfare. Despite these limitations, he still managed to command a dismaying degree of obedience.

I will cite one final variation of the experiment that depicts a dilemma that is more common in everyday life. The subject was not ordered to pull the lever that shocked the victim, but merely to perform a subsidiary task (administering the word-pair test) while another person administered the shock. In this situation, thirty-seven of forty adults continued to the highest level on the shock generator. Predictably, they excused their behavior by saying that the responsibility belonged to the man who actually pulled the switch. This may illustrate a dangerously typical arrangement in a complex society: it is easy to ignore responsibility when one is only an intermediate link in a chain of action.

The problem of obedience is not wholly psychological. The form and shape of society and the way it is developing have much to do with it. There was a time, perhaps, when people were able to give a fully human response to any situation because they were fully absorbed in it as human beings. But as soon as there was a division of labor things changed. Beyond a certain point, the breaking up of society into people carrying out narrow and very special jobs takes away from the human quality of work and life. A person does not get to see the whole situation but only a small part of it, and is thus unable to act without some kind of overall direction. He yields to authority but in doing so is alienated from his own actions.

Even Eichmann was sickened when he toured the concentration camps,   115 but he had only to sit at a desk and shuffle papers. At the same time the man in the camp who actually dropped Cyclon-b into the gas chambers was able to justify *his* behavior on the ground that he was only following orders from above. Thus there is a fragmentation of the total human act; no one is confronted with the consequences of his decision to carry out the evil act. The person who assumes responsibility has evaporated. Perhaps this is the most common characteristic of socially organized evil in modern society.

Questions for Discussion and Writing

1. How is Milgram's experiment designed to test how far people will go in obeying orders from authority figures? Why are terms such as *loyalty, duty, discipline,* and *obligation* important in Milgram's studies?

2. How does Milgram's inclusion of the actual transcript of Mr. Prozi's experience (instead of a summary) enable you to identify with the subject and therefore better understand the entire experiment?

3. Have you ever found yourself in a situation in which you were ordered by an authority figure to do something you thought might be wrong? How did you react? Describe your experience. Did your experience give you insight into Milgram's research?

4. **Rhetorical inquiry:** How does the reference in the last paragraph make clear that Milgram thought of this experiment, in part, to find out why so many remained silent while the Holocaust took place?

DALAI LAMA

Lhamo Dhondup was born in 1935 to a poor farming family in northeastern Tibet. At the age of two, he was renamed Tenzin Gyatso (which means "ocean of wisdom") when he was recognized as the incarnation of the thirteenth Dalai Lama. He underwent eighteen years of religious and philosophical studies leading to the Tibetan equivalent of a Ph.D. in Buddhist studies. In 1950, when he was sixteen, the Chinese army invaded Tibet, and he assumed full political powers and attempted to negotiate with Mao Zedong. He escaped into exile in 1959, along with eighty thousand Tibetans, to Dharamasala in northern India, where he still resides. From there, he has waged a nonviolent campaign to free Tibet from the Chinese; he received the Nobel Peace Prize in 1989. His published works include Freedom in Exile: The Autobiography of the Dalai Lama *(1990) and the best-selling* Ethics for a New Millennium *(1999), in which the following essay first appeared.*

Before You Read

How important is religion in your life and in the lives of people you know?

The Role of Religion in Modern Society

It is a sad fact of human history that religion has been a major source of conflict. Even today, individuals are killed, communities destroyed, and societies destabilized as a result of religious bigotry and hatred. It is no wonder that many question the place of religion in human society. Yet when we think carefully, we find that conflict in the name of religion arises from two principal sources. There is that which arises simply as a result of religious diversity—the doctrinal, cultural, and practical differences between one religion and another. Then there is the conflict that arises in the context of political, economic, and other factors, mainly at the institutional level. Interreligious harmony is the key to overcoming conflict of the first sort. In the case of the second, some other solution must be found. Secularization and in particular the separation of the religious hierarchy from the institutions of the state may go some way to reducing such institutional problems. Our concern in this chapter is with interreligious harmony, however.

This is an important aspect of what I have called universal responsibility. But before examining the matter in detail, it is perhaps worth considering the question of whether religion is really relevant in the modern world. Many people argue that it is not. Now I have observed that religious belief is not a precondition either of ethical conduct or of happiness itself. I have also suggested that whether a person practices religion or not, the spiritual qualities of love and compassion, patience, tolerance, forgiveness, humility, and so on are indispensable. At the same time, I should make it clear that I believe that these are most easily and effectively developed within the context of religious practice. I also believe that when an individual sincerely practices religion, that individual will benefit enormously. People who have developed a firm faith, grounded in understanding and rooted in daily practice, are in general much better at coping with adversity than those who have not. I am convinced, therefore, that religion has enormous potential to benefit humanity. Properly employed, it is an extremely effective instrument for establishing human happiness. In particular, it can play a leading role in encouraging people to develop a sense of responsibility toward others and of the need to be ethically disciplined.

On these grounds, therefore, I believe that religion is still relevant today. But consider this too: some years ago, the body of a Stone Age man was recovered from the ice of the European Alps. Despite being more than five thousand years old, it was perfectly preserved. Even its clothes were largely intact. I remember thinking at the time that were it possible to bring this individual back to life for a day, we would find that we have much in common with him. No doubt we would find that he too was concerned for his family and loved ones, for his health and so on. Differences of culture and expression notwithstanding, we would still be able to identify with one another on the level of feeling. And there could be no reason to suppose any less concern with finding happiness and avoiding suffering on his part than on ours. If religion, with its emphasis on overcoming suffering through the practice of ethical discipline and cultivation of love and compassion, can be conceived of as relevant in the past, it is hard to see why it should not be equally so today. Granted that in the past the value of religion may have been more obvious, in that human suffering was more explicit due to the lack of modern facilities. But because we humans still suffer, albeit today this is experienced more internally as mental and emotional affliction, and because religion in addition to its salvific truth claims is concerned to help us overcome suffering, surely it must still be relevant.

How then might we bring about the harmony that is necessary to overcome interreligious conflict? As in the case of individuals engaged in the discipline of restraining their response to negative thoughts and emotions and cultivating spiritual qualities, the key lies in developing understanding. We must first identify the factors that obstruct it. Then we must find ways to overcome them.

Perhaps the most significant obstruction to interreligious harmony is lack of appreciation of the value of others' faith traditions. Until comparatively recently, communication between different cultures, even different communities, was slow or nonexistent. For this reason, sympathy for other faith traditions was not necessarily very important—except of course where members of different religions lived side by side. But this attitude is no longer viable. In today's increasingly complex and interdependent world, we are compelled to acknowledge the existence of other cultures, different ethnic groups, and, of course, other religious faiths. Whether we like it or not, most of us now experience this diversity on a daily basis.

I believe that the best way to overcome ignorance and bring about understanding is through dialogue with members of other faith traditions. This I see occurring in a number of different ways. Discussions among scholars in which the convergence and perhaps more importantly the divergence between different faith traditions are explored and appreciated are very valuable. On another level, it is helpful when there are encounters between ordinary but practicing followers of different religions in which each shares their experiences. This is perhaps the most effective way of appreciating others' teachings. In my own case, for example, my meetings with the late Thomas Merton, a Catholic monk of the Cistercian order, were deeply inspiring. They helped me develop a profound admiration for the teachings of Christianity. I also feel that occasional meetings between religious leaders joining together to pray for a common cause are extremely useful. The gathering at Assisi in Italy in 1986, when representatives of the world's major religions gathered to pray for peace, was, I believe, tremendously beneficial to many religious believers insofar as it symbolized the solidarity and a commitment to peace of all those taking part.

Finally, I feel that the practice of members of different faith traditions going on joint pilgrimages together can be very helpful. It was in this spirit that in 1993 I went to Lourdes, and then to Jerusalem, a site holy to three of the world's great religions. I have also paid visits to various Hindu, Islamic, Jain, and Sikh shrines both in India and abroad. More recently, following a seminar devoted to discussing and practicing meditation in the Christian and Buddhist traditions, I joined an historic pilgrimage of practitioners of both traditions in a program of prayers, meditation, and dialogue under the Bodhi tree at Bodh Gaya in India. This is one of Buddhism's most important shrines.

When exchanges like these occur, followers of one tradition will find that, just as in the case of their own, the teachings of others' faiths are a source both of spiritual inspiration and of ethical guidance to their followers. It will also become clear that irrespective of doctrinal and other differences, all the major world religions are concerned with helping individuals to become good human beings. All emphasize love and compassion, patience, tolerance, forgiveness, humility, and so on, and all are capable of helping individuals to develop these. Moreover, the example given by the founders of each major religion clearly demonstrates a concern for helping others find happiness through developing these qualities. So far as their own lives were concerned, each conducted themselves with great simplicity. Ethical discipline and love for all others was the hallmark of their lives. They did not live luxuriously like emperors and kings. Instead, they voluntarily accepted suffering—without consideration of the hardships involved—in order to benefit humanity as a whole. In their teachings, all placed special emphasis on developing love and compassion and renouncing selfish desires. And each of them called on us to transform our hearts and minds. Indeed, whether we have faith or not, all are worthy of our profound admiration.

At the same time as engaging in dialogue with followers of other religions, we must, of course, implement in our daily life the teachings of our own religion. Once we have experienced the benefit of love and compassion, and of ethical discipline, we will easily recognize the value of other's teachings. But for this, it is essential to realize that religious practice entails a lot more than merely saying, "I believe" or, as in Buddhism, "I take refuge." There is also more to it than just visiting temples, or shrines, or churches. And taking religious teachings is of little benefit if they do not enter the heart but remain at the level of intellect alone. Simply relying on faith without understanding and without implementation is of limited value. I often tell Tibetans that carrying a *mala* (something like a rosary) does not make a person a genuine religious practitioner. The efforts we make sincerely to transform ourselves spiritually are what make us genuine religious practitioners.

We come to see the overriding importance of genuine practice when we recognize that, along with ignorance, individuals' unhealthy relationships with their beliefs is the other major factor in religious disharmony. Far from applying the teachings of their religion in our personal lives, we have a tendency to use them to reinforce our self-centered attitudes. We relate to our religion as something we own or as a label that separates us from others. Surely this is misguided? Instead of using the nectar of religion to purify the poisonous elements of our hearts and minds, there is a danger when we think like this of using these negative elements to poison the nectar of religion.

Yet we must acknowledge that this reflects another problem, one which is implicit in all religions. I refer to the claims each has of being the one "true" religion. How are we to resolve this difficulty? It is true that from the point of view of the individual practitioner, it is essential to have a single-pointed commitment to one's own faith. It is also true that this depends on the deep conviction that one's own path is the sole mediator of truth. But at the same time, we have to find some means of reconciling this belief with the reality of a multiplicity of similar claims. In practical terms, this involves individual practitioners finding a way at least to accept the validity of the teachings of other religions while maintaining a wholehearted commitment to their own. As far as the validity of the metaphysical truth claims of a

10

given religion is concerned, that is of course the internal business of that particular tradition.

In my own case, I am convinced that Buddhism provides me with the most effective framework within which to situate my efforts to develop spiritually through cultivating love and compassion. At the same time, I must acknowledge that while Buddhism represents the best path for me—that is, it suits my character, my temperament, my inclinations, and my cultural background—the same will be true of Christianity for Christians. For them, Christianity is the best way. On the basis of my conviction, I cannot, therefore, say that Buddhism is best for everyone.

I sometimes think of religion in terms of medicine for the human spirit. Independent of its usage and suitability to a particular individual in a particular condition, we really cannot judge a medicine's efficacy. We are not justified in saying this medicine is very good because of such and such ingredients. If you take the patient and the medicine's effect on that person out of the equation, it hardly makes sense. What is relevant is to say that in the case of this particular patient with its particular illness, this medicine is the most effective. Similarly with different religious traditions, we can say that this one is most effective for this particular individual. But it is unhelpful to try to argue on the basis of philosophy or metaphysics that one religion is better than another. The important thing is surely its effectiveness in individual cases.

My way to resolve the seeming contradiction between each religion's claim to "one truth and one religion" and the reality of the multiplicity of faiths is thus to understand that in the case of a single individual, there can indeed be only one truth, one religion. However, from the perspective of human society at large, we must accept the concept of "many truths, many religions." To continue with our medical analogy, in the case of one particular patient, the suitable medicine is in fact the one medicine. But clearly that does not mean that there may not be other medicines suitable to other patients.

To my way of thinking, the diversity that exists among the various religious traditions is enormously enriching. There is thus no need to try to find ways of saying that ultimately all religions are the same. They are similar in that they all emphasize the indispensability of love and compassion in the context of ethical discipline. But to say this is not to say that they are all essentially one. The contradictory understanding of creation and beginninglessness articulated by Buddhism, Christianity, and Hinduism, for example, means that in the end we have to part company when it comes to metaphysical claims, in spite of the many practical similarities that undoubtedly exist. These contradictions may not be very important in the beginning stages of religious practice. But as we advance along the path of one tradition or another, we are compelled at some point to acknowledge fundamental differences. For example, the concept of rebirth in Buddhism and various other ancient Indian traditions may turn out to be incompatible with the Christian idea of salvation. This need not be a cause for dismay, however. Even within Buddhism itself, in the realm of metaphysics there are diametrically opposing

15

views. At the very least, such diversity means that we have different frameworks within which to locate ethical discipline and the development of spiritual values. That is why I do not advocate a super or a new world religion. It would mean that we would lose the unique characteristics of the different faith traditions.

Some people, it is true, hold that the Buddhist concept of *shunyata*, or emptiness, is ultimately the same as certain approaches to understanding the concept of God. Nevertheless, there remain difficulties with this. The first is that while of course we can interpret these concepts, to what extent can we be faithful to the original teachings if we do so? There are compelling similarities between the Mahayana Buddhist concept of *Dharmakaya, Sambogakaya,* and *Nirmanakaya* and the Christian trinity of God as Father, Son, and Holy Spirit. But to say, on the basis of this, that Buddhism and Christianity are ultimately the same is to go a bit far, I think! As an old Tibetan saying goes, we must beware of trying to put a yak's head on a sheep's body—or vice versa.

What is required instead is that we develop a genuine sense of religious pluralism in spite of the different claims of different faith traditions. This is especially true if we are serious in our respect for human rights as a universal principle. In this regard, I find the concept of a world parliament of religions very appealing. To begin with, the word "parliament" conveys a sense of democracy, while the plural "religions" underlines the importance of the principle of a multiplicity of faith traditions. The truly pluralist perspective on religion which the idea of such a parliament suggests could, I believe be, of great help. It would avoid the extremes of religious bigotry on the one hand, and the urge toward unnecessary syncretism on the other.

Connected with this issue of interreligious harmony, I should perhaps say something about religious conversion. This is a question which must be taken extremely seriously. It is essential to realize that the mere fact of conversion alone will not make an individual a better person, that is to say, a more disciplined, a more compassionate, and a warm-hearted person. Much more helpful, therefore, is for the individual to concentrate on transforming themselves spiritually through the practice of restraint, virtue, and compassion. To the extent that the insights or practices of other religions are useful or relevant to our own faith, it is valuable to learn from others. In some cases, it may even be helpful to adopt certain of them. Yet when this is done wisely, we can remain firmly committed to our own faith. This way is best because it carries with it no danger of confusion, especially with respect to the different ways of life that tend to go with different faith traditions.

Given the diversity to be found among individual human beings, it is of course bound to be the case that out of many millions of practitioners of a particular religion, a handful will find that another religion's approach to ethics and spiritual development is more satisfactory. For some, the concept of rebirth and karma will seem highly effective in inspiring the aspiration to develop love and compassion within the context of responsibility. For others, the concept of a transcendent, loving creator will come to seem more so. In such circumstances, it is crucial for those individuals to question themselves again and again. They must ask, "Am I attracted to this other religion for the right reasons? Is it merely the cultural and ritual aspects that are appealing? Or is it the essential teachings? Do I suppose that if I convert to this new religion it will be less demanding than my present one?" I say this because it has often struck me that when people do convert to a religion outside their own heritage, quite often they adopt certain superficial aspects of the culture to which their new faith belongs. But their practice may not go very much deeper than that.

In the case of a person who decides after a process of long and mature reflection to adopt a different religion, it is very important that they remember the positive contribution to humanity of each religious tradition. The danger is that the individual may, in seeking to justify their decision to others, criticize their previous faith. It is essential to avoid this. Just because that tradition is no longer effective in the case of one individual does not mean it is no longer of benefit to humanity. On the contrary, we can be certain that it has been an inspiration to millions of people in the past, that it inspires millions today, and that it will inspire millions in the path of love and compassion in the future. 20

The important point to keep in mind is that ultimately the whole purpose of religion is to facilitate love and compassion, patience, tolerance, humility, forgiveness, and so on. If we neglect these, changing our religion will be of no help. In the same way, even if we are fervent believers in our own faith, it will avail us nothing if we neglect to implement these qualities in our daily lives. Such a believer is no better off than a patient with some fatal illness who merely reads a medical treatise but fails to undertake the treatment prescribed.

Moreover, if we who are practitioners of religion are not compassionate and disciplined, how can we expect it of others? If we can establish genuine harmony derived from mutual respect and understanding, religion has enormous potential to speak with authority on such vital moral questions as peace and disarmament, social and political justice, the natural environment, and many other matters affecting all humanity. But until we put our own spiritual teachings into practice, we will never be taken seriously. And this means, among other things, setting a good example through developing good relations with other faith traditions.

Questions for Discussion and Writing

1. How does the Dalai Lama suggest that we overcome one of the main obstructions to religious harmony—that is, the claim of each religion of being the one "true" religion? Why is compassion the essential quality in developing interreligious harmony?

2. How does the Dalai Lama use an analogy drawn from medicine to promote tolerance toward the teachings and practices of others' faiths?

How does this image of a 1982 meeting between the Dalai Lama and the Pope illustrate important themes in the Dalai Lama's essay?

3. The Dalai Lama believes that spiritual qualities are "most easily and effectively developed within the context of religious practice"; would it be possible to develop these qualities in a secular context? Would this essay have been as effective if you did not know that the author is a great religious leader? Explain your answers.
4. **Rhetorical inquiry:** Why does the Dalai Lama mention the impact of Thomas Merton on his life and how does this help illustrate his thesis?

JEAN-PAUL SARTRE

Jean-Paul Sartre (1905–1980) the French philosopher and author was born in Paris. In 1929, he met the writer and feminist Simone de Beauvoir with whom he had a lifelong relationship. He taught for many years in secondary schools and briefly served in the Army. Sartre studied in Berlin where he developed his ideas on existentialism, a philosophy that views the individual as a responsible but lonely being. His works include Being and Nothingness *(1943), written while he was a prisoner of war. After Paris was liberated in 1945, Sartre delivered a lecture that was later published as a book,* Existentialism and Humanism *(1946), from which the following selection is drawn. His other works include* The Age of Reason *(1945) and* The Critique of Dialectical Reason *(1960). He declined the 1964 Nobel Prize in Literature.*

Before You Read

Why would disbelief in a predetermined plan for human existence create a greater sense of responsibility for one's own actions?

Existentialism

Atheistic existentialism, which I represent, . . . states that if God does not exist, there is at least one being in whom existence precedes essence, a being who exists before he can be defined by any concept, and that this being is man, or, as Heidegger says, human reality. What is meant here by saying that existence precedes essence? It means that, first of all, man exists, turns up, appears on the scene, and, only afterwards, defines himself. If man, as the existentialist conceives him, is indefinable, it is because at first he is nothing. Only afterward will he be something, and he himself will have made what he will be. Thus, there is no human nature, since there is no God to conceive it. Not only is man what he conceives himself to be, but he is also only what he wills himself to be after this thrust toward existence.

Man is nothing else but what he makes of himself. Such is the first principle of existentialism. It is also what is called subjectivity. But what do we mean by this, if not that man has a greater dignity than a stone or table? For we mean that man first exists, that is, that man first of all is the being who hurls himself toward a future and who is conscious of imagining himself as being in the future. Man is at the start a plan which is aware of itself, rather than a patch of moss, a piece of garbage, or a cauliflower; nothing exists prior to this plan; there is nothing in heaven; man will be what he will have planned to be. Not what he will want to be. Because by the word "will" we generally mean a conscious decision, which is subsequent to what we have already made of ourselves. I may want to belong to a political party, write a book, get married; but all that is only a manifestation of an earlier, more spontaneous choice that is called "will." But if existence really does precede essence, man is responsible for what he is. Thus, existentialism's first move is to make every man aware of what he is and to make the full responsibility of his existence rest on him. And when we say that a man is responsible for himself, we do not only mean that he is responsible for his own individuality, but that he is responsible for all men.

The word "subjectivism" has two meanings. Subjectivism means, on the one hand, that an individual chooses and makes himself; and, on the other, that it is impossible for man to transcend human subjectivity. The second of these is the essential meaning of existentialism. When we say that man chooses his own self, we mean that every one of us does likewise; but we also mean by that that in making this choice he also chooses all men. In fact, in creating the man that we want to be, there is not a single one of our acts which does not at the same time create an image of man as we think he ought to be. To choose to be this or that is to affirm at the same time the value of what we choose, because we can never choose evil. We always choose the good, and nothing can be good for us without being good for all.

If, on the other hand, existence precedes essence, and if we grant that we exist and fashion our image at one and the same time, the image is valid for everybody and for our whole age. Thus, our responsibility is much greater than we might have supposed, because it involves all mankind. If I am a workingman and choose to join a Christian trade union rather than be a Communist, and if by being a member, I want to show that the best thing for a man is resignation, that the kingdom of man is not of this world, I am not only involving my own case—I want to be resigned for everyone. As a result, my action has involved all humanity. To take a more individual matter, if I want to marry, to have children, even if this marriage depends solely on my own circumstances or passion or wish, I am involving all humanity in monogamy and not merely myself. Therefore, I am responsible for myself and for everyone else. I am creating a certain image of man of my own choosing. In choosing myself, I choose man.

The existentialist thinks it very distressing that God does not exist,   5
because all possibility of finding values in a heaven of ideas disappears along with Him; there can no longer be an a priori Good, since there is no infinite and perfect consciousness to think it. Nowhere is it written that the good exists, that we must be honest, that we must not lie; because the fact is we are on a plane where there are only men. Dostoievsky said, "If God didn't exist, everything would be possible." That is the very starting point of existentialism. Indeed, everything is permissible if God does not exist, and as a result man is forlorn, because neither within him or without does he find anything to cling to. He can't start making excuses for himself.

If existence really does precede essence, there is no explaining things away by reference to a fixed and given nature. In other words, there is no determinism, man is free, man is freedom. On the other hand, if God does not exist, we find no values or commands to turn to which legitimize our conduct. So, in the bright realm of values, we have no excuse behind us, nor justification before us. We are alone, with no excuses.

That is the idea I shall try to convey when I say that man is condemned to be free. Condemned, because he did not create himself, yet, in other respects is free; because, once thrown into the world, he is responsible for everything he does.

To give you an example which will enable you to understand forlornness better, I shall cite the case of one of my students who came to see me under the following circumstances: his father was on bad terms with his mother, and, moreover, was inclined to be a collaborationist, his elder brother had been killed in the German offensive of 1940, and the young man, with somewhat immature but generous feelings, wanted to avenge him. His mother lived alone with him, very much upset by the half-treason of her husband and the death of her older son; the boy was her only consolation.

The boy was faced with the choice of leaving for England joining the Free French forces—that is, leaving his mother behind—or remaining with his mother and helping her to carry on. He was fully aware that the woman lived only for him and that his going off—and perhaps his death—would plunge her into despair. He was also aware that every act that he did for his mother's sake was a sure thing, in the sense that it was helping her to carry on, whereas every effort he made toward going off and fighting was an uncertain move which might run aground and prove completely useless; for example, on his way to England he might, while passing through Spain, be detained indefinitely in a Spanish camp; he might reach England or Algiers and be stuck in an office at a desk job. As a result, he was faced with two very different kinds of action: one, concrete, immediate, but concerning only one individual; the other concerned an incomparably vaster group, a national collectivity, but for that very reason was dubious, and might be interrupted en route. And, at the same time, he was wavering between two kinds of ethics. On the one hand, an ethics of sympathy, of personal devotion; on the other, a broader ethics, but one whose efficacy was more dubious. He had to choose between the two.

Who could help him choose? Christian doctrine? No. Christian doctrine says, "Be charitable, love your neighbor, take the more rugged path, etc., etc." But which is the more rugged path? Whom should he love as a brother? The fighting man or his mother? Which does the greater good, the vague act of fighting in a group, or the concrete one of helping a particular human being to go on living? Who can decide a priori? Nobody. No book of ethics can tell him. The Kantian ethics says, "Never treat any person as a means, but as an end." Very well, if I stay with my mother, I'll treat her as an end and not as a means; but by virtue of this very fact, I'm running the risk of treating the people around me who are fighting, as means; and conversely, if I go to join those who are fighting, I'll be treating them as an end, and, by doing that, I run the risk of treating my mother as a means. 10

If values are vague, and if they are always too broad for the concrete and specific case that we are considering, the only thing left for us is to trust our instincts. That's what this young man tried to do; and when I saw him, he said, "In the end, feeling is what counts. I ought to choose whichever pushes me in our direction. If I feel that I love my mother enough to sacrifice everything else for her—my desire for vengeance, for action, for adventure—then I'll stay with her. If, on the contrary, I feel that my love for my mother isn't enough, I'll leave."

But how is the value of a feeling determined? What gives his feeling for his mother value? Precisely the fact that he remained with her. I may say that I like so-and-so well enough to sacrifice a certain amount of money for him, but I may say so only if I've done it. I may say "I love my mother well enough to remain with her" if I have remained with her. The only way to determine the value of this affection is, precisely, to perform an act which confirms and defines it. But, since I require this affection to justify my act, I find myself caught in a vicious circle.

Given that men are free and that tomorrow they will freely decide what man will be, I cannot be sure that, after my death, fellow-fighters will carry on my work to bring it to its maximum perfection. Tomorrow, after my death, some men may decide to set up Fascism, and the others may be cowardly and muddled enough to let them do it. Fascism will then be the human reality, so much the worse for us.

Actually, things will be as man will have decided they are to be. Does that mean that I should abandon myself to quietism? No. First, I should involve myself; then, act on the old saw, "Nothing ventured, nothing gained." Nor does it mean that I shouldn't belong to a party, but rather that I shall have no illusions and shall do what I can. For example, suppose I ask myself, "Will socialization, as such, ever come about?" I know nothing about it. All I Know is that I'm going to do everything in my power to bring it about. Beyond that, I can't count on anything. Quietism is the attitude of people who say, "Let others do what I can't do." The doctrine I am presenting is the very opposite of quietism, since it declares, "There is no reality except in action." Moreover, it goes further, since it adds, "Man is nothing else than his plan; he exists only to the extent that he fulfills himself; he is therefore nothing else than the ensemble of his acts, nothing else than his life."

Now, for the existentialist there is really no love other than one which   15
manifests itself in a person's being in love. There is no genius other than one which is expressed in works of art; the genius of Proust is the sum of Proust's works; the genius of Racine is his series of tragedies. Outside of that, there is nothing. Why say that Racine could have written another tragedy, when he didn't write it? A man is involved in life, leaves his impress on it, and outside of that there is nothing. To be sure, this may seem a harsh thought to someone whose life hasn't been a success. But, on the other hand, it prompts people to understand that reality alone is what counts, that dreams, expectations, and hopes warrant no more than to define a man as a disappointed dream, as miscarried hopes, as vain expectations. In other words, to define him negatively and not positively. However, when we say. "You are nothing else than your life," that does not imply that the artist will be judged solely on the basis of his works of art; a thousand other things will contribute toward summing him up. What we mean is that a man is nothing else than a series of undertakings, that he is the sum, the organization, the ensemble of the relationships which make up these undertakings.

When all is said and done, what we are accused of, at bottom, is not our pessimism, but an optimistic toughness. If people throw up to us our works of fiction in which we write about people who are soft, weak, cowardly, and sometimes even downright bad, it's not because these people are soft, weak, cowardly, or bad; because if we were to say, as Zola did, that they are that way because of heredity, the workings of environment, society, because of biological or psychological determinism, people would be reassured. They would say, "Well, that's what we're like, no one can do anything about it." But when the existentialist writes about a coward, he says that this coward is responsible for his cowardice. He's not like that because he has a cowardly heart or lung or brain; he's not like that on account of his physiological make-up; but he's like that because he has made himself a coward by his acts. There's no such thing as a cowardly constitution; there are nervous constitutions; there is poor blood, as the common people say, or strong constitutions. But the man whose blood is poor is not a coward on that account, for what makes cowardice is the act of renouncing or yielding. A constitution is not an act; the coward is defined on the basis of the acts he performs. People feel, in a vague sort of way, that this coward we're talking about is guilty of being a coward, and the thought frightens them. What people would like is that a coward or a hero be born that way.

Existentialism is nothing else than an attempt to draw all the consequences of a coherent atheistic position. It isn't trying to plunge man into despair at all. But if one calls every attitude of unbelief despair, like the Christians, then the word is not being used in its original sense. Existentialism isn't so atheistic that it wears itself out showing that God doesn't exist. Rather, it declares that even if God did exist, that would change nothing. There you've got our point of view. Not that we believe that God exists, but we think that the problem of His existence is not the issue. In this sense existentialism is optimistic, a doctrine of action, and it is plain dishonesty for Christians to make no distinction between their own despair and ours and then to call us despairing.

Questions for Discussion and Writing

1. What kind of burden does existentialism impose and, correspondingly, what freedoms does it give us?
2. How does Sartre use the example of one of his students faced with a dilemma to illustrate his philosophy?
3. In what respects does existentialism put a premium on the individual's need to choose, without reference to traditional moral codes or conventional value systems?
4. **Rhetorical inquiry:** What aspects of this essay illustrate that Sartre is, in one sense, defending existentialism against the charge that it is against traditional religions? Where does he discuss the idea, that for him, religious belief is either irrelevant or inadequate?

JOHN M. DARLEY AND BIBB LATANÉ

John M. Darley (b. 1938) received a Ph.D. from Harvard in 1965. Since 1972 he has been professor of psychology at Princeton University where the focus of his research concerns the principles of moral judgment in children and adults. With Bibb Latané, Darley has coauthored The Unresponsive Bystander: Why Doesn't He Help? *(1970) and* Help in a Crisis: Bystander Response to an Emergency *(1976). Bibb Latané (b. 1937) received a Ph.D. from the University of Minnesota (1963) and was a professor of psychology at the University of North Carolina–Chapel Hill. This essay, drawn from their prize-winning research, describes an ingenious experiment designed to identify the causes of noninvolvement in bystanders who witness street crimes.*

Before You Read

What factors determine if a bystander is willing to help a victim of street crime?

Why People Don't Help in a Crisis

Kitty Genovese is set upon by a maniac as she returns home from work at 3 A.M. Thirty-eight of her neighbors in Kew Gardens, N.Y., come to their windows when she cries out in terror; not one comes to her assistance, even though her assailant takes half an hour to murder her. No one so much as calls the police. She dies.

Andrew Mormille is stabbed in the head and neck as he rides in a New York City subway train. Eleven other riders flee to another car as the 17-year-old boy bleeds to death; not one comes to his assistance, even though his attackers have left the car. He dies.

Eleanor Bradley trips and breaks her leg while shopping on New York City's Fifth Avenue. Dazed and in shock, she calls for help, but the hurrying stream of people simply parts and flows past. Finally, after 40 minutes, a taxi driver stops and helps her to a doctor.

How can so many people watch another human being in distress and do nothing? Why don't they help?

Since we started research on bystander responses to emergencies, we   5
have heard many explanations for the lack of intervention in such cases. "The megalopolis in which we live makes closeness difficult and leads to the alienation of the individual from the group," says the psychoanalyst. "This sort of disaster," says the sociologist, "shakes the sense of safety and sureness of the individuals involved and causes psychological withdrawal." "Apathy," says others. "Indifference."

All of these analyses share one characteristic: they set the indifferent witness apart from the rest of us. Certainly not one of us who reads about these incidents in horror is apathetic, alienated or depersonalized. Certainly these terrifying cases have no personal implications for us. We needn't feel guilty, or re-examine ourselves, or anything like that. Or should we?

If we look closely at the behavior of witnesses to these incidents, the people involved begin to seem a little less inhuman and a lot more like the rest of us. They were not indifferent. The 38 witnesses of Kitty Genovese's murder, for example, did not merely look at the scene once and then ignore it. They continued to stare out of their windows, caught, fascinated, distressed, unwilling to act but unable to turn away.

Why, then, didn't they act?

There are three things the bystander must do if he is to intervene in an emergency: *notice* that something is happening; *interpret* that event as an emergency; and decide that he has *personal responsibility* for intervention. As we shall show, the presence of other bystanders may at each stage inhibit his action.

THE UNSEEING EYE

Suppose that a man has a heart attack. He clutches his chest, staggers to the nearest building and slumps sitting to the sidewalk. Will a passerby come to his assistance? First, the bystander has to notice that something is happening. He must tear himself away from his private thoughts and pay attention. But Americans consider it bad manners to look closely at other people in public. We are taught to respect the privacy of others, and when among strangers we close our ears and avoid staring. In a crowd, then, each person is less likely to notice a potential emergency than when alone.   10

Experimental evidence corroborates this. We asked college students to an interview about their reactions to urban living. As the students waited to see the interviewer, either by themselves or with two other students, they filled out a questionnaire. Solitary students often glanced idly about while filling out their questionnaires; those in groups kept their eyes on their own papers.

As part of the study, we staged an emergency: smoke was released into the waiting room through a vent. Two thirds of the subjects who were alone noticed the smoke immediately, but only 25 percent of those waiting in groups saw it as quickly. Although eventually all the subjects did become aware of the smoke—when the atmosphere grew so smoky as to make them cough and rub their eyes—this study indicates that the more people present, the slower an individual may be to perceive an emergency and the more likely he is not to see it at all.

SEEING IS NOT NECESSARILY BELIEVING

Once an event is noticed, an onlooker must decide if it is truly an emergency. Emergencies are not always clearly labeled as such; "smoke" pouring into a waiting room may be caused by fire, or it may merely indicate a leak in a steam pipe. Screams in the street may signal an assault or a family quarrel. A man lying in a doorway may be having a coronary—or he may simply be sleeping off a drunk.

A person trying to interpret a situation often looks at those around him to see how he should react. If everyone else is calm and indifferent, he will tend to remain so; if everyone else is reacting strongly, he is likely to become aroused. This tendency is not merely slavish conformity; ordinarily we derive much valuable information about new situations from how others around us behave. It's a rare traveler who, in picking a roadside restaurant, chooses to stop at one where no other cars appear in the parking lot.

But occasionally the reactions of others provide false information. The   15
studied nonchalance of patients in a dentist's waiting room is a poor indication of their inner anxiety. It is considered embarrassing to "lose your cool" in
public. In a potentially acute situation, then, everyone present will appear
more unconcerned than he is in fact. A crowd can thus force inaction on its
members by implying, through its passivity, that an event is not an emergency.
Any individual in such a crowd fears that he may appear a fool if he behaves
as though it were.

To determine how the presence of other people affects a person's interpretation of an emergency, Latané and Judith Rodin set up another experiment.
Subjects were paid $2 to participate in a survey of game and puzzle prefer-
ences conducted at Columbia University by the Consumer Testing Bureau. An
attractive young market researcher met them at the door and took them to the
testing room, where they were given questionnaires to fill out. Before leaving,
she told them that she would be working next door in her office, which was
separated from the room by a folding room-divider. She then entered her
office, where she shuffled papers, opened drawers and made enough noise to
remind the subjects of her presence. After four minutes she turned on a high-
fidelity tape recorder.

On it, the subjects heard the researcher climb up on a chair, perhaps to
reach for a stack of papers on the bookcase. They heard a loud crash and a
scream as the chair collapsed and she fell, and they heard her moan, "Oh,
my foot . . . I . . . I . . . can't move it. Oh, I . . . can't get this . . . thing . . .
off me." Her cries gradually got more subdued and controlled.

Twenty-six people were alone in the waiting room when the "accident"
occurred. Seventy percent of them offered to help the victim. Many pushed
back the divider to offer their assistance; others called out to offer their help.

Among those waiting in pairs, only 20 percent—8 out of 40—offered
to help. The other 32 remained unresponsive. In defining the situation as a
nonemergency, they explained to themselves why the other member of the
pair did not leave the room; they also removed any reason for action themselves. Whatever had happened, it was believed to be not serious. "A mild
sprain," some said. "I didn't want to embarrass her." In a "real" emergency,
they assured us, they would be among the first to help.

THE LONELY CROWD

Even if a person defines an event as an emergency, the presence of other   20
bystanders may still make him less likely to intervene. He feels that his
responsibility is diffused and diluted. Thus, if your car breaks down on a
busy highway, hundreds of drivers whiz by without anyone's stopping to
help—but if you are stuck on a nearly deserted country road, whoever
passes you first is likely to stop.

To test this diffusion-of-responsibility theory, we simulated an emergency
in which people overheard a victim calling for help. Some thought they were

the only person to hear the cries; the rest believed that others heard them, too. As with the witnesses to Kitty Genovese's murder, the subjects could not *see* one another or know what others were doing. The kind of direct group inhibition found in the other two studies could not operate.

For the simulation, we recruited 72 students at New York University to participate in what was referred to as a "group discussion" of personal problems in an urban university. Each student was put in an individual room equipped with a set of headphones and a microphone. It was explained that this precaution had been taken because participants might feel embarrassed about discussing their problems publicly. Also, the experimenter said that he would not listen to the initial discussión, but would only ask for reactions later. Each person was to talk in turn.

The first to talk reported that he found it difficult to adjust to New York and his studies. Then, hesitantly and with obvious embarrassment, he mentioned that he was prone to nervous seizures when he was under stress. Other students then talked about their own problems in turn. The number of people in the "discussion" varied. But whatever the apparent size of the group—two, three or six people—only the subject was actually present; the others, as well as the instructions and the speeches of the victim-to-be, were present only on a pre-recorded tape.

When it was the first person's turn to talk again, he launched into the following performance, becoming louder and having increasing speech difficulties: "I can see a lot of er of er how other people's problems are similar to mine because er I mean er they're not er e-easy to handle sometimes and er I er um I think I I need er if if could er er somebody er er er give me give me a little er give me a little help here because er I er *ub* I've got a a one of the er seiz-er er things coming *on* and and er uh uh (choking sounds) . . ."

Eighty-five percent of the people who believed themselves to be alone with the victim came out of their room to help. Sixty-two percent of the people who believed there was *one* other bystander did so. Of those who believed there were four other bystanders, only 31 percent reported the fit. The responsibility-diluting effect of other people was so strong that single individuals were more than twice as likely to report the emergency as those who thought other people also knew about it.

THE LESSON LEARNED

People who failed to report the emergency showed few signs of the apathy and indifference thought to characterize "unresponsive bystanders." When the experimenter entered the room to end the situation, the subject often asked if the victim was "all right." Many of them showed physical signs of nervousness; they often had trembling hands and sweating palms. If anything, they seemed more emotionally aroused than did those who reported the emergency. Their emotional behavior was a sign of their continuing conflict concerning whether to respond or not.

Thus, the stereotype of the unconcerned, depersonalized *homo urbanus*,[1] blandly watching the misfortunes of others, proves inaccurate. Instead, we find that a bystander to an emergency is an anguished individual in genuine doubt, wanting to do the right thing but compelled to make complex decisions under pressure of stress and fear. His reactions are shaped by the actions of others—and all too frequently by their inaction.

And we are that bystander. Caught up by the apparent indifference of others, we may pass by an emergency without helping or even realizing that help is needed. Once we are aware of the influence of those around us, however, we can resist it. We can choose to see distress and step forward to relieve it.

Questions for Discussion and Writing

1. How is Darley and Latané's experiment designed to disclose the reasons why bystanders were unwilling in some situations to help the victims of street crime? What factors actually determine whether a bystander is willing to help?
2. How did Darley and Latané's experiment disprove the common belief that apathy explains why bystanders fail to help others? What physical signs convinced them that people trying to decide whether or not to intervene were not apathetic?
3. Have you ever observed the "diffusion-of-responsibility" hypothesis in the actual behavior of yourself or others? Describe your experiences.
4. **Rhetorical inquiry:** How were Darley and Latané's findings expressed as statistical laws that describe causal relationships that could presumably be replicated by other social scientists?

Fiction

Joyce Carol Oates

Joyce Carol Oates was born in Lockport, New York, in 1938 and was raised on her grandparents' farm in Erie County, New York. She graduated from Syracuse University in 1960 and earned an M.A. at the University of Wisconsin. She has taught writing and literature at Princeton University since 1978. Oates received the O. Henry Special Award for Continuing Achievement and the National Book Award in 1970 for her novel them. *Oates is a prolific author who has published*

---

[1] City dweller.

(on average) two books a year and has written countless essays and reviews. Her work covers the spectrum from novels and short fiction, poetry, plays, and criticism to nonfiction works on topics ranging from the poetry of D. H. Lawrence to boxing. "Where Are You Going, Where Have You Been?" first appeared in The Wheel of Love *(1965). This story was inspired by an article in* Life *magazine titled "The Pied Piper of Tucson," about a twenty-three-year-old man who frequented teenage hangouts, picked up girls, took them for rides in his gold convertible, and ultimately was convicted for murdering three of them. Her recent works include* I Am No One You Know: Stories *(2004),* Sexy *(2005), and* Black Girl / White Girl: A Novel *(2006).*

Before You Read

Did you ever feel that you were different and better than your family and deserved a more exciting life?

For Bob Dylan[1]

Where Are You Going, Where Have You Been?

Her name was Connie. She was fifteen and she had a quick nervous giggling habit of craning her neck to glance into mirrors, or checking other people's faces to make sure her own was all right. Her mother, who noticed everything and knew everything and who hadn't much reason any longer to look at her own face, always scolded Connie about it. "Stop gawking at yourself, who are you? You think you're so pretty?" she would say. Connie would raise her eyebrows at these familiar complaints and look right through her mother, into a shadowy vision of herself as she was right at that moment: she knew she was pretty and that was everything. Her mother had been pretty once too, if you could believe those old snapshots in the album, but now her looks were gone and that was why she was always after Connie.

"Why don't you keep your room clean like your sister? How've you got your hair fixed—what the hell stinks? Hair spray? You don't see your sister using that junk."

Her sister June was twenty-four and still lived at home. She was a secretary in the high school Connie attended, and if that wasn't bad enough—with her in the same building—she was so plain and chunky and steady that Connie had to hear her praised all the time by her mother and her mother's sisters. June did this, June did that, she saved money and helped clean the house and cooked and Connie couldn't do a thing, her mind was all filled with trashy daydreams. Their father was away at work most of the time and

---

[1] *Bob Dylan (b. 1941):* a composer, author, and singer who created and popularized folk rock during the 1960s.

when he came home he wanted supper and he read the newspaper at supper and after supper he went to bed. He didn't bother talking much to them, but around his bent head Connie's mother kept picking at her until Connie wished her mother was dead and she herself was dead and it was all over. "She makes me want to throw up sometimes," she complained to her friends. She had a high, breathless, amused voice which made everything she said a little forced, whether it was sincere or not.

There was one good thing: June went places with girl friends of hers, girls who were just as plain and steady as she, and so when Connie wanted to do that her mother had no objections. The father of Connie's best girl friend drove the girls the three miles to town and left them off at a shopping plaza, so that they could walk through the stores or go to a movie, and when he came to pick them up again at eleven he never bothered to ask what they had done.

They must have been familiar sights, walking around that shopping   5
plaza in their shorts and flat ballerina slippers that always scuffed the sidewalk, with charm bracelets jingling on their thin wrists; they would lean together to whisper and laugh secretly if someone passed by who amused or interested them. Connie had long dark blond hair that drew anyone's eye to it, and she wore part of it pulled up on her head and puffed out and the rest of it she let fall down her back. She wore a pullover jersey blouse that looked one way when she was at home and another way when she was away from home. Everything about her had two sides to it, one for home and one for anywhere that was not home: her walk that could be childlike and bobbing, or languid enough to make anyone think she was hearing music in her head, her mouth which was pale and smirking most of the time, but bright and pink on these evenings out, her laugh which was cynical and drawling at home—"Ha, ha, very funny"—but high-pitched and nervous anywhere else, like the jingling of the charms on her bracelet.

Sometimes they did go shopping or to a movie, but sometimes they went across the highway, ducking fast across the busy road, to a drive-in restaurant where older kids hung out. The restaurant was shaped like a big bottle, though squatter than a real bottle, and on its cap was a revolving figure of a grinning boy who held a hamburger aloft. One night in midsummer they ran across, breathless with daring, and right away someone leaned out a car window and invited them over, but it was just a boy from high school they didn't like. It made them feel good to be able to ignore him. They went up through the maze of parked and cruising cars to the bright-lit, fly-infested restaurant, their faces pleased and expectant as if they were entering a sacred building that loomed out of the night to give them what haven and what blessing they yearned for. They sat at the counter and crossed their legs at the ankles, their thin shoulders rigid with excitement and listened to the music that made everything so good: the music was always in the background like music at a church service, it was something to depend upon.

A boy named Eddie came in to talk with them. He sat backwards on his stool, turning himself jerkily around in semi-circles and then stopping and turning again, and after a while he asked Connie if she would like something to eat. She said she did and so she tapped her friend's arm on her way out— her friend pulled her face up into a brave droll look—and Connie said she would meet her at eleven, across the way. "I just hate to leave her like that," Connie said earnestly, but the boy said that she wouldn't be alone for long. So they went out to his car and on the way Connie couldn't help but let her eyes wander over the windshields and faces all around her, her face gleaming with the joy that had nothing to do with Eddie or even this place; it might have been the music. She drew her shoulders up and sucked in her breath with the pure pleasure of being alive, and just at that moment she happened to glance at a face just a few feet from hers. It was a boy with shaggy black hair, in a convertible jalopy painted gold. He stared at her and then his lips widened into a grin. Connie slit her eyes at him and turned away, but she couldn't help glancing back and there he was still watching her. He wagged a finger and laughed and said, "Gonna get you, baby," and Connie turned away again without Eddie noticing anything.

She spent three hours with him, at the restaurant where they ate hamburgers and drank Cokes in wax cups that were always sweating, and then down an alley a mile or so away, and when he left her off at five to eleven only the movie house was still open at the plaza. Her girl friend was there, talking with a boy. When Connie came up the two girls smiled at each other and Connie said, "How was the movie?" and the girl said, "*You* should know." They rode off with the girl's father, sleepy and pleased, and Connie couldn't help but look at the darkened shopping plaza with its big empty parking lot and its signs that were faded and ghostly now, and over at the drive-in restaurant where cars were still circling tirelessly. She couldn't hear the music at this distance.

Next morning June asked her how the movie was and Connie said, "So-so."

She and that girl and occasionally another girl went out several times a   10 week that way, and the rest of the time Connie spent around the house—it was summer vacation—getting in her mother's way and thinking, dreaming, about the boys she met. But all the boys fell back and dissolved into a single face that was not even a face, but an idea, a feeling, mixed up with the urgent insistent pounding of the music and the humid night air of July. Connie's mother kept dragging her back to the daylight by finding things for her to do or saying suddenly, "What's this about the Pettinger girl?"

And Connie would say nervously, "Oh, her. That dope." She always drew thick clear lines between herself and such girls, and her mother was simple and kindly enough to believe her. Her mother was so simple, Connie thought, that it was maybe cruel to fool her so much. Her mother went scuffling around the house in old bedroom slippers and complained over the telephone to one sister about the other, then the other called up and the two of them complained about the third one. If June's name was mentioned her mother's tone was approving, and if Connie's name was mentioned it was disapproving. This did not really mean she disliked Connie and actually Connie thought that her mother preferred her to June because she was prettier, but the two of them kept up a pretense of exasperation, a sense that they were tugging and struggling over something of little value to either of them. Sometimes, over coffee, they were almost friends, but something would come up—some vexation that was like a fly buzzing suddenly around their heads—and their faces went hard with contempt.

One Sunday Connie got up at eleven—none of them bothered with church—and washed her hair so that it could dry all day long, in the sun. Her parents and sister were going to a barbecue at an aunt's house and Connie said no, she wasn't interested, rolling her eyes, to let mother know just what she thought of it. "Stay home alone then," her mother said sharply. Connie sat out back in a lawn chair and watched them drive away, her father quiet and bald, hunched around so that he could back the car out, her mother with a look that was still angry and not at all softened through the windshield, and in the back seat poor old June all dressed up as if she didn't know what a barbecue was, with all the running yelling kids and the flies. Connie sat with her eyes closed in the sun, dreaming and dazed with the warmth about her as if this were a kind of love, the caresses of love, and her mind slipped over onto thoughts of the boy she had been with the night before and how nice he had been, how sweet it always was, not the way someone like June would suppose but sweet, gentle, the way it was in movies and promised in songs; and when she opened her eyes she hardly knew where she was, the back yard ran off into weeds and a fenceline of trees and behind it the sky was perfectly blue and still. The asbestos "ranch house" that was now three years old startled her—it looked small. She shook her head as if to get awake.

It was too hot. She went inside the house and turned on the radio to drown out the quiet. She sat on the edge of her bed, barefoot, and listened for an hour and a half to a program called XYZ Sunday Jamboree, record after record of hard, fast, shrieking songs she sang along with, interspersed by exclamations from "Bobby King": "An' look here you girls at Napoleon's— Son and Charley want you to pay real close attention to this song coming up!"

And Connie paid close attention herself, bathed in a glow of slow-pulsed joy that seemed to rise mysteriously out of the music itself and lay languidly about the airless little room, breathed in and breathed out with each gentle rise and fall of her chest.

After a while she heard a car coming up the drive. She sat up at once, startled, because it couldn't be her father so soon. The gravel kept crunching all the way in from the road—the driveway was long—and Connie ran to the window. It was a car she didn't know. It was an open jalopy, painted a bright gold that caught the sun opaquely. Her heart began to pound and her fingers snatched at her hair, checking it, and she whispered "Christ. Christ," wondering how bad she looked. The car came to a stop at the side door and the horn sounded four short taps as if this were a signal Connie knew. 15

She went into the kitchen and approaching the door slowly, then hung out the screen door, her bare toes curling down off the step. There were two boys in the car and now she recognized the driver: he had shaggy, shabby black hair that looked crazy as a wig and he was grinning at her.

"I ain't late, am I?" he said.

"Who the hell do you think you are?" Connie said.

"Toldja I'd be out, didn't I?"

"I don't even know who you are."   20

She spoke sullenly, careful to show no interest or pleasure, and he spoke in a fast bright monotone. Connie looked past him to the other boy, taking her time. He had fair brown hair, with a lock that fell onto his forehead. His sideburns gave him a fierce, embarrassed look, but so far he hadn't even bothered to glance at her. Both boys wore sunglasses. The driver's glasses were metallic and mirrored everything in miniature.

"You wanta come for a ride?" he said.

Connie smirked and let her hair fall loose over one shoulder.

"Don'tcha like my car? New paint job," he said. "Hey."

"What?"   25

"You're cute."

She pretended to fidget, chasing flies away from the door.

"Don'tcha believe me, or what?" he said.

"Look, I don't even know who you are," Connie said in disgust.

"Hey, Ellie's got a radio, see. Mine's broke down." He lifted his friend's   30
arm and showed her the little transistor the boy was holding, and now Connie began to hear the music. It was the same program that was playing inside the house.

"Bobby King?" she said.

"I listen to him all the time. I think he's great."

"He's kind of great," Connie said reluctantly.

"Listen, that guy's *great*. He knows where the action is."

Connie blushed a little, because the glasses made it impossible for her to   35
see just what this boy was looking at. She couldn't decide if she liked him or if he was just a jerk, and so she dawdled in the doorway and wouldn't come down or go back inside. She said, "What's all that stuff painted on your car?"

"Can'tcha read it?" He opened the door very carefully, as if he was afraid it might fall off. He slid out just as carefully, planting his feet firmly on the ground, the tiny metallic world in his glasses slowing down like gelatine hardening and in the midst of it Connie's bright green blouse. "This here is my name, to begin with," he said. ARNOLD FRIEND was written in tar-like black letters on the side, with a drawing of a round grinning face that reminded Connie of a pumpkin, except it wore sunglasses. "I wanta intro-duce myself, I'm Arnold Friend and that's my real name and I'm gonna be your friend, honey, and inside the car's Ellie Oscar, he's kinda shy." Ellie brought his transistor up to his shoulder and balanced it there. "Now these numbers are a secret code, honey," Arnold Friend explained. He read off the numbers 33, 19, 17 and raised his eyebrows at her to see what she thought of that, but she didn't think much of it. The left rear fender had been smashed and around it was written, on the gleaming gold background: DONE BY CRAZY WOMAN DRIVER. Connie had to laugh at that. Arnold Friend was pleased at her laughter and looked up at her. "Around the other side's a lot more—you wanta come and see them?"

"No."

"Why not?"

"Why should I?"

"Don'tcha wanta see what's on the car? Don'tcha wanta go for a ride?"   40

"I don't know."

"Why not?"

"I got things to do."

"Like what?"

"Things."   45

He laughed as if she had said something funny. He slapped his thighs. He was standing in a strange way, leaning back against the car as if he were balancing himself. He wasn't tall, only an inch or so taller than she would be if she came down to him. Connie liked the way he was dressed, which was the way all of them dressed: tight faded jeans stuffed into black, scuffed boots, a belt that pulled his waist in and showed how lean he was, and a white pull-over shirt that was a little soiled and showed the hard small muscles of his arms and shoulders. He looked as if he probably did hard work, lifting and carrying things. Even his neck looked muscular. And his face was a familiar face, somehow: the jaw and chin and cheeks slightly darkened, because he hadn't shaved for a day or two, and the nose long and hawklike, sniffing as if she were a treat he was going to gobble up and it was all a joke.

"Connie, you ain't telling the truth. This is your day set aside for a ride with me and you know it," he said, still laughing. The way he straightened and recovered from his fit of laughing showed that it had been all fake.

"How do you know what my name is?" she said suspiciously.

"It's Connie."

"Maybe and maybe not."   50

"I know my Connie," he said, wagging his finger. Now she remembered him even better, back at the restaurant, and her cheeks warmed at the thought of how she sucked in her breath just at the moment she passed him—how she must have looked to him. And he had remembered her. "Ellie and I come out here especially for you," he said. "Ellie can sit in back. How about it?"

"Where?"

"Where what?"

"Where're we going?"

He looked at her. He took off the sunglasses and she saw how pale the   55 skin around his eyes was, like holes that were not in shadow but instead in light. His eyes were like chips of broken glass that catch the light in an amiable way. He smiled. It was as if the idea of going for a ride somewhere, to some place, was a new idea to him.

"Just for a ride, Connie sweetheart."

"I never said my name was Connie," she said.

"But I know what it is. I know your name and all about you, lots of things," Arnold Friend said. He had not moved yet but stood still leaning back against the side of his jalopy. "I took a special interest in you, such a pretty girl, and found out all about you like I know your parents and sister are gone somewheres and I know where and how long they're going to be gone, and I know who you were with last night, and your best friend's name is Betty. Right?"

He spoke in a simple lilting voice, exactly as if he were reciting the words to a song. His smile assured her that everything was fine. In the car Ellie turned up the volume on his radio and did not bother to look around at them.

"Ellie can sit in the back seat," Arnold Friend said. He indicated his   60
friend with a casual jerk of his chin, as if Ellie did not count and she could not bother with him.

"How'd you find out all that stuff?" Connie said.

"Listen? Betty Schultz and Tony Fitch and Jimmy Pettinger and Nancy Pettinger," he said, in a chant. "Raymond Stanley and Bob Hutter—"

"Do you know all those kids?"

"I know everybody."

"Look, you're kidding. You're not from around here."   65

"Sure."

"But—how come we never saw you before?"

"Sure you saw me before," he said. He looked down at his boots, as if he were a little offended. "You just don't remember."

"I guess I'd remember you," Connie said.

"Yeah?" He looked up at this, beaming. He was pleased. He began to   70
mark time with the music from Ellie's radio, tapping his fists lightly together. Connie looked away from his smile to the car, which was painted so bright it almost hurt her eyes to look at it. She looked at that name, ARNOLD FRIEND. And up at the front fender was an expression that was familiar— MAN THE FLYING SAUCERS. It was an expression kids had used the year before, but didn't use this year. She looked at it for a while as if the words meant something to her that she did not yet know.

"What're you thinking about? Huh?" Arnold Friend demanded. "Not worried about your hair blowing around in the car, are you?"

"No."

"Think I maybe can't drive good?"

"How do I know?"

"You're a hard girl to handle. How come?" he said. "Don't you know I'm   75
your friend? Didn't you see me put my sign in the air when you walked by?"

"What sign?"

"My sign." And he drew an X in the air, leaning out toward her. They were maybe ten feet apart. After his hand fell back to his side the X was still in the air, almost visible. Connie let the screen door close and stood perfectly still inside it, listening to the music from her radio and the boy's blend together. She stared at Arnold Friend. He stood there so stiffly relaxed, pretending to be relaxed, with one hand idly on the door handle as if he were keeping himself up that way and had no intention of ever moving again. She recognized most things about him, the tight jeans that showed his thighs and buttocks and the greasy leather boots and the tight shirt, and even that slippery friendly smile of his, that sleepy dreamy smile that all the boys used to get across ideas they didn't want to put into words. She recognized all this and also the singsong way he talked, slightly mocking, kidding, but serious and a little melancholy, and she recognized the way he tapped one fist against the other in homage to the perpetual music behind him. But all these things did not come together.

She said suddenly, "Hey, how old are you?"

His smile faded. She could see then that he wasn't a kid, he was much older—thirty, maybe more. At this knowledge her heart began to pound faster.

"That's a crazy thing to ask. Can'tcha see I'm your own age?"   80

"Like hell you are."

"Or maybe a coupla years older, I'm eighteen."

"Eighteen?" she said doubtfully.

He grinned to reassure her and lines appeared at the corners of his mouth. His teeth were big and white. He grinned so broadly his eyes became slits and she saw how thick the lashes were, thick and black as if painted with a black tar-like material. Then he seemed to become embarrassed, abruptly, and looked over his shoulder at Ellie. "*Him*, he's crazy," he said. "Ain't he a riot, he's a nut, a real character." Ellie was still listening to the music. His sunglasses told nothing about what he was thinking. He wore a bright orange shirt unbuttoned halfway to show his chest, which was a pale, bluish chest and not muscular like Arnold Friend's. His shirt collar was turned up all around and the very tips of the collar pointed out past his chin as if they were protecting him. He was pressing the transistor radio up against his ear and sat there in a kind of daze, right in the sun.

"He's kinda strange," Connie said.   85

"Hey, she says you're kinda strange! Kinda strange!" Arnold Friend cried. He pounded on the car to get Ellie's attention. Ellie turned for the first time and Connie saw with shock that he wasn't a kid either—he had a fair, hairless face, cheeks reddened slightly as if the veins grew too close to the surface of his skin, the face of a forty-year-old baby. Connie felt a wave of dizziness rise in her at this sight and she stared at him as if waiting for something to change the shock of the moment, make it all right again. Ellie's lips kept shaping words, mumbling along with the words blasting his ear.

"Maybe you two better go away," Connie said faintly.

"What? How come?" Arnold Friend cried. "We come out here to take you for a ride. It's Sunday." He had the voice of the man on the radio now. It was the same voice, Connie thought. "Don'tcha know it's Sunday all day and honey, no matter who you were with last night today you're with Arnold Friend and don't you forget it!—Maybe you better step out here," he said, and this last was in a different voice. It was a little flatter, as if the heat was finally getting to him.

"No. I got things to do."

"Hey." 90

"You two better leave."

"We ain't leaving until you come with us."

"Like hell I am—"

"Connie, don't fool around with me. I mean, I mean, don't fool *around*," he said, shaking his head. He laughed incredulously. He placed his sunglasses on top of his head, carefully, as if he were indeed wearing a wig, and brought the stems down behind his ears. Connie stared at him, another wave of dizziness and fear rising in her so that for a moment he wasn't even in focus but was just a blur, standing there against his gold car, and she had the idea that he had driven up the driveway all right but had come from nowhere before that and belonged nowhere and that everything about him and even the music that was so familiar to her was only half real.

"If my father comes and sees you—" 95

"He ain't coming. He's at a barbecue."

"How do you know that?"

"Aunt Tillie's. Right now they're—uh—they're drinking. Sitting around," he said vaguely, squinting as if he were staring all the way to town and over to Aunt Tillie's back yard. Then the vision seemed to clear and he nodded energetically. "Yeah. Sitting around. There's your sister in a blue dress, huh? And high heels, the poor sad bitch—nothing like you, sweetheart! And your mother's helping some fat woman with the corn, they're cleaning the corn—husking the corn—"

"What fat woman?" Connie cried.

"How do I know what fat woman. I don't know every goddamn fat 100 woman in the world!" Arnold Friend laughed.

"Oh, that's Mrs. Hornby. . . . Who invited her?" Connie said. She felt a little lightheaded. Her breath was coming quickly.

"She's too fat. I don't like them fat. I like them the way you are, honey," he said, smiling sleepily at her. They stared at each other for a while, through the screen door. He said softly, "Now what you're going to do is this: you're going to come out that door. You're going to sit up front with me and Ellie's going to sit in the back, the hell with Ellie, right? This isn't Ellie's date. You're my date. I'm your lover, honey."

"What? You're crazy—"

"Yes, I'm your lover. You don't know what that is but you will," he said. "I know that too. I know all about you. But look: it's real nice and you couldn't ask for nobody better than me, or more polite. I always keep my word. I'll tell you how it is, I'm always nice at first, the first time. I'll hold you so tight you won't think you have to try to get away or pretend anything because you'll know you can't. And I'll come inside you where it's all secret and you'll give in to me and you'll love me—"

"Shut up! You're crazy!" Connie said. She backed away from the door.   105
She put her hands against her ears as if she'd heard something terrible, something not meant for her. "People don't talk like that, you're crazy," she muttered. Her heart was almost too big now for her chest and its pumping made sweat break out all over her. She looked out to see Arnold Friend pause and then take a step toward the porch lurching. He almost fell. But, like a clever drunken man, he managed to catch his balance. He wobbled in his high boots and grabbed hold of one of the porch posts.

"Honey?" he said. "You still listening?"

"Get the hell out of here!"

"Be nice, honey. Listen."

"I'm going to call the police—"

He wobbled again and out of the side of his mouth came a fast spat   110
curse, an aside not meant for her to hear. But even this "Christ!" sounded forced. Then he began to smile again. She watched this smile come, awkward as if he were smiling from inside a mask. His whole face was a mask, she thought wildly, tanned down onto his throat but then running out as if he had plastered make-up on his face but had forgotten about his throat.

"Honey—? Listen, here's how it is. I always tell the truth and I promise you this: I ain't coming in that house after you."

"You better not! I'm going to call the police if you—if you don't—"

"Honey," he said, talking right through her voice, "honey, I'm not coming in there but you are coming out here. You know why?"

She was panting. The kitchen looked like a place she had never seen before, some room she had run inside but which wasn't good enough, wasn't going to help her. The kitchen window had never had a curtain, after three years, and there were dishes in the sink for her to do—probably—and if you ran your hand across the table you'd probably feel something sticky there.

"You listening, honey? Hey?"   115

"—going to call the police—"

"Soon as you touch the phone I don't need to keep my promise and can come inside. You won't want that."

She rushed forward and tried to lock the door. Her fingers were shaking. "But why lock it," Arnold Friend said gently, talking right into her face. "It's just a screen door. It's just nothing." One of his boots was at a strange angle, as if his foot wasn't in it. It pointed out to the left, bent at the ankle. "I mean, anybody can break through a screen door and glass and wood and iron or anything else if he needs to, anybody at all and specially Arnold Friend. If the place got lit up with a fire, honey, you'd come running out into my arms, right into my arms and safe at home—like you knew I was your lover and'd stopped fooling around, I don't mind a nice shy girl but I don't like no fooling around." Part of those words were spoken with a slightly rhythmic lilt, and Connie somehow recognized them—the echo of a song from last year, about a girl rushing into her boy friend's arms and coming home again—

Connie stood barefoot on the linoleum floor, staring at him. "What do you want?" she whispered.

"I want you," he said.

"What?"

"Seen you that night and thought, that's the one, yes sir. I never needed to look any more."

"But my father's coming back. He's coming to get me. I had to wash my hair first—" She spoke in a dry, rapid voice, hardly raising it for him to hear.

"No, your daddy is not coming and yes, you had to wash your hair and you washed it for me. It's nice and shining and all for me, I thank you, sweetheart," he said, with a mock bow, but again he almost lost his balance. He had to bend and adjust his boots. Evidently his feet did not go all the way down; the boots must have been stuffed with something so that he would seem taller. Connie stared out at him and behind him Ellie in the car, who seemed to be looking off toward Connie's right, into nothing. This Ellie said, pulling the words out of the air one after another as if he were just discovering them, "You want me to pull out the phone?"

"Shut your mouth and keep it shut," Arnold Friend said, his face red from bending over or maybe from embarrassment because Connie had seen his boots. "This ain't none of your business."

"What—what are you doing? What do you want?" Connie said. "If I call the police they'll get you, they'll arrest you—"

"Promise was not to come in unless you touch that phone, and I'll keep that promise," he said. He resumed his erect position and tried to force his shoulders back. He sounded like a hero in a movie, declaring something important. He spoke too loudly and it was as if he were speaking to someone behind Connie. "I ain't made plans for coming in that house where I don't belong but just for you to come out to me, the way you should. Don't you know who I am?"

"You're crazy," she whispered. She backed away from the door but did not want to go into another part of the house, as if this would give him permission to come through the door. "What do you. . . . You're crazy, you. . . ."

"Huh? What're you saying, honey?"

Her eyes darted everywhere in the kitchen. She could not remember what it was, this room.

"This is how it is, honey: you come out and we'll drive away, have a nice ride. But if you don't come out we're gonna wait till your people come home and then they're all going to get it."

"You want that telephone pulled out?" Ellie said. He held the radio away from his ear and grimaced, as if without the radio the air was too much for him.

"I toldja shut up, Ellie." Arnold Friend said, "You're deaf, get a hearing aid, right? Fix yourself up. This little girl's no trouble and's gonna be nice to me, so Ellie keep to yourself, this ain't your date—right? Don't hem in on me. Don't hog. Don't crush. Don't bird dog. Don't trail me," he said in a rapid meaningless voice, as if he were running through all the expressions he'd learned but was no longer sure which one of them was in style, then rushing on to new ones, making them up with his eyes closed, "Don't crawl under my fence, don't squeeze in my chipmunk hole, don't sniff my glue, suck my popsicle, keep your own greasy fingers on yourself!" He shaded his eyes and peered in at Connie, who was backed against the kitchen table. "Don't mind him, honey, he's just a creep. He's a dope. Right? I'm the boy for you and like I said you come out here nice like a lady and give me your hand, and nobody else gets hurt, I mean, your nice old bald-headed daddy and your mummy and your sister in her high heels. Because listen: why bring them in this?"

"Leave me alone," Connie whispered.

"Hey, you know that old woman down the road, the one with the   135 chickens and stuff—you know her?"

"She's dead!"

"Dead? What? You know her?" Arnold Friend said.

"She's dead—"

"Don't you like her?"

"She's dead—she's—she isn't here any more—"   140

"But don't you like her, I mean, you got something against her? Some grudge or something?" Then his voice dipped as if he were conscious of rudeness. He touched the sunglasses on top of his head as if to make sure they were still there. "Now you be a good girl."

"What are you going to do?"

"Just two things, or maybe three," Arnold Friend said. "But I promise it won't last long and you'll like me that way you get to like people you're close to. You will. It's all over for you here, so come on out. You don't want your people in any trouble, do you?"

She turned and bumped against a chair or something, hurting her leg, but she ran into the back room and picked up the telephone. Something roared in her ear, a tiny roaring, and she was so sick with fear that she could do nothing but listen to it—the telephone was clammy and very heavy and her fingers groped down to the dial but were too weak to touch it. She began to scream into the phone, into the roaring. She cried out, she cried for her mother, she felt her breath start jerking back and forth in her lungs as if it were something Arnold Friend were stabbing her with again and again with no tenderness. A noisy sorrowful wailing rose all about her and she was locked inside it the way she was locked inside this house.

After a while she could hear again. She was sitting on the floor, with her   145 wet back against the wall.

Arnold Friend was saying from the door, "That's a good girl. Put the phone back."

She kicked the phone away from her.

"No, honey. Pick it up. Put it back right."

She picked it up and put it back. The dial tone stopped.

"That's a good girl. Now you come outside."   150

She was hollow with what had been fear, but what was now just an emptiness. All that screaming had blasted it out of her. She sat, one leg cramped under her, and deep inside her brain was something like a pinpoint of light that kept going and would not let her relax. She thought, I'm not going to see my mother again. She thought, I'm not going to sleep in my bed again. Her bright green blouse was all wet.

Arnold Friend said, in a gentle-loud voice that was like a stage voice. "The place where you came from ain't there any more, and where you had in mind to go is cancelled out. This place you are now—inside your daddy's house—is nothing but a cardboard box I can knock down any time. You know that and always did know it. You hear me?"

She thought, I have got to think. I have to know what to do.

"We'll go out to a nice field, out in the country here where it smells so nice and it's sunny," Arnold Friend said. "I'll have my arms tight around you so you won't need to try to get away and I'll show you what love is like, what it does. The hell with this house! It looks solid all right," he said. He ran a fingernail down the screen and the noise did not make Connie shiver, as it would have the day before. "Now put your hand on your heart, honey. Feel that? That feels solid too but we know better, be nice to me, be sweet like you can because what else is there for a girl like you but to be sweet and pretty and give in?—and get away before her people come back?"

She felt her pounding heart. Her hands seemed to enclose it. She thought   155
for the first time in her life that it was nothing that was hers, that belonged to her, but just a pounding, living thing inside this body that wasn't hers either.

"You don't want them to get hurt," Arnold Friend went on. "Now get up, honey. Get up all by yourself."

She stood.

"Now turn this way. That's right. Come over to me—Ellie, put that away, didn't I tell you? You dope. You miserable creep dope," Arnold Friend said. His words were not angry but only part of an incantation. The incantation was kindly. "Now come out through the kitchen to me honey and let's see a smile, try it, you're a brave sweet little girl and now they're eating corn and hotdogs cooked to bursting over an outdoor fire, and they don't know one thing about you and never did and honey you're better than them because not one of them would have done this for you."

Connie felt the linoleum under her feet; it was cool. She brushed her hair back out of her eyes. Arnold Friend let go of the post tentatively and opened his arms for her, his elbows pointing up toward each other and his wrist limp, to show that this was an embarrassed embrace and a little mocking, he didn't want to make her self-conscious.

She put out her hand against the screen. She watched herself push the   160
door slowly open as if she were safe back somewhere in the other doorway,

watching this body and this head of long hair moving out into the sunlight where Arnold Friend waited.

"My sweet little blue-eyed girl," he said, in a half-sung sigh that had nothing to do with her brown eyes but was taken up just the same by the vast sunlit reaches of the land behind him and on all sides of him, so much land that Connie had ever seen before and did not recognize except to know that she was going to it.

Questions for Discussion and Writing

1. Why is it significant that everything about Connie "had two sides to it"? How does Connie see herself as being different from both her mother and her sister?
2. How does the description of Arnold Friend—his unusual hair, pale skin, awkward way of walking in his boots, out-of-date expressions, and car—suggest he is not what he appears to be? Who do you think he really is, or what do you think he represents?
3. What do you think Friend means when he says at the end, "Not a one of them would have done this for you"? In your opinion, does Connie really have a choice, and if so, what is it?
4. **Rhetorical inquiry:** How does Arnold Friend's ability to describe events at Connie's family's barbecue across town add to his mystery and menace? How does his reference to a woman down the road who Connie knows is dead augment this sensation and make Connie and the reader apprehensive?

Parables

PLATO

Plato (428–347 B.C.), the philosopher who was a pupil of Socrates and the teacher of Aristotle, went into exile after the death of Socrates in 399 B.C. Plato returned to Athens in 380 B.C. to establish his school, known as the Academy, where he taught for the next forty years. Most of Plato's works are cast in the form of dialogues between Socrates and his students. The earliest of these, the Ion, Euthyphro, Protagoras, *and* Gorgias, *illustrate the so-called Socratic method, in which questions are asked until contradictions in the answers disclose the truth. Later in his life, Plato also wrote* Crito, Apology, Phaedo, Symposium, *and* Timaeus, *among other dialogues, as well as his influential treatises* The Republic *and* The Laws. *Plato's formative influence on Western thought can be traced to his belief that the soul and body have distinct and separate existences and that beyond the world of the senses exists an eternal order of ideal Forms.*

In "The Allegory of the Cave," from The Republic, *Plato creates an extended analogy to dramatize the importance of recognizing that the "unreal" world of the senses and physical phenomena are merely shadows cast by the immortal life of the "real" world of ideal Forms.*

Before You Read

How would you define an allegory?

The Allegory of the Cave

Socrates: And now, I said, let me show in a figure[1] how far our nature is enlightened or unenlightened:— Behold! human beings living in an underground den, which has a mouth open towards the light and reaching all along the den: here they have been from their childhood, and have their legs and necks chained so that they cannot move, and can only see before them, being prevented by the chains from turning round their heads. Above and behind them a fire is blazing at a distance, and between the fire and the prisoners there is a raised way; and you will see, if you look, a low wall built along the way, like the screen which marionette players have in front of them, over which they show the puppets.

The den, the prisoners: the light at a distance;

Glaucon: I see.

And do you see, I said, men passing along the wall carrying all sorts of vessels, and statues and figures of animals made of wood and stone and various materials, which appear over the wall? Some of them are talking, others silent.

You have shown me a strange image, and they are strange prisoners.

Like ourselves, I replied; and they see only their own shadows, or the shadows of one another, which the fire throws on the opposite wall of cave?

The low wall, and the moving figures of which the shadows are seen on the opposite wall of the den.

5

True, he said; how could they see anything but the shadows if they were never allowed to move their heads?

---

[1] *figure:* a picture or image.

And of the objects which are being carried in like manner they would only see the shadows?

Yes, he said.

And if they were able to converse with one another, would they not suppose that they were naming what was actually before them?

Very true.

And suppose further that the prison had an echo which came from the other side, would they not be sure to fancy when one of the passers-by spoke that the voice which they heard came from the passing shadow?

No question, he replied.

To them, I said, the truth would be literally nothing but the shadows of the images.

That is certain.

And now look again, and see what will naturally follow if the prisoners are released and disabused of their error. At first, when any of them is liberated and compelled suddenly to stand up and turn his neck round and walk and look towards the light, he will suffer sharp pains; the glare will distress him, and he will be unable to see the realities of which in his former state he had seen the shadows; and then conceive some one saying to him, that what he saw before was an illusion, but that now, when he is approaching nearer to being and his eye is turned towards more real existence, he has a clearer vision,—what will be his reply? And you may further imagine that his instructor is pointing to the objects as they pass and requiring him to name them,—will he not be perplexed? Will he not fancy that the shadows which he formerly saw are truer than the objects which are now shown to him?

Far truer.

And if he is compelled to look straight at the light, will he not have a pain in his eyes which will make him turn away to take refuge in the objects of vision which he can see, and which he will conceive to be in reality clearer than the things which are now being shown to him?

True, he said.

And suppose once more, that he is reluctantly dragged up a steep and rugged ascent, and held fast until he is forced into the presence of the sun himself,

The prisoners would mistake the shadows for realities.   10

And when released, they would still persist in maintaining the superior truth of the shadows.   15

When dragged upwards, they would be dazzled by excess of light.

is he not likely to be pained and irritated. When he approaches the light his eyes will be dazzled, and he will not be able to see anything at all of what are now called realities.

Not all in a moment, he said.

He will require to grow accustomed to the sight of the upper world. And first he will see the shadows best, next the reflections of men and other objects in the water, and then the objects themselves; then he will gaze upon the light of the moon and the stars and the spangled heaven; and he will see the sky and the stars by night better than the sun or the light of the sun by day?

Certainly.

Last of all he will be able to see the sun, and not mere reflections of him in the water, but he will see him in his own proper place, and not in another; and he will contemplate him as he is.

At length they will see the sun and understand his nature.

Certainly.

He will then proceed to argue that this is he who gives the season and the years, and is the guardian of all that is in the visible world, and in a certain way the cause of all things which he and his fellows have been accustomed to behold?

Clearly, he said, he would first see the sun and then reason about him.

And when he remembered his old habitation, and the wisdom of the den and his fellow-prisoners, do you not suppose that he would felicitate himself on the change, and pity them?

They would then pity their old companions of the den.

Certainly, he would.

And if they were in the habit of conferring honours among themselves on those who were quickest to observe the passing shadows and to remark which of them went before, and which followed after, and which were together; and who were therefore best able to draw conclusions as to the future, do you think that he would care for such honours and glories, or envy the possessors of them? Would he not say with Homer, "Better to be the poor servant of a poor master," and to endure anything, rather than think as they do and live after their manner?

Yes, he said, I think that he would rather suffer anything than entertain those false notions and live in this miserable manner.

20

25

30

Imagine once more, I said, such an one coming suddenly out of the sun to be replaced in his old situation; would he not be certain to have his eyes full of darkness?

To be sure, he said.

And if there were a contest, and he had to compete in measuring the shadows with the prisoners who had never moved out of the den, while his sight was still weak, and before his eyes had become steady (and the time which would be needed to acquire this new habit of sight might be very considerable), would he not be ridiculous? Men would say of him that up he went and down he came without his eyes; and that it was better not even to think of ascending; and if any one tried to loose another and lead him up to the light, let them only catch the offender, and they would put him to death.

But when they returned to the den they would see much worse than those who had never left it.

No question, he said.

This entire allegory, I said, you may not append, dear Glaucon, to the previous argument; the prison-house is the world of sight, the light of the fire is the sun, and you will not misapprehend me if you interpret the journey upwards to be the ascent of the soul into the intellectual world according to my poor belief, which, at your desire, I have expressed—whether rightly or wrongly God knows. But, whether true or false, my opinion is that in the world of knowledge the idea of good appears last of all, and is seen only with an effort; and when seen, is also inferred to be the universal author of all things beautiful and right, parent of light and of the lord of light in this visible world, and the immediate source of reason and truth in the intellectual; and that this is the power upon which he who would act rationally either in public or private life must have his eye fixed.

The prison is the world of sight, the light of the fire is the sun.   35

I agree, he said, as far as I am able to understand you.

Questions for Discussion and Writing

1. Why do the prisoners in the cave believe the shadows on the wall are real? Why would a prisoner who was released and allowed to leave the cave be unwilling to believe that what he is seeing is real? After his eyes adjust to the light, what will he think about his former life inside the cave?

2. If the prisoner returns to the cave and is unable to see in the dark as well as the others, how would they respond to his report of a greater light outside? Why would they be unwilling to allow other prisoners to follow him outside?

3. Plato used this **allegory** as a teaching tool. If you were one of his philosophy students, what would the allegorical equivalence or meaning of the cave, the prisoners, the fire, the shadow, and the sun make you realize about the human condition? What do you think Plato means when he says that the sun is like the "idea of good" that "appears last of all, and is seen only with an effort"?

4. **Rhetorical inquiry:** How would you characterize the relationship between Socrates and the person to whom he is speaking, Glaucon? Why does Plato choose the form of an allegory as a teaching technique and how effectively does it communicate his point?

MATTHEW

In the Gospels—that is, in the four biographies of Jesus in the New Testament that are attributed to Matthew, Mark, Luke, and John—parables are short illustrative narratives and figurative statements. The teaching that Christ gives in the New Testament takes different forms. The form in which the language of parables is cast is designed to create a bridge between the part of the mind that responds to the literal and the normally undeveloped capacities for spiritual reflection. The fact that the language in parables can be taken in two ways is meant to stimulate an awareness of this higher dimension. In the thirteenth chapter of Matthew,[1] Christ begins to speak in parables to the multitude. His disciples ask why he suddenly has begun to use parables, and he responds that it is because he is speaking about the kingdom of heaven—that is, about a spiritual reality that would be impossible to grasp otherwise. The Parable of the Sower and the Seed is the starting point of Christ's teaching about the kingdom of heaven. Not surprisingly, this master parable is about the way people differ in their capacity to understand this teaching. Differences in receptivity are presented in the parable by analogy as differences in the kinds of ground or earth into which the seed is sown: the wayside, stony places, ground where the seed does not take root, seed planted among thorns, and varying quantities of harvest grown from the seed. From this analysis of capacity for receiving the teachings, there follow parables about the Grain of Mustard Seed, the Woman and the Leaven, the Wheat and the Tares, the Net, the Pearl of Great Price, and the Net Cast into the Sea. Each in its own way deals with the kingdom

---

[1] The Gospel According to St. Matthew is one of the first four books of the New Testament, a collection of documents from the early Christian community written in the first two centuries after Jesus. The Gospel of St. Matthew, believed to have been written between A.D. 80 and 95, stresses the ways in which Jesus fulfills the prophecies of the Old Testament. This Gospel also contains the Sermon on the Mount.

*of heaven and the teaching concerning it. The twentieth chapter of Matthew, in
the Parable of the Laborers in the Vineyard, presents a seemingly paradoxical
idea that challenges conventional concepts of what is just and what is unjust.
Laborers who have spent a whole day in the scorching heat of the fields are
outraged that those who have simply labored one hour are paid the same. The
parable teaches that the kingdom of heaven cannot be thought of in terms of
conventional rewards. The seeming injustice of the parable—that those who
work longer do not gain a greater reward—hints that the kingdom of heaven
has to do with eternity. The context in which the parable is given suggests that
it is meant as an answer to the disciples who have abandoned all they had to
follow Jesus and now want a reward in the conventional sense.*

Before You Read

When would a parable be more effective than a straight explanation?

Parables in The New Testament

CHAPTER 13

The same day went Jesus out of the house, and sat by the sea side.

2 And great multitudes were gathered together unto him, so that he
went into a ship, and sat; and the whole multitude stood on the shore.

3 And he spake many things unto them in parables, saying, Behold, a
sower went forth to sow:

4 And when he sowed, some seeds fell by the way side, and the fowls
came and devoured them up.

5 Some fell upon stony places, where they had not much earth: and
forthwith they sprung up, because they had no deepness of earth.

6 And when the sun was up, they were scorched; and because they had
no root, they withered away.

7 And some fell among thorns; and the thorns sprung up, and choked
them;

8 But other fell into good ground, and brought forth fruit, some an
hundredfold, some sixtyfold, some thirtyfold.

9 Who hath ears to hear, let him hear.

10 And the disciples came, and said unto him, Why speakest thou unto
them in parables?

11 He answered and said unto them: Because it is given unto you to
know the mysteries of the kingdom of heaven, but to them it is not given.

12 For whosoever hath, to him shall be given, and he shall have more
abundance, but whosoever hath not, from him shall be taken away even
that he hath.

13 Therefore speak I to them in parables: because they seeing see not;
and hearing they hear not, neither do they understand.

14 And in them is fulfilled the prophecy of Esaias[2] which saith: By hearing ye shall hear, and shall not understand; and seeing ye shall see, and shall not perceive.

15 For this people's heart is waxed gross, and their ears are dull of hearing, and their eyes they have closed; lest at any time they should see with their eyes, and hear with their ears, and should understand with their heart, and should be converted, and I should heal them.

16 But blessed are your eyes, for they see; and your ears, for they hear.

17 For verily I say unto you, That many prophets and righteous men have desired to see those things which ye see, and have not seen them; and to hear those things which ye hear, and have not heard them.

18 Hear ye therefore the parable of the sower.

19 When any one heareth the word of the kingdom, and understandeth it not, then cometh the wicked one, and catcheth away that which was sown in his heart. This is he which received seed by the way side.

20 But he that received the seed into stony places, the same is he that heareth the word, and anon with joy receiveth it;

21 Yet hath he not root in himself, but dureth for a while: for when tribulation or persecution ariseth because of the word, by and by he is offended.[3]

22 He also that received seed among the thorns is he that heareth the word; and the care of this world, and the deceitfulness of riches, choke the word, and he becometh unfruitful.

23 But he that received seed into the good ground is he that heareth the word, and understandeth it; which also beareth fruit, and bringeth forth, some an hundredfold, some sixty, some thirty.

CHAPTER 20

For the kingdom of heaven is like unto a man that is an householder, which went out early in the morning to hire labourers into his vineyard.

2 And when he had agreed with the labourers for a penny a day, he sent them into his vineyard.

3 And he went out about the third hour, and saw others standing idle in the marketplace,

4 And said unto them; Go ye also into the vineyard, and whatsoever is right I will give you. And they went their way.

5 Again he went out about the sixth and ninth hour, and did likewise.

6 And about the eleventh hour he went out, and found others standing idle, and saith unto them, Why stand ye here all the day idle?

7 They say unto him, Because no man hath hired us. He saith unto them, Go ye also into the vineyard; and whatsoever is right, that shall ye receive.

---

[2] *Esaias:* Isaiah 5:9–10.   [3] *offended:* falls away.

8 So when even was come, the lord of the vineyard saith unto his steward, Call the labourers, and give them their hire, beginning from the last unto the first.

9 And when they came that were hired about the eleventh hour, they received every man a penny.

10 But when the first came, they supposed that they should have received more; and they likewise received every man a penny.

11 And when they had received it, they murmured against the goodman of the house.

12 Saying, These last have wrought but one hour, and thou hast made them equal unto us, which have borne the burden and heat of the day.

13 But he answered one of them, and said, Friend, I do thee no wrong: didst not thou agree with me for a penny?

14 Take that thine is, and go thy way: I will give unto this last, even as unto thee.

15 Is it not lawful for me to do what I will with mine own? Is thine eye evil, because I am good?

16 So the last shall be first, and the first last: for many be called, but few chosen.

Questions for Discussion and Writing

1. What differences can you discover between the four kinds of ground described in the Parable of the Sower and the Seed and the response to Christ's teaching that is implied by each of these categories? Why would this master parable be an important starting point for an attempt to understand the other parables?
2. How does the Parable of the Laborers in the Vineyard contradict conventional ideas about justice and injustice?
3. Pick any of the parables in the preceding selection or any other in the New Testament, and write an essay exploring how the language of the parable functions as a bridge between literal and spiritual meanings. Create your own parable to express your understanding of what the kingdom of heaven means and how it might be obtained.
4. **Rhetorical inquiry:** Why is the form of the parable useful as a teaching technique and superior to a literal explanation?

THE BUDDHA

The Buddha is the title given to the founder of Buddhism, Siddhartha Gautama (563–483 B.C.), who was born into a family of great wealth and power in southern Nepal. Although reared in luxury, Siddhartha renounced this life of privilege at the age of twenty-nine to become a wandering ascetic and to seek an answer to the problems of death and human suffering. After six years of

*intense spiritual discipline, he achieved enlightenment while meditating under
a pipal tree at Bodh Gaya. He spent the remainder of his life teaching, and he
established a community of monks to carry on his work. In the Buddha's view,
bondage to the repeating cycles of birth and death and the consequent suffering
are caused by desire. The method of breaking this cycle is the eightfold noble
path that encompasses right views, right resolve, right speech, right action, right
livelihood, right effort, right mindfulness, and right concentration. Buddhist
parables are well suited to communicate important lessons or moral truths.*

Before You Read

What attitude toward life do you think Buddhism encompasses?

Parables of Buddha

BUDDHA-NATURE

Once upon a time a king gathered some blind men about an elephant and
asked them to tell him what an elephant was like. The first man felt a tusk
and said an elephant was like a giant carrot; another happened to touch an
ear and said it was like a big fan; another touched its trunk and said it was
like a pestle; still another, who happened to feel its leg, said it was like a
mortar; and another, who grasped its tail, said it was like a rope. Not one of
them was able to tell the king the elephant's real form.

In like manner, one might partially describe the nature of man but would
not be able to describe the true nature of a human being, the Buddha-nature.

There is only one possible way by which the everlasting nature of man,
his Buddha-nature, that can not be disturbed by worldly desires or destroyed
by death, can be realized, and that is by the Buddha and the Buddha's noble
teaching.

THE WAY OF PURIFICATION

At one time there lived in the Himalayas a bird with one body and two heads.
Once one of the heads noticed the other head eating some sweet fruit and felt
jealous and said to itself: "I will then eat poison fruit." So it ate poison and
the whole bird died.

Questions for Discussion and Writing

1. How do the many different conclusions the blind men reach about the
   nature of the elephant reveal the partial, limited, and contradictory
   perceptions that are the result of their being unable to see the whole
   elephant? In this case, what might being blind mean in relation to the
   Buddha-nature of humans?

2. What aspect of human nature is illustrated in the story of the bird with one body and two heads?

3. Have you ever had an experience whose meaning could be understood more clearly in light of either of these parables? Describe this experience and what you learned about yourself from it. To gain more insight into Buddha's first parable find an interesting photo and crop it (electronically using an image editor, or by cutting and pasting) to select at least three different elements as focal points. Describe how the meaning changes according to the way the photo is cropped.

4. **Rhetorical inquiry:** How is the idea of erroneous perceptions and the all-too-human need to identify with whatever captures your attention at the moment the impulse that Buddhism is designed to extinguish as suggested by these parables?

NASREDDIN HODJA

Nasreddin Hodja was born in Sivrihisar, Turkey, in the early thirteenth century and died in 1284 near present-day Konya. His father was the religious leader, the imam, of his village, and Hodja, too, served as imam. Later he traveled to Aksehir, where he became a dervish and was associated with a famous Islamic mystical sect. He also served as a judge and university professor. The stories that have made Hodja immortal blend wit, common sense, ingenuousness, and ridicule to reveal certain aspects of human psychology. Today, Hodja's stories are widely known throughout Turkey, Hungary, Siberia, North Africa, and the Middle East. They are told in teahouses, schools, and caravansaries and are even broadcast on the radio. Each tale is a certain kind of joke, a joke with a moral that has long been associated with the Sufi tradition of Islamic teaching. Unlike the philosophical allegories of Plato or the spiritual parables recorded in the New Testament, Hodja's stories use humor to surreptitiously bypass habitual patterns of thought in order to reveal a central truth about the human condition. Hodja very frequently uses the dervish technique of playing the fool. At other times, he is the embodiment of wisdom. All his stories are designed to sharpen our perceptions.

Before You Read

Can jokes be compatible with spiritual lessons?

Islamic Folk Stories

WE ARE EVEN

One day, Hodja went to a Turkish bath but nobody paid him much attention. They gave him an old bath robe and a towel. Hodja said nothing and on his way out he left a big tip. A week later, when he went back to the same bath, he was very well received. Everybody tried to help him and offered him extra services. On his way out, he left a very small tip.

"But, Hodja," they said, "Is it fair to leave such a small tip for all the attention and extra services you received?"

Hodja answered,

"Today's tip is for last week's services and last week's tip was for today's services. Now we are even."

Do As You Please

Hodja and his son were going to another village. His son was riding the donkey and Hodja was walking along. A few people were coming down the road. They stopped and pointing at his son they muttered, "Look at that! The poor old man is walking and the young boy is riding the donkey. The youth of today has no consideration!" Hodja was irritated. He told his son to come down, and he began to ride the donkey himself. Then, they saw another group of people, who remarked, "Look at that man! On a hot day like this, he is riding the donkey and the poor boy is walking."

So, Hodja pulled his son on the donkey, too. After awhile, they saw a few more people coming down the road.

"Poor animal! Both of them are riding on it and it is about to pass out."

Hodja was fed up. He and his son got down and started walking behind the donkey. Soon, they heard a few people say,

"Look at those stupid people. They have a donkey but won't ride it."

Finally, Hodja lost his patience. He turned to his son and said, "You see, you can never please people and everybody says something behind your back. So, always do as you please."

You Believed That It Gave Birth

Hodja had borrowed his neighbour's cauldron. A few days later, he put a bowl in it and returned it. When his neighbour saw the bowl, he asked,

"What is this?"

Hodja answered,

"Your cauldron gave birth!"

His neighbour was very happy. He thanked Hodja and took the cauldron and the bowl.

A few weeks later, Hodja borrowed the cauldron again but this time he didn't return it. When his neighbour came to ask for it, Hodja said,

"Your cauldron died. I am sorry."

The man was surprised.

"Oh, come on!" he said, "Cauldrons don't die."

Hodja snapped back, "Well, you believed that it gave birth, then why don't you believe that it died?"

How does this statue of Nasreddin Hodja depict his unique perspective?

Questions for Discussion and Writing

1. How does the story "We Are Even" suggest that we should not be concerned about how others view our actions so long as we are aware of what we are doing and why we are doing it?
2. What do the experiences of Hodja and his son in "Do As You Please" tell us about human nature? Have you ever had a similar experience that led you to the same conclusion? Describe the circumstances.
3. In your view, what is the point of "You Believed That It Gave Birth"? Discuss your interpretation in a short essay. How is this or any of Hodja's stories designed to awaken people from the bonds of conditioning?
4. **Rhetorical inquiry:** How does the fact that Hodja blends self-mockery with ridicule of people's need to be guided by self-interest make his stories more effective?

Poetry

LINDA PASTAN

Linda Pastan was born in 1932 in New York and was educated at Radcliffe (B.A., 1954), Simmons College (M.L.S., 1955), and Brandeis University

(M.A., 1957). Her poetry explores the metaphysical implications of ordinary life and the mystery of what we take for granted. Her collected poems include Carnival Evening: New and Selected Poems—1968–1998 *(1998) and* PM/AM: New and Selected Poems *(1981), in which "Ethics" first appeared. Recent collections are* The Last Uncle: Poems *(2002) and* Queen of a Rainy Country *(2006).*

Before You Read

How would you go about evaluating the worth of a great work of art when compared to a human being?

Ethics

In ethics class so many years ago
our teacher asked this question every fall:
if there were a fire in a museum
which would you save, a Rembrandt painting
or an old woman who hadn't many   5
years left anyhow? Restless on hard chairs
caring little for pictures or old age
we'd opt one year for life, the next for art
and always half-heartedly. Sometimes
the woman borrowed my grandmother's face   10
leaving her usual kitchen to wander
some drafty, half-imagined museum.
One year, feeling clever, I replied
why not let the woman decide herself?
Linda, the teacher would report, eschews   15
the burdens of responsibility.
This fall in a real museum I stand
before a real Rembrandt, old woman,
or nearly so, myself. The colors
within this frame are darker than autumn,   20
darker even than winter—the browns of earth,
though earth's most radiant elements burn
through the canvas. I know now that woman
and painting and season are almost one
and all beyond saving by children.   25

Questions for Discussion and Writing

1. How has the speaker's understanding of the hypothetical dilemma proposed to her by her teacher altered with the passage of time?

2. How does Pastan make the theme of the poem more apparent through contrasting situations and time periods? How is the impact of the poem strengthened by the associations of fall and winter?

3. In your opinion, is the speaker's problem a failure to take responsibility when she was young and even now that she is an "old woman"? Why or why not?

4. **Rhetorical inquiry:** Why is it significant that the best the speaker can do is to try to imagine the old woman as her grandmother and to move her from her kitchen to the museum?

ROBERT FROST

Robert Frost (1874–1963) was born in San Francisco and lived there until the age of eleven, although most people think of him as having grown up in New England. He spent his high school years in a Massachusetts mill town and studied at Harvard for two years. He worked a farm in New Hampshire that he had acquired in 1900, took a teaching job at the Pinkerton Academy, and wrote poetry that he had no luck in getting published. In 1912 he moved with his wife and five children to England, rented a farm, and met with success in publishing A Boy's Will *(1913) and* North of Boston *(1914). After the outbreak of World War I, he returned to the United States, where he was increasingly accorded recognition. He taught at Amherst College sporadically for many years. Frost won the Pulitzer Prize for poetry four times. He was a friend of John F. Kennedy, who invited him to read a poem at the presidential inauguration in 1961. Many of the qualities that made Frost's poetry so popular can be seen in "The Road Not Taken" (1916).*

Before You Read

Have you ever reconsidered an important decision you made in the past to determine if it was the right one?

The Road Not Taken

Two roads diverged in a yellow wood,
And sorry I could not travel both
And be one traveler, long I stood
And looked down one as far as I could
To where it bent in the undergrowth;   5

Then took the other, as just as fair,
And having perhaps the better claim,
Because it was grassy and wanted wear;
Though as for that the passing there
Had worn them really about the same,   10

And both that morning equally lay
In leaves no step had trodden black.
Oh, I kept the first for another day!
Yet knowing how way leads on to way,
I doubted if I should ever come back.   15

I shall be telling this with a sigh
Somewhere ages and ages hence:
Two roads diverged in a wood, and I—
I took the one less traveled by,
And that has made all the difference.   20

Questions for Discussion and Writing

1. How does Frost use a simple subject as a springboard to express a profound insight?
2. What prevents the speaker from berating himself for not having chosen a different, possibly easier, road?
3. In what way is it implied that the psychological sensibility of the speaker is more sophisticated than the anecdotal manner in which the poem is written?
4. **Rhetorical inquiry:** In line 18, how does Frost signal the reader that the speaker has resolved his ambivalence by emphasizing the first-person pronoun more pointedly than he has previously?

Connections for Chapter 11: The Ethical Dimension

1. **Philip Wheelwright,** *The Meaning of Ethics*
   Does Linda Pastan's poem point out the limits of the kind of ethical analysis described by Wheelwright? Why or why not?
2. **Marya Mannes,** *The Unwilled*
   How might Mannes meet objections to her argument posed by such noteworthy exceptions as Helen Keller (see "The Day Language Came Into My Life" (in Chapter 4)?
3. **Hans Ruesch,** *Slaughter of the Innocent*
   In what respects is Ruesch's argument and Mark Twain's satire "The Lowest Animal" (in Chapter 5) based on similar assumptions?
4. **Garrett Hardin,** *Lifeboat Ethics*
   To what extent does the conflict between self-preservation and consideration of others that Hardin sees as the crux of the lifeboat dilemma enter into Don DeLillo's essay "In the Ruins of the Future" (in Chapter 7)?

5. **Stanley Milgram,** *The Perils of Obedience*
   How do Milgram's subjects react in similar ways to the characters in
   Kurt Vonnegut's story "Harrison Bergeron" (in Chapter 9)?

6. **Dalai Lama,** *The Role of Religion in Modern Society*
   Compare the mutually exclusive assumptions and surprisingly sim-
   ilar goals in this essay by the Dalai Lama and Jean Paul Sartre's
   "Existentialism."

7. **Jean-Paul Sartre,** *Existentialism*
   In what sense does Connie in Joyce Carol Oates's story face the kind of
   dilemma that Sartre discusses in "Existentialism"?

8. **John M. Darley and Bibb Latané,** *Why People Don't Help in a Crisis*
   Does William Carlos Williams's poem "At the Ball Game" (in Chapter 2)
   offer insights into crowd psychology that match what Darley and Latané
   found?

9. **Joyce Carol Oates,** *Where Are You Going, Where Have You Been?*
   In what sense has Connie evoked her own version of the "rough beast"
   portrayed by W. B. Yeats in "The Second Coming" (in Chapter 7)? What
   role does religious symbolism play in both works?

10. **Plato,** *The Allegory of the Cave*
    Compare Plato's allegory (as a method for teaching about the nature of
    absolute good) with the parables in *The New Testament* as to the
    nature of the Kingdom of Heaven. How do both works convey subtle
    concepts that are hard to grasp?

11. **Matthew,** *Parables in The New Testament*
    What similarities can you discover between any of the parables and Tom
    Wayman's poem "Did I Miss Anything?" (in Chapter 3)?

12. **The Buddha,** *Parables of Buddha*
    How do Buddha's parables illuminate the experiences of Bill and Arlene
    in Raymond Carver's story "Neighbors" (in Chapter 2)?

13. **Nasreddin Hodja –** *Islamic Folk Tales*
    What similarities can you discover between Hodja's teaching methods
    and those of George Gurdjieff as described by Fritz Peters in "Boyhood
    with Gurdjieff" (Chapter 1)?

14. **Linda Pastan,** *Ethics*
    Compare the real moral dilemma of Sabine Reichel (see "Learning What
    Was Never Taught" in Chapter 3) with the choice that confronts the
    speaker in Pastan's poem.

15. **Robert Frost,** *The Road Not Taken*
    Could Linda Pastan's poem be considered a rebuttal to Frost's poem?
    Why or why not?

APPENDIX: The MLA Style of Documentation

The recommended method for documenting sources for the humanities is the Modern Language Association (MLA) style described in the *MLA Handbook for Writers of Research Papers* (6th ed., New York: MLA, 2003) and at <http://mla.org/>. It consists of a brief parenthetical citation in the text and a list of works cited at the end of the paper. The parenthetical citations identify sources briefly; provide page references, including the author's name and a shortened version of the title if necessary; and must follow each occurrence of a source that needs to be documented. A complete description of each source appears in a final alphabetical listing of works cited at the end of the paper.

The paper reprinted below ("Prelude to the Internet") uses this system. For example, notice the following sentence taken from the sample student research paper:

Using electricity, an American named Joseph Henry used Sturgeons's device to ring a bell at the end of a one-mile wire (Bellis "History").

The corresponding entry in the list of works cited gives full information on this source.

Bellis, Mary. "The History of the Telegraph and Telegraphy." Inventors 15 Oct. 2004. <http://inventors.about.com./library/inventors/bltelegraph.htm>.

Sample Student Research Paper in MLA Style

We have included marginal comments that point out how Tara Miles introduces and develops her thesis and combines her own ideas with paraphrases and quotations from her sources.

Tara Miles
Professor Guffey
Economics 20
19 October 2004

Prelude to the Internet

"Ever since the beginnings of time, people have been trying to communicate over distances greater than the human voice could reach" (Perera). Methods for doing so have included smoke signals, mirrors, fires, and flags. On May 24, 1844, a new method was demonstrated. Samuel Morse sent a message from the Supreme Court room in the Capitol to a railroad depot in Baltimore. This message was "What hath God wrought" (Numbers 23:23). What makes this event so momentous in our history is the speed with which this message was carried. It didn't go by boat, horse or wagon, but by an invention called the electric telegraph. Though Morse was not the first to invent the idea, he was the man with the desire and dedication to see it brought to life. Within nine years of this first transmission, Florida was the only state east of the Mississippi that was not connected. Seventeen years later the entire American Continent was linked, and after only twenty-two years, continents spanning the Atlantic Ocean were able to communicate with each other almost simultaneously. We can see the economic impact of the telegraph if we examine its influence on the infrastructure, military, and businesses.

First, it will be helpful to discuss the invention of the telegraph, which was a long process combining the ideas of many different individuals. In 1825, a British inventor named William Sturgeon designed the electromagnet. Using electricity, an American named Joseph Hendry used Sturgeons's device to ring a bell at the end of a one-mile wire (Bellis "History"). In 1832, Dr. Charles T. Jackson of Boston started Samuel Morse's mind on the path of designing a telegraph. While returning from overseas, Jackson shared with Morse the experiments with electromagnetism that were occurring in Europe (Bellis "Timeline"). The following years included many changes to Morse's original ideas for the telegraph. Through collaboration and trial and error, Morse continued to design a working model. He also worked diligently on creating a universal code to be used with the telegraph. This code also underwent many changes, but the final result is still known as Morse code. Morse acquired several partners for his project, but the actual contributions of each partner are still debated today. His most notable partners included Leonard Gale, a science professor; Alfred Vail, a steelworks heir; and Francis O.J. Smith, a politician ("Inventor"). Though Morse was eager to share his discoveries with America, it wasn't until 1843 that he finally received support from society in the form of a grant from the federal government. The grant was passed through the House of Representatives by a vote of 89 to 83 and barely passed the Senate on the last day of its session ("Collection"). This grant was used to construct a forty-mile long wire stretching between Baltimore and Washington that became the carrier of the famous first message, "What hath God wrought." Although there were many improvements and additions to the telegraph from that point forward, the telegraph had been invented and the growth of the economy was quickened in response.

Synthesizes various sources

With the invention of the telegraph, the infrastructures of the United States underwent massive expansion. Morse was already aware of the advantages for the railroad companies long before the unveiling of his telegraph in 1844. According to Library of Congress records, "In 1838 . . . Morse was in Europe attempting to obtain a patent for a telegraph system that would indicate by sound the presence of a railroad train at any chosen point on the track" ("Samuel" 1). Although he wasn't successful at the time, it didn't take long for the railroad companies to understand the benefits of such a system of communication along their tracks. They already had a system of timetables to deal with the sharing of the tracks, but the telegraph allowed the railroad companies to deal efficiently with extra trains, late trains, and disabled trains. The first telegraph train order was sent in 1851 on the Erie Railroad. "The new technology was quickly implemented by the railroads, which sharply decreased the number of accidents, collisions, and derailments" (Hempell). The telegraph was directly responsible for the expansion of the railroads. Within a couple of years, the number of telegraph stations, employees, and miles of wire expanded greatly. This not only created a more efficient and safer

Repeats and develops key ideas

railroad service, but it also added many jobs to the economy. "The telegrapher was as much a part of the railroad as the ties that supported its rails. Without his services trains could not have moved safely any faster than horse-drawn coaches" (Grumbine). With the rise in usage of the telegraph by the railroad, many improvements were designed to further its viability across the states. Because of this improved value, more lines were put up, enlarging their significance to the economy. The expansion of the railroads was tied directly to the growth of the telegraph and vice versa. Increased development furthered the use of railroads to transport goods and people, adding to the growth of the country. It also offered reasonable transportation and increased movement among the citizens of the United States.

Along with the railroads, other common infrastructures also grew because of the telegraph. Concepts from the telegraph were adapted to meet the needs of the growing economy and were modified into communication lines for fires and emergencies, allowing for a quicker response time. Criminals on the run were caught when the speed of the telegraph message allowed the police to be waiting for them at the other end. Services provided by these infrastructures were improved and the costs were lessened, making them more efficient. With early notification of a fire, the response was quicker, reducing the damage. The reduction of damage helped lower the cost to the economy as a whole.

What started as a government-funded project was quickly enlarged by businesses with an eye for profit. "By 1846 private companies, using Morse's patent, had built telegraph lines from Washington reaching to Boston and Buffalo, and were pushing further" (Mabee). Telegraph companies began opening up left and right trying to make revenue from this new invention. The expansion of the telegraph across the country was mainly funded through the entrepreneurship of individual businessmen. Not only did they earn money from its expansion, but they also gained more opportunities to further their business. Within a matter of years, the Pony Express was superseded by the electric telegraph, which was quicker and cheaper. Businesses benefited from readily available communication with each other. "Industry found the telegraph indispensable for the transmission of business related communication including information on stocks and commodities" (Raven). The stock market became easier to participate in from greater distances. Business could create a stable market by

Develops analysis in terms of causes and effects

Provides vivid examples that illustrate thesis

Supplies supporting detail

comparing the costs of items around the United States. Newspapers also realized the benefits of such a quick sending of information. "The proprietors of these newspapers saw that this new instrument was bound to affect all newspaperdom profoundly" (Thompson). With the ability to share news quickly across large areas of land, the newspapers companies found the need to improve their printing services. By encouraging the inventions of new things, the telegraph promoted an increase in the market.

As the market grew, the correlation between the telegraph and the growth was obvious. By October 24, 1861, the first transcontinental telegraph system was completed, providing new business opportunities. By 1866, a telegraph cable had been successfully laid across the Atlantic Ocean, a feat that enabled the growth of the nation through foreign contact and trade. Summarizes previous discussion

While the resources of the United States grew, the social climate underwent turmoil. The Civil War had a negative bearing on the financial system of the time, but that influence was minimized by the telegraph. "The American Civil War was one of the first demonstrations of the military value of the telegraph in the control of troop deployment and intelligence" (Raven). The leaders of the troops were able to communicate with each other to coordinate their actions. Telegraphs were also used to coordinate the transfer of soldiers, weapons, and supplies. When the military wanted to use a train for such transportation, it was essential to have communication along the way to avoid an ambush. Often the lines were tapped by the opposite side in order to glean information. Oftentimes false messages were sent with the knowledge that the enemy was listening. Encryption was also used to safeguard the messages being sent. "The exigencies and experiences of the Civil War demonstrated, among other theorems, the vast utility and indispensable importance of the electric telegraph both as an administrative agent and as a tactical factor in military operations" (Greely). The telegraph is acknowledged as a deciding factor in the early end of the Civil War, allowing the economy to begin recovering quickly. Without the use of the telegraph, the outcome of Civil War would have been very different, creating lasting effects on the economy. Highlights the effect of the telegraph

Before the completion of the telegraph, communication was no faster than the fastest horse available. If people in New York wanted to speak to someone in California, they had no choice but to send a Summarizes key points message by Pony Express. It would take at least 20 days before they heard a response. The concept of instant communication opened up the economy in the United States. Railroads flourished, wars were won, business grew, papers expanded, and people connected. Without this discovery, the growth of the United States would have been seriously hampered by the size of the country. Not only did the government take advantage, but businesses and civilians did too. The rapid expansion of the economy can be attributed to the determination and drive of one man to see the electric telegraph become a reality. "It may be difficult to visualize, but if it had not been for the era of telegraphy we might still be looking over the horizon today for arrival of the Pony Express to bring us the latest news, and be watching for the cow to jump over the moon instead of already having placed our flag upon it. Telegraphy was the basic forerunner of all modern communication" (Grumbine). The Internet is nothing more than a complex telegraph. Also originally government sponsored, it now allows worldwide communication with the touch of a button. The modern day miracles that support our economy would not have been discovered without the initial impetus of the electric telegraph.

Reaches conclusion that links to title

Page numbers continue

1-inch from top of page

1"

1/2"

Miles 6

1/2 inch from top

Heading centered

Works Cited

Beavon, Rod. "Samuel Morse." 7 October 2004.

    <http:// www.rod.beavon.clara.netisamuel.htm>.

Sources listed alphabetically

All lines double-spaced

Bellis, Mary. "The History of the Telegraph and Telegraphy." *Inventors*

    15 Oct. 2004. <http://inventors.about.com/library/inventors/

    bltelegraph.htm>.

—. "Timeline: Biography of Samuel Morse." *Inventors* 15 Oct. 2004.

    <http://inventors.about.com/library/inventors/bl_morse_timeline.

    htm>.

"Collection Highlights." *Samuel F. B. Morse Papers*. Library of

    Congress. 13 Oct. 2004. <http://memory.loc.gov/ammem/sfbmhtml/

First line of each entry not indented

    sfbmhighlightsO1.html>.

Greely, A W. "The Military-Telegraph Service." 17 Sept. 2004.

    <http://www.civilwarhome.com/telegraph.htm>.

Grumbine, Arthur. "The Era of Morse Telegraphy." 15 Sept. 2004.
<http://www.faradic.net1~gsraven/telegraph_tales/grumbine/
grumbine_1.html>.

Hempell, Anthony. "A History of Modern Telecommunications: Part 1:
The Telegraph." 25 Sept. 2004. <http://www.peak.sfu.ca/cmass/
issue1/telegraph.html>.

"Inventor of the Week." *Massachusetts Institute of Technology lact.*
2004. <http://web.mit.edu/inventJiow/morse.html>.

Mabee, Carleton. "Samuel F. B. Morse." 22 Sept. 2004.
<http://www.morsehistoricsite.orgihistory/morse.html>.

Perera, Tom. "History, Theory & Construction of the Electric
Telegraph." *WI TP Telegraph & Scientific Instrument
Museums* 2 October 2004. <http://www.chss.montclair.edu/
pereratipertel.htm>.

Raven, G S. "A Brief History of the Morse Telegraph." 3 Sept. 2004.
<http://www.faradic.net!~gsraven/history.html>.

"Samuel F. Morse Preview." Library of Congress: 1-6
<http://lcweb2.loc.gov/ammern/atthtml/morsel.html>.

Thompson, Holland. "Agents of Communication-Newspaper
Printing." 16 Sept. 2004. <http://inventors.about.com!cs/
inventorsalphabetla/media_2.htm>.

Additional
lines
indented 5
spaces

Although English instructors require papers to be formatted in Modern Language Association (MLA) style, teachers in other disciplines may require different systems of documentation. History and the fine arts use *The Chicago Manual of Style* (CMS), the social sciences, business, and education customarily use the format of the *American Psychological Association* (APA), and the sciences and engineering follow the Council of Science Editors (CSE) format. Here, however, are some universal formatting points to check during proofreading:

- one-inch margins on the top, bottom, and sides of each page
- page number and running head on each page (you can use the "header" function for this)
- five space indentation of the first line of each paragraph double-spaced text in a standard 12-point font (do not put an extra double space between paragraphs)

- works cited (or references) on a separate page at the end of the paper
- your name, the title of the paper, the name of your school or the course, and the date on the title page (if one is required by your instructor) or on the first page of the essay.

GLOSSARY

Advertisement   A public announcement of a product, service, or event designed to promote awareness and sales.   00

Allegory   A type of narrative in which characters, events, and even the setting represent particular qualities, ideas, or concepts. See Fable, Parable, and Symbol.   00

Alliteration   The repetition of similar or identical sounds at the beginning of words or in accented syllables. Alliteration is used to underscore similarities and contrasts. For example, from "stem to stern."   23

Allusion   A brief reference in a literary work to a real or fictional person, place, thing or event that the reader might be expected to recognize. See Context.   26

Ambiguity   A phrase, statement, or situation that may be understood in two or more ways.   7

Analogy   A comparison drawn between two basically different things that have some points in common, often used to explain a more complex idea in terms of a simpler and more familiar one. See Metaphor and Symbol.   10

Antagonist   A character who opposes the protagonist's completion of his or her goal. In Joyce Carol Oates's "Where Are You Going, Where Have You Been?" Arnold Friend is the antagonist to Connie.   24

Argument   A process of reasoning and putting forth evidence to support an interpretation.   14

Assonance   The repetition of vowel sounds in a line, stanza, or sentence.   23

Assumptions   The knowledge, values, and beliefs a reader brings to a text.   16

Audience   The group of spectators, listeners, viewers, or readers that a performance or written work reaches.   1

Autobiography   An author's own life history or memoir. For example, Maya Angelou's "Liked for Myself" is drawn from her memoir *I Know Why the Caged Bird Sings* (1970).   6

Biographical Context   The facts and circumstances of the author's life that are relevant to the work.   25

Case History   An in-depth account of the experience of one person that typifies the experience of many people in the same situation; used to substantiate a claim.   7

Casual Analysis   A method of analysis that seeks to discover why something happened or will happen.   11

Character(s)   Fictional personalities created by the writer.   21

Claim   The assertion or interpretation the writer puts forward and supports with evidence and reasons. See Thesis.   14

Classification/Division   A method of sorting, grouping collecting, and analyzing things by categories based on features shared by all members of a class or group. Division is a method of breaking down an entire whole into separate parts, or sorting a group of items into non-overlapping categories; arguments can use classification as part of the writer's analysis in making a case.   7

Climax   The decisive or turning point of emotional intensity in a work of literature. For example, the climax in Carson McCuller's "Madame Zilensky and the King of Finland" occurs when Mr. Brook confronts Madame Zilensky.   24

Comparison/Contrast   Rhetorical technique for pointing out similarities or differences; writers may use a point-by-point or subject-by-subject approach.   8

Conclusion   The end or closing; the last main division of a discourse, usually containing summation and a statement of opinion or decisions reached.   3

Conflict   The opposition between a character or narrator and an obstacle (another character, society, or fate) or within this person's mind.   24

Connotation   The emotional implications a word may suggest, as opposed to its literal meaning. The word *fireplace*, for example, might connote feelings of warmth, hospitality, and comfort, whereas it denotes the portion of a chimney in which fuel is burned. See Denotation.   7

Consonance   Repetition of the final consonant sounds and stressed syllables that are preceded by a different vowel sound, as in "pain of a thorn."   23

Context   The surrounding situation that affects a literary work, including the writer's life and the political, historical, and social environment. See Biographical Context, Historical Context, and Social Context.   25

Controlling Image   A dominant image or metaphor that determines the theme or organization of an entire poem. For example, Marge Piercy's poem "Barbie Doll" uses this figure as a controlling image. See Figurative Language and Metaphor.   353

Crisis   The point of highest tension in a work that precipitates an irrevocable outcome; often the result of a choice made by the protagonist. For example, in Panos Ioannides's story "Gregory" the narrator chooses to follow orders to shoot his prisoner. See Climax.   24

Culture   The totality of practices and institutions and the entire way of life of the people who produce them. In a narrow sense, specific aesthetic productions of literature, art, and music.   30

Deductive Reasoning   A form of argument that applies a set of principles to specific cases and draws logical conclusions.   2

Definition   A method for specifying the basic nature of any phenomenon, idea, or thing. Dictionaries place the subject to be defined in the context of the general class to which it belongs and give distinguishing features that differentiate it from other things in its class.   7

Denotation   The explicit, primary, or literal meaning of a word as found in the dictionary, as distinct from its associative meanings. See Connotation.   00

Description   Writing that reports how a person, place, or thing is perceived by the senses. *Objective* description recreates the appearance of objects, events, scenes, or people. *Subjective* description emphasizes the writer's feelings and reactions to a subject.   4

Dialogue   A conversation between characters. Dialogue can serve to characterize the speakers, create a mood or atmosphere, advance the plot, or develop the theme or main idea of the work. See Monologue.   23

Division   See Classification and Division.   7

Drama   A literary work written to be acted on a stage.   23

Essay   A relatively brief prose discussion on a particular theme or subject.   1

Evidence   All material, including testimony of experts, statistics, cases (whether real, hypothetical, or analogical), and reasons brought forward to support a claim.   2

Examples   Specific incidents that clarify, illustrate, or support a writer's thesis or claim.   6

Exposition   The presentation of background material about the characters or the situation in a story, play, or poem, which supplies information necessary to understand events that follow: may appear either at the beginning or progressively throughout the work.   24

Fable   A short tale that illustrates a moral and whose characters are frequently animals who speak and act like human beings.   20

Fairy Tale   A story frequently from the oral tradition that involves the help or hindrance of magical persons such as fairies, goblins, trolls, and witches.   20

Farce   A type of comedy, usually satiric, that relies on exaggerated character types, slapstick, and other types of ridiculous behavior and situations resulting from a contrived plot that makes use of surprises and coincidences, as in David Ives's play *Sure Thing*.   361

Fiction   A mode of writing that constructs models of reality in the form of imaginative experiences that are not literally true in the sense that they did not actually occur in the "real" world.   20

Figurative Language   The use of words outside their literal or usual meanings, in order to add freshness, and suggest associations and comparisons that create effective images; includes figures of speech such as metaphor, personification, and simile.   9

First-Person Narrator   A narrator who is part of the story and refers to himself or herself as "I."   5

Flashback   An interruption in the major action of a story, play, or essay to show an episode that happened at an earlier time, used to shed light on characters and events in the present by providing background information. Ambrose Bierce uses a flashback in "An Occurrence at Owl Creek Bridge."   509

Folktale   A traditional story about common people from a culture's oral tradition.   20

Foreshadowing   The technique of giving the reader, listener, or viewer of a story or play a hint or clue about what is to come next.   00

Free Verse   Poetry that follows no set patterns of rhyme, meter, or line length, but uses rhythm and other poetic devices, as in Linda Pastan's "Ethics."   22

Genre   A type of literary work defined by particular characteristics of form or technique—for example, the short story, novel, screenplay, poem, play, or essay.   1

Historical Context   Applies to when the work was written and the time period in which the work is set in terms of economic, social, political, and cultural values.   26

Humor   Writing that expresses the faculty of perceiving or appreciating what is amusing or comical, often consisting of the recognition and expression of incongruities in a situation or character.   00

Hypothesis   (pl.: hypotheses) The reader's provisional conjecture or anticipation of what will happen next; an essential element in the reader's interaction with the text.   21

Imagery   The use of language to convey sensory experience in order to arouse emotions or feelings that abstract language cannot accomplish; most often refers to a creation of pictorial images through figurative language. See Figurative Language.   9

Inductive Reasoning   A form of argument that draws inferences from particular cases to support a generalization. Jonathan Kozol in "The Human Cost of an Illiterate Society" uses inductive reasoning.   2

Introduction   A preliminary part (as of a book) leading to the main part. The function of the introduction is to engage the reader in the central issue and present the thesis regarding the question at hand.   3

Irony, Ironic   (from the Greek *eiron,* a stock comic character who misled his listeners). A contrast between appearance and reality, what is and what ought to be. *Dramatic irony* occurs when the reader or viewer can derive meaning from a character's words or actions that are unintended by the character, as in Raymond Carver's "Neighbors." *Verbal irony* is the contrast between what is said and what is actually meant, frequently used as a device in satire, as in Jonathan Swift's "A Modest Proposal."   16

Literature   A term that has come to stand for imaginative writing of high quality, although it should be recognized that literature is an evaluative designation, not an absolute category.   25

Lyric   A short poem or song expressing an intense, basic personal emotion, such as grief, happiness, or love.   00

Metaphor   A figure of speech that implies comparison between two fundamentally different things without the use of "like" or "as." It works by ascribing the qualities of one to the other, linking different meanings together, such as abstract and concrete, and literal and figurative. See Figurative Language.   9

Meter   Recurrent patterns of accented and unaccented or stressed and unstressed syllables that create patterns of rhythm and emphasis. Meter is measured in units called feet, of which the most typical type in English is *iambic* (in which an accented or stressed syllable is preceded by an unaccented or unstressed syllable). Poetry without a recognizable metrical pattern is called *free-verse.* For example, as in Gregory Corso's "Marriage."   23

Monologue   A long speech by one character in a literary work.   23

Myth   Ancient stories that set out a society's religious or social beliefs, which often embody and express a culture's assumptions and values through characters and images that are universal symbols.   20

Narration   A true or made-up story that relates events and/or experiences in either poetry or prose. Narrations tell what happened, when it happened, and to whom; relate events from a consistent point of view; organize a story with a clear beginning, middle, and end; and use events and incidents to dramatize important moments in the action. See Plot.   5

Narrator   Refers to the ostensible teller of a story, who may be a character in the story as in John Cheever's "Reunion" or an anonymous voice outside the story (as in Kate Chopin's "Désirée's Baby"). The narrator's attitude toward the events gives rise to the work's tone. See Persona and Point of View.   00

Organization   The order of presentation that best fulfills the writer's purpose; may be chronological, least familiar to most familiar, simple to complex, or arranged according to some other rhetorical principle (such as comparison/contrast, classification, definition, cause and effect, process analysis, or problem and solution).   1

Parable   A short, simple story that is designed to teach a lesson, truth, or moral; unlike a fable in which the characters are animals or an allegory where the characters represent abstract qualities. St. Matthew's Parables of "The Sower and the Seed," and "The Laborers in the Vineyard" from *The New Testament* are renowned examples.   20

Paradox   A seemingly self-contradictory statement that may, nevertheless, be true.   3

Parody   A composition that imitates the defining features of a serious piece of writing for comic or satiric effect. W. H. Auden's poem "The Unknown Citizen" parodies bureaucratic memorials.   9

Persona   (literally, "actor's mask") refers to the voice and implied personality the author chooses to adopt in order to tell the story in poetry or fiction. The persona may serve as a projection of views quite different from the author's. Jonathan Swift uses this technique in "A Modest Proposal"; Bruce Springsteen adopts a persona in "Streets of Philadelphia." See Speaker and Voice.   16

Personification   A figure of speech that endows abstractions, ideas, animals, or inanimate objects with human characteristics.   23

Persuasion   The winning of the acceptance of a claim achieved through the combined effects of the audience's confidence in the speaker's character, appeals to reason, and the audience's emotional needs and values.   14

Plot   A series of related events organized around a conflict that builds to a climax followed by a resolution. Conflicts may be between two or more characters (as between Louise and Richard in Andre Dubus's story "The Fat Girl"); between a character and society or the forces of nature; or internal, between opposing emotions, such as duty and conscience (as in Panos Ioannides's story, "Gregory"). See Conflict, Crisis, Exposition, and Structure.   20

Poem   A literary form that emphasizes rhythm and figurative language. Often used to express emotions. (See Lyric, Meter, and Rhyme.)   22

Point of View   The perspective from which the events in a story are related; a story may be related in either the first person ("I") or the third person ("he," "she," or "they"). A first-person *narrator* is a character who tells the story he or she participated in or directly observed, as in Irene Zabytko's "Home Soil." The observations and inferences of such a narrator may be reliable, as far as they go, or unreliable. A third-person *omniscient narrator* stands outside the events of the story, but allows the reader unlimited access to the characters' thoughts and feelings and may comment on the story or characters, as in Kate Chopin's "Désirée's Baby." So too, the third-person *limited omniscient narrator* is not directly involved in the story, but restricts the reader's access to the thoughts of one or two of the characters as does the narrator in Joyce Carol Oates's "Where Are You Going, Where Have You Been?"   5

Popular Culture   Those aspects of a culture—chiefly, the artifacts and icons displayed in its forms of entertainment, consumer goods, and means of communication—that have mass appeal.   00

Post-modernist   Refers to works that undercut or subvert traditional models of unity and coherence, employing irony and allusion to create a sense of discontinuity, as in Raymond Carver's "Neighbors."   22

Premise   An assumption from which deductive reasoning proceeds in an argument.   17

Problem Solving   A process writers use to identify problems, search for solutions, and verify them; an indispensable part of all academic and professional research; an argument that proposes a solution will often incorporate problem solving.   12

Process Analysis A method of clarifying the nature of something by explaining how it works in separate, easy-to-understand steps. 11

Propaganda Information or ideas methodically spread to promote or injure a cause, group, or nation. 12

Protagonist The main character in a short story, play, or novel opposed by an adversary, or antagonist, who may be another character, the forces of fate, chance, nature, or any combination of these. See Antagonist. 24

Pseudonym ("false name") An alias used by a writer who does not desire to use his or her real name. Sometimes called a *nom de plume* or "pen name." 00

Purpose The writer's objective; also, the goals of the four types of prose writing: narration (to tell or relate), description (to represent or delineate), exposition (to explain or clarify), and argument (to persuade). 17

Read In the language of semiotics, to decipher the latent social meanings governing the way people dress, what they eat, how they socialize and speak, and other cultural phenomena. 30

Realism A nineteenth-century literary movement that aims to depict life as it is without artificiality or exaggeration. It uses ordinary language and focuses on ordinary people, events, and settings, all of which are described in great detail, as in Kate Chopin's "Désirée's Baby." 21

Rhetoric, Rhetorical modes In ancient Greece and Rome, rhetoric was the art of using language to influence or persuade others. Today, the term also refers to the specialized literary uses of language to express oneself effectively and the study of elements of visual persuasion. 4

Rhyme The exact repetition of similar or identical sounds to unify parts of a poem to emphasize important words or lines, such as "alone" and "stone" in Sara Teasdale's "The Solitary." 23

Rhythm The arrangement of stressed and unstressed sounds into patterns in speech and writing. Rhythm, or meter, may be regular or it may vary within a line or work. See Meter. 23

Satire A technique that ridicules both people and societal institutions, often in an effort to bring about social reform. Exaggeration, wit, and irony are frequent devices used by satirists. Mark Twain in "The Lowest Animal" and Jonathan Swift in "A Modest Proposal" employ satiric techniques. 16

Scene A division of an act in a play that may be long or short, serve as a transition, or even have an inner dramatic structure. 25

Science Fiction Works of fiction usually set in the future or some remote region of the universe that use scientific discoveries or advanced technology, real or imaginary, in the plot. 00

Script The printed text of a play, including dialogue and stage directions. 23

Semiotics The study of linguistic, cultural, and behavioral sign systems. 30

Setting The time period and location in which the action of a story or play takes place. It may serve simply as a background or it may help create the atmosphere from which the story evolves and may even affect the plot's development. 21

Short Story A short work of narrative prose fiction that generally involves a small number of characters in a limited number of settings. 21

Sign A word, object, image, form of behavior, or anything whose meaning is conditioned by and can be interpreted according to an underlying code. 30

Simile A figure of speech involving a direct comparison between two unlike things and using the words "like" or "as." For example, "passengers crammed *like* sardines in a can." See Metaphor. 9

Social Context The relevant social conditions and the effect of social forces as they influence the depiction of characters and classes of people in literary works; includes economic and political circumstances as well as the effects of culture, race, class, power, and gender. 26

Sonnet A lyric poem of fourteen lines written in iambic pentameter. The English sonnet develops an idea in three stages and brings it to a conclusion in a couplet. 00

Speaker   The narrator of a poem; often a separate character created for the purpose of relating the events in a poem from a consistent point of view. See Persona.   23

Stanza   The grouping of a fixed number of verse lines in a recurring metrical and rhyme pattern.   22

Stereotype   A conventional character, who is defined in terms of one oversimplified, often exaggerated, personality trait.   00

Structure   The fundamental organization or framework of a piece of writing, including both the principles underlying the form and the form itself. For example, in stories, the plot is the structural element; in plays, the divisions into acts and scenes express the inner dramatic structure; and in poetry, the formal arrangement into stanzas that develop a specific sequence of images and ideas forms the structure.   24

Style   The author's characteristic manner of expression. Style includes the types of words used, their placement, and the distinctive features of tone, imagery, figurative language, sound, and rhythm.   23

Support   In argument, all the evidence the writer brings forward to enhance the probability of a claim being accepted; can include evidence in the form of summary, paraphrases, quotations, drawn from the text, examples from personal experience, hypothetical cases, the testimony of experts, appeals to the audience's emotions and values, and the writer's own character or personality.   4

Surrealism   A movement in modern literature and art that emphasizes the expression of the imagination as manifested in dreams; stresses the subconscious, often through the unexpected juxtaposition of symbolic objects in mundane settings.   00

Suspense   The feeling of psychological tension experienced by the reader or spectator in anticipation of learning the outcome of a developing sequence of events.   5

Symbol   Something concrete, such as an object, person, place, or event, that stands for or represents something abstract, such as an idea, quality, concept, or condition.   00

Theme   An underlying important idea, either stated or implied, in a nonfiction or literary work that may be mythical, moral, or psychological. Literary works commonly have more than one theme. The reader's reactions determine in large part which themes are perceived as important. The loss of identify is an important theme in Bruce Springsteen's song lyrics.   00

Thesis   The position taken by a writer, often expressed in a single sentence, that an essay develops or supports. See Claim.   1

Tone   The writer's attitude toward the subject, expressed in style and word choice; the voice the writer chooses to project—for example, serious, lighthearted, matter of fact—to relate to readers.   15

Topic   The subject the writer addresses, as distinct from the writer's thesis (opinion) about the subject.   2

Transition   A signal word or phrase that connects two sentences, paragraphs, or sections of an essay to produce coherence. Can include pronoun references, parallel clauses, conjunctions, restatements of key ideas, and terms such as *furthermore, moreover, by contrast, therefore, consequently, accordingly,* or *thus.*   2

Understatement   A form of verbal irony often used for humorous effect in which an opinion is expressed less emphatically than it might be. See Irony.   585

Values   Moral or ethical principles or beliefs that express standards or criteria for judging actions right or wrong, good or bad, acceptable or unacceptable, appropriate or unseemly; an indispensable component of value arguments.   16

Voice   An imagined projection of a speaker in a literary work (usually in a poem), sometimes identified with the author. See Persona, Speaker, and Tone.   15

Wit   Purely intellectual manifestation of cleverness and quick thinking, chiefly in discovering analogies between things that are unlike each other and expressing them in brief sharp observations.   00

CREDITS

Philip Wheelwright, "The Meaning of Ethics" from *A Critical Introduction To Ethics, Third Edition* by Philip Wheelwright. Copyright © 1959 by Philip Wheelwright. Reprinted with the permission of Pearson Education, Inc., Upper Saddle River, NJ.

Irene Zabytko, "Home Soil" by Irene Zabytko from *The Perimeter of Light: Writings about the Vietnam War* edited by Vivian Vie Balafour. Reprinted with the permission of New Rivers Press, Moorhead, MN 56563.

Photos

Introduction: Page 28 © Pete Stone/CORBIS All Rights Reserved; **p. 29,** © Albert Ferreira/CORBIS All Rights Reserved; **p. 30,** Image courtesy of www.adbusters.org; **p. 32,** Image courtesy of www.adbusters.org.

Chap. 1: Page 50, © Thomas A. Kelly/CORBIS All Rights Reserved; **p. 67,** The Granger Collection, New York; **p. 69,** Jeff MacNelly, reprinted by permission of Tribune Media Services; **p. 75,** © Dean Conger/CORBIS All Rights Reserved.

Chap. 2: Page 146, © CORBIS All Rights Reserved; **p. 157,** © Bettmann/CORBIS All Rights Reserved; **p. 159,** © Duomo/CORBIS All Rights Reserved.

Chap. 3: Page 187, © David Butow/CORBIS SABA All Rights Reserved; **p. 219,** © Reinhard Krause/CORBIS All Rights Reserved.

Chap. 4: Page 235, The Far Side® by Gary Larson © 1983 FarWorks, Inc. All Rights Reserved. The Far Side® and the Larson® signatures are registered trademarks of FarWorks, Inc. Used with Permission; **p. 273,** © The New Yorker Collection 1963 Warren Miller from cartoonbank.com. All Rights Reserved; **p. 274,** Courtesy of Johnson & Johnson/Merck Consumer Pharmaceuticals Co.; **p. 275, top,** Courtesy of Mitsubishi Motors North America, Inc.; **p. 275, bottom,** Courtesy of BBDO Detroit on behalf of Chrysler LLC.; **p. 287,** © Hilary B. Price. King Features Syndicate.

Chap. 5: Page 312, Mobilization Recording Inc.; **p. 327,** © Bettmann/CORBIS All Rights Reserved; **p. 328,** Courtesy of The Coca-Cola Company, Atlanta, GA; **p. 360,** © Peter Dazeley/Zefa Collection/CORBIS All Rights Reserved.

Chap. 6: Page 407, Nina Leen/Time Life Pictures/Getty Images; **p. 415,** © Blue Sky Studios/Twentieth Century Fox/Bureau L.A. Collection/CORBIS All Rights Reserved; **p. 421,** Copley News Service.

Chap. 7: Page 450, Erich Lessing/Art Resource, NY. Deir el-Medina, Tombs of the Nobles, Thebes, Egypt; **p. 459,** The Far Side® by Gary Larson © 1983 FarWorks, Inc. All Rights Reserved. The Far Side® and the Larson® signatures are registered trademarks of FarWorks, Inc. Used with Permission; **p. 500,** From *In The Shadow of No Towers* by Art Spiegelman, copyright © 2004 by Art Spiegelman. Used by permission of Pantheon Books, a division of Random House, Inc.

Chap. 8: Page 537, © Hulton-Deutsch Collection/CORBIS All Rights Reserved; **p. 567,** © Peter Endig/CORBIS All Rights Reserved.

Chap. 9: Page 637, © Peter Yates/CORBIS All Rights Reserved; **p. 643,** © Digital Art/CORBIS All Rights Reserved.

Chap. 10: Page 670, Vatican Museums and Galleries, Vatican City, Italy/The Bridgeman Art Library; **p. 682 left,** Getty Images, Inc.; **p. 682, right,** AP Wide World Photos; **p. 691,** © Peter M. Fisher/CORBIS All Rights Reserved.

Chap. 11: Page 762, © Bettmann/CORBIS All Rights Reserved; **p. 798,** © Chris Hellier/CORBIS All Rights Reserved.

INDEX OF FIRST LINES
OF POETRY

INDEX OF AUTHORS
AND TITLES